REED

Practical
Boat Ow

SMALL CR

ALMANAC

2023

EDITORS

Perrin Towler & Mark Fishwick

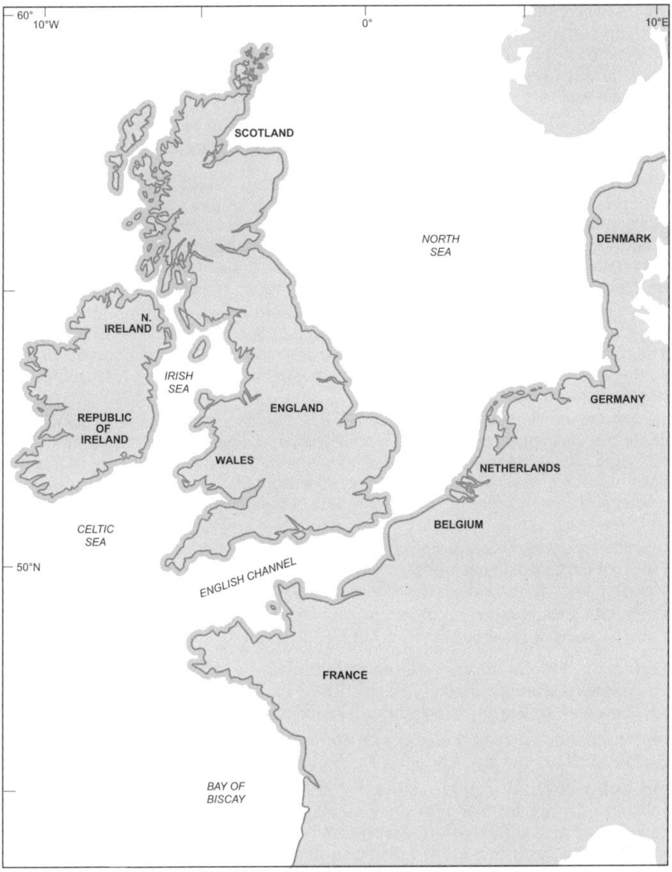

THE UNITED KINGDOM AND IRELAND
PLUS DENMARK TO THE GIRONDE

PLEASE SEE IMPORTANT SAFETY NOTE ON PAGE 2

REEDS

Practical Boat Owner SMALL CRAFT ALMANAC 2023

Editors: Perrin Towler & Mark Fishwick

The Editors would like to thank the many official bodies who have kindly provided essential information in the preparation of this Almanac. They include the UK Hydrographic Office, Trinity House, Northern Lighthouse Board, Irish Lights, HM Nautical Almanac Office, HM Stationery Office, HM Customs, Meteorological Office and the Maritime and Coastguard Agency.

Information from the Admiralty List of Lights, Admiralty Tide Tables and the Admiralty List of Radio Signals is reproduced with the permission of the UK Hydrographic Office and the Controller of HMSO. Extracts from the following are published by permission of the Controller of HM Stationery Office: International Code of Signals, 1969; Meteorological Office Weather Services for Shipping. Phases of the Moon and Sun/Moon rising and setting times are included by permission of HM Nautical Almanac Office. UK and Foreign tidal predictions are supplied by the UK Hydrographic Office, Taunton TA1 2DN. Acknowledgment is also made to the following authorities for permission to use tidal predictions stated: Danmarks Meteorologiske Institut, Denmark: Esbjerg. SHOM, France: Dunkerque, Dieppe, Le Havre, St Malo, Brest, Pointe de Grave, Authorisation (2022-119), Cherbourg (2022-112). Rijkswaterstaat, The Netherlands: Vlissingen, and Hoek van Holland. BSH, Hamburg and Rostock: Helgoland, Wilhelmshaven and Cuxhaven (BSH, Federal Maritime and Hydrographic Agency of Germany) [Licence number 11123/2012-10]. Vlaamse Hydrografie, Belgium: Zeebrugge. **Warning**: The UK Hydrographic Office has not verified the reproduced data and does not accept any liability for the accuracy of reproduction or any modifications made thereafter.

Corrections Any necessary corrections will be published on the website www.reedsalmanacs.co.uk. Data in this almanac is corrected up to Edition 25/2022 of the ***Admiralty Notices to Mariners.***

IMPORTANT SAFETY NOTE AND LEGAL DISCLAIMER

This Almanac provides basic navigational data for planning and executing passages. The tidal prediction data has been reproduced by permission of national hydrographic offices. Chartlets illustrate items in the text, orientate the user and highlight key features; they should not be relied on for navigational purposes and must always be used in conjunction with a current, corrected navigational chart. Any waypoint or position listed in this Almanac must first be plotted on the appropriate chart to assess its accuracy, safety in the prevailing circumstances and relevance to the Skipper's intentions.

Navigational guidance or suggestions are based on the accumulated experience of editors, agents, harbour masters and users. They are generic and in compiling a passage plan or pilotage notebook all other available publications and information should be consulted. They take no account of the characteristics of individual vessels nor the actual or forecast meteorological conditions, sea or tidal state. These need to be checked with appropriate local authorities for the intended area of operation prior to departure.

While every care has been taken in compiling the Almanac, it is a human endeavour with many contributors. Despite rigorous checking there may be inadvertent errors or inaccuracies, and omissions resulting from the time of notification in relation to the publication date. To the extent that the editors or publisher become aware of these, corrections will be published on the website www.reedsalmanacs.co.uk (requires registration). Readers should therefore regularly check the website between January and June for any such corrections. Data in this Almanac is corrected up to Weekly Edition 25/2022 of Admiralty Notices to Mariners.

The publisher, editors and their agents accept no responsibility for any errors or omissions, or for any accident, loss or damage (including without limitation any indirect, consequential, special or exemplary damages) arising from the use or misuse of, or reliance upon, the information contained in this Almanac.

The use of any data in this Almanac is entirely at the discretion of the Skipper or other individual with responsibility for the command, conduct or navigation of the vessel in which it is relied upon.

Correspondence Letters on general matters should be addressed to info@reedsalmanacs.co.uk, or on nautical issues to editor.britishisles@reedsalmanacs.co.uk (British Isles excluding Channel Islands) or editor.continental@reedsalmanacs.co.uk (Denmark to Gironde, including Channel Islands).

Practical Boat Owner is published every four weeks by Future PLC, 161 Marsh Wall, London E14 9AP. For subscription enquiries call +44 (0)330 333 1113 quoting code BL32.

ISBN 978 1 3994 0266 8 A CIP catalogue record for this book is available from the British Library.

Reeds and Adlard Coles are registered trade marks of Bloomsbury Publishing Plc.

Managing editor: Chris Stevens
Cartography & production: Chris Stevens

Adlard Coles
50 Bedford Square, London, WC1B 3DP
29 Earlsfort Terrace, Dublin 2, Ireland
Tel: +44 (0)1865 411010 www.reedsalmanacs.co.uk

Foreword

Welcome to the *Reeds PBO Small Craft Almanac 2023* – your trusty companion for cruising in UK waters, Ireland and the European coast from Denmark to France.

I first came across this guide back in 2001 whilst cruising from Brighton to Conwy in a Westerly GK24. My dad gave it to me, along with some charts and dividers, and tasked me with passage planning. It soon became indispensable for departure times, favourable tides, hazards, pilotage, port entrances and tricky headlands.

Whilst electronic aids to navigation have leapt forward in that time, this is one compact, quick-reference guide, no cruiser can afford to be without. You'll find contact details for harbour authorities and marinas, tidal curves and tables and a full-colour guide to flags, lights and channel markers.

For the small boat sailor, this book has everything you need, compiled using the same trusted data as the full-size Reeds Almanac. Indeed, over 20 years later, I am still using it for passage planning, only this time in our PBO Project Boat, a Maxi 84. Find out more at www.pbo.co.uk

Together with the editors at Reeds, all of us at *Practical Boat Owner* wish you fair winds and sunny skies for the 2023 season.

Ali Wood
Editor
Practical Boat Owner
Britain's biggest-selling boating magazine

Contents

ABBREVIATIONS

AC, ACA	Admiralty chart, chart agent
AC	Shore power (electrical)
ACN	Adlard Coles Nautical
Al	Alternating lt
ALL	Admiralty list of lights
ALRS	Admiralty list of radio signals
ASD	Admiralty sailing directions (Pilot)
ATT	Admiralty tide tables
ATT	Atterisage (landfall/SWM) buoy
Bcn, Bn	Beacon
Bkwtr	Breakwater
BST	British summer time (DST)
CD	Chart datum
Cf	Compare, cross-refer to
CG	Coastguard
Ch	Channel (VHF)
chan.	Channel (navigational)
COG	Course over the ground
CROSS	Centre régional opérationnel de surveillance et sauvetage (MRCC)
CRS	Coast radio station(s)
DF	Direction finding
Dia	Diaphone (fog signal)
Dir Lt	Directional light
DSC	Digital selective calling
DST	Daylight saving time
DZ	Danger zone (buoy)
E	East
ECM	East cardinal mark (buoy/beacon)
ED	Existence doubtful, European datum
EPIRB	Emergency pos'n indicating radio bn
F	Fixed light. Beaufort wind force
FFL	Fixed and flashing lt
Fl	Flashing light
FM	Frequency modulation
FV	Fishing vessel
G	Green. Gravel
GMDSS	Global maritime distress & safety system
H, Hrs, h	Hour(s)
H24	Continuous
HAT	Highest astronomical tide
Hbr	Harbour
Hd	Head, headland
HF	High frequency
HJ	Day service, sunrise to sunset
HO	Office hours, Hydrographic office
ht	Height
HW	High water
HX	No fixed hours
Hz	Hertz
IALA	Int'l association of lt ho authorities
IDM	Isolated danger mark (buoy/bcn)
IMO	Int'l maritime organisation
Inmarsat	Int'l maritime satellite system
IPTS	Int'l port traffic signals
Is, I	Island, Islet
Iso	Isophase light
ITZ	Inshore traffic zone
Kn	Knot(s)
Lanby	Large automatic navigational buoy
Lat	Latitude
LB	Lifeboat
Ldg	Leading (lt)
LF	Low frequency
Long	Longitude
LT	Local time
Lt(s)	Light(s)
Lt F	Light float
Lt Ho	Lighthouse
Lt V	Light vessel
LW	Low water
M	Sea mile(s)
m	Metre(s)
MCA	Maritime & Coastguard Agency
Météo	Météorologie/weather
MF	Medium frequency
MHWN	Mean HW neaps
MHWS	Mean HW springs
MHz	Megahertz
MLWN	Mean LW neaps
MLWS	Mean LW springs
MMSI	Maritime mobile service identity
Mo	Morse
MRCC	Maritime rescue co-ordination centre
MRSC	Maritime rescue sub-centre (not in UK)
MSI	Maritime safety information
N	North
NCM	North cardinal mark (buoy/bcn)
Oc	Occulting light
PHM	Port-hand mark (buoy/bcn)
Pt(e), (a)	Point(e), Punta
Q	Quick flashing
R	Red. River
Ra	Coast radar station
Racon	Radar transponder beacon
RG	Emergency RDF station
R/T	Radiotelephony
S	South
s	second(s) of time
SAR	Search and rescue
SCM	South cardinal mark (buoy/bcn)
SHM	Starboard-hand mark (buoy/bcn)
Sig Stn	Signal station
SMS	Short message service (texting)
SNSM	Société nationale de sauvetage enmer (French LB service)
SOG	Speed over the ground
SOLAS	Safety of life at sea (Convention)
SPM	Special mark (buoy/bcn)
SRR	SAR Region
SSB	Single sideband (radio)
Stn	Station
SWM	Safe water mark, landfall buoy
Tfc	Traffic
TSS	Traffic separation scheme
UQ	Ultra quick flashing lt
UT	Universal time
VHF	Very high frequency
VNF	Voie navigable de France (canals)
VQ	Very quick flashing lt
VTS	Vessel traffic service
W	West, White
WCM	West cardinal mark (buoy/bcn)
WGS	World geodetic system (datum)
WIP	Work in progress
WPT	Waypoint
Y	Yellow, orange, amber

GENERAL VOCABULARY. See also weather vocabulary on page 106

ENGLISH	GERMAN	FRENCH	DUTCH
ASHORE			
Ashore	An Land	A terre	Aan land
Airport	Flughafen	Aéroport	Vliegveld
Bank	Bank	Banque	Bank
Boathoist	Bootskran	Travelift	Botenlift
Boatyard	Bootswerft	Chantier naval	Jachtwerf
Bureau de change	Wechselstelle	Bureau de change	Geldwisselkantoor
Bus	Bus	Autobus	Bus
Chandlery	Yachtausrüster	Shipchandler	Scheepswinkel
Chemist	Apotheke	Pharmacie	Apotheek
Dentist	Zahnarzt	Dentiste	Tandarts
Doctor	Arzt	Médecin	Dokter
Engineer	Motorenservice	Ingénieur/mécanique	Ingenieur
Ferry	Fähre	Ferry/transbordeur	Veer/Pont
Garage	Autowerkstatt	Station service	Garage
Harbour	Hafen	Port	Haven
Hospital	Krankenhaus	Hôpital	Ziekenhuis
Mast crane	Mastenkran	Grue	Masten kraan
Post office	Postamt	Bureau de poste/PTT	Postkantoor
Railway station	Bahnhof	Gare de chemin de fer	Station
Sailmaker	Segelmacher	Voilier	Zeilmaker
Shops	Geschäfte	Boutiques	Winkels
Slip	Slip	Cale	Helling
Supermarket	Supermarkt	Supermarché	Supermarkt
Taxi	Taxi	Taxi	Taxi
Village	Ort	Village	Dorp
Yacht club	Yachtclub	Club nautique	Jacht club
NAVIGATION			
Abeam	Querab	A côté	Naast
Ahead	Voraus	Avant	Voor
Astern	Achteraus	Arrière	Achter
Bearing	Peilung	Cap	Peiling
Buoy	Tonne	Bouée	Boei
Binoculars	Fernglas	Jumelles	Verrekijker
Channel	Kanal	Chenal	Kanaal
Chart	Seekarte	Carte	Zeekaart
Compass	Kompass	Compas	Kompas
Compass course	Kompass Kurs	Cap du compas	Kompas koers
Current	Strömung	Courant	Stroom
Dead reckoning	Koppelnavigation	Estime	Gegist bestek
Degree	Grad	Degré	Graden
Deviation	Deviation	Déviation	Deviatie
Distance	Entfernung	Distance	Afstand
Downstream	Flußabwärts	En aval	Stroom afwaards
East	Ost	Est	Oost
Ebb	Ebbe	Jusant	Eb
Echosounder	Echolot	Sondeur	Dieptemeter
Estimated position	Gegißte Position	Point estimé	Gegiste positie
Fathom	Faden	Une brasse	Vadem
Feet	Fuß	Pieds	Voet
Flood	Flut	Flot	Vloed
Handbearing compass	Handpeilkompass	Compas de relèvement	Handpeil kompas

ENGLISH	GERMAN	FRENCH	DUTCH
Harbour guide	Hafenhandbuch	Guide du port	Havengids
High water	Hochwasser	Pleine mer	Hoog water
Latitude	Geographische Breite	Latitude	Breedte
Leading lights	Feuer in Linie	Alignement	Geleide lichten
Leeway	Abdrift	Dérive	Drift
Lighthouse	Leuchtturm	Phare	Vuurtoren
List of lights	Leuchtfeuer Verzeichnis	Liste des feux	Lichtenlijst
Log	Logge	Loch	Log
Longitude	Geographische Länge	Longitude	Lengte
Low water	Niedrigwasser	Basse mer	Laag water
Metre	Meter	Mètre	Meter
Minute	Minute	Minute	Minuut
Nautical almanac	Nautischer Almanach	Almanach nautique	Almanak
Nautical mile	Seemeile	Mille nautique	Zeemijl
Neap tide	Nipptide	Marée de morte-eau	Dood tij
North	Nord	Nord	Noord
Pilot	Lotse	Pilote	Loods/Gids
Pilotage book	Handbuch	Instructions nautiques	Vaarwijzer
RDF	Funkpeiler	Radio gonio	Radio richtingzoeker
Radar	Radar	Radar	Radar
Radio receiver	Radio, Empfänger	Réceptor radio	Radio ontvanger
Radio transmitter	Sender	Emetteur radio	Radio zender
River outlet	Flußmündung	Embouchure	Riviermond
South	Süd	Sud	Zuid
Spring tide	Springtide	Marée de vive-eau	Springtij/ springvloed
Tide	Tide, Gezeit	Marée	Getijde
Tide tables	Tidenkalender	Annuaire des marées	Getijdetafel
True course	Wahrer Kurs	Vrai cap	Ware Koers
Upstream	Flußaufwärts	En amont	Stroom opwaards
VHF	UKW	VHF	Marifoon
Variation	Mißweisung	Variation	Variatie
Waypoint	Wegpunkt	Point de rapport	Waypoint/Route punt
West	West	Ouest	West
OFFICIALDOM			
Certificate of registry	Schiffszertifikat	Acte de franchisation	Zeebrief
Check in	Einklarieren	Enregistrement	Check-in
Customs	Zoll	Douanes	Douane
Declare	Verzollen	Déclarer	Aangeven
Harbour master	Hafenmeister	Capitaine du port	Havenmeester
Insurance	Versicherung	Assurance	Verzekering
Insurance certificate	Versicherungspolice	Certificat d'assurance	Verzekeringsbewijs
Passport	Paß	Passeport	Paspoort
Police	Polizei	Police	Politie
Pratique	Verkehrserlaubnis	Pratique	Verlof tot ontscheping
Prohibited area	Sperrgebiet	Zone interdite	Verboden gebied
Register	Register	Liste de passagers	Register
Ship's log	Logbuch	Livre de bord	Logboek
Ship's papers	Schiffspapiere	Papiers de bateau	Scheepspapieren
Surveyor	Gutachter	Expert maritime	Opzichter

Chapter 1 – Navigation

PASSAGE PLANNING AND SOLAS V

All passages by any vessel that goes to sea *must* be planned. 'Going to sea' is defined as proceeding beyond sheltered waters. Even in very familiar waters every passage, however short, should be properly planned. Before you set sail you need to determine where you are going, how to get there and what factors may influence the plan.

Full passage planning requirements may be found in Chapter V of the International Convention for Safety of Life at Sea (SOLAS), but more digestible guidance for small craft is in the MCA's Pleasure Craft Information Pack at: **www.dft.gov.uk/mca/pleasure_craft_information_packdec07-2.pdf.**

Although the passage plan does not have to be recorded on paper, in the event of legal action a written plan is clear proof that the required planning has been completed; it can also be referred to during the passage. A suggested passage planning form is overleaf. When completed this would constitute, with due consideration of the points below, a reasonable passage plan. The blank form may be photocopied and modified to suit individual needs.

Although spot checks on small craft are unlikely, the MCA could, following an accident or incident, take action under the Merchant Shipping Act if it could be proved that the skipper did not have a reasonable passage plan.

Passage planning considerations

All passage plans should at least consider the following:

- **Weather.** Before setting out check the weather forecast and know how to get regular updates during the passage.
- **Tides.** Check tidal predictions and determine if there are any limiting depths at your port of departure, during the passage and at the port of arrival (and at alternative ports, if applicable). Tidal streams will almost certainly affect the plan.
- **Vessel.** Confirm she is suitable for the intended trip, is properly equipped, and has sufficient fuel, water and food on board.
- **Crew.** Take into account your crew's experience, expertise and stamina. Cold, tiredness and seasickness can be debilitating – and skippers are not immune.
- **Navigation.** Make sure you are aware of all navigational dangers by consulting up to date charts, pilot books and this Almanac. Never *rely* on GPS for fixing your position.
- **Contingency plan.** Consider bolt holes which can be entered *safely* in an emergency, if the weather deteriorates or mutiny threatens.
- **Information ashore.** Make sure someone ashore knows your plans, when they should become concerned and what action to take if necessary. Be sure to join the Coastguard Voluntary Identification Scheme (Form CG66).

"The winds and waves are always on the side of the ablest navigators." (Edward Gibbon)

Passage planning form

The following notes amplify some of the items on the form:

- The height of tide affects the depth, and tidal streams may hinder sensible progress – off headlands or in narrow passages, for example. On longer passages, which cross main tidal streams, determine the net effect of the streams and calculate a course to steer – more efficient than trying to maintain a track.
- Note which harbours and marinas have restricted times of access due to bars, sills or locks. These may affect your ETA and, probably, your ETD.
- Prepare a detailed pilotage plan for entry/exit of any unfamiliar harbour; a sketch is invaluable.
- Squinting into the setting sun can make pilotage very difficult. At night, light from a full moon can help enormously.
- Know when you expect to see lights at night – a good check on progress. See table of dipping/rising lights.
- Look up and note relevant VHF channels and/or phone numbers for ports of departure and arrival.

PASSAGE PLANNING FORM

DATE:............................ FROM: .... TO: .... DIST: ....M

ALTERNATIVE DESTINATION(S): ....

WEATHER FORECAST: ....

....

FORECASTS AVAILABLE DURING PASSAGE: ....

....

TIDES

DATE:	....		DATE:	....		DATE:	....	
PLACE:	....		PLACE:	....		PLACE:	....	
HW	....	....	HW	....	....	HW	....	....
LW	....	....	LW	....	....	LW	....	....
HW	....	....	HW	....	....	HW	....	....
LW	....	....	LW	....	....	LW	....	....
COEFFICIENT:	....			....			....	
HEIGHT OF TIDE AT:	....			....			....	
..........................hrs	..........................m			..........................hrs	..........................m		..........................hrs	..........................m

DEPTH CONSTRAINTS: ....

TIDAL STREAMS AT: ....

TURNS .... AT .... TOTAL SET (FM .... TO ....): ....° .... M

TURNS .... AT .... TOTAL SET (FM .... TO ....): ....° .... M

NET TIDAL STREAM FOR PASSAGE: ....° .... M

ESTIMATED TIME: ....hrs ETD: .... ETA: ....

SUN/MOON SUNRISE: .... SUNSET: ....

MOONRISE: .... MOONSET: .... PHASE: ....

WAYPOINTS

NO	NAME	TRACK/DISTANCE (TO NEXT WAYPOINT)
....	....	.... / ....
....	....	.... / ....
....	....	.... / ....
....	....	.... / ....
....	....	.... / ....

DANGERS CLEARING BEARINGS/RANGES/DEPTHS

....

....

LIGHTS/MARKS EXPECTED ....

....

....

COMMUNICATIONS

PORT/MARINA .... VHF .... ☎ ....

PORT/MARINA .... VHF .... ☎ ....

NOTES (CHARTS PREPARED & PAGE NUMBERS OF RELEVANT PILOTS/ALMANACS/ETC): ....

....

....

DISTANCES (M) ACROSS THE ENGLISH CHANNEL

ENGLAND / FRANCE/CI	Longships	Falmouth	Fowey	Plymouth bkwtr	Salcombe	Dartmouth	Torbay	Weymouth	Poole Hbr Ent	Needles Lt Ho	Nab Tower	Littlehampton	Shoreham	Brighton	Newhaven	Eastbourne	Folkestone	Dover
Le Conquet	114	118	134	142	139	152	158	181	199	203	236	256	260	264	269	281	313	318
L'Aberwrac'h	101	103	114	120	122	133	142	171	191	197	197	236	246	247	248	258	297	301
Roscoff	110	97	101	97	91	100	107	130	144	149	165	184	193	197	200	211	246	252
Trébeurden	118	105	107	100	95	103	110	128	148	148	168	186	197	201	206	218	257	262
Tréguier	131	114	112	102	93	99	104	116	132	136	153	170	182	187	192	211	252	253
Lézardrieux	139	124	119	107	97	102	105	117	129	133	150	167	179	184	189	208	249	250
St Q.-Portrieux	151	134	128	120	109	114	115	128	133	136	151	174	180	185	188	200	238	242
St Malo	172	152	145	132	118	121	124	125	130	133	148	170	176	182	185	195	235	240
St Helier	156	133	124	110	95	97	100	103	108	110	125	145	155	160	163	175	211	218
St Peter Port	140	113	105	89	75	71	73	81	87	90	105	126	135	139	142	155	190	196
Braye (Alderney)	149	129	107	90	74	72	71	63	68	71	86	108	115	120	123	135	173	178
Cherbourg	173	144	130	111	98	94	93	67	64	63	72	89	99	102	107	120	153	158
St Vaast	194	165	151	134	119	117	119	86	78	72	69	84	91	94	97	104	140	147
Ouistreham	231	203	190	173	158	155	159	121	111	100	88	93	94	94	93	96	132	133
Deauville	238	210	198	181	164	163	160	127	114	103	89	90	89	87	87	89	124	126
Le Havre	239	210	197	180	164	162	165	125	112	98	84	84	83	82	82	83	119	120
Fécamp	246	218	206	188	173	169	165	127	111	98	81	72	69	66	63	63	98	98
Dieppe	273	243	231	214	200	194	191	151	133	121	97	86	76	72	67	62	78	80
Boulogne	294	264	247	231	216	204	202	161	143	132	101	86	77	73	65	54	28	28
Calais	307	276	261	244	229	218	214	174	155	143	114	99	91	86	78	64	29	24

NOTES

1. This Table applies to Areas 1–3, and 14–16, each of which also contains its own internal Distance Table. Approximate distances in nautical miles are by the most direct route, while avoiding dangers and allowing for Traffic Separation Schemes.
2. For ports within the Solent, add the appropriate distances given in Area 2 to those shown above under either Needles Lighthouse or Nab Tower.

AREA 1 *South West England - Isles of Scilly to Anvil Point*

SELECTED LIGHTS, BUOYS & WAYPOINTS

ISLES OF SCILLY TO LAND'S END

Bishop Rock ☆ Fl (2) 15s 44m **20M**; part obsc 204°-211°, obsc 211°-233° and 236°-259°; Gy ○ twr with helo platform; ***Racon T, 18M, 254°-215°***; 49°52'·37N 06°26'·74W; 992351137.
Round Rk 49°53'·10N 06°25'·19W.
Old Wreck VQ; 49°54'·26N 06°22'·81W.

ST AGNES and ST MARY'S

Peninnis Hd ☆ Fl 20s 36m 9M; 231°-117° but part obsc 048°-083° within 5M; W ○ twr on B frame, B cupola; 49°54'·28N 06°18'·21W.
Gugh Fl (5) Y 20s; 49°53'·52N 06°18'·73W.
Spanish Ledge Q (3) 10s; *Bell;* 49°53'·94N 06°18'·86W.
Woolpack Fl G 5s; 49°54'·40N 06°19'·37W.
Bartholomew Ledges QR 12m; 49°54'·37N 06°19'·89W.
N Bartholomew Fl R 5s; 49°54'·49N 06°19'·99W.
Bacon Ledge Fl (4) R 5s; 49°55'·22N 06°19'·26W.
Ldg lts 097·3°: Front, Iso RW (vert) 2s; W △, 49°55'·12N 06°18'·50W. Rear, Oc WR (vert) 10s; Or X on W bcn.
Crow Rock Fl (2) 10s; 49°56'·26N 06°18'·49W.
Hats VQ (6) + L Fl 10s; 49°56'·21N 06°17'·14W.

AROUND TRESCO, BRYHER and ST MARTIN'S

Tresco Flats, Hulman Fl G 4s, 49°56'·29N 06°20'·30W.
Little Rag Ledge Fl (2) R 5s, 49°56'·44N 06°20'·43W.
Bryher, Bar Q (3) 10s, 49°57'·37N 06°20'·84W.
Bryher, Church Quay Q (3) 10s, 49°57'·18N 06°20'·97W.
Spencers Ledge Q (6) + L Fl 15s; 49°54'·78N 06°22'·06W.
Steeple Rock Q (9) 15s; 49°55'·46N 06°24'·24W.
Round Island ☆ Fl 10s 55m **18M**, also shown in reduced vis; 021°-288°; W ○ twr; *Horn (4) 60s*; 49°58'·74N 06°19'·39W.
St Martin's, Higher Town quay ☆ Fl R 5s, 49°57'·45N 06°16'·84W.

SCILLY to LAND'S END

Seven Stones Lt V Fl (3) 30s 12m **15M**; R hull; *Horn (3) 60s*; ***Racon O, 15M***; 50°03'·63N 06°04'·32W; 992351023.
Wolf Rock ☆ Fl 15s 34m **16M**; H24; *Horn 30s*; ***Racon T, 10M***; 49°56'·72N 05°48'·55W; 992351128.
Longships ☆ Fl (2) WR 10s 35m **W15M**, R11M; 189°-R-327°-W- 189°; also shown in reduced vis; Gy ○ twr with helicopter platform; *Horn 10s;* 50°04'·01N 05°44'·81W.
Carn Base Q (9) 15s; 50°01'·48N 05°46'·18W.
Runnel Stone Q (6) + L Fl 15s; *Bell;* 50°01'·18N 05°40'·36W.

LAND'S END TO PLYMOUTH

Tater-du ☆ Fl (3) 15s 34m 12M; 241°-072°; W ○ twr. FR 31m 9M, 060°-072° over Runnel Stone; 50°03'·14N 05°34'·67W.

NEWLYN

Low Lee Q (3) 10s; 50°05'·56N 05°31'·38W.
S Pier ☆ Fl 5s 10m 9M; W ○ twr; 253°-336°; 50°06'·18N 05°32'·57W.
N Pier ☆ F WG 4m 2M; 238°-G-248°, 50°06'·18N 05°32'·62W.

PENZANCE

S Pier ☆ Fl WR 5s 11m **W17M**, R12M; 159°-R (unintens)-224°-R-268°-W-344·5°-R-shore; 50°07'·06N 05°31'·68W.
Mountamopus Q (6) + L Fl 15s; 50°04'·62N 05°26'·25W.
Lizard ☆ Fl 3s 70m **26M**; 250°-120°, partly visible 235°-250°; W 8-sided twr; *Horn 30s;* 49°57'·61N 05°12'·13W.
Manacle Q (3) 10s; *Bell;* 50°02'·81N 05°01'·91W.

FALMOUTH

St Anthony Head ☆ Iso WR 15s 22m, **W16M**, R14M, H24; 295°-W-004°-R (over Manacles)-022°-W-172°; W 8-sided twr; *Horn 30s;* 50°08'·46N 05°00'·96W.
Black Rock Fl(2) 10s 3M; IDM B bn; 50°08'·72N 05°02'·00W.
Black Rock Fl R 2·5s; 50°08'·68N 05°01'·74W.
Castle Fl G 2·5s; 50°08'·99N 05°01'·62W.
St Mawes Q (6) + L Fl 15s; 50°09'·10N 05°01'·42W.
The Governor VQ (3) 5s; 50°09'·15N 05°02'·40W.
West Narrows Fl (2) R 10s; 50°09'·39N 05°02'·07W.
East Narrows Fl (2) G 10s; 50°09'·43N 05°01'·90W.
The Vilt Fl (4) G 15s; 50°09'·99N 05°02'·28W.
Northbank Fl R 4s; 50°10'·34N 05°02'·26W.
St Just QR; 50°10'·44N 05°01'·72W.
Mylor appr chan Fl G 6s; 50°10'·79N 05°02'·70W. Fl R 5s.
Messack Fl G 15s; 50°11'·31N 05°02'·22W.
Carrick Fl (2) G 10s; 50°11'·59N 05°02'·74W.
Pill Fl (3) G 15s; 50°12'·05N 05°02'·40W.
Turnaware Bar Fl G 5s; 50°12'·40N 05°02'·15W.
Dock Basin Dir ☆ 266°: WRG 2s 15m, 10M; 258°-Iso G-226°-Al WG-264°-Iso W-268°-Al WR-270°-Iso R-274°; 50°09'·38N 05°03'·29W.
N Arm ☆ QR 5m 3M; 50°09'·42N 05°03'·20W.
Inner Hbr Dir ☆ 233°: WRG 3s 5m, 9M; 226°-Iso G-231°-Iso W-236°-Iso R-241°; 50°09'·20N 05°03'·94W.
Falmouth Haven Marina ☆ 2 FR (vert); 50°09'·27N 05°03'·91W.
Falmouth Marina VQ (3) 5s; 50°09'·91N 05°04'·99W.

DODMAN POINT and MEVAGISSEY

Naval gunnery targets SSE of Dodman Point:
'A' Fl Y 10s; 50°08'·53N 04°46'·37W.
'B' Fl Y 5s; 50°10'·30N 04°45'·00W.
'C' Fl Y 2s; 50°10'·40N 04°47'·51W.
Gwineas Q (3) 10s; *Bell;* 50°14'·48N 04°45'·40W.
Mevagissey, Victoria Pier ☆ Fl (2) 10s 9m 12M; *Dia 30s;* 50°16'·15N 04°46'·92W.

FOWEY

Cannis Rock Q (6) + L Fl 15s; *Bell;* 50°18'·45N 04°39'·88W.
Fowey ☆ L Fl WR 5s 28m W11M, R9M; 284°-R-295-°-W-028°-R-054°; W 8-sided twr, R lantern; 50°19'·63N 04°38'·83W.
St Catherine's Pt ☆ Fl R 2·5s 15m 2M; vis 150°-295°; 50°19'·69N 04°38'·66W.
Lamp Rock Fl G 5s 3m 2M; vis 357°-214°; 50°19'·70N 04°38'·41W. Whitehouse Pt ☆ Iso WRG 3s 11m W11M, R/G8M; 017°-G-022°- W-032°-R-037°; R col; 50°19'·98N 04°38'·28W.

POLPERRO, LOOE, EDDYSTONE and WHITSAND BAY

Udder Rock VQ (6) + L Fl 10s; *Bell;* 50°18'·93N 04°33'·85W.

POLPERRO, W pier ☆ FW 4m 4M; FR when hbr closed in bad weather; 50°19'·86N 04°30'·96W.

Spy House Pt ☆ Iso WR 6s 30m 7M; W288°-060°, R060°-288°; 50°19'·81N 04°30'·69W.

LOOE, Ranneys Q (6) + L Fl 15s; 50°19'·85N 04°26'·37W.

Mid Main Q (3) 10s 2M; 50°20'·56N 04°26'·94W.

Banjo Pier ☆ Oc WR 3s 8m **W15M**, R12M; 207°-R267°-W-313°-R-332°; 50°21'·06N 04°27'·06W.

White Rock ☆ Fl R 3s 5m 2M; 50°21'·03N 04°27'·09W.

Eddystone ☆ Fl (2) 10s 41m **17M**. Same twr, Iso R 10s 28m 8M; vis 110°-133° over Hand Deeps; Gy twr, helicopter platform; *Horn 30s;* ***Racon T, 10M***; 50°10'·84N 04°15'·94W; 992351125.

Hand Deeps Q (9) 15s; 50°12'·68N 04°21'·10W.

PLYMOUTH

PLYMOUTH SOUND, WESTERN CHANNEL

Draystone Fl (2) R 5s; 50°18'·85N 04°11'·07W.

Knap Fl G 5s; 50°19'·56N 04°10'·02W.

Plymouth bkwtr W head, ☆ Fl WR 10s 19m W12M, R9M; 262°-W-208°-R-262°; W ○ twr. *Horn 15s;* 50°20'·07N 04°09'·52W.

Maker ☆ Fl (2) WRG 10s 29m, W11M, R/G6M; 270°-G330°-W-004°-R-050°; W twr, R stripe; 50°20'·51N 04°10'·87W.

Queens Ground Fl (2) R 10s; 50°20'·29N 04°10'·08W.

New Ground Fl R 2s; 50°20'·47N 04°09'·43W.

Melampus Fl R 4s; 50°21'·15N 04°08'·72W.

PLYMOUTH SOUND, EASTERN CHANNEL

Wembury Pt ☆ Oc Y 10s 45m; occas; 50°19'·01N 04°06'·63W.

West Tinker VQ (9) 10s; 50°19'·25N 04°08'·64W.

East Tinker Q (3) 10s; 50°19'·20N 04°08'·30W.

Whidbey Oc (2) WRG 10s 29m, W8M, R/G6M, H24; 000°-G-137·5°-W-139·5°-R-159°; Or and W col; 50°19'·53N 04°07'·27W.

The Breakwater, E head L Fl WR 10s 9m W8M, R6M; 190°-R-353°-W-001°-R-018°-W-190°; 50°20'·01N 04°08'·24W.

Staddon Pt Oc WRG 10s 15m W8M, R/G5M; H24. 348°-G-038°-W-050°-R-090°; W structure, R bands; 50°20'·17N 04°07'·54W.

Withyhedge Dir ☆ 070° (for W Chan): WRG 13m W13M, R/G5M; H24; 060°-FG-065°-Al WG (W phase inc with brg) -069°-FW-071°-Al WR (R phase inc with brg)-075°-F R-080°; W ▽, orange stripe on col. Same col, Fl (2) Bu 5s; vis 120°-160°; 50°20'·75N 04°07'·44W.

SMEATON PASS (W of Mount Batten and S of The Hoe)

Ldg lts 349°. Front, Mallard Shoal Q WRG 5m W10M, R/G3M;

W △, Or bands; 233°-G-043°-R-067°-G-087°-W-099°-R-108°; 50°21'·60N 04°08'·33W. Fog Lt Fl 5s 232°-Fl W-110°. Rear mark: W Hoe Dir ☆ WRG 315·5° W13 R/G5M, 309°-FG-311°-Al WG (W phase inc with brg)-314°-FW-317°-Al WR (R phase inc with brg)-320°-FR-329°; H24; Or ▽; Fog Lt 232°-W-110°. 50°21'·81N 04°08'·39W.

S Mallard VQ (6) + L Fl 10s; 50°21'·51N 04°08'·30W.

W Mallard QG; 50°21'·57N 04°08'·36W.

S Winter Q (6) + L Fl 15s; 50°21'·40N 04°08'·55W.

NE Winter QR; 50°21'·54N 04°08'·50W.

NW Winter VQ (9) 10s; 50°21'·55N 04°08'·70W.

ENTRANCE TO THE CATTEWATER

QAB (Queen Anne's Battery) ldg lts ☆ 048·5°. Front, FR; Or/W bcn; 50°21'·84N 04°07'·84W. Rear, Oc R 8s 14m 3M; 139m NE.

Fishers Nose ☆ Fl (3) R 10s 6m 4M; 50°21'·80N 04°08'·01W. Also F Bu ≠ 026·5° with F Bu 50°22'·00N 04°07'·86W, for Cobbler Chan.

DRAKE CHANNEL, THE BRIDGE and THE NARROWS

Ravenness Dir ☆ 225°: WRG 11m, W13M, R/G5M; vis 217°-FG-221°-Al WG-224° (W phase inc with brg)-FW-226°-Al WR-229° (R phase inc with bearing)-FR-237°; H24; W ▽, Or stripe col; Fog Lt, 160°-FW-305°; 50°21'·14N 04°10'·07W.

Asia Fl (2) R 5s; 50°21'·47N 04°08'·85W.

St Nicholas QR; 50°21'·55N 04°09'·20W.

N Drakes Is Fl R 4s; 50°21'·52N 04°09'·38W.

E Vanguard QG; 50°21'·47N 04°09'·70W.

W Vanguard Fl G 3s; 50°21'·49N 04°09'·98W.

Devils Point QG 5m 3M; Fl 5s in fog; 50°21'·59N 04°10'·04W. Battery Fl R 2s; 50°21'·52N 04°10'·21W.

The Bridge Channel

No 1, QG 4m; 50°21'·03N 04°09'·53W. No 2, QR 4m. No 3, Fl (3) G 10s 4m. No 4, Fl (4) R 10s 4m; 50°21'·09N 04°09'·63W.

Mount Wise, Dir ☆ 343°: WRG 7m, W13M, R/G5M; 331°-FG-338° Al WG (W phase inc with brg) 342°-FW-344°-Al WR (R phase inc with bearing) 348°-FR-351°; H24; Fog Lt, 341·5°-FW-344·5°; 50°21'·96N 04°10'·33W.

Ocean Court Dir ☆ Q WRG 15m, W11M, R/G3M; 010°-G-080°-W-090°-R-100°; 50°21'·85N 04°10'·11W; 992351357.

PLYMOUTH TO START POINT

RIVER YEALM

Sand bar Fl R 5s; 50°18'·59N 04°04'·12W.

SALCOMBE

Sandhill Pt Dir ☆ 000°: Fl WRG 2s 27m W/R/G 8M; 337·5°-G-357·5°-W-002·5°-R-012·5°; R/W ◇ on W mast, rear daymark; 50°13'·77N 03°46'·67W. Front daymark, Pound Stone R/W.

Bass Rk Fl R 5s; 50°13'·47N 03°46'·71W.

Wolf Rk Fl G 5s; 50°13'·53N 03°46'·58W.

Blackstone Rk; 50°13'·61N 03°46'·51W.

Ldg lts 042·5°, front Fl 2s 5m 8M, 50°14'·53N 03°45'·31W; rear Fl 5s 45m 8M.

Start Pt ☆ Fl (3) 10s 62m **18M**; 184°-068°. Same twr: FR 55m 9M; 210°-255° over Skerries Bank; *Horn 30s;* 50°13'·34N 03°38'·54W.

START POINT TO PORTLAND BILL

DARTMOUTH

Kingswear Dir ☆ 328°: Iso WRG 3s 9m 8M; 318°-G-325°-W-331°-R-340°; W ○ twr; 50°20'·81N 03°34'·09W.

Mewstone VQ (6) + L Fl 10s; 50°19'·92N 03°31'·89W.

West Rock Q (6) + L Fl 15s; 50°19'·86N 03°32'·47W.

Homestone QR; 50°19'·61N 03°33'·55W.

Castle Ledge Fl G 5s; 50°19'·99N 03°33'·11W.

Checkstone Fl (2) R 5s; 50°20'·45N 03°33'·81W.

Dir ☆ 104·5°: F WRG 5m 9M; vis 090°-G-102°-W-107°-R-115°; 50°20'·65N 03°33'·80W.

BRIXHAM

Berry Head ☆ Fl (2) 15s 58m **18M**; vis 100°-023°; W twr; 50°23′·98N 03°29′·01W. R lts on radio mast 5·7M NW, inland of Paignton.

Victoria bkwtr ☆ Oc R 15s 9m 6M; W twr; 50°24′·33N 03°30′·78W.

No 1 Fl G; 50°24′·30N 03°30′·89W.

No 2 Fl R; 50°24′·32N 03°30′·83W.

PAIGNTON and TORQUAY

QG (May-Sep); 50°27′·42N 03°31′·80W, 85m off Haldon Pier.

Haldon Pier (E) ☆ QG 9m 6M; 50°27′·43N 03°31′·73W.

Princess Pier (W) ☆ QR 9m 6M; 50°27′·46N 03°31′·73W.

TEIGNMOUTH

Outfall Fl Y 5s; 50°31′·97N 03°27′·77W, 288°/1·3M to hbr ent.

Bar Fl G 2s; 50°32′·44N 03°29′·25W.

Trng wall, middle Oc R 6s 4m 3M; 50°32′·33N 03°29′·93W.

The Point Oc G 6s 3M & FG (vert); 50°32′·42N 03°30′·05W.

RIVER EXE to SIDMOUTH and AXMOUTH

Exe Mo(A) 10s; 50°35′·86N 03°23′·79W.

No 1 50°36′·03N 03°23′·77W.

No 2 50°36′·01N 03°23′·87W.

Exmouth Dir ☆ 305°: WRG 6m, 6M; 299°-Iso G-304°-Iso W-306°-Iso R-311°; W col, 50°36′·99N 03°25′·34W.

No 10 Fl R 3s; 50°36′·73N 03°24′·77W.

No 12 Warren Pt 50°36′·91N 03°25′·41W.

Sidmouth ☆ Fl R 5s 5m 2M; 50°40′·48′N 03°14′·43W.

Axmouth jetty ☆ Fl G 4s 7m 2M; 50°42′·12N 03°03′·29W.

LYME REGIS

Outfall Q (6) + L Fl 15s; 50°43′·17N 02°55′·66W.

Ldg lts 284°: Front, Victoria Pier ☆ Oc WR 8s 6m, W9M, R7M; 284°-R-104°-W-284°; Bu col; 50°43′·19N 02°56′·17W. Rear, FG 8m 9M.

WEST BAY (BRIDPORT)

W pier root, Dir ☆ 336°: F WRG 5m 4M; 165°-G-331°-W-341°-R-165°; 50°42′·62N 02°45′·89W.

W pier outer limit ☆ Iso R 2s 5m 4M; 50°42′·51N 02°45′·83W.

E pier outer limit ☆ Iso G 2s 5m 4M; 50°42′·53N 02°45′·80W.

PORTLAND BILL TO ANVIL POINT

Portland Bill lt ho ☆ Fl (4) 20s 43m **18M**. vis 221°-141°. W ○ twr; *Dia 30s*; 50°30′·85N 02°27′·38W. Same twr, FR 19m 13M; 265°-291° over Shambles.

W Shambles Q (9) 15s; *Bell;* 50°29′·78N 02°24′·41W.

E Shambles Q (3) 10s; *Bell;* 50°31′·26N 02°20′·08W.

PORTLAND HARBOUR

Outer Bkwtr Fort Head (N end) ☆ QR 14m 5M; 013°-268°; 50°35′·11N 02°24′·87W.

NE Bkwtr (A Hd) ☆ Fl 2·5s 22m 10M; 50°35′·16N 02°25′·07W.

NE Bkwtr (B Hd) ☆ Oc R 15s 11m 5M; 50°35′·65N 02°25′·88W.

N Arm (C Hd) ☆ Oc G 10s 11m 5M; 50°35′·78N 02°25′·95W.

WEYMOUTH

Ldg lts 239·6°: both FR 5/7m 7M; Front 50°36′·46N 02°26′·87W, S Pier hd ☆ Q 10m 9M; 50°36′·58N 02°26′·49W. IPTS 190m SW.

LULWORTH RANGE TO ANVIL POINT

Targets: DZ ‘A’ , Fl Y 2s, 50°33′·34N 02°06′·52W.
off DZ ‘B’ , Fl Y 10s, 50°32′·11N 02°05′·92W.
St Alban’s Hd DZ ‘C’ , Fl Y 5s, 50°32′·76N 02°04′·56W.

Anvil Pt ☆ Fl 10s 45m 9M; vis 237°-076° (H24); W ○ twr and dwelling; 50°35'·51N 01°57'·60W. Measured mile close west.

DISTANCE TABLES

Approx distances in nautical miles are by the most direct route allowing for dangers and TSS.

1	Longships	1																
2	Scilly (Crow Rock)	22	2															
3	Penzance	15	35	3														
4	Lizard Point	23	42	16	4													
5	Falmouth	39	60	32	16	5												
6	Mevagissey	52	69	46	28	17	6											
7	Fowey	57	76	49	34	22	7	7										
8	Looe	63	80	57	39	29	16	11	8									
9	Plymouth (bkwtr)	70	92	64	49	39	25	22	11	9								
10	River Yealm (ent)	72	94	66	51	41	27	24	13	4	10							
11	Salcombe	81	102	74	59	50	40	36	29	22	19	11						
12	Start Point	86	103	80	63	55	45	40	33	24	21	7	12					
13	Dartmouth	95	116	88	72	63	54	48	42	35	32	14	9	13				
14	Torbay	101	118	96	78	70	62	55	50	39	36	24	15	11	14			
15	Exmouth	113	131	107	90	82	73	67	61	51	48	33	27	24	12	15		
16	Lyme Regis	126	144	120	104	96	86	81	74	63	60	48	41	35	30	21	16	
17	Portland Bill	135	151	128	112	104	93	89	81	73	70	55	49	45	42	36	22	17

AREA 2 *South Central England – Anvil Point to Selsey Bill*

SELECTED LIGHTS, BUOYS & WAYPOINTS

SWANAGE TO ISLE OF WIGHT

SWANAGE

Pier Hd 2 FR (vert) 6m 3M; 50°36'·56N 01°56'·95W.
Peveril Ledge QR; 50°36'·41N 01°56'·10W.

POOLE BAR and SWASH CHANNEL

Poole Bar (No 1) QG; 50°39·29N 01°55'·14W.
(Historic wreck) Fl Y 5s; 50°39'·70N 01°54'·86W.
No 2 Fl R 2s; 50°39'·23N 01°55'·24W.
No 3 Fl G 3s; 50°39'·76N 01°55'·49W.
No 4 Fl R 2s; 50°39'·72N 01°55'·60W.
Training Bank 2 FR (vert); 50°39'·82N 01°55'·86W.
No 5 Fl G 5s; 50°40'·19N 01°55'·81W.
No 6 Fl R 4s; 50°40'·14N 01°55'·91W.
Hook Sands (No 7) Fl G 3s; 50°40'·50N 01°56'·16W.
Channel (No 8) Fl R 2s; 50°40'·45N 01°56'·27W.
Swash (No 9) Q (9) 15s; 50°40'·88N 01°56'·70W.
No 10 Fl R 4s; 50°40'·84N 01°56'·86W.

EAST LOOE CHANNEL

East Hook 50°40'·58W 01°55'·23W.
East Looe 1 Fl G 5s; 50°41'·09N 01°55'·82W.
East Looe 2 Fl R 4s; 50°41'·07N 01°55'·83W.
East Looe 3 (Limit 10kn) Fl G 3s; 50°41'·07N 01°56'·17W.
East Looe 4 (Limit 10kn) Fl R 2s; 50°41'·05N 01°56'·17W.
North Hook Fl (2) R 5s; 50°40'·97N 01°56'·51W.

BROWNSEA ROADS

No 12 Q R; 50°40'·94N 01°57'·17W.
No14 Fl R 2s; 50°41'·03N 01°57'·32W.
N Haven Q (9) 15s 5m; 50°41'·15N 01°57'·17W.
Brownsea Q (3) 10s; 50°41'·14N 01°57'·39W.
Brownsea Island Dir lt 299°F WRG; 296·5°-G-297·8°-AltWG-298·8°-W-299·2°-AltWR-300·2°-R-301·5°; 50°41'·16N 01°57'·67W (only shown for commercial vessels); 2FR(vert); 301·5°-296·5° (H24).

MIDDLE SHIP CHANNEL

Bell (No 15) Q (6) + L Fl 15s; 50°41'·36N 01°57'·12W.
No 16 VQ R; 50°41'·43N 01°57'·25W.
No 17 Fl G 3s; 50°41'·68N 01°57'·02W.
Aunt Betty (No 22) Q (3)10s; 50°41'·96N 01°57'·39W.
Diver (No 25) Q (9) 15s; 50°42'·29N 01°58'·32W.

NORTH CHANNEL

Salterns Marina Outer Bkwtr Hd 2 FR (vert) 2M; Tfc sigs; 50°42'·23N 01°57'·10W.
Parkstone YC platform Q 8m 1M; 50°42'·37N 01°58'·08W.
Stakes (No 29) Q (6) + L Fl 15s; 50°42'·43N 01°59'·00W.

POOLE BAY

Flag Hd Chine Fl (2); 50°41'·79N 01°55'·10W.
Bournemouth Rocks 50°42'·32N 01°53'·40W.
Christchurch Ledge 50°41'·57N 01°41'·55W (Apr-Oct).
(x2) Fl(5) Y 20s; 50°37'·98N 01°43'·02W; (265°Needles F'wy).

WESTERN APPROACHES TO THE SOLENT

NEEDLES CHANNEL

Needles Fairway L Fl 10s; *Bell*; 50°38'·24N 01°38'·98W.
SW Shingles Fl R 2·5s; 50°39'·29N 01°37'·52W.
Bridge VQ (9) 10s; **Racon (T) 10M**; 50°39'·63N 01°36'·88W.

NEEDLES ☆ 50°39'·73N 01°35'·50W; Oc (2) WRG 20s 24m **W17M**, R14M, R13M G14M; ○ Twr, R band and lantern; vis: shore-R-300°-W-083°-R (unintens)-212°-W-217°-G-224° (H24). *Horn (2) 30s.*

Shingles Elbow Fl (2) R 5s; 50°40'·37N 01°36'·05W.
Mid Shingles Fl (3) R 10s; 50°41'·21N 01°34'·66W.
Warden Fl G 2·5s; *Bell*; 50°41'·48N 01°33'·55W.
NE Shingles Q (3) 10s; 50°41'·96N 01°33'·41W.

Hurst Point ☆ 50°42'·48N 01°33'·03W; FL (4) WR 15s 23m W13M, R11M; W ○ Twr; vis:080°-W(unintens)-104°, 234°-W-244°-R-250°- W-053°. Same structure, Iso WRG 4s 19m **W21M, R18M, G17M**; vis: 038·8°-G-040·8°-W-041·8°-R- 043·8°; By day W7M, R5M, G5M.

NORTH CHANNEL

North Head Fl (3) G 10s; 50°42'·69N 01°35'·52W.

THE WESTERN SOLENT

Note: Numerous yellow yacht racing buoys are laid throughout the Solent (seasonal, Mar-Dec). Most, but not all, are lit Fl Y 4s.

SOLENT MARKS

Sconce Q; *Bell*; 50°42'·53N 01°31'·43W.
Black Rock Fl G 5s; 50°42'·57N 01°30'·59W.
Lymington Bank Fl (2) R 5s; *Bell*; 50°43'·10N 01°30'·85W.
Solent Bank Fl (3) R 10s; 50°44'·23N 01°27'·37W.
Hamstead Ledge Fl (2) G 5s; 50°43'·87N 01°26'18W.
Newtown River Q (9) 15s; 50°43'·75N 01°24'·96W.
W Lepe Fl R 5s; 50°45'·24N 01°24'·09W.
Salt Mead Fl (3) G 10s; 50°44'·51N 01°23'·04W.
Gurnard Ledge Fl (4) G 15s; 50°45'·51N 01°20'·59W.
E Lepe Fl (2) R 5s; *Bell*; 50°45'·93N 01°21'·07W.
Lepe Spit Q (6) + L Fl 15s; 50°46'·78N 01°20'·64W.
Gurnard Q; 50°46'·22N 01°18'·84W.

YARMOUTH

East Fairway Fl R 2s; 50°42'·62N 01°29'·95W.
Poole Belle Fl Y 5s; 50°42'·54N 01°30'·17W.
Pier Head, centre, 2 FR (vert) 2M; G col. High intensity FW (occas); 50°42'·51N 01°29'·97W.
Ldg Lts 187·6° Front FG 5m 2M; 50°42'·36N 01°30'·06 W. Rear, 63m from front, FG 9m 2M; both W ◇.

LYMINGTON

Ldg Lts 319·5°, Or posts. Front, FR 12m 8M; 50°45'·19N 01°31'·65W. vis: 309·5°-329·5°. Rear, FR 17m 8M.
Jack in the Basket Fl R 2s 9m; 50°44'·27N 01°30'·57W.
No 1 Fl G 2s 2m 3M; G △ on pile; 50°44'·41N 01°30'·48W.
No 2 (Cross Boom) Fl R 2s 4m 3M; 50°44'·36N 01°30'·58W.
Yacht Haven ldg lts 244°. Front FY 4m; R △; 50°45'·09N 01°31'·53W. Rear, 22m from front, FY 6m; R ▽.

BEAULIEU RIVER

Millennium Dir lt 334°. Oc WRG 4s 13m W4M, R3M, G3M; vis: 318°-G-330°-W-337°-R-348°; 50°47'·12N 01°21'·90W.
Beaulieu Spit E Fl R 5s 3M; R dolphin; 50°46'·85N 01°21'·76W.

No 1 50°46′·91N 01°21′·70W.
No 2 50°46′·92N 01°21′·78W.

COWES

Prince Consort VQ; 50°46′·41N 01°17′·56W.
Trinity House Fl Y 5s; 50°46′·31N 01°17′·75W.
No 1 Q G; 50°46′·07N 01°18′·03W.
No 2 Q R; 50°46′·07N 01°17′·87W.
No 2A LFl R 10s; 50°45′·92N 01°17′·70W.
No 4A Tide gauge L Fl R 5s; 50°45′·76N 01°17′·63W.
EC 11 Q (6) + L Fl 15s; 50°45′·80N 01°17′·67W.
E Cowes Bkwtr Hd 2F R; 50°45′·88N 01°17′·52W.
EC 8 Fl R 4s; 50°45′·87N 01°17′·58W.
EC 7 Fl G 4s; 50°45′·90N 01°17′·60W.
EC 3 Q (3) 10s; 50°45′·99N 01°17′·51W.
EC 2 Fl R 3s; 50°46′·06N 01°17′·04W.
EC 1 Fl G 3s; 50°46′·08N 01°17′·05W.
Shrape Bn LFl R 10S 3m 3M; 50°46′·09N 01°16′·90W.

CENTRAL SOLENT AND SOUTHAMPTON WATER

Note: Numerous yellow yacht racing buoys are laid throughout the Solent (seasonal, Mar-Dec). Most, but not all, are lit Fl Y 4s.

SOLENT MARKS

Lepe Spit Q(6) + L Fl 15s; 50°46′·78N 01°20′·64W.
NE Gurnard Fl(3) R 10s; 50°47′·06N 01°19′·42W.
South Bramble Fl G 2·5s; 50°46′·98N 01°17′·72W.
W Bramble VQ(9) 10s; **Racon (T) 3M**; 50°47′·20N 01°18′·65W; AIS.
Thorn Knoll Fl G 5s; 50°47′·50N 01°18′·44W.
Bourne Gap Fl R 3s; 50°47′·83N 01°18′·34W.
West Knoll Fl Y 2·5s; 50°47′·43N 01°17′·84W.
North Thorn QG; 50°47′·92N 01°17′·84W.
East Knoll Fl(2) G 10s; 50°47′·96N 01°16′·86W.
Stanswood Outfall Iso R 10s 6m 5M; 4 FR Lts; 50°48′·26N 01°18′·82W.

CALSHOT REACH

East Knoll 50°47′·96N 01°16′·83W.
CALSHOT SPIT Fl 5s 5m 10M; R hull, Lt Twr amidships; *Horn (2) 60s*; 50°48′·35N 01°17′·64W.
Calshot VQ; 50°48′·44N 01°17′·03W.
Castle Point IQ R 10s; 50°48′·71N 01°17′·67W.
Reach Fl (3) G 10s; 50°49′·05N 01°17′·65W.
Black Jack Fl (2) R 4s; 50°49′·13N 01°18′·09W.
Hook QG; *Horn (1) 15s*; 50°49′·52N 01°18′·30W.
Coronation Fl Y 5s; 50°49′·55N 01°17′·62W.
Bald Head Fl G 2·5s; 50°49′·80N 01°18′·06W.

RIVER HAMBLE

Hamble Pt Q (6) + L Fl 15s; 50°50′·15N 01°18′·66W.
Hamble Common Dir 351·7°, Oc (2) WRG 12s 5m W4M; R4M; G4M; vis: 348·7°-G-350·7°-W-352·7°-R-354·7°; 50°51′·00N 01°18′·84W.
Sailing Club Dir lt 028·9° Iso WRG 6s 5m W4M, R4M, G4M: vis: 025·9°-G-027·9°-W-029·9°-R-031·9°; 50°51′·10N 01°18′·34W.

SOUTHAMPTON WATER

Fawley Terminal SE 2 FR(vert) 9m 10M; 50°50′·06N 01°19′·42W.
Fawley Deep Fl (2) G 4s; 50°50′·42N 01°19′·19W.
Greenland Iso G 2s; 50°51′·11N 01°20′·38W.
Cadland Fl R 3s; 50°51′·02N 01°20′·54W.
After Barn Fl (2) G 4s; 50°51′·53N 01°20′·81W.
Lains Lake Fl (2) R 4s; 50°51′·59N 01°21′·65W.
Hound Fl (3) G 10s; 50°51′·68N 01°21′·52W.
Netley Fl G 3s; 50°52′·03N 01°21′·81W.
Deans Elbow Oc R 4s; 50°52′·20N 01°22′·85W.
NW Netley Q G; 50°52′·31N 01°22′·73W.
Moorhead Q G; 50°52′·55N 01°22′·90W.
Test Fl (2) R 4s; 50°52′·59N 01°23′·45W.
Weston Shelf Fl (2) G 4s; 50°52′·71N 01°23′·26W.

HYTHE

Hythe Pier Hd 2 FR (vert) 12m 5M; 50°52′·49N 01°23′·61W.
Hythe Marina Ent Q (3) 10s; 50°52′·63N 01°23′·88W.
Hythe Knock Fl R 3s; 50°52′·83N 01°23′·81W.

SOUTHAMPTON and RIVER ITCHEN

Swinging Ground No 1 Oc G 4s; 50°53′·00N 01°23′·44W.
E side. No 1 QG; 50°53′·15N 01°23′·40W.
No 2 Fl G 5s 2M; 50°53′·29N 01°23′·38W.
No 3 Fl G 7s; 50°53′·48N 01°23′·28W.
No 4 QG 4m 2M; 50°53′·62N 01°23′·16W.

SOUTHAMPTON and RIVER TEST

QE II Terminal, S end 4 FG (vert) 16m 3M; 50°53′·00N 01°23′·71W.
Gymp QR; 50°53′·07N 01°24′·16W.
Town Quay Ldg Lts 329°, both F 12/22m 3/2M.
Gymp Elbow Oc R 4s; 50°53′·43N 01°24′·61W.
Dibden Bay Q; 50°53′·70N 01°24′·92W.

THE EASTERN SOLENT

Note: Numerous yellow yacht racing buoys are laid throughout the Solent (seasonal, Mar-Dec). Most, but not all, are lit Fl Y 4s.

SOLENT MARKS

West Ryde Middle Q (9) 15s; 50°46′·48N 01°15′·79W.
Norris Fl (3) R 10s; 50°45′·97N 01°15′·51W.
North Ryde Middle Fl (4) R 20s; 50°46′·61N 01°14′·31W.
South Ryde Middle Fl G 5s; 50°46′·13N 01°14′·16W.
Peel Bank Fl (2) R 5s; 50°45′·49N 01°13′·35W.
SE Ryde Middle VQ (6)+L Fl 10s; 50°45′·93N 01°12′·10W.
NE Ryde Middle Fl (2) R 10s; 50°46′·21N 01°11′·88W.
Mother Bank Fl R 3s; 50°45′·49N 01°11′·21W.
Browndown Fl G 15s; 50°46′·57N 01°10′·95W.
Fort Gilkicker Oc G 10s 7M; 50°46′·43N 01°08′·47W.
N Sturbridge VQ; 50°45′·33N 01°08′·23W.
Ryde Sands Fl R 10s; 50°44′·56N 01°07′·26W.
Ryde Sands L Fl R 12s; 50°44′·16N 01°05′·99W.
No Man's Land Fort Iso R 2s 21m 5M; 50°44′·40N 01°05′·70W.
Horse Sand Fort Iso G 2s 21m 5M; 50°45′·01N 01°04′·34W.
Saddle VQ (3) G 10s; 50°45′·05N 01°04′·94W.

NORTH CHANNEL and HILLHEAD

Calshot VQ; *Bell (1) 30s*; 50°48′·44N 01°17′·03W.
Hillhead Fl R 2·5s; 50°48′·07N 01°16′·00W.
E Bramble VQ (3) 5s; 50°47′·23N 01°13′·64W.

WOOTTON CREEK

Wootton Beacon Q 1M; (NB); 50°44′·53N 01°12′·16W.
Dir lt Oc WRG 10s vis: 220·8°-G-224·3°-W-225·8°-R-230·8°; 50°44′·03N 01°12′·86W.

RYDE

Ryde Pier 2 FR (vert) mark corners. In fog FY from N corner, vis: 045°-165°, 200°-320°; 50°44′·34N 01°09′·72W.

Leisure Hbr E side 2 FR (vert) 7m 1M. FY 6m shown when depth of water in Hbr greater than 1m; 2 FY 6m when depth exceeds 1·5m; 50°43′·99N 01°09′·29W.

PORTSMOUTH APPROACHES

Horse Sand Fl G 2·5s; 50°45′·62N 01°05′·12W.
Outer Spit (OSB) Q (6) + L Fl 15s; 50°45′·44N 01°05′·46W.
Mary Rose Fl Y 5s; 50°45′·80N 01°06′·22W.
Boyne Fl G 5s; 50°46′·04N 01°05′·26W.
Spit Refuge Fl R 5s; 50°46′·21N 01°05′·68W.
Spit Sand Fort Fl R 5s; 18m 5M. 50°46′·24N 01°05′·94W.
Castle Fl (2) G 6s; 50°46′·50N 01°05′·40W.
Southsea S Castle Pile Dir 348° WRG 17m 11M day 6M, pile vis: 340°-FG-343°-Al WG (W phase inc with brg)-347°-FW-349°-AlWR(R phase incr with brg)-354°-FR-356°; H24; same structure Fl G 5s; 50°46′·66N 01°05′·65W.
No 1 Bar (NB) Fl (3) G 10s; 50°46′·77N 01°05′·81W.
No 2 Fl (3) R 10s; 50°46′·66N 01°06′·15W.
No 3 QG; 50°47′·08N 01°06′·23W.
No 4 QR; 50°46′·98N 01°06′·48W.
BC Outer Oc R 15s; 50°47′·32N 01°06′·68W.

PORTSMOUTH HARBOUR

Fort Blockhouse Dir 323° WRG 4s 6m WRG 12M; vis: 313°- Oc G-317°-Fl G (phase dec with brg)-321°-Oc W-325°-Fl R (phase inc with brg)-329°-Oc R-333°; 50°47′·37N 01°06′·74W.
Ballast Fl R 2·5s; 50°47′·62N 01°06′·83W.
Hbr Ent Dir 333·75° WRG 2s 2m 12M; vis: 323·75°-Iso G-329·75°-Fl G (phase dec with brg)-332·75°-Iso (main chan)-334·75°-Fl R (phase inc with brg)-337·75°-Iso R-343·75°; H24; same structure Fuel Jetty 2F R (vert) 8m 4M; 50°47′·85N 01°06′·98W.

EASTERN APPROACHES to THE SOLENT

Outer Nab 1 VQ (9) 10s; 50°38′·18N 00°56′·88W.
Outer Nab 2 VQ (3) 5s; 50°38′·43N 00°57′·70W.
Nab Tower Fl 10s 17m 12M; *Horn (2) 30s; RACON T;* 50°40′·08N 00°57′·15W; 992351136.
N 2 Fl Y 2·5s. 6M; 50°41′·03N 00°56′·74W.
N 1 Fl Y (4)10s; 50°41′·26N 00°56′·52W.
N 4 Fl Y 7·5s; 50°41′·86N 00°57′·24W.
N 3 Fl (3) Y 15s; 50°41′·63N 00°56′·74W.
N 5 Fl Y 5s; 50°41′·99N 00°56′·97W.
N 7 Fl Y 2·5s; 50°42′·35N 00°57′·20W.
New Grounds VQ (3) 5s; 50°41′·84N 00°58′·49W.
Nab End Fl R 5s; *Whis*; 50°42′·63N 00°59′·49W.
Dean Tail Fl G 5s; 50°42′·99N 00°59′·17W.
Dean Tail S VQ (6) + L Fl 10s; 50°43′·04N 00°59′·58W.
Dean Tail N Q; 50°43′·13N 00°59′·57W.
Horse Tail Fl (2) G 10s; 50°43′·23N 01°00′·23W.
Nab East Fl (2) R 10s; 50°42′·86N 01°00′·80W.
Dean Elbow Fl (3) G 15s; 50°43′·69N 01°01′·88W.
St Helens Fl (3) R 15s; 50°43′·36N 01°02′·41W.
Horse Elbow QG; 50°44′·26N 01°03′·88W.
Cambrian Wreck 50°44′·43N 01°03′·43W.
Warner QR; *Whis*; 50°43′·87N 01°03′·99W.

BEMBRIDGE

St Helen's Fort (IOW) Fl (3) 10s 16m 5M; large ○ stone structure; 50°42′·30N 01°05′·05W.

SOUTH EAST COAST of the ISLE OF WIGHT

St Catherine's Point 50°34′·54N 01°17′·87W; Fl 5s 41m **18M**; vis: 257°-117°; FR 35m 13M (same Twr) vis: 099°-116°.
Ventnor Haven W Bwtr 2 FR (vert) 3M; 50°35′·50N 01°12′·30W.
Sandown Pier Hd 2 FR (vert) 7m 2M; 50°39′·05N 01°09′·18W.
W Princessa Q (9) 15s; 50°40′·16N 01°03′·65W.
Bembridge Ledge Q (3) 10s; 50°41′·15N 01°02′·81W

LANGSTONE and APPROACHES

Eastney Pt Fraser Trials Range FR, Oc (2) Y 10s, and FY Lts (occas) when firing taking place; 50°47′·19N 01°02′·22W.
Winner ; 50°45′·10N 01°00′·10W.
Roway Wk Fl (2) 5s; 50°46′·11N 01°02′·28W.
Langstone Fairway L Fl 10s; 50°46′·32N 01°01′·36W.
Eastney Pt Outfall QR 2m 2M; 50°47′·23N 01°01′·68W.
East Milton Fl (4) R 10s; 50°48′·16N 01°01′·76W.
NW Sinah Fl G 5s; 50°48′·14N 01°01′·58W.

DISTANCE TABLES

Approx distances in nautical miles are by the most direct route allowing for dangers and TSS.

1	Portland Bill	1																	
2	Weymouth	8	2																
3	Swanage	23	22	3															
4	Poole Hbr ent	28	26	6	4														
5	Needles Lt Ho	35	34	14	14	5													
6	Lymington	42	40	21	21	7	6												
7	Yarmouth (IOW)	40	39	19	19	6	2	7											
8	Beaulieu River ent	46	45	25	25	12	7	7	8										
9	Cowes	49	46	28	28	15	9	9	3	9									
10	Southampton	55	54	34	34	21	15	15	9	9	10								
11	R. Hamble (ent)	53	51	32	32	19	12	12	6	6	4	11							
12	Portsmouth	58	57	37	37	24	18	18	11	9	18	15	12						
13	Langstone Hbr	61	59	40	40	27	22	22	15	12	16	13	5	13					
14	Chichester Bar	63	62	42	42	29	24	24	17	15	20	17	8	5	14				
15	Bembridge	59	58	38	38	25	19	19	12	10	19	15	6	6	8	15			
16	Nab Tower	60	63	39	39	30	25	25	18	16	21	18	10	7	6	6	16		
17	St Catherine's Pt	45	44	25	25	14	18	18	27	25	30	27	19	20	19	17	15	17	
18	Littlehampton	79	79	60	61	46	44	45	38	36	41	38	31	27	24	28	22	35	18

CHICHESTER ENTRANCE
West Pole (tripod) Fl R 5s 14m 7M; 50°45'·45N 00°56'·59W.
Bar Fl(2) R 10s 10m 4M; 50°46'·02N 00°56'·37W.
Eastoke QR; 50°46'·68N 00°56'·11W.
West Winner QG; Tide gauge. 50°46'·88N 00°55'·98W.

EMSWORTH CHANNEL
Fishery Q (6) + L Fl 15s; 50°47'·38N 00°56'·07W.
NW Pilsey Fl G 5s; 50°47'·50N 00°56'·20W.
Verner Fl R 10s; 50°48'·20N 00°56'·63W.
Marker Pt Fl (2) G 10s 8m; 50°48'·91N 00°56'·72W.
Emsworth Q (6) + L Fl 15s; tide gauge; 50°49'·66N 00°56'·76W.

THORNEY CHANNEL
Camber Q (6) + L Fl 15s; 50°47'·87N 00°54'·06W.
Pilsey Fl (2) R 10s ; 50°47'·98N 00°54'·24W.
Thorney Fl G 5s; 50°48'·20N 00°54'·28W.

CHICHESTER CHANNEL
NW Winner Fl G 10s; 50°47'·19N 00°55'·92W.
N Winner Fl (2) G 10s; 50°47'·31N 00°55'·83W.
Mid Winner Fl (3) G 10s; 50°47'·40N 00°55'·72W.
Stocker Fl (3) R 10s; 50°47'·45N 00°55'·52W.
Copyhold Fl (4) R 10s; 50°47'·50N 00°54'·93W.
East Head Spit Fl (4) G 10s; 50°47'·45N 00°54'·82W.
Snowhill Fl G 5s; 50°47'·52N 00°54'·34W.
Sandhead Fl R 10s; 50°47'·67N 00°54'·25W.
Chalkdock Fl (2) G 10s; 50°48'·49N 00°53'·30W.

AREA 3 *South East England – Selsey Bill to North Foreland*

SELECTED LIGHTS, BUOYS & WAYPOINTS

OWERS TO BEACHY HEAD

SELSEY BILL and THE OWERS
S Pullar VQ (6) + L Fl 10s; 50°38'·84N 00°49'·29W.
Pullar Q (9) 15s; 50°40'·47N 00°50'·09W.
Boulder Fl G 2·5s; 50°41'·56N 00°49'·09W.
Street QR; 50°41'·69N 00°48'·89W.
Mixon Bn Q(6) + L Fl 15s; 50°42'·37N 00°46'·32E.
Owers Q (6) + L Fl 15s; *Bell*; **Racon (O) 10M**; 50°38'·59N 00°41'·09W.
E Borough Hd Q (3) 10s *Bell;* 50°41'·54N 00°39'·09W.

LITTLEHAMPTON
West Pier Hd QR 7m 6M; 50°47'·88N 00°32'·46W.
Training Wall Hd QG 10m 2M; 50°47'·87N 00°32'·38W.
Ldg lts 346°. Front, E Pier Hd ☆ FG 6m 7M; B col. Rear, 64m from front, Oc W 7·5s 9m10M; W twr; vis: 290°-W-042°; 50°48'·09N 00°32'·51W.
Outfall Fl Y 5s; 50°46'·27N 00°30'·53W.
Littlehampton ☆ Fl (5) Y 20s 9m 5M; 50°46'·19N 00°29'·54W.

WORTHING and SHOREHAM
Met Mast ☆ Fl Y 5s 12m 2M; 50°41'·29N 00°20'·59W.
Outfall Fl R 2·5s 3m; 50°48'·38N 00°20'·34W.
Express Fl Y 5s; (Apr-Oct); 50°47'·28N 00°17'·09W.
W Bkwtr Head ☆ Fl R 5s 7m 7M; 50°49'·49N 00°14'·89W.
Ldg Lts 355°. Middle Pier Front, Oc 5s 8m 10M; W watch-house, R base; tidal Lts, tfc sigs; *Horn 20s*. Rear, 192m from front, Fl 10s 12m 10M; Gy twr vis: 283°-103°; 50°49'·85N 00°14'·89W.
Outfall 50°49'·47N 00°14'·39W.
Shoreham Outfall Q (6) + L Fl 15s; 50°47'·88N 00°13'·72W.

BRIGHTON and BRIGHTON MARINA
Black Rk Ledge Fl Y 4s; 50°48'·07N 00°06'·46W.
W Bkwtr Hd ☆ QR 10m 7M; W ○ structure, R bands; *Horn (2) 30s*; 50°48'·50N 00°06'·38W.
E Bkwtr Hd ☆ QG 8m 7M.
Saltdean Outfall Fl Y 5s; 50°46'·72N 00°02'·13W.

NEWHAVEN
Bkwtr Head ☆ Oc (2) 10s 17m 12M; 50°46'·56N 00°03'·50E.
E Pier Hd ☆ Iso G 10s 12m 6M; W twr; 50°46'·81N 00°03'·59E.

OFFSHORE MARKS
CS 1 Fl Y 2·5s; *Whis*; 50°33'·69N 00°03'·92W.
GREENWICH 50°24'·54N 00°00'·10E; Fl 5s 12m **15M**; Riding light FW; R hull; **Racon (M) 10M**; *Horn 30s*; 992351032.
CS 2 Fl Y 5s; 50°39'·14N 00°32'·60E.
CS 3 Fl Y 10s; 50°52'·04N 01°02'·18E.

BEACHY HEAD TO DUNGENESS

Beachy Head ☆ 50°44'·03N 00°14'·49E; Fl (2) 20s 31m **16M**; W round twr, R band and lantern; vis: 248°-101°; (H24).
Royal Sovereign Q(6) + L Fl 15s; 50°43'·34N 00°26'·10E, AIS.
Royal Sovereign QR; 50°44'·23N 00°25'·84E.

EASTBOURNE and SOVEREIGN HARBOUR
SH L Fl 10s; 50°47'·40N 00°20'·71E.
Martello Tower ☆ Fl (3) 15s 12m 7M.; 50°47'·24N 00°19'·83E.
Dir lt 258° Fl WRG 5s 4m 1M; vis: 254°-G-257°-W-259°-R-262°; 50°47'·28N 00°19'·71E.
S Bkwtr Hd ☆ Fl (4) R 12s 3m 6M; 50°47'·30N 00°20'·03E.
St Leonard's Outfall Fl Y 5s; 50°49'·31N 00°31'·95E.

HASTINGS
Ldg Lts 356·3°. Front, FR 14m 4M; 50°51'·29N 00°35'·38E.
Rear, West Hill, 357m from front, FR 55m 4M; W twr.

RYE
Rye Fairway, L Fl 10s; 50°54'·04N 00°48'·04E.
W Groyne Hd No 2 ☆ LFl R 7s 7m 6M; 50°55'·58N 00°46'·55E; 992351156.
E Arm Hd No 1 Q (9) 15s 7m 5M; G △; *Horn 7s*; 50°55'·73N 00°46'·46E.
Dungeness Outfall Q (6) + L Fl 15s; 50°54'·45N 00°58'·21E.
Dungeness ☆ 50°54'·81N 00°58'·56E; Fl 10s 40m **21M**; B ○ twr, W bands and lantern, floodlit; Part obsc 078°-shore; (H24). F RG 37m 10M (same twr); vis: 057°-R-073°-G-078°-196°-R-216°; *Horn (1) 30s*; FR Lts shown between 2·4M and 5·2M WNW when firing taking place. QR on radio mast 1·2M NW.

DUNGENESS TO NORTH FORELAND

FOLKESTONE

Hythe Flats Outfall Fl Y 5s; 51°02′·52N 01°05′·32E.

Breakwater Head ☆ Fl (2) 10s 14m **22M**; vis: 210°-W-090°; 51°04′·56N 01°11′·69E.

DOVER

Admiralty Pier Extension Head ☆ 51°06′·69N 01°19′·66E; Fl 7·5s 21m **20M**; W twr; vis: 096°-090°, obsc in The Downs by S Foreland inshore of 226°; *Horn 10s;* Int Port Tfc sigs.

S Bkwtr W Hd ☆ 51°06′·78N 01°19′·80E;Oc R 30s 21m **18M**; W twr.

Knuckle ☆ 51°07′·04N 01°20′·49E; Fl (4) WR 10s 15m **W15M**, R13M; W twr; vis: 059°-R-239°-W-059°.

N Head ☆ Fl R 2·5s 11m 5M; 51°07′·20N 01°20′·61E.

EasternArmHd☆FlG5s12m5M;*Horn(2)30s;*Intporttfcsigs; 51°07′·31N 01°20′·59E.

DOVER STRAIT

Bullock Bank VQ; 50°46′·94N 01°07′·60E.

Ridens SE VQ (3) 5s; 50°43′·47N 01°18′·87E.

Colbart SW VQ (6) + L Fl 10s; 50°48′·86N 01°16′·30E.

South Varne Q (6) + L Fl 15s; 50°55′·64N 01°17′·30E.

Mid Varne VQ(9)10s; 50°58′·94N 01°19′·88E.

East Varne VQ(3)5s; 50°58′·22N 01°20′·90E.

Colbart N VQ; 50°57′·45N 01°23′·29E.

Varne NW Q; 51°00′·80N 01°22′·70E.

Varne NE Q (3) 10s; 50°59′·80N 01°22′·70E.

VARNE 51°01′·29N 01°23′·90E; Fl R 5s 12m **15M**; **Racon (T) 10M**; *Horn 30s*; 992351038.

CS 4 Fl (4) Y 15s; 51°08′·62N 01°33′·92E.

MPC Fl Y 2·5s; **Racon (O) 10M**; 51°06′·12N 01°38′·20E; 992351122.

SW Goodwin Q (6) + LFl 15s; 51°08′·50N 01°28′·88E; 992351036.

S Goodwin Fl (4) R 15s; 51°10′·60N 01°32′·26E.

SE Goodwin Fl (3) R 10s; 51°12′·99N 01°34′·45E.

E GOODWIN 51°13′·26N 01°36′·37E; Fl 15s 12m **23M**; R hull with lt twr amidships; **Racon (T) 10M**; *Horn 30s*; 992351035.

E Goodwin Q (3) 10s; 51°15′·67N 01°35′·69E.

NE Goodwin Q(3) 10s; **Racon (M) 10M**. 51°20′·31N 01°34′·16E.

DEAL and THE DOWNS

Trinity Bay VQ(9) 10s; 51°11′·60N 01°29′·00E.

Deal Bank QR; 51°12′·92N 01°25′·57E.

Goodwin Fork Q(6) + L Fl 15s; *Bell;* 51°14′·38N 01°26′·70E.

Downs Fl (2) R 5s; *Bell;* 51°14′·50N 01°26′·22E.

GULL STREAM

W Goodwin Fl G 5s; 51°15′·61N 01°27′·38E.

S Brake Fl (3) R 10s; 51°15′·77N 01°26′·82E.

NW Goodwin Q (9) 15s; 51°16′·72N 01°28′·47E.

Brake Fl (4) R 15s; 51°16′·98N 01°28′·19E.

N Goodwin Fl G 2·5s; 51°16′·74N 01°28′·40E.

Gull Stream QR; 51°18′·26N 01°29′·69E.

Gull VQ (3) 5s; 51°19′·57N 01°31′·30E.

Goodwin Knoll Fl (2) G 5s; 51°19′·57N 01°32′·20E.

RAMSGATE CHANNEL

B2 Fl (2) G 5s; 51°18′·26N 01°23′·93E.

W Quern Q (9) 15s; 51°18′·98N 01°25′·39E.

RAMSGATE

RA Q(6) + L Fl 15s; 51°19′·60N 01°30′·13E.

E Brake Fl R 5s; 51°19′·47N 01°29′·20E.

No 1 QG; 51°19′·56N 01°27′·29E.

No 2 Fl (4) R 10s; 51°19′·46N 01°27′·28E.

No 3 Fl G 2·5s; 51°19′·56N 01°26′·61E.

No 4 QR; 51°19′·46N 01°26′·60E.

N Quern Q; 51°19′·41N 01°26′·11E.

No 5 Q (6) + L Fl 15s; 51°19′·56N 01°25′·91E.

No 6 Fl (2) R 5s; 51°19′·46N 01°25′·91E.

South Bkwtr Hd VQ R 10m 5M; 51°19′·46N 01°25′·41E.

N Bkwtr Hd QG 10m 5M; 51°19′·56N 01°25′·47E.

W Marine Terminal Dir lt 270°, Oc WRG 10s 10m 5M; B △ Or stripe; vis: 259°-G-269°-W-271°-R-281°; 51°19′·51N 01°24′·85E. Rear 493m fm front Oc 5s 17m 5M; B ▽ Or stripe; vis: 263°-278°.

BROADSTAIRS and NORTH FORELAND

Broadstairs Knoll Fl R 2·5s; 51°20′·88N 01°29′·48E.

Pier SE End ☆ 2 FR (vert) 7m 4M; 51°21′·50N 01°26′·74E.

Elbow Q; 51°23′·23N 01°31′·59E.

North Foreland ☆ 51°22′·49N 01°26′·70E; Fl (5) WR 20s 57m **W19M, R16M, R15M**; W 8-sided twr; vis: shore-W-150°-R(**16M**)-181°-R(**15M**)-200°-W-011°; H24; 992351020.

1	Nab Tower	**1**																
2	Boulder Lt Buoy	5	**2**															
3	Owers Lt Buoy	10	6	**3**														
4	Littlehampton	19	13	12	**4**													
5	Shoreham	32	24	21	13	**5**												
6	Brighton	35	28	24	17	5	**6**											
7	Newhaven	40	34	29	24	12	7	**7**										
8	Beachy Head Lt	46	41	36	30	20	14	8	**8**									
9	Eastbourne	51	45	40	34	24	19	12	7	**9**								
10	Rye	72	67	62	56	46	41	34	25	23	**10**							
11	Dungeness Lt	76	71	66	60	50	44	38	30	26	9	**11**						
12	Folkestone	92	84	81	76	65	60	53	43	40	23	13	**12**					
13	Dover	97	89	86	81	70	65	58	48	45	28	18	5	**13**				
14	Ramsgate	112	104	101	96	85	80	73	63	60	43	33	20	15	**14**			
15	N Foreland Lt	115	107	104	99	88	83	76	66	63	46	36	23	18	3	**15**		
16	Sheerness	146	139	135	132	119	114	107	97	96	79	67	54	49	34	31	**16**	
17	London Bridge	188	184	177	177	161	156	149	139	141	124	109	96	91	76	73	45	**17**

DISTANCE TABLES

Approx distances in nautical miles are by the most direct route allowing for dangers and TSS.

OFFSHORE MARKS

SANDETTIE 51°09'·36N 01°47'·12E; Fl 5s 12m **15M**; R hull with lt twr amidships; *Racon; Horn 30s;* 992351029.
F1 Fl (4) Y 15s; 51°11'·21N 01°44'·91E.
South Falls Q (6) + L Fl 15s; 51°13'·84N 01°43'·93E.
Sandettie W Fl (3) G 12s; 51°15'·09N 01°54'·47E.
Mid Falls Fl (3) R 10s; 51°18'·63N 01°46'·99E.
Inter Bank Fl Y 5s; *Bell;* **Racon (M) 10M**; 51°16'·47N 01°52'·23E. F2 Fl (4) Y 15s; 51°20'·41N 01°56'·19E.

AREA 4 *East England – North Foreland to Berwick-upon-Tweed*

SELECTED LIGHTS, BUOYS & WAYPOINTS

THAMES ESTUARY – SOUTHERN

(Direction of buoyage generally East to West)

APPROACHES to THAMES ESTUARY

Foxtrot 3 51°24'·15N 02°00'·38E; Fl 10s 12m **15M**; **Racon (T) 10M**; *Horn 10s;* 992351033.
Falls Hd Q; 51°28'·23N 01°49'·89E.
Drill Stone Q (3) 10s; 51°25'·88N 01°42'·89E.
Thanet N VQ 15s; 51°28'·28N 01°38'·06E.
NE Spit VQ (3) **Racon (T) 10M**; 51°27'·93N 01°29'·89E; 992351037
East Margate Fl R 2·5s; 51°27'·03N 01°26'·40E.
Elbow Q; 51°23'·23N 01°31'·59E.
Foreness Pt Outfall Fl R 5s; 51°24'·58N 01°26'·12E.
Longnose 51°24'·15N 01°26'·08E.
Longnose Spit Fl R 2·5s 5m 2M; 51°23'·93N 01°25'·68E.

MARGATE and GORE CHANNEL

SE Margate Q (3) 10s; 51°24'·05N 01°20'·40E.
S Margate Fl G 2·5s; 51°23'·83N 01°16'·65E.
Copperas QG; 51°23'·81N 01°11'·18E.
Reculver QR; 51°23'·63N 01°12'·56E.

HERNE BAY

Beltinge Bay Bn Fl Y 5s; 51°22'·73N 01°08'·63E.
Landing Stage ☆ Q 18m 4M, (isolated); 51°22'·91N 01°06'·89E.
N Pier Hd ☆ 2 FR (vert); 51°22'·43N 01°07'·27E.

WHITSTABLE

Whitstable Street ; 51°24'·00N 01°01'·54E.
Oyster Fl (2) R 10s; 51°22'·14N 01°01'·16E.
W Quay Dn ☆ Fl G 5s 2m.

THE SWALE

Whitstable Street Fl R 2s; 51°24'·00N 01°01'·54E.
Columbine Fl G 2s; 51°24'·26N 01°01'·34E.
Columbine Spit Fl (3) G 10s; 51°23'·86N 01°00'·03E.
Ham Gat Q G; 51°23'·08N 00°58'·32E.
Pollard Spit Q R; 51°22'·98N 00°58'·57E.
Sand End Fl G 5s; 51°21'·43N 00°55'·90E.
Receptive Point Fl G 10s; 51°20'·86N 00°54'·41E.
Queenborough Spit Q (3) 10s; 51°25'·81N 00°43'·93E.
South Oaze Fl R 2s; 51°21'·34N 00°56'·01E.

QUEENS CHANNEL and FOUR FATHOMS CHANNEL

E Margate Fl R 2·5s; 51°27'·03N 01°26'·40E.
Spaniard Q (3) 10s; 51°26'·23N 01°04'·00E.
Spile Fl G 2·5s; 51°26'·43N 00°55'·70E.

PRINCES CHANNEL

Tongue Sand E VQ (3) 5s; 51°29'·48N 01°22'·21E.
Tongue Sand N Q; 51°29'·68N 01°22'·03E.
Princes Outer VQ (6) + L Fl 10s; 51°28'·79N 01°19'·87E.
Princes North Q G; 51°29'·25N 01°18'·35E.
Princes South Q R; 51°28'·74N 01°18'·26E.
Princes No 1 Fl (4) G 15s; 51°29'·23N 01°16'·02E.
Princes No 2 Fl (2) R 5s; 51°28'·81N 01°13'·08E.
Princes No 3 Fl (2) G 5s; 51°29'·33N 01°13'·10E.
Princes No 4 Fl (3) R 10s; 51°28'·83N 01°09'·90E.
Princes No 5 Fl (3) G 10s; 51°29'·39N 01°10'·00E.
Princes Mid Fl Y 5s; 51°29'·19N 01°09'·00E.
Shivering Sand Twr N Q; 51°30'·01N 01°04'·76E.
Shivering Sand Twr S Q (6)+L Fl 15s; *Bell*; 51°29'·75N 01°04'·83E.
Princes No 8 Fl (2) R 5s; 51°29'·14N 01°03'·00E.
Princes Inner Fl Y 2·5s; 51°29'·59N 01°03'·47E.

FOULGER'S GAT and KNOB CHANNEL

N Edinburgh Channel is not buoyed. Foulger's Gat, lies within the boundary of the London Array Wind Farm.
Long Sand Outer Iso 2s; 51°34'·61N 01°28'·34E.
Long Sand Middle Iso 5s; 51°35'·60N 01°26'·45E.
Long Sand Inner Iso 2s; 51°38'·78N 01°25'·44E.
SE Knob Fl G 5s; 51°30'·89N 01°06'·41E.
Knob Iso 5s; *Whis*; 51°30'·69N 01°04'·28E.

OAZE DEEP

Oaze Deep Fl (2) G 5s; 51°29'·18N 00°56'·77E.
Red Sand Trs N Fl (3) R 10s; *Bell*; 51°28'·73N 00°59'·32E.
N Oaze QR; 51°30'·03N 00°57'·65E.
Oaze Fl (4) Y 10s; 51°29'·06N 00°56'·93E.
W Oaze Iso 5s; 51°29'·06N 00°55'·43E.
Oaze Bank Q G 5s; 51°29'·18N 00°56'·77E.
Cant (unlit); 51°27'·77N 00°53'·36E.
East Cant QR; 51°28'·53N 00°55'·60E.

MEDWAY, SHEERNESS

Medway Mo (A) 6s; 51°28'·83N 00°52'·81E.
No 1 Fl G 2·5s; 51°28'·55N 00°50'·50E.
No 2 Q; 51°28'·33N 00°50'·52E.
No 7 Fl G 10s; 51°27'·91N 00°47'·52E.
No 9 Fl G 5s; 51°27'·74N 00°46'·61E.
No 11 Fl (3) G 10s; 51°27'·51N 00°45'·80E.
Grain Hard Fl G 5s; 51°26'·98N 00°44'·17E.
Isle of Grain ☆ Q 20m 13M; RW ◇ on R twr; 51°26'·70N 00°43'·38E.
Queenborough Spit Q (3) 10s; 51°25'·81N 00°43'·93E.

RIVER THAMES

SEA REACH, NORE and YANTLET

Sea Reach 1 (N) Fl Y 2·5s; **Racon (T) 10M**; 51°29'·59N 00°52'·71E.
Sea Reach 1 (S) Fl R 2·5s; 51°29'·39N 00°52'·45E.
Sea Reach 2 (N) Fl R 2·5s; 51°29'·49N 00°49'·73E.
Sea Reach 2 (S) Fl R 2·5s; 51°29'·30N 00°49'·75E.
Sea Reach 3 (N) Q G (sync); 51°29'·41N 00°46'·80E.

Sea Reach 3 (S) Q R (sync); 51°29′·22N 00°46′·71E.
Sea Reach 4 (N) Fl (2) G 5s; 51°29′·69N 00°44′·19E.
Sea Reach 4 (S) Fl (2) R 5s; 51°29′·50N 00°44′·12E.
Sea Reach 5 (N) VQ G; 51°30′·04N 00°41′·47E.
Sea Reach 5 (S) VQ R; 51°29′·85N 00°41′·43E.
Sea Reach 6 (N) Fl G 5s; 51°30′·13N 00°39′·87E.
Sea Reach 6 (S) Fl R 5s; 51°29′·93N 00°39′·84E.
Sea Reach 7 (N) Fl Y 2·5s; 51°30′·21N 00°36′·94E.
Sea Reach 7 (S) Fl R 2·5s; **Racon (T) 10M**; 51°30′·01N 00°36′·91E.
Nore Swatch Fl (4) R 15s; 51°28′·28N 00°45′·55E.
Mid Swatch Fl G 5s; 51°28′·68N 00°44′·16E.
W Nore Sand Fl (3) R 10s; 51°29′·48N 00°40′·87E.
East Blyth Q; 51°29′·73N 00°37′·81E.
Mid Blyth Q; 51°30′·08N 00°32′·38E.

LEIGH-ON-SEA and SOUTHEND-ON-SEA

Leigh ; 51°31′·09N 00°42′·72E.
Southend Pier E End 2 FG (vert) 7m; *Horn Mo (N) 30s, Bell (1).*

LOWER HOPE REACH

West Blyth Q R; 51°29′·57N 00°28′·39E.
Mucking 1 Q G; 51°29′·70N 00°37′·28E.
Lower Hope Fl R 5s; 51°29′·32N 00°28′·02E.
Mucking 3 Fl G 2·5s; 51°29′·33N 00°27′·68E.
Mucking 5 Fl (3) G 10s; 51°28′·76N 00°27′·19E.
Mucking 7 Fl G 5s; 51°28′·03N 00°26′·77E.
Bell Ovens Q G; 51°27′·50N 00°26′·35E.
Higham Fl (2) R 5s; 51°27′·40N 00°26′·85E.
Tilbury Q(6) + L Fl 15s; 51°27′·16N 00°25′·50E.

GRAVESEND

Shornmead Fl (2) WR 10s 12m, W11/7M, R11M; vis 070°-W-084°-R(Intens)-089°-W(Intens)-094°-W-250°; 51°26′·92N 00°26′·24E.
Northfleet Upper Oc WRG 10s 30m W10M, R7M, G7M; vis:126°-R-149°-W-159°-G-268°-W-279°; 51°26′·93N 00°20′·06E.

THAMES TIDAL BARRIER

Spans B, C, D, E, F, G are navigable. Spans C – F are for large ships. Eastbound small craft/yachts use Span B (51°29′·73N 00°02′·23E) Westbound small craft/yachts use Span G (51°29′·91N 00°02′·21E) **X** indicates span closed → indicates span open. W lights show either side of open spans in poor visibility.

KENTISH KNOCK

Kentish Knock Q (3) 10s; 51°38′·08N 01°40·43E.
S Knock Q (6) + L Fl 15s; *Bell*; 51°34′·13N 01°34′·29E.

KNOCK JOHN CHANNEL

No 7 Fl (4) G 15s; 51°32′·03N 01°06′·40E.
No 5 Fl (3) G 10s; 51°32′·49N 01°07′·75E.
No 4 QR 10s; 51°32′·40 N 01°08′·08E.
No 2 Fl (3) R 10s; 51°33′·03N 01°09′·63E.
No 3 Q (6) + L Fl 15s; 51°33′·29N 01°09′·83E.
No 1 Fl G 5s; 51°33′·75N 01°10′·72E.
Knock John Fl (2) R 5s; 51°33′·61N 01°11′·37E.

BLACK DEEP

No 12 Fl (4) R 15s; 51°33′·83N 01°13′·50E.
No 11 Fl (3) G 10s; 51°34′·33N 01°13′·40E.
No 10 Fl (3) R 10s; 51°34′·74N 01°15′·60E.
No 9 Q (6) + L Fl 15s; 51°35′·13N 01°15′·09E.
No 8 Q (9) 15s; 51°36′·36N 01°20′·43E.
No 7 QG. 51°37′·08N 01°17′·69E.
No 6 Fl R 2·5s; 51°38′·53N 01°24′·40E.
No 5 VQ (3) 5s; 51°39′·53N 01°23′·00E.
No 4 Fl (2) R 5s; 51°41′·42N 01°28′·49E.
Long Sand Bcn ; 51°41′·48N 01°29′·49E.
No 3 Fl (3) G 15s; 51°42′·39N 01°26′·65E.
No 1 Fl G 5s, 51°44′·03N 01°28′·09E.
No 2 Fl (4) R 15s; 51°45′·66N 01°32′·22E.
SHM Fl Y 2·5s; **Racon (T) 10M**; 51°29′·59N 00°52′·71E.

SUNK

Sunk Head Tower Q; *Bell*; 51°46′·63N 01°30′·51E.
Black Deep QR; 51°48′·32N 01°36′·96E.
Long Sand Head VQ; *Bell*; 51°48′·12N 01°39′·39E.
Sunk Centre Mo (A) 15s, **Racon C 10M** 51°50′·10N 01°46′·02E; 992351034.
Dynamo Fl Y 2·5s; 51°29′·59N 00°52′·71E.
Trinity Q (6) + L Fl 15s; 51°49′·03N 01°36′·39E.
SUNK INNER 51°51′·17N 01°34′·40E; Fl(5) 15s 11m 12M; **Racon (C) 10M**; *Horn 30s*; 992351027.

FISHERMANS GAT

Outer Fisherman Q (3) 10s; 51°34′·02N 01°25′·10E.
Fisherman No 1 Fl G 2·5s (sync); 51°34′·50N 01°23′·52E.
Fisherman No 2 Fl R 2·5s (sync); 51°34′·30N 01°23′·50E.
Fisherman No 3 Fl G 5s; 51°34′·78N 01°22′·65E.
Fisherman No 4 Fl (2) R 5s; 51°34′·77N 01°22′·08E.
Fisherman No 5 Fl (2) G 5s; 51°35′·25N 01°21′·84E.
Fisherman No 6 Fl (3) R 10s; 51°35′·08N 01°21′·56E.
Inner Fisherman Q R; 51°36′·15N 01°20′·08E.

BARROW DEEP

SW Barrow Q(9) 15s; 51°32′·12N 01°00′·12E.
Alice Wk Fl (2) 5s; 51°32′·33N 01°04′·22E.
Barrow No 14 Fl R 2·5s; 51°31′·83N 01°00′·43E.
Barrow No 13 Fl (2) G 5s; 51°32′·82N 01°03′·07E.
Barrow No 12 Fl (2) R 5s; 51°33′·24N 01°05′·94E.
Barrow No 11 Fl (3) G 10s; 51°34′·08N 01°06′·70E.
Barrow No 9 VQ (3) 5s; 51°35′·34N 01°10′·30E.
Barrow No 8 Fl (2) R 5s; 51°35′·05N 01°11′·36E.
Barrow No 7 Fl G 2·5s; 51°37′·49N 01°13′·47E.
Barrow No 6 Fl (4) R 15s; 51°37′·30N 01°14′·68E.
Barrow No 5 Fl G 10s; 51°40′·03N 01°16′·20E.
Barrow No 4 VQ (9) 10s; 51°39′·88N 01°17′·48E.
Barrow No 3 Q (3) 10s; **Racon (M)10M**; 51°42′·02N 01°20′·24E.
Barrow No 2 Fl (2) R 5s; 51°41′·98N 01°22′·89E.

WEST SWIN and MIDDLE DEEP

Blacktail Spit Fl (3) G 10s; 51°31′·47N 00°56′·75E.
Maplin Q G (sync with W Swin); *Bell*; 51°33′·66N 01°01′·40E.
W Swin Q R (sync with Maplin); 51°33′·40N 01°01′·97E.
Maplin Edge Fl G 2.5s; 51°35′·33N 01°03′·64E.
Maplin Bank Fl (3) R 10s; 51°35′·50N 01°04′·70E.
Maplin Middle Fl G 5s; *Bell*; 51°36′·78N 01°05′·50E.
E Maplin 51°38′·29N 01°08′·86E.
Maplin Approach Fl (2) G 10s; 51°39′·54N 01°09′·39E.

EAST SWIN and KING'S CHANNEL

N Middle Q; 51°41′·35N 01°12′·61E.
W Sunk Q (9) 15s; 51°44′·33N 01°25′·80E.
Gunfleet Spit Q (6) + L Fl 15s; *Bell*; 51°45′·33N 01°21′·70E.

WHITAKER CHANNEL and RIVER CROUCH

Whitaker Q (3) 10s; *Bell*; 51°41′·43N 01°10′·51E.
Inner Whitaker VQ (6) + L Fl 10s; 51°40′·76N 01°08′·40E.

Swin Spitway Iso 10s; *Bell;* 51°41'·95N 01°08'·35E.
Whitaker 1 FlG 5s (sync Whit 2), 51° 40'·69N 01° 06'·67E.
Whitaker 2 FlR 5s (sync Whit 1), 51° 40'·41N 01° 06'·78E.
Whitaker 3 Fl(2) G 5s (sync Whit 4) 51° 40'·41N 01° 04'·74E.
Whitaker 4 Fl(2) R 5s (sync Whit 4) 51° 40'·16N 01° 04'·91E.
Whitaker 5 Fl(2) G 5s (sync Whit 6) 51° 40'·03N 01° 03'·22E.
Whitaker 6 Fl(2) R 5s(sync Whit 5) 51° 39'·77N 01° 03'·43E.
Whitaker 7 Fl(3) G 10s(sync Whit 8) 51° 39'·54N 01° 02'·00E.
Whitaker 8 Fl(3) R 10s(sync Whit 7), 51° 39'·35N 01° 02'·00E.
Swallowtail 1 Fl Y 5s, 51° 41'·38N 01° 08'·20E.
Swallowtail 2 Fl Y 10s, 51° 41'·19N 01° 06'·28E.
Swallowtail 3 (2) Y 10s, 51° 40'·52N 01° 03'·47E.
Buxey Edge Fl G 10s, 51° 40'·65N 01° 03'·48E.
Swallowtail VQ (9) 10s, 51° 40'·04N 01° 02'·65E.
Sunken Buxey VQ; 51°39'·59N 01°00'·77E.
Buxey No 1 VQ (6) + L Fl 10s; 51°39'·18N 01°01'·13E.
Buxey No 2 Q; 51°39'·08N 01°00'·23E.
Outer Crouch 1 Fl G 5s (sync Cro 2) 51° 38'·71N 00° 59'·00E.
Outer Crouch 2 Fl R 5s (sync Cro 1) 51° 38'·62N 00° 59'·20E.
Outer Crouch 3 Fl G 10s (sync Cro 4) 51° 38'·10N 00° 57'·83E.
Outer Crouch 4 Fl R 10s (sync Cro 3) 51° 38'·00N 00° 58'·00E.
Crouch Q.Fl, 51° 37.650N 00° 56.582E.
Inner Crouch L Fl 10s, 51° 37'·19N 00° 55'·09E.
Branklet (RGR) **Pref Chan to Stbd,** Comp grp Fl (R) 2+1 10s, 51° 36'·99N 00° 52'·10E.

GOLDMER GAT and WALLET

NE Gunfleet Q (3) 10s; 51°49'·93N 01°27'·79E.
Wallet No 2 Fl R 5s; 51°48'·88N 01°22'·99E.
Wallet No 4 Fl (4) R 10s; 51°46'·53N 01°17'·23E.
Wallet Spitway L Fl 10s; *Bell*; 51°42'·86N 01°07'·30E.
Knoll Q; 51°43'·88N 01°05'·07E.
Eagle QG; 51°44'·10N 01°03'·63E.
N Eagle Q; 51°44'·71N 01°04'·32E.
NW Knoll Fl (2) R 5s; 51°44'·29N 01°02'·14E.
Colne Bar Fl (2) G 5s; 51°44'·61N 01°02'·57E.
Bench Head Fl (3) G 10s; 51°44'·56N 01°01'·18E.

RIVER BLACKWATER

The Nass VQ (3) 5s 6m 2M; 51°45'·83N 00°54'·83E.
Thirslet Fl (3) G 10s; 51°43'·73N 00°50'·39E.
No 1 ; 51°43'·44N 00°48'·02E.

RIVER COLNE and BRIGHTLINGSEA

Inner Bench Head No 2 Fl (2) R 5s; 51°45'·96N 01°01'·74E.
Colne Pt No 1 Fl G 3s; 51°46'·01N 01°01'·92E.
No 8 Fl R 3s; 51°46'·90N 01°01'·30E.
No 9 Fl G 3s; 51°47'·36N 01°01'·07E.

Ldg lts 041°. Front, FR 7m 4M; W □, R stripe on post; vis: 020°-080°; 51°48'·39N 01°01'·20E. Rear, 50m from front, FR 10m 4M; W □, R stripe on post. FR lts are shown on 7 masts between 1·5M and 3M NW when firing occurs.

WALTON BACKWATERS

Pye End L Fl 10s; 51°55'·03N 01°17'·90E.
No 2 Fl (2) 5s; 51°54'·62N 01°16'·80E.
Crab Knoll No 3 Fl G 5s; 51°54'·41N 01°16'·41E.
No 16 51°53'·17N 01°15'·52E.

HARWICH APPROACHES

(Direction of buoyage is North to South)

MEDUSA CHANNEL

Medusa Fl G 5s; 51°51'·23N 01°20'·35E.
Stone Banks FlR 5s; 51°53'·19N 01°19'·23E.
Pennyhole ; 51°53'·55N 01°18'·00E (Mar–Sep).

CORK SAND and ROUGH SHOALS

S Cork Q (6) + L Fl 15s; 51°51'·33N 01°24'·09E.
SE Roughs Tower Q (3) 10s; 51°53'·64N 01°28'·94E.
NW Roughs Tower VQ (9) 10s; 51°53'·81N 01°28'·77E.
Cork Sand Fl (3) R 10s; 51°55'·51N 01°25'·42E.

HARWICH CHANNEL

S Threshold Fl (4) Y 10s; 51°52'·20N 01°33'·14E.
S Shipwash 2 By(s) Q (6) + L Fl 15s; 51°52'·71N 01°33'·97E.
Outer Tidal Bn Mo (U) 15s 2m 3M; 51°52'·85N 01°32'·34E.
E Fort Massac VQ (3) 5s; 51°53'·36N 01°32'·79E.
W Fort Massac VQ (9) 10s; 51°53'·36N 01°32'·49E.
Walker Q (9)15s; 51°53'·79N 01°33'·90E.
N Threshold Fl Y 5s; 51°54'·49N 01°33'·47E.
SW Shipwash Fl Y 2·5s; 51°54'·75N 01°34'·21E.
Haven Mo (A) 5s; 51°55'·76N 01°32'·56E.
W Shipwash Fl (2) R 10s; 51°57'·13N 01°35'·89E.
NW Shipwash Fl R 5s; 51°58'·98N 01°37'·01E.
Harwich App (HA) Iso 5s; 51°56'·75N 01°30'·66E.
Cross Fl (3) Y 10s; 51°56'·23N 01°30'·48E.
Harwich Chan No 1 Fl Y 2·5s; **Racon (T) 10M**; 51°56'·13N 01°27'·06E.
Harwich Chan No 3 Fl (3) Y 10s; 51°56'·04N 01°25'·54E.
Harwich Chan No 5 Fl (5) Y 10s; 51°55'·96N 01°24'·01E.
Harwich Chan No 7 Fl (3) Y 10s; 51°55'·87N 01°22'·49E.
S Bawdsey Q (6) + L Fl 15s; *Whis*; 51°57'·23N 01°30'·19E.
Washington QG; 51°56'·52N 01°26'·59E.
Felixstowe Ledge Fl (3) G 10s; 51°56'·30N 01°23'·72E.
Wadgate Ledge Fl (4) G 15s; 51°56'·16N 01°21'·99E.
Platters Q (6) + L Fl 15s; 51°55'·64N 01°20'·97E.
Rolling Ground QG; 51°55'·55N 01°19'·75E.
Beach End Fl (2) G 5s; 51°55'·62N 01°19'·21E.
Cork Sand Yacht Bn VQ 2M; 51°55'·21N 01°25'·20E.
Rough VQ; 51°55'·19N 01°31'·00E.
Pitching Ground Fl (4) R 15s; 51°55'·43N 01°21'·05E.
Inner Ridge QR; 51°55'·38N 01°20'·20E.
Deane L Fl R 6s; 51°55'·36N 01°19'·28E.
Landguard Q; 51°55'·45N 01°18'·84E.

RIVERS STOUR AND ORWELL

RIVER STOUR and HARWICH

Shotley Spit Q (6) + L Fl 15s; 51°57'·21N 01°17'·69E.
Shotley Marina Lock E side Dir lt 339·5° 3m 1M (uses Moiré pattern); Or structure; 51°57'·46N 01°16'·60E.
Guard Fl R 5s; *Bell*; 51°57'·07N 01°17'·86E.

RIVER ORWELL and IPSWICH

Suffolk Yacht Harbour. Ldg lts Front Iso Y 1M; 51°59'·73N 01°16'·09E. Rear Oc Y 4s 1M.

HARWICH TO ORFORD NESS

FELIXSTOWE, R DEBEN and WOODBRIDGE HAVEN

Woodbridge Haven Mo(A)15s; 51°57'·99N 01°23'·63E.
Deben ; 51°59'·30N 01°23'·53E.

RIVERS ORE and ALDE

Orford Haven L Fl 10s; *Bell*. 52°02'·00N 01°28'·20E.

OFFSHORE MARKS

S Galloper Q (6) L Fl 15s; **Racon (T) 10M**; 51°43'·98N 01°56'·43E.

N Galloper Q; 51°49'·84N 01°59'·99E.
S Inner Gabbard Q (6) + L Fl 15s. 51°49'·92N 01°51'·89E.
N Inner Gabbard Q; 51°59'·20N 01°56'·00E.
NHR-SE Fl G 5s; 51°45'·39N 02°39'·89E.

SHIPWASH and BAWDSEY BANK
E Shipwash VQ (3) 5s; 51°57'·08N 01°37'·89E.
NW Shipwash Fl R 5s; 51°58'·98N 01°37'·01E.
N Shipwash Q 7M; **Racon (M) 10M**; *Bell*; 52°01'·73N 01°38'·27E; 992351069.
S Bawdsey Q (6) + L Fl 15s; *Bell*; 51°57'·23N 01°30'·19E.
Mid Bawdsey Fl (3) G 10s; 51°58'·88N 01°33'·59E.
NE Bawdsey Fl G 10s; 52°01'·73N 01°36'·09E.

CUTLER and WHITING BANKS
Cutler QG; 51°58'·51N 01°27'·48E.
SW Whiting Q (6) + L Fl 10s; 52°00'·96N 01°30'·69E.
Whiting Hook Fl R 10s; 52°02'·98N 01°31'·82E.
NE Whiting Q (3) 10s; 52°03'·61N 01°33'·32E.

ORFORD NESS TO WINTERTON

(Direction of buoyage is South to North)
Orford Ness Lt Ho (dis) 52°05'·04N 01°34'·45E; W ○ twr, R bands.
Aldeburgh Ridge QR; 52°06'·49N 01°36'·95E.

SOUTHWOLD
Southwold ☆ 52°19'·63N 01°40'·89E; Fl 10s 37m **W24M**; vis 204°-W-032·5°, 992351019.

LOWESTOFT and APPR VIA STANFORD CHANNEL
E Barnard Q (3) 10s; 52°25'·14N 01°46'·38E.
Newcome Sand QR; 52°26'·33N 01°47'·16E.
S Holm VQ (6) + L Fl 10s; 52°26'·63N 01°47'·11E.
Stanford Fl R 2·5s; 52°27'·35N 01°46'·67E.
SW Holm Fl (2) G 5s; 52°27'·87N 01°46'·99E.
Kirkley ☆ Dir WRG 17m 10M, vis: 222°-OcG 10s -225°-FlG 2·5s-226°-FlW 2·5s-227°-OcW 10s-229°-FlW 2·5s-230°-FlR 2·5s-231°-OcR 10s-232°; 52°27'·71N 01°44'·54E.
Outer Hbr S Pier Hd ☆ Oc R 5s 12m 6M; *Horn (4) 60s*; tfc sigs; 52°28'·29N 01°45'·36E.
N Newcome Fl (4) R 15s; 52°28'·39N 01°46'·37E.
Lowestoft ☆ 52°29'·22N 01°45'·35; Fl 15s 37m **23M**; W twr; part obscd 347°- shore.

LOWESTOFT NORTH ROAD and CORTON ROAD
Lowestoft Ness SE Q (6) + L Fl 15s; 52°28'·84N 01°46'·25E.
Lowestoft Ness N VQ (3) 5s; *Bell*; 52°28'·89N 01°46'·23E.
W Holm Fl (3) G 10s; 52°29'·50N 01°46'·99E.
NW Holm Fl (4) G 15s; 52°30'·75N 01°46'·46E.

GREAT YARMOUTH APPROACH via HOLM CHANNEL
E Newcome Fl (2) R 5s; 52°28'·51N 01°49'·21E.
Holm Approach Q (3) 10s; 52°30'·88N 01°50'·22E.
Holm Sand Q (9) 15s; 52°33'·28N 01°46'·62E.
S Corton Q (6) + L Fl 15s; *Bell*; 52°33'·37N 01°48'·41E.
NE Holm Fl R 2·5s; 52°33'·16N 01°48'·10E.
Mid Corton Fl G 2·5s; 52°33'·61N 01°47'·98E.
N Holm Q 52°33'·73N 01°47'·29E.
W Corton Fl (3) G 10s; 52°34'·12N 01°47'·50E.

GREAT YARMOUTH and GORLESTON
Gorleston South Pier Hd ☆ Fl R 3s 11m 11M; vis: 235°-340°; 52°34'·33N 01°44'·28E.
N Pier Hd ☆ QG 8m 6M; vis: 176°-078°; *Horn(3) 60s*; 52°34'·38N 01°44'·38E.
Outer Hbr S Pier ☆ Q R 17m 3M; 52°34'·61N 01°44'·73E.
Outer Hbr N Pier ☆ Q G 17m 3M; 52°34'·70N 01°44'·74E.

GREAT YARMOUTH TO THE WASH

(Direction of buoyage South to North)
YARMOUTH and CAISTER ROADS/COCKLE GATEWAY
SW Scroby Fl G 2·5s; 52°35'·13N 01°46'·69E.
Scroby Elbow Fl (2) G 5s; *Bell*; 52°36'·55N 01°46'·26E.
Yarmouth Outfall Q R; 52°37'·58N 01°45'·70E.
Mid Caister Fl (2) R 5s; *Bell*; 52°38'·99N 01°45'·66E.
NW Scroby Fl (3) G 10s; 52°40'·36N 01°46'·31E.
N Caister Fl (3) R 10s; 52°40'·76N 01°45'·76E.
Hemsby Fl R 2·5s; 52°41'·80N 01°46'·00E.
N Scroby VQ; 52°41'·39N 01°46'·47E.
Cockle VQ (3) 5s; *Bell*; 52°44'·03N 01°43'·59E.

OFFSHORE ROUTE
Cross Sand L Fl 10s 5M; **Racon (T) 10M**; 52°40'·33N 01°53'·70E.
Barley Q (6) + L Fl 15s 6M; 52°38'·76N 01°52'·90E.
E Cross Sand Fl (4) R 15s; 52°40'·33N 01°53'·70E.
NE Cross Sand VQ (3) 5s; ***Racon (M) 10M***; 52°44'·22N 01° 53'·80E; 992351264.
Smith's Knoll Q (6) + L Fl 15s 7M; ***Racon (T) 10M***; 52°43'·52N 02°17'·89E.
S Winterton Ridge Q (6) + L Fl 15s; 52°47'·21N 02°03'·44E.
E Hammond Knoll Q (3) 10s; 52°52'·32N 01°58'·64E.
Hammond Knoll Q (9) 15s; 52°49'·68N 01°57'·54E.
S Haisbro Q (6) + L Fl 15s; *Bell*; 52°50'·82N 01°48'·29E.
Mid Haisbro Fl (2) G 5s; 52°54'·22N 01°41'·59E.
N Haisbro Q; ***Racon (T) 10M***; 53°00'·22N 01°32'·29E; 992351031.
Happisburgh ☆ Fl (3) 30s 41m 14M; 52°49'·21N 01°32'·18E.

(Direction of buoyage East to West)
CROMER
Cromer ☆ 52°55'·45N 01°19'·01E; Fl 5s 84m **21M**; W 8-sided twr; vis: 102°-307° H24; ***Racon (O) 25M***; 992351015.
Tayjack Wk Fl R 2·5s; 52°57'·61N 01°15'·37E.
E Sheringham Q (3) 10s; 53°02'·21N 01°14'·84E.
W Sheringham Q (9) 15s; 53°02'·95N 01°06'·72E.

BLAKENEY
Blakeney Fairway ; 52°59'·22N 00°58'·53E.
Blakeney Overfalls Fl (2) R 5s; *Bell*; 53°03'·01N 01°01'·37E.

WELLS-NEXT-THE-SEA/BRANCASTER STAITHE
Wells WCM Q(9) 15s; 52°59'·68N 00°50'·24E.
Bridgirdle Fl R 2·5s; 53°01'·73N 00°43'·95E.

APPROACHES TO THE WASH
S Race Q (6) + L Fl 15s; *Bell*; 53°07'·81N 00°57'·34E.
E Docking Fl R 2·5s; 53°09'·82N 00°50'·39E.
N Race Fl G 5s; *Bell*; 53°14'·98N 00°43'·87E.
N Docking Q; 53°14'·82N 00°41'·49E.
Scott Patch VQ (3) 5s; 53°11'·12N 00°36'·39E.
S Inner Dowsing Q (6) + L Fl 15s; *Bell*; 53°12'·12N 00°33'·69E.
Boygrift Tower Fl (2) 10s 12m 5M; 53°17'·63N 00°19'·24E.
Burnham Flats Q (9) 15s; *Bell*; 53°07'·53N 00°34'·89E.
Lincs WF E Q (3) 10s; 53°07'·61N 00°31'·06E.

THE WASH

West Ridge Q (9) 15s; 53°19′·06N 00°44′·47E.

N Well L Fl 10s; *Whistle*; ***Racon (T) 10M***; 53°03′·02N 00°27′·87E.

Fl(2) 10s; 53°01′·53N 00°25′·63E.

Z9 Fl(2) 6s; 52°59′·73N 00°22′·75E.

ROARING MIDDLE L Fl 10s 7m 8M; 52°58′·64N 00°21′·08E.

KING'S LYNN

Line 1, No 1, Fl Y 3s; 52°56′·00N 00°23′·00E.

Line 2, No 2, Fl(2) R 6s; 52°55′·35N 00°23′·75E.

Line 3, No 3, Fl(2) G 6s; 52°55′·35N 00°23′·26E.

WISBECH CHANNEL/RIVER NENE

W2 Fl Y 6s; 52°54′·93N 00°16′·00E.

Nene Roads *Mo(A) 6s*; 52°53′·85N 01°15′·51E

East Knock VQ (3) 5s; 52°52′·14N 00°14′·69E.

Bob LFl R 5s; 52°52′·05N 00°14′·74E.

Wisbech No 1 Fl G 3s; 52°53′·33N 00°13′·60E.

Tide Gauge DZ6; 52°52′·57N 00°13′·10E.

Beacons are moved as required.

FREEMAN CHANNEL

Boston No 1 Fl G 3s; 52°57′·84N 00°15′·03E.

Alpha Fl R 3s; 52°57′·69N 00°15′·06E.

No 3 Fl G 6s; 52°57′·93N 00°15′·42E.

No 5 Fl G 3s; 52°58′·51N 00°12′·72E.

No 7 Fl G 6s; 52°58′·63N 00°11′·40E.

Delta Fl R 6s; 52°58′·38N 00°11′·25E.

BOSTON LOWER ROAD

Echo Fl R 3s; 52°58′·38N 00°10′·13E.

Foxtrot Fl R 3s; 52°57′·60N 00°08′·94E.

Boston No 9 Fl G 3s; 52°57′·58N 00°08′·36E.

Black Buoy Fl (2) R 6s; 52°56′·82N 00°07′·74E.

Tabs Head Q WG 4m 1M; R □ on W mast; vis: W shore-251°- G-shore; 52°56'·00N 00°04'·91E.

BOSTON, NEW CUT AND RIVER WITHAM

Ent N side, Dollypeg QG 4m 1M; B △; 52°56′·13N 00°05′·03E.

New Cut Fl G 3s; △ on pile; 52°55′·98N 00°04′·67E.

New Cut Ldg Lts 240°. Front, No 1, F 5m 5M; 52°55′·85N 00°04′·40E. Rear, 90m from front, F 8m 5M.

WELLAND CUT/RIVER WELLAND

SE side Iso R 2s; NW side Iso G 2s. Lts QR (to port) and QG (to stbd) mark the chan upstream; 52°55′·72E 00°04′·68E.

THE WASH TO THE RIVER HUMBER

(Direction of buoyage South to North)

Dudgeon Q (9) 15s 7M; ***Racon (O) 10M***; 53°16′·62N 01°16′·90E.

E Dudgeon Q (3) 10s; 53°19′·72N 00°58′·69E.

W Ridge Q (9) 15s; 53°19′·04N 00°44′·50E.

Inner Dowsing Q (3) 10s 7M, ***Racon (T) 10M***; Horn 60s; 53°19′·10N 00°34′·80E.

Mid Outer Dowsing Fl (3) G 10s; 53°24′·82N 01°07′·79E.

N Outer Dowsing Q; 53°33′·52N 00°59′·59E; ***Racon (T) 10M***; 992351031.

B.1D Platform Dowsing 53°33′·68N 00°52′·63E; Fl (2) 10s 28m **22M**; Morse (U) R 15s 28m 3M; *Horn (2) 60s*.

RIVER HUMBER APPROACHES

Protector Fl R 2·5s; 53°24′·84N 00°25′·12E.

DZ No 4 Fl Y 5s; 53°27′·15N 00°19′·06E.

DZ No 3 Fl Y 2·5s 53°29′·30N 00°19′·21E.

Rosse Spit Fl (2) R 5s 53°30′·56N 00°16′·60E.

Outer Sand Q (3) 10s; 53°36′·41N 00°29′·39E; 992351119.

Haile Sand No 2 Fl (3) R 10s; 53°32′·42N 00°13′·18E.

Humber L Fl G 10s; 53°38′·70N 00°21′·24E.

N Binks Fl G 4s; 53°36′·01N 00°18′·28E.

S Binks Fl G 2s 53°34′·74N 00°16′·55E.

SPURN Q (3) 10s 10m 8M; ***Racon (M) 5M***; 53°33′·42N 00°14′·15E.

SE CHEQUER VQ (6)+L Fl 10s 6m 6M; 53°33′·36N 00°12′·86E.

Chequer No 3 Q (6) + L Fl 15s; 53°33′·07N 00°10′·63E.

No 2B Fl R 4s; 53°32′·33N 00°09′·10E.

TETNEY 2 VQ Y (vert); *Horn Mo (A)60s*; QY on 290m floating hose; 53°32′·35N 00°06′·76E.

RIVER HUMBER/GRIMSBY/HULL

Binks No 3A Fl G 4s; 53°33′·92N 00°07′·43E.

Spurn Pt Fl G 3s 11m 5M; 53°34′·37N 00°06′·47E.

BULL VQ 8m 6M; 53°33′·54N 00°05′·70E.

Bull Sand Q R ; 53°34′·45N 00°03′·69E.

North Fort Q; 53°33′·80N 00°04′·19E.

South Fort Q (6) + L Fl 15s; 53°33′·65N 00°03′·96E.

Haile Sand Fort Fl R 5s 21m 3M; 53°32′·07N 00°01′·99E.

Haile Chan No 4 Fl R 4s; 53°33′·64N 00°02′·84E.

Middle No 7 VQ (6) + L Fl 10s; 53°35′·80N 00°01′·50E.

Sunk S8 Fl G 1·5s; 53°37′·10N 00°02′·16E (992351275).

Grimsby Royal Dock ent E side Fl (2) R 6s 10m 8M; Dn; 53°35′·08N 00°04′·04W.

Immingham Bulk Terminal Dir Lt 291° Dir WRG 1s 17m 3M; vis: 288·5°-FG-289·5°-IsoG-290·5-FW-291·5-IsoR-292·5°-FR-295·5; on bldg; 53°38′·41N 00°11′·97W (992351276).

RIVER HUMBER TO WHITBY

Canada & Giorgios Wreck VQ (3) 5s; 53°42′·37N 00°07′·16E.

Albrough intake Q R 17m 2M; 53°49′·01N 00°03′·38W.

BRIDLINGTON

SW Smithic Q (9) 15s; 54°02′·41N 00°09′·21W.

N Pier Hd Fl 2s 12m 9M; *Horn 60s*; (Tidal Lts) Fl R or Fl G; 54°04′·77N 00°11′·19W.

N Smithic VQ; *Bell*; 54°06′·22N 00°03′·90W.

Flamborough Hd ☆ 54°06′·98N 00°04′·96W; Fl (4) 15s 65m **24M**; W ○ twr; *Horn (2) 90s*.

FILEY/SCARBOROUGH/WHITBY

Filey Brigg Q (3) 10s; *Bell*; 54°12′·74N 00°14′·60W.

Scarborough E Pier Hd QG 8m 3M; 54°16′·88N 00°23′·36W.

Scarborough Pier Iso 5s 17m 9M; W ○ twr; vis: 219°-039° (tide sigs); *Dia 60s*; 54°16′·91N 00°23′·40W.

Whitby Q; *Bell*; 54°30′·33N 00°36′·58W.

Whitby High ☆ 54°28′·67N 00°34′·10W; Fl WR 5s 73m **18M**,R16M; W 8-sided twr & dwellings; vis:128°-R-143°-W- 319°.

Whitby E Pier Fl(2) R 4s 16m 5M; 54°29′·57N 00°36′·71W; Twr.

Whitby E Pier Ext Hd ☆ Q R 12m 5M; 54°29′·65N 00°36′·74W.

Whitby W Pier ☆ Fl(2) G 4s 24m 5M; 54°29′·57N 00°36′·78W; Twr.

Whitby W Pier Ext Hd ☆ Q G 12m 5M; 54°29′·65N 00°36′·80W.

WHITBY TO THE RIVER TYNE

RUNSWICK/REDCAR

Salt Scar 54°38′·12N 01°00′·12W VQ; *Bell.*

Luff Way Ldg Lts 197°. Front, on Esplanade, FR 8m 7M; vis: 182°-212°; 54°37′·10N 01°03′·71W. Rear, 115m from front, FR 12m 7M; vis: 182°-212°.

High Stone. Lade Way Ldg Lts 247°. Front, Oc R 2·5s 9m 7M; 54°37′·15N 01°03′·92W. Rear, 43m from front, Oc R 2·5s 11m 7M; vis: 232°-262°.

TEES APPROACHES/HARTLEPOOL

Tees Approach Mo(A) 5s 8M; *Horn*; 54°40′·60N 01°04′·00W; AIS.

Bkwtr Hd S Gare ☆ 54°38′·85N 01°08′·25W; Fl WR 12s 16m 10M; W ○ twr; vis: 020°-W-240°-R-357°; Sig Stn.

Ldg Lts 210·1° Front, FR 18m 13M; 54°37′·22N 01°10′·20W. **Rear**, 560m from front, FR 20m **16M**.

Longscar Q (3) 10s; *Bell*; 54°40′·86N 01°09′·89W.

The Heugh ☆ 54°41′·79N 01°10′·56W; Fl (2) **WR** 10s 19m **19M**; vis: 309°-R-319°-W-190°; W twr.

Hartlepool Marina Lock Dir Lt 308° Dir Fl WRG2s 6m 3M; vis: 305·5°-G-307°-W-309°-R-310·5°; 54°41′·45N 01°11′·92W.

SEAHAM/SUNDERLAND

Seaham N Pier Hd ☆ Fl G 10s 12m 5M; W col, B bands; 54°50′·26N 01°19′·26W.

Sunderland Roker Pier Hd ☆ 54°55′·28N 01°21′·15W; Fl 5s 25m **18M**; W □ twr, 3 R bands and cupola: vis: 211°-357°; *Siren 20s.*

Old N Pier Hd ☆ QG 12m 8M; metal column; 54°55′·13N 01°21′·61W.

DZ 54°57′·04N 01°18′·90W and 54°58′·61N 01°19′·90W; both Fl Y 2·5s.

TYNE ENTRANCE/NORTH SHIELDS

Ent North Pier Hd ☆ 55°00′·88N 01°24′·18W; Fl (3) 10s 26m **26M**; Gy □ twr, W lantern; *Horn 10s.*

Herd Groyne Hd Dir Ldg Lt 249°, Oc 10s 14m **19M**; vis: 246·5°-W-251·5°; R pile structure, R&W lantern. Same structure Oc RG 10s 13m, 11M; vis: 224°-G-246·5°, 251·5°-R-277°; sync with Dir lt FR (unintens) 080°-224°. *Bell (1) 5s*; 55°00′·49N 01°25′·44W.

RIVER TYNE TO BERWICK-UPON-TWEED

CULLERCOATS and BLYTH

Cullercoats Ldg Lts 256°. Front, FR 27m 3M; 55°02′·06N 01°25′·91W. Rear, 38m from front, FR 35m 3M.

Blyth Ldg Lts 324°. Front, F Bu 11m 10M; 55°07′·42N 01°29′·82W. Rear, 180m from front, F Bu 17m 10M. Both Or on twr.

Blyth E Pier Hd ☆ 55°06′·98N 01°29′·21W; Fl (4) 10s 19m **21M**, W twr; same structure FR 13m 13M, vis:152°-249°; Horn (3) 30s.

Met Mast ☆; Mo(U)15s 17m 10M; 55°08′·78N 01°25′·25W; Aero 3 FR (107m), *Horn 30s*.

COQUET ISLAND, AMBLE and WARKWORTH

Coquet ☆ 55°20′·03N 01°32′·39W; Fl (3) WR 20s 25m **W19M, R15M**; W □ twr, turreted parapet, lower half Gy; vis: 330°-R-140°-W-163°-R-180°-W-330°; sector boundaries are indeter-minate and may appear as Alt WR; *Horn 30s*.

Amble N Pier Head ☆ Fl G 6s 12m 6M; 55°20′·39N 01°34′·25W.

SEAHOUSES, BAMBURGH and FARNE ISLANDS

N Sunderland Fl R 2·5s; 55°34′·62N 01°37′·12W.

Bamburgh Black Rocks Point ☆ 55°36′·99N 01°43′·45W; Oc(2) WRG 8s 12m **W14M**, R11M, G11M; W bldg; vis: 122°-G-165°-W- 175°-R-191°-W- 238°-R- 275°-W- 289°-G-300°.

Inner Farne ☆ Fl (2) WR 15s 27m WR 8M; W ○ twr; vis: 119°- R - 280° - W -119°; 55°36′·92N 01°39′·35W.

Longstone ☆ **W side** 55°38′·62N 01°36′·65W; Fl 20s 23m **18M**; R twr, W band; 992351127.

Swedman Fl G 2·5s; 55°37′·65N 01°41′·63W.

HOLY ISLAND

Ridge Q (3) 10s; 55°39′·70N 01°45′·97W.

Plough Rock Q (9) 15s; 55°40′·24N 01°46′·00W.

Old Law E Bn ☆ (Guile Pt) Oc WRG 6s 9m 4M; vis: 180·5°-G-258·5°-W-261·5°-R-300°, 55°39′·49N 01°47′·59W; stone obelisk.

Heugh ☆ Oc WRG 6s 24m 5M; vis: 135°-G-308°-W-311-R-shore; 55°40′·09N 01°47′·99W.

Plough Seat QR; 55°40′·37N 01°44′·97W.

Goldstone QG; 55°40′·25N 01°43′·64W.

BERWICK-UPON-TWEED

Bkwtr Hd ☆ Fl 5s 15m 6M; vis: 201°-009°, (obscured 155°-201°); W ○ twr, R cupola and base; FG (same twr) 8m 1M; vis 009°-G-155°; 55°45'·88N 01°59'·06W.

1	Ramsgate	**1**										
2	Sheerness	34	**2**									
3	Gravesend	56	22	**3**								
4	London Bridge	76	45	23	**4**							
5	Burnham-on-Crouch	44	34	54	77	**5**						
6	Brightlingsea	41	28	48	71	21	**6**					
7	Harwich	40	50	66	93	31	20	**7**				
8	River Deben (ent)	45	55	75	98	36	25	6	**8**			
9	Southwold	62	72	92	115	53	42	25	23	**9**		
10	Lowestoft	72	82	102	125	63	52	35	33	10	**10**	
11	Great Yarmouth	79	87	105	132	70	59	42	40	18	7	**11**

11	31	61	78	91	107	126	189	205	205	232	Berwick-upon-Tweed	**11**
	10	27	42	65	81	102	157	176	185	203	Amble	**10**
		9	16	36	51	70	138	149	156	180	Sunderland	**9**
			8	24	39	58	122	137	140	169	Hartlepool	**8**
				7	16	35	88	114	121	143	Whitby	**7**
					6	20	81	98	105	130	Scarborough	**6**
						5	58	83	87	114	Bridlington	**5**
							4	79	75	113	Hull	**4**
								3	34	83	Boston	**3**
									2	85	King's Lynn	**2**
										1	Great Yarmouth	**1**

AREA 5 *E Scotland – Berwick-upon-Tweed to C Wrath & N Isles*

SELECTED LIGHTS, BUOYS & WAYPOINTS

BERWICK-UPON-TWEED TO BASS ROCK

BURNMOUTH

Ldg lts 241°. Front, FR 29m 4M; 55°50'·53N 02°04'·25W. Rear, 45m from front, FR 35m 4M. Both on W posts (unclear by day).

EYEMOUTH

Blind Buss Q; 55°52'·80N 02°05'·25E.
Ldg Lts 174°. Front, W Bkwtr Hd ☆, FG 9m 6M; 55°52'·47N 02°05'·29W. Rear, elbow 55m from front, FG 10m 6M.

ST ABBS to DUNBAR and BASS ROCK

St Abbs Hd ☆ 55°54'·96N 02°08'·29W; Fl 10s 68m **18M**; W twr; **Racon (T) 18M**.
Barns Ness Tr (Lt ho disused 36m); 55°59'·22N 02°26'·76W.
Torness Pwr Stn Ldg Lts 215°. Front, Iso G 4s 6m 6M; W □ with B vert stripe on plinth; 55°58'·27N 02°24'·86W. Rear, Iso G 4s 22m 3M; W □ with B vert stripe on post; sync with front.
Dunbar Hbr Ldg Lts (Bayswell Hill) 198°. Front, Oc G 6s 15m 3M; 3 Or △ on col; 56°00'·26N 02°31'·21W. Rear, Oc G 6s 22m 3M; 3 Or ▽; sync with front; both lts 188°-G(intens)-208°.
S Carr Q; 56°03'·69N 02°37'·50W.
Bass Rock, S side, ☆ Fl (3) 20s 46m 10M; W twr; vis: 241°-107°; 56°04'·61N 02°38'·48W.

FIRTH OF FORTH AND SOUTH SHORE

(Direction of buoyage East to West)

NORTH BERWICK

Outfall Fl Y; 56°04'·29N 02°40'·89W.
Fidra ☆ 56°04'·39N 02°47'·13W; Fl(4) 30s 34m **15M**; W twr; obsc by Bass Rock, Craig Leith and Lamb Island.

PORT SETON, COCKENZIE, FISHERROW and S CHANNEL

Port Seton, E Pier Hd ☆ Iso WR 4s 10m W9M, R6M; vis: shore-R-105°-W-225°-R-shore; *Bell (occas)*; 55°58'·40N 02°57'·23W.
Fisherrow E Pier Hd ☆ Oc 6s 5m 6M; 55°56'·79N 03°04'·11W.
Narrow Deep Fl(2) R 10s; 56°01'·46N 03°04'·59W.
Herwit Fl(3) G 10s; 56°01'·05N 03°06'·52W.
North Craig Q(3) 10s; 56°01'·02N 03°03'·52W.
Craigh Waugh Fl(2) 10s; 56°00'·26N 03°04'·47W.
Diffuser Hds (Outer) Q; 55°59'·81N 03°07'·84W.
Diffuser Hds (Inner) Q(6) + LFl 15s; 55°59'·38N 03°08'·02W.

LEITH and GRANTON

Leith Approach Fl R 3s; 55°59'·95N 03°11'·51W.
East Bkwtr Hd ☆ Iso R 4s 7m 9M; 55°59'·48N 03°10'·94W.
Granton E Pier Hd ☆ Fl R 2s 5m 6M; 55°59'·28N 03°13'·27W.

NORTH CHANNEL and MIDDLE BANK

Inchkeith Fairway Iso 2s; **Racon (T) 5M**; 56°03'·49N 03°00'·10W.
No 1 Fl G 9s; 56°03'·22N 03°03'·71W.
No 2 Fl R 9s; 56°02'·90N 03°03'·72W.
No 3 Fl G 6s; 56°03'·22N 03°06'·10W.
No 4 Fl R 6s; 56°02'·89N 03°06'·11W.
No 5 Fl G 3s; 56°03'·18N 03°07'·88W.
No 6 Fl R 3s; 56°03'·05N 03°08'·44W.
No 8 Fl R 9s 56°02'·95N 03°09'·62W.
Inchkeith ☆ 56°02'·01N 03°08'·17W; Fl 15s 67m 14M; stone twr.
Pallas Rock VQ (9) 10s 56°01'·50N 03°09'·30W.
East Gunnet Q (3) 10s; 56°01'·41N 03°10'·38W.
West Gunnet Q (9) 15s 56°01'·34N 03°11'·06W.
No 7 QG; **Racon (T) 5M**; 56°02'·80N 03°10'·97W.
No 9 Fl G 6s; 56°02'·32N 03°13'·48W.
No 10 Fl R 6s; 56°02'·07N 03°13'·32W.
No 11 Fl G 3s 56°02'·08N 03°15'·26W.
No 12 Fl R 3s; 56°01'·78N 03°15'·15W.
No 13 Fl G 9s; 56°01'·77N 03°16'·94W.
No 14 Q R; 56°01'·51N 03°16'·90W.
Oxcars ☆ Fl (2) WR 7s 16m W13M, R12M; W twr, R band; vis: 072°-W-087°- R-196°-W-313°-R-072°; 56°01'·36N 03°16'·84W.
Inchcolm E Pt ☆ Fl (3) 15s 20m 10M; Gy twr; part obsc by land 075°-145·5°; 56°01'·72N 03°17'·83W.
No 15 Fl G 6s; 56°01'·39N 03°18'·95W.

MORTIMER'S DEEP

Hawkcraig Point Ldg Lts 292°. Front, Iso 5s 12m 14M; W twr; vis: 282°-302°; 56°03'·03N 03°17'·07W. Rear, 96m from front, Iso 5s 16m 14M; W twr; vis: 282°-302°.
Inchcolm S Lts in line 066°. Front, 84m from rear, Q 7m 7M; W twr; vis: 062·5°-082·5°; 56°01'·78N 03°18'·28W. Common Rear, Iso 5s 11m 7M; W twr; vis: 062·5°-082·5°; 56°01'·80N 03°18'·13W. N Lts in line 076·7°. Front, 80m from rear, Q 7m 7M; W twr; vis: 062·5°-082·5°.

APPROACHES TO FORTH BRIDGES

No 17 Fl G 3s; 56°01'·23N 03°19'·84W.
No 16 Fl R 3s; 56°00'·87N 03°19'·60W.
No 19 Fl G 9s; 56°00'·71N 03°22'·47W.
Rosyth Chan centreline ☆ Iso 4s 56m 8M; 56°00'·44N 03°24'·64W.
Central Twr (Beamer Rk) ☆ Iso 2s 7m 9M; 56°00'·29N 03°24'·75W.
Forth Chan centreline ☆ Iso 8s 56m 8M; 56°00'·12N 03°24'·85W.

PORT EDGAR

W Bkwtr Hd ☆ Fl R 4s 4m 8M; 55°59'·86N 03°24'·78W. W blockhouse.

FIRTH OF FORTH – NORTH SHORE (INWARD)

BURNTISLAND

W Pier Outer Hd ☆ Fl (2) R 6s 7m; W twr; 56°03'·22N 03°14'·26W.
E Pier Outer Hd ☆ Fl (2) G 6s 7m 5M; 56°03'·24N 03°14'·17W.

ABERDOUR, BRAEFOOT BAY and INCHCOLM

Hawkcraig Pt ☆ (see **MORTIMER'S DEEP** above).
Braefoot Bay Terminal, W Jetty. Ldg Lts 247·3°. **Front**, Fl 3s 6m **15M**; W △ on E dolphin; vis: 237·2°-257·2°; 56°02'·16N 03°18'·71W; 4 dolphins with 2 FG (vert). **Rear**, 88m from front, Fl 3s 12m **15M**; W ▽ on appr gangway; vis: 237·2°-257·2°; sync with front.

INVERKEITHING BAY

St David's Fl G 5s 3m 7M; Or □, on pile; 56°01'·37N 03°22'·29W.
Channel QG; 56°01'·43N 03°23'·02W.

ROSYTH

No 2 Q (3) 10s; 56°00'·69N 03°25'·18W.

Main Chan Dir lt 323·5°. Bn 'A' Oc WRG 7m 4M; R □ on W post with R bands; vis: 318°-G-321°-321°-W-326°-R-328° (H24); 56°01'·19N 03°25'·61W.

Dir lt 115°, Bn 'C' Oc WRG 6s 7m 4M; W ▽ on W Bn; vis: 110°- R -113° W -116·5° - G -120°; 56°00'·61N 03°24'·25W.

S Arm Jetty Hd ☆ L Fl (2) WR 12s 5m W9M; R6M; vis: 010°-W-280°-R-010°; 56°01'·09N 03°26'·58W.

RIVER FORTH

ROSYTH to GRANGEMOUTH

Dhu Craig Fl G 5s; 56°00'·74N 03°27'·23W.

Blackness QR; 56°01'·06N 03°30'·30W.

Tancred Bank Fl (2) R 10s; 56°01'·58N 03°31'·91W.

Dods Bank Fl R 3s; 56°02'·03N 03°34'·07W.

Bo'ness Fl R 10s; 56°02'·23N 03°35'·38W.

Torry ☆ Fl G 10s 5m 7M; G ○ structure; 56°02'·46N 03°35'·28W.

Bo'ness Bcns 2 QR 3m 2M; 56°01'·85N 03°36'·22W.

Bo'ness Hbr ; 56°01'·26N 03°36'·46W.

GRANGEMOUTH

Grangemouth App No 1 Fl (3) 10s 4m 6M;56°02'·12N 03°38'·10W.

Hen & Chickens Fl (3) G 10s; 56°02'·35N 03°38'·08W.

FIRTH OF FORTH – NORTH SHORE (OUTWARD)

KIRKCALDY and METHIL

Kirkcaldy W Pier Hd ☆ Fl R 5s 7m 3M; 56°06'·80N 03°08'·97W.

Kirkcaldy E Pier Hd ☆ Fl G 5s 12m 3M; 56°06'·78N 03°08'·90W.

Methil Outer Pier Hd ☆ Oc G 6s 8m 5M; W twr; vis: 280°-100°; 56°10'·76N 03°00'·48W.

ELIE and ST MONANS

Elie Ness ☆ 56°11'·04N 02°48'·77W; Fl 6s 15m **17M**; W twr.

St Monans Bwtr Hd ☆ Fl G 3s 3m 4M; 56°12'·19N 02°45'·94W.

St Monans Inner Lt ☆ Iso 4s 3m 4M; 56°12'·29N 02°45'·95W.

PITTENWEEM and ANSTRUTHER EASTER

Pittenweem, Ldg Lts 037° Middle Pier Hd. Front, FR 4m 5M. Rear, FR 8m 5M. Both Gy Cols, Or stripes; 56°12'·69N 02°43'·69W.

Pittenweem, E Bkwtr Hd ☆ Fl (2) RG 5s 9m R9M, G6M; vis: 265°-R-345°-G-055°; 56°12'·63N 02°43'·74W.

Anstruther, Ldg Lts 019°. Front FG 7m 4M; 56°13'·28N 02°41'·76W. Rear, 38m from front, FG 11m 4M (both W masts).

MAY I, CRAIL, ST ANDREWS and FIFE NESS to MONTROSE

Isle of May ☆ 56°11'·12N 02°33'·46W(Summit); Fl (2) 15s 73m **22M**; □ twr on stone dwelling.

Crail, Ldg Lts 295°. Front, FR 24m 6M (not lit when hbr closed); 56°15'·46N 02°37'·84W. Rear, 30m from front, FR 30m 6M.

Fife Ness ☆ 56°16'·74N 02°35'·19W; Iso WR 10s 12m **W15M**, R12M; W bldg; vis: 143°-W-197°-R-217°-W-023°; 002320798.

N Carr Q (3) 10s 3m 5M; 56°18'·05N 02°32'·94W.

St Andrews ☆ 56°20'·38N 02°47'·07W; Dir lt 277·5; Iso WRG 2s 17m 9M; vis: 272°-G-276°-AlWG-277°-W-278°-AlWR-279°-R-283°. St Andrews N Bkwtr Bn ☆ Fl G 3M 56°20'·36N 02°46'·77W.

Bell Rk ☆ 56°26'·08N 02°23'·21W; Fl 5s 28m **18M; Racon (M) 18M**.

Met Mast ☆ Mo(U) 15s 22m 10M; Aero FR (116m), *Horn Mo(U) 30s;* 56°26'·40N 02°14'·49W; 992351153.

RIVER TAY, TAYPORT, DUNDEE and PERTH

Tay Fairway L Fl 10s; *Bell;* 56°28'·45N 02°36'·60W.

Middle Fl G 3s; 56°28'·08N 02°38'·47W.

Middle Fl (2) R 6s 56°27'·87N 02°37'·95W.

Abertay N Q (3) 10s; 56°27'·61N 02°40'·75W.

Abertay S (Elbow) Fl R 6s 56°27'·18N 02°39'·63W.

Tayport High Lt ☆ Dir lt 268·25°; WRG 3s 23m WRG14M; W twr, vis: 266°- VQG -267·5°- IsoG -268°- IsoW -268·5°- IsoR -269°- VQR -270°; 56°27'·17N 02°53'·94W.

ARBROATH

Ldg lts 299·2°. Front , FR 7m 5M; W col; 56°33'·29N 02°35'·16W. Rear, 50m from front, FR 13m 5M; W col.

MONTROSE

Scurdie Ness ☆ 56°42'·10N 02°26'·24W; Fl (3) 20s 38m **20M**; W twr; **Racon (T) 14-16M**.

Outer Ldg Lts 271·5°; Front, FR 11m 5M; W twin pillars, R bands; 56°42'·21N 02°27'·41W; Rear, 272m from front, FR 18m 5M; W twr, R cupola.

Inner Ldg Lts 265°; Front FG 21m 5M; Rear FG 33m 5M Or ▽ on metal framework tower; vis: 263°-G-264°-AlWG-264°-W-265°-AlWR-265°-R-266° (occas).

MONTROSE TO RATTRAY HEAD

JOHNSHAVEN and GOURDON HARBOUR

Johnshaven, Ldg Lts 316°. Front, FR 5m; 56°47'·62N 02°20'·26W. Rear, 85m from front, FG 20m; shows R when unsafe to ent hbr. Gourdon Hbr, Ldg Lts 358°. Front, FR 5m 5M; W twr; shows G when unsafe to enter; 56°49'·69N 02°17'·24W. Rear, 120m from front, FR 30m 5M; W twr.

Gourdon E B'water ☆ Q 3m 3M; 49°57'·60N 02°17'·19W.

Todhead Lighthouse (disused), white tower, 13m.

STONEHAVEN to GIRDLE NESS

Outer Pier Hd ☆ Iso WRG 4s 7m 5M; vis: 214°-G-246°-W-268°-R-280°; 56°57'·59N 02°12'·00W.

Girdle Ness ☆ Fl (2) 20s 56m **22M**; obsc by Greg Ness when brg > 020°; **Racon (G) 25M**; 57°08'·34N 02°02'·91W.

ABERDEEN

Fairway Mo (A) 5s; **Racon (T) 7M**; 57°09'·31N 02°01'·95W.

Torry Ldg lts 237·2°, Front FR or G 14m 5M; R when ent safe, FG when dangerous to navigate; W twr; 57°08'·38N 02°04'·50W.

Rear, 220m from front, FR or G 19m 5M; R when ent safe, FG when dangerous to navigate; W twr; 57°08'·31N 02°04'·68W.

Aberdeen Harbour Ent ☆ 57°08'·38N 02°04'·48W; Dir lt 237·2° Fl WRG 1s 7m 9M; metal post; vis: 235·2°-QG-236·2°-AlQGW-236·7°-QW-237·7°-AlQRW-238·2°-QR-239·2°.

S Bkwtr Hd ☆ Fl (3) R 8s 23m 7M; 57°08'·69N 02°03'·34W.

N Pier Hd ☆ Iso G 4s 11m 10M; W twr; 57°08'·74N 02°03'·69W. In fog FY 10m (same twr) vis: 136°-336°; *Bell (3) 12s.*

S Skates Nose Jetty Hd ☆ Q R 4m 4M; 57°08'·49N 02°04'·06W.

Abercrombie Jetty Hd ☆ Oc G 4s 5m 4M; 57°08'·53N 02°04'·15W.

BUCHAN NESS TO INVERNESS

PETERHEAD and RATTRAY HEAD

Buchan Ness ☆ Fl 5s 40m **18M**; W twr, R bands; **Racon (O) 14-16M**; 57°28'·23N 01°46'·51W.

Kirktown Ldg lts 314°. Front, Oc R 6s 14m 10M; Or △ on lattice mast; 57°30′·22N 01°47′·21W. Rear, Oc R 6s 21m 10M (sync with front); Or ▽ on lattice mast.

S Bkwtr Hd ☆ Fl (2) R 12s 24m 7M; 57°29′·79N 01°46′·54W.

N Bkwtr Hd ☆ Iso RG 6s 19m 11M; W tripod; vis: 171°-R-236°-G-171°; *Horn 30s;* 57°29′·84N 01°46′·32W.

Rattray Hd ☆ 57°36′·61N 01°49′·03W Fl (3) 30s 28m **18M**; W twr; **Racon (M) 15M**; *Horn (2) 45s*.

Smith Bank Met Mast Mo(U) 15s 17m 10M Mast (101); Horn Mo(U) 30s; 58°10′·93N 02°49′·22W.

FRASERBURGH

Balaclava Bkwtr Head ☆ Fl (2) G 8s 26m 6M; dome on W twr; vis: 178°-326°; 57°41′·51N 01°59′·70W.

N Pier ☆ WRG 2s 7m 8M; metal post; 285°-G-287°-WG-289°-W-293°-WR-295°-R-297°; 57°41′·54N 01°59′·99W.

Kinnaird Hd ☆ 57°41′·87N 02°00′·26W Fl 5s 25m **22M**; vis: 092°-297°.

MACDUFF, BANFF and WHITEHILLS

Macduff Pier Hd ☆ Fl (2) WRG 6s 12m W9M, R7M; W twr; vis: shore-G-115°-W-174°-R-210°; 57°40′·26N 02°30′·01W.

Macduff Ldg Lts 130°, Front FR 28m 3M; 57°40′·18N 02°29′·85W. Rear, 220m from front, FR 55m 3M; both Or △ on mast.

Banff Ldg Lts 295°, Front Fl R 4s; 57°40·30N 02°31·36W. Rear, QR; both vis: 210°-345°.

Whitehills Pier Hd ☆ 57°40′·80N 02°34′·88W Fl WR 3s 7m W9M, R6M; W twr; vis: 132°-R-212°-W-245°.

PORTSOY and FINDOCHTY

Portsoy Pier Ldg Lts 173°, Front Fl G 4s 20m 3M; post; 57°41′·09N 02°41′·40W; Rear Q G 22m 3M; R △ on BW post.

Findochty Middle Pier Ldg Lts 166°, Front FR 6m 3M; 57°41′·90N 02°54′·20W. Rear FR 10m 3M.

BUCKIE

West Muck ☆ QR 5m 7M; tripod; 57°41′·06N 02°58′·01W.

N Pier Ldg Lts 096°, Front, FR 6m 9M; 57°40′·83N 02°57′·71W. **Rear** ☆, 60m from front, Oc R 10s 15m 15M; W twr.

LOSSIEMOUTH, HOPEMAN and BURGHEAD

Lossiemouth S Pier Hd ☆ Fl R 6s 11m 5M; 57°43′·42N 03°16′·69W.

Halliman Skerries Q; **Racon M**, 57°44′·33N 03°18′·57W.

Hopeman Ldg Lts 081°, Front, FR 3m; 57°42′·71N 03°26′·18W. Rear, 10m from front, FR, 4m.

Burghead N Bkwtr Hd ☆ Oc 8s 7m 5M; 57°42′·09N 03°30′·03W.

FINDHORN, NAIRN and INVERNESS FIRTH

Findhorn Landfall LF 10s 57°40′·34N 03°38′·77W.

Nairn E Pier Hd ☆ Oc WRG 4s 6m 5M; 8-sided twr; vis: shore-G-100°-W-207°-R-shore; 57°35′·62N 03°51′·65W.

Riff Bank E Fl Y 10s 3m 5M 57°38′·38N 03°58′·18W; AIS.

SOUTH CHANNEL

Riff Bank S Q (6) + L Fl 15s; 57°36′·73N 04°00′·97W.

Chanonry ☆ 57°34′·45N 04°05′·56W Oc 6s 12m 12M; W twr; vis: 148°-073°.

Munlochy L Fl 10s; 57°32′·91N 04°07′·65W.

Petty Bank Fl R 5s 57°31′·58N 04°08′·98W.

Meikle Mee Fl G 3s 57°30′·26N 04°12′·02W.

Longman Pt Fl WR 2s 7m W5M, R4M; vis: 078°-W-258°-R-078°; 57°29′·99N 04°13′·31W.

Craigton Point ☆ Fl WRG 4s 6m W11M, R7M, G7M; vis: 312°-W-048°-R-064°-W-085°-G-shore; 57°30′·05N 04°14′·09W.

Bridge Centre, Or △; **Racon (K) 6M**; 57°29′·97N 04°13′·79W.

INVERNESS and CALEDONIAN CANAL

R. Ness Outer QR 3m 4M; 57°29′·83N 04°13′·93W.

Carnarc Pt ☆ Fl G 2s 8m 4M; G lattice twr; 57°29′·72N 04°14′·25W.

Clachnaharry, S Tr′ng Wall Hd Iso G 4s 5m 2M; tfc sigs; 57°29′·43N 04°15′·86W.

INVERNESS TO DUNCANSBY HEAD

CROMARTY FIRTH and INVERGORDON

Fairway L Fl 10s; **Racon (M) 5M**; 57°39′·96N 03°54′·19W.

Cromarty Bank Fl (2) G 10s; 57°40′·66N 03°56′·78W.

Buss Bank Fl R 3s 57°40′·97N 03°59′·54W.

The Ness (Lt ho disused W tr 13m); 57°40′·98N 04°02′·20W

Nigg Oil Terminal Pier Hd ☆ Oc G 5s 31m 5M; Gy twr, floodlit; 57°41′·54N 04°02′·60W.

DORNOCH FIRTH to LYBSTER

Tarbat Ness ☆ 57°51′·88N 03°46′·76W Fl (4) 30s 53m **18M**; W twr, R bands; **Racon (T) 14-16M**.

Met Mast ☆ Mo(U) 15s 17m 10M; FR (101m), *Horn Mo(U) 30s;* 58°10′·93N 00°49′·22W.

Helmsdale ☆ Dir lt 313° WRG 2s 7m 6M (1M day); post; vis: 308°-Iso G-311°-Al WG-312°-Iso W-313°-Al WR-314°-Iso R-318°; 58°06′·91N 03°39′·04W.

Lybster, S Pier Hd ☆ Oc R 6s 10m 3M; 58°17′·79N 03°17′·41W.

Clyth Ness Lt Ho (unlit); W twr, R band; 58°18′·64N 03°12′·74W.

WICK

Wick Bay Fl (2)R 6s 2M; 58°26′·24N 03°04′·10W.

S Pier Hd ☆ Fl WRG 3s 12m W12M, R9M, G9M; W 8-sided twr; vis: 253°-G-270°-W-286°-R-329°; 58°26′·34N 03°04′·73W.

Dir lt 288·5° F WRG 9m W10M, R7M, G7M; col, N end of bridge; vis: 283·5°-G-287·2°-W-289·7°-R-293·5°; 58°26′·54N 03°05′·34W

Noss Hd ☆ 58°28′·76N 03°03′·09W Fl 20s 53m **W18M**; W twr; vis: 073°-045° (332°).

DUNCANSBY HEAD TO CAPE WRATH

Duncansby Hd ☆ 58°38′·65N 03°01′·58W Fl 12s 67m **21M**; W twr; **Racon (T)**.

Muckle Skerry ☆ 58°41′·41N 02°55′·49W Fl (3) 30s 52m **23M**; W twr; 992351086.

Lother Rock ☆ Fl 2s 13m 6M; **Racon (M) 10M**; 58°43′·79N 02°58′·69W.

Swona ☆ Fl 8s 17m 9M; vis: 261°-210°; 58°44′·25N 03°04′·24W.

Swona N Hd ☆ Fl (3) 10s 16m 10M; 58°45′·11N 03°03′·10W.

Stroma ☆, Swilkie Point 58°41′·75N 03°07′·01W Fl (2) 20s 32m **20M**; W twr; 992351092.

Dunnet Hd ☆ 58°40′·28N 03°22′·60W Fl (4) 30s 105m **23M**.

THURSO, SCRABSTER and CAPE WRATH

Thurso ☆ FG 5m 4M; Gy post; 58°35′·91N 03°30′·80W.

Scrabster Q. E. Pier Hd ☆ Fl (2) 4s 8m 8M 58°36′·66N 03°32′·31W.

Strathy Pt Lt Ho (disused) W twr on W dwelling; 58°36′·04N 04°01′·12W.

Sule Skerry ☆ 59°05′·09N 04°24′·38W Fl (2) 15s 34m **21M**; W twr; **Racon (T)**.

Sule Stack ⊙; V-AIS; ; 59°01′·45N 04°30′·40W; 992356017.
Nun Rock ⊙; V-AIS; ; 58°52′·65N 04°58′·30W; 992356016.

North Rona ☆ 59°07′·27N 05°48′·91W Fl (3) 20s 114m **22M**.

Sula Sgeir ☆ Fl 15s 74m 11M; □ structure; 59°05′·61N 06°09′·57W.

Loch Eriboll, White Hd ☆ Fl WR10s 18m W13M, R12M; W twr and bldg; vis: 030°-W-172°-R-191°-W-212°; 58°31′·01N 04°38′·90W.

Cape Wrath ☆ 58°37′·52N 04°59′·94W Fl (4) 30s 122m **21M**; W twr 992351087.

ORKNEY ISLANDS

Tor Ness ☆ 58°46′·78N 03°17′·86W Fl 5s 21m **17M**; W twr.

Cantick Hd (S Walls, SE end) ☆ 58°47′·23N 03°07′·88W Fl 20s 35m 13M; W twr.

SCAPA FLOW and APPROACHES

Long Hope, S Ness Pier Hd ☆ Fl WRG 3s 6m W7M, R5M, G5M; vis: 082°-G-242°-W-252°-R-082°; 58°48′·05N 03°12′·35W.

Hoxa Head ☆ Fl WR 3s 15m W9M, R6M; W twr; vis: 026°-W-163°-R-201°-W-215°; 58°49′·31N 03°02′·09W.

Nevi Skerry Fl (2) 6s 7m 6M; 58°50′·67N 03°02′·70W.

Flotta Grinds Fl (2) R; 58°50′·97N 03°00′·77W; 992351083.

Rose Ness ☆ 58°52′·33N 02°49′·97W Fl 6s 24m 8M; W twr.

Copinsay ☆ Fl (5) 30s 79m 14M; W twr; 58°53′·79N 02°40′·33W.

Barrel of Butter ☆ Fl (2) 10s 6m 7M; 58 53′·40N 03°07′·62W.

Cava ☆ Fl WR 3s 11m W10M, R8M; W ○ twr; vis: 351°-W-143°-196°-W-251°-R-271°-R-298°; 58°53′·21N 03°10′·70W .

Holm of Houton ☆ 58°54′·62N 03°10′·97W; Fl R 3s 7m 5M.

Houton Bay Ldg Lts 316°. Front Fl G 3s 8m. Rear , 200m from front, FG 16m; vis: 312°- 320°; 58°54′·97N 03°11′·56W.

CLESTRAN SOUND and HOY SOUND

Graemsay Is Hoy Sound ☆ Ldg Lts 104°. Front Low, Iso 3s 17m 12M; W twr; vis: 070°-255°, 58°56′·42N 03°18′·60W. **High Rear**, 1·2M from front, Oc WR 8s 35m **W19M**, R14M; W twr; vis: 097°-R-112°-W-163°-R-178°-W-332°; obsc on Ldg line within 0·5M.

Skerry of Ness ☆ Fl 4s 7m 7M,180°-W-090°; 58°56′·95N 03°17′·83W.

STROMNESS

Ldg Lts 317°. Front FR 29m 11M; W twr; 58°57′·61N 03°18′·15W. Rear, 55m from front, FR 39m 11M; vis: 307°-327°; H24.

AUSKERRY

Auskerry ☆ 59°01′·51N 02°34′·34W Fl 20s 34m **20M**; W twr.

Helliar Holm, S end ☆ Fl WRG 10s 18m W14M, R11M, G11M; W twr; vis: 256°-G-276°-W-292°-R-098°-W-116°-G-154°; 59°01′·13N 02°54′·09W.

Balfour Pier Shapinsay ☆ Fl (2) WRG 5s 5m W3M, R2M, G2M; vis: 270°-G-010°-W-020°-R-090°; 59°01′·86N 02°54′·49W.

KIRKWALL

Thieves Holm, ☆ Q R 8M; 59°01′·09N 02°56′·21W.

Pier N end ☆ 58°59′·29N 02°57′·72W Iso WRG 5s 8m **W15M**, R13M, G13M; W twr; vis: 153°-G-183°-W-192°-R-210°.

WIDE FIRTH

Linga Skerry Q (3) 10s; 59°02′·39N 02°57′·56W.
Boray Skerries Q (6) + L Fl 15s; 59°03′·65N 02°57′·66W.
Skertours Q; 59°04′·11N 02°56′·72W.
Galt Skerry Q; 59°05′·21N 02°54′·20W.
Seal Skerry ☆ Fl R 3s 5m 3M; platform; 59°05′·21N 02°54′·20W.

Brough of Birsay ☆ 59°08′·19N 03°20′·41W Fl (3) 25s 52m **18M**.

Papa Stronsay NE end, The Ness ☆ Fl(4)20s 8m 9M; W twr; 59°09′·34N 02°34′·93W.

SANDAY ISLAND and NORTH RONALDSAY

Quiabow Fl (2) G 12s; 59°09′·82N 02°36′·30W.

Start Pt ☆ 59°16′·69N 02°22′·71W Fl (2) 20s 24m **18M**.

Kettletoft Pier Hd ☆ Fl WRG 3s 7m W7M, R5M, G5M; vis: 351°-W- 011°-R-180°-G-351°; 59°13′·80N 02°35′·86W.

N Ronaldsay ☆ NE end, 59°23′·34N 02°22′·91W Fl 10s 43m **24M**; R twr, W bands; **Racon (T) 14-17M**.

EDAY and EGILSAY

Calf Sound ☆ Fl (3) WRG 10s 6m W8M, R6M, G6M; W twr; vis: shore-R-215°-W-222°-G-301°-W-305°; 59°14′·21N 02°45′·82W.

Backaland Pier ☆ 59°09′·43N 02°44′·88W Fl R 3s 5m 4M; vis: 192°-250°.

Egilsay Graand Q (6) + L Fl 15s; 59°06′·86N 02°54′·42W.

WESTRAY and PIEROWALL

Noup Head ☆ 59°19′·86N 03°04′·23W Fl 30s 79m **20M**; W twr; vis: about 335°-282° but partially obsc 240°-275°.

Pierowall E Pier Head ☆ Fl WRG 3s 7m W11M, R7M, G7M; vis: 254°-G-276°-W-291°-R-308°-G-215°; 59°19′·35N 02°58′·53W.

Papa Westray, Moclett Bay Pier Head ☆ Fl WRG 5s 7m W5M, R3M, G3M; vis: 306°-G-341°-W-040°-R-074°; 59°19′·60N 02°53′·52W.

SHETLAND ISLES

FAIR ISLE

Skadan South ☆, 59°30′·84N 01°39′·16W Fl (4) 30s 32m **22M**; W twr; vis: 260°-146°, obsc inshore 260°-282°.

Skroo ☆ N end 59°33′·13N 01°36′·58W Fl (2) 30s 80m **22M**; W twr; vis: 086·7°-358°.

MAINLAND, SOUTH

Sumburgh Head ☆ 59°51′·21N 01°16′·58W Fl (3) 30s 91m **23M**.

Lt Ho disused 59°51′·48N 01°16′·28W; W twr.

Mousa, Perie Bard ☆ Fl 3s 20m 10M; 59°59′·84N 01°09′·51W.

BRESSAY and LERWICK

Bressay, Kirkabister Ness ☆ 60°07′·20N 01°07′·31W; Fl (2) 10s 18m 10M. Adjacent Lt Ho disused.

Maryfield Ferry Terminal ☆ Oc WRG 6s 5m 5M; vis: W008°-R013°-G-111°-008°; 60°09′·43N 01°07′·45W.

North Ness ☆ Iso WG 4s 4m 5M; vis: shore-W-158°-G-216°-W-301°; 60°09′·57N 01°08′·77W

Loofa Baa Q (6) + L Fl 15s 4m 5M; 60°09′·72N 01°08′·79W.

Soldian Rock ⚓ Q (6) + L Fl 15s 60°12′·51N 01°04′·73W.

N ent Dir lt 215°, Oc WRG 6s 27m 8M; Y △, Or stripe; vis: 211°-R-214°-W-216°-G-221°; 60°10′·47N 01°09′·53W.

Rova Hd ☆ 60°11′·46N 01°08′·60W; Fl WRG 4s (sync) 12m W12M, R/G9M; W twr; vis: 090°-R-182°-W-191°-G-213°-R-241°-W-261·5°-G-009°-R-040°; same structure: **Dir** ☆ 186·5° Fl WRG 4s (sync) 14m **W16M**, R/G13M; (sync) vis: 176·5°-R-182°-W-191°-G-196·5°.

Dales Voe ☆ Fl (2) WRG 8s 5m W4M, R3M, G3M; vis: 220°-G-227°-W-233°-R-240°; 60°11′·79N 01°11′·23W.

Hoo Stack ☆ Fl (4) WRG 12s 40m W7M, R5M, G5M; W pylon; vis: 169°-R-180°-W-184°-G-193°-W-169°. Same structure, Dir lt 182°. Fl (4) WRG 12s 33m W9M, R6M, G6M; vis: 177°- R-180°-W-184°-W-187°; synch with upper lt; 60°14′·96N 01°05′·38W.

Mull (Moul) of Eswick ☆ Fl WRG 3s 50m W9M, R6M, G6M; W twr; vis: 028°-R-200°-W-207°-G-018°-W-028°; 60°15′·74N 01°05′·90W.

Inner Voder ⚓ Q (9) 15s; 60°16′·44N 01°05′·18W; AIS.

WHALSAY and SKERRIES

Symbister Ness ☆ Fl (2) WG 12s 11m W8M, G6M; W twr; vis: shore-W-203°-G-shore; 60°20′·43N 01°02′·29W.

Suther Ness ☆ Fl WRG 3s 10m W10M, R8M, G7M; vis: shore -W-038°-R-173°-W-206°-G-shore; 60°22′·12N 01°00′·20W.

Bound Skerry ☆ 60°25′·47N 00°43′·72W Fl 20s 44m **20M**; W twr.

South Mouth. Ldg Lts 014°. Front, FY3m 2M; 60°25′·33N 00°45′·01W. Rear, FY 12m 2M.

Muckle Skerry ☆ Fl (2) WRG 10s 15m W7M, R5M, G5M; W twr; vis: 046°-W-192°-R-272°-G-348°-W-353°-R-046°; 60°26′·41N 00°51′·84W.

YELL SOUND

S ent, Lunna Holm ☆ Fl (3) WRG 15s 19m W10M, R7M, G7M; W ◯ twr; vis: shore-R-090°-W-094°-G-209°-W-275°-R-shore; 60°27′·34N 01°02′·52W.

Firths Voe ☆, N shore 60°27′·21N 01°10′·63W Oc WRG 8s 9m **W15M**, R10M, G10M; W twr; vis: 189°-W-194°-G-257°-W-261°-R-339°-W-066°.

Linga Is. Dir lt 150° ☆ Q (4) WRG 8s 10m W9M, R9M, G9M; vis: 145°-R-148°-W-152°-G-155°. Q (4) WRG 8s 10m W7M, R4M, G4M; same structure; vis: 052°-R-146°, 154°-G-196°-W-312°; synch; 60°26′·80N 01°09′·13W.

The Rumble Bn ☆ R Bn; Fl 10s 8m 4M; **Racon (O)**; 60°28′·16N 01°07′·26W.

Yell, Ulsta Ferry Term. Bkwtr Hd ☆ Oc RG 4s 7m R5M, G5M; vis: shore-G-354°, 044°-R-shore. Same structure; Oc WRG 4s 5m W8M, R5M, G5M; vis: shore-G-008°-W-036°-R-shore; 60°29′·74N 01°09′·52W.

Toft Ferry Terminal ☆, Dir lt 241° (H24); Dir Oc WRG 10s 8m **W16M**, R10M, G10M; vis: 236° -G-240°-W-242°-R-246°; by day W2M, R1M, G1M. 60°27′·96N 01°12′·34W.

Ness of Sound, W side ☆ Fl (3) WRG 12s 18m W9M, R6M, G6M; vis: shore-G-345°-W-350°-R-160°-W-165°-G-shore; 60°31′·34N 01°11′·28W.

Brother Is. Dir lt 329°, Fl (4) WRG 8s 16m W10M, R7M, G7M; vis: 323·5°-G-328°-W-330°-R-333·5°; 60°30′·95N 01°14′·11W.

Mio Ness ☆ Q (2) WR 10s 12m W7M, R4M; W ◯ twr; vis: 282°-W-238°-R-282°; 60°29′·66N 01°13′·68W.

Tinga Skerry ☆ Q(2)G 10s 9m 5M. W ◯ twr; 60°30′·48N 01°14′·86W.

YELL SOUND, NORTH ENTRANCE

Bagi Stack ☆ Fl (4) 20s 45m 10M; 60°43′·53N 01°07′·54W.

Gruney Is ☆ Fl WR 5s 53m W8M, R6M; W twr; vis: 064°-R-180°-W-012°; **Racon (T) 14M**; 60°39′·15N 01°18′·17W.

Pt of Fethaland ☆ 60°38′·05N 01°18′·70W Fl (3) WR 15s 65m **W19M, R15M**; vis 080°-R-103°-W-160°-R-206°-W-340°.

Muckle Holm ☆ Fl (4) 10s 32m 10M 60°34′·83N 01°16′·01W.

Little Holm ☆ Iso 4s 12m 6M; W twr; 60°33′·42N 01°15′·88W.

Outer Skerry ☆ Fl 6s 12m 8M; 60°33′·04N 01°18′·32W.

Quey Firth ☆ Oc WRG 6s 22m W12M, R8M, G8M; W twr; vis: shore (through S & W)-W-290°-G-327°-W-334°-W-shore; 60°31′·43N 01°19′·58W.

Lamba, S side ☆Fl WRG 3s 30m W8M, R5M, G5M; W twr; vis: shore-G-288°-W-293°-R-327°-W-044°-R-140°-W-shore. Dir lt 290·5° Fl WRG 3s 24m W10M, R7M, G7M; vis: 285·5°-G-288°-W-293°-W-295·5°; 60°30′·73N 01°17′·84W.

SULLOM VOE

Gluss Is ☆ Ldg Lts 194·7° (H24). **Front**, 60°29′·77N 01°19′·44W F 39m **19M**; ☐ on Gy twr; **Rear**, 0·75M from front, F 69m **19M**; ☐ on Gy twr; both Lts 9M by day.

Little Roe ☆ Fl (3) WR 10s 16m W5M, R4M; W structure, Or band; vis: 036°-R-095·5°-W-036°; 60°29′·99N 01°16′·46W.

Skaw Taing ☆ Ldg Lts 150·5°. Front, Oc WRG 5s 21m W8M, R5M, G5M; Or and W structure; vis: 049°-W-078°-G-147°-W-154°-R-169°-W-288°; 60°29′·10N 01°16′·86W. Rear, 195m from front, Oc 5s 35m 8M; vis: W145°-156°.

Ness of Bardister ☆ Oc WRG 8s 20m W9M, R6M, G6M; Or &W structure; vis: 180·5°- W-240°-R-310·5°-W-314·5°-G-030·5°; 60°28′·19N 01°19′·63W.

Fugla Ness. Lts in line 212·3°. Rear, 60°27′·25N 01°19′·74W Iso 4s 45m 14M. Common front 60°27′·45N 01°19′·57W Iso 4s 27m 14M; synch with rear Lts. Lts in line 203°. Rear, 60°27′·26N 01°19′·81W Iso 4s 45m 14M.

Sella Ness ☆ Dir lt 133·5°; 60°26′·76N 01°16′·66W Oc WRG 10s 19m **W16M**, R3M, G3M; vis: 123·5°-G-130·5°-Al WG (white phase increasing with brg)-132·5°-W-134·5°-Al WR(R phase inc with brg)-136·5°-R-143·5°; H24. By day Oc WRG 10s 19m W2M, R1M,G1M as above.

EAST YELL, UNST and BALTA SOUND

Whitehill ☆ Fl WR 3s 24m W9M, R6M; W clad metal frame twr; vis: 147°-W-163°-R-211°-W-352°-R-003°; 60°34′·80N 01°00′·22W. Fetlar. Hamars Ness ☆ Iso G 6s 5m 3M; 60°37′·78N 00°55′·73W.

Balta Sound ☆Fl WR 10s 17m 10M, R7M; vis: 249°-W-008°-R-058°-W-154°; 60°44′·43N 00°47′·68W.

Holme of Skaw ☆ Fl 5s 8m 8M; white metal framework twr; 60°49′·87N 00°46′·30W.

Muckle Flugga ☆ 60°51′·32N 00°53′·13W Fl (2) 20s 66m **22M**.

Yell. Cullivoe Bkwtr Hd ☆ Fl (2) WRG 10s 3m 4M; vis: 080°-G- 294°-W-355°-R-080°; 60°41′·86N 00°59′·70W.

Unst. Head of Mula ☆ Fl WRG 5s 48m W10M, G7M, R7M; metal framework twr; vis: 292°-G-357°-W-002°-R-157°-W-161·5; 60°40′·76N 00°57′·58W.

MAINLAND, WEST

Esha Ness ☆ 60°29′·34N 01°37′·65W Fl 12s 61m **25M**.

Ness of Hillswick ☆ Fl (4) WR 15s 34m W9M, R6M; vis: 217°-W-093°-R-114°; 60°27′·21N 01°29′·80W.

Muckle Roe, Swarbacks Minn ☆ Fl WR 3s 30m W9M, R6M; vis: 314°-W-041°-R-075°-W-137°; 60°20′·98N 01°27′·07W.

W Burra Firth Outer ☆ Oc WRG 8s 27m W9M, R7M, G7M; vis: 136°-G-142°-W-150°-R-156°. H24; 60°17′·79N 01°33′·56W.

W Burra Firth Inner ☆ 60°17′·78N 01°32′·17W F WRG 9m **W15M**, R9M, G9M; vis: 095°-G-098°-W-102°-105°; H24.

Ve Skerries ☆ Fl (2) 20s 17m 11M; W twr; **Racon (T) 15M**; 60°22′·36N 01°48′·78W.

Papa Stour Housa Voe Dir lt 228° ☆ F WRG 2m W9M, R7M, G7M; vis: 219°- G-226°- W-230°-R-239°; 60°19′·58N 01°40′·47W.

Rams Head ☆ Fl WRG 8s 16m W9M, R6M; G6M; W house; vis: 265°-G-355°-W-012°-R-090°-W-136°, obsc by Vaila I when brg more than 030°; 60°11′·96N 01°33′·47W.

North Havra ☆ Fl(3) WRG 12s 24m W11M, R8M, G8M; W twr; vis: 001°-G-053·5°-W-060·5°-R-144°, 274°-G-334°-W-337·5°-R -001°; 60°09′·85N 01°20′·29W.

SCALLOWAY

Bullia Skerry ☆ Fl 5s 5m 5M; stainless steel pillar & platform 60°06′·55N 01°21′·57W.

Point of the Pund ☆ Fl WRG 5s 20m W7M, R5M, G5M; W GRP twr; vis: 267°-W-350°-R-090°-G-111°-R-135°-W-140°-G-177°; 60°07′·99N 01°18′·31W.

Whaleback Skerry ⍋ Q; 60°07′·95N 01°18′·90W.

Blacks Ness Pier SW corner ☆ Oc WRG 10s 10m W11M, G8M, R8M; vis: 052°-G-063·5°-W-065·5°-R-077°; 60°08′·02N 01°16′·59W.

Fugla Ness ☆ Fl (2) WRG 10s 20m W10M, R7M, G7M; W twr; vis: 014°-G-032°-W-082°-R-134°-W-shore; 60°06′·38N 01°20′·85W.

FOULA

South Ness ☆ 60°06′·75N 02°03′·86W Fl WR (3) 15s 36m **W18M** R14M; W twr; vis: 221°-W-255°-R-277°-W-123°-obscured-221°.

1	Berwick-upon-Tweed	**1**										
2	Eyemouth	10	**2**									
3	Dunbar	26	17	**3**								
4	Port Edgar	58	50	34	**4**							
5	Methil	45	36	20	20	**5**						
6	Fife Ness	38	29	17	34	16	**6**					
7	Dundee	58	49	37	54	36	20	**7**				
8	Montrose	59	51	43	61	43	27	27	**8**			
9	Stonehaven	72	66	60	78	60	44	45	20	**9**		
10	Aberdeen	82	78	73	90	72	56	57	32	13	**10**	
11	Peterhead	105	98	93	108	94	78	80	54	35	25	**11**

11	155	79	47	76	104	144	126	120	125	145	Cape Wrath	**11**
	10	95	124	120	148	190	170	162	156	160	Lerwick	**10**
		9	50	46	74	114	104	90	95	115	Kirkwall	**9**
			8	31	59	99	89	75	80	100	Scrabster	**8**
				7	29	69	58	44	50	72	Wick	**7**
					6	43	32	26	44	74	Helmsdale	**6**
						5	13	34	59	90	Inverness	**5**
							4	23	48	79	Nairn	**4**
								3	25	56	Lossiemouth	**3**
									2	33	Banff/Macduff	**2**
										1	Peterhead	**1**

AREA 6 *NW Scotland – C Wrath to Oban including The Western Isles*

SELECTED LIGHTS, BUOYS & WAYPOINTS

CAPE WRATH TO LOCH TORRIDON

Cape Wrath ☆ 58°37′·52N 04°59′·94W Fl (4) 30s 122m **21M**; W twr; 992351087.

LOCH INCHARD and LOCH LAXFORD

Kinlochbervie Dir lt 327° ☆ 58°27′·49N 05°03′·08W WRG 15m **16M** vis: 326°-FG-326·5°-AlGW-326·8°-FW-327·3°-AlRW-327·5°-FR-328°.

Creag Mhòr Dir lt 147°; Iso WRG 2s 16m 4M; vis: 136·5°-R -146·5°-W-147·5°-G-157·5°; 58°26′·99N 05°02′·45W.

Stoer Head ☆ 58°14′·43N 05°24′·07W Fl 15s 59m **24M**; W twr.

LOCH INVER, SUMMER ISLES and ULLAPOOL

Soyea I ☆ Fl (2) 10s 34m 6M; 58°08′·56N 05°19′·67W.

Glas Leac ☆ Fl WRG 3s 7m 5M; vis: 071°- W-078°-R-090°-G-103°-W-111°, 243°-W-247°-G-071°; 58°08′·68N 05°16′·36W.

Rubha Cadail ☆ Fl WRG 6s 11m W9M, R6M, G6M; W twr; vis: 311°-G-320°-W-325°-R-103°-W-111°-G-118°-W-127°-R-157°-W-199°; 57°55′·51N 05°13′·40W.

Ullapool Pt ☆ Iso R 4s 8m 6M; W twr; vis: 258°-108°; 57°53′·59N 05°09′·93W.

Cailleach Head ☆ Fl (2) 12s 60m 9M; W twr; vis: 015°-236°; 57°55′·81N 05°24′·23W.

LOCH EWE and LOCH GAIRLOCH

Fairway ⍟ L Fl 10s; 57°51′·98N 05°40′·09W.

Rubha Reidh ☆ 57°51′·52N 05°48′·72W Fl (4) 15s 37m **18M**.

Glas Eilean ☆ Fl WRG 6s 9m W6M, R4M; vis: 080°-W-102°-R-296°-W-333°-G-080°; 57°42′·79N 05°42′·42W.

Sgeir Dhubh Mhór ⍋; 57°42′·02N 05°42′·72W.

OUTER HEBRIDES – EAST SIDE

LEWIS

Butt of Lewis ☆ 58°30′·92N 06°15′·72W Fl 5s 52m **25M**; R twr; vis: 056°-320°.

Tiumpan Hd ☆ 58°15′·66N 06°08′·29W Fl (2)15s 55m **18M**; W twr.

Broad Bay Tong ⚓ Ldg Lts 320°, Oc R 8s 8m 4M; 58°14′·48N 06°19′·98W. Rear, 70m from front, Oc R 8s 9m 4M.

STORNOWAY

Arnish Point ☆ Fl WR 10s 17m W9M, R7M; W ○ twr; vis: 088°-W-198°-R-302°-W-013°; 58°11′·50N 06°22′·16W.

Sandwick Bay, NW ☆ Dir WRG 4s 10m 10M; 336°-IsoG -339°- AlWG -341°-IsoW-347°-AlWR-349°-Iso-R-352°; 58°12′·17N 06°22′·15W.

No 1 Pier SW corner ☆ Q WRG 5m 11M; vis: shore-G-335°-W-352°-R-shore; 58°12′·36N 06°23′·43W.

Creed Estuary Dir Lt ☆ 288·5° WRG 4s 23m 5M; 277°-IsoG-282°-Al WG-287°-IsoW-290°-Al WR-292°-R-295°; 58°12'·00N 06°23'·54W.

No 3 Pier ☆ Q (2) G 10s 7m 2M 58°12'·31N 06°23'·28W.

Glumaig Hbr ☆ Iso WRG 3s 8m 3M; 58°11'·29N 06°22'·83W; grey framework twr; vis: 150°-G-174°-W-185°-R-205°.

LOCH ERISORT, LOCH SHELL and EAST LOCH TARBERT

Shiants QG; 57°54'·57N 06°25'·70W.

Sgeir Inoe Fl G 6s; **Racon (M) 5M**; 57°50'·93N 06°33'·93W.

Eilean Glas (Scalpay) ★ 57°51'·41N 06°38'·55W Fl (3) 20s 43m **18M**; W twr, R bands; **Racon (T) 16-18M**; 992356014.

Sgeir Graidach Q (6) + L Fl 15s; 57°50'·36N 06°41'·37W.

Sgeir Ghlas ☆ Iso WRG 4s 9m W9M, R6M, G6M; W ○ twr; vis: 282°-G-319°-W-329°-R-153°-W-164°-G-171°; 57°52'·36N 06°45'·24W.

Tarbert ☆ Dir 301·5° WRG 9m 4M; vis : 290°-Iso G-297°-Al WG-300°-Iso W-303°-Al WR-306°-Iso R306°-313°; 57°53'·80N 06°47'·85W.

SOUND OF HARRIS, LEVERBURGH and BERNERAY

No 1 QG; 57°41'·20N 07°02'·67W.

No 3 Fl G 5s; 57°41'·86N 07°03'·44W.

No 4 Fl R 5s; 57°41'·76N 07°03'·63W.

Suilven Fl (3)R 10s; 57°41'·68N 07°04'·36W.

Cabbage Fl (2) R 6s; **Racon (T) 5M (3cm)**; 57°42'·13N 07°03'·96W.

Leverburgh Ldg Lts 014·7°. Front, Q 10m 4M 57°46'·23N 07°02'·04W. Rear, Oc 3s 12m 4M.

Jane's Tower Q (2) G 5s 6m 4M; vis: obscured 273°-318°; 57°45'·76N 07°02'·11W.

Leverburgh Reef Fl R 2s 4m 57°45'·97N 07°01'·86W.

Laimhrig Mhor ☆ Q G; 57°45'·92N 07°01'·65W.

Leverburg Dir Lt 064·5°; Dir G 4m 6M metal twr; vis: 060°-QG-063°-F G-066°-OcG 2·25s-069°; 57° 46'·00 N 07° 01'·55 W.

NORTH UIST

Fairway L Fl 10s; 57°40'·23N 07°01'·39W.

Griminish Hbr Dir lt 183° ☆ metal post; vis: WRG 4s 6m WRG2M 178°-IsoG-182°-AlWG-182·5°-IsoW-183·5°-AlWR-184°-IsoR-188°; 57°39'·39N 07°26'·72W.

LOCH MADDY and GRIMSAY

Weaver's Pt ☆ Fl 3s 24m 7M; W hut; 57°36'·49N 07°06'·00W.

Glas Eilean Mòr ☆ Fl (2) G 4s 8m 5M; 57°35'·95N 07°06'·70W.

Vallaquie Is Dir lt 207·5°/ 255·5° ☆ W pillar; vis: Fl (3) WRG 8s 11m W5M, R5M, G5M; shore-G-205°-W-210°-R-240°; Fl (3) WRG 8s 11m W8M, R8M, G8M; 249°-G-254°-W-257°-R-262° 57°35'·49N 07°09'·32W.

Lochmaddy Ro-Ro Pier, Dir lt 300° ☆ post; Iso WRG 2s W6M, R4M, G4M; vis: 288°-G-295°-WG-298°-W-302°-WR-305°-R-311° 57°35'·79N 07°09'·46W.

Grimsay No 1 Fl (2) R 8s; 57°28'·26N 07°11'·82W.

SOUTH UIST and LOCH CARNAN

Landfall L Fl 10s.; 57°22'·27N 07°11'·52W.

Ldg Lts 222°. Front Fl R 2s 7m 5M; W ◇ on post; 57°22'·00N 07°16'·34W. Rear, 58m from front, Iso R 10s 11m 5M; W ◇ on post.

Ushenish ★ (S Uist) 57°17'·90N 07°11'·57W Fl W 20s 54m **W19M**; W twr; vis: 193°- 018°.

LOCH BOISDALE

MacKenzie Rk Fl (3) R 15s 3m 4M; 57°08'·24N 07°13'·71W.

Calvay E End ☆ Fl (2) WRG 10s 16m W7M, R7M, G7M; W twr; vis: 111°-W-190°-G-202°-W-286°-R-111°; 57°08'·53N 07°15'·38W; 992351139.

Gasay I ☆ Fl WR 5s 10m W7M, R7M; W twr; vis: 120°-W-284°-R-120°; 57°08'·93N 07°17'·39W.

LochBoisdaleDirlt☆,292·5°;WRG4s4m5M;vis:287·5°-IsoG-290·5°-AlWG-292°-IsoW-293°-AlW-294·5°-IsoR-298·5°; 57°09'·19N 07°18'·24W.

2 FG 8m 3M on dn; 57°09'·13N 07°18'·18W.

LUDAIG and ERISKAY

Ludaig Bwtr ☆ 2 FR (vert) 6m 3M; 57°06'·17N 07°19'·49W.

Acairseid Mhor Ldg Lts 285°. Front, Oc R 6s 9m 4M; 57°03'·89N 07°17'·25W. Rear, 24m from front, Oc R 6s 10m 4M.

BARRA, CASTLEBAY and VATERSAY SOUND

Drover Rocks Q (6) + L Fl 15s; 57°04'·08N 07°23'·54W.

Binch Rock Q (6) + L Fl 15s; 57°01'·60N 07°17'·12W.

Curachan Q (3) 10s; 56°58'·56N 07°20'·51W.

Ardveenish ☆ Oc WRG 6m 9/6M; vis: 300°-G-304°-W-306°-R-310°; 57°00'·21N 07°24'·43W.

Vich Chuan Q(6)+LFl 15s; **Racon (M) 5M**; 56°56'·15N 07°23'·31W.

Channel Rk ☆ Fl WR 6s 4m W6M, R4M; vis: 121·5°-W-277°-R-121·5°; 56°56'·24N 07°28'·94W.

Sgeir a Scape Fl (2) G 8s; 56°56'·25N 07°27'·21W.

Rubha Glas. Ldg Lts 295°. Front FBu 9m 6M; Or △ on W twr; 56°56'·77N 07°30'·64W. Rear, 457m from front, FBu 15m 6M; Or ▽ on W twr; vis: 15° and 8° respectively either side of ldg line.

Barra Hd ★ 56°47'·12N 07°39'·21W Fl 15s 208m **18M**; W twr; obsc by islands to NE; 992351095.

OUTER HEBRIDES – WEST SIDE

Flannan I ★, Eilean Mór Fl (2) 30s 101m **20M**; W twr; 58°17'·29N 07°35'·29W, obsc in places by Is to W of Eilean Mór.

Rockall ☆ Fl 15s 19m 8M (unreliable); 57°35'·76N 13°41'·27W.

Gasker Lt ☆ Fl (3) 10s 38m 10M; 57°59'·05N 07°17'·20W.

Whale Rock Q (3) 10s 5m 5M; **Racon (T)**; 57°54'·40N 07°59·91W.

Haskeir I ★ 57°41'·96N 07°41·31W Fl 20s 44m **24M**; W twr; **Racon (M) 17–15M**; 992351140.

Monach Is ★ Fl (2)15s 47m **18M**; red brick twr; 57°31'·55N 07°41'·68W.

EAST LOCH ROAG

Aird Laimishader Carloway ☆ Fl 6s 63m 8M; W hut; obsc on some brgs; 58°17'·06N 06°49'·50W.

Ardvanich Pt ☆ Fl G 3s 4m 2M; 58°13'·48N 06°47'·68W.

Tidal Rk ☆ Fl R 3s 2m 2M (sync with Ardvanich Pt above); 58°13'·45N 06°47'·57W.

Grèinam ☆ Fl WR 6s 8m W8M, R7M; W bn; vis: R143°-169°, W169°-143°; 58°13'·30N 06°46'·16W.

LOCH ROAG

Rubha Domhain ☆ Fl G 5s 9m 1M; post; 58°12'·96N 06°45'·40W.

Bogha na Muilne Fl (2) 10s; 58°12'·70N 06°54'·23W.

Mia Vaig Bay Fl G 2s 2m 1M; bn; 58°11'·83N 06°56'·60W.

NORTH UIST and SOUTH UIST

Falconet twr ☆ FR 25m 8M (3M by day); shown 1hr before firing, changes to Iso R 2s 15 min before firing until completion; 57°22'·04N 07°23'·58W.

ST KILDA

Ldg Lts 270°. Front, Oc 5s 26m 3M; 57°48'·32N 08°34'·31W. Rear, 100m from front, Oc 5s 38m 3M; sync.

LOCH TORRIDON TO MALLAIG

LITTLE MINCH and W SKYE

Eugenie Rock Q 6 + LF 15s; 57°46'·47N 06°27'·28W.

Eilean Trodday ☆ Fl (2) WRG 10s 52m W12M, R9M, G9M; W Bn; vis: W062°-R088°-130°-W-322°-G-062°; 57°43'·63N 06°17'·93W; 992351084.

Uig, Edward Pier Hd ☆ 57°35'·09N 06°22'·29W Iso WRG 4s 9m W7M, R4M, G4M; vis: 180-W-006°-G-050°-W-073°-R-180°.

Waternish Pt ☆ Fl 20s 21m 8M; W twr; 57°36'·48N 06°37'·99W.

Loch Dunvegan, Uiginish Pt ☆ Fl WRG 3s 16m W7M,R5M,G5M; W lattice twr; vis: 041°-G-132°-W-145°-R-148°-W-253°-R- 263°-W-273°-G-306°, (>148° obsc by Fiadhairt Pt); 57°26'·84N 06°36'·53W.

Neist Point ☆ 57°25'·41N 06°47'·30W Fl 5s 43m **16M**; W twr.

Loch Harport, Ardtreck Pt ☆ 57°20'·38N 06°25'·80W Fl 6s 18m 9M; small W twr.

RONA, LOCH A'BHRAIGE and INNER SOUND

Na Gamhnachain Q; 57°35'·89N 05°57'·71W.

Rona NE Point ☆ 57°34'·69N 05°57'·54W Fl 12s 69m 12M; W twr; vis: 050°-358°; 992351045.

Loch A'Bhraige, Sgeir Shuas ☆ Fl R 2s 6m 3M; vis: 070°-199°; 57°35'·02N 05°58'·61W.

Ldg Lts 136·5°. Front, Q WRG 3m W4M, R3M; vis: 135°-W- 138°-R-318°-G-135°; 57°34'·41N 05°58'·09W. Rear, Iso 6s 28m 5M.

Rubha Ard Ghlaisen Fl R 3s; 57°29'·67N 05°58'·71W.

Screapadal Fl R (2) 5s; 57°25'·54N 06°01'·90W.

SOUND OF RAASAY, PORTREE and CROWLIN ISLANDS

Sgeir Mhór Fl G 5s; 57°24'·57N 06°10'·53W.

Eilean Beag ☆ Fl 6s 32m 6M; W Bn; 57°21'·21N 05°51'·42W.

Eyre Pt ☆ Fl WR 3s 6m W9M R6M; W clad framework twr; vis: 215°-W-267°-R-288°-W-063°; 57°20'·01N 06°01'·28W.

Sgeir Thraid ☆ Q 12m 3M; metal twr; 57°19'·82N 05°56'·50W.

Sgeir Ghobhlach ☆ Fl(3)10s 10m 3M; metal twr; 57°15'·69N 05°52'·25W.

LOCH CARRON

Sgeir Golach ☆ Fl 10s 5m 3M; 57°21'·20N 05°39'·01W.

Eilean a Chait Lt ho (dis) 13M; 57°20'·96N 05°38'·87W.

Bogha Dubh Sgeir Fl (2)R 6s 4m 2M; 57°20'·92N 05°37'·85W.

RAASAY and LOCH SLIGACHAN

Suisnish ☆ 2 FG (vert) 8m 2M; 57°19'·87N 06°03'·91W.

Eyre Point ☆ Fl WR 3s 6m W9M, R6M; W twr; vis: 215°-W-266°-R- 288°-W-063°; 57°20'·01N 06°01'·29W.

KYLEAKIN and KYLE OF LOCH ALSH

Carragh Rk Fl (2) G 12s; **Racon (T) 5M**; 57°17'·18N 05°45'·36W.

Bow Rk Fl (2) R 12s; 57°16'·71N 05°45'·85W.

Fork Rks Fl G 6s; 57°16'·85N 05°44'·93W.

Black Eye Rk Fl R 6s; 57°16'·68N 05°45'·20W.

Eileanan Dubha East ☆ Fl (2) 10s 9m 8M; vis: obscured 104°-146°; 57°16'·56N 05°42'·32W.

8 Metre Rock ☆ Fl G 6s 5m 4M; 57°16'·60N 05°42'·69W.

String Rock Fl R 6s; 57°16'·50N 05°42'·89W.

Sgeir-na-Caillich ☆ Fl (2) R 6s 3m 4M; 57°15'·59N 05°38'·90W.

SOUND OF SLEAT

Kyle Rhea ☆ Fl WRG 3s 7m W8M, R5M, G5M; W Bn; vis: shore-R-219°-W-228°-G-338°-W-346°-R-shore; 57°14'·22N 05°39'·93W.

Sandaig I, NW point ☆ Fl 6s 13m 8M; W twr; 57°10'·05N 05°42'·29W.

Ornsay ☆ Oc 8s 18m 12M; vis: 157°-030°; 57°08'·60N 05°46'·85W.

Pt. of Sleat ☆ Fl 3s 20m9M; W twr; 57°01'·08N 06°01'·08W.

MALLAIG and LOCH NEVIS ENTRANCE

Sgeir Dhearg QG; 57°00'·74N 05°49'·50W.

Northern Pier E end ☆ Iso WRG 4s 6m W9M, R6M, G6M; Gy twr; vis: 181°-G-185°-W-197°-R-201°. Fl G 3s 14m 6M; same structure; 57°00'·47N 05°49'·50W.

Sgeir Dhearg ☆ 57°00'·63N 05°49'·61W Fl (2) WG 8s 6m 5M; Gy Bn; vis: 190°-G-055°-W-190°.

SMALL ISLES AND WEST OF MULL

CANNA and RUM

Sanday ☆ Fl 10s 32m 9M; vis: 152°-061°; 57°02'·82N 06°28'·02W.

Loch Scresort Q; 57°00'·79N 06°14'·61W.

HYSKEIR, EIGG, MUCK and ARISAIG

Humla Fl G 6s 3m 4M 57°00'·46N 06°37'·39W.

Hyskeir ☆ 56°58'·16N 06°40'·83W Fl (3) 30s 41m **24M**; W twr. **Racon (T) 14-17M**; 992351094.

SE point Eigg (Eilean Chathastail) ☆ Fl 6s 24m 8M; W twr; vis: 181°-shore; 56°52'·25N 06°07'·28W.

Eigg, Sgeir nam Bagh (Ferry Terminal) ☆ Dir 245°; Fl WRG 3s 9m W14, R11, G11; H24; steel pole; vis: 242·5°-G-244°-W-246°-R-247·5°. 2FR(vert) on same structure; 56°52'·79N 06°07'·56W.

Isle of Muck ☆ Dir 319·5° Fl WRG 3s 7m W14 RG11, by day WRG1; twr; vis: 317°-G-318·5°-W-320·5°-R-322°; 56°49'·94N 06°13'·71W.

Bogha Ruadh ☆ Fl G 5s 4m 3M; 56°49'·56N 06°13'·04W.

Dubh Sgeir ☆ Fl (2) R 10s 4m 3M; 56°49'·54N 06°13'·13W.

Bo Faskadale Fl (3) G 18s; 56°48'·18N 06°06'·37W.

Ardnamurchan ☆ 56°43'·63N 06°13'·58W Fl (2) 20s 55m **18M**; Gy twr; vis: 002°-217°.

Suil Ghorm ☆ Fl 12s 23m 10M; W twr; 56°42'·26N 06°26'·75W.

TIREE, COLL and ARINAGOUR

Loch Eatharna, Pier Head ☆ Dir 325°; Oc WRG 7s 6m 2M; vis: 316°-G-322°-W-328°-R-334°; 56°36'·86N 06°31'·29W.

Loch Eatharna, Bogha Mór Fl G 6s; 56°36'·65N 06°30'·90W.

Roan Bogha Q (6) + L Fl 15s 3m 5M; 56°32'·23N 06°40'·18W.

Placaid Bogha Fl G 4s; 56°33'·22N 06°44'·06W.

Scarinish ☆ Fl 3s 11m 12M; W □ twr; vis: 210°-030°; S side of ent, 56°30'·02N 06°48'·26W.

Cairn na Burgh More (Treshnish Is), Fl (3) 15s 36m 8M; solar panels on framework tr; 56°31'·05N 06°22'·95W.

Gott Bay Ldg Lts 286·5°. Front FR 8m; 56°30'·61N 06°47'·82W. Rear 30m from front FR 11m.

Skerryvore ☆ Fl 10s 46m **23M**; Gy twr; **Racon (M) 18M**. 56°19'·36N 07°06'·88W; 992351091.

LOCH NA KEAL, LOCH NA LÀTHAICH and IONA

Sgeir a Charraigein Q(6) + LFl 15s; 56°28'·29N 06°07'·71W.
Eileanan na Liathanaich, SE end ☆ Fl WR 6s 12m W8M, R6M; vis: R088°- W108°-088°; 56°20'·56N 06°16'·38W.
Bo na Sliganach Q(6) + LFl 15s; 56°19'·45N 06°23'·12W.
Bogha hun a Chuhoil Q(6) + LFl 15s; 56°16'·57N 06°24'·86W.

DUBH ARTACH

Dubh Artach ☆ 56°07'·94N 06°38'·08W Fl (2) 30s 44m **20M**; Gy twr, R band; 992351088.

SOUND OF MULL

LOCH SUNART, TOBERMORY and LOCH ALINE

Ardmore Pt ☆ Fl (2) 10s 18m 13M; 56°39'·37N 06°07'·70W.
Salen Bay 56°42'·67N 05°46'·57W.
New Rks Q (9) 15s; 56°39'·07N 06°03'·55W; AIS.
Little Stirk Q(6)+L Fl 15s; 56°38'·50N 06°01'·50W.
Rubha nan Gall ☆ 56°38'·33N 06°04'·00W Fl 3s 17m **15M**; W twr.
Tobermory Slip ☆ Iso WRG 3s 5m 4M; vis: 220°-G-232°-W-244°-R-256° (sectors± 2°); metal column; 56°37'·41N 06°03'·77W.
Dearg Sgeir ☆ Fl 6s 7m 8M; W ○ twr; 56°32'·25N 05°54'·80W.
Fiunary Spit Fl G 6s; 56°32'·66N 05°53'·17W.
Fishnish Ferry Slip ☆ Iso WRG 3s 5m 4M; vis: 158°-G-170°-W-195°-R-230° (sectors± 4°); metal column; 56°30'·89N 05°48'·61W.
Loch Aline, ☆ Dir 357°; Oc WRG 6s 2m 4M; vis: 353°-G-356°-W-358°-R-002°; Or concrete plinth; 56°32'·38N 05°46'·47W.
Ardtornish Pt ☆ Fl (2) WRG 10s 8m W8M, R6M, G6M; W twr; vis: G shore- 301°-W-308°-R-342°-W-057°-R-095°-W-108°-G-shore; 56°31'·09N 05°45'·21W.
Craignure Ldg Lts 240·9°. Front, FR 10m; 56°28'·26N 05°42'·28W. Rear, 150m from front, FR 12m; vis: 225·8°-255·8°.

MULL TO CALEDONIAN CANAL AND OBAN

Lismore ☆, SW end 56°27'·34N 05°36'·45W Fl 10s 31m **17M**; W twr; vis: 237°-208°.
Lady's Rk Fl 6s 12m 5M; Red clad lattice tower on W base 56°26'·92N 05°37'·05W; 992351093.
Duart Pt ☆ Fl (3) WR 18s 14m W5M, R3M; vis: 162°-W-261°-R-275°-W-353°-R-shore; 56°26'·84N 05°38'·77W.

LOCH LINNHE

Corran Shoal QR 56°43'·69N 05°14'·39W.
Corran Pt ☆ Iso WRG 4s 12m W10M, R7M, G7M; W twr; vis: shore-R-195°-W-215°-G-020-W-030°-R-shore; 56°43'·25N 05°14'·54W.
Corran Narrows NE ☆ Fl 5s 4m 4M; W twr; vis: S shore-214°; Dir lt 033° Iso WRG 2s 4m 4M (1M day), vis: 028·5°- Iso G -030·5° - Alt W/G -031·5°- Iso W -032·5°- Alt W/R - 033·5°- Iso R -035·5°; co-located 56°43'·62N 05°13'·90W.
Clovullin Spit Fl (2) R 15s; 56°42'·29N 05°15'·56W.
Cuil-cheanna Spit Fl G 6s; 56°41'·17N 05°15'·72W.
Mc Lean Rk QR 56°49'·80N 05°07'·04W.
Eilean na Creiche Fl (2) 5s; 56°50'·25N 05°07'·02W.
Eilean na Craobh Fl (2) R 6s 4m 2M; 56°50'·43N 05°07'·95W.

FORT WILLIAM and CALEDONIAN CANAL

Corpach, Caledonian Canal Lock ent ☆ Iso WRG 4s 6m 5M; W twr; vis: G287°- W310°- R335°-030°; 56°50'·52N 05°07'·44W.
Rubha Cuil-Cheanna ☆ Dir 194°; WRG 2s 12m 5M; vis: 190·5°- Iso R -192·5° - Alt W/R -193·5°- Iso W -194·5°- Alt W/G -195·5°- Iso G -197·5°; W clad framework twr; 56°42'·31N 05°14'·80W.

LYNN OF LORN

Sgeir Bhuidhe Appin Fl (2) WR 7s 8m W9M R6M; W Bn; vis: W013·5°- R184°-220°; 56°33'·63N 05°24'·65W.
Appin Point Fl G 6s; 56°32'·69N 05°25'·97W.
Dearg Sgeir, off Aird's Point Fl WRG 2s 2m W3M, R1M, G1M; vis: 196°-R-246°-W-258°-G-041°-W-058°-R-093°-W-139°; 56°32'·20N 05°25'·22W.
Rubha nam Faoileann (Eriska) QG 2m 2M; G col; vis 128°-329°; 56°32'·20N 05°24'·11W.
Branra Rk ☆ Fl(2) 10s 4m 5M; metal frame on W twr; 56°32'·02N 05°26'·60W.

OBAN

N spit of Kerrera ☆ Fl R 3s 9m 5M; W col; 56°25'·49N 05°29'·56W.
Dunollie ☆ Fl (2) WRG 6s 6m W8M, R6M, G6M; vis: 351°-G- 020°- W-047°-R-120°-W-138°-G-143°; twr; 56°25'·37N 05°29'·05W.
Rubh'a'Chruidh ☆ Q R 3m 2M; W post; 56°25'·32N 05°29'·29W.
Transit Marina ☆ Fl G 2m 2M; post; 56°25'·00N 05°28'·57W.
Oban Bay Q; 56°24'·92N 05°29'·23W.
Sgeir Rathaid Q(6)+L Fl 15s; 56°24'·75N 05°29'·37W.
N Pier 2 F G (vert); metal post; 56°24'·89N 05°28'·49W.
Ro-Ro Jetty 2 F G (vert); post on dn; 56°24'·69N 05°28'·65W.
N Lt Pier 2 FG (vert); metal post; 56°24'·71N 05°28'·91W.

OBAN TO LOCH CRAIGNISH

Heather Is ☆ Fl R 2·5s 11m 2M; 56°24'·41N 05°30'·24W.
Ferry Rks NW Q G; 56°24'·11N 05°30'·69W.
Kerrera Q R; 56°24'·15N 05°30'·81W.
Ferry Rks SE Q (3) 10s; 56°23'·99N 05°30'·53W.

1	Cape Wrath	1																
2	Ullapool	54	2															
3	Stornoway	53	45	3														
4	East Loch Tarbert	75	56	33	4													
5	Portree	83	57	53	42	5												
6	Kyle of Lochalsh	91	63	62	63	21	6											
7	Mallaig	112	82	83	84	42	21	7										
8	Eigg	123	98	97	75	54	35	14	8									
9	Castlebay (Barra)	133	105	92	69	97	76	59	46	9								
10	Tobermory	144	114	115	87	74	53	32	20	53	10							
11	Loch Aline	157	127	128	100	87	66	45	33	66	13	11						
12	Fort William	198	161	162	134	121	98	75	63	96	43	34	12					
13	Oban	169	138	139	111	100	77	56	44	77	24	13	29	13				
14	Loch Melfort	184	154	155	117	114	93	69	61	92	40	27	45	18	14			
15	Craobh Haven	184	155	155	117	114	92	70	60	93	40	27	50	21	5	15		
16	Crinan	187	157	158	129	112	95	74	63	97	42	30	54	25	14	9	16	
17	Mull of Kintyre	232	203	189	175	159	143	121	105	120	89	87	98	72	62	57	51	17

DISTANCE TABLES

Approx distances in nautical miles are by the most direct route allowing for dangers and TSS.

Ferry Pier ☆ 2 FL (vert); 56 23'.92N 005 31'.02W.
Little Horseshoe Fl R 12 s; 56 23'.22N 005 31'.83W.
Sgeirean Dubha ☆ Fl (2) 12s 7m 5M; W ○ twr; 56°22'·81N 05°32'·27W.
Sgeir an Fheuran Fl G 3s; 56°22'·80N 05°31'·94W.
Bogha Nuadh Q(6)+LFl 15s; 56°21'·69N 05°37'·87W; 992351090.
Bogha Ghair Q (3) 10s; 56°16'·50N 05°40'·44W.
Bono Rock Q (9) 15s; 56°16'·21N 05°41'·22W.
Fladda ☆ Fl (2) WRG 9s 13m W11M, R9M, G9M; W twr; vis: 169°-R-186°-W-337°-G-344°-W-356°-R-026°; 56°14'·89N 05°40'·83W.

Dubh Sgeir (Luing) ☆ Fl WRG 6s 9m W6M, R4M. G4M; W twr; vis: W000°-R010°-W025°-G199°-000°; **Racon (M) 5M**; 56°14'·76N 05°40'·20W.
The Garvellachs, Eileach an Naoimh, SW end ☆ Fl 6s 21m 9M; W Bn; vis: 240°-215°; 56°13'·04N 05°49'·06W.

LOCH MELFORT and CRAOBH HAVEN

Melfort Pier ☆ Dir FR 6m 3M; (Apr -Nov); 56°16'·14N 05°30'·19W.
56°12'·88N 05°33'·59W.
Craobh Marina Bkwtr Hd ☆ Iso WRG 5s 10m, W5M, R3M, G3M; vis:114°-G-162°-W-183°-R-200°; 56°12'·78N 05°33'·52W.

AREA 7 *SW Scotland – Colonsay to Kirkcudbright*

SELECTED LIGHTS, BUOYS & WAYPOINTS

COLONSAY TO ISLAY

COLONSAY

Scalasaig, Rubha Dubh ☆ Fl (2) WR 10s 8m W8M, R6M; W bldg; vis: shore-R- 230°-W-337°-R-354°; 56°04'·01N 06°10'·90W.

SOUND OF ISLAY

Rhubh' a Mháil (Ruvaal) ☆ 55°56'·18N 06°07'·46W Fl (3) 15s 45m **19M**; W twr.
Carragh an t'Struith ☆ Fl 3s 8m 9M; W twr; vis: 354°-180°; 55°52'·30N 06°05'·78W.
Carraig Mòr ☆ Fl (2) WR 6s 7m W8M, R6M; W twr; vis: shore-R- 175°-W-347°-R-shore; 55°50'·42N 06°06'·13W.
McArthur's Hd ☆ Fl (2) WR 10s 39m W13M, R10M; W twr; W in Sound of Islay from NE coast, 159°-R-244°-W-E coast of Islay; 55°45'·84N 06°02'·90W.
Orsay Is, **Rhinns of Islay** ☆ 55°40'·40N 06°30'·80W Fl 5s 46m **18M**; W twr; vis: 256°-184°.

PORT ELLEN and LOCH INDAAL

Carraig Fhada ☆ Fl WRG 3s 20m W8M, R6M, G6M; W □ twr; vis: W shore- 248°-G-311°-W-340°-R-shore; 55°37'·22N 06°12'·71W.
Otter Gander VQ (3) 5s; 55°36'·60N 06°12'·34W.
Fhada Q (3) 10s; 55°37'·21N 06°12'·41W.
Sgeir nan Ron Q R; 55°45'·53N 06°17'·32W.
Hbr entrance Q G; 55°37'·55N 06°11'·45W.
Rubh'an Dùin ☆ Fl (2) WR 7s 15m W11M, R8M; W twr; vis: shore-R-218°-W-249°-R-350°-W-shore; 55°44'·70N 06°22'·28 W.
L Indaal, Dir lt 168·5°; Iso WRG 3m 4s WRG 5M, vis: 343°-G-347°-Al WG-348°-Iso W-349°-Al WR-350°-R-354°; 55°46'·01N 06°21'·63W.

JURA TO MULL OF KINTYRE

SOUND OF JURA, CRAIGHOUSE, L SWEEN and GIGHA

Skervuile ☆ Fl 15s 22m 9M; 55°36'·60N 06°12'·34W; W twr.
Nine Foot Rk Q (3) 10s; 55°52'·44N 05°52'·91W.
Goat Rock VQ (3) 5s; 55°50'·12N 05°55'·67W.
Eilean nan Gabhar ☆ Fl 5s 9m 8M; 55°50'·01N 05°56'·25W.
Craighouse ☆ Fl R 6s 3m 5M; 55°49'·98N 05°56'·43W.
Na Cùiltean ☆ Fl 10s 9m 9M; 55°48'·64N 05°54'·90W.
Gamhna Gigha ☆ Fl (2) 6s 7m 5M; 55°43'·78N 05°41'·08W.
Bhanarach Rocks Q (3) 5s; 55°40'·73N 05°43'·29W.
Ardminish Bay, ☆ Q (3) 10s 3m 2M; 55°40'·56N 05°43'·99W.

WEST LOCH TARBERT

Dunskeig Bay ☆ Q (2) 10s 11m 8M; 55°45'·22N 05°35'·00W.
Eileen Tráighe (S side) Fl (2) R 5s 5m 3M; R post; 55°45'·37N 05°35'·75W.

MULL OF KINTYRE

Mull of Kintyre ☆ 55°18'·64N 05°48'·25W Fl (2) 20s 91m **18M**; W twr on W bldg; vis: 347°-178°.

CRINAN CANAL and ARDRISHAIG

Crinan, E of lock ent ☆ Fl WG 3s 8m 4M; W twr, R band; vis: shore-W-146°-G-shore; 56°05'·48N 05°33'·37W.
Ardrishaig Bkwtr Hd ☆ L Fl WRG 6s 9m 4M; vis: 287°-G-339°-W- 350°-R-035°; 56°00'·76N 05°26'·59W.

LOCH FYNE TO SANDA ISLAND

EAST LOCH TARBERT

Eilean na Beithe ☆ Fl WRG 3s 7m 5M; vis: G036°- W065°- R078°-106°; 55°52'·68N 05°19'·62W.

KILBRANNAN SOUND, CRANNAICH and CARRADALE BAY

Port Crannaich Bkwtr Hd ☆ Fl R 10s 5m 6M; vis: 099°-279°; 55°35'·60N 05°27'·84W.
Claonaig Ferry Terminal ☆ Iso WRG 3s 5m 2M (Apr-Oct); vis: 305°-G-350° -W-020°-R-040°; metal column; 55°45'·04N 05°23'·28W.

CAMPBELTOWN LOCH to SANDA ISLAND

Davaar N Pt ☆ 55°25'·69N 05°32'·42W Fl (2) 10s 37m **15M**; W twr; vis: 073°-330°.
Sanda Island ☆ 55°16'·50N 05°35'·01W Fl 10s 50m **15M**; W twr; vis: 242°-121°; 992351116.
Patersons Rock Fl (3) R 18s; 55°16'·90N 05°32'·48W.

KYLES OF BUTE TO RIVER CLYDE

WEST KYLE

Ardlamont Point No 47 Fl R 4s; 55°49'·59N 05°11'·76.
Carry Rk No 46 Fl R 4s; 55°51'·40N 05°12'·14W.

BURNT ISLAND CHANNEL

Fl R 4s; 55°55'·80N 05°10'·46W.
Fl G 3s; 55°55'·79N 05°10'·48W.
Fl R 2s; 55°55'·76N 05°10'·39W.
Fl G 5s; 55°55'·74N 05°10'·38W.
Creyke Rk No 45 ; 55°55'·68N 05°10'·89W.
Beere Rk No 44 ; 55°55'·10N 05°10'·63W.
Wood Fm Rk ; 55°55'·42N 05°10'·31W.

EAST KYLE

Colintrave Pt ☆ Fl R 3s 7m 2M; metal post; 55°55'·39N 05°09'·22W.

Ardmaleish Point No 41 Q; 55°53'·02N 05°04'·70W.

ROTHESAY SOUND

Ardyne Fl G 3s; 55°52'·10N 05°03'·20W.

Bogany Point No 36 Fl R 4s; 55°50'·78N 05°01'·41W.

FIRTH OF CLYDE

Toward Pt ☆ 55°51'·73N 04°58'·78W Fl 10s 21m **22M**; W twr.

No 34 Q (3) 10s; 55°51'·44N 04°59'·11W.

Skelmorlie Iso 5s; 55°51'·65N 04°56'·34W.

WEMYSS and INVERKIP

Cowal L Fl 10s; 55°56'·00N 04°54'·83W.

The Gantocks Fl R 6s 12m 6M; ○ twr; 55°56'·45N 04°55'·08W.

The Gantocks No 31 Q; 55°56'·56N 04°55'·13W.

DUNOON

Cloch Point ☆ Fl 3s 24m 8M; W ○ twr, B band, W dwellings; 55°56'·55N 04°52'·74W.

LOCH LONG and LOCH GOIL

Loch Long Oc 6s; 55°59'·15N 04°52'·42W.

Baron's Pt No 3 ☆ Oc (2) Y 10s 5m 3M; 55°59'·18N 04°51'·12W.

Ravenrock Pt ☆ Fl 4s 12m 10M; W twr on W col. Dir lt 204°, WRG 9m (same twr); vis: 201·5°-F R-203°-Al WR(W phase incr with brg)-203·5°-FW-204·5°-Al WG(G phase incr with brg)-205°-FG-206·5°; 56°02'·14N 04°54'·39W; 992351319

Port Dornaige ☆ Fl 6s 8m 11M; W col; vis: 026°-206°; 56°03·75N 04°53'·65W.

Rubha Ardnahein ☆ Fl R 5s 3m 3M; vis: 132°-312°; 56°06'·15N 04°53'·60W.

The Perch, Dir lt 318°; WRG 3m W8M RG 6M, by day WRG 3M; vis: 314·5°-G-316·5°-Al WG-317·5°-W-318·5°-AlWR-319·5°-R-324·5°; ☆ Fl R 3s 3m 3M (occas); vis: 187°-322°; 56°06'·91N 04°54'·29W.

Cnap Pt Dir lt 024°; WRG 10m W8M RG 6M, by day WRG 3M; vis: 020·5°-G-022·5°-AlWG-023·5°-W-024·5°-AlWR-025·5°-R-027·5°; 56°07'·38N 04°50'·19W.

GOUROCK

Ashton Iso 5s; 55°58'·10N 04°50'·65W.

Rosneath Patch Fl (2) 10s 5m 10M; 55°58'·52N 04°47'·45W.

ROSNEATH, RHU NARROWS and GARELOCH

Ldg Lts 356°. **Front, No 7N** 56°00'·05N 04°45'·36W Dir lt 356°. WRG 5m **W16M**, R13M, G13M; vis: 353°-Al WG- 355°-FW-357°-Al WR-000°-FR-002°.

Dir lt 115° WRG 5m **W16M**, R13M, G13M; vis: 111°-Al WG-114°-FW- 116°-Al WR-119°-FR-121°. Passing lt Oc G 6s 6m 3M; G △ on G pile. Rear, Ardencaple Castle Centre ☆ 56°00'·54N 04°45'·43W 2 FG (vert) 26m 12M; twr on Castle NW corner; vis: 335°-020°.

No 8N Lt Bn 55°59'·09N 04°44'·21W Dir lt 080° WRG 4m; **W16M**, R13M,G13M;vis: 075°-FG-077·5°-Al WG-079·5°-FW-080·5°-AltWR-082·5°-FR-085°. **Dir lt 138°** WRG 4m **W16M**, R13M, G13M; vis: 132°-FG-134°-Al WG-FW137°-139°-Al WR-142°. Passing lt Fl Y 3s 6m 3M.

Gareloch No 1 Lt Bn ☆ VQ (4) Y 5s 9m; Y 'X' on Y structure; 55°59'·12N 04°43'·89W.

No 3N Lt Bn 56°00'·07N 04°46'·72W Dir lt 149° WRG 9m **W16M**, R13M, G13M F & Al; vis: 144°-FG-145°-Al WG-148°-FW-150°-Al WR-153°-FR-154°. Passing lt Oc R 8s 9m 3M.

Rosneath DG Jetty ☆ 2 FR (vert) 5M; W col; vis: 150°-330°; 56°00'·39N 04°47'·51W.

Rhu Pt Dir lt 318° WRG **W16M**, R13M, G13M; vis: 315°-Al WG-317°-F-319°-Al WR-321°-FR-325°; Dir W; vis: 325°-QW-340°-FW-345°-OcW-350°; 56°00'·95N 04°47'·20W.

Limekiln No 2N Lt Bn 56°00'·67N 04°47'·64W Dir lt 295° WRG 5m **W16M**, R13M, G13M F & Al; R □ on R Bn; vis: 291°-Al WG- 294°-FW- 296°-Al WR-299°-FR-301°.

Carraig an Roin ☆ Fl Y 5s 2m 2M; Y post with 'x' topmark; 56°00'·99N 04°48'·40W.

Mambeg Dir lt 331°, Q (4) WRG 8s 10m 14M; vis: 328·5°-G-330°-W- 332°-R-333°; H24; 56°03'·74N 04°50'·47W.

GREENOCK and PORT GLASGOW

Anchorage Lts in line 196°. Front, FG 7m 12M; Y col; 55°57'·62N 04°46'·58W. Rear, 32m from front, FG 9m 12M. Y col.

Lts in line 194·5°. Front, FG 18m; 55°57'·45N 04°45'·91W. Rear, 360m from front, FG 33m.

Steamboat Quay, W end ☆ FG 12m 12M; B&W chequered col; vis 210°-290°; 55°56'·25N 04°41'·44W.

CLYDE TO MULL OF GALLOWAY

HUNTERSTON CHANNEL

'C' Fl G 5s; 55°48'·10N 05°55'·30W.

Hun 1 (Y) Fl (4) Y 15s; 55°48'·10N 04°54'·21W.

Hun 3 Fl R 2s; 55°47'·60N 04°53'·52W.

LARGS and FAIRLIE

Approach L Fl 10s; 55°46'·40N 04°51'·85W.

Fairlie Patch Fl G 1·5s; 55°45'·38N 04°52'·34W.

MILLPORT and GREAT CUMBRAE

Tomont End Daymark 55°47'·56N 04°54'·10W.

Tattie Pier ☆ WRG 3s 5m 4M; vis: 222°-G-234°-W-246°-R-258°; metal column; 55°47'·20N 04°53'·89W.

Ldg Lts 333°. Pier Head front, 55°45'·04N 04°55'·85W FR 7m 5M. Rear, 137m from front, FR 9m 5M.

DISTANCE TABLES

Approx distances in nautical miles are by the most direct route allowing for dangers and TSS.

1	Loch Craignish	1													
2	Crinan	5	2												
3	Ardrishaig	14	9	3											
6	East Loch Tarbert	24	19	10	4										
5	Campbeltown	55	50	39	31	5									
6	Lamlash	48	43	34	25	24	6								
7	Largs	48	43	34	24	39	17	7							
8	Kip Marina	53	48	39	28	50	25	10	8						
9	Greenock	59	54	45	36	53	31	16	6	9					
10	Rhu (Helensburgh)	62	57	48	37	59	33	19	9	4	10				
11	Troon	54	49	40	33	33	16	20	29	34	38	11			
12	Girvan	67	62	53	43	29	20	33	46	49	51	21	12		
13	Stranraer	89	84	75	65	34	39	56	69	65	74	44	23	13	
14	Kirkcudbright	136	131	122	114	88	92	110	116	124	125	97	94	71	14

Mountstuart L Fl 10s; 55°48′·00N 04°57′·57W.
Runnaneun Pt (Rubha'n Eun) ☆ Fl R 6s 8m 12M; W twr; 55°43′·79N 05°00′·23W.
Little Cumbrae Is, Cumbrae Elbow ☆ Fl 6s 28m 14M; W twr; vis: 334°-193°; 55°43′·22N 04°58′·06W.

ARDROSSAN

Approach Dir lt 055°, WRG 15m W14M, R11M, G11M; vis: 050°-F G-051·2°-Alt WG(W phase inc with Brg)-053·8°-FW-056·2°-Alt WR(R phase inc with brg)-058·8°-FR-060°; 55°38′·66N 04°49′·22W. Same structure FR 13m 6M; vis: 325°-145°.
Lt ho Pier Hd ☆ Iso WG 4s 11m 9M; W twr; vis: 035°-W-317°-G-035°; 55°38′·47N 04°49′·57W.

IRVINE

Ldg Lts 051°. Front, FG 10m 5M; 55°36′·40N 04°41′·57W. Rear, 101m from front, FR 15m 5M; G masts, both vis: 019°-120°.

TROON

Troon Approach Fl G 4s; 55°33′·08N 04°41′·42W.
W Pier Hd ☆ Fl (2) WG 5s 11m 9M; W twr; vis: 036°-G-090°-W-036°; 55°33′·07N 04°41′·02W.
Lady I ☆ Fl 2s 19m 11M; W Tr R vert stripes; **Racon (T) 13-11M**; 55°31′·63N 04°44′·05W.

ARRAN, RANZA, LAMLASH and BRODICK

Pillar Rk Pt ☆ (Holy Island), 55°31′·04N 05°03′·65W Fl (2) 20s 38m **18M**; W □ twr.
Holy Is SW end ☆ Fl G 3s 14m 6M; W twr; vis: 282°-147°; 55°30′·73N 05°04′·21W.
Pladda ☆ 55°25′·50N 05°07′·12W Fl (3) 30s 40m **17M**; W twr.

AYR and AILSA CRAIG

S Pier Hd ☆ Q 7m 7M; R twr; vis: 012°-161°. Also Fl G 4s 5m 5M; vis: 012°-082°; 55°28′·17N 04°38′·74W.
Ldg Lts 098°. Front, FR 10m 5M; Tfc sigs; 55°28′·15N 04°38′·38W. Rear, 130m from front Oc R 10s 18m 9M.
Maidens Hbr, E side ☆ Fl G 5s 4m 3M; 55°20′·24N 04°49′·20W.
Maidens Hbr, W side ☆ Fl R 3s 4m 2M; 55°20′·23N 04°49′·19W.
Turnberry Point ☆, near castle ruins 55°19′·57N 04°50′·69W Fl 15s 29m 12M; W twr.
Ailsa Craig ☆ 55°15′·12N 05°06′·52W Fl 4s 18m **17M**; W twr; vis: 145°-028°.

GIRVAN

S Pier Hd ☆ 2 FG (vert) 8m 4M; W twr; 55°14′·72N 04°51′·90W.

LOCH RYAN and STRANRAER

Milleur Point Q; 55°01′·28N 05°05′·66W.
Fairway Iso 4s; 54°59′·77N 05°03′·82W.
Forbes Shoal QR; 54°59′·47N 05°02′·96W.
Loch Ryan W QG; 54°59′·23N 05°03′·24W.
Cairn Pt ☆ Fl (2) R 10s 14m 12M; W twr; 54°58′·46N 05°01′·85W.
Cairnryan ☆ Fl R 5s 5m 5M; 54°57′·77N 05°00′·99W.
Stranraer No 1 Oc G 6s; 54°56′·67N 05°01′·32W.
No 3 QG; 54°55′·87N 05°01′·60W.
No 5 Fl G 3s; 54°55′·08N 05°01′·86W.
E Pier Hd ☆ 2 FR (vert) 9m; 54°54′·61N 05°01′·60W.
Corsewall Point ☆ 55°00′·41N 05°09′·58W Fl (5) 30s 34m **22M**; W twr; vis: 027°-257°.
Black Hd Old Lt Ho; W tower, 22m; 54°51′·70N 05°08′·80W.

PORTPATRICK

Ldg Lts 050·5°. Front, FG (occas); 54°50′·50N 05°07′·02W. Rear, 68m from front, FG 8m (occas).
Crammag Hd ☆ 54°39′·90N 04°57′·92W Fl 10s 35m **18M**; W twr.
Mull of Galloway ☆, SE end 54°38′·11N 04°51′·45W Fl 20s 99m **18M**; W twr; vis: 182°-105°.

MULL OF GALLOWAY and WIGTOWN BAY

Port William Ldg Lts 105°. Front, Pier Hd Fl G 3s 7m 3M; 54°45′·66N 04°35′·28W. Rear, 130m from front, FG 10m 2M.
Isle of Whithorn ☆ Fl WR 3s 20m 6/4M; vis: 310°-W-005°-R-040°; 54°41′·79N 04°21′·54W.
Whithorn Ldg Lts 335°. Front, Oc R 8s 7m 7M; Or ♦; 54°42′·01N 04°22′·05W. Rear, 35m from front, Oc R 8s 9m 7M; Or ♦, synch.
Little Ross ☆ Fl 5s 50m 12M; W twr; obsc in Wigtown B when brg more than 103°; 54°45′·93N 04°05′·10W.

KIRKCUDBRIGHT BAY and KIPPFORD

Little Ross NNE end of Is ☆ Fl (2) 5s 21m 5M; Stone bcn; 54°46′·06N 04°05′·02W.
Hestan I, E end ☆ Fl (2) 10s 42m 9M; 54°49′·95N 03°48′·53W.

AREA 8 *NW England, Isle of Man & N Wales – Solway Firth to Bardsey I*

SELECTED LIGHTS, BUOYS & WAYPOINTS

SOLWAY FIRTH TO BARROW-IN-FURNESS

SILLOTH and MARYPORT

Lees Scar ☆ Fl G 5s 11m 4M; W piles; 54°51′·78N 03°24′·79W.
Groyne Hd ☆ 2 FG (vert) 4m 4M; Fl Bu tfc signals close by; 54°52′·14N 03°23′·93W.
Maryport S Pier Hd ☆ Fl 1·5s 10m 6M; 54°43′·07N 03°30′·64W.

WORKINGTON and HARRINGTON

N Workington Q; 54°40′·10N 03°38′·18W.
S Workington VQ (6) + L Fl 10s; 54°37′·01N 03°38′·58W.
South Pier ☆ Fl 5s 11m 5M; R bldg; 54°39′·12N 03°34′·67W.
Ldg Lts 131·8°. Front, FR 10m 3M; 54°38′·92N 03°34′·19W. Rear, 134m from front, FR 12m 3M.

WHITEHAVEN

W Pier Hd ☆ Fl G 5s 16m 8M; W ○ twr; 54°33′·17N 03°35′·92W.
N Pier Hd ☆ Fl R 5s 8m 10M; W ○ twr; 54°33′·17N 03°35′·75W.
Saint Bees Hd ☆ 54°30′·81N 03°38′·23W Fl (2) 20s 102m **18M**; W ○ twr; obsc shore-340°.

RAVENGLASS

Blockhouse ☆ FG; (Eskdale Range); 54°20′·16N 03°25′·34W.
Selker Fl (3) G 10s; *Bell;* 54°16′·14N 03°29′·58W.

BARROW-IN-FURNESS

Lightning Knoll L Fl 10s; 53°59′·83N 03°14′·28W.
Halfway Shoal QR 19m 10s; R&W chequer Bn; 54°01′·46N 03°11′·88W.
Isle of Walney ☆ Fl 15s 21m 10M; stone twr; obsc 122°-127° within 3M of shore; 54°02′·92N 03°10′·64W.
Walney Chan Ldg Lts 040·7°. No 1 Front , Q 7m 10M; vis: 035·2°-W-046·2°; Or □; 54°03′·19N 03°09′·22W. No 2

Rear, 0·61M from front, Iso 2s 13m 10M; Or □ on Pile. Rampside Sands Ldg Lts 005·1°. No 3 Front, Q 9m10M; W ○ twr; 54°04'·41N 03°09'·79W. No 4 Rear, 0·77M from front, Iso 2s 14m 6M; R col, W face.

ISLE OF MAN

Ballacash Bank VQ (9) 10s; 54°26'·50N 04°16'·70W.

Whitestone Bank Q (9) 15s; 54°24'·58N 04°20'·41W.

Point of Ayre ☆ 54°24'·94N 04°22'·13W Fl (4) 20s 32m **19M**; W twr, two R bands, **Racon (M) 13-15M**.

Low Lt Ho (unlit), RW twr, B base, 54°25'·03N 04°21'·86W.

PEEL

Peel Bkwtr Hd ☆ Oc 7s 11m 6M; W twr; 54°13'·67N 04°41'·69W.

PORT ERIN and PORT ST MARY

Ldg Lts 099·1°. Front, 54°05'·23N 04°45'·57W FR 10m 5M; W twr, R band. Rear, 39m from front, FR 19m 5M; W col, R band.

Calf of Man Lighthouse (disused), white 8-sided tower.

Chicken Rk ☆ Fl 5s 38m **20M**; **Racon (C)** 54°02'·27N 04°50'·32W

Alfred Pier Hd ☆ Oc R 10s 8m 6M; 54°04'·33N 04°43'·82W.

CASTLETOWN and DERBY HAVEN

Dreswick Pt ☆ Fl (2) 30s 23m 12M; W twr; 54°03'·29N 04°37'·45W.

New Pier Hd ☆ Oc R 15s 8m 5M; 54°04'·33N 04°38'·97W.

Derby Haven, Bkwtr SW end ☆ Iso G 2s 5m 5M; W twr, G band; 54°04'·58N 04°37'·06W.

DOUGLAS

Douglas Head ☆ 54°08'·60N 04°27'·95W Fl 10s 32m **15M**; W twr; obsc brg more than 037°. FR Lts on radio masts 1 and 3M West.

No 1 Q (3) G 5s; 54°09'·04N 04°27'·68W.

Princess Alexandra Pier Hd ☆ Fl R 5s 16m 8M; R mast; *Whis (2) 40s;* 54°08'·84N 04°27'·85W.

Ldg Lts 229·3°, Front, Oc Bu 10s 9m 5M; W △ R border on mast; 54°08'·72N 04°28'·25W. Rear, 62m from front, Oc Bu 10s 12m 5M; W ▽ on R border; synch with front.

Victoria Pier Hd ☆ Iso G 10s 6m 10M; Post; Intl Port Tfc Signals; 54°08'·84N 04°28'·08W.

Conister Rk Refuge Q 3M; vis: 234°-312°; 54°09'·03N 04°28'·12W.

LAXEY to RAMSEY

Laxey Pier Hd ☆ Oc R 3s 7m 5M; W twr, R band; obsc when brg less than 318°; 54°13'·50N 04°23'·43W.

Maughold Head ☆ 54°17'·72N 04°18'·58W Fl (3) 30s 65m **15M**.

Bahama VQ (6) + L Fl 10s; 54°20'·01N 04°08'·57W.

Queens Pier Dn ☆ Fl R 5s; 54°19'·28N 04°21'·95W.

King William Bank Q (3) 10s; 54°26'·01N 04°00'·08W.

BARROW TO RIVERS MERSEY AND DEE

MORECAMBE

Met Mast ☆ Fl Y 5s 20m 5M; 54°00'·13N 03°33'·38W; Aero FR (80m), *Horn 30s.*

Lightning Knoll L Fl 10s; 53°59'·84N 03°14'·28W.

Morecambe Q (9) 15s; 53°52'·00N 03°22'·00W.

Lune Deep Q (6) + L Fl 15s; **Racon (T);** 53°56'·07N 03°12·90W.

Lts in line about 090°. Front, FR 10m 2M; G mast; 54°04'·41N 02°52'·63W. Rear, 140m from front, FR 14m 2M; G mast.

HEYSHAM

SW Quay Ldg Lts 102·2°. Front, both F Bu 11/14m 2M; Or & B ♦ on masts; 54°01'·91N 02°55'·22W.

RIVER LUNE, GLASSON DOCK and FLEETWOOD

R Lune Q (9) 15s; 53°58'·63N 03°00'·03W.

Fairway No 1(Fleetwood) 53°57'·67N 03°02'·03W Q; *Bell.*

Fleetwood Esplanade Ldg Lts 156°. Front, Iso G 2s 14m 9M; 53°55'·71N 03°00'·56W. Rear, 320m from front, Iso G 4s 28m 9M. Both vis on Ldg line only. (H24) (chan liable to change).

RIVER RIBBLE

Gut L Fl 10s; 53°41'·74N 03°08'·98W.

Perches show Fl R on N side, and Fl G on S side of chan.

S side, 14¼M Perch ☆ Fl G 5s 6m 3M; 53°42'·75N 03°04'·90W.

Jordan's Spit Q (9) 15s; 53°35'·76N 03°19'·28W.

FT Q; 53°34'·56N 03°13'·20W.

RIVER MERSEY and LIVERPOOL

Bar Fl.5s 12M; **Racon (T) 10M**; 53°32'·02N 03°20'·98W, AIS.

Q1 VQ; 53°31'·01N 03°16'·70W.

Q2 VQ R; 53°31'·48N 03°14'·94W.

Q3 Fl G 3s; 53°30'·97N 03°15'·08W.

Formby Iso 4s; 53°31'·14N 03°13'·48W.

C4 Fl R 3s; 53°31'·83N 03°08'·50W.

CROSBY Oc 5s; 53°30'·74N 03°06'·30W.

C14 Fl R 3s; 53°29'·93N 03°05'·35W.

Brazil QG; G hull,53°26'·85N 03°02'·23W.

RIVER DEE, MOSTYN and CONNAH'S QUAY

HE1 Q (9) 15s; 53°26'·33N 03°18'·08W.

HE2 Fl G 2·5s; 53°24'·90N 03°12'·88W.

HE3 Q G; 53°24'·55N 03°12'·74W.

1.	Portpatrick	1																
2.	Mull of Galloway	16	2															
3.	Kirkcudbright	48	32	3														
4.	Maryport	65	49	26	4													
5.	Workington	63	47	25	6	5												
6.	Ravenglass	70	54	40	30	23	6											
7.	Point of Ayre	38	22	28	37	31	34	7										
8.	Peel	41	26	46	55	49	52	18	8									
9.	Douglas	60	42	46	50	44	39	19	30	9								
10.	Glasson Dock	101	85	74	66	60	37	64	85	63	10							
11.	Fleetwood	95	79	68	59	53	30	58	80	57	10	11						
12.	Liverpool	118	102	97	89	83	60	80	86	70	52	46	12					
13.	Conwy	111	95	95	92	86	58	72	72	59	62	56	46	13				
14.	Beaumaris	109	93	94	95	89	72	71	73	58	66	60	49	12	14			
15.	Caernarfon	117	103	104	105	99	82	81	73	68	76	70	59	22	10	15		
16.	Holyhead	93	81	94	96	90	69	68	62	50	79	73	68	36	32	26	16	
17.	Fishguard	171	158	175	175	169	160	153	140	134	153	147	136	100	88	78	89	17

DISTANCE TABLES

Approx distances in nautical miles are by the most direct route allowing for dangers and TSS.

Mostyn Dir Lt ☆ 194·5°; Iso WRG 2s 11m W 10M R,G 7M, by day W 3M R,G 2M; vis: 192°-G-194°-W-195°-R-197°; H24; Y framework twr; 53°19'·55N 03°15'·69W.
Dee No1 L Fl 10s; 53°20'·70N 03°12'·46W.
Dee Q (6) + L Fl 15s; 53°21'·90N 03°18·20W.
West Hoyle Spit (Earwig) Dir Lt 090. 53°21'·21N 03°24'·07W; Iso WRG 2s W10M, R7M, G7M (day W3M, R2M, G2M); vis: 087·5°-G-089·5°-W-090·5°-R-092·5°; occasional.
S Hoyle Outer Fl R 2·5s; 53°21'·26N 03°26'·95W.

WALES – NORTH COAST AND INNER PASSAGE

South Hoyle Outer Fl R 2·5s; 53°21'·47N 03°24'·70W.
Prestatyn Q; 53°21'·37N 03°29'·00W.
Inner Passage Fl R 5s; 53°21'·91N 03°31'·95W.
Mid Patch Spit QR; 53°22'·25N 03°32'·67W.
Mast ☆ Fl Y 5s 18m 5M; Mast (80); 53°28'·84N 03°30'·50W.
W Constable Q (9) 15s; **Racon (M) 10M**; 53°23'·14N 03°49'·26W.

RHYL, LLANDUDNO and CONWY

River Clwyd Outfall Q R 7m 2M; 53°19'·45N 03°30'·34W.
Llandudno Pier Hd ☆ 2 FG (vert) 8m 4M; 53°19'·90N 03°49'·51W.
Great Ormes Hd Lt Ho, (unlit); 53°20'·56N 03°52'·17W.
Conwy Fairway L Fl 10s; 53°17'·95N 03°55'·58W.
C1 Fl G 10s; 53°17'·83N 03°54'·58W.
C2 Fl (2) R 10s; 53°17'·94N 03°54'·52W.
R Conwy ent, ☆ L Fl G 15s 5m 2M; 53°18'·03N 03°50'·86W.

ANGLESEY

Point Lynas ☆ 53°24'·98N 04°17'·35W Oc 10s 39m **18M**; W castellated twr; vis: 109°-315°; H24.

AMLWCH to HOLYHEAD BAY

Main Bkwtr ☆ Fl G 15s 11m 3M; W mast; vis: 141°-271°; 53°25'·02N 04°19'·91W.
Furlong Fl G 2·5s; 53°25'·41N 04°30'·47W.
Archdeacon Rock Q; 53°26'·71N 04°30'·87W.
Victoria Bank VQ; 53°25'·61N 04°31'·37W.
Coal Rk Q (6) + L Fl 15s; 53°25'·91N 04°32'·79W.
Ethel Rk VQ; 53°26'·64N 04°33'·67W.
The Skerries ☆ 53°25'·27N 04°36'·50W Fl (2) 15s 36m **20M**; W ○ twr, R band; **Racon (T) 25M**. Iso R 4s 26m 10M; same twr; vis: 233°-252°, sector unreliable > 4M; *Horn (2) 60s*. H24 in periods of reduced visibility; 992351084.
Langdon Q (9) 15s; 53°22'·74N 04°38'·74W.
Bolivar FL G 2·5s; 53°21'·51N 04°35'·33W.
Wk Fl (2) R 10s; 53°20'·43N 04°36'·60W.

HOLYHEAD to SOUTH STACK

Bkwtr Head ☆ Fl (3) G 10s 21m 14M; W □ twr, B band; Fl Y vis: 174°-226°; *Siren 20s;* 53°19'·86N 04°37'·16W.
Spit Fl G 3s; 53°19'·79N 04°37'·15W.
South Stack ☆ 53°18'·41N 04°41'·98W Fl 10s 60m **24M**; (H24); W ○ twr; obsc to N by N Stack and part obsc in Penrhos bay; *Horn 30s*. Fog Det lt vis: 145°-325°.

MENAI STRAIT TO BARDSEY ISLAND

Ten Feet Bank QR; 53°19'·47N 04°02'·82W.
Dinmor QG; 53°19'·34N 04°03'·32W.
Trwyn-Du ☆ Fl 5s 19m 12M; W ○ castellated twr, B bands; vis: 101°-023°; *Horn (3) 30s*, sounded continuously; 53°18'·77N 04°02'·45W.

MENAI STRAIT

(Direction of buoyage NE to SW)
Perch Rock Fl R 5s; 53°18'·73N 04°02'·09W.
Port Dinorwic Pier Hd ☆ 53°11'·21N 04°12'·60W F WR 5m 2M; vis: 225°-R-357°-W-225°.
(Direction of buoyage SW to NE)
Caernarfon N Pier ☆ 2 FG(vert) 5m 2M; 53°08'·72N 04°16'·56W.
Abermenai Point ☆ Fl WR 3·5s 6m 3M; W mast; vis: 065°-R-245°-W-065°; 53°07'·62N 04°19'·72W.
C1 Fl G 5s; 53°07'·18N 04°24'·60W.
C2 Fl R 10s; 53°07'·38N 04°24'·33W.
Caernarfon Bar L Fl 10s; 53°07'·00N 04°25'·00W.
Llanddwyn I ☆Fl WR 2·5s 12m W7M, R4M; W twr; vis: 280°-R- 015°-W-120°; 53°08'·05N 04°24'·79W.

PORTH DINLLÄEN

CG Stn ☆ FR when firing 10M N; 52°56'·82N 04°33'·89W.
Careg y Chwislen Fl(2) 10s 2M 52°56'·99N 04°33'·51W.
Bardsey I ☆ 52°44'·97N 04°48'·02W Fl R 10s 39m **18M**; W □ twr, R bands; obsc by Bardsey Is 198°-250° and in Tremadoc B when brg < 260°.

AREA 9 *S Wales & SW England – Cardigan Bay to St Ives*

SELECTED LIGHTS, BUOYS & WAYPOINTS

CARDIGAN BAY

Bardsey I ☆ 52°44'·98N 04°48'·01W Fl R 10s 39m **18M**; W □ twr, R bands; obsc by Bardsey I 198°-250° and in Tremadoc B when brg less than 260°.
St Tudwal's ☆ Fl WR 15s 46m W14, R10M; vis: 349°-W-169°-R- 221°-W-243°-R-259°-W-293°-R-349°; obsc by East I 211°-231°; 52°47'·92N 04°28'·30W.

PWLLHELI and PORTHMADOG

Pwllheli App Iso 2s; 52°53'·03N 04°22'·90W.
Porthmadog Fairway L Fl 10s; 52°52'·97N 04°11'·20W.

BARMOUTH and ABERDOVEY

Diffuser Fl Y 5s; 52°43'·19N 04°05'·38W.
Barmouth Outer L Fl 10s; 52°42'·81N 04°04'·89W.
Aberdovey Outer Iso 4s; 52°32'·00N 04°05'·55W.
Cynfelyn Patches, Patches Q (9) 15s; 52°25'·83N 04°16'·41W.

ABERYSTWYTH, ABERAERON and NEW QUAY

Aberystwyth S Bkwtr Hd ☆ Fl (2) WG 10s 12m 10M; vis: 030°-G- 053°-W-210°; 52°24'·40N 04°05'·52W.
Ldg Lts 133°. Front, FR 4m 5M; 52°24'·37N 04°05'·39W. Rear, 52m from front, FR 7m 6M.
Aberaeron N Pier ☆ Fl (4) WRG 15s 10m 6M; vis: 050°-G-104°-W-178°-R-232°; 52°14'·61N 04°15'·87W.
Carreg Ina Q; 52°13'·19N 04°20'·70W.
New Quay Pier Hd ☆ Fl WG 3s 12m W8M, G5M; G △; vis: 135°-W- 252°-G-295; 52°12'·95N 04°21'·35W.

CARDIGAN and FISHGUARD

Cardigan Channel Fl (2) 5s; 52°06′·44N 04°41′·43W.
Cardigan Cliff Base Bn 1 ☆ Fl R 4s 3M; 52°07′·05N 04°41′·39W.
Cardigan Cliff Base Bn 2 ☆ Fl R 2s 3M; 52°06′·91N 04°41′·34W.
Fishguard N Bkwtr Hd ☆ Fl G 4·5s 18m 13M; *Bell (1) 8s;* 52°00′·76N 04°58′·23W.
Strumble Head ✩ 52°01′·79N 05°04′·43W Fl (4) 15s 45m **26M**; vis: 038°-257°; (H24).

BISHOPS and SMALLS

South Bishop ✩ 51°51′·14N 05°24′·74W Fl 5s 44m **16M**; W ○ twr; *Horn (3) 45s;* **Racon (O)10M**; (H24).
The Smalls ✩ 51°43′·27N 05°40′·19W Fl (3) 15s 36m **18M**; **Racon (T)**; *Horn (2) 60s*. Same twr, Iso R 4s 33m 13M; vis: 253°-285° over Hats & Barrels Rk; both Lts shown H24 in periods of reduced visibility; 992351123.
Skokholm I ☆, 51°41′·64N 05°17′·22W Fl WR 10s 54m W8M, R8M; vis: 301°-W-154°-R-301°; partially obsc 226°-258°.

WALES – SOUTH COAST – BRISTOL CHANNEL

MILFORD HAVEN

St Ann's Head ✩ 51°40′·87N 05°10′·42W Fl WR 5s 48m **W18M, R17M**, R14M; W 8-sided twr; vis: 233°-W-247°-R-332°-W131°, partially obscured 124°-129°; *Horn (2) 60s*.
W Blockhouse Point Ldg Lts 022·5°. Front, F 54m 13M (day 10M); B stripe on W twr; vis: 004·5°-040·5°; intens on lead line. vis: 004·5°-040·5°; **Racon (Q)**; 51°41′·31N 05°09′·56W.
Watwick Point Common Rear ✩, 0·5M from front, F 80m **15M** (day 10M); vis: 013·5°-031·5°; **Racon (Y)**.
W Blockhouse Point Q WR 21m W9M, R7M; R lantern on W base: vis: 220°-W-250°-R-020°-W-036°-R-049°; 51°41′·31N 05°09′·56W.
Dale Fort ☆ Fl (2) WR 5s 20m W5M, R3M; vis: 222°-R-276°-W-019°; 51°42′·16N 05°09′·01W.
Gt Castle Hd F WRG 27m W5M, R3M, G3M; vis: 243°-R-281°-G- 299°-W-029°; 51°42′·68N 05°07′·06W. Co-located Dir WRG (040°); vis: 038·25°-G-039°-AlWG-039·5°-W-040·5°-AlWR-041°-R-041·75° (**not** used in conjunction with the front ldg light below) **Ldg Lts** ≠ 039·7° **Front,** Oc 4s 27m **15M**; vis: 031·2°-048·2°. **Rear**, 890m from front. Oc 8s 53m **15M** (day 10M); vis: 031·2°-048·2°.
St Ann's Fl R 2·5s; 51°40′·25N 05°10′·51W.
Mid Channel Rks Q (9) 15s; 51°40′·18N 05°10′·14W.
Mid Channel Rk ☆ Fl (3) G 7s 18m 8M; 51°40′·31N 05°09′·83W.
Rows Rks Q R; 51°40′·22N 05°09′·02W.
Sheep QG; 51°40′·06N 05°08′·31W.
Millbay Fl (2) R 5s; 51°41′·05N 05°09′·45W.
W Chapel Fl G 10s; 51°40′·98N 05°08′·67W.
E Chapel Fl R 5s; 51°40′·87N 05°08′·15W.
Rat Fl G 5s; 51°40′·80N 05°07′·86W.
Angle VQ; 51°41′·63N 05°08′·27W.
Thorn Rock Q (9) 15s; 51°41′·53N 05°07′·76W.
Turbot Bank VQ (9) 10s; 51°37′·41N 05°10′·08W.
St Gowan Q (6) + L Fl 15s, **Racon (T) 10M**; 51°31′·93N 04°59′·77W; 992351126.

TENBY to SWANSEA BAY

Caldey I ☆ Fl (3) WR 20s 65m W13M, R9M; vis: R173°-W212°- R088°-102°; 51°37′·90N 04°41′·08W.
Woolhouse Q (6) + L Fl 15s; 51°39′·35N 04°39′·69W.
Burry Port Inlet ☆ Fl 5s 7m 6½M; 51°40′·62N 04°15′·06W.
W. Helwick (9) 15s; **Racon (T) 10M**; 51°31′·40N 04°23′·65W.
E. Helwick VQ (3) 5s; *Bell;* 51°31′·80N 04°12′·68W.

SWANSEA BAY and SWANSEA

Ledge VQ (6) + L Fl 10s; 51°29′·93N 03°58′·77W.
Mixon Fl (2) R 5s; *Bell;* 51°33′·12N 03°58′·78W.
Outer Spoil Gnd Fl Y 2·5s; 51°32′·11N 03°55′·73W.
Grounds VQ (3) 5s; 51°32′·81N 03°53′·47W.
Mumbles ✩ 51°34′·01N 03°58′·27W Fl (4) 20s 35m **15M**; W twr; *Horn 3s*.
SW Inner Green Grounds Q(3) 10s; 51°34′·21N 03°57′·12W.
Swansea Lts in line 020°. Front: E Breakwater head, Oc G 4s 5m 2M & 2FG(vert) 10m 6M; 51°36′·38N 03°55′·62W. Rear, 3·1ca from front: FG 6M.

SWANSEA BAY, RIVER NEATH and PORT TALBOT

Neath App Chan Fl G 5s; 51°35′·71N 03°52′·83W.
Cabenda Q (6) + L Fl 15s; **Racon (Q)**; 51°33′·36N 03°52′·23W.
Ldg Lts 059·8° (occas). Front, Oc R 3s 12m 6M; 51°34′·92N 03°48′·10W. Rear, 400m from front, Oc R 6s 32m 6M.

BRISTOL CHANNEL – NORTH SHORE (E PART)

W Scar Q (9) 15s, *Bell*, **Racon (T) 10M**; 51°28′·31N 03°55′·57W.
South Scar (S SCAR) Q (6) + L Fl 15s; 51°27′·61N 03°51′·58W.
E. Scarweather Q (3) 10s; *Bell;* 51°27′·98N 03°46′·76W.

PORTHCAWL

Fairy Q (9) 15s; *Bell;* 51°27′·86N 03°42′·07W.
Bkwtr Hd ☆ 51°28′·39N 03°41′·98W F WRG 10m W6M, R4M, G4M; vis: 302°-G-036°-W-082°-R-116°.
W Nash VQ (9) 10s ; *Bell;* 51°25′·99N 03°45′·95W.
Nash ✩ 51°24′·03N 03°33′·06W Fl (2) WR 15s 56m **W21M, R16M**; vis: 280°-R-290°-W-100°-R-120°-W-128°.
Breaksea L Fl 10s; **Racon (T) 10M**; 51°19′·88N 03°19′·08W; 992351124.

BARRY

W Bkwtr Hd ☆ Fl 2·5s 12m 10M; 51°23′·46N 03°15′·52W.
N. One Fathom Q; 51°20′·94N 03°12′·17W.
Mackenzie QR; 51°21′·75N 03°08′·24W.

CARDIFF and PENARTH ROADS

Lavernock Outfall Fl Y 5s; 51°23′·95N 03°09′·50W.
Ranie Fl (2) R 5s; 51°24′·23N 03°09′·39W.
S Cardiff Q (6) + L Fl 15s; *Bell;* 51°24′·18N 03°08′·57W.
Mid Cardiff Fl (3) G 10s; 51°25′·60N 03°08′·09W.
Cardiff Spit QR; 51°24′·57N 03°07′·12W.
N Cardiff QG; 51°26′·52N 03°07′·19W.
Wrach Chan Dir lt 348·5°. Oc WRG 10s 5m; W3M, R3M, G3M; vis: 344·5°-G-347°-W-350°-R-352°; H24; 51°27′·16N 03°09′·75W.
Outer Wrach Q (9) 15s; 51°26′·20N 03°09′·46W.

FLATHOLM to THE BRIDGE

Flat Holm ✩, SE Pt 51°22′·54N 03°07′·14W Fl (3) WR 10s 50m **W15M**, R12M; W ○ twr; vis: 106°-R-140°-W-151°-R-203°-W-106°; (H24).
Monkstone ☆ Fl 5s 13m 12M; R column on W ○ twr; 51°24′·89N 03°06′·01W.
Tail Patch QG; 51°23′·53N 03°03′·65W.
Hope Q (3) 10s; 51°24′·84N 03°02′·68W.

NW Elbow VQ (9) 10s; *Bell;* 51°26'·28N 02°59'·93W.
EW Grounds L Fl 10s 7M; *Bell;* **Racon (T) 7M**; 51°27'·12N 02°59'·95W.

NEWPORT DEEP, RIVER USK and NEWPORT

Newport Deep Fl (3) G 10s; *Bell;*51°29'·36N 02°59'·12W.
East Usk ☆ 51°32'·40N 02°58'·01W; Oc WRG 10s 10m W11M, R9M, G9M; vis: 011°-G-015°-W- 017°-R-021°.
Julians Pill Ldg Lts 062°. Front, F Bu 5m 5M; 51°33'·32N 02°57'·94W. Rear, `44m from front, F Bu 8m 5M.

BRISTOL CHANNEL – SOUTH SHORE (E PART)

BRISTOL DEEP

N Elbow QG; *Bell;* 51°26'·97N 02°58'·65W.
S Mid Grounds VQ(6) + L Fl 10s; 51°27'·62N 02°58'·68W.
E Mid Grounds Fl R 5s; 51°27'·75N 02°54'·98W.
Clevedon VQ; 51°27'·39N 02°54'·93W.
Welsh Hook Q(6) + L Fl 15s; 51°28'·53N 02°51'·86W.
Avon Fl G 2·5s; 51°27'·92N 02°51'·73W.
Black Nore Pt Lt Ho; W ○ twr on frame; 51°29'·09N 02°48'·05W.
Newcome 51°30'·01N 02°46'·71W Fl (3) R 10s.
Denny Shoal VQ(6) + L Fl 10s; 51°30'·15N 02°45'·45W.
Cockburn 51°30'·45N 02°44'·10W Fl R 2·5s.
W Dock Middle 51°29.95'N 02°44'·20W Q G.
W Dock Outer 51°30'·00N 02°44'·85W Fl G 5s.
Firefly Fl(2) G 5s; 51°29'·96N 02°45'·35W.
Portishead Point ☆ 51°29'·68N 02°46'·42W Q (3) 10s 9m **16M**; B twr, W base; vis: 060°-262°; *Horn 20s.*

PORTISHEAD

Pier Hd ☆ Iso G 2s 5m 3M; 51°29'·69N 02°45'·27W.
Seabank ☆ ldg line 086·8°; W Mast, Q(8) 5M 16m; vis: 070·3°-103·3°; day 1M vis: 076·8°-096·8°; 51°30'·09N 02°43'·36W.
Knuckle Lts in line 099·6°, Oc G 5s 6m 6M; 51°29'·94N 02°43'·67W. Rear, 165m from front, FG 13m 6M; vis: 044°-134°.

AVONMOUTH

Royal Edward Dock N Pier Hd ☆ Fl 4s 15m 10M; vis: 060°-228·5°; 51°30'·49N 02°43'·09W.
King Road Ldg Lts 072·4°. N Pier Hd ☆ Front, Oc R 5s 5m 9M; W obelisk, R bands; vis: 062°-082°; 51°30'·49N 02°43'·09W. Rear ☆, 546m from front, QR 15m 10M; vis: 066°-078°.

RIVER AVON, CUMBERLAND BASIN and AVON BRIDGE

S Pier Hd ☆ Oc RG 30s 9m 10M and FBu 4m 1M; vis: 294°-R-036°-G-194°; 51°30'·37N 02°43'·10W. *Bell(1) 10s.*

Ldg Lts 127·2°. Front, Iso R 2s 6m 3M, vis: 010°-160°; 51°30'·10N 02°42'·59W. Rear, Iso R 2s10m 3M, vis: 048°-138°.

BRISTOL CHANNEL (SOUTH SHORE)

WESTON-SUPER-MARE

Pier Hd ☆ 2 FG (vert) 6m; 51°20'·88N 02°59'·26W.
E Culver Q (3) 10s; 51°18'·00N 03°15'·44W.
W Culver VQ (9) 10s; 51°17'·47N 03°19'·00W.
E Hinkley 51°13.50'N 03°09'·26W Fl(4) G 10s.
W Hinkley 51°13'·67N 03°10'·76W Fl(3) R 10s.

BURNHAM-ON-SEA and RIVER PARRETT

Ent ☆ Fl 7·5s 7m 12M; vis: 074°-164°; 51°14'·89N 03°00'·36W;
Dir lt 080°. F WRG 4m W12M, R10M, G10M; vis: 071°-G-075°-W-085- R-095°.
DZ No 1 Fl Y 2·5s; 51°15'·28N 03°09'·49W.
DZ No 2 Fl Y 10s; 51°13'·77N 03°19'·86W.
DZ No 3 Fl Y 5s; 51°16'·34N 03°14'·98W.

WATCHET, MINEHEAD and PORLOCK WEIR

Watchet W Bkwtr Hd ☆ Oc G 3s 9m 9M; 51°11'·03N 03°19'·74W.
Watchet E Pier ☆ 2 FR (vert) 3M; 51°11'·01N 03°19'·71W.
Minehead Bkwtr Hd ☆ Fl(2) G 5s 4M; vis: 127°-262°; 51°12'·81N 03°28'·35W.
Lynmouth Foreland ☆ 51°14'·73N 03°47'·21W Fl (4) 15s 67m **18M**; W ○ twr; vis: 083°-275°.

LYNMOUTH and WATERMOUTH

River Training Arm ☆ 2 FR (vert) 6m 5M; 51°13'·90N 03°49'·83W.
Harbour Arm ☆ 2 FG (vert) 6m 5M; 51°13'·92N 03°49'·84W.
Sand Ridge Q G; 51°15'·01N 03°49'·77W.
Copperas Rock Fl G 2·5s; 51°13'·78N 04°00'·60W.
Watermouth ☆ Oc WRG 5s 1m 3M; W △; vis: 149·5°-G-151·5°-W- 154·5°-R-156·5°; 51°12'·93N 04°04'·60W.

ILFRACOMBE to BAGGY POINT

Ldg Lts 188°. Front, Oc 10s 8m 3M; 51°12'·53N 04°06'·65W. Rear, Oc 10s 6m 3M.
Horseshoe Q; 51°15'·03N 04°12'·96W; AIS.
Bull Point ☆ 51°11'·94N 04°12'·09W Fl (3) 10s 54m **20M**; W ○ twr, obscd shore-056°. Same twr; FR 48m 12M; vis: 058°-096°.
Morte Stone Fl G 5s; 51°11'·30N 04°14'·95W.
Baggy Leap Fl(2) G 10s; 51°08'·92N 04°16'·97W.

1	Aberystwyth	**1**												**12**	64	66	122	164	192	224	254	286	299	318	361	Kilrush	**12**
2	Fishguard	40	**2**												**11**	13	69	111	139	171	201	233	246	265	308	Dingle	**11**
3	Milford Haven	84	48	**3**												**10**	56	102	131	165	188	227	242	252	295	Valentia	**10**
4	Tenby	107	71	28	**4**												**9**	42	70	102	132	164	177	196	239	Baltimore	**9**
5	Swansea	130	94	55	36	**5**												**8**	35	69	95	135	150	168	202	Kinsale	**8**
6	Cardiff	161	125	86	66	46	**6**												**7**	34	65	100	115	133	172	Youghal	**7**
7	Sharpness	192	156	117	106	75	33	**7**												**6**	32	69	84	102	139	Dunmore East	**6**
8	Avonmouth	175	139	100	89	58	20	18	**8**												**5**	34	47	66	108	Rosslare	**5**
9	Burnham-on-Sea	169	133	94	70	48	53	50	33	**9**												**4**	15	36	75	Arklow	**4**
10	Ilfracombe	128	92	53	35	25	44	74	57	45	**10**												**3**	21	63	Wicklow	**3**
11	Padstow	142	106	70	70	76	97	127	110	98	55	**11**												**2**	48	Dun Laoghaire	**2**
12	Longships	169	133	105	110	120	139	169	152	140	95	50	**12**												**1**	Carlingford Lough	**1**

BIDEFORD, RIVERS TAW and TORRIDGE

Bideford Fairway L Fl 10s; *Bell;* 51°05′·25N 04°16′·25W.

Bideford Bar Q G; 51°04′·89N 04°14′·62W.

Instow ☆ Ldg Lts 118°. **Front**, 51°03′·62N 04°10′·66W Oc 6s 22m **15M**; vis: 103·5°-132°. **Rear**, 427m from front, Oc 10s 38m **15M**; vis: 103°-132·5°; (H24).

Crow Pt Fl WR 2. 5s 8m W6M R5M; vis: 225°-R-232°-W-237°-R-358°-W- 015°-R-045°; 51°03′·96N 04°11′·39W.

LUNDY

North Pt ☆ 51°12′·10N 04°40′·65W Fl 15s 48m **18M**; vis: 009°-285°.

South East Pt ☆ 51°09′·72N 04°39′·37W Fl 5s 53m **15M**; vis: 170°-073°.

Hartland Point 51°01′·3N 04°31′·6W Fl (6) 15s 30m 8M; adjacent to Hartland Point Light House (disused).

NORTH CORNWALL

BUDE, PADSTOW and NEWQUAY

Compass Pt twr 50°49′·71N 04°33′·42W.

Stepper Pt (Padstow) LFl 10s 12m 4M; 50°34′·12N 04°56′·72W.

Middle Gnd (Padstow) Fl(2+1)R 10s; 50°32′·84N 04°55′·96W.

Trevose Head ☆ 50°32′·94N 05°02′·13W Fl 7·5s 62m **21M**.

North Pier Hd (Newquay) 2 FG (vert) 5m 2M; 50°25′·07N 05°05′·19W.

HAYLE and ST IVES

The Stones Q; 50°15′·64N 05°25′·51W.

Godrevy I Fl WR 10s 28m 8M; metal post; vis: 022°-W-101°-R-145°-W-272°; 50°14′·56N 05°24′·01W; adjacent to Godrevy Light House (disused).

Hayle App Q; 50°12′·28N 05°26′·20W.

St Ives App 50°12′·85N 05°28′·42W.

Bann Shoal Fl G 2.5s; **Racon (B) 10M**; 50°20′·03N 05°51′·11W; 992351053.

Pendeen ☆ 50°09′·90N 05°40′·30W Fl (4) 15s 59m **16M**; vis: 042°-240°; between Gurnard Hd and Pendeen it shows to coast.

AREA 10 *Ireland – Clockwise from Lambay Island*

SELECTED LIGHTS, BUOYS & WAYPOINTS

LAMBAY ISLAND TO TUSKAR ROCK

MALAHIDE and LAMBAY ISLAND

Taylor Rks Q; 53°30′·21N 06°01′·87W.

Burren Rocks Fl G 5s; 53°29′·33N 06°02′·37W.

Malahide approach L Fl 10s; 53°27′·12N 06°06′·87W.

HOWTH

Rowan Rocks Q (3) 10s; 53°23′·88N 06°03′·27W.

Howth 53°23.727′N 006°03.593′W; 992501250.

E Pier Hd Fl (2) WR 7·5s 13m W12M, R9M; W twr; vis: W256°- R295°-256°; 53°23′·64N 06°04′·02W.

Baily ☆ 53°21′·69N 06°03′·16W Fl 15s 41m **18M**; twr. Fog Det Lt VQ; 992501010.

Rosbeg E Q (3) 10s; 53°21′·02N 06°03′·45W.

Rosbeg S Q (6) + L Fl 15s; 53°20′·22N 06°04′·17W.

PORT OF DUBLIN

Dublin Bay Iso 4s; **Racon (M);** 53°19′·92N 06°04′·65W; 992351301.

No 1 Fl (3) G 5s; 53°20′·30N 06°05′·56W.

No 3 Q G; 53°20′·59N 06°06′·78W.

No 4 Q R; 53°20′·39N 06°06′·81W.

No 5 Fl G 2s; 53°20′·64N 06°08′·60W.

No 6 Fl R 2s; 53°20′·56N 06°08′·75W.

Great S Wall Hd Poolbeg Fl R 4s 20m 10M *(sync with N.Bull)*; R ○ twr; 53°20′·52N 06°09′·08W.

N Bull Fl G 4s 15m 10M; G ○ twr; 53°20′·70N 06°08′·98W.

N Bank ☆ 53°20′·69N 06°10′·59W Oc G 8s 10m **16M**; G □ twr.

DUN LAOGHAIRE

E Bkwtr Hd Fl (2) R 8s 16m **17M**; granite twr, R lantern 7M; 53°18′·14N 06°07′·62W. Fog Det Lt VQ.

Outfall Fl Y 5s; 53°18′·41N 06°08′·35W.

Muglins Fl R 5s 14m 11M; 53°16′·52N 06°04′·58W; 992501019.

OFFSHORE MARKS

Bennett Bank Q(6)+ L Fl 15s; 53°20′·17N 05°55′·11W; 992501012.

Kish Bank ☆ 53°18′·65N 05°55′·54W Fl (2) 20s 29m **21M** (H24); W twr, R band; **Racon (T) 15M**; 992501017.

N Kish VQ; 53°18′·56N 05°56′·44W.

E Kish Fl (2) R 10s; 53°14′·35N 05°53′·56W; 992501020.

N Burford Q 53°20.51′N 06° 01′.49W; 992501016.

S Burford VQ(6)+L Fl 10s; 53°18′.06N 06° 01.30′W; 992501018.

E Codling Fl (4) R 10s; 53°08′·54N 05°46′·07W; 992501024.

W Codling Fl G 10s; 53°06′·97N 05°54′·51W.

Moulditch Fl R 10s; 53°08′·43N 06°01′·23W; 992501022.

S Codling VQ (6) + L Fl 10s; 53°04′·54N 05°49′·13W.

Codling Q(3) 10s; 53°04.19′N 005°37.36′W, **Racon (G) 10M,** 992501028.

Breaches Shoal Fl (2) R 6s; 53°05′·67N 05°59′·81W.

North India Q; 53°03′·12N 05°53′·46W.

S India Q (6) + L Fl 15s; 53°00′·36N 05°53′·31W; 992501030.

WICKLOW to ARKLOW

Wicklow Fl (4) Y 10s; 52°59′·54N 06°01′·29W.

E Pier Hd Fl WR 5s 11m 6M; W twr, R base and cupola; vis: 136°-R-293°-W-136°; 52°58′·99N 06°02′·07W.

W Packet Quay Hd Fl WG 10s 5m 6M; vis: 076°-G-256°-W-076°; 52°58′·88N 06°02′·08W.

Wicklow Hd ☆ 52°57′·93N 05°59′·93W Fl (3) 15s 37m **18M**; W twr; 992501031.

Horseshoe Fl R 3s; 52°56′·84N 05°58′·47W; 992501032.

N Arklow Q; 52°53′·86N 05°55′·21W; 992501034.

Arklow Bank Wind Farm from 52°48′·47N 05°56′·57W to 52°46′·47N 05°57′·11W, N and S Turbines Fl Y 5s14m 10M. No 7 Turbine 992501302. Other turbines Fl Y 5s.

ARKLOW to WEXFORD

S Pier Hd Fl WR 6s 11m 13M; twr; vis: R shore- W223°-R350°-shore; 52°47'·61N 06°08'·22W.

Roadstone Bkwtr Hd QY; 52°46'·65N 06°08'·23W.

S Arklow Q (6) + LFl 15s; **Racon (O) 10M**; 52°40'·20N 05°58'·89W; 992501040.

2 Glassgorman Fl (4)R 10s; 52°45'·35N 06°05'·34W; 992501038

1 Glassgorman Fl (2) R 6s; 52°37'·69N 06°07'·46W.

Courtown Fl R 5s 2m 3M; twr; 52°38'·61N 06°13'·45W.

Courtown Fl G 5s 2m 3M; twr; 52°38'·61N 06°13'·45W.

Blackwater Q; 52°32'·22N 06°09'·51W; 992501046.

No 6 Rusk Fl R 3s; 52°32'·65N 06°10'·41W.

No 4 Rusk Fl (2) R 5s; 52°31'·07N 06°10'·86W.

No 2 Rusk Fl (2) R 5s (sync); 52°28'·61N 06°12'·66W.

No 1 Rusk Fl (2) G 5s (sync); 52°28'·56N 06°11'·78W; AIS.

W Blackwater Fl G 6s; 52°25'·87N 06°13'·56W.

SE Blackwater Q (3) 10s, 52°25'·64N 06°08'·42W; **Racon (M) 6M**; 992501050.

S Blackwater Q (6) + L Fl 15s; 52°22'·76N 06°12'·87W.

North Long Q; 52°21'·44N 06°17'·04W.

West Long QG; 52°18'·18N 06°17'·96W.

Lucifer VQ (3) 5s; 52°17'·02N 06°12'·67W; 992501054.

ROSSLARE

S Long Fl G 6s (sync with Splaugh); 52°14'·74N 06°15'·80W.

Splaugh Fl R 6s (sync with S Long); 52°14'·36N 06°16'·78W; 992501062.

S Holdens Fl G 3s; 52°15'·15N 06°17'·25W. (sync Calmines).

Calmines Fl R 3s; 52°15'·00N 06°17'·78W. (sync S Holdens).

W Holdens Fl (3) G 9s; 52°15'·76N 06°18'·75W.

Rosslare Pier Hd Oc WRG 5s 15m W13M, R10M, G10M; R twr; vis:098°-G-188°-W-208°-R-246°-G-283°-W-286°-R-320°; 52°15'·43N 06°20'·29W.

Ballygeary Oc WR 1·7s 7m 4M vis: shore-R-152°-W-200°-W(unintens)-205°; 52°15'·25N 06°20'·48W.

TUSKAR ROCK TO OLD HEAD OF KINSALE

Tuskar 52°12'·17N 06°12'·44W Q (2) 7·5s 33m **18M**; W twr; **Racon (T) 18M**; 992501065.

S Rock Q (6)+L Fl 15s; 52°10'·80N 06°12'·84W.

Fundale Fl (2) R 10s; 52°11'·04N 06°19'·78W.

Barrels Q (3) 10s; 52°08'·32N 06°22'·05W; 992501070.

KILMORE

Kilmore Quay SWM Iso 10s; (Apr-Sep); 52°09'·20N 06°35'·30W.

Kilmore Bkwtr Hd Q RG 7m 5M; vis: 269°-R-354°-G-003°-R-077°; 52°10'·20N 06°35'·15W.

Ldg lts 007·9°, Front 52°10'·37N 06°35'·08W Oc 4s 3m 6M. Rear, 100m from front, Oc 4s 6m 6M; sync with front.

Bore Rks Q (3) 10s; 52°06.07'N 006°31.87'W; 992501072.

Coningbeg Q(6)+LFl 15s; 52°03'·20N 06°38'·57W; **Racon (G) 9M**; 992501074.

Red Bank VQ (9) 10s; 52°04.499'N 006°41.652'W; 992501076.

'M5' ODAS 35 51°41'·40N 06°42'·24W; Fl (5) Y 20s.

WATERFORD

Hook Hd 52°07'·42N 06°55'·76W Fl 3s 46m **18M**; W twr, two B bands; **Racon (K) 10M**. Fog Det Lt VQ. 992501079.

Waterford Fl R 3s. Fl (3) R 10s; 52°08'·95N 06°57'·00W.

Duncannon Dir lt F WRG 13m 10M, white tower on fort, 359·5°-FG-001·2°-Alt GW-001·7°-FW-002·4°-Alt WR-002·9°-FR-004·5°; 52°13'·23N 06°56'·25W; Oc WR 4s 13m W 9M R 7M on same tower, 119°-R-149°-W-172°.

Passage Pt Fl WR 5s 7m W6M, R5M; R pile structure; vis: 114°-W-127°-R-180°-W-302°-R-021° (shore); 52°14'·26N 06°57'·77W.

Cheek Pt Q WR 6m 5M; W mast; vis: W007°-R289°-007°; 52°16'·12N 06°59'·38W.

Sheagh Fl R 3s 29m 3M; Gy twr; vis: 090°-318°; 52°16'·29N 06°59'·34W.

Snowhill Point Ldg lts 255°. Front, Fl WR 2·5s 5m 3M; vis: W222°- R020°- W057°-107°; 52°16'·39N 07°00'·91W. Rear, Flour Mill, 750m from front, Q 12m 5M.

Queen's Chan Ldg lts 098°. Front, QR 8m 5M; B twr, W band; vis: 030°-210°;52°15'·32N 07°02'·38W. Rear, 550m from front, Q 15m 5M; W mast.

Beacon Quay Fl G 3s 9m; vis: 255°-086°; 52°15'·50N 07°04'·21W.

Cove Fl WRG 6s 6m 2M; W twr; vis: R111°-G161°-W234°-111°; 52°15'·05N 07°05'·16W.

Smelting Ho Pt Q 8m 3M; W mast; 52°15'·15N 07°05'·27W.

Ballycar Fl RG 3s 5m; vis: G127°-R212°-284°; 52°15'·06N 07°05'·51W.

DUNMORE EAST

East Pier Head 52°08'·93N 06°59'·34W Fl WR 8s 13m **W17M**, R13M; Gy twr, vis: W225°- R310°-004°.

Dunmore East 1 Q G; 52°09'·06N 06°59'·38W.

Dunmore East 2 Fl G 2s; 52°09'·00N 06°59'·47W.

W Wharf Fl G 2s 6m 4M; vis: 165°-246°; 52°08'·97N 06°59'·45W.

DUNGARVAN

Ballinacourty Pt Fl (2) WRG 10s 16m W10M, R8M, G8M; W twr; vis: G245°- W274°- R302°- W325°-117°; 52°04'·69N 07°33'·18W.

Helvick Q (3) 10s; 52°03'·61N 07°32'·25W.

Mine Head 51°59'·56N 07°35'·23W Fl (4) 30s 87m 12M; W twr, B band; vis: 228°-052°; 992501085.

YOUGHAL

Bar Rocks Q (6) + L Fl 15s; 51°54'·85N 07°50'·05W.

Blackball Ledge Q (3) 10s, 51°55'·34N 07°48'·53W.

W side of ent 51°56'·57N 07°50'·53W Fl WR 2·5s 24m **W17M**, R13M; W twr; vis: W183°- R273°- W295°- R307°-W351°-003°.

BALLYCOTTON

Ballycotton 51°49'·50N 07° 59'·13W; Fl WR 10s 59m **W18M**, R14M; B twr, within W walls, B lantern; vis: 238°-W-041°-R-238°; 992501093.

The Smiths Fl (3) R 10s; 51°48'·43N 08°00'·60W.

Power Q (6) + L Fl 15s; 51°45'·59N 08°06'·67W; 992501098.

CORK

Cork L Fl 10s; 51°42'·92N 08°15'·60W; **Racon (T) 7M**; 992501100.

Daunt Rock Fl (2) R 6s; 51°43'·53N 08°17'·50W; 992501102.

Fort Davis Ldg lts 354·5°. Front, 51°48'·83N 08°15'·79W, H24 Dir WRG 25m **17M**; vis: 351·5°-FG-352·5°-QG-353·5°-FW-355·5°-QR-356·5°-FR-357·5°. Rear, Dognose Quay, 203m from front, Oc 5s 37m 10M; Or 3, sync with front.

Roche's Pt ☆ 51°47'·58N 08°15'·29W Fl WR 3s 30m **W18M**, R12M; vis: shore-R-292°-W-016°-R-033°, 033°- W (unintens)-159°-R-shore; 992501099.
Outer Hbr Rk E2 Fl R 2·5s; 51°47'·52N 08°15'·67W.
Chicago Knoll E1 Fl G 5s; 51°47'·66N 08°15'·54W.
W1 Fl G 10s; 51°47'·69N 08°16'·05W.
W2 Fl R 10s; 51°47'·69N 08°16'·34W.
White Bay Ldg lts 034·6°. Front, Oc R 5s 11m 5M; W hut; 51°48'·53N 08°15'·22W. Rear, 113m from front, Oc R 5s 21m 5M; W hut; synch with front.
Spit Bank Pile Iso WR 4s 10m W10M, R7M; W house on R piles; vis: R087°- W196°- R221°- 358°; 51°50'·72N 08°16'·45W.

KINSALE and OYSTER HAVEN
Bulman Q (6) + L Fl 15s; 51°40'·14N 08°29'·74W; 992501104.
Charlesfort Fl WRG 5s 18m W9M, R6M, G7M; vis: G348°- W358°- R004°-168°; H24; 51°41'·75N 08°29'·84W.

OLD HEAD OF KINSALE TO MIZEN HEAD

Old Head of Kinsale ☆, S point 51°36'·29N 08°32'·02W Fl (2) 10s 72m **20M**; B twr, two W bands; 992501107.

COURTMACSHERRY
Barrel Rock 51°37'·01N 08°37'·30W.
Black Tom Fl G 5s; 51°36'·41N 08°37'·95W; 992501110.
Wood Pt (Land Pt) Fl (2) WR 5s 15m 5M; vis: W315°-R332°-315°; 51°38'·16N 08°41'·00W.
Galley Head ☆ summit 51°31'·80N 08°57'·21W Fl (5) 20s 53m **23M**; W twr; vis: 256°-065°.

GLANDORE and CASTLETOWNSHEND
Glandore Dir lt Oc WRG 37m 7M, metal tower, vis: 294°-G-304°-W-312°-R-342°; 51°33'·33N 09°07'·08W.
Reen Point Fl WRG 10s 9m W5M, R3M, G3M; W twr; vis: shore-G-338°-W-001°-R-shore; 51°30'·98N 09°10'·50W.
Kowloon Bridge Q(6)+LFl 15s; 51°27'·58N 09°13'·75W; 992501118.

BALTIMORE and FASTNET
Barrack Pt Fl (2) WR 6s 40m W6M, R3M; vis: R168°- W294°-038°; 51°28'·33N 09°23'·65W.
Loo Rock Fl G 3s; 51°28'·44N 09°23'·46W; 992501119.
Lousy Rks Q(6)+LFl 15s; 51°28'·93N 09°23'·39W.
Wallis Rk Fl (3) R 10s; 51°28'·93N 09°22'·99W.
Lettuce Pt VQ (3) 5s; 51°29'·32N 09°23'·81W.
Mealbeg Q(6) + LFl 15s; 51°29'·68N 09°24'·69W.
Inane Pt Q(6) + LFl 15s; 51°30'·02N 09°23'·66W.
Hare Is Q; 51°30'·17N 09°25'·38W.
Fastnet ☆, W end 51°23'·36N 09°36'·18W Fl 5s 53m **18M**; Gy twr, **Racon (G) 18M**. Fog Det Lt VQ; 992501123.

SCHULL and LONG ISLAND CHANNEL
Amelia ; 51°29.979'N 009°31.461'W; 992501120.
Copper Point 51°30'·25N 09°32'·06W Q (3) 10s 16m 8M. Ldg lts 346° Front, Oc 5s 5m 11M, W mast; 51°31'·68N 09°32'·43W. Rear, 91m from front, Oc 5s 8m11M; W mast.

CROOKHAVEN
Rock Is Pt L Fl WR 8s 20m W13M, R11M; W twr; vis: W over Long Is B to 281°-R-340°; inside harbour 281°-R-348°- towards N shore; 51°28'·59N 09°42'·27W; 992501124.

MIZEN HEAD TO DINGLE BAY

Mizen Head Iso 4s 55m 12M; vis: 313°-133°; 51°26'·99N 09°49'·23W; 992501127.
Sheep's Hd ☆ 51°32'·59N 09°50'·92W Fl (3) WR 15s 83m **W15M** R9M; W bldg; vis: 011·3°-R-016·6°-W-212·5°-(partially obs) 233° (shore); 992501129.

BANTRY BAY, CASTLETOWN BEARHAVEN, WHIDDY IS
Carrigavaddra VQ (3) 5s, 51°38'·72N 09°45'·91W.
Roancarrigmore Fl WR 5s 13m W11M, R9M, R5M; s/ steel twr; vis: 312°-W-050°-R-122°-R(unintens)-207°-obsc-246°-R-312°; 51°39'·18N 09°44'·82W. Old Lt ho W twr, B band; 992501130.
Ardnakinna Pt 51°37'·10N 09°55'·09W Fl (2) WR 10s 62m W14M, R9M; W ○ twr; vis: 319°-R-348°-W-066°-R-shore; 992501131.
Walter Scott Rk Q (6) + L Fl 15s; 51°38'·52N 09°54'·20W; 992501128.
Castletownbere Dir lt 023·25° Oc WRG 5s 5·7m WRG15M; Twr; vis: 020·5°-G-023°-W-023·5°-R-025·5°; 51°38'·73N 09°54'·35W; 992501125.
Castletown Ldg lts 008°. Front, Oc Bu 6s 4m 6M; W col, R stripe; vis: 005°-013°; 51°39'·16N 09°54'·40W. Rear, 80m from front, Oc Bu 6s 7m 6M; W with R stripe; vis: 005°-013°.
Bull Rock ☆ 51°35'·52N 10°18'·07W Fl 15s 91m **18M**; W twr; 992501131.

KENMARE RIVER, DARRYNANE and BALLYCROVANE
Illaunnameanla (Ballycrovane) Fl R 3s; 51°42'·60N 09°57'·50W.
Book Rks Fl(2) R 10s; 51°46'·54N 09°49'·74W.
Cuskeal Fl R 5s; 51°46'·45N 09°48'·85W.
Bunaw Ldg Lts 041°. Front, Oc R 3s 9m 2M; B col, Y bands; 51°46'·80N 09°48'·40W. Rear, 200m from front Iso R 2s 11m 2M.
Maiden Rk Fl G 5s; 51°49'·00N 09°47'·99W; 992501134.
Bat Rk Fl G 5s; 51°50'·89N 09°40'·89W.
Carrignaronebeg Fl R 5s; 51°50'·99N 09°41'·39W.
No1 Fl G 5s; 51°52'·09N 09°36'·35W.
Carrignarone (Seal Rk) Fl 5s 2m 2M; 51°48'·58N 09°52'·65W.
Castlecove Ldg Lts 045°. Front, Oc 2s 5m 6M; concrete post W front; 51°46'·29N 10°02'·04W. Rear, 400m from front Oc 2s 18m 6M.
West Cove Hbr Fl R 3s; post W front; 51°46'·00N 10°02'·93W.
West Cove Hbr Ldg Lts 312°. Front, Fl 2s 2m 6M; concrete post; 51°46'·11N 10°03'·08W. Rear, 200m from front Fl 2s 4m 6M.
Darrynane Ldg lts 034°. Front, Oc 3s 10m 4M; 51°45'·90N 10°09'·20W. Rear, Oc 3s 16m 4M.

SKELLIG ISLANDS
Skelligs Rock Fl (3) 15s 53m 12M; W twr; vis: 262°-115°; part obsc within 6M 110°-115°; 51°46'·11N 10°32'·52W; 992501137.

VALENTIA and PORTMAGEE
Fort (Cromwell) Point ☆ 51°56'·02N 10°19'·27W Fl WR 2s 16m **W17M, R10M**; W twr; vis: 304°-R-351°,104°-W-304°; obsc from seaward by Doulus Head when brg more than 180°; 992501141.

Dir lt 141° ☆ Oc WRG 4s 25m W11M, R8M, G8M (by day: W3M, R2M, G2M); W twr, R stripe; vis:136°-G-140°-W-142°-R-146°; 51°55'·51N 10°18'·42W.
The Foot VQ (3) 5s; 51°55'·72N 10°17'·07W; 992501140.

DINGLE BAY TO LOOP HEAD

DINGLE BAY, VENTRY and DINGLE

Lt Twr ☆ Fl WRG 3s 20m WRG 6M; W metal twr; vis: 310°-G-328°-W-000°-R-024°; 52°07'·30N 10°15'·51W.
Dingle Hbr ☆ Fl (2) 3s 6m 3M, 52 07·24 N 10 15·71 W.
Foheragh Dir Lt ☆ 182° Oc WRG 5s 8 2 Pole; vis:177°-Oc R-181°-Oc W-183°-Oc G-187°, 52 07·43 N 10 16·59 W.
Dingle Dir Lt ☆ 002° Oc WRG 5s 14 3 Mast; vis: 354°-Oc G-001°-Oc W-003°-Oc R-009°, 52 08·34 N 10 16·52 W.
Inishtearaght ☆, W end Blasket Islands 52°04'·54N 10°39'·67W Fl (2) 20s 84m **18M**; W twr; vis: 318°-221°; **Racon (O)**; 992501143.

BRANDON BAY, TRALEE BAY and FENIT HARBOUR

Lit Samphire Is ☆ Fl WRG 5s 17m W14M, RG11M; Bu ○ twr; vis: 262°-R-275°, 280°-R-090°-G-140°-W-152°-R-172°; 52°16'·26N 09°52'·91W.
Gt Samphire Is ☆ QR 15m 3M; vis: 242°-097°; 52°16'·15N 09°51'·81W.
Fenit Hbr Pier Hd ☆ 2 FR (vert) 12m 3M; vis: 148°-058°; 52°16'·24N 09°51'·55W.

SHANNON ESTUARY

Ballybunnion VQ; **Racon (M) 6M**; 52°32'·52N 09°46'·93W; 992501146.
Kilstiffin Fl R 3s; 52°33'·80N 09°43'·83W; 992501148.
Kilcredaun Q R (sync); 52°34'·42N 09°41'·16W.
Tail of Beal Q G (sync); 52°34'·37N 09°40'·71W; 992501150.
Kilcredaun Head, W twr; 52°34'·78N 09°42'·58W.
Carrigaholt Fl (2) R 6s (sync); 52°34'·90N 09°40'·47W.
Beal Spit Fl (2) G 6s (sync); 52°34'·80N 09°39'·94W.
Beal Bar Fl G 3s (sync); 52°35'·18N 09°39'·05W.
Doonaha Fl R 3s (sync); 52°35'·54N 09°39'·01W; 992501154.
Corlis Pt (Ldg lts 046·4° H24) ☆ Front, Iso 4s 9m 7M(day) 10M; hut; 52°37'·10N 09°36'·36W; 992501156.
Querrin Pt ☆ Rear, Iso 4s 28m 7M(day) 10M; lattice mast; 52°37'·69N 09°35'·34W.
Letter Point Fl R 7s; 52°35'·44N 09°35'·89W.
Asdee Fl R 5s; 52°35'·09N 09°34'·55W.
Rineanna QR; 52°35'·59N 09°31'·24W.
North Carraig Q; 52°35'·60N 09°29'·76W.
Scattery Is, Rineanna Pt ☆ Fl (2) 8s 15m 10M; W twr; vis: 208°-092°; 52°36'·35N 09°31'·07W.

KILRUSH

Marina Ent Chan Ldg lts 355°. Front, Oc 3s; 52°37'·99N 09°30'·27W. Rear, 75m from front, Oc 3s.
Tarbert Is N Point ☆ Q WR 4s 18m W14M, R10M; W ○ twr; vis: W069°-R277°-W287°-339°; 52°35'·52N 09°21'·83W.
Tarbert (Ballyhoolahan Pt) Ldg lts 128·2°. Front, Iso 3s 13m 3M; △ on W twr; vis: 123·2°-133·2°; 52°34'·35N 09°18'·80W. Rear, 400m from front, Iso 5s 18m 3M; G stripe on W Bn.
Garraunbaun Pt ☆ Fl (3) WR 10s 16m W8M, R5M; W □ col, vis: R shore - W072°- R242°- shore; 52°35'·62N 09°13'·94W.
Rinealon Pt ☆ Fl 2·5s 4m 7M; B col, W bands; vis: 234°-088°; 52°37'·12N 09°09'·82W.

FOYNES

W Chan Ldg lts 107·9° (may be moved for changes in chan). Front, Oc 4s 34m 12M; 52°36'·91N 09°06'·59W . Rear, Oc 4s 39m 12M.

RIVER SHANNON

Beeves Rock ☆ Fl WR 5s 12m W12M, R9M; vis: 064·5°-W-091°-R-238°-W-265°-W(unintens)-064·5°; 52°39'·01N 09°01'·35W .
North Channel Ldg lts 093°. Front, Tradree Rock Fl R 2s 6m 5M; W Trs; vis: 246°-110°; 52°41'·00N 08°49'·87W. Rear 0·65M from front, Iso 6s 14m 5M; W twr, R bands; vis: 327°-190°.
N side, Ldg lts 061°. Front, 52°40'·72N 08°45'·27W, Crawford Rock 490m from rear, Fl R 3s 6m 5M. Crawford No 2, Common Rear, Iso 6s 10m 5M; 52°40'·85N 08°44'·88W.
Ldg lts 302·1°, Flagstaff Rock, 670m from rear, Fl R 7s 7m 5M; 52°40'·66N 08°44'·40W.
Ldg lts 106·5°. Meelick Rk, Front Iso R 4s 6m 5M; 52°40'·24N 08°42'·32W. Meelick No 2, rear 275m from front Iso R 4s 9m 5M; both W beacons.

LOOP HEAD

Loop Head ☆ 52°33'·67N 09°55'·92W Fl (4) 20s 84m **23M**; vis: 280°-218°; 992501161.
Mal Bay Fl(5) Y 20s 52°46.42'N 009°35.15'W; *AIS.*

LISCANNOR BAY TO SLYNE HEAD

GALWAY BAY and INISHMORE

Eeragh, Rock Is ☆ 53°08'·91N 09°51'·39W Fl 15s 35m **18M**; W twr, two B bands; vis: 297°-262°; 992501172.
Straw Is ☆ Fl (2) 5s 11m 12M; W twr; 53°07'·08N 09°37'·82W.
Killeany Ldg lts 192°. Front, Oc 5s 6m 3M; W col on W □ base; vis: 142°-197°, 53°06'·25N 09°39'·74W. Rear, 43m from front, Oc 5s 8m 2M; W col on W □ base; vis: 142°-197°.
Inishmaan, Ldg lts 199°, Oc 6s 8M; 53°06'·08N 09°34'·77W.
Killeaney Fl G 3s; 53°07.33'N 009°38.37'W; 992501166.
Inisheer ☆ 53°02'·76N 09°31'·61W Iso WR 12s 34m **W16M**, R11M; vis: 225°-W(partially vis >7M)-231°, 231°-W-245°-R-269°-W-115°; **Racon (K) 13M**; 992501165.
Finnis Q (3) 10s; 53°02'·82N 09°29'·14W, 992501164.
Black Hd ☆ Fl WR 5s 20m W11M, R8M, W □ twr; vis: 045°- R268°-276°; 53°09'·25N 09°15'·83W.

GALWAY

Margaretta Shoal Fl G 3s (sync); *Whis;* 53°13'·68N 09°05'·99W, 992501170.
Black Rk Fl R 3s (sync); 53°14'·00N 09°06'·55W.
Leverets ☆ Q WRG 9m 10M; B □ twr, W bands; vis: 015°-G-058°-W-065°-R-103°-G-143·5°-W-146·5°-R-015°; 53°15'·33N 09°01'·90W.
Rinmore ☆ Iso WRG 4s 7m 5M; W □ twr; vis: 359°-G-008°-W-018°-R-027°; 53°16'·12N 09°01'·97W.
Appr Chan Dir lt 325°, WRG 7m 3M; vis: 322·25°-FG-323·75°-AlGW-324·75°-FW-325·25°-AlRW-326·25°-FR-331·25°-FlR-332·25°; 53°16'·12N 09°02'·83W.

GALWAY to SLYNE HEAD

Barna Quay Hd ☆ Fl 2 WRG 5s 6m W8M, R5M, G5M; vis:250°-G-344·5°-W-355·5°-R-090°; 53°14'·93N 09°08'·90W.
Spiddle Pier Hd ☆ Fl WRG 3·5s 11m W8M, R8M, G8M; Y col; vis: 265°-G-308°-W-024°-R-066°; 53°14'·42N 09°18'·54W.
Cashla Bay Ent, W side ☆ Fl (3) WR 10s 8m W6M, R3M; W col on concrete twr; vis: 216°-W-000°-R-069°; 53°14'·23N 09°35'·20W.
Cannon Rk Fl G 5s; 53°14'·08N 09°34'·35W, 992501173.
Lion Pt Dir lt 010°, Iso WRG 5s 6m (H24), G6M, W8M, R6M,(night), G2M, W3M, R2M(day); vis: 005°-G-008·5°-W-011·5°-R-015°; 53°15'·83N 09°33'·98W; 992501171.

Rossaveel Pier Ldg lts 116°. Front, 53°16′·02N 09°33′·38W Oc 3s 7m 3M; W mast. Rear, 90m from front, Oc 3s 8m 3M.

Kiggaul Bay ☆ Fl WRG 3s 5m W5M, R3M, G3M; vis: 310°-G-329°-W-349°-R-059°; 53°14′·03N 09°43′·02W.

Croaghnakeela Is ☆ Fl 3·7s 7m 5M; W col; vis: 034°-045°, 218°-286°, 311°-325°; 53°19′·40N 09°58′·21W.

Inishnee ☆ Fl (2) WRG 10s 9m W5M, R3M, G3M; W col on W □ base; vis: 314°-G-017°-W-030°-R-080°-W-194°; 53°22′·75N 09°54′·53W.

Slyne Head, North twr, Illaunamid ☆ 53°23′·99N 10°14′·05W Fl (2) 15s 35m **19M**; B twr; **Racon (T)**; 992501175.

SLYNE HEAD TO EAGLE ISLAND

CLIFDEN BAY and INISHBOFIN

Carrickrana Rocks Bn, large W Bn; 53°29′·24N 10°09′·48W.

Cleggan Point ☆ Fl (3) WRG 15s 20m W6M, R3M, G3M; W col on W hut; vis: shore-G-091°-W-124°-R-221°; 53°34′·48N 10°07′·69W.

Inishlyon Lyon Head ☆ Fl WR 7·5s 13m W7M, R4M; W post; vis: 036°-W-058°-R-184°-W-325°-R-036°; 53°36′·74N 10°09′·56W.

Gun Rk ☆ Fl (2)6s 8m 4M; W col on W hut; vis: 296°-253°; 53°36′·59N 10°13′·22W.

Inishbofin Dir lt 021°, Oc WRG 6s 10m 11M; W pole; vis: 015·75°-G-020·75°-W-021·25°-R-026·25°; 53°36′·78N 10°13′·16W.

CLEW BAY and WESTPORT

Roonagh Quay Ldg lts 144°. Front 53°45′·75N 09°54′·23W. Rear, 54m from front, both Iso Bu 10s 9/15m.

Inishgort ☆ L Fl 10s 10M; 53°49.59′N 009°40.25′W; 992501179.

Cloughcormick Q (9) 15s; 53°50′·56N 09°43′·20W.

Achillbeg I, S Point ☆ 53°51′·51N 09°56′·84W Fl WR 5s 56m **W16M, R18M**, R11M; W ○ twr on □ building; vis: 262°-R-281°-W-342°-R-060°-W-092°-R(intens)-099°-W-118°; 992501181.

ACHILL SOUND

Ldg lts 330°, 53°52′·50N 09°56′·89W Whitestone Point. Front and rear both 2 Oc Bu 4s 5/6m; W ◊, B stripe.

Achill I Ldg lts 310°, Purteen, 53°57′·81N 10°05′·96W, Iso Bu 6s 5m. Rear, 46m from front Iso Bu 6s 6m.

BLACKSOD BAY

Blacksod Q (3) 10s; 54°05′·89N 10°03′·01W.

Blacksod Pier Root ☆ Fl (2) WR 7·5s 13m W12M, R9M; W twr on bldg; vis: 189°-R-210°-W-018°; 54°05′·92N 10°03′·63W; 992501186.

Carrigeenmore VQ(3) 5s 3M; 54°06′·56N 10°03′·4W.

Black Rock ☆ 54°04′·06N 10°19′·23W Fl WR 12s 86m **W20M, R16M**; W twr; vis: 276°-W-212°-R-276°; 992501183.

Eagle Is, W end ☆ 54°17′·02N 10°05′·56W Fl (3) 15s 67m **18M**; W twr; 992501189.

EAGLE ISLAND TO RATHLIN O'BIRNE

BROAD HAVEN BAY

Rinroe Pt ☆ Fl (2) 10s 5m 3M; 54°17′·83N 09°50′·59W.

Gubacashel Pt ☆ Iso WR 4s 27m **W17M**, R12M; 110°-R-133°-W-355°-R-021° W twr; 54°16′·06N 09°53′·32W; 992501190.

KILLALA

Carrickpatrick Q (3) 10s; 54°15′·56N 09°09′·17W; 992501192.

Inishcrone Pier Root ☆ Fl WRG 1·5s 8m 2M; vis: 098°-W-116°-G- 136°-R-187°; 54°13′·21N 09°05′·79W.

Ldg lts 230°. Rinnaun Point. Front No 1, Oc 10s 7m 5M; □ twr; 54°13′·21N 09°05′·79W. Rear, 150m from front, No 2 Oc 10s 12m 5M; □ twr.

Inch Is Dir lt 215°, Fl WRG 2s 6m 3M; □ twr; vis: 205°-G-213°-W- 217°-R-225°; 54°13′·29N 09°12′·30W.

Ldg lts 196°. Kilroe. Front, 54°12′·63N 09°12′·33W Oc 4s 5m 2M; □ twr. Rear,120m from front, Oc 4s 10m 2M; □ twr.

Pier Ldg lts 236° Front, Iso Bu 2s 5m 2M; W ◊ on twr; 54°13′·02N 09°12′·84W. Rear, 200m fm front, Iso Bu 2s 7m 2M; W ◊ on pole.

SLIGO

Black Rock ☆ Fl WR 5s 24m 10/8M; vis: 130°-W-107°-R-130° (R over Wheat + Seal Rks); W twr, B band; 54°18′·46N 08°37′·06W.

Lower Rosses ☆ Fl (2) WRG 10s 8m 10M; W hut on piles; vis: 061°-G-066°-W-070°-R-075°; shown H24; 54°19′·73N 08°34′·41W.

Ldg lts 125° Fl (3) 6s 7M (sync). Front, Metal Man; 54°18′·24N 08°34′·55W, 3m. Rear, Oyster Is, 365m from front, 13m; H24.

Wheat Rk Q (6) + LFl 15s; 54°18′·84N 08°39′·10W; 992501196.

DONEGAL BAY and KILLYBEGS

St John's Pt ☆ Fl 6s 30m 14M; W twr; 54°34′·16N 08°27′·66W; 992501197.

Bullockmore Q (9) 15s; 54°33′·98N 08°30′·14W; 992501198.

Rotten I ☆ 54°36′·97N 08°26′·41W Fl WR 4s 20m **W15M**, R11M; W twr; vis: W255°- R008°- W039°-208°.

New Landing Dir lt 338°, Oc WRG 8s 17m; vis: 328°-G-334°-Al WG-336°-W-340°-Al WR-342°-R-348°; 54°38′·14N 08°26′·38W.

Killybegs Outer VQ (6) + L Fl 10s; 54°37′·92N 08°29′·15W.

RATHLIN O'BIRNE TO BLOODY FORELAND

S of ARAN and RUTLAND S CHANNEL

Rathlin O'Birne ☆ Fl WR 15s 35m W12M, R10M; W twr; vis: 195°-R-307°-W-195°; **Racon (O) 13M**, vis 284°-203°. 54°39′·82N 08°49′·95W; 992501203.

Dawros Head ☆ L Fl 10s 39m 4M; 54°49′·63N 08°33′·64W.

Wyon Point ☆ Fl (2) WRG 10s 8m W6M, R3M; W □ twr; vis: shore-G-021°-W-042°-R-121°-W-150°-R-shore; 54°56′·51N 08°27′·54W.

BURTONPORT

Ldg lts 068·1°. Front , FG 17m 1M; Gy Bn, W band; 54°58′·95N 08°26′·40W. Rear, 355m from front, FG 23m 1M; Gy Bn, Y band.

N SOUND OF ARAN and RUTLAND N CHANNEL

Rutland I Ldg lts 137·6°. Front, 54°58′·97N 08°27′·68W Oc 6s 8m 1M; W Bn, B band. Rear, 330m from front, Oc 6s 14m 1M.

Inishcoo Ldg lts 119·3°. Front, Iso 6s 6m 1M; W Bn, B band; 54°59′·43N 08°29′·63W. Rear, 248m from front, Iso 6s 11m 1M.

Ldg lts 186°. Front, Oc 8s 8m 3M; B Bn, W band; 54°58'·94N 08°29'·27W. Rear, 395m from front, Oc 8s 17m 3M; B Bn.

Aranmore, Rinrawros Pt ☆ 55°00'·90N 08°33'·69W Fl (2) 20s 71m **18M**; W twr; obsc by land about 234°-007° and about 013°.

Aux lt Fl R 3s 61m 13M, same twr; vis: 203°-234°; 992501205.

OWEY SOUND to INISHSIRRER

Cruit Is. Owey Sound Ldg lts 068·3°. Oc 10s. Front, 55°03'·06N 08°25'·85W. Rear, 107m from front.

Rinnalea Point ☆ 55°02'·59N 08°23'·72W Fl 7·5s 19m 9M; □ twr; vis: 132°-167°.

Gola Is Ldg lts 171·2°. Oc 3s 2M (sync). Front, 9m; W Bn, B band; 55°05'·11N 08°21'·07W. Rear, 86m fm front, 13m; B Bn, W band.

Glassagh. Ldg lts 137·4°. Front, Oc 8s 12m 3M; 55°06'·83N 08°18'·97W. Rear, 46m from front, Oc 8s 17m 3M; synch.

Inishsirrer, NW end ☆ Fl 3·7s 20m 4M; W □ twr vis: 083°-263°; 55°07'·40N 08°20'·93W.

BLOODY FORELAND TO INISHTRAHULL

BLOODY FORELAND to SHEEPHAVEN

Bloody Foreland ☆ Fl WG 7·5s 14m W6M, G4M; vis: 062°-W-232°-G-062°; 55°09'·51N 08°17'·03W.

Tory Island ☆ 55°16'·36N 08°14'·96W Fl (4) 30s 40m **18M**; B twr, W band; vis: 302°-277°; **Racon (M) 12-23M**; 992501211.

West Town Ldg lts 001° ☆ Iso 2s 9m 7M △ on Y structure R stripe; 55°15'·79N 08°13'·50W. Rear Iso 2s 11m 7M ▽ ditto (sync).

Inishbofin Pier ☆ Fl 8s 3m 3M; 55°10'·14N 08°10'·01W.

Ballyness Hbr. Ldg lts 119·5°. Front, Iso 4s 25m 1M; 55°09'·06N 08°06'·98W. Rear, 61m from front, Iso 4s 26m 1M.

Portnablahy Ldg lts 125·3°. Front Oc 6s 7m 2M; B col, W bands; 55°10'·79N 07°55'·65W. Rear, 81m from front, Oc 6s 12m 2M; B col, W bands.

MULROY BAY

Limeburner Q Fl; 55°18'·54N 07°48'·40W; 992501214.

Ravedy Is ☆ Fl 3s 9m 3M; vis 177°-357°; 55°15'·14N 07°46'·90W.

LOUGH SWILLY, BUNCRANA and RATHMULLAN

Fanad Head ☆ 55°16'·57N 07°37'·92W Fl (5) WR 20s 39m **W18M**, R14M; W twr; vis 100°-R-110°-W-313°-R-345°-W-100°; 992501215.

Swillymore Fl G 3s; 55°15'·12N 07°35'·79W; 992501216.

Dunree ☆ Fl (2) WR 5s 49m W12M, R9M; vis: 320°-R-328°-W-183°-R-196°; 55°11'·89N 07°33'·24W; 992501217.

Buncrana Pier near Hd ☆ Iso WR 4s 11m W13M, R10M; R twr, W band; vis: R shore- over Inch spit, 052°-W-139°-R-shore over White Strand Rock; 55°07'·60N 07°27'·88W.

Rathmullan Pier Hd ☆ Fl G 3s 5M; vis: 206°-345°; 55°05'·70N 07°31'·66W.

Inishtrahull ☆ 55°25'·89N 07°14'·63W Fl (3) 15s 59m **19M**; W twr; obscd 256°-261° within 3M; **Racon (T) 24M 060°-310°**. Fog Det Lt VQ; 992501229.

INISHTRAHULL TO RATHLIN ISLAND

LOUGH FOYLE

Foyle L Fl 10s; 55°15'·32N 06°52'·62W; **Racon (M)**; 992501230.

Tuns Fl R 3s; 55°14'·00N 06°53'·46W; 992501232.

Inishowen Dunagree ☆ 55°13'·60N 06°55'·70W Fl (2) WRG 10s 28m **W18M**, R14M, G14M; W twr, 2 B bands; vis: 197°-G-211°-W-249°-R-000°. Fog Det lt VQ 16m vis: 270°.

Greencastle S Bkwtr Dir lt 042·5°. Fl (2) WRG 3s 4m W11M, R9M, G9M; vis 307°-G- 040°-W-045°-R-055°; 55°12'·17N 06°59'·13W.

McKinney's Fl R 5s; 55°10'·9N 07°00'·5W.

Moville Fl WR 2·5s 11m 4M; W house on G piles vis: 240°-W-064°-R-240°; 55°10'·99N 07°02'·12W.

RIVER BANN, COLERAINE and PORTRUSH

River Bann Ldg lts 165°. Front, Oc 5s 6m 2M; W twr; 55°09'·96N 06°46'·23W. Rear, 245m from front, Oc 5s 14m 2M; W □ twr.

W Mole ☆ Fl G 5s 4m 2M; vis: 170°-000°; 55°10'·25N 06°46'·45W.

Portstewart Point ☆ Oc R 10s 21m 5M; R □ hut; vis: 040°-220°; 55°11'·33N 06°43'·26W.

N Pier Hd ☆ Fl R 3s 6m 3M; vis: 220°-160°; 55°12'·34N 06°39'·58W.

Skerries Fl R 5s; 53°13'·90N 06°36'·90W; 992351096.

RATHLIN ISLAND

Rathlin W ☆ (½M NE of Bull Pt) 55°18'·05N 06°16'·82W; Fl R 5s 62m **18M**; W twr, lantern at base; vis: 015°-225°; H24. Fog Det Lt VQ; 992351000.

Drake Wreck 55°17'·00N 06°12'·48W Q (6) + L Fl 15s.

Manor House ☆ Oc WRG 4s 5M; vis: 020°-G-023°-W-026°-R-029°; 55°17'·52N 06°11'·73W.

Rue Pt ☆ Fl(2) 5s 16m 14M; W twr B bands; 55°15'·52N 06°11'·46W; 992351131.

Altacarry Head ☆ 55°18'·11N 06°10'·31W Fl (4) 20s 74m **18M**; W twr, B band; vis: 110°-006° and 036°-058°; **Racon (G) 15-27M**; 992320707.

FAIR HEAD TO LAMBAY ISLAND

RED BAY, CARNLOUGH and LARNE

Red Bay Pier ☆ Fl 3s 10m 5M; 55°03'·93N 06°03'·19W.

Carnlough Hbr N Pier ☆ Fl G 3s 4m 5M; 54°59'·59N 05°59'·29W.

East Maiden ☆ Fl (3) 15s 32m **18M**; **Racon (M) 11-21M;** W twr, B band; 54°55'·74N 05°43'·65W. Aux lt Fl R 5s 15m 8M; same twr vis:142°-182° over Russel and Highland Rks, H24; 992351110.

N Hunter Rock Q; 54°53'·04N 05°45'·13W.

S Hunter Rock VQ(6) + LFl 10s; 54°52'·69N 05°45'·22W; 992351007.

Larne No 1 QG; 54°51'·68N 05°47'·67W; *AIS*.

Chaine Twr ☆ Iso WR 5s 23m **W16M,** R12M; Gy twr; vis: 232°-W-240°-R-000° (shore); 54°51'·27N 05°47'·90W.

Larne Ldg lts 184°, No 11 Front, 54°49'·60N 05°47'·81W Oc 4s 6m 12M; W 2 with R stripe on R pile structure; vis: 179°-189°. No 12 Rear, 610m from front, Oc 4s 14m 12M; W 2 with R stripe on R □ twr; synch with front, vis: 5° either side of Ldg line.

CARRICKFERGUS

Black Hd ☆ 54°46'·02N 05°41'·34W Fl 3s 45m **27M**; W 8-sided twr; 992351002.

Marina Ent Appr ☆ Dir Oc WRG 3s 5m 3M**;** vis: G308°-W317·5°- R322·5°-332°; 54°42'·58N 05°48'·78W.

BELFAST LOUGH and BANGOR

Mew Is ☆ NE end 54°41′·92N 05°30′·82W F Fl (4) 30s 35m **18M**; B twr, W band; **Racon (O) 14M**; 992351109.

Belfast Fairway Iso 4s; 54°42′·32N 05°42′·30W; **Racon (G)**; *AIS*.

Kilroot Fl QG (sync); 54°42′·85N 05°42′·85W.

Helen's Bay QR (sync); 54°41′·86N 05°42′·85W.

No 1 Fl G 2s (sync); 54°41′·67N 05°46′·51W.

No 2 Fl R 2s (sync); 54°41′·55N 05°46′·43W.

Briggs Q; 54°41′·18N 05°53′·73W; 992351133.

DONAGHADEE

Merandoragh Fl (2) G 6s (sync); 54°39′·84N 05°32′·24W.

Foreland Spit Fl (2) R 6s (sync); 54°39′·64N 05°32′·31W.

Governor's Fl G 3s (sync); 54°39′·36N 05°31′·99W; 992351134.

Riggs Bank ⊙ V–AIS PHM; 54°38′·63N 05°27′·10W; 992356011.

Donaghadee ☆, S Pier Hd 54°38′·70N 05°31′·86W Iso WR 4s 17m **W16M**, R10M; twr; vis: shore-W-326°-R-shore; 002320792.

BALLYWATER and PORTAVOGIE

Ballywater, Bkwtr Hd Fl WRG 3s 4m 9M; vis: 240°-G-267°-W-277°-R-314°; 54°32′·68N 05°28′·83W.

Skulmartin Fl (2) R 6s 10s; 54°32′·39N 05°24′·91W; 992351022.

Portavogie Bkwtr Hd ☆ Iso WRG 5s 6m WRG 5M; □ twr; vis: shore-G-262°-W-272°-R-350°; 54°27′·44N 05°26′·14W.

Plough Rock 54°27′·40N 05°25′·12W Fl R 3s.

South Rock Fl (3) R 30s 9M 54°24′·48N 05°21′·99W; **Racon (T)**; 992351004.

STRANGFORD LOUGH

Strangford L Fl 10s; 54°18′·63N 05°28′·69W; 992351028.

Butter Pladdy Q (3) 10s; 54°22′·45N 05°25′·74W.

Bar Q (6) + L Fl 15s; 54°19′·34N 05°30′·51W; 992351135.

Dogtail Pt Ldg lts 341°. Front, Iso 4s 2m 5M; G Bn; 54°20′·79N 05°31′·84W. Rear, Gowlands Rk, 0·8M fm front, Iso 4s 6m 5M; W twr, G top, B base.

Swan Is Q (3) 5m; BYB brick twr; 54°22′·38N 05°33′·16W.

Strangford East Ldg lts 256°. Front, Oc WRG 5s 6m W9M, R6M, G6M: vis: 190°-R-244°-G-252°-W- 260°-R-294°; 54°22′·29N 05°33′·27W. Rear, 46m from front, Oc R 5s 10m 6M; vis: 250°-264°.

Portaferry Pier Hd ☆ Oc WR 10s 9m W9M, R6M; Or mast; vis: W335°-R005°-W017°-128°; 54°22′·82N 05°33′·03W.

ARDGLASS

Inner Pier Hd ☆ Iso WRG 4s 10m W8M, R7M, G5M; twr; vis: shore-G-308°-W-314°-R-shore; 54°15′·79N 05°36′·33W.

DUNDRUM BAY

St John's Point ☆ 54°13′·61N 05°39′·61W Q (2) 7·5s 37m **25M**; B twr, Y bands. **Auxiliary Light** ☆ Fl WR 3s 14m **W15M**, R11M; same twr, vis: 064°-W-078°-R-shore; Fog Det lt VQ 14m vis: 270°; 992351005.

DZ East Fl (2) Y 10s; 54°12′·05N 05°45′·30W.

DZ West Fl Y 5s; 54°11′·84N 05°50′·82W.

ANNALONG

E Bkwtr Hd ☆ Oc WRG 5s 8m 9M; twr; vis: 204°-G-249°-W-309°-R-024°; 54°06′·51N 05°53′·73W.

KILKEEL

Pier Hd ☆ Fl WR 2s 8m 8M; vis: R296°-W313°-017°; 54°03′·46N 05°59′·30W; 992356010 (emergency AIS 992356008).

CARLINGFORD LOUGH and NEWRY RIVER

Hellyhunter Q(6) + LFl 15s; 54°00′·35N 06°02′·10W; 992351009.

Haulbowline ☆ 54°01′·19N 06°04′·74W Fl (3) 10s 32m 10M; Grey twr; 992501235.

Ldg lts 310·4° Front, Oc 3s 7m 11M; R △ on twr; vis: 295°-325°; 54°01′·80N 06°05′·43W; 992501237. Rear, 457m from front, Oc 3s 12m 11M; R ▽ on twr; vis: 295°-325°; both H24.

Newry River Ldg lts 310·4°. Front, 54°06′·37N 06°16′·51W. Rear, 274m from front. Both Iso 4s 5/15m 2M; stone cols.

DUNDALK

Imogene Fl (2) R 10s; 53°57′·41N 06°07′·02W; 992501238.

Pile Light ☆ 53°58′·56N 06°17′·71W Fl WR 15s 10m 10M; W Ho.

Dunany Fl R 3s; 53°53′·56N 06°09′·47W; 992501243.

SKERRIES BAY

Cardy Rks Q(3) 10s; 53°37′·91N 06°10′·86W.

Skerries Pier Hd ☆ Oc R 6s 7m 7M; W col; vis: 103°-R-154°; 53°35′·09N 06°06′·49W.

DROGHEDA to LAMBAY ISLAND

Port Approach Dir lt 53°43′·30N 06°14′·73W WRG 10m **W19M, R15M**, G15M; vis: 268°-FG-269°-Al WG-269·5°-FW-270·5°-Al WR-271°-FR-272°; H24.

Balbriggan ☆ Fl (3) WRG 10s 12m W13M, R10M, G10M; W twr; vis: 159°-G-193°-W-288°-R-305°; 53°36′·76N 06°10′·80W.

Rockabill ☆ 53°35′·81N 06°00′·30W Fl WR 12s 45m **W17M, R13M;** W twr, B band; vis: 178°-W-329°-R-178°; 992501246.

Skerries Bay Pier Hd ☆ Oc R 6s 7m 7M; W col; vis: 103°-154°; 53°35′·09N 06°06′·49W.

1	Strangford Lough	1														
2	Bangor	34	2													
3	Carrickfergus	39	6	3												
4	Larne	45	16	16	4											
5	Carnlough	50	25	26	11	5										
6	Portrush	87	58	60	48	35	6									
7	Lough Foyle	92	72	73	55	47	11	7								
8	L Swilly (Fahan)	138	109	104	96	81	48	42	8							
9	Burtonport	153	130	130	116	108	74	68	49	9						
10	Killybegs	204	175	171	163	148	115	109	93	43	10					
11	Sligo	218	189	179	177	156	123	117	107	51	30	11				
12	Eagle Island	234	205	198	193	175	147	136	123	72	62	59	12			
13	Westport	295	266	249	240	226	193	187	168	120	108	100	57	13		
14	Galway	338	309	307	297	284	253	245	227	178	166	163	104	94	14	
15	Kilrush	364	335	332	323	309	276	270	251	203	191	183	142	119	76	15

DISTANCE TABLES

Approx distances in nautical miles are by the most direct route allowing for dangers and TSS.

AREA 11 *West Denmark – Skagen to Rømø*

SELECTED LIGHTS, BUOYS & WAYPOINTS

SKAGEN TO THYBORØN

SKAGEN

Skagen W ☆ Fl (3) WR 10s 31m **W17M**/R12M; 053°-W-248°-R-323°; W ○ twr; 57°44'·94N 10°35·70E.
Skagen ☆ Fl 4s 44m **23M**; Gy ○ twr; ***Racon G, 20M***; 57°44'·14N 10°37'·81E.
Skagen No 1A L Fl 10s; ***Racon N***; 57°43'·46N 10°53'·55E. (Route T)
Skagen No 2 L Fl 10s; 57°37'·61N 11°05'·51E. (Route T)
Skagens Rev Q; 57°45'·97N 10°43'·74E.
Q (3) 10s; 57°43'·87N 10°42'·31E.
Skagen Harbour S bkwtr root, Dir ☆ Oc WRG 5s 20m W11/RG10M, 263·3°-G-266·3°-W°-270·3°-R-273·3°; Gy lattice twr; 57°42'·77N 10°34'·99E.
S bkwtr head ☆ Fl R 3s 4m 5M; 57°42'·72N 10°35'·99E.
N bkwtr head ☆ Fl G 3s 4m 5M; 57°42'·92N 10°35'·91E.
Inner hbr ent SW side ☆ Fl R 5s
Inner hbr ent NE side ☆ Fl G 5s

HIRTSHALS

Hirtshals ☆ F Fl 30s 57m **F 18M**; **Fl 25M**; W ○ twr, approx 1M SSW of hbr ent; 57°35'·10N 09°56'·55E.
Ldg lts 166°, both 156°-176°. Front, Iso R 2s 10m 11M; R △ on twr; 57°35'·69N 09°57'·64E; marina ent is close N of this lt. Rear, Iso R 4s 18m 11M; R ▽ on twr; 330m from front.
Approach chan Fl (3) G 10s; 57°36'·18N 09°56·94E.
Fl R 3s; 57°36'·44N 09°57'·67E.
Fl (5) Y 20s; 57°36'·43N 09°57'·72E.
Fl G 5s; 57°36'·11N 09°57·14E.
Outer W mole ☆ Fl G 3s 14m 6M; G mast; *Horn 15s*; 57°35'·97N 09°57'·37E.
W mole spur ☆ Fl G 5s 9m 4M; G mast; 57°35'·77N 09°57'·51E.
E mole ☆ Fl R 5s 9m 6M; G mast; 57°35'·85N 09°57'·61E.

LØKKEN

Lee bkwtr ☆ Fl 5s 5m 5M; 57°22'·39N 09°42'·11E.

TRANUM STRAND (Firing ranges)

Tranum No 1 ☆ Al Fl WR 4s 19m W7M, R7M; twr; by day Q 4M; shown when firing in progress; 57°12'·43N 09°30'·34E.
Tranum No 2 ☆ light as per No 1; 57°10'·57N 09°26'·22E.

LILD STRAND

Bragerne Fl G 5s; 57°10'·67N 08°56'·35E.
Ldg lts 138°, three ☆: F 12/22m 7/8M; 127°-149°; 3 masts. Front 57°09'·22N 08°57'·75E.

HANSTHOLM

Hanstholm ☆ Fl (3) 20s 65m **24M**; shown by day in poor vis; W 8-sided twr; 57°06'·77N 08°35'·92E, approx 1M S of the hbr ent.
Hanstholm LFl 10s; 57°08'·24N 08°36'·09E.
Outer bkwtr, W head ☆ Fl G 3s 11m 9M; G post; 57°07'·70N 08° 35'·48E.
Outer bkwtr, E head ☆, Fl R 3s11m 9M, R pillar; 57°07'·61N 08° 35'·57E.
Inner W mole, ldg lts, Oc WRG 5s 13m 13M; 197°-G-205°-W-210°-R-218°; mast; 57°07'·53N 08°35'·42E
Roshage ☆ Fl 5s 7m 5M; 57°07'·75N 08°37'·25E (1M E of hbr).

NØRRE VORUPØR

Mole ☆ Fl G 5s 6m 5M; 56°57'·75N 08°21'·679E.
Ldg lts, both Iso R 4s 20/30m 9M, indicate safest landing place for FVs; vis 22·5° either side of ldg line; synch. Front 57°57'·46N 08°22'·10E. Rear, 80m from front.
Lodbjerg ☆ Fl (2) 20s 48m **23M**; ○ twr; 56°49'·40N 08°15'·76E.

THYBORØN

Landfall L Fl 10s; ***Racon T, 10m***; 56°42'·54N 08°08'·69E.
Agger Tange ldg lts 082°: Front, Iso WRG 4s 8m W11M, R/G8M; 074·5°-G-079·5°-W-084·5°-R-089·5°; R △ on bcn; 56°42'·97N 08°14'·14E. Rear, Iso 4s 17m 11M; 075°-089°; synch; R ▽ on Gy twr; 804m from front.
Off Havmolen 56°43'·25N 08°12'·52E.
Approach ☆ Fl (3) 10s 24m 12M; intens 023·5°-203·5°; also lit by day in poor vis; lattice twr; 56°42'·49N 08°12'·91E (S side of ent).
Langholm ldg lts 120°, both Iso 2s 7/13m 11M; synch; 113°-127°. Front, R △ on R hut, 56°42'·45N 08°14'·54E. Rear, R ▽ on Gy twr.
Thyborøn Havn ☆ Oc (2) WRG 12s 6m W11M, R/G8M; 122·5°-G-146·5°-W-150°-R-211·3°-G-337·5°-W-340°-R-344°; W twr R band; 56°42'·35N 08°13'·39E (680m N of ent to Yderhavn and Basins).
Yderhavn approach ☆ Dir Iso WRG 2s 21m 5M (0.5M by day); 213°-G-218°-W-223°-R-228°; 56°41'·85N 08°13'·32E
N mole ☆ Fl G 3s 6m 4M; G pedestal; 56°42'·02N 08°13'·52E.
S mole ☆ Fl R 3s 6m 4M; R pedestal; 56°41'·97N 08°13'·53E.

LIMFJORD (Limited coverage E, only to 08°42'E)

Sælhundeholm Løb, into Nissum Bredning ('Broad').
No 1 Fl (2) G 5s; 56°41'·14N 08°14'·17E.
No 3 Fl G 3s; 56°40'·75N 08°13'·79E.
No 7 Fl G 3s; 56°40'·31N 08°13'·52E.
No 11 Fl G 3s; 56°39'·83N 08°13'·59E.
No 16 Fl R 3s; 56°38'·51N 08°13'·89E.
No 18 Fl (2) R 5s; 56°38'·20N 08°14'·34E.
No 21 Fl G 3s; 56°38'·98N 08°14'·71E.
No 26 Fl R 3s; 56°38'·71N 08°15'·38E.
No 29 Fl G 3s; 56°38'·40N 08°15'·94E.

APPROACHES TO LEMVIG (Marina and Havn)

Toftum Dir ☆ 120°, Iso WRG 4s 24m, W12M, R/G 8M; 110°-G-120°-W-137°-R-144°; hut; 56°33'·09N 08°18'·33E.
Rønnen Fl G 3s; 56°36'·71N 08°21'·74E.
Søgard Mark ldg lts 243·5°: both FR 20/30m 5M; vis 90° either side of ldg line. Front, R △ on W bcn; 56°34'·39N 08°17'·29E. Rear, R ▽ on W post; 235m from front.
Chan 56°33'·27N 08°18'·31E.
Ldg lts, W of hbr 177·7°, both FR 8/20m 5M; 153°-203°. Front R △ on twr; 56°33'·04N 08°18'·16E. Rear, R ▽ on W post; 184m from front.
Vinkel Hage Marina, N mole ☆ FG 3m 5M; 56°33'·09N 08°18'·33E.
S mole, FR 3m 4M. Marina is 9ca N of the Havn on the W side.
Ostre Havn 56°33'·17N 08°18'·40E. Havn ent, FG/FR 4m 5M.

THISTED HAVN (Marina)
Outer W mole Fl R 3s 4m 2M; 56°57′·10N 08°41′·90E.
Outer E mole Fl G 3s 4m 2M; 56°57′·10N 08°41′·95E.
Thisted Bredning Aero 3 Fl R 1·5s (vert; 45m apart) 183m 10M; TV mast; 56°58′·52N 08°41′·15E, 1·55M NNW of hbr ent.

THYBORØN TO BLÅVANDS HUK

Bovbjerg Fl (2) 15s 62m 16M; 56°30′·79N 08°07′·18E.

THORSMINDE HAVN
(All Lat/Longs for this harbour are approximate)
Lt ho F 30m 13M; Gy twr; 56°22′·34N 08°06′·99E.
Groyne, N Fl 5s 8m 5M; Gy hut; 56°22′·46N 08°06′·82E.
N mole Iso R 2s 9m 4M; R hut; 56°22′·36N 08°06′·62E.
S mole Iso G 2s 9m 4M; G hut; 56°22′·26N 08°06′·92E.
West hbr, W mole FG 5m 2M; Gy post; 56°22′·36N 08°07′·12E.
E mole FR 5m 2M; Gy post; 56°22′·26N 08°07′·18E.
NW dolphin FG 5m 4M; Gy post; 56°22′·26N 08°07′·22E.
SE dolphin FG 5m 4M; Gy post; 56°22′ 26N 08°07′ 26E.
Lock, E side Iso 4s 12m 4M; Gy mast; 020°-160°; 56°22′·36N 08°07′·22E.
Road bridge Iso 4s 5m 4M; 200°-340°; 56°22′·36N 08°07′·26E.

HVIDE SANDE
Lyngvig Fl 5s 53m **23M** W ○ twr; 56°02′·99N 08°06′·22E.
N outer bkwtr Fl R 3s 7m 8M; R hut; 55°59′·94N 08°06′·55E.
Ent, 2 pairs converging Ldg lts: 2Iso 2s 063·2°, 2IsoR 4s 077·8°.
N mole Fl R 5s 10m 6·5M; R floodlit,55°59′·98N 08°06′·84E.
S mole Fl G 5s 10m 6M; 55°59′·96N 08°06′·98E.
Lt ho F 27m 14M; Gy twr; 56°00′·00N 08°07′·35E.
Nordhavn, E pier FG 4m 4M; 56°00′·16N 08°07′·42E.
W pier 2 FR 3m 2M; W posts; 060°-035°; 56°00′·07N 08°07′·12E.
Sydhavn, W pier FG 4m 2M; 56°00′·06N 08°07′·52E.
E Pier FR 4m 2M; Gy post; 56°00′·06N 08°07′·53E.
Lock entrance ldg lts 293·5°: both FR 11/14m 2M; 201·6°-021·6°. Front, R △ on Gy tr, 56°00′·0N 08°07′·8E. Rear, R ▽ on Gy twr, 72m from front.
Fjordhavn ldg lts 246·6° (both vis 7·5° either side of ldg line): Front, Iso G 2s 4m 4M; Or △ on mast; 56°00′·5N 08°07′·9E. Rear, Iso G 4s 6m 4M, Or ▽ on mast, 128m from front.

HORNS REV (marks westward from coast)
Oskbøl firing range. Two lights (4M apart) both AlFl WR 4s 35m **16M**, R13M, (by day Q 10M) are shown when firing is in progress: North 55°37′·24N 08°07′·04E. South 55°33′·53N 08°04′·67E.
Range safety buoys: Fl Y 5s; 55°42′·32N 08°06′·92E. Fl Y 3s; 55°38′·63N 07°50′·91E. Fl Y 3s; 55°37′·35N 07°56′·98E. 55°36′·02N 08°02′·49E.

Blåvands Huk Fl (3) 20s 55m **23M**; W □ twr; 55°33′·46N 08°04′·95E.

Horns Rev is encircled by:
Tuxen Q; 55°34′·22N 07°41′·92E on the N side.
Vyl Q (6) + L Fl 15s; 55°26′·22N 07°49′·99E on the S side.
No 2 L Fl 10s; 55°28′·74N 07°36′·49E on the SW side.
Horns Rev W Q (9) 15s; 55°34′·47N 07°26′·05E, off the W end.

Slugen Channel (crosses Horns Rev ESE/WNW)
L Fl G 10s; 55°33′·99N 07°49′·38E.
Fl G 3s; 55°32′·26N 07°53′·65E.
Fl (2) R 5s; 55°31′·46N 07°52′·88E.
Fl (2) G 5s; 55°30′·52N 07°59′·20E.
Fl (3) R 10s; 55°29′·42N 08°02′·56E.

Søren Bovbjergs Dyb (unlit N/S side channel off Slugen Chan)
55°33′·57N 07°55′·55E.
55°32′·80N 07°55′·30E.
55°32′·19N 07°56′·29E.
55°31′·24N 07°57′·46E.

BLÅVANDS HUK TO RØMØ

APPROACHES TO ESBJERG
Grådyb L Fl 10s; ***Racon G, 10M***; 55°24′·63N 08°11′·59E.
Sædding Strand 053·8° triple ldg lts: valid to buoys 7/8; H24: **Front** Iso 2s 14m **19M**; 052·3°-055·3°; Gy twr, copper roof; 55°29′·74N 08°23′·86E.
Middle Iso 4s 27m **19M**; 052·3°-055·3°; R metal twr, W bands; 55°29′·94N 08°24′·35E, 740m from front.
Rear F 37m **20M**; 052·3°-055·3°; R framework twr; 55°30′·18N 08°24′·92E, 0·75M from front.
No 1 Q; 55°25′·49N 08°13′·89E.
No 2 Fl (3) R 10s; 55°25′·62N 08°13′·73E.
No 3 Fl G 3s; 55°25′·93N 08°14′·84E.
No 4 Fl R 3s; 55°26′·02N 08°14′·72E.
Tide Gauge Fl (5) Y 20s 8m 4M; 55°26′·05N 08°15′·93E.
No 5 Fl G 5s; 55°26′·32N 08°15′·83E.
No 6 Fl R 5s; 55°26′·44N 08°15′·70E.
No 7 Q; 55°26′·76N 08°16′·91E.
No 8 Fl (2) R 5s; 55°26′·89N 08°16′·81E.
Ldg lts 067°, valid up to Nos 9/10 buoys. Both FG 10/25m **16M**, H24. Front, Gy tripod; rear, Gy twr, 55°28′·76N 08°24′·70E.
No 9 Fl (2) G 10s; 55°27′·04N 08°18′·21E.
No 10 Fl (2) R 10s; 55°27′·20N 08°18′·04E.
Ldg lts 049°, valid up to No 16 buoy/Jerg. Both FR 16/27m **16M**, H24. Front, W twr; rear, Gy twr, 55°29′·92N 08°23′·75E.
No 11 Fl G 3s; 55°27′·71N 08°19′·59E.
No 12 Fl R 3s; 55°27′·88N 08°19′·39E.
No 13 Fl G 5s; 55°28′·40N 08°20′·99E.
No 14 Fl R 5s; 55°28′·57N 08°20′·73E.
Jerg Fl G 3s 7m 5M; G twr, Y base; 55°28′·88N 08°22′·00E.
No 16 Q (6) + L Fl 15s; 55°29′·04N 08°21′·80E.
No 15A Fl (2) G 5s; 55°29′·01N 08°22′·47E.
No 18 Fl (2) R 5s; 55°29′·19N 08°22′·71E.
Fovrfelt N Oc (2) WRG 6s 7m W6M, R/G4M; 066·5°-G-073°-W-077°-R-085·5°; 327°-G-331°- W-333·5°-R-342°; Y twr; 55°29′·29N 08°23′·79E.
Fovrfelt Fl (2) R 10s 11m 6M; R twr; 55°29′·03N 08°23′·75E.
No 15B Fl (2) G 10s; 55°28′·83N 08°23′·65E.

ESBJERG HAVN

Marina, N mole head ☆ Fl R 3s, 7m 2·5M, R post, 55°28′·83N 08° 24′·44E

Marina, S mole head ☆ Fl G 3s, 7m 2·5M, G post, 55°28′·82N 08° 24′·46E

Marina, inner entrance, storm gate, 3FR(vert) 11m 2.5M, Gy post, 55°28′·88N 08°24′·52E. SS(Traffic), if lit = gate closed.

Strandby, shelter mole, NW corner ☆ Oc WRG 5s 6m W7·5M, R6M,G6·5M 102·1°-G-105·9°-W-109·7°-R-111·9°; W bldg, R band; 55°28′·76N 08°24′·63E (just south of marina).

Industrifiskerihavn, W mole ☆ Fl R 5s 6m 4M; R structure; 55°28′·57N 08°24′·89E.

E mole ☆ Fl G 5s 7m 4M; G structure; 55°28′·52N 08°25′·03E.

Nordsøkai Q (9) 15s 5m; Y twr, B band; 55°28′·45N 08°25′·04E.

Konsumfiskerihavn, W mole ☆ FlR 3s 6m; 203°-119°; R twr; 55°28′·31N 08°25′·33E.

E mole ☆ Fl G 3s 6m; 023°-256°; G tr; 55°28·31N 08°25·40E.

Trafikhavn, NW corner, ☆ Oc (2) WRG 12s 6m W11M, R/G8M; 118°-G-124·5°-W-129°-R-131°; W bldg, R band; 55°28·22N 08°25·43E.

N mole ☆ FR 8m 5M; 232°-135°; R bldg; 55°28′·13N 08°25′·46E.

S mole ☆ FG 8m 4M; 045°-276°; G bldg; 55°28′·08N 08°25′·51E.

No 22 Fl (2) R 5s; 55°27′·62N 08°25′·50E.

Sønderhavn (industrial) W mole ☆ FR 9m 4M; 55°27′·49N 08°26′·12E. E mole ☆ FG 9m 4M; 55°27′·43N 08°26′·31E.

Aero ☆ 3 x Fl 1·5s (vert, 82m apart) 251m 12M, H24; on chimney; 55°27′·27N 08°27′·32E (1200m ESE of Sønderhavn ent).

FANØ

Slunden outer ldg lts 242°, both Iso 2s 5/8m 3M; 227°-257°. Front, twr; 55°27′·20N 08°24′·53E. Rear, twr, 106m from front.

E shore, reciprocal ldg lts 062°, both FR 10/13m 3M; 047°-077°. Front, twr; 55°27′·65N 08°26′·01E. Rear, twr, 140m from front.

No 1 ☆ Fl (2) G 5s 5m 2M; G pile; 55°27′·45N 08°25′·28E.

No 2 ☆ Fl (2+1) Y 6s 5m 2M; Y pile; 55°27′·41N 08°25′·32E.

No 3 ☆ Fl G 3s 5m 2M; G pile; 55°27′·39N 08°25′·07E.

No 4 ☆ Fl R 3s 5m 2M; R pile; 55°27′·35N 08°25′·10E.

Nordby ldg lts 214°, both FR 7/9m 4M; 123·7°-303·7°. Front, W mast;55°26′·94N 08°24′·44E. Rear, Gy twr, 84m from front.-Kremer Sand ☆ FG 5m 3M; G dolphin; 55°27′·3N 08°24′·9E.

Næs Søjord ☆ FR 5m 3M; R pile; 55°27′·27N 08°24′·86E.

Nordby marina 55°26′·65N 08°24′·53E.

KNUDEDYB

G 55°20′·50N 08°24′·28E.

K 55°18′·92N 08°20′·06E.

No 2 55°18′·82N 08°21′·33E.

No 4 55°18′·81N 08°22′·21E.

No 6 55°18′·38N 08°24′·63E.

No 10 55°18′·68N 08°28′·50E.

Knoben 55°18′·71N 08°30′·60E.

JUVRE DYB

No 4 55°13′·76N 08°24′·73E.

No 6 55°13′·41N 08°26′·60E.

No 8 55°12′·69N 08°26′·83E.

No 10 55°12′·55N 08°28′·72E.

Rejsby Stjært 55°13′·15N 08°30′·55E.

OUTER APPROACH (Lister Tief) TO RØMØ

See also Area 15 for details of lights on Sylt.

Rode Klit Sand, Fl (3) Y 15s, 55°08′·40N 08°07′·25E.

Lister Tief Iso 8s, *Whis;* 55°05′·32N 08°16′·80E.

No 1 55°05′·48N 08°18′·50E.

No 3 Fl G 4s; 55°05′·36E 08°20′·14E.

No 2 Fl (3) R 10s; 55°03′·92N 08°21′·22E.

No 9 Fl (2) G 9s; 55°03′·76N 08°23′·05E.

Lister Landtief No 5 55°03′·68N 08°24′·73E.

No 4 FL (2) R 5s; 55°03′·84N 08°25′·29E.

G1 Fl Y 4s; 55°03′·27N 08°28′·32E.

RØMØ DYB and HAVN

No 1 Fl (2) G 10s; 55°03′·23N 08°30′·30E.

No 10 ☆ Fl (2) R 10s 5m 3M; R pole; 55°03′·50N 08°31′·10E.

No 14 ☆ Fl R 3s 6m 2M; R pole; 55°03′·85N 08°32′·55E.

No 20 ☆ Fl R 5s 5m 2M; R pole; 55°04′·79N 08°34′·13E.

No 9 55°04′·79N 08°34′·63E.

No 11 55°05′·17N 08°34′·69E.

Rømø Havn, S mole ☆ Fl R 3s 7m 2M; Gy twr; 55°05′·19N 08°34′·31E.

N mole ☆ Fl G 3s 7m 2M; Gy twr; 55°05′·23N 08°34′·30E.

Inner S mole ☆ FR 4m 1M; 55°05′·2N 08°34′·2E.

DISTANCE TABLES

Approx distances in nautical miles are by the most direct route allowing for dangers and TSS.

1	Skagen	1																	
2	Hirtshals	33	2																
3	Hanstholm	85	52	3															
4	Thyborøn	114	84	32	4														
5	Torsminde	141	108	56	24	5													
6	Hvide Sande	162	179	77	45	24	6												
7	Esbjerg	200	174	122	90	76	54	7											
8	Fanø	210	177	125	93	79	57	3	8										
9	Rømø	233	200	148	116	94	73	30	33	9									
10	Hörnum	248	215	163	131	108	86	70	73	29	10								
11	Husum	275	247	195	163	152	131	95	98	68	45	11							
12	Kiel/Holtenau	261	233	281	249	232	208	180	183	189	126	129	12						
13	Bremerhaven	306	285	233	201	185	163	127	129	107	83	82	123	13					
14	Wilhelmshaven	414	296	242	310	184	162	125	128	106	82	82	123	45	14				
15	Helgoland	259	238	186	154	141	119	83	85	63	39	47	104	44	43	15			
16	Cuxhaven	304	284	232	200	162	138	110	113	85	56	66	70	58	56	38	16		
17	Wangerooge	283	262	210	178	168	147	109	112	94	68	52	108	38	27	24	42	17	
18	Hamburg	338	317	265	233	216	192	163	167	139	99	113	90	81	110	88	54	61	18

AREA 12 *Germany (North Sea coast) – List to Emden*

SELECTED LIGHTS, BUOYS & WAYPOINTS

DANISH BORDER TO BÜSUM

SYLT

Lister Tief Iso 8s; *Whis;* 55°05′·33N 08°16′·79E.

List West (Ellenbogen) ☆ Oc WRG 6s 19m W14M, R11M, G10M; 040°-R-133°-W-227°-R-266·4°-W-268°-G-285°-W-310°- W(unintens)-040°; W twr, R lantern; 55°03′·15N 08°24′·00E.

List Hafen, S mole ☆ FR 5m 4M; 218°-353°; R mast; 55°01′·01N 08°26′·51E.

Hörnum ☆ Fl (2) 9s 48m **20M**; 54°45′·23N 08°17′·47E.

Vortrapptief Iso 4s; 54°34′·80N 08°14′·36E, toward Hörnum.

S mole ☆ FR 7m 4M; 54°45′·57N 08°17′·97E.

AMRUM ISLAND

Rütergat Iso 8s; 54°30′·08N 08°12′·32E.

Amrum ☆ Fl 7·5s 63m **23M**; R twr, W bands; 54°37′·84N 08°21′·23E.

Wriakhorn Cross ☆ L Fl (2) WR 15s 26m W9M, R7M; 297·5°-W-319·5°-R-330°-W-005·5°-R-034°; 54°37′·62N 08°21′·22E.

FÖHR ISLAND

Nieblum Dir lt showing over Rütergat. ☆ Oc (2) WRG 10s 11m **W19M, R/G15M**; 028°-G-031°-W-032·5°-R-035·5°; R twr, W band; 54°41′·10N 08°29′·20E.

Ohlörn ☆ Oc (4) WR 15s 10m 13/10M, 208°-W-237·5°-R-298°- W-353°- R-080°; R twr, Gy lantern; 54°40′·85N 08°34′·00E (SE Föhr).

Wyk Hbr outer ent, FR 54°41′·55N 08°34′·69E; and FG.

DAGEBÜLL

Dagebüll Iso WRG 8s 23m **W18M, R/G15M**; 042°-G-043°-W-044·5°- R-047°; 54°43′·82N 08°41′·43E. FW lts on ent moles.

LANGENESS ISLAND

Nordmarsch ☆ L Fl (3) WR 20s 13m W14M, R11M; 268°-W-279°-R-306°-W-045°-R-070°-W-218°; dark brown twr; 54°37′·58N 08°31′·85E.

SCHLÜTTSIEL

No 2/SA 26 54°36′·84N 08°38′·95E. Hbr ent 54°40′·89N 08°45′·10E.

RIVER HEVER

Hever Iso 4s; *Whis;* 54°20′·41N 08°18′·82E.

Westerheversand ☆ Oc (3) WRG 15s 41m **W21M, R17M, G16M**; 012·2°-W-069°-G-079·5°-W-081°(ldg sector for Hever) -R-107°-W-150°-R-207°-W-233°-R-248°; R twr, W bands; 54°22′·40N 08°38′·39E.

Norderhever No 1 Fl (2+1) R 15s; 54°22′·46N 08°30′·83E.

PELLWORM ISLAND

Pellworm ☆ Oc WRG 5s 38m **20M, R 16M, G 15M**; 037·5°-G-040°-W-042·5°-R-045°; R twr, W band; 54°29′·78N 08°39′·98E.

NORDSTRAND

Suderhafen, S mole 54°28′·07N 08°55′·62E.

HUSUM

Fl G 4s, 54°28′·80N 08°58′·60E, start of access chan. Ldg lts 090°, both Iso G 8s 7/9m 3M.

RIVER EIDER

Eider Iso 4s; 54°15′·70N 08° 29′·20E.

St Peter ☆ L Fl (2) WR 15s 23m **W16M**, R13M; 280°-R-282°-W-334°-R-052°-W-080°-R-091°-W-120°; 54°17′·24N 08°39′·13E.

Eiderdamm lock, N mole, W end ☆ Oc (2) R 12s 8m 5M; W twr.

BÜSUM

Süderpiep Iso 8s; *Whis;* 54°05′·82N 08°25′·70E.

Büsum ☆ Iso WR 6s 22m **W19M**, R12M; 248°-W-317°-R-024°-W-148°; 54°07′·61N 08°51′·49E.

E mole ☆ Oc (3) G 12s 10m 4M; vis 260°-168°; G twr; 54°07′·19N 08°51′·65E.

GERMAN BIGHT TO RIVER ELBE

GB Light V Iso 8s 12m **17M**; R hull marked G-B; *Horn Mo (R) 30s*; 54°09′·89N 06°20′·84E.

HELGOLAND

Helgoland ☆ Fl 5s 82m **28M**; brown □ twr, B lantern, W balcony; 54°10′·91N 07°52′·93E.

Vorhafen. Ostmole, S elbow ☆ Oc WG 6s 5m W6M, G3M; 203°-W-250°-G-109°; G post; fog det lt; 54°10′·31N 07°53′·94E.

RIVER ELBE (LOWER)

APPROACHES

Nordergründe N VQ; 53°57′·06N 08°00′·12E.

Elbe Iso 10s; 53°59′·96N 08°06′·51E.

No 1 QG; 53°59′·21N 08°13′·20E.

No 25 QG; 53°56′·62N 08°38′·25E.

Neuwerk ☆ S side, L Fl (3) WRG 20s 38m **W16M**, R12M, G11M; 165·3°-G-215·3°-W-238·8°-R-321°; 343°-R-100°; 53°54′·92N 08°29′·73E.

CUXHAVEN

No 31 Fl G 4s; 53°53′·93N 08°41′·21E.

Yacht hbr ent, F WR and F WG lts; 53°52′·43N 08°42′·49E.

OTTERNDORF

No 43 Oc (2) G 9s; 53°50′·23N 08°52′·24E.

Otterndorf 3 Fl (3) G 12s; 53°50′·22N 08°53′·94E.

BRUNSBÜTTEL

Ldg lts, 065·5°, Front, **Schleuseninsel**, Iso W 3s 24m **16M;** 53° 53′·32N 09°08′·47E, Rear, 0·9M from front, Iso W 3s 46m **21M;** 53°53′·69N 09°09′·82E. Both R twrs W bands.

No 57a Fl G 4s; 53°52′·62N 09°07′·93E, 030°/8 cables to lock.

Neuer Vorhafen ent approach VQ (6) + L Fl 10s, 53°53′·25N 09°08′·07E.

Alter Vorhafen ent, mole 1 head ☆ F WG 14m W10M, G6M; 266·3°-W-273·9°-G-088·8° (F in Fog), floodlit; 53°53′·27N 09°08′·59E. Mole 2 ☆ F.WRG 14m W12M RG10M 277°-R-022°-G-082°-W-084°-090°. *Horn (1) 10s.* R twr, W roof, 53°53′·25N 09° 08′·24E.

RIVER ELBE (BRUNSBÜTTEL TO HAMBURG)

FREIBURG

Reede 1 Oc (2) Y 9s; 53°50′·41N 09°19′·45E, off ent.

STÖRLOCH

Stör ldg lts 093·8°, both Fl 3s 7/12m 6M; synch. Front, 53°49′·29N 09°23′·91E; △ on R ○ twr. Rear, 200m east; ▽ on white mast.

GLÜCKSTADT

Glückstadt ldg lts 131·8°, both Iso 8s, front,15m/**19M**, rear 40m/**21M**; intens on ldg line; W twrs, R bands. **Front** ☆, 53°48'·31N 09°24'·24E. **Rear** ☆, 0·68M from front.

Rhinplatte Nord ☆ Oc WRG 6s 11m W6M, R4M, G3M; 122°-G-144°-W-150°-R-177°-W-122°; 53°48'·09N 09°23'·36E.

N mole ☆ Dir Oc WRG 6s 9m W9M R7M, G6M; 330°-R-343°-W-346°-G-008°; 123°-G-145°-W-150°-R-170°; W twr with gallery; 53°47'·12N 09°24'·53E.

N pier hd ☆ FR 5m 5M; 53°47'·10N 09°24'·50E. (S mole hd, FG).

KRUCKAU

S mole Oc WRG 6s 8m, W6M, R4M, G3M; 116·3°-W-120·7° (ldg sector)-R-225°-G-315°-R-331·9°-W-335·4° (ldg sector)-335·4°-G-116·3°; B dolphin; 53°42'·85N 09°30'·72E.

PINNAU

Ldg lts 112·7°, both Iso 4s 8/13m 6M. Front, 53°40'·08N 09°34'·02E.

STADE

Stadersand ☆ Iso 8s 20m 14M; 53°37'·69N 09°31'·64E (at ent).

HAMBURG YACHT HARBOUR, WEDEL

Both entrances show FR & FG, May to Oct; 53°34'·25N 09°40'·77E.

CITY SPORTHAFEN

Brandenburger Hafen Ent ☆ Iso Or 2s; 53°32'·52N 09°58'·81E.

WESER ESTUARY

ALTE WESER

Alte Weser Dir ☆ F WRG 33m **W23M, R19M, G18M**; 288°-FW-352°-FR-003°-FW-017°(ldg sector for Alte Weser) 017°-FG-045°-FW-074°-FG-121°-FW-126°-FR-140°-FG-175°-FW-183°-FR-196°-FW-238°; R ○ twr, 2 W bands, G lantern, B base, floodlit; *Horn Mo (AL) 60s;* 53°51'·80N 08°07'·65E.

16/A15 Fl (2+1) R 15s; 53°49'·66N 08°06'·44E (junction with Neuwe Weser).

NEUE WESER

Tegeler Plate, N end, Dir ☆ Occ (3) WRG 12s 21m **W21M, G17M R18M R17M** ; 329°-W-340°-R-014°-W-100°-G-116°-W-119° (ldg sector for Neue Weser).119°-R-123°-G-148·3°-W-150° (ldg sector for Alte Weser)150°-R-264°; R ○ twr, gallery, W lantern, R roof; Fog det lt; Ra refl; 53°47'·87N 08°11'·46E.

BREMERHAVEN

No 61 QG; 53°32'·26N 08°33'·93E (Km 66·0).

Vorhafen N pier ☆ FR 15m 5M; 245°-166°; F in fog; 53°32'·15N 08°34'·50E.

RIVER JADE

1b/Jade1 Oc G 4s; 53°52'·40N 07°44'·02E.

Mellumplate ☆ FW 28m **24M**; 116·1°-116·4° (ldg sector for outer part of Wangerooger Fahrwasser); R □ twr, W band; 53°46'·28N 08°05'·51E.

No 19 QG; 53°47'·10N 08°01'·83E.

No 31/P-Reede/W Siel 1 Oc (3) G 12s; 53°41'·59N 08°04'·51E.

HOOKSIEL

No 37/Hooksiel 1 IQ G 13s; 53°39'·37N 08°06'·58E.

Vorhafen ent ☆ L Fl R 6s 9m 3M; 53°38'·63N 08°05'·25E.

WILHELMSHAVEN

Fluthafen N mole ☆ F WG 9m,W6M, G3M; 216°-W-280°-G-010°-W-020°-G-130°; G twr; 53°30'·86N 08°09'·32E.

EAST FRISIAN ISLANDS

NORTH EDGE OF INSHORE TRAFFIC ZONE

TG9/Weser 2 Fl (2+1) G 15s; 53°55'·0N 07°44'·60E.

TG13 Oc (3) G 12s; 53°50'·85N 07°15'·43E.

TG7 Fl (2) G 9s; 53°47'·24N 06°49'·65E.

TG1 Oc (3) G 12s; 53°44'·90N 06°33'·20E.

WANGEROOGE

Harle Iso 8s; 53°49'·38N 07°46'·40E.

Wangerooge, W end ☆ Fl R 5s 60m **23M**; R ○ twr, 2 W bands; 53°47'·40N 07°51'·37E.

Dir lt 145·5°, Dir WRG 24m W22M G18M R17M; 119·4°-G-138·8°-W-152·2°-R-159·9°.

Buhne H VQ (9) 10s; 53°46'·86N 07°49'·65E.

W2 ; 53°46'·25N 07°51'·89E, off hbr ent.

SPIEKEROOG

Otzumer Balje Iso 4s; 53°48'·47N 07°37'·55E (often moved).

Spiekeroog ☆ FR 6m 4M; 197°-114°; R mast; 53°45'·0N 07°41'·3E.

LANGEOOG

Accumer Ee Iso 8s; 53°46'·84N 07°25'·85E (frequently moved).

W mole head ☆ Oc WRG 6s 8m W7M, R5M, G4M; 064°-G-070°-W-074°-R-326°-W-330°-G-335°-R-064°; R basket on R mast; *Horn Mo (L) 30s* (0730-1800LT); 53°43'·42N 07°30'·13E.

BALTRUM

Groyne hd ☆ Oc WRG 6s 6m; W6M, R4M, G3M; 074·5°-G-090°-W-095°-R-074·5°; 53°43'·3N 07°21'·7E.

1	Esbjerg	**1**																	
2	Hörnum Lt (Sylt)	47	**2**																
3	Husum	95	48	**3**															
4	Hamburg	163	112	113	**4**														
5	Kiel/Holtenau	179	128	129	90	**5**													
6	Brunsbüttel	126	75	76	37	53	**6**												
7	Cuxhaven	110	63	66	54	70	17	**7**											
8	Bremerhaven	127	80	82	81	131	78	58	**8**										
9	Wilhelmshaven	125	78	82	110	123	70	56	45	**9**									
10	Hooksiel	116	69	73	101	117	64	47	36	9	**10**								
11	Helgoland	83	38	47	88	104	51	38	44	43	35	**11**							
12	Wangerooge	109	60	52	61	108	55	42	38	27	19	24	**12**						
13	Langeoog	119	72	77	114	130	77	60	47	43	34	35	21	**13**					
14	Norderney	123	77	85	81	137	84	69	62	53	44	44	29	18	**14**				
15	Emden	165	129	137	174	190	137	120	115	106	97	85	80	63	47	**15**			
16	Borkum	133	97	105	104	163	110	95	88	80	71	67	55	46	31	32	**16**		
17	Delfzijl	155	119	127	159	173	120	105	100	89	83	81	65	56	41	10	22	**17**	
18	Den Helder	187	192	198	229	245	192	175	180	159	150	153	148	130	115	125	95	115	**18**

DISTANCE TABLES

Approx distances in nautical miles are by the most direct route allowing for dangers and TSS.

NORDERNEY

Norderney ☆ Fl (3) 12s 59m **23M**; unintens 067°-077° and 270°-280°; R 8-sided twr; 53°42'·54N 07°13'·79E.
Dovetief Iso 4s; 53°45'·47N 07°12'·70E.
Schluchter Iso 8s; 53°44'·50N 07°02'·13E.
W mole head ☆ Oc (2) R 9s 13m 4M; 53°41'·9N 07°09'·9E.

JUIST

Juist-N VQ; 53°43'·82N 06°55'·42E.
Training wall, S end ☆ Oc (2) R 9s 7m 3M; 53°39'·65N 06°59'·81E.

MAINLAND HARBOURS: R JADE TO R EMS

HARLESIEL

Carolinensieler Balje, Leitdamm ☆ L Fl 8s 7m 6M; G mast; 53°44'·13N 07°50'·10E.
Ldg lts 138°, both Iso 6s 12/18m 9M, intens on ldg line; Front 53°40'·70N 07°34'·50E. Rear 167m from front.
N mole head ☆ Iso R 4s 6m 7M; 53°42'·58N 07°48'·64E.

NEUHARLINGERSIEL

Training wall head ☆ Oc 6s 6m 5M; 53°43'·22N 07°42'·30E.

BENSERSIEL

E training wall head ☆ Oc WRG 6s 6m W5M, R3M, G2M; 110°-G-119°-W-121°-R-110°; R post & platform; 53° 41'·80N 07°32'·84E.

DORNUMER-ACCUMERSIEL

W bkwtr head, approx 53°41'·04N 07°29'·30E.

NESSMERSIEL

N mole head ☆ Oc 4s 6m 5M; G mast; 53°41'·9N 07°21'·7E.

NORDDEICH

W trng wall head ☆ FG 8m 4M, 021°-327°; G framework twr; 53°38'·62N 07°09'·0E.

GREETSIEL

Meßstation lt bcn, Fl Y 4s 15m 3M; 53°32'·94N 07°02'·18E.

RIVER EMS

APPROACHES

GW/EMS Iso 8s 14m **17M** (H24); Emergency Lt, FR, occas. 2 FR vert; R Lt vessel, floodlit; *Horn Mo (R) 30s (H24);* 54°09'·96N 06°20'·72E.
Borkumriff Oc 4s; 53°47'·48N 06°22'·27E.
Osterems Iso 4s; 53°41'·91N 06°36'·17E.
Riffgat Iso 8s; 53°38'·96N 06°27'·10E.
Westerems Iso 4s; 53°36'·95N 06°17'·74E. 992111104.
H1 53°34'·91N 06°17'·97E.

BORKUM

Borkum Grosser ☆ Fl (2) 12s 63m **24M**; brown ○ twr; 53°35'·32N 06°39'·64E. Same twr, ☆ F WRG 46m **W19M, R/G15M**; 107·4°-G-109°-W-111·2°- R-112·6°.
Fischerbalje ☆ Oc (2) 16s 15m **3M**; 260°-W-123°. Fog det lt; R/W ○ twr on tripod; 53°33'·18N 06°42'·90E.
Schutzhafen, E mole hd ☆ FG10m 4M; 53°33'·48N 06°45'·02E. W mole hd, FR 8m 4M.

RIVER EMS (LOWER)

No 27 Fl G 4s; 53°30'·24N 06°47'·52E.
No 35 Fl G 4s; 53°27'·03N 06°52'·80E.
No 37 QG; 53°26'·01N 06°54'·85E.
No 41 Fl (2) G 9s; 53°24'·25N 06°56'·68E.
No 49 Oc (2) G 9s; 53°19'·95N 06°59'·71E.

KNOCK

Knock ☆ F WRG 28m W12M,R9M, G8M; 270°-W-299°-R-008·3°-G-023°-W-026·8°-R-039°-W-073°-R-119°-W-154°; fog det lt; Gy twr, white conical radar antenna; 53°20'·32N 07°01'·40E.

EMDEN

No 59 Oc (2) G 9s; 53°19'·41N 07°03'·86E.
No 65 Fl (2) G 9s; 53°19'·82N 07°06'·56E.
Outer hbr, W pier ☆ FR 10m 4M; R 8-sided twr; 53°20'·06N 07°10'·49E.
E pier ☆ FG 7m 5M; G mast on pedestal; 53°20'·05N

AREA 13 *Netherlands & Belgium – Delfzijl to Nieuwpoort*

SELECTED LIGHTS, BUOYS & WAYPOINTS

TSS OFF NORTHERN NETHERLANDS

TERSCHELLING-GERMAN BIGHT TSS

TG1/Ems IQ G 13s; 53°43'·33N 06°22'·24E.
TE5 Fl (3) G 10s; 53°37'·79N 05°53'·69E.
TE1 Fl (3) G 10s; 53°29'·58N 05°11'·31E.

OFF VLIELAND TSS

VL-CENTER Fl 5s 12M; ***Racon C, 12–15M***; 53°26'·93N 04°39'·88E. VL7 L Fl G 10s; 53°26'·40N 04°57'·60E.
VL1 Fl (2) G 10s; 53°10'·96N 04°35'·31E.

DELFZIJL TO HARLINGEN

DELFZIJL

PS3/BW26 Fl (2+1) G 12s; 53°19'·25N 07°00'·32E.
W mole ☆ FG; 53°19'·01N 07°00'·27E.
Ldg lts 203° both Iso 4s. Front, 53°18'·63N 07°00'·17E.

SCHIERMONNIKOOG AND LAUWERSOOG

WG (Westgat) Iso 8s; ***Racon N***; 53°31'·96N 06°01'·84E .
WRG Q; 53°32'·87N 06°03'·24E.
AM VQ; 53°30'·95N 05°44'·72E.
Schiermonnikoog ☆ Fl (4) 20s 43m **28M**; dark R ○ twr. Same twr: F WR 29m **W15M**, R12M; 210°-W-221°-R-230°. 53°29'·20N 06°08'·79E.
Lauwersoog W mole ☆ FG; *Horn (2) 30s;* 53°24'·68N 06°12'·00E.

ZEEGAT VAN AMELAND

BR Q; 53°30'·66N 05°33'·52E.
TS VQ; 53°28'·15N 05°21'·53E.
WA 53°28'·35N 05°28'·64E. (Westgat buoys are all unlit)
Ameland, W end ☆ Fl (3) 15s 57m **30M**; 53°26'·89N 05°37'·42E.

NES

VA2-R1 VQ(6) + L Fl 10s; 53°25'·71N 05°45'·88E.
Reegeul R3 ☆ Iso G 4s; 53°25'·80N 05°45'·93E.
R7 ☆ QG; 53°25'·91N 05°46'·21E.

HET VLIE (ZEEGAT VAN TERSCHELLING)

ZS Iso 4s; ***Racon T***; 53°18'·28N 04°56'·23E.

ZS1 VQ G; 53°18′·58N 04°57′·54E.
ZS3 QG; 53° 19′·29N 04° 59′·49E
ZS5 L Fl G 8s; 53°18′·55N 05°00′·83E.
ZS11-VS2 Q (9) 15s; 53°18′·63N 05°05′·94E.

NOORD MEEP/SLENK TO WEST TERSCHELLING

WM3 Iso G 2s; 53°17′·45N 05°12′·28E.
NM 4-S 21 VQ (3) 5s; 53°19′·02N 05°15′·47E.
SG1 Q (9) 15s; 53°20′·44N 05°11′·70E.
Brandaris Twr ☆ Fl 5s 54m **29M**; Y □ twr partly obscured by dunes; 53°21′·62N 05°12′·86E.
W Terschelling W hbr mole ☆ FR 5m 5M; R post, W bands; *Horn 15s;* 53°21′·26N 05°13′·09E. E pier hd ☆ FG 4m 4M.

VLIELAND

VS3 (Vliesloot) VQ G; 53°18′·27N 05°06′·25E.
VS14 Iso R 4s; 53°17′·58N 05°05′62E.
VS16-VB1 Fl (2+1) R 10s; 53°17′·62N 05°05′·19E.
E/W mole hds ☆ FG and ☆ FR; 53°17′·68N 05°05′·51E.
Ldg lts 282° ☆ Iso 4s 10/16m 1M, synch; 53°17′·75N 05°04′·47W (100m apart); mainly for the ferry terminal at E Vlieland.
E Vlieland (Vuurduin) ☆ Iso 4s 54m **20M**; 53°17′·75N 05°03′·49E.

APPROACHES TO HARLINGEN (selected marks):

VLIESTROOM buoys are frequently moved.
VL1 QG; 53°18′·99N 05°08′·82E. VL 2 QR; 53°19′·40N 05°09′·19E.
VL 11 Iso G 8s; 53°16′·42N 05°09′·70E.

BLAUWE SLENK

BS1-IN2 VQ (3) 5s; 53°15′·41N 05°09′·41E.
BS13 QG; 53°13′·31N 05°17′·13E. BS19 VQ G; 53°11′·90N 05°18′·28E.
BS23 L Fl G 8s; 53°11′·42N 05°19′·60E.

POLLENDAM

Ldg lts 112°, both Iso 6s 8/19m 13M (H24); B masts, W bands. Front, 53°10′·52N 05°24′·19E. Use only between P2 and P6.
P2 ; 53°11′·47N 05°20′·38E on the training wall.
P4, Iso R 8s; P6, Iso R 4s; P8, Iso R 8s; and P10, Iso R 2s.
Yachts should keep outboard of P1 thru 7 SHM buoys. P1 Iso G 2s; 53°11′·39N 05°20′·32E. P7 VQ G; 53°10′·68N 05°23′·45E.

HARLINGEN

S mole hd ☆ FG 9m; 53°10′·56N 05°24′·18E.
N mole hd ☆ FR 9m 4M; R/W pedestal; 53°10′·59N 05°24′·32E.

TEXEL AND THE WADDENZEE

TEXEL (from NW and W)

Eierland ☆ Fl (2) 10s 52m **29M**; R ○ twr; 53°10′·93N 04°51′·31E.
TX Q(9) 15s; 53°06′·81N 04°41′·19E

MOLENGAT (from the N)

Note: Positions/depths unreliable, see: Pl Terschelling to Texel and Den Helder.
Zinker-MG VQ(9) 10s; 53°02′·27N 04°40′·95E
MG-A,Y ; 53°02′·61N 04°40′·28E.
MG-B, Y ; 53°01′·99N 04°42′·00E
MG-D, Y ; 53°00′·90N 04°42′·04E;
MG-G, Y ; 52°59′·30N 04°42′·56E;
MG-H, Y ; 52°58′·91N 04°43′·10E.

OUDESCHILD

T12 Iso R 8s; 53°02′·23N 04°51′·52E.
Oudeschild Dir ☆ Oc 6s; intens 291°; 53°02′·40N 04°50′·94E; leads 291° into hbr between N mole head FG 6m; and S mole head ☆ FR 6m; 53°02′·33N 04°51′·17E.

APPROACHES TO KORNWERDERZAND SEALOCK

DOOVE BALG (From Texelstroom eastward)

T23 VQ G; 53°03′·60N 04°55′·85E, 066°/3M from Oudeschild.
T29 53°03′·25N 05°00′·05E.
D1 Iso G 4s; 53°02′·18N 05°03′·42E.
D21 Iso G 8s; 53°03′·55N 05°15′·71E.
BO2-WG1 Q (6) + L Fl 10s; 53°05′·00N 05°17′·91E.

KORNWERDERZAND SEALOCK

W mole ☆ FG 9m 7M; *Horn Mo(N) 30s;* 53°04′·78N 05°20′·03E.
E mole ☆ FR 9m 7M; 53°04′·70N 05°20′·08E.
W mole elbow ☆ Iso G 6s 6m 7M; 53°04′·61N 05°19′·90E.

APPROACHES TO DEN OEVER SEALOCK

MALZWIN and VISJAGERSGAATJE CHANS TO DEN OEVER

MH4-M1 VQ (9) 10s; 52°58′·14N 04°47′·49E, close N Den Helder.
M15 QG; 52°59′·39N 04°55′·48E (thence use DYC 1811.3).
VG1-W2 Fl (2+1) G 10s; 52°59′·00N 04°56′·85E.
O9 Iso G 8s; 52°56′·63N 05°02′·38E.

DEN OEVER SEALOCK

Ldg lts 131°, both Oc 10s 6m 7M; 127°-137°. Front, 52°56′·32N 05°02′·98E. Rear, 280m from front.
E end of swing bridge, ☆ Iso WRG 5s 14m 10/7M; 226°-G-231°-W-235°-R-290°-G-327°-W-335°-R-345°; 52°56′·12N 05°02′·52E.

ZEEGAT VAN TEXEL AND DEN HELDER

OFFSHORE MARKS W and SW OF DEN HELDER

NH (Noorderhaaks) VQ; 53°00′·24N 04°35′·37E.
MR Q (9) 15s; 52°56′·77N 04°33′·82E.
ZH (Zuiderhaaks) VQ (6) + L Fl 10s; 52°54′·65N 04°34′·72E.
Vinca G wreck Q (9) 15s; 52°45′·93N 04°12′·31E.

SCHULPENGAT (from the SSW)

Schulpengat Dir ☆ 026·5°, Dir WRG, Al WR, Al WG, **W22M R/G18M**, church spire; 025.1°-FG- 025.6°-AlWG- 026.3°-FW-026.7°-Al WR- 027.4° -F R- 027.9°; shown H24.
Licht van Troost ☆, delete entry in toto, substitute:
Licht van Troost ☆ FWRG 27m W3M (Green post on Texel), W8M 21m, R8M, G5M; 333°-W-026°-G-033°-W-038°-R-070°; 53°00′·50N 04°45′·70E.
SG Mo (A) 8s; **Racon Z**; 52°52′·90N 04°37′·90E.
S1 Iso G 4s; 52°53′·53N 04°38′·82E.
S7 QG; 52°56′·25N 04°40′·92E. S6A QR; 52°56′·52N 04°40′·51E.
S10 Iso R 8s; 52°57′·59N 04°41′·57E. S14-MG17 , see Molengat.
S11 Iso G 8s; 52°57′·55N 04°43′·25E.
Kijkduin ☆ Fl (4) 20s 56m **30M**; vis 360°, except where obsc'd by dunes on Texel; brown twr; 52°57′·33N 04°43′·58E (mainland).

MARSDIEP and DEN HELDER

T1 Fl (3) G 10s; 52°57′·99N 04°44′·62E.

T3 Iso G 8s; 52°58′·07N 04°46′·42E.

Den Helder ldg lts 191°, both Oc G 5s 16/25m 3M, synch. Front, vis 183·5°-198·5°; B ▽ on bldg; 52°57′·37N 04°47′·08E.

Marinehaven, W bkwtr head QG 11m 8M; *Horn 20s;* 52°57′·95N 04°47′·07E (Harssens Island).

W side, Fl G 5s 9m 4M (H24); 180°-067°; 52°57′·78N 04°47′·08E.

Yacht hbr (KMYC) ent FR & FG; 165m SW of Fl G 5s, above.

E side, MH6 Iso R 4s; 52°57′·99N 04°47′·41E.

Ent E side, QR 9m 4M (H24); 52°57′·77N 04°47′·37E.

DEN HELDER TO AMSTERDAM

Zanddijk Grote Kaap Oc WRG 10s 30m 8M; 041°-G-088°-W-094°-R-120°; brown twr; 52°52′·86N 04°42′·88E.

Petten VQ (9) 10s; 52°47′·33N 04°36′·78E (Power stn outfall).

Egmond-aan-Zee ☆ Iso WR 10s 36m **W18M**, R14M; 010°-W-175°-R-188°; W ○ twr; 52°36′·99N 04°37′·16E.

IJMUIDEN

Baloeran Q (9) 15s; 52°29′·21N 04°32′·00E.

IJmuiden Mo (A) 8s; ***Racon Y, 10M***; 52°28′·45N 04°23′·92E.

Ldg lts 100·5° (FW 5M by day; 090·5°-110·5°). **Front** ☆ F WR 30m **W16M**, R13M; 050°-W-122°-R-145°-W-160°; (Tidal and traffic sigs); dark R ○ twrs; 52°27′·70N 04°34′·47E. **Rear** ☆ Fl 5s 52m **29M**; 019°-199° (FW 5M by day; 090·5°-110·5°); 560m from front.

S bkwtr hd FG 14m 10M (in fog Fl 3s); W twr, G bands; 52°27′·82N 04°31′·93E.

N bkwtr hd FR 15m 10M; 52°28′·05N 04°32′·55E.

IJM1 Iso G 4s; 52°27′·75N 04°33′·59E.

S outer chan Iso G 6s, 52°27′·75N 04°33′·81E. Iso R 6s, 52°27′·84N 04°34′·39E (Forteiland). Kleine Sluis 52°27′·84N 04°35′·43E.

AMSTERDAM

IJ8 Iso R 8s (for Sixhaven marina); 52°22′·86N 04°54′·37E.

Oranjesluizen, N lock 52°22′·93N 04°57′·60E (for IJsselmeer).

AMSTERDAM TO ROTTERDAM

Noordwijk-aan-Zee ☆ Oc (3) 20s 32m **18M**; W □ twr; 52°14′·88N 04°26′·02E.

SCHEVENINGEN

Lighthouse ☆ Fl (2) 10s 48m **29M**; 014°-244°; brown twr; 52°06′·23N 04°16′·13E, 5ca E of hbr ent.

Ldg lts 156°, both Iso 4s 14M, H24; synch; Gy masts. Front 52°05′·99N 04°15′·44E; rear 250m from front. Intens at night.

SCH Iso 4s; 52°07′·76N 04°14′·12E.

KNS Q (9)15s; 52°06′·48N 04°15′·27E.

W mole FG 12m 9M; G twr, W bands; 52°06′·23N 04°15′·16E.

E mole , FR 12m 9M; R twr, W bands; 52°06′·24N 04°15′·37E.

Inner ldg lts 131°: both Iso G 4s synch; Gy posts. Front 52°05′·81N 04°15′·89E. Rear, 34m from front.

NOORD HINDER N & S TSS and JUNCTION

NHR-N L Fl 8s; ***Racon K, 10M***; 52°10′·91N 03°04′·76E.

Noord Hinder Fl (2) 10s; *Horn (2) 30s*; ***Racon T, 12-15M***; 52°00′·10N 02° 51′·11E.

NHR-S Fl Y 10s; 51°49′·53N 02°25′·95E.

NHR-SE Fl G 5s; 51°43′·43N 02°37′·18E.

Birkenfels Q (9) 15s; 51°38′·96N 02°32′·03E.

Twin Fl (3) Y 9s; 51°32′·05N 02°22′·62E.

Garden City Q (9) 15s; 51°29′·12N 02°17′·92E.

APPROACHES TO HOEK VAN HOLLAND

Europlatform Mo (U) 15s; W structure, R bands; helicopter platform; *Horn Mo(U) 30s;* 51°55′·50N 03°40′·10E.

Goeree ☆ Mo(U)15s 32m **28M**; R/W chequered twr on platform; helicopter platform; *Horn Mo(U) 30s*; ***Racon T, 12-15M***; 51°55′·42N 03°40′·03E.

Maasvlakte ☆ Fl (5) 20s 67m **28M**, H24; 340°-267°; W twr, B bands; 51°58′·20N 04°00′·84E, 1·5M SSW of Maas ent.

Maas Center Iso 4s; ***Racon M, 10M***; 52°00′·92N 03°48′·79E.

MO Mo (A) 8s; 52°01′·10N 03°58′·19E.

MN3 Fl (3) G 10s; 52°07′·04N 04°00′·00E.

MN1 Fl G 5s; 52°02′·23N 04°01′·91E.

HOEK VAN HOLLAND

Maasmond ldg lts 112° (for deep draught vessels): both Iso 4s 30/46m **21M**; 101°-123°, synch; W twr, B bands. **Front**, 51°58′·88N 04°04′·88E (NW end of Splitsingsdam). **Rear**, 0·6M from front.

Indusbank N Q, 52°01′·82N 04°03′·60E.

MVN VQ; 51°59′·61N 04°00′·23E.

NETW Q (9) 15s; 51°59′·32N 04°01′·24E.

Maas 1 L Fl G 5s; 51°59′·35N 04°01′·68E.

Nieuwe Waterweg ldg lts 107°: both Iso R 6s 29/43m **18M**; 099.5°-114.5°; R twr, W bands. Front, 51°58′·55N 04°07′·52E. Rear, 450m from front.

Noorderdam Head FR 25m 10M (In fog Al Fl WR 6s; 278°-255°); R twr, W bands; 51°59′·67N 04°02′·80E.

Nieuwe Zuiderdam FG 25m 10M, 330°-307°; (In fog Al Fl WG 6s); G twr, W bands; 51°59′·14N 04°02′·49E.

ROTTERDAM

Maassluis FG 6m; 51°54′·94N 04°14′·81E; and FR.

Vlaardingen FG; 51°53′·99N 04°20′·95E; and FR.

Spuihaven, W ent FR; 51°53′·98N 04°23′·97E.

Veerhaven, E ent FG; 51°54′·42N 04°28′·75E; and FR.

City marina ent, 51°54′·64N 04°29′·76E.

APPROACHES TO HARINGVLIET

Buitenbank , Iso 4s; 51°51′·16N 03°25′·71E.

Hinder Q (9) 15s; 51°54′·55N 03°55′·42E.

SH VQ (9) 10s; 51°49′·49N 03°45′·79E.

Westhoofd ☆ Fl (3) 15s 55m **30M**; R □ tr; 51°48′·79N 03°51′·85E.

Ooster Q (9) 15s; 51°47′·90N 03°41′·27E.

SLIJKGAT

SG Iso 4s; 51°51′·95N 03°51′·42E.

SG 2 Iso R 4s; 51°51′·71N 03°53′·45E.

SG 5 Iso G 4s; 51°50′·00N 03°55′·56E.

SG 11 Iso G 4s; 51°50′·81N 03°58′·52E.

P1 Iso G 4s; 51°51′·30N 04°01′·12E.

P3 Iso G 8s; 51°51'·12N 04°01'·45E.
P9 Iso G 8s; 51°49'·98N 04°02'·15E.

STELLENDAM

N mole FG; *Horn (2) 15s;* 51°49'·88N 04°02'·03E.
Buitenhaven Oc 6s; 51°49'·73N 04°01'·75E.

APPROACHES TO OOSTERSCHELDE

OUTER APPROACHES

Schouwenbank Mo (A) 8s; ***Racon O, 10M***; 51°44'·94N 03°14'·32E.
Middelbank Iso 8s; 51°40'·86N 03°18'·20E.
MW Q (9) 15s; 51°44'·55N 03°24'·04E (Schouwendiep).
MD 3 Fl G 5s; 51°42'·70N 03°26'·98E.
Rabsbank Iso 4s; 51°38'·25N 03°09'·93E.
Westpit Iso 8s; 51°33'·65N 03°09'·92E.
ZSB VQ (9) 10s; 51°36'·57N 03°15'·62E.
OG1 QG; 51°36'·14N 03°20'·08E.

WESTGAT, OUDE ROOMPOT and ROOMPOTSLUIS

West Schouwen ☆ Fl (2+1)15s 57m **30M**; Gy twr, R diagonals on upper part; 51°42'·52N 03°41'·50E, 5·8M N of Roompotsluis.
OG-WG VQ (9) 10s; 51°37'·18N 03°23'·82E.
WG1 Iso G 8s; 51°38'·00N 03°26'·24E.
WG4 L Fl R 8s; 51°38'·62N 03°28'·78E.
WG7 Iso G 4s 51°39'·40N 03°32'·67E.
WG-GB (Geul van de Banjaard) 51°39'·72N 03°32'·69E.
OR1 51°39'·15N 03°33'·59E.
OR5 Iso G 8s; 51°38'·71N 03°35'·53E.
OR11 Iso G 4s; 51°36'·98N 03°38'·40E.
R11A QG 51°36'·74N 03°39'·29E.
R11B Iso G 4s 51°37'·00N 03°39'·82E.
OR12 Iso R 4s; 51°37'·27N 03°39'·25E.
OR13 R14; VQ (3) 5s 51°36'·61N 03°38'·67E.
Roompotsluis ldg lts 073·5°, both Oc G 5s; synch. Front, 51°37'·33N 03°40'·75E. Rear, 280m from front.
N bkwtr FR 7m; 51°37'·31N 03°40'·09E.

WESTKAPELLE TO VLISSINGEN

OOSTGAT

Ldg lts 149·5°: Front, Noorderhoofd Oc WRG 10s 20m; W13M, R/G10M; 353°-R-008°-G-029°-W-169°; R ○ twr, W band; 51°32'·40N 03°26'·21E, 0·73M from rear (Westkapelle).
Westkapelle ☆, rear, Fl 3s 50m **28M**; obsc'd by land on certain brgs; □ twr, R top; 51°31'·75N 03°26'·83E.
Kaloo Iso 8s; 51°35'·55N 03°23'·24E. Chan is well buoyed/lit.
OG5 Iso G 8s; 51°34'·10N 03°23'·88E.
OG 7 VQ G , 51°32'·76N 03° 24'·87E.
Molenhoofd Oc WRG 6s 10m; 311·5°-R-330·5°-W-348·5°-R-008°-G-034·5°-W-036·5°-G-147.5°-W-168.5°-R-198°; W mast R bands; 51°31'·58N 03°26'·05E.
Zoutelande F 22m 12M; 321°-352°; R □ twr; 51°30'·28N 03°28'·41E.
Kaapduinen, ldg lts 130°: both Oc 5s 25/34m 13M; synch; Y □ twrs, R bands. Front, 122·5° - 137·5°; 51°28'·47N 03°30'·99E. Rear, 122·5° - 137·5°; 220m from front.
Fort de Nolle Oc 9s 6m 2M R col, W bands; 51°26'·95N 03°33'·12E.
Ldg lts 117°: Front, Leugenaar, Oc R 5s 6m 5M; intens 108°-126°; W&R pile; 51°26'·43N 03°34'·14E.
Rear, Sardijngeul Oc W 5s 9m 2M ; ▽ on R mast, W bands; Koopmanshaven W Head, 550m from front; 51°26'·30N 03°34'·55E.

OFFSHORE: W HINDER TSS TO SCHEUR CHAN

West Hinder ☆ Fl (4) 30s 23m 13M; *Horn Mo (U) 30s*; ***Racon W***; 51°23'·30N 02°26'·27E.
WH Zuid Q (6) + L Fl 15s; 51°22'·78N 02°26'·25E.
OostdyckBk Q; 51°21'·38N 02°31'·12E.
BerguesBk-N Q; 51°19'·95N 02°24'·50E.
Oost-Dyck West Q (9) 15s; 51°17'·15N 02°26'·32E.
Oostdyck radar twr; Mo (U) 15s 15m 12M on 4 corners; *Horn Mo (U) 30s;* ***Racon O***. R twr, 3 W bands, with adjacent red twr/helipad; 51°16'·49N 02°26'·85E.
A-N Fl (4) R 20s; 51°23'·45N 02°36'·90E.
AS Fl (3) G 10s; 51°21'·15N 02°36'·92E.
KB2 VQ; 51°21'·04N 02°42'·22E.
KB Q; ***Racon K***; 51°21'·03N 02°42'·83E.
MBN Q; 51°20'·82N 02°46'·29E.
Akkaert-SW Q (9) 15s; 51°22'·28N 02°46'·34E.
VG Q ; 51°23'·38N 02°46'·21E, Vaargeul 1.
VG1 VQ G; 51°25'·03N 02°49'·04E.
VG2 Q (6) + L Fl R 15s; ***Racon V***; 51°25'·96N 02°48'·16E.
VG3 QG; 51°25'·05N 02°52'·92E.
VG5 Fl G 5s; 51°24'·63N 02°57'·92E.
SVG Q ; 51°24'·53N 02°59'·92E.
Goote Bank Q (3) 10s; 51°26'·95N 02°52'·72E.
A1 Iso 8s; 51°22'·36N 02°53'·33E.
A1bis L Fl 10s; 51°21'·68N 02°58'·02E.

WESTERSCHELDE APPROACHES

SCHEUR CHANNEL

S1 Fl G 5s; 51°23'·14N 03°00'·12E.
S3 Q; 51°24'·30N 03°02'·92E.
MOW 0 ⊙ Fl (5) Y 20s; ***Racon S, 10M***; 51°23'·67N 03°02'·75E.
S5 Fl G 5s; 51°23'·70N 03°06'·30E.
S7 Fl G 5s; 51°23'·98N 03°10'·42E.
S9 QG; 51°24'·42N 03°14'·99E.
S12 Fl (4) R 10s; 51°24'·67N 03°18'·22E.
S-W Q; 51°24'·13N 03°18'·22E, here Wielingen chan merges.
S14 Fl R 5s; 51°24'·58N 03°19'·67E.

WIELINGEN CHANNEL

BVH Q (6) + L Fl R 15s; 51°23'·15N 03°12'·04E.
MOW3 tide gauge Fl (5) Y 20s; ***Racon H, 10M***; 51°23'·38N 03°11'·92E.
W Fl (3) G 15s; 51°23'·26N 03°14'·90E.
W1 Fl G 5s; 51°23'·46N 03°18'·21E.
Fort Maisonneuve VQ (9) 10s; wreck; 51°24'·20N 03°21'·50E.
W3 Iso G 4s; 51°23'·95N 03°21'·48E.
W5 Iso G 8s; 51°24'·30N 03°24'·50E.
W7 Iso G 8s; 51°24'·59N 03°27'·27E.
W9 Q G; 51°24'·94N 03°30'·43E.
Nieuwe Sluis Oc WRG 10s 26m W14M, R11M, G10M; 055°-R-089°-W-093°-G-105°-R-134°-W-136·5°-G-156·5°-W-236·5°-G-243°-W-254°-R-292°-W-055°; B 8-sided twr, W bands; 51°24'·41N 03°31'·29E.
Songa QG; 51°25'·26N 03°33'·66E.
W10 QR; 51°25'·85N 03°33'·28E.

VLISSINGEN

Koopmanshaven, Boulevard de Ruyter Hd, ☆ Iso R 9s 11m 2M; R metal framework twr; 51°26'·37N 03°34'·52E.

Sardijngeul ☆ Oc W 5s; 51°26'·30N 03°34'·55E: see OOSTGAT last 3 lines.

E mole head, ☆ FG 7m; W mast; 51°26'·32N 03°34'·67E.

Buitenhaven ent, W side ☆ FR 10m 5M; also Iso WRG 4s 6M: W073°-324°, G324°-352°, W352°-017°, G017°-042°, W042°-056°, R056°-073°; W post, R bands; tfc sigs; 51°26'·38N 03°36'·06E.

Buitenhaven ent, E side ☆ FG 7m 4M; 51°26'·41N 03°36'·38E.

Schone Waardin ☆ Oc WRG 9s 10m W13M, R10M, G9M; 235°-R-271°-W-283°-G-335°-R-341°-G-026°-W-079°-R-091°; R mast, W bands; 51°26'·54N 03°37'·91E (1M E of Buitenhaven ent).

BRESKENS TO CADZAND-BAD

Nieuwe Sluis ☆ Oc 10s 28m 14M (priv); B/W banded 8 sided tr; 51°24'·43N 03°31'·26E.

ARV-VH Q; 51°24'·71N 03°33'·89E.

VH2 (Vaarwaterlangs Hoofdplaat) Iso R 2s; 51°24'·41N 03°33'·72E.

Yacht hbr, W mole ☆ FG 7m; in fog FY; Gy post; 51°24'·03N 03°34'·06E. E mole ☆ FR 6m; Gy mast; 51°23'·95N 03°34'·09E.

Cadzand-Bad, marina approach, CZ Mo (A) 8s; 51°23'·08N 03°23'·07E.

WESTERSCHELDE: TERNEUZEN TO PAAL

TERNEUZEN

Nieuw Neuzenpolder ldg lts 125°, both Oc 5s 6/16m 9/13M; intens 117°-133°; synch. Front, W col, B bands; 51°20'·97N 03°47'·24E. Rear, B & W twr; 365m from front.

Oost Buitenhaven E mole ☆ FR 5M; 51°20'·56N 03°49'·19E.

Veerhaven (former ferry hbr, W part) & marinas (E part) W mole head ☆ FG, Gy mast; 51°20'·57N 03°49'·64E. E mole, FR.

W mole ☆ Oc WRG 5s 15m W9M, R7M, G6M; 090°-R-115°-W-120°-G-130°-W-245°-G-249°-W-279°-R-004°; B & W post; 51°20'·54N 03°49'·58E, close SW of ☆ FG.

HANSWEERT

W mole ☆ Oc WRG 10s 9m W6M, R6M, G6M; (in fog FY); 288°-R-311°-G-320°-W-332·5°-G-348·5°-W-042·5°-R-061·5°-W-078°-G-099°-W-114·5°-R-127·5°-W-288°; R twr, W bands; 51°26'·42N 04°00'·53E.

BELGIUM
ZANDVLIET TO ANTWERPEN

ZANDVLIET

Dir ☆ 118·3°,WRG 20m W4M, R/ G3M; 116·63°-Oc G-117·17°- FG-117·58°-Alt GW-118·63°-F-118·63°-Alt RW-119·18°-FR-119·58°- Oc R-120·13°; 51°20'·61N 04°16'·47E, near Zandvliet locks.

ANTWERPEN

No 107 Iso G 8s, 51°14'·12N 04°23'·80E (Kattendijksluis for Willemdok).

Royerssluis, ldg lts 091°, both FR. Ent FR/FG.

No 109 Iso G 8s; 51°13'·88N 04°23'·87E, (off Linkeroever).

Linkeroever marina F WR 9m W3M, R2M; shore-W-283°- R-shore; B ⊙, R lantern; 51°13'·91N 04°23'·70E. Marina ent, FR/FG.

COASTAL MARKS

AW2 Fl (4) R 20s; 51°21'·95N 03°00'·94E; Wandelaar.

AW1 QG; 51°21'·50N 03°02'·59E; Wandelaar.

Oostende Bank N Q; 51°21'·20N 02°52'·93E.

Wenduine Bank E QR; 51°18'·83N 03°01'·64E.

Wenduine Bank W Q (9) 15s; 51°17'·23N 02°52'·76E.

Nautica Ena wreck Q; 51°18'·08N 02°52'·79E.

Oostendebank E Fl G 5s; 51°17'·35N 02°51'·92E.

Oostendebank W Q (9)15s; 51°16'·20N 02°44'·74E.

LST 420 Q (9)15s; 51°15'·45N 02°40'·67E.

MBN Q; 51°20'·82N 02°46'·29E.

Middelkerke Bank Fl G 5s; 51°18'·19N 02°42'·75E.

Middelkerke Bank S Q (9) R 15s; 51°14'·73N 02°41'·89E.

D1 Q (3) 10s; 51°13'·95N 02°38'·59E.

BT Ratel Fl (4) R 15s; 51°11'·63N 02°27'·92E; Buiten Ratel.

ZEEBRUGGE TO THE FRENCH BORDER

ZEEBRUGGE

AW Iso 8s; 51°22'·41N 03°07'·05E.

Ldg lts 136°, both Oc 5s 22/45m 8M; 131°-141°; H24, synch; W cols, R bands. Front, 51°20'·71N 03°13'·11E. Rear, 890m SE.

SZ Q (3) 10s; 51°23'·30N 03°08'·65E (Scheur Channel).

Z QG; 51°22'·48N 03°09'·95E.

WZ Q (9) 15s; 51°22'·57N 03°10'·72E.

W outer mole ☆ Oc G 7s 31m 7M; G vert strip lts visible from seaward; 057°-267°; *Horn (3) 30s;* IPTS; 51°21'·74N 03°11'·17E.

E outer mole ☆ Oc R 7s 31m 7M; R vert strip lts visible from seaward; 087°-281°; *Bell 25s;* 51°21'·78N 03°11'·86E.

Ldg lts 154°: Front, Oc WR 6s 20m 3M, 135°-W-160°-R-169°; W pylon, R bands; 51°20'·33N 03°12'·89E. Rear, Oc 6s 38m 3M, H24, synch; 520m from front.

Leopold II mole ☆ Oc WR 15s 22m, **W20M, R18M;** 068°-W-145°-R-212°-W-296°; IPTS; 51°20'·85N 03°12'·17E.

Entrance to Marina and FV hbr 51°19'·88N 03°11'·85E.

BLANKENBERGE

Promenade pier Fl (3) Y 20s, 8m 4M; 51°19'·28N 03°08'·18E.

Lt ho ☆ Fl (2) 8s 30m **20M**; 065°-245°; W twr, B top; 51°18'·76N 03°06'·87E.

Ldg lts 134°, both FR 5/9m 3/10M, R cross (X) topmarks on masts; front 51°18'·70N 03°08'·82E; rear 81m from front.

E pier ☆ FR 12m 11M; R290°-245°(315°); W ○ twr; 51°18'·91N 03°06'·56E.

W pier ☆ FG 14m 11M; intens 065°-290°, unintens 290°-335°; W ○ twr; 51°18'·89N 03°06'·42E.

OBST 4 – OBST 14 are eleven s Q approx 3ca offshore, marking Spoil Ground between Blankenberge and Oostende.

OOSTENDE

Wenduinebank West Q (9) 15s; 51°17'·23N 02°52'·76E.

Buitenstroombank Q; 51°15'·17N 02°51'·71E.

Binnenstroombank Q (3) 10s; 51°14'·47N 02°53'·65E.

Ldg lts 143°: both Iso 4s (triple vert) 36/46m 4M, 068°-218°; X on metal mast, R/W bands. Front, 51°13'·80N 02°54'·89E.

Oostende lt ho ☆ Fl (3) 10s 65m **27M**; obsc 069·5°-071°; Gy twr, 2 sinusoidal Bu bands; 51°14'·44N 02°55'·84E.
W bkwtr hd ☆ FG 19m 11M, *Horn Mo (U)*; G mast; 51°14'·44N 02° 54'·97E.
E bkwtr hd ☆ FR 9m 3M + QY; R mast; 51°14'·51N 02° 55'·18E and Radar tr, 50m, vert R/W stripes, R top, 51°14'·51N 02°55'·19E.

NIEUWPOORT
Zuidstroombank Fl R 5s; 51°12'·28N 02°47'·37E.
Weststroombank Fl (4) R 20s; 51°11'·34N 02°43'·03E.
Wreck 4 Q (6) + L Fl 15s; 51°10'·98N 02°40'·10E.
Nieuwpoort Bank Q (9) 15s; 51°10'·16N 02°36'·09E.
Whitley Q; 51°09'·15N 02°39'·44E.
Lt ho ☆ Fl (2) R 14s 28m **16M**; R/W twr; 51°09'·28N 02°43'·80E.
E pier ☆ FR 10m 10M; R025°-250°(225°) R307°-347°(40°); W ○ twr; 51°09'·41N 02°43'·08E.
W pier ☆ FG 10m 9M; G025°-250°(225°) G284°-324°(40°); W ○ twr; 51°09'·35N 02°43'·00E.
Storm surge barrier, 51°09'·13N 02°43'·46E; outer and inner approach walls, 3 sequential bcns P+S, FR and FG lts.
☆ QG 51°08'·65N 02°44'·31E marks the Y-junction where the channel forks stbd for KYCN and port for WSKLuM and VVW-N.

WESTDIEP and PASSE DE ZUYDCOOTE
Den Oever wreck 2 Q; 51°08'·11N 02°37'·43E.
Wreck 1 Q; 51°08'·32N 02°35'·03E (adjacent to next line).
Wave recorder Fl (5) Y 20s; 51°08'·25N 02°34'·98E.
Trapegeer Fl G 10s; 51°08'·41N 02°34'·36E.
E12 VQ (6) + L Fl 10s; 51°07'·92N 02°30'·61E.
French waters, for continuity (see also Area 17):
CME Q (3) 10s; 51°07'·30N 02°30'·00E.
E11 Fl G 4s; 51°06'·85N 02°30'·83E.
E10 Fl (2) R 6s; 51°06'·26N 02°30'·40E.
E9 Fl (2) G 6s; 51°05'·61N 02°29'·60E.
E8 Fl (3) R 12s; 51°05'·12N 02°28'·60E.

1	Delfzijl	**1**																
2	Terschelling	85	**2**															
3	Harlingen	102	19	**3**														
4	Den Oever	110	34	21	**4**													
5	Den Helder	115	39	30	11	**5**												
6	Amsterdam	159	83	81	62	51	**6**											
7	IJmuiden	146	70	68	49	38	13	**7**										
8	Scheveningen	171	95	93	74	63	38	25	**8**									
9	Rotterdam	205	129	127	108	97	72	59	34	**9**								
10	Hook of Holland	185	109	107	88	77	52	39	14	20	**10**							
11	Stellendam	201	125	123	104	93	68	55	30	36	16	**11**						
12	Roompotsluis	233	157	155	136	125	100	87	50	68	48	32	**12**					
13	Vlissingen	228	152	150	131	120	99	86	61	67	47	45	24	**13**				
14	Zeebrugge	239	163	161	142	131	106	93	68	74	54	50	28	16	**14**			
15	Blankenberge	244	168	166	147	136	111	98	73	79	59	55	33	21	5	**15**		
16	Oostende	239	163	161	142	131	110	106	81	87	67	72	40	29	13	9	**16**	
17	Nieuwpoort	262	186	184	165	154	129	116	91	97	77	83	51	39	23	18	9	**17**

DISTANCE TABLES
Approx distances in nautical miles are by the most direct route allowing for dangers and TSS.

AREA 14 *North France – Dunkerque to Cap de la Hague*

SELECTED LIGHTS, BUOYS & WAYPOINTS

OFFSHORE MARKS: W Hinder to Dover Strait
Fairy South VQ (6) + L Fl 10s; 51°21'·20N 02°17'·31E.
Fairy West VQ (9) 10s 6M; 51°23'·89N 02°09'·27E. 992271127. Hinder 1 Fl (2) 6s; 51°20'·80N 02°10'·93E.
Bergues Fl G 4s 7m 4M; 51°17'·14N 02°18'·63E.
Bergues S Q (6) + L Fl 15s; 51°15'·09N 02°19'·42E.
Ruytingen E VQ; 51°14'·55N 02°17'·93E.
Ruytingen N VQ 4M; 51°13'·16N 02°10'·28E.
Ruytingen SE VQ (3) 15s; 51°09'·20N 02°08'·94E.992271126.
Ruytingen NW Fl G 4s 3M; 51°09'·11N 01°57'·30E.
Ruytingen W VQ 4M; 51°06'·93N 01°50'·45E.
Ruytingen SW Fl (3) G 12s 3M; 51°04'·33N 01°45'·84E.
Sandettié N VQ 6M; 51°18'·35N 02°04'·73E.
Sandettié E Fl R 4s 7m 3M;51°14'·88N 02°02'·65E.992271119.

DUNKERQUE TO BOULOGNE

PASSE DE ZUYDCOOTE
E12 VQ (6) + L Fl 10s; 51°07'·92N 02°30'·61E. (Belgium)
CME Q (3) 10s; 51°07'·30N 02°30'·00E.
E11 Fl G 4s; 51°06'·85N 02°30'·83E.
E10 Fl (2) R 6s; 51°06'·26N 02°30'·40E.
E9 Fl (2) G 6s; 51°05'·61N 02°29'·60E.
E8 Fl (3) R 12s; 51°05'·12N 02°28'·60E. (E7 does not exist)

PASSE DE L'EST
E6 QR; 51°04'·86N 02°27'·08E.
E4 Fl R 4s; 51°04'·58N 02°24'·52E.
E1 Fl (2) G 6s; 51°04'·12N 02°23'·04E.
E2 Fl (2) R 6s; 51°04'·35N 02°22'·31E.
Q (6) + L Fl 15s; 51°04'·28N 02°21'·73E.

DUNKERQUE PORT EST
E jetty ☆ Fl (2) R 6s 12m 10M; R □, W pylon; 51°03'·59N 02°21'·20E.
W jetty ☆ Fl (2) G 6s 35m 11M; W twr, brown top; 51°03'·63N 02°20'·95E.
Ldg lts 137·5°, front Q7m11M 51°02'·98N 02°22'·05E, rear, Q10m11M, 114m from front, both W cols, R tops, synched.

Inner W jetty Q 11m 9M; 51°03'·33N 02°21'·43E.
Dunkerque lt ho ☆ Fl (2) 10s 59m **26M**; 51°02'·93N 02°21'·86E.

DUNKERQUE INTERMEDIATE CHANNEL

DW30 QR; 51°04'·14N 02°20'·16E.
DW29 QG; 51°03'·85N 02°20'·21E.
DW16 Fl (2) R 6s; 51°03'·52N 02°08'·62E.
DKB VQ (9) 10s; 51°02'·95N 02°09'·26E.
DW12 Fl (3) R 12s; 51°03'·38N 02°05'·36E.
DW11 Fl (3) G 12s; 51°02'·79N 02°05'·53E. (DW10-7 omitted)

GRAVELINES

W jetty ☆ Fl (2) WG 6s 9m W/G4M; 085°-W-224°-G-085°; Y ○ twr, G top; 51°00'·94N 02°05'·49E.

PASSE DE L'OUEST

DW6 VQ R; 51°02'· 81N 02°00'· 80E.
DW5 QG; 51°02'·20N 02°00'·92E.
DKA L Fl 10s; 51°02'·55N 01°56'·96E.
RCE (Ridens de Calais East) Fl G 4s; 51°02'·29N 01°52'·98E.
Dyck Fl R 4s; ***Racon B***; 51° 02'·90N 01°51'·80E.
RCA (Ridens de Calais Approach) Q; 51°01'·00N 01°48'·53E. 992271125.

CALAIS

E Jetty head, ☆ Q(9)W15s 12m 10M, (in fog 2 Fl (2) W (vert) 6s on request); Gry twr, W top. 50°58'·39N 01°50'·46E.
E Jetty root, Dir ☆ WG 12m 1M; 089·4°-FG-093·7°-Al WG-094°·3- FW-098·6°; metal structure; 50°58'·25N 01°51'·20E.
W jetty ☆ Iso G 3s 12m 9M; (in fog Fl 5s on request); W twr, G top; *Bell 5s;* 50°58'·24N 01°50'·40E.
Calais ☆ Fl (4) 15s 59m **22M**; vis 073°-260°; W 8-sided twr, B top; 50°57'·68N 01°51'·21E (440m E of marina entry gate).

CALAIS, WESTERN APPROACH

CA6 Fl (3) R 12s; 50°58'·63N 01°49'·92E.
CA4 Fl (2)R 6s; 50°58'·38N 01°48'·65E.
CA1 Fl G 4s; 50°57'·64N 01°46'·14E (0·5M NNW of Sangatte). Sangatte ☆ Oc WG 4s 13m W8M, G5M; 065°-G-089°-W-152°-G-245°; W pylon, B top; 50°57'·19N 01°46'·50E.
Les Quénocs VQ; 50°56'·85N 01°41'·12E.
Abbeville wreck VQ (9) 10s; 50°56'·08N 01°37'·58E.
Cap Gris-Nez ☆ Fl 5s 72m **29M**; 005°-232°; W twr, B top; 50°52'·09N 01°34'·96E.

OFFSHORE MARKS: DOVER STRAIT TSS, French side

Colbart N Q 6M; 50°57'·50N 01°23'·30E. 992271121.
Colbart SW VQ (6) + L Fl 10s 8m; 50°48'·87N 01°16'·32E.
ZC2 (Zone Cotière) Fl (2+1) Y 15s 5M; 50°53'·54N 01°30'·89E.
ZC1 Fl (4) Y 15s 4MN; 50°44'·99N 01°27'·21E.
Ridens SE VQ (3) 5s 6M; 50°43'·48N 01°18'·87E.
Bassurelle Fl (4) R 15s 6M; ***Racon B, 5-8M***; 50°32'·74N 00°57'·69E.
Vergoyer N VQ 5M; 50°39'·67N 01°22'·21E.
Vergoyer NW Fl (2) G 6s 4M; 50°37'·16N 01°17'·85E.
Vergoyer E VQ (3) 5s 6M; 50°35'·80N 01°19'·70E. 992271132
Vergoyer W Fl G 4s 4M; 50°34'·66N 01°13'·57E.
Vergoyer SW VQ (9) 10s 6M; 50°27'·01N 01°00'·03E.

BOULOGNE TO DIEPPE

BOULOGNE

Bassure de Baas VQ; 50°48'·53N 01°33'·05E.
Approches Boulogne VQ (6) + L Fl 10s 8m 6M; 50°45'·31N 01°31'·07E.
Digue N (detached) ☆ Fl (2) R 6s 10m 7M; 50°44'·71N 01°34'·18E.
Digue S (Carnot) ☆ Fl (2+1) 15s 25m **19M**; W twr, G top; 50°44'·44N 01°34'·05E.
Clearing brg 122·4° : Front, FG in a neon ▽ 4m 5M; 50°43'·71N 01°35'·66E. Rear, FR 44m 11M; intens 113°-133°; 560m from front.
Inner NE jetty ☆ FR 11m 7M; 50°43'·91N 01°35'·24E. Inner SW jetty ☆ FG 17m 5M; W col, G top; *Horn 30s;* 50°43'·90N 01°35'·11E.
Cap d'Alprech ☆ Fl (3) 15s 62m **23M**; W twr, B top; 50°41'·91N 01°33'·75E, 2·5M S of hbr ent.

LE TOUQUET/ÉTAPLES

Pte de Lornel VQ (9) 10s 6m 3M; 50°33'·24N 01°35'·12E.
Mérida wreck 50°32'·85N 01°33'·44E.
Camiers lt ho ☆ Oc (2) WRG 6s 17m W10M, R/G7M; 015°-G-090°-W-105°-R-141°; R pylon; 50°32'·86N 01°36'·28E.
Canche Est groyne Fl R 4s 8m; 50°32'·57N 01°35'·66E.
Le Touquet ☆ Fl (2) 10s 54m **25M**; Or twr, brown band, W&G top; 50°31'·43N 01°35'·52E.
Pointe du Haut-Blanc ☆ Fl 5s 44m **23M**; W twr, R bands, G top; 50°23'·90N 01°33'·67E (Berck).

BAIE DE LA SOMME

ATSO Mo (A) 12s; 50°14'·00N 01°28'·08E (shifts frequently).
Pte du Hourdel ☆ Oc (3) WG 12s 19m, W12M, G9M; 053°-W-248°-G-323°; tidal sigs; *Horn (3) 30s*; W twr, G top; 50°12'·90N 01°33'·98E.
Cayeux-sur-Mer ☆ Fl R 5s 32m **22M**; W twr, R top; 50°11'·65N 01°30'·72E.
Le Crotoy ☆ Oc (2) R 6s 19m 8M; 285°-135°; W pylon; 50°12'·91N 01°37'·40E. Marina ☆ Fl R & Fl G 2s 4m 2M; 50°12'·98N 01°38'·20E.

ST VALÉRY-SUR-SOMME

Trng wall head, Fl G 2.5s 2m 1M; 50°12'·25N 01°35'·85E.
Embankment head ☆ Iso G 4s 9m 9M; 347°-222°; W pylon, G top; 50°12'·25N 01°36'·02E.
La Ferté môle ☆ Fl R 4s 9m 9M; 000°-250°; W pylon, R top; 50°11'·18N 01°38'·14E (ent to marina inlet).

LE TRÉPORT

Ault ☆ Oc (3) WR 12s 95m **W15M**, R11M; 040°-W-175°-R-220°; W twr, R top; 50°06'·28N 01°27'·23E (4M NE of Le Tréport).
W jetty ☆ Fl (2) G 10s 15m **20M**; W twr, G top; 50°03'·88N 01°22'·14E.

DIEPPE

W jetty ☆ Iso G 4s 11m 8M; W twr, G top; *Horn 30s;* 49°56'·27N 01°04'·97E.
Quai de la Marne QR 12m 3M; 49°55'·93N 01°05'·20E, E quay.
Pointe d'Ailly ☆ Fl (3) 20s 95m **31M**; W □ twr, G top; *Horn (3) 60s;* 49°54'·96N 00°57'·50E.

DIEPPE TO LE HAVRE

SAINT VALÉRY-EN-CAUX

W jetty ☆ Fl (2) G 6s 13m 11M; W twr, G top; 49°52'·40N 00°42'·54E.

Paluel power station, restricted area, Paluel 2 Fl Y 4s; 49°52'·33N 00°38'·45E; Wave recorder Fl(5) Y 20s; 49°52'·30N 00°37'·87E; Paluel 1 Fl Y 4s; 49°52'·33N 00°37'·53E.

FÉCAMP

N jetty ☆ Fl (2) 10s 15m **16M**; Gy twr, R top; 49°45'·94N 00°21'·80E.

Fécamp NW, Met Mast FECO1-YO2 ☆ Mo(U) W 15s 13m 10M, Aero F R 36m, Aero UQ R 60m, Aero UQ W 60m(day) Gy pylon,Y platform; Horn Mo(U) 30s; 49°50'·85N 00°13'·14E. 992271122.

PORT DU HAVRE-ANTIFER

Cap d'Antifer ☆ Fl 20s 128m **29M**; 021°-222°; Gy 8-sided twr, G top, on 90m cliffs; 49°41'·01N 00°09'·93E.

A17 Iso G 4s; 49°41'·53N 00°01·75E.

A18 QR; 49°42'·02N 00°02'·18E. Cross the chan W of A17/18.

Ldg lts 127·5°, both Dir Oc 4s 113/135m **22M**; 127°-128°; by day F **33M** 126·5°-128·5° occas. **Front** ☆, 49°38'·31N 00°09'·12E.

LE HAVRE, APPROACH CHANNEL

Cap de la Hève ☆ Fl 5s 123m **24M**; 225°-196°; W 8-sided twr, R top; 49°30'·74N 00°04'·16E.

LHA Mo (A) 12s 10m 6M; R&W; ***Racon, 8-10M*** (a series of 8 dots, or 8 groups of dots; distance between each dot or group represents 0·3M); 49°31'·38N 00°09'·86W. Reserve lt Mo (A).

Ldg lts 106·8°, both Dir F 36/78m **25M** (H24); intens 106°-108°; Gy twrs, G tops. Front, 49°28'·91N 00°06'·50E; rear, 0·73M from front.

LH3 QG; 49°30'·84N 00°04'·02W. (LH1 & 2 buoys do not exist)

LH4 QR; 49°31'·11N 00°03'·90W.

LH7 Iso G 4s; 49°30'·25N 00°00'·82W.

LH8 Fl (2) R 6s; 49°30'·44N 00°00'·70W.

Note the W-E longitude change. (LH9 buoy does not exist)

LH13 Fl G 4s; 49°29'·32N 00°03'·62E (Ent to Port 2000).

LH14 Fl R 4s; 49°29'·67N 00°03'·43E; 1m shoal depth close W.

LH16 Fl (2) R 6s; 49°29'·45N 00°04'·28E.

LH 2000 VQ (9) 10s; 49°29'·14N 00°04'·78E (Ent to Port 2000).

LE HAVRE

Digue N ☆ Fl R 4s 15m 8M; IPTS; W ○ twr, R top; 49°29'·19N 00°05'·44E.

Digue S ☆ Fl G 4s 15m 8M; W twr, G top; 49°29'·05N 00°05'·38E.

Marina ent, W spur ☆ Fl (2) R 6s 3M; 49°29'·22N 00°05'·53E.

THE SEINE ESTUARY UP TO HONFLEUR

CHENAL DE ROUEN

Nord du Mouillage Fl (4) Y 15s; 49°28'·80N 00°00'·22E.

No 2 QR; ***Racon T***; 49°27'·70N 00°00'·60E.

No 4 Fl R 2·5s; 49°27'·19N 00°01'·97E. Yachts keep N of chan.

Amfard SW QR; 49°26'·30N 00°04'·82E.

No 10 Fl R 4s; 49°26'·10N 00°06'·39E.

Digue du Ratier VQ 10m 4M; 49°25'·94N 00°06'·59E.

Falaise des Fonds ☆ Fl (3) WRG 12s 15m, **W17M**, R/G13M; 040°-G-080°-R-084°-G-100°-W-109°-R-162°-G-260°; W twr, G top; 49°25'·47N 00°12'·85E.

No 20 Fl (2) R 6s; 49°25'·85N 00°13'·71E. (over to Honfleur)

HONFLEUR

Digue Ouest ☆ QG 10m 6M; 49°25'·67N 00°13'·83E.

Digue Est ☆ Q 9m 8M; *Horn (5) 40s;* 49°25'·67N 00°13'·95E.

Inner E jetty head, ☆ Fl R 2M; 49°25'·40N 00°14'·10E.

No 22 Fl R 4s; 49°25'·85N 00°15'·37E.

TROUVILLE TO COURSEULLES

CHENAL DE ROUEN TO DEAUVILLE and TROUVILLE

Ratelets Q (9) 15s; 49°25'·29N 00°01'·71E.

Semoy VQ (3) 5s; 49°24'·15N 00°02'·35E, close to 148° ldg line.

Trouville SW VQ (9) 10s; 49°22'·54N 00°02'·56E.

DEAUVILLE and TROUVILLE

Ldg lts 145°, both Oc R 4s 11/17m 12/10M: Front, East inner jetty (*estacade*); 330°-150°; W twr, R top; 49°22'·03N 00°04'·48E.

Rear, Pte de la Cahotte; synch; 120°-170°; 49°21'·93N 00°04'·58E.

W trng wall ☆ Fl WG 4s 10m W9M, G6M; 005°-W-176°-G-005°; B pylon, G top; 49°22'·37N 00°04'·11E. Also 4 unlit SHM bcns.

E trng wall ☆ Fl (4) WR 12s 8m W7M, R4M; 131°-W-175°-R-131°; W pylon, R top; 49°22'·22N 00°04'·33E. Also 3 unlit PHM bcns.

W outer bkwtr ☆ Iso G 4s 9m 5M; 49°22'·11N 00°04'·33E.

West inner jetty (*estacade*) ☆ QG 11m 9M; 49°22'·03N 00°04'·43E.

DIVES-SUR-MER ***Note the E–W longitude change.***

DI Iso 4s; 49°19'·17N 00°05'·86W.

No 1 VQ G; 49°18'·50N 00°05'·67W. Ch bys freq moved.

No 2 VQ R; 49°18'·51N 00°05'·56W.

No 3 QG 7m 4M; W pylon, G top; 49°18'·30N 00°05'·55W.

No 5 Fl G 4s 8m 4M; W pylon, G top; 49°18'·09N 00°05'·50W.

Bcns 3 & 5, if damaged, may be temporarily replaced by buoys.

No 7 Fl G 6s; 49°17'·65N 00°05'·31W.

OUISTREHAM and CAEN

Merville VQ; 49°19'·65N 00°13'·39W; spoil ground buoy.

Ouistreham VQ (3) 5s; wreck buoy; 49°20'·42N 00°14'·81W.

Ldg lts 184·5°, both Dir Oc (3) R 12s 11/30m **17/18M**; intens 183·5°-186·5°, synch. **Front** ☆, E jetty, W mast, R top, 49°16'·99N 00°14'·81W. **Rear** ☆, 610m from front, tripod, R top.

No 1 QG; 49°19'·19N 00°14'·67W.

No 2 QR; 49°19'·17N 00°14'·43W.

Barnabé ☆ QG 7m 5M; W pylon, G top; 49°18'·02N 00°14'·76W.

St-Médard ☆ QR 7m 5M; 49°18'·02N 00°14'·62W.

Riva ☆ Fl G 4s 9m 3M; W pylon, G top; 49°17'·73N 00°14'·79W.

Quilbé ☆ Fl R 4s 9m 3M; W pylon, R top; 49°17'·72N 00°14'·67W.

Ouistreham lt ho ☆ Oc WR 4s 37m **W17M**, R13M; 115°-R-151°-W-115°; W twr, R top; 49°16'·79N 00°14'·87W.

COURSEULLES-SUR-MER

Courseulles Iso 4s; 49°21'·28N 00°27'·68W.

W jetty ☆ Iso WG 4s 7m; W9M, G6M; 135°-W-235°-G-135°; brown pylon on dolphin, G top; 49°20'·41N 00°27'·37W.

E jetty ☆ Oc (2) R 6s 9m 7M; 49°20'·26N 00°27'·39W.

COURSEULLES TO ST VAAST

Ver ☆ Fl (3)15s 42m **26M**; obsc'd by cliffs of St Aubin when brg >275°; conspic lt ho, W twr, Gy top; 49°20'·41N 00°31'·13W.

ARROMANCHES

Ent buoys: 49°21'·35N 00°37'·26W; 49°21'·25N00°37'·30W.

Bombardons wreck buoys; 49°21'·66N 00°38'·97W.

PORT-EN-BESSIN

Ldg lts 204°, both Oc (3) 12s 25/42m 10/11M; synch. Front, 069°-339°, W pylon, G top; 49°20'·96N 00°45'·53W. Rear; 114°-294°, W and Gy ho; 93m from front.

E mole ☆ Oc R 4s 14m 7M, R pylon; 49°21'·12N 00°45'·38W.

W mole ☆ Fl WG 4s 14m, W10M, G7M; G065°-114·5°, W114·5°-065°; G pylon; 49°21'·17N 00°45'·43W.

COASTAL MARKS

Omaha Beach, 1M off : 49°22'·66N 00°50'·28W; 49°23'·17N 00°51'·93W; 49°23'·66N 00°53'·74W.

Broadsword Q (3) 10s, wreck buoy; 49°25'·34N 00°52'·96W.

Est du Cardonnet VQ (3) 5s; 49°26'·83N 01°01'·10W.

GRANDCAMP

Les Roches de Grandcamp: No 1 49°24'·72N 01°01'·75W; No 3 49°24'·92N 01°03'·70W; No 5 49°24'·78N 01°04'·98W.

Ldg lts 146°, both Dir Q 9/12m **15M**, 144·5°-147·5°. **Front** ☆, 49°23'·42N 01°02'·90W. **Rear** ☆,102m from front.

Jetée Est ☆ Oc (2) R 6s 9m 9M; *Horn Mo(N) 30s;* 49°23'·53N 01°02'·96W.

Jetée Ouest ☆ Fl G 4s 9m 6M; 49°23'·47N 01°02'·96W.

ISIGNY-SUR-MER

IS, small B/Y , no topmark (on AC2135); 49°24'·28N 01°06'·37W.

No 1 , Fl R 4s; 49°23'·60N 01°07·27W

Dir lts 173°, both Dir Q WRG 7m 9M; 49°19'·57N 01°06·78W.

Training wall heads Fl G 4s; 49°21'·40N 01°07'·20W; Fl R 4s, 49°21'·40N 01°07'·10W, off Pte du Grouin.

CARENTAN

C-I Iso 4s; 49°25'·44N 01°07'·08W; 210°/1·76M to 1 & 2 bys.

No 1 Fl G 4s; 49°24'·29N 01°08'·57W.

No 2 Fl R 4s; 49°23'·93N 01°08'·32W.

Trng wall Fl (4) G 15s; G △ on G bcn;49°21'·96N 01°09'·95W.

Trng wall Fl (4) R 15s; R □ on R bcn;49°21'·93N 01°09'·878W.

ÎLES SAINT-MARCOUF

Iles St-Marcouf ☆ VQ (3) 5s 18m 8M; □ Gy twr, G top; 49°29'·86N 01°08'·81W.

Ouest-Saint-Marcouf Q (9) 15s; 49°29'·73N 01°11'·97W.

Saint Floxel 49°30'·64N 01°13'·94W.

Quineville Q (9) 10s, wreck buoy; 49°31'·79N 01°12'·38W.

ST VAAST TO POINTE DE BARFLEUR

ST VAAST-LA-HOUGUE

Ldg lts 267°: Front, La Hougue Oc 4s 9m 10M; W pylon, G top; 49°34'·25N 01°16'·37W. Rear, Morsalines Oc (4) WRG 12s 90m, W11M, R/G8M; 171°-W-316°-G-321°-R-342°-W-355°; W 8-sided twr, G top; 49°34'·16N 01°19'·10W, 1·8M from front.

Le Manquet 49°34'·26N 01°15'·56W.

Le Bout du Roc 49°34'·68N 01°15'·27W.

La Dent 49°34'·57N 01°14'·20W.

Le Gavendest Q (6) + L Fl 15s; 49°34'·36N 01°13'·89W.

Jetty ☆ Dir Oc (2) WRG 6s 12m W10M, R/G7M; 219°-R-237°-G-310°-W-350°-R-040°; W 8-sided twr, R top; 49°35'·17N 01°15'·41W.

Pte de Saire ☆ Iso 4s 11m 10M; squat W twr, G top; 49°36'·36N 01°13'·78W.

BARFLEUR

Ldg lts 219·5°, both Oc (3) 12s 7/13m 10M; synch. Front, W □ twr;49°40'·18N 01°15'·61W. Rear, 085°-355°; Gy and W □ twr, G top; 288m from front.

La Grotte 49°41'·06N 01°14'·86W.

Roche-à-l'Anglais 49°40'·78N 01°14'·93W.

La Vimberge 49°40'·54N 01°15'·25W.

W jetty ☆ Fl G 4s 8m 6M; 49°40'·32N 01°15'·57W.

E jetty ☆ Fl R 4s 5m 6M; 49°40'·32N 01°15'·46W.

La Jamette 49°41'·87N 01°15'·59W.

Pte de Barfleur ☆ Fl (2) 10s 72m **25M**; obsc when brg less than 088°; Gy twr, B top; 49°41'·79N 01°15'·95W.

POINTE DE BARFLEUR TO CAP DE LA HAGUE

Les Équets Q 8m 3M; 49°43'·62N 01°18'·36W.

Basse du Rénier VQ 8m 4M; 49°44'·84N 01°22'·09W.

Les Trois Pierres 49°42'·90N 01°21'·80W.

Anse de Vicq, 158° ldg lts; both Iso R 4s 8/14m 6M; front 49°42'·20N 01°23'·95W.

La Pierre Noire Q (9) 15s 8m 4M;49°43'·54N 01°29'·07W.

PORT DU LÉVI

Cap Lévi ☆ Fl R 5s 36m **17M**; Gy □ twr; 49°41'·75N 01°28'·39W.

Port Lévi ☆ Oc (2) WRG 6s 7m 7M; 055°-G-083°-W-105°-R-163°; W & Gy hut, W lantern; 49°41'·24N 01°28'·34W.

PORT DU BECQUET

Ldg lts 186·3°, both intens 183°-189·3°; synch. Front, Dir Oc (3) 12s 8m 10M; W 8-sided twr; 49°39'·23N 01°32'·84W. Rear, Dir Oc (3) 12s 13m 7M. W 8-sided twr, R top; 49m from front.

CHERBOURG, EASTERN ENTRANCES

Passe Collignon ☆ Fl (2) R 6s 5m 4M; 49°39'·59N 01°34'·24W.

Passe de l'Est, ldg lts 183·6°, front, **La Motterie** Q 158m **20M**; Gray metal tripod, 49°37'·50N 01°36'·00W. Rear, 830m from front, **Terres Rouges**, Q 194m **20M**; White water twr; 49°37'·00N 01°36'·00W. Roches du Nord-Ouest Fl R 2·5s; 49°40'·64N 01°35'·28W.

La Truite Fl (4) R 15s; 49°40'·33N 01°35'·49W.

Fort d'Île Pelée ☆ Oc (2) WR 6s 19m; W10M, R7M; 055°-W-120°-R-055°; W and R pedestal; 49°40'·21N 01°35'·08W.
Fort de l'Est ☆ 49°40'·28N 01°35'·92W, Iso G 4s 19m 9M.
Fort Central ☆ VQ (6) + L Fl 10s 5m 4M; 322°-032°; 49°40'·40N 01°37'·04W.

CHERBOURG, PASSE DE L'OUEST

CH1 ⊙; V-AIS; 49°43'·24N 01°42'·09W.
Passe de l'Ouest, Dir Q , lights in line140·3°; Front, Jetée du Homet 5m **17M**; W △; 49° 39'·54N 01°37'·97W. Rear, Gare Maritime, 0.99M from front; 35m **17M**; intens 138·8°-141·8°, shows 24H, sync with front; W △ on Gy pylon; 49°38'·78N 01°37'·00W.
Fort de l'Ouest ★ Fl (3) WR 15s 19m **W24M, R20M**; 122°-W-355°-R-122°; Gy tr, R top; 49°40'·46N 01°38'·87W.
Fort de l'Ouest Fl R 4s; 49°40'·39N 01°38'·89W.
Q (6) + L Fl 15s; 49°40'·34N 01°38'·65W.
Digue de Querqueville ☆ Fl (2) G 6s 8m 6M; W col, G top; 49°40'·30N 01°39'·80W.
Petite Rade approach, **Terre-Pleine des Flamands**, Ldg lts, 120·6°, front, Q 22m **19M** W metal tripod; 49°39'·30N 01°36'·16W. Rear, 500m from front, **Fort des Flamands**, Q 26m **19M** Small W pylon/ concrete base. 49°39'·10N 01°35'·60W
La Ténarde VQ 8m 4M; 49°39'·74N 01°37'·75W.

1. Dunkerque-Est	1																		
2. **Calais**	28	2																	
3. **Boulogne**	49	21	3																
4. St Valéry-sur-Somme	86	58	37	4															
5. Le Tréport	90	62	41	16	5														
6. **Dieppe**	100	74	53	30	15	6													
7. St Valéry-en-Caux	109	81	62	42	28	16	7												
8. **Fécamp**	121	93	76	57	44	32	17	8											
9. **Le Havre**	148	121	103	84	71	61	47	27	9										
10. Honfleur	157	129	108	92	80	67	51	35	13	10									
11. **Deauville/Trouville**	152	125	108	91	79	61	53	34	9	13	11								
12. Dives-sur-Mer	155	129	110	94	83	66	55	38	16	19	9	12							
13. **Ouistreham**	160	138	115	97	85	73	59	41	20	24	15	9	13						
14. Courseulles	162	136	115	100	87	75	60	44	24	30	23	18	14	14					
15. Grandcamp	177	150	130	118	104	94	80	62	47	52	45	41	37	27	15				
16. Carentan	187	159	139	126	112	100	85	69	56	61	55	50	45	36	13	16			
17. **St Vaast**	179	151	131	120	107	96	80	65	54	61	54	50	46	35	16	20	17		
18. Barfleur	175	147	128	118	105	94	78	64	56	62	57	53	48	39	21	26	10	18	
19. **Cherbourg**	188	160	142	131	120	108	94	80	71	77	73	69	66	57	40	44	28	21	19

DISTANCE TABLES

Approx distances in nautical miles are by the most direct route allowing for dangers and TSS.

CHERBOURG, PETITE RADE and MARINA

Entrance, W side, Digue du Homet ☆ QG 10m 8M; intens 114·3°-134·3°; W pylon, G top; 49°39'·48N 01°36'·96W.
E side, Q R, off Jetée des Flamands; 49°39'·44N 01°36'·60W.
Marina ent, E side, ☆ Fl (3) R 12s 6m 6M; W col, R lantern; 49°38'·91N 01°37'·08W.
W mole ☆ Fl (3) G 12s 7m 6M; G pylon; 49°38'·87N 01°37'·15W.
E quay ☆ Fl (4) R 15s 3m 3M; R bcn; 49°38'·79N 01°37'·12W.
Wavescreen pontoon, N end ☆ Fl (4) G 15s 4m 2M; W post, G top.

CHERBOURG TO CAP DE LA HAGUE

Raz de Bannes 49°41'·32N 01°44'·53W.
Omonville Dir lt 257°: Iso WRG 4s13m; W10M, R/G7M; 180°-G-252°-W-262°-R-287°; W pylon, G top; 49°42'·24N 01°50'·15W.
L'Étonnard 49°42'·33N 01°49'·84W.
Basse Bréfort VQ 8m 4M; 49°43'·93N 01°51'·18W.
Jobourg Nuclear plant chimney, R lts; 49°40'·80N 01°52'·91W.
La Plate Fl (2+1) WR 10s 11m; W9M, R6M; 115°-W-272°-R-115°; Y 8-sided twr, with B top; 49°43'·97N 01°55'·74W.
Cap de la Hague (Gros du Raz) ★ Fl 5s 48m **23M**; Gy twr, W top; *Horn 30s;* 49°43'·31N 01° 57'·26W.
La Foraine VQ (9) 10s, 12m 6M; 49°42'·90N 01°58'·31W.

AREA 15 *N Central France (Cap de la Hague to St Quay) & Channel Is*

SELECTED LIGHTS, BUOYS & WAYPOINTS

CAP DE LA HAGUE TO ST MALO

GOURY

La Foraine VQ (9) 10s 12m 6M; 49°42'·90 N 01°58'·32W.
Ldg lts 065·2°: Front, QR 5m 7M; R □ in W □ on pier, 49°42'·89N 01°56'·70W. Rear, 116m from front, Q 11m 7M; W pylon/hut.
Hervieu 49°42'·77N 01°56'·92W.

DIELETTE

W bkwtr Dir lt 140°, Iso WRG 4s 12m W10M, R/G7M; 070°-G-135°-W-145°-R-180°; W twr, G top ;49°33'·18N 01°51'·81W.
E bkwtr ☆ Fl R 4s 6m 2M; 49°33'·21N 01°51'·78W.
Inner N jetty, Fl (2) R 6s. Inner S jetty, Fl (2) G 6s; bth 6m 1M.

Banc des Dious Q (9) 15s; 49°32'·58N 01°54'·02W.

CARTERET

Cap de Carteret ★ Fl (2+1) 15s 81m **26M**; Gy twr, G top; 49°22'·41N 01°48'·41W. .
W bkwtr ☆ Oc R 4s 7m 7M; W post, R top; 49°22'·07N 01°47'·32W.
E training wall ☆ Fl G 2·5s 4m 2M; W post, G top; 49°22'·17N 01°47'·30W.
Outer sill N side ☆ Fl (3) R 12s 5m 1M; R pylon; 49°22'·58N 01°47'·24W. S side ☆ Fl (3) G 12s 5m 1M; G pylon; 49°22'·56N 01°47'·20W.

PORTBAIL

PB 49°18'·37N 01°44'·75W.

Ldg lts 042°: Front, QW 14m 10M; W pylon, R top, 49°19'·75N 01°42'·50W. Rear, 870m frm front, Oc 4s 20m 10M; ch belfry.
49°19'·32N 01°43'·16W.
49°19'·20N 01°43'·00W.
Training wall head Fl (2) R 5s 5m 4M; W mast, R top; 49°19'·43N 01°42'·99W.

REGNÉVILLE
La Catheue Q (6) + L Fl 15s, 48°57'·67N 01°42'·23W.
Le Ronquet Fl (2) WR 6s, W6M, R4M; 100°-R-293°-W-100°; 49°00'·11N 01°38'·07W.
Pte d'Agon Oc (2) WR 6s 12m, W10M, R7M; 063°-R-110°-W-063°; W twr, R top, W dwelling; 49°00'·18N 01°34'·63W.
Dir lt 028°, Oc WRG 4s 9m, W12M, R/G9M; 024°-G-027°-W-029°-R-033°; house; 49°00'·63N 01°33'·36W.

PASSAGE DE LA DÉROUTE
Les Trois-Grunes Q (9) 15s, 49°21'·84N 01°55'·21W.
Écrévière Q (6) + L Fl 15s; *Bell;* 49°15'·27N 01°52'·16W.
Basse Jourdan Q (3) 10s; 49°06'·85N 01°43'·96W.
Le Boeuf 49°06'·56N 01°47'·17W.
Les Boeuftins 49°07'·03N 01°45'·96W.
La Basse du Sénéquet 49°05'·96N 01°41'·11W.
Le Sénéquet Fl (3) WR 12s 18m W13M, R10M; 083·5°-R-116·5°-W-083·5°; W twr; 49°05'·48N 01°39'·73W.
Les Nattes 49°03'·46N 01°41'·81W.
International F 49°02'·16N 01°42'·98W.
International E 49°02'·08N 01°47'·21W.
Basse le Marié Q (9) 15s; 49°01'·79N 01°48'·57W.
NE Minquiers VQ (3) 5s; *Bell;* 49°00'·85N 01°55'·30W.
Les Ardentes Q (3) 10s; 48°57'·89N 01°51'·53W.
SE Minquiers Q (3) 10s; *Bell;* 48°53'·42N 02°00'·09W.
S Minquiers Q (6) + L Fl 15s; 48°53'·09N 02°10'·10W.

ÎLES CHAUSEY
La Pointue 48°54'·44N 01°50'·92W.
L'Enseigne, W twr, B top; 48°53'·67N 01°50'·37W.
L'Etat, BW, 48°54'·67N 01°46'·21W.
Anvers wreck 48°53'·91N 01°41'·07W.
Le Founet Q (3) 10s; 48°53'·25N 01°42'·34W.
Le Pignon Fl (2) WR 6s 10m, W9M, R6M; 005°-R-150°-W-005°; B twr, W band; 48°53'·49N 01°43'·36 W.
La Haute Foraine 48°52'·89N 01°43'·66W.
Grande Île ☆ Fl 5s 39m **23M**; Gy □ twr, G top; *Horn 30s;* 48°52'·17N 01°49'·34W.
Channel Fl G 2s; 48°52'·07N 01°49'·08W.
La Crabière Est Dir Oc(3)WRG 12s 5m, W9M, R/G6M;079°-W-291°-G-329°-W-335°-R-079°; B beacon, Y top; 48°52'·46N 01°49'·39W.
La Cancalaise 48°51'·90N 01°51'·11W.

GRANVILLE
Le Videcoq VQ (9) 10s; 48°49'·66N 01°42'·06W.
La Fourchie 48°50'·15N 01°37'·00W.
Pointe du Roc ☆ Fl (4) 15s 49m **23M;** 48°50'·06N 01°36'·78W.
Le Loup Fl (2) 6s 8m 11M; 48°49'·57N 01°36'·24W.
Avant Port, E jetty Fl G 2·5s 11m 4M; 48°49'·93N 01°36'·19W.
W jetty Fl R 2·5s 12m 4M; 48°49'·86N 01°36'·23W.

Marina S bkwtr Fl (2) R 6s 12m 5M; W post, R top; *Horn (2) 40s;* 48°49'·89N 01°35'·90W.
N bkwtr Fl (2) G 6s 4m 5M; 48°49'·93N 01°35'·90W.
Sill, W side, QR 2M, E side QG 2M; Gy pylons topped R (W) and G (E).

CANCALE
La Fille 48°44'·16N 01°48'·46W.
Pierre-de-Herpin ☆ Oc (2) 6s 20m 13M; W twr, B top and base; 48°43'·77N 01°48'·92W.
Ruet *Bell;* 48°43'·44N 01°50'·11W.
Grande Bunouze 48°43'·17N 01°50'·95W.
Barbe Brûlée 48°42'·11N 01°50'·57W.
Jetty hd Oc (3) G 12s 9m 3M; W pylon B top; 48°40'·10N 01°51'·11W.

ST MALO AND RIVER RANCE

CHENAL DE LA BIGNE
Basse Rochefort (aka Basse aux Chiens) 48°42'·69N 01°57'·31W.
La Petite Bigne 48°41'·66N 01°58'·72W.
La Crolante ; 48°41'·01N 01°59'·51W, off Pte de la Varde.
Les Létruns ; *Bell;* 48°40'·71N 02°00'·61W.
Roches-aux-Anglais Fl G 4s; 48°39'·65N 02°02'·27W.
Les Crapauds-du-Bey Fl R 4s; 48°39'·37N 02°02'·57W.

CHENAL DES PETITS POINTUS
Dinard ch spire (74m) brg 203° to right of Le Petit Bé rocks.
La Saint-Servantine Fl G 2·5s; *Bell;* 48°41'·93N 02°00'·94W.
Les Petits Pontus 48°41'·30N 02°00'·86W.

CHENAL DE LA GRANDE CONCHÉE
Villa Brisemoulin 181·5°, on with LH edge of Le Petit Bé rocks.
La Plate Q WRG 11m, W10M, R/G7M; 140°-W-203°-R-210°-W-225°-G-140°; 48°40'·78N 02°01'·91W.
Le Bouton 48°40'·59N 02°01'·85W.

CHENAL DU BUNEL
St Énogat ldg lts 158·2°; both Iso 4s 3/85m 7/10M, sync. Front 48°38'·29N 02°04'·11W, vis 126°-236°. Rear, on white water twr, Dinard, vis 143°-210°; 48°36'·97N 02°03'·31W.
Bunel Q (9) 15s; 48°40'·84N 02°05'·38W.

CHENAL DE LA PETITE PORTE
Outer ldg lts 129·7°: **Front, Le Grand Jardin** ☆ Fl (2) R 10s 24m **15M,** 48°40'·20N 02°04'·97W. Rear, **La Balue** ☆ FG 20m **22M**; 3·1M from front; intens 128°-129·5°; Gy □ twr; 48°38'·16N 02°01'·30W.
Vieux-Banc E Q; 48°42'·38N 02°09'·12W.
Vieux-Banc W VQ (9) 10s; 48°41'·84N 02°10'·20W.
St Malo Atterrisage (Fairway) Iso 4s; 48°41'·39N 02°07'·28W.
Les Courtis Fl G 4s 14m 7M; 48°40'·46N 02°05'·80W.
Nearing Le Grand Jardin, move stbd briefly onto Ch du Bunel 152·8° ldg lts to pick up: Inner ldg lts 128·6°, both Dir FG 20/69m **22/25M**; H24. Front, **Les Bas Sablons** ☆, intens 127·2°-130·2°; W □ twr, B top; 48°38'·16N 02°01'·30W. Rear, **La Balue** ☆, 0·9M from front; intens 128°-129·5°; Gy □ twr; 48°37'·60N 02°00'·24W.
Basse du Nord No 5 48°39'·98N 02°05'·04W.
Les Pierres-Garnier No 8 48°39'·98N 02°04'·41W.

Les Patouillets Fl (3) G 12s, 48°39'·68N 02°04'·30W.
Clef d'Aval No 10 48°39'·72N 02°03'·91W.
Basse du Buron No 12 Fl (4) R 15s, 48°39'·42N 02°03'·51W.
Le Buron Fl (4) G 15s 15m 7M; G twr, 48°39'·32N 02°03'·66W.
Les Grelots VQ (6) + L Fl 10s, 48°39'·16N 02°03'·03W.

CHENAL DE LA GRANDE PORTE
Banchenou VQ, 48°40'·44N 02°11'·48W.
Outer ldg lts 089·1°: **Front, Le Grand Jardin** ☆ Fl (2) R 10s 24m **15M,** 48°40'·20N 02°04'·97W.
Rear, **Rochebonne** ☆ Dir FR 40m **24M**; intens 088·2°-089·7°; Gy □ twr, R top, 4·2M from front; 48°40'·26N 01°58'·71W. .
Buharats W No 2 Fl R 2·5s, 48°40'·22N 02°07'·50W.
Buharats E No 4 *Bell;* 48°40'·24N 02°07'·20W.
Bas du Boujaron No 1 Fl (2) G 6s, 48°40'·17N 02°05'·97W.
Le Sou VQ (3) 5s; 48°40'·11N 02°05'·30W.
Continue on inner 128·6° ldg line: see Chenal de la Petite Porte.

RADE DE ST MALO
Plateau Rance Nord VQ, 48°38'·64N 02°02'·35W.
Plateau Rance Sud Q (6) + L Fl 15s, 48°38'·43N 02°02'·28W.
Crapaud de la Cité QG, 48°38'·34N 02°02'·01W.

ST MALO
Môle des Noires hd ☆ VQ R 11m 6M; W twr, R top; *Horn (2) 20s*; 48°38'·52N 02°01'·91W.
Écluse du Naye ldg lts 070·4°, both FR 7/23m 3/7M. Front, 48°38'·58N 02°01'·48W. Rear, 030°-120°.
Ferry jetty hd, ☆ VQ G 6M; 48°38'·44N 02°01'·82W (128·6° ldg line). Ferry jetty, ☆ Fl R 4s 3m 1M; 260°-080°; 48°38'·44N 02°01'·76W.
Bas-Sablons marina, mole head ☆ Fl G 4s 7m 5M; Gy mast; 48°38'·42N 02°01'·70W.

LA RANCE BARRAGE
La Jument Fl G 4s 6m 4M; G twr, 48°37'·44N 02°01'·76W.
ZI 12 Fl R 4s, 48°37'·47N 02°01'·62W.
NE dolphin ☆ Fl (2) R 6s 6m 5M; 040°-200°, 48°37'·09N 02°01'·71W.
Barrage lock, NW wall ☆ Fl (2) G 6s 6m 5M,191°-291°; G pylon, 48°37'·06N 02°01'·73W.
Barrage lock, SW wall, ☆ Fl (3) G 12s, 48°37'·00N 02°01'·70W.
SE dolphin ☆ Fl (3) R 12s, 48°36'·97N 02°01'·66W.
ZI 24 Fl (2) R 6s, 48°36'·63N 02°01'·33W.

ST MALO TO ST QUAY-PORTRIEUX

ST BRIAC
R. Frémur mouth. Dir lt 125° Iso WRG 4s 10m 12M; 121·5°-G-124·5°-W-125·5°-R-129·5°; W mast on hut, 48°37'·07N 02°08'·20W.

ST CAST
Les Bourdinots 48°39'·01N 02°13'·48W.
St Cast môle ☆ Iso WG 4s 12m, W9M, G6M; 180°-G-206°-W-217°-G-235°-W-245°-G-340°; G&W structure; 48°38'·41N 02°14'·61W.

Laplace, 48°39'·73N 2°16'·45W; 5ca SE of Pte de la Latte.
Cap Fréhel ☆ Fl (2) 10s 85m **29M**; Gy □ twr, G lantern; 48°41'·05N 02°19'·13W. Reserve lt range **15M**.

CHENAL and PORT D'ERQUY
Les Justières Q (6) + L Fl 15s; 48°40'·56N 02°26'·48W.
Basses du Courant VQ (6) + L Fl 10s; 48°39'·21N 02°29'·16W.
L'Evette 48°38'·51N 02°31'·45W.
S môle ☆ Fl (2) WRG 6s 11m W10M, R/G7M; 055°-R-081°-W-094°-G-111°-W-120°-R-134°; W twr; 48°38'·06N 02°28'·68W.
Inner jetty ☆ Fl (3) R 12s 10m 3M; R/W twr; 48°38'·09N 02°28'·39W.

DAHOUET
Petit Bignon 48°36'·82N 02°35'·06W.
Le Dahouet 48°35'·15N 02°35'·43W.
La Petite Muette Fl WRG 4s 10m W9M, R/G6M; 055°-G-114°-W-146°-R-196°; W twr, G band; 48°34'·82N 02°34'·30W.
Entry chan, Fl (2) G 6s 5m 1M; 156°-286°; 48°34'·71N 02°34'·19W.

BAIE DE ST BRIEUC
Grand Léjon ☆ Fl (3) WR 12s 17m W11M, R10M; 015°-R-058°-W-190°-R-253°-W-283°-R-350°-W-015°; R truncated conical twr, W bands; 48°44'·91N 02°39'·88W.
Les Landas Q, 48°41'·43N 02°31'·29W.
Le Rohein Q (9) WRG 15s 13m, W8M, R/G5M; 072°-R-105°-W-180°-G-193°-W-237°-G-282°-W-301°-G-330°-W-072°; Y twr, B band; 48°38'·80N 02°37'·77W.

SAINT-BRIEUC LE LÉGUÉ
Tra-Hillion 48°33'·38N 02°38'·50W.
Le Légué Mo (A)10s; 48°34'·32N 02°41'·15W.
No 1 Fl G 2·5s; 48°32'·42N 02°42'·51W.
No 2 Fl R 2·5s; 48°32'·37N 02°42'·40W.
No 3 Fl (2) G 6s; 48°32'·27N 02°42'·78W.
No 4 Fl (2) R 6s; 48°32'·23N 02°42'·70W.
No 5 Fl (3) G 12s; 48°32'·18N 02°42'·92W.
No 6 Fl (3) R 12s; 48°32'·14N 02°42'·90W.
NE jetty ☆ VQ R 4M; 48°32'·12N 02°42'·88W.
Pte à l'Aigle jetty ☆ VQ G 13m 8M; 160°-070°; W twr, G top; 48°32'·12N 02°43'·11W.
No 7 Fl (4) G 15s; 48°32'·11N 02°43'·08W.
No 8 Fl R 2·5s; 48°32'·01N 02°43'·16W.
No 9 Fl (2) G 6s; 48°31'·96N 02°43'·29W.
No 10 Fl (2) R 6s; 48°31'·91N 02°43'·31W.
Jetty☆ Iso G 4s 6m 2M; W cols, G top; 48°31'·90N 02°43'·43W.
No 11 Fl (3) G 12s; 48°31'·90N 02°43'·43W.
No 13 Fl (4) G 15s; 48°31'·76N 02°43'·56W.
No 14 Fl (4) R 15s; 48°31'·70N 02°43'·61W.

BINIC
N Môle hd ☆ Fl (4) G 15s12m 6M; unintens 020°-110°; W twr, G lantern; 48°36'·07N 02°48'·92W.

ST QUAY-PORTRIEUX
Les Hors 48°39'·60N 02°44'·04W.
Caffa Q (3) 10s; 48°37'·82N 02°43'·08W.
La Longue 48°37'·88N 02°44'·68W.

La Roselière VQ (6) + L Fl 10s; 48°37′·31N 02°46′·19W.
Herflux Dir ☆ 130°, Fl (2) WRG 6s 10m, W 8M, R/G 5M; 115°-G-125°-W-135°-R-145°; 48°39′·07N 02°47′·95W.
Île Harbour (Roches de Saint-Quay) ☆ Fl WRG 4s 16m, W9M, R/G 6M; 011°-R-133°-G-270°-R-306°-G-358°-W-011°; W twr and dwelling, R top; 48°39′·99N 02°48′·49W.
Madeux 48°40′·41N 02°48′·81W.
Grandes Moulières de St Quay 48°39′·76N 02°49′·91W.
Moulières de Portrieux 48°39′·26N 02°49′·21W.
Les Noirs 48°39′·09N 02°48·46W.
Marina, **NE mole elbow**, Dir lt 318·2°: Iso WRG 4s 16m **W15M**, R/G11M; W159°-179°, G179°-316°, W316°-320·5°, R320·5° -159°; Reserve lt ranges 11/8M; 48°38′·99N 02°49′·09W.
NE môle hd ☆ Fl (3) G 12s 10m 2M; 48°38′·84N 02°48′·91W.
S môle hd ☆ Fl (3) R 12s 10m 2M; 48°38′·83N 02°49′·03W.
Old hbr ent: N side, Fl G 2.5s 11m 2M; 48°38′·71N 02°49′·36W.
S side, Fl R 2.5s 8m 2M; 48°38′·67N 02°49′·35W.

MID-CHANNEL MARK

Channel L Fl 10s, 10M, RW vert stripes, R topmark, **Racon O,10M;** 49°54′·45N 02°53′·74W; 992351028 .

COTENTIN PENINSULA (NW COAST)

La Plate Fl (2+1) WR 10s 11m; W9M, R6M; 115°-W-272°-R-115°; Y 8-sided twr, with B top; 49°43′·98N 01°55′·76W.
Cap de la Hague (Gros du Raz) ☆ Fl 5s 48m **23M**; Gy twr, W top; *Horn 30s;* 49°43′·31N 01° 57′·27W.
La Foraine VQ (9) 10s 12m 6M; 49°42′·90 N 01°58′·32W.
Cap de Carteret ☆ Fl (2+1) 15s 81m **26M**; Gy twr, G top; 49°22′·41N 01°48′·41W.

THE CASQUETS AND ALDERNEY

Casquets ☆ Fl (5) 30s 37m **18M**, H24; W twr, 2 R bands; NW'most of three; ***Racon T, 25M***; 49°43′·32N 02°22′·63W. 992351121.
Ortac rock, unlit; 49°43′·40N 02°17′·44W.
Pierre au Vraic, unmarked rk 1·2m; 49°41′·61N 02°16′·94W.
Quenard Pt (Alderney) ☆ Fl (4) 15s 37m 12M; 085°-027°; W ○ twr, B band; 49°43′·75N 02°09′·86W.
Château à L'Étoc Pt ☆ Iso WR 4s 20m W10M, R7M; 071·1°-R- 111·1°-W-151·1°; 49°43′·94N 02°10′·63W.

BRAYE

Ldg bns 142° (to clear the submerged Adm'ty bkwtr). Front, W, 49°43′·90N 02°10′·97W. Rear, BW; 720m from front.
Ldg lts 215°: both Q 8/17m 9/12M, synch; 210°-220°; orange △s. Front, old pier elbow, 49°43′·40N 02°11′·91W. Rear, 215°/335m.
Admiralty bkwtr head ☆ L Fl 10s 7m 5M; 49°43′·82N 02°11′·67W.
Fairway No 1 QG; 49°43′·72N 02°11′·72W.
No 2 QR; 49°43′·60N 02°11′·75W.
Inner fairway Q (2) G 5s; 49°43′·58N 02°11′·98W.
Braye quay ☆ 2 FR (vert) 8m 5M; 49°43′·53N 02°12′·00W.
Little Crabby hbr ent ☆ FG & FR 5m 2M; 49°43′·45N 02°12′·12W.

GUERNSEY, NORTHERN APPROACHES

LITTLE RUSSEL CHANNEL

Grande Amfroque, two unlit bcn twrs: larger, BW-banded; smaller, white; 49°30′·57N 02°24′·62W.
Tautenay ☆ Q (3) WR 6s 7m W7M, R6M; 050°-W-215°-R-050°; B & W striped bcn 49°30′·11N 02°26′·84W.
Platte Fougère ☆ Fl WR 10s 15m **16M**; 155°-W-085°-R-155°; W 8-sided twr, B band. *Horn 45s* **TD 2021**; 49°30′·83N 02°29′·14W.
Corbette d'Amont Y bcn twr, topmark; 49°29′·64N 02°29′·38W.
Roustel ☆ Q 8m 7M; BW chequered base, W framework col; 49°29′·23N 02°28′·79W.
Rousse, Y bcn twr, topmark; 49°28′·98N 02°28′·36W.
Platte ☆, Fl WR 3s 6m, W7M, R5M; 024°-R-219°-W-024°; G conical twr; 49°29′·08N 02°29′·57W.
Vivian bcn twr, BW bands, 49°28′·45N 02°30′·66W.
Brehon ☆ Iso 4s 19m 9M; bcn on ○ twr, 49°28′·28N 02°29′·28W.
Demie Flieroque, Y bcn twr, topmark F; 49°28′·13N 02°31′·38W.

BIG RUSSEL

Noire Pute ☆ Fl (2) WR 15s 8m 6M; 220°-W-040°-R-220°; on 2m high rock; 49°28′·21N 02°25′·02W; unreliable.
Fourquies Q; 49°27′·34N 02°26′·47W.
Lower Heads Q (6) + L Fl 15s; *Bell;* 49°25′·85N 02°28′·55W.

GUERNSEY, HERM AND SARK

BEAUCETTE MARINA

Petite Canupe Q (6) + L Fl 15s; 49°30′·20N 02°29′·14W.
Ldg lts 277°: Both FR. Front, W □, R stripe; 49°30′·19N 02°30′·23W. Rear, R □, W stripe; 185m from front.
Appr chan buoys: SWM L Fl 10s 49°30′·15N 02°29′·66W. SHM Fl G 5s, PHM Fl R 5s & Fl (3) R 5s. NCM perch Q 49°30′·165N 02°30′·06W. SHM perch Q (3) G 5s at ent; 49°30′·18N 02°30′·24W.

ST SAMPSON

Ldg lts 286°: Front, FR 3m 5M; 230°-340°; tfc sigs; 49°28′·90N 02°30′·74W. Rear, FG 13m; clock twr, 390m from front.
N Pier ☆ FG 3m 5M; 230°-340°; 49°28′·92N 02°30′·71W.
Crocq pier ☆ FR 11m 5M; 250°-340°; 49°28′·98N 02°31′·00W.

ST PETER PORT

Outer ldg lts 220°: **Front**, Castle bkwtr, Al WR 10s 14m **16M**; 187°-007°; dark ○ twr, W on NE side; *Horn 15s;* 49°27′·31N 02°31′·45W.
Rear 220° ldg lt, Belvedere, Oc 10s 61m 14M; 179°-269°; intens 217°-223°; W □ on W twr; 980m from front. The lts are synchronised so that the rear lt is on when the front is W, and the off when the front is R.
Queen Elizabeth II marina, 270° Dir Oc ☆ WRG 3s 5m 6M; 258°-G-268°-W-272°-R-282°; 49°27′·73N 02°31′·87W.
Reffée Q (6) + L Fl 15s; 49°27′·74N 02°31′·27W.
Appr buoys: outer pair QG; 49°27′·83N 02°31′·54W. QR; 49°27′·71N 02°31′·52W. Inner pair: QG; 49°27′·76N 02°31′·74W. QR; 49°27′·72N 02°31′·74W.
The Pool ldg lts 265° (*not* into moorings): Front, Victoria marina, S Pier, ☆ Oc R 5s 10m 14M; 49°27′·32N 02°32′·03W.

Rear, ☆ Iso R 2s 22m 3M; 260°-270°; on Creasey's bldg, 160m from front.
White Rock pier ☆ Oc G 5s 11m 14M; intens 174°-354°; ○ twr; tfc sigs; 49°27'·38N 02°31'·59W.
S Fairway ▲ QG; 49°27'·30N 02°31'·76W; N of fuel pontoon W of buoy 3 x Fl R; 49°27'·28N 02°31'·74W. 49°27'·27N 02°31'·80W. 49°27'·27N 02°31'·86W.

HAVELET BAY
Oyster Rock Y bcn, topmark 'O'; 49°27'·09N 02°31'·46W.
Oyster Rock ▲ QG; 49°27'·04N 02°31'·47W.
Moulinet QR; 49°26'·97N 02°31'·54W.
Moulinet Y bcn, topmark 'M'; 49°26'·95N 02°31'·58W.

GUERNSEY, SOUTH-EAST and SOUTH COASTS
Anfré, Y bcn, topmark 'A'; 49°26'·45N 02°31'·48W.
Longue Pierre, Y bcn, topmark 'LP'; 49°25'·36N 02°31'·48W.
St Martin's Pt ☆ Fl (3) WR 10s 15m 14M; 185°-R-191°-W-011°-R-061·5°; flat-topped, W bldg. *Horn (3) 30s;* 49°25'·30N 02°31'·70W.

GUERNSEY, NORTH-WEST COAST
Les Hanois ☆ Fl (2) 13s 33m **20M**; 294°-237°; Gy ○ twr, B lantern, helicopter platform; *Horn (2) 60s;* 49°26'·10N 02°42'·15W.
4 FR on mast 1·3M ESE of Les Hanois lt ho.
Portelet Hbr, bkwtr bcn, 49°26'·16N 02°39'·84W.
Cobo Bay, Grosse Rock, B bcn 11m; 49°29'·02N 02°36'·19W.
Grand Havre, Rousse Point bkwtr, B bcn; 49°29'·92N 02°33'·05W.

HERM
Corbette de la Mare, Wh disc (W side) and R disc (E side) on Y pole, 49°28'·48N 02°28'·72W.
Petit Creux ☆ QR; red 'C' on red pole; 49°28'·09N 02°28'·72W.
Alligande ☆ Fl (3) G 5s; B pole, Or 'A'; 49°27'·86N 02°28'·78W.
Épec ☆ Fl G 3s; black 'E' on G mast; 49°27'·98N 02°27'·89W.
Vermerette ☆ Fl (2) Y 5s; Or 'V' on bcn; 49°28'·12N 02°27'·75W.
Gate Rock (Percée Pass) Q (9) 15s; 49°27'·88N 02°27'·54W.
Hbr ldg lts 078°: White drums. ☆ 2F occas; 49°28'·25N 02°27'·11W.
Hbr pier, N end ☆ 2 FG; G □ on G bcn; 49°28'·21N 02°27'·26W.

SARK
Courbée du Nez ☆ Fl (4) WR 15s 14m 8M; 057°-W-230°-R-057°; W structure on rock; 49°27'·09N 02°22'·17W.
Noir Pierre , Y bcn, topmark radar refl, 49°26'·67N 02°20'·92W. **Point Robert** ☆ Fl 15s 65m **18M**; vis 138°-353°; W 8-sided twr; *Horn (1) 30s;* 49°26'·19N 02°20'·75W.
Founiais , topmark 'F'; 49°26'·02N 02°20'·36W.
Blanchard Q (3) 10s; *Bell;* 49°25'·36N 02°17'·42W.
Pilcher monument (070° appr brg); 49°25'·71N 02°22'·44W.

JERSEY, WEST AND SOUTH COASTS

Desormes Q (9) 15s; 49°18'·94N 02°17'·98W.
Grosnez Point ☆ Fl (2) WR 15s 50m10M; 081°-W-188°-R-241°; W hut; 49°15'·50N 02°14'·80W.
La Rocco twr (conspic) 15m; 49°11'·90N 02°14'·05W.
La Frouquie (seasonal); 49°11'·30N 02°15'·38W.
La Corbière ☆ Iso WR 10s 36m **W18M**, R14M; shore-W-294°-R-328°-W-148°-R-shore; W ○ twr; *Horn Mo (C) 60s;* 49°10'·79N 02°15'·01W.
Pt Corbière ☆ FR; R □, W stripe; 49°10'·87N 02°14'·38W.

WESTERN PASSAGE
Ldg lts 082°. Front, La Gréve d'Azette Oc 5s 23m 14M; 034°-129°; 49°10'·16N 02°05'·09W. Rear, Mont Ubé, Oc R 5s 46m 12M; 250°-095°; 1M from front.
Passage Rock VQ; 49°09'·54N 02°12'·26W.
Les Fours Q; 49°09'·59N 02°10'·16W.
Noirmont Pt ☆ Fl (4) 12s 18m 10M; B twr, W band; 49°09'·91N 02°10'·08W.
Pignonet 49°09'·88N 02°09'·70W.
Ruaudière Rock ▲ Fl G 3s; *Bell;* 49°09'·74N 02°08'·62W.

ST AUBIN'S BAY and HARBOUR
Les Grunes du Port 49°10'·02N 02°09'·14W.
Diamond Rock Fl (2) R 6s; 49°10'·12N 02°08'·64W.
Castle pier ☆ Fl R 4s 8m 1M; 49°11'·13N 02°09'·634W.
North pier, Dir lt 254° ☆ F WRG 5m, 248°-G-253°-W-255°-R-260°; 49°11'·22N 02°10'·03W. Same col, Iso R 4s 12m 10M.
Beach Rock 49°11'·29N 02°08'·42W, (Apr-Oct).
Rocquemin 49°10'·64N 02°07'·95W.
Baleine ▲ 49°10'·41N 02°08'·23W.

ST HELIER
Elizabeth marina, west appr: Dir ☆ 106°: F WRG 4m 1M; 096°-G-104°-W-108°-R-119°; R dayglo □, B stripe; 49°10'·76N 02°07'·12W.
La Vrachiére 49°10'·90N 02°07'·59W, Fl (2) 5s 1M.
Fort Charles North 49°10'·81N 02°07'·50W.
Marina ent ☆ Oc G & Oc R, both 4s 2M; 49°10'·83N 02°07'·13W.
Red & Green Passage, ldg lts 022° on dayglo R dolphins: Front, Elizabeth E berth Dn ☆ Oc G 5s 10m 11M; 49°10'·63N 02°06'·94W. Rear, Albert Pier root ☆ Oc R 5s 18m 12M; synch; 230m SSW.
East Rock ▲ QG; 49°09'·96N 02°07'·28W.
Dog's Nest Rk Fl Y 3s 3M; Y cross on bcn; 49°09'·99N 02°06'·95W.
Oyster Rocks, R/W bcn, topmark 'O'; 49°10'·10N 02°07'·49W.
Platte Rock Fl R 1·5s 6m 5M; R col; 49°10'·16N 02°07'·34W.
Small Road No 2 QR; 49°10'·39N 02°07'·24W.
No 4 QR; 49°10'·53N 02°07'·12W.
Elizabeth marina, S appr: E1 ▲ Fl G 3s; 49°10'·59N 02°07'·09W.
E2 Fl R 2s; 49°10'·58N 02°07'·13W.
E5 ▲ Fl G 5s; 49°10'·70N 02°07'·17W.
E6 Fl R 2s; 49°10'·69N 02°07'·21W.
Fort Charles East Q (3) 5s 2m 1M; 49°10'·74N 02°07'·26W.
La Collette basin QR; 49°10'·54N 02°06'·91W. 49°10'·52N 02°06'·90W.
St Helier Hbr, ldg lts 078°, both FG on W cols. Front, 49°10'·62N 02°06'·66W. Rear, 80m from front.

Victoria pier hd, Port control twr; IPTS; 49°10′·57N 02°06′·88W.

JERSEY, SOUTH-EAST AND EAST COASTS

Hinguette QR; 49°09′·33N 02°07′·32W.
Hettich Fl Y 5s; 49°08′·10N 02°09′·00W.
South Pier Marine Fl Y 5s; 49°09′·10N 02°06′·30W.
Demie de Pas Mo (D) WR 12s 11m, WR 8M; 130°-R-303°-W-130°; *Horn (3) 60s*; ***Racon T, 10M***; B bn twr, Y top; 49°09′·01N 02°06′·15W. Icho Tower (conspic, 14m) 49°08′·89N 02°02′·90W.
Canger Rock Q (9) 15s; 49°07′·35N 02°00′·38W.
La Conchière Q (6) + L Fl 15s 2M; 49°08′·22N 02°00′·17W.
Frouquier Aubert Q (6) + L Fl 15s; 49°06′·08N 01°58′·84W.
Violet L Fl 10s; 49°07′·81N 01°57′·14W.
Petite Anquette; SCM; 49°08′·47N 01°56′·29W.
Grande Anquette VQ(9) 10s; 49°08′·32N 01°55′·20W.
Le Cochon 49°09′·77N 01°58′·80W.
La Noire 49°10′·13N 01°59′·23W.
Le Giffard Fl R 3s 49°10′·59N 01°58′·99W.

GOREY

Pier Hd ☆ Occ WRG 5s 8m 8M; 228°-G-296·5°-W-299·5°-R-299·5°-008°; W twr on pierhead; 49°11′·81N 02°01′·33W.
Horn Rock, topmark 'H'; 49°10′·96N 01°59′·85W.
Les Burons, R bcn, topmark 'B'; 49°11′·33N 02°00′·81W.
Fairway QG; 49°11′·50N 02°00′·34W.
Écureuil Rock 49°11′·67N 02°00′·78W.
Equerrière Rk, bcn 'fishtail' topmark; 49°11′·80N 02°00′·67W.
Les Arch, BW bcn, 'A' topmark; 49°12′·02N 02°00′·60W.

ST CATHERINE BAY

St Catherine Bay, Le Fara Q (3) 10s 3M; 49°12′·85N 02°00′·48W.
Archirondel Twr (conspic, 16m) 49°12′·72N 02°01′·42W.
Verclut bkwtr ☆ Fl 1·5s 18m 13M; 49°13′·34N 02°00′·64W,in line 315° with unlit turret, La Coupe Pt, 49°13′·96N 02°01′·57W,

JERSEY, NORTH COAST

Rozel Bay Dir lt 245°, F WRG 11m 5M; 240°-G-244°-W-246°-R-250°; W col; 49°14′·21N 02°02′·76W.
Bonne Nuit Bay ldg lts 223°: both FG 7/34m 6M. Front, Pier 49°15′·10N 02°07′·17W. Rear, 170m from front.
Demie Rock 49°15′·56N 02°07′·36W.
Sorel Point ☆ L Fl WR 7·5s 50m **15M**; 095°-W-112°-R-173°-W-230°-R-269°-W-273°; W ○ twr, only 3m high; 49°15'·60N 02°09'·54W.

OFFLYING ISLANDS

LES ÉCREHOU

Écrevière Q (6) + L Fl 15s; 49°15′·26N 01°52′·15W.
Maître Ile 49°17′·08N 01°55′·60W.

PLATEAU DES MINQUIERS

N Minquiers Q; 49°01′·64N 02°00′·58W.
NE Minquiers VQ (3) 5s; *Bell;* 49°00′·85N 01°55′·30W.
SE Minquiers Q (3) 10s; *Bell;* 48°53′·42N 02°00′·09W.
S Minquiers Q (6) + L Fl 15s; 48°53′·09N 02°10′·10W.
SW Minquiers Q (9) 15s 5M; *Bell;* 48°54′·34N 02°19′·38W.
NW Minquiers Q 5M; *Whis;* 48°59′·63N 02°20′·59W.
Refuge; B/W bcn; 49°00′·13N 02°10′·16W.
Demie de Vascelin Fl G 3s, 49°00′·81N 02°05′·17W.
Grand Vascelin, BW bcn 48°59′·97N 02°07′·26W.
Maitresse Ile, Puffin B&W bcn twr 48°58′·33N 02°03′·65W.
Le Coq Reef, Q (3) 10s 6m 3M; 48°57′·88N 02°01′·29W.

FRENCH MARKS NORTH OF ILE DE BRÉHAT

Roches Douvres ☆ Fl 5s 60m **24M**; pink twr on dwelling with G roof; 49°06′·30N 02°48′·87W. (16M NNE of Ile de Bréhat).
Barnouic VQ (3) 5s 15m 7M; 49°01′·64N 02°48′·41W.
Roche Gautier VQ (9) 10s; 49°02′·013N 02°54′·36W.
Les Héaux de Bréhat ☆ Fl (4) WRG 15s 48m, **W15M**, R/G11M; 227°-R-247°-W-270°-G-302°-W-227°; Gy twr; 48°54'·50N 03°05'·18W (4·7M WNW of Ile de Bréhat).

1	Cherbourg	**1**																
2	Omonville	10	**2**															
3	Braye (Alderney)	25	15	**3**														
4	St Peter Port	44	34	23	**4**													
5	Creux (Sark)	37	29	22	10	**5**												
6	St Helier	64	51	46	29	24	**6**											
7	Carteret	41	29	28	31	23	26	**7**										
8	Portbail	49	33	32	35	27	25	5	**8**									
9	Iles Chausey	69	61	58	48	43	25	33	30	**9**								
10	Granville	75	67	66	55	50	30	38	35	9	**10**							
11	Dinan	102	91	85	66	64	50	62	59	29	35	**11**						
12	St Malo	90	79	73	54	52	38	50	47	17	23	12	**12**					
13	Dahouet	88	80	72	54	52	41	60	59	37	45	41	29	**13**				
14	Le Légué/St Brieuc	96	86	76	57	56	46	69	69	41	49	45	33	8	**14**			
15	Binic	95	84	75	56	55	46	70	70	43	51	45	33	10	8	**15**		
16	St Quay-Portrieux	88	80	73	56	51	46	64	64	47	54	47	35	11	7	4	**16**	
17	Lézardrieux	88	80	68	48	38	47	68	71	53	54	61	49	33	32	30	21	**17**

DISTANCE TABLES

Approx distances in nautical miles are by the most direct route allowing for dangers and TSS.

AREA 16 *N & S Brittany – Paimpol to Le Guilvinec*

SELECTED LIGHTS, BUOYS & WAYPOINTS

OFFSHORE MARKS

Roches Douvres ☆ Fl 5s 60m **24M**; pink twr on dwelling with G roof; 49°06'·30N 02°48'·87W.
Barnouic VQ (3) 5s 15m 7M; 49°01'·63N 02°48'·41W.
Roche Gautier VQ (9) 10s; 49°02'·00N 02°54'·73W.

PAIMPOL TO ÎLE DE BRÉHAT

PAIMPOL

Les Calemarguiers 48°46'·98N 02°54'·84W.
L'Ost Pic ☆ Fl(4)WR 15s 20m, W9M, R6M; 105°-W-116°-R-221°-W-253°-R-291°-W-329°; obsc by islets near Bréhat when brg < 162°; W twr/turret, R top; 48°46'·77N 02°56'·42W.
Les Charpentiers 48°47'·89N 02°56'·01W.
Pte de Porz-Don ☆ Oc (2) WR 6s 13m **W15M**, R11M; 269°-W-272°-R-279°; W house; 48°47'·48N 03°01'·55W.
El Bras Fl G 2·5s; 48°47'·21N 03°01'·50W.
Fl R 2·5s; 48°47'·17N 03°01'·49W.
Ldg lts 262·2°, both QR 5/12m 7/10M. Front, Kernoa jetty; W & R hut; 48°47'·09N 03°02'·44W. Rear, Dir QR, intens 260·2°-264·2°; W pylon, R top; 360m from front. ☆ QG 48°47'·12N 03°02'·47W.

CHENAL DU FERLAS (277°-257°-271°)

Lel Ar Serive 48°49'·98N 02°58'·76W.
Loguivy Dir lt 257°: Q WRG 12m 10/8M; 254°-G-257°-W-257·7°-R-260·7°; Gy twr; 48°49'·37N 03°03'·67W.
Les Piliers 48°49'·77N 02°59'·99W.
Kermouster Dir ☆ 271°: Fl WRG 2s 16m, W 10M, R/G 8M; 267°-G-270°-W-272°- R-274°; W col; 48°49'·55N 03°05'·19W (R. Trieux).

ÎLE DE BRÉHAT

Le Paon ☆ Oc WRG 4s 22m W10M, R/G6M; 033°-W-078°-G-181°-W-196°- R-307°-W-316°-R-348°; Y twr; 48°51'·92N 02°59'·15W.
Roche Guarine 48°51'·63N 02°57'·63W, Chenal de Bréhat.
Rosédo ☆ Fl 5s 29m **20M**; W twr; vis 006°-340° (334°); 48°51'·45N 03°00'·29W.
La Chambre 48°50'·16N 02°59'·58W.
Men-Joliguet Fl (2) WRG 6s 6m W11M, R/G8M; 255°-R-279°-W-283°-G-175°; 48°50'·12N 03°00'·20W.

LÉZARDRIEUX TO TRÉGUIER

LE TRIEUX RIVER to LÉZARDRIEUX

Nord Horaine VQ, 7M; 48°54'·53N 02°55'·42W.
La Horaine Fl (3) 12s 13m 7M; Gy 8-sided twr on B hut; 48°53'·50N 02°55'·22W.
Men-Marc'h 48°53'·17N 02°51'·82W.
Ldg lts 224·8°: Front, **La Croix** ☆ Q 15m **18M**; intens 215°-235°; two Gy ○ twrs joined, W on NE side, R tops; 48°50'·23N 03°03'·25W. Rear **Bodic** ☆ Dir Q 55m **22M**; intens 221°-229°; W ho with G gable; 2·1M from front.
Les Sirlots *Whis;* 48°52'·95N 02°59'·58W.
Coatmer ldg lts 218·7°. Front, Q RG 16m R/G7M; 200°-R-250°-G-053°; W gable; 48°48'·26N 03°05'·75W. Rear, QR 50m 7M; vis 197°-242°; W gable; 660m from front.
Les Perdrix Fl (2) WG 6s 5m, W6M, G3M; 165°-G-197°-W-202·5°-G-040°; G twr; 48°47'·74N 03°05'·79W.

CHENAL DE LA MOISIE (339·4°); PASSE DE LA GAINE (241·5°)

La Vieille du Tréou 48°52'·00N 03°01'·09W.
An Ogejou Bihan 48°53'·37N 03°01'·91W.
La Moisie 48°53'·83N 03°02'·22W.
Les Héaux de Bréhat ☆ Fl (4) WRG 15s 48m, **W15M**, R/G11M; 227°-R-247°-W-270°-G-302°-W-227°; Gy ○ twr; 48°54'·50N 03°05'·17W.
Basse des Héaux 48°54'·07N 03°05'·28W.
Pont de la Gaine 48°53'·12N 03°07'·40W.

JAUDY RIVER TO TRÉGUIER

La Jument des Héaux VQ 7m 4M; 48°55'·42N 03°08'·04W.
Grande Passe, Port de la Chaine, Dir Oc WRG 12m W12M R/G11M; 131°·8G136°·8 W137°·8 R142°·8. Red and white house, 48°51'·55N 03° 07'·88W.(Mark is hard to see by day).
Basse Crublent QR; 3m 2M; *Whis;* 48°54'·29N 03°11'·16W.
Le Corbeau Fl R 4s; 48°53'·35N 03°10'·26W.
Pierre à l'Anglais Fl G 4s; 48°53'·21N 03°10'·46W.
Petit Pen ar Guézec Fl (2) G 6s 1M; 48°52'·52N 03°09'·44W.
La Corne ☆ Dir Fl (3) WRG 12s 14m W8M R/G6M; 052°-W-059°-R-173°-G-213°-W-220°-R-052°; W twr, R base; 48°51'·35N 03°10'·62W.

TRÉGUIER TO TRÉBEURDEN

PORT BLANC

Le Voleur Dir ☆ 150°: Fl WRG 4s 17m, W14M, R/G 11M; 140°-G-148°-W-152°-R-160°; W twr; 48°50'·20N 03°18'·52W.
Basse Guazer ; 48°51'·58N 03°20'·96W.

PERROS-GUIREC

Passe de l'Est, ldg lts 224·8°. Front, Le Colombier ☆ Dir Q 28m 14M; intens 214·5°-234·5°; W house; 48°47'·87N 03°26'·66W. Rear, **Kerprigent** ☆, Dir Q 79m **21M**; intens 221°-228°; W twr, 1·5M from front.
Pierre du Chenal 48°49'·29N 03°24'·67W.
Passe de l'Ouest. Kerjean ☆ Dir lt 143·6°, Oc (2+1) WRG 12s 78m, W10M, R/G 8M; 133·7°-G-143·2°-W-144·8°-R-154·3°; W twr, B top; 48°47'·79N 03°23'·40W.
Les Couillons de Tomé 48°50'·90N 03°25'·75W.
La Horaine 48°49'·89N 03°27'·26W.
Roche Bernard 48°49'·43N 03°25'·46W.
Gommonénou VQ R 1M; 48°48'·27N 03°25'·83W.
Jetée du Linkin ☆ Fl (2) G 6s 4m 6M; W pile, G top; 48°48'·20N 03°26'·31W.

PLOUMANAC'H

Mean-Ruz ☆ Oc WR 4s 26m W12M, R9M; 226°-W-242°-R-226°; obsc by Pte de Trégastel when brg <080°; partly obsc by Les Sept-Îles 156°-207° and partly by Île Tomé 264°-278°; pink □ twr; 48°50'·25N 03°29'·00W.

LES SEPT ÎLES

Île-aux-Moines ☆ Fl (3) 20s 59m **24M**; obsc by Îliot Rouzic and E end of Île Bono 237°-241°, and in Baie de Lannion when brg <039°; Gy twr/dwelling; 48°52'·72N 03°29'·40W.
Les Dervinis 48°52'·35N 03°27'·32W.

TRÉGASTEL-PLAGE
Île Dhu 48°50′·37N 03°31′·24W.
Les Triagoz ☆ Fl (2) WR 6s 31m W14M, R11M; 010°-W-339°-R-010°; obsc in places 258°-268° by Les Sept-Îles; Gy □ twr, R lantern; 48°52′·28N 03°38′·80W.
Bar-ar-Gall VQ (9) 10s; 48°49′·79N 03°36′·22W.
Le Crapaud Q (9) 15s; 48°46′·67N 03°40′·59W.

TRÉBEURDEN
Pte de Lan Kerellec ☆ Iso WRG 4s; W8M, R/G5M; 058°-G-064°-W-069°-R-130°; Gy twr; 48°46′·74N 03°35′·06W.
Ar Gouredec VQ (6) + L Fl 10s 3M; 48°46′·41N 03°36′·59W.
An Ervennou Fl (2) R 6s 1m 1M; 48°46′·48N 03°35′·96W.
NW bkwtr ☆ Fl G 2·5s 8m 2M; IPTS; 48°46′·33N 03°35′·21W.

TRÉBEURDEN TO MORLAIX

LÉGUER RIVER
An Taro Braz Q (6)+L Fl 15s 1M 48° 44′·70N 03°39′· 64W.
Beg-Léguer ☆ Oc (4) WRG 12s 60m W12M, R/G9M; 007°-G-084°-W-098°-R-129°; W face of W house, R lantern; 48°44′·31N 03°32′·91W.
Kinierbel; *Bell;* 48°44′·15N 03°35′·18W.

LOCQUÉMEAU
Locquémeau Dir Lt 121° Q, WRG, 39m W12M, R/G 8M, QG115·5°-120·5°QW-121°5-R-126·5°; White gabled house, 48°43′·28N 03°34′·11W.
Ldg lts 121°: Front, ☆ QR 21m 7M; 068°-228°; W pylon, R top; 48°43′·41N 03°34′·44W. Rear, ☆ QR 39m 7M; 016°-232°; W gabled house; 484m from front.
Locquémeau *Whis;* 48°43′·86N 03°35′·93W.
Locquémeau approach Fl G 2.5s; 48°43′·62N 03°34′·96W.

LOCQUIREC
Gouliat 48°42′·57N 03°38′·97W.

PRIMEL-TRÉGASTEL
Méloine 48°45′·56N 03°50′·68W.
Ldg lts 152°, both ☆ QR 35/56m 7M. Front, 134°-168°; W □, R stripe, on pylon; 48°42′·45N 03°49′·19W. Rear, R vert stripe on W wall; 172m from front.
W bkwtr ☆ Fl G 4s 6m 7M; 48°42′·77N 03°49′·52W.

BAIE DE MORLAIX
Chenal de Tréguier ldg lts 190·5°: Front, ☆ Île Noire Oc (2) WRG 6s 15m, W11M, R/G8M; 051°-G-135°-R-211°-W-051°; obsc in places; W □ twr, R top; 48°40′·35N 03°52′·54W. Common Rear, **La Lande** ☆ Fl 5s 85m **23M**; obsc by Pte Annelouesten when brg >204°; W □ twr, B top; 48°38′·20N 03°53′·14W.
La Pierre Noire 48°42′·56N 03°52′·20W.
La Chambre 48°40′·74N 03°52′·51W.
Grande Chenal ldg lts 176·4°: Front, Île Louet ☆ Oc (3) WG 12s 17m W12M,G8M; 305°-W (except where obsc by islands)-244°-G-305°; W □ twr, B top; 48°40′·41N 03°53′·34W. Common Rear, **La Lande** as above.
Pot de Fer *Bell;* 48°44′·23N 03°54′·02W.
Stolvezen 48°42′·64N 03°53′·41W.
Ricard 48°41′·54N 03°53′·51W.
Vieille 48°42′·60N 03°54′·11W. (Ch Ouest de Ricard 188·8°)
La Noire 48°41′·65N 03°54′·06W.
Corbeau 48°40′·63N 03°53′·33W.

MORLAIX RIVER
Barre de-Flot No 1 48°40′·18N 03°52′·95W.
No 2 Fl R 2·5s; 1m 2M 48°39′·88N 03°52′·53W.
No 3 Fl G 2·5s; 1m 2M 48°39′·25N 03°52′·32W.
No 4 Fl R 2·5s; 1m 2M 48°38′·62N 03°51′·62W.
No 5 Fl G 2·5s; 1m 2M 48°38′·04N 03°51′·34W.
No 7 48°37′·68N 03°51′·03W.

PENZÉ RIVER
Cordonnier 48°42′·93N 03°56′·59W.
Guerhéon 48°42′·73N 03°57′·18W.
Trousken 48°42′·26N 03°56′·54W.
Pte Fourche 48°42′·14N 03°56′·76W.
Ar Tourtu 48°41′·99N 03°56′·57W.
An Nehou (Caspari) 48°41′·56N 03°56′·45W.
Le Figuier 48°40′·46N 03°56′·16W.

ROSCOFF TO ÎLE VIERGE

BLOSCON/ROSCOFF
Astan VQ (3) 5s 4m 4M; 48°44′·91N 03°57′·66W.
Le Menk Q (9) WR 15s 6m W6M, R4M; 160°-W-188°-R-160°; 48°43′·28N 03°56′·71W.
Basse de Bloscon VQ 3m 4M 48°43′·71N 03°57′·55W.
Bloscon pier ☆ Fl WG 4s 9m W10M, G7M (in fog Fl 2s); 200°-W-210°-G-200°; W twr, G top; 48°43′·21N 03°57′·69W.
Roscoff Marina ent, E side, ☆ Fl (2) R 6s 4M; 48°43′·11N 03°57′·89W. Ent W side ☆ Fl (2) G 6s 4M; 48°43′·11N 03°57′·94.
Ar Pourven Q 2m 3M; 48°43′·04N 03°57′·70W.
Ar-Chaden Q (6) + L Fl WR 15s 14m, W8M, R6M; 262°-R-289·5°-W-293°-R-326°- W-110°; YB twr; 48°43′·94N 03°58′·26W.
Men-Guen-Bras Q WRG 14m, W9M, R/ G6M; 068°-W-073°-R-197°-W-257°-G-068°; BY twr; 48°43′·76N 03°58′·07W.
Roscoff ldg lts 209°: Front, N môle ☆ Oc (3) G 12s 7m 7M; synch; 078°-318°; W col, G top; 48°43′·56N 03°58′·67W. **Rear** ☆ Oc (3) 12s 24m **15M**; 062°-242°; Gy □ twr, W on NE side; 430m from front.

CANAL DE L'ÎLE DE BATZ
Roc'h Zu 48°43′·88N 03°58′·59W.
Jetty hd (LW landing) ☆ Q 5m 1M; BY col; 48°43′·92N 03°58′·97W.
Run Oan 48°44′·10N 03°59′·30W.
Perroch 48°44′·10N 03°59′·71W.
Tec'hit Bihan 48°44′·02N 04°00′·88W.
La Croix 48°44′·19N 04°01′·30W.
L'Oignon 48°44′·04N 04°01′·35W.
Basse Plate 48°44′·25N 04°02′·53W.

ÎLE DE BATZ
Île aux Moutons VQ (6)+ L Fl 10s 3m 7M; 48°44′·25N 04°00′·52W; landing stage, S end and ent to hbr.
Malvoch 48°44′·26N 04°00′·67W, W side of ent.
Lt ho ☆ Fl (4) 25s 69m **23M**; Gy twr; 48°44′·71N 04°01′·62W. Same twr, auxiliary lt, FR 65m 7M; 024°-059°.

MOGUÉRIEC
Ldg lts 162°: Front ☆ Iso WG 4s 9m W11M, G6M; 158°-W-166°-G-158°; W twr, G top; jetty 48°41′·34N 04°04′·47W. Rear ☆ Iso G 4s 25m 9M, synch; 142°-182°; W col, G top; 440m from front.

PONTUSVAL
Pointe de Pontusval 48°41′·42N 04°19′·32W.
Ar Peich 48°40′·90N 04°19′·16W.
Pte de Beg-Pol ☆ Oc (3) WR 12s 15m W10M, R7M; Shore-W-056°-R-096°-W-shore; W twr, B top, W dwelling; 48°40′·67N 04°20′·76W. QY and FR lts on towers 2·4M S.
Aman-ar-Ross Q 5m 4M; 48°41′·88N 04°27′·03W.

Lizen Ven VQ (9) 10s 6m 4M; 48°40′·53N 04°33′·63W.
Île-Vierge ☆ Fl 5s 77m **27M**; 337°-325°; Gy twr; 48°38′·33N 04°34′·05W.

ÎLE VIERGE TO L'ABER-ILDUT

L'ABER WRAC'H

Libenter Q (9) 15s 5m 4M; 48°37′·45N 04°38′·46W.
Outer ldg lts 100·1°: Front, Île Wrac'h ☆ QR 20m 7M; W □ twr, Or top; 48°36′·88N 04°34′·56W. Rear, Lanvaon ☆ Q 55m 12M; intens 090°-110°; W □ twr, Or △ on top; 1·63M from front.
Grand Pot de Beurre 48°37′·21N 04°36′·48W.
Petit Pot de Beurre 48°37′·12N 04°36′·23W.
Basse de la Croix Fl (3) G 12s 3M; 48°36′·92N 04°35′·99W.
Breac'h Ver Fl (2) G 2·5s 6m 3M; △ on twr; 48°36′·63N 04°35′·38W.Île Enez Terc'h Fl (2) R 6s 1m 2M; 48°36′·20N 04°34′·40W.
Dir ☆ 128°, Oc (2) WRG 6s 5m W13M, R/G11M; 125·7°-G-127·2°-W-128·7°-R-130·2°; 48°35′·89N 04°33′·82W, root of W bkwtr.
Marina ent: QG 3m 2M; vis 186°-167° (341°); 48°35′·97N 04°33′·64W. QR 3m 2M; vis 244°-226° (342°).

L'ABER BENOÎT

Petite Fourche 48°36′·99N 04°38′·75W.
Rusven Est 48°36′·30N 04°38′·63W.
Rusven Ouest *Bell;* 48°36′·07N 04°39′·43W.
Basse du Chenal Abers 48°35′·81N 04°38′·53W.
Poul Orvil 48°35′·52N 04°38′·29W.
La Jument 48°35′·10N 04°37′·41W.
Ar Gazel 48°34′·90N 04°37′·27W.
Le Chien 48°34′·67N 04°36′·88W.

ROCHES DE PORTSALL

Le Relec 48°35′·99N 04°40′·84W.
Corn-Carhai ☆ Fl (3) 12s 19m 9M; W 8-sided twr, B top; 48°35′·19N 04°43′·94W.
Grande Basse de Portsall VQ (9) 10s 6m 4M; 48°36′·70N 04°46′·13W.
Basse Paupian 48°35′·31N 04°46′·27W.
Bosven Aval 48°33′·82N 04°44′·27W.
Men ar Pic 48°33′·65N 04°44′·03W.
Portsall ☆ Oc (4) WRG 12s 9m W13M, R/G10M; 058°-G-084°-W-088°-R-058°; W col, R top; 48°33′·84N 04°42′·26W.

ARGENTON to L'ABER-ILDUT

Le Taureau 48°31′·46N 04°47′·34W.
Argenton, Île Dolvez, front ldg bcn 086° 48°31′·25N 04°46′·23W.
Le Four ☆ Fl (5) 15s 28m **22M**; Gy ○ twr; 48°31′·38N 04°48′·32W.
L'Aber-Ildut ☆ Dir Oc (2) WRG 6s 12m W10M, R10M, G10M; 078°-G-081°-W- 085°-R- 088° ; W bldg; 48°28′·26N 04°45′·56W.
Le Lieu Fl R 2·5s 5m 4M; R twr, 48°28′·25N 04°46′·65W.
Beg ar Groaz FL G 2·5s 1M; 48°28′·22N 04°45′·3W.

CHENAL DU FOUR AND CHENAL DE LA HELLE

Ldg lts 158·5°. Front, **Kermorvan** ☆ Fl 5s 20m **22M**; obsc'd by Pte de St Mathieu when brg <341°; W □ twr; *Horn 60s*; 48°21′·72N 04°47′·40W. 992271316.
Rear, **Pte de St Mathieu** ☆ Fl 15s 56m **24M**; W twr, R top; 48°19′·79N 04°46′·26W. Same twr: Dir F 54m **28M**; intens 157·5°-159·5°.
☆ Q WRG 26m, W12M, R/G 8M; 085°-G-107°-W-116°-R-134°; W twr 54 m WNW of previous entry; 48°19′·80N 04°46′·30W.
Plâtresses N Fl G 2·5s 3m 4M; 48°26′·46N 04°50′·71W.
Valbelle Fl (2) R 2·5s 8m 4M; 48°26′·43N 04°50′·03W.
Plâtresses SE Fl (2) G 6s 7m 2M; 48°25′·96N 04°50′·52W.
Saint Paul Fl (2) R 6s 7m 4M; 48°24′·82N 04°49′·16W.
Pte de Corsen ☆ Dir Q WRG 33m **W12M**, R/G8M; 008°-R-012°-W-015° (ldg sector)- G-021°; W hut; 48°24′·89N 04°47′·61W.

CHENAL DE LA HELLE

Ldg lts 137·9°: Front, **Kermorvan** ☆ see above. Rear, **Lochrist** ☆ Dir Oc (3) 12s 49m **22M**; intens 135°-140°; W 8-sided twr, R top; 48°20′·55N 04°45′·82W.
Luronne ; 48°26′·61N 04°53′·78W.
Ldg lts 293·5° astern (to join Ch du Four S of St Paul): Front, Le Faix VQ 16m 8M; 48°25′·73N 04°53′·91W. Rear, **Le Stiff** ☆ (below at Ouessant); 6·9M from front.
Ldg line 142·5°, optional day only (to join Chenal du Four SE of St Pierre): Front, **Kermorvan** ☆ see above. Rear, two W gables (Les Pignons de Kéravel, 48m) 48°20′·10N 04°45′·55W
Pourceaux Q 7m 4M; 48°24′·00N 04°51′·31W.
Saint-Pierre Fl (3) G 12s; 48°23′·09N 04°49′·09W.
Rouget Fl G 4s 7m 4M; 48°22′·04N 04°48′·88W (Ch du Four).
Grande Vinotière Fl R 4s 12m 5M; R 8-sided twr; 48°21′·94N 04°48′·42W.
Le Conquet, Môle Ste Barbe ☆ Fl G 2·5s 5m 6M; 48°21′·57N 04°46′·98W.
Les Renards 48°21′·00N 04°47′·48W.
Tournant et Lochrist Fl (2) R 6s7m 4M; 48°20′·64N 04°48′·12W,
Ar Christian Braz 48°20′·68N 04°50′·14W, E of Ile de Béniguet.
Ldg line 325°: Front, Grand Courleau ; rear, La Faix (above).
Ldg lts 007°: Front, **Kermorvan** ☆ above. Rear, **Trézien** ☆ Dir Oc (2) 6s 84m **20M**; intens 003°-011°; Gy twr, W on S side; 48°25′·41N 04°46′·74W.
Les Vieux-Moines Fl R 4s 16m 5M; 280°-133°; R 8-sided twr; 48°19′·33N 04°46′·63W, 5ca SSW of Pte de St Mathieu.
La Fourmi Fl G 4s; 48°19′·02N 04°48′·01W.

OUESSANT AND ÎLE MOLÉNE

OFF USHANT TSS

Ouessant NE ⨀; V-AIS; 48°59′·51N 05°24′·00W.
Ouessant SW ⨀; V-AIS 48°30′·00N 05°45′·00W.

ÎLE D'OUESSANT

Le Stiff ☆ Fl (2) R 20s 85m **22M**; two adjoining W twrs; 48°28′·47N 05°03′·41W. Radar twr, conspic, 340m NE, ☆ Q (day); ☆ FR (night).
Port du Stiff, E môle ☆ Dir Q WRG 11m W10M, R/G7M; 251°-G-254°-W-264°-R-267°; W twr, G top; 48°28′·12N 05°03′·25W.
Baie du Stiff: Gorle Vihan 48°28′·32N 05°02′·60W.
Men-Korn VQ (3) WR 5s 21m 8M; 145°-W-040°-R-145°; BYB twr; 48°27′·96N 05°01′·32W.
Men ar Froud 48°26′·62N 05°03′·67W.
La Jument ☆ Fl (3) R 12s 36m 10M; 241°-199°; Gy 8-sided twr, R top; 48°25′·33N 05°08′·04W.

Nividic VQ (9) 10s 28m 10M; 290°-225°; Gy 8-sided twr, helicopter platform; 48°26′·74N 05°09′·06W.
Créac'h ☆ Fl (2) 10s 70m **30M**; obsc 247°-255°; W twr, B bands; 48°27′·55N 05°07′·76W.

ÎLE MOLÈNE and ARCHIPELAGO
Kéréon Oc (3) WR 12s 38m 10M; 019°-W-248°-R-019°; Gy twr; 48°26′·24N 05°01′·59W; unreliable.
Les Trois-Pierres Iso WRG 4s 15m W9M, R/G6M; 070°-G-147°-W-185°-R-191°-G-197°-W-213°-R-070°; W col; 48°24′·70N 04°56′·84W.
Molène, Old môle Dir 191°, Fl (3) WRG 12s 6m W9M, R/G7M; 183°-G-190°-W-192°-R-203°; 48°23′·85N 04°57′·29W.
Same structure: Chenal des Laz , Dir 261°: Fl (2) WRG 6s 9m W9M, R/G7M ; 252·5°-G-259·5°-W-262·5°-R-269·5°.
Pierres-Vertes VQ (9) 10s 9m 4M; 48°22′·19N 05°04′·76W.
Pierres Noires ; 48°18′·47N 04°58′·15W.
Les Pierres Noires ☆ Fl R 5s 27m **19M**; W twr, R top; 48°18′·67N 04°54′·88W.

BREST AND APPROACHES

Basse Royale Q (6) + L Fl 15s; 48°17′·45N 04°49′·61W.
Vandrée VQ (9) 10s 7m 4M; *Whis;* 48°15′·21N 04°48′·24W.
Goëmant ; 48°15′·12N 04°46′·34W.
La Parquette Fl RG 4s 17m R6M, G6M; 244°-R-285°-G-244°; W 8-sided twr, B diagonal stripes; 48°15′·90N 04°44′·29W.
Coq Iroise 48°19′·07N 04°43′·99W.
Charles Martel Fl (4) R 15s 7m 4M; 48°18′·95N 04°41′·92W.
Trépied 48°16′·73N 04°41′·50W.

GOULET DE BREST
Le Chat 48°20′·29N 04°41′·72W (Anse de Bertheaume).
Pte du Petit-Minou ☆ Fl (2) WR 6s 32m **W17M,** R13M; Shore-R-252°-W-260°-R-307°-W(unintens)-015°-W-065·5°; 036·5°-R(intens)- 039·5°; 70·5°-W-shore; Gy twr, R top; 48°20′·19N 04°36′·86W.
Ldg lts 068°, both Dir Q 30/54m **22M. Front, Pte du Petit-Minou,** intens 067·3°-068·8°. **Rear, Pte du Portzic** ☆, Aux Dir Q 54m; intens 065°-071° (see below).
Fillettes VQ (9) 10s 7m 4M; 48°19′·75N 04°35′·66W.
Kerviniou Fl R 2·5s 7m 4M; 48°19′·77N 04°35′·25W.
Basse Goudron Fl (2) R 6s 7m 3M; 48°20′·03N 04°34′·86W.
Mengam Fl (3) WR 12s 10m W9M, R6M; 034°-R-054°-W-034°; R twr, B bands; 48°20′·32N 04°34′·56W.
Pte du Portzic ☆ Oc (2) WR 12s 56m **W19M, R15M**; 219°-R-259°-W-338°-R-000°-W-065·5° (vis 041°-069° west of Goulet)-W-219°; Gy twr; 48°21′·49N 04°32′·05W. Same lt ho, Aux Dir Q, rear 068° ldg lt. Aux ☆ Dir Q (6) + L Fl 15s 54m **23M**; intens 045°-050°.

BREST
Pénoupèle Fl R 2·5s 4m 4M; 48°21′·45N 04°30′·53W.
S jetty QR 10m 6M; 094°-048°; W/R twr; 48°22′·10N 04°29′·46W.
E jetty QG 10m 6M; W/G twr; 48°22′·15N 04°29′·22W.
Ldg lts 343·1°: Front Dir Q WRG 24m W9M, R/G6M; G333·5°-341·5°-W-345°-R-023·5°; 48°22′·80N 04°29′·62W. Rear Dir Q 32m 9M; intens 342°-346°; 110m from front.
Le Château Marina, S Jetty hd, Fl G 2·5s 8m 4M; 48°22′·66N 04°29′·49W.
Le Château Marina, N Jetty hd, Fl R 2·5s 8m 4M; 48°22′·67N 04°29′·45W.
Port de Commerce, E ent: N jetty Oc (2) G 6s 8m 6M; W/G pylon; 48°22′·76N 04°28′·53W. S jetty Oc (2) R 6s 8m 6M; W pylon, R top; 48°22′·69N 04°28′·48W.
R2 Fl (2) R 6s 3m 3M; 48°22′·01N 04°28′·75W.
R1 Fl (2) G 6s 3m 3M; 48°21′·83N 04°28′·29W.
R4 Fl (3) R 12s 3m 4M; 48°22′·29N 04°27′·92W.
R6 Fl R 4s 3m 3M; 48°22′·55N 04°27′·86W.

LE MOULIN BLANC MARINA
Moulin Blanc Fl (2) R 6s 3m 3M; 48°22′·80N 04°25′·91W
MBA Q(3) 10s 3m 2M; pontoon elbow; 48°23′·54N 04°25′·74W.

CAMARET
N môle Iso WG 4s 7m W12M, G9M; 135°-W-182°-G-027°; W pylon, G top; 48°16′·85N 04°35′·31W.
Port Vauban wavebreak, S end, Fl (2) G 6s 2m 2M; 48°16′·74N 04° 35′·33W.
S môle Fl (2) R 6s 9m 5M; R pylon; 48°16′·63N 04°35′·33W.
Styvel QR 2M; 46°16′·73N 04°35′·74W.

POINTE DU TOULINGUET TO RAZ DE SEIN

Pte du Toulinguet ☆ Oc (3) WR 12s 49m **W15M**, R11M; Shore-W-028°-R-090°-W-shore; W □ twr; 48°16′·81N 04°37′·72W.
La Louve 48°16′·76N 04°38′·03W.
Mendufa 48°16′·05N 04°39′·43W.
Basse du Lis Q (6) + L Fl 15s 6m 4M; 48°12′·99N 04°44′·53W.
Le Chevreau 48°13′·30N 04°36′·98W.
Le Bouc Q (9) 15s 5m 4M; 48°11′·51N 04°37′·37W.
Basse Vieille Fl (2) 6s 8m 4M; 48°08′·22N 04°35′·75W.

DISTANCE TABLES
Approx distances in nautical miles are by the most direct route allowing for dangers and TSS.

1	Lézardrieux	**1**											
2	Tréguier	22	**2**										
3	Perros-Guirec	28	21	**3**									
4	Trébeurden	40	32	17	**4**								
5	Morlaix	60	46	36	23	**5**							
6	Roscoff	54	41	28	17	12	**6**						
7	L'Aberwrac'h	84	72	60	49	48	32	**7**					
8	Le Conquet	106	98	83	72	68	55	29	**8**				
9	Brest (marina)	114	107	92	83	79	67	42	18	**9**			
10	Morgat	126	118	103	92	88	75	49	20	24	**10**		
11	Douarnenez	131	123	108	97	93	80	54	25	29	11	**11**	
12	Audierne	135	128	113	102	98	86	55	30	34	27	30	**12**

12	16	18	24	42	43	45	72	97	100	105	124	Pornic	**12**
	11	12	24	39	40	41	66	87	90	95	113	St Nazaire	**11**
		10	13	30	30	34	55	78	80	85	106	La Baule/Pornichet	**10**
			9	18	22	27	48	73	75	79	100	Le Croisic	**9**
				8	28	36	57	78	80	84	105	Arzal/Camöel	**8**
					7	16	37	58	60	64	85	Crouesty	**7**
						6	26	47	48	54	74	Le Palais (Belle Ile)	**6**
							5	32	33	38	61	Lorient	**5**
								4	4	12	37	Concarneau	**4**
									3	12	36	Port-la-Forêt	**3**
										2	30	Loctudy	**2**
											1	Audierne	**1**

MORGAT

Pointe de Morgat ☆ Oc (4) WRG 12s 77m **W15M**, R11M, G10M; Shore-W-281°-G-301°-W-021°-R-043°; W □ twr, R top, W dwelling; 48°13'·17N 04°29'·80W.
Hbr approach Q R 1·2s 3m 2M; 48°13'·60N 04°29'·55W.
Hbr ent, E side, Fl R 2·5s 4s 2M; 48°13'·58N 04°29'·72W'.
Hbr ent, W side, ☆ Fl G 2·5s 4s 2M; 48°13'·57N 04°29'·79W'.

DOUARNENEZ to RAZ DE SEIN

Île Tristan ☆ Fl (3) WR 12s 35m, W6M, R6M; Shore-W-138°-R-153°-W-shore; Gy twr, W band, B top; 48°06'·14N 04°20'·24W.

Pointe du Millier ☆ Oc (2) WRG 6s 34m **W16M**, R12M, G11M; 080°-G-087°-W-113°-R-120°-W-129°-G-148°-W-251°-R-258°; W house; 48°05'·92N 04°27'·93W.
Basse Jaune 48°04'·70N 04°42'·45W.

RAZ DE SEIN TO POINTE DE PENMARC'H

Tévennec ☆ Q WR 28m W9M R6M; 090°-W-345°-R-090°; W □ twr and dwelling; 48°04'·28N 04°47'·73W. Same twr, Dir ☆ Fl 4s 24m 12M; intens 324°-332° (through Raz de Sein).
La Vieille ☆ Iso WRG 4s 33m WRG10M; 290°-W-298°-R-325°-W-355°-G-017°-W-035°-G-105°-W-123°-R-158°-W-205°; Gy □ twr; 48°02'·44N 04°45'·40W.
La Plate VQ (9) 15s 10m 8M; 48°02'·37N 04°45'·58W.
Le Chat Fl (2) WRG 6s 20m W9M RG6M; 096°-G-215°-W-230°-R-271°-G-286°-R-096°; YB twr; 48°01'·43N 04°48'·86W.

CHAUSSÉE DE SEIN and ÎLE DE SEIN

Cornoc-An-Ar-Braden Fl G 4s 7m 4M; 48°03'·23N 04°50'·84W.
Men-Brial ☆ Oc (2) WRG 6s 16m, W12M, R9M, G7M; 149°-G-186°-W-192°-R-221°-W-227°-G-254°; G&W twr; 48°02'·28N 04°50'·97W.
Île de Sein ☆ Fl (4) 25s 49m **28M**; W twr, B top; 48°02'·62N 04°52'·02W. Same twr, Dir Q WRG, W8M, R/G 6M; 267°-G-269°-W-271°-R-275°. **Ar-Men** ☆ Fl (3) 20s 29m **21M**; W twr, B top; 48°03'·01N 04°59'·87W.
Chaussée de Sein VQ (9) 10s 9m 4M; ***Racon O (3cm), 10M***; 48°03'·75N 05°08'·13W.

AUDIERNE

Pointe de Lervily ☆ Fl WR 4s 20m W14M, R11M; 236°-W-269°-R-294°-W-087°-R-109°; W twr, R top; 48°00'·04N 04°33'·94W. Gamelle W , VQ (9) 10s 6m 4M; 47°59'·46N 04°32'·85W.
Jetée de Ste-Évette ☆ Fl (2) R 6s 2m 7M; R lantern; 090°-000° (270°); 48°00'·31N 04°33'·07W.
Passe de l'Est ldg lts 331°: Front, Jetée de Raoulic ☆ Fl (3) RG 12s 11m, R/G6M; 034°-G-085°-R-034°; 48°00'·55N 04°32'·46W.
Kergadec ☆ 006°: Dir Q WRG 43m W12M, R/G9M; 000°-G-005·3°-W-006·7°-R-017°; W 8-sided twr, R top; 48°00'·96N 04°32'·78W.
Gamelle E ; 47°59'·46N 04°32'·05W.

POINTE DE PENMARC'H

Eckmühl ☆ Fl 5s 60m **23M**; Gy 8-sided twr; 47°47'·89N 04°22'·36W.
Men-Hir ☆ Fl (2) WG 6s 19m, W7M, G4M; G135°-315°, W315°-135°; W twr, B band; 47°47'·74N 04°23'·99W.
Cap Caval Q (9) 15s 6m 4M; 47°46'·47N 04°22'·68W.
Locarec ☆ Iso WRG 4s 11m, W9M, R/G6M; 063°-G-068°-R-271°-W-285°-R-298°-G-340°-R-063°; iron col on rk; 47°47'·29N 04°20'·31W.

AREA 17 *South Biscay – River Loire to Bordeaux*

SELECTED LIGHTS, BUOYS & WAYPOINTS

PTE DE PENMARC'H TO CONCARNEAU GUILVINEC

LE GUILVINEC

Névez Fl G 2·5s 7m 4M; 47°45'·84N 04°20'·08W.
Ldg lts (triple Q) 053°, synch: **Front**, ☆ Q 7m 8M; 233°-066°; W pylon; Môle de Léchiagat, spur; 47°47'·43N 04°17'·07W. Middle, ☆ Q WG 12m W14M, G11M; 006°-W-293°-G-006°; synch; R □ on R col; Rocher Le Faoutés, 210m from front. Rear, ☆ Q 26m 8M, 051·5°-054·5°, R h on W twr; 0·58M from front.
Spineg Q (6) + L Fl 15s 7m 4M; 47°45'·19N 04°18'·90W.

LESCONIL

Karek Greis Q (3) 10s; 47°46'·03N 04°11'·36W.
Q (6) + LFl 15s; 47°46'·53N 04°10'·63W
Men-ar-Groas ☆ Fl (3) WRG 12s 14m, W10M, R/G7M; 268°-G-313°-W-333°-R-050°; W lt ho, G top; 47°47'·79N 04°12'·68W. Rostolou 47°46'·64N 04°07'·29W.
Boulanger VQ (6) + L Fl 10s;47°47'·38N 04°09'·13W.
Chenal de Bénodet 47°48'·53N 04°07'·04W.
Bilien VQ (3) 5s; 47°49'·10N 04°08'·09W.

LOCTUDY

Pte de Langoz ☆ Fl (4) WRG 15s 12m, **W15M**, R11M G12M; 115°-G-243°-W-257°-G-284°-W-295°-R-318°-W-328°-R-025°; W twr, R top; 47°49'·88N 04°09'·55W.
Karek-Saoz Fl R 2·5s 3m 1M; R twr; 47°50'·02N 04°09'·38W.
Men Audierne 47°50'·22N 04°09'·05W.
No 2 (Karek-Croisic) Fl (2) R 6s; 47°50'·19N 04°09'·49W.
No 1 Fl (2) G 6s; 47°50'·22N 04°09'·73W.
No 3 Fl (3) G 12s; 47°50'·22N 04°09'·99W.
Groyne head ☆ Q 3m 10M; 47°50'·21N 04°10'·34W.
Le Blas Fl (4) G 15s 5m 1M; 47°50'·28N 04°10'·23W.

BENODET

Ldg lts 345·5°: Front, Pte du Coq ☆ Dir Oc (3) G 12s 11m 10M; intens 345°-347°; W ○ twr, G stripe; 47°52'·31N 04°06'·70W. Pyramide ☆ Oc (3) 12s 48m 14M; 338°-016°, synch; W twr, G top; common rear, 348m from front.
Lts in line 000·5°: Front, Pte de Combrit ☆ Oc (2) WR 6s 19m, W12M, R9M; 325°-W-017°-R-325°; W □ twr, Gy corners 47°51'·86N 04°06'·78W. Common rear, Pyramide; see above.
Rousse 47°51'·55N 04°06'·47W. La Potée 47°51'·78N 04°06'·55W.
Pte du Toulgoët ☆ Fl R 2·5s 2m 1M; 47°52'·30N 04°06'·86W.
Le Taro 47°50'·51N 04°04'·83W.
La Voleuse Q (6) + L Fl 15s; 47°48'·76N 04°02'·49W.

ILE AUX MOUTONS and LES POURCEAUX

Île-aux-Moutons ☆ Iso WRG 2s 18m, **W15M**, R/G11M;

035°-W-050°-G-063°-W-081°-R-141°-W-292°-R-035°; W □ twr and dwelling; 47°46′·48N 04°01′·66W.
Rouge de Glénan VQ (9) 10s 8m 8M; 47°45′·48N 04°03′·95W.
Grand Pourceaux Q; 47°45′·98N 04°00′·80W.

ÎLES DE GLÉNAN
Penfret ☆ Fl R 6s 36m **19M**; W □ twr, R top; 47°43′·26N 03°57′·18W. Same twr: auxiliary ☆ Dir Q 34m 11M; 295°-315°.
La Pie Fl (2) 6s 9m 3M; 47°43′·75N 03°59′·76W.
Pte de la Baleine VQ (3) 5s 2M; 47°43′·26N 03°59′·20W.
Les Bluiniers 47°43′·35N 04°03′·81W.
Offlying marks, anticlockwise from the west:
Basse Pérennès Q (9) 15s 8m 4M; 47°41′·06N 04°06′·14W.
Jument de Glénan Q (6) + L Fl 15s 10m 4M; 47°38′·76N 04°01′·41W.
Laoennou 47°39′·65N 03°54′·70W.
Jaune de Glénan Q (3) 10s 4M; 47°42′·56N 03°49′·83W.

PORT-LA-FORÊT
Linuen Q (3) 10s; 47°50′·76N 03°57′·31W.
Laouen Pod 47°51′·23N 03°58′·00W.
Cap Coz mole ☆ Fl (2) WRG 6s 5m, W7M, R/G5M; Shore-R-335°-G-340°-W-346°-R-shore; 47°53′·49N 03°58′·28W.
Le Scoré 47°52′·75N 03°57′·56W.
Les Ormeaux 47°53′·27N 03°58′·34W.
Entry channel Fl G 2·5s; 47°53′·39N 03°58′·12W.
Fl R 2·5s; 47°53′·39N 03°58′·22W.
Kerleven mole ☆ Fl G 4s 8m 6M; 47°53′·60N 03°58′·37W.

CONCARNEAU
Ldg lts 028·5°: Front, La Croix ☆ Q 14m 13M; 006·5°-093°; R&W twr; 47°52′·16N 03°55′·08W. **Rear, Beuzec** ☆ Dir Q 87m **23M**; synch, intens 026·5°-030·5°; spire, 1·34M from front.
QR; 47°51′·40N 03°55′·75W.
Le Cochon Fl (3) WRG 12s 5m W9M, R/G6M; 230°-R-352°-W-048°-G-207°-Obsc'd-230°; G twr; 47°51′·47N 03°55′·55W.
Basse du Chenal Fl R 4s; 47°51′·54N 03°55′·66W.
Men Fall Fl (2) G 6s; 47°51′·76N 03°55′·28W.
Kersos 47°51′·80N 03°54′·93W (Anse de Kersos).
Lanriec ☆ QG 13m 8M; 063°-078°; G window on W gable end; 47°52′·01N 03°54′·64W.
La Medée Fl (3) R 12s 9m 4M; 47°52′·07N 03°54′·80W.
Ville-Close ☆ Q WR, W9M, R6M; 209°-R-354°-W-007°-R-018°; R turret; 47°52′·27N 03°54′·76W.
No 1 ☆ Fl (4) G 15s 4m 5M; G turret; 47°52′·16N 03°54′·72W.
Marina wavescreen ☆ Fl (4) R 15s 3m 1M; 47°52′·23N 03°54′·79W. No 2 ☆ Fl R 4s 4m 5M; G turret; 47°52′·31N 03°54′·71W.
Ville-Close (NE end) ☆ Fl (2) R 6s; R twr; 47°52′·37N 03°54′·68W.
Ent to FV basin ☆ Fl (2) G 6s; G twr; 47°52′·36N 03°54′·63W.
Pouldohan ☆ Fl G 4s 6m 8M; 053°-065°; W □ twr, G top; 47°50′·97N 03°53′·69W.
Roché Tudy 47°50′·52N 03°54′·49W.

CONCARNEAU TO ÎLE DE GROIX

PTE DE TRÉVIGNON TO PORT MANEC'H
Les Soldats VQ (9) 10s 6M; 47°47′·86N 03°53′·42W.
Trévignon mole ☆ Fl G 4s 5m 6M; 47°47′·69N 03°51′·30W.
Trévignon bkwtr root ☆ Fl (2) WRG 6s 11m, W10/7M, R/G7M; 004°-W-051°-G-085°-W-092°-R-127°; 322°-R-351°; W □ twr, G top; 47°47′·59N 03°51′·33W.
Men Du 47°46′·41N 03°50′·50W.
Men an Tréas 47°45′·77N 03°49′·66W.

PORT MANEC'H (Aven and Bélon rivers)
Port Manech ☆ Oc (4) WRG 12s 38m, W10M, R/G7M; obscd by Pte de Beg-Morg when brg <299°; 050°-W (unintens)-140°-W-296°-G-303°-W-311°-R (over Les Verrès)-328°-W-050°; W & R twr; 47°47′·99N 03°44′·34W.
Les Verrès 47°46′·65N 03°42′·71W.

BRIGNEAU
Brigneau 47°46′·11N 03°40′·10W.
W mole, ☆ Oc (2) WRG 6s 7m, W12M, R/G9M; R col, W top; 280°-G-329°-W-339°-R-034°; 47°46′·86N 03°40′·18W. In line 331° with W □ daymark behind, Hard to see, rear beacon unlit.

MERRIEN
☆ Dir QR 26m 7M; 004°-009°; W □ twr, R top; 47°47′·04N 03°38′·97W.
Ent, W side. E side 47°46′·45N 03°38′·89W.

DOËLAN
Ldg lts 013·8°: Front ☆ Oc (3) WG 12s 20m, W13M, G10M; W shore-305°, G305°-314°, W314°-shore; W lt ho, G band and top; 47°46′·32N 03°36′·51W. Rear ☆ Oc (3)R 12s 27m 9M; W lt ho, R band & top; 326m from front.

LE POULDU
Ent 47°45′·74N 03°32′·25W.
Grand Cochon 47°43′·03N 03°30′·81W.
Pte de Kerroc'h ☆ Oc (2) WRG 6s 22m W11M, R/G8M; 096·5°-R-112°·5-G-132°-R-302°-W-096·5°; W twr, R top; 47°41′·97N 03°27′·66W.

ÎLE DE GROIX
Pen Men ☆ Fl (4) 25s 60m **29M**; 309°-275°; W □ twr, B top; 47°38′·84N 03°30′·56W.
Speerbrecker, 47°39′·10N 03°26′·33W.
Port Tudy, N môle ☆ Fl (2) G 6s 12m 7M; W twr, G top; 47°38′·72N 03°26′·73W.
E môle ☆ Fl (2) R 6s 11m 6M; 112°-226°; W twr R top; 47°38′·68N 03°26′·78W.
Basse Melité 47°38′·84N 03°25′·54W.
Pte de la Croix ☆ Oc WR 4s 16m, W12M, R9M; 169°-W-336°-R-345°-W-353°; W pedestal, R lantern; 47°38′·05N 03°25′·02W.
Edouard de Cougy 47°37′·93N 03°23′·90W.
Pointe des Chats ☆ Fl R 5s 16m **19M**; W □ twr and dwelling; 47°37′·24N 03°25′·30W.
Les Chats Q (6) + L Fl 15s; 47°35′·70N 03°23′·57W.

LORIENT AND RIVER ÉTEL

LORIENT, PASSE DE L'OUEST
Passe de l'Ouest ldg lts 057°: both Dir Q 11/22m 13/**18M**. Front, Les Sœurs; (intens 042·5°-058·5°, 058·5°-042·5°, 4M range only); R twr, W bands; 47°42′·13N 03°21′·84W. Rear **Port Louis** ☆, W pylon, R bands; 47°42′·35N 03°21′·34W.
Banc des Truies Q (9) 15s; 47°40′·76N 03°24′·48W.
Loméner, Anse de Stole, Dir ☆ 357·2°: Q WRG 13m, W10M, R/G8M; 349·2°-G-355·2°-W-359·2°-R-005·2°; W twr, R top; 47°42′·30N 03°25′·54W.
A2 Fl R 2·5s; 47°40′·94N 03°24′·98W.

Les Trois Pierres Q RG 11m R/G6M; 060°-G-196°-R-002°; B twr, W bands; 47°41'·53N 03°22'·47W.
A8 Fl R 2·5s; 47°41'·90N 03°22'·52W.

PASSE DU SUD

Bastresses Sud QG; 47°40'·77N 03°22'·09W.
Les Errants Fl (2) R 6s; 47°41'·10N 03°22'·38W.
Bastresses Nord Fl (2) G 6s; 47°41'·11N 03°22'·20W.
Locmalo Fl (3) G 12s; 47°41'·67N 03°22'·13W.

SOUTH OF PORT LOUIS

La Paix ; 47°41'·97N 03°21'·84W.
Île aux Souris ☆ Dir Q WG 6m, W3M, G2M; 041·5°-W-043·5°-G-041·5°; G twr; 47°42'·15N 03°21'·52W.
Fl G 2·5s; 47°42'·13N 03°21'·21W.
Ban-Gâvres FV/yacht hbr, W jetty ☆ Fl (2) G 6s 3M; 47°42'·06N 03°21'·11W. E jetty ☆ Fl (2) R 6s 3M; 47°42'·06N 03°21'·06W.

ENTRANCE CHANNEL

Ldg lts 016·5°, both Dir QG 8/14m 13M; intens 014·5°-017·5°; synch; W twrs, G tops. Front ☆, 47°43'·47N 03°21'·63W (Île St Michel). Rear ☆, 306m from front.
La Citadelle Oc G 4s 6m 6M; 012°-192°; 47°42'·59N 03°21'·94W.
Secondary yacht chan, RGR, 47°42'·49N 03°22'·12W.
La Petite Jument Oc R 4s 5m 6M; 182°-024°; R twr; 47°42'·58N 03°22'·07W.
Le Cochon Fl R 4s 5m 5M; RGR twr; 47°42'·80N 03°22'·00W.
No 1 47°42'·80N 03°21'·84W.

PORT LOUIS (Port de la Pointe)

D 1 47°42'·76N 03°21'·52W.
Jetty ☆ Fl G 2·5s 7m 6M; W twr, G top; 47°42'·71N 03°21'·37W.
Anse du Driasker Stage Head Fl R 2·5s 2M, metal mast.

KERNEVEL

Kéroman ldg lts 350°, both Dir Oc (2) R 6s 25/31m **15M**; synch; intens 349°-351°: **Front** ☆, 47°43'·60N 03°22'·02W, R ho, W bands. **Rear** ☆ R&W topmark on Gy pylon, R top; 91m from front.
Banc du Turc Fl G 2·5s; 47°43'·33N 03°21'·85W.
Kernével marina, ent: ☆ QR 1M; 47°43'·39N 03°22'·10W.
Ldg lts 217°, both Dir QR 10/18m **15M**; intens 215°-219°; synch: **Front, Kernével** ☆ R&W twr; 47°43'·02N 03°22'·32W. **Rear** ☆ W □ twr, R top; 290m from front.
Q (3) 10s; marks wreck; 47°43'·49N 03°22'·05W.

NORTHERN PART OF LORIENT HARBOUR

Grand Bassin (FV hbr) E side of ent, ☆ Fl RG 4s 7m 6M; 000°-G-235°-R-000°; W twr, G top; 47°43'·63N 03°21'·87W.
Ste Catherine marina ent ☆ QG 5m 3M; 47°43'·52N 03°21'·12W.
N side of marina ent ☆ QR 2m 2M 47°43'·53N 03°21'·10W.
Pengarne Fl G 2·5s 3m 3M; G twr; 47°43'·88N 03°21'·23W.
No 9 Fl (2) G 6s; 47°43'·95N 03°21'·16W.
No 11 Fl (3) G 12s; 47°44'·04N 03°21'·01W.
Pen-Mané marina, bkwtr elbow ☆ Fl (2) G 6s 4M; 47°44'·11N 03°20'·86W.
Blavet River, No 1 Fl (2+1)G 10s; 47°44'·20N 03°20'·78W.
No 2 Fl R 2·5s; 47°44'·26N 03°20'·74W.
Pointe de l'Espérance, Dir ☆ 037°, Q WRG 8m W10M, R/G8M; 034·2°-G-036·7°-W-037·2°-R-047·2°; W twr, G top; 47°44'·51N 03°20'·66W.
Ro-Ro jetty ☆ QR 7m 2M; 47°44'·42N 03°20'·96W.
No 8 Fl R 2·5s; 47°44'·56N 03°20'·98W, ent to Lorient marina.

RIVIÈRE D'ÉTEL

Roheu 47°38'·54N 03°14'·70W.
Épi de Plouhinec ☆ Fl R 2·5s 7m 2M; 47°38'·59N 03°12'·86W.
W side ent ☆ Oc (2) WRG 6s 13m W9M, R/G6M; 022°-W-064°-R-123°-W-330°-G-022°; R twr; 47°38'·69N 03°12'·83W.
Conspic R/W radio mast (CROSS Étel) 47°39'·73N 03°12'·11W.
Les Pierres Noires 47°35'·53N 03°13'·29W.

BELLE ÎLE AND QUIBERON BAY (W OF 2° 50'W)

PLATEAU DES BIRVIDEAUX (6M NNW of Belle Île)

Fl (2) 6s 24m 10M; BRB twr; 47°29'·15N 03°17'·46W.

BELLE ÎLE

Pte des Poulains ☆ Fl 5s 34m **23M**; 023°-291°; W □ twr and dwelling; 47°23'·31N 03°15'·11W.
Les Poulains 47°23'·44N 03°16'·68W.
N Poulains 47°23'·68N 03°14'·88W.
Sauzon, NW jetty ☆ Fl G 4s 8m 8M; 47°22'·49N 03°13'·04W.
SE jetty ☆ Fl R 4s 8m 8M; 315°-272°; W twr, R top; 47°22'·45N 03°13'·00W. Inner hbr, W jetty ☆, QG 9m 5M; 194°-045°; W twr, G top; 47°22'·37N 03°13'·13W.
Le Palais, N jetty ☆ QG 11m 7M; obsc 298°-170° by Ptes de Kerdonis and Taillefer; W twr, G top; 47°20'·84N 03°09'·04W.
No 1 Fl (2) G 6s; 47°20'·82N 03°08'·96W;
No 2 Fl R 4s; 47°20'·71N 03°08'·89W;
No 4 Fl (2) R 6s; 47°20'·78N 03°09'·01W.
S jetty ☆ QR 11m 7M; obsc'd 298°-170° (see N jetty); W twr, R lantern; 47°20'·82N 03°09'·07W.
Pointe de Kerdonis ☆ Fl (3) R 15s 49m **15M**; obsc'd 225°-320°
(095°) by vegetation, 004°-155° (151°) by land. W □ twr, R top and W dwelling; 47°18'·60N 03°03'·58W.
Les Galères VQ(3)5s; 47°18'·77N 03°02'·76W.
SW coast of Belle Île: La Truie 47°17'·11N 03°11'·79W.
Goulphar ☆ Fl (2) 10s 87m **27M**; Gy twr; 47°18'·65N 03°13'·63W.

PORT MARIA (Quiberon ferry port)

Light ho ☆ Q WRG 28m W14M, R/ G10M; 246°-W-252°-W-297°-G-340°-W-017°-R-051°-W-081°-G-098°-W-143°; W twr, G lantern; 47°28'·78N 03°07'·45W.
Le Pouilloux 47°27'·88N 03°08'·01W.
An Tréac'h Fl (2)10s; 47°27'·92N 03°07'·20W.
Ldg lts 006·5°, both Dir QG 5/13m **16/17M**; intens 005°-008°; W twrs, B bands: **Front**, 47°28'·63N 03°07'·18W. **Rear**, 230m north.
Les Deux Frères Fl R 2·5s; 175°-047°;47°28'·34N 03°07'·29W.
S bkwtr ☆ Oc (2) R 6s 9m 7M; W twr, R top; 47°28'·54N 03°07'·31W.

CHAUSSÉE and PASSAGE DE LA TEIGNOUSE

Le Four 47°27'·78N 03°06'·54W.
Les Trois Pierres 47°27'·46N 03°05'·24W.
Roc er Vy 47°27'·70N 03°04'·40W; Chenal en Toull Bras.
Roc er Vy 47°27'·86N 03°04'·35W.
Basse Cariou 47°26'·94N 03°06'·38W.

Basse du Chenal 47°26'·66N 03°05'·77W.
Goué Vaz S Q (6) + L Fl 15s; 47°25'·76N 03°04'·93W.
La Teignouse ☆ Fl WR 4s 20m **W15M**, R11M; 033°-W-039°-R-033°; W ○ twr, R top; 47°27'·44N 03°02'·75W.
Basse du Milieu Fl (2) G 6s 9m 2M; 47°25'·91N 03°04'·12W.
Goué Vaz E Fl (3) R 12s; 47°26'·23N 03°04'·28W.
NE Teignouse Fl (3) G 12s; 47°26'·55N 03°01'·87W.
Basse Nouvelle Fl R 2·5s; 47°26'·98N 03°01'·99W.

CHAUSSÉE and PASSAGE DU BÉNIGUET
Les Esclassiers 47°25'·68N 03°03'·05W.
Le Grand Coin 47°24'·45N 03°00'·26W.
Bonen Bras 47°24'·26N 02°59'·88W.

ÎLE DE HOUAT
Le Rouleau 47°23'·67N 03°00'·31W.
Port St-Gildas N môle ☆ Fl (2) WG 6s 8m W9M, G6M; 168°-W-198°-G-210°-W-240°-G-168°; W twr, G top; 47°23'·57N 02°57'·34W.
Mussel beds, 1 -1.5M NNE of above ☆ and in its G sector (198°-210°) marked by 2 at S end, and VQ (3) 5s & VQ at N end.
Bcns SE and S of Houat: Men Groise 47°22'·77N 02°55'·00W.
Er Spernec Bras 47°22'·09N 02°55'·23W.
Men er Houteliguet 47°22'·54N 02°56'·38W.

ÎLE DE HOËDIC
Les Sœurs 47°21'·14N 02°54'·74W.
La Chèvre 47°21'·08N 02°52'·55W.
Port de l'Argol bkwtr ☆ Fl WG 4s 10m W9M, G6M; 143°-W-163°-G-183°-W-194°-G-143°; W twr, G top; 47°20'·66N 02°52'·48W.
Er Gurranic'h 47°20'·51N 02°50'·44W.
Cohfournik 47°19'·49N 02°49'·69W.
Grands Cardinaux ☆ Fl (4) 15s 28m 13M; R and W twr; 47°19'·27N 02°50'·10W. 2·1M SE of Argol.
Le Chariot 47°18'·76N 02°52'·95W.
Er Palaire 47°20'·16N 02°55'·01W.

PORT HALIGUEN
Banc de Quiberon S Q (6) + L Fl 15s; 47°28'·04N 03°02'·34W.
Banc de Quiberon N 47°29'·65N 03°02'·58W.
E bkwtr hd ☆ Fl (2) WR 6s 10m, W10M, R7M; 233°-W-240·5°-R-299°-W-306°-R-233°; W twr, R top; 47°29'·36N 03°05'·94W.
Port Haliguen 47°29'·38N 03°05'·55W; marks 1·7m patch.
NW bkwtr hd ☆ Fl (2) G 6s 10m 6M; 47°29'·34N 03°06'·02W.
Bugalet wreck 47°31'·19N 03°05'·45W.
Men er Roué 47°32'·25N 03°06'·06W.

LA TRINITÉ-SUR-MER
Rivière de Crac'h ☆ Q WRG 11m W10M, R/G7M; 321°-G-345°-W-013·5°-R-080°; W twr, G top; 47°34'·09N 03°00'·37W.
Buissons de Méaban 47°31'·66N 02°58'·49W.
Le Petit Buisson 47°32'·14N 02°58'·57W.
Roche Révision 47°32'·63N 02°59'·36W.
Petit Trého Fl R 2·5s; 47°33'·47N 03°00'·71W.
R. de Crac'h Dir ☆ 347°: Oc WRG 4s 9m W13M, R/G 11M; 345°-G-346°-W-348°-R-349°; W twr; 47°35'·03N 03°00'·98W.
S pier ☆ Q WR 6s 6m, W9M, R6M; 090°-R-293·5°-W-300·5°-R-329°; W twr, R top; 47°35'·09N 03°01'·50W.
Marina wavebreak/pier ☆ Iso R 4s 8m 5M; 47°35'·28N 03°01'·46W.

GOLFE DU MORBIHAN
Méaban 47°30'·77N 02°56'·23W.
Outer ldg marks 001°: Front, Petit Vezid ; W obelisk; 47°34'·17N 02°55'·23W. Rear, Baden ch spire (83m) 47°37'·20N 02°55'·14W.
Pointe de Port-Navalo ☆ Oc (3) WRG 12s 32m, **W15M**, R/G11M; 155°-W-220°; 317°-G-359°-W-015°-R-105°; W twr and dwelling; 47°32'·87N 02°55'·11W.
Ldg marks 359°: Front, Grégan Q (6) + L Fl 15s 3m 8M; 47°33'·91N 02°55'·05W. Rear, Baden ch spire (5 lines above).
Auray river: Catis 47°36'·14N 02°57'·23W.
César 47°38'·36N 02°58'·22W.
No 13 47°39'·48N 02°58'·64W (last bcn before 14m bridge).
Morbihan: Grand Mouton QG; 47°33'·71N 02°54'·85W.
Gavrinis 47°34'·21N 02°54'·05W.
Jument 47°34'·29N 02°53'·43W.
Creizic S 47°34'·63N 02°52'·84W.
Creizic N 47°34'·93N 02°52'·20W.
Les Rechauds, two 47°36'·18N 02°51'·30W.
Truie d'Arradon 47°36'·58N 02°50'·27W.
Logoden 47°36'·70N 02°49'·91W.
Drenec 47°36'·84N 02°48'·39W.
Bœdic 47°36'·85N 02°47'·59W.
Roguédas Fl G 2·5s 4m 4M; G twr; 47°37'·12N 02°47'·28W.

CROUESTY
Ldg lts 058°, both Dir Q 10/27m 8M; intens 056·5°-059·5°: Front ☆ R panel, W stripe; 47°32'·53N 02°53'·95W. Rear ☆, W twr; 315m from front.
No 1 QG; 47°32'·26N 02°54'·76W.
No 2 47°32'·26N 02°54'·76W.
N jetty ☆ Fl R 4s 9m 7M; R&W □ twr; 47°32'·47N 02°54'·14W.
S jetty ☆ Fl G 4s 9m 7M; G&W □ twr; 47°32'·45N 02°54'·10W.

PLATEAU DU GRAND MONT
Chimère 47°28'·83N 02°53'·98W.
L'Epieu 47°29'·51N 02°52'·91W.
St Gildas 47°29'·78N 02°52'·87W.
Grand Mont 47°28'·98N 02°51'·12W.

QUIBERON BAY (E OF 2° 50'W) TO PTE DU CROISIC

PLATEAU DE SAINT JACQUES
Le Bauzec 47°28'·90N 02°49'·40W.
St Jacques 47°28'·17N 02°47'·52W.
Port St Jacques, jetty ☆ Oc (2) R 6s 5m 6M; W 8-sided twr, R top; 47°29'·24N 02°47'·41W.

PLATEAU DE LA RECHERCHE
Recherche Q (9) 15s; 47°25'·56N 02°50'·39W.
Locmariaquer 47°25'·82N 02°47'·36W.

PÉNERF
Outer Rade Fl (5) Y 20s; 47°27'·58N 02°39'·56W.
Penvins 47°28'·93N 02°40'·09W.
Borenis 47°29'·21N 02°38'·35W.
Tour des Anglais W bcn; 47°30'·21N 02°37'·94W; appr brg 031·4°.
Pignon Fl (3) WR 12s 6m W9M, R6M; 028·5°-R-167°-W-175°-R-349·5°-W-028·5°; R twr; 47°30'·03N 02°38'·89W.

VILAINE RIVER
Pte de Penlan ☆ Oc (2) WRG 6s 26m, **W15M**, R/G11M; 292·5°-R-025°-G-052°-W-060°-R-138°-G-180°; W sector defines Passe de la Grande Accroche; W twr, R bands; 47°30'·97N 02°30'·11W.
Bertrand Iso WG 4s 6m, W9M, G6M; 040°-W-054°-G-227°-W-234°-G-040°; G twr; 47°31'·06N 02°30'·72W.
Basse de Kervoyal Dir Q WR W8M, R5M; 269°-W-271°-R-269°; W sector leads to/from Nos 1 & 2 buoys; 47°30'·37N 02°32'·62W.
No 1 Fl G 2·5s; 47°30'·32N 02°28'·73W.
No 2 Fl R 2·5s; 47°30'·41N 02°28'·71W.
Pointe du Scal ☆ QG 8m 4M; 47°29'·67N 02°26'·87W.

ÎLE DUMET
Fort ☆ Fl (3) WRG 15s 14m, W7M, R/G4M; 090°-G-272°-W-285°-R-335°-W-090°; W col, G top; 47°24'·69N 02°37'·21W.
Basse-Est Île Dumet Q (3) 10s; 47°25'·20N 02°34'·93W.
Île Dumet Q; 47°25'·90N 02°36'·05W.

MESQUER
Laronesse 47°25'·96N 02°29'·50W.
Basse Normande 47°25'·47N 02°29'·80W.
Jetty ☆ Oc WRG 4s 7m W10M, R/G7M; 067°-W-072°-R-102°-W-118°-R-293°-W-325°-G-067°; W col & bldg; 47°25'·31N 02°28'·05W.

PIRIAC-SUR-MER
Grand Norven Q; 47°23'·55N 02°32'·89W.
Inner mole ☆ Oc (2) WRG 6s 8m, W10M, R/G7M; 066°-R-148°-G-194°-W-201°-R-221°; W col; 47°22'·93N 02°32'·71W. *Siren 120s (occas), 35m SW.* E bkwtr ☆ Fl R 4s 4m 5M; W pylon, R top; 47°23'·00N 02°32'·67W.
Les Bayonnelles Q (9) 15s;47°22'·56N 02°35'·23W.

LA TURBALLE
Ldg lts 006·5°, both Dir Iso R 4s 11/19m 3M; intens 004°-009°: Front, 47°20'·70N 02°30'·87W. Rear, 275m N of the front lt.
Ouest Jetée de Garlahy ☆ Fl (4) WR 12s 13m, W10M, R7M; 060°-R-315°-W-060°; W pylon, R top; 47°20'·70N 02°30'·93W.
Digue Tourlandroux ☆ Fl G 4s 4m 2M; G post, E side of access chan; 47°20'·75N 02°30'·88W.

LE CROISIC
Basse Hergo Fl G 2·5s 5m 3M; 47°18'·62N 02°31'·69W.
Jetée du Tréhic ☆ Iso WG 4s 12m W14M, G11M; 042°-G-093°-W-137°-G-345°; Gy twr, G top; 47°18'·49N 02°31'·42W. F Bu fog det lt, 100m SE.
Outer ldg lts 155·5°, both Dir Q 10/14m 13M; intens 154°-158°: Front ☆ 47°17'·96N 02°30'·99W . Rear ☆, 116m from front.
Middle ldg lts 174°, both QG 5/8m 11M; 170·5°-177·5°: Front 47°18'·06N 02°31'·07W. Rear, 48m from front.
Le Grand Mabon Fl (3) R 12s 6m 2M; 47°18'·05N 02°31'·03W.
Inner ldg lts 134·7°, both QR 6/10m 8M; intens 132·5°-143·5°; synch.
Basse Castouillet Q (9) 15s; 47°18'·12N 02°34'·37W.
Basse Lovre 47°15'·87N 02°29'·58W, Chenal du Nord.

PLATEAU DU FOUR/BANC DE GUÉRANDE
Bonen du Four Q; 47°18'·53N 02°39'·29W.
Le Four ☆ Fl 5s 23m **18M**; W twr, B diagonal stripes; 47°17'·87N 02°38'·05W. 992271016.
Ouest Basse Capella Q (9) 15s; *Whis;* 47°15'·66N 02°42'·78W.
Goué-Vas-du-Four Q (6) + L Fl 15s; 47°14'·91N 02°38'·20W.
Sud Banc Guérande VQ (6) + L Fl 10s; 47°08'·80N 02°42'·81W.
Le Croisic, Mo(U)15s R Lt 14m 5M, and Wavegem electricity generator) Oc(3)Y 10s, (both floating), 2x SPM Fl (5) Y 20s 4x SPM Fl Y 4s centred on 47°14'·37N 02°46'·61W. 992271051.

PLATEAU DE LA BANCHE
NW Banche Q 8m 4M; 47°12'·86N 02°31'·02W.
W Banche VQ (9) 10s; 47°11'·64N 02°32'·41W.
La Banche ☆ Fl (2) WR 6s 22m **W15M**, R11M; 266°-R-280°-W-266°; B twr, W bands; 47°10'·62N 02°28'·08W. 992271020.
SE Banche 47°10'·40N 02°26'·10W.

PLATEAU DE LA LAMBARDE
NW Lambarde 47°10'·84N 02°22'·93W.
SE Lambarde Q (6) + L Fl 15s; 47°10'·04N 02°20·80W.

BAIE DU POULIGUEN (or Baie de la Baule)
Penchateau Fl R 2·5s; 47°15'·24N 02°24'·35W.
Les Guérandaises Fl G 2·5s; 47°15'·03N 02°24'·29W.
47°15'·24N 02°23'·50W.
Les Evens 47°14'·32N 02°22'·55W.
Les Troves 47°14'·23N 02°22'·41W.
NNW Pierre Percée 47°13'·63N 02°20'·63W.
La Vieille 47°14'·03N 02°19'·51W.
Sud de la Vieille 47°13'·75N 02°19'·54W.
Le Caillou 47°13'·65N 02°19'·18W.
Le Petit Charpentier 47°13'·34N 02°18'·95W.
Le Grand Charpentier ☆ Q WRG 22m, W14M, R/G10M; 020°-G-054°-W-062°-R-092°-W-111°-R-310°-W-020°; Gy lt ho, G lantern; 47°12'·83N 02°19'·13W.

LE POULIGUEN
Basse Martineau 47°15'·54N 02°24'·34W.
La Vieille ,Fl (2) G 6s 2M, 47°15'· 83N 02°24'·43W.
Petits Impairs Fl (3) G 12s 6m 2M; 47°15'·99N 02°24'·61W.
SW jetty ☆ QR 13m 9M; 171°-081°; W col; 47°16'·39N 02°25'·39W.

PORNICHET (La Baule)
S bkwtr ☆ Iso WRG 4s 11m, W10M, R/G7M; 303°-G-081°-W-084°-R-180°; W twr, G top; 47°15'·49N 02°21'·14W.
Ent,W side ☆ QG 3m 1M; B perch, G top; 47°15'·51N 02°21'·12W.
E side ☆ QR 4m 1M; B perch, R top; 47°15'·50N 02°21'·10W.

ST NAZAIRE APPROACH (Chenal du Sud)
S-N1 L Fl 10s 8m 5M; ***Racon Z (3cm), 3–8M***; 47°00'·07N 02°39'·84W.
S-N2 Iso 4s 8m 5M; 47°02'·08N 02°33'·47W.
Les Chevaux Fl G 2·5s; 47°03'·53N 02°26'·37W.

Thérèsia Fl R 2·5s; 47°04′·84N 02°27′·27W.
La Couronnée Fl (2) G 6s; ***Racon T, 3–5M***; 47°07′·60N 02°20′·05W. 992271001.
Lancastria Fl (2) R 6s;47°08′·88N 02°20′·37W.

PASSE DES CHARPENTIERS

Portcé ☆ ldg lts 025·5°, both Dir Q 6/36m **22/24M**: **Front**, intens 024·7°-026·2°; synch; W col; 47°14′·57N 02°15′·44W. 992271021. **Rear** ☆ (H24); intens 024°-027°; W twr; 0·75M from front.
Wreck (Y) Fl (3) R 12s; 47°09′·87N 02°19′·46W.
No 1 VQ G; 47°09′·94N 02°18′·40W.
No 2 VQ R; 47°10′·06N 02°18′·72W.
No 6 Fl (3) R 12s; 47°12′·05N 02°17′·31W.
No 5 Fl (4) G 15s; 47°12′·65N 02°16′·57W.
No 8 Fl (4) R 15s; 47°12′·75N 02°16′·86W.
No 7 VQ G; 47°13′·30N 02°16′·11W.
No 10 VQ R; 47°13′·62N 02°16′·16W. (Buoys 9–18 not listed).
Pointe d'Aiguillon ☆ Oc (3) WR 12s 27m, W13M, R10M; 207°-R-233°-W-293°; 297°-W-300°-R-327°-W-023°; 027°-R-089°; W lt ho, conspic; 47°14′·54N 02°15′·79W.
Ville-ès-Martin jetty Fl (2) 6s 10m 10M; W twr, R top; 47°15′·33N 02°13′·66W.
Morées Fl (3) WR 12s 12m, W6M, R4M; W058°-224°, R300°-058°; G twr; 47°15′·00N 02°13′·02W.

SAINT NAZAIRE

W jetty Oc (4) R 12s 11m 8M; W twr, R top; 47°15′·97N 02°12′·25W.
E jetty Oc (4) G 12s 11m 11M; W twr, G top; 47°15′·99N 02°12′·14W. (Ent lock for big ships into Bassin St Nazaire)
No 20 QR; 47°16′·19N 02°11′·37W.
Sud Basse Nazaire Q (6) + L Fl 15s; 47°16′·21N 02°11′·51W.
Basse Nazaire Fl G 2·5s; 47°16′·24N 02°11′·63W.
Old Môle Q (3) 10s 18m 11M; 153·5°-063·5°; W twr, R top; weather signals; 47°16′·27N 02°11′·82W.
Fl (2) R 6s 5m 1M; R dolphin ; 47°16′·37N 02°11′·80W.
Entrée Est Fl (3) R 12s 9m 9M; R pylon; 47°16′·47N 02°11′·85W.
Ldg lts 280° (into E lock) 2 VQ Vi; front 47°16′·49N 02°11′·92W.

EAST SIDE OF RIVER, SOUTH TO PTE DE ST GILDAS

Le Pointeau, Digue S Fl WG 4s 4m, W10M, G7M; 050°-G-074°-W-149°-G-345°-W-050°; G&W ○ hut; 47°14′·02N 02°10′·96W.
Port de Comberge La Truie 47°12′·06N 00°13′·36W.
S jetty Oc WG 4s 7m W9M, G6M; 123°-W-140°-G-123°; W twr, G top; 47°10′·70N 02°09′·90W.
La Gravette 47°09′·81N 02°13′·06W.
La Gravette bkwtr Fl (3) WG 12s 7m, W8M, G5M; 183°-W-188°-G-124°-W-138°-G-183°; W/G top; 47°09′·64N 02°12′·70W.
Anse du Boucau bkwtr Fl (2) G 6s 3M; 47°08′·41N 02°14′·80W.
Pte de Saint Gildas Q WRG 20m, W14M, R/G10M; 264°-R-308°-G-078°-W-088°-R-174°-W-180°-G-264°; W house, G top; 47°08′·02N 02°14′·74W. 992271017.

RIVER LOIRE TO NANTES

Buoyed/lit to Île de Bois, then G lts, S side; R lts N side.
No 21 VQ G; 47°16′·96N 02°10′·25W.
Suspension bridge, Iso 4s 55m, 47°17′·10N 02°10′·24W;
MA Fl (2) G 6s; 47°17′·50N 02°09′·22W.
MB Fl (3) G 12s; 47°17′·95N 02°07′·53W.
Fernais-25 Fl (4) G 15s; 47°18′·10N 02°06′·60W.
Paimboeuf, môle root Oc (3) WG 12s 9m, W10M, G7M; Shore-G-123°-W-shore; W twr, G top; 47°17′·42N 02°01′·95W.
Île de Bois (upstream) Fl (2) G 6s; 47°12′·79N 01°48′·27W.
Ldg lts 064° Rear Dir VQ R; 47°12′·00N 01°34′·35W, Y-junction with Bras de la Madeleine.

POINTE DE SAINT GILDAS TO FROMENTINE

Pte de Saint Gildas Q WRG 20m, W14M, R/G10M; 264°-R-308°-G-078°-W-088°-R-174°-W-180°-G-264°; 47°08′·02N 02°14′·75W.
Nord Couronnée Q; 47°07′·34N 02°17′·78W.
Notre Dame VQ (9) 10s 7m 3M; 47°05′·42N 02°08′·26W.

PORNIC

Approaches Fl G 4s; 47°06′·39N 02°06′·60W; Fl R 4s; 47°06′·40N 02°06′·64W
Marina ent, S side Fl (2) R 6s 4m 2M; 47°06′·47N 02°06′·67W.
Pte de Noëveillard Oc (4) WRG 12s 22m W13M, R/G10M; Shore-G-051°-W-079°-R-shore; W □ twr, G top, W house; 47°06′·62N 02°06′·92W.

ÎLE DE NOIRMOUTIER anti-clockwise from the East

Pte des Dames ☆ Oc (3) WRG 12s 34m, **W19M, R/G15M**; 016·5°-G-057°-R-124°-G-165°-W-191°-R191°-267°-W-357°-R-016·5°; W □ twr; 47°00′·67N 02°13′·26W. La Chaise 47°01′·21N 02°12′·64W.
L'Herbaudière, ldg lts 187·5°, both Q 5/21m 7M, Gy masts. Front, 47°01′·59N 02°17′·84W. Rear, 310m from front.
Martroger , Q WRG 11m W9M, R/G6M; 033°-G-055°-W-060°-R-095°-G-124°-W-153°-R-201°-W-240°-R-033°; 47°02′·61N 02°17′·11W.
W jetty Oc (2+1) WG 12s 9m W10M, G7M; 187·5°-W-190°-G-187·5°; W col and hut, G top; 47°01′·63N 02°17′·84W.
E jetty Fl (2) R 6s 8m 4M; 47°01′·61N 02°17′·81W.
Île du Pilier ☆ Fl (3) 20s 33m **29M**; Gy twr; 47°02′·55N 02°21′·60W. Same twr, aux QR 10m 11M, 321°-034°.
Passe de la Grise Q (6) + L Fl 15s; 47°01′·66N 02°19′·97W.
Les Boeufs VQ (9) 10s; 46°55′·04N 02°27′·99W.
Réaumur Q (9) 15s; 46°57′·46N 02°24′·22W.
Le Bavard VQ (6) + L Fl 10s; 46°56′·79N 02°23′·34W.
Pte du Devin (Morin) Oc (4) WRG 12s 10m W11M, R/G8M; 314°-G-028°-W-035°-R-134°; W col & hut, G top; 46°59′·15N 02°17′·60W.

GOULET DE FROMENTINE

Fromentine L Fl 10s 3m 6M; 46°53′·38N 02°11′·90W
Milieu Fl (2) R 6s 6m 2M; 46°53′·59N 02°09′·63W.
Pte de Notre Dame-de-Monts Dir Oc (2) WRG 6s 21m, W13M, R/G10M; 000°-G-043°-W-063°-R-073°-W-094°-G-113°-W-116°-R-175°-G-196°-R-230°; W twr, B top; 46°53′·33N 02°08′·54W.

ÎLE D'YEU TO BOURGENAY

ÎLE D'YEU

Feu principal ☆ Fl 5s 56m **24M**; W □ twr, G lantern; 46°43′·05N 02°22′·92W.

Les Chiens Perrins Q (9) WG 15s 16m W7M, G4M; 330°-G-350°-W-200°; 46°43′·60N 02°24′·58W.

Pont d'Yeu 46°45′·81N 02°13′·81W.

La Sablaire Q (6) + L Fl 15s; 46°43′·62N 02°19′·49W.

Port Joinville ldg lts 219°, both QR 11/16m 6M, 169°-269°: Front, Quai du Canada 46°43′·61N 02°20′·94W. Rear, 85m from front.

NW jetty ☆ Oc (3) WG 12s 7m, W11M, G8M; Shore-G-150°-W-232°-G-279°-W-285°-G-shore; W 8-sided twr, G top; 46°43′·77N 02°20′·82W. La Galiote 46°43′·73N 02°20′·71W.

Pte des Corbeaux ☆ Fl (2+1) R 15s 25m **20M**; 083°-143° obsc by Île de Yeu; W □ twr, R top; 46°41′·41N 02°17′·08W.

Port de la Meule ☆ Oc WRG 4s 9m, W9M, R/G6M; 007·5°-G-018°-W-027·5°-R-041·5°; Gy twr, R top; 46°41′·62N 02°20′·72W.

SAINT GILLES-CROIX-DE-VIE

Pte de Grosse Terre ☆ QW 7m **15M**, W square tower, R top, 46°41′·86 01°56′·76, W033·5°- 053·5° (20°). Ldg lts 043·7°, Front as above, rear 260m from front, 28m,**15M** sync with front. W pyramid tower, R top 46°41′·96N 01°56′·61

Pilours Q (6) + L Fl 15s; 46°40′·99N 01°58′·09W.

Jetée de la Garenne ☆ Fl G 4s 8m 6M; 46°41′·46N 01°57′·25W.

Jetée de Boisvinet ☆ Fl R 4s 8m 6M; 46°41′·62N 01°57′·16W.

LES SABLES D'OLONNE

Les Barges ☆ Fl (2) R 10s 25m 13M; Gy twr; 46°29′·70N 01°50′·50W.

Petite Barge Q (6) + L Fl 15s 3M; 46°28′·90N 01°50′·61W.

L'Armandèche ☆ Fl (2+1) 15s 42m **24M**; 295°-130°; W 6-sided twr, R top; 46°29′·39N 01°48′·29W.

Nouch Sud Q (6) + L Fl 15s; 46°28′·55N 01°47′·41W.

Nouch Nord 46°28′·88N 01°47′·36W.

SW Pass, ldg lts 032·5°, Iso 4s 12/33m **16M**, **Front** ☆, 46°29′·42N 01°46′·37W. 992271024. **Rear** ☆, **La Potence**, W □ twr.

SE Pass, ldg lts 320°: Front, E jetty ☆ QG 11m 8M; W twr, G top; 46°29′·44N 01°47′·51W. 992271032. Rear, Tour d'Arundel ☆ Q 33m 13M, synch; large Gy □ twr; 46°29′·63N 01°47′·74W.

Jetée St Nicolas (W jetty) ☆ QR 1·2s 16m 8M; 143°-094°; W twr, R top; 46°29′·23N 01°47′·52W.

BOURGENAY

Ldg lts 040°, both QG 9/19m 7M. Front, 020°-060°; on S bkwtr; 46°26′·34N 01°40′·62W. Rear, 010°-070°; 162m from front.

Landfall L Fl 10s; 46°25′·26N 01°41′·93W.

Ent ☆ Fl R 4s 8m 9M & ☆ Iso G 4s 6m 5M; 46°26′·29N 01°40′·75W.

PLATEAU DE ROCHEBONNE (Shoal 32M offshore)

NW Q (9) 15s; *Whis;* 46°12′·92N 02°31′·58W.

NE Iso G 4s; 46°12′·64N 02° 25′·08W; at end of entry add: 992271045.

SE Q (3) 10s; *Bell;* 46°09′·20N 02°21′·13W.

SW Fl (2) R 6s; 46°10′·11N 02°27′·04W.

PERTUIS BRETON

JARD-SUR-MER and LA TRANCHE-SUR-MER

Ldg marks 036°, two unlit W bcns; 46°24′·47N 01°34′·16W.

Pte du Grouin du Cou ☆ Fl WRG 5s 29m, **W20M, R/G16M**; 034°-R-061°-W-117°-G-138°-W-034°; W 8-sided twr, B top; 46°20′·67N 01°27′·83W.

La Tranche pier ☆ Fl (2) R 6s 6m 6M; R col; 46°20′·55N 01°25′·63W.

Mussel farm, No entry, marked by: Q, 46°17′·17N 01°22′·19W.

Q (3) 10s, 46°15′·73N 01°18′·42W. Q (6) + L Fl 15s, 46°15′·16N 01°19′·98W. Q (9) 15s, 46°16′·28N 01°22′·88W.

L'AIGUILLON and LA FAUTE-SUR-MER

Le Lay Q (6) + L Fl 15s; 46°16′·10N 01°16′·53W.

No 1 46°16′·65N 01°16′·25W. Many mussel beds.

ANSE DE L'AIGUILLON (for La Sèvre Niortaise & Marans)

ATT de L'Aiguillon L Fl 10s; 46°15′·33N 01°11′·50W.

Inner fairway 46°17′·19N 01°09′·65W.

Port du Pavé ☆ Fl G 4s 9m 7M; W col, G top; 46°18′·15N 01°08′·01W.

ÎLE DE RÉ

Les Baleineaux ☆ VQ 23m 7M; pink twr, R top; 46°15′·81N 01°35′·22W.

Les Baleines ☆ Fl (4) 15s 53m **27M**; conspic Gy 8-sided twr, R lantern; 46°14′·64N 01°33′·69W.

ARS-EN-RÉ

Dir ☆ 268° WRG, W10M, R/G 7M, 275·5°-G-267·5°-W-268·5°-R-274·5°; W on W □ with R stripe, R on wooden mast; 46°14′·05N 01°28′·60W.

Les Islattes Q 13m 3M; NCM bcn twr 46°14′·03N 01°23′·32W.

Bûcheron No 1 Fl G 2·5s; 46°14′·21N 01°25′·98W.

Bûcheron No 3 Fl (2) G 6s; 46°14′·14N 01°26′·94W.

Le Fier d'Ars, inner ldg lts 232·5°, both Q 5/13m 9/11M: Front ☆ R/W frame on W col; 46°12′·75N 01°30′·59W. Rear ☆ 142°-322°; B vert rectangle on W mast, 370m from front.

ST MARTIN DE RÉ

Lt ho, E of ent ☆ Oc (2) WR 6s 18m W10M, R7M; Shore-W-245°-R-281°-W-shore; W twr, R top; 46°12′·44N 01°21′·89W.

W mole ☆ Fl G 2·5s 10m 5M; obsc'd by Pte du Grouin when brg <124°; W post, G top; 46°12′·49N 01°21′·91W.

LA FLOTTE

N bkwtr ☆ Fl WG 4s 10m W12M, G9M; 130°-G-205°-W-220°-G-257°; W ○ twr, G top; 46°11′·33N 01°19′·30W.

Dir lt 212·5°, Moiré effect, is next to the main lt twr.

ÎLE DE RÉ (South coast, from the W, inc bridge)

Chanchardon ☆ Fl WR 4s 15m W11M, R8M; 118°-R-290°-W-118°; B 8-sided twr, W base; 46°09′·71N 01°28′·41W.

Chauveau ☆ Oc (3) WR 12s 27m **W15M**, R11M; 057°-W-094°-R-104°-W-342°-R-057°; W ○ twr, R top; 46°08′·03N 01°16′·42W.

Bridge span (30m cl'nce) for SE-bound vessels, ☆ Iso 4s 34m 8M; 46°10′·18N 01°14′·75W . Span (30m cl'nce) for NW-bound vessels, ☆ Iso 4s 34m 8M; 46°10′·26N 01°14′·52W.

La Pallice, W mole, ☆ Fl G 4s 5m 6M; 46°09′·78N 01°14′·45W. S end, ☆ Q (6) + L Fl 15s 6m 9M; 46°09′·36N 01°14′·52W.

LA ROCHELLE AND LA CHARENTE TO ROCHEFORT

LA ROCHELLE

Chauveau VQ (6) + L Fl 10s; 46°06′·56N 01°16′·06W.

Roche du Sud Q (9) 15s; 46°06′·37N 01°15′·22W.

La Rochelle ldg lts 059°, both Dir Q 15/25m 13/14M; synch; by day Fl 4s. Front; intens 056°-062°; R ○ twr, W bands; 46°09′·35N 01°09′·16W. Rear, 044°-074°, obsc'd 061°-065°; W 8-sided twr, G top, 235m from front.

Lavardin Fl (2) 6s 14m 7M; BRB IDM twr; 46°08′·09N 01°14′·52W.

Les Minimes Q (9) 15s; 46°08′·01N 01°11′·60W.

Pte des Minimes ☆ Fl (3) WG 12s 8m; W8M, G5M; 059°-W-213°; 313°-G-059°; 8-sided twr on piles; 46°08′·27N 01°10′·76W.

Chan buoy QG; 46°08′·53N 01°10′·87W; marking hbr limit.

Tour Richelieu Fl (2)R 6s 0m 6M; R twr; 46°08′·90N 01°10′·34W.

Port des Minimes, W bkwtr ☆ Fl G 2·5s; W twr, G top; 46°08′·88N 01°10′·18W.

E bkwtr ☆ VQ(9) 10s 3M; Y/B band, 46°08′·92N 01°10′·09W.

LA CHARENTE

Fort Boyard twr ☆ Q (9) 15s; 45°59′·97N 01°12′·86W.

Ldg lts 115°, both Dir QR 8/21m **19/20M**; intens 113°-117°; W □ twr, R top: **Front** ☆, 45°57′·96N 01°04′·38W. **Rear, Soumard** ☆, 600m from front. Same twr: ☆ QR 21m 8M; vis 322°-067°.

Île d'Aix ☆ Fl WR 5s 24m **W24M, R20M**; 103°-R-118°-W-103°; two conspic W ○ twrs, R top; 46°00′·60N 01°10′·67W.

Pte Ste Catherine, jetty hd Q (6) + L Fl 15s 5m 4M; 45°59′·05N 01°07′·85W. Les Palles Q; 45°59′·54N 01°09′·56W.

Fouras, Port Sud bkwtr ☆ Fl WR 4s 6m 9/6M; 115°-R-177°-W-115°; 45°58′·97N 01°05′·72W.

ROCHEFORT

Night passage by yachts is not advised.

☆ Fl (2) G 6s; bcn 45°55′·21N 00°56′·98W, 1·4M S of Rochefort.

ÎLE D'OLÉRON

Pte de Chassiron ☆ Fl 10s 50m, **28M**; conspic W twr, B bands; 46°02′·80N 01°24′·62W, NW tip of island.

Antioche Q 20m 11M; 46°03′·94N 01°23′·71W.

ST DENIS

Dir ☆ 205°, Iso WRG 4s 14m, W11M, R/G8M; 190°-G-204°-W-206°-R-220°; 46°01′·61N 01°21′·92W.

E jetty ☆ Fl (2) WG 6s 6m, W9M, G6M; 205°-G-277°-W-292°-G-165°; □ hut; 46°02′·10N 01°22′·06W.

PORT DU DOUHET and PASSAGE DE L'OUEST

Seaweed farm VQ; 46°00′·65N 01°17′·38W.

N ent 46°00′·10N 01°19′·20W.

Fish farm Q; 46°00′·24N 01°15′·34W. Q (3) 10s; 45°59′·84N 01°14′·79W.

BOYARDVILLE

Mole ☆ Fl (2) R 6s 8m 5M; obsc'd by Pte des Saumonards when brg <150°; W twr, R top; 45°58′·24N 01°13′·83W.

COUREAU D'OLÉRON and LE CHÂTEAU D'OLÉRON

Juliar Q (3) WG 10s 12m, W11M; G8M; 147°-W-336°-G-147°; 45°54′·11N 01°09′·48W.

Chateau d'Oléron, ldg lts 318·5°, both QR 11/24m 7M; synch. Front, 191°-087°; R line on W twr; 45°53′·03N 01°11′·45W. Rear, W twr, R top; 240m from front.

St Trojan-les-Bains bridge (limits of nav width, 18m clearance) Fl G 4s 4M, 45°51′·42N 01°11′·20W; Fl R 4s 4M, 45°51′·40N 01°11′·7W.

LA SEUDRE RIVER

Pte du Mus de Loup ☆ Oc G 4s 8m 6M; 118°-147°; 45°47′·70N 01°08′·60W.

Pertuis de Maumusson. Depths & buoys subject to change.

ATT Maumusson L Fl 10s; 45°43′·90N 01° 16′·98W.

La Barre 45°46′·59N 01°16′·25W.

Tabouret 45°46′·93N 01°16′·15W.

Mattes 45°46′·93N 01°15′·29W.

Gatseau 45°47′·36N 01°14′·70W.

LA COTINIÈRE (SW side of island)

Entrance Ldg lts, 336·6° both ☆ Dir Oc(2)6s,10M, 329°-349° (20°). Front, 6m R octagonal metal structure, 45°54′·72N 01°19′· 71W. Rear, 403m from front, 14m W pylon/ R bands 45°54′·92N 01°19′·83W.

W bkwtr head ☆ Fl R 4s 10m 6M, 45°54′·58N 01°19′·66W.

GIRONDE APPROACHES AND TO BORDEAUX

GRANDE PASSE DE L'OUEST

Pte de la Coubre ☆ Fl (2) 10s 64m **28M**; W twr, R top; 45°41′·78N 01°13′·99W. Same twr, Q R 42m10M; 030°-R-110°.

BXA Iso 4s 8m 7M; ***Racon B***; 45°34′·10N 01°26′·63W. 992271005.

La Palmyre Wtr Twr Dir ☆ 056·7°, WRG 54m **W25M R/G20M**; 055·25°-FG-055·95°-AlWG-056·58°-FW-057·42°-AlWR-058·02-FR-058·72°; Gy Wtr Twr; 45°41′·65N 01°10′·18W.

Duc d'Albe ☆ Fl(2) 6s 10m 2M; W pylon on dolphin; 45°39′·56N 01°08′·77W.

No 1 QG; 45°36′·17N 01°21′·70W; 992271036.

No 6 VQ (6) + L Fl 10s; 45°38′·27N 01°17′·91W.

No 7a Fl G 4s; 45°38′·96N 01°14′·85W.

No 9 Q; 45°39′·43N 01°12′·79W.

No 11 Iso G 4s; 45°39′·06N 01°10′·60W.

No 11A Fl G 2·5s; 45°38'·37N 01°07'·90W.

No 13 Fl (2) G 6s; 45°37'·34N 01°06'·41W.

No 13A Fl (3) G 12s; 45°35'·68N 01°04'·19W.

No 13B QG; 45°34'·65N 01°02'·99W.

Ldg lts 327° (down-river): Front, Terre-Nègre ☆, Oc (3) WRG 12s 39m W14M, R/G11M; 304°-R-319°-W-327°-G-000°-W-004°-G-097°-W-104°-R-116°; W twr, R top on W side; 45°38'·77N 01°06'·39W. Rear, **La Palmyre** Oc (3) R 12s 57m 17M; W radar Twr; 45°39'·72N 01° 07'·25W. 1.1M from front (Terre Nègre) above.

Cordouan ☆ Oc (2+1) WRG 12s 60m, **W19M, R16M, G15M**; 014°-W-126°-G-178·5°-W-250°-W (unintens) -267°-R (unintens)-294·5°-R-014°; obsc'd in estuary when brg >285°; W twr, Gy band; 45°35'·18N 01°10'·40W.

PASSE SUD (or DE GRAVE)

Ldg lts 063°: **Front, St Nicolas** ☆ Dir QG 22m **16M**; intens 061·5°-064·5°; W □ twr; 45°33'·73N 01°05'·01W.

Rear, Pte de Grave ☆ Oc WRG 4s 26m, **W17M, R/G13M**; 033°-W(unintens)-054°-W-233·5°-R-303°-W-312°-G-330°-W-341°- W(unintens)-025°; W □ twr, B corners and top, 0·84M from front.

G 45°30'·33N 01°15'·55W. G3 45°32'·79N 01°07'·72W.

Ldg lts 041°, both Dir QR 33/61m **18M**. **Front, Le Chay** ☆ 45°37'·31N 01°02'·43W. **Rear, St Pierre** ☆, 0·97M from front.

G4 45°34'·70N 01°05'·80W. G6 45°34'·88N 01°04'·80W.

ROYAN

R1 Iso G 4s; 45°36'·56N 01°01'·96W.

S jetty ☆ Fl (2) R 10s 11m 9M; 45°37'·00N 01°01'·81W.

Hbr ent, W jetty ☆ Fl (3) R 12s 8m 6M; 45°37'·12N 01°01'·53W.

PORT BLOC and PORT-MÉDOC

Pte de Grave, jetty Q 6m 2M; 45°34'·42N 01°03'·68W.

Port Bloc, ent N side ☆ Fl G 4s 9m 4M; 45°34'·14N 01°03'·74W.

Port-Médoc, N bkwtr head ☆ QG 4M; 45°33'·40N 01°03'·39W.

MESCHERS, MORTAGNE, PORT MAUBERT, PAUILLAC and BLAYE

Meschers ldg lts 354·4°: QG (privately maintained). Front 45°33'·20N 00°56'·63W, on E bkwtr head. Rear, 130m from front.

Mortagne ent VQ (9) 10s; 45°28'·24N 00°49'·02W.

Port Maubert, ldg lts 024·5°, both QR 5/9m 5M; 45°25'·56N 00°45'·47W.

Pauillac, No 43 Fl (2) G 6s; 45°12'·44N 00°44'·27W.

NE elbow ☆ Fl G 4s 7m 5M; 45°11'·95N 00°44'·59W.

Ent E side ☆ QG 7m 4M; 45°11'·83N 00°44'·59W.

Blaye, No S9 45°09'·35N 00°40'·27W; 1·8M N of Blaye.

N quay ☆ Q (3) R 5s 6m 3M; 45°07'·49N 00°39'·99W.

D6 Fl (2) R 6s; 45°06'·91N 00°39'·93W, 0.6M S of Blaye.

Bec d'Ambés QG 5m 5M; 45°02'·53N 00°36'·47W (here Rivers Dordogne and Garonne flow into River Gironde).

BORDEAUX

Pont d'Aquitaine ☆ 4 F Vi; 44°52'·82N 00°32'·28W.

No 73 Iso G 4s; 44°52'·72N 00°32'·24W.

Lormont Iso R 4s, S end of Ⓥ pontoon; 44°52'·62N 00°32'·12W.

Lock ent to Bassins Nos 1 and 2, 44°51'·72N 00°33'·07W.

Pont de Pierre, 44°50'·30N 00°33'·78W, Km 0.

DISTANCE TABLES

Approx distances in nautical miles are by the most direct route allowing for dangers and TSS.

		1	2	3	4	5	6	7	8	9	10	11	12	13	14	15	16
1	Port Joinville	1															
2	St Gilles-C-de-Vie	18	2														
3	Sables d'Olonne	31	16	3													
4	Bourgenay	40	25	9	4												
5	St Martin (I de Ré)	55	44	27	20	5											
6	La Rochelle	66	51	36	29	12	6										
7	Rochefort	84	75	61	54	36	26	7									
8	R La Seudre	89	71	58	52	33	24	30	8								
9	Port St Denis	59	48	33	30	21	13	26	22	9							
10	Port Bloc/Royan	97	85	71	60	56	52	68	27	42	10						
11	Bordeaux	152	140	126	115	111	107	123	82	97	55	11					
12	Cap Ferret	138	130	113	110	102	98	114	75	88	68	123	12				
13	Capbreton	192	186	169	166	165	156	172	131	145	124	179	58	13			
14	Anglet/Bayonne	200	195	181	178	177	168	184	143	157	132	187	70	12	14		
15	Santander	212	210	204	204	206	202	218	184	192	180	235	133	106	103	15	
16	Cabo Finisterre	377	395	393	394	406	407	423	399	397	401	456	376	370	373	274	16

Times are UT - add 1 hour in non-shaded months to convert to Summer Time

SUN RISE/SET LATITUDE 56°N – 2023

	JANUARY		FEBRUARY		MARCH		APRIL		MAY		JUNE	
	Rise	Set	Rise	Set	Rise	Set	Rise	Set	Rise	Set	Rise	Set
1	0831	1536	0755	1632	0652	1733	0532	1838	0417	1939	0322	2034
4	0830	1540	0750	1639	0645	1740	0524	1844	0410	1945	0319	2038
7	0829	1544	0743	1645	0637	1746	0516	1850	0404	1951	0317	2041
10	0826	1549	0737	1652	0629	1752	0508	1856	0358	1957	0315	2044
13	0824	1554	0730	1659	0621	1759	0500	1902	0352	2002	0314	2047
16	0820	1559	0724	1705	0614	1805	0453	1908	0346	2008	0313	2049
19	0817	1605	0717	1712	0606	1811	0445	1914	0341	2013	0313	2050
22	0812	1611	0710	1718	0558	1817	0438	1920	0336	2019	0313	2051
25	0808	1617	0702	1725	0550	1823	0431	1927	0331	2024	0314	2051
28	0803	1624	0655	1731	0542	1829	0424	1933	0327	2028	0316	2050
31	0757	1630			0534	1836			0323	2033		

	JULY		AUGUST		SEPTEMBER		OCTOBER		NOVEMBER		DECEMBER	
1	0318	2049	0403	2008	0504	1855	0602	1736	0706	1620	0806	1531
4	0321	2047	0409	2002	0509	1848	0608	1728	0713	1614	0811	1529
7	0324	2045	0415	1956	0515	1840	0614	1720	0719	1608	0815	1527
10	0328	2042	0420	1949	0521	1832	0620	1713	0725	1602	0819	1526
13	0332	2039	0426	1942	0527	1824	0626	1705	0732	1556	0823	1525
16	0336	2035	0432	1935	0533	1816	0633	1658	0738	1551	0826	1525
19	0341	2031	0438	1928	0539	1808	0639	1650	0744	1546	0828	1526
22	0345	2026	0444	1921	0545	1800	0645	1643	0750	1542	0830	1527
25	0351	2021	0450	1913	0550	1752	0651	1636	0756	1538	0831	1529
28	0356	2016	0456	1906	0556	1744	0658	1629	0801	1534	0832	1531
31	0401	2010	0502	1858			0704	1622			0831	1534

SUN RISE/SET LATITUDE 48°N – 2023

	JANUARY		FEBRUARY		MARCH		APRIL		MAY		JUNE	
	Rise	Set	Rise	Set	Rise	Set	Rise	Set	Rise	Set	Rise	Set
1	0750	1617	0728	1659	0642	1744	0539	1830	0443	1913	0405	1951
4	0750	1620	0724	1704	0636	1748	0533	1834	0438	1917	0403	1954
7	0749	1624	0720	1709	0630	1753	0527	1838	0433	1921	0402	1956
10	0748	1627	0715	1714	0624	1757	0521	1843	0429	1925	0401	1958
13	0746	1631	0710	1719	0618	1802	0515	1847	0424	1929	0400	2000
16	0744	1635	0705	1723	0612	1806	0509	1851	0421	1933	0400	2002
19	0742	1639	0700	1728	0606	1811	0504	1856	0417	1937	0400	2003
22	0739	1644	0655	1733	0600	1815	0458	1900	0414	1940	0401	2003
25	0736	1648	0649	1738	0553	1819	0453	1904	0411	1944	0401	2004
28	0733	1653	0644	1742	0547	1824	0448	1908	0408	1947	0403	2004
31	0729	1658			0541	1828			0406	1950		

	JULY		AUGUST		SEPTEMBER		OCTOBER		NOVEMBER		DECEMBER	
1	0404	2003	0436	1936	0517	1842	0559	1740	0644	1642	0728	1609
4	0406	2002	0440	1932	0522	1836	0603	1734	0649	1638	0732	1608
7	0409	2001	0444	1927	0526	1830	0607	1728	0654	1633	0735	1607
10	0411	1959	0448	1922	0530	1824	0611	1722	0658	1629	0738	1607
13	0414	1957	0452	1917	0534	1817	0616	1716	0703	1625	0741	1607
16	0417	1955	0456	1912	0538	1811	0620	1710	0707	1622	0744	1607
19	0420	1952	0500	1907	0542	1805	0625	1705	0712	1618	0746	1608
22	0423	1949	0504	1901	0546	1759	0629	1659	0716	1616	0747	1610
25	0427	1945	0508	1855	0550	1752	0634	1654	0720	1613	0749	1611
28	0431	1942	0512	1850	0554	1746	0638	1649	0724	1611	0749	1613
31	0434	1938	0516	1844			0643	1644			0750	1616

SUN RISE/SET LATITUDE 40°N – 2023

	JANUARY Rise	JANUARY Set	FEBRUARY Rise	FEBRUARY Set	MARCH Rise	MARCH Set	APRIL Rise	APRIL Set	MAY Rise	MAY Set	JUNE Rise	JUNE Set
1	0722	1645	0709	1719	0634	1751	0545	1824	0501	1854	0433	1923
4	0722	1648	0706	1722	0629	1755	0540	1827	0457	1857	0432	1925
7	0722	1651	0703	1726	0625	1758	0535	1830	0453	1900	0431	1927
10	0722	1653	0659	1729	0620	1801	0530	1833	0450	1903	0431	1928
13	0721	1657	0656	1733	0615	1804	0526	1836	0447	1906	0431	1930
16	0720	1700	0652	1737	0611	1807	0521	1839	0444	1909	0431	1931
19	0718	1703	0648	1740	0606	1811	0517	1842	0442	1912	0431	1932
22	0717	1707	0644	1744	0601	1814	0513	1845	0439	1915	0431	1932
25	0715	1710	0640	1747	0556	1817	0508	1848	0437	1917	0432	1933
28	0712	1714	0635	1750	0551	1820	0504	1851	0435	1920	0433	1933
31	0710	1717			0546	1823			0434	1922		

	JULY Rise	JULY Set	AUGUST Rise	AUGUST Set	SEPTEMBER Rise	SEPTEMBER Set	OCTOBER Rise	OCTOBER Set	NOVEMBER Rise	NOVEMBER Set	DECEMBER Rise	DECEMBER Set
1	0435	1933	0458	1914	0527	1832	0556	1743	0629	1658	0702	1635
4	0436	1932	0501	1911	0530	1827	0559	1738	0632	1655	0705	1635
7	0438	1932	0504	1907	0533	1822	0602	1733	0635	1651	0708	1635
10	0440	1930	0506	1904	0536	1818	0605	1729	0639	1648	0711	1635
13	0442	1929	0509	1900	0539	1813	0608	1724	0642	1646	0713	1635
16	0444	1927	0512	1856	0541	1808	0611	1720	0646	1643	0715	1636
19	0447	1926	0515	1852	0544	1803	0614	1715	0649	1641	0717	1637
22	0449	1923	0518	1847	0547	1758	0618	1711	0653	1639	0719	1638
25	0452	1921	0521	1843	0550	1753	0621	1707	0656	1638	0720	1640
28	0454	1918	0524	1838	0553	1748	0624	1703	0659	1636	0721	1642
31	0457	1915	0526	1834			0627	1659			0722	1644

MOON RISE/SET LATITUDE 56°N – 2023

	JANUARY Rise	JANUARY Set	FEBRUARY Rise	FEBRUARY Set	MARCH Rise	MARCH Set	APRIL Rise	APRIL Set	MAY Rise	MAY Set	JUNE Rise	JUNE Set
1	1217	0247	1140	0556	1018	0452	1244	0459	1421	0334	1725	0207
4	1307	0652	1440	0809	1343	0636	1642	0524	1825	0351	2204	0252
7	1538	0938	1836	0851	1740	0708	2048	0542	2302	0426	****	0603
10	1930	1033	2229	0910	2139	0726	****	0622	0123	0652	0051	1056
13	2322	1055	0117	0935	0034	0756	0323	0905	0233	1137	0112	1521
16	0207	1117	0542	1106	0437	0958	0423	1355	0256	1609	0143	1943
19	0646	1229	0743	1542	0604	1445	0446	1831	0322	2036	0325	2246
22	0923	1643	0816	2036	0630	1932	0515	2302	0440	****	0706	2343
25	1001	2138	0840	****	0657	****	0649	0130	0804	0111	1059	****
28	1024	0032	0937	0346	0810	0242	1024	0306	1200	0143	1457	0015
31	1109	0442			1125	0443			1558	0200		

	JULY Rise	JULY Set	AUGUST Rise	AUGUST Set	SEPTEMBER Rise	SEPTEMBER Set	OCTOBER Rise	OCTOBER Set	NOVEMBER Rise	NOVEMBER Set	DECEMBER Rise	DECEMBER Set
1	1933	0051	2049	0232	1937	0643	1807	0853	1740	1221	1846	1224
4	2226	0333	2122	0743	2001	1127	1905	1329	2108	1423	2246	1302
7	2307	0836	2145	1220	2110	1545	2208	1558	****	1453	0118	1317
10	2328	1309	2236	1641	****	1753	0048	1637	0339	1508	0521	1338
13	****	1730	0010	1922	0304	1827	0440	1653	0749	1532	0947	1459
16	0119	2046	0358	2009	0654	1842	0841	1712	1203	1710	1149	1918
19	0452	2151	0749	2027	1056	1903	1303	1819	1343	2135	1219	****
22	0845	2212	1144	2045	1512	2022	1520	2214	1410	0045	1240	0303
25	1236	2229	1607	2143	1714	****	1554	0131	1432	0521	1331	0735
28	1702	2314	1850	****	1745	0403	1615	0616	1533	0957	1625	1024
31	2023	0100	1930	0503			1702	1101			2028	1109

MOON RISE/SET LATITUDE 48°N – 2023

	JANUARY Rise	JANUARY Set	FEBRUARY Rise	FEBRUARY Set	MARCH Rise	MARCH Set	APRIL Rise	APRIL Set	MAY Rise	MAY Set	JUNE Rise	JUNE Set
1	1241	0226	1240	0456	1121	0349	1321	0420	1431	0320	1659	0226
4	1401	0559	1530	0718	1426	0551	1648	0514	1805	0405	2100	0346
7	1634	0841	1854	0829	1752	0652	2024	0559	2204	0513	2341	0659
10	1955	1005	2219	0915	2122	0737	****	0713	0019	0755	0031	1112
13	2319	1053	0046	1009	****	0839	0222	1006	0205	1202	0123	1504
16	0144	1144	0438	1211	0332	1103	0359	1416	0259	1559	0225	1851
19	0545	1330	0706	1617	0532	1513	0453	1818	0356	1952	0430	2146
22	0839	1724	0813	2033	0632	1924	0555	2212	0544	2307	0745	2313
25	0953	2141	0908	****	0730	2320	0754	0025	0850	0023	1107	****
28	1045	0014	1036	0248	0913	0139	1105	0223	1214	0126	1436	0029
31	1201	0351			1212	0354			1543	0209		

	JULY Rise	JULY Set	AUGUST Rise	AUGUST Set	SEPTEMBER Rise	SEPTEMBER Set	OCTOBER Rise	OCTOBER Set	NOVEMBER Rise	NOVEMBER Set	DECEMBER Rise	DECEMBER Set
1	1834	0139	2006	0327	1936	0649	1834	0830	1845	1116	1938	1131
4	2137	0434	2116	0755	2034	1058	2007	1228	2155	1334	2305	1240
7	2255	0856	2210	1159	2214	1442	2301	1503	0013	1435	0118	1322
10	2346	1255	2334	1544	0007	1701	0119	1613	0334	1516	0450	1412
13	0029	1641	0114	1825	0331	1806	0441	1656	0712	1611	0840	1606
16	0223	1944	0433	1942	0652	1848	0812	1744	1055	1818	1107	1958
19	0534	2117	0754	2027	1023	1939	1157	1925	1305	2211	1212	****
22	0856	2206	1119	2113	1405	2130	1432	2259	1405	0056	1303	0243
25	1219	2250	1506	2245	1631	****	1542	0149	1459	0457	1429	0638
28	1608	****	1800	0055	1739	0416	1635	0559	1635	0855	1721	0927
31	1927	0205	1918	0522			1800	1005			2050	1044

MOON RISE/SET LATITUDE 40°N – 2023

	JANUARY Rise	JANUARY Set	FEBRUARY Rise	FEBRUARY Set	MARCH Rise	MARCH Set	APRIL Rise	APRIL Set	MAY Rise	MAY Set	JUNE Rise	JUNE Set
1	1258	0211	1317	0419	1201	0310	1346	0354	1438	0310	1640	0239
4	1436	0525	1602	0645	1455	0521	1652	0507	1751	0415	2021	0422
7	1710	0805	1907	0813	1801	0641	2006	0612	2127	0545	2311	0734
10	2013	0945	2212	0918	2109	0745	2339	0747	****	0834	0017	1123
13	2317	1052	0024	1033	****	0908	0144	1043	0145	1219	0130	1452
16	0127	1203	0358	1251	0251	1143	0342	1430	0302	1553	0254	1817
19	0508	1408	0639	1641	0510	1533	0459	1808	0421	1922	0509	2109
22	0809	1752	0810	2032	0634	1918	0623	2140	0624	2227	0811	2252
25	0947	2144	0927	****	0754	2251	0834	****	0920	****	1113	2358
28	1100	0002	1113	0212	0953	0100	1133	0154	1224	0113	1421	0040
31	1235	0318			1244	0321			1532	0216		

	JULY Rise	JULY Set	AUGUST Rise	AUGUST Set	SEPTEMBER Rise	SEPTEMBER Set	OCTOBER Rise	OCTOBER Set	NOVEMBER Rise	NOVEMBER Set	DECEMBER Rise	DECEMBER Set
1	1757	0211	1937	0402	1936	0654	1853	0813	1926	1036	2011	1057
4	2104	0512	2112	0804	2056	1038	2046	1150	2226	1301	2318	1224
7	2246	0910	2228	1143	2254	1403	2336	1427	0030	1422	0117	1325
10	2359	1245	****	1508	0045	1628	0141	1556	0331	1523	0428	1436
13	0056	1609	0153	1748	0350	1752	0442	1658	0647	1639	0759	1647
16	0303	1905	0456	1923	0651	1853	0752	1807	1014	1859	1038	2024
19	0602	2054	0757	2027	1000	2004	1117	2006	1238	2235	1206	****
22	0904	2202	1102	2132	1324	2211	1400	2330	1402	0104	1320	0229
25	1207	2305	1428	2324	1602	0028	1534	0203	1518	0441	1506	0602
28	1534	0004	1726	0134	1734	0425	1650	0547	1714	0817	1757	0851
31	1850	0245	1910	0536			1836	0929			2106	1026

SPEED, TIME AND DISTANCE (NAUTICAL MILES)

Time in minutes	Speed in knots 1	2	3	4	5	6	7	8	9	10	15	20
1	0·0	0·0	0·1	0·1	0·1	0·1	0·1	0·1	0·2	0·2	0·3	0·3
2	0·0	0·1	0·1	0·1	0·2	0·2	0·2	0·3	0·3	0·3	0·5	0·7
3	0·1	0·1	0·2	0·2	0·3	0·3	0·4	0·4	0·5	0·5	0·8	1·0
4	0·1	0·1	0·2	0·3	0·3	0·4	0·5	0·5	0·6	0·7	1·0	1·3
5	0·1	0·2	0·3	0·3	0·4	0·5	0·6	0·7	0·8	0·8	1·3	1·7
6	0·1	0·2	0·3	0·4	0·5	0·6	0·7	0·8	0·9	1·0	1·5	2·0
7	0·1	0·2	0·4	0·5	0·6	0·7	0·8	0·9	1·1	1·2	1·8	2·3
8	0·1	0·3	0·4	0·5	0·7	0·8	0·9	1·1	1·2	1·3	2·0	2·7
9	0·2	0·3	0·5	0·6	0·8	0·9	1·1	1·2	1·4	1·5	2·3	3·0
10	0·2	0·3	0·5	0·7	0·8	1·0	1·2	1·3	1·5	1·7	2·5	3·3
11	0·2	0·4	0·6	0·7	0·9	1·1	1·3	1·5	1·7	1·8	2·8	3·7
12	0·2	0·4	0·6	0·8	1·0	1·2	1·4	1·6	1·8	2·0	3·0	4·0
13	0·2	0·4	0·7	0·9	1·1	1·3	1·5	1·7	2·0	2·2	3·3	4·3
14	0·2	0·5	0·7	0·9	1·2	1·4	1·6	1·9	2·1	2·3	3·5	4·7
15	0·3	0·5	0·8	1·0	1·3	1·5	1·8	2·0	2·3	2·5	3·8	5·0
16	0·3	0·5	0·8	1·1	1·3	1·6	1·9	2·1	2·4	2·7	4·0	5·3
17	0·3	0·6	0·9	1·1	1·4	1·7	2·0	2·3	2·6	2·8	4·3	5·7
18	0·3	0·6	0·9	1·2	1·5	1·8	2·1	2·4	2·7	3·0	4·5	6·0
19	0·3	0·6	1·0	1·3	1·6	1·9	2·2	2·5	2·9	3·2	4·8	6·3
20	0·3	0·7	1·0	1·3	1·7	2·0	2·3	2·7	3·0	3·3	5·0	6·7
21	0·4	0·7	1·1	1·4	1·8	2·1	2·5	2·8	3·2	3·5	5·3	7·0
22	0·4	0·7	1·1	1·5	1·8	2·2	2·6	2·9	3·3	3·7	5·5	7·3
23	0·4	0·8	1·2	1·5	1·9	2·3	2·7	3·1	3·5	3·8	5·8	7·7
24	0·4	0·8	1·2	1·6	2·0	2·4	2·8	3·2	3·6	4·0	6·0	8·0
25	0·4	0·8	1·3	1·7	2·1	2·5	2·9	3·3	3·8	4·2	6·3	8·3
30	0·5	1·0	1·5	2·0	2·5	3·0	3·5	4·0	4·5	5·0	7·5	10·0
35	0·6	1·2	1·8	2·3	2·9	3·5	4·1	4·7	5·3	5·8	8·8	11·7
40	0·7	1·3	2·0	2·7	3·3	4·0	4·7	5·3	6·0	6·7	10·0	13·3
45	0·8	1·5	2·3	3·0	3·8	4·5	5·3	6·0	6·8	7·5	11·3	15·0
50	0·8	1·7	2·5	3·3	4·2	5·0	5·8	6·7	7·5	8·3	12·5	16·7

DISTANCE (NAUTICAL MILES) OFF RISING/DIPPING LIGHTS

Height of light in metres	Height of eye in feet 2	3	4	5	6	7	8	9	10	20	30	40	50
2	4·6	4·9	5·2	5·5	5·7	6·0	6·2	6·4	6·6	8·1	9·2	10·2	11·0
3	5·2	5·6	5·9	6·2	6·4	6·6	6·8	7·0	7·2	8·7	9·9	10·8	11·7
4	5·8	6·1	6·4	6·7	6·9	7·2	7·4	7·6	7·8	9·3	10·4	11·4	12·2
5	6·3	6·6	6·9	7·2	7·4	7·7	7·9	8·1	8·3	9·8	10·9	11·9	12·7
6	6·7	7·1	7·4	7·6	7·9	8·1	8·3	8·5	8·7	10·2	11·3	12·3	13·2
7	7·1	7·5	7·8	8·0	8·3	8·5	8·7	8·9	9·1	10·6	11·8	12·7	13·6
8	7·5	7·8	8·2	8·4	8·7	8·9	9·1	9·3	9·5	11·0	12·1	13·1	14·0
9	7·8	8·2	8·5	8·8	9·0	9·2	9·5	9·7	9·8	11·3	12·5	13·5	14·3
10	8·2	8·5	8·8	9·1	9·4	9·6	9·8	10·0	10·2	11·7	12·8	13·8	14·6
11	8·5	8·9	9·2	9·4	9·7	9·9	10·1	10·3	10·5	12·0	13·1	14·1	15·0
12	8·8	9·2	9·5	9·7	10·0	10·2	10·4	10·6	10·8	12·3	13·4	14·4	15·3
13	9·1	9·5	9·8	10·0	10·3	10·5	10·7	10·9	11·1	12·6	13·7	14·7	15·6
14	9·4	9·7	10·0	10·3	10·6	10·8	11·0	11·2	11·4	12·9	14·0	15·0	15·8
15	9·6	10·0	10·3	10·6	10·8	11·1	11·3	11·5	11·6	13·1	14·3	15·3	16·1
16	9·9	10·3	10·6	10·8	11·1	11·3	11·5	11·7	11·9	13·4	14·6	15·5	16·4
17	10·2	10·5	10·8	11·1	11·3	11·6	11·8	12·0	12·2	13·7	14·8	15·8	16·6
18	10·4	10·8	11·1	11·4	11·6	11·8	12·0	12·2	12·4	13·9	15·1	16·0	16·9
19	10·7	11·0	11·3	11·6	11·8	12·1	12·3	12·5	12·7	14·2	15·3	16·3	17·1
20	10·9	11·3	11·6	11·8	12·1	12·3	12·5	12·7	12·9	14·4	15·5	16·5	17·3
25	12·0	12·3	12·6	12·9	13·2	13·4	13·6	13·8	14·0	15·5	16·6	17·6	18·4
30	13·0	13·3	13·6	13·9	14·1	14·4	14·6	14·8	15·0	16·5	17·6	18·6	19·4
40	14·7	15·1	15·4	15·7	15·9	16·1	16·3	16·5	16·7	18·2	19·4	20·3	21·2
50	16·3	16·6	16·9	17·2	17·4	17·7	17·9	18·1	18·3	19·8	20·9	21·9	22·7
60	17·7	18·0	18·3	18·6	18·8	19·1	19·3	19·5	19·7	21·2	22·3	23·3	24·1

CONVERSION TABLE

Sq inches to sq millimetres *multiply by* **645.20**	**Sq millimetres to sq inches** *multiply by* **0.0016**
Inches to millimetres *multiply by* **25.40**	**Millimetres to inches** *multiply by* **0.0394**
Sq feet to square metres *multiply by* **0.093**	**Sq metres to sq feet** *multiply by* **10.7640**
Inches to centimetres *multiply by* **2.54**	**Centimetres to inches** *multiply by* **0.3937**
Feet to metres *multiply by* **0.305**	**Metres to feet** *multiply by* **3.2810**
Nautical miles to kilometres *multiply by* **1.852**	**Kilometres to nautical miles** *multiply by* **0.5400**
Statute miles to kilometres *multiply by* **1.609**	**Kilometres to statute miles** *multiply by* **0.6214**
Statute miles to nautical miles *multiply by* **0.8684**	**Nautical miles to statute miles** *multiply by* **1.1515**
HP to metric HP *multiply by* **1.014**	**Metric HP to HP** *multiply by* **0.9862**
Pounds per sq inch to kg per sq centimetre *multiply by* **0.0703**	**Kg per sq centimetre to pounds per sq inch** *multiply by* **14.2200**
HP to kilowatts *multiply by* **0.746**	**Kilowatts to HP** *multiply by* **1.341**
Cu inches to cu centimetres *multiply by* **16.39**	**Cu centimetres to cu inches** *multiply by* **0.0610**
Imperial gallons to litres *multiply by* **4.540**	**Litres to imperial gallons** *multiply by* **0.2200**
Pints to litres *multiply by* **0.5680**	**Litres to pints** *multiply by* **1.7600**
Pounds to kilogrammes *multiply by* **0.4536**	**Kilogrammes to pounds** *multiply by* **2.2050**

LIGHT CHARACTERISTICS

CLASS OF LIGHT		International abbreviations	National abbreviations
FIXED		F	
OCCULTING *(total duration of light longer than dark)*			
Single-occulting			Oc Occ
Group-occulting	eg	Oc(2)	Gp Occ(2)
Composite group-occulting	eg	Oc(2+3)	Gp Occ(2+3)
ISOPHASE *(light and dark equal)*			Iso
FLASHING *(total duration of light shorter than dark)*			
Single-flashing		Fl	
Long-flashing *(flash 2s or longer)*			L Fl
Group-flashing	eg	Fl(3)	Gp Fl(3)
Composite group-flashing	eg	Fl(2+1)	Gp Fl(2+1)
QUICK *(50 to 79, usually either 50 or 60, flashes per min.)*			
Continuous quick		Q	Qk Fl
Group quick	eg	Q(3)	Qk Fl(3)
Interrupted quick		IQ	Int Qk Fl
VERY QUICK *(80 to 159, usually either 100 or 120, flashes per min.)*			
Continuous very quick		VQ	V Qk Fl
Group very quick	eg	VQ(3)	V Qk Fl(3)
Interrupted very quick		IVQ	Int V Qk Fl
ULTRA QUICK *(160 or more, usually 240 to 300, flashes per min.)*			
Continuous ultra quick		UQ	
Interrupted ultra quick		IUQ	
MORSE CODE	eg	Mo(K)	
FIXED AND FLASHING		F Fl	
ALTERNATING	eg	Al. WR	Alt. WR

Illustration
Period shown ├──────┤

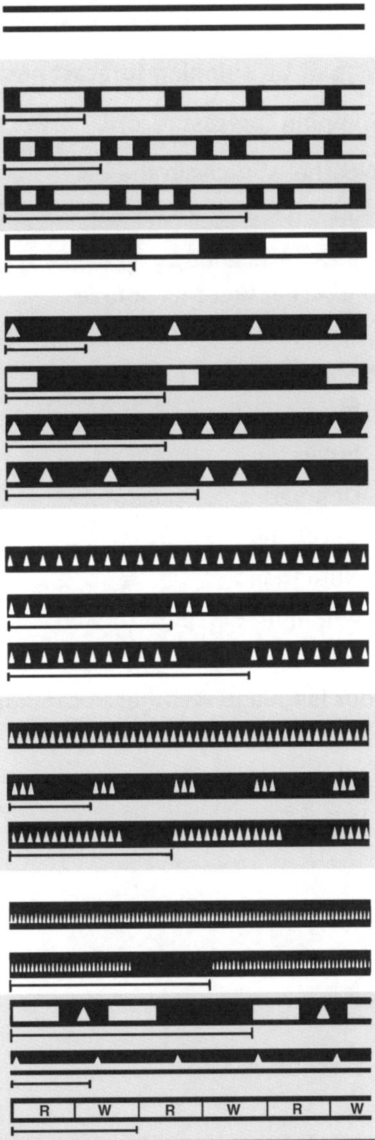

COLOUR	International abbreviations
White	W *(may be omitted)*
Red	R
Green	G
Blue	Bu
Violet	Vi
Yellow	Y
Orange	Y
Amber	Y

NOMINAL RANGE in miles		International abbreviations
Light with single range	eg	15M
Light with two different ranges	eg	15/10M
Light with three or more ranges	eg	15-7M
PERIOD is given in seconds	eg	90s
DISPOSITION horizontally disposed		(hor)
VERTICALLY DISPOSED		(vert)
SYNCHRONISED with (an)other light(s)		(sync)
ELEVATION is given in metres (m) or feet (ft) above MHWS		

Chapter 2 – Weather

Beaufort scale

Force	Wind speed (knots)	(km/h)	(m/sec)	Description	State of sea	Probable wave ht(m)
0	0–1	0–2	0–0·5	Calm	Like a mirror	0
1	1–3	2–6	0·5–1·5	Light airs	Ripples like scales are formed	0
2	4–6	7–11	2–3	Light breeze	Small wavelets, still short but more pronounced, not breaking	0·1
3	7–10	13–19	4–5	Gentle breeze	Large wavelets, crests begin to break; a few white horses	0·4
4	11–16	20–30	6–8	Moderate breeze	Small waves growing longer; fairly frequent white horses	1
5	17–21	31–39	8–11	Fresh breeze	Moderate waves, taking more pronounced form; many white horses, perhaps some spray	2
6	22–27	41–50	11–14	Strong breeze	Large waves forming; white foam crests more extensive; probably some spray	3
7	28–33	52–61	14–17	Near gale	Sea heaps up; white foam from breaking waves begins to blow in streaks	4
8	34–40	63–74	17–21	Gale	Moderately high waves of greater length; edge of crests break into spindrift; foam blown in well-marked streaks	5·5

Terminology used in forecasts

Pressure systems' speed of movement

Slowly	< 15 knots
Steadily	15–25 knots
Rather quickly	25–35 knots
Rapidly	35–45 knots
Very rapidly	> 45 knots

Visibility

Good	> 5 miles
Moderate	2–5 miles
Poor	1000 metres–2 miles
Fog	< 1000 metres

Barometric pressure tendency

Rising/falling slowly: Change of 0·1 to 1·5 hPa/mb in the preceding 3 hours.
Rising/falling: Change of 1·6 to 3·5 hPa/mb in the preceding 3 hours.
Rising/falling quickly: Change of 3·6 to 6 hPa/mb in the preceding 3 hours.
Rising/falling very rapidly: Change of > 6 hPa/mb in the preceding 3 hours.
Now rising/falling: Pressure has been falling (rising) or steady in the preceding 3 hours, but was definitely rising (falling) at the time of observation.

Gale warnings

A ***Gale*** warning means that winds of at least F8 (34-40kn) or gusts up to 43-51kn are expected somewhere within the area, but not necessarily over the whole area

Severe Gale means winds of at least F9 (41-47kn) or gusts reaching 52-60kn

Storm means winds of F10 (48-55kn) or gusts of 61-68kn

Violent Storm means winds of F11 (56-63kn) or gusts of 69+ kn

Hurricane Force means winds of F12 (64+ kn)

Gale warnings remain in force until amended or cancelled. If a gale persists for >24 hours the warning is re-issued.

Timing of gale warnings from time of issue

Imminent	<6 hrs
Soon	6–12 hrs
Later	>12 hrs

Strong wind warnings

Issued, if possible 6 hrs in advance, when winds F6 or more are expected up to 5M offshore; valid for 12 hrs.

MAP OF UK SHIPPING FORECAST AREAS

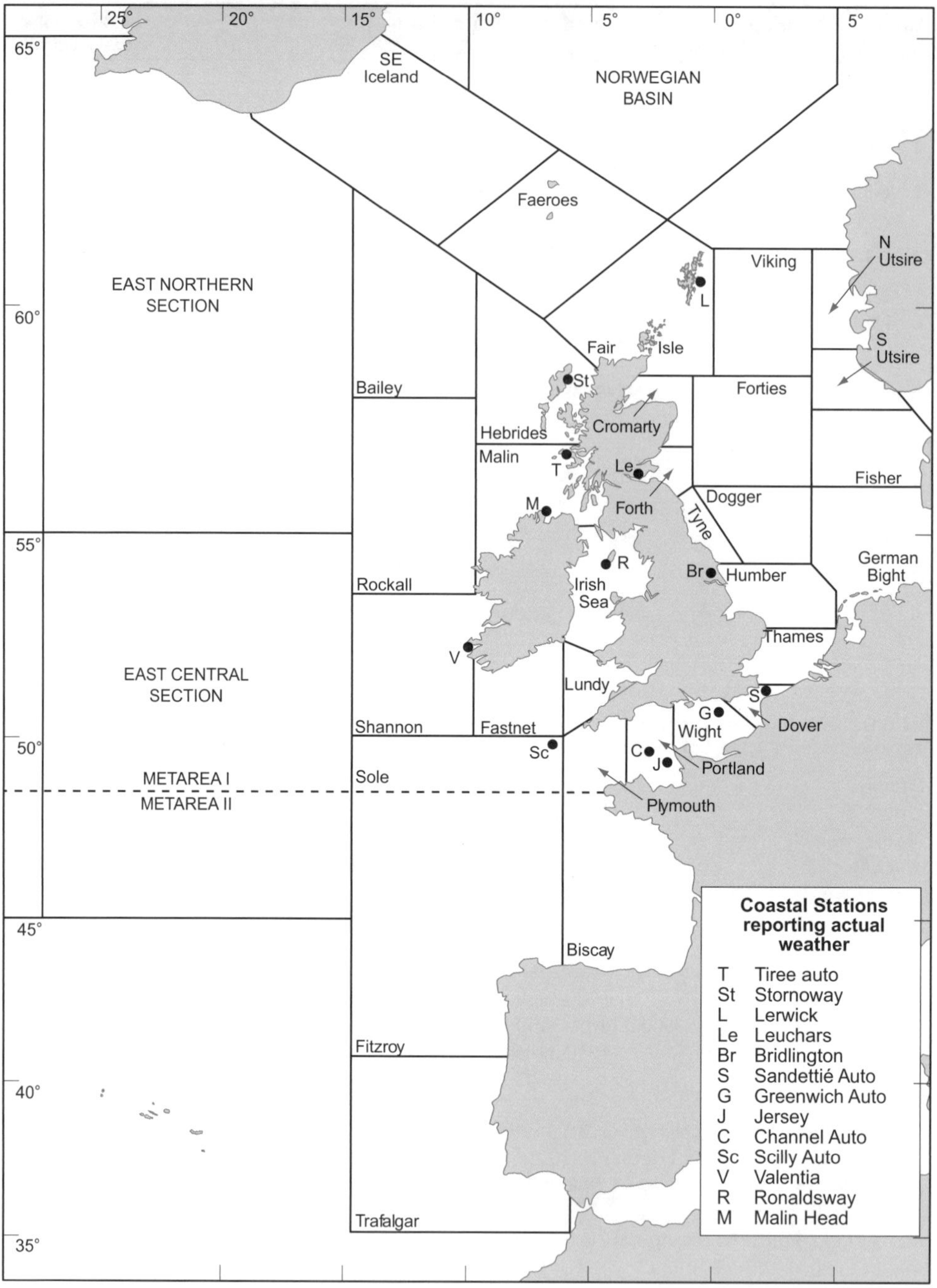

SHIPPING FORECAST RECORD TIME/DAY/DATE ....

GENERAL SYNOPSIS At 0048, 0520, 1201, 1754 LT

System	Present position	Movement	Forecast position	At

Gales	SEA AREA FORECAST	Wind (At first)	Wind (Later)	Weather	Visibility
	VIKING				
	NORTH UTSIRE				
	SOUTH UTSIRE				
	FORTIES				
	CROMARTY				
	FORTH				
	TYNE				
	DOGGER				
	FISHER				
	GERMAN BIGHT				
	HUMBER				
	THAMES				
	DOVER				
	WIGHT				
	PORTLAND				
	PLYMOUTH				
	BISCAY				
	TRAFALGAR (0048)				
	FITZROY				
	SOLE				
	LUNDY				
	FASTNET				
	IRISH SEA				
	SHANNON				
	ROCKALL				
	MALIN				
	HEBRIDES				
	BAILEY				
	FAIR ISLE				
	FAEROES				
	S E ICELAND				

COASTAL REPORTS at .... UT BST	Wind Direction	Wind Force	Weather	Visibility	Pressure	Change
Tiree auto (T)						
Stornoway (St)						
Lerwick (L)						
Leuchars (Le)						
Bridlington (Br)						
Sandettié auto (S)						

COASTAL REPORTS	Wind Direction	Wind Force	Weather	Visibility	Pressure	Change
Greenwich auto (G)						
Jersey (J)						
Channel auto (C)						
Scilly auto (Sc)						
Valentia (V)						
Ronaldsway (R)						
Malin Head (M)						

SOURCES OF WEATHER INFORMATION IN THE UK

BBC Radio 4 Shipping forecasts are at:

0048 LT[1]	LW FM
0520 LT[1]	LW FM
1201 LT	weekdays only, LW FM
1754 LT	weekdays LW only
0048, 0520,1754 LT	Sat/Sun, LW, FM

[1]includes weather reports from coastal stations

Frequencies

LW		198 kHz
FM	**England**	92·4–94·6 MHz
	Scotland	91·3–96·1 MHz
		103·5–104·9 MHz
	Wales	92·8–96·1 MHz
		103·5–104·9 MHz
	N Ireland	93·2–96·0 MHz
		103·5–104·6 MHz
	Channel Islands	94·8 MHz

The Shipping forecast contains:

Time of issue; summary of gale warnings in force at that time; a general synopsis of weather systems and their expected development and movement over the next 24 hours; sea area forecasts for the same 24 hours, including wind direction/force, weather and visibility in each; and an outlook for the following 24 hours.

Gale warnings for all affected areas are broadcast at the earliest break in Radio 4 programmes after receipt, as well as after the next news bulletin.

Shipping forecasts cover large sea areas, and rarely include the detailed variations that may occur near land. The inshore waters forecast can be more helpful on coastal passages.

Weather reports from coastal stations follow the 0048 and 0520 shipping forecasts. They include wind direction and force, present weather, visibility, and sea-level pressure and tendency, if available. The stations are shown on the previous page.

BBC Radio 4 Inshore waters forecast

A forecast for inshore waters (up to 12M offshore) in 17 areas around the UK and N Ireland, valid for 24 hrs, is broadcast after the 0048 and 0520 coastal station reports.

It includes forecasts of wind direction and force, weather, visibility and sea state. The 17 inshore areas are defined by the following well-known places and headlands, clockwise around the UK: Cape Wrath, Orkney, Rattray Hd, Berwick-upon-Tweed, Whitby, Gibraltar Point, N Foreland, Selsey Bill, Lyme Regis, Land's End, St David's Head, Great Ormes Head, Isle of Man, Mull of Galloway, Carlingford Lough, Lough Foyle, Mull of Kintyre, Ardnamurchan Pt and Shetland.

Strong wind warnings are issued by the Met Office whenever winds of Force 6 or more are expected over coastal waters up to 5M offshore.

Reports of actual weather are broadcast from all the coastal stations below after the 0048 inshore waters forecast and also after the 0520 forecast, except those in italics: Tiree*, Stornoway, Lerwick, *Wick*, Aberdeen,* Leuchars, *Boulmer*, Bridlington, Sandettie LV*, Greenwich LV*, *St Catherines Point**, Jersey, Channel LV*, Scilly*, *Milford Haven, Aberporth, Valley, Liverpool (Crosby),* Valentia, Ronaldsway, Malin Head, *Macrihanish**. An asterix* denotes an automatic station.

BBC general (land) forecasts

Land area forecasts may include an outlook up to 48 hours beyond the shipping forecast, plus more details of frontal systems and weather along the coasts. The most comprehensive land area forecasts are broadcast by Radio 4 on the frequencies above.

Land area forecasts – Wind strength

Wind descriptions used in land forecasts, with their Beaufort scale equivalents, are:

Calm	0	Fresh	5
Light	1–3	Strong	6–7
Moderate	4	Gale	8

Land area forecasts – Visibility

The following visibility definitions are used in land forecasts:

Mist	2000m–1000m
Fog	<1000m
Dense fog	< 50m

NAVTEX

NAVTEX is the prime method of disseminating MSI to at least 200 miles offshore. A dedicated aerial and receiver with an LCD screen (or integrated printer) are required. The user selects which stations and message categories are recorded for automatic display or printing.

Two frequencies are used. On the international frequency, 518kHz, messages are always available in English with excellent coverage of Europe. Interference between stations is minimised by scheduling time slots and and by limiting transmission power; see Fig 6(3). NAVTEX information applies only to the geographical area for which each station is responsible.

490 kHz (for clarity shown in italics throughout this chapter) is used abroad for transmissions in the national language. In the UK it is used for inshore waters forecasts in English. Identification letters for 490 kHz stations differ from 518 kHz stations.

Message categories

A*	Navigational warnings
B*	Meteorological warnings
C	Ice reports
D*	SAR info and piracy warnings
E	Weather forecasts
F	Pilot service
H	Loran-C
J	Satellite navigation
K	Other electronic navaids
L	Subfacts and Gunfacts (UK)
V	Amplifies Navwarnings initially sent under A; plus weekly oil/gas rig moves.
W-Y	Special service, trials
Z	No messages on hand at scheduled time

Missing category letters are unallocated.

*The receiver cannot reject these categories.

WEATHER

NAVTEX is convenient and particularly useful when preoccupied handling your vessel as you will not miss potentially important information.

Messages

Each message is prefixed by a four-character group:

The first character is the code letter of the transmitting station (eg **E** for Niton).

The second character is the message category, see below.

The third and fourth are message serial numbers, running from 01 to 99 and then re-starting at 01.

The serial number 00 denotes urgent messages which are always printed.

Messages which are corrupt or have already been printed are rejected. Weather messages, and certain other message types, are dated and timed.

NAVTEX stations/areas – UK & W Europe

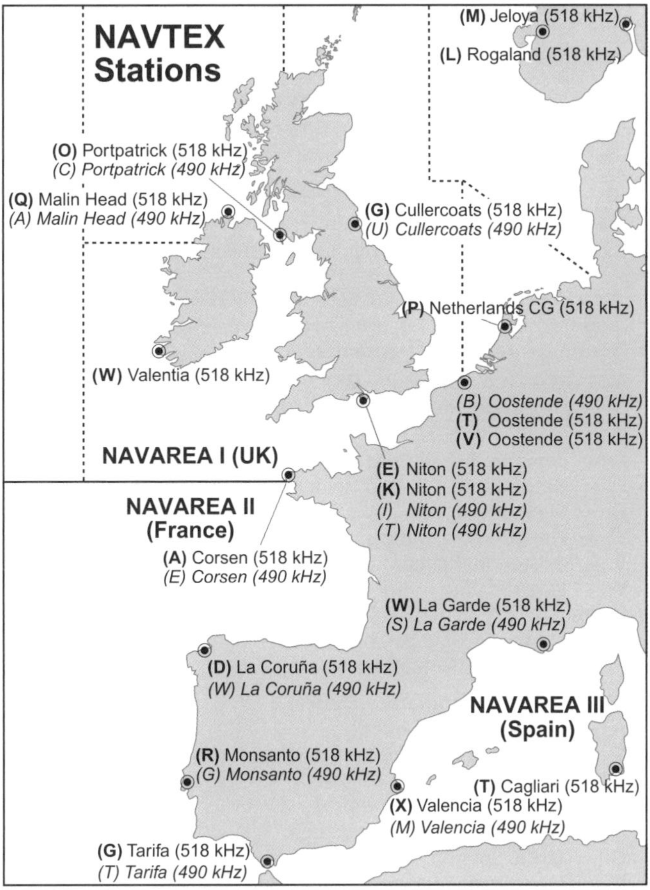

UK Sea area forecasts on 518 kHz

The times (UT) of weather messages are in bold; the times of an extended outlook (a further 2 or 3 days beyond the shipping forecast period) are in italics.

G – **Cullercoats** *0100* 0500 **0900** 1300 1700 **2100**
Viking, Forties, Cromarty, Forth, Tyne, Dogger, Humber, Thames, Fair Isle .

O – **Portpatrick** *0220* **0620** 1020 1420 **1820** 2220
Lundy clockwise to SE Iceland, excluding Shannon.

E – **Niton** *0040* 0440 **0840** 1240 1640 **2040**
Thames clockwise to Fastnet, excluding Trafalgar.

Q – **Malin Head** Shannon, Rockall, Malin, Hebrides **0640** **1840**

T – **Oostende** Thames, Dover 0710, 1910

UK490 kHz broadcasts (in italic) provide forecasts for UK inshore waters, a national 3 day outlook for inshore waters and, at times in bold, reports of actual weather at some or all of the places listed below. To receive these reports select message category 'V' on the receiver. Times (UT) are listed in chronological order. Reports include some or all of: Sea level pressure (hPa/mb), wind direction and speed (kn), weather, visibility (M), air and sea temperatures (°C), dewpoint temperature (°C) and mean wave height (m).

A – **Malin Head** **0000** **0400** 0800 **1200** **1600** 2000
Lough Foyle to Carlingford Lough, Mull of Galloway to Cape Wrath, the Minch.

Note times of forecasts and actuals not known at time of going to press.

C – **Portpatrick** Land's End to Shetland **0020** **0420** 0820 **1220** **1620** 2020
N Rona, Stornoway, S Uist, Lusa (Skye), Tiree, Campbeltown Airport, Macrihanish, Belfast, Malin Hd, Belmullet, St Bees Hd, Ronaldsway, Crosby, Valley, Aberporth, Milford Haven, Roches Pt, Valentia, St Mawgan .

I – **Niton** The Wash to St David's Head **0120** 0520 **0920** **1320** 1720 **2120**
Sandettie Lt V, Greenwich Lt V, Bournmouth Airport, Guernsey airport, Jersey airport, Plymouth (Mountbatten), Culdrose, Seven Stones Lt V, Roches Point(Cork).

U – **Cullercoats** Cape Wrath to N Foreland **0320** 0720 **1120** **1520** 1920 **2320**
Sandettie Lt V, Manston, Shoeburyness, Weybourne, Donna Nook, Boulmer, Leuchars, Aberdeen, Lossiemouth, Wick, Kirkwall, Lerwick, Foula, K7 Met buoy, Sule Skerry.

NAVTEX coverage abroad: Selected NAVTEX stations in Metareas I and II, with identity codes and transmission times, are listed below. Times of weather messages are shown in **bold**. Gale warnings are usually transmitted 4 hourly.

METAREA I (Co-ordinator – UK)	**Transmission times (UT)**					
B – **Oostende**, *Belgium (mostly Dutch)*	***0010***	***0410***	*0810*	*1210*	***1610***	***2010***
K – **Niton** (Note 1)	0140	0540	0940	1340	1740	2140
L – **Pinneberg**, *Hamburg*	***0150***	***0550***	*0950*	*1350*	***1750***	***2150***
P – **Netherlands CG**, Den Helder	**0230**	0630	1030	**1430**	1830	2230
Q – **Malin Head**, Eire	0240	**0640**	**1040**	1440	**1840**	**2240**
S – **Pinneberg**, Hamburg	**0300**	**0700**	**1100**	**1500**	**1900**	**2300**
V – **Oostende,** Belgium (Note 2)	0330	0730	1130	1530	1930	2330
W – **Valentia**, Eire	0340	**0740**	**1140**	1540	**1940**	**2340**

Notes:
1 In English, no weather; only Nav warnings for waters from Cap Gris Nez to Île de Bréhat.
2 No weather information, only Nav warnings.

METAREA II (Co-ordinator – France)						
A – **Corsen**, Le Stiff, France	**0000**	0400	0800	**1200**	1600	2000
E – ***Corsen**, Le Stiff, France (In French)*	*0040*	*0440*	***0840***	*1240*	*1640*	***2040***
D – **Coruña**, Spain	0030	0430	**0830**	1230	1630	**2030**
W – ***Coruña**, Spain (in Spanish)*	*0340*	*0740*	***1140***	*1540*	***1940***	*2340*
F – **São Miguel ,** Açores, Portugal	**0050**	**0450**	**0850**	**1250**	**1650**	**2050**
G – **Tarifa,** Spain	0100	0500	**0900**	1300	1700	**2100**
R – **Monsanto**, Portugal	**0250**	**0650**	**1050**	**1450**	**1850**	**2250**

INTERNET WEATHER SOURCES

The Internet provides a useful back-up for GMDSS services,and information not available by conventional means.

www.metoffice.gov.uk/weather/marine/ has texts of all marine forecasts, warnings and weather from coastal stations, light vessels and data buoys. www.bbc.co.uk/weather/coast/ has texts of NAVTEX broadcasts.

Other websites include: www.metmarine.com
www.weatheronline.com / www.mailasail.com
www.grib.us / www.saildocs.com
www.passageweather.com
www.windfinder.com / www.xcweather.co.uk/
www.windguru.com / www.theyr.com /
www.wetterzentrale.de/topkarten/tknf.html
www.weatherweb.net/marine
www.weather.mailasail.com/Franks-Weather

Broadcasts of shipping and inshore waters forecasts by HM Coastguard

HM MRCC broadcast MSI every 3 hours at the times shown below* (LT). The VHF working channel, either 10,62,63, or 64, is announced on VHF Ch 16 prior to each broadcast which will use one of 3 different Groups of MSI: **Group A**, the full broadcast, contains the Shipping forecast, a new Inshore waters forecast and 24 hrs outlook, Gale warnings, a 3 day forecast for Fishermen in the winter months, Navigational (WZ) warnings and Subfacts & Gunfacts where relevant ‡. '**A**' broadcast times are in **bold type**.

Group B contains a new Inshore waters forecast, plus the previous outlook, and Gale warnings. '**B**' broadcast times are in plain type.

Group C is a repeat of the Inshore forecast and Gale warnings (as per the previous Group A or B) plus new Strong wind warnings. '**C**' broadcast times are *italicised.*

Note: ‡ indicates Subfacts & Gunfacts.

Coastguard	Shipping forecast areas	Inshore areas	Broadcast times, LT*							
East Coast			B	*C*	**A**	*C*	B	*C*	**A**	*C*
Aberdeen‡	Cromarty, Forties, Forth, Fair Isle, Tyne	1,2	0130	*0430*	**0730**	*1030*	1330	*1630*	**1930**	*2230*
Humber	Tyne Dogger Fisher, Humber, German Bight	3,4,5	0150	*0450*	**0750**	*1050*	1350	*1650*	**1950**	*2250*
South Coast			B	*C*	**A**	*C*	B	*C*	**A**	*C*
Dover	Humber, Thames, Dover, Wight	5,6	0110	*0410*	**0710**	*1010*	1310	*1610*	**1910**	*2210*
Solent	Dover, Wight, Portland, Plymouth	5, 6,7	0130	*0430*	**0730**	*1030*	1330	*1630*	**1930**	*2230*
Falmouth‡	Portland, Plymouth, Sole, Lundy, Fastnet.	8,9	0110	*0410*	**0710**	*1010*	1310	*1610*	**1910**	*2210*
West Coast			B	*C*	**A**	*C*	B	*C*	**A**	*C*
Milford Haven	Lundy, Fastnet, Irish Sea	9, 10	0150	*0450*	**0750**	*1050*	1350	*1650*	**1950**	*2250*
Holyhead A	Irish Sea	10,11	0150	*0450*	**0750**	*1050*	1350	*1650*	**1950**	*2250*
Holyhead B	Irish Sea	11,12	0130	*0430*	**0730**	*1030*	1330	*1630*	**1930**	*2230*
Belfast‡	Irish Sea, Rockall, Malin, Hebrides	12,13,14	0210	*0510*	**0810**	*1110*	1410	*1710*	**2010**	*2310*
Stornoway‡	Rockall, Malin, Hebrides, Bailey, Fair Is, Faeroes, SE Iceland	15,16,17	0110	*0410*	**0710**	*1010*	1310	*1610*	**1910**	*2210*
Shetland	Cromarty, Viking, Fair Isle	18	0110	*0410*	**0710**	*1010*	1310	*1610*	**1910**	*2210*

*HMCG endeavour to broadcast at the times shown but this can vary depending on the level of operational activity during busy times and emergencies.

NOTE: Readers are advised to check for changes in the MCA Maritime safety leaflet information (MCA/064) available at www.mcga.gov.uk. See also our free monthly updates from January to June available for download www.reedsnauticalalmanac.co.uk/update.

Remote CG transmitters and their VHF working channels

MSI broadcasts are transmitted every 3 hours from the start times (LT) shown via remote aerial sites giving optimum coverage at the positions listed below. The VHF broadcast channel, either 10, 62, 63 or 64 is usually announced first on Ch 16.

To avoid missing a broadcast, pre-select Ch 16 on Dual watch with the relevant (clearest) channel. **MF frequencies** (*kHz*), as quoted below, are also used for the broadcasts, primarily for fishermen.

INSHORE WATER FORECAST AREAS, MSI TRANSMITTERS, WORKING CHANNELS AND START TIMES

1 Cape Wrath to Rattray Head inc Orkney, 0130

Durness (Loch Eriboll)	63	58°34'N 04°44'W
Noss Head (Wick)	62	58°29'N 03°03'W
Rosemarkie (Cromarty)	64	57°38'N 04°05'W
Windyheads Hill	63	57°39'N 02°14'W

2 Rattray Head to Berwick-upon-Tweed, 0130

Gregness *2226kHz*,	64	57°08'N 02°03'W
Inverbervie	63	56°51'N 02°16'W
Fife Ness	62	56°17'N 02°35'W
Craigkelly (Burntisland)	63	56°04'N 03°14'W
St Abbs Head/Cross Law	64	55°54'N 02°12'W

3 Berwick-upon-Tweed to Whitby, 0150

Newton	63	55°31'N 01°37'W
Cullercoats(Blyth) *1925kHz*,	64	55°04'N 01°28'W
Boulby	63	54°34'N 00°51'W

4 Whitby to Gibraltar Point, 0150

Ravenscar	64	54°24'N 00°30'W
Flamborough	63	54°07'N 00°05'W
Easington (Spurn Hd)	64	53°39'N 00°06'E
Mablethorpe	62	53°21'N 00°16'E

5 Gibraltar Point to North Foreland, 0110

Guy's Head (Wisbech)	63	52°48'N 00°13'E
Langham (Blakeney)	64	52°57'N 00°58'E
Trimingham (Cromer)	63	52°54'N 01°21'E
Caister (Great Yarmouth)	64	52°36N 01°43E
Lowestoft	63	52°29'N 01°46'E
Bawdsey (R Deben)	62	52°00'N 01°25'E
Walton-on-the-Naze	63	51°51'N 01°17'E
Bradwell (R Blackwater)	64	51°44'N 00°53'E
Shoeburyness	63	51°31'N 00°47'E

6 North Foreland to Selsey Bill, 0110

Langdon (Dover)	64	51°08'N 01°21'E
Fairlight (Hastings)	62	50°52'N 00°39'E

7 Selsey Bill to Lyme Regis, 0130

Newhaven (in Area 6)	62	50°47'N 00°03'E
Boniface (Ventnor, IoW)	63	50°36'N 01°12'W
Needles	62	50°39'N 01°35'W
Portland Bill	63	50°33'N 02°25'W
Beer Head (E Lyme Bay)	62	50°41'N 03°05'W

8 Lyme Regis to Land's End inc Isles of Scilly, 0110

Berry Head	63	50°24'N 03°29'W
Dartmouth	10	50°21'N 03°35'W
Prawle (Salcombe)	62	50°13'N 03°42'W
Rame Head	64	50°19'N 04°13'W
Fowey	10	50°20'N 04°38'W
Falmouth	62	50°09'N 05°03'W
Lizard	63	49°58'N 05°12'W
St Marys, Scilly *1880kHz*,	64	49°56'N 06°18'W
Trevose Head (in Area 9)	62	50°33'N 05°02'W

9 Land's End to St David's Head inc the Bristol Channel, 0150

Hartland Point	64	51°01'N 04°31'W
Combe Martin	63	51°12'N 04°03'W
Severn Bridges	64	51°36'N 02°38'W
St Hilary (Barry)	63	51°27'N 03°25'W
Mumbles (Swansea)	64	51°42'N 04°41'W
Tenby	62	51°41'N 05°10'W
St Ann's Head	62	51°40'N 05°11'W

10 St David's Head to Great Orme Head, inc St George's Channel, 0150

Dinas Hd (Fishguard)	64	52°00'N 04°54'W
Blaenplwyf (Aberystwyth)	62	52°22'N 04°06'W
South Stack (Holyhead)	63	53°19'N 04°41'W
Great Orme Head	64	53°20'N 03°51'W

11 Great Orme Head to the Mull of Galloway, 0130

Moel-y-Parc (NE Wales)	63	53°13'N 04°28'W
Langthwaite (Lancaster)	62	54°02'N 02°46'W
Caldbeck (Carlisle)	63	54°46'N 03°07'W

12 Isle of Man, 0130

Snaefell (Isle of Man)	64	54°16'N 04°28'W

13 Lough Foyle to Carlingford Lough, 0210

Slievemartin (Rostrevor)	64	54°06'N 06°10'W
Orlock Head (Bangor)	62	54°40'N 05°35'W
Black Mountain (Belfast)	63	54°35'N 06°01'W
West Torr (Fair Head)	64	55°12'N 06°06'W
Limavady (Lough Foyle)	10	55°06'N 06°53'W
Navar (Lower L Erne)	64	54°28'N 07°54'W

14 Mull of Galloway to Mull of Kintyre inc the Firth of Clyde and North Channel, 0210

Rhu Staffnish (Kintyre)	10	55°22'N 05°32'W
Lawhill (Ardrossan)	64	55°42'N 04°50'W
Clyde (Greenock)	62	55°58'N 04°48'W

15 Mull of Kintyre to Ardnamurchan Point, 0210

Kilchiaran (W Islay)	62	55°46'N 06°27'W
S Knapdale (Loch Fyne)	63	55°55'N 05°28'W

16 The Minch, 0110

Torosay (E Mull)	10	56°27'N 05°43'W
Glengorm (N Mull)	62	56°38'N 06°08'W
Tiree *1883kHz*,	63	56°31'N 06°57'W
Arisaig (S of Mallaig)	64	56°55'N 06°50'W
Drumfearn (SE Skye)	63	57°12'N 05°48'W
Skriag (Portree, Skye)	10	57°23'N 06°15'W
Rodel (S Harris)	62	57°45'N 06°57'W
Melvaig (Loch Ewe)	64	5°50'N 05°47'W
Portnaguran (Stornoway)	63	58°15'N 06°10'W

17 Ardnamurchan Point to Cape Wrath, 0110

Barra	10	57°01'N 07°30'W
Clettreval (N Uist)	63	57°37'N 07°26'W
Forsnaval (W Lewis)	62	58°13'N 07°00'W
Butt of Lewis *1743kHz*,	10	58°28'N 06°14'W

18 Shetland Isles and 60 NM radius, 0110

Fitful Head (Sumburgh)	63	59°54'N 01°23'W
Saxavord (Unst)	63	60°42'N 00°51'W
Lerwick (Shetland)	62	60°10'N 01°08'W
Collafirth *1770kHz*,	64	60°32'N 01°23'W
Wideford Hill (Kirkwall)	64	58°59'N 03°01'W

NOTE: This Information can change. Check MCGA MSI leaflet (MCA/064) at www.mcga.gov.uk, and download our free monthly pdf updates from January to June at www.reedsnauticalalmanac.co.uk

Inshore waters forecast area boundaries used by the UK Coastguard

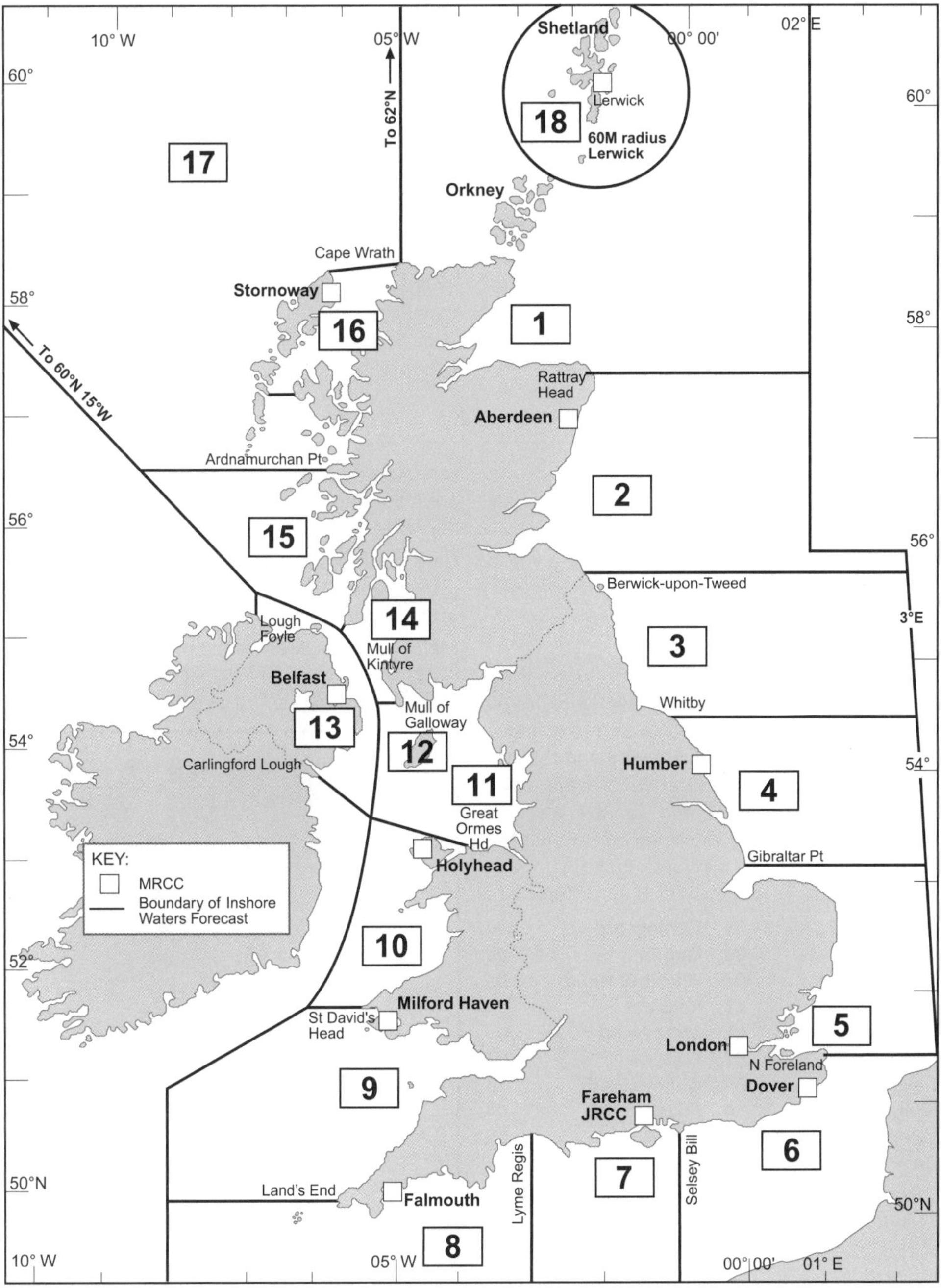

CHANNEL ISLANDS

Jersey Meteorological department

From the CI and UK call ☎ 0900 669 0022 (60p per min) for the Channel Islands recorded shipping forecast. From Guernsey only, call ☎ 12080; it is chargeable. For more detailed info call ☎ +44 1534 448770, www.gov.je/weather.

Forecasts include:general situation, 24hr forecast for wind, weather, vis, sea state, swell, sea temperature, plus 2 & 4 day outlooks and St Helier tide times/heights. The area is bounded by 50°N, 03°W and the mainland from Cap de la Hague to Ile de Bréhat.

Weather by public service radio

BBC Radio Guernsey 93·2 MHz, 99.0 MHz 1116 kHz broadcasts a weather bulletin for the waters around Guernsey, Herm and Sark at 0630 LT. It contains a synopsis, warnings, coastal forecast and coastal reports from Jersey, Guernsey, Alderney, Cap de la Hague, Cherbourg and Portland. ☎ 01481 200600. www.bbc.co.uk/guernseyguernsey@bbc.co.uk.

BBC Radio Jersey 1026 kHz, 88·8 MHz.
Storm warnings on receipt. Wind info for Jersey waters: Mon-Fri 0725, 0825, 1325, 1725 LT; Sat/Sun 0725, 0825. ☎ 01534 870000

Shipping forecast for local waters: Mon-Fri @ H+00 (0600-1900, after the news) and 0625 & 1625 LT; Sat/Sun @ H+00 (0700-1300, after the news) and 0725 LT.

Jersey Coastguard broadcasts gale warnings, synopsis, 24h forecast, outlook for next 24 hrs and reports from observation stations on VHF Ch 82 (after prior announcement on Ch 16) at 0645 LT, 0745 LT, 0845 LT 1245 UT 1845 UT 2245 UT and on request on VHF Ch's 25 and 82. Gale warnings are also broadcast at 0307, 0907, 1507 and 2107 UT. Jersey Coastguard is part of CG and SAR services at St Helier. www.jersey-harbours.com ☎ 01534 447705.

REPUBLIC OF IRELAND (ROI)

Met Éireann (Irish Met Office) is at Glasnevin Hill, Dublin 9, Ireland. ☎ +353 1806 4200, ℻ +353 1 806 4247, www.met.ie. General forecasting division: ☎ 1806 4255, ℻ 1806 4275 (H24, charges may apply).

Irish Coast radio stations

CRS and their VHF channels are listed below and shown opposite, (see: also www.malinheadcoastguardradio.com/index.htm). Weather bulletins for 30M offshore and the Irish Sea are broadcast on VHF at 0103, 0403, 0703, 1003, 1303, 1603, 1903 and 2203UT after an announcement on Ch 16. Broadcasts are made 1 hour earlier when DST is in force. Bulletins include gale warnings, synopsis and a 24-hour forecast.

Malin Head	01,05	**Carlingford**	04
Glen Head	03	**Dublin**	03
Donegal Bay	02	**Wicklow Head**	02
Belmullet	63	**Rosslare**	05
Clew Bay	05	**Mine Head**	03
Clifden	03	**Cork**	02
Galway	04	**Galley Head**	16
Shannon	64	**Mizen Head**	04
Valentia	62	**Bantry**	05

Gale warnings are broadcast on these VHF channels on receipt and at 0033, 0633, 1233 and 1833 LT, after an announcement Ch 16.

MF Valentia Radio broadcasts forecasts for sea areas Shannon and Fastnet on 1752 kHz at 0833 & 2033 UT, and on request.

Gale warnings are broadcast on 1752 kHz on receipt and at 0303, 0903, 1503 and 2103 (UT) after an announcement on 2182 kHz.

Malin Head does not broadcast weather information on 1677 kHz. At Dublin there is no MF transmitter.

Radio Telefís Éireann (RTE) Radio 1

RTE Radio 1 broadcasts weather bulletins daily at 0602, 1253 & 2355LT on 252kHz (LW) Summerhill (15M W ofDublin airport) and FM (88·2-95·2MHz).

Bulletins contain a situation, forecast and coastal reports. Forecasts include: wind, weather, vis, swell (if higher than 4m) and a 24 hrs outlook.

Gale warnings are included in hourly news bulletins on FM & MF.

Coastal reports include wind, weather, visibility, pressure and pressure tendency. The change over the last 3 hrs is described as:

Steady	=	0–0·4hPa
Rising/falling slowly	=	0·5–1·9
Rising/falling	=	2·0–3·4
Rising/falling rapidly	=	3·5–5·9
Rising/falling very rapidly	=	> 6·0

Weather by telephone

The latest sea area forecast and gale warnings are available as recorded messages H24 from Weatherdial. but only from Republic of Ireland landline or mobile numbers.

Dial ☎ 1550 123 plus the suffixes below:

850	Munster
851	Leinster
852	Connaught
853	Ulster
854	Dublin (plus winds in Dublin Bay and HW times)
855	Coastal waters and Irish Sea.

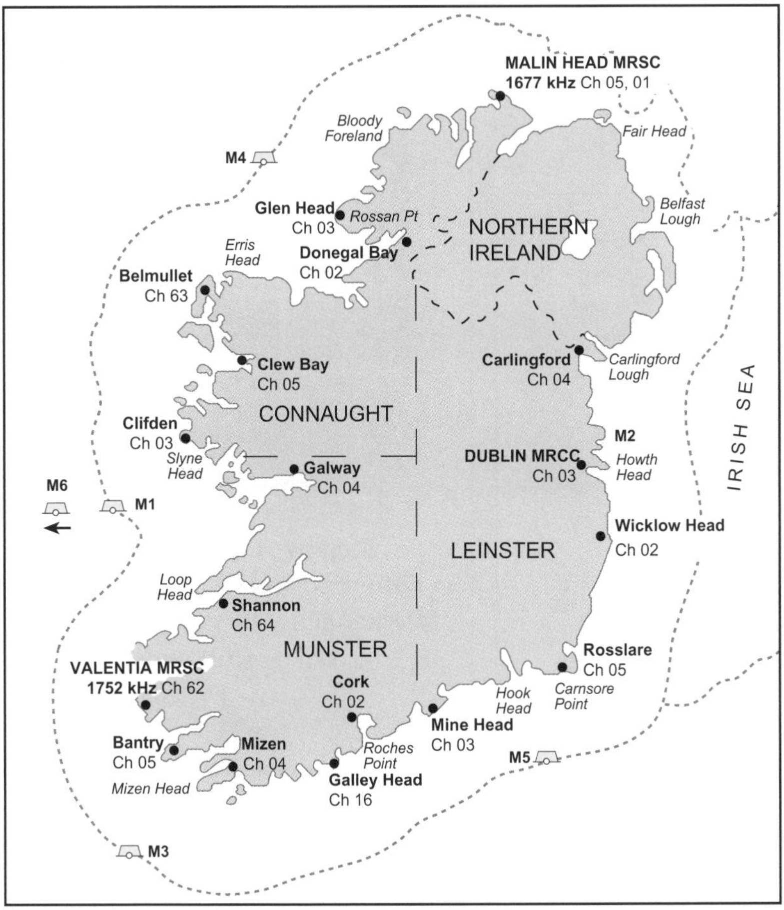

Provinces, headlands, sea areas and coastal stations referred to in weather broadcasts are shown here. Forecasts for coastal waters cover areas within 30M of the shore.

DENMARK

Lyngby Radio broadcasts, in Danish and English on MF/SSB1,734 kHz (Blåvand), 2,586 kHz (Rønne) and on VHF Blåvand, Ch 07. Gale warnings for Skagerrak, Fisher and German Bight are issued on receipt after announcement on 2187.5 kHz and Ch 16 with repeats on 2 182 kHz and Ch16. Forecasts will be provided on request.

Danish sea area forecasts in English are at: http://www.dmi.dk/products-in-english/

Weather bulletins and gale/storm warnings for Danish coastal waters and sea areas 2 to 6, 8 and 9 are broadcast in Danish on 243kHz AM, at 0545, 0845,1145 (plus 5 day forecast) and 1745 (plus 7 day forecast for coastal waters). Navigational warnings are broadcast at 1803 and Firing practice warnings at 1745 after the weather forecast. All LT.

Danmarks Meteorologiske Institut (DM)

Provides marine forecasts in **English** on www.dmi.dk/products-in-english/

'Wetter und warnfunk', a www.bsh/de/DE PDF document in German gives useful, clear information on GMDSS, and other forecasts from Denmark, Germany and the Netherlands.

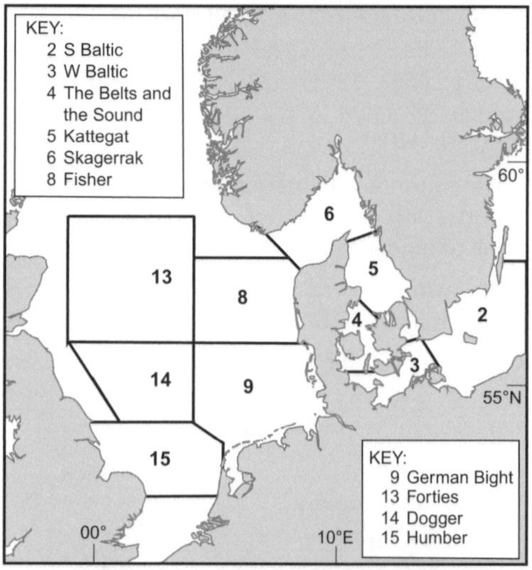

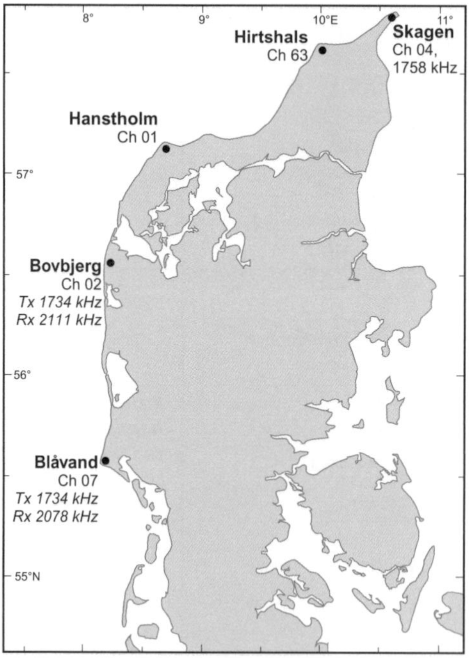

GERMANY

Deutscher Wetterdienst (DWD)

DWD provides a weather service for leisure and commercial sailors, SEEWIS and KUESTE. Current weather data and forecasts can be obtained by telephone/modem/DSL/WLAN and displayed on a PC or tablet. Users choose from an extensive range of information. Details, ☎ (+ 49) (0)69 8062 6190, ☎ (+ 49) (0)69 8062 6193, or seewis-online@dwd.de. Find English texts of marine forecasts on the dwd/de site at Wetter und Klima - Deutscher Wetterdienst - North and Baltic Sea.

Traffic Centres

Broadcast local storm/navigational warnings, weather, and visibility in German or **English.** North Sea Traffic also provides them on request.

Traffic Centre	VHF Ch	Every
Westcoast Traffic	15	H+20
North Sea Traffic	11	H+20
German Bight Traffic	79 (West) 80 (East)	H+00
Cuxhaven-Elbe Traffic	71 (outer Elbe)	H+35
Brunsbüttel-Elbe Traffic	68 (lower Elbe)	H+05
Kiel Kanal I+II (W part)	02,13	H+15 & H+45
Kiel Kanal III+IV (E part)	03,12	H+20 & H+50
Bremerhaven-Weser Traffic	02, 04, 05, 07, 21, 22, 82	H+20
Bremen-Weser Traffic	19, 78, 81	H+30
Hunte Traffic	63	H+30
Jade Traffic	20, 63	H+10
Ems Traffic	15, 18, 20, 21	H+50

Coast Radio Stations

DP07 (Seefunk) commercial CRS, below, at: **Nordfriesland (Sylt)** Ch 26. **Elbe-Weser** Ch 24. **Hamburg** (Control centre) Ch 83. **Bremen** Ch 25. **Borkum** Ch 28. For Fisher, German Bight and Humber DPO7 broadcasts from late March to early October, in German. Gale and strong wind warnings on receipt. Forecasts for 12 hour with 12 hour outlook at 0745, 0945, 1245, 1645 and 1945 LT, 4–5 day outlook at 0945, 1645 and 1945.

Hamburg Ch 83, Accumersiel Ch 28, Borkum Ch 61, Bremen Ch 25, Elbe-Weser Ch 24, Nordfriesland Ch 26.

Public Service Radio

Deutschlandfunk (DLF)

Gale and strong wind warnings, weather situation, forecast for 12 hours, 12 hour outlook, 3-day outlook and weather actuals for the North Sea after the news.

DAB+ Bremerhaven; Kiel; At 0105 0640 1810 LT. Also telephone +49 (0) 221 34 52 99 18.

Norddeutscher Rundfunk (NDR)

Gale and strong wind warnings, weather situation, forecast for 12 hours, 12 hour outlook, 3-day outlook and weather actuals for the North Sea.

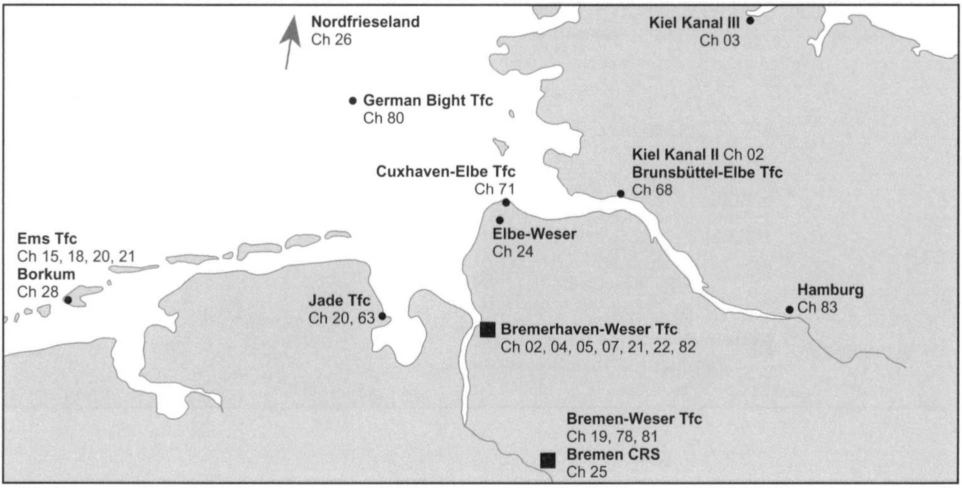

On FM at 0005 LT. **Eutin** 101·9 MHz; **Flensburg/Eckernförde** 103·3 MHz; **Hamburg/Pinneberg** 88·7 MHz; **Heide** 104·4 MHz; **Helgoland** 107·4 MHz; **Itzehoe** 102·2MHz; **St Peter-Ording** 102·3 MHz; **Westerland** 90·3 MHz; **Aurich** 101·8 MHz; **Bremen**107·1 MHz; **Bremerhaven** 103·4 MHz; **Cuxhaven** 101·6 MHz. Also at 0005 0830 2205 LT on **NDR Info Spezial**.

Digital radio DAB+, satellite DVB-S radio, the **NDR radio app** and as livestream.

Recorded Telephone forecasts

Call ☎+49(0)69 8062 5799 (standard rates); after voice prompt select from the following table:

1	for the general situation report.
2	for the SW North Sea, German Bight and Fisher.
3	for the Skagerrak and Kattegat.
4	for the Baltic Sea (South and West).
5	for the German N Sea coast.
6	for the German Baltic coast.

NETHERLANDS

VHF MSI broadcasts

For coastal waters 30M out to sea and inland waters, in English and Dutch. Wind warnings (F6+) at 0333, 0733, 1133, 1533, 1933, 2333. Weather forecasts at 0805,1305, 1905, 2305, after prior announcement on Chs 16/70.

VHF Ch 23: Schiermonnikoog, Kornwerderzand, Wezep, Huisduinen (Den Helder), IJmuiden, Renesse, Woensdrecht.

VHF Ch 83: Appingedam, West Terschelling, Hoorn, Schoorl, Westkapelle.

All stations monitor Ch 16.

Weather bulletins for specifically for the Westerschelde are also broadcast by **Vlissingen Traffic Centre** VHF Ch 14 every H+50 UTC. and **Terneuzen Traffic Centre** VHF Ch 11, every H+00 All times UTC.

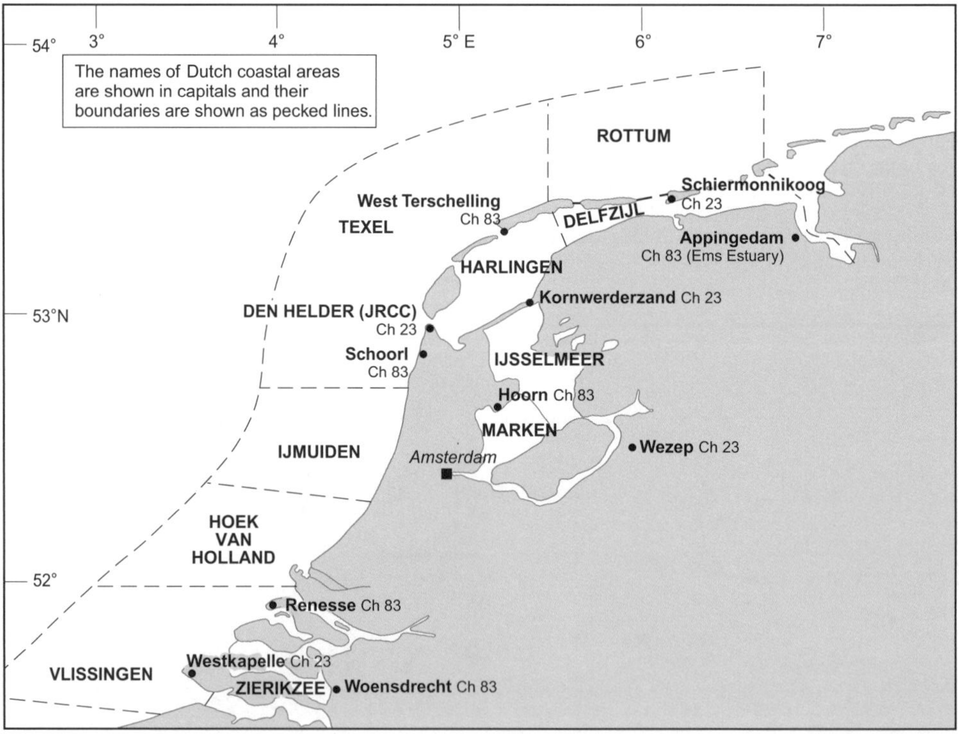

MF/SSB weather broadcasts in English

On 1890 kHz (Appingedam) and 3673 kHz (Scheveningen) after call on 2187·5 kHz. Wind warnings (F7+) for Dogger, Humber, Thames and German Bight at 0333, 7333, 1533, 1933, 2333. Forecasts at 0940, 2140, all UTC.

Radio Noord-Holland (FM)

Northern coastal area, gale warnings/wind strength in Dutch, Mon-Fri at 0730, 0838, 1005, 1230 and 1705LT; Sat/Sun 1005, by: **Haarlem** 97.6 MHz and **Wieringermeer** 93.9 MHz.

Omroep Zeeland (FM)

Southern coastal areas, synopsis, gale warnings / wind strength broadcast in Dutch, Mon-Fri at 0715, 0915, 1215 and 1715LT; Sat/Sun 1015, by:

Philippine 97.8 MHz and **Goes** 101.9 MHz.

BELGIUM, Coast radio stations

Oostende Radio, after prior notice on VHF 16, 24, DSC 70 and 2182kHz, broadcasts in **English** and Dutch on VHF 27, MF 2256, 2376 and 2761 kHz: Strong wind warnings on receipt and after the next 2 silent periods. Forecasts for Thames, Dover and the Belgian coast at 0720 LT and 0820, 1720 UT.

Oostende Radio broadcasts in **English** and Dutch on VHF Ch 24 for the Schelde estuary: Gale warnings on receipt and at every H+48 LT. Also strong wind warnings (F6+) on receipt and at every H+48 LT.

Zeebrugge Traffic Centre broadcasts weather for the Westeschelde on VHF Ch 69 every H+10 LT.

FRANCE

Le Guide Marine a free annual booklet which summarises French weather forecasts, warnings and broadcasts is usually available from marinas or from www.meteofrance.fr/publications/nos-collections/guides-pratiques/guide-marine.

CROSS VHF and MF broadcasts

CROSS broadcasts Met bulletins in French, after an announcement on Ch 16. In the English Channel broadcasts can be given in English, on request Ch 16. Broadcasts include: Any gale warnings, general situation, 24 hrs forecast (actual weather, wind, sea state and vis) and further trends for coastal waters, which extend 20M offshore. VHF channels, remote stations and local times are shown below. A useful source of texts for all Météo France marine forecasts is www.meteo-marine.com/meteo-marine

French forecast areas

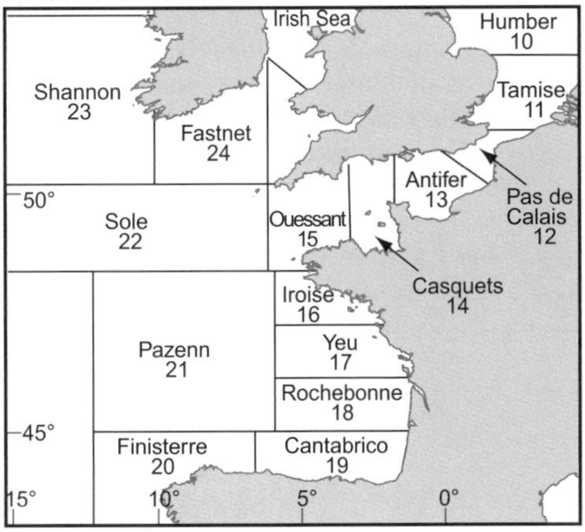

Gale warnings feature in Special Met Bulletins (*Bulletins Météorologique Spéciaux* or BMS). They are broadcast in French by all CROSS on VHF at H+03 and at other times on MF frequencies as shown below.

CROSS GRIS-NEZ Ch 79

Belgian border to Baie de la Somme

Dunkerque	0720, 1603, 1920
St Frieux	0710, 1545, 1910

Baie de la Somme to Cap de la Hague

St Valéry-en-Caux

0703, 1533, 1903

Gale warnings for areas 12-13 are broadcast in French on MF 1650 & 2677 kHz at 0833 & 2033LT

CROSS JOBOURG Ch 80

Baie de la Somme to Cap de la Hague

Antifer	0803, 1633, 2003
Port-en-Bessin	0745, 1615, 1945
Jobourg	0733, 1603, 1933

Cap de la Hague to Pointe de Penmarc'h

Jobourg	0715, 1545, 1915
Granville	0703, 1533, 1903

Gale warnings for areas 13-14 in **English** on receipt and at H+20 and H+50. No gale warnings on MF.

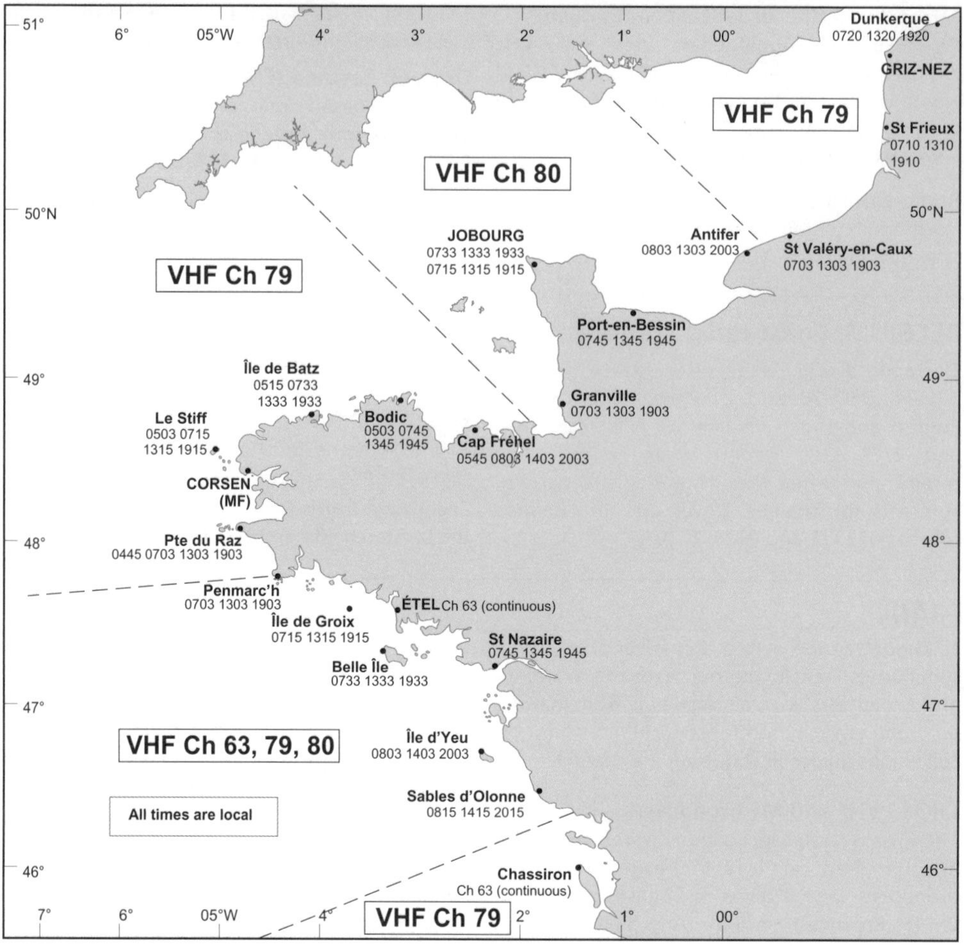

CROSS CORSEN Ch 79

Cap de la Hague to Pte de Penmarc'h (Times in bold = 1 May to 30 Sep only).

Cap Fréhel 0545, 0803, **1203**, 1633, 2003 **Bodic** 0533, 0745, **1145**, 1615, 1945

Ile de Batz	0515, 0733, **1133**, 1603, 1933
Le Stiff	0503, 0715, **1115**, 1545, 1915
Pte du Raz	0445, 0703, **1103**, 1533, 1903

Corsen broadcasts gale warnings for areas 13-22 in French at 0815 and 2015LT on MF 1650 & 2677 kHz.

CROSS ÉTEL Chs 63, 80

Pte de Penmarc'h to l'Anse de l'Aiguillon (46° 15'N 01°10'W). Étel has no MF freqs

Penmarc'h	0703, 1533, 1903
Ile de Groix	0715, 1545, 1915
Belle Ile	0733, 1603, 1933
Saint-Nazaire	0745, 1615, 1945
Ile d'Yeu	0803, 1633, 2003
Les Sables d'Olonne	0815, 1645, 2015

CROSS ÉTEL Ch 79 L'Anse de l'Aiguillon to Spanish border

Chassiron every 20 minutes

Local radio (FM)

Radio Bretagne 5 provides the only MW broadcasts of Météo France marine forecast on 1593kHz/188m. All LT, in French. For the North Sea and Atlantic sea areas at 0740, and 2205. For coastal areas from Cap de la Hague to Anse de l'Aiguillon at 1330. This can be heard over a wide area but signal strength may be poor south of Brest.

Forecasts by telephone

Automatic service ☎ 08·99·71·08·08 (€2·99 plus call charge). The menu provides:

Bulletin Rivage, (2 miles out to sea) Nine day forecasts updated 3 times daily.

Bulletin Côtier, (20 miles out to sea) Seven day forecast updated 3 times daily.

Bulletin Large, (Offshore sea area) Seven day forecast updated twice daily.

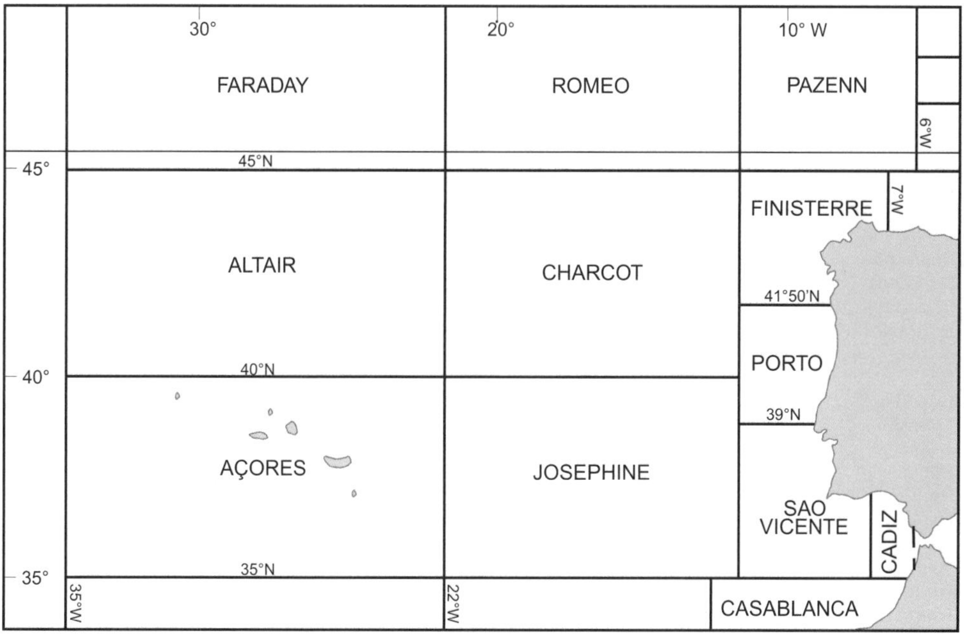

Forecast areas for the Eastern Atlantic and Coastal/Offshore Areas off France, Spain, Portugal and North West Africa

WEATHER VOCABULARY

ENGLISH	GERMAN	FRENCH	DUTCH
Air mass	Luftmasse	Masse d'air	Luchtmassa
Anticyclone	Antizyklonisch	Anticyclone	Hogedrukgebied
Area	Gebiet	Zone	Gebied
Backing wind	Rückdrehender Wind	Vent reculant	Krimpende wind
Barometer	Barometer	Baromètre	Barometer
Breeze	Brise	Brise	Bries
Calm	Flaute	Calme	Kalmte
Centre	Zentrum	Centre	Centum
Clouds	Wolken	Nuages	Wolken
Cold	Kalt	Froid	Koud
Cold front	Kaltfront	Front froid	Kou front
Cyclonic	Zyklonisch	Cyclonique	Cycloonachtig
Decrease	Abnahme	Affaiblissement	Afnemen
Deep	Tief	Profond	Diep
Deepening	Vertiefend	Approfondissant	Verdiepend
Depression	Sturmtief	Dépression	Depressie
Direction	Richtung	Direction	Richting
Dispersing	Auflösend	Se dispersant	Oplossend
Disturbance	Störung	Perturbation	Verstoving
Drizzle	Niesel	Bruine	Motregen
East	Ost	Est	Oosten
Extending	Ausdehnung	S'étendant	Uitstrekkend
Extensive	Ausgedehnt	Etendu	Uitgebreid
Falling	Fallend	Descendant	Dalen
Filling	Auffüllend	Secomblant	Vullend
Fog	Nebel	Brouillard	Nevel
Fog bank	Nebelbank	Ligne de brouillard	Mist bank
Forecast	Vorhersage	Prévision	Vooruitzicht
Frequent	Häufig	Fréquent	Veelvuldig
Fresh	Frisch	Frais	Fris
Front	Front	Front	Front
Gale	Sturm	Coup de vent	Storm
Gale warning	Sturmwarnung	Avis de coup de vent	Stormwaarschuwing
Good	Gut	Bon	Goed
Gradient	Druckunterschied	Gradient	Gradiatie
Gust, squall	Bö	Rafalle	Windvlaag
Hail	Hagel	Grêle	Hagel
Haze	Diesig	Brume	Nevel
Heavy	Schwer	Abondant	Zwaar
High	Hoch	Anticyclone	Hoog
Increasing	Zunehmend	Augmentant	Toenemend
Isobar	Isobar	Isobare	Isobar
Isolated	Vereinzelt	Isolé	Verspreid
Lightning	Blitze	Eclair de foudre	Bliksem
Local	Örtlich	Locale	Plaatselijk
Low	Tief	Dépression	Laag
Mist	Dunst	Brume légere	Mist
Moderate	Mäßig	Modéré	Matig
Moderating	Abnehmend	Se modérant	Matigend
Moving	Bewegend	Se déplacant	Bewegend
North	Nord	Nord	Noorden
Occluded	Okklusion	Couvert	Bewolkt
Poor	Schlecht	Mauvais	Slecht
Precipitation	Niederschlag	Précipitation	Neerslag
Pressure	Druck	Pression	Druk
Rain	Regen	Pluie	Regen
Ridge	Hochdruckbrücke	Crête	Rug
Rising	Ansteigend	Montant	Stijgen
Rough	Rauh	Agitée	Ruw
Sea	See	Mer	Zee
Seaway	Seegang	Haute mer	Zee

ENGLISH	GERMAN	FRENCH	DUTCH
Scattered	Vereinzelt	Sporadiques	Verspreid
Shower	Schauer	Averse	Bui
Slight	Leicht	Un peu	Licht
Slow	Langsam	Lent	Langzaam
Snow	Schnee	Neige	Sneeuw
South	Süd	Sud	Zuiden
Storm	Sturm	Tempête	Storm
Sun	Sonne	Soleil	Zon
Swell	Schwell	Houle	Deining
Thunder	Donner	Tonnerre	Donder
Thunderstorm	Gewitter	Orage	Onweer
Trough	Trog, Tiefausläufer	Creux	Trog
Variable	Umlaufend	Variable	Veranderlijk
Veering	Rechtdrehend	Virement de vent	Ruimende wind
Warm front	Warmfront	Front chaud	Warm front
Weather	Wetter	Temps	Weer
Wind	Wind	Vent	Wind
Weather report	Wetterbericht	Météo	Weer bericht meteorologica

Chapter 3 – Communications

RADIO OPERATION

Avoiding interference

Before transmitting, first listen on the VHF channel. If occupied, wait for a break before transmitting, or choose another channel. If you cause interference you must comply immediately with any request from a Coastguard or Coast radio station to stop transmitting.

Control of communications

Ship-to-Shore: Communications between ship and shore stations are controlled by the latter, except in distress, urgency or safety cases.

Intership: The ship *called* controls communication. If you call another ship, then it has control. If you are called by a ship, you assume control. If a shore-based station breaks in, both ships must comply with instructions given.

Radio confidentiality

Private conversations heard on the radio must not be reproduced, passed on or otherwise used.

Making yourself understood

Clear R/T speech is vital. If a message cannot be understood by the receiver it is useless. Messages which have to be written down at the receiving station should be spoken slowly. This gives time for it to be written down by the receiving operator. If the transmitting operator himself writes it down all should be well. The average reading speed is 250 words a minute, whilst average writing speed is only 20.

When speaking, consider the following:

- **What** to say, ie *voice Procedure*
- **How** to say it, ie *voice Technique*

Voice Procedure is discussed below and overleaf. It includes procedural words, callsigns, making contact etc.

Voice Technique depends on a few simple rules:

Hold the microphone a few inches in front of the mouth and speak directly into it at a normal level. Speak clearly so that there can be no confusion. The voice should be pitched up at a higher level than normal. Do not drop the voice pitch at the end of a phrase or sentence. Emphasise words with weak syllables; 'Tower', if badly pronounced, could sound like 'tar'. Non Anglophones, or people with strong regional accents must try to pronounce words as clearly as possible.

Difficult words may be spelled phonetically, preceded with 'I spell'. If the word can be pronounced, include it before and after it has been spelt. For example, the message 'I will berth on the yacht *Coila*' would be sent as: 'I will berth on the yacht *Coila* – I spell – Charlie Oscar India Lima Alfa – *Coila*'.

The phonetic alphabet (ITU)

The syllables to emphasise are underlined

Letter	*Morse*	*Phonetic*	*Spoken as*
A	•–	Alfa	<u>AL</u>-fah
B	–•••	Bravo	<u>BRAH</u>-voh
C	–•–•	Charlie	<u>CHAR</u>-lee
D	–••	Delta	<u>DELL</u>-tah
E	•	Echo	<u>ECK</u>-oh
F	••–•	Foxtrot	<u>FOKS</u>-trot
G	––•	Golf	<u>GOLF</u>
H	••••	Hotel	hoh-<u>TELL</u>
I	••	India	<u>IN</u>-dee-ah
J	•–––	Juliett	<u>JEW</u>-lee-ett
K	–•–	Kilo	<u>KEY</u>-loh
L	•–••	Lima	<u>LEE</u>-mah
M	––	Mike	<u>MIKE</u>
N	–•	November	no-<u>VEM</u>-ber
O	–––	Oscar	<u>OSS</u>-car
P	•––•	Papa	pa-<u>PAH</u>
Q	––•–	Quebec	keh-<u>BECK</u>
R	•–•	Romeo	<u>ROW</u>-me-oh
S	•••	Sierra	see-<u>AIR</u>-rah
T	–	Tango	<u>TANG</u>-go
U	••–	Uniform	<u>OO</u>-nee-form
V	•••–	Victor	<u>VIK</u>-tah
W	•––	Whiskey	<u>WISS</u>-key
X	–••–	X-ray	<u>ECKS</u>-ray
Y	–•––	Yankee	<u>YANG</u>-key
Z	––••	Zulu	<u>ZOO</u>-loo

Phonetic numerals

When numerals are transmitted, the following pronunciations make them easier to understand.

No	*Morse*	*Spoken*	*No*	*Morse*	*Spoken*
1	•––––	WUN	6	–••••	SIX
2	••–––	TOO	7	––•••	SEV-EN
3	•••––	TREE	8	–––••	AIT
4	••••–	FOW-ER	9	––––•	NIN-ER
5	•••••	FIFE	0	–––––	ZERO

Numerals are transmitted digit by digit except that multiples of thousands may be spoken as follows:

Numeral	*Spoken as*
44	FOW-ER FOW-ER
90	NIN-ER ZERO
136	WUN TREE SIX
500	FIFE ZERO ZERO
1478	WUN FOW-ER SEV-EN AIT
7000	SEV-EN THOU-SAND

Punctuation
Punctuation marks should be used only where their omission would cause confusion.

Mark	*Word*	*Spoken as*
.	Decimal	DAY-SEE-MAL
,	Comma	COMMA
.	Stop	STOP

Procedural words or 'prowords'
These are used to shorten transmissions

All after and **All before.** Used after proword *'say again'* to request repetition of a part of a message

Correct Reply to repeat of message that was preceded by prowords *'read back for check'* when it has been correctly repeated. Often said twice

Correction Cancel the last word or group of words. The correct word or group follows. Spoken when an error has been made in a transmission.

I say again I repeat the transmission or the part indicated (see 'All after' and 'All before').

I spell I shall spell the next word or group of letters phonetically

Out This is the end of working to you

Over Invitation to reply

Read back If the receiver is doubtful about accuracy of all or part of message he may repeat it back to the sending station, preceding the repetition with prowords *'I read back'*

Station calling Used when a station is uncertain of the calling station's identification/callsign

This is This transmission is from the station whose callsign or name immediately follows

Wait If a called station cannot accept traffic immediately, it will reply **'WAIT.......MINUTES'**, with reason if delay may exceed 10 minutes

Word after or Word before Used after the proword *'say again'* to request repetition

Wrong Reply to repetition of message preceded by prowords *'read back'* when it has been incorrectly repeated

Calls, calling and callsigns
Shore stations normally use a callsign of their geographic name followed by Coastguard or Radio, eg Solent Coastguard, Dublin Radio etc. Vessels usually identify themselves by the ship's name but the International callsign may be used in certain cases. If two yachts have the same or confusingly similar names, give your International callsign when starting communications, and thereafter use your ship's name as callsign.

'All ships' broadcast
Address used by Coastguard Radio where broadcast information is to be received or used by all who intercept it, eg gale warnings etc. No reply is needed.

Communicating with a coast radio station
Call initially on a working channel or very briefly on channel 16 to establish a working channel.

- Pause to check the working channel is clear before transmitting
- Use low power *(1 watt)* if close enough , ie up to 10 miles away. High power *(25 watts)* drains more from the battery
- The callsign of calling station up to three times only, and prowords 'This is'
- Say how many R/T calls you have to make
- Proword 'Over'

Using high power decreases battery state and the range your VHF will achieve. Continued calling also clutters up the channel and denies access to other users.

Aerial faults commonly reduce your transmitting range. Possibly the station aerial for the channel chosen is directionally orientated and you are on the wrong side. Try another channel or station. Call again when closer.

RADIO DATA

SHORT, MEDIUM and LONG RANGE RADIO COMMUNICATIONS

A suitable radio receiver on board will provide weather forecasts and time signals at scheduled times on a number of frequencies in various wavebands. With a maritime receiver you are not limited to the familiar BBC and commercial broadcasts. HM Coastguard transmit navigation warnings, storm warnings and weather messages for shipping in their respective sea areas.

Short range radiotelephony (RT) transmits and receives on VHF channels in the marine VHF (Very High Frequency) band. The equipment and procedures are simple, but range is normally limited to about 20 miles from ship to shore, rather less from ship to ship. Interconnection with national telephone systems is possible on certain VHF/RT channels when a yacht is within range of a Coast Radio Station, although there are now no such stations on the mainland of the UK, France or the Netherlands. Mobile telephones are now by far the most common form of ship to shore communication.

Medium range two-way communication operate in the marine MF (medium frequency) RT band, the 2MHz 'trawler band'. Single sideband techniques are employed on these medium frequencies and SSB equipment is essential. The effective range depends on the power of the transmitter and the sensitivity of the associated receiver; in general this might be up to 200 miles from certain (but not all) Coast Radio Stations.

THE MARINE VHF BAND

VHF is used by most vessels, Coast Radio Stations, CG centres and other rescue services. Its range is slightly better than the line of sight between the transmitting and receiving aerials. A good aerial, as high as possible, is most important.

In the Marine VHF band (156·00–174·00 MHz) the individual frequencies are separated from their neighbours by exactly 25kHz 'elbow-room' to eliminate mutual interference. Each frequency is given a channel number, not necessarily consecutive. Thus 55 channels are available, plus some with special purposes (see below).

VHF Channel Grouping

Channels are grouped for three main purposes, but some can be used for more than one purpose. They are listed below in their preferred order of usage:

- **Public correspondence** (ie link calls via CRS into the shore telephone system): Ch 26, 27, 25, 24, 23, 28, 04, 01, 03, 02, 07, 05, 84, 87, 86, 83, 85, 88, 61, 64, 65, 62, 66, 63, 60, 82, 78, 81.

- **Inter-ship:** Ch 06, 08, 10, 13, 09, 72, 73, 67, 69, 77, 15, 17. Remember these, so that if another vessel calls you, you can swiftly nominate a working channel from within this group.

- **Port Operations:**
Ch 12, 14, 11, 13, 09, 68, 71, 74, 69, 73, 17, 15, 20, 22, 18, 19, 21, 05, 07, 02, 03, 01, 04, 78, 82, 79, 81, 80, 60, 63, 66, 62, 65, 64, 61, 84.

Special purposes. The following channels have one specific purpose only:

Ch 0 (156·00 MHz): SAR ops, not available to yachts.

Ch's 10 (156·50 MHz), **62** (160·725 MHz), **63** (160·775 MHz) and **64** (160·825 MHz): HMCG MSI broadcasts, (after prior announcement Ch 16).

Ch 13 (156·650 MHz): Intership safety of navigation (sometimes referred to as bridge-to-bridge); a possible channel for calling a merchant ship if no contact on Ch 16.

Ch 16 (156·80 MHz): Distress, Safety and calling. *See Chapter 4 for Distress and Safety.* Ch 16 is monitored by UK and Irish CG rescue centres (speaker based listening watch) along with DSC Ch 70. Commercial vessels are required to monitor DSC Ch 70. Although vessels are no longer required to monitor Ch 16 it is always advised and good seamanship too. After an initial call, the stations concerned **must** switch to a working channel, except for Distress and Safety matters.

Ch 67 (156·375 MHz): the Small Craft Safety channel in the UK, accessed via Ch 16.

Ch 70 (156·525 MHz): exclusively for digital selective calling for Distress and Safety purposes.

Ch 80 (157·025 MHz): the primary working channel between yachts and UK marinas.

Ch M (157·85 MHz): the secondary working channel between yachts and UK marinas. For use in UK territorial waters only.

Ch M2 (161·425 MHz): for race control, with Ch M as stand-by. YCs often use Ch M2. For use in UK territorial waters only.

SILENCE PERIODS

The periods are the 3 minutes immediately after the whole and half hours, ie H to H+03 and H+30 to H+33, when no transmissions should be made.

MEDIUM RANGE MF RADIO

Single sideband MF/RT provides communications in the offshore waters of the UK and Western Europe where small craft may be out of VHF contact. A receiver alone gives the ability to hear weather bulletins, storm and navigation warnings for local sea areas broadcast from CRS in the 1.6 to 4.0MHz maritime band, ie on frequencies from 1605 to 4200 kHz.

MF transmissions tend to follow the curvature of the earth, which makes them suitable for direction-finding. For this reason, and because of their good range, the marine Distress R/T frequency (2182 kHz) is in the MF band.

TRAFFIC LISTS

If a Coast Radio station has messages for a vessel, but is unable to contact her, that vessel's name will be added to the Traffic List broadcast at (usually) two hour intervals. This is not a system much used by yachts and small craft.

LONG RANGE HF RADIO

HF radios use short wave frequencies in the 4, 8, 12, 16 and 22 MHz bands, as chosen to suit propagation conditions. HF is more expensive than MF and requires more power, but can provide worldwide coverage. A good installation and skilled operating techniques are essential for satisfactory results.

GLOBAL COMMUNICATIONS

Once out of range of VHF/MF or wireless telephony/broadband service, the yachtsman's communications options are limited to MF/HF radio and satellite systems (Satcoms).

A yachtsman embarking on an extended offshore venture would usually choose a mix of equipment for sensible reasons of redundancy, this will allow a choice of listening and transmitting, via terrestrial and satellite radio systems, to meet his needs at various times and in different circumstances. A typical setup might include a fixed or handheld satcoms transceiver, a HF SSB transceiver and receiver. For data capability, these would be interfaced to an on-board PC.

HF/single sideband radio (HF-SSB)

HF SSB radios use frequencies in the 4, 8, 12, 16 and 22 MHz bands (short wave), provide worldwide coverage and usually include MF frequencies as well.

Despite rapid growth in marine satellite communications, HF SSB remains a popular choice amongst long-distance cruisers, providing a cost-free voice (and limited email) capability for cruisers, sometimes operating over vast distances. Operators have the Long Range Certificate (LRC) or General Operators Certificate (GOC). To use Amateur (ham) bands (giving more frequencies and higher power, therefore range) operators must take the ham examination.

Using HF SSB radio for email requires a radio modem, often proprietary to the supplier. Though slow and requiring some skill to operate effectively, the almost-nil operating costs appeal to many and SSB radio has a strong following amongst blue-water cruisers. Established suppliers include Sailmail and Globe Wireless.

HF SSB radio is also extensively used for receipt of weatherfax images, although a receive-only SSB radio (with an adequate, grounded antenna installation) may be used rather than a full transceiver. Though declining in popularity, several useful weatherfax transmitting stations remain, including Northwood, UK and Offenbach, Germany.

Satellite Communications (Satcoms)

Satellite communications systems operate over **Ultra High Frequency (UHF)** radio using digital technology that makes them simpler-to-operate and more reliable for voice (and data) communications than HF SSB radio; they operate with either a dedicated ship installation or a standalone handheld terminal. Apart from the equipment purchase (and installation if necessary), ongoing costs usually include a monthly service fee and usage charges that will be related to either the amount of satellite time used, or the volume of data transmitted and received.

For two-way voice communications, the 'Ship Station' (aka 'Mobile Earth Station') transmits to a visible satellite that is simultaneously in sight of a 'Land Earth Station', eg Goonhilly, Cornwall. From there, the call is routed to its destination through the normal terrestrial telephone network.

The satellite 'constellations' have different architectures. Inmarsat for example has four geostationary (GEO) satellites, one each positioned over the Pacific and Indian oceans and two over the Atlantic. Because they are comparatively high up 19,400M (36,000km), each satellite has a large signal 'footprint', overlapping the next one and thus world-wide coverage is provided (although not in the polar regions above about 70°N and 70°S).

Other systems employ many more Low Earth Orbit (LEO) satellites orbiting the Earth about 540M (1,000km) above the surface.

The smaller, low-data rate, handheld voice terminals incorporate an omni-directional antenna that works best with an unobstructed view of the satellite. Fixed installations use an external gyro-stabilised antenna (to keep it pointing at the satellite as the boat moves); more powerful systems that support higher data rates employ antenna radomes that are really too large for installation aboard a 10–15m yacht.

The GMDSS provides automatic distress, urgency and safety communications, with some satcom systems (eg Inmarsat C) providing a red button that alerts a Maritime Rescue Coordination Centre (MRCC) when pressed.

There are several service providers, each offering an array of capabilities. The table opposite provides a useful summary of systems that might be used aboard a 10–20m yacht.

This is a fast moving market place and you should check with manufacturers/retailers for up-to-date specifications and prices.

[1] typical, if in coverage area [2] using VOIP [3] Likely to be expensive	Wired Broadband	Wi-Fi	Cellular GSM	Cellular GPRS	Cellular 3G	Wi-Max
Range offshore[1] (NM)	0	0-1	0-15	0-15	0-15	0-30
Voice communication	Y [2]	Y [2]	Y	Y	Y	Y [2]
Text messages	Y	Y	Y	Y	Y	Y
Light email traffic	Y	Y	Y [3]	Y	Y	Y
Text weather forecasts	Y	Y	Y [3]	Y	Y	Y
Heavy email traffic	Y	Y	×	Y [3]	Y	Y
Graphical weather forecasts	Y	Y	×	Y [3]	Y	Y
Full web browsing	Y	Y	×	Y [3]	Y	Y

SATELLITE COMMUNICATION SERVICES

System	Antenna	Satellites	Coverage	GMDSS	Phone (voice)	Fax	SMS text	Position tracking	Data rate
INMARSAT C	Omni-directional	4 GEO	Global excepting polar regions	Yes	No	Yes	Yes	Yes (GPS)	Very low, uneconomic for email
Iridium Certus	Omni-directional	66 LEO	Global	Yes	Yes	Yes	Yes	No	352kpbs to 704kbps (1408kbps planned)
Globalstar	Omni-directional	40 LEO	Global excepting polar regions	No	Yes	Yes	Yes	To 10km	9.6kbps uncom-pressed, 38.6kbps compressed, 56k with data kit
Fleet Broadband	Gyro-stabilised 40cms diameter	GEO	Global excepting polar regions	Yes	Yes	Yes	Yes	No	To 284kpbs
Thuraya	Omni-directional	2 GEO	Europe, N Africa & Middle East	No	Yes	Yes	Yes	Yes (GPS)	Satphone 60kbps download 15kbps upload or 384kbps-444kbpsvia high speed IP+ data terminal

PORT AND/OR MARINA VHF CHANNELS AND TELEPHONE DETAILS

In larger ports it is sensible to monitor the VTS channel (if any) or the primary port channel (in bold) before changing to a marina channel. Times are local, unless marked UT. Abbreviations are at the front of the book. Telephone codes are shown only once unless more than one applies.

ENGLAND – SOUTH COAST

ISLES OF SCILLY, St Mary's HM Ch 14 (0800-1700); ☎ 01720 422768. *Falmouth CG* covers Scilly and the TSS off Land's End on Ch 23.
Tresco HM ☎ 07778 601237.

NEWLYN HM Ch 09, **12** (M-F: 0800-1700, Sat: 0800-1200). ☎ 01736 362523.

PENZANCE HM Ch 09, **12** (M-F: 0830-1730 and HW –2 to +1). ☎ 01736 366113.

FALMOUTH *Falmouth Hbr Radio* Ch 11, **12**, 14 (M-F 0800-1700). ☎ 01326 310991.

Ch 80: Falmouth ☎ 316620 and Port Pendennis marinas ☎ 311113. **Ch 12**: Falmouth Haven ☎ 310991; St Mawes HM ☎ 270553. **Ch M** (HO): Mylor Yacht Hbr ☎ 372121.

TRURO HM *Carrick One* Ch 12. ☎ 01872 272130. **Ch M** (HO): Malpas Marine ☎ 271260.

MEVAGISSEY HM Ch 14 (Summer: 0900-2100, Winter: 0900-1700). ☎ 01726 842496.

CHARLESTOWN HM Ch 14, HW –2 to +1, only when a vessel is expected. ☎ 01726 70241.

FOWEY HM Ch 12 (0900-1700); also Hbr Patrol (0900-2000). ☎ 01726 832471. Water taxi: Ch 06.

LOOE. HM Ch 16, occas. ☎ 01503 262839.

PLYMOUTH *Long Room Port Control* Ch 14 H24, ☎ 01752 836528. **QAB** Ch 80, ☎ 671142. **Sutton Hbr lock**: Ch 12 H24, ☎ 204702. **Cattewater HM** Ch 14 (M-F 0900-1700), ☎ 836528. **Plymouth Yacht Haven**, Ch 80, M; ☎ 404231. **King Point Marina** ☎ 424297. **Mayflower Marina**, Ch 80; ☎ 556633.

SALCOMBE HM & launch: Ch 14, May to mid-Sep: 7/7, 0600-2100; otherwise: M-F 0900-1600; ☎ 01548 843791. *Hbr Taxi* Ch 12. Fuel barge Ch 06, ☎ 07801 798862. **Island CC** ☎ 531776.

DARTMOUTH HM *Dartnav* Ch 11, 7/7 0730-dusk; ☎ 01803 832337. Darthaven marina Ch 80, ☎ 752242. Dart marina Ch 80, ☎ 837161. Noss marina ☎ 839087. Fuel barge Ch 06. Yacht taxi Ch 69.

TORBAY HBRS Brixham Marina Ch 80, ☎ 01803 882929; YC, ☎ 853332, & Water taxi *Shuttle* Ch M. Torquay Marina Ch 80, ☎ 200210. Fuel Ch M.

EXETER Exmouth Marina Ch 14, ☎ 01395 269314. **Retreat BY**: Ch M, ☎ 01392 874720. **Port of Exeter** HM Ch 12, M-F: 0730-1730 and when vessel due; ☎ 07864 958658.

LYME REGIS HM Ch 14. Summer 0800-2000, winter 1000-1500. ☎ 01297 442137.

BRIDPORT HM Ch 11. ☎ 01308 423222.

PORTLAND PORT Port Control Ch 74 (H24). ☎ 01305 824044. **Marina** ☎ 01305 866190 Ch 80.

WEYMOUTH HM & Town Bridge: Ch 12, M-F 0800-2000 summer & when vessel due; ☎ 01305 838423. **Marina** Ch 80, ☎ 767576. **Fuel** Ch 60.

POOLE
HM Ch 14 (H24); Code 01202 ☎ 440233.
Poole Bridge Ch12.
Marinas Ch 80 M: Salterns ☎ 709971. Parkstone YC ☎ 743610. Poole Quay ☎ 649488. Cobbs Quay ☎ 674299.

YARMOUTH (IoW)
HM & Yar bridge **Ch 68** H24. ☎ 01983 760321. Water taxi **Ch 15.**

LYMINGTON
Marinas Ch 80, M: Yacht Haven ☎ 01590 677071. Berthon Marina ☎ 01590 673312.

COWES
Harbour Radio, Chain Ferry & Folly Inn Ch 69 Mon-Fri: 0800-1700. Marinas **Ch 80, M.** Tel code 01983: Yacht Haven ☎ 299975. Shepards ☎ 297821. East Cowes ☎ 293983. Island Hbr **Ch 80,** ☎ 822999. Water Taxi **Ch 06.**

NEWPORT HM & Yacht Hbr Ch 69 0800-1600. ☎ 01983 823885.

RYDE HM Ch 80. Summer 0900-2000, Winter HX. ☎ 01983 613903. Access HW±2.

BEMBRIDGE Marina **Ch 80,** ☎ 01983 872828. Water Taxi **Ch 80.**

SOUTHAMPTON
Port Ops and VTS Ch 12 14. Marinas **Ch 80, M.** Tel code 02380: Hythe ☎ 207073. Ocean Village ☎ 229385. Shamrock Quay ☎ 229461. Kemp's ☎ 632323. Town Quay ☎ 234397.

HAMBLE
Hbr Radio Ch 68 Apr-Sep daily 0600-2200; Oct-Mar 0700-1830. Marinas **Ch 80, M.** Tel code 02380: Hamble Pt ☎ 452464. Port Hamble ☎ 452741. Mercury ☎ 455994. Water Taxi **Ch 77,** ☎ 454512. Tel code 01489: Universal ☎ 574272. Swanwick ☎ 884081.

PORTSMOUTH
VTS **Ch 11** (& *QHM* if essential). Marinas **80**. Tel code 02392: Haslar ☎ 601201. Gosport ☎ 524811. Royal Clarence ☎ 523810. Port Solent ☎ 210765. THE CAMBER (Commercial Hbr): *Portsmouth Hbr Radio* **Ch 11** 14 (H24).

LANGSTONE HBR
HM **Ch 12**. Summer, daily 0830-1700; Winter, M-F 0830-1700; Sat/Sun 0830-1300. Southsea Marina **Ch 80, M,** ☎ 02392 822719.

CHICHESTER
HM *Chichester Hbr Radio* **Ch 14**. 1 Apr-Sep: M-Fri: 0830-1700. Sat: 0900-1300. 1 Oct - 31 Mar: 0900-1300, 1400-1700. Marinas **Ch 80, M**. Sparkes ☎ 02392 463572. Tel code 01243: Northney ☎ 466321. Emsworth Yacht Hbr ☎ 377727. Thornham ☎ 375335. Birdham Pool ☎ 512310. Chichester ☎ 512731. Water taxi **Ch 08** 0900-1800, mobile 07970 378350

LITTLEHAMPTON HM/Bridge **Ch 71** 0900-1700. Marina **Ch 80, M**; ☎ 01903 241663.

SHOREHAM HM & lock *Shoreham Hbr Radio* **Ch 14** (H24). Marina ☎ 01273 593801.

BRIGHTON
Marina *Brighton Control* **Ch M 80**; ☎ 01273 819919.

NEWHAVEN HM & Bridge *Newhaven Radio* **Ch 12.** HM / Port Control 612926 (H24). Marina **Ch 80, M;** ☎ 01273 513881.

EASTBOURNE
Sovereign Hbr, inc lock/berthing**: Ch 17.** ☎ 01323 470099.

RYE *Hbr Radio,* **Ch 14** 0900-1700 or when ship due. ☎ 01797 225225.

FOLKESTONE
Port Control **Ch 15** for entry; ☎ 01303 254597.

DOVER
Port Control **Ch 74** for entry. Marina Ch 80; ☎ 01304 241663.

RAMSGATE
Port Control **Ch 14**. Marina **Ch 80**; ☎ 01843 572110.

ENGLAND – EAST COAST

WHITSTABLE
Hbr Radio Ch 09 12, Mon-Fri: 0830-1700 and –3HW+1. ☎ 01227 274086.

MEDWAY
Medway VTS **Ch 74**. Kingsferry Bridge (W Swale) **Ch 10** H24. Marinas **Ch 80, M**. Tel code 01634: Gillingham ☎ 280022. Hoo ☎ 250311. Chatham ☎ 899200.

PORT OF LONDON
LONDON VTS: Ch 69 from sea to Sea Reach No 4 buoy. **Ch 68** Sea Reach No 4 to Crayford Ness. **Ch 14**, 22, W of Crayford Ness.
Thames Barrier Ch 14. ☎ 020 8855 0315.

RIVER THAMES
Patrol Launches *Thames Patrol* **Ch 06, 13, 14, 68**
King George V Dock lock *KG Control* **Ch 13.**
West India Dock lock **Ch 13**
Greenwich Yacht Club **Ch M**
Thames lock (Brentford) **Ch 74** Summer 0800-1800; Winter 0800-1630.
Cadogan Pier **Ch 14** 0900-1700.
Marinas Ch 80, M; Tel code 0207: Gallions Point ☎ 4767054. Poplar Dock ☎ 5151046. South Dock ☎ 2522244. Limehouse Basin ☎ 3089930. St Katherine Haven ☎ 2645312. Chelsea Hbr ☎ 2259100. Brentford Dock ☎ 0208 2328941.

RIVER ROACH Havengore Bridge **Ch 72** *Shoe Bridge* HW±2. ☎ 01702 383436.

BURNHAM-ON-CROUCH
Ch 80: HM Launch 0900-1700. Yacht Hbr ☎ 01621 782150. Essex Marina ☎ 01702 258531.

RIVER BLACKWATER
Marinas **Ch 80, M**; Tel code 01621: Tollesbury ☎ 869202. Bradwell ☎ 776235. **Ch M**: Blackwater ☎ 740264. Heybridge Lock, **Ch 80** ☎ 853506.

RIVER COLNE
Brightlingsea Hbr **Ch 68** 0800-2000. Tel code 01206 ☎ 302200. Waterside Marina Ch 68 ☎ 308709.

WALTON BACKWATERS
Titchmarsh Marina **Ch 80,** ☎ 01255 672185.

RIVERS STOUR AND ORWELL
HARWICH VTS **Ch 71**, 11, 20, H24
SUNK VTS **Ch 14,** H24
Orwell Navigation Service **Ch 68,** H24, ☎ 211066.
Marinas **Ch 80, M**. Tel code 01473: Shotley ☎ 788982. Suffolk Hbr ☎ 659240. Woolverstone ☎ 780206. Fox's ☎ 689111. Neptune ☎ 215204. Ipswich Haven ☎ 236644.

RIVER DEBEN HM ☎ 07803 476621.
Tidemill Yacht Hbr ☎ 01394 385745.

SOUTHWOLD *Port Radio* **Ch** 09 **12**. HM ☎ 01502 724712.

LOWESTOFT
Hbr Control **Ch** 11, **14**. HM ☎ 01502 572286.
Royal Norfolk & Suffolk YC **Ch 80.** ☎ 566726.
Haven Marina **Ch 80** ☎ 580300.
Mutford Bridge & Lock Ch 73 ☎ 531778.

GREAT YARMOUTH
Yarmouth Radio **Ch 12**. HM ☎ 01493 335511. *Haven & Breydon bridges* **Ch 12.**

WELLS-NEXT-THE-SEA
Wells Hbr **Ch 12,** HJ, HW±2 and when vessel expected. HM ☎ 01328 711646.

WISBECH Ch 09 HW–3 when vessel expected. HM 01945 588059. Sutton Bridge **Ch 09**

KING'S LYNN
Harbour Radio **Ch 14** 11 Mon-Fri: 0800-1700 and –3HW+1. HM ☎ 01553 773411.

BOSTON
Port Control **Ch 12** Mon-Fri 0800-1700 and HW HW -2½ to HW + 1½. HM ☎ 01205 362328.
Grand Sluice **Ch 74** only when lock operates.
Marina ☎ 07480 525230.

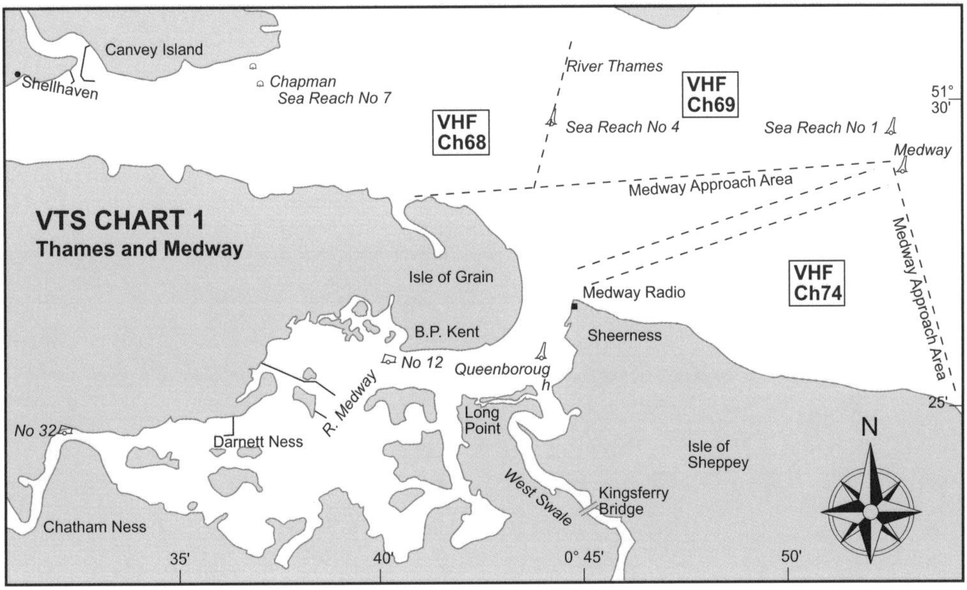

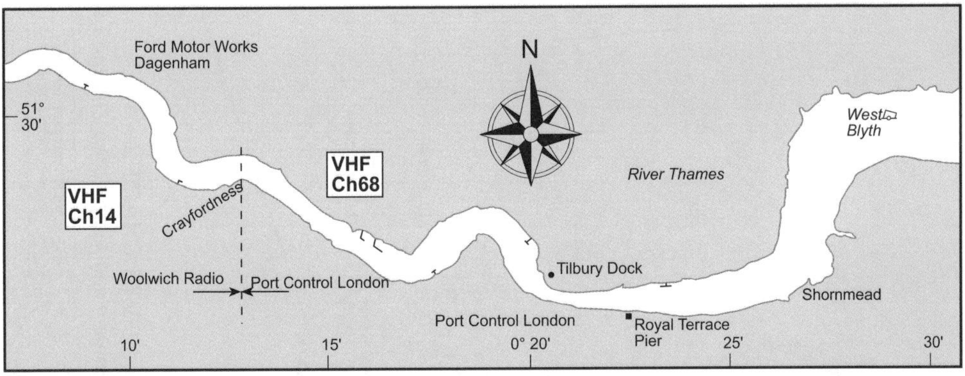

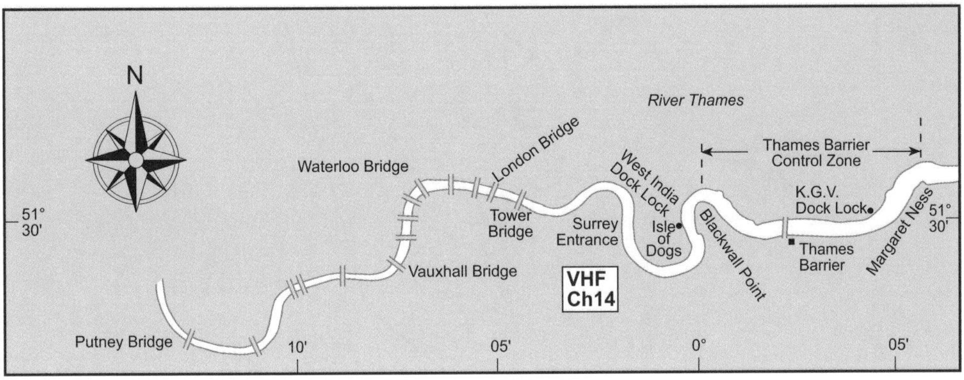

COMMUNICATIONS

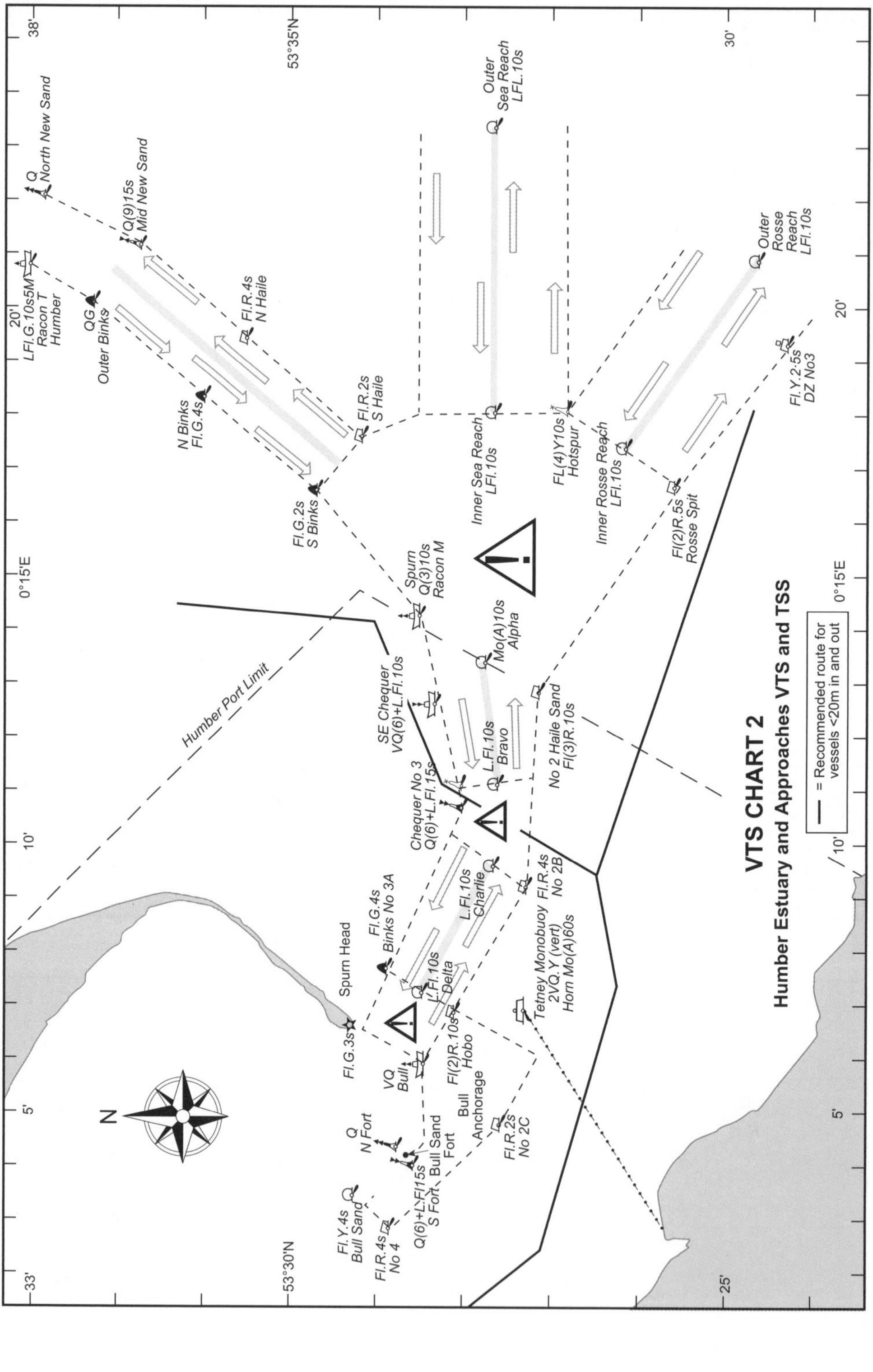
VTS CHART 2
Humber Estuary and Approaches VTS and TSS
= Recommended route for vessels <20m in and out
Humber Port Limit
Spurn Head
N
Q
North New Sand
Q(9)15s
Mid New Sand
20'
LFl.G.10s5M
Racon T
Humber
QG
Outer Binks
Fl.R.4s
N Haile
N Binks
Fl.G.4s
Fl.R.2s
S Haile
Fl.G.2s
S Binks
Outer
Sea Reach
LFL.10s
Inner Sea Reach
LFl.10s
FL(4)Y10s
Hotspur
Inner Rosse Reach
LFl.10s
Outer
Rosse
Reach
LFl.10s
Fl.Y.2·5s
DZ No3
Fl(2)R.5s
Rosse Spit
Spurn
Q(3)10s
Racon M
Mo(A)10s
Alpha
SE Chequer
VQ(6)+L.Fl.10s
No 2 Haile Sand
Fl(3)R.10s
L.Fl.10s
Bravo
Chequer No 3
Q(6)+L.Fl.15s
Fl.G.4s
Binks No 3A
L.Fl.10s
Charlie
Fl.R.4s
No 2B
Tetney Monobuoy
2VQ.Y (vert)
Horn Mo(A)60s
L.Fl.10s
Delta
Fl.G.3s
VQ
Bull
Fl(2)R.10s
Hobo
Bull
Anchorage
Fl.R.2s
No 2C
Q
N Fort
Bull Sand
Fort
Q(6)+L.Fl.15s
S Fort
Fl.Y.4s
Bull Sand
Fl.R.4s
No 4
38'
53°35'N
30'
20'
0°15'E
10'
5'
33'
53°30'N
25'

RIVER HUMBER
VTS 1, Ch 14 to seaward of Clee Ness Lt F
VTS 2, Ch 12 Clee Ness–Gainsborough (R Trent) & Goole (R Ouse). MSI broadcasts Ch 12 & 14 every 2 hrs from 0103LT.
Grimsby Docks Radio **Ch 74**; 18 79 H24
Marinas: Grimsby, Meridian Quay **Ch 74,** ☎ 01472 268424. **Hull, Ch 80,** ☎ 01482 330508.
South Ferriby, Sluice **Ch 74. Brough,** Humber Yawl club ☎ 01482 667224. **Goole** Boathouse ☎ 01405 763985.

BRIDLINGTON
HM, call Ch 16; work **Ch 12.** ☎ 01262 670148.

SCARBOROUGH
HM *Scarborough Port Control* **Ch 12** H24. ☎ 01723 373530.

WHITBY HM, Bridge & Marina **Ch 11,** 12 H24. ☎ 01947 602354.

RIVER TEES and HARTLEPOOL
Monitor *Tees Port control* **Ch 14,** 08, 11, 12, 22.
Hartlepool Marina **Ch 80, M** H24. ☎ 01429 865744.

SEAHAM
HM **Ch 12,** M-F 0800-1700. ☎ 0191 5161700.

SUNDERLAND
Hbr Radio **Ch 14** (H24). Marina **Ch 80, M.** ☎ 0191 5144721.

RIVER TYNE
Tyne VTS **Ch 12,** 08, 11, inc Info service.
Royal Quays Marina **Ch 80** ☎ 0191 2728282.
St Peter's Marina **Ch 80** ☎ 0191 2654472.
Newcastle City Marina ☎ 0191 2211348.

BLYTH
Port control **Ch 12,** 11. ☎ 01670 357025. Marina ☎ 01670 353636 (R Northumberland YC).

WARKWORTH HARBOUR (Amble)
HM Ch 16, work **Ch 14.** ☎ 01665 710306. Marina **Ch 80,** ☎ 01665 712168.

BERWICK-UPON-TWEED
HM **Ch 12,** M-F 0800-1700. ☎ 01289 307404.

SCOTLAND

EYEMOUTH HM **Ch 12,** 06 HO. ☎ 01890 750223.

FIRTH OF FORTH
Forth and Tay Navigation **Ch 71**; may work 12, 20.

PORT EDGAR Marina **Ch 80, M.** ☎ 0131 313330.

GRANTON, Royal Forth YC, Call *Boswell* **Ch M.** ☎ 0131 5523006.

GRANGEMOUTH Docks **Ch 14.** ☎ 01324 498566.

FORTH & CLYDE CANAL *Carron Sea Lock* **Ch 74.** ☎ 01324 483034.

METHIL Docks **Ch 14.** ☎ 01324 4426725.

ANSTRUTHER Ch 11. ☎ 01333 312591.

DUNDEE *Harbour Radio* **Ch 12.** ☎ 01382 224121.
Royal Tay YC Ch M. ☎ 01382 477516.

PERTH *Perth Harbour* **Ch 09.** ☎ 01738 624056.

ARBROATH *Port Control* **Ch 11.** ☎ 01241 872166.

MONTROSE *Port Control* **Ch 12.** ☎ 01674 672302.

STONEHAVEN HM **Ch 11.** ☎ 01569 762741.

ABERDEEN VTS **Ch 12,** ☎ 01224 597000.

PETERHEAD *Peterhead Hbrs* **Ch 14** for cl'nce to enter/exit. Marina ☎ 01779 477868.

FRASERBURGH Ch 12 H24, ☎ 01346 515858.

MACDUFF Ch 12 H24, ☎ 01261 832236.

BANFF Ch 12, ☎ 01261 815544.

WHITEHILLS *Whitehills Hbr Radio* **Ch 14,** ☎ 01261 861291.

BUCKIE Ch 12, 16 (H24), ☎ 01542 831700.

LOSSIEMOUTH
HM **Ch 12** 0700-1700. Marina, ☎ 01343 813066.

HOPEMAN and BURGHEAD
Same HM: *Burghead Radio* **Ch 14** HX, ☎ 01343 835337.

NAIRN HM/Marina ☎ 01667 454330. No VHF.

INVERNESS
HM **Ch 12,** M-Fri 0900-1700; Tel code 01463: ☎ 715715.
Clachnaharry Sealock **Ch 74,** ☎ 713896. HW ±4.
Inverness Marina **Ch 12.**
Seaport Marina ☎ 239745.
Caley Marina ☎ 236539.

HELMSDALE Ch 13, ☎ 01431 821692.

WICK Ch 14 HM, ☎ 01955 602030.

SCRABSTER HM **Ch 12** H24, Call on arr/dep. ☎ 01847 892779.

ORKNEY HARBOURS NAVIGATION SERVICE
Orkney Harbour Radio **Ch** 09 **11** 12
Stromness HM **Ch 14** M-Fri 0900-1700; ☎ 07810 465825. Marina, ☎ 465825.
Kirkwall *Hbr Radio* **Ch 14,** ☎ 872292. M-Fri, 0800-1700. Marina, ☎ 871313.
Westray Pier, *Pierowall Hbr* **Ch 14** expected,☎ 01857 677216. Marina, ☎ 07787 364934.

SHETLAND
Lerwick Hbr Radio **Ch 12** ☎ 01595 692991.
Scalloway Hbr Radio **Ch** 09, **12,** M-F 0700-1800, Sat 0900-1230. Piermaster ☎ 01595 744221.
Sullom Voe VTS **Ch 14** for tfc info, weather & radar assistance on request. ☎ 01806 242551.
Balta Sound Harbour **Ch 16, 20** HO

OUTER HEBRIDES
STORNOWAY HM **Ch 12** H24, ☎ 01851 702688.

Loch Maddy, N Uist Ch 12, ☎ 01876 500337.

St Kilda, *Kilda Radio* **Ch 16,** ☎ 01870 604406.

MAINLAND
Kinlochbervie Ch 14 HX, ☎ 01971 521235.

Loch Inver Ch 09 HX, ☎ 01571 844247.

ULLAPOOL Ch 14, ☎ 01854 612724.

Loch Gairloch Hbr Ch 16, ☎ 01445 712140.

ISLE OF SKYE

Portree Ch 12 (occas), ☎ 01478 612926.

Kyle Akin Ch 11, ☎ 01599 534167.

KYLE OF LOCH ALSH Ch 11, ☎ 01599 534589.

Mallaig Ch 09 HO, ☎ 01687 462154.

Tiree, Gott Bay Pier, **Ch 31,** ☎ 01879 230337.

Coll, Arinagour Pier, **Ch 31,** ☎ 01879 230347.

L Sunart, Salen Bay, **Ch 16,** ☎ 01967 431510.

ISLAND OF MULL

Tobermory, Ch 12, M HJ, ☎ 01688 302876.

Loch Lathaich; Sound of Iona; Craignure Pier.

Corpach basin & lock/Caledonian Canal Ch 74, ☎ 01397 772249, mob 07917 348025.

DUNSTAFFNAGE Marina, Ch M, ☎ 01631 566555.

Oban *North Bay* **Ch 12. Marina,** ☎ 01631 565333.

L Melfort, Kilmelford Haven, **Ch M,** ☎ 01852 200248.

L Shuna, Craobh Marina, **Ch M,** ☎ 01852 500222.

L Craignish, Ardfern **Ch 80, M,** ☎ 01852 500247.

CRINAN CANAL, Ch 74. BWB, ☎ 01546 603210.

Islay, Port Ellen, Marina ☎ 07464 151200; no VHF.

Tarbert, Loch Fyne Ch 14, ☎ 01880 820344.

Portavadie Marina Ch 80, ☎ 01700 811075.

CAMPBELTOWN Ch 12, 13, ☎ 07798 524821.

ROTHESAY, Bute Ch 12, ☎ 07799 724225.

LARGS Yacht Haven **Ch 80, M,** ☎ 01475 675333.

KIP Marina **Ch 80, M,** ☎ 01475 521485.

HOLY LOCH Marina **Ch 80, M,** ☎ 01369 701800.

RHU Marina **Ch 80, M,** ☎ 01436 820238.

ARDROSSAN Marina **Ch 80, M,** ☎ 01294 607077.

IRVINE HM/Bridge **Ch 12,** ☎ 01292 487286.

TROON Ch 14. Marina **Ch 80, M,** ☎ 01294 315553.

GIRVAN HM **Ch 12,** ☎ 01465 713648.

STRANRAER Ch 14, ☎ 01776 707500.

KIRKCUDBRIGHT HM **Ch 12,** ☎ 01557 331135.

ENGLAND W COAST AND WALES

MARYPORT Marina **Ch 80,** ☎ 01900 814431.

WORKINGTON HM **Ch 14,** ☎ 01900 602301.

WHITEHAVEN Marina **Ch 12,** ☎ 01946 692435.

ISLE OF MAN (Tel code 01624) If unable to contact IoM hbrs below, call Douglas.

Douglas *Hbr Control* **Ch 12** H24.

Port St Mary HM **Ch 12** HJ, ☎ 833205.

Peel HM **Ch 12** HJ, ☎ 842338.

Ramsey HM **Ch 12** 0800-1600. HO, ☎ 812245.

MAINLAND

GLASSON DOCK Marina **Ch 69,** ☎ 01524 751491.

FLEETWOOD *Fleetwood Dock Radio* (HW±2) **Ch 12** for Marina, ☎ 01253 879062.

PRESTON Lock *Riversway* **Ch 14.** Marina **Ch 80,** ☎ 01772 733595.

LIVERPOOL *Mersey Radio* **Ch 12.** Info **Ch 09.** Radar **Ch 18.** Liverpool Marina (Brunswick Dock) **Ch M,** ☎ 0151 7076777. Albert Dock **Ch M,** ☎ 0151 7096558; access via Canning Dock lock.

CONWY HM **Ch 14.** Marinas, both **Ch 80:** Conwy, ☎ 01492 593000. Deganwy 576888.

MENAI STRAIT and ANGLESEY

Beaumaris/Menai HM **Ch 69,** ☎ 01248 712312.

Caernarfon, HM & Victoria Dock **Ch 80,** ☎ 01286 672118. Mon-Fri: 0900-1700 Sat: 0900-1200

HOLYHEAD *Port Control* **Ch 14,** ☎ 01407 606700. Marina 764242.

MAINLAND

PWLLHELI, HM **Ch 12,** ☎ 701219 . Marina **Ch 80, M,** ☎ 01758 704081.

PORTHMADOG *Hbr* **Ch 12,** ☎ 01766 512927.

BARMOUTH HM *Barmouth Hbr* **Ch 12,** ☎ 01341 280671.

ABERDOVEY *Aberdovey Hbr* **Ch 12,** ☎ 01654 767626.

ABERYSTWYTH HM **Ch 14.** Marina **Ch 80,** ☎ 01970 611422.

FISHGUARD HM **Ch 14.**

MILFORD HAVEN Monitor *Port Control* (and *Patrol launch*) **Ch 12,** whilst under way. **Milford Docks** *Pierhead* **Ch 18.** Milford Dock Marina **Ch 14,** ☎ 01646 696312. Neyland Yacht Haven **Ch 80, M,** ☎ 01646 601601.

Tenby Ch 80, ☎ 01834 842717.

Saundersfoot Ch 11

SWANSEA Tawe Lock Ch 18. Marina **Ch 80,** ☎ 01792 470310.

BARRY *Barry Radio* **Ch 11.** HM ☎ 01446 732665.

CARDIFF *Cardiff Radio* **Ch 14.** Barrage control **Ch 18.** Penarth Marina **Ch 80,** ☎ 02920 705021.

NEWPORT HM **Ch 71,** ☎ 0870 6096699.

SHARPNESS *Sharpness Radio* **Ch 13** for lock. Marina, ☎ 01453 811476. Canal **Ch 74**

BRISTOL *Bristol VTS* **Ch 12** ☎ 0117 980 2638. *City Docks Radio* **Ch 14** (low power) to confirm. *Bristol Floating Hbr* **Ch 73.** Bristol Marina **Ch 80,** ☎ 0117 9213198.

PORTISHEAD Marina **Ch 80,** ☎ 0198 4631264.

BURNHAM-ON-SEA HM **Ch 08,** ☎ 01938 822666.

WATCHET Marina **Ch 80,** ☎ 01984 631264.

ILFRACOMBE HM **Ch 80,** ☎ 01271 862108.

APPLEDORE-BIDEFORD HM *Two Rivers* **Ch 12,** Appledore ☎ 01237 428700.

BUDE HM **Ch 12,** ☎ 01288 353111.

PADSTOW HM **Ch 12,** ☎ 01841 532239.

ST IVES HM **Ch 12,** ☎ 07816 077755.

IRELAND

ROSSAVEEL Ch 12, ☎ 091 572108.

GALWAY, HM **Ch 12,** ☎ 091 561874.

SHANNON ESTUARY *Shannon Ports Radio* **Ch 11** (HO), ☎ 087 2560427.

KILRUSH Marina Ch 80, ☎ 06590 52072.

LIMERICK HBR Ch 12 13, ☎ 061 315377.

MFENIT HM **Ch 14, M,** ☎ 066 7136231.

DINGLE HM **Ch 14** (no calls req'd), ☎ 087 9254115.

CAHERSIVEEN (Valentia) Marina Ch 80, ☎ 066 9472777.

BANTRY BAY, Lawrence Cove Marina **Ch M,** ☎ 027 75044.

CASTLETOWN BEARHAVEN ⚓, ☎ 027 70220.

CROOKHAVEN ⚓, ☎ 028 35319.

SCHULL ⚓, mobile ☎ 086 1039105.

BALTIMORE Ch 09, mobile 087 2351485.

GLANDORE HM **Ch 06,** ☎ 028 34737.

COURTMACSHERRY HM ☎ 08610 40812.

KINSALE HM **Ch 14** ☎ 021 4772503. Marinas **Ch M**: KYC ☎ 4772196. Castlepark ☎ 4774959.

CORK *Cork Hbr Radio* **Ch 12,** 14 H24. HM ☎ 021 4273125. Marinas **Ch M**: Crosshaven ☎ 4831161. Salve ☎ 4831145. Royal Cork YC ☎ 4831023. East Ferry ☎ 4813390. Cork Hbr ☎ (087) 3669009.

YOUGHAL HM/Pilots **Ch 14** Mon-Fri 0900-1700 and when ships expected. ☎ 024 92577.

DUNMORE EAST HM/Pilots **Ch 14** ☎ 051 383166.

WATERFORD & NEW ROSS Ch 12, **14.** ☎ 051 873501.

KILMORE QUAY Ch 09. Marina, ☎ 053 29955.

ROSSLARE HM **Ch 12** H24, ☎ 053 33114.

WEXFORD Hbr Boat club. **Ch 16,** ☎ 053 22039.

ARKLOW HM **Ch 12,** ☎ 0402 32466. Marina 39901.

WICKLOW HM **Ch 14** 12, ☎ 0404 67455.

DUN LAOGHAIRE HM **Ch 14,** ☎ 01 2801130. Marina **Ch M,** ☎ 2020040. YCs: National 2805725; R. St George 2801811; R. Irish 2809452; DL Motor 2801371.

Greystones Marina, ☎ 353 (086) 2718161

DUBLIN HM and VTS *Dublin VTS* **Ch 12,** 13. Poolbeg Marina **Ch M,** ☎ 01 6689983. Lifting bridge *Eastlink* **Ch 12, 13.** City moorings, ☎ 01 8183300.

HOWTH HM **Ch 11.** Marina Ch M, 80, ☎ 01 8392777.

MALAHIDE Marina **Ch 80, M,** ☎ 01 8454129.

CARLINGFORDFORD LOUGH
Carlingford Marina Ch M, ☎ 042 9373072.

Warrenpoint Ch 12, ☎ 028 41752878.

Kilkeel Ch 12, ☎ 028 41762287.

ARDGLASS (Phennick Cove) HM **Ch 12.** Marina **Ch M, 80,** ☎ 028 44842332.

STRANGFORD LOUGH
HM **Ch 12 14,** ☎ 028 44881637.

Portaferry Marina Ch 80, M, ☎ 07703 209780.

Donaghadee Copelands Marina, ☎ 028 91882184.

BELFAST VTS *Belfast Hbr Radio* **Ch 12. Marinas Ch 80, M:** Carrickfergus, ☎ 028 93366666. Bangor, ☎ 028 91453217.

LARNE *Port Control* **Ch 14,** 11.

Glenarm HM/Marina, mobile ☎ 07703 606763.

Ballycastle HM/Marina, mob ☎ 07803 505084.

PORTRUSH HM **Ch 12,** ☎ 028 70822307.

COLERAINE HM **Ch 12.** Marina, ☎ 028 70832086.

LONDONDERRY *Hbr radio* **Ch 14,** ☎ 028 71860313.

L SWILLY Fahan Marina, ☎ 074 9360008.

KILLYBEGS HM **Ch 14,** ☎ 07497 31032.

Burton Port HM **Ch** 06, 12, **14,** ☎ 075 42155.

SLIGO HM **Ch 12,** 14, ☎ 071 9153819.

DENMARK

Skagen HM **Ch 12** 13 HX, ☎ 98 941346.

Hirtshals HM **Ch 12** 13 HX, ☎ 98 941422.

Torup Strand HM **Ch 12** 13 HX.

Hanstholm HM **Ch 12** 13 HX, ☎ 97 961833/ 96550710.

THYBORØN HM **Ch 12** 13 H24, ☎ 97 831188.

Thisted (Limfjord) Ch 12 13 HX, ☎ 97 911400.

Torsminde HM **Ch 13** 16, ☎ 97 497044.

Hvide Sande HM **Ch 12** (0700-1700), ☎ 97 311633 H24.

ESBJERG *Hbr Control* **Ch 12** 13 14 H24, ☎ 75 124000. **Fanø** HM, ☎ 75 163100.

Rømø HM **Ch 10, 12, 13** HX, ☎ 74 755245.

GERMANY

HELGOLAND HM **Ch 67,** ☎ 04725 81593583.
May-Aug Mon-Thu 0700-1200, 1300-2000. Fri-Sun 0700-1200.

COMMUNICATIONS

Sep-Apr Mon-Thu 0700-1200, 1300-1600. Fri 0700-1200.
List HM **Ch 11,** ☎ 046 51870374.
Hörnum HM **67,** ☎ 046 51881027.
Wyk HM **Ch 11,** ☎ 046 81500430.
Pellworm HM **Ch 11,** ☎ 048 44726.
Husum HM **Ch 11,** ☎ 048 16670.
R. Eider sealock **Ch 14,** ☎ 04833 4535211.
Büsum HM **Ch 11,** ☎ 048 413607.

INNER DEUTSCHE BUCHT (GERMAN BIGHT) VTS, Eastern part **Ch 80,** ☎ 04421 489282. VTS, Western part **Ch 79**

BRUNSBÜTTEL WSA (hbr info) ☎ 04852 8850.

NORD-OSTSEE KANAL (KIEL CANAL)

VTS Canal I	**Ch 13,**	☎ 04852 885371.
VTS Canal II	**Ch 02,**	☎ 04852 885369.
VTS Canal III	**Ch 03,**	☎ 0431 3603456.
VTS Canal IV	**Ch 12,**	☎ 0431 3603465.

Brieholz, Ch 73. Ostermoor, Ch 73.
Kiel-Holtenau, HM ☎ **0431 363830.**

RIVER ELBE
CUXHAVEN HM **Ch 69** HX, ☎ 04721 500150. **Lock Ch 69,** ☎ 500120. **Cuxhaven** Marina, ☎ 175 90 20015. **YC** Marina, ☎ 34111. **R. Stör Lock Ch 09** Bridge opens on request. **Glückstadt** HM **Ch 08,** ☎ 04124 913200.

HAMBURG Port HM **Ch 12,** ☎ 040 7411540. **VTS** *Hamburg Port Traffic* **Ch** 13, **14, 74**. Wedel Yacht Hbr, ☎ 040 1034438. City Sporthafen, ☎ 040 364297.Lloyd & R Geeste Marinas ☎

BREMERHAVEN *Weser VTS* **Ch 22. Port Ch 12,** ☎ 0471 59613401. **HM,** ☎ 59613416. **Locks Ch 69, 10. Marinas** Weser YC, ☎ 23531. NYC, ☎ 77555. WVW, ☎ 73268.Lloyds/Geeste ☎1428690.

BREMEN *Port Radio* **Ch 03,** ☎ 0421 3618504.

JADE VTS *Jade Traffic* **Ch 63, 20.**

WILHEMSHAVEN
Port Ch 11, ☎ 04421 154580. **Sealock Ch 13. Bridges Ch 11. Marinas** Nassauhafen, ☎ 41439. Wiking Sportsboothafen, ☎ 41301.

HOOKSIEL Ch 63. Alterhafen Marina.

WANGEROOGE HM **Ch 17,** ☎ 04469 1322.

SPIEKEROOG HM No VHF, ☎ 04976 9193133.

DORNUMER-ACCUMERSIEL HM No VHF, ☎ 04933 2510. YC ☎ 2240.

LANGEOOG HM **Ch 17,** ☎ 04972 301.

NORDERNEY HM **Ch 17,** ☎ 04932 82826.

NORDDEICH HM **Ch 17,** ☎ 04931 81317.

BORKUM HM **Ch 14,** ☎ 04922 81317.

EMS VTS *Ems Traffic* **Ch** 15, 18, 20, 21

EMDEN HM & locks **Ch 13,** ☎ 04921 897260. YC Marina, ☎ 997147. Mariners' Club, ☎ 953795. City Marina, ☎ 8907211.

NETHERLANDS

DELFZIJL/EEMSHAVEN VTS is not compulsory for leisure craft. **Delfzijl Radar** Ch 03 gives radar assistance when visibility falls below 2000m. **Eemshaven Radar** Ch 01. **Port Control** Ch 66 broadcasts info every even H+10.

DELFZIJL HBR. HM Ch 14; ☎ 0596 640400. **Locks** Ch 26, M-Sat H24, Sun & hols on request; ☎ 693293. **Bridges:** Weiwerder Ch 11. Heemskes & Handelshaven Ch 14. **Farmsumerhaven,** Ch 66, ☎ 640494.

EEMSHAVEN HM Ch 14; ☎ 516142. Radar Ch 19.

LAUWERSOOG. HM, *Havendienst*, Ch 09; ☎ 0519 39023. Mon 0000-1700; Tu-Wed 0800-1700; Th-Sat 0700-1500.

TERSCHELLING VTS Call/monitor *Brandaris* Ch 02; ☎ 0562 443100. **Marina**, Ch 31; ☎ 443337.

VLIELAND. HM Ch 12. **Marina**, Ch 31; ☎ 0562 451729.

HARLINGEN HM Ch 11 (not on Sun); ☎ 0517 723300. **Locks** Ch 22.

OUDESCHILD HM Ch 12; ☎ 0222 312710. **Marina**, Ch 31; ☎ 0222 321227. See Den Helder VTS.

DEN HELDER VTS. Monitor *Tfc Centre* Ch 62, H24; broadcasts info and gives radar surveillance. **PORT CONTROL** Ch 14; ☎ 0223 62770. **Marina** ☎ 652645. **Bridge**: Moormanbrug Ch 18. **Lock**: Koopvaarders Ch 22.

IJSSELMEER Den Oever lock Ch 20, ☎ 0227 511789. **Port** Ch 11, ☎ 511303. Marina ☎ 511789. **Kornwerderzand lock** Ch 18, ☎ 0517 57441.

ENKHUIZEN Naviduct (also Krabbersgat) Ch 22.

IJMUIDEN VTS. Traffic Centre Ch 07, Roads (W of IJmuiden buoy). Thence **Port Control** Ch 61 to Noordzeesluizen (locks).

Seaport Marina Ch 75, ☎ 0255 560300.

NORDZEEKANAAL VTS
Noordzeesluizen. *Sluis IJmuiden* Ch 22. **Noordzeekanaal.** Ch 03, from locks to km 11·2.

AMSTERDAM Port Control Ch 68 (Km 11·2 to Oranjesluisen). **Port Info** Ch 14. Access to Standing Mast route: **Westerkeersluis** Ch 22. **Haarlem hbr** Ch 18. **Westerdoksbrug** ☎ 6241457, Ch 22. **Marinas: Amsterdam Marina** ☎ 6310767. **City Marina IJdock** ☎ 0687478290. **Marina Het Realeneiland,** ☎ 6238855. **Sixhaven,** ☎ 020 6329429. **WV Aeolus,** ☎ 6360791. **Aquadam,** ☎ 6320616. Access to Markermeer: **Oranjesluisen** Ch 18.

SCHEVENINGEN. Traffic Centre & Port Ch 21; ☎ 070 3527711. **Marina** Ch 31; ☎ 070 3520017.

HOEK VAN HOLLAND ROADSTEAD
To cross the mouth of the Maas, call *Maas Entrance* **Ch 03**, with vessel's name, position and course. Track close W of a line joining buoys MV, MVN and Indusbank N. See VTS Chart No 4. Maintain continuous listening watch and lookout.

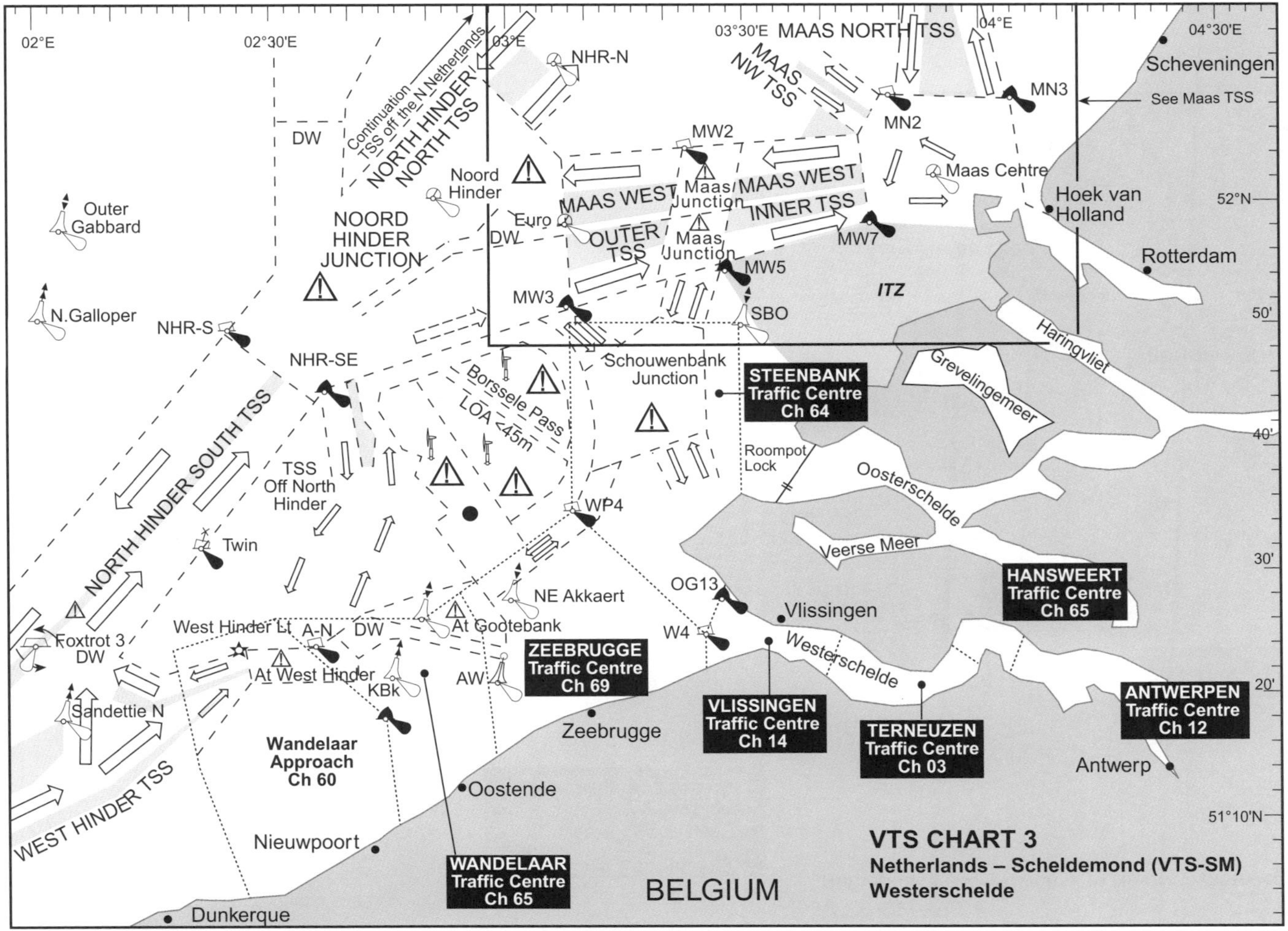

COMMUNICATIONS

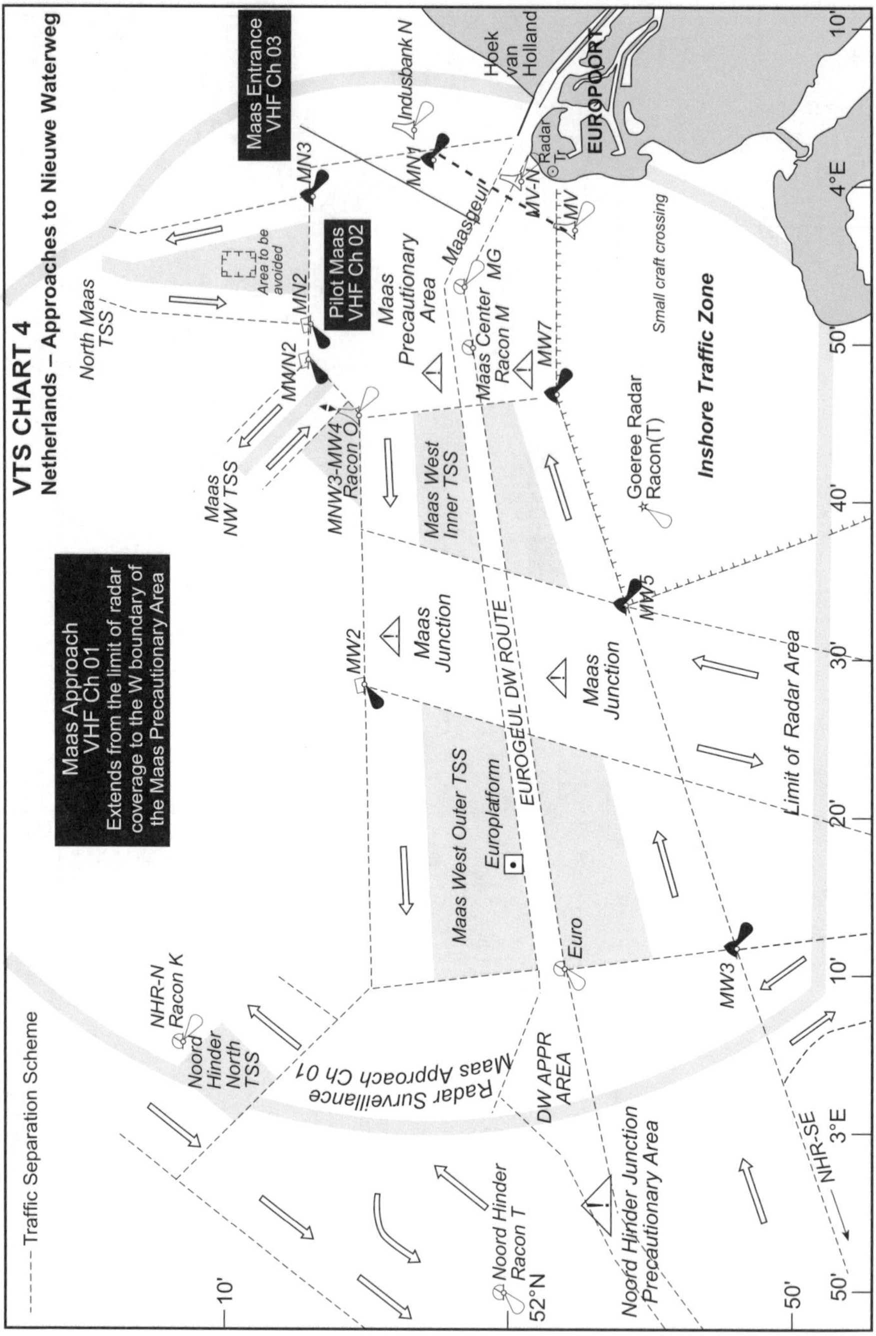
VTS CHART 4
Netherlands – Approaches to Nieuwe Waterweg
Traffic Separation Scheme
Maas Approach
VHF Ch 01
Extends from the limit of radar coverage to the W boundary of the Maas Precautionary Area
Maas Entrance
VHF Ch 03
Pilot Maas
VHF Ch 02
North Maas TSS
Area to be avoided
Maas NW TSS
MN3
MN2
MWN2
MN1
Indusbank N
MNW3-MW4
Racon O
Maas Precautionary Area
Maasgeul
MV-N
MV
MG
Maas Center
Racon M
MW7
Hoek van Holland
EUROPOORT
Radar Tr
Small craft crossing
Maas West Inner TSS
Goeree Radar
Racon(T)
Inshore Traffic Zone
MW2
Maas Junction
MW5
EUROGEUL DW ROUTE
Maas West Outer TSS
Europlatform
Limit of Radar Area
Euro
MW3
NHR-N
Racon K
Noord Hinder North TSS
Maas Approach Ch 01
Radar Surveillance
DW APPR AREA
Noord Hinder
Racon T
Noord Hinder Junction
Precautionary Area
NHR-SE
52°N
3°E
4°E
10'
50'
20'
30'
40'

NIEUWE WATERWEG VTS. Outer areas as shown on VTS Charts 3 & 4: **Maas Approach** Ch 01. **Pilot Maas** Ch 02. **Maas Entrance** Ch 03. **HCC** *Central Traffic Control* Ch 14 19. Report to/ monitor continuously the relevant Tfc Centre, as listed from seaward to City Marina: Rozenburg Ch 65; Maassluis Ch 80; Botlek Ch 61; Eemhaven Ch 63; Waalhaven Ch 60; Maasbruggen Ch 81.

ROTTERDAM Rotterdam Tfc Centre Ch 11. **Hbr Coordination Centre** (HCC) Ch 19. **Marinas/ Yacht hbrs: Vlaardingen** ☎ 010 2484333; Lock Ch 20. **Spuihaven** ☎ 4667765, mob 0644326722. Coolhaven ☎ 4764146. **Veerhaven** ☎ 4365446, mob 0653536107. **City Marina** ☎ 48540986, via Erasmus bridge Ch 18.

STELLENDAM Haringvliet lock & lifting bridge: *Goereese Sluis* Ch 20, ☎ 0187 497350. Opening hrs: M-F 0000-2200. 1 Nov - 1 Apr: Sat 0800-2200; Sun 0800-1000, 1600-1800. 1 Apr - 1 Nov: Sat & Sun 0800-2000. **Marina** Ch 31, ☎ 493769.

OOSTERSCHELDE Lock *Roompotsluis* Ch 18, ☎ 0111 659265. Opening hours: Mon & Thu, 0000-2200; Tue & Sun, 0600-0000; Wed H24; Fri & Sat: 0600-2200. **Roompot Marina** Ch 31.

WESTERSCHELDE VTS See VTS Chart No 3. Reporting not compulsory for leisure craft, but monitor the VHF channel for appropriate Traffic Area. Each Traffic Area is controlled by a Traffic Centre and bounded by buoys. *In emergency call the relevant Traffic Centre: Ch 67.*
Tfc Centre Steenbank & Radar Ch 64.
Tfc Centre Vlissingen Ch 14. **Radar** Ch 21. **Info broadcast** Ch 14 H+55.
Tfc Centre Terneuzen & Radar Ch 03. **Info broadcast** Ch 11 H+00.
Tfc Centre Hansweert Ch 65.
Antwerpen, Zeebrugge and Wandelaar Traffic Areas are listed under Belgium.

VLISSINGEN De Ruyter Marina no VHF, ☎ 0118 414498, mobile 06 5353 7181. *Flushing Port Control* Ch 09. **Sealocks & canal bridge** Ch 22. **VVW Schelde Marina** Ch 14, ☎ 465912 / 0615538515.

BRESKENS Marina, Ch 31, ☎ 0117 381902.

TERNEUZEN Port control Ch 11. **Marina**, ☎ 0115 697089. **Oostsluis** (E lock, small craft) Ch 18.

CADZAND-BAD, Jachthaven Cadzand, Ch 31 ☎ +31 611410975.

BELGIUM

ANTWERPEN, Tfc Centre Zandvliet Ch 12. **Info broadcast** Ch 12 H+35.

ANTWERPEN PORT Calling and safety Ch 74. **Kattendijksluis** Ch 69. **Siberia & Londen bridges** Ch 62. **Willemdok Marina** Ch 23, ☎ 03 2315066. **Linkeroever Marina** Ch 09, ☎ 03 2190895.

ZEEBRUGGE Tfc Centre Zeebrugge Ch 69. **Info broadcasts** Ch 69 H+15.

ZEEBRUGGE Port Control Ch 71 H24, ☎ 050 546867/550801. **Marinas VZW** ☎ 544903; **BZYC** ☎, 734738. **E lock** Ch 68.

BLANKENBERGE Marinas: VNZ, ☎ 050 429150, **& SYCB,** ☎ 411420, Ch 31. **VVW** ☎ 417536, Ch 23.

WANDELAAR Tfc Centre Wandelaar Ch 65. **Wandelaar Approach** Ch 60.

OOSTENDE Port Control Ch 09 H24, ☎ 059 340711. **Mercator lock,** ☎ 321669, **& marina,** ☎ 705762: Ch 14 H24. **Marinas**: RNSYC, ☎ 505912. RYCO, ☎ +32 59702754 .

NIEUWPOORT Port HM Ch 60 H24, ☎ 058 233000. **Marinas: KYCN**, Ch 23, ☎ 234413. **WSKLuM**, Ch 72, ☎ 5233641. **VVW-N**, Ch 08, ☎ 235232.

NORTH FRANCE

DUNKERQUE Port & VTS Ch 73, H24. The VTS does not affect leisure craft, but monitor Ch 73. **Marinas** Ch 09: Grande Large ☎ 03.28.63.23.00. YCMN ☎ 03.28.66.79.90. **Trystram lock** Ch 14.

GRAVELINES HM/Marina, Ch 09, ☎ 03·59·73·42·42.

CALAIS VTS, Port Control & Marina Ch 17 H24, ☎ 03.21.34.55.23.

BOULOGNE Boulogne Port, ☎ 03.21.31.52.43, Ch 12, H24. **Marina** Ch 09, ☎ 06.76.98.74.98 / 03.21.99.66.50.

LE TOUQUET/ÉTAPLES-SUR-MER Ch 09, 77. **Étaples Marina,** ☎ 03.21.84.54.03.

LE TRÉPORT Marina/lock Ch 12, 72, ☎ 02.35.50.63.06

DIEPPE Port HM Ch 12, HO. **Marina** Ch 09, ☎ 02.35.40.19.79.

ST VALÉRY-EN-CAUX Entry gate & marina Ch 09, ☎ 02.35.97.01.30.

FÉCAMP Port HM, Ch 10, **12**, ☎ 02.35.28.25.53. **Marina & Bérigny lock**, Ch 09, ☎ 02.35.28.13.58.

LE HAVRE Control Tower Ch **12**, 20. **Port Ops** Ch 67, 69. **Marina**, Ch 09, ☎ 02.35.21.23.95.

LA SEINE VTS Rouen Port Control Ch 73 (Estuary), 68 (River). **Honfleur radar** Ch 15, 19, **73.**

HONFLEUR HM Ch **17,** 73 HX, ☎ 02.31.14.61.09. **Lock,** ☎ 02.31.98.72.82, **& Bridge** Ch 17 H24.

ROUEN Port HM Ch **73,** 68 H24. **Halte Nautique,** ☎ 02.35.07.33.94. **Marina** ☎ 02.35.08.30.59.

ROUEN – PARIS, LOCKS Amfreville Ch 18. **Notre-Dame-de-la-Garenne** Ch 22. **Mericourt** Ch 18. **Andrésy** Ch 22. **Bougival** Ch 22. **Chatou** Ch 18. **Suresnes** Ch 22. **PARIS-ARSENAL Marina** Ch 09, ☎ 01.43.41.39.32.

DEAUVILLE Port Deauville lock, ☎ 02.31.88.95.66; Marina ☎ 02.31.98.30.01, Ch 09 0800-1730. **Port Morny** gate ☎ 02.31.88.57.89; Marina, Ch 09, ☎ 02.31.98.50.40.

DIVES-SUR-MER. Marina Ch 09, ☎ 02.31.24.48.00.

OUISTREHAM Port Ch74; **lock** Ch74, ☎ 02.31.36.22.00. **Marina** Ch 09, ☎ 02.31.96.91.37. **Canal** Ch 68. **CAEN** HM/Marina Ch 74, ☎ 02.31.95.24.47.

COURSEULLES-SUR-MER Marina Ch 09, ☎ 02.31.37.51.69.

PORT-EN-BESSIN HM, ☎ 02.31.21.70.49. **Gate/ bridge** Ch 18, ☎ 02.31.21.71.77.

GRANDCAMP Marina Ch 09, ☎ 02.31.22.63.16.

CARENTAN Lock Ch 09, ☎ 02.33.71.10.85. **Marina** Ch 09, ☎ 02.33.42.24.44.

ST VAAST-LA-HOUGUE Marina Ch 09, ☎ 02.33.21.61.00.

BARFLEUR HM, ☎ 02.33.54.08.29. No VHF.

CHERBOURG VTS (yachts to monitor) *Vigie du Homet* Ch 12 H24. **Marina** *Chantereyne* Ch 09, ☎ 02.33.87.65.70. **Gate** (B du Commerce) Ch 12

OMONVILLE-LA-ROGUE No VHF/Tel. 6 W ⚓s.

DIÉLETTE Marina Ch 09, ☎ 02.33.53.68.78.

CARTERET Marina Ch 09, ☎ 02.33.04.70.84.

PORTBAIL Yacht hbr Ch 09, ☎ 02.33.04.83.48.

GRANVILLE Port HM Ch 12. **Marina** Ch 09, ☎ 02.33.50.20.06.

ST MALO Port HM Ch 12 H24. **Marinas** Ch 09: **Bas Sablons,** ☎ 02.99.81.71.34. **Bassin Vauban,** ☎ 02.99.56.51.91. **DINARD,** ☎ 02.99.46.65.55.

R RANCE barrage lock Ch 13, ☎ 02.99.46.21.87. **Chatelier lock** Ch 14, ☎ 02.99.39.55.66.

ST CAST-LE-GUILDO Marina ☎ 02 96 81 04 43

DAHOUËT Marina Ch 09, ☎ 02.96.72.82.85.

LE LÉGUÉ HM/Marina Ch 12, ☎ 02.96.77.49.85.

BINIC Marina Ch 09, ☎ 02.96.73.61.86.

ST QUAY-PORTRIEUX Marina ☎ 02.96.70.81.30. Ch 09.

PAIMPOL Lock/Marina Ch 09, ☎ 02.96.20.47.65.

LÉZARDRIEUX Marina Ch 09, ☎ 02.96.20.14.22.

PONTRIEUX Lock/Marina Ch 12, ☎ 02.96.95.34.87.

TRÉGUIER Marina Ch 09, ☎ 02.96.92.42.37.

PERROS-GUIREC Marina Ch 09, ☎ 02.96.49.80.50.

PLOUMANAC'H Marina Ch 09, ☎ 02.96.91.44.31.

TRÉBEURDEN Marina Ch 09, ☎ 02.96.23.64.00.

MORLAIX Lock, ☎ 06.77.50.15.90 / 02.98.88.15.10. **Marina** Ch 09, ☎ 02.98.62.13.14.

ROSCOFF HM/S Basin Ch 09, ☎ 02.98.69.76.37.

ROSCOFF Marina *Plaisance Roscoff* Ch 09, ☎ 02.98.79.79.49. **Ferry Port** Ch 12, ☎ 02.98.61.27.84.

L'ABERWRACH Marina Ch 09, ☎ 02.98.04.91.62.

CHANNEL ISLANDS

ALDERNEY, Braye Hbr, *Alderney Coastguard* Ch 67, ☎ 01481 822620, or *Guernsey Coastguard. Alderney Port Control* Ch 74.

GUERNSEY Beaucette Marina, Ch 80, ☎ 01481 245000. **St Sampson** Ch 12 H24 via **St Peter Port** Control Ch 12 H24, ☎ 720229. **Victoria Marina** Ch 80 HO, ☎ 725987. *Guernsey Coastguard* Ch 20 H24 (Ch 62 for emergecy link calls).

JERSEY St Helier Port Control Ch 14 H24; 8M max range. **St Helier Marina,** ☎ 01534 447730/447708, has no VHF; call Ch 14 only if essential.
Gorey Ch 74, ☎ 853616.

WEST FRANCE

BREST VTS *Brest Port* Ch 08 H24. **Marinas** Ch 09. **Marina du Chateau,** ☎ 02·98·33·12·50. **Port du Moulin Blanc,** ☎ 02·98·33·12·50.

CAMARET Marina Ch 09, ☎ 02.98.27.95.99.

MORGAT Marina Ch 09, ☎ 02.98.27.01.97.

DOUARNENEZ HM Ch 12. **Marinas** Ch 09: Tréboul ☎ 02.98.74.02.56; Port Rhu ☎ 02.98.92.00.67.

AUDIERNE HM Ch 09. **Marina** ☎ 02.98.74.04.93. **Ste Evette** ☎ 02.98.70.00.28.

LOCTUDY Marina Ch 09, ☎ 02.98.87.51.36.

BENODÉT Marinas Ch 09: Penfoul ☎ 02.98.57.05.78. **Ste Marine** ☎ 02.98.56.38.72.

PORT-LA-FORÊT Marina Ch 09, ☎ 02.98.56.98.45.

CONCARNEAU Marina Ch 09, ☎ 02.98.97.57.96.

LORIENT Port Ch 12. **Marinas** Ch 09: Ban-Gâvres ☎ 02.97.65.48.25. Kernével ☎ 02.97.65.48.25. Port Louis ☎ 02.97.83.59.55. Locmiquélic ☎ 02.97.33.59.51. Lorient ☎ 02.97.21.10.14.

PORT TUDY Marina Ch 09, ☎ 02.97.86.54.62.

RIVER ÉTEL Marina Ch 13, ☎ 02.97.55.46.62.

BELLE ILE Sauzon HM Ch 09, ☎ 02.97.31.63.40. **Le Palais** HM Ch 09, ☎ 02.97.31.42.90.

PORT HALIGUEN Marina Ch 09, ☎ 02.97.50.20.56.

LA TRINITÉ Marina Ch 09, ☎ 02.97.55.71.49.

VANNES Marina Ch 09 (0800-1200, 1500-1900 July-Aug), ☎ 02.97.01.55.20.

CROUESTY Marina Ch 09, ☎ 02.97.53.73.33.

LA VILAINE Arzal Marina Ch 09, ☎ 02.97.45.02.97.

PIRIAC Marina Ch 09, ☎ 02.40.23.52.32.

LA TURBALLE Marina Ch 09, ☎ 02.40.23.41.65.

LE CROISIC Marina Ch 09, ☎ 09.81.12.75.92.

LE POULIGUEN Marina Ch 09, ☎ 02.40.11.97.97.

PORNICHET Marina Ch 09, ☎ 02.40.61.03.20.

ST-NAZAIRE VTS *Loire Ports Control* Ch 14. **Port HM** Ch 14, ☎ 02.40.00.45.89.

PORNIC Marina Ch 09, ☎ 02.40.82.05.40.

L'HERBAUDIÈRE Marina Ch 09, ☎ 02.51.39.05.05.

PORT JOINVILLE Marina Ch 09, ☎ 02.51.58.38.11.

ST GILLES CROIX DE VIE Marina Ch 09, ☎ 02.51.55.30.83.

LES SABLES D'OLONNE Port HM Ch 12, ☎ 02.51.95.11.79. **Marina** Ch 09, ☎ 02.51.32.51.16.

BOURGENAY Marina Ch 09, ☎ 02.51.22.20.36.

ILE DE RÉ Ars-en-Ré Ch 09, ☎ 05.46.29.08.52. **St Martin** Ch 09, ☎ 05.46.09.26.69.

LA ROCHELLE Marinas Ch 09: **Port des Minimes** ☎ 05.46.44.41.20. **Vieux Port** ☎ 05.46.41.32.05.

ROCHEFORT Marina Ch 09, ☎ 05.46.83.99.06.

ILE D'OLÉRON St Denis Ch 09, ☎ 05.46.47.97.97. **Boyardville** Ch 09, ☎ 05.46.76.48.56.

LA GIRONDE VTS Ch 12 (yachts to monitor). **Radar** *Bordeaux Port Control* Ch 12 on request. Depths in Gironde broadcast Ch 17 every 5 mins.

ROYAN Marina Ch 09, ☎ 05.46.38.72.22.

COAST RADIO STATIONS

Coast Radio Stations (CRS) deal with public correspondence (and a few other things). They enable a yachtsman to be linked by radio into the public telephone system to converse with a subscriber ashore, to make or receive a Link call.

However the mobile 'phone has to a great extent rendered Link calls obsolescent. Thus there are no longer any CRS in the UK, France and Netherlands. In Germany a limited service is provided by a commercial company (see below).

CRS still operate in the Channel Islands, Ireland*, Denmark, Belgium, Spain and Portugal; see below. But they too may gradually be withdrawn. *In Ireland CRS no longer handle commercial link calls, but Medico link calls are still available on both VHF and MF.

The CG does **not** handle Link calls, except in Denmark and Belgium where the functions of CG and CRS have always been co-located.

CHANNEL ISLANDS

GUERNSEY COASTGUARD 49°27'·00N 02°32'00W ☎ 01481 720672 📠 01534 714177
VHF **Ch 20** (primary working Ch for pilotage/ navigation). Link calls, Ch 62.

JERSEY COAST GUARD 49°10'·85N 02°14'30W ☎ 01534 447705 📠 01534 499089
VHF Ch 82 (primary working Ch for pilotage/ navigation). Emergency link calls **Ch 25.**

REPUBLIC OF IRELAND

A Coast Radio service is provided by the Dept of the Marine, Leeson Lane, Dublin 2, Eire. ☎ +353 (0)1 662 0922; ext 670 for enquiries. Broadcasts are made on a working channel/frequency following a prior announcement on Ch 16 and 2182 kHz. Ch 67 is used for Safety messages only.
VHF calls to an Irish Coast Radio Station should be made on a working channel. Only use Ch 16 in case of difficulty or in emergency.

NW, NE and SE Ireland

Weather broadcasts are at 0103, 0403, 0703, 1003, 1303, 1603, 1903, 2203 LT and at 0033, 0633, 1233, 1833 LT on the VHF Channels below. Nav warnings are broadcast at 0033, 0433, 0833, 1233, 1633 and 2033 LT.

Clifden CG	53°30'N 09°56'W	Ch 03
Clew Bay CG	53°46'·N 09°32'W	Ch 05
Belmullet CG	54°16'N 10°03'W	Ch 63
Donegal Bay CG	54°22'N 08°31'W	Ch 02
Glen Head CG	54°44'N 08°43'W	Ch 03
MALIN HEAD CG	55°22'N 07°21'W	Chs 01 and 05.

MF 1677 kHz, ☎ +353 (0) 77 70103
MMSI 002500100 DSC: 2187·5 kHz

Carlingford CG	54°05'N 06°19'W	Ch 04
DUBLIN CG	53°23'N 06°04'W	Ch 03
Wicklow Hd CG	52°58'N 06°00'W	Ch 02
Rosslare CG	52°15'N 06°20'W	Ch 05
Mine Hd CG	52°00'N 07°35'W	Ch 03

SW and W Ireland

Broadcasts at 0103, 0403, 0703, 1003, 1303, 1603, 1903, 2203 and at 0033, 0633, 1233, 1833 LT on VHF Channels listed. below
Nav warnings are at 0033, 0633,1233,1833 LT.

Cork CG	51°51'N 08°29'W	Ch 02
Galley Hd CG	51°31'N 08°57'W	Ch 16
Mizen Hd CG	51°34'N 09°33'W	Ch 04
Bantry CG	51°38'N 10°00'W	Ch 05
VALENTIA CG	51°56'N 10°21'W	Ch 62

MF 1752 kHz, ☎ + 353 (0) 66947 6109
MMSI 002500200, DSC: 2187·5 kHz

Shannon CG	52°31'N 09°36'W	Ch 64
Galway Bay CG	53°18'N 09°07'W	Ch 04

DENMARK

All VHF/MF CRS are remotely controlled from Lyngby Radio (55°50N 11°25'E) (MMSI 002191000). Use callsign *Lyngby Radio* on working frequencies The stations listed below monitor Ch 16 H24 and Ch 70 DSC. The MF stations do not monitor 2182 kHz. Traffic lists are broadcast on all VHF channels every odd H+05. Blåvand, Skagen and Lyngby monitor MF 2187·5 kHz DSC.

Skagen	57°44'N 10°35'E MF: Tx 1758, Rx 2102	Ch 04,
Hirtshals	57°31'N 09°57'E	Ch 63
Hanstholm	57°07'N 08°39'E	Ch 01
Bovbjerg	56°32'N 08°10'E MF: Tx 1734, Rx 2111	Ch 02
Blåvand	55°33'N 08°07'E MF: Tx 1734, Rx 2078	Ch 07

GERMANY

CRS: DPO7 – Seefunk (Hamburg) *(MMSI 002113100).* All stns monitor DSC Ch 70 and 16. Traffic lists are broadcast (LT): 0745, 0945, 1245, 1645, 1945 and H & H+30 on request Ch 16.

Nordfriesland	54°31'N 08°41'E	Ch 26
Elbe-Weser	53°50'N 08°39'E	Ch 24
Hamburg	53°33'N 09°58'E	Ch 83
Bremen	53°05'N 08°48'E	Ch 25
Accumersiel	53°40'N 07°29'E	Ch 28
Borkum	53°35'N 06°40'E	Ch 61

SHAPES

◆	Towing vessel - length of tow > 200m	**Rule 24**
▼	Yacht under sail *and* power	**Rule 25**
⧗	Vessel fishing or trawling	**Rule 26**
⧗ + ▲	Vessel fishing with outlying gear >150m long	**Rule 26**
● ◆ ●	Vessel restricted in her ability to manoeuvre	**Rule 27**
● ●	Vessel not under command	**Rule 27**
▮	Vessel constrained by her draught	**Rule 28**
●	Vessel at anchor	**Rule 30**

SOUND SIGNALS

MANOEUVRING AND WARNING Rule 34

•	A short blast = about 1 second.
–	A prolonged blast = 4 – 6 seconds.
•	I am altering course to **Starboard**
••	I am altering course to **Port**
•••	My engines are going **Astern**
•••••	I do not understand your intentions/ actions

Note: The above sound signals may be supplemented by light signals flashed on an all-round white light with least range of 5 miles.

In a narrow channel

– – •	I intend to overtake on your starboard side.
– – ••	I intend to overtake on your port side.
– • – •	I agree with your overtaking signal
–	Warning by vessel nearing a bend where other vessels may not be seen
–	Approaching vessel acknowledges.

VESSELS IN RESTRICTED VISIBILITY Rule 35

–	Power-driven vessel making way.
– –	Power-driven vessel underway, but stopped and not making way.
– ••	**A sailing vessel**; vessels not under command; restricted in ability to manoeuvre; constrained by draught; engaged in fishing, towing or pushing.
– •••	Vessel being towed or, if more than one vessel is towed, the last vessel in the tow.

VESSELS AT ANCHOR

🔔	Bell, ring for 5 seconds every minute
🔔 \	Vessel >100m: Bell forward, ring for 5 seconds every minute; plus
⊙	Gong aft, for 5 seconds every minute.
• – •	Optional extra to warn any approaching vessel

Sailing vessels < 12m at ⚓ do not have to sound the above fog signals. But if they do not, they *must* make an efficient noise every 2 minutes.

INTERNATIONAL PORT TRAFFIC SIGNALS (IPTS)

IPTS are widely used on the Continent, but less so around the UK. They may also be used to control traffic at locks and bridges.

No	Lights		Main message
1	Ⓡ Ⓡ Ⓡ	Flashing	Serious emergency – all vessels to stop or divert according to instructions
2	Ⓡ Ⓡ Ⓡ	Fixed or Slow Occulting	Vessels shall not proceed (*Note:* Some ports may use an exemption signal, as in 2a below)
3	Ⓖ Ⓖ Ⓖ	Fixed or Slow Occulting	Vessels may proceed. One-way traffic
4	Ⓖ Ⓖ Ⓦ	Fixed or Slow Occulting	Vessels may proceed. Two-way traffic
5	Ⓖ Ⓦ Ⓖ	Fixed or Slow Occulting	A vessel may proceed only when she has received specific orders to do so. (*Note:* Some ports may use an exemption signal, as in 5a below)
			Exemption signals and messages
2a	Ⓨ Ⓡ Ⓡ Ⓡ	Fixed or Slow Occulting	Vessels shall not proceed, except that vessels which navigate outside the main channel need not comply with the main message
5a	Ⓨ Ⓖ Ⓦ Ⓖ	Fixed or Slow Occulting	A vessel may proceed when she has received specific orders to do so, except that vessels which navigate outside the main channel need not comply with the main message
			Auxiliary signals and messages
White and/or yellow lights, displayed with the main lights			

- The main movement signal is always 3 lights in a vertical column, to which no extra light shall be added. Thus it is always recognisable as IPTS, as distinct from some kind of navigational lights.
- Red lights Ⓡ indicate ***Do not proceed.***
- Green lights Ⓖ indicate ***Proceed, subject to the conditions stipulated***. To avoid confusion Ⓡ and Ⓖ lights are never displayed together.
- Signals may be omni-directional ie seen by all vessels simultaneously; or directional, ie seen only from outside or from inside the harbour.
- Some ports may only use signals 2 and 4, or only Signal 1 when necessary
- Signal 1 ***Serious Emergency*** must show at least 60 flashes/minute.
- All other signals may be fixed or slow occulting, eg every 10s (helpful when background glare poses a problem), but never a mixture of both.
- Signal 5 assumes that VHF, signal lamp, loud-hailer, auxiliary signal or other means of communication will specifically inform a vessel that she may proceed.
- Exemption signals. A single Ⓨ light, shown to the left of signals 2 or 5 and level with the upper light, means ***Vessels which can safely navigate outside the main channel need not comply with the main message.*** This signal is obviously important to small craft, which nevertheless have a clear duty to keep clear of manoeuvring vessels.
- Auxiliary signals (only Ⓦ and/or Ⓨ lights) may be locally authorised and displayed to the right of the main signal. Their meanings must be promulgated.

Chapter 4 – Safety

DISTRESS, URGENCY, SAFETY

MAYDAY (Distress) must only be used if a ship or person is in ***grave and imminent danger and requires immediate assistance.*** The initial call may be made by voice or DSC, but only with the skipper's authority. It is appropriate for a man overboard if not quickly recovered.

PAN-PAN (Urgency) is used for ***very urgent messages concerning the safety*** of a vessel or person.

SÉCURITÉ (Safety) is usually used by coast stations to transmit navigational or weather warnings. It may also be used by vessels to report a hazard.

MAYDAY call by voice

A voice MAYDAY call is usually sent on VHF Ch 16 – the calling and distress channel. A distress call has priority over all other transmissions. The MAYDAY format below should be displayed by the radio.

Check the radio is ON, that HIGH POWER (25 watts) and Ch 16 are selected.

Press and hold down the transmit button, and say slowly and distinctly:

> **MAYDAY MAYDAY MAYDAY**
>
> **THIS IS** ....
> (name of boat, spoken three times)
>
> **MAYDAY** ....
> (name of boat spoken once & MMSI No)
>
> **MY POSITION IS** ....
> (latitude and longitude or true bearing and distance *from* a known point)
>
> **Nature of distress** ....
> (sinking, on fire etc)
>
> **Help required** ....
> (immediate assistance)
>
> **Number of persons on board** ....
> **Any other important, helpful information** ..
> (you are taking to the liferaft; distress rockets are being fired etc)
>
> **OVER**

Release the transmit button and listen. If an acknowledgement is not received, check the set and repeat the distress call.

False alerts

If a distress alert is inadvertently transmitted, an All Stations voice message on VHF Ch 16 cancelling the false alert must be sent at once: 'Cancel my Distress Alert of (date/time (GMT/UT)'.

Distress alert by DSC

A distress alert is typically sent as follows:

> Briefly press the red, guarded Distress button. The set will automatically switch to Ch 70. Press ***again*** for 5 seconds to transmit a basic distress alert* with position and time. The set then reverts to Ch 16.
>
> *If time permits, select the nature of the distress from the menu (eg Collision, Fire, Flooding) then press the Distress button for 5 seconds to send a full distress alert.

CG/CRS automatically send acknowledgements on Ch 70 before replying on Ch 16. Ships in range should reply directly on Ch 16. If a distress acknowledgement is not received from a CG/CRS, the distress alert will automatically be repeated by the radio every four minutes.

> When a DSC distress acknowledgement has been received, or after about 15 seconds, the vessel in distress should transmit a MAYDAY message by voice on Ch 16, including its MMSI and callsign.

MAYDAY acknowledgement

An acknowledgement should be expected:

> **MAYDAY** ....
> (name of vessel sending the distress message, spoken three times)
>
> **THIS IS** ....
> (name of station acknowledging, spoken three times)
>
> **RECEIVED MAYDAY**

On hearing a MAYDAY call, immediately cease all transmissions, listen on the frequency concerned and note down the details. If you can help, acknowledge accordingly but only after giving an opportunity for the nearest Coastguard Station or more suitable vessel to do so.

MAYDAY relay

If you hear a distress message from a vessel which is not acknowledged, you should pass on the message as follows:

> **MAYDAY RELAY** ....
> (spoken three times)
>
> **THIS IS** ....
> (name of vessel re-transmitting the distress message, spoken three times), followed by the intercepted message.

HELICOPTER RESCUE

- **COMMUNICATE ON CHANNEL 16**
- Use flares or smoke when helicopter is seen or heard
- Helicopter may ask you to drop sails and motor on a specific course
- You may be asked to stream the casualty astern in the dinghy
- Brief your crew early (too noisy when helicopter is close)
- **MAINTAIN YOUR COURSE** and do not get distracted
- Weighted line lowered
- Let it touch boat or water first (to earth any static charge)
- Take in slack line only
- **PULL LINE IN AS DIRECTED**
- **DO NOT SECURE IT TO THE BOAT**
- **DO EXACTLY AS YOU ARE TOLD**

Note: The text and sketch relate to a Hi-line transfer, one of several techniques which may be used

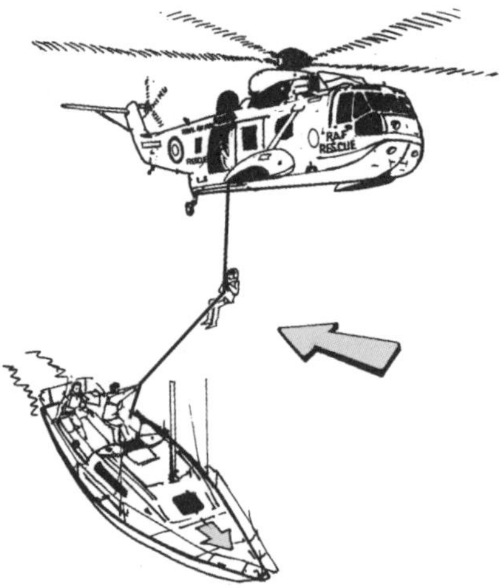

URGENT MEDICAL HELP - PAN PAN

- **Send an URGENCY call by DSC**, if possible, and/or...
- **Make a PAN PAN voice call:**
- **CHANNEL 16, HIGH POWER (25W) (**if necessary, turn off dual watch)
- **PAN PAN** .... (repeat 3 times)
- **ALL STATIONS** .... (repeat 3 times)
- **THIS IS** .... (vessel's name; repeat 3 times)
- **OVER**

Next message should include:
Yacht's name, callsign, nationality
Yacht's position and nearest harbour
Patient's details, symptoms and advice wanted
The medication you have on board

FIRST AID

The objectives of First Aid at sea are to:

- **Preserve life** • **Prevent further damage**
- **Relieve pain and distress**
- **Deliver a live casualty ashore**

With any casualty be calm, reassuring and methodical. First ensure your own safety and that of the vessel. If in doubt call for advice and assistance.

Completion of a First Aid Course is strongly recommended. In the UK, RYA approved, one-day, basic training is available through sailing clubs and schools. The St Johns Ambulance and British Red Cross provide a variety of recognised courses.

MEDICAL ADVICE can be obtained almost anywhere in European waters by making an All Stations 'PAN PAN' call or a DSC Urgency Alert to the Coastguard or to a Coast Radio Station. You will then be connected to a doctor or to the nearest hospital.

The Urgency signal 'PAN PAN' is always advised, especially abroad, because it is internationally understood and eliminates most language problems; it is also free.

If you are not qualified to judge how serious the casualty's condition is, get the best possible advice and/or help as quickly as possible. **Urgent help needed** is shown against the more serious medical problems.

Be ready to describe the patient's symptoms, eg consciousness, pulse rate, breathing rate, temperature, skin colour, site and type of injury, any pain, amount of blood lost etc. If a doctor needs to come aboard, or a casualty has to be landed, the Coastguard will arrange.

If non-urgent, wait until in harbour. Consider calling the port authority before arrival so that a doctor or paramedic can meet you on arrival.

MEDICAL CARE ABROAD It is advisable for each person on board to carry the European Health Insurance Card (EHIC) which entitles you to medical treatment on a reciprocal basis, although it may not cover the full charge. See *www.dh.gov.uk* for full details.

EMERGENCY RESUSCITATION (ABC)

The immediate procedure for any collapsed or apparently unconscious person is: Assess whether or not the casualty is conscious. Carefully shake his/her shoulders and ask loudly 'What's happened?' or 'Are you all right?' or give a command such as 'Open your eyes'. An unconscious casualty will not respond.

A = Airway

Remove any visible obstruction from the casualty's mouth (leave well-fitting dentures in place). Listen at the mouth for breathing. Tilt the head backwards, using head tilt and chin lift to maintain a clear airway.

Look, listen and feel for ***no more than 10 seconds*** to determine if the casualty is breathing normally. If in any doubt, act as if it is ***not*** normal.

If breathing, place casualty in recovery position. Check the area is clear of danger.

B = Breathing and C = Circulation

If not breathing and the airway is clear, start chest compressions. This situation is called **cardiac arrest**. The casualty will be unconscious and may appear very pale, grey or bluish in colour. An artificial circulation will have to be provided by chest compression. If the circulation stops, the breathing will also stop. Casualties with cardiac arrest will need both rescue breathing and chest compression, a combination known as Cardio Pulmonary Resuscitation (**CPR**).

External chest compression

To start external chest compression, lay the casualty face up on a hard, flat surface. Kneel beside casualty. Place the heel of your hand on top of the other hand and interlock your fingers. Apply pressure at the centre of the chest.

Depress breastbone 5–6cm (2-2½in) then release.

With either one or two operators give 30 chest compressions and continue cycles of 2 breaths to 30 compressions. Use a compression rate of 100 per minute. Chest compression should be combined with rescue breaths; after 30 compressions, give 2 effective rescue breaths (2 breaths should not take more than 5 seconds). *Do not stop.*

Action plan for the resuscitation of adults

Casualty unconscious but is breathing normally:

- ***Urgent help needed***
- Turn casualty into the recovery position
- Check for continued breathing

Casualty is unconscious and not breathing:

- ***Urgent help needed***
- Start chest compressions
- After 30 compressions, give 2 rescue breaths

Continue with chest compressions and rescue breaths in a ratio of 30:2. If you are untrained, or are unwilling to give rescue breaths, give chest compressions only. Stop to re-check casualty only if he/she starts to show signs of regaining consciousness; coughing, opening eyes, speaking or moving purposefully ***and*** starts to breath normally. If so place the casualty in the recovery position. Otherwise, ***do not interrupt resuscitation***.

BITES AND STINGS Injected poison from bites and stings usually only causes local swelling and discomfort, but some people may react severely. For insect stings, resuscitate if collapse occurs; otherwise give rest, painkillers, antihistamines (eg chlorpheniramine).

BLEEDING – OPEN WOUND Bleeding is often very dramatic, but is virtually always controllable.

- Apply firm continuous direct pressure; bandage on a large pad. If bleeding continues, bandage more pads on top of initial pads; then press directly over wound for at least 10 minutes (blood takes this long to clot).
- Elevate if wound is on a limb.
- Do *not* apply a tourniquet. This practice is out of date due to the danger of losing a limb.

BLEEDING – INTERNAL (CLOSED INJURY)
Follows fractured bones, crush injuries, or rupture of organs such as the liver or spleen. Treat for shock which may appear rapidly. ***Urgent help needed***.

BURNS AND SCALDS Move the victim into fresh air to avoid inhaling smoke.

ABC – Airway, Breathing, Circulation

- Stop further injury: dip the whole of the burnt part into cold water for 10–15 minutes. Seawater is excellent but may be very painful.
- Remove only loose clothing. Do not pull off clothing stuck to the skin.
- Cover with sterile dressing. If skin is broken or blistered, use sterile paraffin gauze beneath the dressing. Separate burnt fingers with paraffin gauze. Never use adhesive dressings.
- Do not prick blisters or apply ointments.
- Elevate burnt limb and immobilise.
- Give strong painkillers.
- Treat for shock: give frequent and copious drinks of water.
- Start giving antibiotics for major burns. If burns extensive or deep, ***urgent help needed***.

CHOKING If blockage by some object (eg a peanut) is suspected, turn the casualty on his side and give up to 5 sharp back slaps with the flat of the hand between the shoulder blades. Check mouth and remove any obstruction.

If unsuccessful, wrap both arms around the victim's waist from behind, and give 5 sharp upward thrusts with both fists into the abdomen above the navel but below the ribs so as to cause coughing. Clear object from mouth.

CUTS AND WOUNDS Often dramatic but only potentially serious if nerves, tendons or blood vessels are severed.

Clean thoroughly with antiseptic. Remove dirt or other foreign bodies. Small clean cuts can be closed using as many Steristrips as necessary to keep the skin edges together. Skin must be dry. Leave for 5 days at least. Larger deep cuts may require stitches; apply a dressing and seek help. Do not try amateur surgery at sea.

Ragged lacerations or very dirty wounds – do not attempt to close these. Clean as well as possible, sprinkle antibiotic powder in wound and apply a dressing. Seek help. If in doubt a wound is best left open and lightly covered to keep it clean and dry.

Fingers and toes Blood may collect under the nail following an injury. Release the blood by piercing the nail with a red hot needle or paper clip. It will not hurt!

DENTAL PAIN seems worse at sea; prevention is better than cure. Dentanurse is an emergency treatment pack which enables an amateur to make temporary repairs, eg replacing crowns, lost fillings. It contains zinc oxide and Eugenol.

Throbbing toothache made worse by hot or cold or when bitten on. Clean out any cavity and apply temporary filling. Take painkiller.

Dull toothache tender to bite on; gum swollen or red with possible discharge. Treat as above but also take an antibiotic.

Broken tooth or filling Cover exposed surfaces with zinc oxide paste. Teeth knocked out should be put in a clean container with milk or moist gauze for a dentist to re-implant asap. This can be attempted onboard - ideally within 1 hour

Bleeding gums Clean teeth more thoroughly. Use regular hot salt water rinses and antibiotics.

Pain round wisdom tooth Clean area with toothbrush; use hot salt water rinses; take antibiotics and painkillers.

Mouth ulcers Hot salt water rinses.

DIARRHOEA Can become serious, especially in young children if much fluid is lost. Stop food, give plenty of fluid. Plain water is usually sufficient, or add salt (1 teaspoonful/litre) and sugar (4–5 teaspoons/litre). Lomotil or Imodium tablets are very effective in adults.

DROWNING ABC Clear seaweed, dentures. If not breathing start mouth to mouth ventilation as soon as possible and in the water if practicable. If no pulse, start chest compression as soon as on board. Keep the head low so that vomit is not inhaled and water can drain.

If stomach is bulging, turn casualty on to side to empty water and avoid inhaling it. Prevent cooling. Remove wet clothes; wrap casualty in blankets to warm him/her.

Continue resuscitation until the casualty revives or death is certain. Hypothermia may mimic death. Do not abandon resuscitation until the casualty has been warmed or signs of death persist despite attempts at warming.

Once revived, put in the recovery position.

Any person rescued from drowning may collapse in the next 24 hours as the lungs react to inhaled water. ***Urgent help needed***.

EYE INJURIES are potentially serious. Never put old or previously opened ointment or drops into an eye; serious infection could result.

Foreign object Flush with clean water, pull the lower lid out to inspect, remove object with a clean tissue. For objects under upper eyelid, ask casualty to grasp lashes and pull the upper lid over the lower lid. An eye-bath is very effective. Blinking under water may help. After removal of object, insert sterile antibiotic ointment inside pulled out lower lid. Cover with pad.

Corrosive fluid Flush continuously with water for 15 minutes. Give painkillers and chloramphenicol ointment; cover with pad. ***Seek help asap***.

Conjunctivitis Sticky, weeping eye with yellow discharge. Chloramphenicol 4 times a day.

FISH HOOKS Push the hook round until the point and barb can be cut off; withdraw the hook. Dress the holes and give an antibiotic.

FRACTURES AND DISLOCATIONS Fracture is a broken bone. Dislocation is a displaced joint. Both produce pain (aggravated by attempted movement), localised swelling, abnormal shape, and a grating feeling on movement (if it is a fracture). Blood vessels or nerves around the fracture or dislocation may also be damaged causing a cold, pale, or numb limb below the site of the injury.

Fractures of large bones such as the femur (upper leg) will result in major internal bleeding and may cause shock. When complications occur ***urgent help is needed***.

Early application of a splint and raising the injured limb where possible will reduce pain and complications. Treat for shock and pain.

Specific fractures and dislocations

Cheek Caused by a direct blow. Rarely serious but requires specialist care.

Jaw Beware of associated brain or spinal injury. Remove blood and teeth fragments; leave loose teeth in place; protect broken teeth. Ensure airway is clear. Start regular antiseptic mouth washes and antibiotics. Support jaw with bandage over top of the head. Give only fluids by mouth.

Neck May result from a direct blow, a fall or a whiplash type injury. If conscious, casualty may complain of pain, tingling, numbness or weakness in limbs below the injury. ***Mishandling may damage the spinal cord, causing paralysis or death***. Avoid movement and support the head. Immobilise by wrapping a folded towel around the neck. If movement is necessary then lift the victim as one rigid piece, never allowing the neck to bend. ***Urgent help needed.***

Nose Control bleeding by pinching.

Ribs Very painful. Strapping is not advised.

Spine Fracture of the spine below the neck, may cause ***paralysis or death***. Mishandling of the victim may greatly worsen the damage. Avoid movement if possible. Lift the casualty without allowing the spine to sag. ***Urgent help needed.***

Collar bone Support arm in sling.

Dislocated shoulder If this has happened before, the casualty may remedy the dislocation himself; otherwise do not attempt to remedy it in case a fracture exists.

Upper arm Support the arm with a collar and cuff inside the shirt, ie tie a clove hitch around the wrist and loop the ends behind the neck.

Forearm and wrist Splint (eg with battens or wood). Do not bandage tightly. Elevate or support in a sling.

Fingers Elevate hand and, unless badly crushed, leave unbandaged; keep moving. If very wobbly, bandage to adjacent finger.

Lower limb

Thigh Shock may be considerable. Strap to other leg with padding between. Gently straighten the lower leg. If necessary apply traction at the ankle to help straighten the leg. Do not bandage too tightly.

Knee Twisting injuries or falls damage the ligaments and cartilages of the knee. Very painful and swollen. Treat as for fracture.

Lower leg Pad very well. Splint using oar, broom handle or similar pieces of wood.

Ankle Fracture or severe sprain may be indistinguishable. Immobilise in neutral position with foot at right angles. Raise the limb.

HEART ATTACK Severe 'crushing' chest pain; may spread to shoulders, neck or arms. Sweating, then bluish lips, then collapse. Breathing and heart may stop. Give one 300mg aspirin tablet (to chew) ***Urgent help needed***.

Rest, reassure. If unconscious: recovery position; observe breathing and pulse. If breathing stops or no pulse, start mouth to mouth ventilation and chest compression immediately; do not stop.

STROKE Symptoms: if a person develops **sudden** onset weakness on one side of the body, problems with speech &/or visual problems: ***think of stroke***.

Recognise a stroke using the FAST test:

- Face – Has side of face fallen; can they smile?
- Arms – Can both arms be raised and kept up?
- Speech – Is it slurred or muddled?
- Time – To call for help.

Place in recovery position and check airway. ***Urgent help needed*** – specialist treatment within 4½ hours can reverse the effects of a stroke. If you are more than 4½ hours from help, and the casualty is conscious and able to swallow, give 300mg of asprin even if he/she is improving.

HEAT STROKE Cool casualty by spraying with cold water or wrap the casualty in a cold wet sheet until their temperature under the tongue falls to 38°C. Encourage drinking (1 teaspoon of salt/half litre of water). If casualty stops sweating, has a rapid pounding pulse and is becoming unconscious: ***Urgent help needed***.

HYPOTHERMIA Symptoms: unreasonable behaviour, apathy and confusion; unsteady gait, stumbling; slurring of speech; pale, cold skin; slow, weak pulse; slow breathing; shivering. It leads to collapse, unconsciousness and ultimately death.

ABC Put in recovery position. If not breathing, start mouth to mouth ventilation. Be prepared to use chest compressions.

Remove wet clothing. Avoid wind chill. Dry and wrap in blankets or sleeping bag plus warm hat and cover, if available, in foil survival bag. ***Urgent help needed***.

Give hot sweet drinks if conscious. Do not give alcohol, rub or place very hot objects against skin.

SEASICKNESS is aggravated by anxiety, fatigue and boredom. Symptoms: lethargy, dizziness, headache and nausea/vomiting. Help prevent with anti-seasickness pills, avoiding rich foods and alcohol. Take frequent small amounts of fluid and food. Keep warm; keep busy. Prolonged seasickness may cause serious loss of fluid – seek advice.

SHOCK can result from almost any accident or medical emergency; it can lead to collapse.

Signs and symptoms Thirst, apathy, nausea, restlessness. Pale, cold, clammy skin, sweating. Rapid, weak pulse. Rapid, shallow breathing. Dull, sunken eyes, bluish lips.

ABC Control any bleeding. Lay the casualty flat or in recovery position; raise legs 20°. Splint any fractures; avoid movement. Avoid chilling, keep warm. Give pain killers. Reassure the casualty. Do not let the casualty eat, drink, smoke or move unnecessarily. If complaining of thirst, moisten the lips with a little water. Note: Fluids may be life saving in cases of dehydration (eg diarrhoea, vomiting, severe burns).

FIRST AID KIT

Stow the following items in a waterproof container, readily accessible and clearly marked:

Triangular bandage x 2 (doubles as a sling)

Crepe bandage 75mm x 2

Gauze bandage 50mm x 2

Elastoplast 75mm x 1

Band Aids (or similar) various shapes and sizes

Wound dressings, 1 large, 1 medium

Sterile non-adhesive dressing (Melolin) x 5

Steristrips x 5 packs

Cotton wool. Safety pins. Thermometer.

Scissors and forceps, good quality stainless steel

Disposable gloves

Antiseptic solution (eg Savlon)

Sunscreen with high protection factor

Antifungal powder or cream (athlete's foot)

Insect repellent (DEET, diethyltoluamide)

Individual choice of anti-seasick tablets

Antibiotic eye ointment (prescription only)

Additional items for extended cruising

Vaccinations – a course may need to start as much as 6 months before departure.

Syringes 2ml x 2 (if carrying injections)

Dental kit – see Dental pain.

DRUGS AND MEDICATION

Paracetamol, painkiller. 1-2 500mg tablets 4 hrly.

Asprin, blood thiner. 300mg single dose for heart attack or stroke.

Ibuprofen, anti-inflammatory. 400mg every 8 hours (avoid if history of asthma or stomach ulcer).

**Dihydrocodeine*, strong painkiller. 1-2 30mg tablets 4 hourly.

Certirizine, antihistamine. 10mg once a day.

Aludrox, indigestion. 1-2 before meals.

Loperamide, diarrhoea. 2 x 2mg capsules initially, then 1 after each loose stool; max 8 day.

Senokot, constipation. 2-4 tablets per day.

**Amoxycillin*, antibiotic. 2 x 250mg capsules 8 hourly (beware penicillin allergy)

**Erythromycin*, antibiotic for penicillin-allergic adults. 4 x 250mg tablets daily.

Cinnarizine, seasickness. 2 x 15mg tablets before sailing, then 1 every 8 hours.

**Scopolamine patches*, seasickness. 1 patch behind ear 5-6 hours before voyage; replace after 72 hrs if necessary.

Chloramphenicol ointment 1%, eye infection, apply 3-4 times/day

* Only available on prescription.

OBSERVATION FORM

The information recorded by you on this form will be invaluable in helping doctors and/or paramedics ashore to diagnose the problem and arrange the best possible treatment for your casualty.

This is particularly important if there may be a considerable time lapse between requesting medical help and the casualty reaching hospital.

- Keep photocopies of this form in your First Aid kit so as to preserve the original.
  Whilst awaiting help, record your careful observations by ticking or annotating the various boxes at 10 minute intervals. This will help doctors detect any improvement or deterioration in the casualty's condition.
- If within radio range of shore attempt to pass the observations via the Coastguard to a medical authority; or ask a ship to relay.
- Before the casualty is taken off the yacht ensure that this form and personal documents (money, passport, EHIC and mobile 'phone) are securely tied to him/her.

DATE .... CASUALTY'S NAME .... AGE .... M/F ....

Times of observations @ 10 minute intervals:		10	20	30	40	50	60
EYES Observe for reactions whilst testing other responses	Open spontaneously						
	Open when spoken to						
	Open to painful stimulus						
	Nil response						
MOVEMENT Apply painful stimulus: Pinch ear lobe or skin on back of hand	Obeys commands						
	Responds						
	Nil response						
SPEECH Speak clearly and directly, close to the casualty's ear	Responds sensibly to queries						
	Seems confused						
	Uses inappropriate words						
	Incomprehensible sounds						
	Nil response						
PULSE (Beats per minute) Take adult's pulse at wrist or neck. Note rate and whether beats are: weak (w); strong (s); regular (reg) or irregular (irreg)	Over 110						
	101-110						
	91-100						
	81-90						
	71-80						
	61-70						
	Below 61						
BREATHING (Breaths per minute) Note rate and whether breathing is: quiet (q); noisy (n); easy (e); or difficult (d)	Over 40						
	31-40						
	21-30						
	11-20						
	Below 11						

GMDSS

The Global Maritime Distress and Safety System (GMDSS) is a sophisticated, but complex, semi-automatic, third-generation communications system. Although not compulsory for yachts, its potential for saving life, particularly when far offshore and out of VHF range, is so great that every yachtsman should seriously consider it. Equipment costs continue to fall. Training courses, leading to the award of the Short Range Certificate (SRC) of Competence, are widely available. The Long Range Certificate covers MF, HF, SatCom, EPIRBs and SART.

Recommended reading:

- *ALRS, Vol 5* (UK Hydrographic Office)
- *GMDSS: a User's Handbook* (Bréhaut/ACN)
- *GMDSS for small craft* (Clemmetsen/ Fernhurst)
- *Reeds VHF/DSC Handbook* (Fletcher/ACN)

Purpose

GMDSS enables a coordinated SAR operation to be mounted rapidly and reliably anywhere at sea. To this end, terrestrial and satellite communications and navigation equipment is used to alert SAR authorities ashore and ships in the vicinity to a Distress incident or Urgency situation. GMDSS also promulgates Maritime Safety Information.

Sea areas

For the purposes of GMDSS, the world's sea areas are divided into 4 categories (A1-4), defined mainly by the range of radio communications. These are:

A1 An area within R/T coverage of at least one VHF Coastguard or Coast radio station in which continuous VHF alerting is available via DSC. Range: 20–50M from the CG/CRS.

A2 An area, excluding sea area A1, within R/T coverage of at least one MF CG/ CRS in which continuous DSC alerting is available. Range: approx 50–250M from the CG/CRS.

A3 An area between 76°N and 76°S, excluding sea areas A1 and A2, within coverage of HF or an Inmarsat satellite in which continuous alerting is available.

A4 An area outside sea areas A1, A2 and A3, ie the polar regions, within coverage of HF.

The radio equipment to be carried by GMDSS vessels for each sea area category is specified: in

- A1 – VHF DSC;
- A2 – VHF and MF DSC;
- A3 – VHF, MF + HF/SatCom;
- A4 VHF, MF and HF.

Most UK yachtsmen will operate in A1 areas (the English Channel, for example, is an A1 area) where a simple VHF radio and a NAVTEX receiver will initially meet GMDSS requirements. As equipment becomes more affordable, yachtsmen may decide to fit GMDSS. This will become increasingly necessary as the present system for sending and receiving Distress calls is run down. The CG will continue a loudspeaker watch on VHF Ch 16 until further notice.

Functions

Regardless of the sea areas in which they operate, vessels complying with GMDSS must be able to perform certain functions:

- transmit ship-to-shore Distress alerts by two independent means
- receive shore-to-ship Distress alerts
- transmit & receive ship-to-ship Distress alerts
- transmit signals for locating incidents
- transmit and receive communications for SAR co-ordination
- transmit/receive maritime safety info, eg navigation and weather warnings

Distress alerts

A Distress alert is simply a Distress call using DSC. It is transmitted on Ch 70 and is automatically repeated five times. Whenever possible, a Distress alert should always include the last known position and time in UT. The position is normally entered automatically from an interfaced GPS, but can be entered manually if required. The nature of the distress can also be selected from the receiver's menu. The vessel's identity (MMSI number) is automatically included.

GMDSS requires participating ships to be able to send Distress alerts by two out of three independent means. These are:

- Digital Selective Calling (DSC) using terrestrial communications, ie VHF Ch 70, MF 2187·5 kHz, or HF distress and alerting frequencies in the 4, 6, 8,12 and 16 MHz bands.
- Emergency Position Indicating Radio Beacons (EPIRBs). See below.
- Inmarsat, via ship terminals.

Digital Selective Calling

DSC is an essential component of GMDSS.

Information is sent by a burst of digital code, which can be selectively addressed to a specific DSC-equipped vessel or group of vessels.

Every vessel and relevant shore station has a 9-digit identification number, or MMSI (Maritime Mobile Service Identity), which is in effect an automatic, electronic callsign.

DSC is used to transmit Distress alerts from ships, to receive Distress acknowledgements from ships or shore stations; to send Urgency and Safety alerts; to relay Distress alerts; and for routine calling & answering.

Maritime Safety Information (MSI)

MSI consists of the vital navigational, weather and safety messages sent to vessels at sea by R/T on VHF, MF broadcasts and GMDSS. For navigation and weather warnings see this and Chapter 2 respectively.

GMDSS transmits MSI in English by two independent but complementary means, NAVTEX and SafetyNet.

- NAVTEX on MF (518 kHz and 490 kHz) which can be received out to about 300 miles offshore, see Chapter 2.
- SafetyNet uses Inmarsat-C satellites to cover beyond MF range, except Area A4. Enhanced Group Calling (EGC) is a part of SafetyNet which enables MSI to be sent to selected groups of users in any of the four oceans.

Personal Locator Beacons (PLB) operate on the same principle. They must also be registered but they do not have a vessel-specific MMSI.

Emergency Position Indicating Radio Beacons (EPIRB) may be hand-held or float-free, they transmit on 406 MHz. Most EPIRBs have a built in GPS and about 48 hours of battery life. They communicate via the Cospas-Sarsat (C/S) network of geostationary and polar orbit satellites. Although C/S will relay an EPIRB signal to earth with no delay, the position of a non-GPS EPIRB may take several hours to determine.

An EPIRB transmits uniquely coded data to identify the individual beacon and it must be registered. It is important that any changes are immediately notified. The UK registration centre is:-

The EPIRB Registry, The Maritime and Coastguard Agency, CGOC Falmouth, Pendennis Point, Castle Drive, Falmouth, Cornwall TR11 4WZ; ☎ 01326 211569; email: epirb@mcga.gov.uk.

False alerts caused by inadvertent or incorrect use of EPIRBs put a significant burden on SAR Centres and may coincide with an actual distress situation. If an EPIRB is activated accidentally, advise the nearest CG/CRS as soon as possible.

All crew members should be aware of the proper use of the EPIRB onboard. Ensure that testing is adequately supervised; that the EPIRB is correctly installed and maintained; and that it is not activated if assistance is already available.

Search And Rescue Transponders (SART) are radar transceivers which operate on 9 GHz and respond to 3 cm (X-band) radars, like a small portable Racon (see Chapter 3). They are primarily intended for use in liferafts to help searching ships and aircraft find survivors. The transmitted signal shows on a radar screen as 12 dots radiating out from the SART's position.

HM COASTGUARD – CONTACT DETAILS

SCOTLAND & NORTHERN IRELAND

†SHETLAND MRCC
60°09'N 01°08'W. MMSI 002320001
Knab Road, Lerwick ZE1 0AX.
☎ 01595 692976. 📠 01595 694810.
Area: Orkney, Fair Isle and Shetland and mainland from C Wrath to S of Brora, incl Pentland Firth

†ABERDEEN MRCC
57°08'N 02°05'W. MMSI 002320004
Marine House, Blaikies Quay, Aberdeen AB11 5PB.
☎ 01224 592334. 📠 01224 212862.
Area: English border to Cape Wrath, incl Pentland Firth. .

†*STORNOWAY MRCC
58°12'N 06°22'W. MMSI 002320024
Battery Pt, Stornoway, Isle of Lewis H51 2RT.
☎ 01851 702013. 📠 01851 704387.
Area: Cape Wrath to Mull, Western Isles and St Kilda.

†*BELFAST MRCC
54°40'N 05°40'W. MMSI 002320021
Bregenz House, Quay St, Bangor, Co Down BT20 5ED.
☎ 02891 463933. 📠 02891 465886.
Area: Carlingford Lough to Lough Foyle and Firth of Clyde, incl islands.

EASTERN REGION

†HUMBER MRCC
54°06'N 00°11'W. MMSI 002320007
Lime Kiln Lane, Bridlington,
N Humberside YO15 2LX.
☎ 01262 672317. 📠 01262 606915.
Area: Southwold to the Scottish border.

LONDON MRSC
51°30'N 00°03'E MMSI 002320063 ☎ 0208 3127380 📠 0208 3098196. Thames Barrier Navigation Centre, Unit 28, 34 Bowater Road, Woolwich, London SE18 5TF.
Area: River Thames from Shell Haven Pt (N bank) and Egypt Bay (S bank), up-river to Teddington Lock.

DOVER MRCC
50°08'N 01°20'E DSC MMSI 002320010
☎ 01304 210008 📠 01304 225762
Langdon Battery, Swingate, Dover CT15 5NA.
Area: Beachy Head to Southwold Note: In this area, use call signs *Thames Coastguard* or *Dover Coastguard*, both VHF Ch 16. Also operates Channel Navigation Information Service (CNIS)

JOINT RESCUE COORDINATION CENTRE FAREHAM, (JRCC)
50°51'·50N 01°14'·90W DSC MMSI, 002320011 ☎ 02392 552100 📠 02392 554131/01305 760451. Kites Croft, Fareham PO14 4LW.
Area: South Coast: Topsham (River Exe) to Beachy Head (Note: in this area make initial calls to *Solent Coastguard* on Ch 67 (H24) to avoid congestion on Ch 16).

WESTERN REGION

†*FALMOUTH MRCC
50°09'N 05°03'W. MMSI 002320014
Pendennis Point, Castle Drive,
Falmouth TR11 4WZ.
☎ 01326 317575. 📠 01326 318342.
Area: Marsland Mouth to Topsham (R. Exe).
NOTES: †Monitors DSC MF 2187.5 kHz.
*Broadcasts Gunfacts/Subfacts.

†MILFORD HAVEN MRCC
51°42'N 05°03'W. MMSI 002320017
Gorsewood Drive, Hakin,
Milford Haven, SA73 2HD.
☎ 01646 690909. 📠 01646 692176.
Area: Friog to Marsland Mouth (nr Bude).

†HOLYHEAD MRCC
53°19'N 04°38'W. MMSI 002320018
Prince of Wales Rd, Holyhead,
Anglesey LL65 1ET.
☎ 01407 762051. 📠 01407 764373.
Area: Area: Mull of Galloway to Friog (1·6M S of Barmouth) inc Isle of Man.

THE SEA SAFETY GROUP – www.seasafetygroup.org – a charity, is an association of independent coastal watch stations, each authorised by HM CG (MCA) to provide additional lookout and communications cover around the UK. They are similar in ethos but separate from the NCI. Stations are:

Pakefield	07367 096492
Happisburgh	07500 628299
Winterton	01493 393989
Sheringham	01263 821200
Hartlepool	07946 036793
Redcar	01642 491606
Sunderland	01915 672579
Berwick	07738 269071
St Monans	07706 664839
Tay	07849 184354
Irvine	01294 271855

NATIONAL COASTWATCH INSTITUTION (NCI) www.nci.org.uk, a national charity, is a voluntary organisation keeping visual watch along the coast of England and Wales, assisting the preservation and protection of life at sea. The National Office is 17 Dean St, Liskeard, Cornwall, PL14 4AB ☎(01579) 347392. There are 56 operational stations (2021) manned by over 2600 volunteers. They are marked on the Area maps by the symbol © and maintain direct contact with HM CG.

Stations monitor VHF Ch **65** 16, HM CG channels and local operational VHF channels. **65** is the NCI dedicated channel. Seafarers can call directly for radio/AIS checks, actual weather, sea state, hazards and local info.

South West and South Coast	
Gwennap Head	01736 871351
Penzance	01736 367063
Bass Point (Lizard)	01326 290212
Nare Point (Helford)	01326 231113
Portscatho (w/ends only)	01872 580180
Charlestown	01726 817068
Polruan (Fowey)	01726 870291
Rame Head (Plymouth)	01752 823706
Prawle Point (Salcombe)	01548 511259
Froward Pt (Dartmouth)	07976 505649
Torbay	01803 411145
Teignmouth	01626 772377
Exmouth	01395 222492
Lyme Bay	07745 756872
Charmouth	01308 897778
Portland Bill	01305 860178
St Alban's Head	01929 439220
South West and South Coast	
Peveril Pt (Swanage)	01929 422596
Hengistbury Hd	07851 672540
Needles	01983 754321
Calshot	02380 893562
Lee on Solent	02392 556758
Gosport	02392 765194
Shoreham	01273 463292
Newhaven	01273 516464
Folkestone (Copt Pt)	01303 227132
Herne Bay (w/ends only)	01227 744454
Whitstable (w/ends only)	07864 646209
East Anglia	
Holehaven (Canvey Is)	01268 696971
Southend (w/ends only)	0781 5945210
Felixstowe	01394 670808
Gorleston (Gt Yarmouth)	01493 440384
Caister	07527 977613
Mundesley	01263 722399
Runton	01263 513725
Wells-next-the-Sea	01328 710587
East Coast	
Skegness	07902 076605
Chapel Pt	01754 874311
Mablethorpe	07958 038564
Hornsea	01964 668248
North West Coast	
Rossall Pt (Fleetwood)	01253 681378
Great Orme	07384 276604
Wales	
Point Lynas	No landline
Rhoscolyn	07887 955496
Porth Dinllean	07773 362005
Wooltack Point (St Brides)	01646 636802
Worms Head (Gower)	01792 390167
Porthcawl	01656 782936
St Donat's Bay	07747 410135
Nells Point (Barry)	01446 420746
South West, North Coast	
Boscastle	01840 250965
Stepper Point (Padstow)	01841 530039
St Agnes Head	01872 552073
St Ives	01736 799398
Cape Cornwall	01736 787890

ROYAL NATIONAL LIFEBOAT INSTITUTION

The RNLI is a registered charity which saves life at sea providing a lifeboat service H24 up to 50M off the UK and Irish coasts. There are 237 lifeboat stations, and a combined fleet of over 340 all-weather boats (ALB's) and inshore craft (ILB's).

On active service, lifeboats >10m keep watch on VHF and MF DSC as well as VHF Ch 16. They use alternative frequencies to contact shore agencies, SAR aircraft, and HMCG. All show a quick-flashing blue light.

The RNLI actively promotes safety at sea by providing a free safety service both to members and the general public including help, advice, publications and demonstrations, to prevent accidents by helping people to be better prepared through water safety awareness.

If you wish to help support the RNLI financially, ☎ 0300 300 9990, visit www.rnli.org.uk or supporter_care@rnli.gov.uk for details of membership options.

Their website page 'Safety' covers emergencies, first aid, seamanship, navigation, weather, and engines, with contact details for safety checks.

Their headquarters are at: RNLI, West Quay Road, Poole, Dorset BH15 1HZ.

THE CHANNEL ISLANDS

Guernsey and Jersey Coastguard stations direct SAR operations in the North and South of the CI area respectively, they also provide communications on VHF and DSC.

Close liaison is maintained with adjacent French SAR authorities. A distress situation may be controlled by the Channel Islands or France, whichever is more appropriate. For example a British yacht in difficulty in French waters may be handled by St Peter Port or Jersey so as to avoid language problems; and vice versa for a French yacht.

GUERNSEY CG 49°27'·00N 02°32'00W. DSC MMSI 002320064. ☎ 01481 720672. 📠 714177.
Area: Channel Islands North.

JERSEY CG 49°10'·85N 02°14'30W.
DSC MMSI 002320060. ☎: 01534 447705.
📠: 499089. Area: Channel Islands South.

SEARCH AND RESCUE ABROAD
THE IRISH REPUBLIC

The Irish CG co-ordinates SAR operations around the coast of Ireland via Dublin MRCC, Malin Head and Valentia MRSCs and remote sites. It may liaise with the UK and France during any rescue operation within 100M of the Irish coast.

It is part of the Dept of Marine, Leeson Lane, Dublin 2. ☎ (01) 678 3454; 📠 (01) 662 0795. The Irish EPIRB Registry is co-located; ☎ (01) 6199280; 📠 (01) 6621571.

The MRCC/MRSCs are co-located with the Coast radio stations of the same name and manned by the same staff. All stations keep watch H24 on VHF Ch 16 and DSC Ch 70. If ashore dial 999 or 112 in an emergency and ask for Marine Rescue.

Details of the MRCC/MRSCs are as follows:

DUBLIN (MRCC)
53°20'N 06°15W. DSC MMSI 002500300 (+2187·5 kHz).
☎ +353 1 662 0922/3; 📠 +353 1 662 0795.
Area: Carlingford Lough to Youghal.

VALENTIA (MRSC)
51°56'N 10°21'W.DSC MMSI 002500200 (+2187·5 kHz).
☎ +353 669 476 109; 📠 +353 669 476 289.
Area: Youghal to Slyne Head.

MALIN HEAD (MRSC)
55°22'N 07°20W. DSC MMSI 002500100 (+2187·5 kHz).
☎ +353 749 370103; 📠 +353 749 370221.
Area: Slyne Head to Lough Foyle.

SAR resources

The Irish CG provides some 50 units around the coast and is on call H24. The RNLI maintains 4 stations around the coast and operates 42 lifeboats; six community-run inshore rescue boats are also available.

Sikorsky S-61 helicopters, based at Dublin, Waterford, Shannon and Sligo, can respond within 15 to 45 minutes and operate to a radius of 200M. They are equipped with infrared search equipment and can uplift 30 survivors.

Military and civilian aircraft and vessels, together with the Garda and lighthouse service, can also be called upon.

Some stations provide specialist cliff climbing services. They are manned by volunteers, who are trained in first aid and equipped with inflatables, breeches buoys, cliff ladders, etc. Their ☎ numbers (the Leader's residence) are given, where appropriate, under each port.

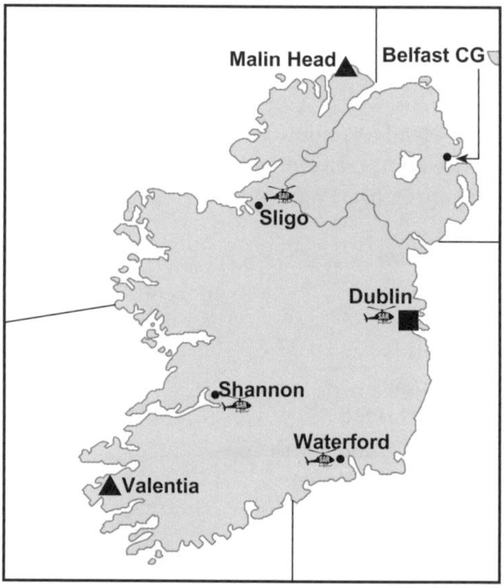

Irish Coastguard centres

DENMARK

The national SAR agency is: JRCC Defence Command Denmark, Defence Command Denmark, JOC Herningvej 30, Karup J, Denmark. ☎ +45 72850380 (switchboard) 📠 +45 72850384.
The SAR coordinator for Denmark is: **JRCC Denmark**, ☎+45 72850450 switchboard; 📠+45 72850384; jrcc@sok.dk MMSI 002191000

JRCC Denmark has no direct communications with vessels in distress, but operates via two Maritime Operations Centres (MOC's) and

Coast Radio Station (CRS) Lyngby Radio. **MOC North** (MRSC) ☎ +45 992 21520; 📠 +45 992 21538, mocn-orum@mil.dk, covers the W coast of Denmark.

Lyngby Radio

This is the main Danish CRS and is DSC VHF/MF/HF equipped. ☎ +45 72198410; 📠 +45 458 82485, vfk-ktp-joc-lyngbyradio@fiin.dk MMSI 002191000.

Its remote sites at Skagen, Hirtshals, Hantsholm, Bovbjerg and Blavand, all monitor Ch 16 H24 and use callsign *Lyngby Radio*. Their VHF and MF frequencies are shown in the chartlet below.

Firing practice areas

There are four such areas on the W coast as in the chartlet and listed below. Firing times are broadcast daily by Danmarks Radio 1 (243 kHz LW) after the weather at 1745LT. Times can also be obtained from the Range office Ch 16 or ☎.

Ⓐ Tranum & Blokhus ☎+45 728 39699 or call *Tranum.*

Ⓑ Nymindegab ☎+45 728 39550 or call *Nymindegab.*

Ⓒ Oksbøl ☎+45 728 39550 call *Oksbøl,* or see:www.forsvaret.dk/oksbol

Ⓓ Rømø E ☎+45 728 39550 (☎+45 737 55219/2148290 during firing) or call *Fly Rømø.* Rømø W ☎ +45 728 48121 .

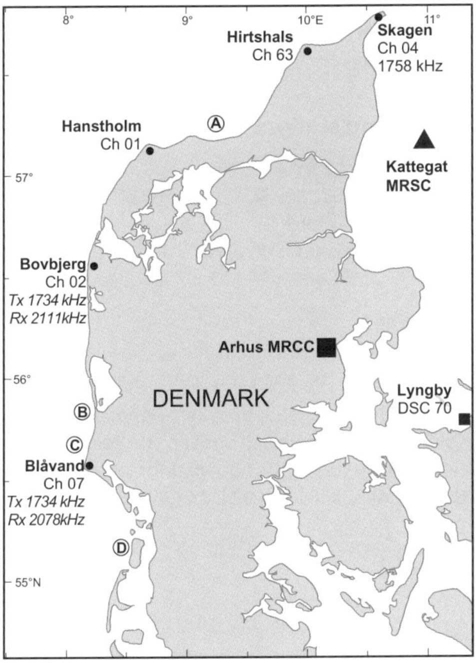

Danish Coastguard centres

GERMANY

The national SAR agency is: *Deutsche Gesellschaft zur Rettung Schiffbrüchiger* (DGzRS), the German Sea Rescue Service. Werderstrasse 2, Hermann-Helms-Haus, D-28199 Bremen. info@seenotretter.de. ☎ +49 421 536870 (emergency), 421 53707-0 (ops); 📠 421 537 07690.

DGzRS is responsible for coordinating SAR operations, supported by ships and SAR helicopters of the German Navy.

Bremen MRCC (☎ +49 421 536870; mail@mrcc-bremen.de, MMSI 002111240), using call sign *Bremen Rescue Radio,* maintains an H24 watch on Ch 16 and DSC Ch 70 via remote Coast radio stations at: Blumenthal / Borkum / Cuxhaven / Helgoland / kampen / Norderney / Stade / Wangerooge / Westerhever.

DGzRS has a total of 20 offshore lifeboats 20-26m LOA and 40 <11m LOA along the German seaboard with 12 large and 16 small based on their North Sea coast at: List, Amrum, Helgoland, Cuxhaven, Bremerhaven, Wilhelmshaven, Langeoog, Norderney and Borkum. There are also many inshore lifeboats.

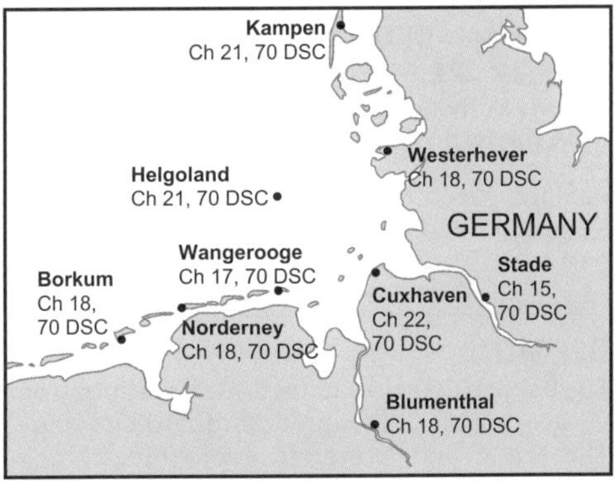

German Coastguard stations

THE NETHERLANDS

The national SAR agency is: SAR Commission, Directorate Transport Safety (DGG), PO Box 20904, 2500 EX The Hague, Netherlands.

The Netherlands CG at Den Helder, co-located with the Navy HQ, coordinates SAR operations as the Dutch JRCC for A1 and A2 Sea Areas. (JRCC = Joint Rescue Coordination Centre – marine & aeronautical.) Callsign is *Netherlands Coastguard,* but *Den Helder Rescue* during SAR operations.

The JRCC keeps a listening watch H24 on DSC Ch 70, and MF DSC 2187·5 kHz (but not on 2182 kHz); MMSI 002442000.

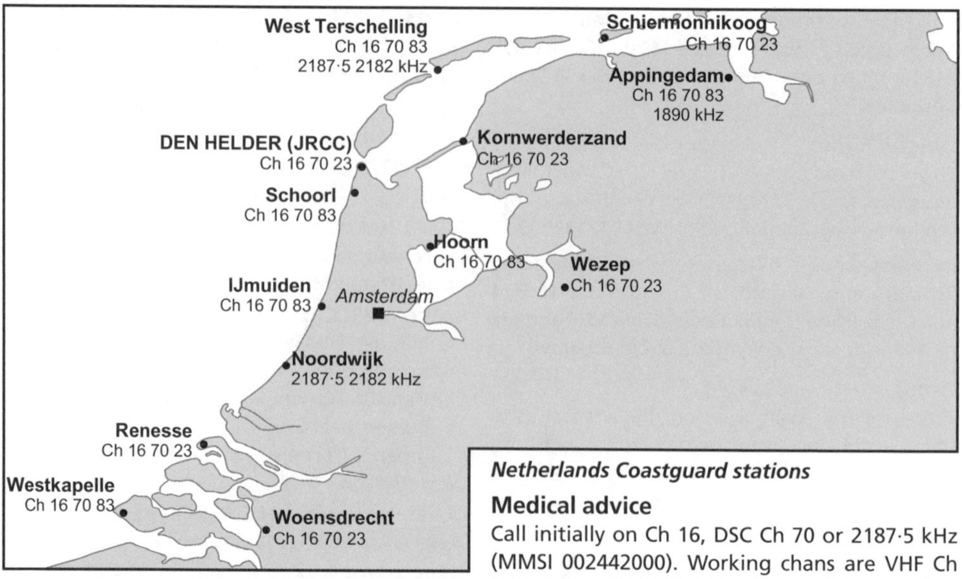

Netherlands Coastguard stations

Coastguard Operations can be contacted H24 via:

Emergency and Operations contact details:
☎ + 31 223 542300. 📠 + 31 223 658358; ccc@kustwacht.nl

Admin/info (HO)
☎+ 31 223 658300. 📠+31 223 658303.
www.kustwacht.nl info@kustwacht.nl
PO Box 10000, 1780 CA Den Helder.

Remote CG stations are shown above. Working chans are VHF 23 and 83.

Medical advice

Call initially on Ch 16, DSC Ch 70 or 2187·5 kHz (MMSI 002442000). Working chans are VHF Ch 23 & 83 or MF 2824 kHz (transmit), 2520 kHz (receive).

Resources

The Dutch Lifeboat Ass'n (KNRM) manages 26 lifeboat stations and 13 inshore lifeboat stations along the coast. The 60 lifeboats include 13m LOA water-jet, rigid inflatables capable of 36 kn. Helicopters, fixed wing aircraft and ships of the RNLN can be called upon; also Air Force helos at Leeuwarden. The area of activity is from the Dutch Continental Shelf into the Waddenzee, IJsselmeer and estuaries of Zuid Holland and Zeeland.

BELGIUM

The Belgian CG coordinates SAR operations from Oostende MRCC, callsign *Coastguard Oostende*. The MRCC and *Oostende Radio* (Coast radio station) both keep listening watch H24 on Ch 16, 67, 2182 kHz and DSC Ch 70 and 2187·5 kHz.

Coast Radio stations

OOSTENDE RADIO
☎ +32 59 255493 📠 +32 59 255467 rmd@mil.be
MMSI 002050480 Ch 16, MF 2182 kHz, DSC Ch 70 and 2187·5 kHz (H24)
MF: Tx 2484, Rx 3178 kHz. VHF Ch 07, 24, 27, 63, 78, 81 85
Zeebrugge Ch 27, 63
Middelkerke (Oostende)Ch 27
De Panne (French border) Ch 78
Antwerp Ch 07, 27
Ghent Ch 81
Rest of Belgium Ch 24.

Coastguard stations

MRCC OOSTENDE
☎ +32 59 701000; 📠 +32 59 703605.
MMSI 002059981.
RCC Brussels (COSPAS/SARSAT agency)
☎ +32 2 751 4615; 📠 +32 2 7524201.

Resources

Offshore and inshore lifeboats are based at Nieuwpoort, Oostende and Zeebrugge.

The Belgian Air Force provides helicopters from Koksijde near the French border. The Belgian Navy also participates in SAR operations as required, ☎ +32 2 4430350; 📠 +32 2 4439658; mik@mil.be

FRANCE – CROSS

Four CROSS (Centres Régionaux Opérationnels de Surveillance et de Sauvetage, ie an MRCC) provide a permanent, H24, all weather operational presence along the N and W coasts and liaise with foreign CGs.

CROSS' main functions include:

- Co-ordinating SAR operations.
- Navigational surveillance.
- Broadcasting navigational warnings.
- Broadcasting weather information.
- Anti-pollution control.
- Marine and fishery surveillance.

All centres keep watch on VHF Ch 16 as well as Ch 70 (DSC) and co-ordinate SAR on Ch 15, 67, 68, 73. They also broadcast gale warnings, weather forecasts and local navigational warnings.

CROSS Étel specialises in medical advice and responds to alerts from Cospas/Sarsat satellites.

CROSS can be contacted by R/T, by ☎ dial 112, through Coast Radio Stations, via the National Gendarmerie or Affaires Maritimes, or via a Semaphore station. Call *Semaphore* stations on Ch 16 (working Ch 10) or by ☎ as listed later in this section. If a nautical emergency *is witnessed from the land*, ☎ dial196.

CROSS also monitor TSS in the Dover Strait, off Casquets and off Ouessant using, for example, the callsign *Corsen Traffic*.

For medical advice call CROSS which will contact a doctor or SAMU (Service d'Aide Médicale Urgente). In harbour/marina SAMU responds faster in emergency than calling a doctor. Simply dial 15.

CROSS stations (Emergency ☎ 112).

CROSS Gris-Nez
50°52'N 01°35'E MMSI 002275100
☎ 03 21 87 21 87; 📠 03 21 87 78 55
Belgian border to Cap d'Antifer.

NavWarnings Ch 79 at every H+10 via Dunkerque, Saint-Frieux and L'Ailly. CROSS Gris-Nez responds to COSPAS/SARSAT alerts.

CROSS Jobourg
49°41'N 01°54'W MMSI 002275200
☎ 02 33 52 16 16; 📠 02 33 52 71 72
Cap de la Hague to Mont St Michel

NavWarnings Ch 80 every H+20 and H+50 via Antifer, Ver-sur-Mer, Gatteville, Jobourg, Granville and Roche Douvres.

CROSS Corsen
48°24'N 04°47'W MMSI 002275300
☎ 02 98 89 31 31; 📠 02 98 89 65 75
Mont St Michel to Pointe de Penmarc'h.

NavWarnings Ch 79 every H+10 and H+40 via Cap Fréhel, Bodic, Ile de Batz, Le Stiff and Pte du Raz.

CROSS Étel
47°39'N 03°12'W MMSI 002275000
☎ 02 97 55 35 35; 📠 02 97 55 49 34
Pte de Penmarc'h to the Spanish border

NavWarnings Ch 79 for Landes range activity via Chassiron 1903.

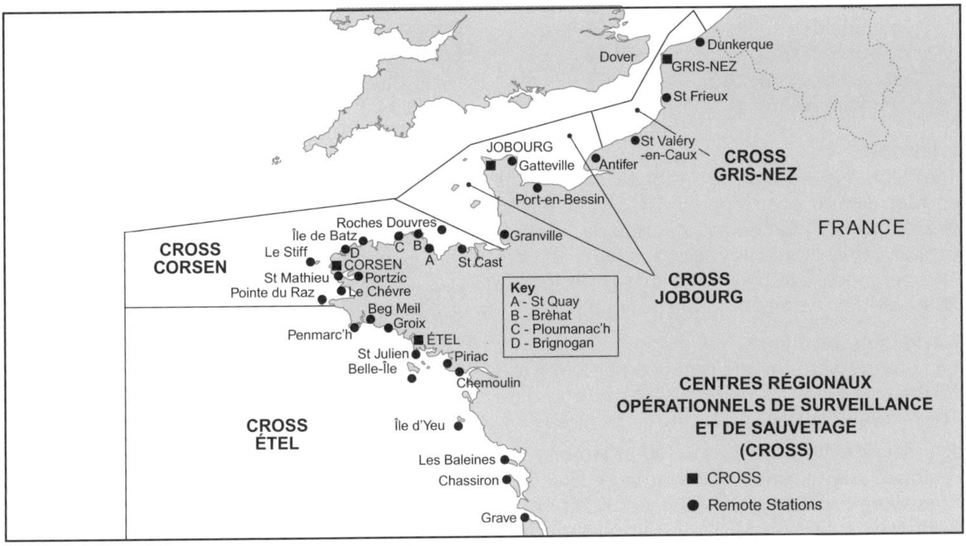

CROSS locations and areas of responsibility

Semaphore stations keep visual, radar and radio watch (Ch 16); are equipped with VHF DF; relay emergency calls to CROSS; show gale warning signals, repeat forecasts and offer local weather reports. Hours sunrise-sunset, but * H24.

* Dunkerque	03·28·66·86·18
* Boulogne	03·21·31·32·10
* Ault	03·22·60·47·33
* Dieppe	02·35·84·23·82
* Fécamp	02·35·28·00·91
* La Hève	02·35·46·07·81
* Villerville	02·31·88·11·13
* Port-en-Bessin	02·31·21·81·51
* St-Vaast	02·33·54·44·50
* Barfleur	02·33·54·04·37
* Le Homet	02·33·92·60·08
* La Hague	02·33·52·71·07
* Barneville-Carteret	02·33·53·85·08
* Granville Le Roc	02·33·50·05·85
St-Cast	02·96·41·85·30
* St Quay-Portrieux	02·96.70.42.18
Bréhat	02·96·20·00·12
* Ploumanac'h	02·96·91·46·51
Batz	02·98·61·76·06
* Brignogan	02·98·83·50·84
* Ouessant Stiff	02·98·48·81·50
* St-Mathieu	02·98·89·01·59
* Portzic (Ch 08)	02·98·22·21·47
Toulinguet	02·98·27·90·02
Cap-de-la-Chèvre	02·98·27·09·55
* Pointe-du-Raz	02·98·70·66·57
* Penmarc'h	02·98·58·61·00
Beg Meil	02·98·94·98·92
Étel Mât Fenoux	02·97·55·35·39
* Beg Melen (Groix)	02·97·86·80·13
Talut (Belle-Île)	02·97·31·85·07
* St-Julien	02·97·50·09·35
Piriac-sur-Mer	02·40·23·59·87
* Chemoulin	02·40·91·99·00
* St-Sauveur (Yeu)	02·51·58·31·01
Les Baleines (Ré)	05·46·29·42·06
* Chassiron (Oléron)	05·46·47·85·43

Lifeboats

The lifeboat service Société National de Sauvetage en Mer (SNSM) comes under CROSS, At sea all vessels must call CROSS to call upon the services of SNSM, they should not be contacted directly in an emergency. A hefty charge may be levied if a SNSM lifeboat attends a vessel not in distress.

Navigation warnings

Long-range warnings are broadcast by SafetyNet for Navarea II, which includes the W coast of France. The N coast is in Navarea I.

Avurnavs (AVis URgents aux NAVigateurs) are regional, coastal and local warnings issued by Cherbourg and Brest and broadcast by Niton and Brest Navtex and on MF. Warnings are prefixed by '*Sécurité Avurnav*'.

EMERGENCY VHF DF SERVICE

A yacht in emergency can call CROSS on VHF Ch 16, 11 or 67 to obtain a true bearing of the yacht *from* the DF station. These monitor Ch 16 and other continuously scanned frequencies, which include Ch 1-29, 36, 39, 48, 50, 52, 55, 56 and 60-88. The Semaphore stations overleaf are also equipped with VHF DF.

HJ = Day service only.

VHF DF stations, are listed below geographically from NE to W then S:

Station	Lat/Long	Hrs
Dunkerque	51°03′.40N 02°20′.40E	H24
*Gris-Nez	50°52′.20N 01°35′.01E	H24
Boulogne	50°44′.00N 01°36′.00E	H24
Ault	50°06′.50N 01°27′.50E	H24
Dieppe	49°56′.00N 01°05′.20E	H24
Fécamp	49°46′.10N 00°22′.20E	H24
La Hève	49°30′.60N 00°04′.20E	H24
Villerville	49°23′.20N 00°06′.50E	H24
Port-en-Bessin	49°21′.10N 00°46′.30W	H24
Saint-Vaast	49°34′.50N 01°16′.50W	H24
Barfleur	49°41′.90N 01°15′.90W	H24
Levy	49°41′.70N 01°28′.20W	H24
†Homet	49°39′.50N 01°37′.90W	H24
*Jobourg	49°41′.50N 01°54′.50W	H24
La Hague	49°43′.60N 01°56′.30W	H24
Carteret	49°22′.40N 01°48′.30W	H24
Le Roc	48°50′.10N 01°36′.90W	H24
Grouin/Cancale	48°42′.60N 01°50′.60W	**HJ**
Saint-Cast	48°38′.60N 02°14′.70W	H24
St-Quay-Port'x	48°39′.30N 02°49′.50W	**HJ**
Bréhat	48°51′.30N 03°00′.10W	H24
Ploumanac'h	48°49′.50N 03°28′.20W	**HJ**
Batz	48°44′.80N 04°00′.60W	H24
Brignogan	48°40′.60N 04°19′.70W	**HJ**
Creac'h (Ushant)	48°27′.60N 05°07′.70W	H24
*Creac'h	48°27′.60N 05°07′.80W	H24
†Saint-Mathieu	48°19′.80N 04°46′.20W	H24
Toulinguet	48°16′.80N 04°37′.50W	**HJ**
Cap de la Chèvre	48°10′.20N 04°33′.00W	**HJ**
Pointe du Raz	48°02′.30N 04°43′.80W	H24
Penmarc'h	47°47′.90N 04°22′.40W	H24
Beg-Meil	47°51′.30N 03°58′.40W	**HJ**
Beg Melen	47°39′.20N 03°30′.10W	H24
*Etel	47°39′.80N 03°12′.00W	H24
Saint-Julien	47°29′.70N 03°07′.50W	**HJ**
Taillefer	47°21′.80N 03°09′.00W	H24
Le Talut	47°17′.70N 03°13′.00W	H24
Piriac	47°22′.50N 02°33′.40W	H24
Chemoulin	47°14′.10N 02°17′.80W	H24
Saint-Sauveur	46°41′.70N 02°18′.80W	H24
Les Baleines	46°14′.60N 01°33′.70W	**HJ**
Chassiron	46°02′.80N 01°24′.50W	H24

Chapter 5 – Tides

2023 TIDAL COEFFICIENTS

Date	Jan		Feb		Mar		Apr		May		June		July		Aug		Sept		Oct		Nov		Dec	
	am	pm	am	pm	am	pm	am	pm	am	pm	am	pm	am	pm	am	pm	am	pm	am	pm	am	pm	am	pm
1	51	50	40	43	29	28	36	42	45	51	61	66	62	67	82	88	110	112	111	108	84	77	69	64
2	51	52	47	52	30	34	49	55	57	63	71	75	72	77	93	98	112	110	104	98	71	63	60	---
3	54	57	56	61	40	46	61	67	68	73	79	82	81	85	102	104	107	---	91	---	56	---	54	50
4	59	62	65	69	52	58	73	78	78	82	84	86	88	90	104	---	101	95	83	75	48	42	45	41
5	65	67	72	75	64	69	82	86	85	88	87	88	92	93	104	101	87	79	66	57	36	31	38	36
6	69	71	78	80	74	78	88	91	90	90	87	86	93	---	97	92	70	61	48	40	29	29	35	35
7	73	74	81	82	81	85	92	93	90	90	84	---	92	89	86	79	52	44	33	28	31	35	36	39
8	74	74	82	82	87	89	92	91	88	85	81	77	86	83	72	64	37	32	26	28	40	45	43	47
9	74	74	81	80	90	90	89	---	81	---	73	70	78	74	57	50	30	31	32	38	51	56	51	56
10	73	71	78	75	90	88	85	81	76	71	66	63	69	64	44	40	35	40	44	50	62	66	61	65
11	69	67	72	---	86	83	76	70	65	60	60	58	59	56	38	39	47	53	57	62	71	75	70	73
12	65	---	68	63	79	74	63	57	54	51	57	57	53	51	41	45	59	64	68	73	79	82	77	80
13	62	59	59	54	69	---	50	44	48	48	58	60	50	51	49	54	69	73	77	81	84	86	82	84
14	56	53	49	45	63	57	40	39	50	54	62	64	52	54	59	63	77	80	84	86	87	87	85	86
15	50	47	41	40	50	44	42	48	59	64	66	68	57	59	67	70	83	85	88	89	86	84	85	84
16	45	44	42	46	39	37	56	64	70	74	70	71	62	65	74	76	86	87	89	88	82	79	83	80
17	44	46	52	60	38	43	72	80	79	82	72	73	67	69	78	80	87	87	87	85	75	71	77	---
18	49	54	69	77	51	60	87	92	85	86	74	74	71	72	81	81	85	83	82	78	66	---	74	71
19	59	66	86	93	70	79	97	100	87	87	74	73	73	73	81	80	80	---	73	---	61	56	67	64
20	72	79	100	105	88	95	101	102	87	85	72	70	73	73	79	---	77	72	68	62	52	49	61	59
21	85	91	109	111	102	106	101	99	83	80	69	66	72	---	77	74	67	61	56	50	48	49	57	57
22	96	100	112	110	109	111	95	91	77	73	64	---	71	69	71	68	56	49	44	40	52	56	57	59
23	103	105	107	103	110	108	86	80	69	---	61	58	67	65	64	59	43	38	38	40	61	67	61	63
24	105	103	97	---	105	100	74	---	65	60	56	53	62	59	54	49	35	35	45	52	72	77	66	69
25	101	97	90	82	94	87	67	60	55	50	50	47	56	52	44	40	39	47	60	69	81	85	71	74
26	91	---	73	65	79	---	53	46	46	41	45	43	49	46	37	37	55	65	77	85	88	89	75	77
27	85	78	56	47	71	63	40	34	38	35	42	41	44	42	40	45	75	84	91	97	90	90	78	78
28	71	64	40	33	54	46	29	27	34	34	42	43	42	43	52	61	93	100	101	103	89	87	78	78
29	57	50			38	31	27	29	35	38	46	49	45	50	70	79	105	110	104	104	85	82	77	75
30	45	40			26	24	34	39	42	46	53	58	55	62	87	95	112	112	102	99	78	74	73	71
31	38	38			26	30			51	56			68	75	102	107			95	90			68	65

Tidal coefficients indicate the magnitude of the tide on any particular day without having to look up and calculate the range, and thus determine whether it is springs, neaps or somewhere in between. This table, which is based on Cherbourg, is valid for all areas covered by this Almanac. Typical values are:

120	Very big spring tide
95	**Mean spring tide**
70	Average tide
45	**Mean neap tide**
20	Very small neap tide

TIDAL CALCULATIONS

Find the height at a given time (STANDARD PORT)

1. On Standard Curve diagram, plot heights of HW and LW occuring either side of required time and join by sloping line.
2. Enter HW Time and sufficient others to bracket required time.
3. From required time, proceed vertically to curves, using heights plotted in (1) to help interpolation between Spring and Neaps. Do NOT extrapolate.
4. Proceed horizontally to sloping line, thence vertically to Height scale.
5. Read off height.

EXAMPLE:

Find the height of tide at ULLAPOOL at 1900 on 6th January

Find the time for a given height (STANDARD PORT)

From tables	JANUARY	
ULLAPOOL	**6** 0420	4.6
	1033	1.6
	1641	4.6
	F 2308	1.2

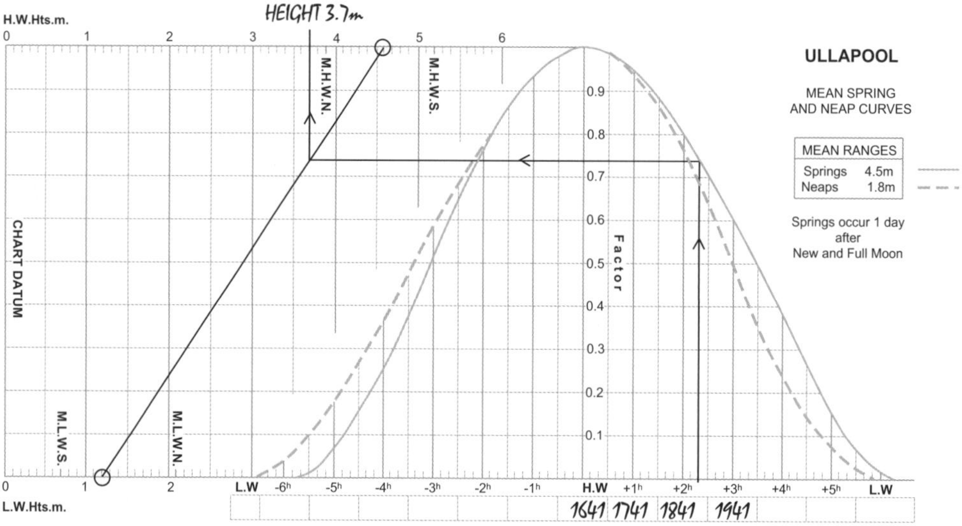

1. On Standard Curve diagram, plot heights of HW and LW occurring either side of required event and join by sloping line.
2. Enter HW time and those for half-tidal cycle covering required event.
3. From required height, proceed vertically to sloping line, thence horizontally to curves, using heights plotted in (1) to assist interpolation between Spring and Neaps. Do NOT extrapolate.
4. Proceed vertically to Time scale.
5. Read off time.

EXAMPLE:

Find the time at which the afternoon tide at ULLAPOOL falls to 3.7m on 6 January

From tables		JANUARY	
		0420	4.6
ULLAPOOL	6	1033	1.6
		1641	4.6
	F	2308	1.2

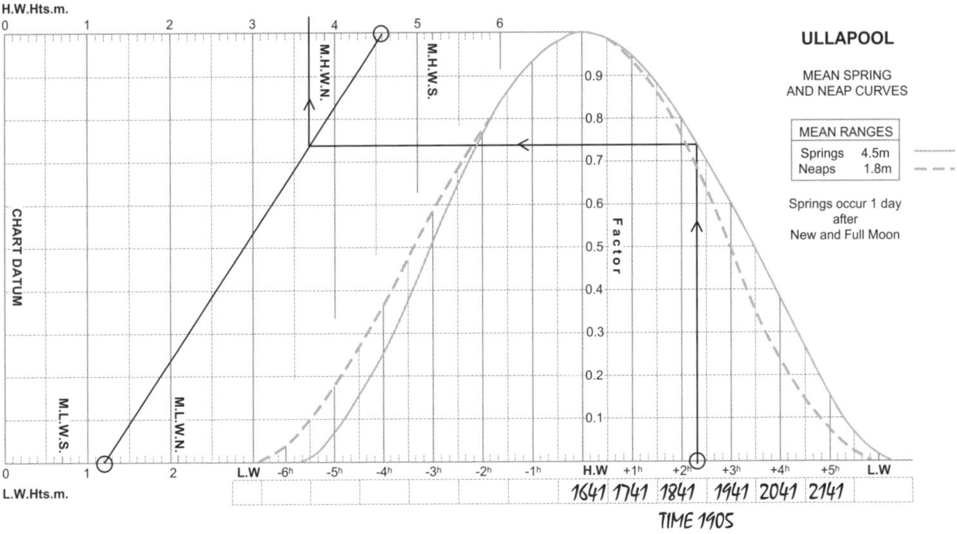

Find the time and height of HW and LW at a Secondary Port

EXAMPLE:

Find the time and height of the afternoon HW and LW at ST MARY's (Isles of Scilly) on 14th July (BST)

Note: *The data used in this example do not refer to the year of these tables.*

From tables		JULY	
		0309	1.0
PLYMOUTH (DEVONPORT)	14	0927	5.3
		1532	1.1
	SA	2149	5.0

From tables Location	Lat	Long	High Water		Low Water		MHWS	MHWN	MLWN	MLWS
			0000 and 1200	0600 and 1800	0000 and 1200	0600 and 1800				
DEVONPORT *Standard port*	50°22'N	4°11'W					5.5	4.4	2.2	0.8
St Mary's, *Scilly*	49° 55'N	6°19'W	–0035	–0100	–0040	–0025	+0.2	–0.1	–0.2	–0.1

TIDAL PREDICTION FORM (NP 204)

STANDARD PORT *Devonport* TIME/HEIGHT REQUIRED *pm*

SECONDARY PORT *St Mary's* DATE *14 July* TIME ZONE *B.S.T*

	TIME		HEIGHT		
STANDARD PORT	HW	LW	HW	LW	RANGE
	1 2149	2 1532	3 5·0	4 1·1	5 3·9
Seasonal change	Standard Ports -		6 0·0	6 0·0	
DIFFERENCES	7* -0044	8 -0032	9 0·1	10 -0·1	
Seasonal change *	Secondary Ports +		11 0·0	11 0·0	
SECONDARY PORT	12 2105	13 1500	14 5·1	15 1·0	
Duration	16 0605		LW 1500 UT = 1600 BST HW 2105 UT = 2205 BST		

* The seasonal changes are generally less than ± 0.1m and for most purposes can be ignored. See Admiraly Tide Tables Vol 1. for details

CLEARANCE BELOW BRIDGES AND OVERHEAD POWER LINES

Vertical clearance heights are above the level of HAT (Highest Astronomical Tide) instead of MHWS as in the past. HAT is always a higher level than MHWS, as shown in the diagram on the back cover flap. It helps to draw such a diagram and insert the relevant dimensions when calculating overhead clearances. The Height of HAT above Chart Datum is stated at the foot of each page of Standard port tide tables. New editions of Admiralty charts are referenced to HAT; earlier editions to MHWS. Check the title block under **Heights**.

INTERMEDIATE TIMES/HEIGHTS (SECONDARY PORT)

These are the same as the appropriate calculations for a Standard Port except that the Standard Curve diagram for the Standard Port must be entered with HW and LW heights and times for the Secondary Port obtained on Form N.P. 204. When interpolating between the Spring and Neap curves the Range at the Standard Port must be used.

EXAMPLE:

Find the height of the tide at PADSTOW at 1100 on 28th February. Find the time at which the morning tide at PADSTOW falls to 4.9m on 28th February.

Note: The data in these examples do not refer to the year of these tables.

From tables

MILFORD HAVEN — **FEBRUARY**

Day	Time	Height
28	0315	1.1
	0922	6.6
	1538	1.3
TU	2145	6.3

From tables

Location	Lat	Long	High Water		Low Water		MHWS	MHWN	MLWN	MLWS
			0100 and 1300	0700 and 1900	0100 and 1300	0700 and 1900				
MILFORD HAVEN *Standard port*	51°42′N	5°03′W					**7.0**	**5.2**	**2.5**	**0.7**
River Camel										
Padstow	50°33′N	4°56′W	−0055	−0050	−0040	−0050	+0.3	+0.4	+0.1	+0.1
Wadebridge	50°31′N	4°50′W	−0052	−0052	+0235	+0245	−3.8	−3.8	−2.5	−0.4

TIDAL PREDICTION FORM (NP 204)

STANDARD PORT Milford Haven TIME/HEIGHT REQUIRED 1100 : 4.9

SECONDARY PORT Padstow DATE 28 Feb TIME ZONE UT

	TIME		HEIGHT		
	HW	LW	HW	LW	RANGE
STANDARD PORT	1 0922	2 1538	3 6·6	4 1·3	5 5·3
Seasonal change	Standard Ports +		6 0·0	6 0·0	
DIFFERENCES	7* -0052	8 –	9 +0·3	10 +0·1	
Seasonal change *	Secondary Ports -		11 0·0	11 0·0	
SECONDARY PORT	12 0830	13 –	14 6·9	15 1·4	
Duration	16 –				

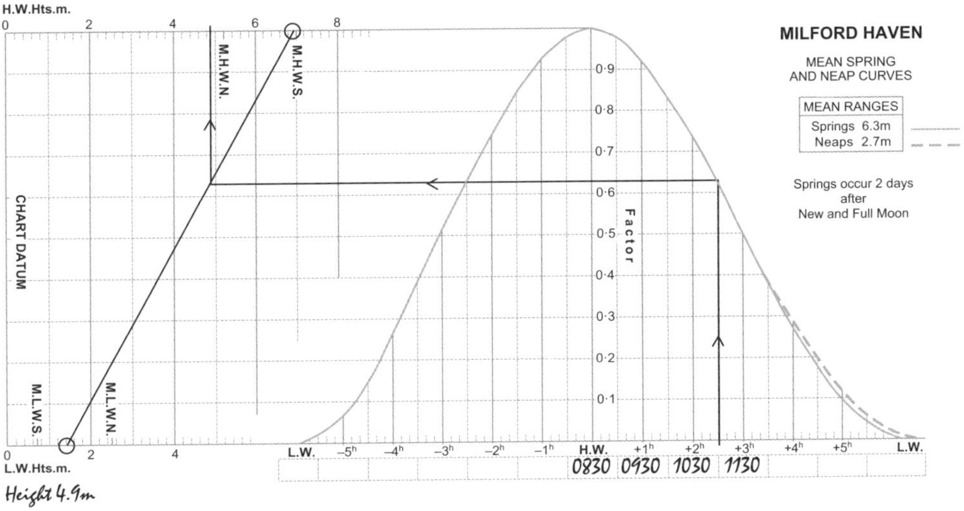

SPECIAL INSTRUCTIONS FOR PLACES BETWEEN BOURNEMOUTH AND SELSEY BILL

• Owing to the rapid change of tidal characteristics and distortion of the tidal curve in this area, curves are shown for individual ports. It is a characteristic of the tide here that Low Water is more sharply defined than High Water and these curves have therefore been drawn with their times relative to that of Low Water.

• Apart from differences caused by referring the times to Low Water the procedure for obtaining intermediate heights at places whose curves are shown is identical to that used for normal Secondary Ports.

• The **height** differences for ports between Bournemouth and Yarmouth always refer to the higher High Water, i.e. that which is shown as reaching a factor of 1.0 on the curves. Note that the **time** differences, which are not required for this calculation, also refer to the higher High Water.

• The tide at ports between Bournemouth and Christchurch shows considerable change of shape and duration between Springs and Neaps and it is not practical to define the tide with only two curves. A third curve has therefore been drawn for the range at Portsmouth at which the two High Waters are equal at the port concerned – this range being marked on the body of the graph. Interpolation here should be between this 'critical' curve and either the Spring or Neap curve as appropriate.
Note that while the critical curve extends throughout the tidal cycle the Spring and Neap curves stop at the higher High Water. Thus for a range at Portsmouth of 3.5m the factor for 7 hours after LW at Bournemouth should be referred to the following Low Water, whereas had the range at Portsmouth been 2.5, it should be referred to the preceding Low Water.

NOTES

1. NEWPORT. Owing to the constriction of the River Medina, Newport requires slightly different treatment since the harbour dries out at 1.4m. The calculation should be performed using the Low Water Time and Height Differences for Cowes and the High Water Height Differences for Newport. Any calculated heights which fall below 1.4m should be treated as 1.4m
2. CHRISTCHURCH (Tuckton). Low Waters do not fall below 0.7m except under very low river flow conditions.

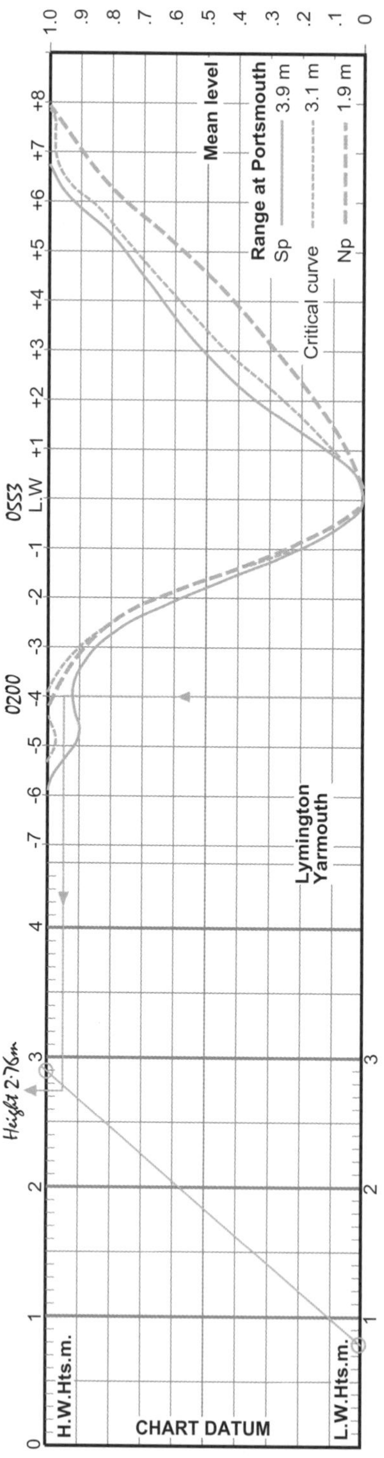

To find the Height of tide at a given time at any Secondary Port between Bournemouth and Selsey Bill

1. Complete top section of N.P. 204 (as below). Omit HW time column (Boxes 1,7,12)
2. On Standard Curve diagram (previous page), plot Secondary Port HW and LW heights and join by sloping line.
3. From the time required, using Secondary Port LW time, proceed vertically to curve, interpolating as necessary using Range at Portsmouth. Do NOT extrapolate.
4. Proceed horizontally to sloping line, thence vertically to Height Scale.
5. Read off height.

EXAMPLE:
Find the height of tide at LYMINGTON at 0200 UT on 18th November

From tables	**NOVEMBER**		
		0110	4.6
PORTSMOUTH	**18**	0613	1.1
		1318	4.6
	SA	1833	1.0

From tables Location	Lat	Long	High Water		Low Water		MHWS	MHWN	MLWN	MLWS
PORTSMOUTH	50°48′N	1°07′W	**0000** and **1200**	**0600** and **1800**	**0500** and **1700**	**1100** and **2300**	**4.7**	**3.8**	**1.9**	**0.8**
Standard port										
Lymington	50°46′N	1°32′W	–0110	+0005	–0020	–0020	–1.7	–1.2	–0.5	–0.1

STANDARD PORT Portsmouth TIME/~~HEIGHT~~ REQUIRED 0200

SECONDARY PORT Lymington DATE 18 Nov TIME ZONE UT

	TIME		HEIGHT		
	HW	LW	HW	LW	RANGE
STANDARD PORT	1 –	2 0613	3 4.6	4 1.1	5 3.5
Seasonal change	Standard Ports -		6 0.0	6 0.0	
DIFFERENCES	7* –	8 –0020	9 –1.7	10 –0.2	
Seasonal change *	Secondary Ports +		11 0.0	11 0.0	
SECONDARY PORT	12 –	13 0553	14 2.9	15 0.9	
Duration	16 –				

* *The Seasonal changes are generally less than ± 0.1m and for most purposes can be ignored. See Admiralty Tide Tables Vol 1 for full details.*

TIDAL CURVES - BOURNEMOUTH TO FRESHWATER

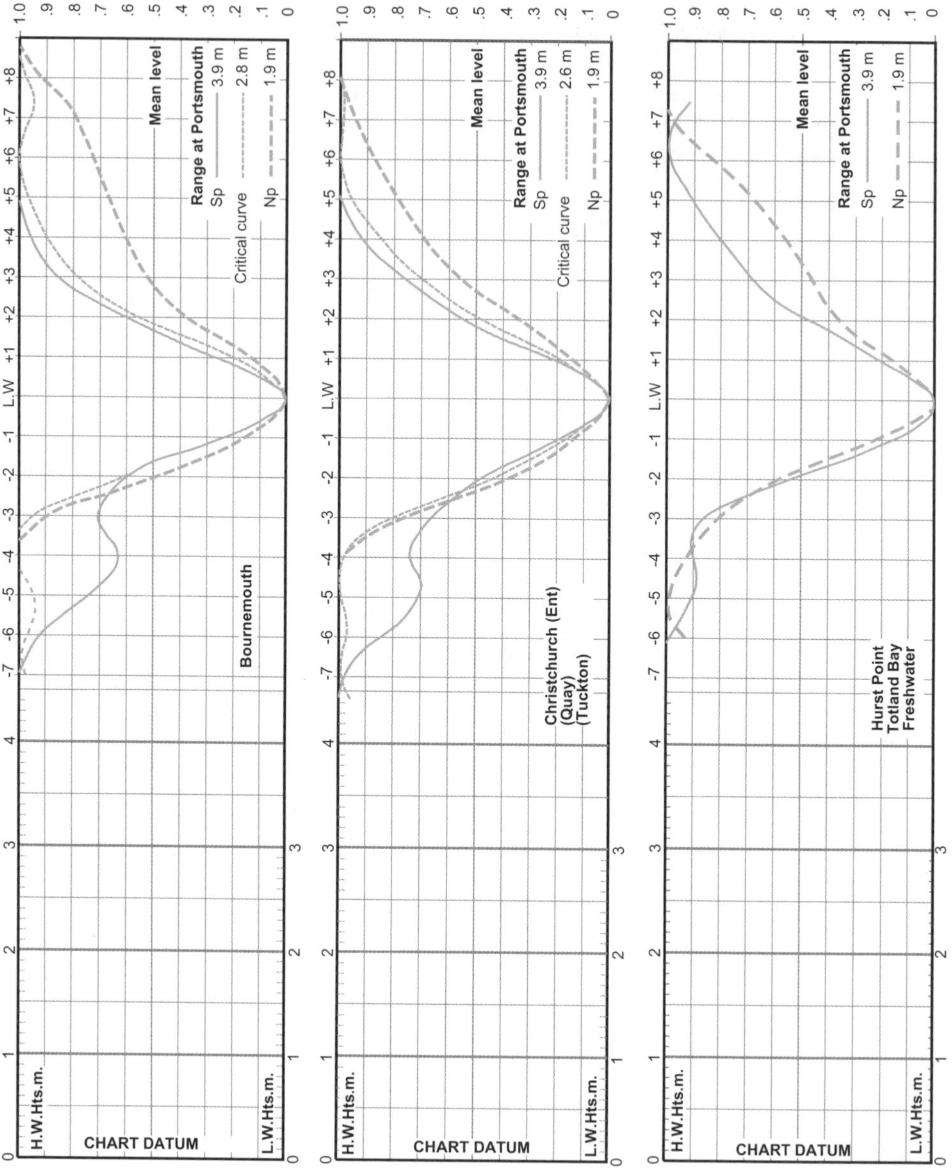

Note: The curves for Lymington and Yarmouth are on page 154, together with a worked example.

TIDAL CURVES - BUCKLERS HARD TO SELSEY BILL

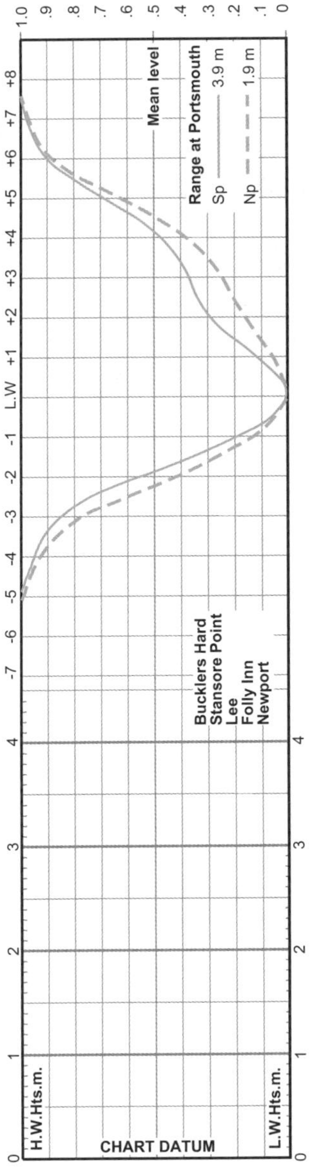

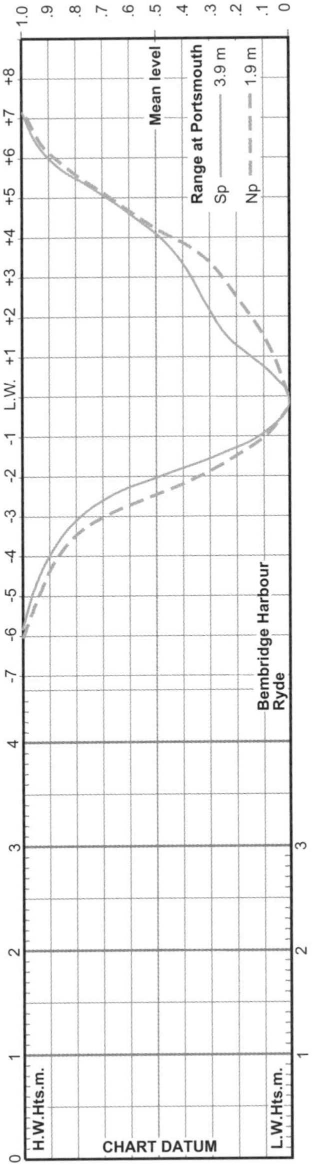

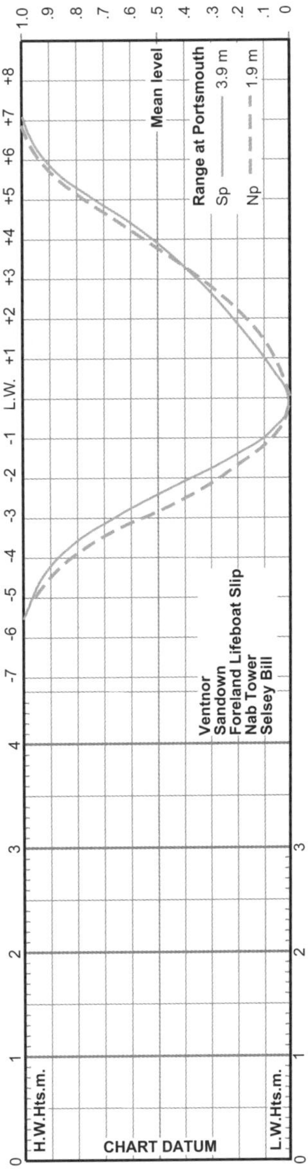

TIDES

ENGLISH CHANNEL AND SOUTH BRITTANY

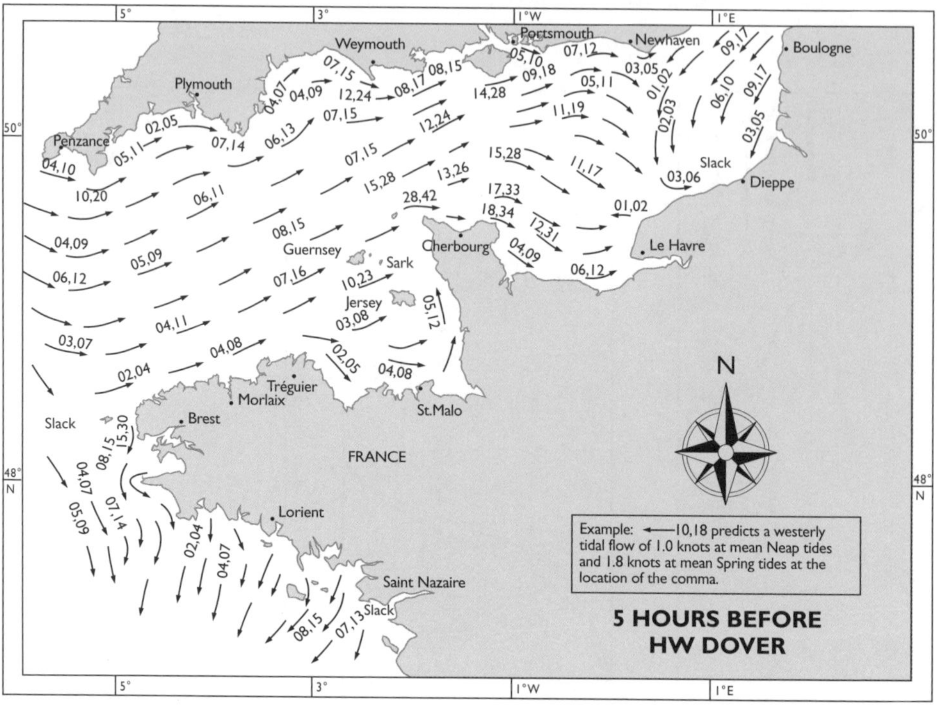

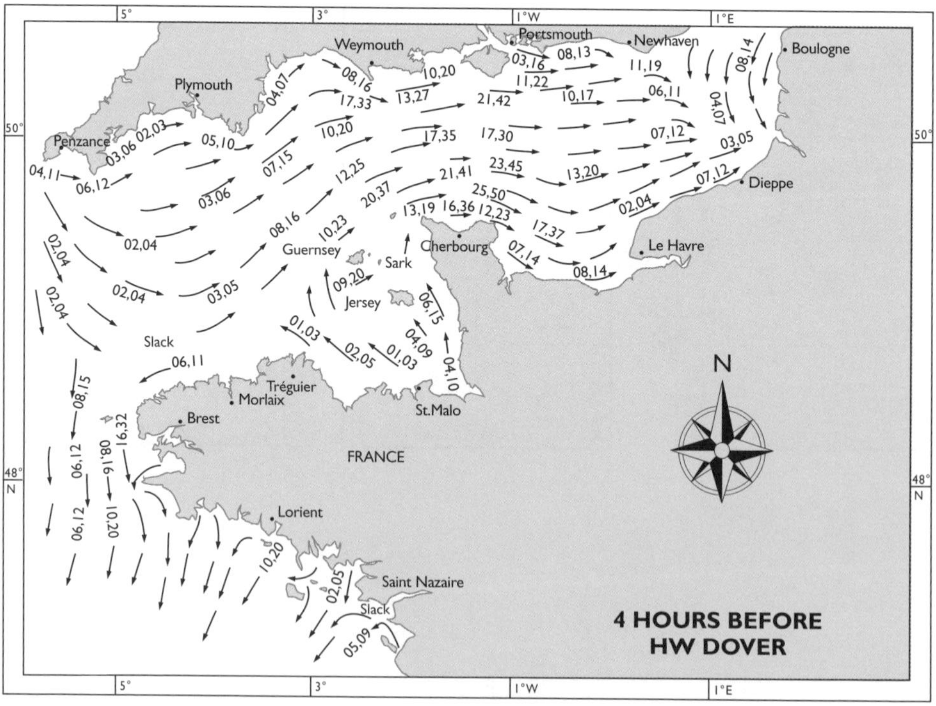

ENGLISH CHANNEL AND SOUTH BRITTANY

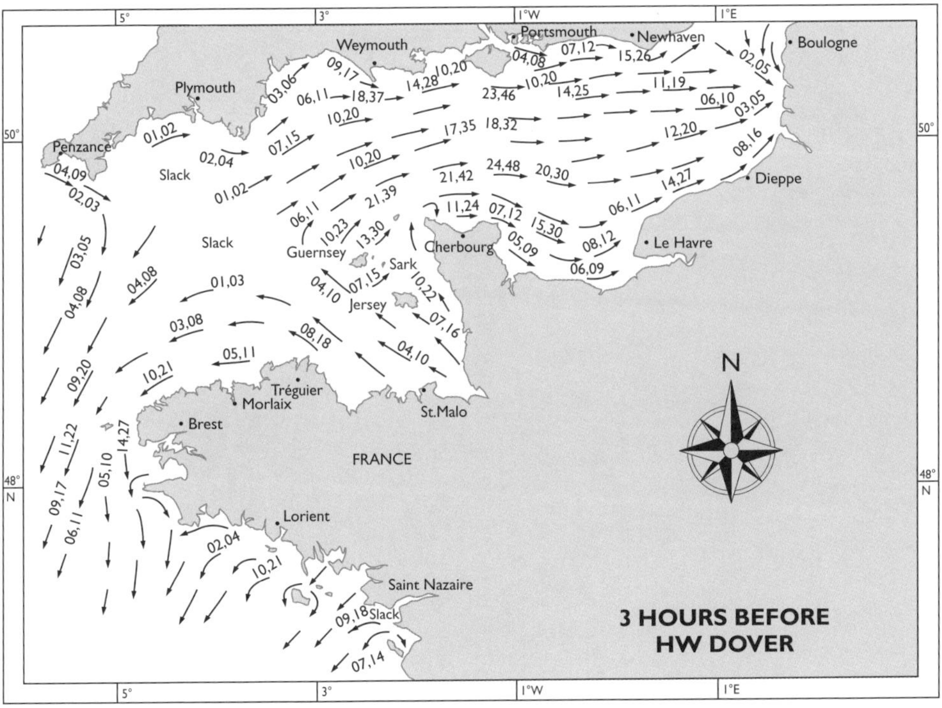

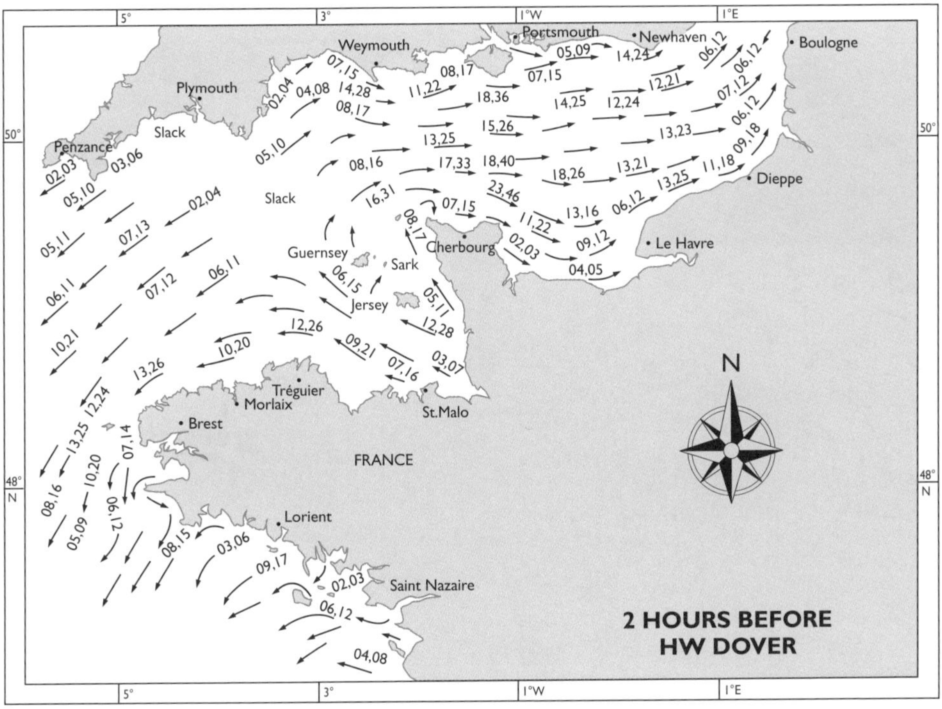

ENGLISH CHANNEL AND SOUTH BRITTANY

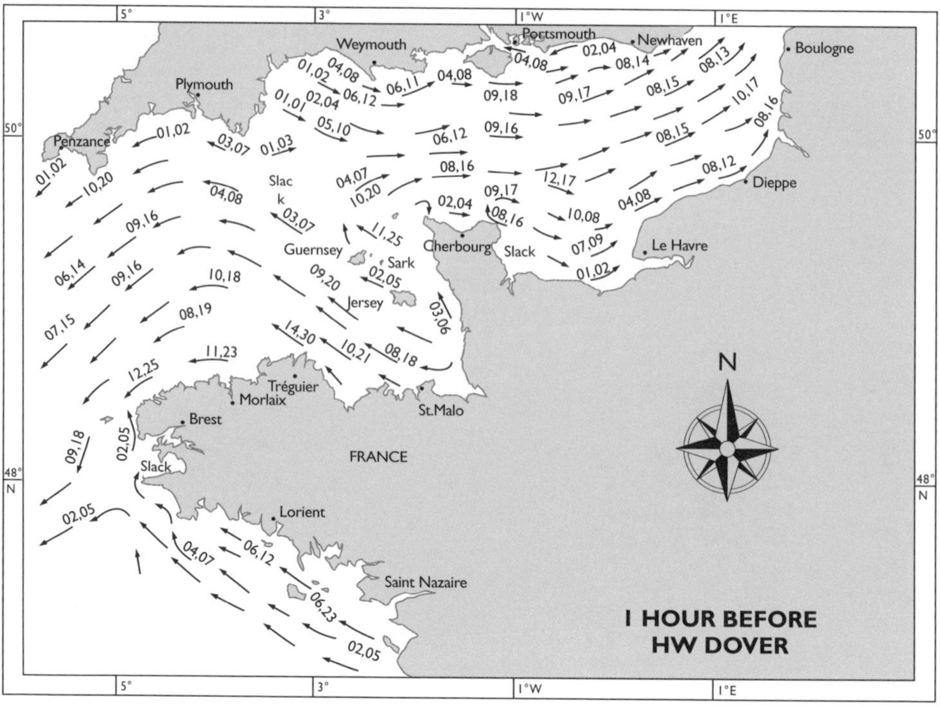

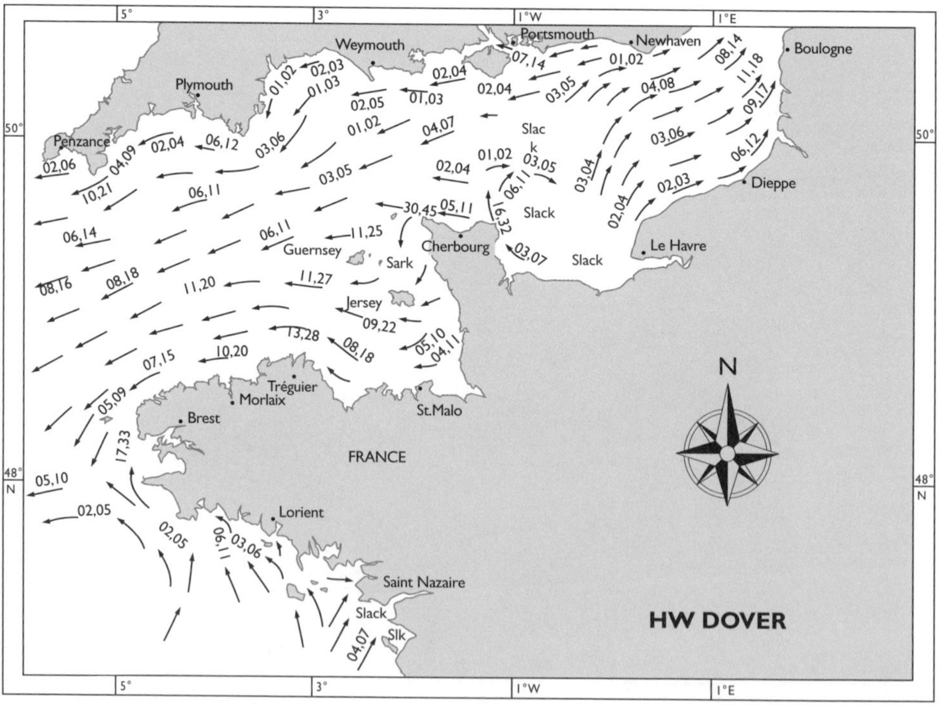

ENGLISH CHANNEL AND SOUTH BRITTANY

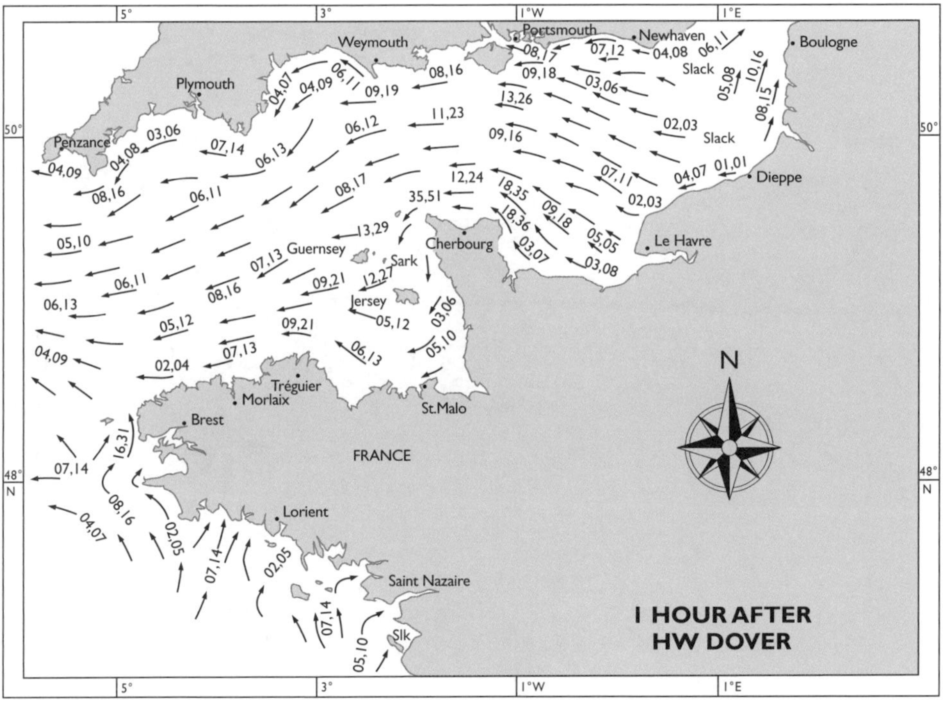

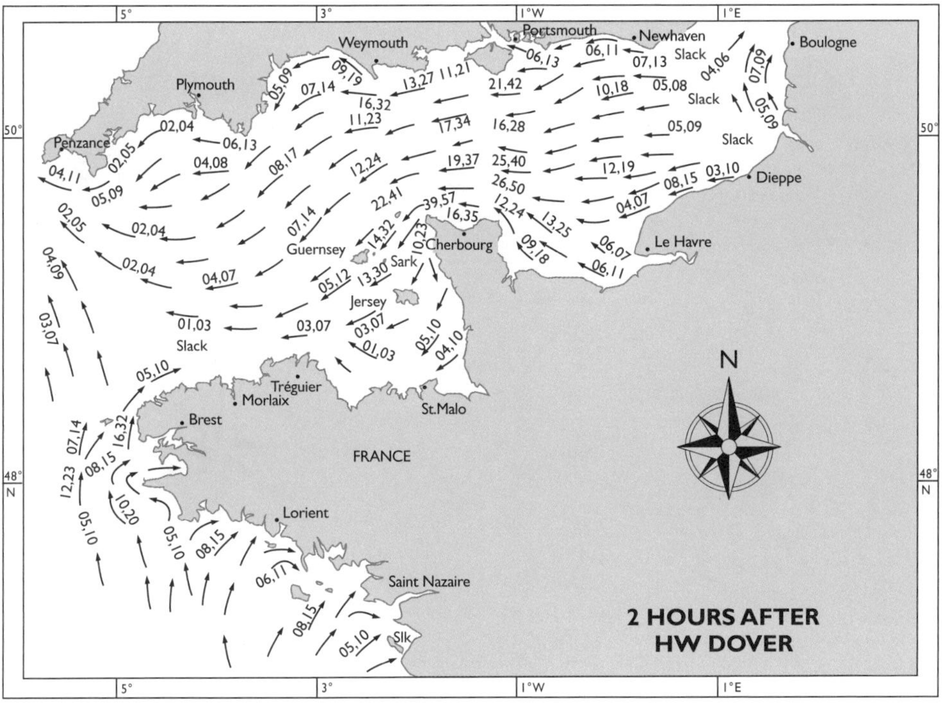

ENGLISH CHANNEL AND SOUTH BRITTANY

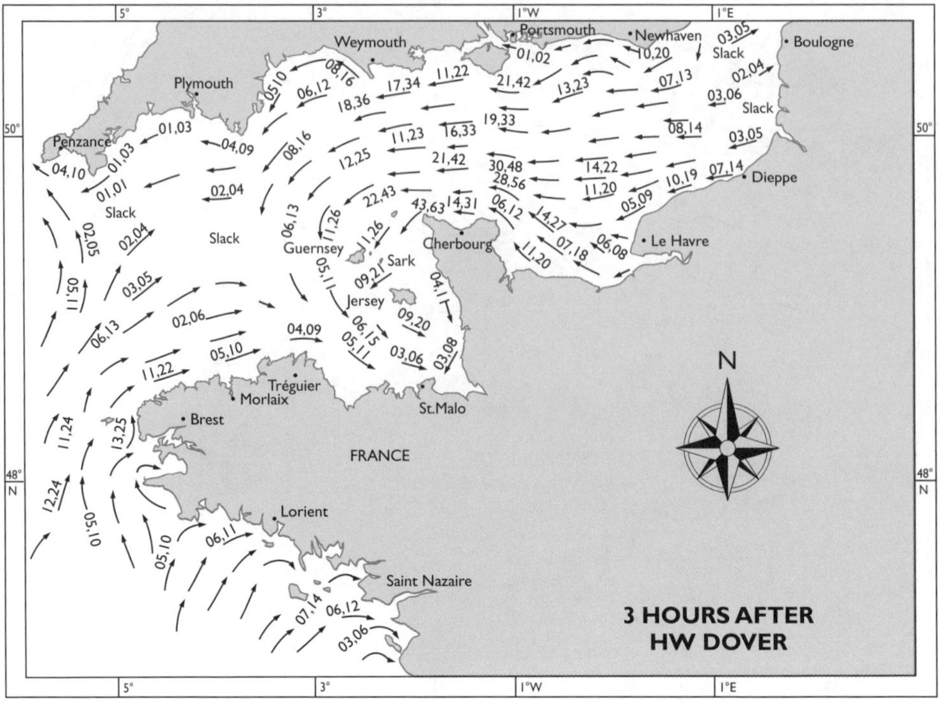

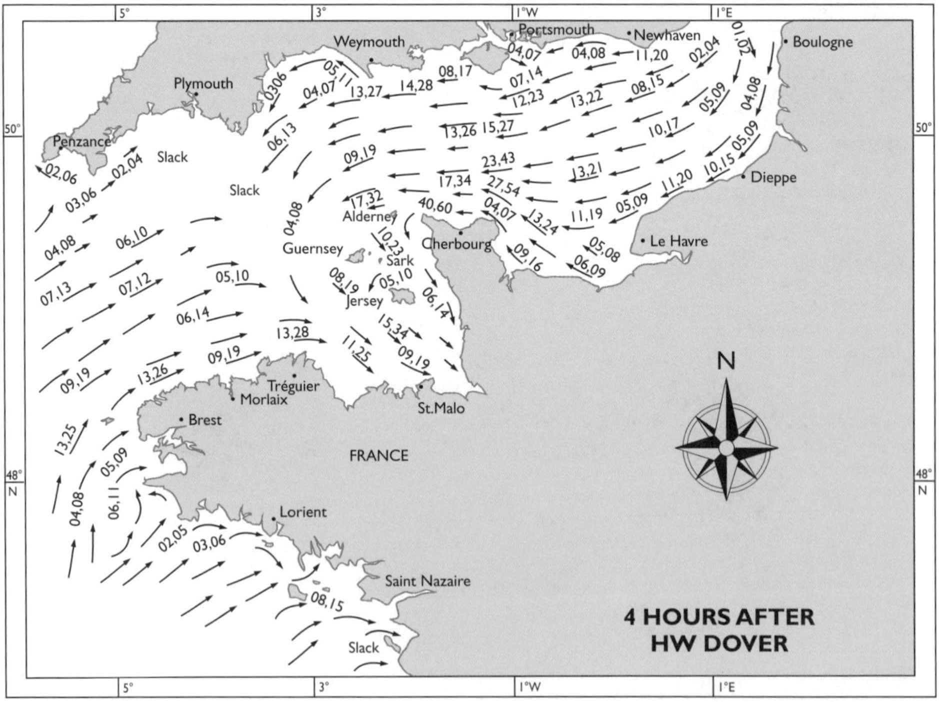

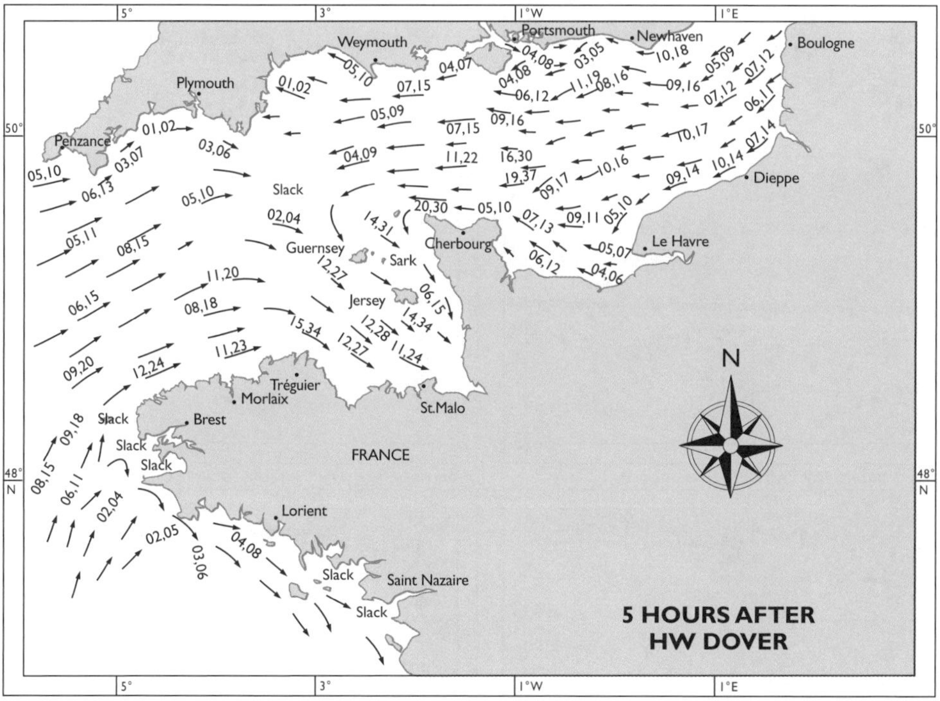
Weymouth
Portsmouth
Newhaven
Boulogne
Plymouth
Penzance
Dieppe
Le Havre
Cherbourg
Guernsey
Sark
Jersey
Tréguier
Morlaix
St.Malo
Brest
FRANCE
Lorient
Saint Nazaire
Slack
N
5 HOURS AFTER
HW DOVER

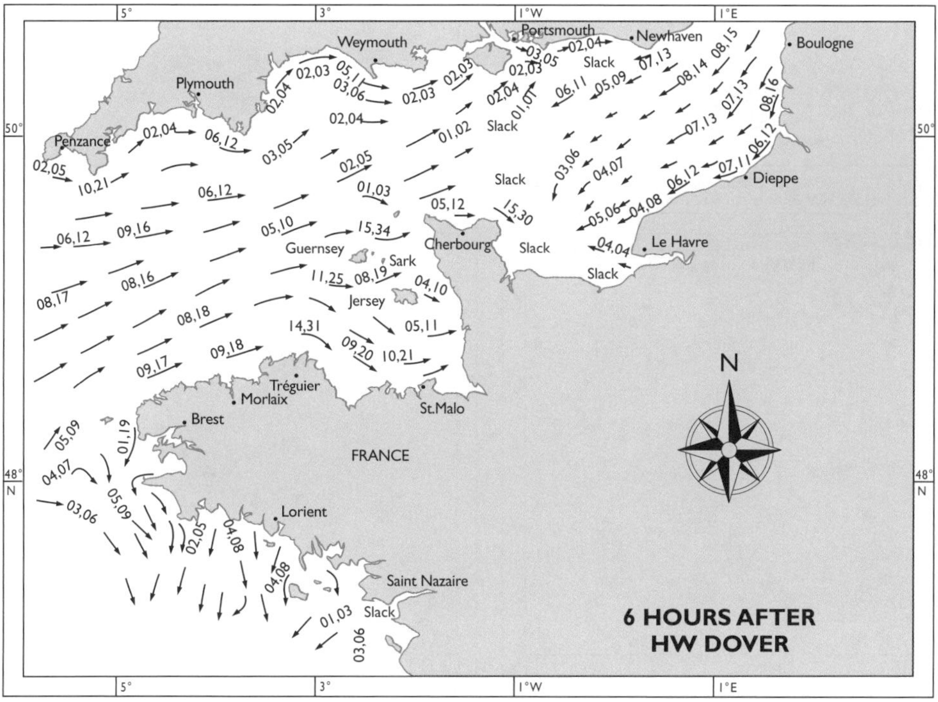
Weymouth
Portsmouth
Newhaven
Boulogne
Plymouth
Penzance
Dieppe
Le Havre
Cherbourg
Guernsey
Sark
Jersey
Tréguier
Morlaix
St.Malo
Brest
FRANCE
Lorient
Saint Nazaire
Slack
N
6 HOURS AFTER
HW DOVER

PORTLAND

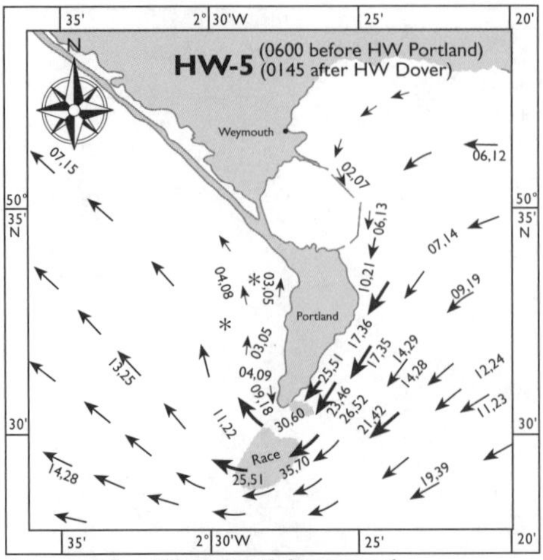

5 hours before HW Plymouth (Devonport)

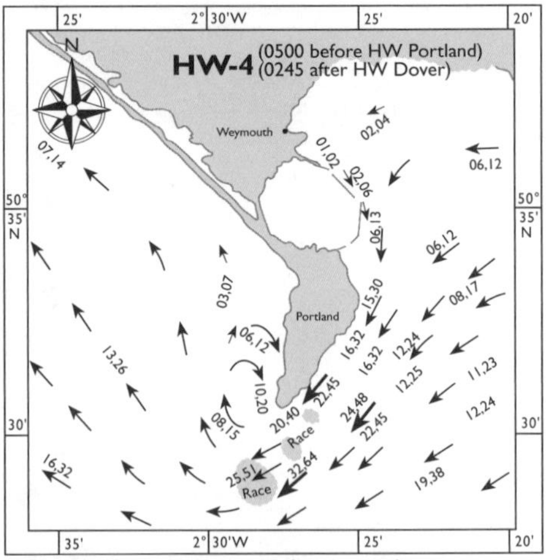

4 hours before HW Plymouth (Devonport)

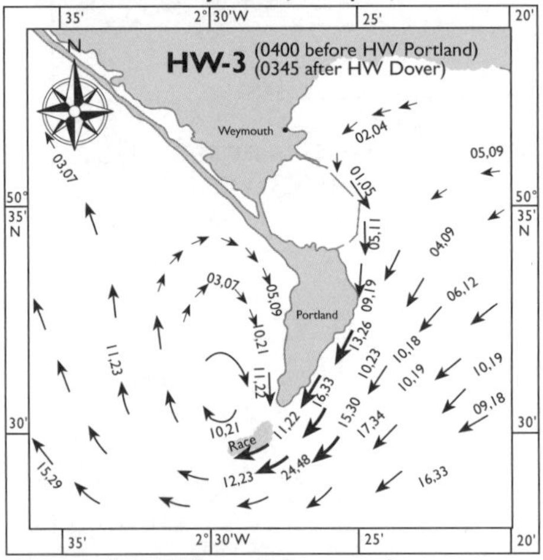

3 hours before HW Plymouth (Devonport)

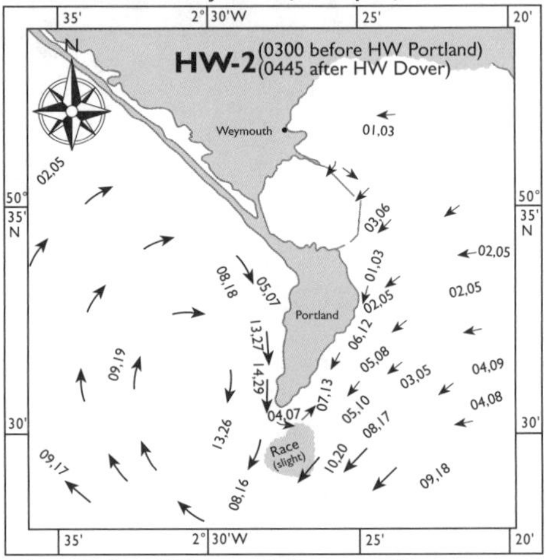

2 hours before HW Plymouth (Devonport)

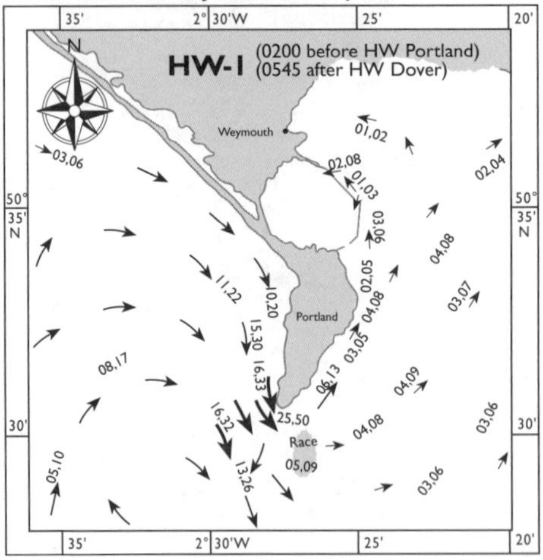

1 hour before HW Plymouth (Devonport)

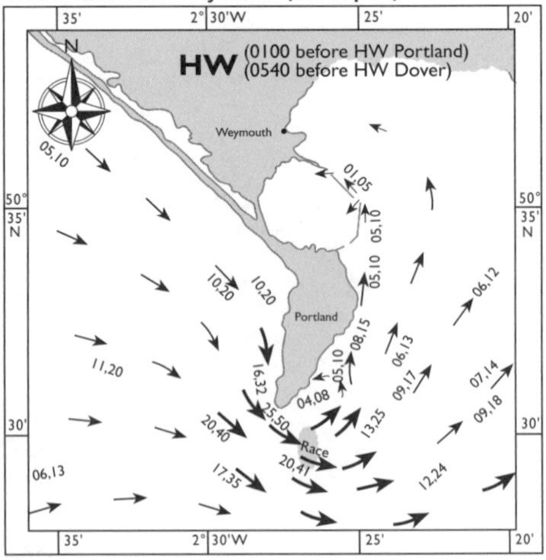

HW Plymouth (Devonport)

PORTLAND

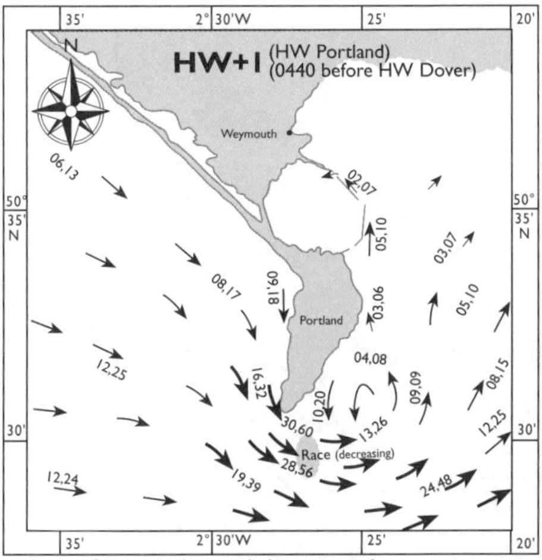

1 hour after HW Plymouth (Devonport)

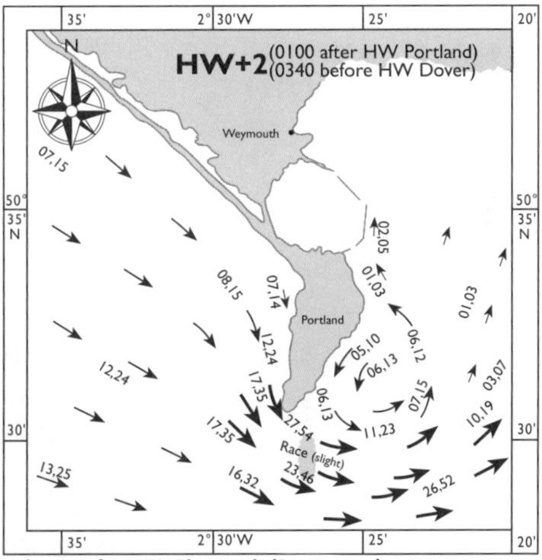

2 hours after HW Plymouth (Devonport)

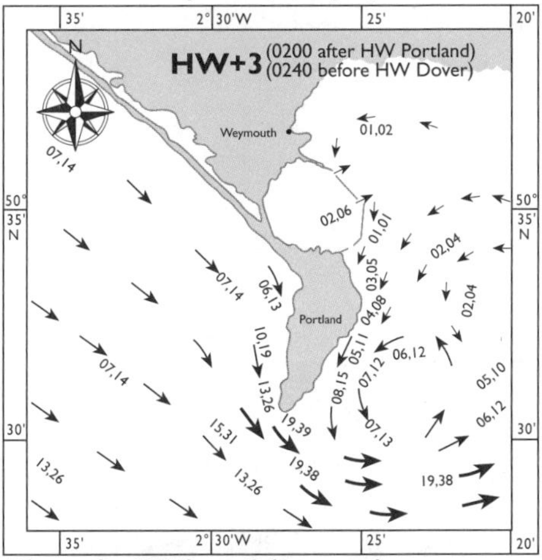

3 hours after HW Plymouth (Devonport)

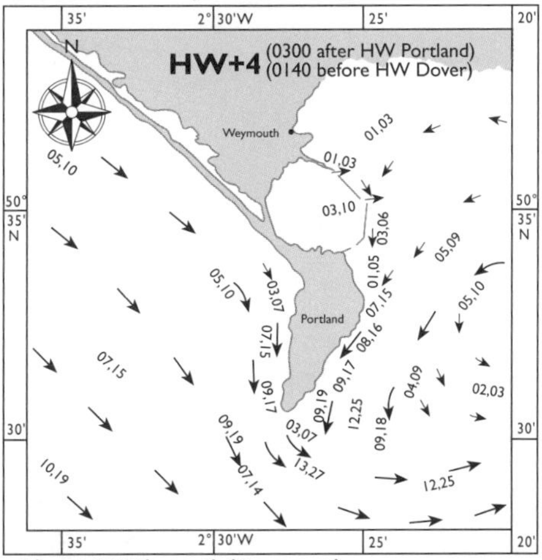

4 hours HW Plymouth (Devonport)

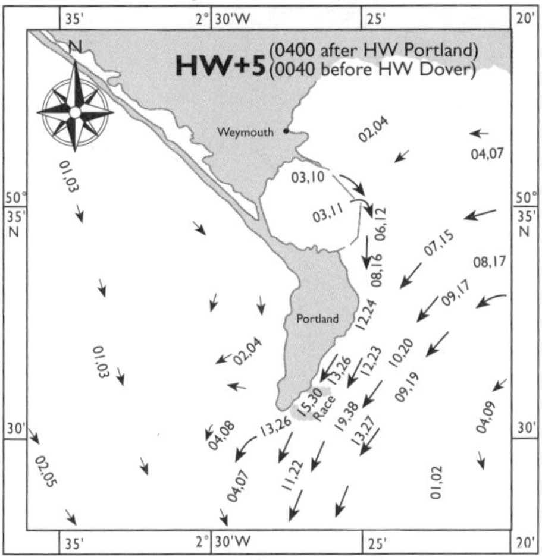

5 hours after HW Plymouth (Devonport)

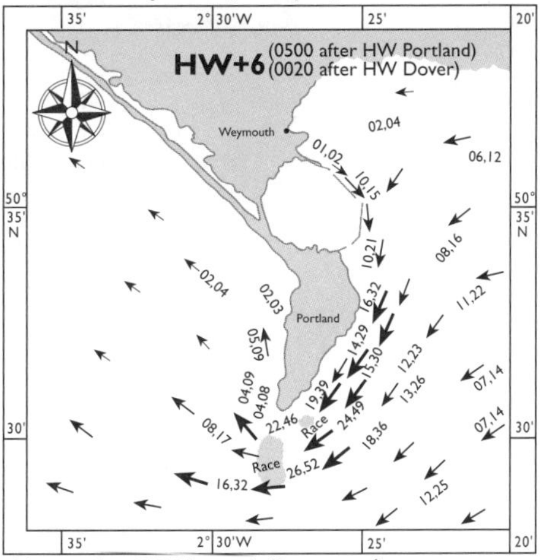

6 hours after HW Plymouth (Devonport)

TIDES

ISLE OF WIGHT

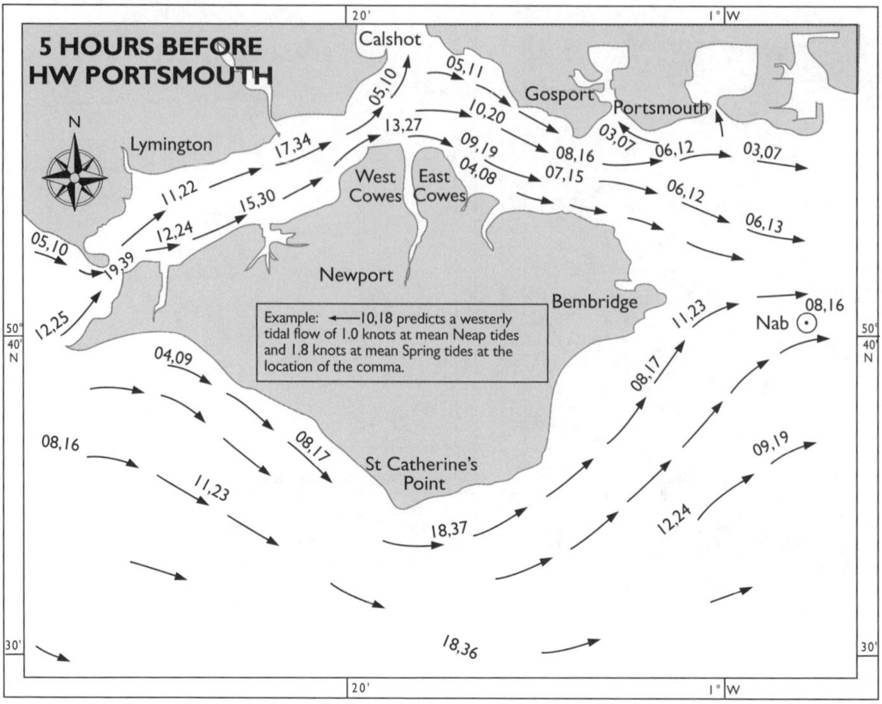

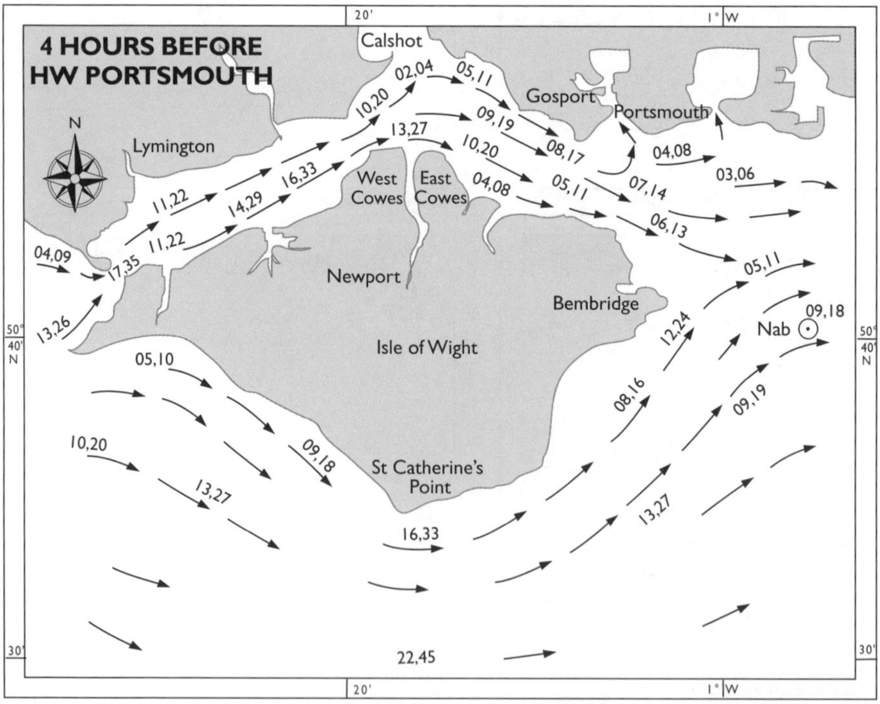

ISLE OF WIGHT

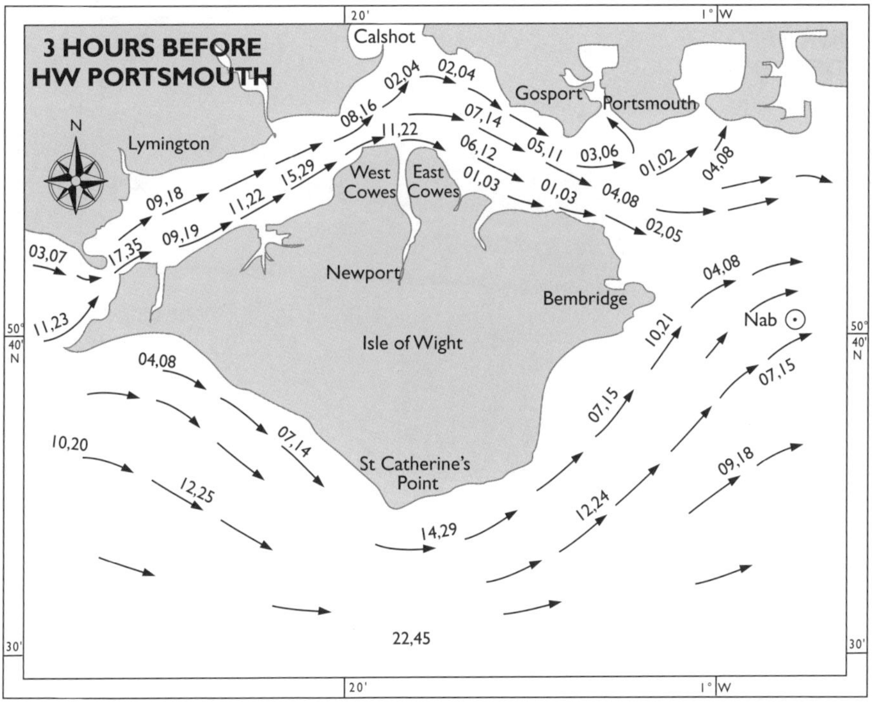

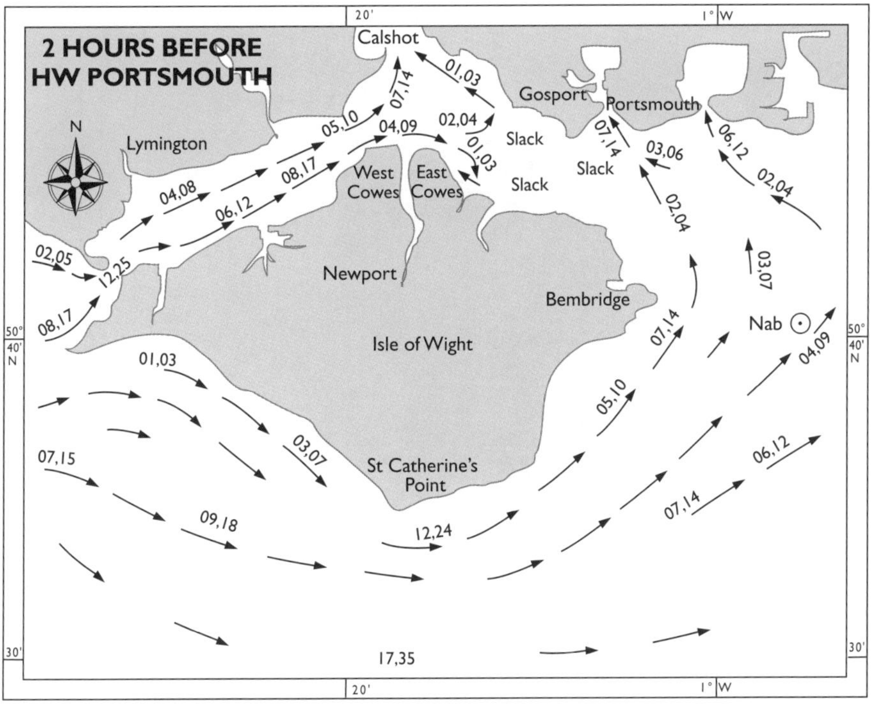

ISLE OF WIGHT

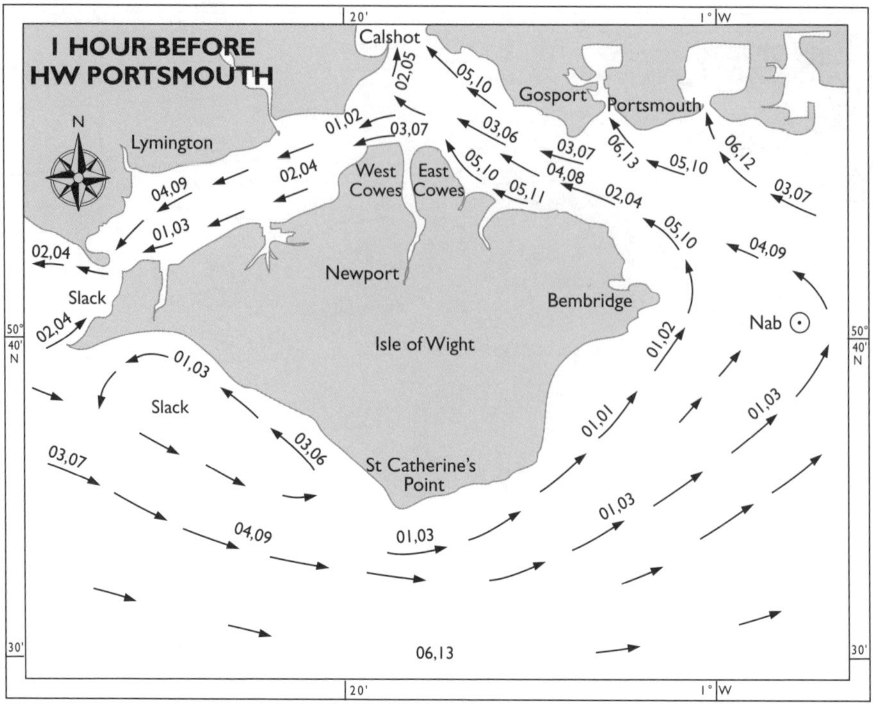

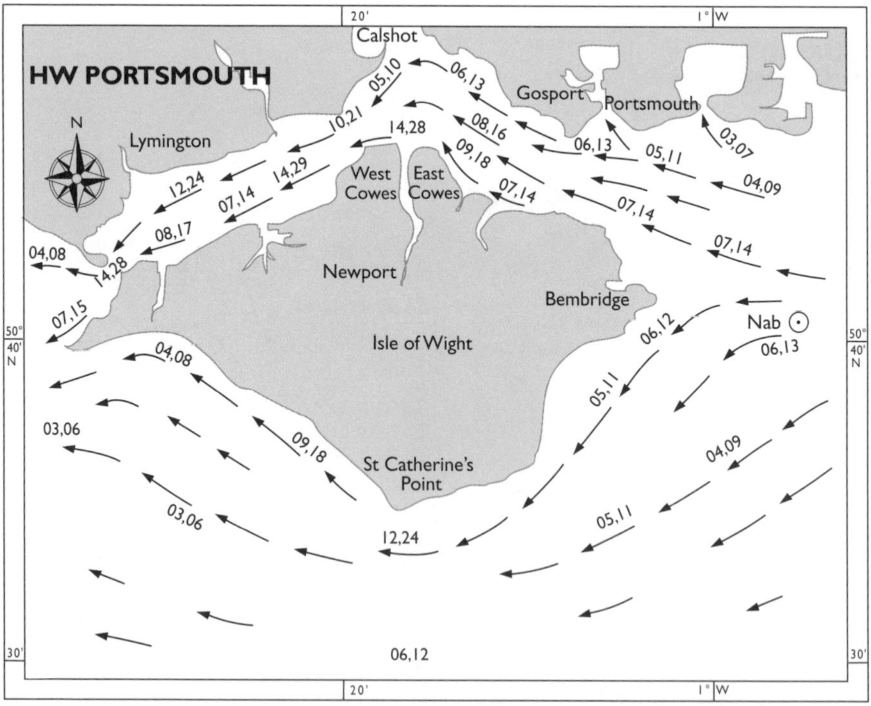

ISLE OF WIGHT

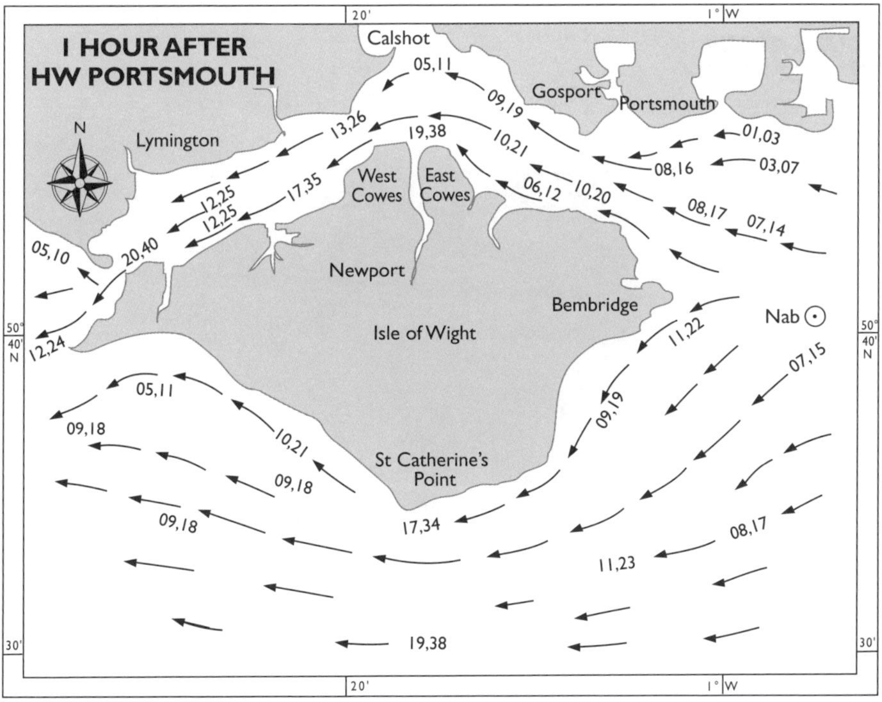

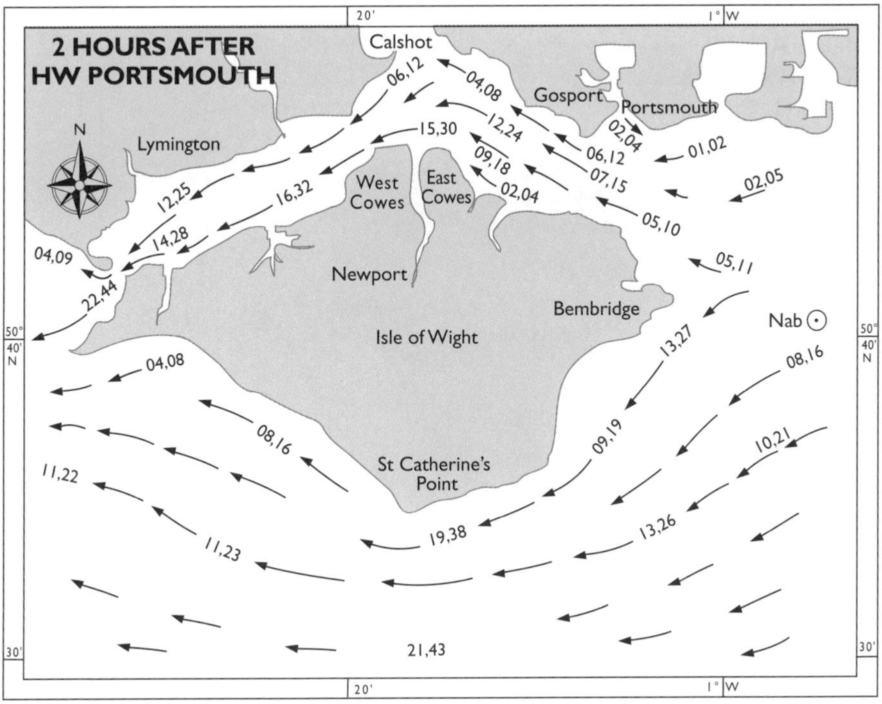

TIDES

ISLE OF WIGHT

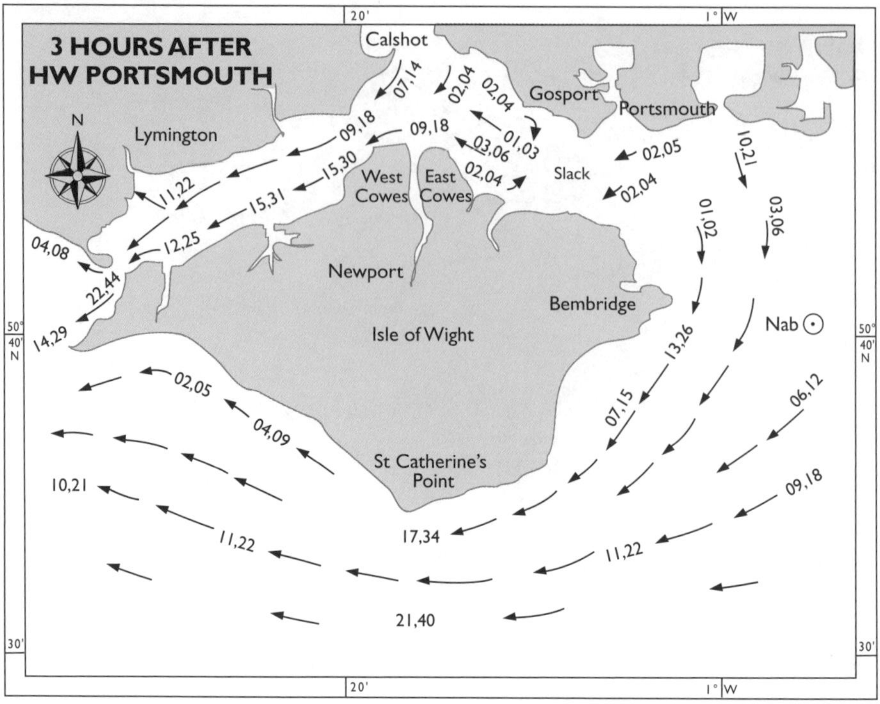

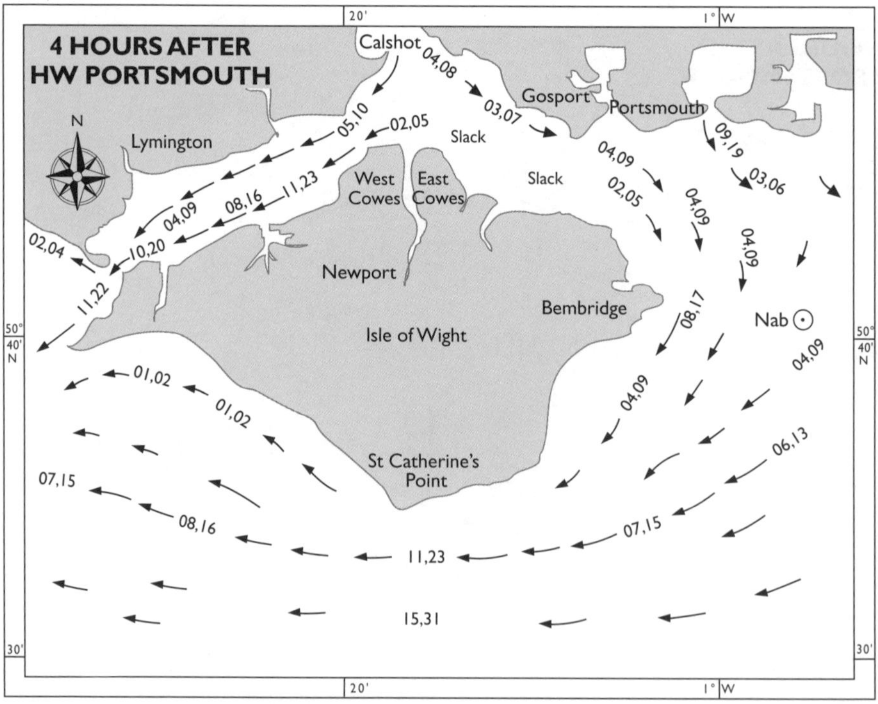

ISLE OF WIGHT

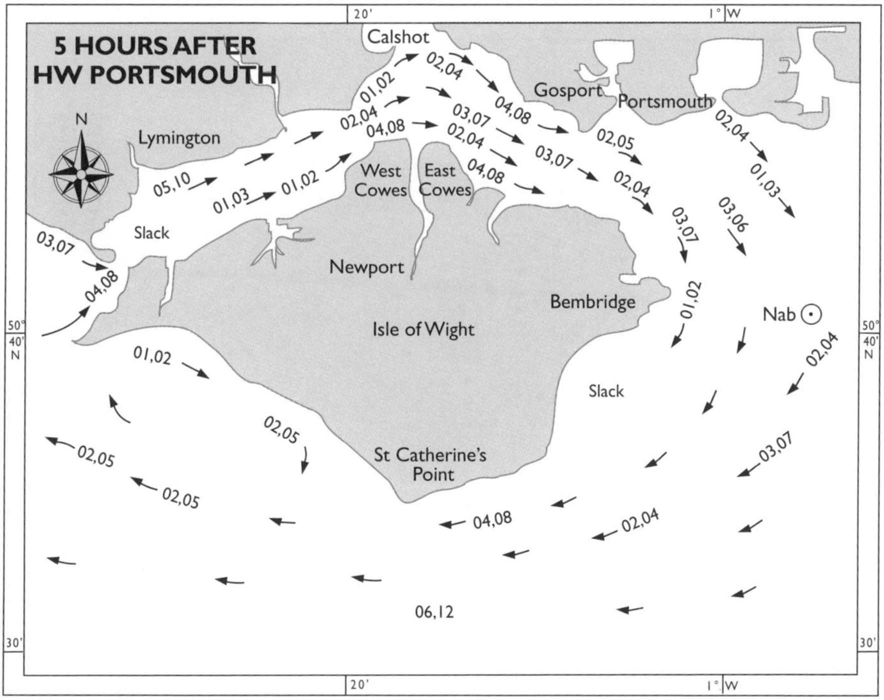

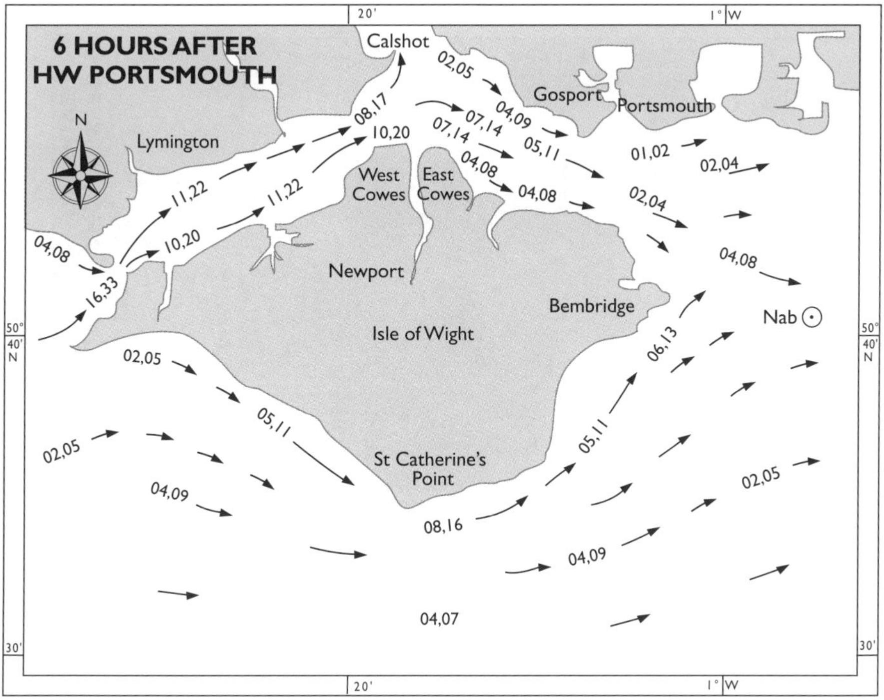

CHANNEL ISLANDS

Example: ⟵10,18 predicts a westerly tidal flow of 1.0 knots at mean Neap tides and 1.8 knots at mean Spring tides at the location of the comma.

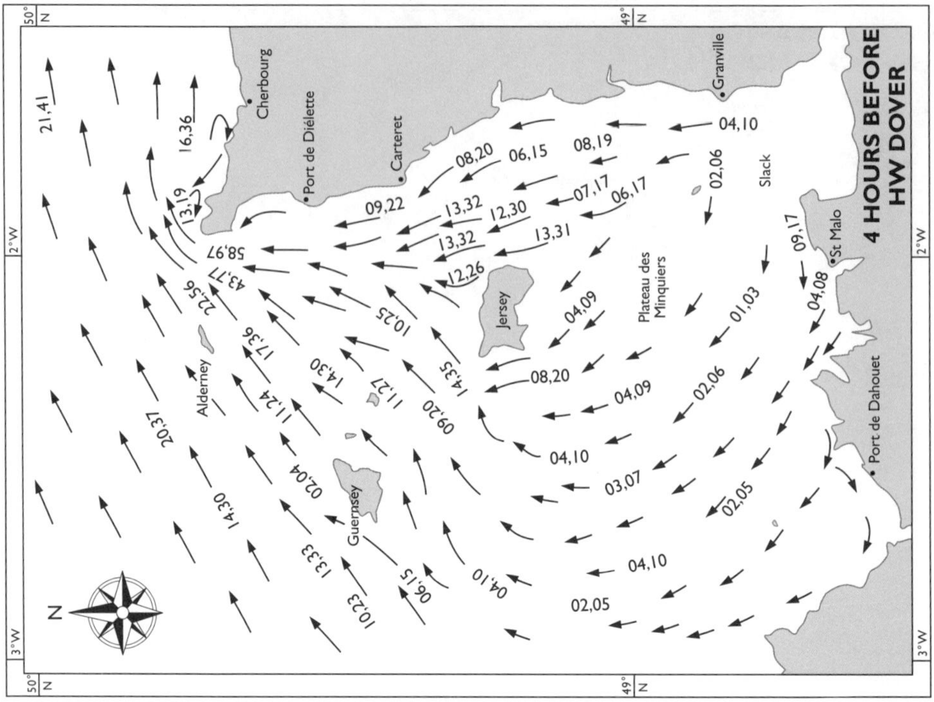

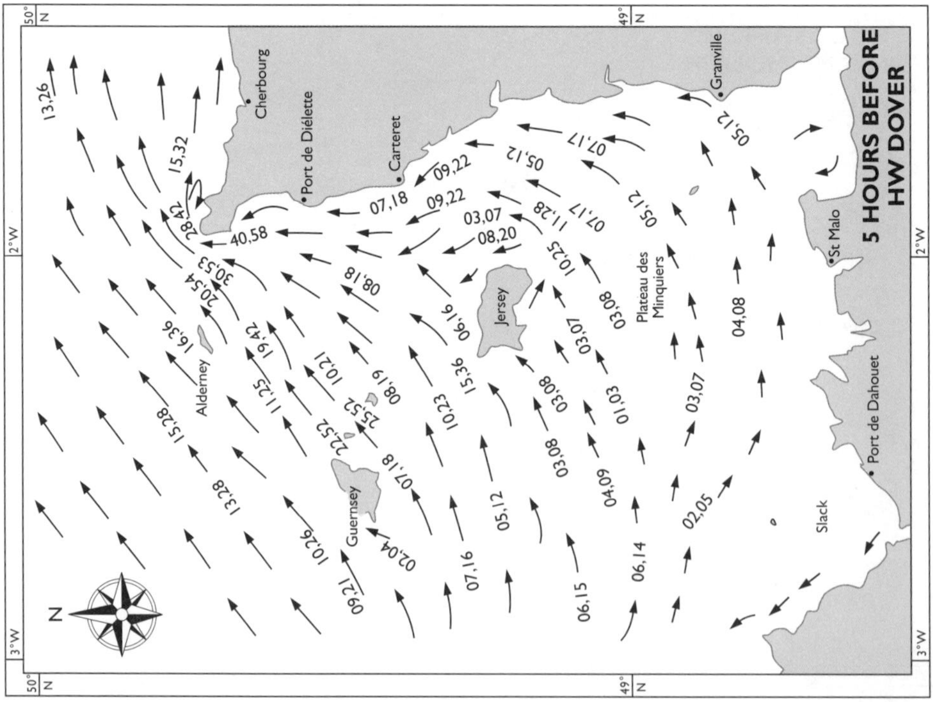

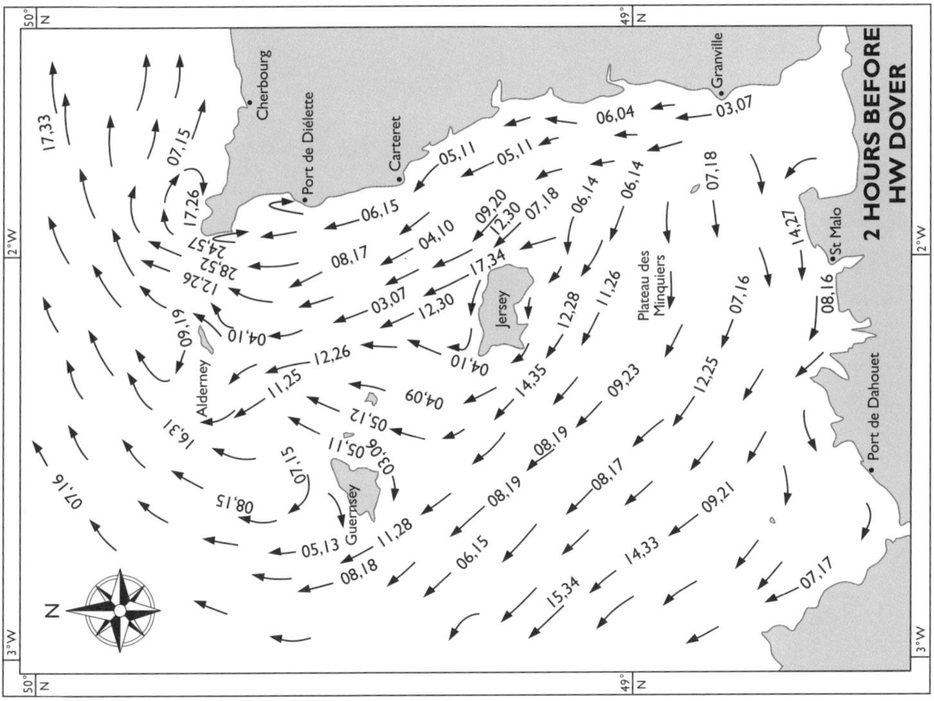
2 HOURS BEFORE HW DOVER
Cherbourg
Port de Diélette
Carteret
Granville
St Malo
Port de Dahouet
Jersey
Guernsey
Alderney
Plateau des Minquiers
50° N
49° N
2° W
3° W
N

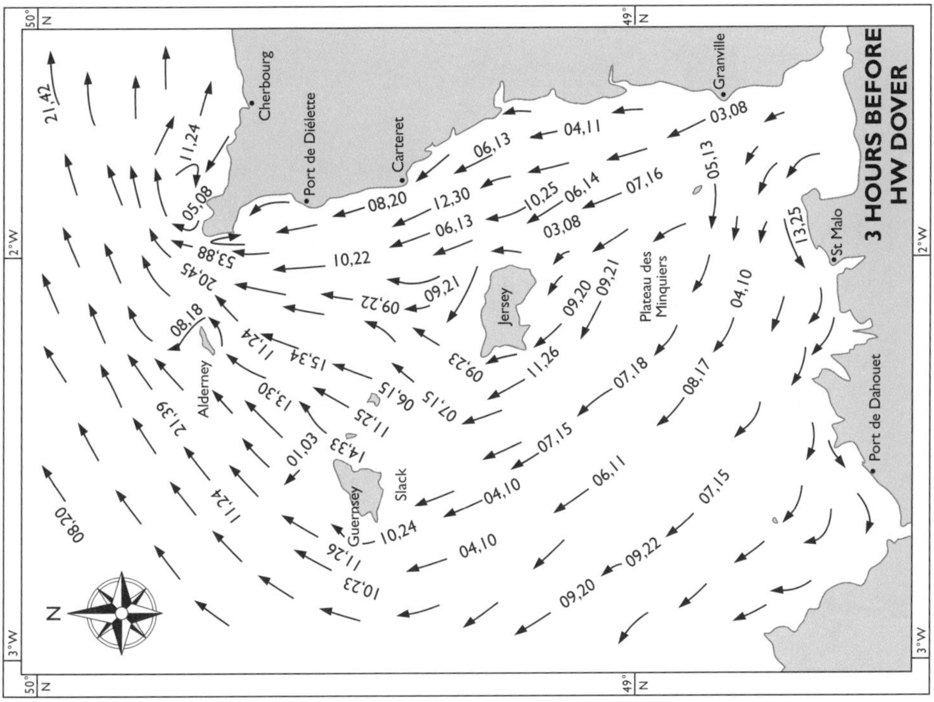
3 HOURS BEFORE HW DOVER
Cherbourg
Port de Diélette
Carteret
Granville
St Malo
Port de Dahouet
Jersey
Guernsey
Alderney
Plateau des Minquiers
Slack
50° N
49° N
2° W
3° W
N

TIDES

CHANNEL ISLANDS

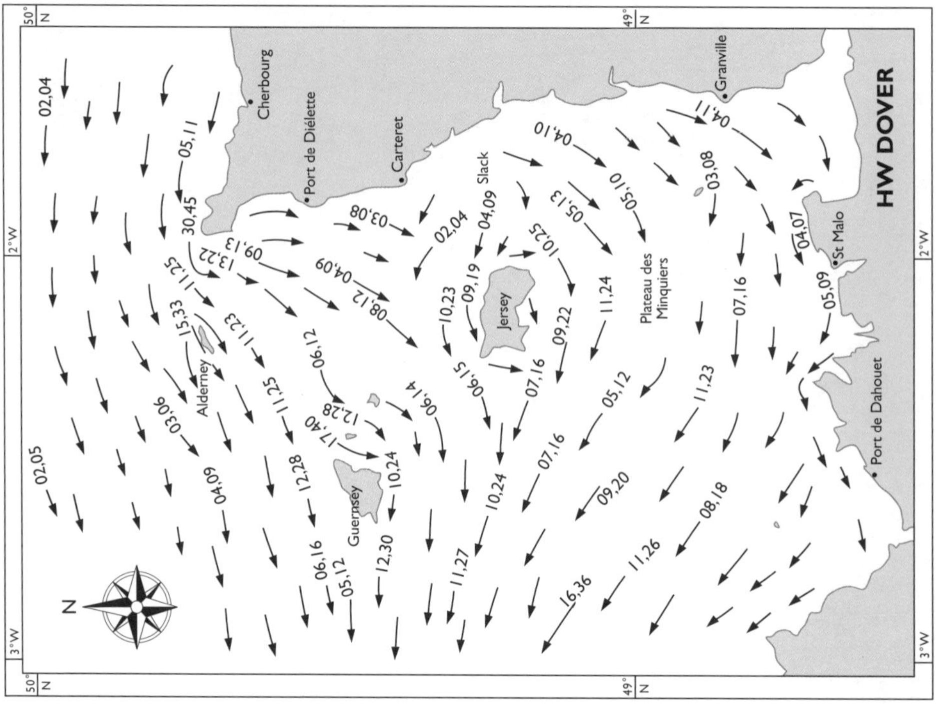

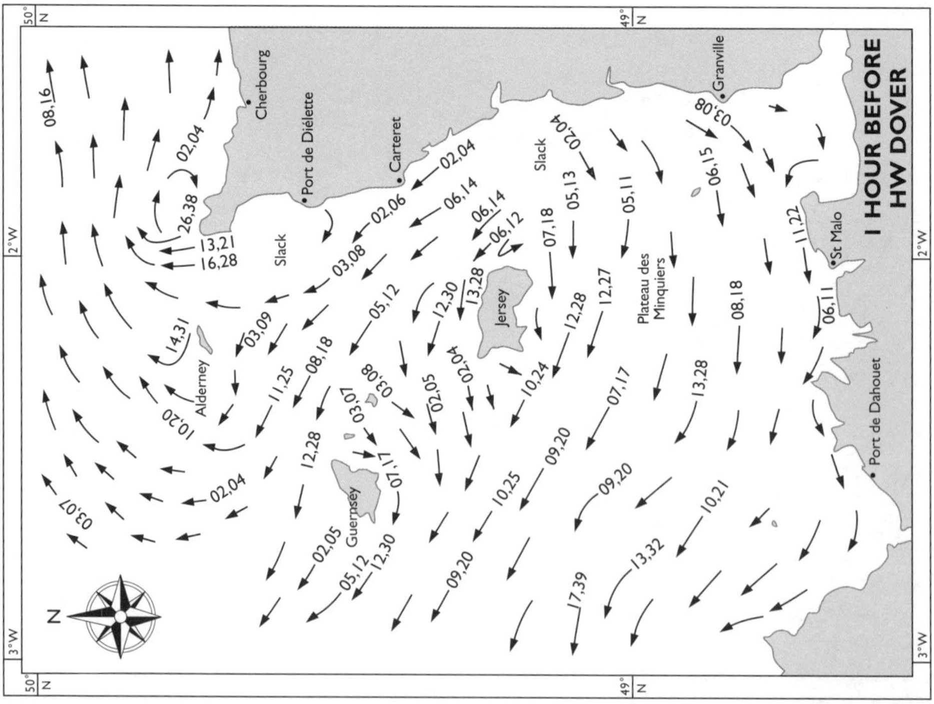

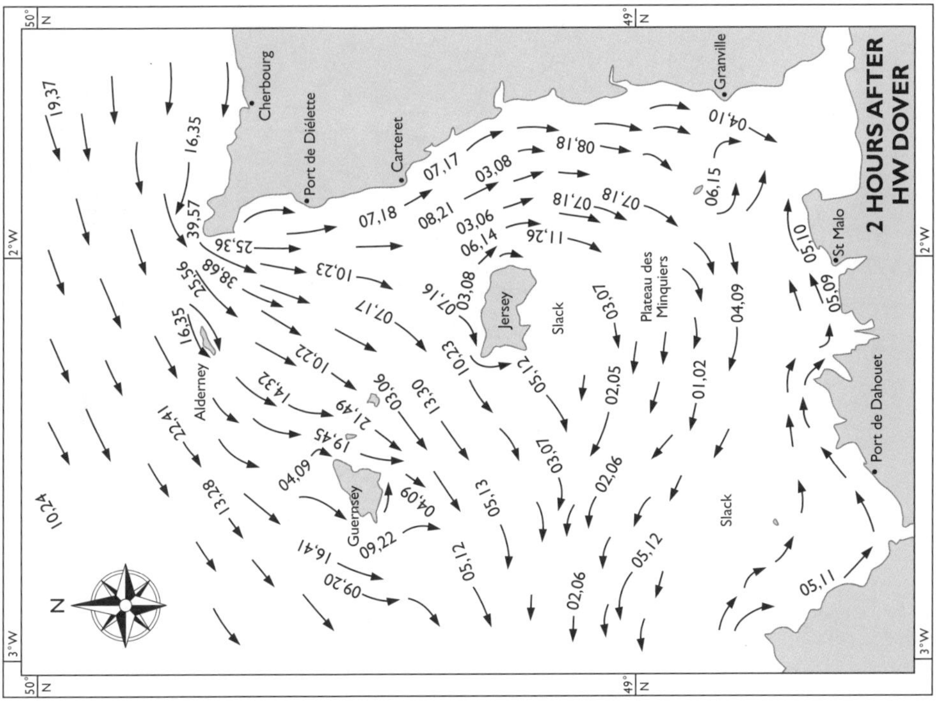
2 HOURS AFTER
HW DOVER
Cherbourg
Port de Diélette
Carteret
Granville
Alderney
Guernsey
Jersey
Slack
Plateau des Minquiers
St Malo
Port de Dahouet
Slack
50° N
49° N
2° W
3° W
N

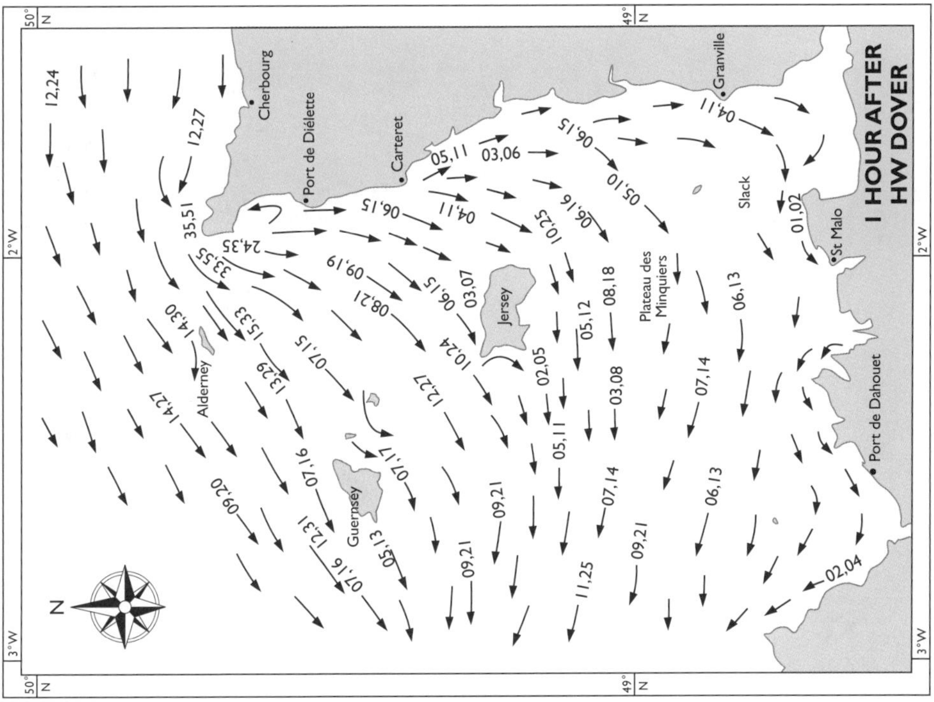
1 HOUR AFTER
HW DOVER
Cherbourg
Port de Diélette
Carteret
Granville
Alderney
Guernsey
Jersey
Plateau des Minquiers
Slack
St Malo
Port de Dahouet
50° N
49° N
2° W
3° W
N

TIDES

CHANNEL ISLANDS

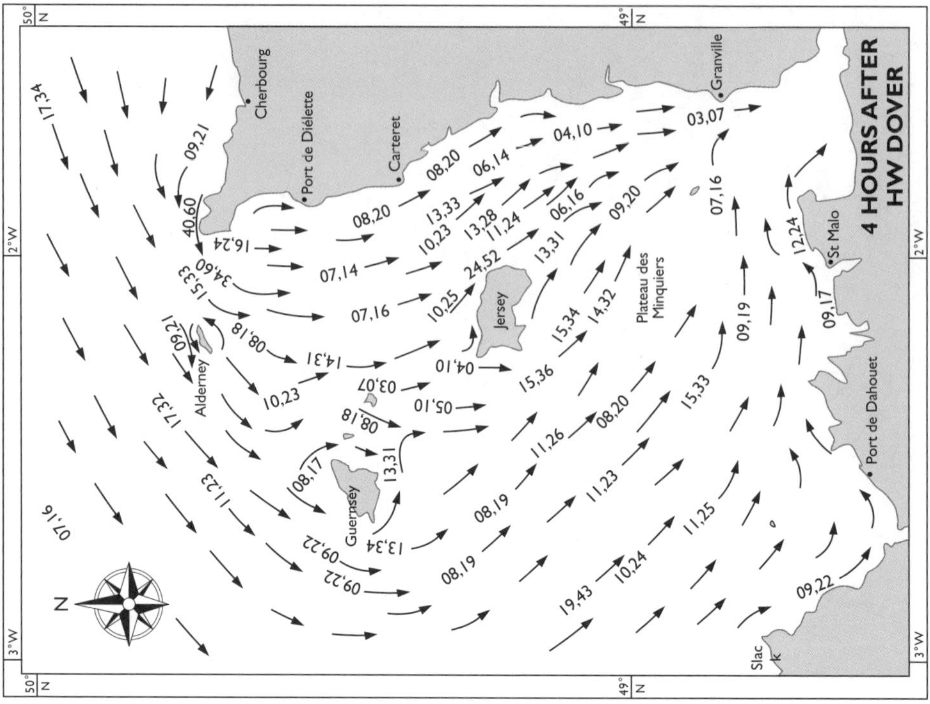

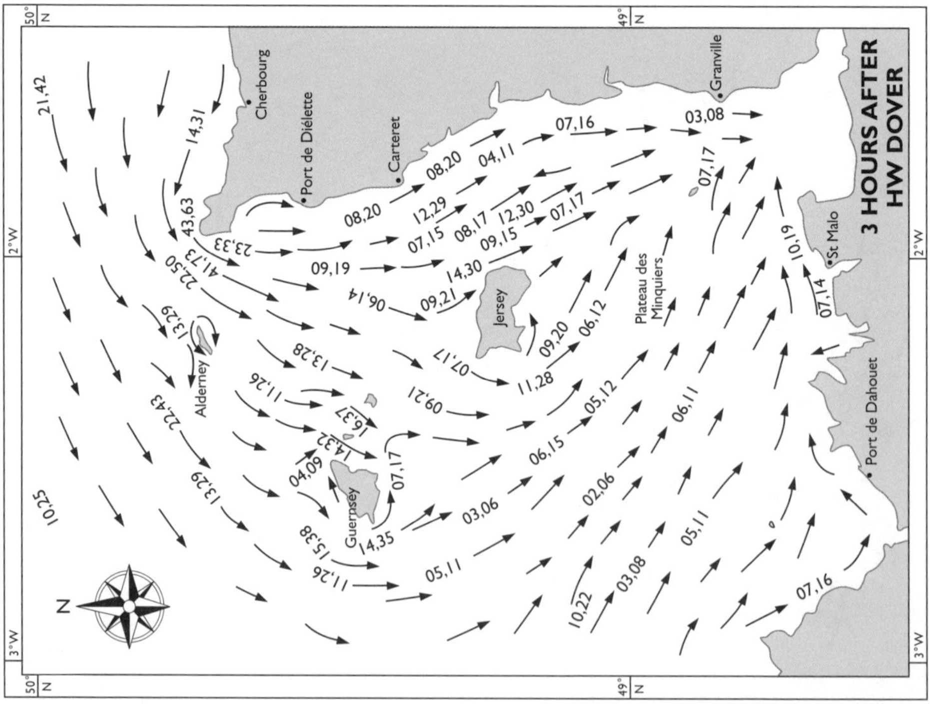

CHANNEL ISLANDS

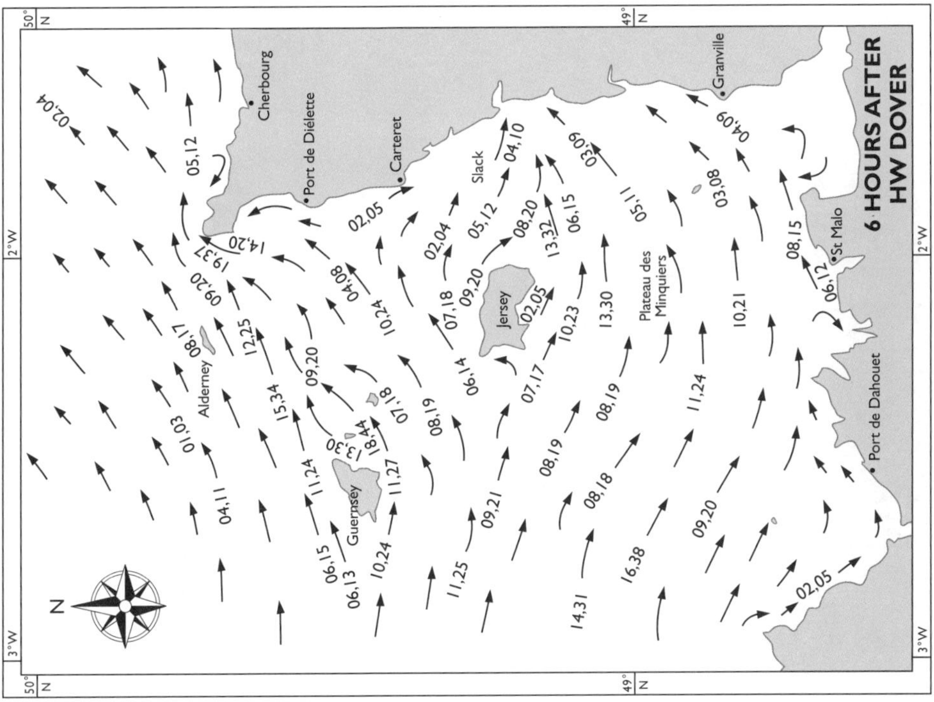

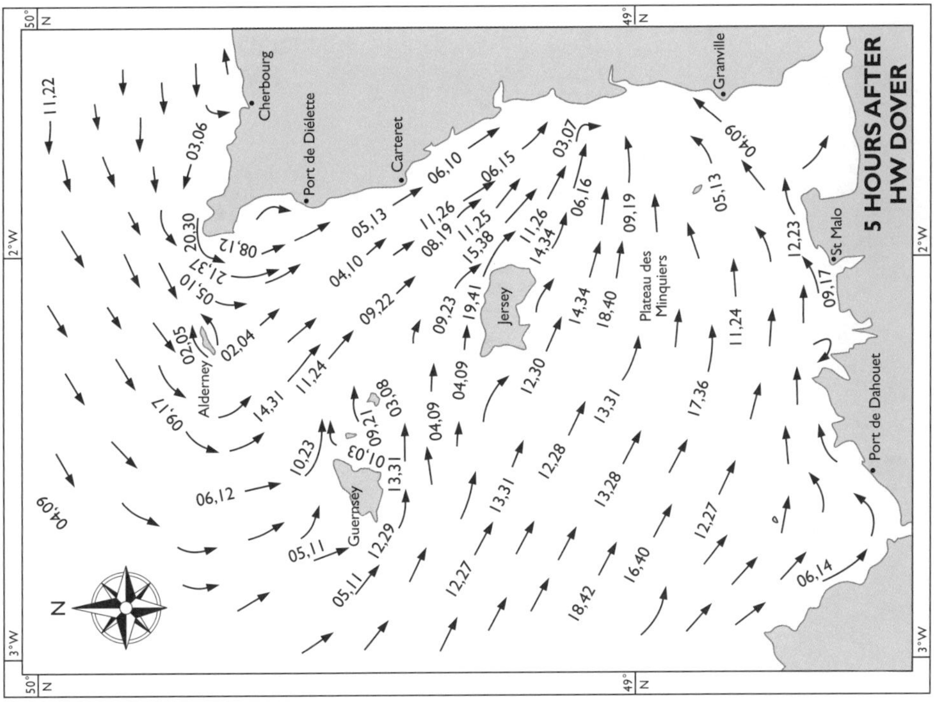

TIDES

NORTH SEA

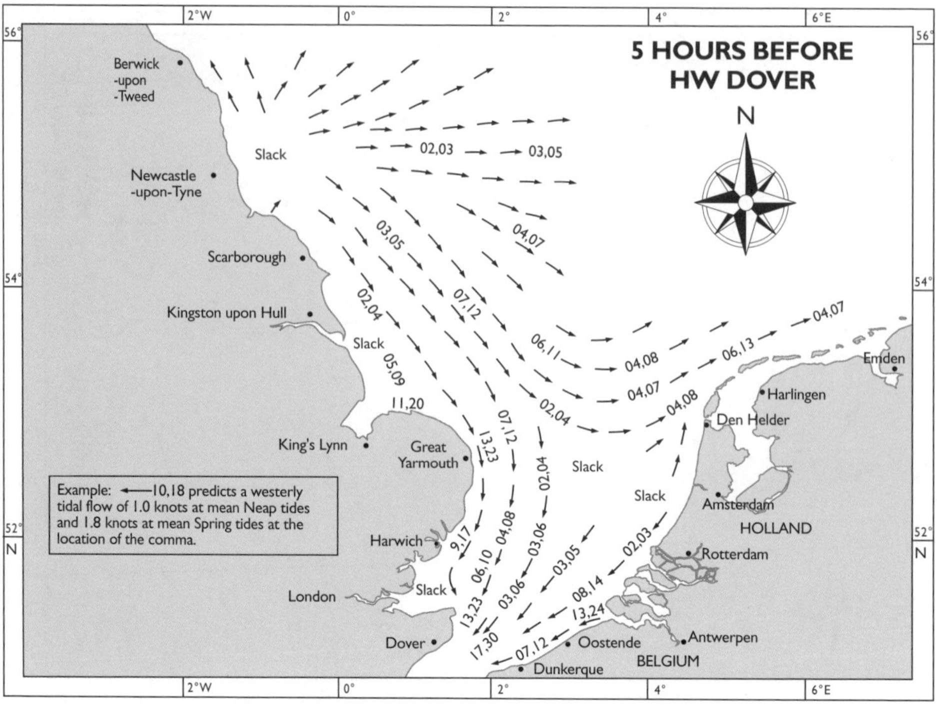
5 HOURS BEFORE HW DOVER
N
2°W
0°
2°
4°
6°E
56°
54°
52° N
Berwick -upon -Tweed
Newcastle -upon-Tyne
Scarborough
Kingston upon Hull
King's Lynn
Great Yarmouth
Harwich
London
Dover
Oostende
Dunkerque
BELGIUM
Antwerpen
Rotterdam
HOLLAND
Amsterdam
Den Helder
Harlingen
Emden
Slack
02,03
03,05
03,05
04,07
02,04
07,12
05,09
11,20
06,11
04,08
04,07
06,13
04,07
04,08
02,04
07,12
13,23
02,04
Slack
Slack
9,17
06,10
04,08
03,06
03,06
03,05
02,03
08,14
13,24
13,23
17,30
07,12
Slack
Example: ⟵10,18 predicts a westerly tidal flow of 1.0 knots at mean Neap tides and 1.8 knots at mean Spring tides at the location of the comma.

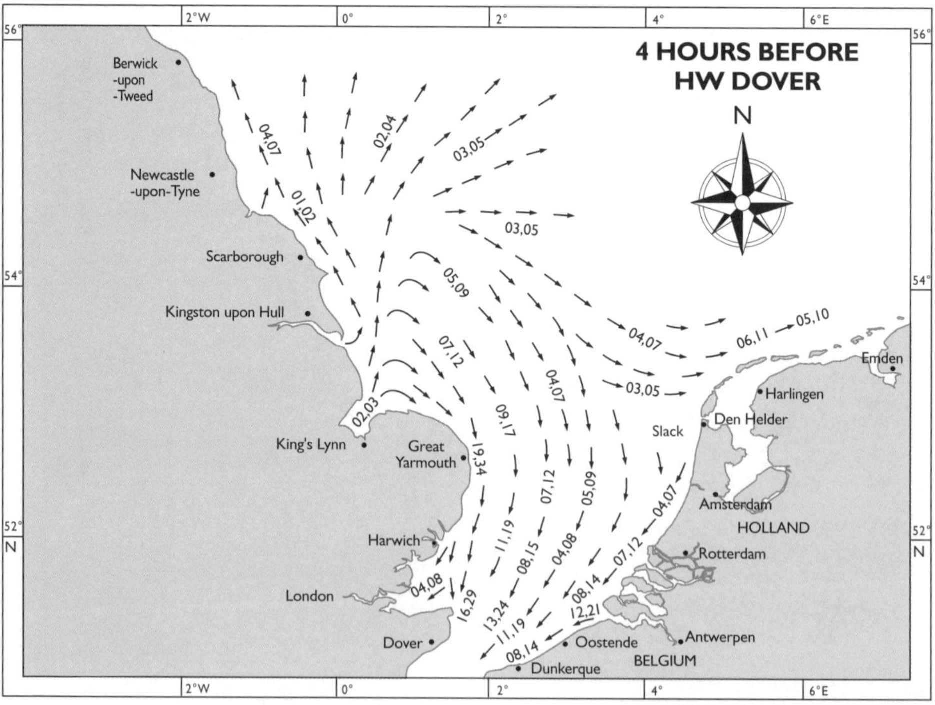
4 HOURS BEFORE HW DOVER
N
2°W
0°
2°
4°
6°E
56°
54°
52° N
Berwick -upon -Tweed
Newcastle -upon-Tyne
Scarborough
Kingston upon Hull
King's Lynn
Great Yarmouth
Harwich
London
Dover
Oostende
Dunkerque
BELGIUM
Antwerpen
Rotterdam
HOLLAND
Amsterdam
Den Helder
Harlingen
Emden
04,07
01,02
02,04
03,05
03,05
05,09
04,07
06,11
05,10
07,12
02,03
09,17
04,07
03,05
Slack
19,34
07,12
05,09
04,07
11,19
08,15
04,08
07,12
04,08
16,29
13,24
11,19
08,14
12,21
08,14

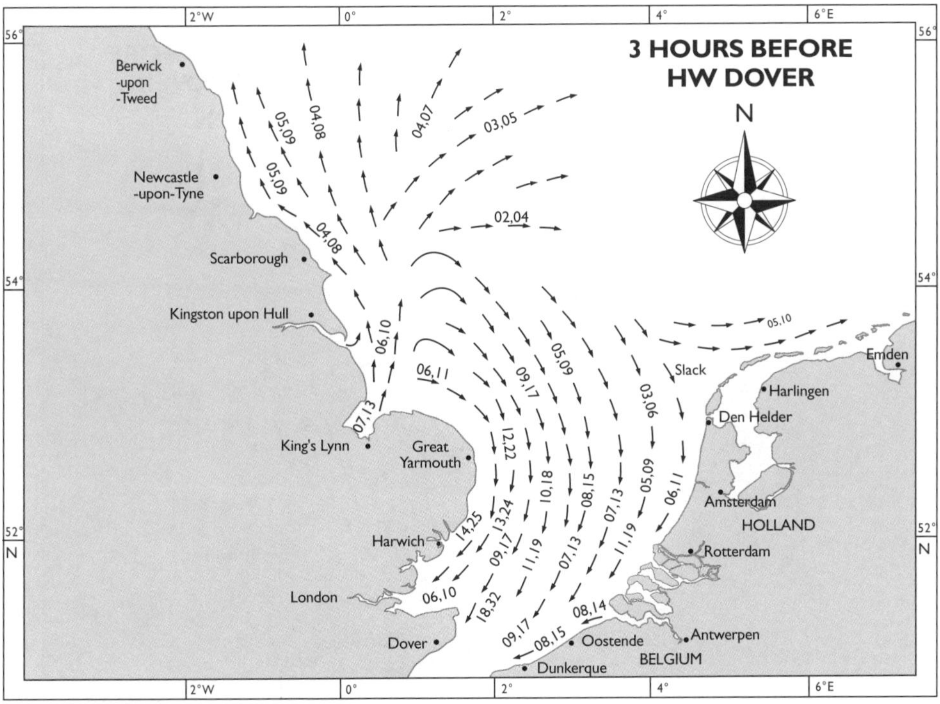
3 HOURS BEFORE HW DOVER
N
Berwick -upon -Tweed
Newcastle -upon-Tyne
Scarborough
Kingston upon Hull
King's Lynn
Great Yarmouth
Harwich
London
Dover
Dunkerque
Oostende
BELGIUM
Antwerpen
Rotterdam
HOLLAND
Amsterdam
Den Helder
Harlingen
Emden
Slack
2°W
0°
2°
4°
6°E
56°
54°
52°
N
05,09
04,08
04,07
03,05
02,04
06,10
06,11
07,13
09,17
05,09
03,06
05,10
12,22
10,18
08,15
07,13
05,09
06,11
14,25
13,24
09,17
11,19
07,13
11,19
06,10
18,32
08,14
09,17
08,15

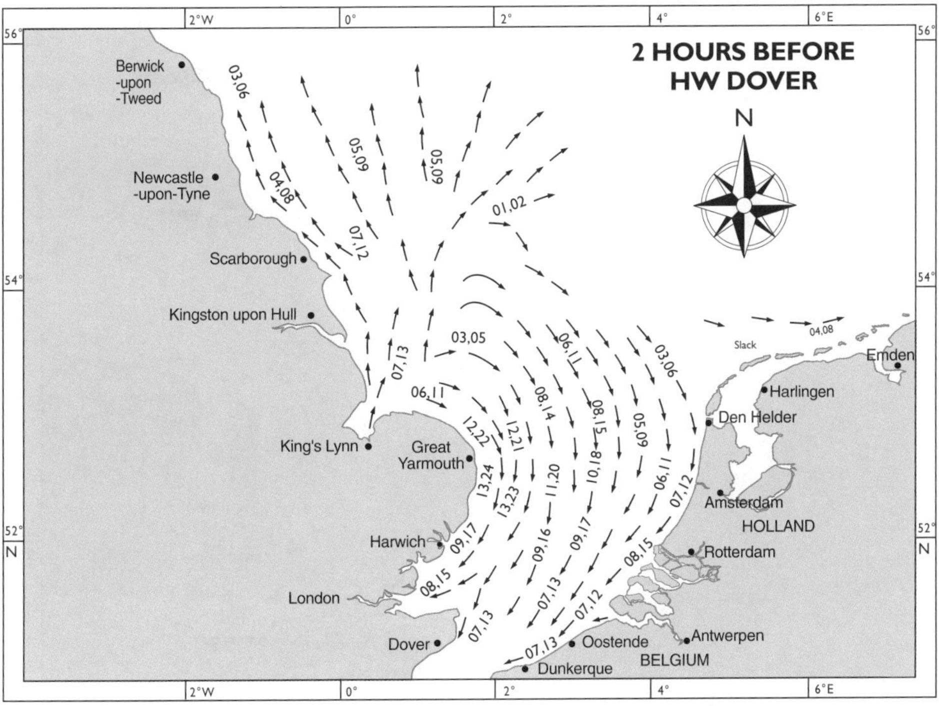
2 HOURS BEFORE HW DOVER
N
Berwick -upon -Tweed
Newcastle -upon-Tyne
Scarborough
Kingston upon Hull
King's Lynn
Great Yarmouth
Harwich
London
Dover
Dunkerque
Oostende
BELGIUM
Antwerpen
Rotterdam
HOLLAND
Amsterdam
Den Helder
Harlingen
Emden
Slack
2°W
0°
2°
4°
6°E
56°
54°
52°
N
03,06
05,09
05,09
04,08
07,12
01,02
04,08
07,13
03,05
06,11
03,06
06,11
12,22
12,21
08,14
08,15
05,09
13,24
13,23
11,20
10,18
06,11
07,12
09,17
09,16
09,17
08,15
08,15
07,13
07,13
07,12
07,13

NORTH SEA

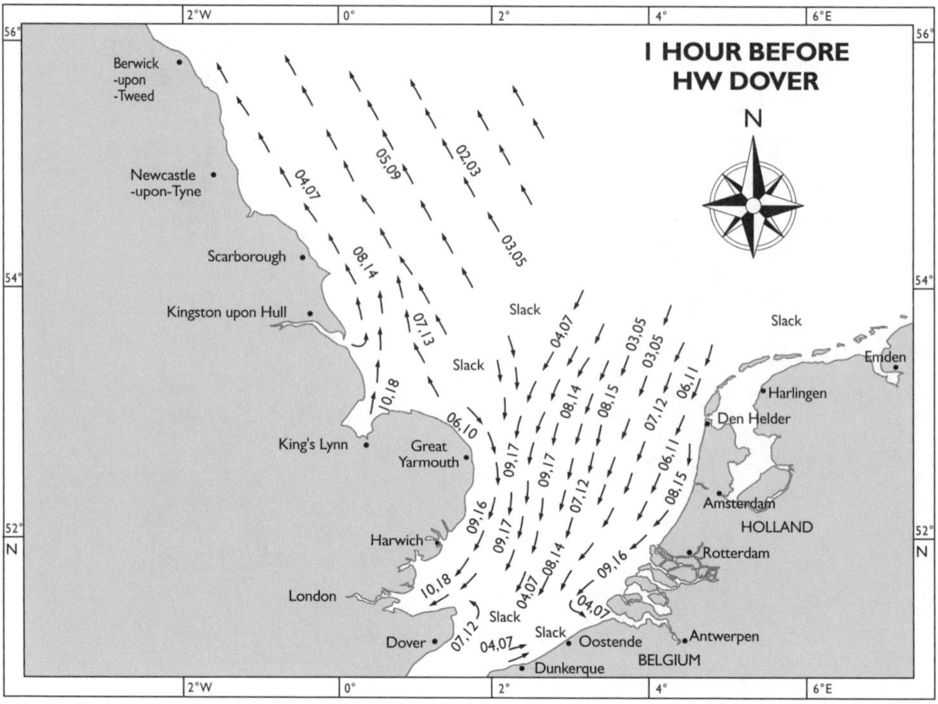
I HOUR BEFORE HW DOVER
N
2°W
0°
2°
4°
6°E
56°
54°
52°
N
Berwick -upon -Tweed
Newcastle -upon-Tyne
Scarborough
Kingston upon Hull
King's Lynn
Great Yarmouth
Harwich
London
Dover
Dunkerque
Oostende
BELGIUM
Antwerpen
Rotterdam
HOLLAND
Amsterdam
Den Helder
Harlingen
Emden
Slack
04,07
05,09
02,03
03,05
08,14
07,13
10,18
06,10
09,17
09,16
10,18
07,12
04,07
08,14
08,15
06,11
09,16
04,07

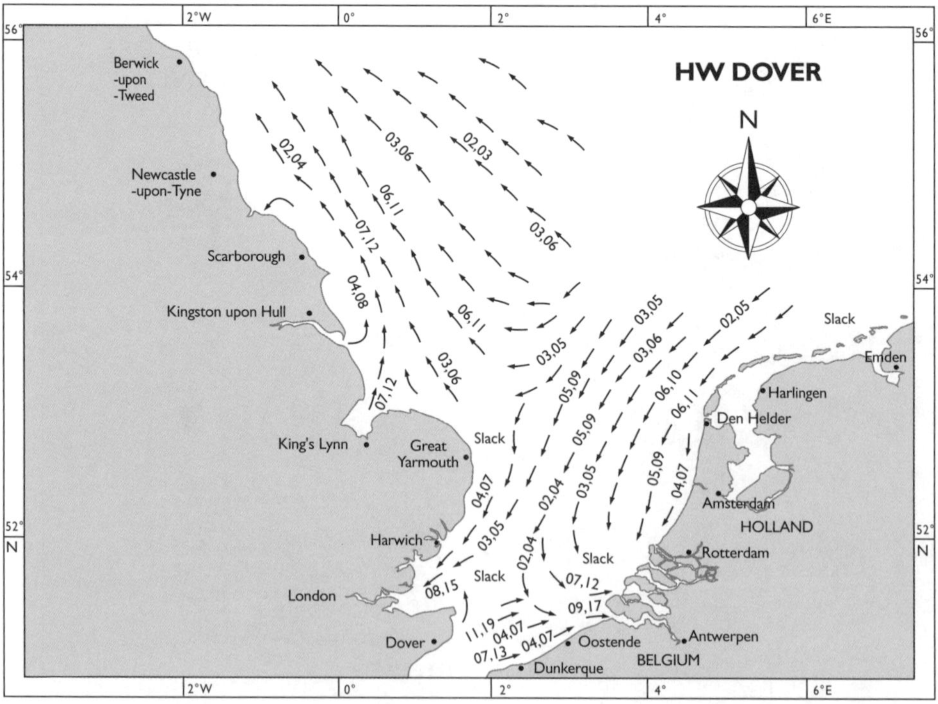
HW DOVER
N
2°W
0°
2°
4°
6°E
56°
54°
52°
N
Berwick -upon -Tweed
Newcastle -upon-Tyne
Scarborough
Kingston upon Hull
King's Lynn
Great Yarmouth
Harwich
London
Dover
Dunkerque
Oostende
BELGIUM
Antwerpen
Rotterdam
HOLLAND
Amsterdam
Den Helder
Harlingen
Emden
Slack
02,04
03,06
02,03
06,11
07,12
04,08
06,11
03,06
07,12
03,05
05,09
03,06
06,10
02,05
04,07
02,04
08,15
11,19
07,13
09,17

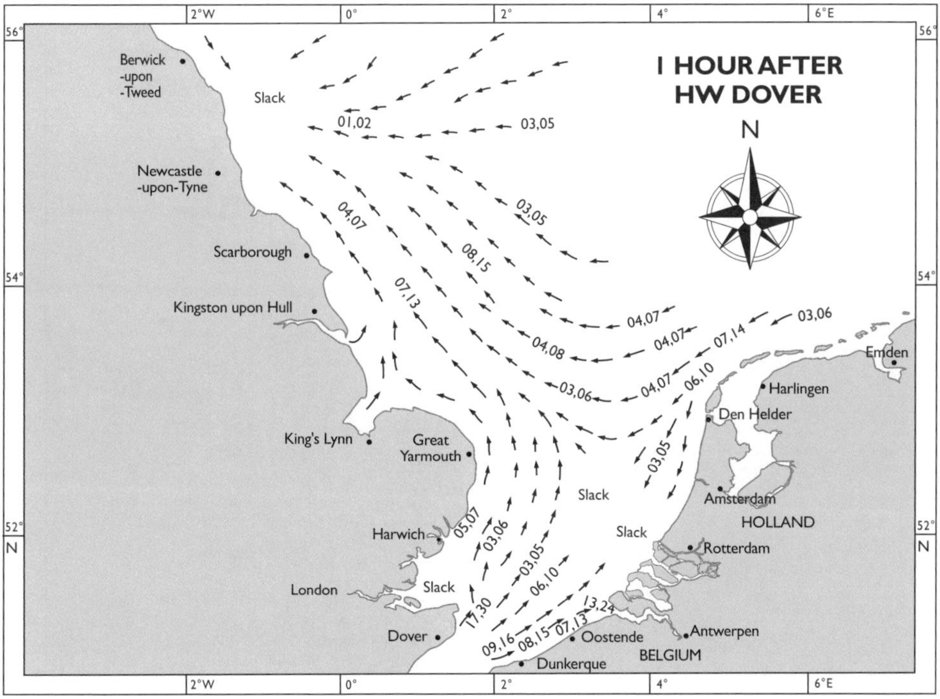
1 HOUR AFTER HW DOVER
N
Berwick -upon -Tweed
Newcastle -upon-Tyne
Scarborough
Kingston upon Hull
King's Lynn
Great Yarmouth
Harwich
London
Dover
Dunkerque
Oostende
BELGIUM
Antwerpen
Rotterdam
HOLLAND
Amsterdam
Den Helder
Harlingen
Emden
Slack
01,02
03,05
04,07
03,05
08,15
07,13
04,07
04,08
04,07
07,14
03,06
03,06
04,07
06,10
03,05
05,07
03,06
03,05
06,10
13,24
07,13
08,15
09,16
17,30
2°W
0°
2°
4°
6°E
56°
54°
52°
N

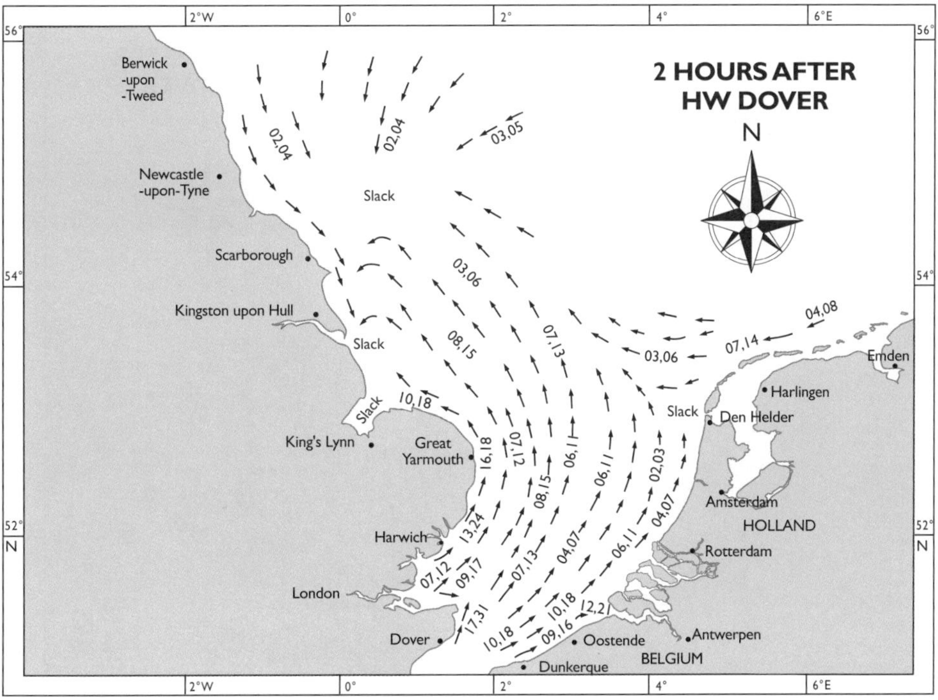
2 HOURS AFTER HW DOVER
N
Berwick -upon -Tweed
Newcastle -upon-Tyne
Scarborough
Kingston upon Hull
King's Lynn
Great Yarmouth
Harwich
London
Dover
Dunkerque
Oostende
BELGIUM
Antwerpen
Rotterdam
HOLLAND
Amsterdam
Den Helder
Harlingen
Emden
Slack
02,04
02,04
03,05
03,06
08,15
07,13
04,08
07,14
03,06
10,18
16,18
07,12
08,15
06,11
06,11
02,03
04,07
06,11
04,07
07,13
13,24
07,12
09,17
17,31
10,18
10,18
09,16
12,21
2°W
0°
2°
4°
6°E
56°
54°
52°
N

NORTH SEA

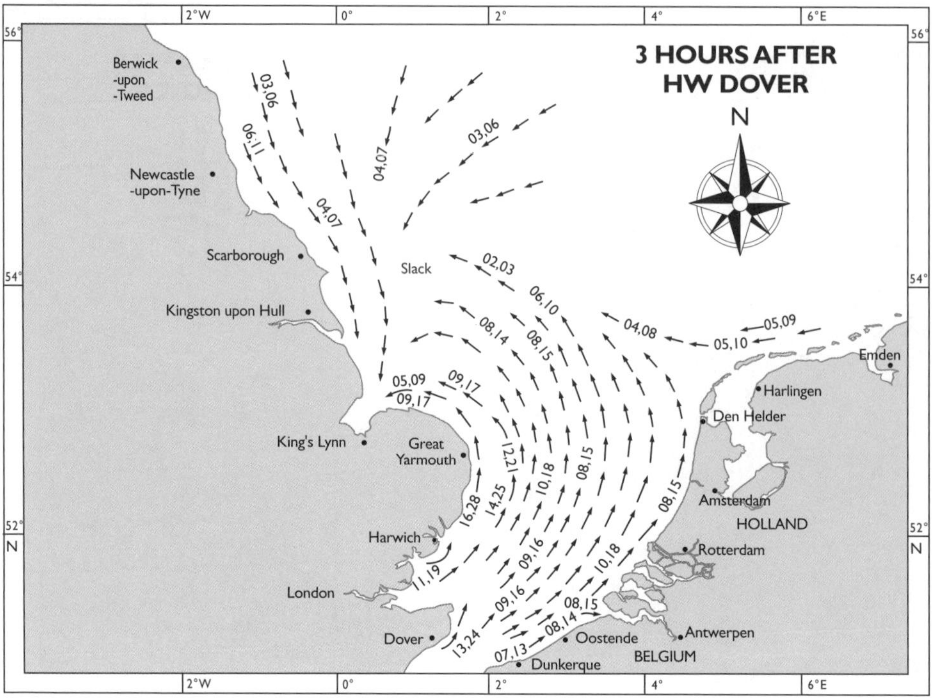
3 HOURS AFTER
HW DOVER
N
2°W
0°
2°
4°
6°E
56°
54°
52°
N
Berwick
-upon
-Tweed
Newcastle
-upon-Tyne
Scarborough
Kingston upon Hull
King's Lynn
Great
Yarmouth
Harwich
London
Dover
Dunkerque
Oostende
BELGIUM
Antwerpen
Rotterdam
HOLLAND
Amsterdam
Den Helder
Harlingen
Emden
Slack
03,06
06,11
04,07
04,07
03,06
02,03
06,10
08,14
08,15
04,08
05,10
05,09
05,09
09,17
09,17
12,21
10,18
08,15
16,28
14,25
08,15
11,19
09,16
10,18
09,16
08,15
13,24
08,14
07,13

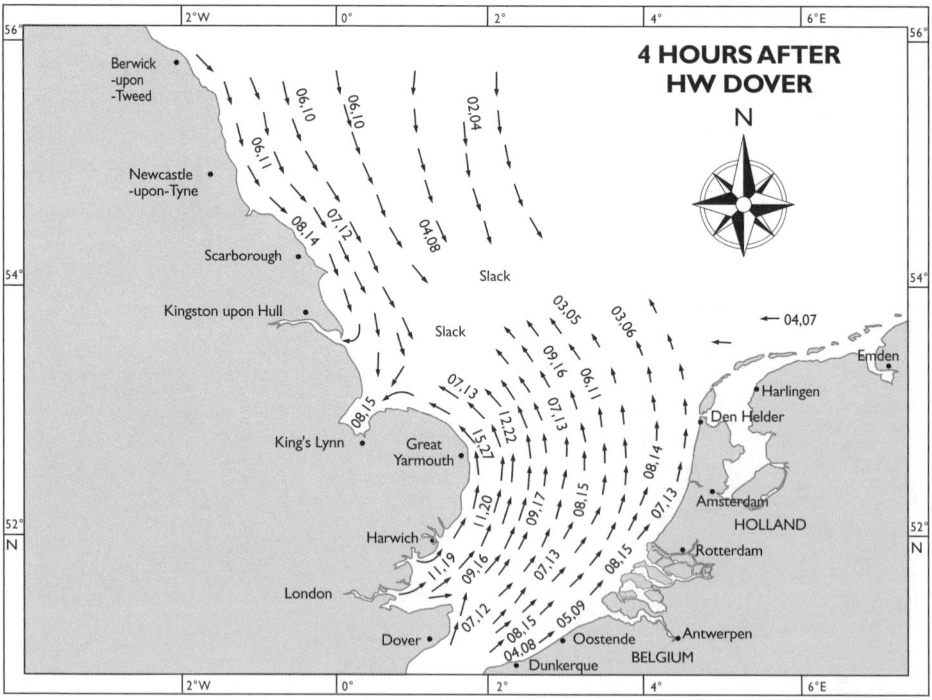
4 HOURS AFTER
HW DOVER
N
2°W
0°
2°
4°
6°E
56°
54°
52°
N
Berwick
-upon
-Tweed
Newcastle
-upon-Tyne
Scarborough
Kingston upon Hull
King's Lynn
Great
Yarmouth
Harwich
London
Dover
Dunkerque
Oostende
BELGIUM
Antwerpen
Rotterdam
HOLLAND
Amsterdam
Den Helder
Harlingen
Emden
Slack
Slack
06,10
06,10
02,04
06,11
07,12
08,14
04,08
03,05
03,06
04,07
09,16
06,11
07,13
07,13
12,22
15,27
08,15
08,14
11,20
09,17
08,15
07,13
11,19
09,16
07,13
08,15
07,12
08,15
05,09
04,08

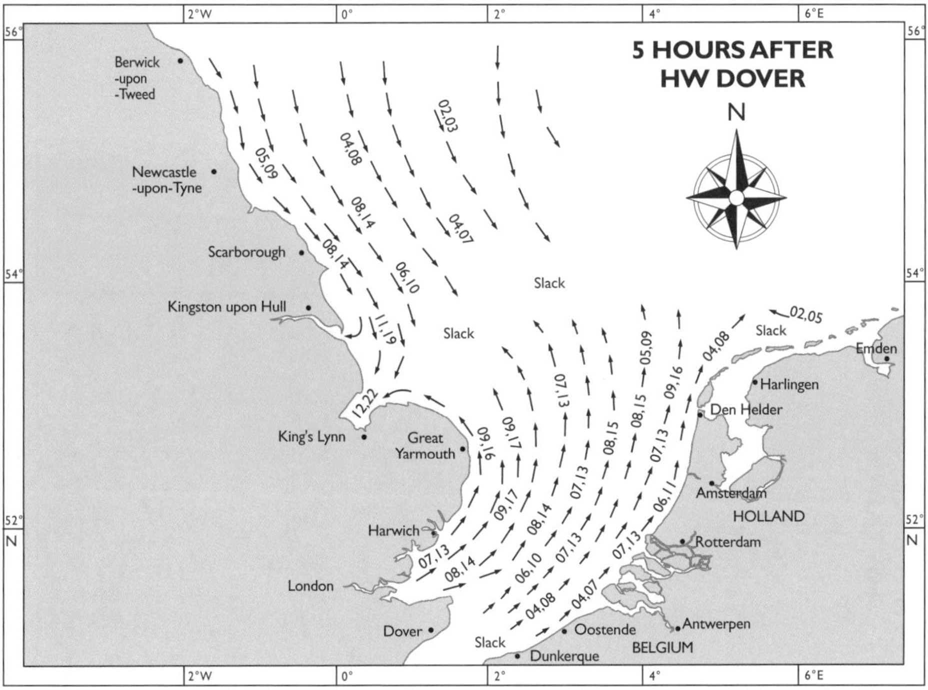
5 HOURS AFTER HW DOVER
N
2°W
0°
2°
4°
6°E
56°
54°
52°
N
Berwick -upon -Tweed
Newcastle -upon-Tyne
Scarborough
Kingston upon Hull
King's Lynn
Great Yarmouth
Harwich
London
Dover
Dunkerque
Oostende
Antwerpen
BELGIUM
Rotterdam
HOLLAND
Amsterdam
Den Helder
Harlingen
Emden
Slack
02,03
04,08
05,09
08,14
04,07
06,10
11,19
12,22
09,16
09,17
07,13
08,15
05,09
09,16
04,08
02,05
07,13
06,11
08,14
06,10
04,08
04,07

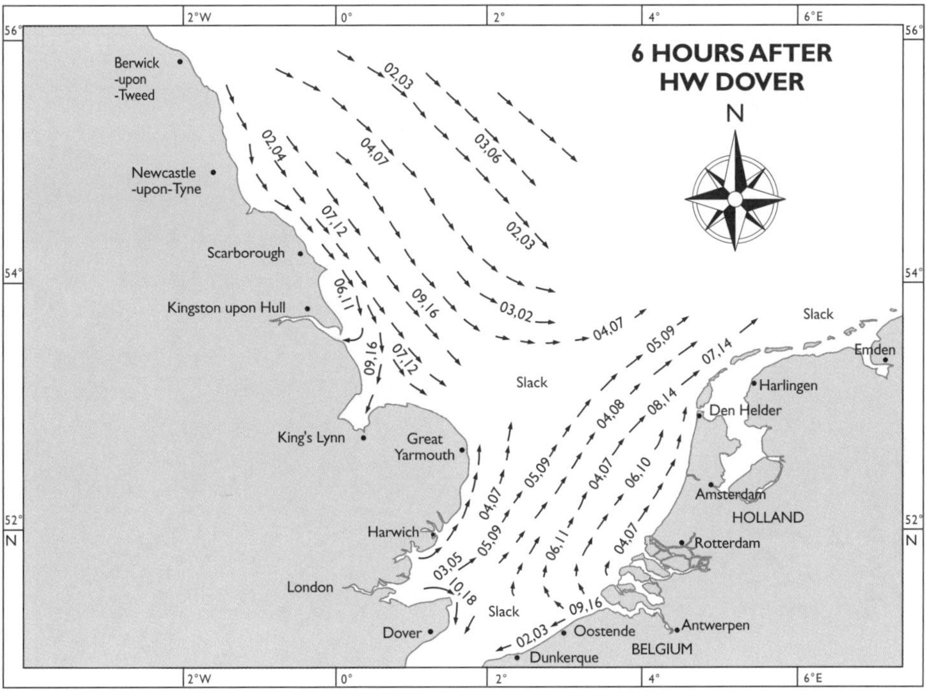
6 HOURS AFTER HW DOVER
N
2°W
0°
2°
4°
6°E
56°
54°
52°
N
Berwick -upon -Tweed
Newcastle -upon-Tyne
Scarborough
Kingston upon Hull
King's Lynn
Great Yarmouth
Harwich
London
Dover
Dunkerque
Oostende
Antwerpen
BELGIUM
Rotterdam
HOLLAND
Amsterdam
Den Helder
Harlingen
Emden
Slack
02,03
02,04
04,07
03,06
07,12
02,03
06,11
09,16
03,02
04,07
05,09
07,14
07,12
08,14
04,08
05,09
04,07
06,10
03,05
05,09
06,11
04,07
10,18
09,16
02,03

SCOTLAND

Example: ⟵10,18 predicts a westerly tidal flow of 1.0 knots at mean Neap tides and 1.8 knots at mean Spring tides at the location of the comma.

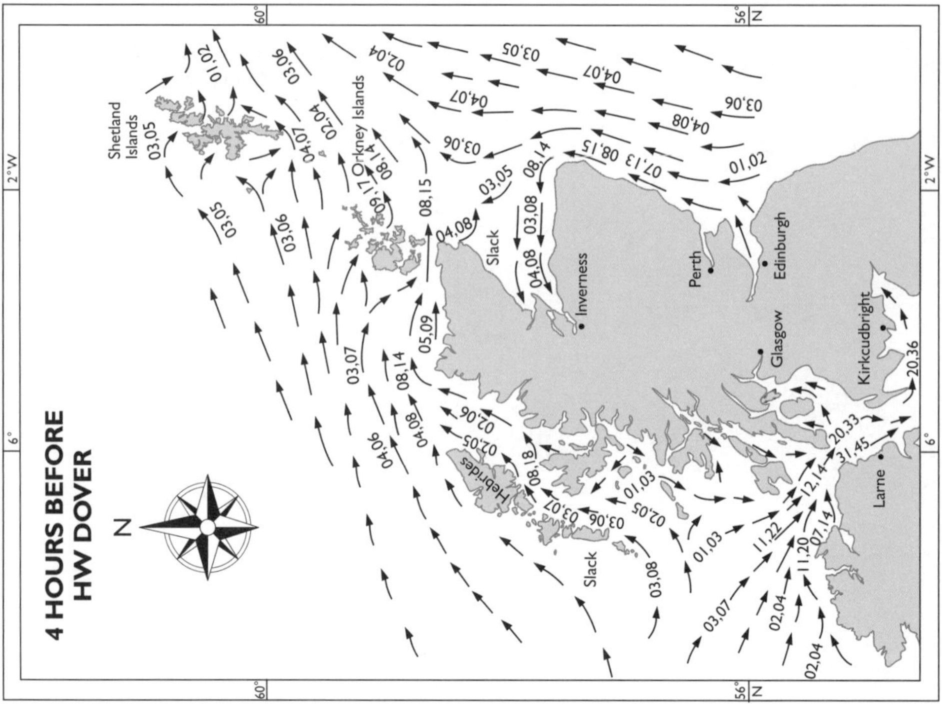

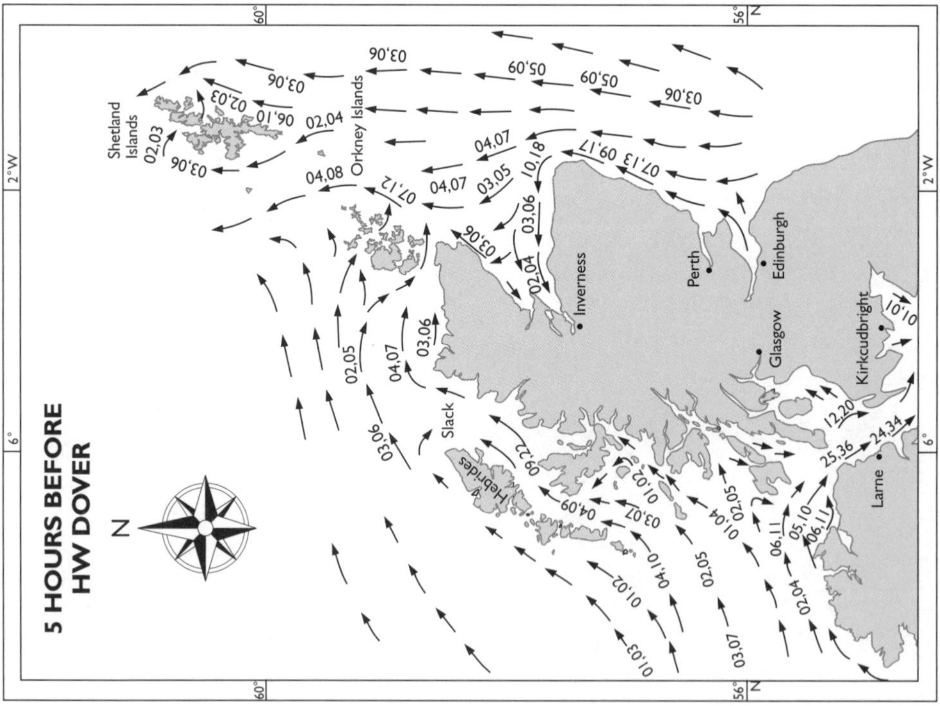

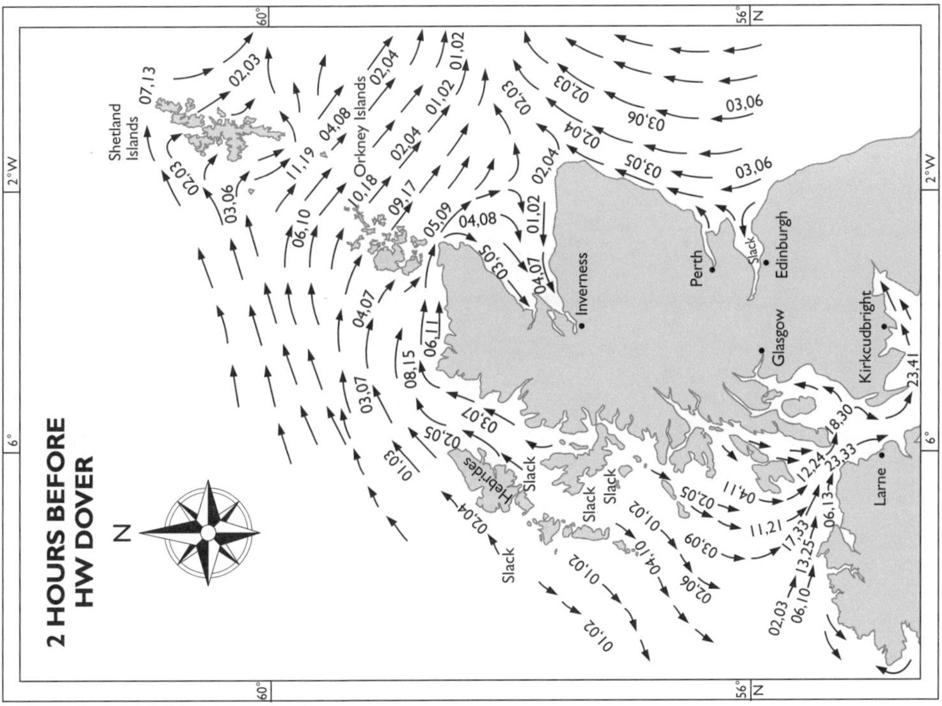
2 HOURS BEFORE
HW DOVER
N
Shetland Islands
Orkney Islands
Inverness
Perth
Edinburgh
Glasgow
Kirkcudbright
Larne
Hebrides
Slack
60°
56°N
2°W
6°

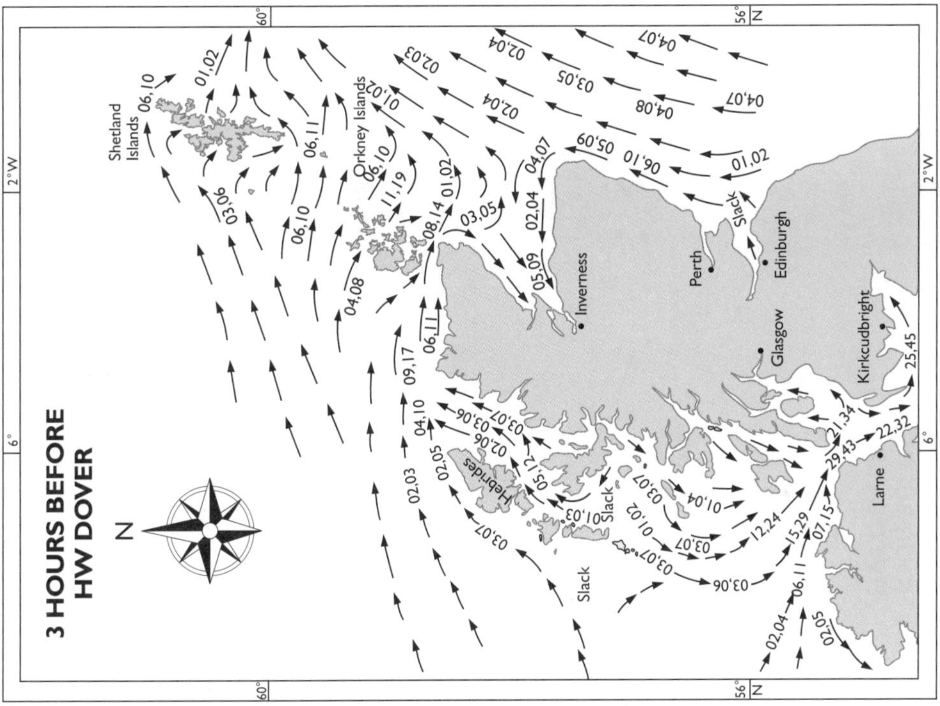
3 HOURS BEFORE
HW DOVER
N
Shetland Islands
Orkney Islands
Inverness
Perth
Edinburgh
Glasgow
Kirkcudbright
Larne
Hebrides
Slack
60°
56°N
2°W
6°

SCOTLAND

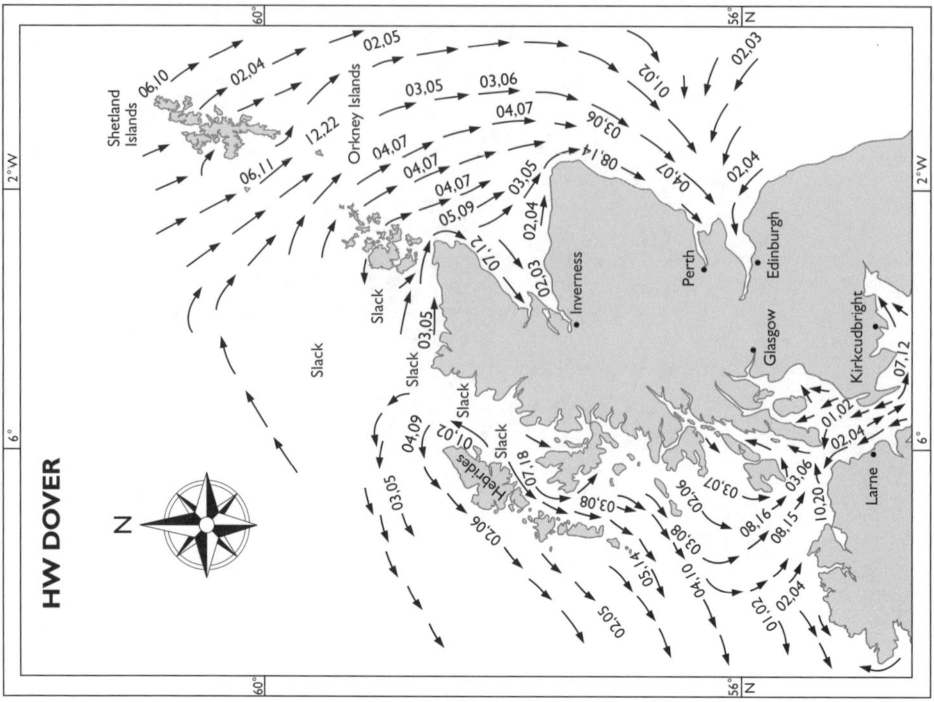
HW DOVER
Shetland Islands
Orkney Islands
Hebrides
Inverness
Perth
Edinburgh
Glasgow
Kirkcudbright
Larne
Slack
60°
56°N
2°W
6°

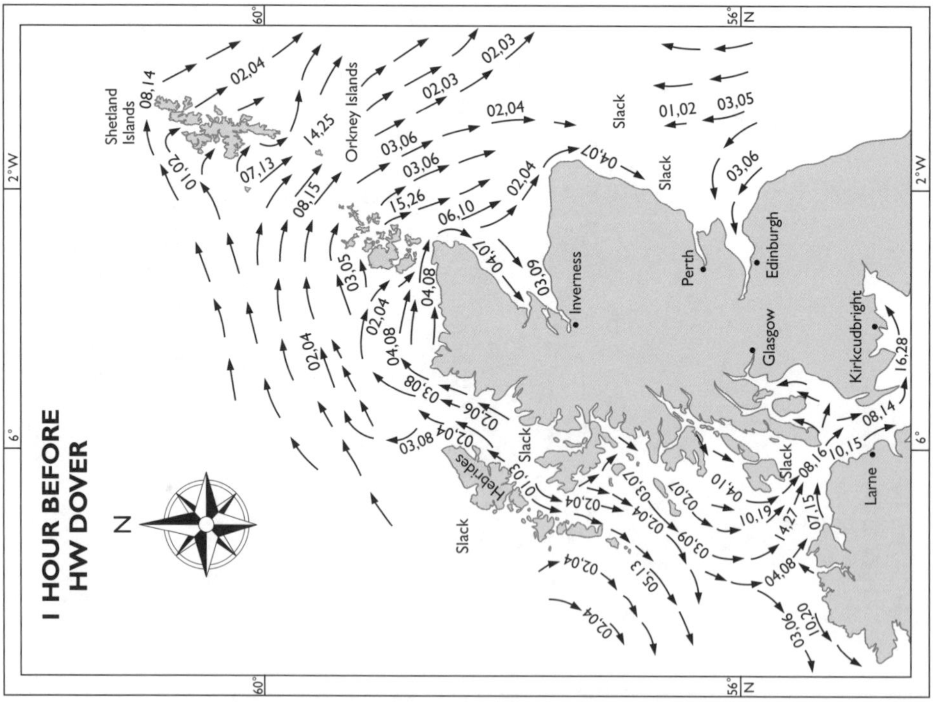
1 HOUR BEFORE HW DOVER
Shetland Islands
Orkney Islands
Hebrides
Inverness
Perth
Edinburgh
Glasgow
Kirkcudbright
Larne
Slack
60°
56°N
2°W
6°

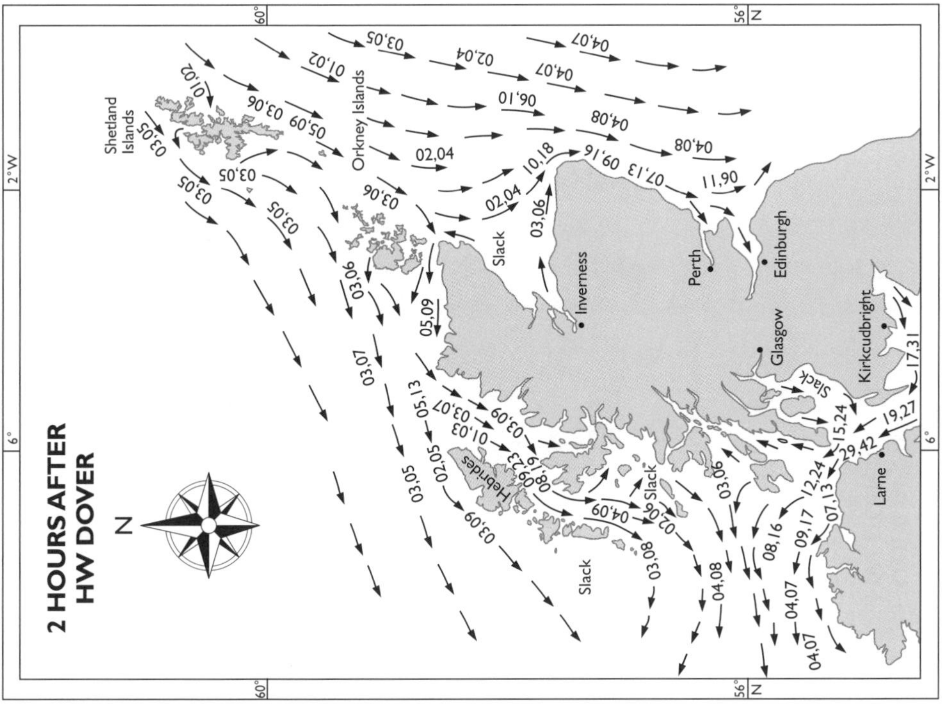
2 HOURS AFTER HW DOVER
N
Shetland Islands
Orkney Islands
Inverness
Perth
Edinburgh
Glasgow
Kirkcudbright
Larne
Hebrides
Slack
60°
56°N
2°W
6°

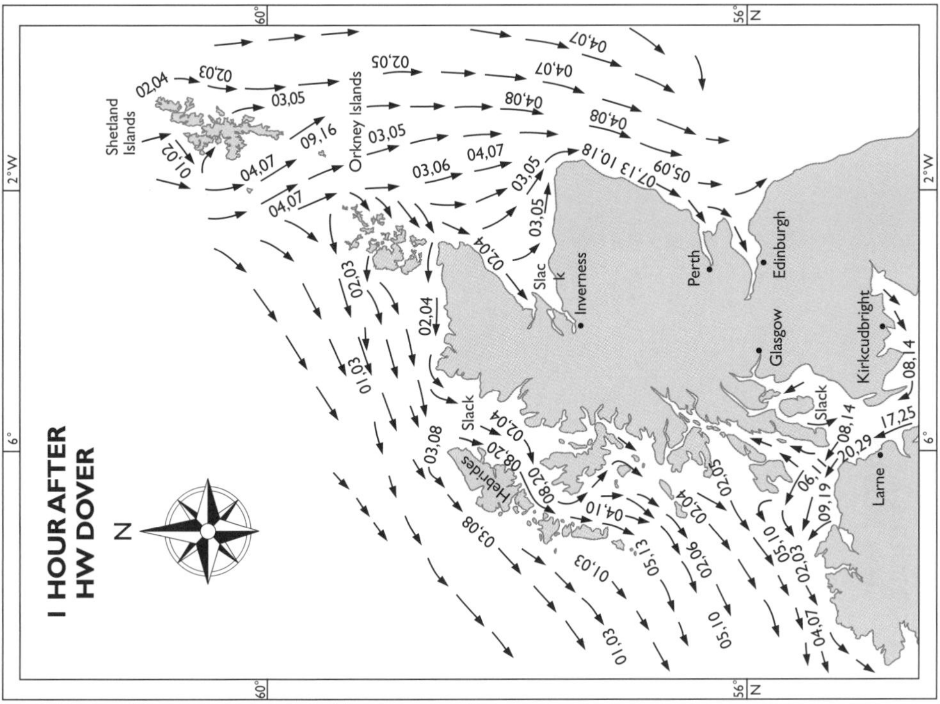
1 HOUR AFTER HW DOVER
N
Shetland Islands
Orkney Islands
Inverness
Perth
Edinburgh
Glasgow
Kirkcudbright
Larne
Hebrides
Slack
60°
56°N
2°W
6°

TIDES

SCOTLAND

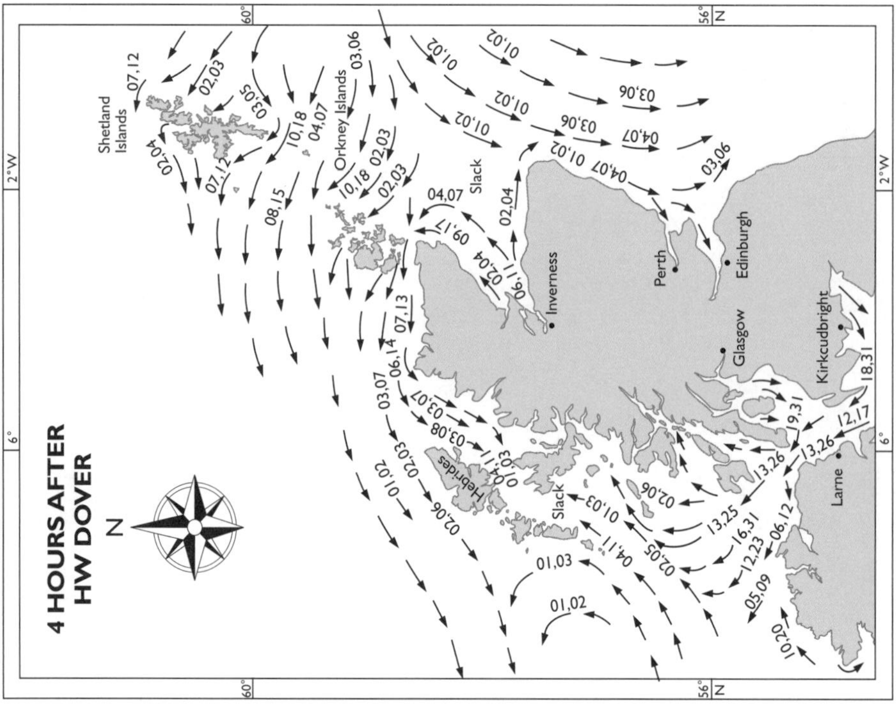
4 HOURS AFTER HW DOVER
N
Shetland Islands
Orkney Islands
Hebrides
Inverness
Perth
Edinburgh
Glasgow
Kirkcudbright
Larne
Slack
Slack
60°
56°N
2°W
6°

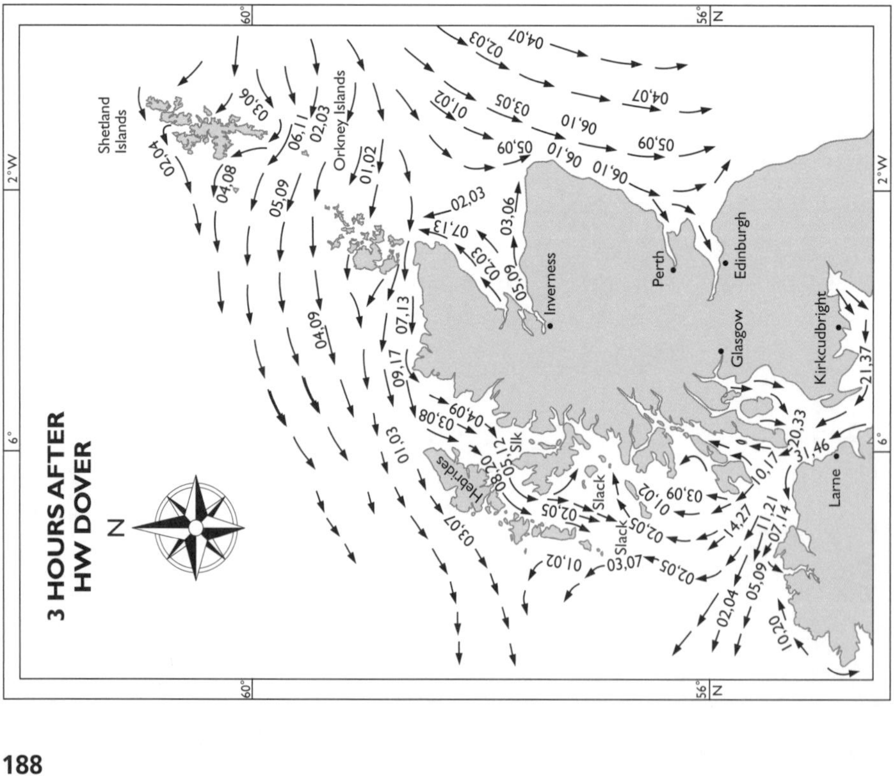
3 HOURS AFTER HW DOVER
N
Shetland Islands
Orkney Islands
Hebrides
Inverness
Perth
Edinburgh
Glasgow
Kirkcudbright
Larne
Slack
Slack
Slk
60°
56°N
2°W
6°

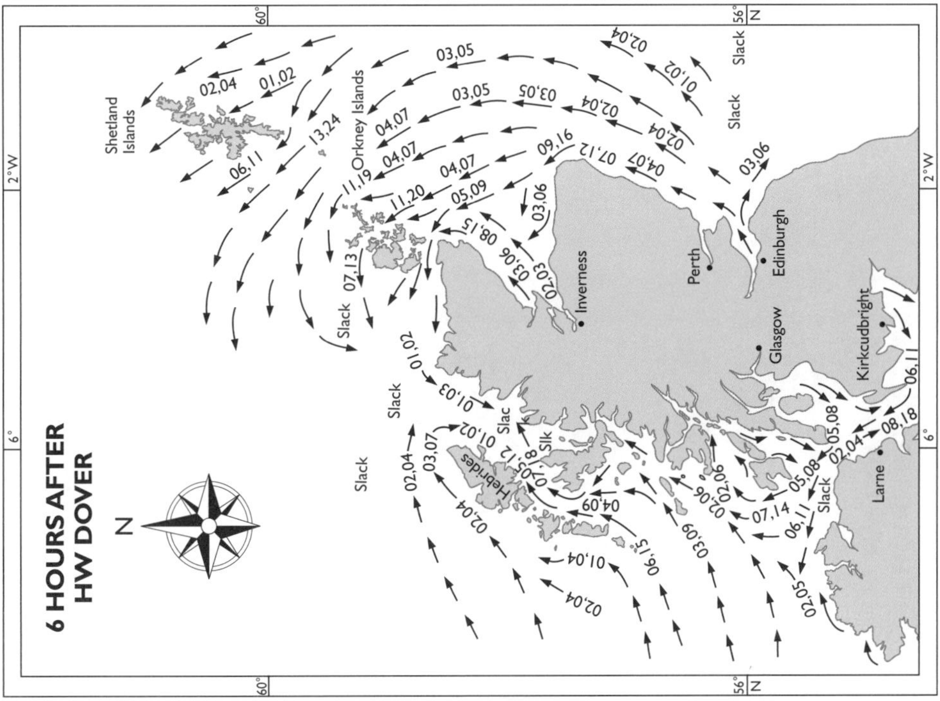
6 HOURS AFTER
HW DOVER
N
Shetland Islands
Orkney Islands
Inverness
Perth
Edinburgh
Glasgow
Kirkcudbright
Larne
Hebrides
Slack
60°
56° N
2°W
6°

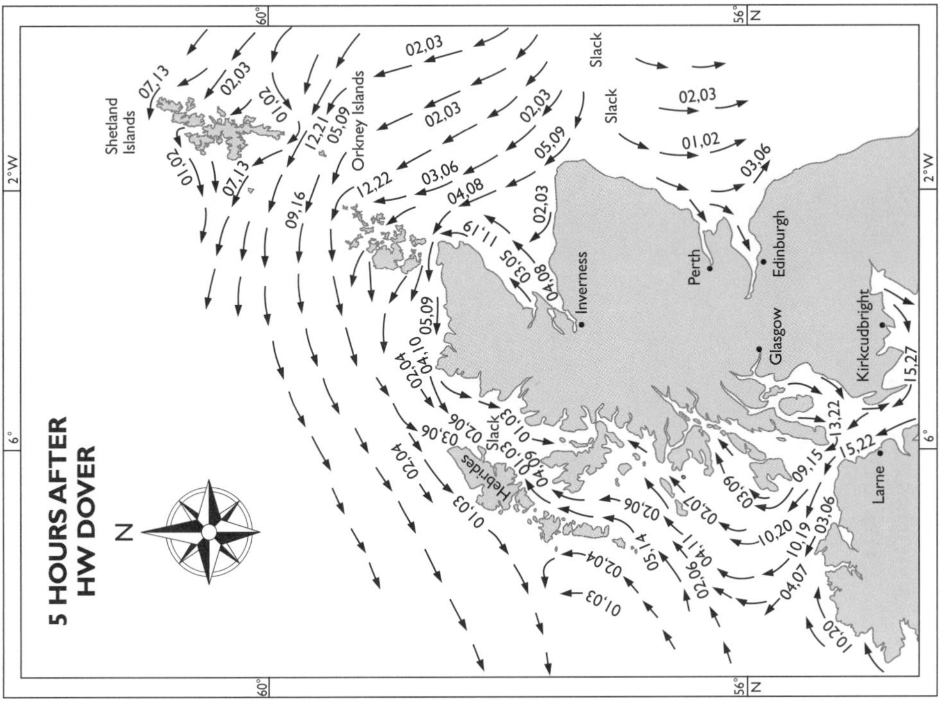
5 HOURS AFTER
HW DOVER
N
Shetland Islands
Orkney Islands
Inverness
Perth
Edinburgh
Glasgow
Kirkcudbright
Larne
Hebrides
Slack
60°
56° N
2°W
6°

TIDES

WEST UK AND IRELAND

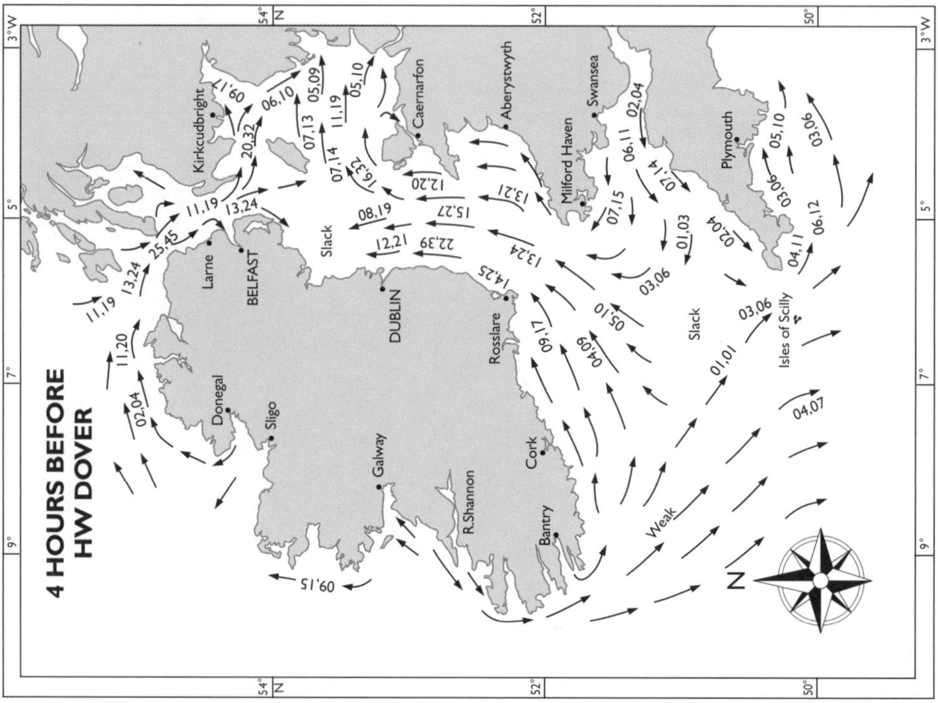

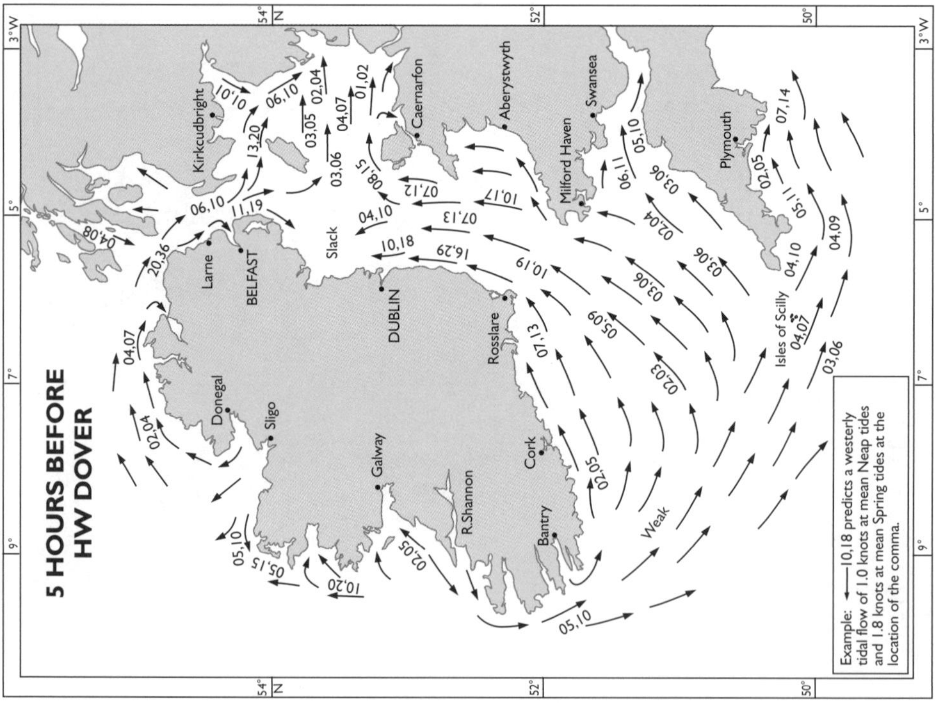

WEST UK AND IRELAND

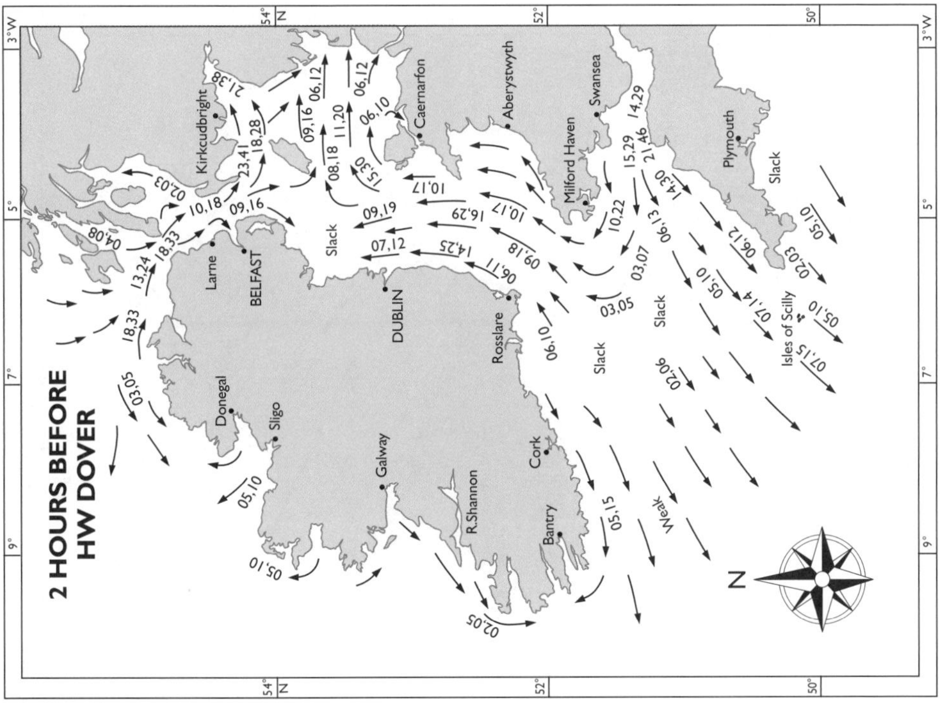

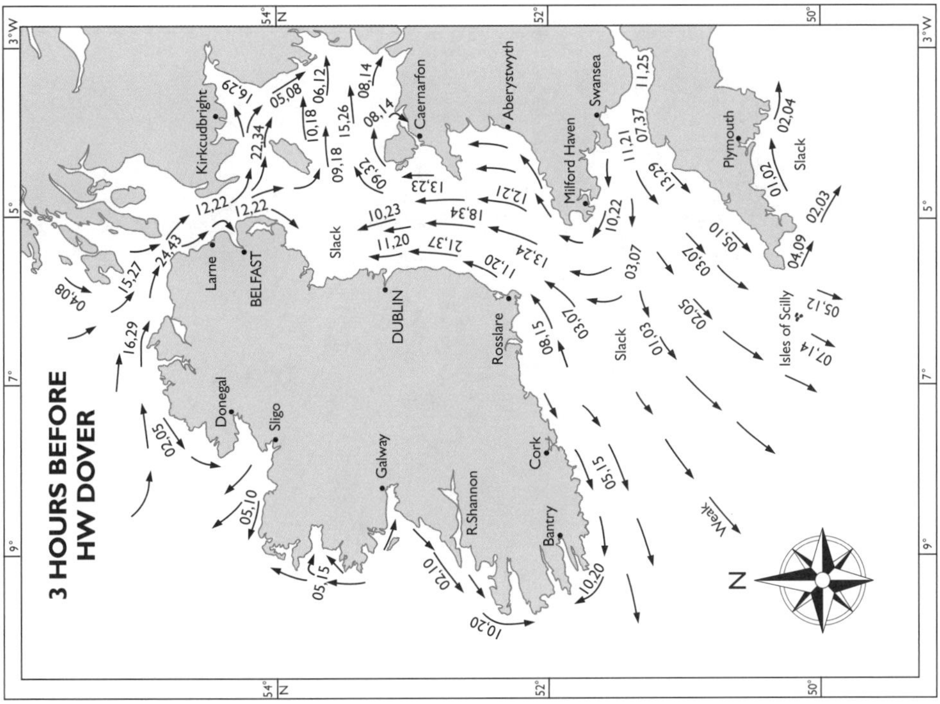

TIDES

WEST UK AND IRELAND

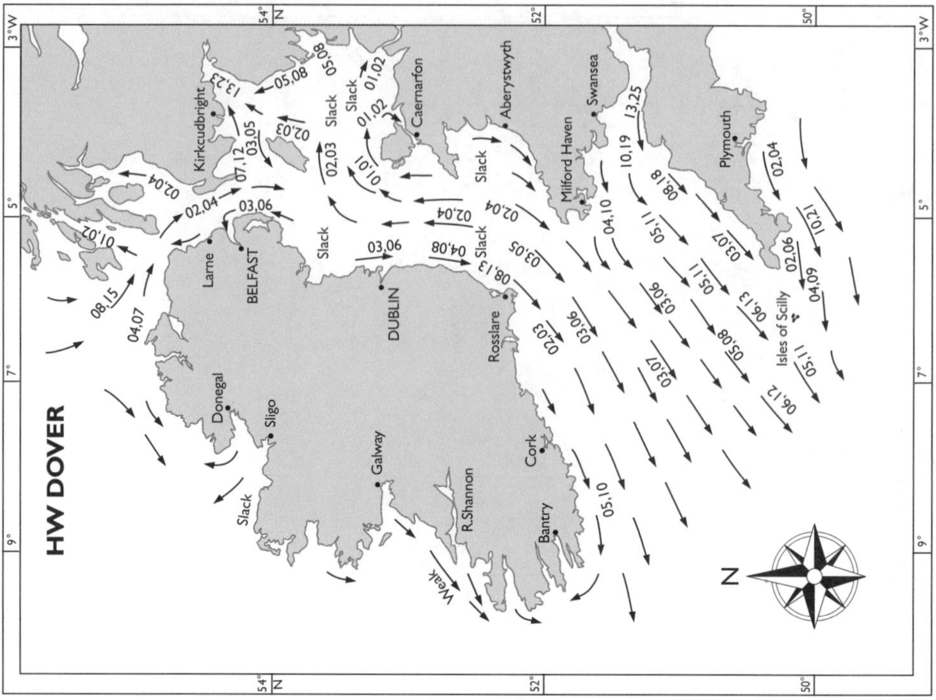

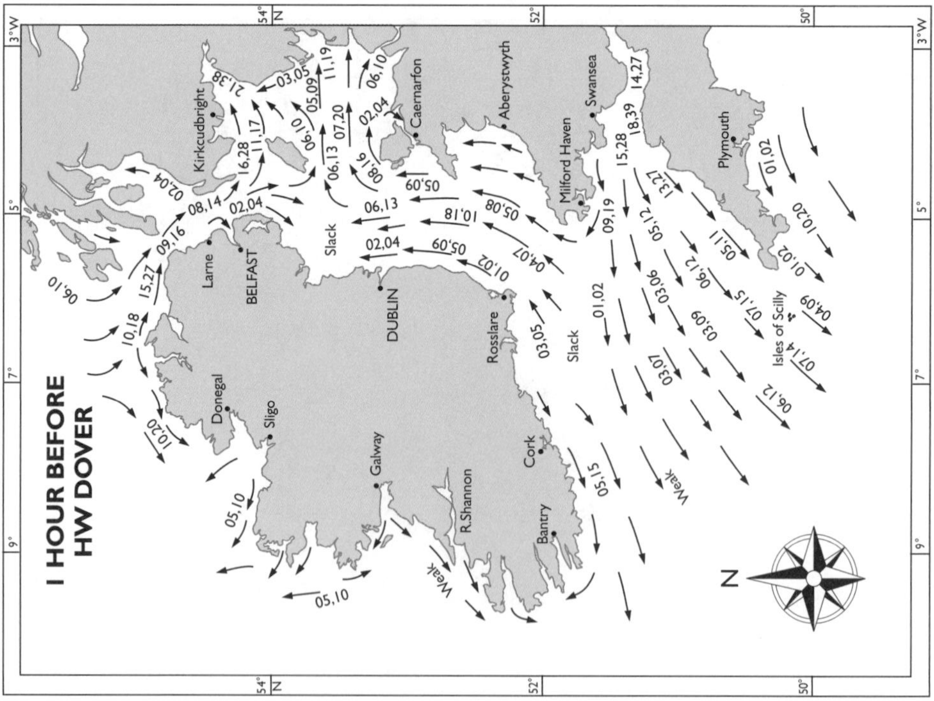

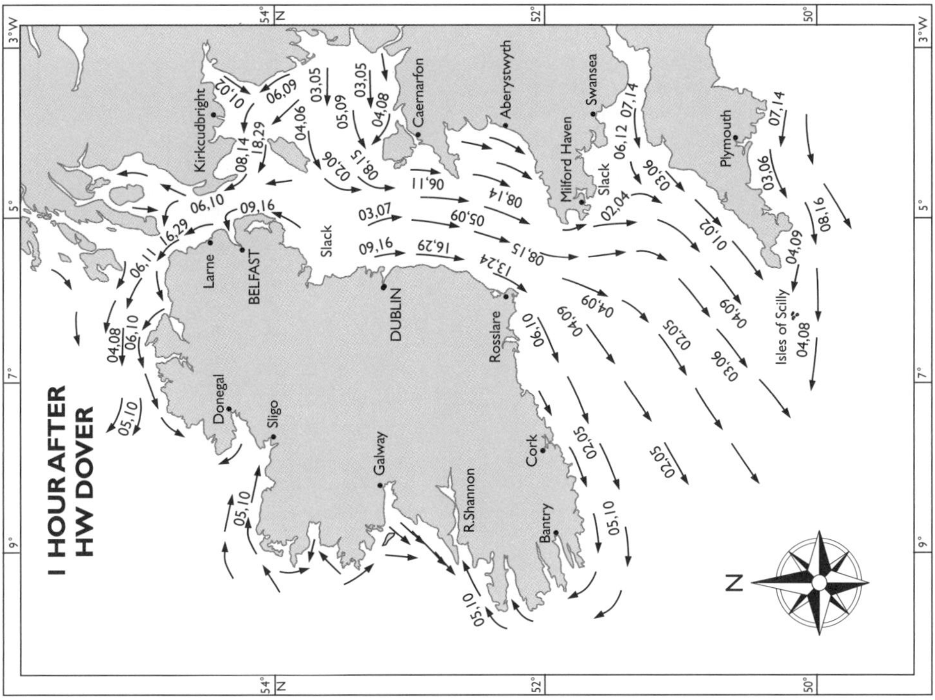
1 HOUR AFTER HW DOVER
Kirkcudbright
Larne
BELFAST
DUBLIN
Caernarfon
Aberystwyth
Milford Haven
Swansea
Plymouth
Rosslare
Isles of Scilly
Donegal
Sligo
Galway
R.Shannon
Cork
Bantry
Slack
N

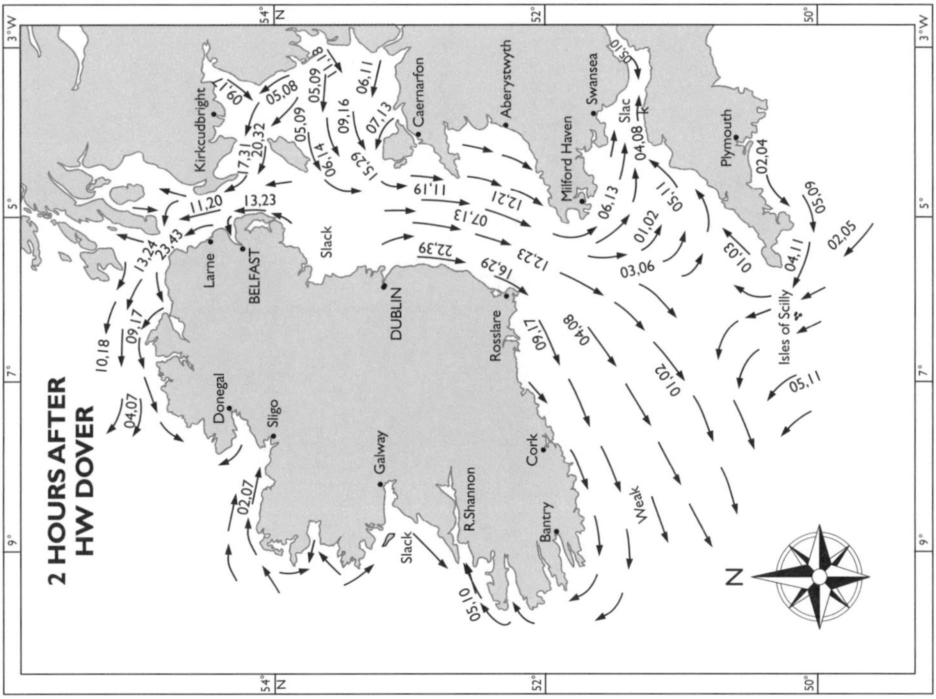
2 HOURS AFTER HW DOVER
Kirkcudbright
Larne
BELFAST
DUBLIN
Caernarfon
Aberystwyth
Milford Haven
Swansea
Plymouth
Rosslare
Isles of Scilly
Donegal
Sligo
Galway
R.Shannon
Cork
Bantry
Slack
Weak
N

TIDES

WEST UK AND IRELAND

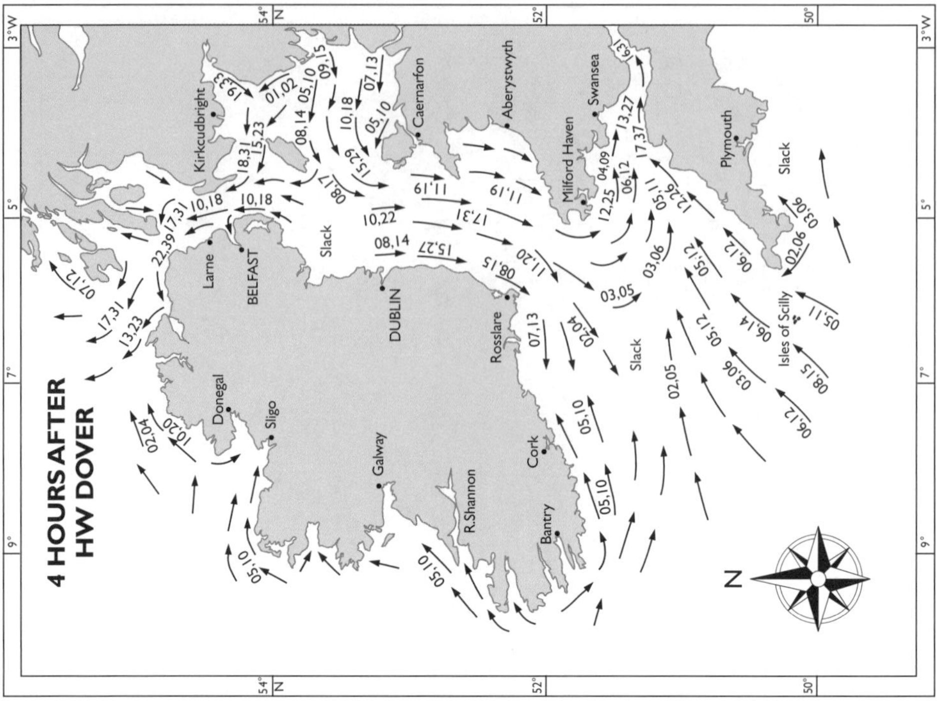

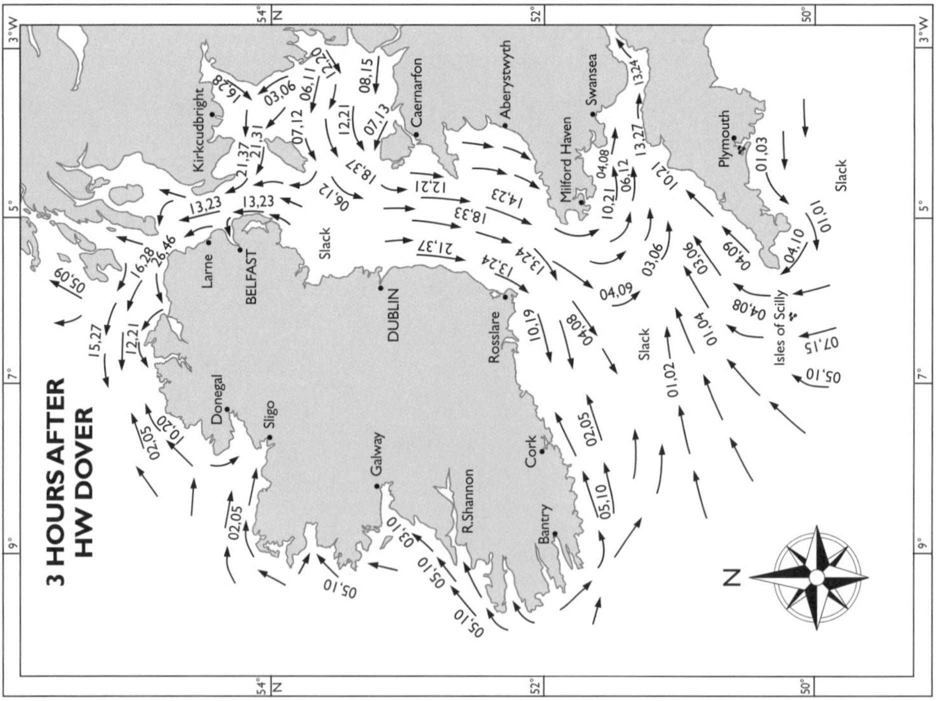

WEST UK AND IRELAND

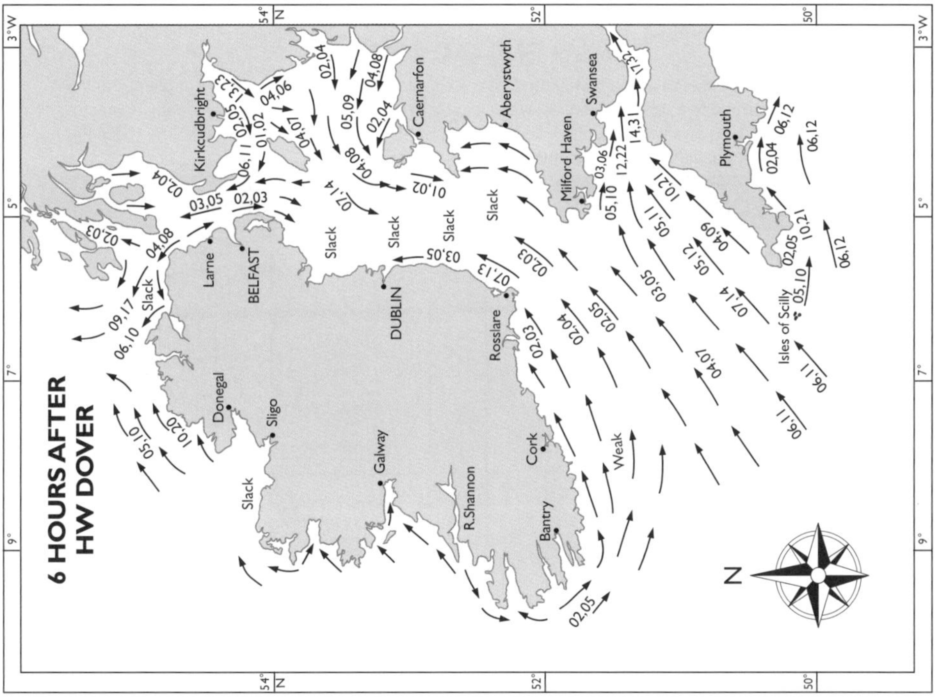

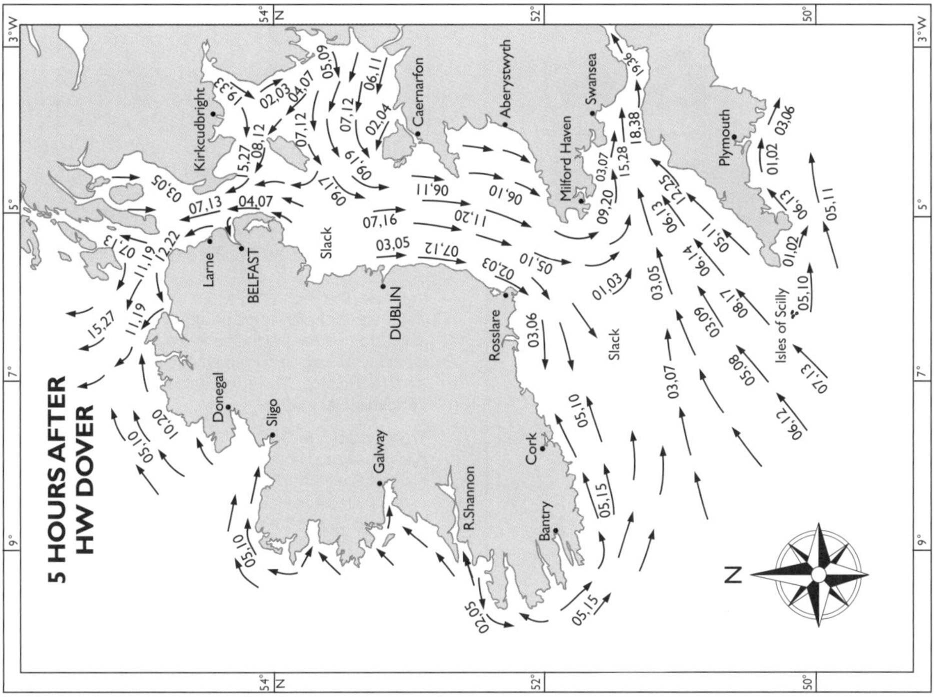

TIDES

TIDAL GATES – SOUTHERN ENGLAND

A guide to the time of tide turn at tidal gates, the approximate maximum strength of the tidal flow (spring rates shown - neaps are approximately 60% of these), and the position and timing of races, counter tides, etc.

LAND'S END (AC 1148)

Tidal streams set hard north/south round Land's End, and east/west around Gwennap and Pendeen. But the inshore currents run counter to the tidal streams. By staying close inshore, this tidal gate favours a N-bound passage. With careful timing nearly 9½hrs of fair tide can be carried, from HWD–3 to HWD+5. The chartlets, referenced to HW Dover, depict both tidal streams and inshore currents.

FLOOD

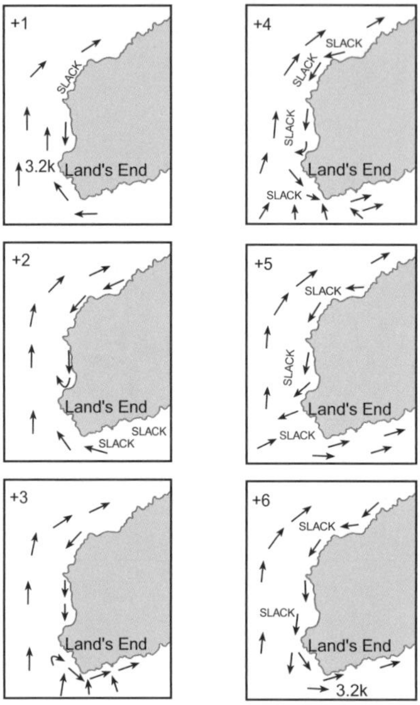

Example N-bound: At HWD+1 the N-going flood starts off Gwennap and does not turn NE along the N Cornish coast until HWD+3. But as early as HWD–3 an inshore current is beginning to set north. Utilise this by arriving off Runnel Stone at HWD–2 and then keeping within ¼M of the shore. If abeam the Brisons at HWD, the tide and current should serve for the next 6 or 7 hours to make good St Ives, or even Newquay and Padstow.

EBB

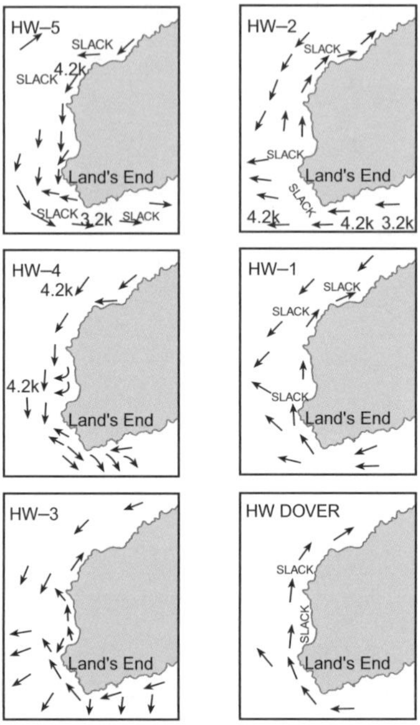

Example S-bound: If S-bound from St Ives to Newlyn, aim to reach the Runnel Stone by HWD+5, ie with 2hrs of E-going tide in hand for the remaining 9M to Newlyn. To achieve this 20M passage, leave St Ives 5 hours earlier, ie at HWD. Buck a foul tide for the first 3 hours, then use the S-going inshore current, keeping as close inshore as is prudent, only moving seaward to clear the Wra and the Brisons. This timing would also suit a passage from S Wales or the Bristol Channel, going inshore of Longships if conditions allow.

From Ireland, ie Cork or further W, the inshore passage would not benefit. But aim to be off the Runnel Stone at HWD+5 if bound for Newlyn; or at HWD+3 if bound for Helford/Falmouth, with the W-going stream slackening and 5hrs of fair tide to cover the remaining 20M past the Lizard.

With acknowledgements to the Royal Cruising Club Pilotage Foundation for their kind permission to use the tidal stream chartlets and text written by Hugh Davies, as first published in Yachting Monthly magazine.

TIDAL GATES – SOUTHERN ENGLAND

A guide to the time of tide turn at tidal gates, the approximate maximum strength of the tidal flow (spring rates shown - neaps are approximately 60% of these), and the position and timing of races, counter tides, etc.

FLOOD	EBB

THE LIZARD (AC 777, 2345)

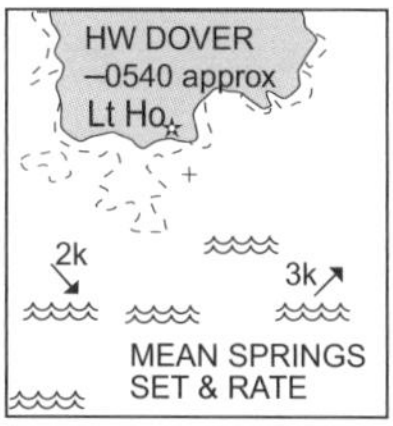

Drying rocks lie approx 5 cables S of the Lizard lt ho and extend westwards. 49°57'N is about as far N as yachts may safely pass inshore of the Race, which extends 2-3M to seaward of these rocks. Race conditions may also exist SE of the Lizard with short, heavy seas in westerlies. If passing S of the Race, route via 49°55'N 05°13'W to clear the worst of the Race.

Inshore the E-going Channel flood, 2kn max @ springs, begins at HW Dover +0145; and outside the Race at approx HWD +0300.

Inshore the W-going Channel ebb, 3kn max @ springs, begins at HW Dover –0345; and outside the Race at HWD –0240.

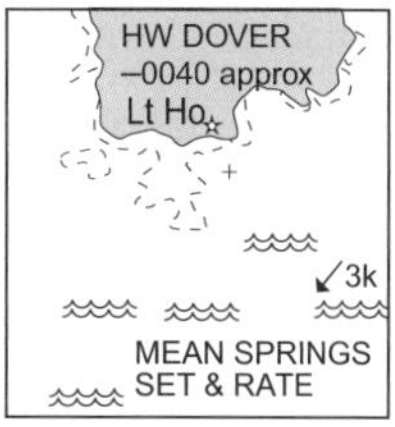

START POINT (AC 1634)

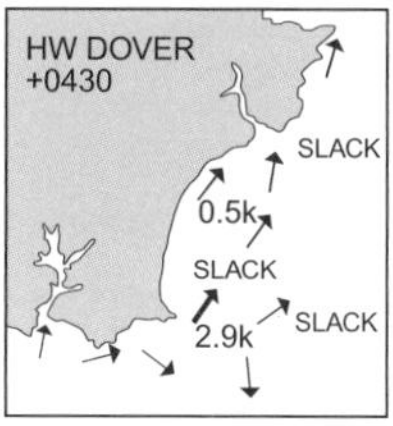

Start Pt, and to a lesser extent Prawle Pt (3.3M WSW), can be slow to round when W-bound with a fair tide against a W'ly wind raising a bad sea. Drying rocks extend 3 cables SSE of the lt ho and a Race may extend up to 1.7M ESE and 1.0M S of the lt ho. It is safe to pass between the Race and the rocks, but in bad weather wiser to go outside the Race. The Skerries Bank (least depth 2.1m) lies 8 cables NE of Start Pt. On both the flood and the ebb back eddies form between Start Pt and Hallsands, 1M NW.

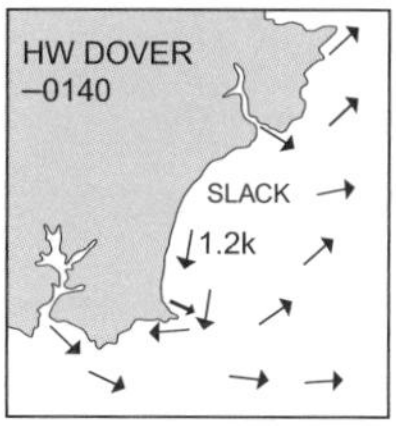

The NE-going Channel flood, 3.1kn max @ springs, begins at HW Dover +0430.

The SW-going Channel ebb, 2.2kn max @ springs, begins at HW Dover –0140, but an hour earlier it is possible to round Start Pt close inshore using the back eddy.

PORTLAND (AC 2255)

Tidal streams off Portland Bill run very strongly. The notorious Portland Race is caused by the almost constant strong southerly flow down both sides of the Bill meeting the main E and W-going streams in the English Channel. The violence of the race is increased by the sudden decrease in depth on Portland Ledge. The tidal stream chartlets on Pages 164–165 show that the race shifts to the E on the flood, and to the W on the ebb. Even in calm weather the race can be dangerous for small craft; in heavy weather or with wind against tide the whole area should be given a wide berth. In such conditions, pass at least 3 miles S of the Bill and do not pass between Portland and The Shambles bank.

In settled weather, with winds <F4/5, but not at springs nor with wind against tide, passage may be made very close S of the Bill in the narrow stretch of relatively smooth water N of the race. Night passage should not be attempted due to numerous fishing floats which may be semi-submerged.

Seaward of the race the Channel flood sets east from HW Plymouth -1 to HW +5; the ebb sets west from HW Plymouth +5 to HW -1.

Inshore passage

E-bound across Lyme Bay timing is critical to be close inshore about 2M north of the Bill by HW Plymouth –2 to achieve passage around the Bill between HW Plymouth –2 to HW+1.

W-bound timing is easier if starting from Portland Hbr, Weymouth or Lulworth Cove. Aim to be close inshore about 2M north of the Bill at HW Plymouth +4, and make the passage between HW Plymouth +5 and HW–5.

When using the inshore passage be particularly wary of being set S into the race itself.

ST ALBAN'S HEAD (AC 2610)

A sometimes vicious Race forms over St Alban's Ledge, a rocky dorsal ridge (least depth 8.5m) which extends approx 4M SW from St Alban's Head. Three yellow naval target buoys (DZ A, B and C) straddle the middle and outer sections, but are only occasionally used. In settled weather and at neaps the Race may be barely perceptible in which case it can be crossed with impunity. Avoid it either by keeping to seaward via 50°31'.40N 02°07'.80W; or by using the narrow inshore passage at the foot of St Alban's Head.

Based on a position 1M S of St Alban's Head, the tidal stream windows are:

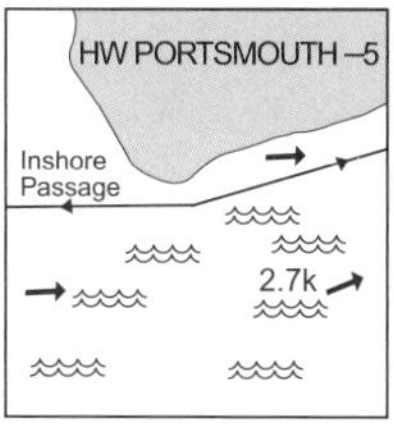

ESE-going stream starts at HW Portsmouth +0530. Spring rates are the same, max 4kn. Along the W side of St Alban's Head the stream runs almost continuously SE due to a back eddy.

WNW-going stream starts at HW Portsmouth. Overfalls extend 2.5M further SW than on the E-going stream and are more dangerous to small craft. Slack water lasts barely half an hour.

The inshore passage lies as close to the foot of St Alban's Head as feels comfortable. It may be hard to see the width of clear water in the inshore passage until committed to it, but except in onshore gales when it is better to stay offshore, the passage will be swiftly made with only a few, if any, overfalls. The NCI station on the Head (☎ 01929 439220) may advise on conditions.

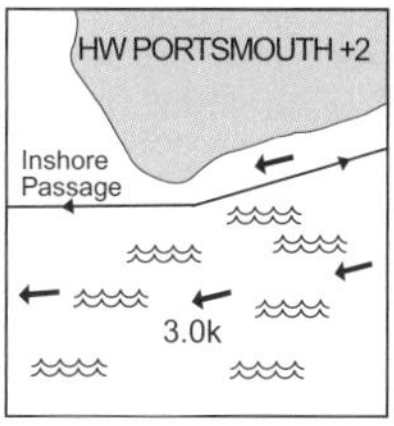

TIDAL GATES – SOUTHERN ENGLAND

A guide to the time of tide turn at tidal gates, the approximate maximum strength of the tidal flow (spring rates shown - neaps are approximately 60% of these), and the position and timing of races, counter tides, etc.

FLOOD	EBB

THE NEEDLES CHANNEL (AC 2035)

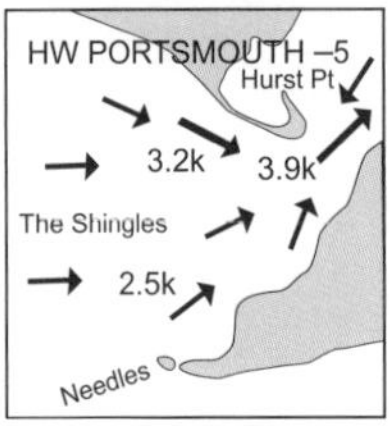

The Needles Channel lies between the SW Shingles PHM buoy and the Bridge WCM buoy. Once through this narrow section the channel widens with the Island shore to starboard and the long, drying 1.2m, Shingles bank to port. Abeam Hurst Castle the channel again narrows (assisted by The Trap, a shoal spit south of Hurst Castle) before opening out into the west Solent.

Study carefully the hourly tidal stream chartlets for the Isle of Wight on pp.166-171 and the values shown on AC 2035 at tidal diamonds B, C, D and E.

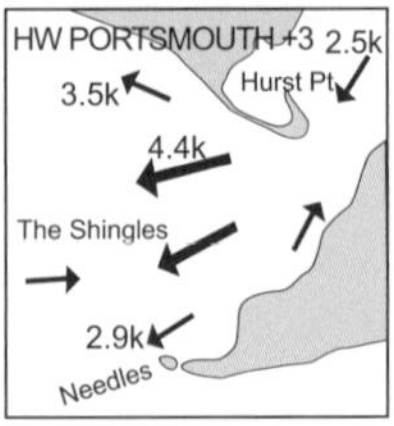

The ENE-going flood runs from HW Portsmouth +5 until HW P –1½, at springs reaching 3.1kn at The Bridge and 3.9kn at Hurst.

The WSW-going ebb runs from HW P –1 until HW P +4½, reaching 4.4kn at Hurst and 3.4kn at The Bridge, both spring rates. The ebb sets strongly WSW across the Shingles which with adequate rise is routinely crossed by racing yachts; but cruisers should stay clear even in calm conditions when any swell causes the sea to break heavily.

Prevailing W/SW winds, even if only F4, against the ebb raise dangerous breaking seas in the Needles Channel and at The Bridge, a shallow ridge extending 9 cables west from the Needles light. Worst conditions are often found just after LW slack. In such conditions it is safer to go via the North Channel to Hurst. In W/SW gales avoid the Needles altogether by sheltering at Poole or going east-about via Nab Tower.

ON PASSAGE UP CHANNEL

The following 3 tidal gates (Looe Channel, Beachy Head and Dungeness) are components in the tidal conveyor belt which, if stepped onto at the outset, can enable a fastish yacht to carry a fair tide for 88M from Selsey Bill to Dover.
Go through the Looe at slackish water, HW Portsmouth +4½ (HW Dover +5). Based on a mean SOG of 7 knots, Beachy Head will be passed at HW D –1, Dungeness at HW D +3 and Dover at HW +5½, only bucking the first of the ebb in the last hour. A faster boat could make Ramsgate. The down-Channel passage is less rewarding and many yachts will pause at Brighton.

LOOE CHANNEL (AC 2045, 1652)

This channel is little shorter than the detour south of the Owers, but is much used by yachts on passage from/to points east of the Solent. Although adequately lit, it is best not attempted at night due to many lobster floats; nor in onshore gales as searoom is limited by extensive shoals on which the sea breaks.

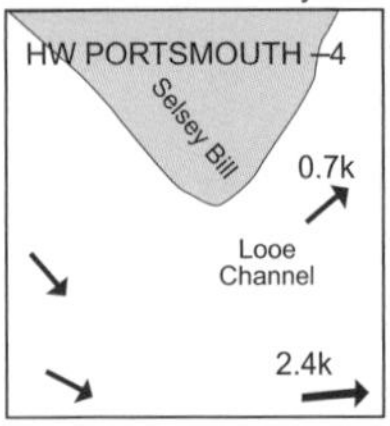

The E-going flood runs from HW Portsmouth +4½ (HW Dover +5) until HW P –1½ (HW D –1), at springs reaching 2.4kn near the Boulder and Street light buoys which mark its narrow western end; they may be hard to see in other than good visibility. Max neap rate is 1.2kn.

The W-going ebb runs from HW P –1½(HW D –1) until HW P +4½ (HW D +5), at springs reaching 2.6kn near Boulder and Street. Max neap rate is 1.3kn.

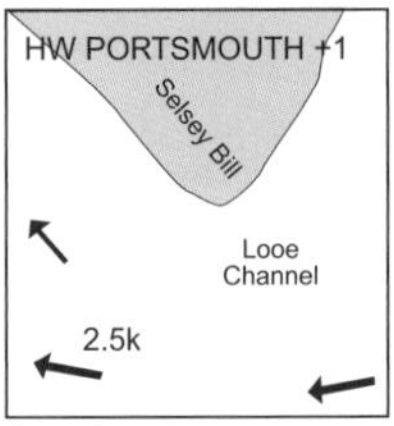

At the wider eastern end of the channel (near E Borough Head buoy) rates are greatly reduced.

BEACHY HEAD (AC 1652, 536)

Stay at least 5 cables to seaward of the towering chalk cliffs to avoid isolated boulders and rocky, part-drying ridges such as Head Ledge. The lt ho stands on a drying rock ledge. Close inshore many fishing floats are a trap for the unwary. In bad weather stay 2M offshore to avoid overfalls caused by a ridge of uneven ground which extends 1M SSE from Beachy Head.

2M south of Beachy Head the E-going flood starts at HW Dover -0530, max spring rate 2.6kn.

The W-going ebb starts at HW Dover +0030, max spring rate 2.0kn.

Between 5M and 7M east of Beachy Head avoid breakers and eddies caused by the Horse of Willingdon, Royal Sovereign and other shoals.

DUNGENESS (AC 536, 1892)

Tidal stream atlases: Dungeness is on the east and west edges respectively of NP 250 (English Channel) and NP 233 (Dover Strait). The nearest tidal stream diamond (2.2M SE of Dungeness) is 'H' on AC 536 and 'B' on AC 1892; their positions and values are the same.

The NE-going flood starts at HW Dover –0100, max spring rate 1.9kn.

The SW-going ebb starts at HW Dover +0430, max spring rate 2.1kn.

TIDAL GATES – NORTH EAST SCOTLAND

A guide to the time of tide turn at tidal gates, and in straits and estuaries, showing the approximate strength of the tidal flow (spring rates shown - neaps are approximately 60% of these), and the pos ition and timing of races, counter tides etc.

FLOOD	EBB

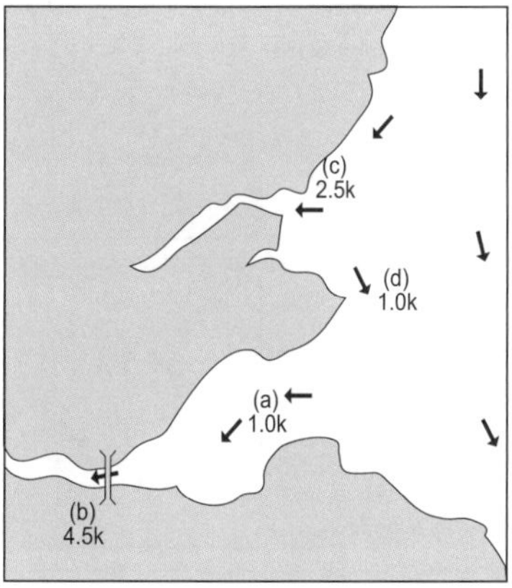

FIRTHS of FORTH (AC 175) & TAY (AC 1481)

Tidal streams are quite weak in the outer partof the Firth, increasing as the narrows at islands and the bridges are approached.

Apart from the stream of the Tay, which attains 5 knots in most places, the coastwise tidal streams between Fife Ness and Arbroath are weak.

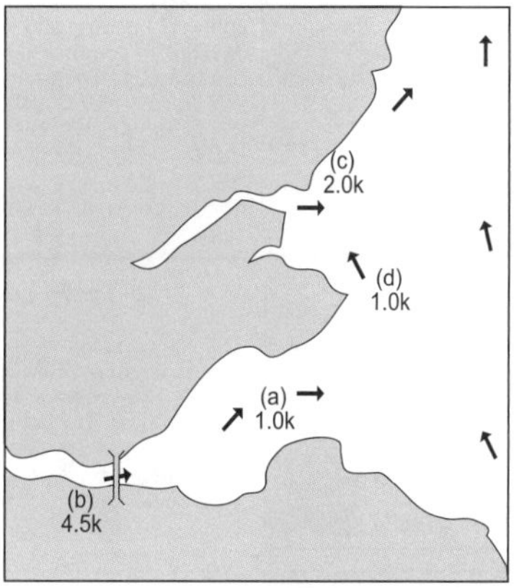

(a) Dover –0225 to Dover +0330
(b) Dover –0200 to Dover +0400
(c) Dover –0210 to Dover +0420
(d) Dover –0110 to Dover +0520

(a) Dover +0330 to Dover –0225
(b) Dover +0400 to Dover –0200
(c) Dover +0420 to Dover –0210
(d) Dover +0520 to Dover –0110

PASSAGES FROM FORTH & TAY

Northbound. Leave before HW (Dover +0400) to be at N Carr at Dover +0600. Bound from Forth to Tay aim to arrive at Abertay By at LW slack (Dover –0200).

Southbound. Leave before LW (Dover -0200) to be at Bass Rk at HW Dover. Similar timings if bound from Tay to Forth, leave late in ebb to pick up early flood off St Andrews to N Carr and into Forth.

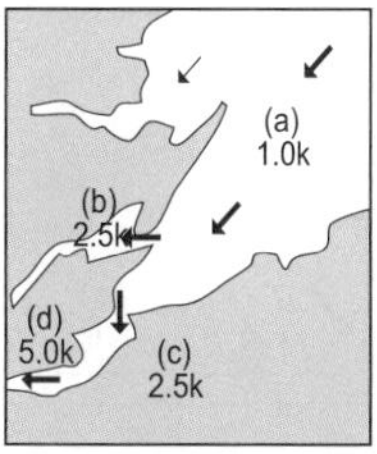

INVERNESS & CROMARTY FIRTHS (AC 1077)

Tidal streams in the Inverness Firth and approaches are not strong, except in the Cromarty Firth Narrows, the Fort George Narrows and the Kessock Road, including off the entrance to the Caledonian Canal.

Flood	Ebb
(a) Dover –0555 to Dover +0030	(a) Dover +0030 to Dover –0555
(b) Dover –0400 to Dover +0115	(b) Dover +0115 to Dover –0400
(c) Dover –0400 to Dover HW	(c) Dover +0115 to Dover –0525
(d) Dover –0430 to Dover +0100	(d) Dover +0130 to Dover +0545

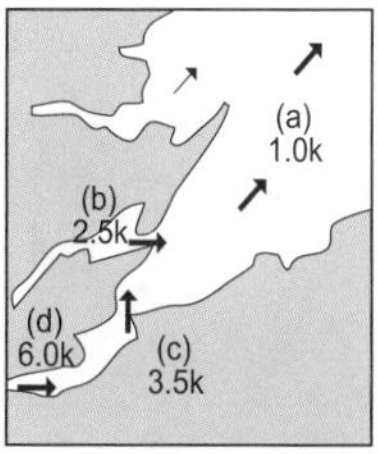

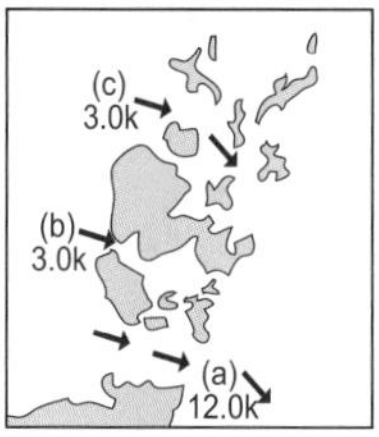

PENTLAND FIRTH & ORKNEYS (AC 1954)

The tide flows strongly around and through the Orkney Islands. The Pentland Firth is a dangerous area for all craft, tidal flows reach 12 knots between Duncansby Head and S Ronaldsay. W of Dunnet Hd & Hoy is less violent. There is little tide within Scapa Flow.

Flood	Ebb
(a) Dover –0500 to Dover +0100	(a) Dover +0115 to Dover –0535
(b) Dover +0530 to Dover –0110	(b) Dover –0110 to Dover +0530
(c) Dover –0530 to Dover +0040	(c) Dover +0040 to Dover –0530

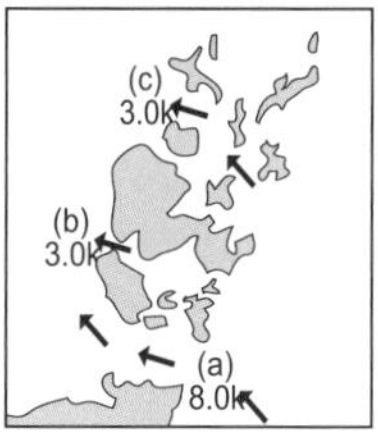

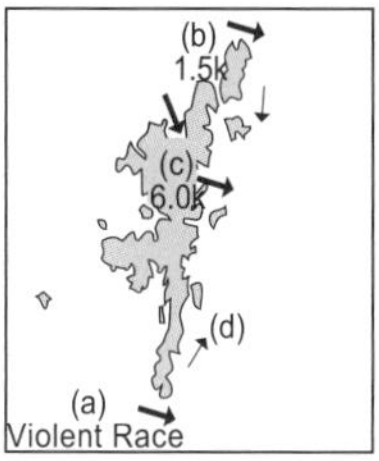

SHETLAND ISLANDS (AC 219)

The tidal flow around the Shetland Islands rotates as the cycle progresses. When the flood begins, at –0400 HW Dover, the tidal flow is to the E, at HW Dover it is S, at Dover +0300 it is W, and at –0600 Dover it is N.

Flood	Ebb
(a) Dover –0410 to Dover +0020	(a) Dover +0050 to Dover –0410
(b) Dover –0400 to Dover +0030	(b) Dover +0130 to Dover –0500
(c) Dover –0530 to Dover +0100	(c) Dover +0100 to Dover –0530
(d) Dover –0400 to Dover –0200	(d) Dover +0200 to Dover +0500

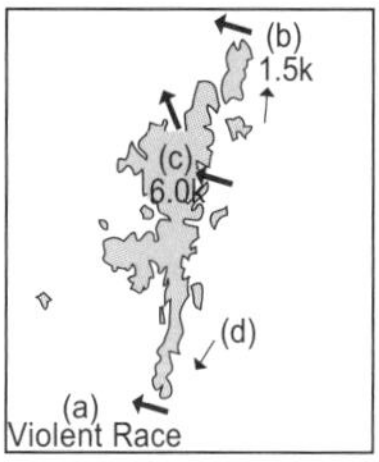

TIDAL GATES – NORTH WEST SCOTLAND

A guide to the time of tide turn at tidal gates, the approximate maximum strength of the tidal flow (spring rates shown – neaps are approximately 60% of these), and the position and timing of races, counter tides, etc.

FLOOD	EBB

SOUND OF HARRIS (AC 2802)

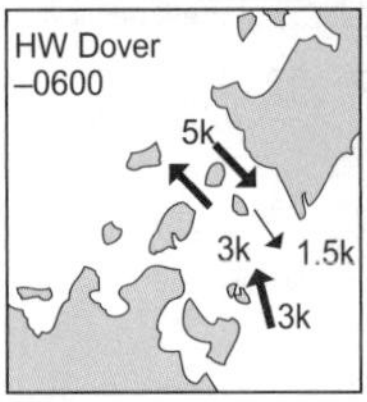

The behaviour of tidal streams in the Sd of Harris varies from day to night, springs to neaps, and winter to summer. The following data applies to daylight, in summer at spring tides in the Cope Channel. Further information can be sought in the Admiralty West of Scotland Pilot.
HW Dover - HW D +0200: SE stream.
HW D +0300 - HW D +0600: Incoming stream from both ends.
HW D –0600 - HW D –0500: NW stream.
HW D –0500 - HW Dover: Outgoing stream from both ends.
At neaps in summer the stream will run SE for most of the day.
Tide rates shown are the maxima likely to be encountered at any time.

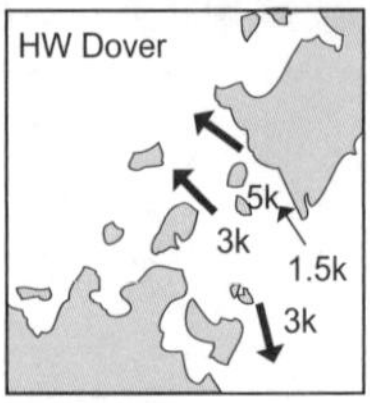

THE LITTLE MINCH (AC 1795)

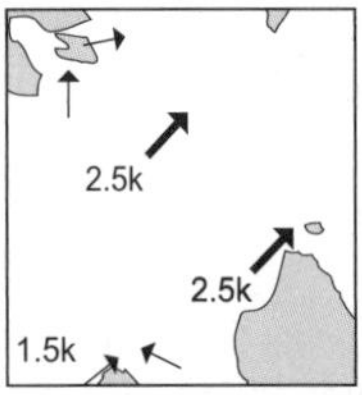

The N going stream on both shores begins at HW Dover +0430 (HW Ullapool -0345), with the strongest flow from mid channel to the Skye coast. There is a W going counter tide E of Vaternish Point.

The S going stream on both shores begins at HW Dover –0130 (HW Ullapool +0240), with the strongest flow from mid channel to the Skye coast. The E going stream in Sound of Scalpay runs at up to 2k.The E going flood and W going ebb in Sound of Scalpay run at up to 2k.

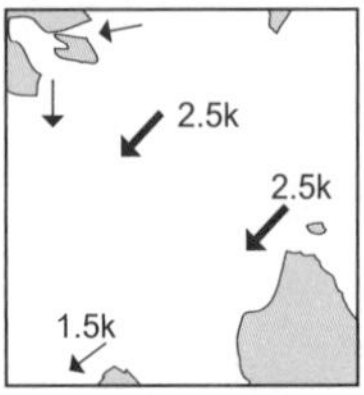

KYLE OF LOCHALSH & KYLERHEA (AC 2540)

NOTE: THESE STREAMS ARE SUBJECT TO VARIATION

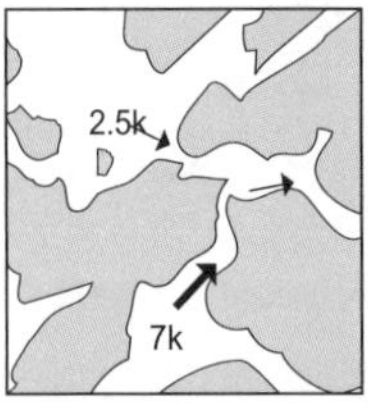

N going stream in Kyle Rhea begins HW Dover +0140 (HW Ullapool +0555) and runs for 6 hours. The E going stream in Kyle Akin begins (Sp) HW Dover +0350 (HW Ullapool –0415). (Nps) HW Dover –0415 (HW Ullapool).

S going stream in Kyle Rhea begins HW Dover -0415 (HW Ullapool) and runs for 6 hours. The W going stream in Kyle Akin begins (Sp) HW Dover –0015 (HW Ullapool +0400). (Nps) HW Dover +0140 (HW Ullapool +0555).

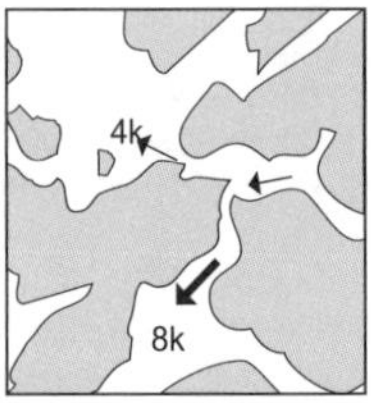

ARDNAMURCHAN POINT (AC 2171)

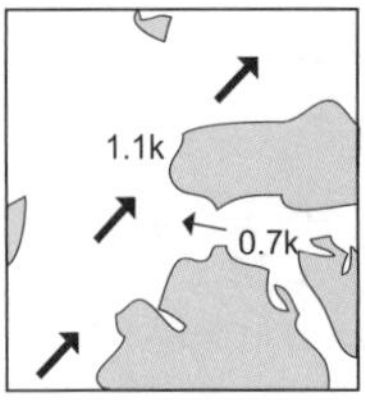

The N going stream off Ardnamurchan begins at HW Dover +0130 (HW Oban –0525). The E going stream in the Sound of Mull begins at HW Dover +0555 (HW Oban –0100).

The S going stream off Ardnamurchan begins at HW Dover –0430 (HW Oban +0100). The W going stream in the Sound of Mull begins at HW Dover –0130 (HW Oban +0400).

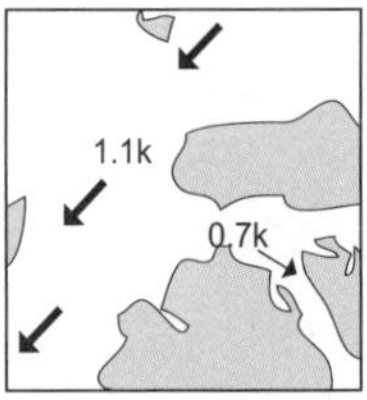

SOUND OF MULL – EAST (AC 2171)

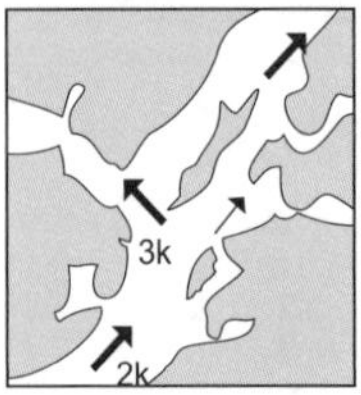

The N going stream in the Firth of Lorne begins at HW Dover –0100 (HW Oban +0430). The W going stream in the Sound of Mull begins at HW Dover +0105 (HW Oban –0550). The ingoing tides at Lochs Feochan, Etive and Creran begin at HW Dover +0300, –0100 & +0030.

The S going stream in the Firth of Lorne begins at HW Dover +0500 (HW Oban –0155). The E going stream in the Sound of Mull begins at HW Dover +0555 (HW Oban –0025). The outgoing tides at Lochs Feochan, Etive and Creran begin at HW Dover –0500, –0520 & –0505.

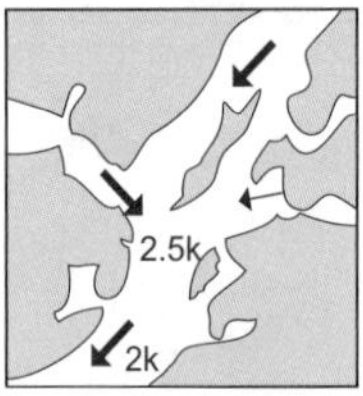

SOUND OF LUING & DORUS MOR (AC 2343)

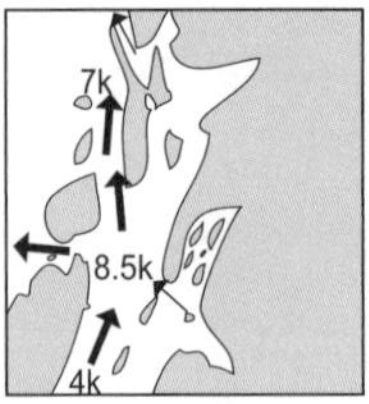

The N or W going stream begins as follows:

Dorus Mor:	HW Dover –0200 (HW Oban +0330). Springs: 8 knots.
Corryvreckan:	HW D –0120 (HW O +0410). Sp: 8.5 knots.
Cuan Sound:	HW D –0110 (HW O +0420). Sp: 6 knots.
Sound of Jura:	HW D –0130 (HW O +0400). Sp: 4 knots.
Sound of Luing:	HW D –0100 (HW O +0430). Sp: 7 knots.

The S or E going stream begins as follows:

Dorus Mor:	HW Dover +0440 (HW Oban –0215). Springs: 8 knots.
Corryvreckan:	HW D +0445 (HW O –0210). Sp: 8.5 knots.
Cuan Sound:	HW D +0455 (HW O –0200). Sp: 6 knots.
Sound of Jura:	HW D +0450 (HW O –0205). Sp: 4 knots.
Sound of Luing:	HW D +0500 (HW O –0155). Sp: 7 knots.

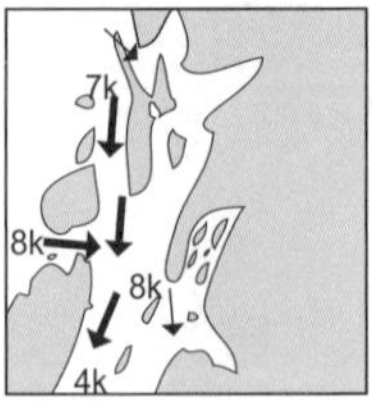

TIDAL GATES – SOUTH WEST SCOTLAND

A guide to the time of tide turn at tidal gates, the approximate maximum strength of the tidal flow (spring rates shown - neaps are approximately 60% of these), and the position and timing of races, counter tides, etc.

FLOOD	EBB

SOUNDS OF ISLAY AND GIGHA (AC 2168)

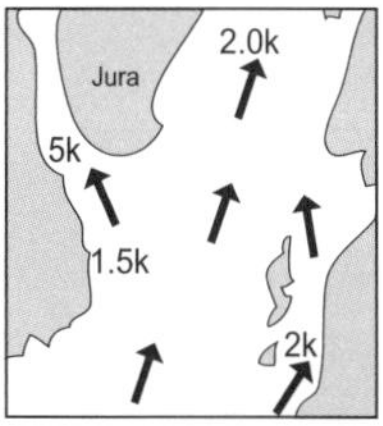

Flood: Main flood begins +0015 HW Dover (HW Oban +0545). Streams turn approx 1 hr earlier in Gigha Sd and at Kintyre and Jura shores. S going stream for 9hrs close inshore between Gigha and Machrihanish starting HW Dover (HW Oban –0530).

Ebb: Main ebb begins HW Dover –0545 (HW Oban –0015). Streams turn 1 hr earlier in Gigha Sd, Kintyre & Jura shores. Overfalls off McArthur's Hd.

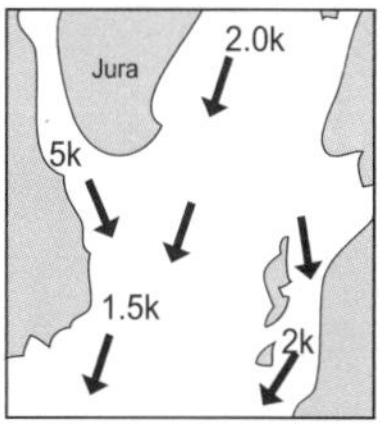

NORTH CHANNEL – NORTH (AC 2798)

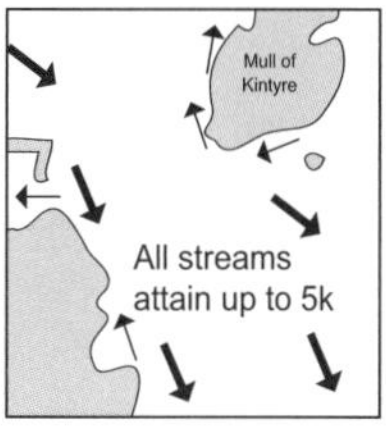

Flood: Main flood begins HW Dover –0600 (HW Greenock +0505). Races off Mull of Kintyre, Altacarry Hd & Fair Hd. Counter tides in bays of Antrim coast. W-going streams in Rathlin Sd, counter tide from Sanda Sd to Machrihanish last 1h30 - 2 hrs.

Ebb: Main ebb begins HW Dover (HW Greenock –0120). Races off Mull of Kintyre & Altacarry Hd. Counter tides in bays of Antrim coast, counter tide from Macrihanish to Sanda Sd last 1h30 - 2 hrs.

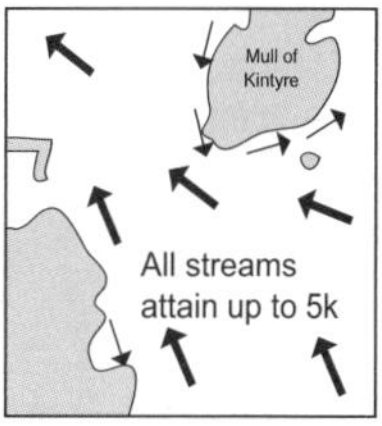

NORTH CHANNEL – SOUTH (AC 2198)

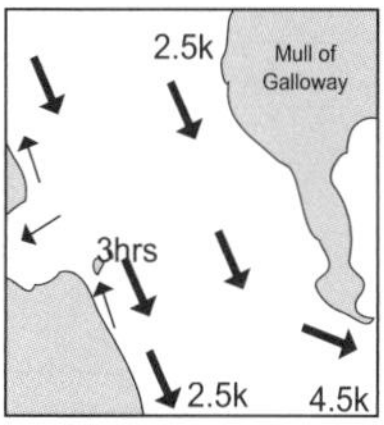

Flood: Irish coast - flood begins HW Dover +0610 (HW Belfast –0600). Scottish coast - HW Dover +0430 (HW Greenock +0310). Races off Copeland Is. & Mull of Galloway. Counter tide off Donaghadee and Island Magee last 3 hrs of flood.

Ebb: Irish coast - ebb begins HW Dover –0015 (HW Belfast). Scottish coast - HW Dover –0130 (HW Greenock –0250). Races off Copeland Is. & Mull of Galloway. Flood begins 2 hrs early close inshore N of Mull of Galloway.

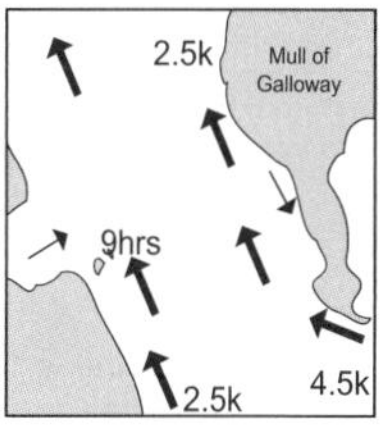

APPROACHES TO STRANGFORD LOUGH (AC 2156)

The tide cycle is approx 3 hours later than in the N Channel

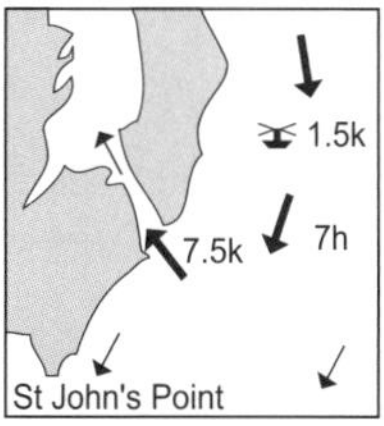

Flood: Flood runs for 6 hours from HW Dover –0345 (HW Belfast –0330), with a maximum rate of 7.5 knots at Rue Point. The strong flow flattens the sea in onshore winds and entrance can be made in strong winds.

Ebb: Ebb runs for 6 hours from HW Dover +0215 (HW Belfast +0230), max rate 7.5k, E of Angus Rk. If entering against ebb use West Channel with care. Smoothest water near Bar Pladdy Buoy when leaving.

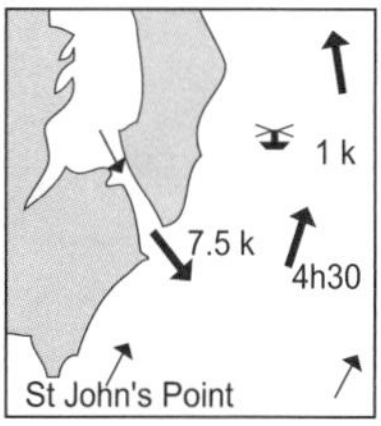

ISLE OF MAN – NORTH (AC 2094)

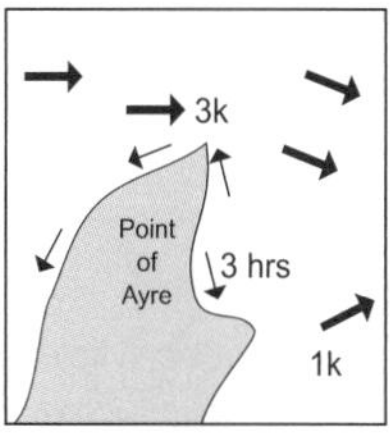

Flood: E going stream at Point of Ayre begins HW Dover –0545 (HW Liverpool –0600). Counter tide inside banks E of Point.
In Ramsey Bay the S Going tide runs for 3h from +0530 Dover (+0515 Liverpool).

Ebb: W going stream at Point of Ayre begins HW Dover +0015 (HW Liverpool). Counter tide inside banks W of Point.
In Ramsey Bay the N going tide runs for 9h from –0330 Dover (–0345 Liverpool).

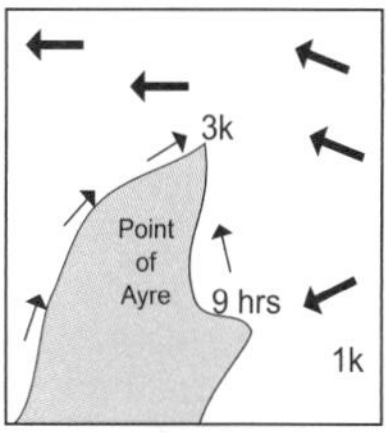

ISLE OF MAN – SOUTH (AC 2094)

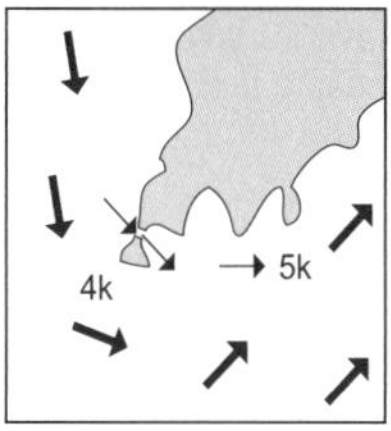

Flood: E going stream begins –0600 Dover (Liverpool +0610). Overfalls and race E of Chicken Rock.
Calf Sound: The E going stream begins earlier, at approximately Dover +0400 (Liverpool +0345).

Ebb: W going stream begins +0015 Dover (HW Liverpool). Overfalls and race N of Chicken Rock.
Calf Sound:The W going stream begins earlier, at approximately –0130 Dover (–0145 Liverpool).
Note: all times may vary due to weather conditions.

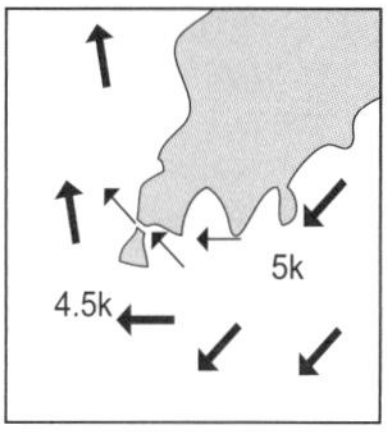

MENAI STRAIT (AC 1464) – TIDAL GATES

FLOOD

(T): turning → : < 2k ➡ : 2-4k ➡ : 4k +

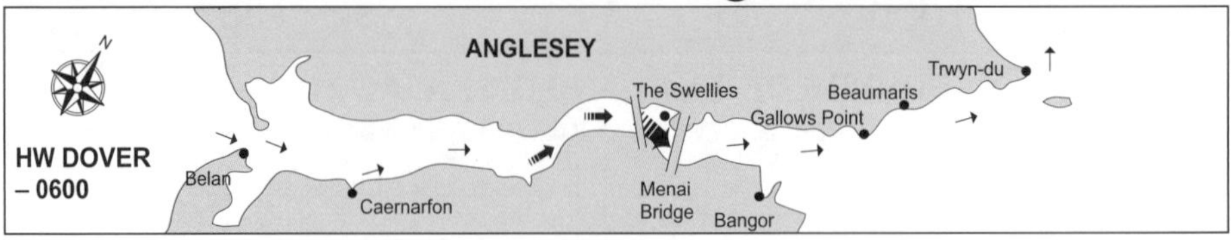

LOCAL LW: Caernarfon: HW Dover –0555. Port Dinorwic: –0620. Menai: –0540. Beaumaris: –0605.

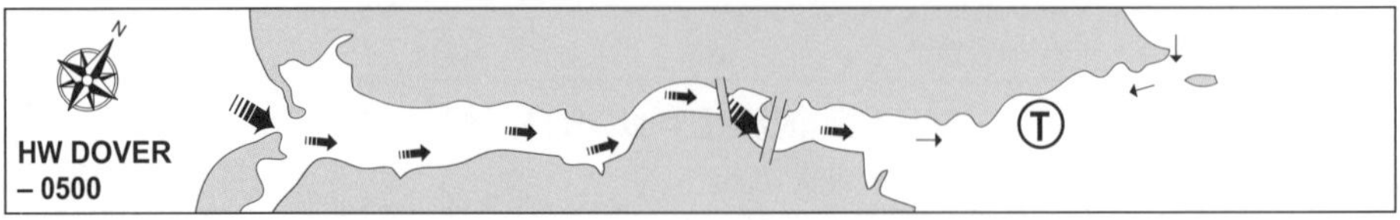

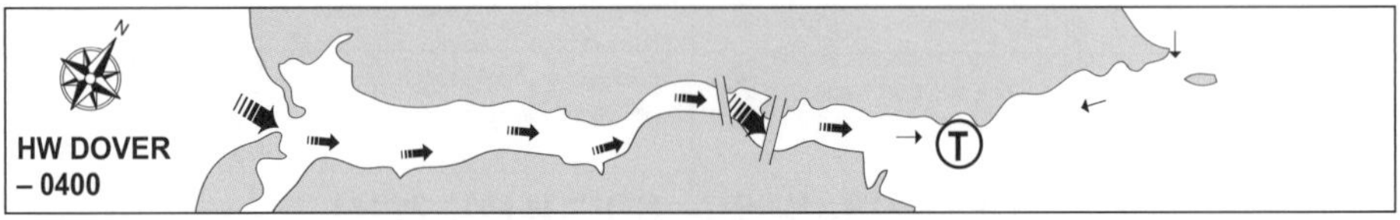

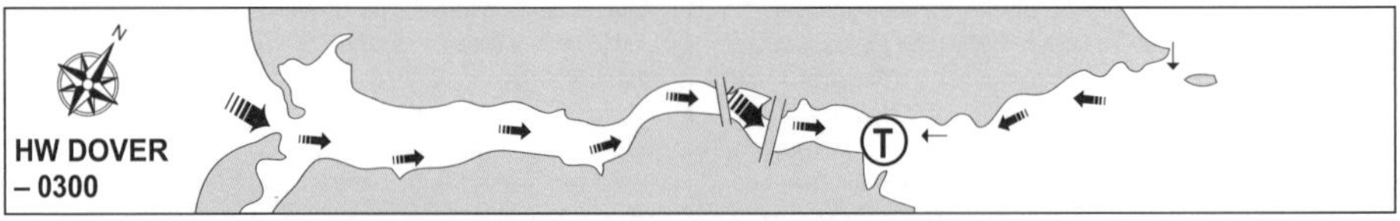

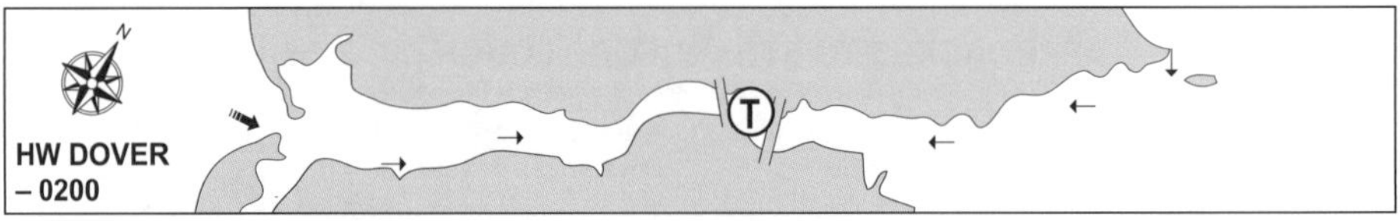

SLACK WATER IN THE SWELLIES: HW Dover –0200 to –0230.

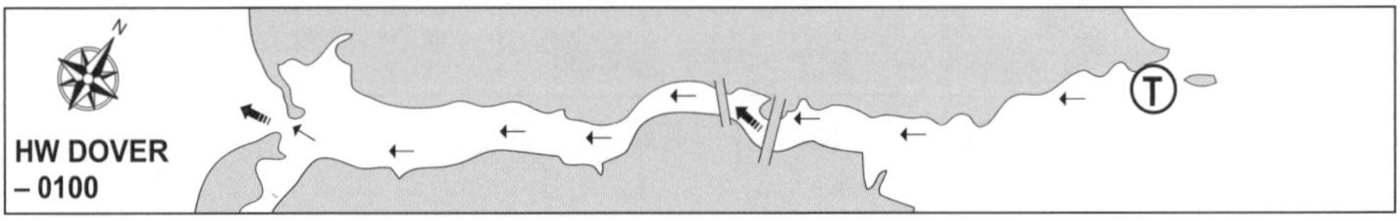

LOCAL HW: Belan: HW Dover –0115. Caernarfon: –0105. Port Dinorwic: –0050.

THE SWELLIES

WESTBOUND: Leave or pass Beaumaris in time to arrive at the Swellies by HW Dover –0230 to –0200. If in doubt about passage speed, leave early; the adverse tide will check your progress. For a first time passage this is useful, as the yacht's speed over the ground is reduced. Late arrival will mean a faster passage, but with perhaps less control.

EASTBOUND: Leave or pass Port Dinorwic in time to arrive at Menai Bridge by HW Dover –0230 to –0200. Progress towards the Swellies should be closely monitored, as you are travelling with the last of the flood. Early arrival will mean a fast, perhaps dangerous passage, being late may make it impossible.

EBB

Ⓣ: turning → : < 2k ➡ : 2-4k ⇛ : 4k +

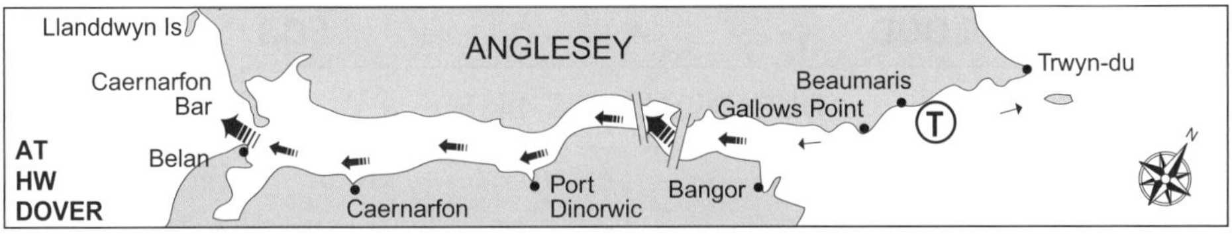

LOCAL HW TIMES: Menai: Dover – 0005. Beaumaris: Dover – 0010

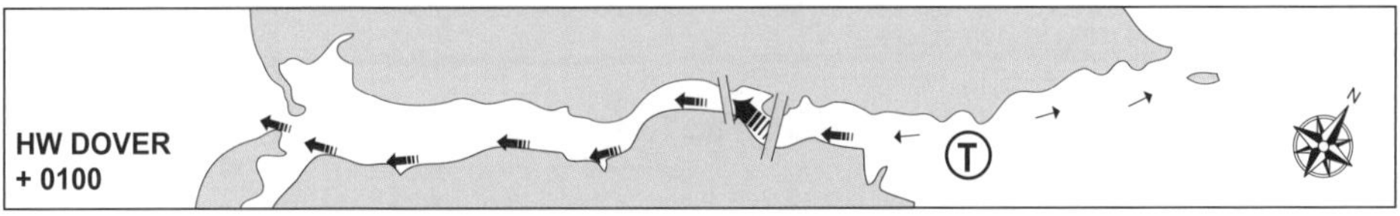

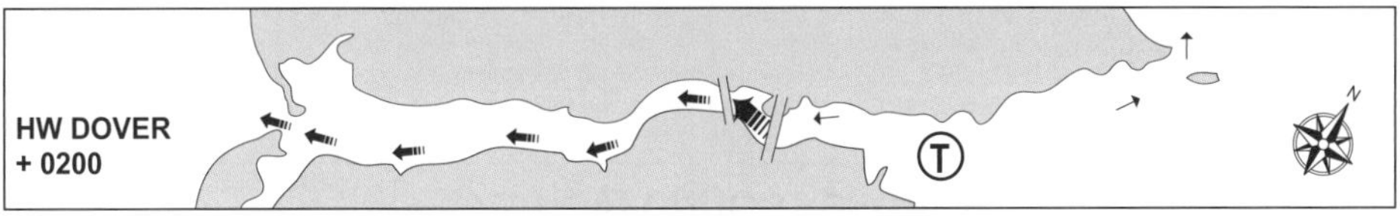

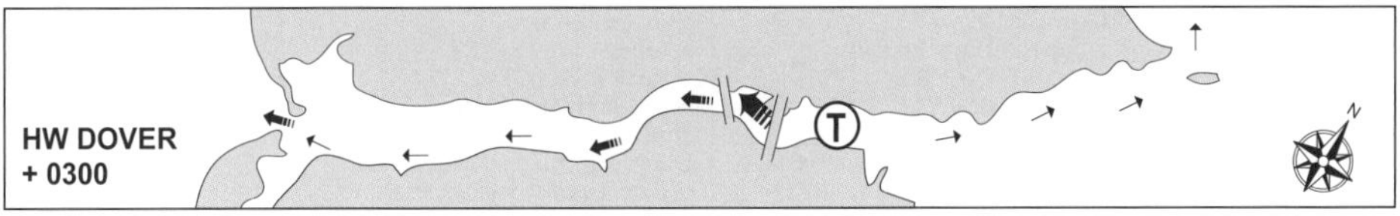

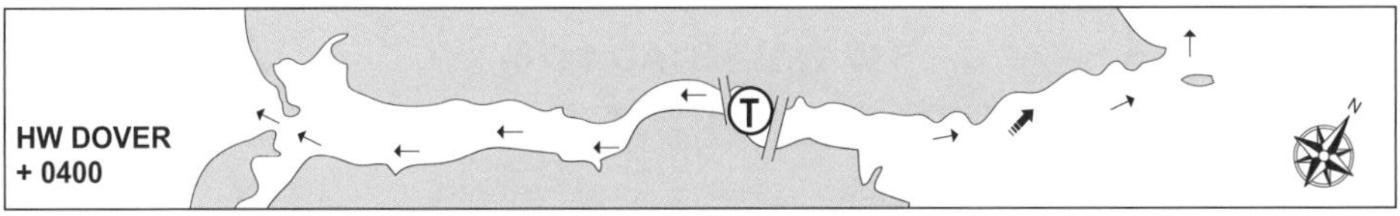

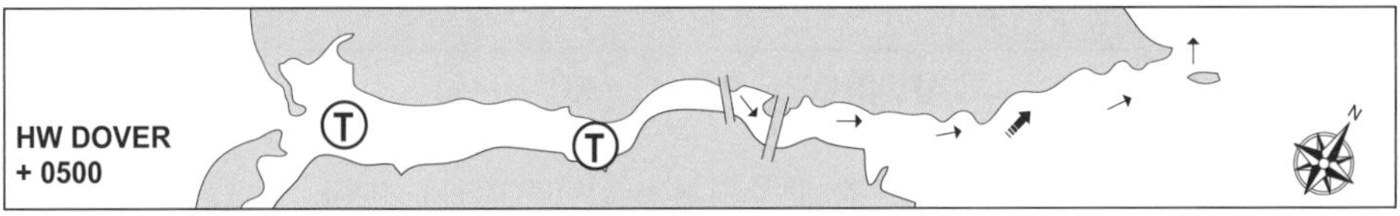

LOCAL LW TIMES: Belan: Dover + 0520.

CAERNARFON BAR

CAERNARFON BAR is without question highly dangerous in certain conditions. Buoys are located to suit changing channel; positions obtainable from Caernarfon Port Radio - VHF Ch 16; 06, 12: 2h–HW, or when vessel expected. Beware cross track tides near high water. Bar impassable during or after fresh or strong onshore weather. Keep strictly in channel.

OUTWARD BOUND: Do not leave Belan Narrows after half tide, better as soon as possible after the ebb commences, which gives maximum depth and duration of fair tide if bound S & W.

INWARD BOUND: Locating the bar buoys may be difficult; head for Llanddwyn I. until they are located. Only cross after half tide (HW Dover –0400), which inevitably limits onward passage to max of 3 hours.

TIDAL GATES – IRISH SEA

A guide to the time of tide turn at tidal gates, the approximate strength of the tidal flow (spring rates shown – neaps are approximately 60% of these), and the position and timing of races, counter tides, etc.

FLOOD	EBB

DUBLIN BAY (AC 1415)

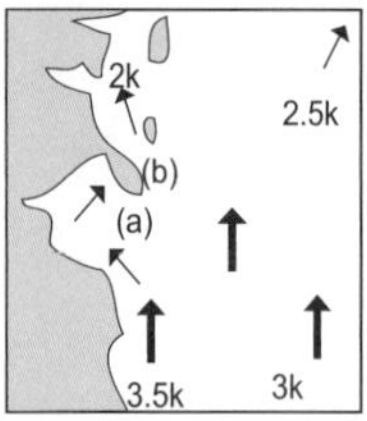

Tide between Rosbeg bank and Howth Hd (a) runs NE from HW Dublin +0300 for 9h30. In Howth Sd (b) the stream is NW going from +0430 to –0130.
New flood and ebb tides begin close to the S shore and N of Baily up to 1h before HW Dublin.

The tide between Rosbeg bank and Howth Hd (a) runs SW from HW Dublin for 3h. In Howth Sd (b) the stream is SE going from –0130 to +0430.
Strengths of streams increase S of Dublin Bay, and decrease N of it.

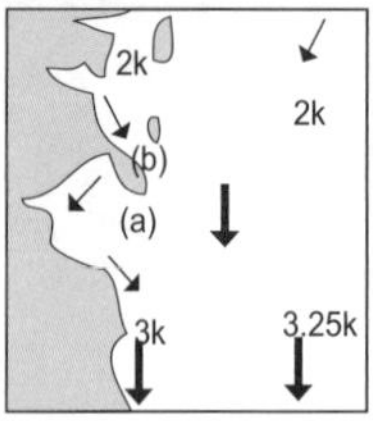

N W ANGLESEY (AC 1977)

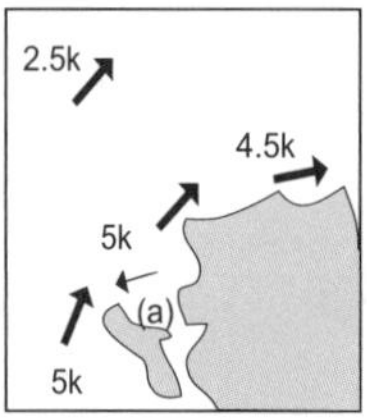

Flood tide close to the coast runs at over 5k springs, and at about 2.5k 7 miles offshore. The brief period of slack water offshore is 1h before HW Dover (1h15 before HW L'pool). Slack water lasts longer in Holyhead Bay.

Ebb tide close to the coast runs at over 5k springs, and at about 2.5k 7 miles offshore. Slack water is 5h after HW Dover (4h45 after HW L'pool). There is no significant counter tide in Holyhead Bay, but the ebb starts first there, giving about 9h W-going tide N of the harbour (a).

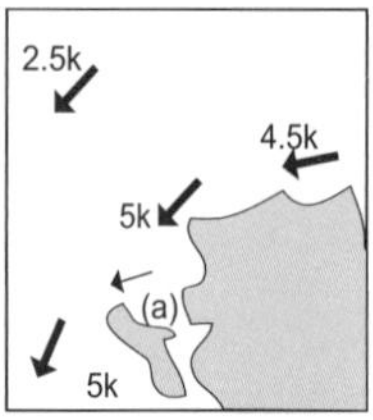

BARDSEY SOUND (AC 1971)

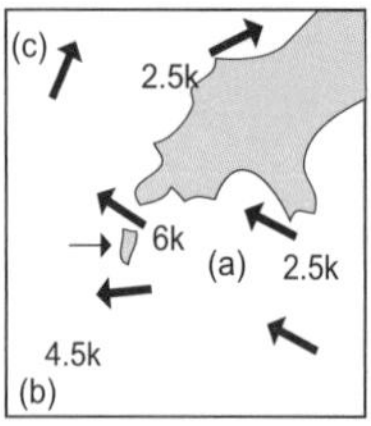

The tide turns to the NW or NE (flood) as follows:
at (a): HW Dover +0300;
at (b): HW D +0500;
at (c): –0545 HW D.
These times are approximate.
There is a strong eddy down tide of Bardsey Island and overfalls throughout the area.

The tide turns to the SW or SE (ebb) as follows:
at (a): HW Dover –0300;
at (b): HW D –0100 ;
at (c): at HW D –0030.
These times are approximate.
There is a strong eddy down tide of Bardsey Island and overfalls throughout the area.

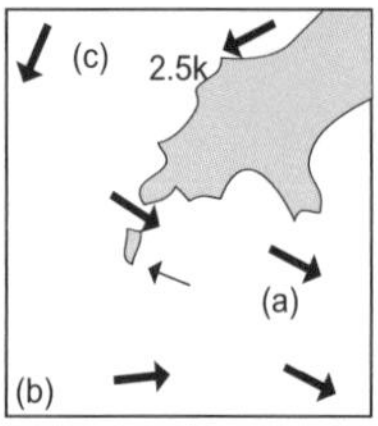

S W WALES (AC 1478)

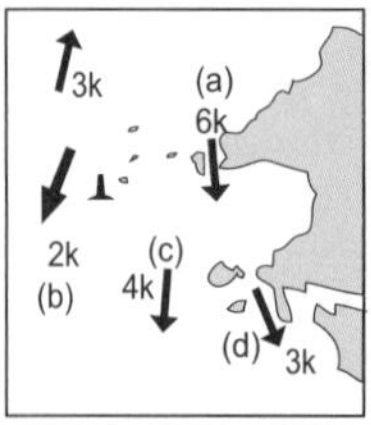

The tide turns to the S or SE (Bristol Channel flood) as follows:
at (a): HW Dover –0200;
at (b) & (c): HW D –0100 ;
at (d): –0300 HW D

The tide turns to the N or NW (Bristol Channel ebb) as follows:
at (a): HW Dover +0400;
at (b) & (c): HW D +0500 ;
at (d): +0300 HW D

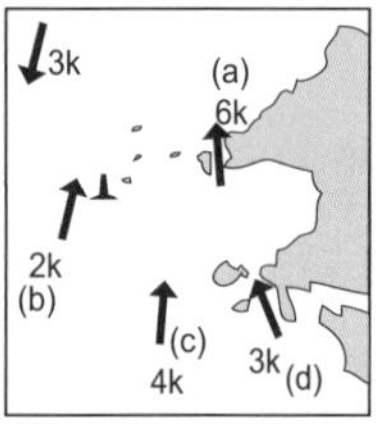

CARNSORE POINT (AC 2049)

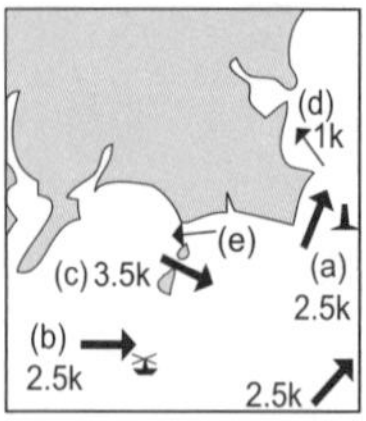

The tide turns to the NE or N (Irish Sea flood) as follows:
at (a): HW Dover +0500; at (b): HW D +0520; at (c): HW D +0600; at (d): –0600 HW D. NE going streams are shorter in duration and weaker than SE going - careful passage planning is essential.

The tide turns to the SW or S as follows:
at (a): –0200 HW D ; at (b): HW D –0020; at (c): –0015 HW D; at (d): –0300 HW Dover. Leaving Rosslare at –0300 HW D a yacht can carry a fair tide for about 8h until HW D +0515 off Hook Head.

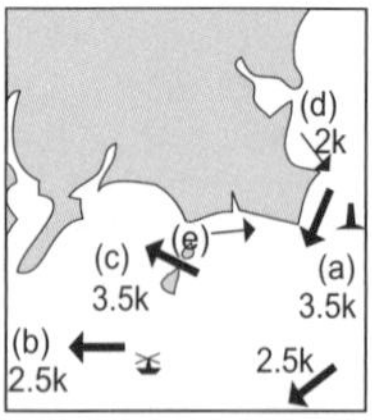

NOTE: The tide turns on St Patrick's Bridge (e) up to 2 hours earlier than in Saltee Sound

CORK COAST (AC 2049)

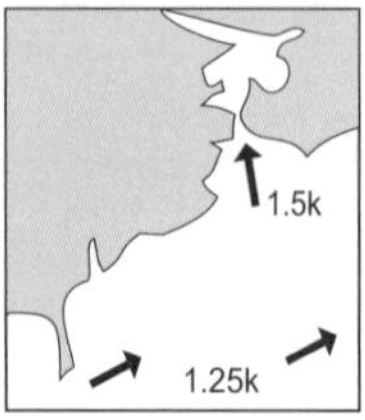

The tide, which flows coastwise, turns to the NE at HW Dover +0045. There is an eddy 5 miles ESE of Old Head of Kinsale at HW Dover +0400. The ingoing Cork Harbour tide begins at HW Dover +0055.

The tide turns SW at HW Dover +0500. The outgoing Cork Harbour tide begins at HW Dover –0540.

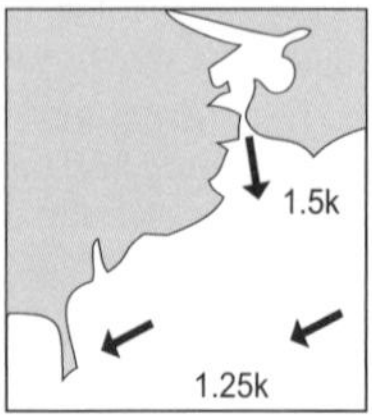

SECONDARY PORTS: TIME & HEIGHT DIFFERENCES
SOUTH COAST OF ENGLAND *Time zone UT*

Location	Lat	Long	High Water		Low Water		MHWS	MHWN	MLWN	MLWS
			0000	**0600**	**0000**	**0600**				
PLYMOUTH (DEVONPORT)	50 22N	4 11W	and	and	and	and	**5.5**	**4.4**	**2.2**	**0.8**
Standard port			**1200**	**1800**	**1200**	**1800**				
Isles of Scilly, St Mary's	49 55N	6 19W	–0052	–0103	–0048	–0045	+0.2	–0.1	–0.2	–0.1
Penzance & Newlyn	50 06N	5 33W	–0053	–0108	–0035	–0036	0.0	–0.1	–0.2	0.0
Porthleven	50 05N	5 19W	–0045	–0105	–0030	–0025	0.0	–0.1	–0.2	0.0
Lizard Point	49 57N	5 12W	–0045	–0100	–0030	–0030	–0.2	–0.2	–0.3	–0.2
Coverack	50 01N	5 05W	–0030	–0050	–0020	–0015	–0.2	–0.2	–0.3	–0.2
Helford River Entrance	50 05N	5 05W	–0030	–0035	–0015	–0010	–0.2	–0.2	–0.3	–0.2
FALMOUTH	50 09N	5 03W	*Standard port (no Secondaries)*							
River Fal, Truro	50 16N	5 03W	–0020	–0025	*Dries*	*Dries*	–2.0	–2.0	*Dries*	
Mevagissey	50 16N	4 47W	–0015	–0020	–0010	–0005	–0.1	–0.1	–0.2	–0.1
Par	50 21N	4 42W	–0010	–0015	–0010	–0005	–0.4	–0.4	–0.4	–0.2
River Fowey, Fowey	50 20N	4 38W	–0010	–0015	–0010	–0005	–0.1	–0.1	–0.2	–0.2
Lostwithiel	50 24N	4 40W	+0005	–0010	*Dries*	*Dries*	–4.1	–4.1	*Dries*	
Looe	50 21N	4 27W	–0010	–0010	–0005	–0005	–0.1	–0.2	–0.2	–0.2
Whitsand Bay	50 20N	4 15W	0000	0000	0000	0000	0.0	+0.1	–0.1	+0.2
River Tamar										
Saltash	50 24N	4 12W	0000	+0010	0000	–0005	+0.1	+0.1	+0.1	+0.1
Cargreen	50 26N	4 12W	0000	+0010	+0020	+0020	0.0	0.0	–0.1	0.0
Cotehele Quay	50 29N	4 13W	0000	+0020	+0045	+0045	–0.9	–0.9	–0.8	–0.4
River Tavy, Lopwell	50 28N	4 09W	*No data*	*No data*	*Dries*	*Dries*	–2.6	–2.7	*Dries*	
River Lynher, Jupiter Point	50 23N	4 14W	+0010	+0005	0000	–0005	0.0	0.0	+0.1	0.0
St Germans	50 23N	4 18W	0000	0000	+0020	+0020	–0.3	–0.1	0.0	+0.2
Turnchapel	50 22N	4 07W	0000	0000	+0010	–0015	0.0	+0.1	+0.2	+0.1
Bovisand Pier	50 20N	4 08W	–0010	–0010	–0008	–0009	–0.1	0.0	+0.2	+0.2
River Yealm, Entrance	50 18N	4 04W	+0006	+0006	+0002	+0002	–0.1	–0.1	–0.1	–0.1
			0100	**0600**	**0100**	**0600**				
PLYMOUTH (DEVONPORT)	50 22N	4 11W	and	and	and	and	**5.5**	**4.4**	**2.2**	**0.8**
Standard port			**1300**	**1800**	**1300**	**1800**				
Salcombe	50 13N	3 47W	0000	+0010	+0005	–0005	–0.2	–0.3	–0.1	–0.1
Start Point	50 13N	3 39W	+0015	+0015	+0005	+0010	–0.1	–0.2	+0.1	+0.2
River Dart										
DARTMOUTH	50 21N	3 34W	*Standard port (no Secondaries)*							
Greenway Quay	50 23N	3 35W	+0030	+0045	+0025	+0005	–0.6	–0.6	–0.2	–0.2
Totnes	50 26N	3 41W	+0030	+0040	+0115	+0030	–2.0	–2.1	*Dries*	
Torquay	50 28N	3 31W	+0025	+0045	+0010	0000	–0.6	–0.7	–0.2	–0.1
Teignmouth, Approaches	50 33N	3 29W	+0020	+0050	+0025	0000	–0.9	–0.8	–0.2	–0.1
Teignmouth, New Quay	50 33N	3 30W	+0025	+0055	+0040	+0005	–0.8	–0.8	–0.2	+0.1
Exmouth Approaches	50 36N	3 23W	+0030	+0050	+0015	+0005	–0.9	–1.0	–0.5	–0.3
River Exe										
Exmouth Dock	50 37N	3 25W	+0035	+0055	+0050	+0020	–1.5	–1.6	–0.9	–0.5
Starcross	50 38N	3 27W	+0040	+0100	+0055	+0025	–1.4	–1.5	–0.8	–0.1
Turf Lock	50 40N	3 28W	+0045	+0100	+0034	*No data*	– 1.6	–1.6	–1.2	–0.4
Topsham	50 41N	3 28W	+0045	+0105	*No data*	*No data*	– 1.5	–1.6	*No data*	
Lyme Regis	50 43N	2 56W	+0040	+0100	+0005	–0005	–1.2	–1.3	–0.5	–0.2
Bridport (West Bay)	50 42N	2 45W	+0025	+0040	0000	0000	–1.4	–1.4	–0.6	–0.1
Chesil Beach	50 37N	2 33W	+0040	+0055	–0005	+0010	–1.6	–1.5	–0.5	0.0
Chesil Cove	50 34N	2 28W	+0035	+0050	–0010	+0005	–1.5	–1.6	–0.5	–0.2
			0100	**0700**	**0100**	**0700**				
PORTLAND	50 34N	2 26W	and	and	and	and	**2.1**	**1.4**	**0.8**	**0.1**
Standard port			**1300**	**1900**	**1300**	**1900**				
Lulworth Cove, Mupe Bay	50 37N	2 14W	+0005	+0015	–0005	0000	+0.1	+0.1	+0.2	+0.1
			—	—	**0500**	**1100**				
POOLE HARBOUR	50 42N	1 59W			and	and	**2.2**	**1.7**	**1.2**	**0.6**
Standard port			—	—	**1700**	**2300**				
Swanage	50 37N	1 57W	—	—	–0045	+0050	–0.1	+0.1	+0.2	+0.2
Poole Harbour Entrance	50 41N	1 57W	—	—	–0025	–0010	0.0	0.0	0.0	0.0
Ro-Ro terminal	50 42N	1 59W	*Standard port*							
Pottery Pier	50 42N	1 59W	—	—	+0010	+0010	–0.2	0.0	+0.1	+0.2
Wareham, River Frome	50 41N	2 06W	—	—	+0130	+0045	0.0	0.0	0.0	+0.3
Cleavel Point	50 40N	2 00W	—	—	–0005	–0005	–0.1	–0.2	0.0	–0.1
			0000	**0600**	**0500**	**1100**				
PORTSMOUTH	50 48N	1 07W	and	and	and	and	**4.7**	**3.8**	**1.9**	**0.8**
Standard port			**1200**	**1800**	**1700**	**2300**				
Bournemouth	50 43N	1 52W	–0240	+0055	–0050	–0030	–2.6	–2.0	–0.6	–0.2
Christchurch Entrance	50 43N	1 45W	–0230	+0030	–0035	–0035	–2.9	–2.4	–1.2	–0.2

Location	Lat	Long	High Water		Low Water		MHWS	MHWN	MLWN	MLWS
Christchurch Quay	50 44N	1 47W	–0210	+0100	+0105	+0055	–2.9	–2.4	–1.0	0.0
Christchurch, Tuckton	50 44N	1 47W	–0205	+0110	+0110	+0105	–3.0	–2.5	–1.0	+0.1
Hurst Point	50 42N	1 33W	–0115	–0005	–0030	–0025	–2.0	–1.5	–0.5	–0.1
Lymington	50 46N	1 32W	–0110	+0005	–0020	–0020	–1.6	–1.2	–0.4	–0.1
Bucklers Hard	50 48N	1 25W	–0040	–0010	+0010	–0010	–1.0	–0.8	–0.2	–0.3
Stansore Point	50 47N	1 20W	–0030	–0010	–0005	–0015	–0.8	–0.5	–0.3	–0.3
Isle of Wight										
Yarmouth	50 42N	1 30W	–0105	+0005	–0025	–0030	–1.7	–1.2	–0.3	0.0
Totland Bay	50 41N	1 33W	–0130	–0045	–0035	–0045	–2.2	–1.7	–0.4	–0.1
Freshwater	50 40N	1 31W	–0210	+0025	–0040	–0020	–2.1	–1.5	–0.4	0.0
Ventnor	50 36N	1 12W	–0025	–0030	–0025	–0030	–0.8	–0.6	–0.2	+0.2
Sandown	50 39N	1 09W	0000	+0005	+0010	+0025	–0.6	–0.5	–0.2	0.0
Foreland Lifeboat Slip	50 41N	1 04W	–0005	0000	+0005	+0010	+0.1	+0.1	0.0	+0.1
Bembridge Harbour	50 42N	1 07W	+0020	0000	+0100	+0020	–1.5	–1.4	–1.3	–1.0
Ryde	50 44N	1 10W	–0010	–0010	–0005	–0005	–0.1	0.0	0.0	0.0
Medina River										
Cowes	50 46N	1 18W	–0015	+0015	0000	–0020	–0.5	–0.3	–0.1	0.0
Folly Inn	50 44N	1 17W	–0015	+0015	0000	–0020	–0.6	–0.4	–0.1	+0.2
Newport	50 42N	1 17W	*No data*	*No data*	*No data*	*No data*	–0.6	–0.4	+0.1	+0.8
			0400	**1100**	**0000**	**0600**				
SOUTHAMPTON	50 53N	1 24W	and	and	and	and	**4.5**	**3.7**	**1.8**	**0.5**
Standard port			**1600**	**2300**	**1200**	**1800**				
Calshot Castle	50 49N	1 18W	0000	+0025	0000	0000	0.0	0.0	+0.2	+0.3
Redbridge	50 55N	1 28W	–0020	+0005	0000	–0005	–0.1	–0.1	–0.1	–0.1
River Hamble										
Warsash	50 51N	1 18W	+0020	+0010	+0010	0000	0.0	+0.1	+0.1	+0.3
Bursledon	50 53N	1 18W	+0020	+0020	+0010	+0010	+0.1	+0.1	+0.2	+0.2
			0500	**1000**	**0000**	**0600**				
PORTSMOUTH	50 48N	1 07W	and	and	and	and	**4.7**	**3.8**	**1.9**	**0.8**
Standard port			**1700**	**2200**	**1200**	**1800**				
Lee-on-the-Solent	50 48N	1 12W	–0005	+0005	–0015	–0010	–0.2	–0.1	+0.1	+0.2
Chichester Harbour Entrance	50 47N	0 56W	–0010	+0005	+0015	+0020	+0.2	+0.2	0.0	+0.1
Northney	50 50N	0 58W	+0020	+0010	0000	+0005	0.0	–0.2	–0.2	–0.4
Bosham	50 50N	0 52W	+0010	+0005	*No data*	*No data*	0.0	–0.1	*No data*	
Itchenor	50 48N	0 52W	+0005	0000	–0010	+0005	–0.1	–0.2	–0.2	–0.3
Dell Quay	50 49N	0 49W	+0015	+0010	*no data*	*No data*	0.0	–0.1	*No data*	
Selsey Bill	50 43N	0 47W	+0010	–0010	+0035	+0020	+0.5	+0.3	–0.1	–0.2
Nab Tower	50 40N	0 57W	+0015	0000	+0015	+0015	–0.2	0.0	+0.2	0.0
			0500	**1000**	**0000**	**0600**				
SHOREHAM	50 50N	0 15W	and	and	and	and	**6.3**	**4.8**	**1.9**	**0.6**
Standard port			**1700**	**2200**	**1200**	**1800**				
Pagham	50 46N	0 43W	+0015	0000	–0015	–0025	–0.7	–0.5	–0.1	–0.1
Bognor Regis	50 47N	0 40W	+0010	–0005	–0005	–0020	–0.6	–0.5	–0.2	–0.1
River Arun										
Littlehampton Entrance	50 48N	0 33W	+0010	0000	–0005	–0010	–0.4	–0.4	–0.2	–0.2
Littlehampton UMA wharf	50 49N	0 33W	+0015	+0005	0000	+0045	–0.7	–0.7	–0.3	+0.2
Arundel	50 51N	0 33W	*No data*	+0120	*No data*	*No data*	–3.1	–2.8	*No data*	
Worthing	50 48N	0 22W	+0010	0000	–0005	–0010	–0.1	–0.2	0.0	0.0
Brighton	50 49N	0 08W	–0002	–0002	0000	0000	+0.2	+0.2	+0.1	+0.1
Newhaven	50 47N	0 04E	–0003	–0005	0000	+0005	+0.5	+0.4	+0.2	+0.2
Eastbourne	50 46N	0 17E	–0010	–0005	+0015	+0020	+1.1	+0.6	+0.2	+0.1
			0000	**0600**	**0100**	**0700**				
DOVER	51 07N	1 19E	and	and	and	and	**6.8**	**5.3**	**2.1**	**0.8**
Standard port			**1200**	**1800**	**1300**	**1900**				
Hastings	50 51N	0 36E	0000	–0010	–0030	–0030	+0.8	+0.5	+0.1	–0.1
Rye Approaches	50 55N	0 47E	+0005	–0010	*No data*	*No data*	+1.0	+0.7	*No data*	
Rye Harbour	50 56N	0 48E	+0005	–0010	*Dries*	*Dries*	–1.4	–1.7	*Dries*	
Dungeness	50 55N	0 58E	–0010	–0015	–0020	–0010	+1.0	+0.6	+0.4	+0.1
Folkestone	51 05N	1 12E	–0020	–0005	–0010	–0010	+0.4	+0.4	0.0	–0.1
Deal	51 13N	1 25E	+0012	+0010	+0004	+0002	–0.5	–0.3	0.0	+0.1
Richborough	51 18N	1 21E	+0015	+0015	+0030	+0030	–3.4	–2.6	–1.7	–0.7
Ramsgate	51 20N	1 25E	+0030	+0030	+0017	+0007	–1.6	–1.3	–0.7	–0.2

EAST COAST ENGLAND *Time Zone UT*

Location	Lat	Long	High Water		Low Water		MHWS	MHWN	MLWN	MLWS
			0100	**0700**	**0100**	**0700**				
MARGATE	51 23N	1 23E	and	and	and	and	**4.8**	**3.9**	**1.4**	**0.5**
Standard port			**1300**	**1900**	**1300**	**1900**				
Herne Bay	51 23N	1 07E	+0022	+0020	+0019	+0017	+0.6	+0.3	+0.2	+0.1
Whitstable approaches	51 22N	1 02E	+0042	+0029	+0025	+0050	+0.6	+0.6	+0.1	0.0

Location	Lat	Long	High Water		Low Water		MHWS	MHWN	MLWN	MLWS
SHEERNESS	51 27N	0 45E	**0200 and 1400**	**0800 and 2000**	**0200 and 1400**	**0700 and 1900**	**5.8**	**4.7**	**1.5**	**0.6**
Standard port										
River Swale										
Grovehurst Jetty	51 22N	0 46E	–0007	0000	0000	+0016	0.0	0.0	0.0	–0.1
Faversham	51 19N	0 54E	*No data*	*No data*	*No data*	*No data*	–0.2	–0.2	*No data*	
River Medway										
Bee Ness	51 25N	0 39E	+0002	+0002	0000	+0005	+0.2	+0.1	0.0	0.0
Bartlett Creek	51 23N	0 38E	+0016	+0008	*No data*	*No data*	+0.1	0.0	*No data*	
Darnett Ness	51 24N	0 36E	+0004	+0004	0000	+0010	+0.2	+0.1	0.0	–0.1
Chatham, Lock approaches	51 24N	0 33E	+0010	+0012	+0012	+0018	+0.3	+0.1	–0.1	–0.2
Upnor	51 25N	0 32E	+0015	+0015	+0015	+0025	+0.2	+0.2	–0.1	–0.1
Rochester, Strood Pier	51 24N	0 30E	+0018	+0018	+0018	+0028	+0.2	+0.2	–0.2	–0.3
Wouldham	51 21N	0 27E	+0030	+0025	+0035	+0120	–0.2	–0.3	–1.0	–0.3
New Hythe	51 19N	0 28E	+0035	+0035	+0220	+0240	–1.6	–1.7	–1.2	–0.3
Allington Lock	51 17N	0 30E	+0050	+0035	*No data*	*No data*	–2.1	–2.2	–1.3	–0.4
River Thames										
Southend–on–Sea	51 31N	0 43E	–0005	–0005	–0005	–0005	+0.1	0.0	–0.1	–0.1
Coryton	51 30N	0 31E	+0005	+0010	+0010	+0010	+0.4	+0.3	0.0	0.0
LONDON BRIDGE	51 30N	0 05W	**0300 and 1500**	**0900 and 2100**	**0400 and 1600**	**1100 and 2300**	**7.1**	**5.9**	**1.3**	**0.5**
Standard port										
Tilbury	51 27N	0 22E	–0055	–0040	–0050	–0115	–0.7	–0.5	+0.1	0.0
North Woolwich	51 30N	0 05E	–0020	–0020	–0035	–0045	–0.1	0.0	+0.2	0.0
Albert bridge	51 29N	0 10W	+0025	+0020	+0105	+0110	–0.9	–0.8	–0.7	–0.4
Hammersmith bridge	51 29N	0 14W	+0040	+0035	+0205	+0155	–1.4	–1.3	–1.0	–0.5
Kew bridge	51 29N	0 17W	+0055	+0050	+0255	+0235	–1.8	–1.8	–1.2	–0.5
Richmond lock	51 28N	0 19W	+0105	+0055	+0325	+0305	–2.2	–2.7	–0.9	–0.5
SHEERNESS	51 27N	0 45E	**0200 and 1400**	**0700 and 1900**	**0100 and 1300**	**0700 and 1900**	**5.8**	**4.7**	**1.5**	**0.6**
Standard port										
Thames Estuary Shivering Sand	51 30N	1 05E	–0025	–0019	–0008	–0026	–0.6	–0.6	–0.1	–0.1
WALTON-ON-THE-NAZE	51 51N	1 17E	**0000 and 1200**	**0600 and 1800**	**0500 and 1700**	**1100 and 2300**	**4.2**	**3.4**	**1.1**	**0.4**
Standard port										
Whitaker Beacon	51 40N	1 06E	+0022	+0024	+0033	+0027	+0.6	+0.5	+0.2	+0.1
Holliwell Point	51 38N	0 56E	+0034	+0037	+0100	+0037	+1.1	+0.9	+0.3	+0.1
River Roach Rochford	51 35N	0 43E	+0050	+0040	*Dries*	*Dries*	–0.8	–1.1	*Dries*	
River Crouch										
Burnham-on-Crouch	51 37N	0 48E	+0050	+0035	+0115	+0050	+1.0	+0.8	–0.1	–0.2
North Fambridge	51 38N	0 41E	+0115	+0050	+0130	+0100	+1.1	+0.8	0.0	–0.1
Hullbridge	51 38N	0 38E	+0115	+0050	+0135	+0105	+1.1	+0.8	0.0	–0.1
Battlesbridge	51 37N	0 34E	+0120	+0110	*Dries*	*Dries*	–1.8	–2.0	*Dries*	
River Blackwater										
Bradwell Waterside	51 45N	0 54E	+0035	+0023	+0047	+0004	+1.0	+0.8	+0.2	0.0
Osea Island	51 43N	0 46E	+0057	+0045	+0050	+0007	+1.1	+0.9	+0.1	0.0
Maldon	51 44N	0 42E	+0107	+0055	*No data*	*No data*	–1.3	–1.1	*No data*	
West Mersea	51 47N	0 54E	+0035	+0015	+0055	+0010	+0.9	+0.4	+0.1	+0.1
River Colne										
Brightlingsea	51 48N	1 00E	+0025	+0021	+0046	+0004	+0.8	+0.4	+0.1	0.0
Colchester	51 53N	0 56E	+0035	+0025	*Dries*	*Dries*	0.0	–0.3	*Dries*	
Clacton–on–Sea	51 47N	1 10E	+0012	+0010	+0025	+0008	+0.3	+0.1	+0.1	+0.1
Bramble Creek	51 53N	1 14E	+0010	–0007	–0005	+0010	+0.3	+0.3	+0.3	+0.3
Sunk Head	51 47N	1 30E	0000	+0002	–0002	+0002	–0.3	–0.3	–0.1	–0.1
Harwich	51 57N	1 17E	+0007	+0002	–0010	–0012	–0.2	0.0	0.0	0.0
Mistley	51 57N	1 05E	+0032	+0027	–0010	–0012	0.0	0.0	–0.1	–0.1
Ipswich	52 03N	1 10E	+0022	+0027	0000	–0012	0.0	0.0	–0.1	–0.1
WALTON–ON–THE–NAZE	51 51N	1 17E	**0100 and 1300**	**0700 and 1900**	**0100 and 1300**	**0700 and 1900**	**4.2**	**3.4**	**1.1**	**0.4**
Standard port										
Felixstowe Pier	51 57N	1 21E	–0005	–0007	–0018	–0020	–0.5	–0.4	0.0	0.0
River Deben										
Woodbridge Haven	51 59N	1 24E	0000	–0005	–0020	–0025	–0.5	–0.5	–0.1	+0.1
Woodbridge	52 05N	1 19E	+0045	+0025	+0025	–0020	–0.2	–0.3	–0.2	0.0
Bawdsey	52 01N	1 26E	–0016	–0020	–0030	–0032	–0.8	–0.6	–0.1	–0.1
Orford Haven										
Bar	52 02N	1 28E	–0026	–0030	–0036	–0038	–1.0	–0.8	–0.1	0.0
Orford Quay	52 05N	1 32E	+0040	+0040	+0055	+0055	–1.4	–1.1	0.0	+0.2
Slaughden Quay	52 08N	1 36E	+0105	+0105	+0125	+0125	–1.3	–0.8	–0.1	+0.2
Iken Cliffs	52 09N	1 31E	+0130	+0130	+0155	+0155	–1.3	–1.0	0.0	+0.2

Location	Lat	Long	High Water		Low Water		MHWS	MHWN	MLWN	MLWS
			0300	**0900**	**0200**	**0800**				
LOWESTOFT	52 28N	1 45E	and	and	and	and	**2.4**	**2.1**	**1.0**	**0.5**
Standard port			**1500**	**2100**	**1400**	**2000**				
Orford Ness	52 05N	1 35E	+0135	+0135	+0135	+0125	+0.4	+0.6	–0.1	0.0
Aldeburgh	52 09N	1 36E	+0130	+0130	+0115	+0120	+0.3	+0.2	–0.1	–0.2
Minsmere Sluice	52 14N	1 38E	+0110	+0110	+0110	+0110	0.0	–0.1	–0.2	–0.2
Southwold	52 19N	1 40E	+0105	+0105	+0055	+0055	0.0	0.0	–0.1	0.0
Great Yarmouth										
Gorleston-on-Sea	52 34N	1 44E	–0035	–0035	–0030	–0030	0.0	0.0	0.0	0.0
Britannia Pier	52 36N	1 45E	–0105	–0100	–0040	–0055	+0.1	+0.1	0.0	0.0
Caister-on-Sea	52 39N	1 44E	–0120	–0120	–0100	–0100	0.0	–0.1	0.0	0.0
Winterton-on-Sea	52 43N	1 42E	–0225	–0215	–0135	–0135	+0.8	+0.5	+0.2	+0.1
			0100	**0700**	**0100**	**0700**				
IMMINGHAM	53 38N	0 11W	and	and	and	and	**7.3**	**5.8**	**2.6**	**0.9**
Standard port			**1300**	**1900**	**1300**	**1900**				
Cromer	52 56N	1 18E	+0044	+0032	+0108	+0059	–2.3	–1.8	–0.7	0.0
Blakeney Bar	52 59N	0 59E	+0035	+0025	+0030	+0040	–1.6	–1.3	*No data*	
Blakeney	52 57N	1 01E	+0115	+0055	*No data*	*No data*	–3.9	–3.8	*No data*	
Wells Bar	52 59N	0 49E	+0020	+0020	+0020	+0020	–1.3	–1.0	*No data*	
Wells	52 57N	0 51E	+0035	+0045	+0340	+0310	–3.8	–3.8	*Not below CD*	
Burnham Overy Staithe	52 58N	0 48E	+0045	+0055	*No data*	*No data*	–5.0	–4.9	*No data*	
The Wash										
Hunstanton	52 56N	0 29E	+0010	+0020	+0105	+0025	+0.1	–0.2	–0.1	0.0
West Stones	52 50N	0 21E	+0025	+0025	+0115	+0040	–0.3	–0.4	–0.3	+0.2
King's Lynn	52 45N	0 24E	+0030	+0030	+0305	+0140	–0.5	–0.8	–0.8	+0.1
Outer Westmark Knock	52 53N	0 13E	+0010	+0015	+0040	+0020	–0.2	–0.5	–0.6	–0.4
Wisbech Cut	52 48N	0 13E	+0020	+0010	+0120	+0055	–0.3	–0.7	–0.4	*No data*
Port Sutton bridge	52 46N	0 12E	+0030	+0020	+0130	+0105	–0.3	–0.6	–0.6	+0.3
Wisbech	52 40N	0 09E	+0055	+0040	*Dries*	*Dries*	–0.2	–0.6	*Dries*	*Dries*
Lawyer's Creek	52 53N	0 05E	+0010	+0020	*No data*	*No data*	–0.3	–0.6	*No data*	
Tabs Head	52 56N	0 05E	0000	+0005	+0125	+0020	+0.2	–0.2	–0.2	–0.2
Boston	52 58N	0 01W	0000	+0010	+0140	+0050	–0.5	–1.0	–0.9	–0.5
Skegness	53 09N	0 21E	+0010	+0015	+0030	+0020	–0.4	–0.5	–0.1	0.0
Inner Dowsing Light Tower	53 19N	0 35E	0000	0000	+0010	+0010	–0.9	–0.7	–0.1	+0.3
River Humber										
Bull Sand Fort	53 34N	0 04E	–0020	–0030	–0035	–0015	–0.4	–0.3	+0.1	+0.2
Grimsby	53 35N	0 04W	–0012	–0012	–0015	–0013	–0.3	–0.2	+0.1	+0.4
Hull, King George Dock	53 44N	0 16W	+0010	+0010	+0021	+0017	+0.3	+0.2	–0.1	–0.2
Hull, Albert Dock	53 44N	0 21W	+0019	+0019	+0033	+0027	+0.3	+0.1	–0.1	–0.2
Humber Bridge	53 43N	0 27W	+0027	+0022	+0049	+0039	–0.1	–0.4	–0.7	–0.6
River Trent										
Burton Stather	53 39N	0 42W	+0105	+0050	+0240	+0205	–2.0	–2.7	–2.2	–1.1
Flixborough Wharf	53 37N	0 42W	+0100	+0115	+0305	+0220	–2.1	–2.8	–2.2	–0.9
Keadby	53 36N	0 44W	+0130	+0115	+0320	+0235	–2.8	–3.3	–2.3	–0.9
Owston Ferry	53 29N	0 46W	+0155	+0145	*Dries*	*Dries*	–3.5	–3.9	*Dries*	
River Ouse										
Blacktoft	53 42N	0 43W	+0100	+0055	+0325	+0255	–1.6	–1.8	–2.2	–1.1
Goole	53 42N	0 52W	+0130	+0115	+0355	+0350	–1.6	–2.1	–1.9	–0.6
			0000	**0600**	**0000**	**0600**				
R TEES ENTRANCE	54 38N	1 09W	and	and	and	and	**5. 5**	**4.3**	**2.0**	**0.9**
Standard port			**1200**	**1800**	**1200**	**1800**				
Bridlington	54 05N	0 11W	+0100	+0050	+0055	+0050	+0.6	+0.4	+0.3	+0.2
Filey Bay	54 13N	0 16W	+0042	+0042	+0047	+0034	+0.3	+0.6	+0.4	+0.1
Scarborough	54 17N	0 23W	+0040	+0040	+0030	+0030	+0.2	+0.3	+0.3	0.0
Whitby	54 29N	0 37W	+0020	+0020	+0018	+0017	+0.1	+0.1	+0.2	+0.1
Middlesborough Dock ent	54 35N	1 13W	0000	+0002	0000	–0003	+0.1	+0.2	+0.1	–0.1
Tees (Newport) Bridge	54 34N	1 16W	–0002	+0004	+0005	–0003	+0.1	+0.2	0.0	–0.1
Hartlepool	54 42N	1 12W	–0004	–0004	–0006	–0006	–0.1	–0.1	–0.2	–0.1
Seaham	54 50N	1 19W	–0015	–0015	–0015	–0015	–0.3	–0.2	0.0	–0.2
Sunderland	54 55N	1 22W	–0017	–0017	–0016	–0016	–0.2	–0.1	0.0	0.0
			0200	**0800**	**0100**	**0800**				
R TYNE, NORTH SHIELDS	55 00N	1 26W	and	and	and	and	**5. 0**	**3.9**	**1.8**	**0.7**
Standard port			**1400**	**2000**	**1300**	**2000**				
Newcastle-upon-Tyne	54 58N	1 36W	+0003	+0003	+0008	+0008	+0.3	+0.2	+0.1	+0.1
Blyth	55 07N	1 29W	+0005	–0007	–0001	+0009	0.0	0.0	–0.1	+0.1
Coquet Island	55 20N	1 32W	–0010	–0010	–0020	–0020	+0.1	+0.1	0.0	+0.1
Amble	55 20N	1 34W	–0013	–0013	–0016	–0020	0.0	0.0	+0.1	+0.1

Location	Lat	Long	High Water		Low Water		MHWS	MHWN	MLWN	MLWS
North Sunderland	55 35N	1 39W	–0048	–0044	–0058	–0102	–0.2	–0.2	–0.2	0.0
Holy Island	55 40N	1 48W	–0043	–0039	–0105	–0110	–0.2	–0.2	–0.3	–0.1
Berwick	55 46N	1 59W	–0053	–0053	–0109	–0109	–0.3	–0.1	–0.5	–0.1
SCOTLAND *Time Zone UT*										
LEITH *Standard port*	55 59N	3 11W	**0300 and 1500**	**0900 and 2100**	**0300 and 1500**	**0900 and 2100**	**5.6**	**4.4**	**2.0**	**0.8**
Eyemouth	55 52N	2 05W	–0005	+0007	+0012	+0008	–0.4	–0.3	0.0	+0.1
Dunbar	56 00N	2 31W	–0005	+0003	+0003	–0003	–0.3	–0.3	0.0	+0.1
Fidra	56 04N	2 47W	–0001	0000	–0002	+0001	–0.2	–0.2	0.0	0.0
Cockenzie	55 58N	2 57W	–0007	–0015	–0013	–0005	–0.2	0.0	*No data*	
Granton	55 59N	3 13W	0000	0000	0000	0000	0.0	0.0	0.0	0.0
River Forth Grangemouth	56 02N	3 41W	+0015	+0010	–0050	–0045	0.0	–0.1	–0.2	–0.2
Kincardine	56 04N	3 43W	+0015	+0030	–0030	–0030	0.0	–0.2	–0.5	–0.3
Alloa	56 06N	3 48W	+0040	+0040	+0025	+0025	–0.2	–0.5	*No data*	–0.7
Stirling	56 07N	3 56W	+0100	+0100	*No data*		–2.9	–3.1	–2.3	–0.7
Firth of Forth										
Burntisland	56 03N	3 14W	+0013	+0004	–0002	+0007	+0.1	0.0	+0.1	+0.2
Kirkcaldy	56 09N	3 09W	+0005	0000	–0004	–0001	–0.3	–0.3	–0.2	–0.2
Methil	56 11N	3 00W	–0005	–0001	–0001	–0001	–0.1	–0.1	–0.1	–0.1
Anstruther Easter	56 13N	2 42W	–0018	–0012	–0006	–0008	–0.3	–0.2	0.0	0.0
ABERDEEN *Standard port*	57 09N	2 04W	**0000 and 1200**	**0600 and 1800**	**0100 and 1300**	**0700 and 1900**	**4.3**	**3.4**	**1.6**	**0.6**
River Tay										
Bar	56 28N	2 38W	+0100	+0100	+0050	+0110	+0.9	+0.8	+0.3	+0.1
Dundee	56 27N	2 58W	+0140	+0120	+0055	+0145	+1.2	+1.0	+0.5	+0.4
Newburgh	56 21N	3 14W	+0215	+0200	+0250	+0335	–0.2	–0.4	–1.1	–0.5
Perth	56 24N	3 25W	+0220	+0225	+0510	+0530	–0.9	–1.4	–1.2	–0.3
Arbroath	56 33N	2 35W	+0056	+0037	+0034	+0055	+1.0	+0.8	+0.4	+0.2
Montrose	56 42N	2 28W	+0050	+0045	+0035	+0030	+0.6	+0.4	+0.3	+0.2
Stonehaven	56 58N	2 12W	+0013	+0008	+0013	+0009	+0.2	+0.2	+0.1	0.0
Peterhead	57 30N	1 46W	–0035	–0045	–0035	–0040	–0.3	–0.2	0.0	+0.1
Fraserburgh	57 41N	2 00W	–0122	–0118	–0115	–0115	–0.5	–0.4	–0.1	+0.2
ABERDEEN *Standard port*	57 09N	2 04W	**0200 and 1400**	**0900 and 2100**	**0400 and 1600**	**0900 and 2100**	**4.3**	**3.4**	**1.6**	**0.6**
Banff	57 40N	2 31W	–0100	–0150	–0150	–0050	–0.4	–0.2	–0.1	+0.2
Whitehills	57 41N	2 35W	–0122	–0137	–0117	–0127	–0.4	–0.3	+0.1	+0.1
Buckie	57 41N	2 57W	–0130	–0145	–0125	–0140	–0.2	–0.2	0.0	+0.1
Lossiemouth	57 43N	3 18W	–0125	–0200	–0130	–0130	–0.2	–0.2	0.0	0.0
Burghead	57 42N	3 29W	–0120	–0150	–0135	–0120	–0.2	–0.2	0.0	0.0
Nairn	57 36N	3 52W	–0120	–0150	–0135	–0130	0.0	–0.1	0.0	+0.1
McDermott Base	57 36N	3 59W	–0110	–0140	–0120	–0115	–0.1	–0.1	+0.1	+0.3
ABERDEEN *Standard port*	57 09N	2 04W	**0300 and 1500**	**1000 and 2200**	**0000 and 1200**	**0700 and 1900**	**4.3**	**3.4**	**1.6**	**0.6**
Inverness Firth										
Fortrose	57 35N	4 08W	–0125	–0125	–0125	–0125	0.0	0.0	*No data*	
Inverness	57 30N	4 15W	–0050	–0150	–0200	–0150	+0.5	+0.3	+0.2	+0.1
Cromarty Firth										
Cromarty	57 42N	4 03W	–0120	–0155	–0155	–0120	0.0	0.0	+0.1	+0.2
Invergordon	57 41N	4 10W	–0105	–0200	–0200	–0110	+0.1	+0.1	+0.1	+0.1
Dingwall	57 36N	4 25W	–0045	–0145	*No data*	*No data*	+0.1	+0.2	*No data*	
ABERDEEN *Standard port*	57 09N	2 04W	**0300 and 1500**	**0800 and 2000**	**0200 and 1400**	**0800 and 2000**	**4.3**	**3.4**	**1.6**	**0.6**
Dornoch Firth										
Portmahomack	57 50N	3 50W	–0120	–0210	–0140	–0110	–0.2	–0.1	+0.1	+0.1
Meikle Ferry	57 51N	4 08W	–0100	–0140	–0120	–0055	+0.1	0.0	–0.1	0.0
Golspie	57 58N	3 59W	–0130	–0215	–0155	–0130	–0.3	–0.3	–0.1	0.0
WICK *Standard port*	58 26N	3 05W	**0000 and 1200**	**0700 and 1900**	**0200 and 1400**	**0700 and 1900**	**3.5**	**2.8**	**1.4**	**0.7**
Helmsdale	58 07N	3 39W	+0025	+0015	+0035	+0030	+0.5	+0.3	+0.1	–0.1
Duncansby Head	58 39N	3 02W	–0115	–0115	–0110	–0110	–0.4	–0.4	*No data*	
Orkney Islands										
Muckle Skerry	58 41N	2 55W	–0025	–0025	–0020	–0020	–0.9	–0.8	–0.4	–0.3

Location	Lat	Long	High Water		Low Water		MHWS	MHWN	MLWN	MLWS
Burray Ness	58 51N	2 52W	+0005	+0005	+0015	+0015	−0.2	−0.3	−0.1	−0.1
Deer Sound	58 58N	2 50W	−0040	−0040	−0035	−0035	−0.3	−0.3	−0.1	−0.1
Kirkwall	58 59N	2 58W	−0042	−0042	−0041	−0041	−0.5	−0.4	−0.1	−0.1
Egilsay	59 09N	2 57W	−0125	−0125	−0125	−0125	−0.1	0.0	+0.2	+0.1
Whitehall	58 09N	2 36W	−0030	−0030	−0025	−0030	−0.1	0.0	+0.2	+0.2
Loth	59 11N	2 42W	−0045	−0045	−0055	−0105	−0.4	−0.3	+0.1	+0.2
Kettletoft Pier	59 14N	2 36W	−0030	−0025	−0025	−0025	0.0	0.0	+0.2	+0.2
Rapness	59 15N	2 52W	−0205	−0205	−0205	−0200	+0.1	+0.1	+0.2	0.0
Pierowall	59 19N	2 59W	−0150	−0150	−0145	−0145	+0.2	0.0	0.0	−0.1
Tingwall	59 05N	3 03W	−0200	−0125	−0145	−0125	−0.4	−0.4	−0.1	−0.1
Stromness	58 58N	3 18W	−0225	−0135	−0205	−0205	+0.1	−0.1	0.0	0.0
St Mary's	58 54N	2 55W	−0140	−0140	−0140	−0140	−0.2	−0.2	0.0	−0.1
Widewall Bay	58 49N	3 01W	−0155	−0155	−0150	−0150	+0.1	−0.1	−0.1	−0.3
Bur Wick	58 44N	2 58W	−0100	−0100	−0150	−0150	−0.1	−0.1	+0.2	+0.1
LERWICK	60 09N	1 08W	**0000** and **1200**	**0600** and **1800**	**0100** and **1300**	**0800** and **2000**	**2.1**	**1.7**	**0.9**	**0.5**
Standard port										
Fair Isle	59 32N	1 36W	−0006	−0015	−0031	−0037	+0.1	0.0	+0.1	+0.1
Shetland Islands										
Sumburgh (Grutness Voe)	59 53N	1 17W	+0006	+0008	+0004	−0002	−0.3	−0.3	−0.2	−0.1
Dury Voe	60 21N	1 10W	−0015	−0015	−0010	−0010	0.0	−0.1	0.0	−0.2
Out Skerries	60 25N	0 45W	−0025	−0025	−0010	−0010	+0.1	0.0	0.0	−0.1
Toft Pier	60 28N	1 12W	−0105	−0100	−0125	−0115	+0.2	+0.1	−0.1	−0.1
Burra Voe (Yell Sound)	60 30N	1 03W	−0025	−0025	−0025	−0025	+0.2	+0.1	0.0	−0.1
Mid Yell	60 36N	1 03W	−0030	−0020	−0035	−0025	+0.3	+0.2	+0.2	+0.1
Balta Sound	60 46N	0 50W	−0040	−0045	−0040	−0045	+0.3	+0.2	+0.1	0.0
Burra Firth	60 48N	0 52W	−0110	−0110	−0115	−0115	+0.4	+0.2	0.0	0.0
Bluemull Sound	60 42N	1 00W	−0135	−0135	−0155	−0155	+0.5	+0.2	+0.1	0.0
Sullom Voe	60 27N	1 18W	−0135	−0125	−0135	−0120	0.0	0.0	−0.2	−0.2
Hillswick	60 29N	1 29W	−0220	−0220	−0200	−0200	−0.1	−0.1	−0.1	−0.1
Scalloway	60 08N	1 16W	−0150	−0150	−0150	−0150	−0.5	−0.4	−0.3	0.0
Bay of Quendale	59 54N	1 21W	−0025	−0025	−0030	−0030	−0.4	−0.3	0.0	+0.1
Foula	60 07N	2 03W	−0140	−0140	−0130	−0130	−0.1	−0.1	0.0	0.0
WICK	58 26N	3 05W	**0200** and **1400**	**0700** and **1900**	**0100** and **1300**	**0700** and **1900**	**3.5**	**2.8**	**1.4**	**0.7**
Standard port										
Stroma	58 40N	3 08W	−0115	−0115	−0110	−0110	−0.4	−0.5	−0.1	−0.2
Gills Bay	58 38N	3 10W	−0150	−0150	−0202	−0202	+0.7	+0.7	+0.6	+0.3
Scrabster	58 37N	3 33W	−0255	−0225	−0240	−0230	+1.5	+1.2	+0.8	+0.3
Sule Skerry	59 05N	4 24W	−0320	−0255	−0315	−0250	+0.4	+0.3	+0.2	+0.1
Loch Eriboll Portnancon	58 30N	4 42W	−0340	−0255	−0315	−0255	+1.6	+1.3	+0.8	+0.4
Kyle of Durness	58 36N	4 47W	−0350	−0350	−0315	−0315	+1.1	+0.7	+0.4	−0.1
Rona	59 08N	5 49W	−0350	−0350	−0350	−0340	−0.3	−0.4	−0.2	−0.4
STORNOWAY	58 12N	6 23W	**0100** and **1300**	**0700** and **1900**	**0300** and **1500**	**0900** and **2100**	**4.8**	**3.7**	**2.0**	**0.7**
Standard port										
Outer Hebrides										
Loch Shell	58 00N	6 25W	−0013	0000	0000	−0017	0.0	−0.1	−0.1	0.0
E Loch Tarbert	57 54N	6 48W	−0025	−0010	−0010	−0020	+0.2	0.0	+0.1	+0.1
Leverburgh	57 46N	7 02W	−0041	−0020	−0015	−0025	−0.2	−0.2	−0.2	−0.1
Bays Loch	57 43N	7 10W	−0038	−0013	−0014	−0027	−0.1	−0.2	−0.2	−0.1
Loch Maddy	57 36N	7 09W	−0044	−0014	−0016	−0030	0.0	−0.1	−0.1	0.0
Loch Carnan	57 22N	7 16W	−0050	−0010	−0020	−0040	−0.3	−0.5	−0.1	−0.1
Loch Skiport	57 20N	7 16W	−0100	−0025	−0024	−0024	−0.2	−0.4	−0.3	−0.2
Loch Boisdale	57 09N	7 16W	−0055	−0030	−0020	−0040	−0.7	−0.7	−0.3	−0.2
Barra (North Bay)	57 00N	7 24W	−0103	−0031	−0034	−0048	−0.6	−0.5	−0.2	−0.1
Castle Bay	56 57N	7 29W	−0115	−0040	−0045	−0100	−0.5	−0.6	−0.3	−0.1
Barra Head	56 47N	7 38W	−0115	−0040	−0045	−0055	−0.8	−0.7	−0.2	+0.1
Shillay	57 32N	7 42W	−0103	−0043	−0047	−0107	−0.6	−0.7	−0.7	−0.3
Balivanich	57 29N	7 23W	−0103	−0017	−0031	−0045	−0.7	−0.6	−0.5	−0.2
Scolpaig	57 39N	7 29W	−0033	−0033	−0040	−0040	−1.0	−0.9	−0.5	0.0
W Loch Tarbert	57 55N	6 55W	−0015	−0015	−0046	−0046	−1.1	−0.9	−0.5	0.0
Little Bernera	58 16N	6 52W	−0021	−0011	−0017	−0027	−0.5	−0.6	−0.4	−0.2
Carloway	58 17N	6 47W	−0040	+0020	−0035	−0015	−0.7	−0.5	−0.3	0.0
St Kilda Village Bay	57 48N	8 34W	−0040	−0040	−0045	−0045	−1.4	−1.1	−0.8	−0.3
Flannan Isles	58 17N	7 35W	−0026	−0016	−0016	−0026	−0.9	−0.7	−0.6	−0.2
Rockall	57 36N	13 41W	−0055	−0055	−0105	−0105	−1.8	−1.5	−0.9	−0.2

Location	Lat	Long	High Water		Low Water		MHWS	MHWN	MLWN	MLWS
ULLAPOOL *Standard port*	57 54N	5 09W	**0000** and **1200**	**0600** and **1800**	**0300** and **1500**	**0900** and **2100**	**5.2**	**3.9**	**2.1**	**0.7**
Loch Bervie	58 27N	5 03W	+0017	+0020	+0015	+0015	–0.4	–0.2	–0.1	+0.1
Loch Laxford	58 24N	5 05W	+0015	+0015	+0005	+0005	–0.3	–0.4	–0.2	0.0
Eddrachillis Bay										
Badcall Bay	58 19N	5 08W	+0005	+0005	+0005	+0005	–0.7	–0.5	–0.5	+0.2
Loch Nedd	58 14N	5 10W	0000	0000	0000	0000	–0.3	–0.2	–0.2	0.0
Loch Inver	58 09N	5 18W	–0005	–0005	–0005	–0005	–0.2	0.0	0.0	+0.1
Summer Isles Tanera Mor	58 01N	5 24W	–0005	–0005	–0010	–0010	–0.1	+0.1	0.0	+0.1
Loch Ewe Mellon Charles	57 51N	5 38W	–0005	–0010	–0005	–0005	–0.1	–0.1	–0.1	+0.1
Loch Gairloch Gairloch	57 43N	5 41W	–0012	–0011	–0011	–0011	–0.2	+0.1	–0.2	+0.2
Loch Torridon Shieldaig	57 31N	5 39W	–0020	–0020	–0015	–0015	+0.4	+0.3	+0.1	0.0
Inner Sound Applecross	57 26N	5 49W	–0010	–0015	–0010	–0010	0.0	0.0	0.0	+0.1
Loch Carron Plockton	57 21N	5 39W	+0005	–0025	–0005	–0010	+0.5	+0.5	+0.5	+0.2
Rona Loch a' Bhraige	57 35N	5 58W	–0020	0000	–0010	0000	–0.1	–0.1	–0.1	–0.2
Skye										
Broadford Bay	57 15N	5 54W	–0015	–0015	–0010	–0015	+0.2	+0.1	+0.1	0.0
Portree	57 24N	6 11W	–0025	–0025	–0025	–0025	+0.1	–0.2	–0.2	0.0
Loch Snizort (Uig Bay)	57 35N	6 22W	–0045	–0020	–0005	–0025	+0.1	–0.4	–0.2	0.0
Loch Dunvegan	57 27N	6 38W	–0105	–0030	–0020	–0040	0.0	–0.1	0.0	0.0
Loch Harport	57 20N	6 25W	–0115	–0035	–0020	–0100	–0.1	–0.1	0.0	+0.1
Soay Camus nan Gall	57 09N	6 13W	–0055	–0025	–0025	–0045	–0.4	–0.2	*No data*	
Loch Alsh										
Kyle of Lochalsh	57 17N	5 43W	–0040	–0020	–0005	–0025	+0.1	0.0	0.0	–0.1
Dornie Bridge	57 17N	5 31W	–0040	–0010	–0005	–0020	+0.1	–0.1	0.0	0.0
Kyle Rhea Glenelg Bay	57 13N	5 38W	–0105	–0035	–0035	–0055	–0.4	–0.4	–0.9	–0.1
Loch Hourn	57 06N	5 34W	–0125	–0050	–0040	–0110	–0.2	–0.1	–0.1	+0.1
OBAN *Standard port*	56 25N	5 29W	**0000** and **1200**	**0600** and **1800**	**0100** and **1300**	**0700** and **1900**	**4.0**	**2.9**	**1.8**	**0.7**
Loch Nevis										
Inverie Bay	57 02N	5 41W	+0030	+0020	+0035	+0020	+1.0	+0.9	+0.2	0.0
Mallaig	57 00N	5 50W	+0017	+0017	+0030	+0024	+1.0	+0.7	+0.3	+0.1
Eigg Bay of Laig	56 55N	6 10W	+0015	+0030	+0040	+0005	+0.7	+0.6	–0.2	– 0.2
Loch Moidart	56 47N	5 53W	+0015	+0015	+0040	+0020	+0.8	+0.6	– 0.2	–0.2
Coll Loch Eatharna	56 37N	6 31W	+0025	+0010	+0015	+0025	+0.4	+0.3	*No data*	
Tiree Gott Bay	56 31N	6 48W	0000	+0010	+0005	+0010	0.0	+0.1	0.0	0.0
OBAN *Standard port*	56 25N	5 29W	**0100** and **1300**	**0700** and **1900**	**0100** and **1300**	**0800** and **2000**	**4.0**	**2.9**	**1.8**	**0.7**
Mull										
Carsaig Bay	56 19N	5 58W	–0015	–0005	–0030	+0020	+0.1	+0.2	0.0	–0.1
Iona	56 20N	6 23W	–0010	–0005	–0020	+0015	0.0	+0.1	–0.3	–0.2
Bunessan	56 19N	6 14W	–0015	–0015	–0010	–0015	+0.3	+0.1	0.0	–0.1
Ulva Sound	56 29N	6 08W	–0010	–0015	0000	–0005	+0.4	+0.3	0.0	–0.1
Loch Sunart Salen	56 43N	5 47W	–0015	+0015	+0010	+0005	+0.6	+0.5	–0.1	–0.1
Sound of Mull										
Tobermory	56 37N	6 04W	+0025	+0010	+0015	+0025	+0.5	+0.6	+0.1	+0.2
Salen	56 31N	5 57W	+0045	+0015	+0020	+0030	+0.2	+0.2	–0.1	0.0
Loch Aline	56 32N	5 46W	+0012	+0012	*No data*	*No data*	+0.5	+0.3	*No data*	
Craignure	56 28N	5 42W	+0030	+0005	+0010	+0015	0.0	+0.1	–0.1	–0.1
Loch Linnhe										
Corran	56 43N	5 14W	+0007	+0007	+0004	+0004	+0.4	+0.4	–0.1	0.0
Corpach	56 51N	5 07W	0000	+0020	+0040	0000	0.0	0.0	–0.2	–0.2
Loch Eil Head	56 51N	5 20W	+0025	+0045	+0105	+0025	*No data*		*No data*	
Loch Leven Head	56 43N	5 00W	+0045	+0045	+0045	+0045	*No data*		*No data*	
Loch Linnhe Port Appin	56 33N	5 25W	–0005	–0005	–0030	0000	+0.2	+0.2	+0.1	+0.1
Loch Creran										
Barcaldine Pier	56 32N	5 19W	+0010	+0020	+0040	+0015	+0.1	+0.1	0.0	+0.1
Loch Creran Head	56 33N	5 16W	+0015	+0025	+0120	+0020	–0.3	–0.3	–0.4	–0.3
Loch Etive										
Dunstaffnage Bay	56 27N	5 26W	+0005	0000	0000	+0005	+0.1	+0.1	+0.1	+0.1
Connel	56 27N	5 24W	+0020	+0005	+0010	+0015	–0.3	–0.2	–0.1	+0.1
Bonawe	56 27N	5 13W	+0150	+0205	+0240	+0210	–2.0	–1.7	–1.3	–0.5
Seil Sound	56 18N	5 35W	–0035	–0015	–0040	–0015	–1.3	–0.9	–0.7	–0.3
Colonsay Scalasaig	56 04N	6 11W	–0020	–0005	–0015	+0005	–0.3	–0.2	–0.3	0.0
Jura Glengarrisdale Bay	56 07N	5 47W	–0020	0000	–0010	0000	–0.4	–0.2	0.0	–0.2

Location	Lat	Long	High Water		Low Water		MHWS	MHWN	MLWN	MLWS
Islay										
Rubha A'Mhail	55 56N	6 07W	–0020	0000	+0005	–0015	–0.3	–0.1	–0.3	–0.1
Ardnave Point	55 52N	6 20W	–0035	+0010	0000	–0025	–0.4	–0.2	–0.3	–0.1
Orsay	55 41N	6 31W	–0110	–0110	–0040	–0040	–1.4	–0.6	–0.5	–0.2
Bruichladdich	55 46N	6 22W	–0105	–0035	–0110	–0110	–1.8	–1.3	–0.4	+0.3
Port Ellen	55 38N	6 11W	–0530	–0050	–0045	–0530	–3.1	–2.1	–1.3	–0.4
Port Askaig	55 51N	6 06W	–0030	–0035	–0015	–0025	–1.8	–1.3	–0.7	–0.2
Sound of Jura										
Craighouse	55 50N	5 57W	–0230	–0250	–0150	–0230	–3.0	–2.4	–1.3	–0.6
Loch Melfort	56 15N	5 29W	–0055	–0025	–0040	–0035	–1.2	–0.8	–0.5	–0.1
Loch Beag	56 09N	5 36W	–0110	–0045	–0035	–0045	–1.6	–1.2	–0.8	–0.4
Carsaig Bay	56 02N	5 38W	–0105	–0040	–0050	–0050	–2.1	–1.6	–1.0	–0.4
Sound of Gigha	55 41N	5 44W	–0450	–0210	–0130	–0410	–2.5	–1.6	–1.0	–0.1
Machrihanish	55 25N	5 45W	–0520	–0350	–0340	–0540	*Mean range 0.5 metres*			
GREENOCK	55 57N	4 46W	**0000** and **1200**	**0600** and **1800**	**0000** and **1200**	**0600** and **1800**	**3.4**	**2.8**	**1.0**	**0.3**
Standard port										
Firth of Clyde										
Southend, Kintyre	55 19N	5 38W	–0030	–0010	+0005	+0035	–1.3	–1.2	–0.5	–0.2
Campbeltown	55 25N	5 36W	–0025	–0005	–0015	+0005	–0.5	–0.3	+0.1	+0.2
Carradale	55 36N	5 28W	–0015	–0005	–0005	+0005	–0.3	–0.2	+0.1	+0.1
Loch Ranza	55 43N	5 18W	–0015	–0005	–0010	–0005	–0.4	–0.3	–0.1	0.0
Loch Fyne										
East Loch Tarbert	55 52N	5 24W	–0005	–0005	0000	–0005	+0.2	+0.1	0.0	0.0
Inveraray	56 14N	5 04W	+0011	+0011	+0034	+0034	–0.1	+0.1	–0.5	–0.2
Kyles of Bute										
Rubha a'Bhodaich	55 55N	5 09W	–0020	–0010	–0007	–0007	–0.2	–0.1	+0.2	+0.2
Tighnabruich	55 55N	5 13W	+0007	–0010	–0002	–0015	0.0	+0.2	+0.4	+0.5
Firth of Clyde – continued										
Millport	55 45N	4 56W	–0005	–0025	–0025	–0005	0.0	–0.1	0.0	+0.1
Rothesay Bay	55 50N	5 03W	–0020	–0015	–0010	–0002	+0.2	+0.2	+0.2	+0.2
Wemyss Bay	55 53N	4 53W	–0005	–0005	–0005	–0005	0.0	0.0	+0.1	+0.1
Loch Long										
Coulport	56 03N	4 53W	–0011	–0011	–0008	–0008	0.0	0.0	0.0	0.0
Lochgoilhead	56 10N	4 54W	+0015	0000	–0005	–0005	–0.2	–0.3	–0.3	–0.3
Arrochar	56 12N	4 45W	–0005	–0005	–0005	–0005	0.0	0.0	–0.1	–0.1
Gare Loch										
Rhu Marina	56 01N	4 46W	–0007	–0007	–0007	–0007	–0.1	–0.1	–0.1	–0.2
Faslane	56 04N	4 49W	+0003	+0003	+0003	+0003	+0.1	+0.1	+0.1	0.0
Garelochhead	56 05N	4 50W	0000	0000	0000	0000	0.0	0.0	0.0	–0.1
River Clyde										
Helensburgh	56 00N	4 44W	0000	0000	0000	0000	0.0	0.0	0.0	0.0
Port Glasgow	55 56N	4 41W	+0010	+0005	+0010	+0020	+0.2	+0.1	0.0	0.0
Bowling	55 56N	4 29W	+0020	+0010	+0030	+0055	+0.6	+0.5	+0.3	+0.1
Clydebank (Rothesay Dock)	55 54N	4 24W	+0025	+0015	+0035	+0100	+1.1	+0.9	+0.6	+0.3
Glasgow	55 51N	4 16W	+0025	+0015	+0035	+0105	+1.4	+1.1	+0.8	+0.4
Firth of Clyde – continued										
Brodick Bay	55 35N	5 08W	–0013	–0013	–0008	–0008	–0.2	–0.1	0.0	+0.1
Lamlash	55 32N	5 07W	–0016	–0036	–0024	–0004	–0.2	–0.2	*No data*	
Ardrossan	55 38N	4 49W	–0020	–0010	–0010	–0010	–0.2	–0.2	+0.1	+0.1
Irvine	55 36N	4 42W	–0020	–0020	–0030	–0010	–0.3	–0.3	–0.1	0.0
Troon	55 33N	4 41W	–0025	–0025	–0020	–0020	–0.2	–0.2	0.0	0.0
Ayr	55 28N	4 39W	–0025	–0025	–0030	–0015	–0.4	–0.3	+0.1	+0.1
Girvan	55 15N	4 52W	–0025	–0040	–0035	–0010	–0.3	–0.3	–0.1	0.0
Loch Ryan Stranraer	54 55N	5 02W	–0030	–0025	–0010	–0010	–0.2	–0.1	0.0	+0.1
LIVERPOOL	53 27N	3 01W	**0000** and **1200**	**0600** and **1800**	**0200** and **1400**	**0800** and **2000**	**9.4**	**7.5**	**3.2**	**1.1**
Standard port										
Portpatrick	54 51N	5 07W	+0038	+0032	+0009	–0008	–5.5	–4.4	–2.0	–0.6
Luce Bay										
Drummore	54 42N	4 53W	+0035	+0045	+0010	+0015	–3.5	–2.6	–1.2	–0.5
Port William	54 46N	4 35W	+0035	+0035	+0020	–0005	–3.0	–2.3	–1.1	*Nodata*
Wigtown Bay										
Isle of Whithorn	54 42N	4 22W	+0025	+0030	+0020	0000	–2.5	–2.1	–1.1	–0.4
Garlieston	54 47N	4 22W	+0030	+0040	+0025	0000	–2.4	–1.8	–0.8	*Nodata*
Solway Firth										
Kirkcudbright Bay	54 48N	4 04W	+0020	+0020	+0005	–0005	–1.9	–1.6	–0.8	–0.3
Hestan Islet	54 50N	3 48W	+0030	+0030	+0015	+0020	–1.1	–1.2	–0.8	–0.2
Southerness Point	54 52N	3 36W	+0035	+0035	+0025	+0005	–0.8	–0.8	*No data*	

Location	Lat	Long	High Water		Low Water		MHWS	MHWN	MLWN	MLWS
Annan Waterfoot	54 58N	3 16W	+0055	+0110	+0215	+0305	–2.3	–2.7	–3.0	
Torduff Point	54 58N	3 09W	+0110	+0145	+0515	+0405	–4.2	–5.0	*Not below CD*	
Redkirk	54 59N	3 06W	+0115	+0220	+0710	+0440	–5.6	–6.3	*Not below CD*	
WEST COAST OF ENGLAND										
Silloth	54 52N	3 24W	+0035	+0045	+0040	+0050	–0.2	–0.4	–0.9	–0.3
Maryport	54 43N	3 30W	+0021	+0036	+0017	+0002	–0.8	–0.9	–0.7	–0.2
Workington	54 39N	3 34W	+0029	+0027	+0014	+0004	–1.1	–1.1	–0.5	–0.1
Whitehaven	54 33N	3 36W	+0010	+0020	+0005	0000	–1.4	–1.2	–0.8	–0.1
Tarn Point	54 17N	3 25W	+0010	+0010	+0005	–0005	–1.1	–1.1	–0.7	–0.2
Duddon Bar	54 09N	3 20W	+0007	+0007	+0005	–0001	–0.9	–0.9	–0.6	–0.2
			0000	**0600**	**0200**	**0700**				
LIVERPOOL	53 27N	3 01W	and	and	and	and	**9.4**	**7.5**	**3.2**	**1.1**
Standard port			**1200**	**1800**	**1400**	**1900**				
Barrow-in-Furness	54 06N	3 12W	+0020	+0020	+0010	+0010	+0.1	–0.2	–0.2	0.0
Ulverston	54 11N	3 04W	+0025	+0045	*No data*	*no data*	–0.1	–0.2	*No data*	
Arnside	54 12N	2 51W	+0105	+0140	*No data*	*no data*	+0.4	+0.1	*No data*	
Morecambe	54 04N	2 53W	+0010	+0015	+0025	+0010	+0.1	–0.1	–0.3	0.0
Heysham	54 02N	2 55W	+0014	+0012	+0002	–0003	+0.2	–0.1	–0.2	0.0
River Lune Glasson Dock	54 00N	2 51W	+0025	+0035	+0215	+0235	–2.8	–3.1	*No data*	
Lancaster	54 03N	2 49W	+0115	+0035	*Dries*	*Dries*	–5.1	–5.0	*Dries*	
River Wyre										
Wyre Lighthouse	53 57N	3 02W	–0005	–0005	0000	–0005	–0.2	–0.2	*No data*	
Fleetwood	53 56N	3 00W	–0004	–0004	–0006	–0006	–0.2	–0.2	–0.1	+0.1
Blackpool	53 49N	3 04W	–0010	0000	–0010	–0020	–0.5	–0.5	–0.4	–0.1
River Ribble Preston	53 45N	2 45W	+0015	+0015	+0330	+0305	–4.1	–4.2	–3.1	–1.0
Liverpool Bay										
Southport	53 39N	3 01W	–0015	–0005	*No data*	*No data*	–0.4	–0.4	*No data*	
Formby	53 32N	3 07W	–0010	–0005	–0025	–0025	–0.4	–0.2	–0.3	–0.1
River Mersey										
Alfred Dock	53 24N	3 01W	+0007	+0007	0000	0000	–0.1	–0.1	–0.3	–0.2
Eastham	53 19N	2 57W	+0014	+0014	+0006	+0006	+0.2	0.0	–0.4	–0.5
Hale Head	53 19N	2 48W	+0035	+0030	*No data*	*No data*	–2.5	–2.6	*No data*	
Widnes	53 21N	2 44W	+0045	+0050	+0355	+0340	–4.3	–4.5	–2.8	–0.6
Fiddler's Ferry	53 22N	2 40W	+0105	+0120	+0535	+0445	–6.0	–6.4	–2.7	–0.6
River Dee										
Hilbre Island	53 23N	3 14W	–0011	–0008	–0013	–0018	–0.4	–0.3	–0.1	+0.2
Chester	53 12N	2 54W	+0110	+0110	+0455	+0455	–5.4	–5.5	*Dries*	
Connah's Quay (Wales)	53 13N	3 03W	+0005	+0020	+0350	+0335	–4.7	–4.5	*Dries*	
Mostyn Docks (Wales)	53 19N	3 16W	–0015	–0010	–0025	–0025	–0.9	–0.8	*No data*	
Isle of Man Peel	54 14N	4 42W	+0010	+0010	–0020	–0030	–4.2	–3.2	–1.7	–0.7
Ramsey	54 19N	4 22W	+0010	+0020	–0010	–0020	–2.0	–1.6	–0.9	–0.2
Douglas	54 09N	4 28W	+0010	+0020	–0020	–0030	–2.5	–2.1	–0.8	–0.3
Port St Mary	54 04N	4 44W	+0010	+0020	–0015	–0035	–3.5	–2.7	–1.6	–0.6
Calf Sound	54 04N	4 48W	+0010	+0010	–0020	–0030	–3.3	–2.7	–1.2	–0.5
Port Erin	54 05N	4 46W	+0018	+0010	–0013	–0028	–4.1	–3.3	–1.6	–0.6
WALES										
Colwyn Bay	53 18N	3 43W	–0015	–0015	*No data*	*No data*	–1.6	–1.4	*No data*	
Llandudno	53 20N	3 50W	–0019	–0021	–0031	–0038	–1.7	–1.6	–0.9	–0.6
			0000	**0600**	**0500**	**1100**				
HOLYHEAD	53 19N	4 37W	and	and	and	and	**5.6**	**4.4**	**2.0**	**0.7**
Standard port			**1200**	**1800**	**1700**	**2300**				
Conwy	53 17N	3 50W	+0025	+0035	+0120	+0105	+2.3	+1.8	+0.6	+0.4
Menai Strait										
Beaumaris	53 16N	4 05W	+0025	+0010	+0055	+0035	+2.0	+1.6	+0.5	+0.1
Menai Bridge	53 13N	4 10W	+0030	+0010	+0100	+0035	+1.7	+1.4	+0.3	0.0
Port Dinorwic	53 11N	4 13W	–0015	–0025	+0030	0000	0.0	0.0	0.0	+0.1
Caernarfon	53 09N	4 16W	–0030	–0030	+0015	–0005	–0.4	–0.4	–0.1	–0.1
Fort Belan	53 07N	4 20W	–0040	–0015	–0025	–0005	–1.0	–0.9	–0.2	–0.1
Trwyn Dinmor	53 19N	4 03W	+0025	+0015	+0050	+0035	+1.9	+1.5	+0.5	+0.2
Moelfre	53 20N	4 14W	+0025	+0020	+0050	+0035	+1.9	+1.4	+0.5	+0.2
Amlwch	53 25N	4 20W	+0020	+0010	+0035	+0025	+1.6	+ 1.3	+0.5	+0.2
Cemaes Bay	53 25N	4 27W	+0020	+0025	+0040	+0035	+1.0	+0.7	+0.3	+0.1
Trearddur Bay	53 16N	4 37W	–0045	–0025	–0015	–0015	–0.4	–0.4	0.0	+0.1
Porth Trecastell	53 12N	4 30W	–0045	–0025	–0005	–0015	–0.6	–0.6	0.0	0.0
Llanddwyn Island	53 08N	4 25W	–0115	–0055	–0030	–0020	–0.7	–0.5	–0.1	0.0
Trefor	53 00N	4 25W	–0115	–0100	–0030	–0020	–0.8	–0.9	–0.2	–0.1
Porth Dinllaen	52 57N	4 34W	–0120	–0105	–0035	–0025	–1.0	–1.0	–0.2	–0.2
Porth Ysgaden	52 54N	4 39W	–0125	–0110	–0040	–0035	–1.1	–1.0	–0.1	–0.1
Bardsey Island	52 46N	4 47W	–0220	–0240	–0145	–0140	–1.2	–1.2	–0.5	–0.1

Location	Lat	Long	High Water		Low Water		MHWS	MHWN	MLWN	MLWS
MILFORD HAVEN *Standard port*	51 42N	5 03W	**0100** and **1300**	**0800** and **2000**	**0100** and **1300**	**0700** and **1900**	**7.0**	**5.2**	**2.5**	**0.7**
Cardigan Bay										
Aberdaron	52 48N	4 43W	+0210	+0200	+0240	+0310	–2.4	–1.9	–0.6	–0.2
St Tudwal's Roads	52 49N	4 29W	+0155	+0145	+0240	+0310	–2.2	–1.9	–0.7	–0.2
Pwllheli	52 53N	4 24W	+0210	+0150	+0245	+0320	–1.9	–1.6	–0.6	–0.1
Criccieth	52 55N	4 14W	+0210	+0155	+0255	+0320	–2.0	–1.8	–0.7	–0.3
Porthmadog	52 55N	4 08W	+0235	+0210	*No data*	*No data*	–1.9	–1.8	*No data*	
Barmouth	52 43N	4 03W	+0207	+0200	+0300	+0233	–2.0	–1.5	–0.6	0.0
Aberdovey	52 33N	4 03W	+0215	+0200	+0230	+0305	–2.0	–1.7	–0.5	0.0
Aberystwyth	52 24N	4 05W	+0145	+0130	+0210	+0245	–2.0	–1.7	–0.7	0.0
New Quay	52 13N	4 21W	+0150	+0125	+0155	+0230	–2.1	–1.8	–0.6	–0.1
Aberporth	52 08N	4 33W	+0135	+0120	+0150	+0220	–2.1	–1.8	–0.6	–0.1
Port Cardigan	52 07N	4 41W	+0140	+0120	+0220	+0130	–2.3	–1.8	–0.5	0.0
Cardigan (Town)	52 05N	4 40W	+0220	+0150	*No data*	*No data*	–2.2	–1.6	*No data*	
Fishguard	52 01N	4 59W	+0115	+0100	+0110	+0135	–2.2	–1.8	–0.5	+0.1
Porthgain	51 57N	5 11W	+0055	+0045	+0045	+0100	–2.5	–1.8	–0.6	0.0
Ramsey Sound	51 53N	5 19W	+0030	+0030	+0030	+0030	–1.9	–1.3	–0.3	0.0
Solva	51 52N	5 12W	+0015	+0010	+0035	+0015	–1.5	–1.0	–0.2	0.0
Little Haven	51 46N	5 07W	+0010	+0010	+0025	+0015	–1.1	–0.8	–0.2	0.0
Martin's Haven	51 44N	5 15W	+0010	+0010	+0015	+0015	–0.8	–0.5	+0.1	+0.1
Skomer Island	51 44N	5 17W	–0005	–0005	+0005	+0005	–0.4	–0.1	0.0	0.0
Dale Roads	51 42N	5 09W	–0005	–0005	–0008	–0008	0.0	0.0	0.0	–0.1
Cleddau River										
Neyland	51 42N	4 57W	+0002	+0010	0000	0000	0.0	0.0	0.0	0.0
Black Tar	51 45N	4 54W	+0010	+0020	+0005	0000	+0.1	+0.1	0.0	–0.1
Haverfordwest	51 48N	4 58W	+0010	+0025	*Dries*	*Dries*	–4.8	–4.9	*Dries*	
Stackpole Quay	51 37N	4 54W	–0005	+0025	–0010	–0010	+0.9	+0.7	+0.2	+0.3
Tenby	51 40N	4 42W	–0015	–0010	–0015	–0020	+1.4	+1.1	+0.5	+0.2
Towy River										
Ferryside	51 46N	4 22W	0000	–0010	+0220	0000	–0.3	–0.7	–1.7	–0.6
Carmarthen	51 51N	4 18W	+0010	0000	*Dries*	*Dries*	–4.4	–4.8	*Dries*	
Burry Inlet										
Burry Port	51 41N	4 15W	+0003	+0003	+0007	+0007	+1.6	+1.4	+0.5	+0.4
Llanelli	51 40N	4 10W	–0003	–0003	+0150	+0020	+0.8	+0.6	*No data*	
Mumbles	51 34N	3 58W	+0001	+0003	–0012	–0005	+2.5	+2.0	+0.8	+0.4
River Neath Entrance	51 37N	3 51W	+0002	+0011	*Dries*	*Dries*	+2.7	+2.2	*Dries*	
Port Talbot	51 35N	3 49W	0000	+0005	–0010	–0005	+2.7	+2.1	+1.0	+0.4
Porthcawl	51 28N	3 42W	+0005	+0010	–0010	–0005	+2.9	+2.3	+0.8	+0.3
BRISTOL, AVONMOUTH *Standard port*	51 30N	2 44W	**0600** and **1800**	**1100** and **2300**	**0300** and **1500**	**0800** and **2000**	**13.2**	**9.8**	**3.8**	**1.0**
Barry	51 23N	3 16W	–0025	–0025	–0130	–0045	–1.5	–1.1	0.0	+0.2
Flat Holm	51 23N	3 07W	–0015	–0015	–0035	–0035	–1.4	–1.0	–0.5	0.0
Steep Holm	51 20N	3 06W	–0020	–0020	–0040	–0040	–1.7	–1.1	–0.5	–0.4
Cardiff	51 27N	3 10W	–0015	–0015	–0035	–0030	–0.9	–0.7	+0.2	+0.2
Newport	51 33N	2 59W	–0005	–0010	–0015	–0015	–0.9	–0.9	–0.2	–0.2
River Wye Chepstow	51 39N	2 40W	+0020	+0020	*No data*	*No data*	*No data*		*No data*	
BRISTOL, AVONMOUTH *Standard port*	51 30N	2 44W	**0000** and **1200**	**0600** and **1800**	**0000** and **1200**	**0700** and **1900**	**13.2**	**9.8**	**3.8**	**1.0**
WEST COAST OF ENGLAND										
River Severn										
Sudbrook	51 35N	2 43W	+0010	+0010	+0025	+0015	+0.2	+0.1	–0.1	+0.1
Beachley (Aust)	51 36N	2 38W	+0010	+0015	+0040	+0025	–0.2	–0.2	–0.5	–0.3
Inward Rocks	51 39N	2 37W	+0020	+0020	+0105	+0045	–1.0	–1.1	–1.4	–0.6
Narlwood Rocks	51 39N	2 36W	+0025	+0025	+0120	+0100	–1.9	–2.0	–2.3	–0.8
White House	51 40N	2 33W	+0025	+0025	+0145	+0120	–3.0	–3.1	–3.6	–1.0
Berkeley	51 42N	2 30W	+0030	+0045	+0245	+0220	–3.8	–3.9	–3.4	–0.5
Sharpness Dock	51 43N	2 29W	+0035	+0050	+0305	+0245	–3.9	–4.2	–3.3	–0.4
Wellhouse Rock	51 44N	2 29W	+0040	+0055	+0320	+0305	–4.1	–4.4	–3.1	–0.2
Epney	51 42N	2 24W	+0130	*No data*	*No data*	*No data*	–9.4	*No data*	*No data*	
Minsterworth	51 50N	2 23W	+0140	*No data*	*No data*	*No data*	–10.1	*No data*	*No data*	
Llanthony	51 51N	2 21W	+0215	*No data*	*No data*	*No data*	–10.7	*No data*	*No data*	
BRISTOL, AVONMOUTH *Standard port*	51 30N	2 44W	**0200** and **1400**	**0800** and **2000**	**0300** and **1500**	**0800** and **2000**	**13.2**	**9.8**	**3.8**	**1.0**
River Avon										
Shirehampton	51 29N	2 41W	0000	0000	+0035	+0010	–0.7	–0.7	–0.8	0.0
Sea Mills	51 29N	2 39W	+0005	+0005	+0105	+0030	–1.4	–1.5	–1.7	–0.1
Cumberland Basin Entrance	51 27N	2 37W	+0010	+0010	*Dries*	*Dries*	–2.9	–3.0	*Dries*	
Portishead	51 30N	2 45W	–0002	0000	*No data*	*No data*	–0.1	–0.1	*No data*	

Location	Lat	Long	High Water		Low Water		MHWS	MHWN	MLWN	MLWS
Clevedon	51 27N	2 52W	–0010	–0020	–0025	–0015	–0.4	–0.2	+0.2	0.0
St Thomas Head	51 24N	2 56W	0000	0000	–0030	–0030	–0.4	–0.2	+0.1	+0.1
English & Welsh Grounds	51 28N	2 59W	–0008	–0008	–0030	–0030	–0.5	–0.8	–0.3	0.0
Weston-super-Mare	51 21N	2 59W	–0020	–0030	–0130	–0030	–1.2	–1.0	–0.8	–0.2
River Parrett										
Burnham-on-Sea	51 14N	3 00W	–0020	–0025	–0030	0000	–2.3	–1.9	–1.4	–1.1
Bridgwater	51 08N	3 00W	–0015	–0030	+0305	+0455	–8.6	–8.1	*Dries*	
Hinkley Point	51 13N	3 08W	–0032	–0028	–0055	–0049	–1.4	–1.1	–0.1	0.0
Minehead	51 13N	3 28W	–0037	–0052	–0155	–0045	–2.6	–1.9	–0.2	0.0
Porlock Bay	51 13N	3 38W	–0045	–0055	–0205	–0050	–3.0	–2.2	–0.1	–0.1
Lynmouth	51 14N	3 50W	–0055	–0115	*No data*	*No data*	–3.6	–2.7	*No data*	
			0100	**0700**	**0100**	**0700**				
MILFORD HAVEN	51 42N	5 03W	and	and	and	and	**7.0**	**5.2**	**2.5**	**0.7**
Standard port			**1300**	**1900**	**1300**	**1900**				
Ilfracombe	51 13N	4 07W	–0016	–0016	–0041	–0031	+2.3	+1.8	+0.6	+0.3
Rivers Taw & Torridge										
Appledore	51 03N	4 12W	–0020	–0025	+0015	–0045	+0.5	0.0	–0.9	–0.5
Yelland Marsh	51 04N	4 10W	–0010	–0015	+0100	–0015	+0.1	–0.4	–1.2	–0.6
Fremington	51 05N	4 07W	–0010	–0015	+0030	–0030	–1.1	–1.8	–2.2	–0.5
Barnstaple	51 05N	4 04W	0000	–0015	–0155	–0245	–2.9	–3.8	–2.2	–0.4
Bideford	51 01N	4 12W	–0020	–0025	0000	0000	–1.1	–1.6	–2.5	–0.7
Clovelly	51 00N	4 24W	–0030	–0030	–0020	–0040	+1.3	+1.1	+0.2	+0.2
Lundy	51 10N	4 39W	–0025	–0025	–0035	–0030	+1.0	+0.8	+0.2	+0.1
Bude	50 50N	4 33W	–0040	–0040	–0035	–0045	+0.7	+0.6	*No data*	
Boscastle	50 41N	4 42W	–0045	–0010	–0110	–0100	+0.3	+0.4	+0.2	+0.2
Port Isaac	50 35N	4 50W	–0100	–0100	–0100	–0100	+0.5	+0.6	0.0	+0.2
River Camel										
Padstow	50 33N	4 56W	–0055	–0050	–0040	–0050	+0.3	+0.4	+0.1	+0.1
Wadebridge	50 31N	4 50W	–0052	–0052	+0235	+0245	–3.8	–3.8	–2.5	–0.4
Newquay	50 25N	5 05W	–0100	–0110	–0105	–0050	0.0	+0.1	0.0	–0.1
Perranporth	50 21N	5 09W	–0100	–0110	–0110	–0050	–0.1	0.0	0.0	+0.1
St Ives	50 13N	5 29W	–0050	–0115	–0105	–0040	–0.4	–0.3	–0.1	+0.1
Cape Cornwall	50 08N	5 42 W	–0130	–0145	–0120	–0120	–1.0	–0.9	–0.5	–0.1
Sennen Cove	50 05N	5 42W	–0130	–0145	–0125	–0125	–0.9	–0.4	*No data*	
IRELAND			**0000**	**0700**	**0000**	**0500**				
DUBLIN, NORTH WALL	53 21N	6 13W	and	and	and	and	**4.1**	**3.4**	**1.5**	**0.7**
Standard port			**1200**	**1900**	**1200**	**1700**				
Courtown	52 39N	6 13W	–0328	–0242	–0158	–0138	–2.8	–2.4	–0.5	0.0
Arklow	52 48N	6 08W	–0315	–0201	–0140	–0134	–2.7	–2.2	–0.6	–0.1
Wicklow	52 59N	6 02W	–0019	–0019	–0024	–0026	–1.4	–1.1	–0.4	0.0
Greystones	53 09N	6 04W	–0008	–0008	–0008	–0008	–0.5	–0.4	*No data*	
Dun Laoghaire	53 18N	6 08W	0000	0000	+0002	+0003	0.0	+0.1	0.0	0.0
Dublin Bar	53 21N	6 09W	–0006	–0001	–0002	–0003	0.0	0.0	0.0	0.0
Howth	53 23N	6 04W	–0007	–0005	+0001	+0005	0.0	–0.1	–0.2	–0.2
Malahide	53 27N	6 09W	+0002	+0003	+0009	+0009	+0.1	–0.2	–0.4	–0.2
Balbriggan	53 37N	6 11W	–0021	–0015	+0010	+0002	+0.3	+0.2	*No data*	
River Boyne Bar	53 43N	6 14W	–0005	0000	+0020	+0030	+0.4	+0.3	–0.1	–0.2
Dunany Point	53 52N	6 14W	–0028	–0018	–0008	–0006	+0.7	+0.9	*No data*	
Dundalk Soldiers Point	54 00N	6 21W	–0010	–0010	0000	+0045	+1.0	+0.8	+0.1	–0.1
NORTHERN IRELAND										
Carlingford Lough										
Cranfield Point	54 01N	6 04W	–0027	–0011	+0005	–0010	+0.7	+0.9	+0.3	+0.2
Warrenpoint	54 06N	6 15W	–0020	–0010	+0025	+0035	+1.0	+0.7	+0.2	+0.0
Newry (Victoria Lock)	54 09N	6 19W	+0005	+0015	+0045	*Dries*	+1.2	+0.9	+0.1	*Dries*
			0100	**0700**	**0000**	**0600**				
BELFAST	54 36N	5 55W	and	and	and	and	**3.5**	**3.0**	**1.1**	**0.4**
Standard port			**1300**	**1900**	**1200**	**1800**				
Kilkeel	54 03N	5 59W	+0040	+0030	+0010	+0010	+1.2	+1.1	+0.4	+0.4
Newcastle	54 12N	5 53W	+0025	+0035	+0020	+0040	+1.6	+1.1	+0.4	+0.1
Killough Harbour	54 15N	5 38W	0000	+0020	*No data*	*No data*	+1.8	+1.6	*No data*	
Ardglass	54 16N	5 36W	+0010	+0015	+0005	+0010	+1.7	+1.2	+0.6	+0.3
Strangford Lough										
Killard Point	54 19N	5 31W	+0011	+0021	+0005	+0025	+1.0	+0.8	+0.1	+0.1
Strangford	54 22N	5 33W	+0147	+0157	+0148	+0208	+0.1	+0.1	–0.2	0.0
Quoile Barrier	54 22N	5 41W	+0150	+0200	+0150	+0300	+0.2	+0.2	–0.3	–0.1
Killyleagh	54 24N	5 39W	+0157	+0207	+0211	+0231	+0.3	+0.3	*No data*	
South Rock	54 24N	5 25W	+0023	+0023	+0025	+0025	+1.0	+0.8	+0.1	+0.1
Portavogie	54 27N	5 26W	+0010	+0020	+0010	+0020	+1.2	+0.9	+0.3	+0.2
Donaghadee	54 39N	5 32W	+0020	+0020	+0023	+0023	+0.5	+0.4	0.0	+0.1
Carrickfergus	54 43N	5 48W	+0005	+0005	+0005	+0005	–0.3	–0.3	–0.2	–0.1
Larne	54 51N	5 48W	+0005	0000	+0010	–0005	–0.7	–0.5	–0.3	0.0
Red Bay	55 04N	6 03W	+0022	–0010	+0007	–0017	–1.9	–1.5	–0.8	–0.2

Location	Lat	Long	High Water		Low Water		MHWS	MHWN	MLWN	MLWS
Cushendun	55 08N	6 02W	+0010	–0030	0000	–0025	–1.7	–1.5	–0.6	–0.2
Portrush	55 12N	6 40W	–0433	–0433	–0433	–0433	–1.6	–1.6	–0.3	0.0
Coleraine	55 08N	6 40W	–0403	–0403	–0403	–0403	–1.3	–1.2	–0.2	0.0
GALWAY	53 16N	9 03W	**0200** and **1400**	**0900** and **2100**	**0200** and **1400**	**0800** and **2000**	**5.1**	**3.9**	**2.0**	**0.8**
Standard port										
Londonderry	55 00N	7 19W	+0254	+0319	+0322	+0321	–2.4	–1.8	–0.8	–0.1
IRELAND										
Inishtrahull	55 26N	7 14W	+0100	+0100	+0115	+0200	–1.8	–1.4	–0.4	–0.4
Bulbinbeg	55 22N	7 20W	+0120	+0120	+0135	+0135	–1.3	–1.1	–0.4	–0.3
Trawbreaga Bay	55 19N	7 23W	+0115	+0059	+0109	+0125	–1.1	–0.8	*No data*	
Lough Swilly										
Rathmullan	55 06N	7 32W	+0125	+0050	+0126	+0118	–0.8	–0.7	–0.1	–0.3
Fanad Head	55 17N	7 38W	+0115	+0040	+0125	+0120	–1.1	–0.9	–0.5	–0.3
Mulroy Bay Bar	55 15N	7 46W	+0108	+0052	+0102	+0118	–1.2	–1.0	*No data*	
Fanny's Bay	55 12N	7 49W	+0145	+0129	+0151	+0207	–2.2	–1.7	*No data*	
Seamount Bay	55 11N	7 44W	+0210	+0154	+0226	+0242	–3.1	–2.3	*No data*	
Cranford Bay	55 09N	7 42W	+0329	+0313	+0351	+0407	–3.7	–2.8		
No data										
Sheephaven Downies Bay	55 11N	7 50W	+0057	+0043	+0053	+0107	–1.1	–0.9	*No data*	
Inishbofin Bay	55 10N	8 10W	+0040	+0026	+0032	+0046	–1.2	–0.9	*No data*	
GALWAY	53 16N	9 03W	**0600** and **1800**	**1100** and **2300**	**0000** and **1200**	**0700** and **1900**	**5.1**	**3.9**	**2.0**	**0.8**
Standard port										
Gweedore Harbour	55 04N	8 19W	+0048	+0100	+0055	+0107	–1.3	–1.0	–0.5	–0.3
Burtonport	54 59N	8 26W	+0042	+0055	+0115	+0055	–1.2	–1.0	–0.6	–0.3
Loughros More Bay	54 47N	8 30W	+0042	+0054	+0046	+0058	–1.1	–0.9	*No data*	
Donegal Bay										
Killybegs	54 38N	8 26W	+0040	+0050	+0055	+0035	–1.0	–0.9	–0.5	–0.2
Donegal Hbr, Salt Hill Quay	54 38N	8 12W	+0038	+0050	+0052	+0104	–1.2	–0.9	*No data*	
Mullaghmore	54 28N	8 27W	+0036	+0048	+0047	+0059	–1.4	–1.0	–0.4	–0.4
Sligo Hbr (Oyster Island)	54 18N	8 34W	+0043	+0055	+0042	+0054	–1.0	–0.9	–0.5	–0.3
Ballysadare Bay, Culleenamore	54 16N	8 36W	+0059	+0111	+0111	+0123	–1.2	–0.9	*No data*	
Killala Bay (Inishcrone)	54 13N	9 06W	+0035	+0055	+0030	+0050	–1.3	–1.2	–0.7	–0.4
Broadhaven	54 16N	9 53W	+0035	+0035	+0040	+0040	–1.4	–1.0	–0.6	–0.2
Blacksod Bay										
Blacksod Quay	54 06N	10 04W	+0025	+0035	+0040	+0040	–1.2	–1.0	–0.6	–0.4
Inishbiggle	54 00N	9 53W	+0055	+0100	+0125	+0110	–1.3	– 0.9	–0.5	–0.2
Clare Island	53 48N	9 57W	+0015	+0021	+0039	+0027	–0.6	–0.4	–0.1	0.0
Clew Bay Inishgort	53 50N	9 40W	+0035	+0045	+0115	+0100	–0.7	–0.5	–0.2	0.0
Killary Harbour	53 38N	9 53W	+0021	+0015	+0035	+0029	–1.0	–0.8	–0.4	–0.3
Inishbofin Bofin Harbour	53 37N	10 12W	+0013	+0009	+0021	+0017	–1.0	–0.8	–0.4	–0.3
Clifden Bay	53 29N	10 04W	+0005	+0005	+0016	+0016	–0.7	–0.5	*No data*	
Slyne Head	53 24N	10 14W	+0002	+0002	+0010	+0010	–0.7	–0.5	*No data*	
Roundstone Bay	53 23N	9 55W	+0003	+0003	+0008	+0008	–0.7	–0.5	–0.3	–0.3
Kilkieran Cove	53 19N	9 44W	+0005	+0005	+0016	+0016	–0.3	–0.2	–0.1	–0.2
Aran Islands Killeany Bay	53 07N	9 40W	0000	0000	+0001	–0001	–0.1	+0.1	+0.1	+0.2
Liscannor	52 56N	9 23W	–0003	–0007	+0006	+0002	–0.4	–0.3	*No data*	
Seafield Point	52 48N	9 30W	–0006	–0014	+0004	–0004	–0.5	–0.4	*No data*	
Kilrush	52 38N	9 30W	–0006	+0027	+0057	–0016	–0.1	–0.2	–0.3	–0.1
Limerick Dock	52 40N	8 38W	+0135	+0141	+0141	+0219	+1.0	+0.7	–0.8	–0.2
COBH	51 51N	8 18 W	**0500** and **1700**	**1100** and **2300**	**0500** and **1700**	**1100** and **2300**	**4.1**	**3.2**	**1.3**	**0.4**
Standard port										
Tralee Bay Fenit Pier	52 16N	9 52W	–0057	–0017	–0029	–0109	+0.5	+0.2	+0.3	+0.1
Smerwick Harbour	52 12N	10 24W	–0107	–0027	–0041	–0121	–0.3	–0.4	*No data*	
Dingle Harbour	52 07N	10 15W	–0111	–0041	–0049	–0119	–0.1	0.0	+0.3	+0.4
Castlemaine Hbr Cromane Pt	52 08N	9 54W	–0026	–0006	–0017	–0037	+0.4	+0.2	+0.4	+0.2
Valentia Harbour										
Knights Town	51 56N	10 18W	–0118	–0038	–0056	–0136	–0.6	–0.4	–0.1	0.0
Ballinskelligs Bay Castle	51 49N	10 16W	–0119	–0039	–0054	–0134	–0.5	–0.5	–0.1	0.0
Kenmare River										
West Cove	51 46N	10 03W	–0113	–0033	–0049	–0129	–0.6	–0.5	–0.1	0.0
Dunkerron Harbour	51 52N	9 39W	–0117	–0027	–0050	–0140	–0.2	–0.3	+0.1	0.0
Coulagh Bay										
Ballycrovane Hbr	51 43N	9 57W	–0116	–0036	–0053	–0133	–0.6	–0.5	–0.1	0.0
Black Ball Harbour	51 36N	10 02W	–0115	–0035	–0047	–0127	–0.7	–0.6	–0.1	+0.1
Bantry Bay										
Castletown Bearhaven	51 39N	9 54W	–0048	–0012	–0025	–0101	–0.8	–0.6	–0.2	0.0
Bantry	51 41N	9 28W	–0045	–0025	–0040	–0105	–0.7	–0.6	–0.2	+0.1

Location	Lat	Long	High Water		Low Water		MHWS	MHWN	MLWN	MLWS
Dunmanus Bay										
Dunbeacon Harbour	51 37N	9 33W	–0057	–0025	–0032	–0104	–0.8	–0.7	–0.3	–0.1
Dunmanus Harbour	51 32N	9 40W	–0107	–0031	–0044	–0120	–0.7	–0.6	–0.2	0.0
Crookhaven	51 28N	9 44W	–0057	–0033	–0048	–0112	–0.8	–0.6	–0.4	–0.1
Skull	51 31N	9 32W	–0040	–0015	–0015	–0110	–0.9	–0.6	–0.2	0.0
Baltimore	51 29N	9 23W	–0025	–0005	–0010	–0050	–0.6	–0.3	+0.1	+0.2
Castletownshend	51 32N	9 10W	–0020	–0030	–0020	–0050	–0.4	–0.2	+0.1	+0.3
Clonakilty Bay	51 35N	8 50W	–0033	–0011	–0019	–0041	–0.3	–0.2	*No data*	
Courtmacsherry	51 38N	8 43W	–0025	–0008	–0008	–0015	–0.1	–0.1	–0.0	+0.1
Kinsale	51 42N	8 31W	–0019	–0005	–0009	–0023	–0.2	0.0	+0.1	+0.2
Roberts Cove	51 45N	8 19W	–0005	–0005	–0005	–0005	–0.1	0.0	0.0	+0.1
Cork Harbour										
Ringaskiddy	51 50N	8 19W	+0005	+0020	+0007	+0013	+0.1	+0.1	+0.1	+0.1
Marino Point	51 53N	8 20W	0000	+0010	0000	+0010	+0.1	+0.1	0.0	0.0
Cork City	51 54N	8 27W	+0005	+0010	+0020	+0010	+0.4	+0.4	+0.3	+0.2
Ballycotton	51 50N	8 01W	–0011	+0001	+0003	–0009	0.0	0.0	–0.1	0.0
Youghal	51 57N	7 51W	0000	+0010	+0010	0000	–0.2	–0.1	–0.1	–0.1
Dungarvan Harbour	52 05N	7 34W	+0004	+0012	+0007	–0001	0.0	+0.1	–0.2	0.0
Waterford Harbour										
Dunmore East	52 09N	6 59W	+0008	+0003	0000	0000	+0.1	0.0	+0.1	+0.2
Cheekpoint	52 16N	7 00W	+0026	+0021	+0019	+0022	+0.5	+0.4	+0.3	+0.2
Kilmokea Point	52 17N	7 00W	+0026	+0022	+0020	+0020	+0.2	+0.1	+0.1	+0.1
Waterford	52 16N	7 07W	+0053	+0032	+0015	+0100	+0.6	+0.6	+0.4	+0.2
New Ross	52 24N	6 57W	+0100	+0030	+0055	+0130	+0.3	+0.4	+0.3	+0.4
Baginbun Head	52 10N	6 50W	+0003	+0003	–0008	–0008	–0.2	–0.1	+0.2	+0.2
Great Saltee	52 07N	6 37W	+0019	+0009	–0004	+0006	–0.3	–0.4	*No data*	
Carnsore Point	52 10N	6 22W	+0029	+0019	–0002	+0008	–1.1	–1.0	*No data*	
Rosslare Europort	52 15N	6 21W	+0045	+0035	+0015	–0005	–2.2	–1.8	–0.5	–0.1
Wexford Harbour	52 20N	6 27W	+0126	+0126	+0118	+0108	–2.1	–1.7	–0.3	+0.1

DENMARK *Time zone –0100*

Location	Lat	Long	High Water		Low Water		MHWS	MHWN	MLWN	MLWS
ESBJERG *Standard port*	55 28N	8 27E	**0300** and **1500**	**0700** and **1900**	**0100** and **1300**	**0800** and **2000**	**2.0**	**1.6**	**0.6**	**0.2**
Hirtshals	57 36N	9 58E	+0055	+0320	+0340	+0100	–1.7	–1.4	–0.5	–0.2
Hanstholm	57 07N	8 36E	+0100	+0340	+0340	+0130	–1.7	–1.3	–0.5	–0.2
Thyborøn	56 42N	8 13E	+0120	+0230	+0410	+0210	–1.6	–1.3	–0.5	–0.2
Thorsminde	56 22N	8 07E	+0045	+0050	+0040	+0010	–1.4	–1.1	–0.5	–0.2
Hvide Sande	56 00N	8 08E	0000	+0010	–0015	–0025	–1.2	–0.9	–0.4	–0.2
Blavands Huk	55 33N	8 05E	–0120	–0110	–0050	–0100	–0.2	–0.2	–0.3	–0.2
Esbjerg, Gradyb Bar	55 26N	8 15E	–0130	–0115	*No data*	*No data*	–0.5	–0.4	–0.3	–0.2
Havneby (Rømø)	55 05N	8 34E	–0040	–0005	0000	–0020	-0.1	0.0	–0.3	–0.3
Hojer	54 58N	8 40E	–0020	+0015	*No data*	*No data*	+0.4	+0.5	–0.2	–0.2

GERMANY *Time zone –0100*

Location	Lat	Long	High Water		Low Water		MHWS	MHWN	MLWN	MLWS
HELGOLAND *Standard port*	54 11N	7 53E	**0100** and **1300**	**0600** and **1800**	**0100** and **1300**	**0800** and **2000**	**3.1**	**2.8**	**0.8**	**0.4**
Lister Tief, List	55 01N	8 26E	+0252	+0240	+0201	+0210	–0.7	–0.6	–0.1	0.0
Hörnum	54 45N	8 18E	+0223	+0218	+0131	+0137	–0.4	–0.3	–0.1	-0.1
Amrum - Hafen	54 38N	8 23E	+0138	+0137	+0128	+0134	+0.3	+0.3	0.0	0.0
Dagebüll	54 44N	8 41E	+0226	+0217	+0211	+0225	+0.7	+0.8	+0.1	+0.1
Suderoogsand	54 25N	8 30E	+0116	+0102	+0038	+0122	+0.6	+0.5	+0.1	+0.1
River Hever, Husum	54 28N	9 01E	+0205	+0152	+0118	+0200	+1.2	+1.2	+0.1	+0.1
Suederhoeft	54 16N	8 42E	+0103	+0056	+0051	+0112	+0.7	+0.6	–0.2	0.0
Eidersperrwerk	54 16N	8 51E	+0120	+0115	+0130	+0155	+0.6	+0.5	–0.1	0.0
Linnenplate	54 13N	8 40E	+0047	+0046	+0034	+0046	+0.7	+0.6	0.0	0.0
Büsum	54 07N	8 52E	+0054	+0049	–0001	+0027	+0.9	+0.9	–0.1	0.0

Location	Lat	Long	High Water		Low Water		MHWS	MHWN	MLWN	MLWS
CUXHAVEN *Standard port*	53 52N	8 43E	**0200** and **1400**	**0800** and **2000**	**0200** and **1400**	**0900** and **2100**	**3.7**	**3.3**	**0.8**	**0.4**
River Elbe Großer Vogelsand	54 00N	8 29E	–0044	–0046	–0101	–0103	+0.1	0.0	+0.1	+0.1
Scharhörn	53 58N	8 28E	–0045	–0047	–0101	–0103	0.0	0.0	0.0	0.0
Otterndorf	53 50N	8 52E	+0029	+0029	+0027	+0027	0.0	–0.1	0.0	+0.1
Brunsbüttel	53 53N	9 08E	+0057	+0105	+0121	+0112	–0.1	–0.2	–0.1	+0.1
Glückstadt	53 47N	9 25E	+0205	+0214	+0220	+0213	–0.1	0.0	0.0	+0.1
Stadersand	53 38N	9 32E	+0241	+0245	+0300	+0254	+0.1	+0.2	–0.1	+0.1
Schulau	53 34N	9 42E	+0304	+0315	+0337	+0321	+0.3	+0.3	–0.2	0.0
Seemannshoeft	53 32N	9 53E	+0324	+0332	+0403	+0347	+0.4	+0.5	–0.3	–0.1
Hamburg	53 33N	9 58E	+0338	+0346	+0422	+0406	+0.5	+0.5	–0.3	–0.2

Location	Lat	Long	High Water		Low Water		MHWS	MHWN	MLWN	MLWS
			0200	0800	0200	0900				
WILHELMSHAVEN	53 31N	8 09E	and	and	and	and	**4.8**	**4.3**	**1.1**	**0.5**
Standard port			1400	2000	1400	2100				
River Weser										
Alte Weser lt ho	53 32N	8 08E	–0055	–0048	–0015	–0029	–1.1	–1.0	–0.2	0.0
Dwarsgat	53 43N	8 18E	–0015	+0002	–0006	–0001	–0.6	–0.5	–0.2	0.0
Bremerhaven	53 33N	8 34E	+0029	+0046	+0033	+0038	–0.1	0.0	–0.1	0.0
Nordenham	53 28N	8 29E	+0051	+0109	+0055	+0058	0.0	0.1	–0.2	–0.1
Brake	53 19N	8 29E	+0120	+0119	+0143	+0155	–0.2	–0.1	–0.4	–0.2
Elsfleth	53 16N	8 29E	+0137	+0137	+0206	+0216	–0.2	–0.1	–0.4	–0.2
Vegesack	53 10N	8 37E	+0208	+0204	+0250	+0254	-0.1	–0.1	–0.4	–0.1
Bremen	53 07N	8 43E	+0216	+0211	+0311	+0314	0.0	0.0	–0.5	–0.2
River Jade										
Wangerooge East	53 46N	7 59E	–0058	–0053	–0024	–0034	–1.0	–0.9	–0.2	–0.1
Wangerooge West	53 47N	7 52E	–0101	–0058	–0035	–0045	–1.1	–1.0	–0.2	–0.1
Schillig	53 42N	8 03E	–0031	–0025	–0006	–0014	–0.7	–0.6	–0.1	0.0
Hooksiel	53 39N	8 05E	–0023	–0022	–0008	–0012	–0.5	–0.4	–0.1	0.0
			0200	0700	0200	0800				
HELGOLAND	54 11N	7 53E	and	and	and	and	**3.1**	**2.8**	**0.8**	**0.4**
Standard port			1400	1900	1400	2000				
East Frisian Islands and coast										
Spiekeroog	53 45N	7 41E	+0003	–0003	–0031	–0012	+0.4	+0.4	+0.1	+0.1
Neuharlingersiel	53 42N	7 42E	+0014	+0008	–0024	–0013	+0.6	+0.5	+0.1	+0.1
Langeoog	53 43N	7 30E	+0003	–0001	–0034	–0018	+0.4	+0.3	+0.1	0.0
Norderney (Riffgat)	53 42N	7 09E	–0024	–0030	–0056	–0045	+0.1	+0.1	0.0	0.0
Norddeich Hafen	53 39N	7 09E	–0018	–0017	–0029	–0012	+0.2	+0.2	+0.1	0.0
Juist	53 40N	7 00E	–0026	–0032	–0019	–0008	+0.1	+0.1	0.0	0.0
River Ems										
Memmert	53 38N	6 54E	–0032	–0038	–0114	–0103	+0.2	+0.2	+0.1	0.0
Borkum (Fischerbalje)	53 33N	6 45E	–0048	–0052	–0124	–0105	0.0	0.0	0.0	0.0
Emshorn	53 30N	6 50E	–0037	–0041	–0108	–0047	+0.2	+0.2	0.0	0.0
Knock	53 20N	7 02E	+0018	+0005	–0028	+0004	+0.7	+0.7	+0.1	0.0
Emden	53 20N	7 11E	+0041	+0028	–0011	+0022	+0.8	+0.8	–0.1	–0.1
NETHERLANDS *Time zone –0100*										
			0200	0700	0200	0800				
HELGOLAND	54 11N	7 53E	and	and	and	and	**3.1**	**2.8**	**0.8**	**0.4**
Standard port			1400	1900	1400	2000				
Delfzijl	53 20N	6 56E	+0020	–0005	–0040	0000	+0.6	+0.6	0.0	0.0
Eemshaven	53 27N	6 50E	–0025	–0045	–0115	–0045	0.0	+0.1	–0.1	–0.1
Huibertgat	53 35N	6 24E	–0150	–0150	–0210	–0210	–0.5	–0.4	–0.2	–0.2
Schiermonnikoog	53 28N	6 12E	–0120	–0130	–0240	–0220	–0.2	–0.3	–0.1	–0.1
Waddenzee										
Lauwersoog	53 25N	6 12E	–0130	–0145	–0235	–0220	–0.3	–0.2	–0.2	0.0
Nes	53 26N	5 47E	–0135	–0150	–0245	–0225	–0.3	–0.2	–0.2	0.0
West Terschelling	53 22N	5 13E	–0220	–0250	–0335	–0310	–0.7	–0.7	–0.2	–0.1
Vlieland-Haven	53 18N	5 06E	–0250	–0320	–0355	–0330	–0.7	–0.7	–0.2	–0.1
Harlingen	53 10N	5 25E	–0155	–0245	–0210	–0130	–0.8	–0.7	–0.4	–0.1
Kornwerderzand	53 04N	5 20E	–0210	–0315	–0300	–0215	–1.0	–0.8	–0.4	–0.2
Den Oever	52 56N	5 02E	–0245	–0410	–0400	–0305	–1.2	–1.0	–0.5	–0.2
Oudeschild	53 02N	4 51E	–0310	–0420	–0445	–0400	–1.4	–1.1	–0.4	–0.2
Den Helder	52 58N	4 45E	–0410	–0520	–0520	–0430	–1.3	–1.1	–0.4	–0.2
Noordwinning (Platform K13–A)	53 13N	3 13E	–0420	–0430	–0520	–0530	–1.3	–1.4	–0.1	–0.1
			0300	0900	0400	1000				
VLISSINGEN	51 27N	3 36E	and	and	and	and	**5.0**	**4.1**	**1.1**	**0.5**
Standard port			1500	2100	1600	2200				
IJmuiden	52 28N	4 33E	+0145	+0140	+0305	+0325	–2.8	–2.4	–0.7	–0.3
Scheveningen	52 06N	4 16E	+0105	+0100	+0220	+0245	–2.7	–2.3	–0.7	–0.2
Europlatform	52 00N	3 17E	+0005	–0005	–0030	–0055	–2.8	–2.3	–0.6	–0.2
Nieuwe Waterweg										
HOEK VAN HOLLAND		*Standard port, no Secondaries*								
Maassluis	51 55N	4 15E	+0155	+0115	+0100	+0310	–2.9	–2.4	–0.8	–0.3
Nieuwe Maas, Vlaardingen	51 54N	4 21E	+0150	+0120	+0130	+0330	–2.9	–2.4	–0.9	–0.3
Haringvlietsluizen	51 50N	4 03E	+0015	+0015	+0015	–0020	–2.1	–1.9	–0.7	–0.3
Ooster Schelde										
Roompot Buiten	51 37N	3 40E	–0015	+0005	+0005	–0020	–1.3	–1.1	–0.4	–0.1
Walcheren, Westkapelle	51 32N	3 26E	–0025	–0015	–0010	–0025	–0.7	–0.6	–0.2	–0.1
Westerschelde										
Terneuzen	51 20N	3 50E	+0020	+0020	+0020	+0030	+0.4	+0.3	+0.1	0.0
Hansweert	51 27N	4 00E	+0100	+0050	+0040	+0100	+0.6	+0.6	0.0	0.0
Bath	51 24N	4 13E	+0125	+0115	+0115	+0140	+1.1	+1.0	0.0	0.0

BELGIUM *Time zone –0100*

Location	Lat	Long	High Water		Low Water		MHWS	MHWN	MLWN	MLWS
Antwerpen	51 21N	4 14E	+0128	+0116	+0121	+0144	+1.2	+1.0	+0.1	+0.1
ZEEBRUGGE *Standard port*	51 21N	3 12E	**0300** and **1500**	**0900** and **2100**	**0300** and **1500**	**0900** and **2100**	**4.8**	**4.0**	**1.2**	**0.5**
Cadzand	51 23N	3 23E	+0005	-0010	+0000	+0010	0.0	0.0	-0.1	0.0
Blankenberge	51 19N	3 07E	*No data*	*No data*	*No data*	*No data*	+0.1	0.0	-0.1	0.0
Oostende	51 14N	2 56E	–0019	–0019	–0008	–0008	+0.4	+0.2	+0.2	+0.1
Nieuwpoort	51 09N	2 43E	–0031	–0031	–0010	–0010	+0.7	+0.5	+0.2	+0.1

FRANCE *Time zone –0100*

Location	Lat	Long	High Water		Low Water		MHWS	MHWN	MLWN	MLWS
DUNKERQUE *Standard port*	51 03N	2 22E	**0200** and **1400**	**0800** and **2000**	**0200** and **1400**	**0900** and **2100**	**6.0**	**5.0**	**1.5**	**0.6**
Gravelines	51 01N	2 06E	–0010	–0015	–0010	–0005	+0.5	+0.3	+0.1	0.0
Sandettie Bank	51 15N	2 03E	–0010	–0015	–0015	–0010	–0.6	–0.6	–0.2	–0.1
Calais	50 58N	1 51E	–0020	–0030	–0015	–0005	+1.2	+0.9	+0.6	+0.3
Wissant	50 53N	1 40E	–0035	–0050	–0030	–0010	+2.0	+1.5	+0.9	+0.4
Boulogne	50 44N	1 35E	–0045	–0100	–0045	–0025	+2.8	+2.2	+1.1	+0.5
DIEPPE *Standard port*	49 56N	1 05E	**0100** and **1300**	**0600** and **1800**	**0100** and **1300**	**0700** and **1900**	**9.3**	**7.4**	**2.5**	**0.8**
Le Touquet, Étaples	50 31N	1 35E	+0010	+0015	+0030	+0030	+0.2	+0.2	+0.3	+0.4
Berck	50 24N	1 34E	+0005	+0015	+0025	+0030	+0.4	+0.5	+0.3	+0.4
La Somme										
Le Hourdel	50 13N	1 34E	+0020	+0020	*No data*	*No data*	+0.8	+0.6	*No data*	
St Valéry	50 11N	1 37E	+0035	+0035	*No data*	*No data*	+0.9	+0.7	*No data*	
Cayeux	50 11N	1 29E	0000	+0005	+0015	+0010	+0.5	+0.6	+0.4	+0.4
Le Tréport	50 04N	1 22E	+0005	0000	+0005	+0015	+0.3	+0.2	+0.1	+0.1
St Valéry–en–Caux	49 52N	0 42E	–0005	–0005	–0015	–0015	–0.5	–0.4	–0.1	–0.1
Fécamp	49 46N	0 22E	–0015	–0010	–0030	–0040	–1.0	–0.6	+0.3	+0.4
Etretat	49 42N	0 12E	–0020	–0015	–0050	–0050	–1.2	–0.8	+0.3	+0.4
LE HAVRE *Standard port*	49 29N	0 07E	**0000** and **1200**	**0500** and **1700**	**0000** and **1200**	**0700** and **1900**	**7.9**	**6.6**	**2.8**	**1.2**
Antifer (Le Havre)	49 39N	0 09E	+0025	+0015	+0005	–0005	+0.1	0.0	0.0	0.0
La Seine										
Chenal du Rouen	49 26N	0 07E	0000	0000	0000	+0015	+0.1	0.0	+0.1	–0.1
Honfleur	49 25N	0 14E	–0150	–0135	+0025	+0040	+0.1	+0.1	+0.1	+0.3
Tancarville	49 28N	0 28E	–0135	–0120	+0030	+0145	+0.2	+0.2	+0.4	+1.0
Quilleboeuf	49 28N	0 32E	–0055	–0110	+0105	+0210	+0.2	+0.2	+0.6	+1.4
Vatteville	49 29N	0 40E	+0015	–0040	+0205	+0240	0.0	0.0	+0.1	+2.2
Caudebec	49 32N	0 44E	–0005	–0030	+0220	+0300	0.0	0.0	+1.1	+2.3
Heurteauville	49 27N	0 49E	+0055	+0005	+0250	+0330	–0.1	0.0	+1.3	+2.6
Duclair	49 29N	0 53E	+0210	+0145	+0350	+0410	–0.1	+0.1	+1.6	+3.2
Rouen	49 27N	1 06E	+0305	+0240	+0505	+0515	0.0	+0.3	+1.7	+3.3
Trouville	49 22N	0 05E	–0100	–0010	0000	+0005	+0.4	+0.3	+0.3	+0.1
Dives	49 18N	0 05W	–0100	–0010	0000	0000	+0.3	+0.2	+0.2	+0.1
Ouistreham	49 17N	0 15W	–0045	–0010	–0005	0000	–0.3	–0.3	–0.2	–0.3
Courseulles-sur-Mer	49 20N	0 27W	–0100	–0005	–0015	–0025	–0.5	–0.5	–0.1	–0.1
Arromanches	49 21N	0 37W	–0055	–0025	–0025	–0035	–0.5	–0.5	–0.1	–0.2
Port-en-Bessin	49 21N	0 45W	–0055	–0030	–0030	–0035	–0.7	–0.7	–0.2	–0.1
Alpha-Baie de Seine	49 49N	0 20W	+0030	+0020	–0005	–0020	–0.9	–0.8	–0.3	–0.2
CHERBOURG *Standard port*	49 39N	1 38W	**0300** and **1500**	**1000** and **2200**	**0400** and **1600**	**1000** and **2200**	**6.4**	**5.1**	**2.6**	**1.1**
Rade de la Capelle	49 25N	1 05W	+0125	+0055	+0125	+0110	+0.8	+0.8	+0.1	+0.2
Iles Saint Marcouf	49 30N	1 08W	+0130	+0055	+0120	+0110	+0.5	+0.5	+0.2	0.0
Vaast-la-Hougue	49 34N	1 16W	+0115	+0045	+0120	+0110	+0.4	+0.4	-0.1	–0.1
Barfleur	49 40N	1 15W	+0115	+0050	+0045	+0050	+0.1	+0.3	0.0	+0.1
Omonville	49 42N	1 50W	–0015	–0010	–0015	–0015	–0.3	–0.3	–0.3	–0.1
Goury	49 43N	1 57W	–0100	–0040	–0105	–0120	+1.7	+1.6	+0.9	+0.3

CHANNEL ISLANDS *Time zone UT*

Location	Lat	Long	High Water		Low Water		MHWS	MHWN	MLWN	MLWS
ST HELIER *Standard port*	49 11N	2 07W	**0300** and **1500**	**0900** and **2100**	**0200** and **1400**	**0900** and **2100**	**11.0**	**8.1**	**4.0**	**1.4**
Alderney, Braye	49 43N	2 12W	+0050	+0040	+0025	+0105	–4.8	–3.4	–1.5	–0.5
Sark, Maseline Pier	49 26N	2 21W	+0005	+0015	+0005	+0010	–2.1	–1.5	–0.6	–0.3
Guernsey, ST PETER PORT	49 27N	2 31W	*Standard port (no Secondaries)*							

Location	Lat	Long	High Water		Low Water		MHWS	MHWN	MLWN	MLWS
Jersey										
St Catherine Bay	49 13N	2 01W	0000	+0010	+0010	+0010	0.0	–0.1	0.0	+0.1
Bouley Bay	49 15N	2 05W	+0002	+0002	+0004	+0004	–0.3	–0.3	–0.1	–0.1
Les Ecrehou	49 17N	1 56W	+0005	+0009	+0011	+0009	–0.2	+0.1	–0.2	0.0
Les Minquiers	48 57N	2 08W	–0014	–0018	–0001	–0008	+0.5	+0.6	+0.1	+0.1
FRANCE *Time zone –0100*										
ST MALO *Standard port*	48 38N	2 02W	**0100** and **1300**	**0800** and **2000**	**0300** and **1500**	**0800** and **2000**	**12.2**	**9.2**	**4.4**	**1.5**
Les Ardentes	48 58N	1 52W	+0010	+0010	+0020	+0010	0.0	0.0	-0.2	–0.1
Iles Chausey	48 52N	1 49W	+0005	+0005	+0015	+0015	+0.8	+0.8	+0.5	+0.3
Diélette	49 33N	1 52W	+0045	+0035	+0020	+0035	–2.5	–1.8	–0.7	–0.3
Carteret	49 22N	1 47W	+0030	+0020	+0015	+0030	–1.6	–1.1	–0.9	–0.3
Portbail	49 18N	1 45W	+0030	+0025	+0025	+0030	–0.8	–0.5	–0.4	–0.1
St Germain sur Ay	49 14N	1 36W	+0025	+0025	+0035	+0035	–0.7	–0.4	–0.2	+0.1
Le Sénéquet	49 05N	1 40W	+0015	+0015	+0025	+0025	–0.3	–0.2	–0.1	+0.1
Regnéville sur Mer	49 01N	1 33W	+0010	+0010	+0030	+0020	+0.5	+0.5	0.0	0.0
Granville	48 50N	1 36W	+0010	+0005	+0025	+0015	+0.7	+0.5	+0.1	0.0
Cancale	48 40N	1 51W	0000	0000	+0010	+0010	+0.8	+0.7	+0.1	+0.1
Ile des Hebihens	48 37N	2 11W	0000	0000	–0005	–0005	–0.2	–0.1	–0.3	–0.1
St Cast	48 38N	2 15W	0000	0000	–0005	–0005	–0.2	–0.1	–0.3	–0.1
Erquy	48 38N	2 28W	0000	–0005	–0020	–0010	–0.6	–0.4	–0.2	0.0
Dahouët	48 35N	2 34W	–0005	0000	–0025	–0010	–0.9	–0.6	–0.4	–0.2
Le Légué (Buoy)	48 34N	2 41W	–0010	–0005	–0020	–0015	–0.8	–0.4	–0.4	–0.1
Binic	48 36N	2 49W	–0005	–0005	–0025	–0015	–0.8	–0.6	–0.4	–0.2
St Quay-Portrieux	48 38N	2 49W	–0010	–0010	–0030	–0010	–1.0	–0.6	–0.4	–0.1
Paimpol	48 47N	3 02W	–0010	–0005	–0035	–0025	–1.4	–0.8	–0.6	–0.1
Ile de Bréhat	48 50N	3 00W	–0015	–0005	–0040	–0030	–1.8	–1.2	–0.6	–0.2
Les Héaux de Bréhat	48 55N	3 05W	–0015	–0010	–0010	–0045	–2.4	–1.6	–0.8	–0.2
Lézardrieux	48 47N	3 06W	–0020	–0015	–0055	–0045	–1.7	–1.2	–0.7	–0.2
Port-Béni	48 51N	3 10W	–0020	–0020	–0105	–0050	–2.4	–1.5	–0.7	–0.1
Tréguier	48 47N	3 13W	–0020	–0020	–0100	–0045	–2.3	–1.5	–0.8	–0.2
Perros-Guirec	48 49N	3 28W	–0035	–0035	–0115	–0100	–2.9	–1.8	–1.0	–0.2
Ploumanac'h	48 50N	3 29W	–0035	–0040	–0120	–0100	–2.9	–1.8	–0.8	–0.1
BREST *Standard port*	48 23N	4 30W	**0000** and **1200**	**0600** and **1800**	**0000** and **1200**	**0600** and **1800**	**7.0**	**5.5**	**2.7**	**1.1**
Trébeurden	48 46N	3 35W	+0100	+0110	+0120	+0100	+2.2	+1.8	+0.8	+0.3
Locquirec	48 42N	3 38W	+0100	+0110	+0125	+0100	+2.2	+1.8	+0.7	+0.4
Anse de Primel	48 43N	3 50W	+0100	+0110	+0120	+0100	+2.0	+1.6	+0.8	+0.2
Chateau du Taureau (Morlaix)	48 41N	3 53W	+0055	+0105	+0115	+0055	+1.9	+1.6	+0.7	+0.2
Roscoff	48 43N	3 58W	+0055	+0105	+0115	+0055	+1.9	+1.6	+0.7	+0.2
Ile de Batz	48 44N	4 00W	+0045	+0100	+0105	+0055	+1.9	+1.5	+0.8	+0.3
Brignogan	48 40N	4 19W	+0040	+0045	+0100	+0040	+1.4	+1.1	+0.5	+0.1
L'Aber Wrac'h	48 36N	4 34W	+0030	+0030	+0040	+0035	+0.9	+0.6	+0.2	0.0
Aber Benoit	48 35N	4 37W	+0022	+0025	+0035	+0020	+1.1	+0.9	+0.3	0.0
Portsall	48 34N	4 43W	+0015	+0020	+0025	+0015	+0.6	+0.4	+0.1	- 0.1
L'Aber-Ildut	48 28N	4 45W	+0010	+0010	+0020	+0010	+0.3	+0.2	+0.1	-0.1
Ouessant, Baie de Lampaul	48 27N	5 06W	+0010	+0010	–0005	+0005	- 0.1	–0.2	–0.2	- 0.1
Molene	48 24N	4 58W	+0015	+0010	+0020	+0020	+0.3	+0.2	+0.1	0.0
Le Conquet	48 22N	4 47W	0000	0000	+0005	+0005	–0.2	–0.2	–0.2	–0.1
Le Trez Hir	48 21N	4 42W	–0005	–0005	–0015	–0010	–0.4	–0.4	–0.2	0.0
Camaret	48 17N	4 35W	–0010	–0010	–0015	–0010	–0.4	–0.4	–0.2	–0.1
Morgat	48 13N	4 30W	–0005	–0010	–0020	–0005	–0.5	–0.4	–0.2	0.0
Douarnenez	48 06N	4 19W	–0010	–0010	–0020	–0010	–0.4	–0.4	–0.2	–0.1
Ile de Sein	48 02N	4 51W	–0005	–0005	–0015	–0010	–0.9	–0.7	–0.4	–0.2
Anse de Feunteun Aod	48 02N	4 42W	–0030	–0040	–0035	–0025	–1.4	–1.2	–0.6	–0.2
Audierne	48 01N	4 33W	–0035	–0030	–0035	–0030	–1.8	–1.4	–0.7	–0.3
Le Guilvinec	47 48N	4 17W	–0010	–0025	–0025	–0015	–1.9	–1.5	–0.7	–0.2
Lesconil	47 48N	4 13W	–0010	–0030	–0030	–0020	–2.0	–1.5	–0.7	–0.2
Pont l'Abbe River, Loctudy	47 50N	4 10W	–0010	–0030	–0035	–0020	–2.1	–1.7	–0.9	–0.4
Odet River										
Bénodet	47 53N	4 07W	–0010	–0025	–0030	–0020	–1.7	–1.4	–0.6	–0.1
Corniguel	47 58N	4 06W	+0015	+0010	–0015	–0010	–2.1	–1.7	–1.1	–0.8

Location	Lat	Long	High Water		Low Water		MHWS	MHWN	MLWN	MLWS
Concarneau	47 52N	3 55W	–0010	–0030	–0030	–0020	–1.9	–1.5	–0.7	–0.2
Iles de Glenan, Ile de Penfret	47 44N	3 57W	–0005	–0030	–0030	–0020	–2.0	–1.5	–0.8	–0.3
Port Louis	47 42N	3 21W	+0005	–0020	–0020	–0010	–1.8	–1.5	–0.6	–0.2
Lorient	47 45N	3 21W	+0005	–0020	–0020	–0010	–1.9	–1.5	–0.7	–0.3
Hennebont	47 48N	3 17W	+0015	–0015	+0005	+0005	–2.0	–1.6	–0.9	–0.3
Ile de Groix, Port Tudy	47 39N	3 27W	0000	–0025	–0025	–0015	–1.9	–1.5	–0.6	–0.2
Port d'Etel	47 39N	3 12W	+0020	–0010	+0030	+0010	–2.1	–1.4	–0.5	+0.4
Port Haliguen	47 29N	3 06W	+0010	–0020	–0015	–0010	–1.7	–1.3	–0.7	–0.3
Port Maria	47 29N	3 08W	+0010	–0025	–0025	–0015	–1.7	–1.4	–0.7	–0.2
Belle Ile, Le Palais	47 21N	3 09W	–0005	–0025	–0025	–0010	–1.8	–1.4	–0.7	–0.3
Crac'h River, La Trinité	47 35N	3 01W	+0025	–0020	–0015	–0010	–1.6	–1.2	–0.6	–0.3
Golfe du Morbihan										
Port Navalo	47 33N	2 55W	+0030	–0005	–0010	–0005	–2.0	–1.5	–0.8	–0.4
Auray	47 40N	2 59W	+0035	0000	+0015	–0005	–2.3	–1.9	–1.2	–0.5
Arradon	47 37N	2 50W	+0135	+0145	+0140	+0115	–3.9	–3.1	–1.9	–0.8
Vannes	47 39N	2 46W	+0200	+0150	+0140	+0120	–3.8	–3.0	–2.1	–0.9
St Armel (Le Passage)	47 36N	2 43W	+0200	+0200	+0210	+0135	–3.8	–3.0	–2.0	–0.9
Le Logeo	47 33N	2 51W	+0140	+0140	+0145	+0115	–4.1	–3.2	–2.1	–0.9
Port du Crouesty	47 32N	2 54W	+0010	–0025	–0015	–0010	–1.6	–1.2	–0.7	–0.3
Ile de Houat	47 24N	2 57W	+0005	–0025	–0025	–0010	–1.8	–1.4	–0.7	–0.4
Ile de Hoëdic	47 20N	2 52W	+0010	–0035	–0025	–0020	–1.9	–1.5	–0.8	–0.4
Pénerf	47 31N	2 37W	+0015	–0025	–0015	–0015	–1.6	–1.2	–0.7	–0.4
Tréhiguier	47 30N	2 27W	+0035	–0020	–0005	–0010	–1.5	–1.1	–0.6	–0.4
Le Croisic	47 18N	2 31W	+0015	–0040	–0020	–0015	–1.6	–1.3	–0.7	–0.4
Le Pouliguen	47 17N	2 25W	+0020	–0025	–0020	–0025	–1.6	–1.2	–0.7	–0.4
Le Grand-Charpentier	47 13N	2 19W	+0015	–0045	–0025	–0020	–1.6	–1.2	–0.7	–0.4
Pornichet	47 16N	2 21W	+0020	–0045	–0022	–0022	–1.5	–1.1	–0.6	–0.3
La Loire										
St Nazaire	47 16N	2 12W	+0030	–0040	–0010	–0010	–1.2	–0.9	–0.5	–0.3
Donges	47 18N	2 05W	+0035	–0040	+0005	+0005	–1.1	–0.8	–0.6	–0.5
Cordemais	47 17N	1 54W	+0055	–0005	+0105	+0030	–0.8	–0.6	–0.8	–0.5
Le Pellerin	47 12N	1 46W	+0110	+0010	+0145	+0100	–0.8	–0.6	–1.0	–0.5
Nantes (Chantenay)	47 12N	1 35W	+0135	+0055	+0215	+0125	–0.7	–0.4	–0.9	–0.2
BREST *Standard port*	48 23N	4 30W	**0500** and **1700**	**1100** and **2300**	**0500** and **1700**	**1100** and **2300**	**7.0**	**5.5**	**2.7**	**1.1**
Pointe de Saint–Gildas	47 08N	2 15W	–0030	+0025	–0005	–0020	–1.4	–1.1	–0.6	–0.3
Pornic	47 06N	2 07W	–0050	+0030	–0010	–0010	–1.2	–0.9	–0.5	–0.3
Ile de Noirmoutier, L'Herbaudière	47 02N	2 18W	–0045	+0025	–0020	–0020	–1.5	–1.1	–0.6	–0.3
Fromentine	46 54N	2 10W	–0045	+0020	–0015	+0005	–1.8	–1.3	–0.8	–0.1
Ile de Yeu, Port Joinville	46 44N	2 21W	–0040	+0015	–0030	–0035	–2.0	–1.5	–0.8	–0.4
St Gilles-Croix-de-Vie	46 41N	1 56W	–0030	+0015	–0030	–0030	–1.9	–1.4	–0.7	–0.4
Les Sables d'Olonne	46 30N	1 48W	–0030	+0015	–0035	–0035	–1.8	–1.4	–0.7	–0.4
POINTE DE GRAVE *Standard port*	45 34N	1 04W	**0000** and **1200**	**0600** and **1800**	**0000** and **1200**	**0500** and **1700**	**5.3**	**4.4**	**2.1**	**1.0**
Ile de Ré, St Martin	46 12N	1 22W	+0005	–0030	–0025	–0030	+0.7	+0.6	+0.3	–0.1
La Pallice	46 10N	1 13W	+0015	–0030	–0020	–0025	+0.7	+0.6	+0.3	–0.1
La Rochelle	46 09N	1 09W	+0015	–0030	–0020	–0025	+0.7	+0.6	+0.3	–0.2
Ile d'Aix	46 01N	1 10W	+0015	–0040	–0025	–0030	+0.9	+0.7	+0.3	0.0
La Charente, Rochefort	45 57N	0 58W	+0035	–0015	+0125	+0030	+1.2	+1.0	+0.1	–0.2
Le Chapus	45 51N	1 11W	+0015	–0040	–0015	–0025	+0.7	+0.7	+0.4	+0.1
La Cayenne	45 47N	1 08W	+0030	–0015	–0005	–0010	+0.3	+0.3	+0.3	0.0
Pointe de Gatseau	45 48N	1 14W	+0015	0000	–0020	–0015	0.0	0.0	+0.2	0.0
Cordouan	45 35N	1 10W	–0010	–0010	–0025	–0015	–0.3	–0.3	–0.3	–0.1
La Gironde										
Royan	45 37N	1 01W	0000	–0005	0000	0000	+0.1	+0.1	+0.1	0.0
Richard	45 27N	0 56W	+0020	+0020	+0035	+0030	0.0	0.0	–0.4	–0.5
Lamena	45 20N	0 48W	+0035	+0045	+0125	+0100	+0.3	+0.2	–0.5	–0.3
Pauillac	45 12N	0 45W	+0100	+0100	+0205	+0135	+0.2	+0.1	–1.0	–0.4
La Reuille	45 03N	0 36W	+0135	+0145	+0305	+0230	–0.1	–0.2	–1.3	–0.7
La Garonne										
Le Marquis	45 00N	0 33W	+0145	+0150	+0320	+0245	–0.2	–0.3	– 1.5	–0.9
Bordeaux	44 52N	0 33W	+0200	+0225	+0405	+0330	0.0	–0.1	–1.7	–1.0

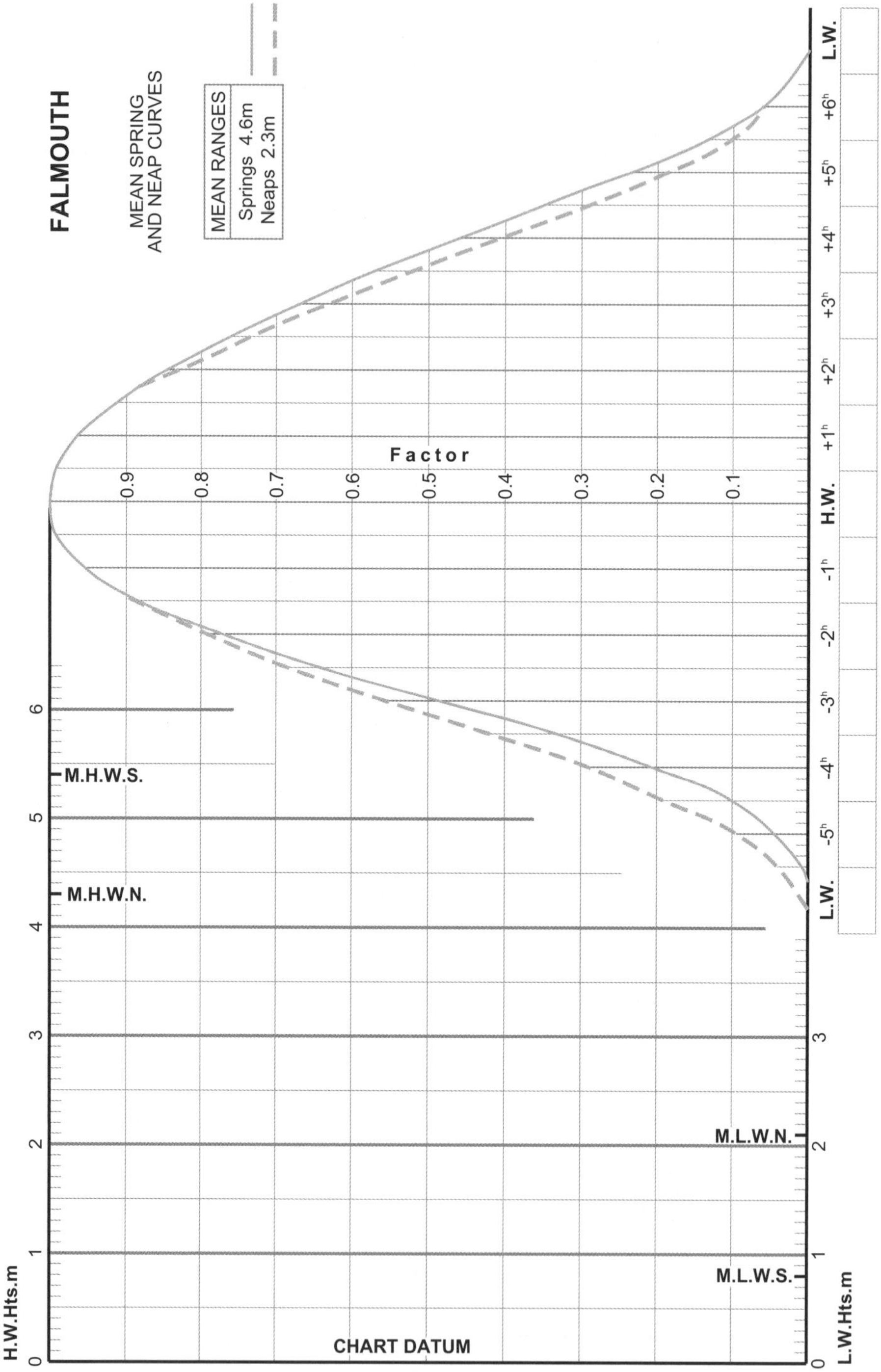
FALMOUTH
MEAN SPRING AND NEAP CURVES
MEAN RANGES
Springs 4.6m
Neaps 2.3m
Factor
0.9
0.8
0.7
0.6
0.5
0.4
0.3
0.2
0.1
L.W.
-5h
-4h
-3h
-2h
-1h
H.W.
+1h
+2h
+3h
+4h
+5h
+6h
L.W.
H.W.Hts.m
0
1
2
3
4
5
6
M.H.W.S.
M.H.W.N.
CHART DATUM
M.L.W.N.
M.L.W.S.
L.W.Hts.m

TIME ZONE (UT)
For Summer Time add ONE hour in **non-shaded areas**

FALMOUTH

LAT 50°09′N LONG 5°03′W

TIMES AND HEIGHTS OF HIGH AND LOW WATERS

Dates in amber are **SPRINGS**
Dates in grey are **NEAPS**

2023

JANUARY

Date	Day	Time	m	Time	m	Time	m	Time	m	Moon
1	SU	0024	4.1	0638	1.6	1245	4.3	1920	1.5	
2	M	0131	4.1	0747	1.6	1352	4.2	2027	1.4	
3	TU	0230	4.3	0855	1.5	1450	4.3	2125	1.3	
4	W	0319	4.4	0951	1.3	1539	4.4	2215	1.2	
5	TH	0402	4.6	1040	1.1	1623	4.5	2259	1.1	
6	F	0442	4.8	1123	1.0	1703	4.6	2339	1.0	○
7	SA	0521	4.9	1203	1.0	1742	4.7			
8	SU	0014	1.0	0559	4.9	1238	0.9	1819	4.7	
9	M	0047	1.0	0635	5.0	1310	1.0	1854	4.6	
10	TU	0117	1.1	0708	4.9	1339	1.0	1928	4.6	
11	W	0146	1.1	0739	4.8	1407	1.1	1959	4.5	
12	TH	0216	1.2	0810	4.7	1439	1.2	2031	4.4	
13	F	0249	1.3	0843	4.6	1515	1.3	2106	4.3	
14	SA	0329	1.5	0923	4.5	1559	1.5	2152	4.2	
15	SU	0417	1.6	1016	4.4	1654	1.6	2255	4.1	◑
16	M	0520	1.7	1121	4.3	1803	1.7			
17	TU	0004	4.1	0636	1.7	1233	4.3	1921	1.6	
18	W	0117	4.2	0756	1.6	1348	4.3	2035	1.4	
19	TH	0228	4.4	0909	1.3	1459	4.5	2142	1.2	
20	F	0331	4.7	1014	1.0	1601	4.7	2242	0.9	
21	SA	0427	5.0	1114	0.7	1657	4.9	2339	0.6	●
22	SU	0519	5.2	1209	0.4	1750	5.0			
23	M	0030	0.4	0611	5.4	1258	0.2	1841	5.1	
24	TU	0117	0.3	0659	5.5	1344	0.1	1928	5.0	
25	W	0201	0.3	0744	5.4	1427	0.2	2010	4.9	
26	TH	0242	0.4	0826	5.3	1508	0.4	2051	4.8	
27	F	0321	0.7	0907	5.0	1548	0.7	2131	4.5	
28	SA	0402	1.0	0949	4.7	1630	1.1	2215	4.3	◐
29	SU	0449	1.3	1036	4.3	1719	1.5	2309	4.0	
30	M	0544	1.6	1135	4.0	1818	1.7			
31	TU	0022	3.9	0652	1.8	1301	3.9	1931	1.8	

FEBRUARY

Date	Day	Time	m	Time	m	Time	m	Time	m	Moon
1	W	0152	4.0	0810	1.8	1424	3.9	2048	1.7	
2	TH	0256	4.2	0925	1.6	1522	4.1	2151	1.5	
3	F	0344	4.4	1022	1.3	1608	4.3	2241	1.3	
4	SA	0426	4.7	1107	1.1	1649	4.5	2323	1.1	
5	SU	0506	4.8	1147	0.9	1728	4.7			○
6	M	0000	0.9	0544	5.0	1223	0.8	1805	4.7	
7	TU	0032	0.9	0620	5.0	1253	0.8	1840	4.7	
8	W	0100	0.9	0652	5.0	1320	0.8	1911	4.7	
9	TH	0127	0.9	0720	4.9	1346	0.8	1937	4.7	
10	F	0155	0.9	0744	4.9	1415	0.9	1957	4.6	
11	SA	0226	1.0	0805	4.8	1446	1.0	2012	4.5	
12	SU	0259	1.1	0828	4.7	1522	1.2	2044	4.4	
13	M	0339	1.3	0909	4.5	1606	1.4	2137	4.2	◑
14	TU	0432	1.6	1018	4.2	1707	1.7	2309	4.0	
15	W	0546	1.8	1156	4.1	1834	1.8			
16	TH	0045	4.1	0724	1.7	1327	4.1	2011	1.7	
17	F	0209	4.3	0855	1.4	1448	4.3	2131	1.3	
18	SA	0318	4.6	1006	1.0	1553	4.6	2235	0.9	
19	SU	0415	5.0	1106	0.6	1647	4.9	2330	0.5	
20	M	0506	5.3	1159	0.2	1737	5.1			●
21	TU	0019	0.2	0555	5.5	1245	0.0	1824	5.2	
22	W	0103	0.0	0640	5.6	1327	-0.1	1906	5.2	
23	TH	0143	0.0	0722	5.5	1406	0.0	1943	5.1	
24	F	0219	0.2	0759	5.3	1440	0.3	2016	5.0	
25	SA	0253	0.5	0833	5.1	1513	0.7	2049	4.7	
26	SU	0327	0.9	0906	4.7	1546	1.1	2125	4.4	
27	M	0405	1.3	0943	4.3	1626	1.6	2210	4.1	◐
28	TU	0455	1.7	1033	3.9	1722	1.9	2312	3.8	

MARCH

Date	Day	Time	m	Time	m	Time	m	Time	m	Moon
1	W	0605	2.0	1150	3.6	1839	2.1			
2	TH	0106	3.8	0731	2.1	1403	3.7	2011	2.0	
3	F	0233	4.0	0904	1.8	1504	4.0	2130	1.7	
4	SA	0324	4.3	1003	1.4	1550	4.3	2221	1.4	
5	SU	0406	4.6	1047	1.1	1630	4.5	2302	1.1	
6	M	0445	4.8	1125	0.9	1707	4.7	2338	0.9	
7	TU	0522	5.0	1159	0.7	1743	4.8			○
8	W	0009	0.8	0557	5.0	1228	0.6	1817	4.8	
9	TH	0038	0.7	0628	5.0	1255	0.6	1847	4.8	
10	F	0105	0.7	0655	5.0	1322	0.6	1910	4.8	
11	SA	0133	0.7	0717	4.9	1350	0.7	1923	4.8	
12	SU	0202	0.8	0732	4.8	1420	0.8	1939	4.7	
13	M	0234	0.9	0755	4.7	1453	1.1	2012	4.5	
14	TU	0312	1.2	0835	4.4	1534	1.4	2103	4.3	
15	W	0402	1.5	0944	4.1	1633	1.7	2241	4.0	◑
16	TH	0519	1.8	1142	3.9	1807	1.9			
17	F	0028	4.0	0712	1.8	1321	3.9	2002	1.8	
18	SA	0157	4.3	0850	1.4	1443	4.2	2123	1.3	
19	SU	0305	4.6	0957	0.9	1543	4.6	2223	0.8	
20	M	0359	5.0	1052	0.4	1632	4.9	2315	0.4	
21	TU	0447	5.3	1140	0.1	1717	5.1			●
22	W	0000	0.1	0533	5.5	1224	-0.1	1759	5.2	
23	TH	0042	0.0	0616	5.5	1303	-0.1	1838	5.3	
24	F	0119	0.0	0655	5.4	1339	0.1	1912	5.2	
25	SA	0152	0.2	0730	5.2	1410	0.4	1944	5.0	
26	SU	0223	0.5	0801	4.9	1438	0.8	2014	4.8	
27	M	0254	0.9	0831	4.6	1507	1.2	2047	4.5	
28	TU	0327	1.4	0905	4.2	1539	1.6	2128	4.2	
29	W	0411	1.8	0953	3.9	1629	2.0	2226	3.9	◐
30	TH	0524	2.1	1104	3.6	1756	2.2	2356	3.7	
31	F	0653	2.1	1334	3.6	1928	2.2			

APRIL

Date	Day	Time	m	Time	m	Time	m	Time	m	Moon
1	SA	0159	3.9	0826	1.9	1438	3.9	2052	1.8	
2	SU	0254	4.2	0928	1.5	1523	4.2	2146	1.4	
3	M	0337	4.5	1012	1.1	1602	4.5	2227	1.1	
4	TU	0416	4.8	1050	0.9	1638	4.7	2304	0.9	
5	W	0451	4.9	1125	0.7	1713	4.8	2338	0.7	
6	TH	0525	5.0	1157	0.6	1745	4.9			○
7	F	0010	0.6	0558	5.0	1227	0.5	1815	4.9	
8	SA	0040	0.6	0628	5.0	1257	0.5	1841	4.9	
9	SU	0111	0.6	0653	4.9	1328	0.6	1901	4.9	
10	M	0143	0.7	0715	4.8	1359	0.8	1926	4.8	
11	TU	0217	0.9	0745	4.6	1434	1.1	2005	4.6	
12	W	0257	1.2	0834	4.3	1519	1.4	2107	4.3	
13	TH	0352	1.5	1002	4.0	1624	1.8	2244	4.1	◑
14	F	0517	1.7	1143	3.8	1803	1.9			
15	SA	0019	4.1	0709	1.6	1316	4.0	1951	1.7	
16	SU	0143	4.3	0836	1.2	1430	4.3	2105	1.2	
17	M	0247	4.7	0937	0.8	1524	4.6	2202	0.8	
18	TU	0339	5.0	1029	0.4	1610	4.9	2251	0.4	
19	W	0425	5.2	1115	0.2	1651	5.1	2336	0.2	
20	TH	0508	5.3	1158	0.1	1731	5.2			●
21	F	0016	0.1	0550	5.3	1236	0.1	1808	5.2	
22	SA	0052	0.2	0628	5.2	1310	0.3	1842	5.1	
23	SU	0126	0.4	0703	5.0	1341	0.6	1915	5.0	
24	M	0157	0.7	0734	4.8	1409	0.9	1946	4.8	
25	TU	0228	1.0	0804	4.5	1437	1.3	2020	4.6	
26	W	0300	1.4	0840	4.2	1507	1.7	2101	4.3	
27	TH	0340	1.8	0928	3.9	1554	2.0	2155	4.0	◐
28	F	0448	2.0	1033	3.7	1715	2.2	2306	3.9	
29	SA	0611	2.1	1221	3.6	1840	2.1			
30	SU	0054	3.9	0729	1.9	1353	3.9	1954	1.9	

Chart Datum: 2·91 metres below Ordnance Datum (Newlyn)
HAT is 5·7 metres above Chart Datum

TIME ZONE (UT)
For Summer Time add ONE hour in **non-shaded areas**

FALMOUTH

LAT 50°09′N LONG 5°03′W

TIMES AND HEIGHTS OF HIGH AND LOW WATERS

Dates in amber are **SPRINGS**
Dates in grey are **NEAPS**

2023

MAY

Date	Day	Time	m	Time	m	Time	m	Time	m
1	M	0208	4.2	0833	1.6	1443	4.2	2053	1.6
2	TU	0256	4.4	0923	1.2	1523	4.4	2141	1.2
3	W	0335	4.6	1006	1.0	1559	4.6	2223	1.0
4	TH	0412	4.8	1045	0.8	1634	4.8	2303	0.8
5	F ○	0448	4.9	1123	0.6	1708	4.9	2341	0.6
6	SA	0525	5.0	1200	0.6	1743	5.0		
7	SU	0017	0.6	0603	5.0	1236	0.6	1818	5.0
8	M	0054	0.6	0641	4.9	1312	0.7	1854	5.0
9	TU	0131	0.7	0719	4.8	1349	0.8	1934	4.8
10	W	0212	0.9	0804	4.5	1430	1.1	2023	4.7
11	TH	0259	1.1	0901	4.3	1522	1.4	2126	4.4
12	F ◑	0401	1.4	1014	4.1	1632	1.6	2243	4.3
13	SA	0523	1.5	1139	4.0	1757	1.6		
14	SU	0005	4.3	0650	1.4	1259	4.1	1922	1.5
15	M	0120	4.4	0805	1.1	1405	4.3	2033	1.2
16	TU	0222	4.7	0907	0.8	1458	4.6	2131	0.9
17	W	0314	4.9	0959	0.6	1543	4.8	2222	0.6
18	TH	0400	5.0	1046	0.5	1624	4.9	2308	0.5
19	F ●	0444	5.0	1130	0.4	1703	5.0	2350	0.5
20	SA	0525	5.0	1209	0.5	1741	5.0		
21	SU	0027	0.5	0604	4.9	1245	0.7	1817	5.0
22	M	0103	0.7	0640	4.8	1318	0.9	1852	4.9
23	TU	0137	0.9	0714	4.6	1348	1.1	1926	4.8
24	W	0209	1.1	0747	4.4	1418	1.4	2001	4.6
25	TH	0242	1.4	0823	4.2	1451	1.6	2040	4.4
26	F	0321	1.6	0908	4.0	1533	1.8	2128	4.2
27	SA ◐	0413	1.8	1005	3.9	1633	2.0	2227	4.1
28	SU	0519	1.9	1113	3.8	1744	2.0	2334	4.1
29	M	0627	1.8	1227	3.9	1852	1.9		
30	TU	0043	4.1	0730	1.6	1334	4.1	1954	1.7
31	W	0147	4.3	0827	1.4	1426	4.3	2049	1.4

JUNE

Date	Day	Time	m	Time	m	Time	m	Time	m
1	TH	0240	4.5	0918	1.1	1510	4.5	2139	1.1
2	F	0326	4.7	1005	0.9	1552	4.7	2227	0.9
3	SA	0412	4.8	1051	0.8	1634	4.9	2314	0.7
4	SU ○	0458	4.9	1137	0.7	1719	5.0		
5	M	0000	0.6	0546	4.9	1221	0.7	1805	5.1
6	TU	0044	0.6	0635	4.9	1304	0.7	1852	5.1
7	W	0130	0.6	0723	4.8	1349	0.8	1940	5.0
8	TH	0217	0.7	0813	4.6	1437	0.9	2031	4.9
9	F	0309	0.9	0908	4.5	1530	1.1	2127	4.7
10	SA ◑	0407	1.0	1010	4.3	1630	1.3	2231	4.6
11	SU	0510	1.2	1118	4.2	1735	1.3	2339	4.5
12	M	0615	1.2	1227	4.2	1841	1.3		
13	TU	0047	4.5	0723	1.2	1331	4.3	1949	1.2
14	W	0150	4.5	0827	1.1	1427	4.4	2053	1.1
15	TH	0247	4.6	0925	1.0	1516	4.6	2150	1.0
16	F	0337	4.6	1017	0.9	1600	4.7	2241	0.9
17	SA	0423	4.7	1104	0.9	1641	4.8	2327	0.8
18	SU ●	0505	4.7	1147	0.9	1721	4.9		
19	M	0008	0.9	0546	4.7	1225	0.9	1800	4.9
20	TU	0047	0.9	0625	4.6	1301	1.0	1837	4.9
21	W	0122	1.0	0701	4.6	1333	1.2	1912	4.8
22	TH	0155	1.1	0735	4.5	1404	1.3	1947	4.7
23	F	0227	1.3	0810	4.4	1434	1.4	2022	4.6
24	SA	0259	1.4	0848	4.3	1509	1.6	2101	4.5
25	SU	0338	1.5	0932	4.1	1551	1.7	2147	4.3
26	M ◐	0426	1.6	1024	4.1	1645	1.8	2241	4.3
27	TU	0523	1.7	1121	4.0	1747	1.8	2340	4.2
28	W	0626	1.7	1222	4.1	1854	1.7		
29	TH	0042	4.3	0731	1.6	1323	4.2	1959	1.6
30	F	0147	4.4	0833	1.4	1424	4.4	2101	1.3

JULY

Date	Day	Time	m	Time	m	Time	m	Time	m
1	SA	0249	4.5	0931	1.2	1519	4.7	2159	1.1
2	SU	0346	4.7	1027	1.0	1612	4.9	2255	0.9
3	M ○	0441	4.8	1121	0.8	1703	5.1	2349	0.7
4	TU	0536	4.9	1213	0.7	1755	5.2		
5	W	0041	0.5	0629	4.9	1303	0.6	1846	5.3
6	TH	0131	0.4	0720	4.9	1351	0.6	1936	5.3
7	F	0219	0.4	0809	4.9	1437	0.6	2024	5.2
8	SA	0306	0.5	0858	4.7	1523	0.7	2114	5.0
9	SU	0353	0.7	0948	4.6	1611	0.9	2205	4.8
10	M ◑	0443	0.9	1042	4.4	1703	1.2	2301	4.6
11	TU	0536	1.2	1141	4.3	1759	1.4		
12	W	0004	4.4	0636	1.4	1248	4.2	1903	1.5
13	TH	0115	4.2	0742	1.5	1356	4.2	2014	1.5
14	F	0223	4.2	0851	1.4	1454	4.4	2123	1.4
15	SA	0319	4.3	0952	1.3	1543	4.5	2222	1.3
16	SU	0408	4.4	1045	1.2	1626	4.7	2312	1.1
17	M ●	0451	4.5	1131	1.1	1706	4.8	2356	1.0
18	TU	0532	4.6	1211	1.1	1745	4.9		
19	W	0034	1.0	0611	4.6	1247	1.1	1823	4.9
20	TH	0109	1.0	0648	4.6	1318	1.1	1858	4.9
21	F	0138	1.0	0722	4.6	1346	1.2	1930	4.9
22	SA	0205	1.1	0754	4.6	1412	1.2	2000	4.8
23	SU	0232	1.2	0823	4.5	1440	1.3	2030	4.7
24	M	0303	1.3	0853	4.4	1514	1.4	2103	4.6
25	TU ◐	0340	1.4	0930	4.3	1555	1.6	2146	4.4
26	W	0426	1.6	1021	4.2	1648	1.7	2245	4.3
27	TH	0526	1.7	1127	4.1	1757	1.8	2356	4.2
28	F	0640	1.7	1239	4.2	1917	1.8		
29	SA	0111	4.3	0757	1.6	1353	4.4	2033	1.5
30	SU	0227	4.4	0908	1.4	1500	4.6	2142	1.2
31	M	0333	4.6	1013	1.1	1558	4.9	2245	0.9

AUGUST

Date	Day	Time	m	Time	m	Time	m	Time	m
1	TU ○	0431	4.8	1112	0.8	1652	5.2	2343	0.6
2	W	0526	5.0	1207	0.6	1743	5.4		
3	TH	0035	0.3	0618	5.1	1256	0.4	1834	5.5
4	F	0123	0.2	0707	5.2	1341	0.3	1921	5.5
5	SA	0207	0.1	0752	5.1	1423	0.3	2006	5.4
6	SU	0248	0.3	0834	5.0	1503	0.5	2048	5.2
7	M	0328	0.6	0913	4.8	1543	0.8	2129	4.9
8	TU ◑	0409	0.9	0954	4.5	1627	1.2	2213	4.5
9	W	0454	1.3	1043	4.3	1719	1.5	2309	4.2
10	TH	0549	1.7	1151	4.1	1822	1.8		
11	F	0036	3.9	0657	1.9	1328	4.0	1941	1.9
12	SA	0206	3.9	0822	1.9	1438	4.2	2112	1.7
13	SU	0307	4.1	0939	1.7	1529	4.4	2215	1.5
14	M	0355	4.3	1033	1.4	1611	4.7	2302	1.2
15	TU	0436	4.5	1117	1.2	1650	4.9	2342	1.0
16	W ●	0514	4.7	1155	1.1	1728	5.0		
17	TH	0017	0.9	0552	4.8	1228	1.0	1805	5.0
18	F	0048	0.9	0629	4.8	1257	1.0	1839	5.0
19	SA	0114	0.9	0702	4.8	1321	1.0	1908	5.0
20	SU	0137	0.9	0730	4.8	1345	1.0	1933	4.9
21	M	0202	1.0	0752	4.7	1411	1.1	1954	4.8
22	TU	0230	1.1	0808	4.6	1442	1.2	2014	4.7
23	W	0302	1.3	0829	4.5	1517	1.4	2045	4.5
24	TH ◐	0341	1.5	0913	4.3	1603	1.7	2144	4.3
25	F	0434	1.8	1039	4.2	1711	1.9	2324	4.1
26	SA	0555	2.0	1211	4.1	1848	1.9		
27	SU	0054	4.1	0735	1.9	1336	4.3	2022	1.7
28	M	0219	4.3	0858	1.6	1449	4.7	2136	1.2
29	TU	0327	4.6	1005	1.1	1547	5.0	2237	0.8
30	W	0422	4.9	1103	0.7	1638	5.4	2332	0.4
31	TH ○	0512	5.1	1154	0.4	1727	5.6		

Chart Datum: 2·91 metres below Ordnance Datum (Newlyn)
HAT is 5·7 metres above Chart Datum

TIME ZONE (UT)
For Summer Time add ONE hour in **non-shaded areas**

FALMOUTH

LAT 50°09'N LONG 5°03'W

TIMES AND HEIGHTS OF HIGH AND LOW WATERS

Dates in amber are **SPRINGS**
Dates in grey are **NEAPS**

2023

SEPTEMBER

Date	Day	Time	m	Time	m	Time	m	Time	m
1	F	0020	0.1	0601	5.3	1240	0.2	1815	5.7
2	SA	0105	0.0	0645	5.4	1322	0.1	1859	5.7
3	SU	0145	0.0	0725	5.3	1400	0.2	1940	5.5
4	M	0222	0.2	0801	5.2	1436	0.4	2017	5.2
5	TU	0256	0.6	0834	4.9	1511	0.8	2051	4.9
6	W	0331	1.1	0909	4.6	1550	1.3	◑ 2127	4.4
7	TH	0411	1.6	0952	4.3	1639	1.8	2214	4.0
8	F	0504	2.0	1052	4.0	1745	2.1	2341	3.7
9	SA	0618	2.2	1300	3.9	1915	2.2		
10	SU	0152	3.7	0800	2.2	1418	4.1	2109	1.9
11	M	0252	4.0	0928	1.8	1509	4.4	2200	1.5
12	TU	0336	4.3	1015	1.5	1551	4.7	2240	1.2
13	W	0415	4.6	1054	1.2	1628	4.9	2316	1.0
14	TH	0451	4.8	1129	1.0	1704	5.1	2349	0.8
15	F	0527	4.9	1201	0.9	1739	5.1	●	
16	SA	0018	0.8	0602	5.0	1228	0.9	1812	5.1
17	SU	0043	0.8	0634	5.0	1253	0.9	1841	5.1
18	M	0108	0.8	0701	4.9	1318	0.9	1904	5.0
19	TU	0134	0.9	0719	4.8	1345	1.0	1921	4.9
20	W	0202	1.0	0730	4.8	1415	1.1	1937	4.7
21	TH	0232	1.2	0753	4.6	1449	1.4	2010	4.5
22	F	0309	1.5	0839	4.4	1533	1.7	◐ 2114	4.2
23	SA	0401	1.9	1019	4.2	1643	2.0	2314	4.0
24	SU	0530	2.1	1157	4.1	1839	2.0		
25	M	0050	4.0	0728	2.0	1325	4.3	2018	1.6
26	TU	0216	4.3	0851	1.5	1437	4.7	2127	1.1
27	W	0318	4.7	0953	1.1	1533	5.1	2223	0.6
28	TH	0407	5.0	1046	0.6	1621	5.4	2313	0.3
29	F	0452	5.3	1134	0.3	1707	5.6	○ 2358	0.1
30	SA	0536	5.4	1218	0.1	1751	5.7		

OCTOBER

Date	Day	Time	m	Time	m	Time	m	Time	m
1	SU	0040	0.0	0617	5.4	1257	0.1	1833	5.6
2	M	0118	0.1	0654	5.4	1334	0.3	1911	5.4
3	TU	0152	0.4	0728	5.2	1407	0.6	1945	5.1
4	W	0224	0.8	0800	5.0	1441	1.0	2016	4.7
5	TH	0255	1.3	0833	4.7	1517	1.4	2050	4.3
6	F	0331	1.7	0914	4.4	1603	1.9	◑ 2137	3.9
7	SA	0422	2.1	1011	4.0	1712	2.2	2253	3.6
8	SU	0542	2.4	1155	3.9	1843	2.3		
9	M	0126	3.7	0720	2.3	1346	4.0	2035	2.0
10	TU	0225	4.0	0851	2.0	1440	4.4	2125	1.6
11	W	0309	4.3	0939	1.6	1522	4.7	2203	1.2
12	TH	0347	4.6	1017	1.2	1559	4.9	2238	1.0
13	F	0422	4.8	1053	1.0	1635	5.0	2312	0.8
14	SA	0457	5.0	1126	0.9	1709	5.1	● 2343	0.8
15	SU	0531	5.0	1157	0.8	1741	5.1		
16	M	0011	0.7	0602	5.0	1225	0.8	1812	5.1
17	TU	0040	0.8	0630	5.0	1254	0.8	1840	5.0
18	W	0109	0.9	0654	4.9	1324	0.9	1904	4.8
19	TH	0139	1.0	0717	4.8	1356	1.1	1928	4.7
20	F	0212	1.2	0749	4.7	1433	1.3	2011	4.4
21	SA	0252	1.6	0850	4.4	1522	1.6	2138	4.1
22	SU	0350	1.9	1018	4.2	1641	1.9	◐ 2312	3.9
23	M	0526	2.1	1146	4.2	1833	1.9		
24	TU	0043	4.0	0714	1.9	1309	4.4	2002	1.5
25	W	0202	4.3	0832	1.4	1418	4.8	2106	1.0
26	TH	0259	4.7	0931	1.0	1512	5.1	2159	0.6
27	F	0345	5.0	1022	0.6	1559	5.3	2247	0.4
28	SA	0428	5.2	1109	0.4	1644	5.4	○ 2332	0.2
29	SU	0509	5.3	1152	0.3	1726	5.4		
30	M	0012	0.2	0548	5.3	1231	0.3	1807	5.3
31	TU	0050	0.4	0624	5.3	1308	0.4	1844	5.1

NOVEMBER

Date	Day	Time	m	Time	m	Time	m	Time	m
1	W	0124	0.7	0659	5.2	1342	0.7	1918	4.9
2	TH	0156	1.0	0732	5.0	1416	1.1	1950	4.6
3	F	0228	1.4	0807	4.7	1452	1.5	2026	4.3
4	SA	0303	1.7	0848	4.4	1535	1.8	2113	4.0
5	SU	0350	2.1	0941	4.2	1638	2.1	◑ 2220	3.7
6	M	0502	2.3	1053	4.0	1757	2.2		
7	TU	0024	3.7	0625	2.3	1242	4.0	1919	2.0
8	W	0139	3.9	0743	2.0	1352	4.2	2024	1.7
9	TH	0229	4.2	0843	1.7	1441	4.5	2112	1.4
10	F	0310	4.5	0929	1.4	1522	4.7	2153	1.1
11	SA	0347	4.7	1010	1.1	1559	4.9	2231	0.9
12	SU	0423	4.9	1049	1.0	1635	5.0	2307	0.8
13	M	0457	5.0	1125	0.8	1711	5.0	● 2342	0.8
14	TU	0531	5.0	1201	0.8	1747	5.0		
15	W	0017	0.8	0606	5.1	1236	0.8	1824	4.9
16	TH	0052	0.8	0642	5.0	1312	0.8	1902	4.8
17	F	0128	1.0	0720	4.9	1350	1.0	1944	4.6
18	SA	0207	1.2	0805	4.8	1434	1.2	2036	4.4
19	SU	0253	1.4	0902	4.6	1530	1.5	2143	4.2
20	M	0356	1.7	1011	4.4	1645	1.6	◐ 2301	4.1
21	TU	0517	1.8	1126	4.4	1810	1.6		
22	W	0021	4.1	0642	1.7	1241	4.5	1928	1.3
23	TH	0132	4.3	0756	1.4	1348	4.7	2033	1.1
24	F	0230	4.6	0859	1.1	1445	4.9	2129	0.8
25	SA	0319	4.8	0953	0.8	1535	5.0	2219	0.6
26	SU	0403	5.0	1042	0.6	1621	5.1	2305	0.6
27	M	0444	5.1	1127	0.6	1704	5.1	○ 2348	0.6
28	TU	0524	5.1	1209	0.6	1745	5.0		
29	W	0027	0.7	0602	5.1	1248	0.7	1824	4.9
30	TH	0103	0.9	0638	5.1	1324	0.9	1900	4.7

DECEMBER

Date	Day	Time	m	Time	m	Time	m	Time	m
1	F	0137	1.1	0714	4.9	1400	1.1	1934	4.5
2	SA	0210	1.3	0750	4.8	1435	1.4	2011	4.3
3	SU	0244	1.6	0829	4.6	1513	1.6	2054	4.1
4	M	0323	1.8	0915	4.4	1600	1.8	2149	3.9
5	TU	0414	2.0	1010	4.2	1659	2.0	◑ 2256	3.9
6	W	0521	2.1	1116	4.1	1807	1.9		
7	TH	0012	3.9	0631	2.1	1226	4.1	1913	1.8
8	F	0122	4.0	0737	1.9	1333	4.3	2013	1.6
9	SA	0217	4.3	0835	1.6	1429	4.4	2104	1.4
10	SU	0304	4.5	0926	1.4	1517	4.6	2150	1.1
11	M	0345	4.7	1013	1.1	1601	4.8	2234	1.0
12	TU	0425	4.9	1058	0.9	1644	4.9	● 2318	0.8
13	W	0506	5.0	1142	0.8	1728	4.9		
14	TH	0000	0.8	0550	5.1	1225	0.7	1814	4.9
15	F	0043	0.8	0633	5.1	1309	0.7	1900	4.8
16	SA	0126	0.8	0719	5.1	1354	0.8	1947	4.7
17	SU	0210	0.9	0806	5.0	1441	0.9	2037	4.6
18	M	0258	1.1	0857	4.9	1533	1.0	2132	4.4
19	TU	0352	1.2	0954	4.7	1631	1.2	◐ 2235	4.3
20	W	0453	1.4	1056	4.6	1734	1.3	2342	4.2
21	TH	0559	1.5	1203	4.5	1841	1.3		
22	F	0050	4.2	0709	1.4	1311	4.4	1951	1.3
23	SA	0155	4.3	0819	1.3	1415	4.5	2055	1.2
24	SU	0252	4.5	0923	1.2	1513	4.6	2152	1.0
25	M	0342	4.7	1019	1.0	1603	4.6	2243	0.9
26	TU	0426	4.8	1109	0.9	1649	4.7	2329	0.9
27	W	0507	4.9	1154	0.8	1731	4.7	○	
28	TH	0011	0.9	0547	5.0	1235	0.8	1811	4.7
29	F	0049	0.9	0625	5.0	1312	0.9	1848	4.7
30	SA	0123	1.0	0702	5.0	1347	1.0	1923	4.6
31	SU	0155	1.1	0737	4.9	1418	1.1	1958	4.5

Chart Datum: 2·91 metres below Ordnance Datum (Newlyn)
HAT is 5·7 metres above Chart Datum

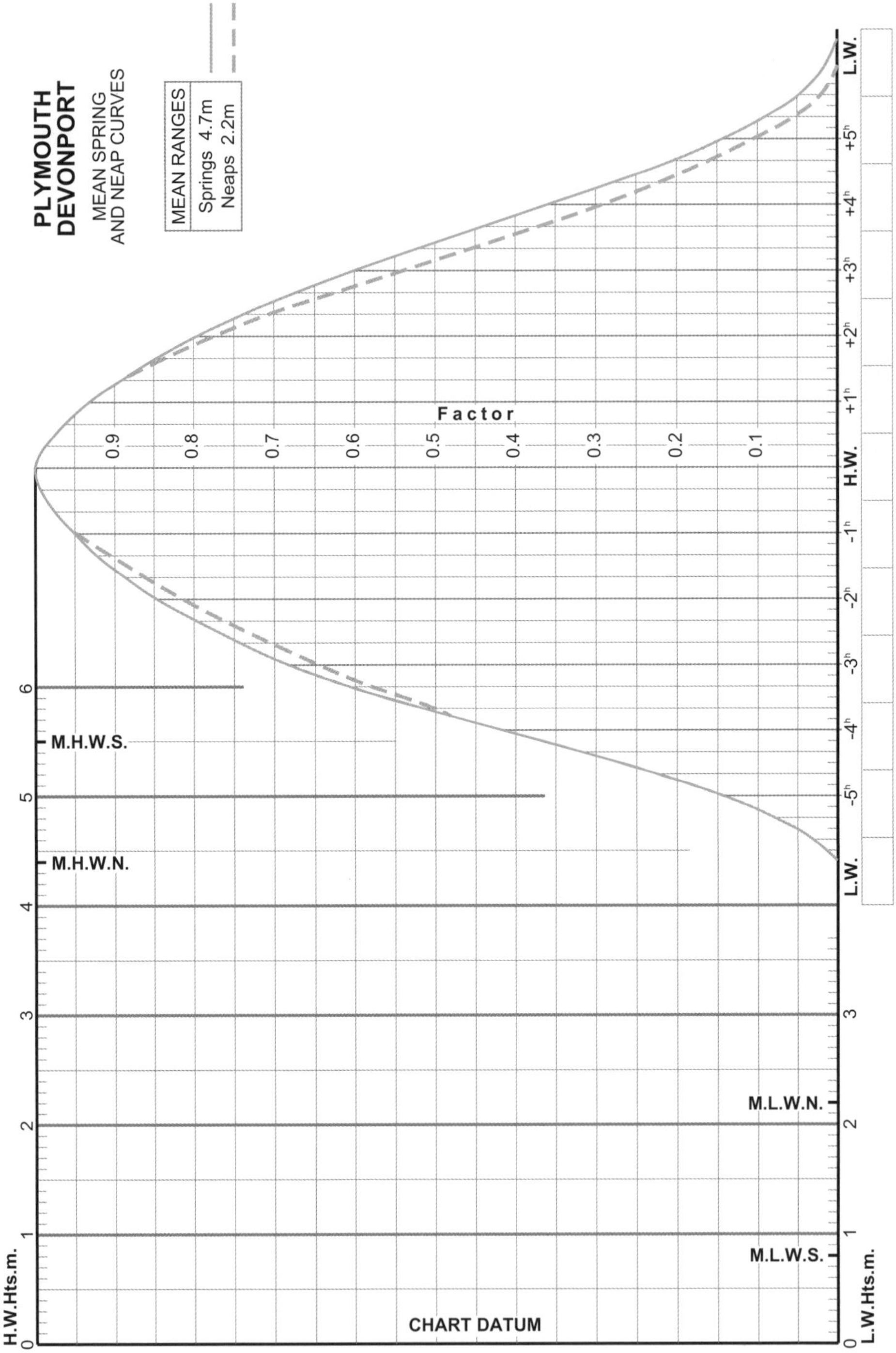
PLYMOUTH
DEVONPORT
MEAN SPRING
AND NEAP CURVES
MEAN RANGES
Springs 4.7m
Neaps 2.2m
Factor
0.9
0.8
0.7
0.6
0.5
0.4
0.3
0.2
0.1
L.W.
-5h
-4h
-3h
-2h
-1h
H.W.
+1h
+2h
+3h
+4h
+5h
L.W.
H.W.Hts.m.
0
1
2
3
4
5
6
M.H.W.S.
M.H.W.N.
CHART DATUM
M.L.W.N.
M.L.W.S.
L.W.Hts.m.

TIME ZONE (UT)
For Summer Time add ONE hour in **non-shaded areas**

PLYMOUTH (DEVONPORT)

LAT 50°22′N LONG 4°11′W

TIMES AND HEIGHTS OF HIGH AND LOW WATERS

Dates in amber are **SPRINGS**
Dates in grey are **NEAPS**

2023

JANUARY

Date	Time	m	Date	Time	m
1 SU	0047	4.6	16 M	0522	2.1
	0651	2.0		1140	4.6
	1311	4.7		1804	2.1
	1930	2.0			
2 M	0149	4.6	17 TU	0022	4.4
	0803	2.1		0644	2.2
	1414	4.7		1252	4.6
	2036	1.9		1929	2.1
3 TU	0248	4.7	18 W	0141	4.5
	0908	1.9		0809	2.0
	1513	4.7		1414	4.6
	2135	1.8		2046	1.9
4 W	0341	4.8	19 TH	0257	4.8
	1003	1.8		0922	1.7
	1605	4.8		1530	4.8
	2225	1.7		2154	1.6
5 TH	0428	5.0	20 F	0403	5.1
	1052	1.6		1027	1.4
	1651	4.9		1635	5.0
	2309	1.5		2254	1.3
6 F	0509	5.2	21 SA	0501	5.4
	1135	1.5		1125	1.0
	1732	5.0		1733	5.2
	○ 2349	1.4		● 2350	1.0
7 SA	0547	5.3	22 SU	0554	5.6
	1214	1.4		1219	0.7
	1810	5.0		1826	5.4
8 SU	0025	1.4	23 M	0040	0.8
	0624	5.3		0646	5.7
	1249	1.4		1309	0.5
	1847	5.0		1918	5.4
9 M	0058	1.4	24 TU	0128	0.6
	0700	5.3		0735	5.8
	1321	1.4		1355	0.5
	1922	5.0		2006	5.4
10 TU	0128	1.5	25 W	0212	0.6
	0734	5.2		0822	5.8
	1351	1.5		1439	0.5
	1957	4.9		2051	5.4
11 W	0158	1.5	26 TH	0254	0.8
	0808	5.1		0907	5.6
	1421	1.5		1520	0.7
	2031	4.8		2133	5.2
12 TH	0227	1.6	27 F	0334	1.0
	0841	5.0		0948	5.4
	1450	1.6		1600	1.1
	2104	4.7		2212	5.0
13 F	0259	1.7	28 SA	0413	1.3
	0914	4.9		1028	5.1
	1524	1.7		1640	1.5
	2139	4.6		◐ 2251	4.7
14 SA	0335	1.8	29 SU	0456	1.7
	0952	4.8		1111	4.7
	1604	1.8		1725	1.8
	2221	4.5		2338	4.5
15 SU	0421	2.0	30 M	0548	2.1
	1040	4.7		1207	4.4
	1655	2.0		1821	2.2
	◑ 2315	4.4			
			31 TU	0045	4.3
				0657	2.3
				1326	4.3
				1936	2.3

FEBRUARY

Date	Time	m	Date	Time	m
1 W	0204	4.3	16 TH	0105	4.4
	0825	2.3		0738	2.2
	1442	4.3		1353	4.4
	2100	2.2		2024	2.1
2 TH	0311	4.5	17 F	0236	4.6
	0943	2.1		0909	1.8
	1544	4.4		1520	4.6
	2206	2.0		2144	1.7
3 F	0406	4.7	18 SA	0350	5.0
	1038	1.8		1020	1.4
	1635	4.7		1628	4.9
	2255	1.7		2247	1.3
4 SA	0452	5.0	19 SU	0450	5.3
	1123	1.5		1118	0.9
	1718	4.8		1725	5.2
	2337	1.5		2341	0.8
5 SU	0532	5.2	20 M	0542	5.6
	1203	1.3		1209	0.5
	1757	5.0		1816	5.4
	○			●	
6 M	0014	1.3	21 TU	0029	0.5
	0610	5.3		0632	5.8
	1238	1.2		1255	0.2
	1834	5.0		1904	5.5
7 TU	0046	1.2	22 W	0113	0.3
	0647	5.3		0719	5.9
	1309	1.1		1338	0.1
	1910	5.0		1947	5.6
8 W	0116	1.2	23 TH	0154	0.3
	0722	5.3		0802	5.8
	1337	1.1		1417	0.3
	1944	5.0		2025	5.5
9 TH	0143	1.2	24 F	0231	0.5
	0754	5.2		0841	5.6
	1403	1.2		1453	0.5
	2014	5.0		2059	5.3
10 F	0210	1.2	25 SA	0306	0.8
	0823	5.1		0914	5.4
	1429	1.3		1527	0.9
	2041	4.9		2128	5.0
11 SA	0238	1.3	26 SU	0339	1.2
	0851	5.0		0943	5.0
	1458	1.4		1600	1.4
	2107	4.8		2155	4.8
12 SU	0309	1.5	27 M	0414	1.6
	0921	4.9		1013	4.6
	1531	1.5		1636	1.9
	2139	4.7		◐ 2228	4.5
13 M	0347	1.7	28 TU	0458	2.1
	1001	4.7		1054	4.3
	1613	1.8		1726	2.3
	◑ 2227	4.5		2322	4.2
14 TU	0437	1.9			
	1059	4.5			
	1711	2.0			
	2337	4.4			
15 W	0552	2.2			
	1219	4.4			
	1840	2.2			

MARCH

Date	Time	m	Date	Time	m
1 W	0603	2.4	16 TH	0528	2.2
	1214	4.0		1203	4.2
	1838	2.5		1816	2.3
2 TH	0113	4.1	17 F	0047	4.3
	0734	2.5		0727	2.2
	1417	4.0		1349	4.2
	2018	2.5		2016	2.2
3 F	0244	4.3	18 SA	0226	4.6
	0928	2.2		0904	1.8
	1524	4.2		1517	4.6
	2148	2.1		2136	1.7
4 SA	0343	4.6	19 SU	0340	5.0
	1022	1.8		1010	1.2
	1615	4.5		1620	4.9
	2237	1.7		2235	1.1
5 SU	0429	4.9	20 M	0436	5.3
	1105	1.5		1104	0.7
	1657	4.8		1711	5.3
	2318	1.4		2325	0.7
6 M	0510	5.1	21 TU	0525	5.6
	1142	1.2		1151	0.3
	1735	5.0		1757	5.5
	2354	1.2		●	
7 TU	0548	5.2	22 W	0010	0.4
	1216	1.0		0612	5.8
	1812	5.1		1234	0.1
	○			1840	5.6
8 W	0025	1.0	23 TH	0051	0.2
	0626	5.3		0655	5.8
	1246	0.9		1314	0.1
	1848	5.1		1919	5.6
9 TH	0055	1.0	24 F	0129	0.2
	0701	5.3		0734	5.7
	1314	0.9		1350	0.3
	1921	5.1		1953	5.5
10 F	0122	0.9	25 SA	0204	0.4
	0733	5.3		0809	5.5
	1340	0.9		1423	0.6
	1950	5.1		2021	5.3
11 SA	0149	1.0	26 SU	0236	0.8
	0801	5.2		0837	5.2
	1406	1.0		1453	1.0
	2015	5.0		2044	5.1
12 SU	0216	1.1	27 M	0306	1.2
	0829	5.1		0901	4.9
	1434	1.2		1522	1.5
	2041	5.0		2110	4.8
13 M	0247	1.2	28 TU	0337	1.6
	0859	4.9		0930	4.5
	1505	1.4		1554	1.9
	2112	4.8		2144	4.5
14 TU	0323	1.5	29 W	0418	2.1
	0938	4.7		1011	4.2
	1545	1.7		1641	2.3
	2159	4.6		◐ 2233	4.2
15 W	0412	1.8	30 TH	0524	2.4
	1038	4.4		1118	3.9
	1642	2.1		1757	2.6
	◑ 2311	4.4		2357	4.0
			31 F	0652	2.5
				1347	3.9
				1928	2.6

APRIL

Date	Time	m	Date	Time	m
1 SA	0210	4.2	16 SU	0214	4.7
	0850	2.3		0848	1.6
	1455	4.2		1504	4.6
	2109	2.2		2117	1.6
2 SU	0311	4.5	17 M	0321	5.0
	0949	1.8		0949	1.1
	1545	4.5		1600	5.0
	2202	1.8		2213	1.1
3 M	0358	4.8	18 TU	0414	5.3
	1030	1.5		1040	0.7
	1627	4.8		1647	5.3
	2243	1.4		2301	0.7
4 TU	0439	5.0	19 W	0502	5.5
	1107	1.2		1125	0.4
	1706	5.0		1730	5.4
	2320	1.2		2345	0.5
5 W	0519	5.2	20 TH	0546	5.6
	1142	1.0		1207	0.3
	1743	5.1		1810	5.5
	2354	1.0		●	
6 TH	0557	5.3	21 F	0025	0.4
	1214	0.9		0627	5.6
	1819	5.2		1245	0.3
	○			1847	5.5
7 F	0026	0.9	22 SA	0102	0.4
	0634	5.3		0704	5.5
	1245	0.8		1321	0.5
	1853	5.2		1918	5.4
8 SA	0057	0.8	23 SU	0136	0.6
	0708	5.3		0736	5.3
	1315	0.8		1353	0.8
	1924	5.2		1945	5.3
9 SU	0128	0.9	24 M	0208	1.0
	0740	5.2		0803	5.1
	1344	0.9		1423	1.2
	1953	5.2		2010	5.1
10 M	0158	1.0	25 TU	0238	1.3
	0812	5.1		0830	4.8
	1415	1.1		1451	1.6
	2023	5.1		2039	4.9
11 TU	0232	1.2	26 W	0309	1.7
	0847	4.9		0903	4.5
	1449	1.4		1522	2.0
	2100	4.9		2115	4.6
12 W	0312	1.5	27 TH	0349	2.1
	0933	4.6		0946	4.2
	1533	1.8		1608	2.3
	2150	4.7		◐ 2204	4.4
13 TH	0406	1.8	28 F	0452	2.3
	1035	4.3		1049	4.0
	1635	2.1		1722	2.5
	◑ 2301	4.4		2312	4.2
14 F	0530	2.1	29 SA	0612	2.4
	1203	4.2		1249	3.9
	1816	2.3		1843	2.5
15 SA	0039	4.4	30 SU	0108	4.2
	0723	2.0		0734	2.2
	1348	4.3		1409	4.2
	2005	2.0		2001	2.3

Chart Datum: 3·22 metres below Ordnance Datum (Newlyn)
HAT is 5·9 metres above Chart Datum

TIDES

TIME ZONE (UT)
For Summer Time add ONE hour in **non-shaded areas**

PLYMOUTH (DEVONPORT)

LAT 50°22'N LONG 4°11'W

TIMES AND HEIGHTS OF HIGH AND LOW WATERS

Dates in amber are **SPRINGS**
Dates in grey are **NEAPS**

2023

MAY

Date	Day	Time	m	Time	m	Time	m	Time	m
1	M	0223	4.4	0844	1.9	1502	4.4	2104	1.9
2	TU	0315	4.7	0936	1.6	1547	4.7	2154	1.6
3	W	0400	4.9	1020	1.3	1628	4.9	2238	1.3
4	TH	0443	5.1	1100	1.1	1708	5.1	2318	1.1
5	F	0524	5.2	1139	0.9	1747	5.2	○ 2356	0.9
6	SA	0604	5.3	1216	0.9	1824	5.3		
7	SU	0033	0.8	0644	5.3	1252	0.9	1900	5.3
8	M	0110	0.8	0722	5.2	1328	1.0	1936	5.3
9	TU	0147	1.0	0802	5.1	1405	1.2	2014	5.2
10	W	0228	1.2	0845	4.9	1447	1.4	2058	5.0
11	TH	0315	1.4	0936	4.7	1537	1.7	2151	4.8
12	F	0416	1.7	1040	4.4	1644	2.0	◑ 2300	4.6
13	SA	0534	1.9	1203	4.3	1810	2.1		
14	SU	0028	4.6	0703	1.8	1327	4.5	1937	1.9
15	M	0149	4.8	0818	1.5	1434	4.7	2045	1.6
16	TU	0252	5.0	0918	1.2	1528	5.0	2142	1.2
17	W	0345	5.2	1010	0.9	1616	5.2	2232	1.0
18	TH	0434	5.3	1056	0.8	1659	5.3	2317	0.8
19	F	0518	5.4	1139	0.7	1739	5.4	● 2358	0.7
20	SA	0559	5.3	1218	0.8	1815	5.4		
21	SU	0036	0.8	0637	5.2	1254	0.9	1848	5.3
22	M	0112	1.0	0710	5.1	1327	1.1	1917	5.2
23	TU	0145	1.2	0740	4.9	1358	1.4	1947	5.1
24	W	0217	1.4	0812	4.7	1429	1.7	2020	4.9
25	TH	0251	1.7	0848	4.5	1503	1.9	2057	4.7
26	F	0329	1.9	0932	4.3	1544	2.1	2143	4.6
27	SA	0421	2.1	1027	4.2	1643	2.3	◐ 2238	4.4
28	SU	0526	2.2	1138	4.1	1753	2.4	2349	4.3
29	M	0635	2.1	1259	4.2	1902	2.2		
30	TU	0109	4.4	0740	2.0	1403	4.4	2005	2.0
31	W	0217	4.6	0838	1.7	1456	4.6	2102	1.7

JUNE

Date	Day	Time	m	Time	m	Time	m	Time	m
1	TH	0312	4.8	0931	1.5	1545	4.8	2154	1.5
2	F	0403	4.9	1020	1.3	1631	5.0	2243	1.2
3	SA	0451	5.1	1106	1.1	1715	5.2	2329	1.0
4	SU ○	0538	5.2	1151	1.0	1758	5.3		
5	M	0014	0.9	0625	5.2	1235	0.9	1842	5.4
6	TU	0058	0.9	0711	5.2	1319	1.0	1926	5.4
7	W	0144	0.9	0758	5.1	1405	1.1	2011	5.4
8	TH	0232	1.0	0848	5.0	1452	1.3	2100	5.2
9	F	0323	1.2	0941	4.8	1544	1.5	2153	5.1
10	SA	0418	1.4	1040	4.7	1641	1.6	◑ 2254	4.9
11	SU	0520	1.5	1145	4.6	1746	1.8		
12	M	0003	4.8	0628	1.6	1252	4.6	1856	1.8
13	TU	0113	4.8	0737	1.6	1354	4.7	2005	1.7
14	W	0216	4.8	0840	1.5	1450	4.8	2107	1.5
15	TH	0313	4.9	0936	1.3	1542	4.9	2201	1.4
16	F	0405	5.0	1027	1.2	1629	5.0	2251	1.2
17	SA	0453	5.0	1113	1.2	1712	5.1	2335	1.2
18	SU ●	0536	5.0	1155	1.2	1751	5.2		
19	M	0016	1.1	0616	5.0	1233	1.2	1826	5.2
20	TU	0054	1.2	0652	4.9	1308	1.3	1900	5.2
21	W	0130	1.3	0727	4.9	1342	1.4	1934	5.1
22	TH	0203	1.4	0802	4.7	1414	1.6	2008	5.0
23	F	0235	1.6	0839	4.6	1446	1.7	2044	4.9
24	SA	0309	1.7	0918	4.5	1520	1.9	2123	4.7
25	SU	0346	1.8	1001	4.4	1600	2.0	2206	4.6
26	M	0431	1.9	1050	4.3	1651	2.1	◐ 2256	4.5
27	TU	0528	2.0	1147	4.3	1756	2.2	2355	4.5
28	W	0636	2.0	1251	4.4	1907	2.1		
29	TH	0104	4.5	0743	1.9	1357	4.5	2014	1.9
30	F	0217	4.6	0846	1.7	1459	4.7	2116	1.7

JULY

Date	Day	Time	m	Time	m	Time	m	Time	m
1	SA	0324	4.8	0945	1.5	1556	4.9	2214	1.4
2	SU	0423	4.9	1041	1.3	1649	5.2	2309	1.1
3	M ○	0518	5.1	1134	1.1	1739	5.4		
4	TU	0001	0.9	0612	5.2	1225	1.0	1829	5.5
5	W	0052	0.8	0704	5.2	1315	0.9	1919	5.6
6	TH	0142	0.7	0755	5.3	1403	0.9	2008	5.6
7	F	0230	0.7	0845	5.2	1450	0.9	2057	5.5
8	SA	0317	0.8	0934	5.1	1536	1.1	2145	5.3
9	SU	0404	1.0	1022	4.9	1622	1.3	2234	5.1
10	M	0452	1.3	1113	4.8	1712	1.5	◑ 2328	4.9
11	TU	0545	1.5	1209	4.6	1809	1.8		
12	W	0029	4.7	0646	1.8	1309	4.5	1917	1.9
13	TH	0136	4.5	0755	1.9	1412	4.5	2029	1.9
14	F	0242	4.5	0903	1.8	1511	4.7	2135	1.8
15	SA	0341	4.6	1003	1.7	1604	4.8	2232	1.6
16	SU	0434	4.7	1054	1.5	1651	5.0	2321	1.4
17	M ●	0519	4.8	1139	1.4	1732	5.1		
18	TU	0004	1.3	0600	4.9	1219	1.3	1811	5.2
19	W	0043	1.3	0638	4.9	1256	1.3	1847	5.2
20	TH	0118	1.2	0714	4.9	1328	1.3	1922	5.2
21	F	0148	1.3	0750	4.9	1357	1.4	1956	5.1
22	SA	0216	1.4	0824	4.8	1425	1.5	2029	5.0
23	SU	0243	1.5	0857	4.7	1452	1.6	2100	4.9
24	M	0310	1.6	0930	4.6	1522	1.7	2132	4.8
25	TU	0343	1.7	1005	4.5	1559	1.9	◐ 2211	4.7
26	W	0426	1.8	1051	4.4	1649	2.0	2302	4.5
27	TH	0524	2.0	1150	4.4	1802	2.2		
28	F	0009	4.4	0646	2.1	1304	4.4	1931	2.1
29	SA	0133	4.4	0810	2.0	1422	4.6	2048	1.9
30	SU	0257	4.6	0921	1.7	1531	4.9	2156	1.5
31	M	0407	4.8	1026	1.4	1631	5.2	2257	1.1

AUGUST

Date	Day	Time	m	Time	m	Time	m	Time	m
1	TU	0506	5.1	1124	1.1	1726	5.4	○ 2353	0.8
2	W	0601	5.3	1217	0.8	1817	5.6		
3	TH	0044	0.5	0653	5.4	1306	0.6	1908	5.8
4	F	0132	0.4	0743	5.4	1351	0.5	1956	5.8
5	SA	0216	0.4	0829	5.4	1434	0.6	2041	5.7
6	SU	0258	0.5	0912	5.3	1514	0.8	2123	5.5
7	M	0338	0.8	0952	5.1	1554	1.1	2203	5.2
8	TU	0417	1.2	1031	4.9	1634	1.5	◑ 2243	4.8
9	W	0500	1.6	1116	4.6	1722	1.9	2333	4.5
10	TH	0553	2.0	1217	4.4	1826	2.2		
11	F	0054	4.2	0704	2.3	1336	4.3	1953	2.3
12	SA	0219	4.2	0836	2.3	1448	4.4	2122	2.1
13	SU	0326	4.3	0950	2.0	1546	4.7	2222	1.8
14	M	0419	4.6	1042	1.7	1634	4.9	2310	1.5
15	TU	0503	4.8	1126	1.5	1715	5.1	2351	1.3
16	W ●	0542	4.9	1205	1.3	1753	5.2		
17	TH	0027	1.2	0619	5.0	1239	1.2	1829	5.3
18	F	0059	1.1	0655	5.0	1308	1.2	1904	5.3
19	SA	0126	1.1	0729	5.0	1334	1.2	1937	5.2
20	SU	0150	1.2	0801	5.0	1359	1.3	2006	5.1
21	M	0213	1.3	0829	4.9	1423	1.4	2033	5.0
22	TU	0238	1.4	0856	4.8	1450	1.5	2100	4.9
23	W	0307	1.5	0924	4.7	1522	1.7	2132	4.7
24	TH	0343	1.8	1005	4.5	1606	2.0	◐ 2223	4.5
25	F	0433	2.0	1107	4.4	1711	2.2	2337	4.3
26	SA	0554	2.3	1229	4.4	1900	2.3		
27	SU	0110	4.3	0748	2.2	1400	4.5	2034	2.0
28	M	0247	4.5	0911	1.9	1518	4.9	2147	1.5
29	TU	0359	4.8	1017	1.4	1619	5.3	2248	1.0
30	W	0456	5.2	1113	1.0	1712	5.6	2341	0.6
31	TH ○	0547	5.4	1203	0.6	1802	5.8		

Chart Datum: 3·22 metres below Ordnance Datum (Newlyn)
HAT is 5·9 metres above Chart Datum

TIME ZONE (UT)
For Summer Time add ONE hour in **non-shaded areas**

PLYMOUTH (DEVONPORT)

LAT 50°22′N LONG 4°11′W

TIMES AND HEIGHTS OF HIGH AND LOW WATERS

Dates in amber are **SPRINGS**
Dates in grey are **NEAPS**

2023

SEPTEMBER

Date	Day	Time	m	Time	m	Time	m	Time	m
1	F	0028	0.3	0636	5.6	1248	0.4	1850	5.9
2	SA	0112	0.2	0721	5.6	1331	0.3	1934	5.9
3	SU	0153	0.2	0803	5.6	1410	0.4	2015	5.7
4	M	0231	0.5	0840	5.4	1446	0.7	2052	5.5
5	TU	0306	0.9	0913	5.2	1521	1.1	2124	5.1
6	W ◑	0340	1.3	0943	4.9	1557	1.6	2153	4.7
7	TH	0416	1.8	1015	4.6	1640	2.1	2229	4.3
8	F	0505	2.3	1105	4.3	1743	2.5	2340	4.0
9	SA	0618	2.6	1302	4.2	1920	2.6		
10	SU	0202	4.0	0818	2.5	1428	4.3	2114	2.3
11	M	0310	4.3	0936	2.2	1527	4.6	2207	1.9
12	TU	0400	4.6	1024	1.8	1612	4.9	2249	1.5
13	W	0441	4.8	1104	1.4	1652	5.2	2326	1.2
14	TH	0518	5.0	1140	1.2	1729	5.3		
15	F ●	0000	1.1	0554	5.1	1212	1.1	1805	5.4
16	SA	0030	1.0	0629	5.2	1240	1.1	1839	5.4
17	SU	0056	1.0	0702	5.2	1306	1.1	1912	5.3
18	M	0120	1.1	0733	5.2	1331	1.2	1941	5.2
19	TU	0144	1.2	0759	5.1	1356	1.3	2007	5.1
20	W	0209	1.3	0824	5.0	1423	1.4	2034	5.0
21	TH	0238	1.5	0853	4.8	1456	1.7	2109	4.7
22	F ◐	0313	1.8	0936	4.7	1539	2.0	2204	4.5
23	SA	0403	2.2	1042	4.5	1647	2.3	2321	4.3
24	SU	0529	2.5	1208	4.4	1849	2.4		
25	M	0103	4.2	0740	2.3	1349	4.6	2028	2.0
26	TU	0245	4.6	0903	1.9	1508	5.0	2137	1.4
27	W	0350	5.0	1003	1.3	1605	5.4	2232	0.9
28	TH	0441	5.3	1055	0.9	1655	5.7	2321	0.5
29	F ○	0527	5.6	1142	0.5	1741	5.9		
30	SA	0005	0.3	0611	5.7	1225	0.3	1826	5.9

OCTOBER

Date	Day	Time	m	Time	m	Time	m	Time	m
1	SU	0047	0.2	0653	5.7	1305	0.3	1907	5.9
2	M	0125	0.4	0731	5.7	1342	0.5	1945	5.7
3	TU	0201	0.7	0804	5.5	1417	0.8	2018	5.4
4	W	0233	1.1	0832	5.2	1450	1.3	2044	5.0
5	TH	0304	1.5	0858	5.0	1524	1.7	2111	4.6
6	F ◑	0338	2.0	0930	4.7	1605	2.2	2149	4.3
7	SA	0425	2.5	1018	4.4	1709	2.6	2252	4.0
8	SU	0541	2.8	1151	4.1	1844	2.7		
9	M	0136	4.0	0732	2.7	1357	4.3	2044	2.4
10	TU	0242	4.3	0903	2.3	1456	4.6	2134	1.9
11	W	0331	4.6	0950	1.9	1542	4.9	2214	1.6
12	TH	0411	4.9	1029	1.5	1621	5.1	2250	1.3
13	F	0448	5.1	1104	1.3	1659	5.3	2323	1.1
14	SA ●	0524	5.2	1137	1.1	1736	5.4	2354	1.0
15	SU	0559	5.3	1208	1.1	1811	5.4		
16	M	0023	1.0	0633	5.3	1237	1.1	1846	5.4
17	TU	0051	1.1	0704	5.3	1306	1.1	1917	5.3
18	W	0119	1.2	0733	5.2	1335	1.2	1947	5.2
19	TH	0147	1.3	0803	5.1	1406	1.4	2020	5.0
20	F	0219	1.6	0838	5.0	1442	1.7	2102	4.7
21	SA	0258	1.9	0926	4.8	1531	2.0	2159	4.5
22	SU ◐	0354	2.3	1031	4.6	1648	2.3	2316	4.3
23	M	0530	2.5	1157	4.5	1842	2.3		
24	TU	0101	4.3	0727	2.3	1335	4.7	2011	1.9
25	W	0230	4.7	0843	1.8	1448	5.1	2115	1.4
26	TH	0329	5.0	0941	1.4	1543	5.4	2208	1.0
27	F	0418	5.4	1030	0.9	1632	5.7	2255	0.6
28	SA ○	0502	5.6	1116	0.7	1717	5.8	2339	0.5
29	SU	0543	5.7	1159	0.6	1800	5.8		
30	M	0019	0.5	0623	5.7	1238	0.6	1840	5.7
31	TU	0057	0.7	0659	5.6	1316	0.8	1916	5.5

NOVEMBER

Date	Day	Time	m	Time	m	Time	m	Time	m
1	W	0132	1.0	0731	5.5	1350	1.1	1947	5.2
2	TH	0204	1.3	0758	5.3	1424	1.5	2015	4.9
3	F	0235	1.7	0827	5.0	1459	1.8	2046	4.6
4	SA	0309	2.1	0903	4.8	1540	2.2	2127	4.3
5	SU ◑	0354	2.5	0952	4.5	1639	2.5	2228	4.1
6	M	0504	2.7	1101	4.3	1757	2.6		
7	TU	0032	4.0	0629	2.7	1256	4.3	1926	2.5
8	W	0154	4.2	0754	2.5	1407	4.5	2035	2.1
9	TH	0247	4.5	0854	2.1	1458	4.8	2122	1.8
10	F	0330	4.8	0940	1.8	1543	5.0	2203	1.5
11	SA	0411	5.0	1021	1.5	1624	5.2	2241	1.3
12	SU	0450	5.2	1059	1.3	1705	5.3	2317	1.2
13	M ●	0528	5.3	1136	1.2	1744	5.3	2353	1.1
14	TU	0605	5.4	1212	1.1	1821	5.3		
15	W	0027	1.1	0640	5.4	1247	1.1	1859	5.3
16	TH	0101	1.2	0715	5.4	1323	1.2	1936	5.2
17	F	0137	1.4	0752	5.3	1402	1.4	2017	5.0
18	SA	0216	1.6	0834	5.2	1446	1.6	2104	4.8
19	SU	0302	1.9	0925	5.0	1541	1.9	2201	4.6
20	M ◐	0403	2.1	1027	4.8	1653	2.0	2313	4.5
21	TU	0524	2.3	1144	4.8	1819	2.0		
22	W	0040	4.5	0655	2.1	1306	4.8	1939	1.8
23	TH	0156	4.7	0810	1.9	1416	5.0	2043	1.5
24	F	0257	5.0	0910	1.5	1514	5.2	2138	1.2
25	SA	0348	5.2	1003	1.2	1606	5.4	2227	1.0
26	SU	0434	5.4	1050	1.0	1653	5.5	2312	0.9
27	M ○	0517	5.5	1135	0.9	1737	5.5	2354	0.9
28	TU	0557	5.5	1216	1.0	1818	5.4		
29	W	0033	1.0	0634	5.5	1255	1.1	1855	5.2
30	TH	0109	1.2	0707	5.4	1332	1.3	1928	5.1

DECEMBER

Date	Day	Time	m	Time	m	Time	m	Time	m
1	F	0143	1.5	0738	5.3	1407	1.5	2000	4.9
2	SA	0216	1.7	0811	5.1	1443	1.8	2035	4.7
3	SU	0251	2.0	0849	4.9	1521	2.0	2116	4.5
4	M	0331	2.2	0933	4.7	1607	2.3	2207	4.3
5	TU ◑	0422	2.4	1027	4.6	1705	2.4	2312	4.2
6	W	0527	2.5	1133	4.5	1811	2.4		
7	TH	0029	4.3	0639	2.5	1248	4.5	1918	2.3
8	F	0140	4.4	0745	2.3	1356	4.6	2018	2.0
9	SA	0237	4.6	0844	2.1	1453	4.8	2111	1.8
10	SU	0328	4.8	0936	1.8	1545	4.9	2159	1.6
11	M	0414	5.1	1023	1.5	1633	5.1	2244	1.4
12	TU ●	0458	5.2	1108	1.3	1719	5.2	2328	1.3
13	W	0541	5.4	1153	1.2	1803	5.3		
14	TH	0010	1.2	0623	5.5	1236	1.1	1848	5.3
15	F	0053	1.2	0705	5.5	1321	1.1	1932	5.2
16	SA	0137	1.2	0749	5.5	1406	1.2	2019	5.1
17	SU	0222	1.4	0836	5.4	1454	1.3	2108	5.0
18	M	0310	1.5	0926	5.3	1545	1.4	2200	4.9
19	TU ◐	0403	1.7	1020	5.1	1641	1.6	2258	4.7
20	W	0502	1.9	1121	5.0	1743	1.7		
21	TH	0003	4.7	0610	2.0	1228	4.9	1853	1.8
22	F	0111	4.7	0724	1.9	1337	4.9	2003	1.8
23	SA	0216	4.8	0834	1.8	1441	4.9	2106	1.6
24	SU	0315	4.9	0935	1.6	1540	5.0	2201	1.5
25	M	0408	5.1	1029	1.5	1633	5.1	2251	1.4
26	TU	0456	5.2	1118	1.3	1720	5.1	2337	1.3
27	W ○	0539	5.3	1202	1.2	1803	5.1		
28	TH	0018	1.3	0618	5.4	1243	1.2	1842	5.1
29	F	0056	1.3	0654	5.4	1321	1.3	1918	5.0
30	SA	0131	1.4	0728	5.3	1356	1.4	1952	4.9
31	SU	0204	1.6	0802	5.2	1429	1.6	2027	4.8

Chart Datum: 3·22 metres below Ordnance Datum (Newlyn)
HAT is 5·9 metres above Chart Datum

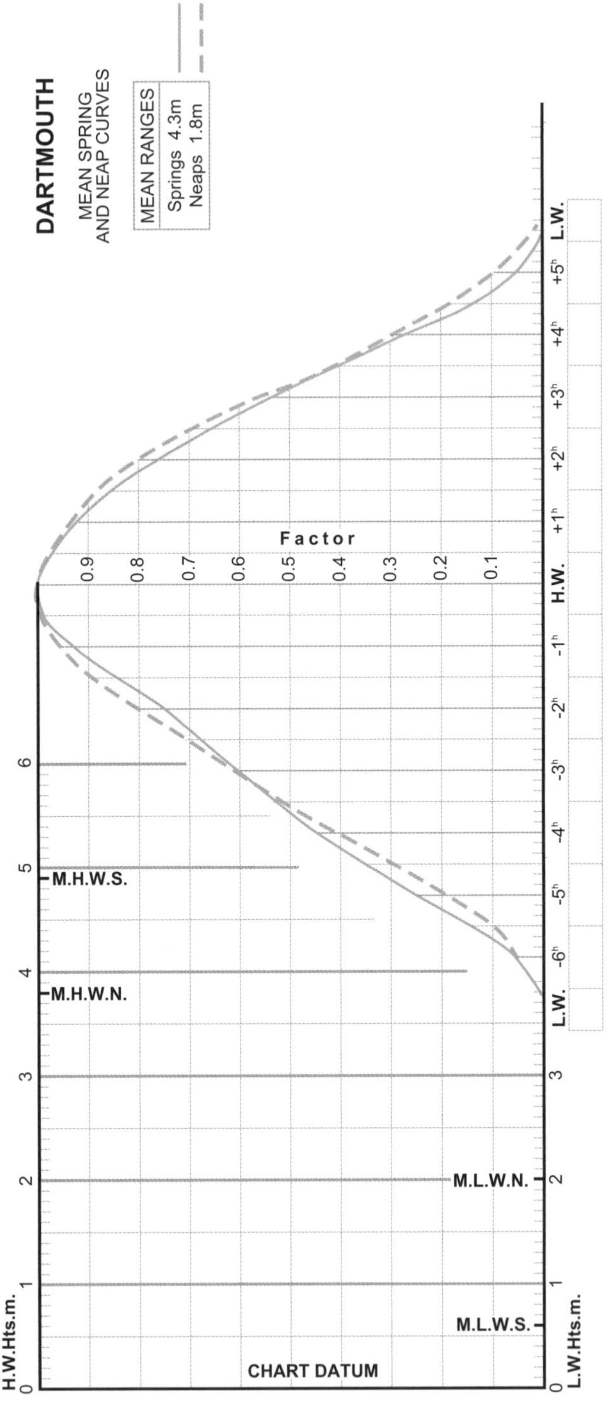
DARTMOUTH
MEAN SPRING AND NEAP CURVES
MEAN RANGES
Springs 4.3m
Neaps 1.8m
Factor
0.9
0.8
0.7
0.6
0.5
0.4
0.3
0.2
0.1
L.W.
-6h
-5h
-4h
-3h
-2h
-1h
H.W.
+1h
+2h
+3h
+4h
+5h
L.W.
H.W.Hts.m.
0
1
2
3
4
5
6
M.H.W.S.
M.H.W.N.
M.L.W.N.
M.L.W.S.
CHART DATUM
L.W.Hts.m.

TIME ZONE (UT)
For Summer Time add ONE hour in **non-shaded areas**

DARTMOUTH

LAT 50°21′N LONG 3°35′W

TIMES AND HEIGHTS OF HIGH AND LOW WATERS

Dates in amber are **SPRINGS**
Dates in grey are **NEAPS**

2023

JANUARY

Date	Day	Time	m	Time	m	Time	m	Time	m	Moon
1	SU	0102	4.0	0646	1.8	1326	4.1	1926	1.8	
2	M	0205	4.0	0759	1.9	1431	4.1	2032	1.7	
3	TU	0306	4.1	0905	1.7	1532	4.1	2132	1.6	
4	W	0401	4.2	1000	1.6	1626	4.2	2223	1.5	
5	TH	0449	4.4	1050	1.4	1713	4.3	2307	1.3	
6	F	0532	4.6	1134	1.3	1756	4.4	2348	1.2	○
7	SA	0611	4.7	1213	1.2	1834	4.4			
8	SU	0024	1.2	0648	4.7	1248	1.2	1910	4.4	
9	M	0057	1.2	0723	4.7	1320	1.2	1945	4.4	
10	TU	0127	1.3	0756	4.6	1350	1.3	2019	4.3	
11	W	0157	1.3	0829	4.5	1419	1.3	2052	4.2	
12	TH	0225	1.4	0902	4.4	1448	1.4	2124	4.1	
13	F	0257	1.5	0934	4.3	1521	1.5	2158	4.0	
14	SA	0332	1.6	1011	4.2	1600	1.6	2239	3.9	
15	SU	0417	1.8	1058	4.1	1651	1.8	2332	3.8	◑
16	M	0517	1.9	1156	4.0	1759	1.9			
17	TU	0037	3.8	0639	2.0	1307	4.0	1925	1.9	
18	W	0157	3.9	0805	1.8	1431	4.0	2042	1.7	
19	TH	0315	4.2	0919	1.5	1550	4.2	2151	1.4	
20	F	0424	4.5	1025	1.2	1657	4.4	2252	1.1	
21	SA	0524	4.8	1123	0.8	1757	4.6	2349	0.8	●
22	SU	0618	5.0	1218	0.5	1850	4.8			
23	M	0039	0.6	0709	5.1	1308	0.3	1941	4.8	
24	TU	0127	0.4	0757	5.2	1354	0.3	2027	4.8	
25	W	0210	0.4	0843	5.2	1437	0.3	2111	4.8	
26	TH	0252	0.6	0927	5.0	1517	0.5	2152	4.6	
27	F	0331	0.8	1007	4.8	1557	0.9	2230	4.4	
28	SA	0409	1.1	1046	4.5	1636	1.3	2309	4.1	◐
29	SU	0452	1.5	1128	4.1	1720	1.6	2354	3.9	
30	M	0543	1.9	1223	3.8	1816	2.0			
31	TU	0100	3.7	0652	2.1	1341	3.7	1932	2.1	

FEBRUARY

Date	Day	Time	m	Time	m	Time	m	Time	m	Moon
1	W	0221	3.7	0821	2.1	1500	3.7	2057	2.0	
2	TH	0330	3.9	0940	1.9	1604	3.8	2203	1.8	
3	F	0427	4.1	1036	1.6	1657	4.1	2253	1.5	
4	SA	0514	4.4	1121	1.3	1741	4.2	2336	1.3	
5	SU	0556	4.6	1202	1.1	1821	4.4			○
6	M	0013	1.1	0634	4.7	1237	1.0	1858	4.4	
7	TU	0045	1.0	0710	4.7	1308	0.9	1933	4.4	
8	W	0115	1.0	0745	4.7	1336	0.9	2006	4.4	
9	TH	0142	1.0	0816	4.6	1401	1.0	2035	4.4	
10	F	0208	1.0	0844	4.5	1427	1.1	2102	4.3	
11	SA	0236	1.1	0911	4.4	1456	1.2	2127	4.2	
12	SU	0306	1.3	0941	4.3	1528	1.3	2158	4.1	
13	M	0344	1.5	1020	4.1	1609	1.6	2245	3.9	◑
14	TU	0433	1.7	1116	3.9	1706	1.8	2353	3.8	
15	W	0547	2.0	1234	3.8	1835	2.0			
16	TH	0120	3.8	0734	2.0	1409	3.8	2020	1.9	
17	F	0254	4.0	0906	1.6	1539	4.0	2141	1.5	
18	SA	0410	4.4	1018	1.2	1649	4.3	2245	1.1	
19	SU	0512	4.7	1116	0.7	1748	4.6	2340	0.6	
20	M	0606	5.0	1208	0.3	1840	4.8			●
21	TU	0028	0.3	0656	5.2	1254	0.0	1927	4.9	
22	W	0112	0.1	0742	5.3	1337	-0.1	2009	5.0	
23	TH	0153	0.1	0824	5.2	1415	0.1	2046	4.9	
24	F	0229	0.3	0902	5.0	1451	0.3	2119	4.7	
25	SA	0303	0.6	0934	4.8	1524	0.7	2148	4.4	
26	SU	0336	1.0	1002	4.4	1557	1.2	2214	4.2	
27	M	0410	1.4	1031	4.0	1632	1.7	2246	3.9	◐
28	TU	0454	1.9	1111	3.7	1721	2.1	2339	3.6	

MARCH

Date	Day	Time	m	Time	m	Time	m	Time	m	Moon
1	W	0558	2.2	1230	3.4	1833	2.3			
2	TH	0128	3.5	0730	2.3	1434	3.4	2014	2.3	
3	F	0302	3.7	0925	2.0	1543	3.6	2145	1.9	
4	SA	0403	4.0	1020	1.6	1636	3.9	2235	1.5	
5	SU	0450	4.3	1103	1.3	1719	4.2	2316	1.2	
6	M	0533	4.5	1141	1.0	1759	4.4	2353	1.0	
7	TU	0612	4.6	1215	0.8	1836	4.5			○
8	W	0024	0.8	0650	4.7	1245	0.7	1911	4.5	
9	TH	0054	0.8	0724	4.7	1313	0.7	1944	4.5	
10	F	0121	0.7	0755	4.7	1339	0.7	2012	4.5	
11	SA	0148	0.8	0823	4.6	1404	0.8	2036	4.4	
12	SU	0214	0.9	0850	4.5	1432	1.0	2102	4.4	
13	M	0245	1.0	0919	4.3	1502	1.2	2132	4.2	
14	TU	0320	1.3	0957	4.1	1542	1.5	2218	4.0	
15	W	0408	1.6	1056	3.8	1638	1.9	2328	3.8	◑
16	TH	0523	2.0	1219	3.6	1811	2.1			
17	F	0102	3.7	0723	2.0	1405	3.6	2012	2.0	
18	SA	0243	4.0	0901	1.6	1536	4.0	2133	1.5	
19	SU	0400	4.4	1007	1.0	1641	4.3	2233	0.9	
20	M	0458	4.7	1102	0.5	1734	4.7	2323	0.5	
21	TU	0548	5.0	1150	0.1	1821	4.9			●
22	W	0009	0.2	0636	5.2	1233	-0.1	1904	5.0	
23	TH	0050	0.0	0718	5.2	1313	-0.1	1942	5.0	
24	F	0128	0.0	0756	5.1	1349	0.1	2015	4.9	
25	SA	0202	0.2	0830	4.9	1421	0.4	2042	4.7	
26	SU	0234	0.6	0858	4.6	1451	0.8	2105	4.5	
27	M	0303	1.0	0921	4.3	1519	1.3	2130	4.2	
28	TU	0334	1.4	0949	3.9	1551	1.7	2203	3.9	
29	W	0414	1.9	1030	3.6	1637	2.1	2251	3.6	◐
30	TH	0519	2.2	1135	3.3	1752	2.4			
31	F	0013	3.4	0647	2.3	1403	3.3	1924	2.4	

APRIL

Date	Day	Time	m	Time	m	Time	m	Time	m	Moon
1	SA	0227	3.6	0847	2.1	1513	3.6	2106	2.0	
2	SU	0330	3.9	0946	1.6	1605	3.9	2159	1.6	
3	M	0418	4.2	1028	1.3	1648	4.2	2241	1.2	
4	TU	0501	4.4	1105	1.0	1729	4.4	2318	1.0	
5	W	0542	4.6	1141	0.8	1807	4.5	2353	0.8	
6	TH	0621	4.7	1213	0.7	1843	4.6			○
7	F	0025	0.7	0658	4.7	1244	0.6	1916	4.6	
8	SA	0056	0.6	0731	4.7	1314	0.6	1946	4.6	
9	SU	0127	0.7	0802	4.6	1343	0.7	2015	4.6	
10	M	0157	0.8	0833	4.5	1413	0.9	2044	4.5	
11	TU	0230	1.0	0908	4.3	1447	1.2	2120	4.3	
12	W	0309	1.3	0952	4.0	1530	1.6	2209	4.1	
13	TH	0402	1.6	1053	3.7	1631	1.9	2318	3.8	◑
14	F	0525	1.9	1219	3.6	1811	2.1			
15	SA	0054	3.8	0718	1.8	1404	3.7	2001	1.8	
16	SU	0231	4.1	0845	1.4	1523	4.0	2114	1.4	
17	M	0340	4.4	0946	0.9	1621	4.4	2211	0.9	
18	TU	0435	4.7	1038	0.5	1709	4.7	2259	0.5	
19	W	0525	4.9	1123	0.2	1754	4.8	2344	0.3	
20	TH	0610	5.0	1206	0.1	1834	4.9			●
21	F	0024	0.2	0651	5.0	1244	0.1	1910	4.9	
22	SA	0101	0.2	0727	4.9	1320	0.3	1941	4.8	
23	SU	0135	0.4	0758	4.7	1352	0.6	2007	4.7	
24	M	0206	0.8	0825	4.5	1421	1.0	2031	4.5	
25	TU	0236	1.1	0851	4.2	1449	1.4	2100	4.3	
26	W	0306	1.5	0923	3.9	1519	1.8	2135	4.0	
27	TH	0346	1.9	1005	3.6	1604	2.1	2223	3.8	◐
28	F	0448	2.1	1107	3.4	1717	2.3	2329	3.6	
29	SA	0607	2.2	1304	3.3	1838	2.3			
30	SU	0123	3.6	0730	2.0	1426	3.6	1957	2.1	

Chart Datum: 2·62 metres below Ordnance Datum (Newlyn)
HAT is 5·3 metres above Chart Datum

TIME ZONE (UT)
For Summer Time add ONE hour in **non-shaded areas**

DARTMOUTH

LAT 50°21′N LONG 3°35′W

TIMES AND HEIGHTS OF HIGH AND LOW WATERS

Dates in amber are **SPRINGS**
Dates in grey are **NEAPS**

2023

MAY

Date	Day	Time	m	Time	m	Time	m	Time	m
1	M	0240	3.8	0840	1.7	1521	3.8	2101	1.7
2	TU	0334	4.1	0933	1.4	1607	4.1	2151	1.4
3	W	0421	4.3	1018	1.1	1649	4.3	2236	1.1
4	TH	0505	4.5	1058	0.9	1731	4.5	2316	0.9
5	F ○	0547	4.6	1138	0.7	1811	4.6	2355	0.7
6	SA	0628	4.7	1215	0.7	1848	4.7		
7	SU	0032	0.6	0707	4.7	1251	0.7	1923	4.7
8	M	0109	0.6	0745	4.6	1327	0.8	1958	4.7
9	TU	0146	0.8	0824	4.5	1403	1.0	2035	4.6
10	W	0226	1.0	0906	4.3	1445	1.2	2118	4.4
11	TH	0312	1.2	0955	4.1	1534	1.5	2210	4.2
12	F ◑	0412	1.5	1058	3.8	1640	1.8	2317	4.0
13	SA	0529	1.7	1219	3.7	1805	1.9		
14	SU	0043	4.0	0658	1.6	1342	3.9	1933	1.7
15	M	0205	4.2	0814	1.3	1452	4.1	2041	1.4
16	TU	0310	4.4	0915	1.0	1547	4.4	2139	1.0
17	W	0405	4.6	1007	0.7	1637	4.6	2230	0.8
18	TH	0456	4.7	1054	0.6	1721	4.7	2315	0.6
19	F ●	0541	4.8	1138	0.5	1803	4.8	2357	0.5
20	SA	0623	4.7	1217	0.6	1839	4.8		
21	SU	0035	0.6	0701	4.6	1253	0.7	1911	4.7
22	M	0111	0.8	0733	4.5	1326	0.9	1940	4.6
23	TU	0144	1.0	0802	4.3	1357	1.2	2009	4.5
24	W	0215	1.2	0833	4.1	1427	1.5	2041	4.3
25	TH	0249	1.5	0908	3.9	1500	1.7	2117	4.1
26	F	0326	1.7	0951	3.7	1541	1.9	2202	4.0
27	SA ◐	0417	1.9	1045	3.6	1639	2.1	2256	3.8
28	SU	0521	2.0	1154	3.5	1748	2.2		
29	M	0005	3.7	0630	1.9	1314	3.6	1857	2.0
30	TU	0124	3.8	0736	1.8	1420	3.8	2001	1.8
31	W	0234	4.0	0834	1.5	1514	4.0	2059	1.5

JUNE

Date	Day	Time	m	Time	m	Time	m	Time	m
1	TH	0331	4.2	0928	1.3	1605	4.2	2151	1.3
2	F	0424	4.3	1018	1.1	1653	4.4	2241	1.0
3	SA	0513	4.5	1104	0.9	1738	4.6	2327	0.8
4	SU ○	0602	4.6	1150	0.8	1822	4.7		
5	M	0013	0.7	0649	4.6	1234	0.7	1905	4.8
6	TU	0057	0.7	0734	4.6	1318	0.8	1948	4.8
7	W	0143	0.7	0820	4.5	1403	0.9	2032	4.8
8	TH	0230	0.8	0908	4.4	1450	1.1	2120	4.6
9	F	0320	1.0	1000	4.2	1541	1.3	2212	4.5
10	SA ◑	0414	1.2	1058	4.1	1637	1.4	2311	4.3
11	SU	0515	1.3	1201	4.0	1741	1.6		
12	M	0019	4.2	0623	1.4	1307	4.0	1851	1.6
13	TU	0128	4.2	0733	1.4	1410	4.1	2001	1.5
14	W	0233	4.2	0836	1.3	1508	4.2	2104	1.3
15	TH	0332	4.3	0933	1.1	1602	4.3	2158	1.2
16	F	0426	4.4	1025	1.0	1650	4.4	2249	1.0
17	SA	0515	4.4	1111	1.0	1735	4.5	2334	1.0
18	SU ●	0600	4.4	1154	1.0	1815	4.6		
19	M	0015	0.9	0640	4.4	1232	1.0	1850	4.6
20	TU	0053	1.0	0715	4.3	1307	1.1	1923	4.6
21	W	0129	1.1	0749	4.3	1341	1.2	1956	4.5
22	TH	0201	1.2	0824	4.1	1412	1.4	2029	4.4
23	F	0233	1.4	0900	4.0	1444	1.5	2105	4.3
24	SA	0306	1.5	0938	3.9	1517	1.7	2143	4.1
25	SU	0343	1.6	1020	3.8	1557	1.8	2225	4.0
26	M ◐	0427	1.7	1108	3.7	1647	1.9	2313	3.9
27	TU	0523	1.8	1203	3.7	1751	2.0		
28	W	0011	3.9	0631	1.8	1306	3.8	1902	1.9
29	TH	0119	3.9	0739	1.7	1413	3.9	2010	1.7
30	F	0234	4.0	0842	1.5	1517	4.1	2113	1.5

JULY

Date	Day	Time	m	Time	m	Time	m	Time	m
1	SA	0343	4.2	0942	1.3	1616	4.3	2212	1.2
2	SU	0444	4.3	1039	1.1	1711	4.6	2307	0.9
3	M ○	0541	4.5	1132	0.9	1803	4.8		
4	TU	0000	0.7	0636	4.6	1224	0.8	1853	4.9
5	W	0051	0.6	0727	4.6	1314	0.7	1942	5.0
6	TH	0141	0.5	0817	4.7	1401	0.7	2029	5.0
7	F	0228	0.5	0906	4.6	1448	0.7	2117	4.9
8	SA	0314	0.6	0953	4.5	1533	0.9	2204	4.7
9	SU	0400	0.8	1040	4.3	1618	1.1	2252	4.5
10	M ◑	0448	1.1	1130	4.2	1707	1.3	2345	4.3
11	TU	0540	1.3	1225	4.0	1804	1.6		
12	W	0044	4.1	0641	1.6	1324	3.9	1912	1.7
13	TH	0152	3.9	0751	1.7	1429	3.9	2025	1.7
14	F	0300	3.9	0900	1.6	1530	4.1	2132	1.6
15	SA	0401	4.0	1000	1.5	1625	4.2	2230	1.4
16	SU	0456	4.1	1052	1.3	1713	4.4	2319	1.2
17	M ●	0542	4.2	1138	1.2	1756	4.5		
18	TU	0003	1.1	0625	4.3	1218	1.1	1835	4.6
19	W	0042	1.1	0702	4.3	1255	1.1	1910	4.6
20	TH	0117	1.0	0737	4.3	1327	1.1	1945	4.6
21	F	0147	1.1	0812	4.3	1356	1.2	2018	4.5
22	SA	0214	1.2	0845	4.2	1423	1.3	2050	4.4
23	SU	0241	1.3	0917	4.1	1450	1.4	2120	4.3
24	M	0307	1.4	0949	4.0	1519	1.5	2151	4.2
25	TU ◐	0340	1.5	1024	3.9	1556	1.7	2230	4.1
26	W	0422	1.6	1109	3.8	1645	1.8	2319	3.9
27	TH	0519	1.8	1206	3.8	1757	2.0		
28	F	0025	3.8	0641	1.9	1319	3.8	1927	1.9
29	SA	0149	3.8	0806	1.8	1439	4.0	2045	1.7
30	SU	0315	4.0	0918	1.5	1551	4.3	2153	1.3
31	M	0428	4.2	1024	1.2	1653	4.6	2255	0.9

AUGUST

Date	Day	Time	m	Time	m	Time	m	Time	m
1	TU ○	0529	4.5	1122	0.9	1749	4.8	2352	0.6
2	W	0625	4.7	1216	0.6	1841	5.0		
3	TH	0043	0.3	0716	4.8	1305	0.4	1931	5.2
4	F	0131	0.2	0805	4.8	1350	0.3	2018	5.2
5	SA	0214	0.2	0850	4.8	1432	0.4	2102	5.1
6	SU	0256	0.3	0932	4.7	1511	0.6	2143	4.9
7	M	0335	0.6	1011	4.5	1551	0.9	2222	4.6
8	TU ◑	0413	1.0	1049	4.3	1630	1.3	2301	4.2
9	W	0456	1.4	1133	4.0	1717	1.7	2350	3.9
10	TH	0548	1.8	1233	3.8	1821	2.0		
11	F	0109	3.6	0659	2.1	1352	3.7	1949	2.1
12	SA	0236	3.6	0832	2.1	1506	3.8	2119	1.9
13	SU	0345	3.7	0947	1.8	1606	4.1	2220	1.6
14	M	0440	4.0	1040	1.5	1656	4.3	2308	1.3
15	TU	0526	4.2	1124	1.3	1738	4.5	2350	1.1
16	W ●	0606	4.3	1204	1.1	1817	4.6		
17	TH	0026	1.0	0643	4.4	1238	1.0	1853	4.7
18	F	0058	0.9	0718	4.4	1307	1.0	1927	4.7
19	SA	0125	0.9	0751	4.4	1333	1.0	1959	4.6
20	SU	0149	1.0	0823	4.4	1358	1.1	2027	4.5
21	M	0211	1.1	0850	4.3	1421	1.2	2054	4.4
22	TU	0236	1.2	0916	4.2	1448	1.3	2120	4.3
23	W	0304	1.3	0944	4.1	1519	1.5	2151	4.1
24	TH ◐	0340	1.6	1024	3.9	1602	1.8	2241	3.9
25	F	0429	1.8	1124	3.8	1706	2.0	2353	3.7
26	SA	0549	2.1	1244	3.8	1855	2.1		
27	SU	0125	3.7	0744	2.0	1417	3.9	2030	1.8
28	M	0305	3.9	0908	1.7	1537	4.3	2144	1.3
29	TU	0419	4.2	1015	1.2	1640	4.7	2246	0.8
30	W	0518	4.6	1111	0.8	1735	5.0	2340	0.4
31	TH ○	0611	4.8	1202	0.4	1826	5.2		

Chart Datum: 2·62 metres below Ordnance Datum (Newlyn)
HAT is 5·3 metres above Chart Datum

TIME ZONE (UT)
For Summer Time add ONE hour in **non-shaded areas**

DARTMOUTH

LAT 50°21′N LONG 3°35′W

TIMES AND HEIGHTS OF HIGH AND LOW WATERS

Dates in amber are **SPRINGS**
Dates in grey are **NEAPS**

2023

SEPTEMBER

Date	Day	Moon	Time	m	Time	m	Time	m	Time	m
1	F		0027	0.1	0700	5.0	1247	0.2	1913	5.3
2	SA		0111	0.0	0744	5.0	1330	0.1	1956	5.3
3	SU		0152	0.0	0825	5.0	1408	0.2	2036	5.1
4	M		0229	0.3	0901	4.8	1444	0.5	2112	4.9
5	TU		0303	0.7	0933	4.6	1518	0.9	2144	4.5
6	W	◑	0337	1.1	1002	4.3	1554	1.4	2212	4.1
7	TH		0412	1.6	1033	4.0	1636	1.9	2247	3.7
8	F		0500	2.1	1122	3.7	1738	2.3	2356	3.4
9	SA		0613	2.4	1317	3.6	1915	2.4		
10	SU		0219	3.4	0814	2.3	1445	3.7	2111	2.1
11	M		0329	3.7	0933	2.0	1546	4.0	2204	1.7
12	TU		0421	4.0	1022	1.6	1633	4.3	2247	1.3
13	W		0503	4.2	1102	1.2	1714	4.6	2324	1.0
14	TH		0541	4.4	1139	1.0	1752	4.7	2359	0.9
15	F	●	0618	4.5	1211	0.9	1829	4.8		
16	SA		0029	0.8	0653	4.6	1239	0.9	1903	4.8
17	SU		0055	0.8	0725	4.6	1305	0.9	1935	4.7
18	M		0119	0.9	0755	4.6	1330	1.0	2003	4.6
19	TU		0143	1.0	0821	4.5	1355	1.1	2028	4.5
20	W		0207	1.1	0845	4.4	1421	1.2	2055	4.4
21	TH		0236	1.3	0913	4.2	1454	1.5	2129	4.1
22	F	◐	0310	1.6	0955	4.1	1536	1.8	2223	3.9
23	SA		0359	2.0	1100	3.9	1643	2.1	2338	3.7
24	SU		0524	2.3	1224	3.8	1844	2.2		
25	M		0118	3.6	0736	2.1	1405	4.0	2024	1.8
26	TU		0303	4.0	0900	1.7	1527	4.4	2134	1.2
27	W		0410	4.4	1000	1.1	1626	4.8	2230	0.7
28	TH		0503	4.7	1053	0.7	1717	5.1	2319	0.3
29	F	○	0550	5.0	1141	0.3	1805	5.3		
30	SA		0004	0.1	0635	5.1	1224	0.1	1850	5.3

OCTOBER

Date	Day	Moon	Time	m	Time	m	Time	m	Time	m
1	SU		0046	0.0	0716	5.1	1304	0.1	1930	5.3
2	M		0124	0.2	0753	5.1	1341	0.3	2007	5.1
3	TU		0159	0.5	0826	4.9	1415	0.6	2039	4.8
4	W		0231	0.9	0853	4.6	1448	1.1	2105	4.4
5	TH		0301	1.3	0918	4.4	1521	1.5	2131	4.0
6	F	◑	0335	1.8	0949	4.1	1601	2.0	2208	3.7
7	SA		0421	2.3	1036	3.8	1704	2.4	2310	3.4
8	SU		0536	2.6	1207	3.5	1839	2.5		
9	M		0152	3.4	0728	2.5	1413	3.7	2040	2.2
10	TU		0300	3.7	0900	2.1	1514	4.0	2131	1.7
11	W		0351	4.0	0947	1.7	1602	4.3	2212	1.4
12	TH		0432	4.3	1027	1.3	1642	4.5	2248	1.1
13	F		0510	4.5	1102	1.1	1721	4.7	2321	0.9
14	SA	●	0547	4.6	1136	0.9	1800	4.8	2353	0.8
15	SU		0623	4.7	1207	0.9	1835	4.8		
16	M		0022	0.8	0657	4.7	1236	0.9	1909	4.8
17	TU		0050	0.9	0727	4.7	1305	0.9	1940	4.7
18	W		0118	1.0	0755	4.6	1334	1.0	2009	4.6
19	TH		0146	1.1	0825	4.5	1404	1.2	2041	4.4
20	F		0217	1.4	0859	4.4	1440	1.5	2122	4.1
21	SA		0256	1.7	0946	4.2	1528	1.8	2218	3.9
22	SU	◐	0351	2.1	1049	4.0	1644	2.1	2333	3.7
23	M		0525	2.3	1213	3.9	1837	2.1		
24	TU		0116	3.7	0723	2.1	1351	4.1	2007	1.7
25	W		0248	4.1	0839	1.6	1506	4.5	2112	1.2
26	TH		0348	4.4	0938	1.2	1603	4.8	2205	0.8
27	F		0439	4.8	1028	0.7	1654	5.1	2253	0.4
28	SA	○	0525	5.0	1114	0.5	1740	5.2	2338	0.3
29	SU		0607	5.1	1158	0.4	1825	5.2		
30	M		0018	0.3	0647	5.1	1237	0.4	1904	5.1
31	TU		0056	0.5	0722	5.0	1315	0.6	1939	4.9

NOVEMBER

Date	Day	Moon	Time	m	Time	m	Time	m	Time	m
1	W		0131	0.8	0753	4.9	1349	0.9	2009	4.6
2	TH		0202	1.1	0820	4.7	1422	1.3	2036	4.3
3	F		0233	1.5	0848	4.4	1457	1.6	2107	4.0
4	SA		0306	1.9	0923	4.2	1537	2.0	2147	3.7
5	SU	◑	0351	2.3	1011	3.9	1635	2.3	2246	3.5
6	M		0459	2.5	1118	3.7	1752	2.4		
7	TU		0047	3.4	0624	2.5	1311	3.7	1922	2.3
8	W		0210	3.6	0750	2.3	1424	3.9	2031	1.9
9	TH		0305	3.9	0851	1.9	1516	4.2	2119	1.6
10	F		0350	4.2	0937	1.6	1603	4.4	2200	1.3
11	SA		0432	4.4	1019	1.3	1645	4.6	2239	1.1
12	SU		0512	4.6	1057	1.1	1728	4.7	2315	1.0
13	M	●	0551	4.7	1135	1.0	1808	4.7	2352	0.9
14	TU		0629	4.8	1211	0.9	1845	4.7		
15	W		0026	0.9	0704	4.8	1246	0.9	1922	4.7
16	TH		0100	1.0	0738	4.8	1322	1.0	1958	4.6
17	F		0136	1.2	0814	4.7	1400	1.2	2038	4.4
18	SA		0214	1.4	0855	4.6	1444	1.4	2124	4.2
19	SU		0259	1.7	0945	4.4	1538	1.7	2220	4.0
20	M	◐	0359	1.9	1045	4.2	1649	1.8	2330	3.9
21	TU		0519	2.1	1200	4.2	1814	1.8		
22	W		0055	3.9	0650	1.9	1321	4.2	1935	1.6
23	TH		0212	4.1	0806	1.7	1433	4.4	2039	1.3
24	F		0315	4.4	0907	1.3	1533	4.6	2135	1.0
25	SA		0408	4.6	1000	1.0	1627	4.8	2225	0.8
26	SU		0456	4.8	1048	0.8	1715	4.9	2310	0.7
27	M	○	0540	4.9	1134	0.7	1801	4.9	2353	0.7
28	TU		0621	4.9	1215	0.8	1842	4.8		
29	W		0032	0.8	0658	4.9	1254	0.9	1918	4.6
30	TH		0108	1.0	0730	4.8	1331	1.1	1950	4.5

DECEMBER

Date	Day	Moon	Time	m	Time	m	Time	m	Time	m
1	F		0142	1.3	0800	4.7	1405	1.3	2022	4.3
2	SA		0214	1.5	0832	4.5	1441	1.6	2056	4.1
3	SU		0249	1.8	0909	4.3	1518	1.8	2136	3.9
4	M		0328	2.0	0952	4.1	1603	2.1	2226	3.7
5	TU	◑	0418	2.2	1045	4.0	1700	2.2	2329	3.6
6	W		0522	2.3	1150	3.9	1806	2.2		
7	TH		0044	3.7	0634	2.3	1303	3.9	1913	2.1
8	F		0156	3.8	0741	2.1	1412	4.0	2014	1.8
9	SA		0255	4.0	0840	1.9	1511	4.2	2108	1.6
10	SU		0347	4.2	0933	1.6	1605	4.3	2156	1.4
11	M		0435	4.5	1021	1.3	1655	4.5	2242	1.2
12	TU	●	0520	4.6	1106	1.1	1742	4.6	2326	1.1
13	W		0605	4.8	1152	1.0	1827	4.7		
14	TH		0009	1.0	0647	4.9	1235	0.9	1911	4.7
15	F		0052	1.0	0728	4.9	1320	0.9	1954	4.6
16	SA		0136	1.0	0811	4.9	1404	1.0	2040	4.5
17	SU		0220	1.2	0857	4.8	1452	1.1	2128	4.4
18	M		0307	1.3	0946	4.7	1542	1.2	2219	4.3
19	TU	◐	0359	1.5	1038	4.5	1637	1.4	2315	4.1
20	W		0457	1.7	1138	4.4	1738	1.5		
21	TH		0019	4.1	0605	1.8	1243	4.3	1848	1.6
22	F		0126	4.1	0720	1.7	1353	4.3	1959	1.6
23	SA		0233	4.2	0830	1.6	1459	4.3	2103	1.4
24	SU		0334	4.3	0932	1.4	1600	4.4	2158	1.3
25	M		0429	4.5	1027	1.3	1655	4.5	2249	1.2
26	TU		0518	4.6	1116	1.1	1743	4.5	2336	1.1
27	W	○	0603	4.7	1201	1.0	1827	4.5		
28	TH		0017	1.1	0642	4.8	1242	1.0	1905	4.5
29	F		0055	1.1	0717	4.8	1320	1.1	1941	4.4
30	SA		0130	1.2	0750	4.7	1355	1.2	2014	4.3
31	SU		0202	1.4	0824	4.6	1427	1.4	2048	4.2

Chart Datum: 2·62 metres below Ordnance Datum (Newlyn)
HAT is 5·3 metres above Chart Datum

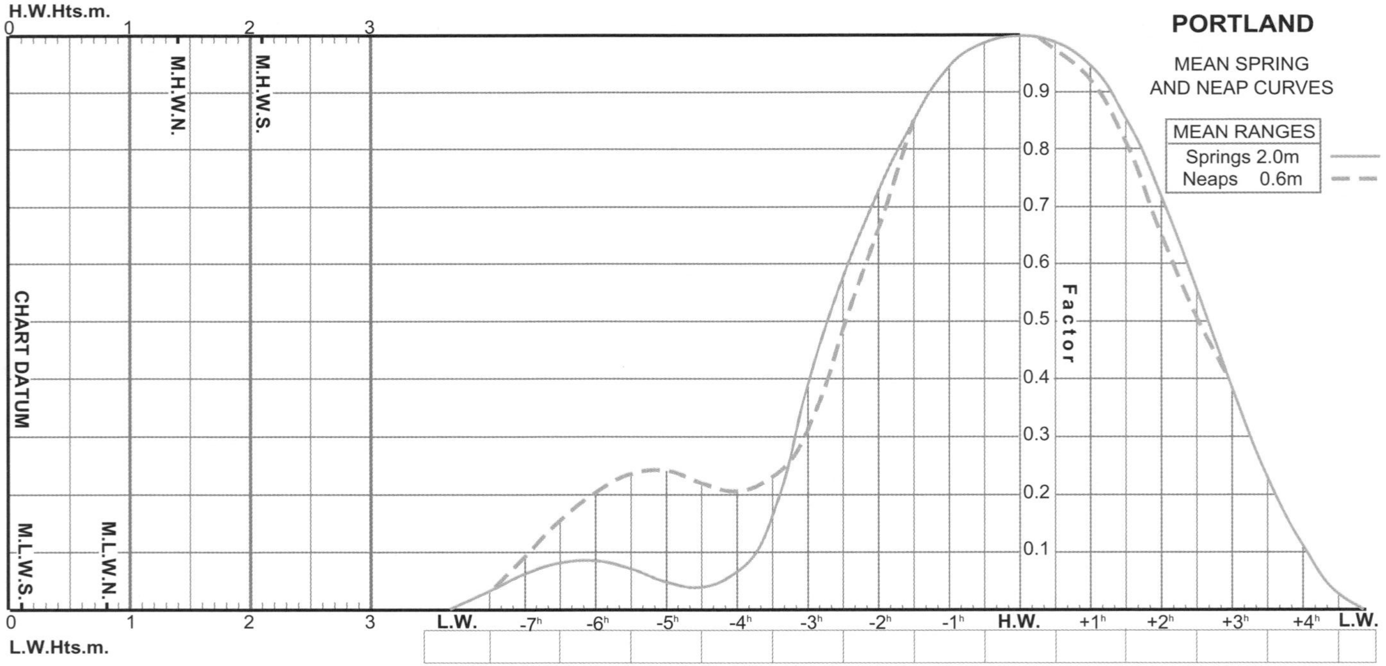

Note - Double LWs occur at Portland. The predictions are for the first LW. The second LW occurs from 3 to 4 Hrs later and may, at Springs, on occasions be lower than the first.

TIME ZONE (UT)
For Summer Time add ONE hour in **non-shaded areas**

PORTLAND

LAT 50°34′N LONG 2°26′W

TIMES AND HEIGHTS OF HIGH AND LOW WATERS

Dates in amber are **SPRINGS**
Dates in grey are **NEAPS**

2023

JANUARY

Date	Day	Time	m	Time	m	Time	m	Time	m
1	SU	0145	1.5	0615	0.9	1408	1.5	1904	0.7
2	M	0249	1.5	0725	0.9	1513	1.5	2004	0.7
3	TU	0346	1.6	0829	0.9	1613	1.5	2058	0.7
4	W	0438	1.7	0926	0.8	1709	1.6	2149	0.6
5	TH	0525	1.9	1020	0.7	1757	1.7	2238	0.5
6	F	0608	2.0	1109	0.6	1840	1.8	○ 2322	0.5
7	SA	0645	2.0	1153	0.5	1918	1.8		
8	SU	0003	0.5	0722	2.0	1232	0.5	1954	1.8
9	M	0039	0.5	0758	2.0	1307	0.4	2028	1.8
10	TU	0111	0.5	0833	1.9	1338	0.4	2101	1.7
11	W	0141	0.5	0905	1.9	1407	0.4	2130	1.6
12	TH	0211	0.5	0934	1.8	1437	0.4	2158	1.6
13	F	0243	0.5	1002	1.7	1513	0.4	2229	1.5
14	SA	0320	0.6	1038	1.6	1555	0.5	2310	1.4
15	SU	0408	0.6	1125	1.5	1647	0.5	◑	
16	M	0007	1.4	0512	0.7	1227	1.5	1750	0.6
17	TU	0127	1.4	0623	0.8	1348	1.4	1859	0.6
18	W	0249	1.5	0739	0.8	1510	1.5	2015	0.6
19	TH	0357	1.7	0900	0.7	1623	1.6	2130	0.6
20	F	0459	1.9	1011	0.6	1730	1.8	2233	0.5
21	SA	0555	2.1	1110	0.4	1830	1.9	● 2327	0.4
22	SU	0649	2.2	1201	0.3	1929	2.0		
23	M	0014	0.3	0743	2.3	1247	0.2	2029	2.1
24	TU	0059	0.2	0837	2.4	1331	0.1	2115	2.1
25	W	0142	0.2	0924	2.4	1414	0.1	2151	2.1
26	TH	0223	0.3	1004	2.2	1457	0.2	2225	1.9
27	F	0302	0.4	1040	2.0	1540	0.3	2259	1.8
28	SA	0341	0.5	1115	1.8	1622	0.4	◐ 2334	1.6
29	SU	0420	0.7	1155	1.6	1708	0.6		
30	M	0018	1.4	0507	0.8	1253	1.4	1808	0.7
31	TU	0139	1.3	0633	0.9	1430	1.3	1922	0.8

FEBRUARY

Date	Day	Time	m	Time	m	Time	m	Time	m
1	W	0309	1.4	0800	0.9	1549	1.3	2027	0.8
2	TH	0414	1.5	0906	0.8	1652	1.4	2125	0.7
3	F	0505	1.7	1004	0.7	1743	1.5	2219	0.6
4	SA	0550	1.8	1056	0.6	1827	1.7	2308	0.5
5	SU	0632	1.9	1142	0.4	1909	1.8	○ 2350	0.4
6	M	0712	2.0	1222	0.3	1947	1.8		
7	TU	0028	0.3	0750	2.0	1256	0.3	2023	1.9
8	W	0100	0.3	0825	2.0	1324	0.3	2053	1.8
9	TH	0130	0.3	0855	1.9	1350	0.3	2116	1.8
10	F	0159	0.3	0917	1.9	1419	0.3	2134	1.7
11	SA	0228	0.3	0938	1.8	1449	0.3	2156	1.6
12	SU	0258	0.4	1009	1.7	1522	0.3	2231	1.6
13	M	0331	0.5	1051	1.6	1603	0.4	◑ 2319	1.5
14	TU	0420	0.6	1145	1.4	1701	0.5		
15	W	0024	1.4	0538	0.7	1304	1.3	1817	0.6
16	TH	0213	1.4	0712	0.8	1455	1.3	1959	0.7
17	F	0338	1.6	0928	0.7	1616	1.5	2131	0.6
18	SA	0446	1.8	1019	0.5	1725	1.7	2229	0.5
19	SU	0545	2.0	1107	0.3	1829	1.9	2318	0.3
20	M	0641	2.2	1151	0.1	1930	2.1	●	
21	TU	0003	0.2	0736	2.4	1233	0.0	2020	2.2
22	W	0044	0.1	0827	2.4	1313	0.0	2057	2.2
23	TH	0123	0.0	0908	2.4	1352	0.0	2128	2.2
24	F	0200	0.1	0942	2.3	1428	0.1	2156	2.0
25	SA	0233	0.2	1010	2.0	1503	0.2	2218	1.8
26	SU	0303	0.4	1034	1.8	1534	0.4	2241	1.6
27	M	0331	0.6	1102	1.5	1601	0.6	◐ 2311	1.5
28	TU	0357	0.7	1140	1.3	1625	0.8	2353	1.3

MARCH

Date	Day	Time	m	Time	m	Time	m	Time	m
1	W	0437	0.9	1241	1.1	1843	0.9		
2	TH	0114	1.2	0744	0.9	1538	1.1	2003	0.9
3	F	0355	1.4	0846	0.8	1640	1.3	2101	0.7
4	SA	0447	1.5	0940	0.6	1727	1.5	2155	0.6
5	SU	0531	1.7	1031	0.5	1809	1.7	2245	0.4
6	M	0613	1.9	1118	0.3	1850	1.8	2330	0.3
7	TU	0654	2.0	1159	0.2	1930	1.9	○	
8	W	0008	0.2	0734	2.1	1233	0.2	2007	2.0
9	TH	0040	0.2	0810	2.1	1300	0.2	2037	1.9
10	F	0109	0.2	0837	2.0	1326	0.2	2057	1.9
11	SA	0138	0.2	0853	1.9	1354	0.2	2107	1.8
12	SU	0207	0.2	0913	1.8	1423	0.2	2129	1.7
13	M	0235	0.3	0945	1.7	1453	0.3	2203	1.7
14	TU	0305	0.4	1027	1.6	1527	0.4	2248	1.5
15	W	0347	0.5	1122	1.4	1618	0.6	◑ 2350	1.4
16	TH	0508	0.7	1251	1.2	1748	0.7		
17	F	0159	1.3	0950	0.7	1455	1.3	2026	0.7
18	SA	0328	1.5	1155	0.5	1611	1.5	2126	0.6
19	SU	0434	1.7	1013	0.4	1716	1.7	2216	0.4
20	M	0533	2.0	1052	0.2	1814	1.9	2302	0.2
21	TU	0627	2.2	1134	0.0	1904	2.1	● 2346	0.1
22	W	0718	2.3	1213	-0.1	1949	2.2		
23	TH	0024	0.0	0804	2.4	1250	-0.1	2027	2.3
24	F	0100	0.0	0843	2.3	1324	0.0	2058	2.2
25	SA	0132	0.1	0912	2.2	1355	0.1	2120	2.0
26	SU	0201	0.2	0934	1.9	1424	0.3	2139	1.8
27	M	0229	0.4	0958	1.7	1450	0.5	2204	1.7
28	TU	0254	0.5	1028	1.5	1509	0.6	2235	1.5
29	W	0318	0.7	1106	1.2	1530	0.8	◐ 2313	1.4
30	TH	0357	0.8	1200	1.1	1618	0.9		
31	F	0012	1.2	0720	0.9	1535	1.1	1935	0.9

APRIL

Date	Day	Time	m	Time	m	Time	m	Time	m
1	SA	0321	1.3	0818	0.7	1621	1.3	2033	0.8
2	SU	0417	1.5	0910	0.6	1701	1.5	2125	0.6
3	M	0500	1.7	0959	0.4	1740	1.7	2215	0.5
4	TU	0543	1.8	1046	0.3	1820	1.8	2300	0.3
5	W	0626	2.0	1127	0.2	1900	2.0	2340	0.2
6	TH	0707	2.1	1201	0.2	1938	2.0	○	
7	F	0013	0.2	0744	2.1	1230	0.1	2012	2.0
8	SA	0043	0.2	0811	2.1	1258	0.1	2031	2.0
9	SU	0114	0.2	0826	2.0	1329	0.2	2042	1.9
10	M	0145	0.2	0853	1.9	1400	0.2	2110	1.9
11	TU	0217	0.3	0931	1.7	1433	0.3	2148	1.7
12	W	0254	0.4	1018	1.5	1510	0.5	2238	1.6
13	TH	0346	0.6	1121	1.3	1609	0.7	◑ 2347	1.4
14	F	0518	0.7	1315	1.2	1752	0.8		
15	SA	0154	1.4	0939	0.6	1451	1.3	2004	0.8
16	SU	0314	1.6	1134	0.4	1557	1.5	2104	0.6
17	M	0416	1.8	0949	0.3	1654	1.8	2154	0.4
18	TU	0512	2.0	1029	0.2	1746	2.0	2240	0.3
19	W	0604	2.1	1110	0.1	1833	2.1	2323	0.2
20	TH	0652	2.2	1148	0.0	1916	2.2	●	
21	F	0000	0.1	0735	2.3	1221	0.0	1953	2.2
22	SA	0032	0.1	0811	2.2	1252	0.1	2023	2.1
23	SU	0103	0.2	0837	2.0	1322	0.2	2045	2.0
24	M	0133	0.3	0902	1.8	1351	0.4	2109	1.8
25	TU	0203	0.4	0931	1.6	1416	0.5	2139	1.7
26	W	0229	0.6	1006	1.4	1435	0.6	2214	1.5
27	TH	0255	0.7	1048	1.3	1501	0.8	◐ 2256	1.4
28	F	0340	0.8	1143	1.1	1557	0.9	2352	1.3
29	SA	0648	0.8	1326	1.1	1859	0.9		
30	SU	0133	1.3	0746	0.7	1537	1.3	1958	0.8

Chart Datum: 0·93 metres below Ordnance Datum (Newlyn)
HAT is 2·5 metres above Chart Datum

TIME ZONE (UT)
For Summer Time add ONE hour in **non-shaded areas**

PORTLAND

LAT 50°34'N LONG 2°26'W

TIMES AND HEIGHTS OF HIGH AND LOW WATERS

Dates in amber are **SPRINGS**
Dates in grey are **NEAPS**

2023

MAY

Date	Day	Time	m	Time	m	Time	m	Time	m
1	M	0313	1.4	0837	0.5	1616	1.5	2051	0.6
2	TU	0412	1.6	0924	0.4	1659	1.6	2138	0.5
3	W	0502	1.7	1009	0.3	1742	1.8	2224	0.4
4	TH	0549	1.9	1048	0.3	1825	2.0	2304	0.3
5	F	0632	2.0	1124	0.2	1905	2.1	○ 2341	0.3
6	SA	0710	2.1	1157	0.2	1940	2.1		
7	SU	0016	0.2	0738	2.0	1232	0.2	2003	2.1
8	M	0052	0.2	0805	2.0	1308	0.2	2027	2.0
9	TU	0129	0.2	0842	1.9	1345	0.3	2104	1.9
10	W	0210	0.3	0929	1.7	1426	0.4	2150	1.8
11	TH	0259	0.4	1024	1.5	1516	0.6	2245	1.7
12	F	0404	0.6	1132	1.4	1624	0.7	◑ 2356	1.5
13	SA	0528	0.6	1311	1.3	1744	0.8		
14	SU	0134	1.5	0946	0.5	1431	1.4	1913	0.8
15	M	0249	1.6	0840	0.5	1530	1.6	2028	0.7
16	TU	0348	1.7	0916	0.4	1623	1.8	2124	0.5
17	W	0443	1.9	0958	0.3	1714	1.9	2212	0.4
18	TH	0535	2.0	1039	0.2	1801	2.0	2255	0.3
19	F	0623	2.0	1116	0.2	1843	2.1	● 2332	0.3
20	SA	0705	2.0	1150	0.2	1920	2.1		
21	SU	0005	0.3	0741	2.0	1223	0.2	1951	2.1
22	M	0040	0.3	0810	1.9	1256	0.3	2020	2.0
23	TU	0114	0.4	0840	1.7	1328	0.4	2051	1.9
24	W	0147	0.5	0914	1.6	1356	0.6	2126	1.7
25	TH	0218	0.6	0952	1.4	1421	0.6	2202	1.6
26	F	0250	0.7	1034	1.3	1454	0.7	2243	1.5
27	SA	0335	0.7	1122	1.2	1548	0.8	◐ 2331	1.4
28	SU	0442	0.7	1228	1.2	1701	0.8		
29	M	0033	1.4	0706	0.7	1402	1.3	1903	0.8
30	TU	0158	1.4	0758	0.6	1513	1.4	2005	0.7
31	W	0309	1.5	0842	0.5	1608	1.6	2053	0.6

JUNE

Date	Day	Time	m	Time	m	Time	m	Time	m
1	TH	0408	1.7	0922	0.4	1657	1.8	2140	0.5
2	F	0502	1.8	1003	0.3	1745	1.9	2225	0.4
3	SA	0551	1.9	1046	0.3	1828	2.0	2310	0.4
4	SU	0634	2.0	1129	0.3	1906	2.1	○ 2355	0.3
5	M	0714	2.0	1213	0.2	1943	2.2		
6	TU	0039	0.3	0757	2.0	1256	0.3	2024	2.1
7	W	0125	0.3	0845	1.9	1340	0.3	2109	2.1
8	TH	0213	0.3	0938	1.8	1428	0.4	2159	2.0
9	F	0306	0.4	1032	1.7	1520	0.5	2250	1.9
10	SA	0404	0.4	1131	1.6	1616	0.6	◑ 2348	1.7
11	SU	0504	0.5	1243	1.5	1716	0.7		
12	M	0058	1.6	0609	0.5	1354	1.5	1821	0.7
13	TU	0210	1.6	0721	0.5	1454	1.6	1932	0.7
14	W	0311	1.6	0826	0.5	1548	1.7	2038	0.7
15	TH	0410	1.7	0916	0.5	1641	1.8	2135	0.6
16	F	0506	1.7	1002	0.4	1730	1.9	2226	0.5
17	SA	0557	1.8	1045	0.4	1815	2.0	2311	0.5
18	SU	0642	1.8	1126	0.4	1854	2.0	● 2351	0.4
19	M	0721	1.8	1204	0.4	1930	2.0		
20	TU	0029	0.4	0755	1.8	1241	0.4	2005	2.0
21	W	0107	0.4	0829	1.7	1316	0.4	2040	1.9
22	TH	0143	0.5	0904	1.6	1349	0.5	2116	1.8
23	F	0216	0.5	0940	1.5	1419	0.6	2151	1.7
24	SA	0247	0.5	1016	1.4	1451	0.6	2225	1.6
25	SU	0322	0.5	1054	1.4	1533	0.7	2300	1.5
26	M	0406	0.5	1140	1.3	1625	0.7	◐ 2346	1.5
27	TU	0500	0.6	1241	1.3	1727	0.7		
28	W	0045	1.4	0603	0.6	1359	1.4	1836	0.7
29	TH	0157	1.5	0711	0.5	1506	1.5	1946	0.7
30	F	0307	1.5	0819	0.5	1606	1.7	2053	0.6

JULY

Date	Day	Time	m	Time	m	Time	m	Time	m
1	SA	0413	1.6	0920	0.4	1702	1.8	2154	0.5
2	SU	0515	1.8	1018	0.4	1754	2.0	2253	0.5
3	M	0612	1.9	1113	0.3	1843	2.1	○ 2347	0.4
4	TU	0706	1.9	1203	0.3	1932	2.2		
5	W	0036	0.3	0800	2.0	1250	0.3	2024	2.3
6	TH	0123	0.2	0857	2.0	1336	0.3	2114	2.2
7	F	0209	0.2	0946	1.9	1421	0.3	2200	2.2
8	SA	0257	0.2	1029	1.8	1507	0.4	2243	2.0
9	SU	0345	0.3	1113	1.7	1554	0.5	2327	1.9
10	M	0434	0.4	1202	1.6	1643	0.6	◑	
11	TU	0017	1.7	0526	0.5	1303	1.5	1738	0.7
12	W	0122	1.5	0625	0.6	1411	1.5	1844	0.8
13	TH	0233	1.4	0731	0.7	1514	1.5	1956	0.8
14	F	0341	1.4	0834	0.7	1613	1.6	2107	0.8
15	SA	0444	1.5	0930	0.6	1707	1.8	2210	0.7
16	SU	0539	1.6	1022	0.5	1754	1.9	2303	0.6
17	M	0626	1.7	1109	0.5	1836	2.0	● 2347	0.5
18	TU	0708	1.7	1152	0.4	1916	2.0		
19	W	0026	0.4	0747	1.8	1231	0.4	1954	2.0
20	TH	0102	0.3	0822	1.8	1307	0.4	2030	2.0
21	F	0135	0.3	0855	1.7	1339	0.4	2104	1.9
22	SA	0204	0.4	0925	1.6	1408	0.4	2134	1.8
23	SU	0229	0.4	0953	1.6	1437	0.5	2159	1.7
24	M	0258	0.4	1020	1.5	1509	0.5	2226	1.6
25	TU	0333	0.4	1053	1.4	1549	0.6	◐ 2303	1.5
26	W	0417	0.4	1139	1.4	1643	0.6	2354	1.5
27	TH	0514	0.5	1243	1.4	1749	0.7		
28	F	0101	1.4	0620	0.6	1410	1.4	1902	0.7
29	SA	0226	1.4	0735	0.6	1528	1.6	2028	0.7
30	SU	0349	1.5	0859	0.6	1634	1.8	2150	0.6
31	M	0501	1.6	1009	0.5	1734	2.0	2251	0.4

AUGUST

Date	Day	Time	m	Time	m	Time	m	Time	m
1	TU	0604	1.8	1105	0.4	1829	2.1	○ 2342	0.3
2	W	0702	1.9	1155	0.3	1922	2.3		
3	TH	0028	0.1	0804	2.1	1240	0.2	2017	2.4
4	F	0112	0.0	0858	2.1	1323	0.1	2107	2.4
5	SA	0155	0.0	0937	2.1	1405	0.1	2147	2.3
6	SU	0236	0.1	1010	2.0	1445	0.2	2223	2.2
7	M	0318	0.2	1043	1.8	1524	0.4	2258	1.9
8	TU	0359	0.4	1117	1.7	1603	0.6	◑ 2334	1.7
9	W	0441	0.5	1158	1.5	1648	0.7		
10	TH	0023	1.4	0534	0.7	1310	1.4	1758	0.9
11	F	0159	1.3	0651	0.8	1447	1.4	1936	0.9
12	SA	0326	1.3	0806	0.8	1555	1.5	2052	0.8
13	SU	0433	1.4	0907	0.7	1650	1.7	2152	0.7
14	M	0526	1.5	1001	0.6	1737	1.8	2243	0.6
15	TU	0611	1.7	1051	0.5	1820	1.9	2329	0.4
16	W	0653	1.8	1135	0.4	1900	2.0	●	
17	TH	0009	0.3	0733	1.9	1215	0.3	1939	2.1
18	F	0046	0.2	0809	1.9	1250	0.3	2015	2.0
19	SA	0116	0.2	0840	1.9	1320	0.3	2047	2.0
20	SU	0140	0.3	0905	1.8	1347	0.3	2111	1.9
21	M	0204	0.3	0923	1.7	1414	0.4	2128	1.8
22	TU	0229	0.3	0940	1.6	1441	0.4	2150	1.7
23	W	0257	0.4	1009	1.6	1511	0.5	2226	1.6
24	TH	0331	0.4	1052	1.5	1553	0.6	◐ 2316	1.5
25	F	0422	0.5	1151	1.4	1707	0.7		
26	SA	0023	1.3	0539	0.7	1326	1.4	1835	0.8
27	SU	0214	1.3	0711	0.7	1510	1.5	2309	0.7
28	M	0345	1.4	0905	0.7	1620	1.7	2159	0.5
29	TU	0455	1.6	1003	0.5	1720	2.0	2246	0.3
30	W	0557	1.9	1054	0.3	1815	2.2	2330	0.2
31	TH	0653	2.0	1141	0.2	1908	2.4	○	

Chart Datum: 0·93 metres below Ordnance Datum (Newlyn)
HAT is 2·5 metres above Chart Datum

TIME ZONE (UT)
For Summer Time add ONE hour in **non-shaded areas**

PORTLAND

LAT 50°34′N LONG 2°26′W

TIMES AND HEIGHTS OF HIGH AND LOW WATERS

Dates in amber are **SPRINGS**
Dates in grey are **NEAPS**

2023

SEPTEMBER

Date	Day	Time	m	Time	m	Time	m	Time	m
1	F	0013	0.0	0748	2.2	1223	0.1	2000	2.5
2	SA	0053	-0.1	0833	2.3	1304	0.0	2046	2.5
3	SU	0132	0.0	0909	2.2	1341	0.1	2124	2.4
4	M	0209	0.1	0940	2.1	1416	0.2	2156	2.1
5	TU	0243	0.2	1004	1.9	1449	0.4	2222	1.9
6	W	0315	0.4	1026	1.7	1521	0.6	◑ 2249	1.6
7	TH	0344	0.7	1058	1.5	1553	0.8	2327	1.3
8	F	0410	0.8	1141	1.4	1647	1.0		
9	SA	0033	1.1	0624	1.0	1426	1.3	1924	1.0
10	SU	0330	1.2	0743	1.0	1546	1.4	2028	0.8
11	M	0428	1.4	0842	0.8	1635	1.6	2122	0.7
12	TU	0511	1.6	0935	0.7	1718	1.8	2212	0.5
13	W	0551	1.7	1025	0.5	1758	1.9	2259	0.4
14	TH	0631	1.9	1111	0.4	1838	2.1	2343	0.2
15	F ●	0709	2.0	1152	0.3	1916	2.1		
16	SA	0019	0.2	0745	2.0	1226	0.2	1952	2.1
17	SU	0047	0.2	0815	2.0	1255	0.3	2022	2.1
18	M	0110	0.2	0838	2.0	1321	0.3	2041	2.0
19	TU	0133	0.3	0847	1.9	1348	0.3	2054	1.9
20	W	0158	0.3	0904	1.8	1414	0.4	2120	1.8
21	TH	0223	0.4	0935	1.7	1440	0.5	2159	1.6
22	F	0251	0.5	1018	1.6	1516	0.6	◐ 2250	1.4
23	SA	0329	0.7	1118	1.4	1637	0.8		
24	SU	0007	1.3	0520	0.8	1309	1.4	2103	0.8
25	M	0224	1.3	0803	0.9	1501	1.5	2225	0.6
26	TU	0344	1.5	0859	0.7	1608	1.8	2149	0.4
27	W	0447	1.7	0949	0.5	1705	2.0	2228	0.3
28	TH	0541	2.0	1036	0.3	1758	2.2	2310	0.1
29	F	0630	2.2	1121	0.2	1847	2.4	○ 2351	0.0
30	SA	0716	2.3	1202	0.1	1935	2.5		

OCTOBER

Date	Day	Time	m	Time	m	Time	m	Time	m
1	SU	0029	0.0	0758	2.3	1239	0.1	2018	2.4
2	M	0103	0.0	0833	2.3	1313	0.2	2053	2.3
3	TU	0135	0.2	0859	2.1	1345	0.3	2119	2.1
4	W	0204	0.4	0920	2.0	1415	0.5	2144	1.8
5	TH	0232	0.6	0947	1.8	1445	0.6	2216	1.5
6	F	0253	0.8	1021	1.6	1513	0.8	◑ 2256	1.3
7	SA	0301	0.9	1104	1.4	1610	1.0	2355	1.1
8	SU	0315	1.1	0910	1.3	1858	0.9		
9	M	0340	1.2	0714	1.0	1529	1.4	1956	0.8
10	TU	0412	1.4	0812	0.9	1610	1.6	2048	0.6
11	W	0447	1.6	0903	0.7	1648	1.8	2137	0.5
12	TH	0523	1.8	0953	0.6	1727	1.9	2224	0.4
13	F	0559	2.0	1039	0.4	1807	2.0	2308	0.3
14	SA	0636	2.1	1121	0.4	1846	2.1	● 2344	0.3
15	SU	0712	2.1	1156	0.3	1922	2.1		
16	M	0011	0.3	0744	2.1	1225	0.3	1952	2.1
17	TU	0037	0.3	0803	2.1	1253	0.3	2008	2.0
18	W	0104	0.3	0815	2.0	1323	0.4	2029	1.9
19	TH	0133	0.4	0840	1.9	1354	0.4	2103	1.8
20	F	0202	0.5	0915	1.8	1428	0.5	2147	1.6
21	SA	0231	0.6	1003	1.7	1514	0.7	2248	1.4
22	SU ◐	0308	0.8	1111	1.5	1647	0.8		
23	M	0020	1.3	0506	1.0	1308	1.4	2042	0.7
24	TU	0222	1.4	0735	0.9	1446	1.6	2105	0.6
25	W	0332	1.6	0837	0.8	1548	1.8	2123	0.4
26	TH	0426	1.8	0927	0.6	1642	2.0	2203	0.3
27	F	0516	2.0	1013	0.4	1734	2.2	2244	0.2
28	SA	0601	2.2	1057	0.3	1822	2.3	○ 2324	0.1
29	SU	0645	2.3	1137	0.3	1907	2.3	2359	0.1
30	M	0723	2.3	1212	0.3	1946	2.3		
31	TU	0031	0.2	0755	2.3	1244	0.3	2019	2.1

NOVEMBER

Date	Day	Time	m	Time	m	Time	m	Time	m
1	W	0102	0.3	0821	2.2	1317	0.4	2047	1.9
2	TH	0133	0.5	0849	2.0	1350	0.5	2118	1.7
3	F	0201	0.7	0922	1.8	1423	0.7	2155	1.5
4	SA	0221	0.8	1000	1.6	1455	0.8	2239	1.3
5	SU	0235	0.9	1045	1.5	1719	0.9	◑ 2335	1.2
6	M	0308	1.1	1145	1.4	1825	0.9		
7	TU	0305	1.2	0638	1.1	1328	1.3	1921	0.8
8	W	0338	1.4	0737	1.0	1511	1.5	2013	0.7
9	TH	0408	1.6	0830	0.8	1559	1.6	2101	0.5
10	F	0443	1.8	0917	0.7	1645	1.8	2146	0.5
11	SA	0520	1.9	1003	0.6	1729	1.9	2227	0.4
12	SU	0559	2.1	1044	0.5	1811	2.0	2302	0.4
13	M	0637	2.2	1120	0.5	1849	2.1	● 2334	0.4
14	TU	0709	2.2	1155	0.4	1919	2.1		
15	W	0007	0.4	0731	2.2	1229	0.4	1945	2.0
16	TH	0042	0.4	0756	2.1	1307	0.4	2018	1.9
17	F	0118	0.4	0832	2.1	1347	0.5	2101	1.8
18	SA	0157	0.5	0916	1.9	1434	0.5	2153	1.6
19	SU	0240	0.7	1010	1.8	1534	0.6	2255	1.5
20	M ◐	0341	0.8	1116	1.6	1650	0.7		
21	TU	0019	1.4	0502	0.9	1246	1.6	2027	0.7
22	W	0157	1.5	0626	0.9	1415	1.6	2014	0.6
23	TH	0301	1.6	0754	0.8	1517	1.8	2048	0.5
24	F	0354	1.8	0855	0.7	1613	1.9	2130	0.4
25	SA	0444	2.0	0944	0.6	1707	2.0	2212	0.4
26	SU	0531	2.1	1029	0.5	1757	2.1	2252	0.3
27	M	0614	2.2	1110	0.5	1842	2.1	○ 2330	0.3
28	TU	0653	2.2	1148	0.4	1922	2.1		
29	W	0005	0.4	0727	2.2	1224	0.5	1957	2.0
30	TH	0039	0.5	0800	2.1	1301	0.5	2030	1.8

DECEMBER

Date	Day	Time	m	Time	m	Time	m	Time	m
1	F	0114	0.6	0834	2.0	1339	0.6	2105	1.7
2	SA	0146	0.7	0910	1.9	1417	0.7	2143	1.6
3	SU	0213	0.8	0949	1.7	1456	0.7	2223	1.4
4	M	0238	0.9	1030	1.6	1541	0.8	2308	1.3
5	TU ◑	0318	0.9	1116	1.5	1738	0.8		
6	W	0007	1.3	0426	1.0	1214	1.4	1841	0.8
7	TH	0135	1.3	0648	1.0	1336	1.4	1935	0.7
8	F	0253	1.5	0748	0.9	1449	1.5	2021	0.6
9	SA	0346	1.6	0836	0.8	1549	1.6	2101	0.6
10	SU	0434	1.8	0920	0.7	1643	1.7	2140	0.5
11	M	0519	2.0	1003	0.6	1733	1.9	2221	0.5
12	TU	0600	2.1	1048	0.6	1817	1.9	● 2305	0.4
13	W	0638	2.2	1133	0.5	1858	2.0	2349	0.4
14	TH	0713	2.2	1218	0.4	1937	2.0		
15	F	0032	0.4	0752	2.2	1303	0.4	2021	1.9
16	SA	0116	0.4	0836	2.2	1350	0.4	2109	1.9
17	SU	0201	0.5	0924	2.1	1440	0.4	2159	1.8
18	M	0249	0.6	1015	2.0	1533	0.4	2252	1.7
19	TU	0341	0.7	1110	1.8	1629	0.5	◐ 2353	1.6
20	W	0438	0.8	1213	1.7	1735	0.6		
21	TH	0107	1.5	0541	0.8	1328	1.6	1834	0.6
22	F	0216	1.6	0651	0.9	1436	1.6	1946	0.6
23	SA	0315	1.7	0807	0.8	1539	1.6	2048	0.6
24	SU	0411	1.8	0915	0.8	1639	1.7	2139	0.6
25	M	0504	1.9	1010	0.7	1737	1.8	2226	0.5
26	TU	0551	2.0	1100	0.6	1826	1.8	2310	0.5
27	W	0634	2.1	1141	0.6	1910	1.9	○ 2351	0.5
28	TH	0713	2.1	1219	0.5	1948	1.9		
29	F	0028	0.5	0750	2.1	1257	0.5	2024	1.8
30	SA	0105	0.5	0826	2.0	1335	0.5	2057	1.7
31	SU	0140	0.5	0902	1.9	1412	0.5	2130	1.6

Chart Datum: 0·93 metres below Ordnance Datum (Newlyn)
HAT is 2·5 metres above Chart Datum

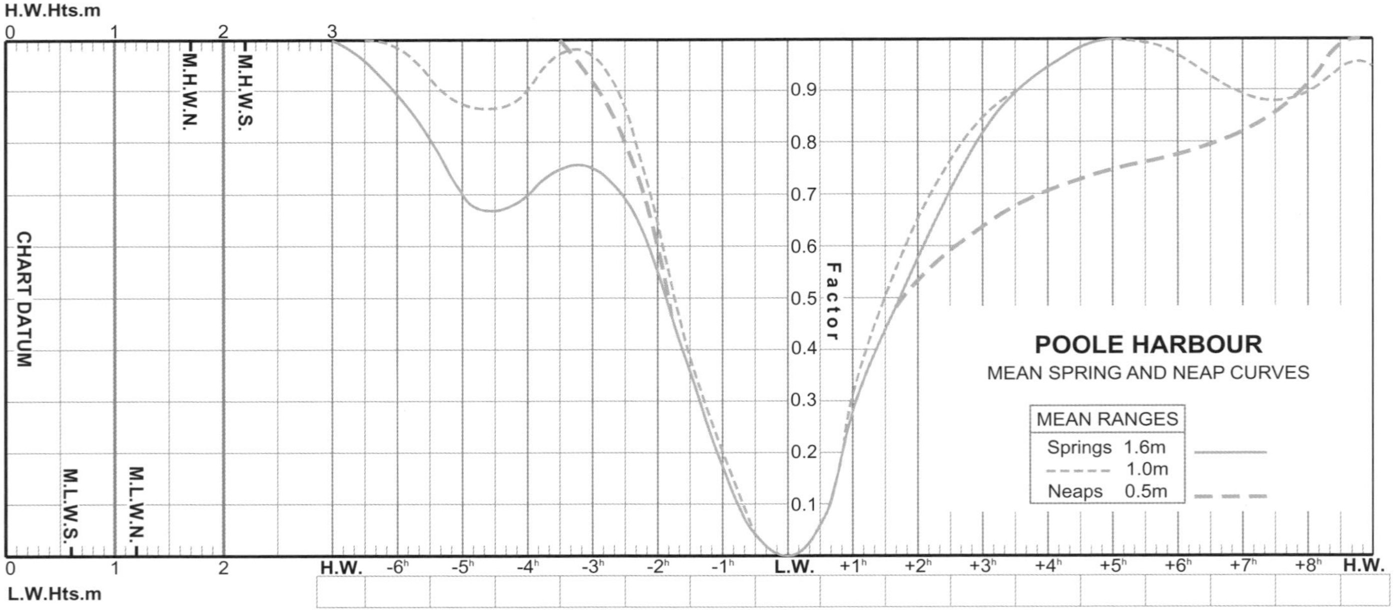

Note - Sea level is above mean tide level from 2 hrs after LW to 2 hrs before the next LW. HW occurs between 5 hrs after LW and 3 hrs before the next LW, the time shown is approximate and should be checked for suitability.

TIME ZONE (UT)
For Summer Time add ONE hour in **non-shaded areas**

POOLE HARBOUR

LAT 50°43′N LONG 1°59′W

TIMES AND HEIGHTS OF HIGH AND LOW WATERS

Dates in amber are **SPRINGS**
Dates in grey are **NEAPS**

2023

JANUARY

Day	Time	m	Day	Time	m
1 SU	0805	2.0	16 M	0114	1.6
	1149	1.2		1044	1.2
	1509	1.6		1331	1.7
				2312	1.0
2 M	0011	1.0	17 TU	0819	1.9
	0908	2.0		1151	1.1
	1249	1.1		1542	1.6
	1612	1.6			
3 TU	0109	1.0	18 W	0017	1.0
	0719	1.8		0628	1.8
	1344	1.0		1256	1.0
	1721	1.6		1848	1.7
4 W	0202	1.0	19 TH	0120	0.9
	0748	1.9		0703	1.9
	1434	0.9		1357	0.8
	2005	1.8		1936	1.8
5 TH	0251	1.0	20 F	0220	0.8
	0639	1.9		0748	2.1
	1519	0.8		1453	0.6
	2034	1.8		2025	2.0
6 F	0336	1.0	21 SA	0316	0.7
	0730	2.0		0837	2.2
	1602	0.8		1546	0.4
	○ 2054	1.9		● 2112	2.1
7 SA	0418	1.0	22 SU	0408	0.6
	0828	2.1		0924	2.3
	1641	0.7		1634	0.3
	2128	1.9		2156	2.2
8 SU	0456	1.0	23 M	0457	0.5
	0921	2.1		1008	2.4
	1715	0.7		1721	0.2
	2210	1.9		2239	2.2
9 M	0531	1.0	24 TU	0544	0.5
	1006	2.1		1049	2.4
	1748	0.7		1806	0.2
	2253	1.9		2319	2.2
10 TU	0604	1.0	25 W	0631	0.6
	1043	2.0		1127	2.3
	1821	0.7		1852	0.3
	2336	1.8		2358	2.1
11 W	0640	1.0	26 TH	0718	0.7
	1027	1.9		1202	2.2
	1856	0.7		1937	0.4
	2359	1.7			
12 TH	0718	1.0	27 F	0033	1.9
	1039	1.9		0806	0.8
	1936	0.8		1227	2.0
	2304	1.7		2025	0.7
13 F	0759	1.1	28 SA	0101	1.7
	1102	1.8		0858	1.0
	2019	0.8		1240	1.8
	2324	1.6		◐ 2118	0.9
14 SA	0846	1.1	29 SU	0118	1.6
	1138	1.8		0958	1.1
	2108	0.9		1313	1.7
				2222	1.1
15 SU	0007	1.6	30 M	0202	1.6
	0941	1.1		1110	1.2
	1226	1.7		1411	1.5
	◑ 2207	1.0		2338	1.2
			31 TU	0311	1.5
				1223	1.2
				1530	1.5

FEBRUARY

Day	Time	m	Day	Time	m
1 W	0049	1.2	16 TH	0618	1.8
	0933	1.9		1231	1.0
	1326	1.1		1901	1.7
	1944	1.7			
2 TH	0150	1.2	17 F	0103	1.0
	0527	1.7		0655	1.9
	1421	1.0		1343	0.8
	2021	1.7		1941	1.8
3 F	0241	1.1	18 SA	0211	0.9
	0613	1.8		0743	2.0
	1507	0.9		1443	0.6
	2053	1.7		2024	2.0
4 SA	0326	1.0	19 SU	0308	0.7
	0706	1.9		0829	2.2
	1549	0.8		1534	0.4
	2109	1.8		2104	2.1
5 SU	0406	0.9	20 M	0358	0.5
	0818	2.0		0912	2.3
	1626	0.7		1621	0.2
	○ 2121	1.9		● 2143	2.2
6 M	0442	0.9	21 TU	0443	0.4
	0912	2.1		0953	2.4
	1659	0.6		1704	0.1
	2153	2.0		2221	2.3
7 TU	0514	0.8	22 W	0526	0.4
	0955	2.1		1031	2.5
	1729	0.6		1746	0.1
	2230	2.0		2256	2.3
8 W	0545	0.8	23 TH	0609	0.4
	1032	2.1		1106	2.4
	1800	0.5		1827	0.2
	2306	2.0		2330	2.1
9 TH	0617	0.8	24 F	0651	0.5
	1104	2.0		1138	2.2
	1832	0.6		1908	0.4
	2341	1.9		2359	2.0
10 F	0651	0.8	25 SA	0733	0.7
	1114	1.9		1202	2.0
	1907	0.6		1950	0.7
	2359	1.8			
11 SA	0728	0.8	26 SU	0009	1.8
	1039	1.9		0817	0.9
	1946	0.7		1159	1.8
	2253	1.7		2035	1.0
12 SU	0808	0.9	27 M	0000	1.7
	1109	1.9		0907	1.1
	2029	0.8		1218	1.6
	2331	1.7		◐ 2127	1.2
13 M	0856	1.0	28 TU	0027	1.6
	1153	1.8		1015	1.3
	2121	0.9		1257	1.5
	◑			2302	1.4
14 TU	0021	1.7			
	0956	1.1			
	1247	1.7			
	2228	1.1			
15 W	0133	1.6			
	1112	1.1			
	1545	1.6			
	2346	1.1			

MARCH

Day	Time	m	Day	Time	m
1 W	0114	1.5	16 TH	0057	1.6
	1158	1.3		1040	1.1
	2045	1.8		1930	1.8
				2331	1.3
2 TH	0040	1.4	17 F	0609	1.7
	0726	1.7		1219	1.0
	1311	1.2		2007	1.8
	2201	1.8			
3 F	0141	1.3	18 SA	0100	1.1
	0749	1.7		0644	1.8
	1403	1.0		1333	0.8
	2018	1.7		1941	1.9
4 SA	0227	1.2	19 SU	0204	0.9
	0608	1.7		0730	2.0
	1448	0.9		1429	0.6
	2041	1.7		2012	2.0
5 SU	0309	1.0	20 M	0255	0.7
	0656	1.8		0813	2.1
	1527	0.7		1516	0.3
	2051	1.8		2047	2.1
6 M	0347	0.9	21 TU	0341	0.5
	0807	1.9		0853	2.3
	1603	0.6		1600	0.2
	2058	1.9		● 2122	2.3
7 TU	0420	0.8	22 W	0424	0.4
	0854	2.0		0931	2.4
	1635	0.5		1642	0.1
	○ 2127	2.1		2155	2.3
8 W	0450	0.7	23 TH	0504	0.3
	0934	2.1		1007	2.4
	1704	0.5		1721	0.2
	2202	2.1		2228	2.3
9 TH	0520	0.6	24 F	0544	0.4
	1011	2.2		1042	2.3
	1734	0.5		1800	0.3
	2237	2.1		2259	2.2
10 F	0551	0.6	25 SA	0623	0.5
	1045	2.2		1113	2.2
	1806	0.5		1839	0.6
	2310	2.1		2324	2.0
11 SA	0623	0.6	26 SU	0702	0.7
	1115	2.1		1138	2.0
	1838	0.5		1919	0.8
	2339	1.9		2314	1.9
12 SU	0657	0.7	27 M	0742	0.9
	1025	1.9		1124	1.8
	1915	0.7		2000	1.1
	2230	1.9		2317	1.8
13 M	0735	0.8	28 TU	0825	1.1
	1047	1.9		1141	1.6
	1956	0.8		2047	1.3
	2305	1.8		2346	1.7
14 TU	0819	0.9	29 W	0917	1.2
	1129	1.8		1219	1.5
	2044	1.0		2155	1.5
	2353	1.8		◐	
15 W	0914	1.0	30 TH	0026	1.6
	1222	1.6		1122	1.3
	2149	1.2		1840	1.8
	◑				
			31 F	0021	1.5
				0637	1.7
				1241	1.2
				1926	1.8

APRIL

Day	Time	m	Day	Time	m
1 SA	0117	1.3	16 SU	0047	1.1
	0711	1.6		0618	1.8
	1333	1.1		1311	0.8
	1951	1.8		1918	1.9
2 SU	0201	1.2	17 M	0144	0.9
	0721	1.6		0705	1.9
	1417	0.9		1404	0.6
	2005	1.8		1949	2.0
3 M	0241	1.0	18 TU	0233	0.7
	0648	1.7		0749	2.1
	1456	0.8		1451	0.4
	2002	1.9		2022	2.1
4 TU	0317	0.9	19 W	0318	0.6
	0742	1.9		0829	2.2
	1531	0.7		1535	0.3
	2023	2.0		2054	2.2
5 W	0350	0.8	20 TH	0400	0.4
	0828	2.0		0906	2.3
	1603	0.5		1617	0.3
	2056	2.1		● 2126	2.3
6 TH	0421	0.6	21 F	0440	0.4
	0908	2.2		0942	2.3
	1635	0.5		1656	0.4
	○ 2131	2.2		2157	2.3
7 F	0452	0.6	22 SA	0519	0.5
	0946	2.2		1016	2.2
	1706	0.5		1735	0.6
	2206	2.2		2226	2.2
8 SA	0524	0.5	23 SU	0557	0.6
	1022	2.2		1049	2.1
	1739	0.5		1814	0.8
	2240	2.2		2250	2.1
9 SU	0558	0.5	24 M	0636	0.7
	1057	2.1		1120	1.9
	1813	0.6		1853	1.0
	2312	2.1		2236	1.9
10 M	0633	0.6	25 TU	0715	0.9
	1132	2.0		1059	1.7
	1851	0.8		1935	1.2
	2222	2.0		2249	1.8
11 TU	0712	0.7	26 W	0757	1.0
	1038	1.9		1118	1.6
	1934	1.0		2023	1.4
	2253	1.9		2322	1.7
12 W	0758	0.9	27 TH	0845	1.2
	1121	1.7		1158	1.5
	2026	1.2		2124	1.5
	2344	1.8		◐	
13 TH	0857	1.0	28 F	0005	1.6
	1235	1.6		0947	1.2
	2148	1.3		1810	1.9
	◑			2334	1.5
14 F	0252	1.7	29 SA	0605	1.6
	1036	1.1		1147	1.2
	1912	1.9		1913	1.8
	2334	1.3			
15 SA	0535	1.8	30 SU	0035	1.4
	1205	1.0		0624	1.6
	2004	1.9		1247	1.1
				1932	1.8

Chart Datum: 1·40 metres below Ordnance Datum (Newlyn)
HAT is 2·6 metres above Chart Datum

TIME ZONE (UT)
For Summer Time add ONE hour in **non-shaded areas**

POOLE HARBOUR

LAT 50°43'N LONG 1°59'W

TIMES AND HEIGHTS OF HIGH AND LOW WATERS

Dates in amber are **SPRINGS**
Dates in grey are **NEAPS**

2023

MAY

Date	Day	Time	m
1	M	0121 0558 1333 1906	1.3 1.6 1.0 1.8
2	TU	0200 0631 1412 1918	1.1 1.7 0.9 1.9
3	W	0236 0715 1449 1947	1.0 1.9 0.8 2.1
4	TH	0312 0759 1526 2021	0.8 2.0 0.6 2.2
5	F	0347 0841 1602 ○ 2058	0.7 2.1 0.6 2.3
6	SA	0423 0921 1639 2134	0.6 2.2 0.6 2.3
7	SU	0459 1001 1716 2212	0.5 2.2 0.6 2.3
8	M	0537 1042 1755 2250	0.5 2.2 0.7 2.2
9	TU	0617 1124 1839 2327	0.6 2.0 0.9 2.1
10	W	0702 1213 1929	0.7 1.9 1.1
11	TH	0007 0756 1315 2035	2.0 0.9 1.8 1.2
12	F	0112 0905 1816 ◑ 2158	1.9 1.0 2.0 1.3
13	SA	0222 1026 1916 2314	1.8 1.0 2.0 1.2
14	SU	0324 1137 2020	1.8 0.9 2.0
15	M	0018 0548 1239 1852	1.1 1.8 0.8 1.9
16	TU	0114 0639 1333 1923	1.0 1.9 0.7 2.0
17	W	0205 0725 1423 1956	0.8 2.0 0.6 2.1
18	TH	0251 0805 1508 2027	0.7 2.1 0.6 2.2
19	F	0335 0842 1552 ● 2055	0.6 2.1 0.6 2.2
20	SA	0417 0918 1633 2124	0.6 2.1 0.7 2.2
21	SU	0457 0953 1713 2155	0.6 2.1 0.8 2.2
22	M	0536 1030 1753 2224	0.7 2.0 1.0 2.1
23	TU	0615 1109 1834 2218	0.8 1.9 1.1 2.0
24	W	0654 1200 1916 2233	0.9 1.8 1.3 1.9
25	TH	0735 1105 2003 2306	1.0 1.7 1.4 1.8
26	F	0820 1141 2054 2347	1.1 1.6 1.4 1.7
27	SA	0910 1230 2152 ◐	1.1 1.5 1.4
28	SU	0036 1008 1907 2258	1.6 1.1 1.9 1.4
29	M	0140 1113 2017	1.6 1.1 1.9
30	TU	0004 0312 1218 1828	1.3 1.6 1.1 1.8
31	W	0059 0442 1314 1847	1.2 1.7 1.0 1.9

JUNE

Date	Day	Time	m
1	TH	0146 0649 1402 1914	1.0 1.8 0.9 2.0
2	F	0230 0732 1447 1946	0.9 1.9 0.8 2.1
3	SA	0314 0817 1531 2026	0.7 2.1 0.7 2.2
4	SU	0357 0902 1615 ○ 2111	0.6 2.1 0.7 2.3
5	M	0439 0948 1659 2156	0.5 2.2 0.7 2.3
6	TU	0523 1034 1745 2242	0.5 2.2 0.8 2.3
7	W	0610 1121 1835 2328	0.6 2.1 0.9 2.2
8	TH	0700 1210 1931	0.6 2.0 1.0
9	F	0013 0755 1301 2033	2.1 0.7 1.9 1.1
10	SA	0100 0855 1356 ◑ 2138	2.0 0.8 1.8 1.1
11	SU	0147 0959 1906 2242	1.9 0.8 2.1 1.1
12	M	0235 1103 2001 2344	1.8 0.9 2.1 1.1
13	TU	0327 1205 2100	1.8 0.9 2.0
14	W	0042 0423 1302 1905	1.0 1.8 0.9 1.9
15	TH	0137 0710 1356 1938	1.0 1.8 0.9 2.0
16	F	0227 0752 1445 2008	0.9 1.9 0.9 2.0
17	SA	0314 0829 1532 2029	0.8 1.9 0.9 2.1
18	SU	0359 0903 1617 ● 2052	0.7 2.0 0.9 2.1
19	M	0441 0937 1659 2130	0.7 2.0 1.0 2.2
20	TU	0521 1016 1739 2210	0.7 2.0 1.1 2.1
21	W	0559 1058 1818 2247	0.8 1.9 1.1 2.0
22	TH	0635 1146 1857 2229	0.8 1.9 1.2 1.9
23	F	0712 1246 1937 2252	0.9 1.8 1.2 1.9
24	SA	0752 1127 2020 2326	0.9 1.7 1.2 1.8
25	SU	0836 1202 2108	1.0 1.6 1.3
26	M	0006 0926 1250 ◐ 2202	1.7 1.0 1.6 1.3
27	TU	0056 1022 1410 2300	1.7 1.1 1.6 1.2
28	W	0200 1122 1812	1.7 1.1 1.8
29	TH	0000 0324 1222 1824	1.2 1.7 1.0 1.9
30	F	0059 0445 1320 1848	1.1 1.8 1.0 2.0

JULY

Date	Day	Time	m
1	SA	0154 0558 1415 1917	0.9 1.8 0.9 2.1
2	SU	0246 0805 1507 2011	0.8 2.0 0.8 2.2
3	M	0336 0855 1558 ○ 2103	0.6 2.1 0.7 2.3
4	TU	0425 0944 1647 2153	0.5 2.2 0.7 2.4
5	W	0513 1030 1737 2238	0.4 2.2 0.7 2.4
6	TH	0601 1114 1827 2322	0.4 2.2 0.8 2.4
7	F	0649 1157 1918	0.4 2.1 0.8
8	SA	0002 0739 1238 2011	2.3 0.5 2.0 0.9
9	SU	0040 0831 1318 2107	2.1 0.6 1.9 1.0
10	M	0114 0926 1354 ◑ 2207	2.0 0.8 1.8 1.1
11	TU	0148 1028 1431 2311	1.8 0.9 1.7 1.2
12	W	0236 1133 1522	1.7 1.1 1.7
13	TH	0013 0336 1236 2128	1.1 1.7 1.1 2.0
14	F	0114 0442 1336 1935	1.1 1.6 1.1 1.9
15	SA	0209 0755 1431 2005	1.0 1.8 1.1 1.9
16	SU	0300 0834 1520 2022	0.9 1.8 1.1 2.0
17	M	0347 0906 1606 ● 2026	0.8 1.9 1.0 2.1
18	TU	0429 0932 1648 2113	0.7 2.0 1.0 2.1
19	W	0507 1003 1726 2158	0.7 2.0 1.0 2.2
20	TH	0542 1040 1800 2238	0.7 2.0 1.0 2.1
21	F	0614 1118 1832 2312	0.7 2.0 1.0 2.0
22	SA	0646 1157 1906 2252	0.7 1.9 1.0 1.9
23	SU	0721 1231 1945 2304	0.8 1.8 1.1 1.9
24	M	0800 1134 2028 2330	0.8 1.8 1.1 1.8
25	TU	0845 1200 2117 ◐	0.9 1.7 1.2
26	W	0008 0938 1245 2215	1.8 1.0 1.7 1.2
27	TH	0102 1039 1401 2319	1.7 1.1 1.7 1.2
28	F	0217 1143 1609	1.7 1.1 1.8
29	SA	0023 0420 1248 1835	1.1 1.7 1.1 1.9
30	SU	0127 0713 1352 1916	1.0 1.8 1.0 2.0
31	M	0227 0805 1452 2009	0.8 1.9 0.9 2.2

AUGUST

Date	Day	Time	m
1	TU	0322 0853 1546 ○ 2100	0.6 2.1 0.8 2.4
2	W	0412 0938 1636 2145	0.4 2.2 0.6 2.5
3	TH	0459 1019 1723 2227	0.2 2.3 0.6 2.5
4	F	0545 1059 1809 2307	0.2 2.3 0.6 2.5
5	SA	0629 1137 1855 2345	0.3 2.3 0.7 2.4
6	SU	0714 1213 1941	0.4 2.1 0.8
7	M	0018 0800 1243 2032	2.2 0.6 2.0 1.0
8	TU	0043 0850 1302 ◑ 2129	2.0 0.9 1.8 1.1
9	W	0106 0949 1332 2238	1.8 1.1 1.7 1.2
10	TH	0152 1103 1432 2351	1.7 1.3 1.7 1.2
11	F	0303 1219 1554	1.6 1.3 1.7
12	SA	0059 0956 1327 1938	1.2 1.9 1.3 1.9
13	SU	0158 0806 1423 2005	1.1 1.8 1.2 1.9
14	M	0248 0839 1510 1854	0.9 1.8 1.1 1.9
15	TU	0332 0906 1553 2004	0.8 1.9 1.0 2.0
16	W	0412 0921 1631 ● 2054	0.7 2.0 1.0 2.2
17	TH	0448 0941 1705 2138	0.6 2.1 0.9 2.2
18	F	0519 1013 1735 2217	0.6 2.1 0.9 2.2
19	SA	0548 1048 1804 2252	0.6 2.1 0.9 2.2
20	SU	0616 1122 1834 2318	0.6 2.1 0.9 2.1
21	M	0648 1149 1909 2246	0.7 2.0 0.9 2.0
22	TU	0724 1102 1947 2251	0.8 1.9 1.0 1.9
23	W	0804 1113 2032 2328	0.9 1.9 1.1 1.9
24	TH	0852 1155 2128 ◐	1.0 1.8 1.2
25	F	0017 0954 1252 2241	1.8 1.2 1.8 1.2
26	SA	0125 1110 1800 2358	1.6 1.3 1.8 1.2
27	SU	0842 1229 1827	1.8 1.2 1.9
28	M	0112 0721 1342 1912	1.0 1.8 1.1 2.1
29	TU	0216 0803 1443 2002	0.8 2.0 0.9 2.2
30	W	0309 0844 1534 2048	0.5 2.2 0.7 2.4
31	TH	0357 0923 1620 ○ 2129	0.3 2.3 0.5 2.6

Chart Datum: 1·40 metres below Ordnance Datum (Newlyn)
HAT is 2·6 metres above Chart Datum

TIME ZONE (UT)
For Summer Time add ONE hour in **non-shaded areas**

POOLE HARBOUR

LAT 50°43′N LONG 1°59′W

TIMES AND HEIGHTS OF HIGH AND LOW WATERS

Dates in amber are **SPRINGS**
Dates in grey are **NEAPS**

2023

SEPTEMBER

Date	Time	m	Date	Time	m
1	0440	0.1	16	0450	0.6
	1001	2.4		0941	2.2
F	1703	0.4	SA	1705	0.8
	2209	2.6		2151	2.3
2	0522	0.1	17	0518	0.6
	1037	2.4		1016	2.3
SA	1746	0.5	SU	1733	0.8
	2247	2.6		2226	2.3
3	0604	0.2	18	0546	0.6
	1112	2.4		1049	2.2
SU	1828	0.6	M	1803	0.8
	2323	2.4		2258	2.2
4	0645	0.4	19	0617	0.7
	1144	2.2		1117	2.1
M	1910	0.7	TU	1835	0.8
	2354	2.2		2318	2.0
5	0728	0.7	20	0650	0.8
	1208	2.0		1023	2.0
TU	1956	1.0	W	1911	0.9
				2220	2.0
6	0014	2.0	21	0728	0.9
	0814	1.0		1040	2.0
W	1209	1.9	TH	1953	1.0
◑	2050	1.2		2257	1.9
7	0024	1.8	22	0813	1.1
	0910	1.3		1122	1.9
TH	1232	1.7	F	2044	1.2
	2204	1.3	◐	2347	1.7
8	0104	1.6	23	0910	1.3
	1041	1.5		1219	1.8
F	1323	1.6	SA	2207	1.2
	2335	1.3			
9	0822	1.9	24	0102	1.6
	1212	1.5		1052	1.4
SA	1845	1.9	SU	1749	1.9
				2346	1.2
10	0045	1.2	25	0749	1.9
	0940	2.0		1227	1.3
SU	1317	1.4	M	1814	1.9
	1911	1.8			
11	0140	1.1	26	0102	1.0
	0748	1.8		0714	1.9
M	1407	1.3	TU	1335	1.1
	1940	1.8		1858	2.1
12	0226	0.9	27	0200	0.7
	0817	1.8		0747	2.0
TU	1450	1.1	W	1428	0.9
	1846	1.9		1944	2.2
13	0308	0.8	28	0249	0.5
	0837	1.9		0824	2.2
W	1530	1.0	TH	1515	0.7
	1940	2.0		2028	2.4
14	0347	0.7	29	0334	0.3
	0844	2.0		0900	2.4
TH	1606	0.9	F	1559	0.5
	2029	2.2	○	2108	2.5
15	0421	0.6	30	0416	0.2
	0907	2.2		0936	2.4
F	1638	0.8	SA	1639	0.4
●	2112	2.3		2147	2.6

OCTOBER

Date	Time	m	Date	Time	m
1	0457	0.2	16	0447	0.6
	1010	2.5		0941	2.3
SU	1720	0.4	M	1704	0.7
	2223	2.5		2200	2.3
2	0537	0.3	17	0518	0.7
	1043	2.4		1014	2.3
M	1800	0.6	TU	1736	0.7
	2259	2.4		2235	2.2
3	0617	0.6	18	0551	0.7
	1113	2.2		1044	2.2
TU	1841	0.7	W	1809	0.8
	2332	2.1		2308	2.1
4	0659	0.9	19	0626	0.9
	1128	2.0		1104	2.1
W	1924	1.0	TH	1846	0.9
	2353	1.9		2203	1.9
5	0743	1.2	20	0706	1.0
	1121	1.9		1023	2.0
TH	2013	1.2	F	1929	1.0
	2343	1.7		2243	1.8
6	0836	1.4	21	0753	1.2
	1145	1.8		1108	1.9
F	2123	1.3	SA	2024	1.1
◑				2338	1.7
7	0018	1.6	22	0858	1.4
	1025	1.6		1218	1.8
SA	1226	1.7	SU	2158	1.2
	2310	1.3	◐		
8	0801	1.9	23	0641	1.9
	1153	1.5		1056	1.4
SU	1800	1.8	M	1717	1.9
				2333	1.1
9	0017	1.2	24	0739	1.9
	0639	1.9		1215	1.3
M	1251	1.4	TU	1751	1.9
	1831	1.8			
10	0110	1.1	25	0040	0.9
	0711	1.9		0650	2.0
TU	1339	1.3	W	1314	1.1
	1851	1.8		1836	2.0
11	0155	1.0	26	0134	0.7
	0736	1.9		0722	2.1
W	1421	1.1	TH	1404	0.9
	1836	1.9		1921	2.2
12	0236	0.8	27	0223	0.5
	0744	2.0		0758	2.2
TH	1459	1.0	F	1450	0.7
	1917	2.0		2004	2.3
13	0314	0.7	28	0308	0.4
	0758	2.1		0833	2.3
F	1534	0.9	SA	1534	0.5
	2002	2.1	○	2044	2.4
14	0347	0.7	29	0351	0.4
	0831	2.2		0908	2.4
SA	1605	0.8	SU	1615	0.5
●	2044	2.2		2123	2.4
15	0417	0.6	30	0431	0.4
	0906	2.3		0941	2.4
SU	1634	0.7	M	1655	0.5
	2123	2.3		2200	2.4
			31	0512	0.6
				1013	2.3
			TU	1735	0.6
				2237	2.2

NOVEMBER

Date	Time	m	Date	Time	m
1	0553	0.8	16	0532	0.8
	1041	2.2		1018	2.2
W	1816	0.8	TH	1754	0.7
	2313	2.0		2300	2.1
2	0635	1.0	17	0613	0.9
	1046	2.0		1055	2.1
TH	1859	0.9	F	1836	0.8
	2353	1.8		2350	1.9
3	0720	1.3	18	0659	1.1
	1046	1.9		1132	2.0
F	1945	1.1	SA	1925	0.9
	2315	1.7			
4	0813	1.4	19	0052	1.8
	1115	1.8		0756	1.2
SA	2041	1.2	SU	1240	1.9
	2350	1.6		2027	1.0
5	0935	1.5	20	0547	2.0
	1156	1.7		0912	1.3
SU	2214	1.3	M	1353	1.9
◑			◐	2147	1.0
6	0053	1.5	21	0644	2.0
	1112	1.5		1036	1.3
M	1732	1.8	TU	1500	1.8
	2334	1.2		2304	1.0
7	0617	1.9	22	0746	2.0
	1213	1.4		1145	1.2
TU	1801	1.7	W	1725	1.9
8	0029	1.1	23	0007	0.8
	0644	1.9		0630	2.0
W	1301	1.3	TH	1244	1.1
	1808	1.7		1815	1.9
9	0116	1.1	24	0104	0.7
	0656	1.9		0700	2.0
TH	1343	1.2	F	1336	0.9
	1824	1.8		1901	2.0
10	0156	1.0	25	0154	0.6
	0703	2.0		0736	2.1
F	1421	1.0	SA	1425	0.8
	1858	1.9		1945	2.1
11	0232	0.9	26	0241	0.6
	0725	2.1		0811	2.2
SA	1455	0.9	SU	1510	0.6
	1937	2.0		2025	2.2
12	0307	0.8	27	0327	0.6
	0755	2.2		0843	2.2
SU	1529	0.8	M	1554	0.6
	2017	2.1	○	2103	2.2
13	0342	0.7	28	0410	0.7
	0829	2.3		0915	2.3
M	1604	0.7	TU	1636	0.6
●	2057	2.2		2141	2.2
14	0418	0.7	29	0453	0.8
	0904	2.3		0946	2.2
TU	1639	0.6	W	1717	0.6
	2136	2.2		2219	2.1
15	0454	0.7	30	0535	0.9
	0942	2.3		1017	2.2
W	1715	0.6	TH	1758	0.7
	2217	2.2		2300	2.0

DECEMBER

Date	Time	m	Date	Time	m
1	0618	1.1	16	0609	0.9
	1037	2.0		1101	2.2
F	1840	0.9	SA	1833	0.6
	2349	1.8		2347	2.0
2	0702	1.2	17	0659	1.0
	1029	1.9		1149	2.1
SA	1922	1.0	SU	1923	0.7
3	0441	2.0	18	0037	1.9
	0749	1.3		0754	1.1
SU	1054	1.8	M	1235	2.0
	2007	1.1		2019	0.7
4	0000	1.6	19	0131	1.8
	0838	1.4		0855	1.1
M	1132	1.8	TU	1323	1.9
	2055	1.1	◐	2120	0.8
5	0012	1.5	20	0633	2.0
	0933	1.4		1002	1.2
TU	1216	1.7	W	1413	1.9
◑	2150	1.2		2227	0.9
6	0637	1.9	21	0726	2.0
	1041	1.4		1109	1.2
W	1313	1.6	TH	1506	1.8
	2257	1.2		2333	0.9
7	0736	1.9	22	0823	2.0
	1155	1.4		1212	1.1
TH	1439	1.6	F	1610	1.7
8	0004	1.1	23	0033	0.9
	0906	1.9		0650	1.9
F	1246	1.3	SA	1310	1.0
	1814	1.7		1852	1.8
9	0057	1.1	24	0129	0.9
	0641	1.9		0724	2.0
SA	1330	1.1	SU	1403	0.9
	1842	1.8		1936	1.9
10	0143	1.0	25	0221	0.8
	0701	2.0		0758	2.0
SU	1413	1.0	M	1452	0.8
	1916	1.9		2017	1.9
11	0227	0.9	26	0310	0.8
	0717	2.1		0830	2.1
M	1455	0.8	TU	1539	0.7
	1954	2.0		2055	2.0
12	0311	0.8	27	0357	0.9
	0741	2.2		0858	2.1
TU	1537	0.7	W	1623	0.6
●	2038	2.1	○	2131	2.0
13	0354	0.7	28	0441	0.9
	0831	2.2		0928	2.1
W	1619	0.6	TH	1705	0.6
	2124	2.1		2207	2.0
14	0437	0.7	29	0523	0.9
	0924	2.3		1003	2.1
TH	1702	0.6	F	1745	0.7
	2211	2.1		2246	2.0
15	0522	0.8	30	0604	1.0
	1014	2.3		1040	2.1
F	1746	0.6	SA	1823	0.7
	2258	2.1		2328	1.9
			31	0642	1.1
				1113	2.0
			SU	1858	0.8

Chart Datum: 1·40 metres below Ordnance Datum (Newlyn)
HAT is 2·6 metres above Chart Datum

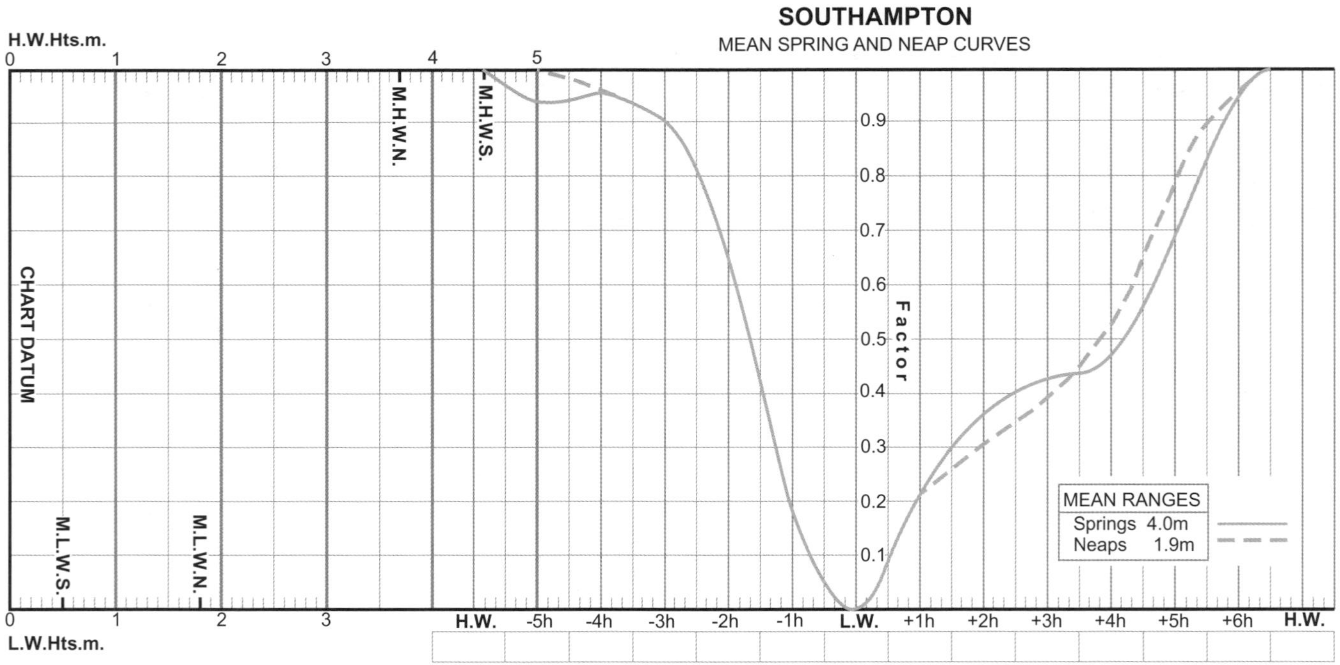

Note - Double HWs occur at Southampton. The predictions are for the first HW.

TIME ZONE (UT)
For Summer Time add ONE hour in **non-shaded areas**

SOUTHAMPTON

LAT 50°53'N LONG 1°24'W

TIMES AND HEIGHTS OF HIGH AND LOW WATERS

Dates in amber are **SPRINGS**
Dates in grey are **NEAPS**

2023

JANUARY

Date	Day	Time	m	Time	m	Time	m	Time	m
1	SU	0541	4.0	1159	1.8	1806	3.7		
2	M	0025	1.8	0637	3.9	1303	1.8	1906	3.7
3	TU	0125	1.7	0733	4.0	1359	1.6	2004	3.8
4	W	0218	1.7	0826	4.0	1449	1.5	2054	3.9
5	TH	0308	1.5	0917	4.1	1535	1.3	2147	4.0
6	F	0354	1.4	1002	4.2	1619	1.2	○ 2231	4.1
7	SA	0438	1.4	1046	4.2	1701	1.1	2311	4.2
8	SU	0520	1.3	1125	4.3	1740	1.1	2350	4.2
9	M	0557	1.4	1157	4.2	1814	1.2		
10	TU	0024	4.2	0628	1.4	1230	4.2	1841	1.2
11	W	0138	4.3	0654	1.4	1304	4.1	1908	1.2
12	TH	0128	4.2	0726	1.5	1338	4.1	1942	1.3
13	F	0238	4.2	0803	1.5	1419	4.0	2022	1.3
14	SA	0251	4.1	0849	1.6	1506	3.9	2110	1.5
15	SU	0341	4.0	0943	1.7	1600	3.8	◑ 2208	1.6
16	M	0433	3.9	1048	1.8	1657	3.7	2318	1.8
17	TU	0532	3.9	1200	1.8	1801	3.7		
18	W	0031	1.7	0638	3.9	1311	1.6	1914	3.8
19	TH	0141	1.6	0751	4.1	1417	1.4	2031	4.1
20	F	0243	1.4	0858	4.3	1514	1.0	2131	4.3
21	SA	0339	1.1	0950	4.5	1607	0.7	● 2249	4.5
22	SU	0430	0.8	1038	4.6	1656	0.5	2332	4.6
23	M	0518	0.7	1147	4.7	1741	0.3		
24	TU	0018	4.7	0604	0.6	1232	4.7	1826	0.3
25	W	0105	4.6	0648	0.6	1319	4.6	1910	0.4
26	TH	0157	4.5	0732	0.8	1409	4.4	1954	0.7
27	F	0218	4.3	0817	1.0	1508	4.2	2040	1.0
28	SA	0309	4.2	0906	1.3	1525	3.9	◐ 2131	1.4
29	SU	0404	4.0	1003	1.7	1623	3.7	2231	1.7
30	M	0501	3.9	1111	1.9	1726	3.6	2344	2.0
31	TU	0556	3.7	1231	2.0	1831	3.5		

FEBRUARY

Date	Day	Time	m	Time	m	Time	m	Time	m
1	W	0100	2.0	0700	3.7	1340	1.9	1935	3.5
2	TH	0204	1.9	0800	3.7	1436	1.7	2041	3.7
3	F	0256	1.7	0859	3.9	1522	1.4	2134	3.9
4	SA	0342	1.5	0947	4.0	1605	1.2	2220	4.1
5	SU	0424	1.3	1030	4.2	1645	1.0	○ 2257	4.2
6	M	0503	1.2	1110	4.2	1722	0.9	2333	4.2
7	TU	0539	1.1	1142	4.2	1755	0.9		
8	W	0002	4.2	0608	1.1	1210	4.2	1822	0.9
9	TH	0034	4.3	0633	1.1	1242	4.3	1847	0.9
10	F	0130	4.4	0702	1.0	1315	4.3	1917	0.9
11	SA	0204	4.4	0735	1.0	1354	4.2	1952	0.9
12	SU	0220	4.2	0816	1.1	1437	4.1	2035	1.1
13	M	0307	4.1	0902	1.3	1524	4.0	◑ 2125	1.4
14	TU	0356	4.0	0959	1.6	1618	3.7	2228	1.7
15	W	0452	3.8	1116	1.8	1817	3.7	2357	1.9
16	TH	0601	3.7	1255	1.8	1850	3.6		
17	F	0139	1.8	0737	3.9	1417	1.5	2025	4.0
18	SA	0245	1.5	0848	4.2	1512	1.0	2121	4.2
19	SU	0336	1.1	0940	4.4	1600	0.6	2241	4.5
20	M	0422	0.7	1029	4.6	1644	0.3	● 2319	4.6
21	TU	0505	0.4	1131	4.7	1727	0.1		
22	W	0001	4.7	0547	0.3	1213	4.7	1808	0.1
23	TH	0044	4.6	0628	0.4	1257	4.6	1847	0.3
24	F	0131	4.5	0708	0.5	1344	4.4	1927	0.5
25	SA	0228	4.4	0747	0.8	1438	4.3	2007	0.9
26	SU	0232	4.1	0830	1.2	1447	3.9	2052	1.4
27	M	0314	3.9	0918	1.6	1535	3.7	◐ 2146	1.8
28	TU	0404	3.6	1021	1.9	1628	3.4	2303	2.1

MARCH

Date	Day	Time	m	Time	m	Time	m	Time	m
1	W	0503	3.4	1157	2.1	1754	3.4		
2	TH	0043	2.2	0621	3.4	1324	2.0	1911	3.4
3	F	0154	2.1	0732	3.5	1419	1.8	2014	3.6
4	SA	0243	1.8	0834	3.7	1503	1.5	2109	3.9
5	SU	0324	1.5	0925	3.9	1543	1.2	2156	4.1
6	M	0403	1.2	1008	4.1	1620	0.9	2232	4.2
7	TU	0439	1.0	1042	4.2	1656	0.8	○ 2308	4.3
8	W	0512	0.9	1119	4.3	1728	0.7	2337	4.3
9	TH	0542	0.8	1147	4.3	1756	0.7		
10	F	0007	4.4	0608	0.8	1240	4.4	1821	0.7
11	SA	0101	4.5	0636	0.7	1313	4.5	1852	0.7
12	SU	0135	4.5	0709	0.7	1352	4.4	1926	0.8
13	M	0155	4.4	0747	0.9	1411	4.2	2006	1.0
14	TU	0236	4.2	0831	1.2	1457	4.0	2053	1.4
15	W	0321	3.9	0924	1.6	1551	3.7	◑ 2154	1.9
16	TH	0412	3.6	1048	1.9	1657	3.5		
17	F	0011	2.1	0537	3.5	1311	1.8	1850	3.6
18	SA	0150	1.8	0728	3.8	1413	1.4	2018	4.0
19	SU	0239	1.4	0834	4.1	1500	1.0	2109	4.3
20	M	0324	1.0	0925	4.3	1544	0.6	2226	4.6
21	TU	0406	0.6	1031	4.6	1626	0.3	● 2302	4.7
22	W	0446	0.3	1111	4.6	1705	0.1	2341	4.7
23	TH	0525	0.2	1152	4.6	1744	0.2		
24	F	0022	4.6	0604	0.3	1235	4.5	1822	0.3
25	SA	0104	4.5	0642	0.5	1318	4.4	1859	0.6
26	SU	0150	4.4	0718	0.8	1410	4.2	1937	1.0
27	M	0151	4.1	0755	1.2	1408	3.9	2016	1.5
28	TU	0224	3.8	0837	1.5	1444	3.6	2106	1.9
29	W	0300	3.5	0935	1.9	1522	3.3	◐ 2227	2.2
30	TH	0440	3.4	1113	2.1	1730	3.4		
31	F	0016	2.3	0635	3.4	1246	2.1	1936	3.5

APRIL

Date	Day	Time	m	Time	m	Time	m	Time	m
1	SA	0126	2.2	0747	3.5	1345	1.9	1942	3.6
2	SU	0215	1.9	0802	3.6	1431	1.6	2035	3.8
3	M	0256	1.5	0853	3.8	1511	1.2	2124	4.1
4	TU	0333	1.2	0937	4.1	1548	0.9	2202	4.3
5	W	0408	1.0	1016	4.2	1623	0.8	2233	4.3
6	TH	0440	0.8	1048	4.3	1656	0.7	○ 2308	4.4
7	F	0510	0.7	1118	4.4	1725	0.6	2336	4.4
8	SA	0540	0.6	1214	4.5	1755	0.6		
9	SU	0033	4.6	0611	0.6	1251	4.5	1828	0.7
10	M	0050	4.5	0647	0.7	1331	4.5	1904	0.8
11	TU	0126	4.3	0726	0.9	1352	4.2	1946	1.1
12	W	0209	4.1	0810	1.2	1440	4.0	2035	1.6
13	TH	0257	3.8	0908	1.6	1539	3.7	◑ 2151	2.0
14	F	0359	3.5	1105	1.9	1705	3.6		
15	SA	0022	2.0	0540	3.5	1250	1.7	1845	3.8
16	SU	0127	1.7	0710	3.8	1348	1.4	1959	4.1
17	M	0216	1.4	0811	4.0	1435	1.0	2050	4.3
18	TU	0300	1.0	0900	4.2	1518	0.7	2133	4.5
19	W	0341	0.7	1012	4.4	1559	0.4	2242	4.6
20	TH	0422	0.5	1051	4.5	1640	0.4	● 2320	4.6
21	F	0501	0.4	1132	4.4	1719	0.4	2359	4.5
22	SA	0539	0.5	1215	4.4	1756	0.6		
23	SU	0038	4.4	0616	0.7	1259	4.3	1833	0.9
24	M	0117	4.3	0652	0.9	1301	4.1	1911	1.2
25	TU	0200	4.2	0727	1.2	1338	3.9	1949	1.6
26	W	0153	3.8	0806	1.5	1422	3.7	2036	1.9
27	TH	0228	3.6	0900	1.8	1506	3.5	◐ 2153	2.2
28	F	0301	3.2	1025	2.1	1611	3.4	2325	2.3
29	SA	0555	3.4	1148	2.1	1742	3.5		
30	SU	0039	2.2	0606	3.3	1254	1.9	1854	3.6

Chart Datum: 2·74 metres below Ordnance Datum (Newlyn)
HAT is 5·0 metres above Chart Datum

TIME ZONE (UT)
For Summer Time add ONE hour in **non-shaded areas**

SOUTHAMPTON

LAT 50°53′N LONG 1°24′W

TIMES AND HEIGHTS OF HIGH AND LOW WATERS

Dates in amber are **SPRINGS**
Dates in grey are **NEAPS**

2023

MAY

Date	Time	m	Date	Time	m
1 M	0134 0807 1346 1955	2.0 3.6 1.7 3.9	16 TU	0142 0741 1401 2017	1.4 4.0 1.2 4.3
2 TU	0217 0816 1430 2043	1.7 3.8 1.4 4.1	17 W	0229 0830 1448 2104	1.1 4.1 1.0 4.4
3 W	0254 0859 1508 2121	1.3 4.0 1.1 4.3	18 TH	0313 0953 1531 2224	0.9 4.3 0.8 4.5
4 TH	0329 0939 1545 2158	1.1 4.2 0.9 4.4	19 F	0356 1035 1613 ● 2302	0.7 4.3 0.8 4.5
5 F	0403 1017 1620 ○ 2235	0.8 4.3 0.8 4.5	20 SA	0436 1121 1654 2342	0.7 4.3 0.8 4.4
6 SA	0438 1050 1655 2308	0.7 4.4 0.7 4.5	21 SU	0516 1121 1734	0.8 4.2 1.0
7 SU	0514 1152 1732 2350	0.6 4.5 0.7 4.6	22 M	0020 0555 1203 1814	4.3 0.9 4.1 1.2
8 M	0552 1232 1811	0.6 4.5 0.8	23 TU	0057 0632 1240 1852	4.2 1.1 4.0 1.4
9 TU	0031 0631 1318 1852	4.5 0.7 4.5 1.0	24 W	0052 0709 1324 1931	4.0 1.3 4.0 1.6
10 W	0112 0715 1411 1940	4.3 0.9 4.3 1.3	25 TH	0132 0747 1406 2015	3.9 1.5 3.9 1.9
11 TH	0157 0806 1521 2039	4.1 1.2 4.1 1.7	26 F	0210 0833 1450 2110	3.7 1.7 3.7 2.0
12 F	0253 0917 1544 ◑ 2206	3.8 1.6 3.8 1.9	27 SA	0253 0935 1545 ◐ 2215	3.5 1.9 3.7 2.1
13 SA	0409 1047 1704 2333	3.7 1.7 3.9 1.9	28 SU	0348 1040 1640 2318	3.4 1.9 3.6 2.1
14 SU	0528 1204 1819	3.7 1.6 4.0	29 M	0453 1143 1751	3.3 1.9 3.7
15 M	0045 0637 1308 1922	1.7 3.8 1.4 4.1	30 TU	0019 0613 1241 1858	2.0 3.5 1.8 3.8
			31 W	0114 0723 1334 1953	1.8 3.7 1.6 4.0

JUNE

Date	Time	m	Date	Time	m
1 TH	0201 0816 1421 2041	1.5 3.9 1.3 4.2	16 F	0246 0943 1505 2117	1.2 4.1 1.2 4.2
2 F	0245 0858 1505 2120	1.2 4.1 1.1 4.3	17 SA	0332 1034 1551 2159	1.1 4.1 1.2 4.2
3 SA	0328 0944 1548 2206	0.9 4.3 0.9 4.5	18 SU	0417 1024 1636 ● 2241	1.0 4.0 1.2 4.2
4 SU	0410 1027 1631 ○ 2245	0.7 4.4 0.8 4.5	19 M	0500 1109 1720 2323	1.0 4.1 1.2 4.2
5 M	0454 1135 1715 2328	0.6 4.5 0.8 4.5	20 TU	0542 1152 1802 2358	1.0 4.1 1.3 4.1
6 TU	0538 1221 1800	0.6 4.5 0.9	21 W	0621 1230 1841	1.1 4.1 1.4
7 W	0018 0624 1311 1849	4.5 0.7 4.5 1.0	22 TH	0038 0657 1307 1916	4.0 1.2 4.0 1.6
8 TH	0103 0714 1407 1941	4.4 0.9 4.4 1.2	23 F	0115 0730 1345 1950	4.0 1.4 4.0 1.7
9 F	0224 0807 1516 2039	4.3 1.1 4.3 1.4	24 SA	0149 0805 1426 2029	3.8 1.5 4.0 1.8
10 SA	0253 0908 1538 ◑ 2143	4.0 1.3 4.1 1.6	25 SU	0232 0847 1507 2116	3.7 1.6 3.9 1.8
11 SU	0356 1013 1643 2250	3.9 1.4 4.1 1.6	26 M	0320 0939 1554 ◐ 2211	3.7 1.7 3.8 1.9
12 M	0459 1119 1745 2358	3.8 1.5 4.1 1.6	27 TU	0411 1038 1646 2312	3.6 1.8 3.8 1.9
13 TU	0605 1224 1847	3.8 1.5 4.1	28 W	0506 1139 1744	3.5 1.8 3.8
14 W	0101 0707 1323 1941	1.5 3.9 1.4 4.1	29 TH	0012 0612 1239 1846	1.8 3.6 1.7 3.9
15 TH	0157 0802 1416 2032	1.4 3.9 1.3 4.2	30 F	0112 0721 1338 1951	1.6 3.8 1.5 4.1

JULY

Date	Time	m	Date	Time	m
1 SA	0208 0823 1433 2051	1.3 4.0 1.3 4.2	16 SU	0317 1039 1538 2143	1.4 4.1 1.5 4.1
2 SU	0301 0918 1525 2142	1.1 4.2 1.1 4.4	17 M	0404 1016 1624 ● 2231	1.2 4.0 1.4 4.1
3 M	0352 1010 1616 ○ 2230	0.8 4.4 1.0 4.5	18 TU	0448 1101 1708 2307	1.1 4.1 1.3 4.1
4 TU	0442 1124 1706 2320	0.7 4.5 0.9 4.6	19 W	0529 1139 1749 2346	1.0 4.1 1.3 4.1
5 W	0531 1211 1754	0.5 4.6 0.8	20 TH	0607 1214 1825	1.0 4.2 1.3
6 TH	0025 0619 1259 1843	4.6 0.5 4.6 0.8	21 F	0019 0640 1248 1855	4.1 1.1 4.2 1.4
7 F	0114 0706 1351 1931	4.5 0.6 4.5 0.9	22 SA	0050 0706 1359 1920	4.0 1.2 4.2 1.4
8 SA	0205 0754 1452 2020	4.4 0.7 4.4 1.1	23 SU	0126 0733 1352 1952	4.0 1.2 4.1 1.4
9 SU	0303 0844 1516 2114	4.3 1.0 4.3 1.3	24 M	0202 0807 1434 2031	4.0 1.3 4.1 1.5
10 M	0412 0939 1613 ◑ 2212	4.1 1.2 4.2 1.5	25 TU	0245 0849 1518 ◐ 2118	3.9 1.4 4.1 1.6
11 TU	0432 1038 1711 2316	3.9 1.5 4.1 1.7	26 W	0335 0940 1604 2216	3.8 1.6 3.9 1.7
12 W	0532 1143 1808	3.8 1.6 4.0	27 TH	0425 1043 1657 2324	3.7 1.7 3.8 1.8
13 TH	0024 0633 1249 1906	1.7 3.7 1.7 3.9	28 F	0523 1154 1801	3.6 1.8 3.8
14 F	0129 0738 1351 2005	1.7 3.7 1.7 4.0	29 SA	0034 0634 1306 1911	1.8 3.6 1.8 3.9
15 SA	0227 0946 1448 2057	1.5 4.0 1.6 4.0	30 SU	0145 0756 1416 2029	1.6 3.8 1.6 4.1
			31 M	0249 0906 1517 2127	1.3 4.1 1.3 4.3

AUGUST

Date	Time	m	Date	Time	m
1 TU	0345 0959 1610 ○ 2218	0.9 4.4 1.0 4.5	16 W	0430 1041 1650 ● 2251	1.0 4.2 1.2 4.2
2 W	0435 1114 1658 2305	0.6 4.6 0.7 4.6	17 TH	0508 1117 1728 2325	0.9 4.2 1.1 4.2
3 TH	0521 1156 1744	0.4 4.7 0.6	18 F	0544 1154 1801 2356	0.9 4.3 1.1 4.2
4 F	0008 0606 1241 1828	4.7 0.3 4.7 0.5	19 SA	0615 1220 1827	1.0 4.3 1.2
5 SA	0054 0649 1329 1911	4.6 0.3 4.6 0.6	20 SU	0029 0638 1318 1849	4.2 1.0 4.4 1.2
6 SU	0142 0732 1424 1955	4.5 0.5 4.5 0.9	21 M	0058 0701 1347 1918	4.2 1.0 4.4 1.2
7 M	0236 0816 1442 2042	4.3 0.8 4.3 1.2	22 TU	0132 0733 1423 1953	4.2 1.1 4.4 1.2
8 TU	0347 0904 1536 ◑ 2134	4.2 1.2 4.1 1.5	23 W	0213 0811 1441 2036	4.1 1.2 4.2 1.4
9 W	0355 1001 1635 2238	3.8 1.6 4.0 1.8	24 TH	0301 0856 1527 ◐ 2128	4.0 1.5 4.0 1.7
10 TH	0459 1108 1731 2354	3.7 1.9 3.8 2.0	25 F	0352 0954 1616 2239	3.8 1.8 3.8 1.9
11 F	0605 1225 1831	3.6 2.1 3.7	26 SA	0531 1118 1719	3.7 2.1 3.7
12 SA	0111 0714 1338 1938	1.9 3.6 2.1 3.7	27 SU	0014 0601 1300 1848	2.0 3.5 2.1 3.7
13 SU	0215 0819 1437 2035	1.8 3.7 1.9 3.8	28 M	0145 0751 1419 2021	1.7 3.9 1.7 4.1
14 M	0305 0913 1526 2129	1.5 3.9 1.6 4.0	29 TU	0248 0900 1513 2115	1.3 4.2 1.3 4.4
15 TU	0349 1001 1609 2211	1.3 4.1 1.4 4.1	30 W	0337 0949 1600 2202	0.8 4.5 0.9 4.6
			31 TH	0422 1058 1644 ○ 2306	0.5 4.7 0.6 4.8

Chart Datum: 2·74 metres below Ordnance Datum (Newlyn)
HAT is 5·0 metres above Chart Datum

TIME ZONE (UT)
For Summer Time add ONE hour in **non-shaded areas**

SOUTHAMPTON

LAT 50°53'N LONG 1°24'W

TIMES AND HEIGHTS OF HIGH AND LOW WATERS

Dates in amber are **SPRINGS**
Dates in grey are **NEAPS**

2023

SEPTEMBER

Date	Day	Time	m	Time	m	Time	m	Time	m
1	F	0504	0.2	1138	4.8	1726	0.4	2348	4.8
2	SA	0545	0.2	1219	4.8	1807	0.4		
3	SU	0031	4.7	0626	0.3	1305	4.7	1847	0.5
4	M	0117	4.6	0706	0.5	1356	4.6	1927	0.8
5	TU	0208	4.4	0746	0.9	1409	4.3	2010	1.2
6	W	0223	4.0	0831	1.3	1452	4.0	◑ 2058	1.6
7	TH	0309	3.8	0925	1.8	1547	3.8	2202	2.0
8	F	0414	3.5	1040	2.2	1652	3.6	2332	2.2
9	SA	0536	3.5	1210	2.3	1801	3.5		
10	SU	0053	2.1	0645	3.5	1323	2.2	1910	3.5
11	M	0155	1.9	0755	3.6	1419	2.0	2011	3.7
12	TU	0242	1.6	0848	3.9	1504	1.6	2200	4.0
13	W	0324	1.3	0935	4.1	1545	1.3	2145	4.1
14	TH	0403	1.0	1014	4.3	1624	1.1	2223	4.2
15	F	0440	0.9	1048	4.4	1659	1.0	● 2302	4.3
16	SA	0515	0.9	1124	4.4	1730	1.0	2332	4.3
17	SU	0543	0.9	1150	4.4	1754	1.0	2358	4.4
18	M	0606	1.0	1244	4.5	1818	1.0		
19	TU	0053	4.5	0631	1.0	1314	4.5	1847	1.0
20	W	0128	4.5	0702	1.0	1330	4.4	1923	1.1
21	TH	0209	4.4	0740	1.2	1409	4.3	2003	1.3
22	F	0232	4.1	0824	1.5	1449	4.0	◐ 2052	1.7
23	SA	0316	3.8	0918	2.0	1541	3.7	2205	2.1
24	SU	0417	3.5	1116	2.3	1649	3.5		
25	M	0033	2.1	0553	3.5	1317	2.1	1841	3.7
26	TU	0143	1.7	0746	4.0	1412	1.7	2006	4.1
27	W	0234	1.2	0846	4.4	1458	1.2	2058	4.4
28	TH	0318	0.8	0932	4.6	1541	0.8	2143	4.6
29	F	0401	0.5	1039	4.8	1623	0.5	○ 2245	4.8
30	SA	0441	0.3	1116	4.9	1702	0.4	2326	4.8

OCTOBER

Date	Day	Time	m	Time	m	Time	m	Time	m
1	SU	0521	0.3	1157	4.8	1741	0.4		
2	M	0008	4.7	0600	0.4	1238	4.7	1820	0.6
3	TU	0052	4.6	0638	0.7	1324	4.6	1859	0.9
4	W	0141	4.4	0717	1.1	1329	4.2	1938	1.3
5	TH	0147	4.0	0759	1.5	1407	4.0	2023	1.7
6	F	0227	3.7	0853	2.0	1446	3.6	◑ 2128	2.1
7	SA	0314	3.4	1019	2.3	1716	3.7	2306	2.2
8	SU	0555	3.7	1146	2.4	1811	3.6		
9	M	0019	2.2	0606	3.5	1252	2.3	1920	3.6
10	TU	0119	2.0	0715	3.6	1348	2.0	1936	3.6
11	W	0208	1.7	0811	3.9	1434	1.7	2028	3.9
12	TH	0251	1.4	0859	4.1	1514	1.4	2115	4.1
13	F	0330	1.2	0939	4.3	1551	1.2	2153	4.3
14	SA	0406	1.0	1018	4.4	1625	1.0	● 2231	4.4
15	SU	0439	0.9	1049	4.5	1654	1.0	2302	4.4
16	M	0508	0.9	1121	4.5	1721	0.9	2356	4.5
17	TU	0535	0.9	1214	4.6	1750	0.9		
18	W	0028	4.6	0605	1.0	1227	4.5	1823	1.0
19	TH	0106	4.5	0640	1.1	1301	4.4	1859	1.1
20	F	0149	4.4	0719	1.3	1341	4.3	1941	1.4
21	SA	0211	4.1	0805	1.7	1426	4.0	2032	1.8
22	SU	0302	3.8	0907	2.1	1519	3.7	◐ 2215	2.1
23	M	0418	3.7	1141	2.3	1651	3.6		
24	TU	0017	1.9	0554	3.8	1254	2.0	1827	3.8
25	W	0117	1.6	0724	4.1	1346	1.6	1938	4.1
26	TH	0207	1.3	0820	4.4	1432	1.2	2033	4.4
27	F	0251	0.9	0904	4.6	1515	0.9	2117	4.5
28	SA	0333	0.7	1019	4.8	1557	0.7	○ 2225	4.7
29	SU	0415	0.5	1054	4.8	1637	0.6	2305	4.7
30	M	0454	0.6	1134	4.7	1716	0.6	2348	4.6
31	TU	0533	0.7	1214	4.6	1755	0.8		

NOVEMBER

Date	Day	Time	m	Time	m	Time	m	Time	m
1	W	0033	4.5	0613	1.0	1256	4.5	1834	1.0
2	TH	0129	4.3	0652	1.3	1345	4.3	1912	1.3
3	F	0123	4.1	0735	1.7	1337	4.0	1956	1.7
4	SA	0206	3.8	0828	2.0	1415	3.7	2056	2.0
5	SU	0258	3.6	0947	2.3	1453	3.4	◑ 2222	2.2
6	M	0414	3.6	1109	2.4	1733	3.6	2335	2.2
7	TU	0616	3.8	1214	2.3	1834	3.6		
8	W	0034	2.1	0627	3.7	1310	2.1	1942	3.7
9	TH	0126	1.9	0728	3.9	1356	1.8	2039	3.9
10	F	0211	1.6	0819	4.1	1436	1.6	2038	4.0
11	SA	0250	1.4	0901	4.3	1512	1.3	2119	4.2
12	SU	0327	1.2	0939	4.4	1545	1.1	2158	4.4
13	M	0401	1.1	1016	4.5	1619	1.0	● 2230	4.4
14	TU	0435	1.0	1052	4.6	1653	0.9	2333	4.6
15	W	0510	1.0	1125	4.6	1729	0.9		
16	TH	0010	4.6	0547	1.0	1203	4.5	1807	0.9
17	F	0052	4.5	0627	1.2	1246	4.5	1849	1.1
18	SA	0141	4.4	0712	1.4	1330	4.3	1936	1.4
19	SU	0239	4.3	0805	1.7	1421	4.0	2036	1.7
20	M	0358	4.1	0920	2.0	1525	3.8	◐ 2206	1.8
21	TU	0419	3.9	1055	2.0	1645	3.8	2331	1.8
22	W	0536	4.0	1211	1.9	1800	3.9		
23	TH	0037	1.6	0648	4.2	1310	1.6	1907	4.0
24	F	0132	1.4	0745	4.4	1401	1.3	2001	4.2
25	SA	0220	1.2	0833	4.5	1447	1.1	2054	4.3
26	SU	0305	1.0	0916	4.5	1531	0.9	2211	4.5
27	M	0349	0.9	1038	4.6	1614	0.8	○ 2255	4.5
28	TU	0431	0.9	1119	4.6	1655	0.8	2345	4.4
29	W	0513	1.0	1200	4.5	1737	0.9	2342	4.3
30	TH	0556	1.2	1200	4.3	1817	1.1		

DECEMBER

Date	Day	Time	m	Time	m	Time	m	Time	m
1	F	0026	4.2	0638	1.4	1237	4.2	1857	1.3
2	SA	0111	4.1	0720	1.7	1318	4.0	1938	1.5
3	SU	0151	4.0	0805	1.9	1359	3.8	2024	1.8
4	M	0241	3.9	0857	2.1	1445	3.7	2121	2.0
5	TU	0329	3.8	1000	2.2	1537	3.5	◑ 2225	2.1
6	W	0425	3.7	1106	2.3	1642	3.5	2329	2.1
7	TH	0528	3.7	1208	2.2	1751	3.5		
8	F	0027	2.0	0633	3.9	1301	2.0	1858	3.7
9	SA	0118	1.8	0730	4.0	1345	1.8	1954	3.9
10	SU	0203	1.6	0823	4.2	1427	1.5	2045	4.1
11	M	0246	1.4	0906	4.3	1509	1.2	2126	4.2
12	TU	0328	1.2	0946	4.4	1551	1.0	● 2206	4.3
13	W	0410	1.1	1026	4.5	1633	0.9	2319	4.5
14	TH	0454	1.0	1109	4.6	1717	0.8		
15	F	0000	4.6	0538	1.0	1152	4.6	1802	0.8
16	SA	0046	4.6	0624	1.1	1237	4.5	1848	0.9
17	SU	0135	4.5	0712	1.2	1327	4.4	1937	1.1
18	M	0231	4.4	0805	1.4	1448	4.3	2031	1.3
19	TU	0339	4.3	0904	1.6	1519	4.1	◐ 2133	1.4
20	W	0401	4.1	1011	1.7	1620	3.9	2242	1.6
21	TH	0503	4.1	1122	1.8	1724	3.9	2352	1.6
22	F	0610	4.1	1232	1.7	1833	3.9		
23	SA	0056	1.6	0711	4.2	1331	1.5	1935	4.0
24	SU	0152	1.5	0805	4.2	1424	1.4	2030	4.0
25	M	0243	1.4	0853	4.3	1512	1.2	2212	4.2
26	TU	0331	1.3	0941	4.3	1558	1.1	2307	4.3
27	W	0417	1.2	1027	4.3	1643	1.0	○ 2255	4.2
28	TH	0502	1.2	1106	4.3	1726	1.0	2336	4.2
29	F	0546	1.3	1147	4.2	1807	1.0		
30	SA	0015	4.2	0627	1.3	1227	4.2	1845	1.2
31	SU	0053	4.1	0704	1.5	1304	4.1	1920	1.3

Chart Datum: 2·74 metres below Ordnance Datum (Newlyn)
HAT is 5·0 metres above Chart Datum

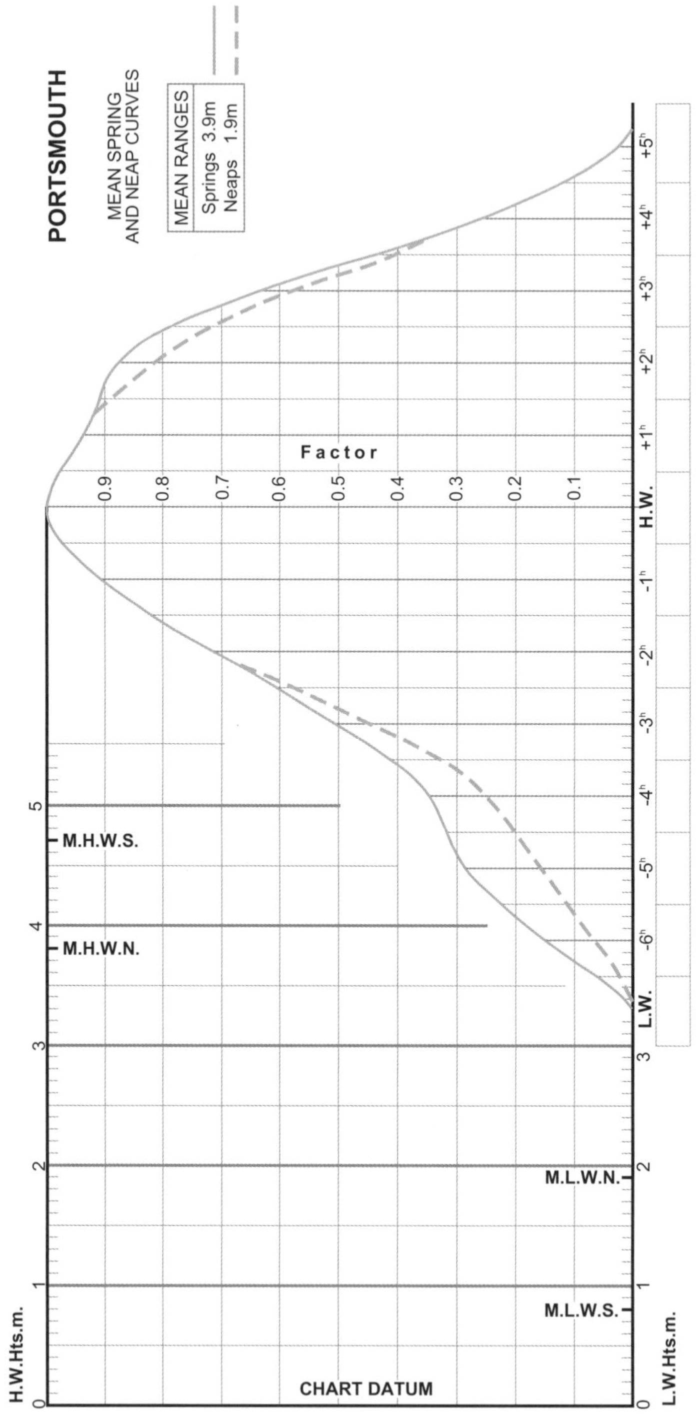
PORTSMOUTH
MEAN SPRING AND NEAP CURVES
MEAN RANGES
Springs 3.9m
Neaps 1.9m
Factor
0.9
0.8
0.7
0.6
0.5
0.4
0.3
0.2
0.1
L.W.
-6h
-5h
-4h
-3h
-2h
-1h
H.W.
+1h
+2h
+3h
+4h
+5h
H.W.Hts.m.
0
1
2
3
4
5
M.H.W.S.
M.H.W.N.
CHART DATUM
L.W.Hts.m.
M.L.W.S.
M.L.W.N.

TIME ZONE (UT)
For Summer Time add ONE hour in **non-shaded areas**

PORTSMOUTH

LAT 50°48'N LONG 1°07'W

TIMES AND HEIGHTS OF HIGH AND LOW WATERS

Dates in amber are **SPRINGS**
Dates in grey are **NEAPS**

2023

JANUARY

Day	Time	m	Time	m	Time	m	Time	m
1 SU	0655	4.3	1221	1.8	1913	4.0		
2 M	0042	1.7	0753	4.2	1320	1.7	2015	4.0
3 TU	0138	1.7	0849	4.2	1412	1.6	2116	4.1
4 W	0230	1.6	0938	4.3	1501	1.5	2210	4.2
5 TH	0318	1.6	1022	4.4	1546	1.3	2254	4.3
6 F	0404	1.5	1102	4.4	1630	1.2	○ 2335	4.4
7 SA	0447	1.4	1141	4.4	1710	1.1		
8 SU	0013	4.4	0527	1.4	1219	4.4	1747	1.1
9 M	0051	4.5	0603	1.4	1254	4.4	1819	1.1
10 TU	0126	4.4	0634	1.4	1327	4.3	1849	1.2
11 W	0200	4.4	0704	1.4	1358	4.3	1920	1.2
12 TH	0233	4.3	0736	1.4	1433	4.2	1953	1.3
13 F	0310	4.3	0813	1.5	1513	4.1	2032	1.3
14 SA	0353	4.2	0857	1.6	1600	4.0	2119	1.5
15 SU	0442	4.1	0950	1.7	1656	3.9	◑ 2215	1.6
16 M	0538	4.0	1056	1.8	1802	3.8	2326	1.7
17 TU	0642	4.0	1212	1.7	1913	3.9		
18 W	0042	1.7	0750	4.1	1322	1.6	2024	4.0
19 TH	0149	1.5	0854	4.3	1424	1.3	2129	4.2
20 F	0249	1.3	0951	4.5	1521	1.1	2225	4.5
21 SA	0345	1.1	1040	4.6	1613	0.8	● 2315	4.6
22 SU	0437	0.9	1127	4.8	1702	0.6		
23 M	0003	4.8	0525	0.8	1212	4.8	1749	0.5
24 TU	0054	4.8	0611	0.7	1300	4.8	1834	0.5
25 W	0149	4.8	0656	0.8	1351	4.7	1919	0.6
26 TH	0250	4.8	0742	0.9	1446	4.6	2004	0.8
27 F	0342	4.7	0830	1.2	1543	4.4	2053	1.1
28 SA	0427	4.5	0923	1.4	1636	4.2	◐ 2148	1.4
29 SU	0513	4.3	1026	1.7	1731	4.0	2255	1.7
30 M	0605	4.1	1138	1.8	1833	3.8		
31 TU	0005	1.9	0708	3.9	1248	1.9	1944	3.7

FEBRUARY

Day	Time	m	Time	m	Time	m	Time	m
1 W	0112	1.9	0814	3.9	1352	1.8	2055	3.8
2 TH	0215	1.9	0915	4.0	1447	1.6	2155	4.0
3 F	0309	1.7	1003	4.1	1534	1.4	2238	4.2
4 SA	0354	1.5	1045	4.2	1616	1.2	2316	4.3
5 SU	0435	1.3	1123	4.3	1654	1.0	○ 2354	4.4
6 M	0511	1.2	1200	4.4	1729	1.0		
7 TU	0029	4.5	0545	1.1	1235	4.4	1800	0.9
8 W	0103	4.5	0614	1.1	1306	4.4	1829	0.9
9 TH	0135	4.4	0642	1.1	1336	4.3	1857	0.9
10 F	0205	4.4	0711	1.1	1405	4.3	1927	0.9
11 SA	0236	4.4	0744	1.1	1439	4.3	2001	1.0
12 SU	0311	4.3	0823	1.2	1520	4.2	2042	1.1
13 M	0355	4.2	0909	1.3	1612	4.0	◑ 2132	1.4
14 TU	0451	4.0	1007	1.6	1719	3.8	2235	1.7
15 W	0601	3.9	1127	1.8	1845	3.7		
16 TH	0012	1.8	0726	3.9	1306	1.7	2015	3.9
17 F	0143	1.7	0844	4.1	1419	1.4	2124	4.1
18 SA	0248	1.4	0941	4.3	1516	1.1	2217	4.4
19 SU	0342	1.1	1029	4.6	1605	0.7	2304	4.6
20 M	0429	0.8	1113	4.7	1651	0.4	● 2350	4.8
21 TU	0513	0.6	1157	4.8	1734	0.3		
22 W	0036	4.9	0555	0.5	1242	4.8	1816	0.3
23 TH	0126	4.8	0637	0.5	1330	4.7	1856	0.4
24 F	0220	4.8	0717	0.7	1420	4.6	1936	0.7
25 SA	0305	4.7	0758	1.0	1510	4.4	2017	1.0
26 SU	0344	4.5	0841	1.3	1558	4.2	2102	1.4
27 M	0424	4.2	0932	1.6	1648	3.9	◐ 2200	1.8
28 TU	0512	3.9	1051	1.9	1752	3.7	2331	2.1

MARCH

Day	Time	m	Time	m	Time	m	Time	m
1 W	0620	3.6	1218	2.0	1914	3.5		
2 TH	0051	2.1	0744	3.6	1331	2.0	2033	3.6
3 F	0203	2.0	0852	3.7	1430	1.7	2135	3.9
4 SA	0256	1.8	0943	3.9	1515	1.5	2217	4.1
5 SU	0337	1.5	1024	4.1	1553	1.2	2253	4.3
6 M	0413	1.3	1101	4.3	1629	1.0	2328	4.4
7 TU ○	0447	1.1	1137	4.4	1702	0.9		
8 W	0002	4.5	0519	1.0	1210	4.4	1733	0.8
9 TH	0034	4.5	0548	0.9	1240	4.4	1803	0.8
10 F	0104	4.5	0616	0.8	1309	4.4	1831	0.8
11 SA	0132	4.5	0646	0.8	1338	4.4	1901	0.8
12 SU	0201	4.5	0718	0.8	1412	4.4	1935	0.9
13 M	0235	4.4	0755	1.0	1453	4.3	2014	1.1
14 TU	0318	4.2	0839	1.2	1545	4.1	2102	1.4
15 W	0417	4.0	0934	1.6	1658	3.8	◑ 2206	1.8
16 TH	0537	3.8	1104	1.8	1839	3.7		
17 F	0025	2.0	0717	3.8	1309	1.7	2010	3.9
18 SA	0148	1.7	0833	4.0	1414	1.4	2113	4.2
19 SU	0243	1.4	0927	4.3	1504	1.0	2202	4.5
20 M	0330	1.0	1012	4.5	1549	0.7	2247	4.7
21 TU	0413	0.7	1055	4.7	1632	0.4	● 2330	4.8
22 W	0454	0.5	1137	4.7	1713	0.3		
23 TH	0013	4.8	0534	0.4	1221	4.7	1753	0.4
24 F	0057	4.8	0613	0.5	1306	4.7	1831	0.5
25 SA	0141	4.7	0651	0.7	1352	4.6	1908	0.8
26 SU	0220	4.6	0727	0.9	1437	4.4	1945	1.1
27 M	0257	4.4	0804	1.2	1520	4.2	2023	1.5
28 TU	0335	4.1	0845	1.6	1604	3.9	2111	1.9
29 W	0418	3.8	0945	1.9	1700	3.7	◐ 2258	2.2
30 TH	0516	3.5	1143	2.1	1838	3.5		
31 F	0023	2.2	0707	3.4	1257	2.0	2004	3.6

APRIL

Day	Time	m	Time	m	Time	m	Time	m
1 SA	0135	2.1	0824	3.6	1357	1.8	2106	3.9
2 SU	0228	1.8	0917	3.8	1442	1.6	2148	4.1
3 M	0307	1.5	0957	4.1	1520	1.3	2224	4.3
4 TU	0341	1.3	1034	4.2	1554	1.0	2257	4.4
5 W	0414	1.1	1108	4.4	1628	0.9	2330	4.5
6 TH ○	0446	0.9	1140	4.4	1701	0.8		
7 F	0001	4.6	0518	0.8	1211	4.5	1733	0.7
8 SA	0031	4.6	0549	0.7	1242	4.5	1805	0.7
9 SU	0101	4.6	0621	0.7	1315	4.5	1838	0.8
10 M	0133	4.5	0656	0.8	1354	4.5	1914	0.9
11 TU	0212	4.4	0735	1.0	1441	4.3	1956	1.2
12 W	0300	4.2	0821	1.3	1543	4.1	2048	1.6
13 TH	0406	4.0	0922	1.6	1704	3.9	◑ 2208	2.0
14 F	0531	3.8	1130	1.8	1836	3.9		
15 SA	0024	1.9	0705	3.8	1253	1.6	1956	4.1
16 SU	0131	1.7	0815	4.0	1352	1.3	2056	4.4
17 M	0223	1.3	0907	4.3	1441	1.0	2144	4.6
18 TU	0308	1.0	0951	4.5	1526	0.8	2226	4.7
19 W	0350	0.8	1033	4.6	1607	0.6	2306	4.8
20 TH	0430	0.6	1115	4.6	1648	0.6	● 2347	4.8
21 F	0510	0.6	1159	4.6	1727	0.6		
22 SA	0026	4.7	0548	0.7	1243	4.6	1805	0.8
23 SU	0105	4.7	0625	0.8	1328	4.5	1841	1.0
24 M	0143	4.5	0700	1.0	1411	4.4	1918	1.3
25 TU	0220	4.3	0736	1.3	1452	4.2	1956	1.6
26 W	0258	4.1	0815	1.6	1535	4.0	2043	1.9
27 TH	0342	3.9	0909	1.9	1625	3.8	◐ 2215	2.2
28 F	0435	3.6	1057	2.0	1739	3.7	2342	2.2
29 SA	0600	3.4	1209	2.0	1918	3.7		
30 SU	0048	2.1	0741	3.5	1307	1.9	2023	3.9

Chart Datum: 2·73 metres below Ordnance Datum (Newlyn)
HAT is 5·1 metres above Chart Datum

TIME ZONE (UT)
For Summer Time add ONE hour in **non-shaded areas**

PORTSMOUTH

LAT 50°48′N LONG 1°07′W

TIMES AND HEIGHTS OF HIGH AND LOW WATERS

Dates in amber are **SPRINGS**
Dates in grey are **NEAPS**

2023

MAY

Date	Day	Time	m	Time	m	Time	m	Time	m
1	M	0143	1.9	0839	3.8	1355	1.7	2109	4.1
2	TU	0224	1.6	0923	4.0	1435	1.4	2147	4.3
3	W	0300	1.4	1000	4.2	1513	1.2	2221	4.5
4	TH	0335	1.1	1033	4.3	1550	1.0	2253	4.5
5	F	0411	0.9	1107	4.4	1627	0.9	○ 2326	4.6
6	SA	0446	0.8	1142	4.5	1704	0.8	2359	4.7
7	SU	0523	0.7	1219	4.6	1741	0.8		
8	M	0035	4.7	0601	0.7	1259	4.6	1820	0.9
9	TU	0114	4.6	0641	0.8	1346	4.5	1903	1.1
10	W	0200	4.5	0726	1.0	1444	4.4	1951	1.4
11	TH	0257	4.3	0818	1.3	1553	4.3	2052	1.7
12	F	0406	4.1	0930	1.5	1706	4.1	◑ 2229	1.8
13	SA	0523	3.9	1110	1.6	1821	4.1	2355	1.8
14	SU	0641	3.9	1222	1.5	1933	4.3		
15	M	0059	1.6	0748	4.1	1320	1.4	2032	4.4
16	TU	0153	1.4	0841	4.3	1411	1.2	2120	4.6
17	W	0240	1.2	0927	4.4	1457	1.0	2201	4.7
18	TH	0323	1.0	1011	4.5	1540	0.9	2240	4.7
19	F	0405	0.9	1055	4.5	1622	0.9	● 2320	4.7
20	SA	0445	0.9	1141	4.5	1702	1.0		
21	SU	0000	4.6	0525	0.9	1227	4.5	1742	1.1
22	M	0038	4.5	0603	1.0	1311	4.5	1821	1.2
23	TU	0117	4.4	0640	1.2	1353	4.4	1859	1.4
24	W	0155	4.3	0717	1.3	1434	4.3	1939	1.6
25	TH	0233	4.1	0756	1.5	1515	4.1	2023	1.8
26	F	0316	4.0	0843	1.7	1600	4.0	2120	2.0
27	SA	0405	3.8	0947	1.9	1652	3.9	◐ 2238	2.1
28	SU	0505	3.6	1104	1.9	1759	3.8	2345	2.1
29	M	0623	3.6	1207	1.9	1917	3.9		
30	TU	0041	1.9	0741	3.7	1258	1.7	2015	4.1
31	W	0128	1.7	0834	3.9	1345	1.5	2058	4.2

JUNE

Date	Day	Time	m	Time	m	Time	m	Time	m
1	TH	0212	1.5	0915	4.1	1429	1.3	2136	4.4
2	F	0254	1.2	0955	4.3	1512	1.2	2214	4.5
3	SA	0336	1.0	1035	4.4	1555	1.0	2254	4.6
4	SU	0419	0.9	1118	4.5	1639	0.9	○ 2335	4.7
5	M	0502	0.8	1203	4.6	1723	0.9		
6	TU	0017	4.7	0547	0.7	1251	4.6	1809	1.0
7	W	0102	4.7	0633	0.8	1345	4.6	1857	1.1
8	TH	0153	4.5	0722	0.9	1448	4.6	1950	1.3
9	F	0252	4.4	0817	1.1	1552	4.5	2051	1.5
10	SA	0358	4.2	0922	1.3	1654	4.4	◑ 2201	1.6
11	SU	0504	4.1	1033	1.4	1756	4.4	2312	1.6
12	M	0610	4.1	1141	1.5	1857	4.4		
13	TU	0018	1.6	0713	4.1	1242	1.4	1955	4.4
14	W	0117	1.5	0810	4.2	1336	1.4	2046	4.4
15	TH	0209	1.4	0902	4.2	1427	1.3	2133	4.5
16	F	0256	1.3	0954	4.3	1514	1.3	2216	4.5
17	SA	0342	1.2	1044	4.3	1600	1.3	2259	4.5
18	SU	0426	1.1	1131	4.4	1644	1.3	● 2340	4.5
19	M	0509	1.1	1216	4.4	1727	1.3		
20	TU	0020	4.4	0549	1.1	1257	4.4	1808	1.3
21	W	0059	4.4	0627	1.2	1338	4.4	1846	1.4
22	TH	0136	4.3	0703	1.3	1417	4.3	1922	1.5
23	F	0213	4.2	0737	1.4	1454	4.3	1958	1.6
24	SA	0252	4.1	0814	1.5	1533	4.2	2038	1.7
25	SU	0335	4.0	0857	1.6	1615	4.1	2125	1.8
26	M	0424	3.9	0948	1.7	1703	4.0	◐ 2221	1.9
27	TU	0519	3.8	1048	1.7	1757	4.0	2325	1.9
28	W	0621	3.8	1153	1.7	1856	4.0		
29	TH	0027	1.8	0726	3.9	1253	1.6	1956	4.1
30	F	0124	1.6	0827	4.0	1348	1.5	2053	4.3

JULY

Date	Day	Time	m	Time	m	Time	m	Time	m
1	SA	0217	1.4	0923	4.2	1441	1.3	2144	4.4
2	SU	0309	1.1	1015	4.4	1533	1.2	2232	4.6
3	M	0400	0.9	1105	4.5	1624	1.0	○ 2318	4.7
4	TU	0449	0.8	1154	4.7	1713	0.9		
5	W	0004	4.7	0538	0.7	1244	4.7	1802	0.9
6	TH	0051	4.7	0626	0.6	1338	4.7	1850	0.9
7	F	0142	4.6	0713	0.7	1439	4.7	1939	1.0
8	SA	0239	4.5	0803	0.8	1539	4.7	2031	1.2
9	SU	0340	4.4	0856	1.1	1632	4.6	2128	1.4
10	M	0439	4.3	0956	1.3	1723	4.5	◑ 2231	1.5
11	TU	0537	4.1	1100	1.5	1816	4.3	2337	1.6
12	W	0637	4.0	1204	1.6	1913	4.2		
13	TH	0041	1.7	0740	4.0	1305	1.7	2013	4.2
14	F	0141	1.6	0844	4.0	1403	1.7	2109	4.2
15	SA	0237	1.5	0947	4.1	1457	1.6	2159	4.3
16	SU	0327	1.4	1038	4.2	1548	1.5	2243	4.3
17	M	0414	1.2	1120	4.3	1634	1.4	● 2324	4.4
18	TU	0457	1.1	1159	4.4	1716	1.3		
19	W	0003	4.4	0536	1.1	1238	4.4	1755	1.3
20	TH	0041	4.4	0612	1.1	1317	4.4	1830	1.3
21	F	0117	4.3	0644	1.1	1353	4.4	1900	1.3
22	SA	0151	4.3	0713	1.2	1427	4.4	1929	1.4
23	SU	0224	4.2	0743	1.3	1500	4.3	2002	1.4
24	M	0300	4.1	0817	1.3	1536	4.2	2040	1.5
25	TU	0341	4.0	0858	1.4	1618	4.2	◐ 2127	1.6
26	W	0431	3.9	0948	1.6	1707	4.1	2224	1.7
27	TH	0529	3.8	1051	1.7	1805	4.0	2333	1.8
28	F	0638	3.8	1206	1.8	1912	4.0		
29	SA	0046	1.7	0756	3.9	1319	1.7	2026	4.1
30	SU	0155	1.5	0910	4.1	1424	1.6	2129	4.3
31	M	0256	1.3	1007	4.4	1523	1.3	2220	4.5

AUGUST

Date	Day	Time	m	Time	m	Time	m	Time	m
1	TU	0351	0.9	1056	4.6	1616	1.0	○ 2305	4.7
2	W	0441	0.7	1143	4.7	1705	0.8	2350	4.8
3	TH	0527	0.5	1230	4.8	1750	0.7		
4	F	0035	4.8	0612	0.4	1321	4.9	1835	0.7
5	SA	0124	4.8	0656	0.5	1418	4.9	1920	0.8
6	SU	0217	4.7	0740	0.7	1515	4.8	2006	1.0
7	M	0314	4.5	0827	0.9	1602	4.7	2055	1.2
8	TU	0410	4.4	0919	1.3	1647	4.5	◑ 2153	1.5
9	W	0505	4.1	1022	1.6	1737	4.2	2301	1.7
10	TH	0605	3.9	1133	1.9	1836	4.0		
11	F	0012	1.9	0716	3.8	1242	2.0	1945	3.9
12	SA	0121	1.9	0833	3.8	1349	2.0	2051	4.0
13	SU	0224	1.7	0943	4.0	1449	1.8	2144	4.1
14	M	0315	1.5	1027	4.2	1537	1.6	2226	4.2
15	TU	0359	1.3	1102	4.3	1620	1.4	2305	4.3
16	W	0439	1.1	1138	4.4	1658	1.2	● 2343	4.4
17	TH	0515	1.0	1214	4.5	1733	1.1		
18	F	0019	4.4	0548	1.0	1250	4.5	1805	1.1
19	SA	0053	4.4	0617	1.0	1323	4.5	1832	1.2
20	SU	0123	4.3	0644	1.0	1353	4.5	1859	1.2
21	M	0151	4.3	0711	1.1	1422	4.4	1928	1.2
22	TU	0221	4.3	0742	1.1	1453	4.3	2002	1.3
23	W	0259	4.2	0818	1.3	1531	4.2	2044	1.4
24	TH	0346	4.0	0904	1.5	1621	4.1	◐ 2136	1.6
25	F	0447	3.9	1002	1.8	1724	3.9	2248	1.9
26	SA	0607	3.7	1131	2.0	1844	3.8		
27	SU	0030	1.9	0748	3.8	1315	1.9	2017	4.0
28	M	0151	1.6	0905	4.1	1424	1.7	2118	4.3
29	TU	0251	1.3	0956	4.4	1518	1.3	2205	4.5
30	W	0341	0.9	1041	4.7	1606	0.9	2249	4.7
31	TH	0427	0.6	1125	4.9	1650	0.7	○ 2331	4.8

Chart Datum: 2·73 metres below Ordnance Datum (Newlyn)
HAT is 5·1 metres above Chart Datum

TIME ZONE (UT)
For Summer Time add ONE hour in **non-shaded areas**

PORTSMOUTH

LAT 50°48′N LONG 1°07′W

TIMES AND HEIGHTS OF HIGH AND LOW WATERS

Dates in amber are **SPRINGS**
Dates in grey are **NEAPS**

2023

SEPTEMBER

Date	Day	Time	m	Time	m	Time	m	Time	m
1	F	0510	0.4	1210	5.0	1732	0.5		
2	SA	0015	4.9	0552	0.3	1256	5.0	1814	0.5
3	SU	0101	4.8	0633	0.4	1348	4.9	1855	0.7
4	M	0150	4.7	0714	0.7	1440	4.8	1937	0.9
5	TU	0243	4.6	0755	1.0	1524	4.6	2021	1.2
6	W ◑	0337	4.4	0841	1.4	1606	4.4	2113	1.6
7	TH	0430	4.1	0942	1.8	1653	4.1	2229	1.9
8	F	0532	3.8	1110	2.1	1756	3.8	2350	2.1
9	SA	0652	3.7	1225	2.2	1919	3.7		
10	SU	0101	2.0	0821	3.7	1335	2.2	2035	3.8
11	M	0205	1.9	0956	4.0	1433	1.9	2130	4.0
12	TU	0254	1.6	1016	4.2	1517	1.6	2207	4.2
13	W	0335	1.3	1040	4.4	1556	1.4	2243	4.3
14	TH	0412	1.1	1113	4.5	1632	1.2	2319	4.4
15	F ●	0446	1.0	1146	4.6	1705	1.1	2353	4.5
16	SA	0518	0.9	1220	4.6	1734	1.0		
17	SU	0025	4.5	0547	0.9	1250	4.6	1802	1.0
18	M	0053	4.5	0614	1.0	1317	4.5	1829	1.0
19	TU	0119	4.5	0641	1.0	1343	4.5	1857	1.1
20	W	0149	4.4	0711	1.1	1412	4.4	1931	1.2
21	TH	0226	4.3	0748	1.3	1450	4.3	2011	1.4
22	F ◐	0315	4.1	0832	1.6	1543	4.1	2101	1.7
23	SA	0423	3.9	0930	2.0	1657	3.8	2219	2.0
24	SU	0600	3.8	1157	2.2	1835	3.8		
25	M	0039	1.9	0744	3.9	1320	2.0	2005	4.0
26	TU	0145	1.6	0851	4.3	1417	1.6	2102	4.3
27	W	0237	1.2	0940	4.6	1504	1.2	2147	4.6
28	TH	0323	0.8	1022	4.8	1547	0.9	2228	4.8
29	F ○	0406	0.6	1104	5.0	1629	0.6	2310	4.9
30	SA	0447	0.4	1146	5.0	1710	0.5	2352	4.9

OCTOBER

Date	Day	Time	m	Time	m	Time	m	Time	m
1	SU	0528	0.4	1229	5.0	1750	0.6		
2	M	0036	4.9	0607	0.6	1312	4.9	1829	0.7
3	TU	0122	4.7	0646	0.8	1355	4.8	1908	1.0
4	W	0211	4.6	0725	1.2	1438	4.6	1948	1.3
5	TH	0301	4.4	0807	1.6	1520	4.3	2034	1.7
6	F ◑	0353	4.1	0903	2.0	1607	4.0	2154	2.0
7	SA	0455	3.8	1049	2.3	1707	3.7	2324	2.2
8	SU	0620	3.7	1201	2.3	1843	3.6		
9	M	0031	2.1	0754	3.7	1307	2.2	2009	3.7
10	TU	0132	2.0	0928	4.0	1404	2.0	2107	3.9
11	W	0221	1.7	0947	4.3	1447	1.7	2143	4.2
12	TH	0301	1.4	1012	4.5	1524	1.4	2218	4.3
13	F	0337	1.2	1043	4.6	1558	1.2	2252	4.5
14	SA ●	0411	1.1	1115	4.6	1630	1.1	2325	4.5
15	SU	0443	1.0	1146	4.7	1701	1.0	2355	4.6
16	M	0514	1.0	1215	4.7	1731	1.0		
17	TU	0023	4.6	0545	1.0	1243	4.6	1801	1.0
18	W	0054	4.6	0615	1.1	1311	4.6	1833	1.0
19	TH	0128	4.5	0649	1.2	1345	4.5	1909	1.2
20	F	0210	4.4	0728	1.4	1428	4.3	1952	1.4
21	SA	0306	4.2	0816	1.7	1527	4.1	2046	1.7
22	SU ◐	0426	4.0	0923	2.1	1650	3.9	2237	2.0
23	M	0558	3.9	1159	2.1	1825	3.9		
24	TU	0024	1.8	0726	4.1	1302	1.9	1944	4.1
25	W	0123	1.5	0830	4.4	1355	1.6	2039	4.4
26	TH	0213	1.2	0919	4.7	1440	1.2	2124	4.6
27	F	0258	0.9	1000	4.9	1523	0.9	2205	4.7
28	SA ○	0340	0.8	1040	5.0	1604	0.8	2247	4.8
29	SU	0422	0.7	1120	5.0	1645	0.7	2331	4.8
30	M	0502	0.7	1200	4.9	1725	0.7		
31	TU	0015	4.8	0542	0.9	1240	4.8	1804	0.9

NOVEMBER

Date	Day	Time	m	Time	m	Time	m	Time	m
1	W	0100	4.7	0621	1.1	1321	4.7	1843	1.1
2	TH	0147	4.6	0700	1.4	1402	4.5	1922	1.4
3	F	0235	4.4	0742	1.7	1444	4.3	2006	1.7
4	SA	0324	4.2	0836	2.0	1530	4.0	2110	2.0
5	SU ◑	0419	3.9	1015	2.3	1625	3.7	2246	2.1
6	M	0530	3.8	1126	2.3	1746	3.6	2352	2.1
7	TU	0658	3.8	1229	2.2	1919	3.6		
8	W	0049	2.0	0810	4.0	1324	2.0	2023	3.8
9	TH	0137	1.8	0857	4.2	1407	1.8	2108	4.1
10	F	0218	1.6	0935	4.4	1444	1.6	2146	4.3
11	SA	0255	1.4	1009	4.5	1519	1.3	2221	4.4
12	SU	0332	1.2	1041	4.6	1553	1.2	2254	4.5
13	M ●	0407	1.1	1112	4.7	1628	1.1	2326	4.6
14	TU	0443	1.1	1144	4.7	1703	1.0		
15	W	0000	4.6	0520	1.1	1216	4.7	1740	1.0
16	TH	0037	4.7	0557	1.1	1252	4.7	1818	1.0
17	F	0119	4.6	0637	1.3	1333	4.6	1900	1.2
18	SA	0210	4.5	0722	1.5	1423	4.4	1948	1.4
19	SU	0315	4.3	0816	1.8	1526	4.2	2049	1.6
20	M ◐	0428	4.2	0936	2.0	1643	4.0	2226	1.8
21	TU	0543	4.2	1124	2.0	1801	4.0	2350	1.7
22	W	0656	4.3	1230	1.8	1911	4.1		
23	TH	0049	1.5	0800	4.5	1324	1.6	2009	4.3
24	F	0142	1.3	0851	4.6	1412	1.3	2058	4.5
25	SA	0229	1.2	0934	4.8	1457	1.1	2144	4.6
26	SU	0313	1.1	1015	4.8	1540	1.0	2229	4.6
27	M ○	0357	1.0	1056	4.8	1622	0.9	2316	4.6
28	TU	0439	1.1	1138	4.8	1704	0.9		
29	W	0002	4.6	0522	1.1	1218	4.7	1746	1.0
30	TH	0049	4.6	0603	1.3	1258	4.6	1826	1.2

DECEMBER

Date	Day	Time	m	Time	m	Time	m	Time	m
1	F	0134	4.5	0644	1.5	1339	4.4	1906	1.4
2	SA	0218	4.4	0726	1.7	1420	4.3	1947	1.6
3	SU	0302	4.3	0812	1.9	1503	4.1	2033	1.8
4	M	0348	4.1	0909	2.1	1550	3.9	2133	1.9
5	TU ◑	0439	4.0	1027	2.2	1647	3.7	2249	2.0
6	W	0540	3.9	1134	2.2	1800	3.7	2351	2.0
7	TH	0655	3.9	1230	2.1	1920	3.7		
8	F	0043	1.9	0758	4.1	1316	1.9	2020	3.9
9	SA	0128	1.8	0848	4.2	1357	1.7	2108	4.1
10	SU	0211	1.6	0929	4.4	1437	1.5	2149	4.2
11	M	0253	1.4	1006	4.5	1518	1.3	2227	4.4
12	TU ●	0336	1.3	1043	4.6	1600	1.1	2306	4.5
13	W	0419	1.2	1120	4.7	1643	1.0	2346	4.6
14	TH	0502	1.1	1159	4.7	1726	0.9		
15	F	0029	4.7	0547	1.1	1240	4.7	1811	0.9
16	SA	0117	4.7	0632	1.2	1326	4.6	1857	0.9
17	SU	0211	4.6	0721	1.3	1418	4.5	1946	1.1
18	M	0313	4.5	0814	1.5	1518	4.4	2042	1.3
19	TU ◐	0416	4.5	0917	1.6	1625	4.2	2148	1.4
20	W	0517	4.4	1032	1.7	1730	4.1	2302	1.5
21	TH	0618	4.4	1146	1.7	1834	4.1		
22	F	0009	1.5	0718	4.4	1248	1.6	1935	4.2
23	SA	0108	1.5	0814	4.4	1343	1.5	2033	4.2
24	SU	0201	1.5	0907	4.5	1433	1.4	2129	4.3
25	M	0251	1.4	0956	4.5	1521	1.2	2224	4.4
26	TU	0339	1.4	1041	4.5	1607	1.1	2313	4.4
27	W ○	0426	1.3	1123	4.5	1652	1.1	2358	4.5
28	TH	0510	1.3	1203	4.5	1734	1.1		
29	F	0039	4.5	0553	1.3	1243	4.5	1815	1.1
30	SA	0120	4.5	0633	1.4	1322	4.4	1852	1.2
31	SU	0200	4.4	0710	1.5	1400	4.3	1926	1.3

Chart Datum: 2·73 metres below Ordnance Datum (Newlyn)
HAT is 5·1 metres above Chart Datum

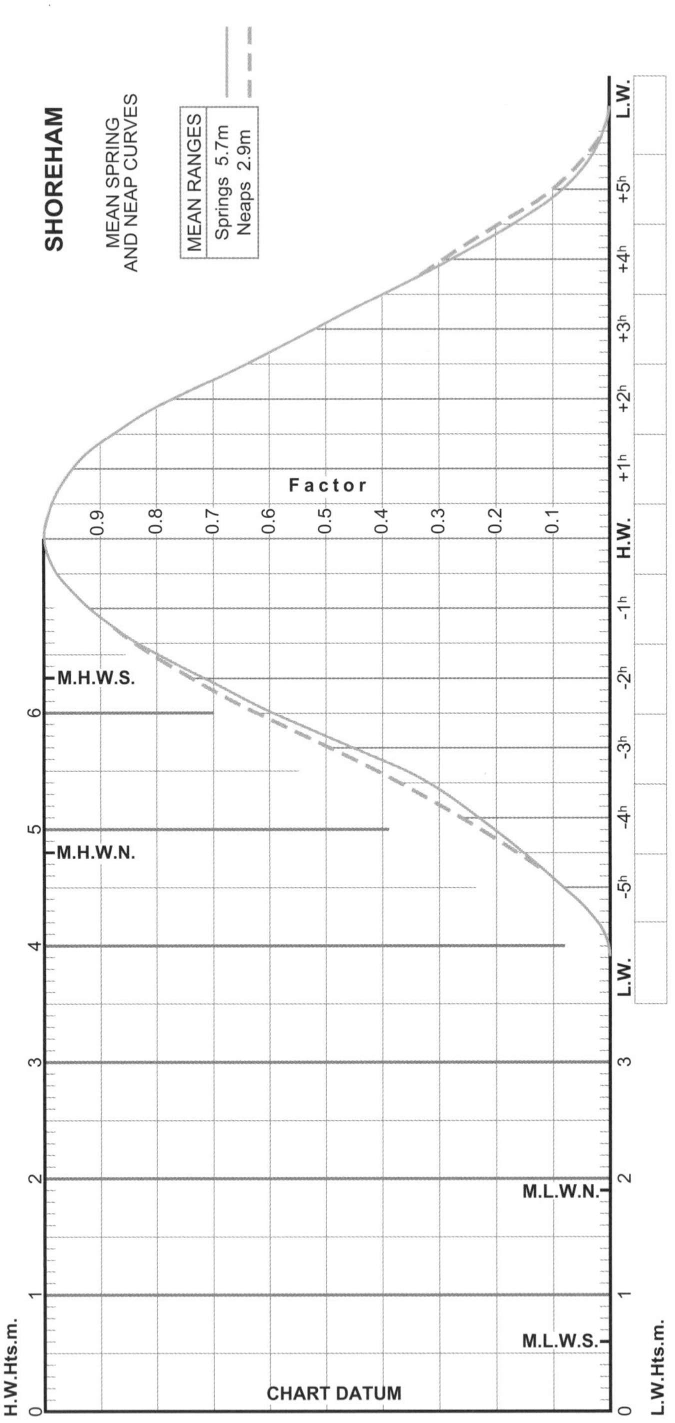
SHOREHAM
MEAN SPRING
AND NEAP CURVES
MEAN RANGES
Springs 5.7m
Neaps 2.9m
M.H.W.S.
M.H.W.N.
M.L.W.N.
M.L.W.S.
CHART DATUM
H.W.Hts.m.
L.W.Hts.m.
0
1
2
3
4
5
6
Factor
0.9
0.8
0.7
0.6
0.5
0.4
0.3
0.2
0.1
L.W.
-5h
-4h
-3h
-2h
-1h
H.W.
+1h
+2h
+3h
+4h
+5h
L.W.

TIME ZONE (UT)
For Summer Time add ONE hour in **non-shaded areas**

SHOREHAM

LAT 50°50′N LONG 0°15′W

TIMES AND HEIGHTS OF HIGH AND LOW WATERS

Dates in amber are **SPRINGS**
Dates in grey are **NEAPS**

2023

JANUARY

Date	Time	m	Date	Time	m
1 SU	0018	1.6	16 M	0500	5.2
	0628	5.4		1128	1.9
	1255	1.6		1731	4.9
	1901	5.1		2354	1.9
2 M	0121	1.7	17 TU	0616	5.1
	0733	5.3		1243	1.8
	1356	1.6		1856	5.0
	2009	5.1			
3 TU	0220	1.7	18 W	0113	1.8
	0834	5.4		0734	5.3
	1451	1.5		1355	1.6
	2107	5.3		2010	5.2
4 W	0314	1.6	19 TH	0225	1.6
	0927	5.5		0839	5.6
	1541	1.4		1500	1.3
	2157	5.5		2114	5.6
5 TH	0401	1.4	20 F	0328	1.3
	1012	5.7		0937	5.9
	1625	1.2		1557	1.0
	2241	5.6		2211	5.9
6 F	0443	1.3	21 SA	0422	1.0
	1052	5.8		1031	6.2
	1705	1.1		1649	0.7
	○ 2320	5.8		● 2305	6.2
7 SA	0522	1.3	22 SU	0514	0.8
	1128	5.8		1123	6.4
	1742	1.1		1740	0.5
	2356	5.8		2357	6.4
8 SU	0558	1.2	23 M	0603	0.7
	1201	5.8		1213	6.5
	1818	1.0		1829	0.4
9 M	0028	5.9	24 TU	0046	6.5
	0633	1.2		0653	0.6
	1232	5.8		1302	6.5
	1853	1.1		1919	0.4
10 TU	0059	5.8	25 W	0134	6.5
	0707	1.3		0741	0.6
	1302	5.7		1349	6.4
	1927	1.1		2007	0.5
11 W	0128	5.8	26 TH	0219	6.4
	0741	1.3		0829	0.7
	1333	5.6		1435	6.2
	1959	1.2		2053	0.6
12 TH	0159	5.7	27 F	0303	6.2
	0814	1.4		0917	0.9
	1407	5.5		1520	5.9
	2031	1.3		2139	0.9
13 F	0233	5.6	28 SA	0348	5.9
	0850	1.5		1005	1.2
	1444	5.4		1607	5.5
	2106	1.5		◐ 2227	1.3
14 SA	0312	5.5	29 SU	0435	5.5
	0931	1.7		1058	1.5
	1528	5.2		1659	5.1
	2149	1.6		2322	1.7
15 SU	0400	5.3	30 M	0529	5.1
	1023	1.8		1204	1.8
	1622	5.1		1802	4.8
	◑ 2244	1.8			
			31 TU	0034	2.0
				0635	4.9
				1320	2.0
				1921	4.7

FEBRUARY

Date	Time	m	Date	Time	m
1 W	0151	2.0	16 TH	0041	2.0
	0755	4.8		0706	4.9
	1428	1.9		1332	1.8
	2044	4.8		1954	5.0
2 TH	0254	1.9	17 F	0212	1.8
	0906	5.0		0827	5.3
	1523	1.6		1450	1.4
	2143	5.1		2107	5.4
3 F	0346	1.7	18 SA	0321	1.4
	0958	5.3		0932	5.7
	1610	1.4		1549	1.0
	2229	5.4		2207	5.9
4 SA	0429	1.4	19 SU	0415	1.0
	1040	5.5		1027	6.1
	1650	1.2		1640	0.6
	2307	5.7		2300	6.3
5 SU	0507	1.2	20 M	0504	0.6
	1116	5.7		1117	6.4
	1726	1.0		1728	0.3
	○ 2342	5.8		● 2348	6.6
6 M	0542	1.1	21 TU	0550	0.4
	1148	5.8		1204	6.5
	1801	0.9		1814	0.2
7 TU	0012	5.9	22 W	0033	6.7
	0616	1.1		0636	0.4
	1216	5.8		1249	6.6
	1835	0.9		1859	0.2
8 W	0040	5.9	23 TH	0115	6.7
	0649	1.0		0720	0.4
	1244	5.8		1331	6.5
	1907	0.9		1942	0.3
9 TH	0106	5.9	24 F	0155	6.6
	0719	1.1		0802	0.5
	1313	5.8		1410	6.3
	1935	1.0		2022	0.5
10 F	0133	5.9	25 SA	0232	6.3
	0747	1.1		0842	0.8
	1343	5.8		1448	6.0
	2001	1.0		2100	0.9
11 SA	0204	5.9	26 SU	0309	5.9
	0816	1.1		0920	1.1
	1417	5.7		1528	5.5
	2031	1.1		2138	1.3
12 SU	0239	5.8	27 M	0349	5.4
	0852	1.3		1001	1.5
	1455	5.6		1614	5.1
	2110	1.3		◐ 2222	1.8
13 M	0321	5.5	28 TU	0439	5.0
	0938	1.5		1053	1.9
	1541	5.3		1715	4.6
	◑ 2200	1.6		2325	2.2
14 TU	0412	5.2			
	1037	1.7			
	1642	5.0			
	2307	1.9			
15 W	0523	5.0			
	1158	1.9			
	1814	4.8			

MARCH

Date	Time	m	Date	Time	m
1 W	0545	4.6	16 TH	0455	4.8
	1230	2.2		1135	1.9
	1833	4.4		1803	4.6
2 TH	0121	2.3	17 F	0030	2.1
	0710	4.4		0655	4.7
	1404	2.1		1323	1.8
	2022	4.5		1949	4.9
3 F	0234	2.1	18 SA	0207	1.8
	0848	4.7		0821	5.1
	1503	1.8		1441	1.4
	2127	4.9		2102	5.4
4 SA	0327	1.8	19 SU	0311	1.3
	0943	5.1		0925	5.6
	1549	1.4		1537	0.9
	2210	5.3		2158	6.0
5 SU	0409	1.4	20 M	0402	0.8
	1022	5.4		1016	6.1
	1627	1.2		1624	0.5
	2246	5.6		2246	6.4
6 M	0445	1.2	21 TU	0447	0.5
	1056	5.7		1103	6.4
	1702	0.9		1709	0.3
	2319	5.8		● 2330	6.6
7 TU	0518	1.0	22 W	0531	0.3
	1126	5.8		1147	6.5
	1736	0.8		1752	0.2
	○ 2348	6.0			
8 W	0551	0.9	23 TH	0011	6.7
	1153	5.9		0613	0.3
	1809	0.8		1228	6.6
				1833	0.2
9 TH	0013	6.0	24 F	0050	6.7
	0624	0.9		0654	0.3
	1221	6.0		1307	6.5
	1840	0.8		1913	0.4
10 F	0039	6.1	25 SA	0126	6.5
	0653	0.8		0732	0.5
	1250	6.0		1343	6.3
	1907	0.8		1949	0.6
11 SA	0107	6.1	26 SU	0159	6.2
	0720	0.8		0807	0.7
	1320	6.0		1417	5.9
	1933	0.8		2023	0.9
12 SU	0138	6.0	27 M	0231	5.8
	0749	0.9		0840	1.1
	1353	5.9		1453	5.5
	2005	0.9		2058	1.3
13 M	0212	5.9	28 TU	0305	5.4
	0826	1.0		0918	1.5
	1430	5.7		1536	5.1
	2045	1.2		2140	1.8
14 TU	0252	5.6	29 W	0350	4.9
	0910	1.3		1007	1.9
	1515	5.4		1637	4.6
	2134	1.6		◐ 2239	2.2
15 W	0342	5.2	30 TH	0502	4.4
	1010	1.7		1119	2.3
	1616	4.9		1754	4.4
	◑ 2245	1.9			
			31 F	0030	2.5
				0627	4.2
				1329	2.2
				1934	4.5

APRIL

Date	Time	m	Date	Time	m
1 SA	0206	2.2	16 SU	0153	1.6
	0812	4.5		0807	5.2
	1432	1.9		1423	1.3
	2054	4.9		2045	5.6
2 SU	0259	1.8	17 M	0253	1.2
	0912	4.9		0907	5.6
	1518	1.5		1516	0.9
	2137	5.3		2137	6.0
3 M	0339	1.4	18 TU	0341	0.8
	0950	5.3		0957	6.0
	1555	1.2		1602	0.6
	2212	5.6		2223	6.4
4 TU	0414	1.2	19 W	0425	0.5
	1022	5.6		1042	6.3
	1630	1.0		1644	0.4
	2243	5.9		2305	6.5
5 W	0448	1.0	20 TH	0506	0.4
	1053	5.8		1125	6.4
	1704	0.8		1726	0.4
	2312	6.0		● 2345	6.6
6 TH	0521	0.8	21 F	0547	0.4
	1123	5.9		1205	6.4
	1738	0.8		1805	0.4
	○ 2341	6.1			
7 F	0554	0.8	22 SA	0022	6.5
	1154	6.0		0627	0.5
	1809	0.7		1242	6.3
				1844	0.6
8 SA	0010	6.2	23 SU	0056	6.3
	0625	0.7		0703	0.6
	1226	6.1		1317	6.1
	1840	0.7		1919	0.8
9 SU	0042	6.2	24 M	0127	6.0
	0656	0.7		0737	0.9
	1259	6.1		1350	5.8
	1911	0.8		1953	1.1
10 M	0115	6.1	25 TU	0158	5.7
	0731	0.8		0811	1.1
	1334	6.0		1426	5.5
	1948	0.9		2029	1.4
11 TU	0152	5.9	26 W	0232	5.3
	0810	1.0		0849	1.5
	1415	5.7		1508	5.1
	2032	1.2		2112	1.8
12 W	0234	5.6	27 TH	0315	4.9
	0859	1.3		0937	1.8
	1504	5.3		1606	4.8
	2127	1.6		◐ 2209	2.2
13 TH	0329	5.1	28 F	0425	4.5
	1003	1.6		1042	2.1
	1614	4.9		1718	4.5
	◑ 2244	2.0		2328	2.4
14 F	0453	4.7	29 SA	0546	4.3
	1132	1.9		1213	2.2
	1805	4.8		1833	4.6
15 SA	0028	2.0	30 SU	0115	2.2
	0647	4.8		0703	4.4
	1312	1.7		1342	2.0
	1937	5.1		1947	4.8

Chart Datum: 3·27 metres below Ordnance Datum (Newlyn)
HAT is 6·9 metres above Chart Datum

TIDES

TIME ZONE (UT)
For Summer Time add ONE hour in **non-shaded areas**

SHOREHAM

LAT 50°50′N LONG 0°15′W

TIMES AND HEIGHTS OF HIGH AND LOW WATERS

Dates in amber are **SPRINGS**
Dates in grey are **NEAPS**

2023

MAY

Date	Day	Time	m	Time	m	Time	m	Time	m
1	M	0215	1.9	0810	4.8	1433	1.6	2042	5.2
2	TU	0259	1.5	0858	5.1	1514	1.4	2122	5.5
3	W	0336	1.2	0937	5.5	1552	1.1	2158	5.8
4	TH	0412	1.0	1014	5.7	1628	1.0	2233	6.0
5	F	0447	0.9	1051	5.9	1704	0.9	○ 2308	6.1
6	SA	0522	0.8	1128	6.1	1739	0.8	2344	6.2
7	SU	0559	0.7	1205	6.1	1817	0.8		
8	M	0020	6.2	0638	0.7	1243	6.1	1857	0.8
9	TU	0058	6.1	0720	0.8	1325	6.0	1941	1.0
10	W	0141	5.9	0806	1.0	1412	5.7	2031	1.2
11	TH	0230	5.6	0900	1.2	1509	5.4	2132	1.5
12	F	0333	5.2	1006	1.5	1625	5.2	◑ 2248	1.7
13	SA	0457	4.9	1127	1.6	1752	5.1		
14	SU	0013	1.7	0627	5.0	1248	1.5	1911	5.3
15	M	0126	1.5	0740	5.2	1354	1.2	2015	5.6
16	TU	0225	1.1	0840	5.6	1447	1.0	2108	5.9
17	W	0314	0.9	0931	5.8	1535	0.8	2155	6.2
18	TH	0359	0.7	1017	6.0	1619	0.7	2238	6.3
19	F	0442	0.6	1100	6.1	1701	0.7	● 2318	6.3
20	SA	0523	0.7	1141	6.1	1741	0.8	2355	6.2
21	SU	0602	0.7	1219	6.0	1819	0.9		
22	M	0030	6.0	0640	0.8	1255	5.9	1856	1.0
23	TU	0102	5.8	0715	1.0	1330	5.8	1932	1.2
24	W	0135	5.6	0750	1.2	1407	5.5	2009	1.5
25	TH	0210	5.3	0829	1.4	1447	5.3	2052	1.7
26	F	0252	5.0	0915	1.7	1537	5.0	2144	2.0
27	SA	0348	4.7	1010	1.9	1637	4.8	◐ 2247	2.1
28	SU	0459	4.5	1115	2.0	1742	4.8	2357	2.1
29	M	0607	4.6	1225	1.9	1844	4.9		
30	TU	0106	1.9	0709	4.8	1328	1.8	1940	5.1
31	W	0202	1.7	0803	5.0	1421	1.6	2030	5.4

JUNE

Date	Day	Time	m	Time	m	Time	m	Time	m
1	TH	0249	1.4	0852	5.4	1507	1.3	2115	5.7
2	F	0331	1.2	0937	5.6	1550	1.1	2157	5.9
3	SA	0413	1.0	1021	5.9	1633	1.0	2239	6.1
4	SU	0455	0.8	1105	6.0	1716	0.9	○ 2322	6.2
5	M	0540	0.7	1150	6.1	1801	0.8		
6	TU	0005	6.2	0626	0.7	1235	6.1	1849	0.9
7	W	0051	6.1	0714	0.7	1324	6.1	1938	0.9
8	TH	0140	6.0	0805	0.8	1416	5.9	2032	1.1
9	F	0234	5.7	0901	1.0	1514	5.8	2131	1.3
10	SA	0335	5.5	1002	1.1	1617	5.6	◑ 2238	1.4
11	SU	0442	5.3	1109	1.3	1724	5.5	2347	1.4
12	M	0553	5.2	1216	1.3	1832	5.5		
13	TU	0052	1.4	0703	5.2	1319	1.3	1937	5.5
14	W	0152	1.3	0806	5.3	1416	1.2	2034	5.7
15	TH	0246	1.1	0903	5.5	1508	1.2	2126	5.8
16	F	0335	1.0	0953	5.6	1556	1.1	2212	5.9
17	SA	0421	1.0	1040	5.7	1641	1.1	2255	5.9
18	SU	0504	1.0	1123	5.8	1723	1.1	● 2335	5.9
19	M	0545	1.0	1202	5.8	1802	1.1		
20	TU	0011	5.8	0623	1.0	1239	5.8	1839	1.2
21	W	0045	5.7	0659	1.1	1314	5.7	1916	1.3
22	TH	0118	5.6	0735	1.2	1349	5.6	1953	1.4
23	F	0152	5.4	0812	1.3	1424	5.5	2032	1.5
24	SA	0228	5.2	0852	1.4	1501	5.3	2115	1.7
25	SU	0308	5.0	0935	1.6	1544	5.2	2203	1.8
26	M	0357	4.9	1024	1.7	1636	5.0	◐ 2259	1.9
27	TU	0458	4.8	1120	1.8	1738	5.0	2359	1.9
28	W	0607	4.8	1222	1.8	1842	5.1		
29	TH	0101	1.8	0712	4.9	1325	1.7	1943	5.3
30	F	0201	1.6	0812	5.2	1425	1.6	2038	5.5

JULY

Date	Day	Time	m	Time	m	Time	m	Time	m
1	SA	0256	1.3	0906	5.5	1520	1.3	2129	5.8
2	SU	0347	1.1	0959	5.8	1611	1.1	2219	6.0
3	M	0437	0.9	1050	6.0	1701	0.9	○ 2308	6.2
4	TU	0527	0.7	1141	6.2	1751	0.8	2358	6.2
5	W	0616	0.6	1232	6.3	1841	0.8		
6	TH	0048	6.2	0708	0.6	1323	6.3	1933	0.7
7	F	0138	6.2	0759	0.6	1413	6.3	2025	0.8
8	SA	0229	6.0	0851	0.7	1503	6.1	2118	0.9
9	SU	0321	5.8	0944	0.8	1554	6.0	2214	1.1
10	M	0415	5.6	1039	1.1	1648	5.7	◑ 2313	1.3
11	TU	0512	5.3	1138	1.3	1745	5.5		
12	W	0015	1.5	0616	5.1	1241	1.5	1849	5.3
13	TH	0120	1.6	0728	5.0	1346	1.6	1959	5.2
14	F	0221	1.5	0837	5.1	1446	1.6	2102	5.3
15	SA	0317	1.4	0936	5.3	1540	1.5	2155	5.5
16	SU	0406	1.3	1026	5.5	1627	1.4	2241	5.6
17	M	0450	1.2	1110	5.7	1708	1.3	● 2321	5.7
18	TU	0530	1.1	1149	5.8	1747	1.2	2357	5.7
19	W	0606	1.0	1225	5.8	1823	1.2		
20	TH	0030	5.7	0642	1.0	1257	5.8	1858	1.2
21	F	0100	5.7	0717	1.1	1327	5.8	1933	1.2
22	SA	0129	5.6	0750	1.1	1355	5.7	2007	1.3
23	SU	0159	5.5	0823	1.2	1424	5.6	2040	1.4
24	M	0232	5.4	0854	1.4	1457	5.5	2116	1.5
25	TU	0310	5.3	0931	1.5	1538	5.4	◐ 2159	1.7
26	W	0357	5.1	1017	1.7	1629	5.2	2255	1.8
27	TH	0455	4.9	1118	1.9	1736	5.0		
28	F	0005	1.9	0618	4.8	1235	1.9	1859	5.1
29	SA	0122	1.8	0740	5.0	1355	1.8	2012	5.3
30	SU	0233	1.5	0848	5.3	1503	1.5	2113	5.6
31	M	0333	1.2	0948	5.7	1600	1.2	2209	6.0

AUGUST

Date	Day	Time	m	Time	m	Time	m	Time	m
1	TU	0426	0.8	1042	6.1	1651	0.9	○ 2301	6.2
2	W	0516	0.6	1134	6.3	1741	0.7	2351	6.4
3	TH	0605	0.4	1224	6.5	1829	0.6		
4	F	0040	6.5	0654	0.3	1311	6.6	1918	0.5
5	SA	0127	6.4	0742	0.4	1357	6.6	2006	0.6
6	SU	0212	6.3	0829	0.5	1440	6.4	2053	0.7
7	M	0257	6.1	0915	0.7	1524	6.1	2141	1.0
8	TU	0342	5.7	1001	1.1	1609	5.7	◑ 2231	1.3
9	W	0432	5.3	1053	1.5	1700	5.3	2331	1.7
10	TH	0531	4.9	1159	1.9	1802	5.0		
11	F	0048	1.9	0648	4.7	1321	2.0	1923	4.8
12	SA	0202	1.9	0820	4.8	1431	2.0	2047	4.9
13	SU	0303	1.7	0927	5.1	1527	1.7	2145	5.2
14	M	0352	1.5	1016	5.4	1612	1.5	2229	5.5
15	TU	0434	1.2	1056	5.7	1652	1.3	2307	5.7
16	W	0511	1.1	1132	5.8	1728	1.1	● 2341	5.8
17	TH	0545	1.0	1205	5.9	1802	1.1		
18	F	0010	5.8	0620	0.9	1233	5.9	1835	1.1
19	SA	0036	5.8	0652	1.0	1258	5.9	1907	1.1
20	SU	0102	5.8	0723	1.0	1322	5.9	1937	1.1
21	M	0130	5.8	0749	1.1	1349	5.9	2003	1.2
22	TU	0200	5.7	0815	1.2	1421	5.8	2034	1.3
23	W	0234	5.6	0849	1.4	1458	5.6	2114	1.5
24	TH	0316	5.3	0934	1.6	1544	5.3	◐ 2207	1.8
25	F	0410	5.0	1035	2.0	1647	4.9	2321	2.0
26	SA	0534	4.7	1201	2.1	1830	4.8		
27	SU	0057	2.0	0725	4.8	1341	2.0	2000	5.1
28	M	0223	1.7	0840	5.3	1456	1.6	2106	5.6
29	TU	0325	1.2	0941	5.8	1551	1.1	2201	6.0
30	W	0415	0.8	1033	6.2	1639	0.8	2251	6.4
31	TH	0502	0.5	1121	6.6	1725	0.5	○ 2338	6.6

Chart Datum: 3·27 metres below Ordnance Datum (Newlyn)
HAT is 6·9 metres above Chart Datum

TIME ZONE (UT)
For Summer Time add ONE hour in **non-shaded areas**

SHOREHAM

LAT 50°50′N LONG 0°15′W

TIMES AND HEIGHTS OF HIGH AND LOW WATERS

Dates in amber are **SPRINGS**
Dates in grey are **NEAPS**

2023

SEPTEMBER

Date	Day	Time	m
1	F	0547 1207 1810	0.3 6.8 0.4
2	SA	0023 0633 1250 1856	6.6 0.2 6.8 0.4
3	SU	0107 0717 1332 1939	6.6 0.3 6.7 0.5
4	M	0148 0759 1411 2021	6.4 0.5 6.5 0.7
5	TU	0227 0839 1449 2102	6.1 0.8 6.1 1.1
6	W	0308 0919 1530 ◑ 2144	5.7 1.2 5.6 1.5
7	TH	0354 1004 1619 2237	5.2 1.7 5.1 1.9
8	F	0454 1106 1723	4.8 2.2 4.7
9	SA	0010 0613 1258 1850	2.3 4.5 2.4 4.5
10	SU	0143 0807 1414 2036	2.2 4.6 2.2 4.7
11	M	0245 0913 1509 2131	1.9 5.0 1.8 5.1
12	TU	0332 0956 1552 2211	1.5 5.4 1.5 5.5
13	W	0411 1033 1629 2246	1.2 5.8 1.2 5.7
14	TH	0446 1106 1702 2316	1.0 5.9 1.1 5.9
15	F	0519 1136 1735 ● 2342	0.9 6.0 1.0 5.9
16	SA	0551 1202 1807	0.9 6.1 1.0
17	SU	0007 0623 1225 1838	6.0 0.9 6.1 1.0
18	M	0033 0651 1250 1905	6.0 1.0 6.1 1.0
19	TU	0102 0716 1318 1931	6.0 1.0 6.0 1.1
20	W	0132 0744 1350 2004	5.9 1.2 5.9 1.3
21	TH	0205 0821 1426 2045	5.7 1.4 5.6 1.5
22	F	0246 0908 1512 ◐ 2140	5.4 1.7 5.2 1.8
23	SA	0342 1013 1618 2259	5.0 2.1 4.8 2.1
24	SU	0522 1150 1822	4.7 2.3 4.7
25	M	0046 0718 1335 1951	2.1 4.9 2.0 5.1
26	TU	0214 0832 1444 2056	1.7 5.4 1.5 5.6
27	W	0311 0928 1535 2148	1.1 6.0 1.0 6.1
28	TH	0358 1016 1620 2234	0.7 6.4 0.6 6.5
29	F	0441 1101 1703 ○ 2319	0.4 6.7 0.4 6.6
30	SA	0524 1143 1746	0.3 6.8 0.3

OCTOBER

Date	Day	Time	m
1	SU	0001 0607 1223 1829	6.7 0.3 6.8 0.4
2	M	0042 0648 1302 1909	6.6 0.4 6.6 0.6
3	TU	0120 0727 1338 1948	6.4 0.7 6.4 0.8
4	W	0157 0804 1413 2025	6.1 1.0 6.0 1.2
5	TH	0235 0842 1451 2104	5.7 1.4 5.5 1.6
6	F	0321 0925 1539 ◑ 2153	5.2 1.9 5.0 2.1
7	SA	0422 1025 1648 2310	4.8 2.3 4.5 2.4
8	SU	0539 1223 1813	4.5 2.5 4.4
9	M	0112 0729 1348 2006	2.4 4.6 2.3 4.6
10	TU	0216 0840 1442 2101	2.0 5.0 1.9 5.0
11	W	0303 0924 1524 2140	1.7 5.4 1.5 5.4
12	TH	0341 0959 1559 2212	1.3 5.8 1.3 5.7
13	F	0415 1030 1632 2240	1.1 6.0 1.1 5.9
14	SA	0448 1058 1704 ● 2308	1.0 6.1 1.0 6.0
15	SU	0520 1124 1737 2337	1.0 6.1 0.9 6.1
16	M	0552 1152 1807	1.0 6.2 0.9
17	TU	0006 0621 1221 1837	6.1 1.0 6.2 1.0
18	W	0037 0650 1252 1908	6.1 1.1 6.1 1.1
19	TH	0110 0724 1326 1945	6.0 1.2 5.9 1.2
20	F	0147 0805 1406 2031	5.8 1.4 5.6 1.5
21	SA	0233 0857 1456 2130	5.4 1.8 5.2 1.9
22	SU	0336 1008 1612 ◐ 2252	5.0 2.1 4.8 2.1
23	M	0527 1146 1812	4.8 2.2 4.8
24	TU	0034 0702 1318 1934	2.0 5.1 1.9 5.2
25	W	0152 0811 1422 2036	1.6 5.6 1.4 5.7
26	TH	0248 0905 1512 2126	1.1 6.1 1.0 6.1
27	F	0334 0952 1556 2212	0.8 6.4 0.7 6.4
28	SA	0417 1035 1639 ○ 2256	0.6 6.6 0.5 6.5
29	SU	0459 1116 1721 2337	0.5 6.7 0.5 6.6
30	M	0540 1156 1802	0.6 6.6 0.6
31	TU	0017 0621 1232 1842	6.5 0.7 6.5 0.7

NOVEMBER

Date	Day	Time	m
1	W	0055 0659 1308 1920	6.3 0.9 6.2 1.0
2	TH	0132 0736 1342 1956	6.0 1.2 5.8 1.3
3	F	0210 0814 1420 2036	5.7 1.6 5.4 1.6
4	SA	0255 0858 1507 2124	5.3 1.9 5.0 2.0
5	SU	0353 0955 1614 ◑ 2229	4.9 2.3 4.6 2.3
6	M	0503 1114 1731	4.7 2.5 4.4
7	TU	0004 0618 1259 1851	2.4 4.7 2.3 4.6
8	W	0127 0737 1359 2005	2.2 5.0 2.0 4.9
9	TH	0219 0831 1444 2050	1.9 5.3 1.7 5.2
10	F	0301 0910 1522 2125	1.6 5.6 1.4 5.5
11	SA	0338 0944 1557 2159	1.3 5.9 1.2 5.8
12	SU	0413 1016 1632 2234	1.2 6.0 1.1 6.0
13	M	0448 1049 1706 ● 2309	1.1 6.1 1.0 6.1
14	TU	0522 1123 1741 2344	1.1 6.2 1.0 6.1
15	W	0557 1158 1817	1.1 6.2 1.0
16	TH	0020 0634 1234 1856	6.1 1.1 6.1 1.0
17	F	0059 0715 1314 1939	6.0 1.2 5.9 1.2
18	SA	0142 0802 1400 2029	5.8 1.4 5.7 1.4
19	SU	0235 0858 1457 2130	5.6 1.7 5.3 1.6
20	M	0343 1008 1614 ◐ 2245	5.3 1.9 5.1 1.8
21	TU	0511 1130 1746	5.2 1.9 5.0
22	W	0007 0632 1247 1903	1.7 5.3 1.7 5.3
23	TH	0118 0739 1351 2005	1.5 5.6 1.4 5.6
24	F	0216 0835 1444 2059	1.2 5.9 1.1 5.9
25	SA	0307 0924 1531 2148	1.0 6.2 0.9 6.1
26	SU	0353 1009 1616 2233	0.9 6.3 0.8 6.2
27	M	0437 1051 1700 ○ 2316	0.8 6.4 0.7 6.3
28	TU	0519 1131 1742 2358	0.9 6.3 0.8 6.2
29	W	0600 1209 1822	1.0 6.2 0.9
30	TH	0036 0640 1245 1901	6.1 1.1 6.0 1.1

DECEMBER

Date	Day	Time	m
1	F	0114 0717 1321 1938	5.9 1.3 5.8 1.3
2	SA	0153 0756 1359 2017	5.7 1.5 5.5 1.5
3	SU	0234 0838 1442 2101	5.5 1.8 5.2 1.8
4	M	0322 0927 1535 2154	5.2 2.0 4.9 2.0
5	TU	0419 1026 1641 ◑ 2255	5.0 2.2 4.7 2.1
6	W	0521 1134 1747	4.9 2.2 4.6
7	TH	0002 0623 1243 1850	2.2 4.9 2.1 4.7
8	F	0109 0721 1345 1946	2.0 5.1 1.9 5.0
9	SA	0206 0813 1435 2036	1.9 5.4 1.7 5.3
10	SU	0254 0858 1518 2121	1.6 5.6 1.4 5.6
11	M	0338 0940 1600 2204	1.4 5.9 1.2 5.8
12	TU	0419 1021 1640 ● 2246	1.3 6.0 1.1 6.0
13	W	0459 1101 1721 2328	1.2 6.2 0.9 6.1
14	TH	0541 1143 1804	1.1 6.2 0.9
15	F	0011 0625 1225 1849	6.2 1.1 6.2 0.9
16	SA	0056 0711 1311 1937	6.1 1.1 6.1 0.9
17	SU	0145 0801 1401 2028	6.0 1.2 5.9 1.1
18	M	0237 0855 1456 2125	5.9 1.3 5.7 1.2
19	TU	0336 0956 1558 ◐ 2227	5.7 1.4 5.5 1.3
20	W	0440 1103 1707 2333	5.6 1.5 5.3 1.5
21	TH	0548 1211 1818	5.5 1.5 5.3
22	F	0039 0655 1315 1927	1.5 5.5 1.5 5.3
23	SA	0142 0759 1415 2030	1.5 5.6 1.4 5.4
24	SU	0240 0856 1510 2127	1.4 5.8 1.2 5.6
25	M	0333 0947 1600 2217	1.3 5.9 1.1 5.8
26	TU	0421 1034 1646 2303	1.2 6.0 1.0 5.9
27	W	0506 1116 1729 ○ 2346	1.1 6.0 1.0 6.0
28	TH	0547 1156 1809	1.1 6.0 1.0
29	F	0025 0626 1232 1847	6.0 1.2 5.9 1.0
30	SA	0102 0703 1307 1923	5.9 1.3 5.8 1.1
31	SU	0137 0739 1341 1959	5.8 1.4 5.6 1.3

Chart Datum: 3·27 metres below Ordnance Datum (Newlyn)
HAT is 6·9 metres above Chart Datum

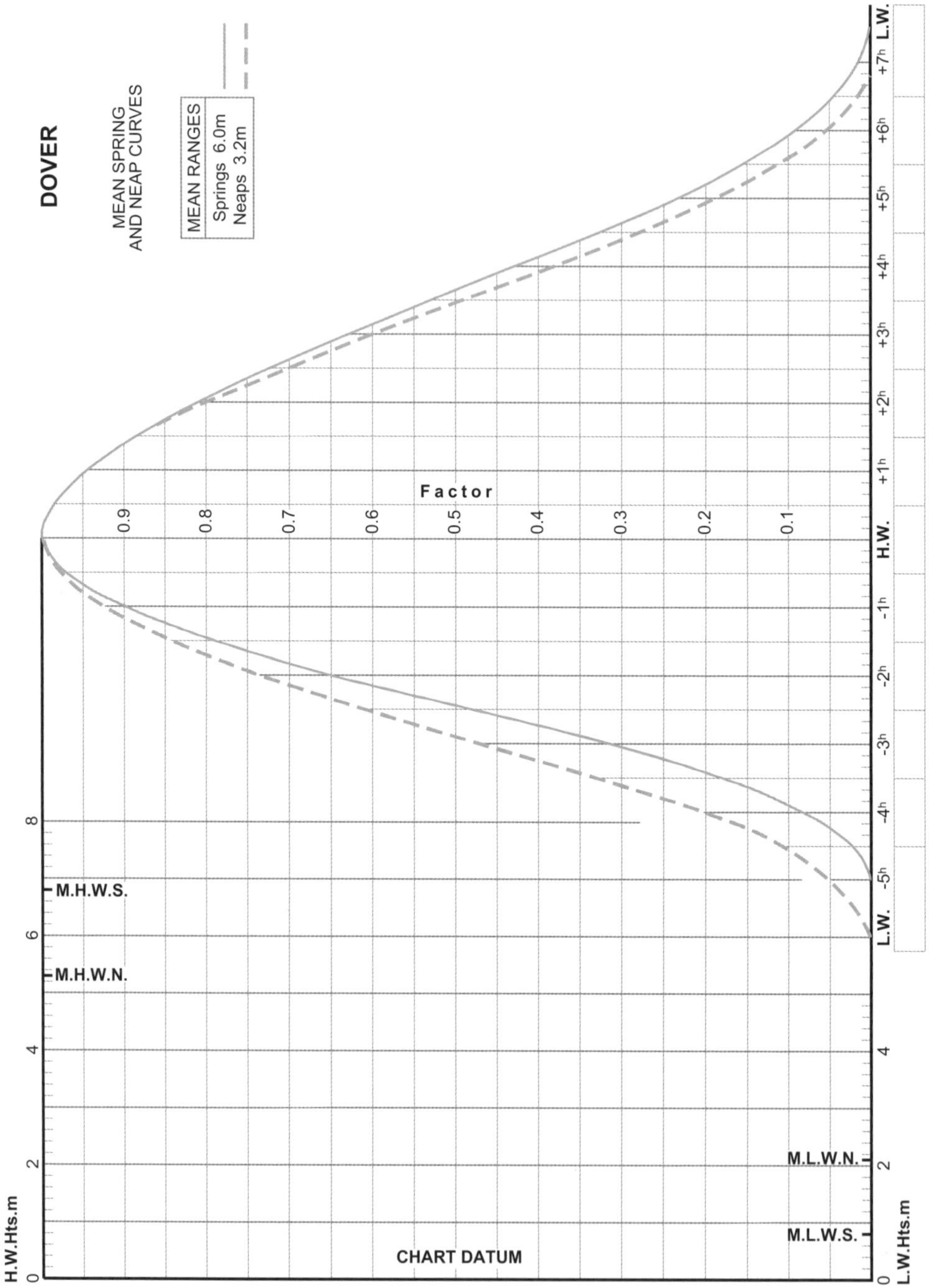
DOVER
MEAN SPRING
AND NEAP CURVES
MEAN RANGES
Springs 6.0m
Neaps 3.2m
Factor
0.9
0.8
0.7
0.6
0.5
0.4
0.3
0.2
0.1
L.W.
-5h
-4h
-3h
-2h
-1h
H.W.
+1h
+2h
+3h
+4h
+5h
+6h
+7h
L.W.
H.W.Hts.m
0
2
4
6
8
M.H.W.S.
M.H.W.N.
CHART DATUM
M.L.W.N.
M.L.W.S.
L.W.Hts.m
0
2
4

TIME ZONE (UT)
For Summer Time add ONE hour in **non-shaded areas**

DOVER

LAT 51°07′N LONG 1°19′E

TIMES AND HEIGHTS OF HIGH AND LOW WATERS

Dates in amber are **SPRINGS**
Dates in grey are **NEAPS**

2023

JANUARY

Date	Day	Time	m	Time	m	Time	m	Time	m
1	SU	0053	2.0	0615	5.8	1331	1.7	1908	5.5
2	M	0156	2.0	0724	5.7	1433	1.8	2009	5.6
3	TU	0300	1.9	0827	5.8	1536	1.7	2103	5.7
4	W	0400	1.8	0921	5.9	1632	1.6	2150	5.9
5	TH	0452	1.6	1009	6.0	1717	1.5	2232	6.1
6	F	0536	1.5	1051	6.1	1756	1.5	○ 2310	6.3
7	SA	0614	1.4	1128	6.2	1830	1.5	2347	6.3
8	SU	0648	1.4	1202	6.2	1902	1.4		
9	M	0020	6.4	0722	1.4	1234	6.1	1935	1.5
10	TU	0052	6.3	0756	1.4	1304	6.1	2008	1.5
11	W	0120	6.3	0831	1.4	1331	6.0	2043	1.5
12	TH	0147	6.2	0907	1.5	1400	5.9	2118	1.6
13	F	0220	6.1	0944	1.6	1435	5.8	2154	1.8
14	SA	0300	6.0	1024	1.7	1519	5.7	2236	1.9
15	SU	0348	5.9	1111	1.8	1614	5.5	◑ 2327	2.1
16	M	0449	5.7	1211	2.0	1726	5.4		
17	TU	0036	2.2	0605	5.6	1325	2.0	1854	5.4
18	W	0159	2.1	0722	5.7	1439	1.8	2004	5.7
19	TH	0313	1.9	0827	6.0	1547	1.6	2104	5.9
20	F	0418	1.6	0927	6.2	1651	1.3	2200	6.3
21	SA	0520	1.2	1023	6.5	1753	1.1	● 2251	6.6
22	SU	0620	1.0	1115	6.7	1852	0.9	2339	6.8
23	M	0717	0.7	1204	6.7	1945	0.8		
24	TU	0025	6.9	0810	0.6	1250	6.7	2032	0.7
25	W	0110	6.9	0856	0.5	1337	6.6	2113	0.8
26	TH	0156	6.9	0939	0.6	1423	6.4	2152	1.0
27	F	0242	6.7	1019	0.8	1511	6.2	2229	1.2
28	SA	0329	6.4	1059	1.2	1601	5.9	◐ 2310	1.6
29	SU	0421	6.0	1145	1.6	1659	5.5		
30	M	0000	2.0	0520	5.7	1239	1.9	1806	5.3
31	TU	0102	2.2	0633	5.4	1343	2.2	1923	5.2

FEBRUARY

Date	Day	Time	m	Time	m	Time	m	Time	m
1	W	0214	2.3	0753	5.3	1451	2.2	2036	5.3
2	TH	0325	2.1	0906	5.5	1557	2.0	2134	5.6
3	F	0427	1.8	1000	5.7	1653	1.8	2220	5.9
4	SA	0517	1.6	1041	5.9	1737	1.6	2257	6.2
5	SU	0558	1.4	1115	6.1	1815	1.4	○ 2330	6.3
6	M	0634	1.3	1145	6.2	1849	1.4		
7	TU	0000	6.4	0709	1.2	1213	6.2	1922	1.3
8	W	0029	6.4	0743	1.2	1240	6.2	1955	1.3
9	TH	0054	6.4	0816	1.1	1305	6.2	2026	1.3
10	F	0120	6.4	0848	1.2	1331	6.2	2057	1.3
11	SA	0150	6.4	0919	1.2	1403	6.2	2128	1.4
12	SU	0225	6.4	0952	1.4	1442	6.1	2203	1.6
13	M	0308	6.2	1031	1.6	1529	5.8	◑ 2247	1.9
14	TU	0401	5.8	1123	1.9	1630	5.5	2348	2.2
15	W	0514	5.5	1238	2.1	1813	5.2		
16	TH	0119	2.3	0703	5.4	1410	2.1	1954	5.4
17	F	0249	2.0	0825	5.7	1530	1.8	2101	5.8
18	SA	0405	1.6	0930	6.1	1645	1.4	2158	6.2
19	SU	0516	1.2	1026	6.4	1751	1.0	2247	6.6
20	M	0618	0.8	1115	6.7	1847	0.8	● 2332	6.9
21	TU	0712	0.5	1158	6.8	1935	0.6		
22	W	0013	7.0	0759	0.3	1238	6.8	2016	0.5
23	TH	0054	7.1	0839	0.3	1317	6.8	2052	0.6
24	F	0134	7.0	0915	0.4	1356	6.6	2124	0.8
25	SA	0214	6.8	0948	0.7	1437	6.3	2155	1.1
26	SU	0255	6.5	1020	1.2	1521	6.0	2227	1.5
27	M	0340	6.0	1056	1.7	1612	5.5	◐ 2306	2.0
28	TU	0435	5.5	1145	2.1	1717	5.1		

MARCH

Date	Day	Time	m	Time	m	Time	m	Time	m
1	W	0008	2.4	0547	5.1	1258	2.5	1837	5.0
2	TH	0135	2.5	0717	5.0	1416	2.5	2007	5.1
3	F	0255	2.3	0855	5.2	1529	2.2	2116	5.5
4	SA	0403	2.0	0949	5.6	1630	1.9	2201	5.8
5	SU	0457	1.6	1026	5.9	1718	1.6	2236	6.1
6	M	0539	1.3	1054	6.1	1757	1.4	2306	6.3
7	TU	0615	1.2	1120	6.2	1830	1.2	○ 2334	6.4
8	W	0648	1.1	1147	6.3	1902	1.2		
9	TH	0000	6.5	0722	1.0	1212	6.4	1933	1.1
10	F	0026	6.5	0754	1.0	1237	6.4	2004	1.1
11	SA	0053	6.6	0824	1.0	1304	6.5	2034	1.1
12	SU	0122	6.6	0853	1.1	1336	6.5	2104	1.2
13	M	0157	6.5	0925	1.3	1415	6.3	2138	1.5
14	TU	0239	6.3	1003	1.6	1501	5.9	2222	1.8
15	W	0331	5.8	1055	1.9	1603	5.4	◑ 2324	2.2
16	TH	0451	5.3	1211	2.3	1809	5.1		
17	F	0059	2.3	0704	5.3	1356	2.2	1946	5.3
18	SA	0237	2.0	0825	5.6	1523	1.8	2053	5.8
19	SU	0359	1.5	0928	6.1	1639	1.4	2148	6.3
20	M	0509	1.0	1020	6.5	1740	1.0	2234	6.7
21	TU	0606	0.6	1104	6.7	1830	0.7	● 2316	7.0
22	W	0655	0.4	1142	6.8	1913	0.5	2355	7.1
23	TH	0737	0.2	1218	6.9	1950	0.5		
24	F	0033	7.1	0814	0.3	1253	6.8	2023	0.6
25	SA	0110	7.0	0846	0.5	1329	6.6	2052	0.8
26	SU	0146	6.7	0914	0.9	1406	6.4	2120	1.1
27	M	0223	6.4	0941	1.3	1447	6.0	2146	1.5
28	TU	0305	5.9	1008	1.8	1536	5.6	2219	2.0
29	W	0359	5.4	1046	2.2	1640	5.2	◐ 2312	2.4
30	TH	0511	5.0	1207	2.6	1756	5.0		
31	F	0057	2.6	0637	4.9	1344	2.6	1924	5.0

APRIL

Date	Day	Time	m	Time	m	Time	m	Time	m
1	SA	0223	2.4	0823	5.1	1457	2.3	2041	5.4
2	SU	0330	2.0	0918	5.5	1557	1.9	2127	5.8
3	M	0423	1.6	0951	5.8	1646	1.6	2201	6.1
4	TU	0505	1.3	1018	6.1	1725	1.4	2231	6.3
5	W	0543	1.1	1046	6.2	1800	1.2	2259	6.4
6	TH	0619	1.0	1114	6.4	1834	1.1	○ 2328	6.5
7	F	0654	0.9	1142	6.5	1907	1.0	2357	6.6
8	SA	0727	0.9	1210	6.5	1939	1.0		
9	SU	0026	6.7	0800	0.9	1240	6.6	2012	1.0
10	M	0059	6.7	0831	1.0	1316	6.5	2045	1.2
11	TU	0137	6.5	0906	1.3	1358	6.3	2123	1.4
12	W	0222	6.2	0947	1.6	1449	5.9	2211	1.8
13	TH	0322	5.7	1042	2.0	1605	5.4	◑ 2318	2.1
14	F	0510	5.3	1205	2.3	1802	5.2		
15	SA	0056	2.2	0658	5.3	1348	2.1	1929	5.5
16	SU	0228	1.8	0814	5.7	1510	1.7	2035	5.9
17	M	0345	1.4	0913	6.1	1618	1.3	2128	6.3
18	TU	0450	0.9	1001	6.4	1715	1.0	2213	6.7
19	W	0544	0.6	1042	6.6	1802	0.7	2254	6.9
20	TH	0629	0.5	1119	6.7	1843	0.6	● 2332	6.9
21	F	0709	0.5	1154	6.7	1919	0.7		
22	SA	0009	6.9	0744	0.6	1228	6.7	1952	0.8
23	SU	0046	6.8	0814	0.8	1304	6.6	2022	1.0
24	M	0121	6.5	0841	1.1	1342	6.3	2048	1.2
25	TU	0158	6.2	0904	1.5	1422	6.1	2115	1.6
26	W	0239	5.8	0931	1.8	1509	5.7	2149	1.9
27	TH	0334	5.4	1009	2.2	1608	5.4	◐ 2239	2.3
28	F	0441	5.1	1110	2.5	1717	5.1		
29	SA	0010	2.5	0557	4.9	1259	2.6	1832	5.1
30	SU	0139	2.4	0715	5.1	1414	2.4	1943	5.4

Chart Datum: 3·67 metres below Ordnance Datum (Newlyn)
HAT is 7·4 metres above Chart Datum

TIME ZONE (UT)
For Summer Time add ONE hour in **non-shaded areas**

DOVER

LAT 51°07′N LONG 1°19′E

TIMES AND HEIGHTS OF HIGH AND LOW WATERS

Dates in amber are **SPRINGS**
Dates in grey are **NEAPS**

2023

MAY

Date	Day	Time	m	Time	m	Time	m	Time	m
1	M	0242	2.0	0818	5.4	1511	2.0	2034	5.7
2	TU	0334	1.7	0859	5.7	1600	1.7	2113	6.0
3	W	0420	1.4	0934	6.0	1644	1.5	2147	6.2
4	TH	0504	1.2	1007	6.2	1724	1.3	2220	6.4
5	F	0545	1.0	1039	6.4	1803	1.1	○ 2254	6.5
6	SA	0625	0.9	1112	6.5	1841	1.0	2328	6.6
7	SU	0703	0.9	1146	6.6	1918	1.0		
8	M	0004	6.7	0740	0.9	1223	6.6	1956	1.0
9	TU	0043	6.6	0816	1.1	1306	6.5	2035	1.2
10	W	0128	6.4	0856	1.3	1355	6.3	2120	1.4
11	TH	0223	6.1	0944	1.6	1457	5.9	2214	1.7
12	F	0337	5.7	1044	1.9	1614	5.7	◑ 2326	1.9
13	SA	0511	5.5	1208	2.0	1739	5.6		
14	SU	0051	1.8	0639	5.5	1330	1.9	1900	5.7
15	M	0207	1.6	0750	5.8	1440	1.6	2006	6.0
16	TU	0316	1.3	0847	6.0	1544	1.4	2059	6.3
17	W	0419	1.0	0934	6.2	1640	1.1	2146	6.5
18	TH	0514	0.9	1016	6.4	1729	1.0	2229	6.6
19	F	0600	0.8	1054	6.5	1812	0.9	● 2310	6.6
20	SA	0639	0.8	1130	6.5	1850	0.9	2348	6.6
21	SU	0714	1.0	1208	6.5	1924	1.0		
22	M	0026	6.5	0745	1.1	1245	6.4	1956	1.2
23	TU	0102	6.3	0813	1.3	1323	6.3	2025	1.4
24	W	0140	6.1	0838	1.6	1403	6.1	2055	1.6
25	TH	0221	5.8	0908	1.8	1446	5.8	2132	1.8
26	F	0310	5.5	0948	2.1	1535	5.6	2219	2.1
27	SA	0408	5.2	1039	2.3	1632	5.4	◐ 2323	2.2
28	SU	0512	5.1	1152	2.4	1735	5.3		
29	M	0040	2.2	0618	5.2	1312	2.3	1839	5.4
30	TU	0145	2.0	0717	5.3	1415	2.1	1934	5.6
31	W	0242	1.8	0806	5.6	1510	1.9	2020	5.8

JUNE

Date	Day	Time	m	Time	m	Time	m	Time	m
1	TH	0334	1.5	0848	5.8	1600	1.6	2102	6.1
2	F	0424	1.3	0928	6.1	1648	1.4	2143	6.3
3	SA	0512	1.1	1007	6.3	1734	1.2	2224	6.5
4	SU	0559	1.0	1048	6.4	1819	1.1	○ 2306	6.6
5	M	0644	1.0	1131	6.5	1903	1.0	2351	6.6
6	TU	0728	1.0	1216	6.6	1948	1.0		
7	W	0038	6.5	0813	1.1	1305	6.5	2036	1.1
8	TH	0130	6.4	0900	1.2	1359	6.4	2127	1.2
9	F	0230	6.2	0952	1.4	1457	6.2	2224	1.3
10	SA	0337	5.9	1050	1.6	1600	6.1	◑ 2326	1.4
11	SU	0450	5.8	1153	1.7	1707	5.9		
12	M	0030	1.5	0605	5.7	1258	1.7	1819	5.9
13	TU	0134	1.5	0713	5.7	1400	1.7	1927	5.9
14	W	0237	1.4	0812	5.8	1502	1.6	2027	6.0
15	TH	0340	1.3	0904	5.9	1602	1.4	2119	6.2
16	F	0439	1.3	0950	6.1	1656	1.3	2208	6.2
17	SA	0529	1.2	1032	6.2	1743	1.2	2252	6.3
18	SU	0611	1.2	1112	6.3	1825	1.2	● 2333	6.3
19	M	0648	1.3	1151	6.3	1902	1.2		
20	TU	0011	6.2	0722	1.4	1229	6.3	1937	1.3
21	W	0048	6.1	0752	1.5	1306	6.3	2009	1.4
22	TH	0124	6.0	0821	1.6	1343	6.2	2042	1.5
23	F	0200	5.8	0854	1.7	1419	6.0	2118	1.6
24	SA	0238	5.7	0931	1.8	1455	5.9	2159	1.7
25	SU	0319	5.5	1012	1.9	1537	5.7	2245	1.9
26	M	0409	5.4	1100	2.1	1628	5.6	◐ 2339	2.0
27	TU	0510	5.3	1159	2.2	1728	5.5		
28	W	0043	2.0	0614	5.3	1310	2.2	1831	5.5
29	TH	0148	1.9	0714	5.5	1418	2.0	1930	5.7
30	F	0250	1.7	0807	5.7	1520	1.8	2024	5.9

JULY

Date	Day	Time	m	Time	m	Time	m	Time	m
1	SA	0349	1.5	0857	5.9	1617	1.6	2115	6.2
2	SU	0445	1.3	0947	6.2	1711	1.3	2206	6.4
3	M	0539	1.2	1036	6.4	1804	1.1	○ 2257	6.5
4	TU	0633	1.0	1124	6.6	1856	1.0	2347	6.6
5	W	0726	1.0	1213	6.7	1949	0.8		
6	TH	0037	6.6	0818	0.9	1301	6.7	2042	0.8
7	F	0129	6.5	0906	1.0	1351	6.7	2131	0.8
8	SA	0223	6.4	0951	1.0	1443	6.6	2219	0.9
9	SU	0318	6.2	1036	1.2	1535	6.4	2306	1.1
10	M	0415	6.0	1124	1.4	1631	6.2	◑ 2358	1.3
11	TU	0516	5.8	1217	1.7	1732	5.9		
12	W	0053	1.6	0624	5.6	1316	1.8	1841	5.7
13	TH	0154	1.7	0732	5.5	1420	1.9	1953	5.7
14	F	0258	1.8	0835	5.6	1526	1.8	2058	5.8
15	SA	0404	1.7	0930	5.8	1628	1.7	2155	5.9
16	SU	0502	1.6	1017	6.0	1721	1.5	2242	6.0
17	M	0549	1.5	1059	6.2	1806	1.4	● 2322	6.1
18	TU	0629	1.5	1137	6.3	1846	1.3	2358	6.1
19	W	0703	1.5	1213	6.4	1921	1.3		
20	TH	0031	6.1	0735	1.5	1247	6.4	1954	1.3
21	F	0103	6.1	0805	1.5	1318	6.3	2026	1.3
22	SA	0132	6.0	0836	1.5	1346	6.2	2059	1.4
23	SU	0158	5.9	0909	1.5	1414	6.1	2133	1.5
24	M	0226	5.8	0943	1.7	1446	6.1	2209	1.6
25	TU	0302	5.7	1020	1.8	1528	5.9	◐ 2249	1.8
26	W	0348	5.6	1103	2.0	1620	5.7	2340	1.9
27	TH	0450	5.4	1201	2.2	1728	5.5		
28	F	0050	2.1	0619	5.3	1325	2.3	1850	5.5
29	SA	0211	2.0	0739	5.5	1446	2.1	2002	5.7
30	SU	0322	1.8	0843	5.8	1553	1.7	2105	6.0
31	M	0426	1.5	0939	6.1	1655	1.4	2202	6.3

AUGUST

Date	Day	Time	m	Time	m	Time	m	Time	m
1	TU	0527	1.2	1031	6.4	1755	1.1	○ 2255	6.5
2	W	0627	1.0	1119	6.7	1853	0.8	2344	6.7
3	TH	0723	0.8	1205	6.9	1947	0.6		
4	F	0030	6.8	0812	0.7	1249	7.0	2035	0.5
5	SA	0116	6.7	0854	0.7	1334	7.0	2118	0.5
6	SU	0201	6.6	0932	0.8	1420	6.9	2157	0.6
7	M	0247	6.4	1008	1.0	1506	6.6	2236	1.0
8	TU	0336	6.1	1047	1.4	1555	6.3	◑ 2319	1.4
9	W	0430	5.8	1133	1.8	1650	5.9		
10	TH	0010	1.8	0534	5.4	1232	2.1	1758	5.5
11	F	0114	2.1	0650	5.2	1345	2.3	1921	5.3
12	SA	0225	2.2	0811	5.3	1500	2.2	2049	5.5
13	SU	0339	2.1	0917	5.6	1611	1.9	2151	5.7
14	M	0445	1.9	1006	5.9	1708	1.6	2235	5.9
15	TU	0534	1.7	1045	6.2	1753	1.4	2310	6.1
16	W	0614	1.5	1120	6.4	1830	1.3	● 2340	6.2
17	TH	0646	1.4	1152	6.5	1902	1.3		
18	F	0008	6.2	0715	1.4	1221	6.5	1933	1.2
19	SA	0035	6.2	0743	1.4	1248	6.4	2003	1.2
20	SU	0058	6.2	0812	1.3	1311	6.4	2033	1.2
21	M	0120	6.2	0842	1.4	1336	6.4	2103	1.3
22	TU	0146	6.2	0912	1.5	1407	6.3	2134	1.5
23	W	0220	6.1	0944	1.7	1444	6.2	2209	1.7
24	TH	0303	5.9	1023	1.9	1532	5.9	◐ 2254	2.0
25	F	0357	5.5	1115	2.2	1638	5.5	2359	2.3
26	SA	0531	5.2	1238	2.4	1832	5.3		
27	SU	0140	2.3	0728	5.3	1422	2.3	1958	5.6
28	M	0305	2.0	0836	5.7	1538	1.8	2104	6.0
29	TU	0415	1.6	0932	6.2	1645	1.4	2200	6.4
30	W	0519	1.2	1021	6.6	1747	0.9	2249	6.7
31	TH	0617	0.9	1106	6.9	1842	0.6	○ 2333	6.9

Chart Datum: 3·67 metres below Ordnance Datum (Newlyn)
HAT is 7·4 metres above Chart Datum

TIME ZONE (UT)
For Summer Time add ONE hour in **non-shaded areas**

DOVER

LAT 51°07′N LONG 1°19′E

TIMES AND HEIGHTS OF HIGH AND LOW WATERS

Dates in amber are **SPRINGS**
Dates in grey are **NEAPS**

2023

SEPTEMBER

Date	Day	Time	m	Time	m	Time	m	Time	m
1	F	0707	0.7	1149	7.1	1932	0.4		
2	SA	0014	6.9	0751	0.6	1230	7.2	2015	0.3
3	SU	0053	6.9	0829	0.6	1311	7.2	2052	0.4
4	M	0133	6.8	0902	0.8	1352	7.0	2127	0.7
5	TU	0214	6.5	0935	1.0	1434	6.7	2200	1.1
6	W	0259	6.2	1009	1.5	1520	6.2	◑ 2237	1.6
7	TH	0351	5.7	1048	1.9	1615	5.7	2323	2.2
8	F	0454	5.3	1147	2.4	1723	5.3		
9	SA	0035	2.6	0612	5.1	1314	2.6	1852	5.1
10	SU	0200	2.6	0746	5.2	1441	2.4	2044	5.3
11	M	0322	2.3	0901	5.6	1557	2.0	2139	5.7
12	TU	0428	2.0	0947	6.0	1652	1.7	2217	6.0
13	W	0514	1.7	1023	6.3	1733	1.4	2247	6.2
14	TH	0551	1.5	1054	6.5	1806	1.3	2312	6.3
15	F	0620	1.4	1123	6.5	1835	1.2	● 2337	6.4
16	SA	0647	1.3	1149	6.6	1903	1.1		
17	SU	0001	6.4	0715	1.3	1213	6.5	1934	1.1
18	M	0023	6.4	0744	1.3	1237	6.6	2004	1.2
19	TU	0046	6.4	0814	1.3	1303	6.6	2033	1.3
20	W	0114	6.4	0843	1.4	1333	6.5	2102	1.4
21	TH	0149	6.3	0916	1.6	1411	6.3	2138	1.7
22	F	0232	6.0	0956	1.9	1459	5.9	◐ 2224	2.1
23	SA	0327	5.5	1050	2.3	1610	5.4	2329	2.4
24	SU	0533	5.1	1215	2.5	1833	5.3		
25	M	0123	2.5	0716	5.3	1408	2.3	1953	5.6
26	TU	0255	2.1	0823	5.8	1527	1.8	2056	6.1
27	W	0404	1.6	0917	6.3	1633	1.2	2148	6.5
28	TH	0504	1.2	1004	6.8	1731	0.8	2233	6.8
29	F	0556	0.9	1047	7.1	1822	0.5	○ 2313	7.0
30	SA	0641	0.7	1127	7.2	1907	0.4	2351	7.0

OCTOBER

Date	Day	Time	m	Time	m	Time	m	Time	m
1	SU	0721	0.6	1206	7.3	1946	0.4		
2	M	0026	6.9	0757	0.7	1244	7.2	2021	0.6
3	TU	0104	6.8	0830	0.9	1323	6.9	2053	0.9
4	W	0143	6.5	0901	1.2	1404	6.6	2123	1.4
5	TH	0227	6.2	0932	1.6	1449	6.1	2153	1.9
6	F	0319	5.8	1007	2.1	1545	5.6	◑ 2232	2.4
7	SA	0421	5.4	1100	2.5	1654	5.2	2350	2.8
8	SU	0535	5.1	1243	2.7	1818	5.0		
9	M	0132	2.8	0705	5.2	1415	2.5	2015	5.2
10	TU	0253	2.5	0826	5.5	1526	2.1	2108	5.6
11	W	0353	2.1	0913	5.9	1616	1.7	2143	5.9
12	TH	0438	1.7	0948	6.2	1655	1.4	2210	6.2
13	F	0514	1.5	1018	6.4	1728	1.3	2234	6.3
14	SA	0545	1.4	1045	6.5	1800	1.2	● 2300	6.4
15	SU	0614	1.3	1112	6.6	1832	1.1	2326	6.5
16	M	0646	1.2	1139	6.6	1904	1.1	2351	6.5
17	TU	0717	1.2	1206	6.6	1936	1.2		
18	W	0018	6.6	0749	1.3	1235	6.6	2007	1.3
19	TH	0050	6.5	0821	1.4	1310	6.5	2039	1.5
20	F	0129	6.4	0857	1.6	1351	6.2	2118	1.8
21	SA	0216	6.0	0941	1.9	1445	5.8	2207	2.1
22	SU	0322	5.5	1040	2.3	1626	5.3	◐ 2316	2.5
23	M	0526	5.3	1212	2.4	1823	5.4		
24	TU	0110	2.4	0654	5.5	1353	2.1	1938	5.7
25	W	0236	2.0	0800	6.0	1507	1.6	2038	6.1
26	TH	0341	1.6	0854	6.4	1611	1.2	2128	6.5
27	F	0437	1.2	0940	6.8	1706	0.8	2210	6.7
28	SA	0527	0.9	1023	7.0	1755	0.7	○ 2249	6.9
29	SU	0611	0.8	1103	7.1	1838	0.6	2325	6.9
30	M	0651	0.8	1142	7.1	1916	0.7		
31	TU	0002	6.9	0727	0.9	1220	6.9	1950	0.9

NOVEMBER

Date	Day	Time	m	Time	m	Time	m	Time	m
1	W	0039	6.7	0801	1.1	1258	6.7	2021	1.2
2	TH	0119	6.5	0833	1.4	1339	6.4	2049	1.6
3	F	0202	6.2	0903	1.7	1424	6.0	2117	2.0
4	SA	0252	5.9	0938	2.1	1520	5.5	2154	2.4
5	SU	0350	5.5	1026	2.4	1625	5.2	◑ 2251	2.7
6	M	0457	5.3	1154	2.6	1738	5.0		
7	TU	0041	2.8	0611	5.3	1325	2.5	1902	5.2
8	W	0201	2.6	0726	5.5	1430	2.2	2009	5.5
9	TH	0301	2.2	0821	5.8	1522	1.8	2050	5.8
10	F	0349	1.9	0900	6.0	1605	1.6	2122	6.0
11	SA	0429	1.7	0933	6.2	1645	1.4	2153	6.2
12	SU	0507	1.5	1004	6.4	1724	1.2	2223	6.4
13	M	0543	1.3	1035	6.5	1802	1.2	● 2254	6.5
14	TU	0619	1.3	1108	6.6	1838	1.1	2325	6.6
15	W	0655	1.2	1142	6.6	1914	1.2		
16	TH	0000	6.6	0732	1.3	1218	6.6	1950	1.3
17	F	0039	6.6	0809	1.4	1259	6.4	2028	1.5
18	SA	0124	6.4	0851	1.5	1349	6.1	2111	1.7
19	SU	0220	6.1	0941	1.8	1454	5.8	2204	2.0
20	M	0332	5.8	1044	2.0	1628	5.6	◐ 2316	2.2
21	TU	0458	5.7	1206	2.0	1758	5.6		
22	W	0045	2.2	0620	5.8	1326	1.8	1910	5.8
23	TH	0200	1.9	0727	6.0	1435	1.5	2010	6.0
24	F	0305	1.6	0824	6.3	1538	1.3	2100	6.3
25	SA	0403	1.4	0913	6.5	1636	1.1	2145	6.4
26	SU	0455	1.2	0958	6.7	1727	1.0	2226	6.6
27	M	0542	1.1	1041	6.7	1811	1.0	○ 2305	6.6
28	TU	0624	1.0	1122	6.7	1850	1.1	2344	6.6
29	W	0703	1.1	1202	6.6	1924	1.2		
30	TH	0022	6.6	0740	1.2	1241	6.4	1957	1.4

DECEMBER

Date	Day	Time	m	Time	m	Time	m	Time	m
1	F	0103	6.5	0813	1.4	1322	6.2	2026	1.7
2	SA	0144	6.3	0846	1.7	1404	5.9	2056	1.9
3	SU	0228	6.0	0921	1.9	1453	5.6	2132	2.2
4	M	0316	5.8	1004	2.1	1548	5.4	2218	2.4
5	TU	0411	5.5	1101	2.3	1651	5.2	◑ 2320	2.5
6	W	0512	5.4	1212	2.3	1757	5.1		
7	TH	0041	2.6	0617	5.4	1321	2.2	1900	5.3
8	F	0152	2.4	0716	5.5	1420	2.0	1951	5.5
9	SA	0250	2.2	0804	5.8	1513	1.8	2034	5.7
10	SU	0342	1.9	0846	6.0	1604	1.5	2114	6.0
11	M	0430	1.6	0926	6.2	1651	1.4	2152	6.2
12	TU	0515	1.4	1006	6.4	1736	1.2	● 2230	6.4
13	W	0558	1.3	1046	6.5	1819	1.2	2310	6.5
14	TH	0640	1.2	1129	6.6	1901	1.2	2353	6.6
15	F	0723	1.2	1213	6.6	1944	1.2		
16	SA	0038	6.6	0809	1.2	1300	6.5	2029	1.3
17	SU	0127	6.5	0857	1.3	1353	6.3	2116	1.4
18	M	0221	6.4	0949	1.4	1453	6.1	2208	1.6
19	TU	0320	6.2	1045	1.5	1601	5.9	◐ 2306	1.8
20	W	0424	6.1	1146	1.6	1715	5.7		
21	TH	0009	1.9	0534	5.9	1249	1.6	1828	5.7
22	F	0115	1.9	0645	5.9	1353	1.6	1933	5.7
23	SA	0220	1.8	0750	6.0	1457	1.5	2030	5.9
24	SU	0324	1.7	0848	6.1	1603	1.5	2122	6.0
25	M	0426	1.5	0940	6.2	1701	1.4	2209	6.2
26	TU	0519	1.4	1028	6.3	1750	1.3	2252	6.3
27	W	0606	1.3	1112	6.3	1831	1.3	○ 2332	6.4
28	TH	0647	1.3	1152	6.3	1908	1.4		
29	F	0011	6.5	0726	1.3	1230	6.3	1942	1.5
30	SA	0049	6.4	0801	1.4	1307	6.1	2012	1.6
31	SU	0126	6.3	0834	1.5	1344	6.0	2041	1.7

Chart Datum: 3·67 metres below Ordnance Datum (Newlyn)
HAT is 7·4 metres above Chart Datum

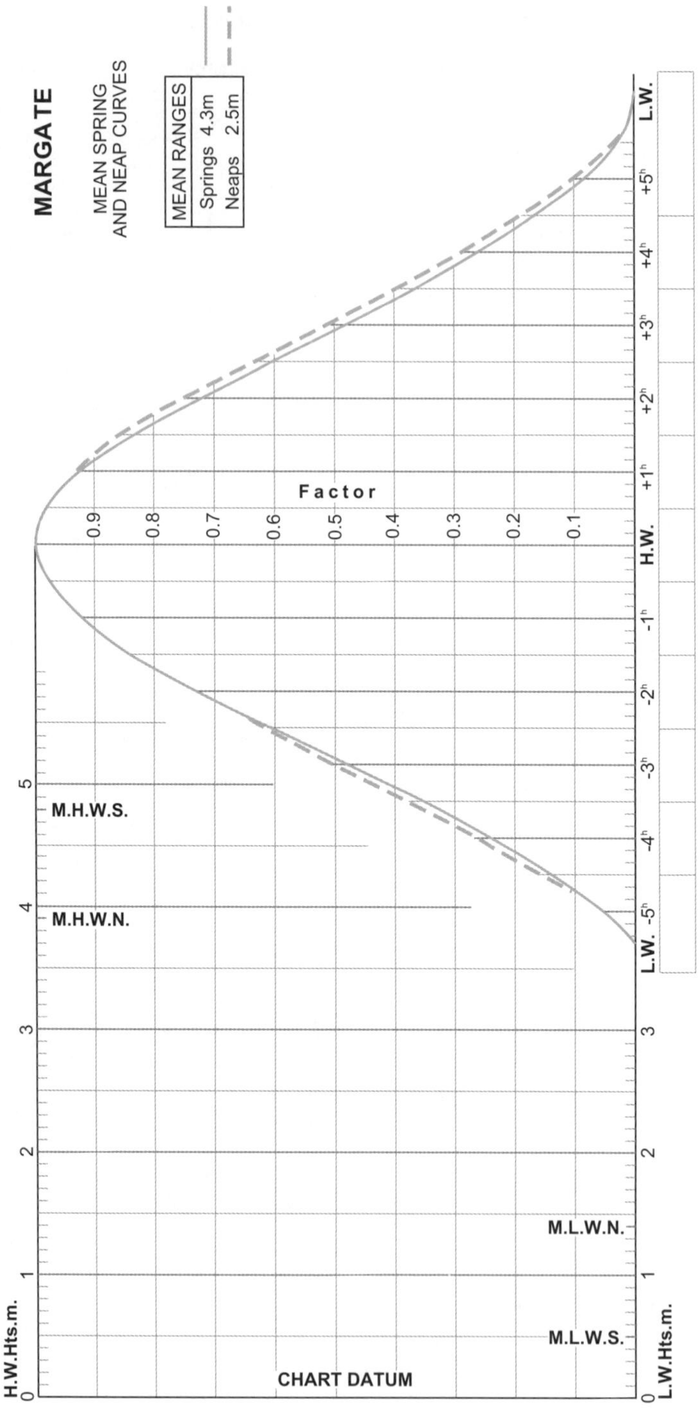
MARGATE
MEAN SPRING AND NEAP CURVES
MEAN RANGES
Springs 4.3m
Neaps 2.5m
Factor
0.9
0.8
0.7
0.6
0.5
0.4
0.3
0.2
0.1
L.W.
-5h
-4h
-3h
-2h
-1h
H.W.
+1h
+2h
+3h
+4h
+5h
L.W.
H.W.Hts.m.
L.W.Hts.m.
M.H.W.S.
M.H.W.N.
M.L.W.N.
M.L.W.S.
CHART DATUM
0
1
2
3
4
5

TIME ZONE (UT)
For Summer Time add ONE hour in **non-shaded areas**

MARGATE

LAT 51°23'N LONG 1°23'E

TIMES AND HEIGHTS OF HIGH AND LOW WATERS

Dates in amber are **SPRINGS**
Dates in grey are **NEAPS**

2023

JANUARY

Date	Day	Time	m	Time	m	Time	m	Time	m	Moon
1	SU	0058	1.4	0708	4.2	1346	0.9	2003	4.2	
2	M	0206	1.4	0811	4.2	1444	1.0	2103	4.2	
3	TU	0307	1.3	0913	4.2	1536	1.1	2158	4.2	
4	W	0405	1.2	1011	4.3	1624	1.1	2245	4.3	
5	TH	0457	1.0	1100	4.3	1707	1.1	2324	4.4	
6	F	0544	0.9	1143	4.4	1747	1.1	2359	4.5	○
7	SA	0625	0.8	1221	4.4	1823	1.0			
8	SU	0031	4.5	0702	0.7	1256	4.5	1856	1.0	
9	M	0105	4.5	0735	0.7	1332	4.5	1928	1.0	
10	TU	0141	4.5	0806	0.7	1408	4.4	2000	1.0	
11	W	0217	4.5	0839	0.7	1445	4.4	2035	1.1	
12	TH	0252	4.4	0914	0.7	1521	4.3	2113	1.2	
13	F	0326	4.3	0951	0.8	1558	4.2	2152	1.3	
14	SA	0403	4.3	1032	0.9	1637	4.1	2236	1.4	
15	SU	0446	4.2	1119	1.0	1724	4.0	2330	1.4	◑
16	M	0538	4.1	1217	1.1	1822	4.0			
17	TU	0037	1.5	0642	4.1	1327	1.1	1937	4.0	
18	W	0202	1.4	0801	4.1	1440	1.1	2057	4.1	
19	TH	0318	1.2	0919	4.2	1545	1.0	2202	4.3	
20	F	0423	1.0	1027	4.4	1644	0.9	2259	4.4	
21	SA	0524	0.8	1127	4.6	1739	0.8	2350	4.6	●
22	SU	0621	0.6	1222	4.8	1831	0.8			
23	M	0038	4.7	0714	0.4	1314	4.9	1919	0.8	
24	TU	0126	4.8	0804	0.3	1405	4.9	2004	0.8	
25	W	0213	4.8	0851	0.3	1454	4.8	2047	0.9	
26	TH	0258	4.8	0935	0.3	1541	4.7	2129	1.0	
27	F	0342	4.7	1018	0.5	1627	4.5	2212	1.1	
28	SA	0426	4.6	1101	0.7	1715	4.3	2300	1.2	◐
29	SU	0517	4.4	1150	0.9	1811	4.0			
30	M	0000	1.4	0618	4.2	1250	1.1	1914	3.9	
31	TU	0116	1.5	0729	4.0	1356	1.3	2021	3.9	

FEBRUARY

Date	Day	Time	m	Time	m	Time	m	Time	m	Moon
1	W	0232	1.4	0842	4.0	1502	1.4	2127	4.0	
2	TH	0345	1.3	0953	4.0	1604	1.3	2225	4.1	
3	F	0449	1.1	1051	4.2	1657	1.2	2311	4.3	
4	SA	0536	0.9	1136	4.3	1738	1.2	2349	4.4	
5	SU	0614	0.8	1212	4.4	1812	1.1			○
6	M	0020	4.5	0647	0.7	1244	4.4	1842	1.0	
7	TU	0052	4.5	0717	0.6	1315	4.5	1912	1.0	
8	W	0125	4.6	0746	0.6	1349	4.5	1944	0.9	
9	TH	0200	4.6	0817	0.6	1423	4.5	2017	0.9	
10	F	0232	4.5	0848	0.6	1456	4.4	2050	1.0	
11	SA	0302	4.5	0920	0.7	1527	4.3	2123	1.1	
12	SU	0331	4.4	0953	0.8	1559	4.2	2200	1.2	
13	M	0408	4.3	1031	0.9	1641	4.1	2246	1.3	◑
14	TU	0458	4.2	1122	1.1	1736	4.0	2350	1.4	
15	W	0602	4.1	1240	1.2	1851	3.8			
16	TH	0125	1.4	0731	4.0	1413	1.3	2031	3.9	
17	F	0258	1.3	0907	4.1	1531	1.2	2148	4.1	
18	SA	0415	1.0	1024	4.4	1637	1.0	2251	4.4	
19	SU	0521	0.7	1125	4.6	1732	0.9	2343	4.6	
20	M	0615	0.4	1218	4.8	1821	0.8			●
21	TU	0030	4.7	0704	0.3	1306	4.9	1905	0.7	
22	W	0115	4.9	0748	0.2	1352	4.9	1947	0.7	
23	TH	0157	4.9	0828	0.2	1435	4.8	2026	0.7	
24	F	0237	4.9	0905	0.3	1514	4.6	2103	0.8	
25	SA	0314	4.8	0937	0.5	1549	4.4	2140	0.9	
26	SU	0351	4.6	1010	0.7	1623	4.2	2220	1.1	
27	M	0433	4.4	1050	1.0	1705	4.0	2310	1.3	◐
28	TU	0527	4.1	1146	1.3	1811	3.7			

MARCH

Date	Day	Time	m	Time	m	Time	m	Time	m	Moon
1	W	0025	1.5	0644	3.8	1307	1.6	1937	3.7	
2	TH	0155	1.5	0813	3.7	1431	1.6	2054	3.8	
3	F	0323	1.4	0935	3.9	1546	1.5	2200	4.0	
4	SA	0430	1.1	1035	4.1	1642	1.3	2251	4.2	
5	SU	0516	0.9	1120	4.2	1721	1.2	2330	4.3	
6	M	0551	0.7	1155	4.3	1753	1.1			
7	TU	0002	4.5	0622	0.6	1224	4.4	1823	1.0	○
8	W	0032	4.5	0651	0.6	1252	4.5	1852	0.9	
9	TH	0103	4.6	0719	0.5	1324	4.5	1923	0.8	
10	F	0136	4.7	0749	0.5	1357	4.5	1955	0.8	
11	SA	0207	4.6	0818	0.5	1428	4.4	2027	0.9	
12	SU	0235	4.6	0848	0.6	1455	4.3	2059	0.9	
13	M	0302	4.5	0918	0.7	1525	4.2	2135	1.0	
14	TU	0340	4.4	0956	0.9	1608	4.1	2221	1.1	
15	W	0432	4.2	1050	1.1	1707	3.9	2328	1.3	◑
16	TH	0544	4.0	1215	1.4	1831	3.7			
17	F	0111	1.4	0727	3.9	1400	1.4	2017	3.8	
18	SA	0250	1.2	0905	4.1	1522	1.2	2136	4.1	
19	SU	0409	0.8	1020	4.4	1626	1.0	2239	4.4	
20	M	0509	0.5	1117	4.6	1716	0.9	2329	4.6	
21	TU	0558	0.3	1204	4.8	1800	0.8			●
22	W	0012	4.8	0642	0.2	1247	4.8	1842	0.7	
23	TH	0052	4.9	0721	0.2	1328	4.8	1922	0.6	
24	F	0131	5.0	0756	0.3	1406	4.7	2001	0.7	
25	SA	0209	4.9	0827	0.4	1439	4.6	2037	0.7	
26	SU	0245	4.8	0856	0.6	1508	4.4	2112	0.8	
27	M	0321	4.6	0926	0.8	1539	4.2	2148	1.0	
28	TU	0400	4.3	1002	1.1	1618	4.0	2233	1.2	
29	W	0448	4.0	1053	1.5	1711	3.7	2339	1.4	◐
30	TH	0558	3.7	1212	1.7	1842	3.6			
31	F	0114	1.5	0739	3.6	1355	1.8	2013	3.6	

APRIL

Date	Day	Time	m	Time	m	Time	m	Time	m	Moon
1	SA	0244	1.4	0902	3.8	1515	1.6	2121	3.9	
2	SU	0351	1.1	1002	4.0	1610	1.4	2214	4.1	
3	M	0437	0.9	1046	4.2	1650	1.2	2256	4.3	
4	TU	0514	0.7	1122	4.3	1724	1.0	2330	4.4	
5	W	0546	0.6	1152	4.4	1755	0.9			
6	TH	0001	4.5	0617	0.5	1221	4.5	1827	0.8	○
7	F	0033	4.6	0647	0.5	1253	4.5	1900	0.8	
8	SA	0106	4.7	0717	0.5	1327	4.6	1933	0.8	
9	SU	0139	4.7	0748	0.5	1359	4.5	2007	0.8	
10	M	0211	4.6	0820	0.6	1430	4.4	2042	0.8	
11	TU	0245	4.5	0855	0.8	1506	4.3	2123	0.9	
12	W	0330	4.4	0940	1.0	1554	4.1	2215	1.0	
13	TH	0430	4.2	1041	1.2	1658	3.9	2330	1.2	◑
14	F	0549	4.0	1210	1.4	1827	3.8			
15	SA	0111	1.2	0729	4.0	1350	1.4	2001	3.9	
16	SU	0241	0.9	0858	4.2	1506	1.2	2116	4.1	
17	M	0352	0.6	1005	4.5	1604	1.0	2215	4.4	
18	TU	0447	0.4	1057	4.6	1652	0.9	2303	4.6	
19	W	0532	0.3	1142	4.7	1734	0.8	2345	4.8	
20	TH	0611	0.3	1221	4.7	1815	0.7			●
21	F	0023	4.9	0646	0.3	1257	4.7	1857	0.6	
22	SA	0102	4.9	0719	0.4	1331	4.6	1937	0.6	
23	SU	0141	4.8	0751	0.5	1403	4.5	2015	0.7	
24	M	0219	4.7	0822	0.7	1434	4.4	2050	0.8	
25	TU	0256	4.5	0853	1.0	1507	4.2	2124	0.9	
26	W	0335	4.2	0928	1.2	1546	4.1	2205	1.1	
27	TH	0420	4.0	1015	1.5	1634	3.8	2303	1.3	◐
28	F	0519	3.7	1120	1.7	1740	3.6			
29	SA	0025	1.4	0648	3.6	1254	1.8	1919	3.6	
30	SU	0152	1.3	0812	3.7	1425	1.6	2030	3.8	

Chart Datum: 2·50 metres below Ordnance Datum (Newlyn)
HAT is 5·2 metres above Chart Datum

TIME ZONE (UT)
For Summer Time add ONE hour in **non-shaded areas**

MARGATE

LAT 51°23'N LONG 1°23'E

TIMES AND HEIGHTS OF HIGH AND LOW WATERS

Dates in amber are **SPRINGS**
Dates in grey are **NEAPS**

2023

MAY

Date	Day	Time	m	Time	m	Time	m	Time	m	Moon
1	M	0258	1.1	0911	3.9	1523	1.4	2125	4.0	
2	TU	0347	0.9	0958	4.1	1608	1.2	2210	4.2	
3	W	0429	0.7	1037	4.3	1646	1.0	2249	4.4	
4	TH	0506	0.6	1112	4.4	1723	0.9	2325	4.5	
5	F	0541	0.6	1147	4.5	1759	0.8			○
6	SA	0000	4.6	0615	0.6	1222	4.5	1837	0.8	
7	SU	0038	4.7	0648	0.6	1259	4.6	1914	0.7	
8	M	0117	4.7	0724	0.6	1337	4.5	1953	0.7	
9	TU	0158	4.6	0802	0.7	1417	4.4	2035	0.7	
10	W	0244	4.5	0845	0.8	1502	4.3	2123	0.8	
11	TH	0337	4.4	0937	1.0	1554	4.2	2223	0.9	
12	F	0439	4.2	1042	1.3	1657	4.0	2340	0.9	◑
13	SA	0555	4.1	1204	1.4	1818	4.0			
14	SU	0105	0.9	0721	4.1	1330	1.3	1938	4.1	
15	M	0221	0.7	0835	4.3	1439	1.2	2045	4.3	
16	TU	0324	0.6	0937	4.4	1536	1.0	2143	4.4	
17	W	0416	0.5	1029	4.5	1624	0.9	2233	4.6	
18	TH	0500	0.5	1113	4.5	1708	0.8	2316	4.7	
19	F	0537	0.5	1151	4.5	1752	0.7	2357	4.7	●
20	SA	0612	0.6	1226	4.6	1835	0.6			
21	SU	0037	4.7	0648	0.6	1300	4.5	1918	0.6	
22	M	0118	4.7	0723	0.7	1334	4.5	1957	0.7	
23	TU	0158	4.5	0756	0.9	1409	4.4	2033	0.8	
24	W	0236	4.4	0829	1.0	1445	4.3	2107	0.9	
25	TH	0315	4.2	0905	1.2	1524	4.2	2147	1.0	
26	F	0358	4.0	0948	1.4	1607	4.0	2236	1.1	
27	SA	0447	3.8	1042	1.5	1659	3.9	2337	1.2	◐
28	SU	0548	3.7	1147	1.6	1804	3.8			
29	M	0048	1.2	0705	3.8	1304	1.6	1925	3.8	
30	TU	0158	1.1	0811	3.9	1423	1.5	2027	4.0	
31	W	0254	0.9	0904	4.1	1519	1.3	2119	4.2	

JUNE

Date	Day	Time	m	Time	m	Time	m	Time	m	Moon
1	TH	0343	0.8	0951	4.2	1606	1.1	2206	4.3	
2	F	0426	0.7	1035	4.3	1651	1.0	2250	4.5	
3	SA	0507	0.7	1117	4.4	1735	0.9	2333	4.6	
4	SU	0548	0.7	1158	4.5	1818	0.8			○
5	M	0017	4.7	0629	0.7	1240	4.5	1903	0.7	
6	TU	0104	4.7	0711	0.7	1325	4.6	1949	0.6	
7	W	0154	4.7	0756	0.8	1411	4.5	2038	0.6	
8	TH	0246	4.6	0844	0.9	1500	4.5	2131	0.6	
9	F	0341	4.5	0937	1.0	1552	4.4	2230	0.6	
10	SA	0440	4.4	1037	1.1	1651	4.3	2336	0.6	◑
11	SU	0548	4.3	1145	1.2	1758	4.3			
12	M	0045	0.6	0658	4.3	1258	1.3	1907	4.3	
13	TU	0151	0.6	0804	4.3	1405	1.2	2010	4.3	
14	W	0249	0.7	0904	4.3	1504	1.1	2109	4.4	
15	TH	0342	0.7	0958	4.3	1557	1.0	2204	4.4	
16	F	0427	0.8	1046	4.4	1648	0.9	2254	4.5	
17	SA	0508	0.8	1127	4.4	1736	0.8	2339	4.5	
18	SU	0547	0.8	1203	4.4	1821	0.7			●
19	M	0020	4.6	0626	0.9	1238	4.5	1904	0.7	
20	TU	0101	4.5	0703	0.9	1314	4.5	1943	0.7	
21	W	0140	4.5	0737	1.0	1351	4.4	2019	0.7	
22	TH	0219	4.4	0811	1.1	1428	4.4	2053	0.8	
23	F	0257	4.3	0847	1.1	1506	4.3	2129	0.8	
24	SA	0336	4.2	0926	1.2	1545	4.2	2210	0.9	
25	SU	0417	4.0	1010	1.3	1626	4.1	2256	1.0	
26	M	0502	3.9	1100	1.4	1712	4.0	2349	1.0	◐
27	TU	0553	3.9	1158	1.5	1807	4.0			
28	W	0049	1.1	0657	3.9	1306	1.5	1913	4.0	
29	TH	0154	1.0	0806	4.0	1423	1.4	2023	4.1	
30	F	0256	1.0	0908	4.1	1527	1.2	2124	4.2	

JULY

Date	Day	Time	m	Time	m	Time	m	Time	m	Moon
1	SA	0351	0.9	1003	4.3	1623	1.1	2221	4.4	
2	SU	0441	0.8	1053	4.4	1716	0.9	2314	4.5	
3	M	0530	0.8	1141	4.5	1808	0.7			○
4	TU	0006	4.7	0618	0.8	1228	4.6	1859	0.6	
5	W	0058	4.8	0706	0.8	1316	4.6	1950	0.5	
6	TH	0151	4.8	0753	0.8	1405	4.7	2040	0.4	
7	F	0244	4.8	0841	0.8	1454	4.7	2130	0.4	
8	SA	0336	4.7	0929	0.9	1542	4.7	2222	0.4	
9	SU	0429	4.6	1019	1.0	1633	4.6	2315	0.5	
10	M	0525	4.4	1114	1.1	1728	4.5			◑
11	TU	0010	0.6	0625	4.3	1216	1.2	1829	4.4	
12	W	0110	0.8	0726	4.2	1325	1.3	1932	4.3	
13	TH	0209	0.9	0827	4.1	1431	1.3	2037	4.2	
14	F	0307	1.0	0928	4.1	1536	1.2	2142	4.3	
15	SA	0402	1.1	1024	4.2	1636	1.0	2241	4.3	
16	SU	0452	1.1	1111	4.3	1729	0.9	2330	4.4	
17	M	0535	1.1	1150	4.4	1814	0.8			●
18	TU	0011	4.4	0614	1.0	1224	4.5	1854	0.7	
19	W	0048	4.4	0648	1.0	1258	4.5	1929	0.7	
20	TH	0124	4.4	0721	1.0	1333	4.5	2001	0.7	
21	F	0200	4.4	0754	1.0	1409	4.5	2033	0.7	
22	SA	0235	4.4	0828	1.0	1445	4.5	2105	0.7	
23	SU	0311	4.3	0903	1.1	1520	4.4	2140	0.8	
24	M	0346	4.2	0940	1.2	1554	4.3	2216	0.9	
25	TU	0422	4.1	1019	1.3	1632	4.2	2258	1.0	◐
26	W	0504	4.0	1106	1.4	1718	4.2	2349	1.1	
27	TH	0555	3.9	1207	1.5	1814	4.1			
28	F	0056	1.2	0703	3.9	1330	1.5	1929	4.0	
29	SA	0214	1.2	0827	4.0	1453	1.3	2052	4.1	
30	SU	0323	1.1	0938	4.1	1602	1.1	2203	4.3	
31	M	0424	1.0	1037	4.3	1704	0.9	2305	4.6	

AUGUST

Date	Day	Time	m	Time	m	Time	m	Time	m	Moon
1	TU	0519	0.9	1130	4.5	1801	0.7			○
2	W	0000	4.7	0611	0.8	1218	4.7	1853	0.5	
3	TH	0053	4.9	0658	0.8	1306	4.8	1942	0.3	
4	F	0143	4.9	0743	0.8	1353	4.9	2028	0.3	
5	SA	0232	4.9	0827	0.8	1439	4.9	2113	0.3	
6	SU	0319	4.8	0909	0.9	1522	4.9	2155	0.4	
7	M	0404	4.6	0952	1.0	1604	4.8	2237	0.6	
8	TU	0449	4.4	1036	1.1	1650	4.6	2322	0.8	◑
9	W	0539	4.2	1131	1.3	1745	4.4			
10	TH	0018	1.1	0641	4.0	1241	1.4	1855	4.2	
11	F	0127	1.3	0750	3.9	1400	1.4	2011	4.0	
12	SA	0238	1.4	0901	4.0	1520	1.3	2130	4.1	
13	SU	0348	1.4	1006	4.1	1631	1.1	2235	4.2	
14	M	0445	1.3	1058	4.3	1722	0.9	2324	4.4	
15	TU	0527	1.2	1138	4.4	1802	0.8			
16	W	0002	4.4	0602	1.1	1211	4.5	1836	0.7	●
17	TH	0034	4.5	0632	1.1	1241	4.6	1907	0.7	
18	F	0104	4.5	0703	1.0	1312	4.6	1936	0.6	
19	SA	0135	4.5	0733	1.0	1346	4.6	2005	0.6	
20	SU	0208	4.5	0805	1.0	1420	4.6	2035	0.7	
21	M	0241	4.4	0837	1.0	1451	4.5	2105	0.8	
22	TU	0312	4.3	0909	1.1	1520	4.4	2135	0.9	
23	W	0342	4.2	0942	1.2	1552	4.4	2208	1.0	
24	TH	0418	4.1	1023	1.3	1636	4.2	2253	1.2	◐
25	F	0508	4.0	1120	1.5	1735	4.1			
26	SA	0003	1.4	0617	3.8	1250	1.5	1856	4.0	
27	SU	0142	1.4	0757	3.8	1431	1.4	2035	4.1	
28	M	0307	1.3	0920	4.1	1549	1.1	2155	4.3	
29	TU	0413	1.1	1024	4.3	1654	0.8	2259	4.6	
30	W	0508	0.9	1118	4.6	1749	0.5	2352	4.8	
31	TH	0555	0.8	1205	4.8	1837	0.3			○

Chart Datum: 2·50 metres below Ordnance Datum (Newlyn)
HAT is 5·2 metres above Chart Datum

TIME ZONE (UT)
For Summer Time add ONE hour in **non-shaded areas**

MARGATE

LAT 51°23′N LONG 1°23′E

TIMES AND HEIGHTS OF HIGH AND LOW WATERS

Dates in amber are **SPRINGS**
Dates in grey are **NEAPS**

2023

SEPTEMBER

Date	Day	Time	m	Time	m	Time	m	Time	m	Moon
1	F	0040	4.9	0640	0.8	1248	4.9	1922	0.2	
2	SA	0126	5.0	0723	0.7	1331	5.0	2003	0.2	
3	SU	0210	4.9	0804	0.7	1413	5.0	2042	0.3	
4	M	0251	4.8	0843	0.8	1453	5.0	2116	0.5	
5	TU	0328	4.6	0921	0.9	1531	4.8	2150	0.8	
6	W	0402	4.3	1002	1.1	1613	4.6	2229	1.1	◑
7	TH	0443	4.1	1051	1.3	1705	4.3	2322	1.4	
8	F	0544	3.9	1201	1.5	1817	4.0			
9	SA	0042	1.7	0711	3.7	1330	1.5	1949	3.9	
10	SU	0213	1.7	0832	3.8	1503	1.4	2116	4.0	
11	M	0333	1.6	0942	4.0	1614	1.1	2220	4.2	
12	TU	0429	1.4	1036	4.3	1701	0.9	2306	4.4	
13	W	0508	1.2	1116	4.4	1737	0.8	2342	4.5	
14	TH	0540	1.1	1148	4.5	1807	0.7			
15	F	0010	4.5	0610	1.1	1216	4.6	1836	0.7	●
16	SA	0035	4.6	0639	1.0	1245	4.7	1905	0.6	
17	SU	0104	4.6	0710	0.9	1317	4.7	1933	0.6	
18	M	0136	4.6	0741	0.9	1350	4.7	2001	0.7	
19	TU	0208	4.5	0812	1.0	1419	4.6	2028	0.8	
20	W	0235	4.4	0842	1.1	1445	4.5	2057	0.9	
21	TH	0301	4.3	0915	1.1	1517	4.4	2131	1.1	
22	F	0337	4.1	0956	1.3	1606	4.2	2219	1.3	◐
23	SA	0434	4.0	1057	1.4	1713	4.0	2335	1.6	
24	SU	0550	3.8	1234	1.5	1846	3.9			
25	M	0124	1.6	0737	3.8	1417	1.3	2028	4.1	
26	TU	0253	1.4	0902	4.1	1536	1.0	2147	4.4	
27	W	0357	1.1	1006	4.4	1637	0.6	2245	4.7	
28	TH	0448	0.9	1057	4.7	1727	0.4	2334	4.9	
29	F	0533	0.8	1141	4.8	1811	0.3			○
30	SA	0017	4.9	0615	0.7	1221	5.0	1852	0.3	

OCTOBER

Date	Day	Time	m	Time	m	Time	m	Time	m	Moon
1	SU	0058	4.9	0657	0.7	1302	5.1	1930	0.3	
2	M	0138	4.9	0738	0.7	1343	5.1	2004	0.5	
3	TU	0214	4.7	0817	0.8	1423	4.9	2036	0.7	
4	W	0246	4.5	0855	0.9	1502	4.7	2108	1.0	
5	TH	0319	4.3	0933	1.0	1543	4.5	2144	1.3	
6	F	0358	4.1	1019	1.2	1633	4.2	2233	1.6	◑
7	SA	0451	3.8	1124	1.5	1741	3.9	2350	1.9	
8	SU	0619	3.6	1255	1.6	1919	3.8			
9	M	0137	1.9	0753	3.7	1426	1.4	2044	3.9	
10	TU	0301	1.7	0903	3.9	1534	1.2	2146	4.2	
11	W	0356	1.5	0957	4.2	1621	1.0	2231	4.3	
12	TH	0436	1.3	1039	4.4	1658	0.8	2305	4.5	
13	F	0509	1.1	1113	4.5	1730	0.7	2334	4.5	
14	SA	0541	1.0	1143	4.6	1800	0.7			●
15	SU	0000	4.6	0612	1.0	1213	4.7	1830	0.7	
16	M	0030	4.6	0644	0.9	1246	4.7	1858	0.7	
17	TU	0102	4.6	0716	0.9	1319	4.7	1927	0.7	
18	W	0134	4.6	0749	0.9	1350	4.6	1958	0.8	
19	TH	0203	4.5	0823	1.0	1422	4.5	2031	1.0	
20	F	0235	4.4	0900	1.0	1503	4.4	2112	1.2	
21	SA	0319	4.2	0948	1.1	1559	4.2	2207	1.4	
22	SU	0420	4.0	1055	1.3	1712	4.1	2326	1.6	◐
23	M	0539	3.8	1229	1.3	1845	4.0			
24	TU	0107	1.6	0718	3.9	1402	1.1	2016	4.2	
25	W	0231	1.4	0836	4.1	1514	0.8	2127	4.5	
26	TH	0332	1.2	0938	4.4	1611	0.6	2222	4.7	
27	F	0422	1.0	1028	4.7	1659	0.4	2308	4.8	
28	SA	0506	0.8	1112	4.8	1740	0.4	2349	4.8	○
29	SU	0549	0.7	1153	5.0	1818	0.4			
30	M	0027	4.8	0632	0.7	1234	5.0	1855	0.5	
31	TU	0103	4.8	0715	0.6	1316	5.0	1930	0.7	

NOVEMBER

Date	Day	Time	m	Time	m	Time	m	Time	m	Moon
1	W	0138	4.7	0756	0.7	1358	4.8	2003	0.9	
2	TH	0212	4.5	0834	0.8	1439	4.6	2036	1.1	
3	F	0247	4.4	0912	1.0	1520	4.4	2112	1.4	
4	SA	0326	4.2	0954	1.2	1607	4.1	2158	1.6	
5	SU	0413	3.9	1050	1.3	1705	3.8	2300	1.9	◑
6	M	0518	3.7	1208	1.4	1832	3.7			
7	TU	0031	2.0	0658	3.7	1332	1.4	1953	3.8	
8	W	0208	1.8	0810	3.8	1439	1.2	2053	4.0	
9	TH	0308	1.6	0905	4.0	1529	1.0	2140	4.2	
10	F	0353	1.4	0951	4.2	1611	0.9	2219	4.4	
11	SA	0432	1.2	1031	4.4	1649	0.8	2254	4.5	
12	SU	0509	1.1	1107	4.5	1723	0.8	2326	4.6	
13	M	0544	1.0	1142	4.6	1756	0.8			●
14	TU	0000	4.6	0619	0.9	1217	4.7	1828	0.8	
15	W	0034	4.6	0656	0.8	1254	4.7	1902	0.8	
16	TH	0110	4.6	0733	0.8	1334	4.7	1938	0.9	
17	F	0147	4.5	0813	0.8	1417	4.6	2019	1.0	
18	SA	0229	4.4	0858	0.9	1507	4.5	2107	1.2	
19	SU	0318	4.3	0951	0.9	1605	4.3	2205	1.4	
20	M	0417	4.1	1059	1.0	1713	4.2	2317	1.5	◐
21	TU	0528	4.0	1220	1.0	1834	4.2			
22	W	0041	1.5	0652	4.1	1338	0.9	1953	4.3	
23	TH	0159	1.4	0803	4.2	1444	0.7	2058	4.5	
24	F	0301	1.2	0904	4.4	1540	0.6	2154	4.6	
25	SA	0353	1.1	0958	4.6	1628	0.6	2241	4.6	
26	SU	0441	0.9	1046	4.7	1709	0.6	2323	4.7	
27	M	0527	0.8	1130	4.8	1748	0.7			○
28	TU	0000	4.7	0613	0.7	1214	4.8	1827	0.8	
29	W	0036	4.7	0658	0.6	1257	4.8	1904	0.9	
30	TH	0113	4.6	0740	0.7	1340	4.7	1940	1.0	

DECEMBER

Date	Day	Time	m	Time	m	Time	m	Time	m	Moon
1	F	0149	4.5	0820	0.8	1421	4.5	2014	1.2	
2	SA	0226	4.4	0857	0.9	1501	4.3	2050	1.3	
3	SU	0305	4.2	0935	1.0	1544	4.1	2132	1.5	
4	M	0347	4.1	1021	1.1	1631	3.9	2222	1.7	
5	TU	0436	3.9	1116	1.2	1727	3.8	2321	1.8	◑
6	W	0536	3.8	1222	1.3	1842	3.8			
7	TH	0032	1.8	0658	3.8	1332	1.2	1950	3.9	
8	F	0200	1.7	0805	3.9	1433	1.1	2045	4.0	
9	SA	0302	1.5	0900	4.1	1523	1.0	2133	4.2	
10	SU	0351	1.3	0948	4.2	1608	1.0	2216	4.3	
11	M	0436	1.1	1033	4.4	1649	0.9	2257	4.4	
12	TU	0519	1.0	1115	4.5	1729	0.9	2337	4.5	●
13	W	0601	0.9	1157	4.6	1807	0.9			
14	TH	0016	4.6	0643	0.8	1241	4.7	1848	0.9	
15	F	0057	4.6	0726	0.7	1328	4.7	1930	0.9	
16	SA	0141	4.6	0812	0.6	1418	4.7	2016	1.0	
17	SU	0227	4.6	0901	0.6	1510	4.6	2105	1.1	
18	M	0316	4.5	0955	0.6	1605	4.5	2159	1.2	
19	TU	0410	4.4	1055	0.7	1705	4.4	2259	1.3	◐
20	W	0510	4.3	1159	0.7	1812	4.3			
21	TH	0006	1.4	0619	4.3	1305	0.8	1920	4.2	
22	F	0119	1.4	0727	4.3	1408	0.8	2024	4.3	
23	SA	0225	1.3	0830	4.3	1505	0.8	2123	4.3	
24	SU	0326	1.2	0931	4.4	1558	0.9	2217	4.4	
25	M	0422	1.0	1028	4.5	1646	0.9	2304	4.4	
26	TU	0515	0.9	1119	4.5	1730	1.0	2345	4.5	
27	W	0604	0.7	1205	4.6	1810	1.0			○
28	TH	0021	4.5	0650	0.7	1246	4.6	1849	1.0	
29	F	0058	4.5	0731	0.7	1327	4.5	1925	1.1	
30	SA	0134	4.5	0808	0.7	1405	4.4	1958	1.1	
31	SU	0211	4.5	0841	0.8	1443	4.3	2032	1.2	

Chart Datum: 2·50 metres below Ordnance Datum (Newlyn)
HAT is 5·2 metres above Chart Datum

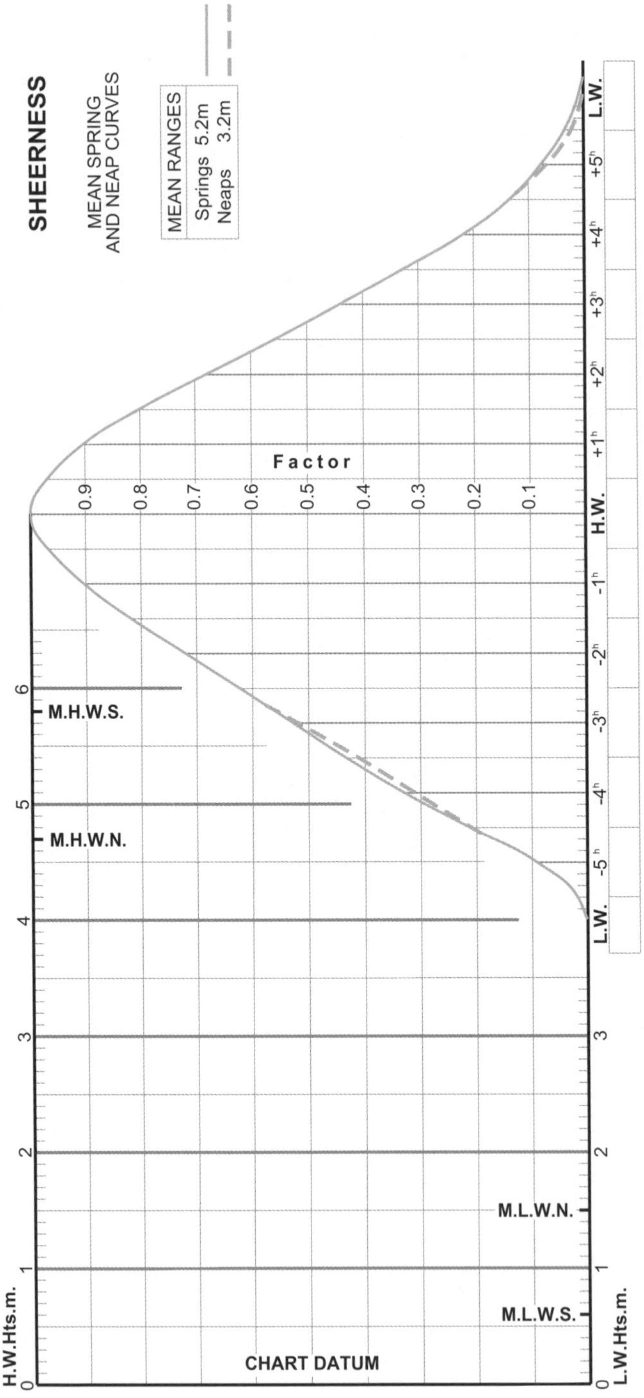
SHEERNESS
MEAN SPRING AND NEAP CURVES
MEAN RANGES
Springs 5.2m
Neaps 3.2m
Factor
0.9
0.8
0.7
0.6
0.5
0.4
0.3
0.2
0.1
L.W.
-5h
-4h
-3h
-2h
-1h
H.W.
+1h
+2h
+3h
+4h
+5h
L.W.
M.H.W.S.
M.H.W.N.
M.L.W.N.
M.L.W.S.
CHART DATUM
H.W.Hts.m.
L.W.Hts.m.
0
1
2
3
4
5
6

TIME ZONE (UT)
For Summer Time add ONE hour in **non-shaded areas**

SHEERNESS

LAT 51°27′N LONG 0°45′E

TIMES AND HEIGHTS OF HIGH AND LOW WATERS

Dates in amber are **SPRINGS**
Dates in grey are **NEAPS**

2023

JANUARY

Date	Day	Time	m	Time	m	Time	m	Time	m
1	SU	0107	1.5	0733	5.1	1406	1.1	2022	5.0
2	M	0213	1.6	0840	5.0	1507	1.2	2125	5.0
3	TU	0318	1.5	0943	5.0	1604	1.2	2222	5.1
4	W	0419	1.3	1041	5.1	1653	1.2	2313	5.2
5	TH	0514	1.2	1132	5.2	1736	1.2	2357	5.3
6	F ○	0602	1.0	1217	5.3	1814	1.2		
7	SA	0035	5.4	0646	0.9	1256	5.4	1849	1.1
8	SU	0110	5.4	0724	0.9	1333	5.4	1922	1.1
9	M	0143	5.4	0758	0.9	1407	5.4	1954	1.1
10	TU	0214	5.4	0831	0.9	1440	5.4	2027	1.1
11	W	0246	5.3	0904	0.9	1514	5.3	2101	1.1
12	TH	0319	5.3	0939	0.9	1550	5.3	2135	1.2
13	F	0354	5.2	1013	1.0	1628	5.1	2211	1.3
14	SA	0432	5.1	1049	1.1	1711	5.0	2250	1.4
15	SU	0516	5.0	1129	1.2	1801	4.9	◑ 2339	1.5
16	M	0610	4.9	1221	1.3	1902	4.8		
17	TU	0041	1.6	0721	4.8	1333	1.3	2014	4.9
18	W	0204	1.6	0840	4.9	1502	1.3	2125	5.0
19	TH	0330	1.4	0952	5.1	1615	1.1	2230	5.2
20	F	0442	1.2	1058	5.4	1717	1.0	2329	5.4
21	SA ●	0547	0.9	1157	5.7	1814	0.9		
22	SU	0022	5.6	0650	0.7	1251	5.9	1907	0.8
23	M	0111	5.7	0745	0.4	1341	6.0	1956	0.7
24	TU	0158	5.8	0836	0.3	1429	6.1	2041	0.7
25	W	0243	5.8	0922	0.2	1516	6.0	2122	0.8
26	TH	0327	5.8	1005	0.3	1602	5.8	2201	0.9
27	F	0411	5.7	1045	0.5	1649	5.6	2239	1.1
28	SA	0456	5.5	1124	0.8	1737	5.3	◐ 2321	1.3
29	SU	0545	5.3	1206	1.0	1830	5.0		
30	M	0011	1.5	0644	5.0	1300	1.3	1931	4.8
31	TU	0118	1.6	0754	4.8	1410	1.5	2040	4.7

FEBRUARY

Date	Day	Time	m	Time	m	Time	m	Time	m
1	W	0237	1.6	0911	4.7	1521	1.5	2151	4.7
2	TH	0353	1.5	1023	4.9	1625	1.5	2252	4.9
3	F	0501	1.3	1121	5.1	1718	1.4	2341	5.1
4	SA	0554	1.1	1206	5.3	1800	1.3		
5	SU	0021	5.3	0637	0.9	1245	5.4	○ 1836	1.2
6	M	0056	5.4	0712	0.8	1318	5.4	1908	1.1
7	TU	0128	5.4	0745	0.8	1350	5.5	1940	1.0
8	W	0159	5.5	0818	0.7	1421	5.5	2013	0.9
9	TH	0229	5.5	0851	0.7	1453	5.5	2046	0.9
10	F	0259	5.5	0923	0.7	1526	5.5	2116	1.0
11	SA	0330	5.4	0951	0.8	1559	5.4	2143	1.1
12	SU	0403	5.3	1016	0.9	1637	5.2	2213	1.2
13	M	0442	5.2	1044	1.0	1720	5.1	◑ 2253	1.3
14	TU	0530	5.1	1129	1.2	1816	4.8	2352	1.5
15	W	0637	4.9	1239	1.4	1930	4.7		
16	TH	0118	1.6	0806	4.8	1431	1.5	2054	4.7
17	F	0309	1.4	0934	5.0	1556	1.3	2212	5.0
18	SA	0431	1.1	1050	5.3	1705	1.1	2317	5.3
19	SU	0545	0.8	1151	5.7	1806	0.9		
20	M	0011	5.6	0646	0.5	1242	6.0	● 1858	0.7
21	TU	0058	5.8	0737	0.2	1329	6.1	1943	0.6
22	W	0142	5.9	0822	0.1	1413	6.1	2024	0.6
23	TH	0223	6.0	0903	0.1	1455	6.0	2102	0.7
24	F	0303	6.0	0940	0.3	1535	5.9	2136	0.8
25	SA	0342	5.8	1011	0.5	1615	5.6	2208	0.9
26	SU	0421	5.6	1039	0.8	1654	5.3	2241	1.1
27	M	0504	5.3	1111	1.1	1738	4.9	◐ 2323	1.3
28	TU	0555	4.9	1156	1.5	1832	4.6		

MARCH

Date	Day	Time	m	Time	m	Time	m	Time	m
1	W	0022	1.6	0706	4.6	1309	1.8	1947	4.4
2	TH	0158	1.7	0839	4.5	1444	1.8	2116	4.4
3	F	0331	1.6	1004	4.7	1600	1.7	2228	4.7
4	SA	0444	1.3	1103	5.0	1659	1.5	2319	5.0
5	SU	0536	1.0	1147	5.3	1743	1.3	2359	5.2
6	M	0616	0.9	1223	5.4	1818	1.1		
7	TU	0033	5.4	0651	0.8	1255	5.5	○ 1850	1.0
8	W	0105	5.5	0723	0.7	1325	5.6	1922	0.9
9	TH	0135	5.6	0756	0.6	1356	5.7	1955	0.8
10	F	0204	5.6	0829	0.6	1427	5.7	2027	0.8
11	SA	0234	5.6	0900	0.6	1458	5.6	2056	0.9
12	SU	0305	5.6	0926	0.8	1531	5.5	2120	1.0
13	M	0339	5.5	0946	0.9	1607	5.3	2147	1.1
14	TU	0418	5.4	1013	1.1	1649	5.1	2228	1.2
15	W	0508	5.1	1101	1.3	1743	4.8	◑ 2330	1.4
16	TH	0616	4.8	1219	1.6	1900	4.6		
17	F	0105	1.5	0750	4.7	1418	1.6	2034	4.6
18	SA	0303	1.3	0927	5.0	1544	1.4	2159	4.9
19	SU	0428	1.0	1042	5.4	1654	1.1	2303	5.3
20	M	0539	0.6	1139	5.8	1752	0.9	2354	5.6
21	TU ●	0632	0.3	1227	6.0	1839	0.7		
22	W	0038	5.8	0718	0.2	1310	6.1	1922	0.6
23	TH	0118	6.0	0759	0.1	1350	6.1	2000	0.6
24	F	0157	6.0	0835	0.2	1428	6.0	2036	0.6
25	SA	0235	6.0	0907	0.4	1504	5.8	2109	0.7
26	SU	0312	5.8	0934	0.6	1539	5.6	2139	0.9
27	M	0349	5.6	0959	0.9	1613	5.3	2208	1.1
28	TU	0429	5.2	1027	1.2	1651	4.9	2245	1.3
29	W	0517	4.8	1109	1.6	1738	4.6	◐ 2338	1.6
30	TH	0623	4.5	1216	1.9	1852	4.3		
31	F	0113	1.7	0758	4.3	1404	2.0	2031	4.3

APRIL

Date	Day	Time	m	Time	m	Time	m	Time	m
1	SA	0301	1.6	0929	4.6	1527	1.8	2150	4.6
2	SU	0410	1.3	1030	4.9	1627	1.5	2244	4.9
3	M	0502	1.0	1114	5.2	1712	1.3	2326	5.2
4	TU	0543	0.9	1151	5.4	1748	1.1		
5	W	0001	5.4	0619	0.7	1223	5.5	1823	1.0
6	TH	0033	5.5	0653	0.7	1255	5.6	○ 1857	0.9
7	F	0105	5.6	0727	0.6	1327	5.7	1932	0.8
8	SA	0137	5.7	0802	0.6	1359	5.7	2006	0.8
9	SU	0209	5.7	0834	0.7	1432	5.7	2037	0.8
10	M	0244	5.7	0902	0.8	1507	5.6	2106	0.9
11	TU	0322	5.6	0928	1.0	1545	5.4	2139	1.0
12	W	0405	5.4	1004	1.2	1629	5.1	2225	1.1
13	TH	0500	5.1	1059	1.4	1727	4.8	◑ 2333	1.3
14	F	0614	4.9	1224	1.7	1848	4.6		
15	SA	0120	1.4	0748	4.9	1408	1.6	2022	4.7
16	SU	0259	1.1	0917	5.1	1527	1.4	2141	5.0
17	M	0417	0.8	1026	5.5	1633	1.1	2241	5.4
18	TU	0520	0.5	1119	5.8	1728	0.9	2330	5.6
19	W	0609	0.4	1205	5.9	1813	0.8		
20	TH	0012	5.8	0651	0.3	1245	5.9	● 1854	0.6
21	F	0052	5.9	0728	0.3	1323	5.9	1933	0.6
22	SA	0131	6.0	0802	0.4	1359	5.9	2010	0.6
23	SU	0209	5.9	0833	0.6	1433	5.7	2044	0.7
24	M	0246	5.7	0900	0.8	1506	5.5	2115	0.9
25	TU	0324	5.5	0926	1.1	1539	5.2	2143	1.0
26	W	0403	5.2	0955	1.4	1614	4.9	2217	1.2
27	TH	0449	4.8	1035	1.6	1658	4.6	◐ 2306	1.5
28	F	0548	4.5	1134	1.9	1803	4.4		
29	SA	0022	1.6	0709	4.4	1303	2.0	1935	4.3
30	SU	0212	1.6	0832	4.5	1437	1.9	2055	4.5

Chart Datum: 2·90 metres below Ordnance Datum (Newlyn)
HAT is 6·3 metres above Chart Datum

TIME ZONE (UT)
For Summer Time add ONE hour in **non-shaded areas**

SHEERNESS

LAT 51°27'N LONG 0°45'E

TIMES AND HEIGHTS OF HIGH AND LOW WATERS

Dates in amber are **SPRINGS**
Dates in grey are **NEAPS**

2023

MAY

Date	Day	Time	m	Time	m	Time	m	Time	m	Moon
1	M	0321	1.3	0938	4.8	1538	1.6	2154	4.8	
2	TU	0414	1.1	1027	5.1	1627	1.3	2241	5.1	
3	W	0459	0.9	1108	5.4	1709	1.2	2321	5.3	
4	TH	0539	0.8	1146	5.5	1748	1.0	2358	5.5	
5	F	0618	0.7	1222	5.7	1828	0.9			○
6	SA	0034	5.6	0657	0.7	1258	5.7	1908	0.8	
7	SU	0111	5.7	0734	0.7	1334	5.7	1947	0.8	
8	M	0149	5.7	0811	0.7	1411	5.7	2026	0.8	
9	TU	0229	5.7	0846	0.9	1449	5.5	2104	0.8	
10	W	0313	5.6	0923	1.0	1532	5.3	2147	0.9	
11	TH	0404	5.4	1008	1.2	1622	5.1	2241	1.0	
12	F	0504	5.2	1107	1.4	1724	4.9	2354	1.1	◑
13	SA	0617	5.1	1225	1.6	1842	4.8			
14	SU	0124	1.1	0739	5.1	1348	1.5	2003	4.9	
15	M	0243	0.9	0855	5.3	1458	1.3	2114	5.1	
16	TU	0352	0.7	0959	5.5	1600	1.2	2213	5.4	
17	W	0451	0.6	1052	5.6	1655	1.0	2302	5.5	
18	TH	0539	0.6	1138	5.7	1743	0.9	2347	5.6	
19	F	0619	0.6	1219	5.7	1826	0.8			●
20	SA	0028	5.7	0655	0.7	1257	5.7	1908	0.7	
21	SU	0109	5.7	0729	0.7	1333	5.7	1947	0.7	
22	M	0149	5.7	0801	0.9	1408	5.6	2024	0.8	
23	TU	0227	5.6	0831	1.0	1441	5.4	2057	0.9	
24	W	0306	5.4	0900	1.2	1514	5.2	2127	1.0	
25	TH	0345	5.1	0931	1.4	1549	5.0	2201	1.2	
26	F	0428	4.9	1010	1.6	1631	4.8	2245	1.3	
27	SA	0518	4.7	1100	1.7	1725	4.6	2344	1.4	◐
28	SU	0618	4.6	1204	1.9	1835	4.5			
29	M	0059	1.4	0727	4.6	1321	1.9	1949	4.6	
30	TU	0216	1.3	0832	4.8	1434	1.7	2054	4.8	
31	W	0316	1.2	0930	5.0	1533	1.5	2149	5.0	

JUNE

Date	Day	Time	m	Time	m	Time	m	Time	m	Moon
1	TH	0409	1.0	1021	5.3	1624	1.3	2238	5.2	
2	F	0457	0.9	1108	5.5	1713	1.1	2324	5.4	
3	SA	0543	0.8	1152	5.6	1800	1.0			
4	SU	0008	5.6	0628	0.8	1233	5.7	1848	0.9	○
5	M	0052	5.7	0712	0.8	1315	5.7	1935	0.8	
6	TU	0136	5.8	0755	0.8	1357	5.6	2022	0.7	
7	W	0223	5.8	0838	0.9	1441	5.6	2110	0.6	
8	TH	0312	5.7	0923	1.0	1528	5.4	2201	0.7	
9	F	0406	5.6	1012	1.1	1621	5.3	2256	0.7	
10	SA	0504	5.5	1106	1.3	1719	5.2	2359	0.8	◑
11	SU	0608	5.3	1208	1.4	1825	5.1			
12	M	0105	0.8	0717	5.3	1315	1.4	1933	5.1	
13	TU	0212	0.8	0824	5.3	1420	1.4	2040	5.2	
14	W	0315	0.8	0926	5.3	1522	1.3	2141	5.3	
15	TH	0413	0.9	1022	5.4	1621	1.2	2236	5.3	
16	F	0504	0.9	1112	5.4	1715	1.1	2326	5.4	
17	SA	0547	1.0	1157	5.5	1804	0.9			
18	SU	0012	5.5	0626	1.0	1237	5.5	1850	0.8	●
19	M	0055	5.5	0702	1.0	1315	5.5	1932	0.8	
20	TU	0136	5.5	0737	1.1	1351	5.4	2011	0.8	
21	W	0215	5.4	0809	1.1	1424	5.3	2045	0.9	
22	TH	0252	5.3	0841	1.2	1458	5.2	2117	1.0	
23	F	0329	5.2	0913	1.3	1532	5.1	2150	1.0	
24	SA	0407	5.1	0950	1.4	1610	5.0	2228	1.1	
25	SU	0448	5.0	1031	1.5	1653	4.9	2311	1.2	
26	M	0534	4.9	1118	1.6	1742	4.8			◐
27	TU	0001	1.3	0628	4.8	1213	1.7	1842	4.7	
28	W	0101	1.3	0730	4.8	1319	1.7	1950	4.8	
29	TH	0211	1.3	0834	4.9	1434	1.6	2057	4.9	
30	F	0319	1.2	0936	5.1	1542	1.4	2159	5.1	

JULY

Date	Day	Time	m	Time	m	Time	m	Time	m	Moon
1	SA	0419	1.1	1033	5.3	1642	1.2	2256	5.3	
2	SU	0514	1.0	1126	5.5	1739	1.0	2349	5.5	
3	M	0606	0.9	1216	5.6	1835	0.9			○
4	TU	0040	5.7	0657	0.9	1303	5.7	1929	0.7	
5	W	0130	5.9	0746	0.8	1349	5.7	2022	0.5	
6	TH	0219	5.9	0833	0.8	1435	5.7	2113	0.4	
7	F	0309	5.9	0920	0.9	1522	5.7	2202	0.4	
8	SA	0359	5.9	1005	1.0	1610	5.6	2251	0.4	
9	SU	0451	5.7	1050	1.1	1701	5.5	2339	0.6	
10	M	0545	5.5	1139	1.2	1755	5.4			◑
11	TU	0030	0.8	0644	5.3	1233	1.4	1856	5.2	
12	W	0128	1.0	0745	5.1	1336	1.5	2002	5.1	
13	TH	0230	1.1	0849	5.1	1444	1.5	2110	5.1	
14	F	0332	1.2	0952	5.1	1552	1.4	2215	5.1	
15	SA	0431	1.3	1050	5.2	1657	1.2	2314	5.2	
16	SU	0522	1.3	1141	5.3	1754	1.1			
17	M	0004	5.3	0606	1.2	1224	5.3	1842	0.9	●
18	TU	0048	5.4	0645	1.2	1303	5.4	1923	0.9	
19	W	0127	5.4	0719	1.2	1338	5.4	1959	0.8	
20	TH	0202	5.5	0752	1.2	1410	5.4	2032	0.8	
21	F	0236	5.4	0824	1.2	1442	5.4	2104	0.8	
22	SA	0308	5.4	0856	1.2	1513	5.4	2135	0.9	
23	SU	0342	5.3	0929	1.2	1546	5.3	2207	0.9	
24	M	0417	5.2	1003	1.3	1620	5.2	2240	1.1	
25	TU	0455	5.1	1038	1.5	1659	5.1	2315	1.2	◐
26	W	0539	5.0	1120	1.6	1747	4.9	2359	1.3	
27	TH	0633	4.9	1215	1.7	1849	4.8			
28	F	0102	1.4	0741	4.8	1332	1.7	2008	4.8	
29	SA	0233	1.4	0855	4.9	1505	1.6	2126	5.0	
30	SU	0350	1.3	1005	5.1	1619	1.3	2236	5.2	
31	M	0453	1.1	1107	5.3	1725	1.0	2337	5.6	

AUGUST

Date	Day	Time	m	Time	m	Time	m	Time	m	Moon
1	TU	0552	1.0	1203	5.6	1828	0.8			○
2	W	0031	5.8	0647	0.9	1252	5.7	1925	0.5	
3	TH	0122	6.0	0737	0.8	1338	5.9	2016	0.3	
4	F	0209	6.1	0823	0.7	1422	5.9	2103	0.2	
5	SA	0255	6.1	0906	0.8	1505	6.0	2147	0.2	
6	SU	0341	6.0	0946	0.9	1548	5.9	2228	0.4	
7	M	0426	5.8	1024	1.0	1632	5.7	2306	0.6	
8	TU	0512	5.5	1103	1.2	1719	5.5	2345	0.9	◑
9	W	0602	5.2	1149	1.4	1814	5.2			
10	TH	0032	1.2	0701	4.9	1249	1.6	1922	4.9	
11	F	0139	1.5	0809	4.8	1409	1.6	2042	4.8	
12	SA	0255	1.6	0924	4.8	1533	1.5	2201	4.9	
13	SU	0407	1.6	1032	5.0	1649	1.3	2305	5.1	
14	M	0507	1.5	1126	5.2	1747	1.1	2354	5.3	
15	TU	0553	1.4	1210	5.3	1830	1.0			
16	W	0035	5.5	0630	1.3	1247	5.4	1907	0.9	●
17	TH	0110	5.5	0702	1.2	1319	5.5	1939	0.8	
18	F	0142	5.5	0733	1.1	1349	5.6	2010	0.8	
19	SA	0212	5.6	0804	1.0	1419	5.6	2041	0.7	
20	SU	0242	5.6	0836	1.1	1448	5.6	2112	0.8	
21	M	0312	5.5	0907	1.1	1517	5.5	2140	0.9	
22	TU	0344	5.4	0934	1.3	1548	5.4	2206	1.1	
23	W	0418	5.3	1000	1.4	1624	5.3	2230	1.2	
24	TH	0457	5.1	1034	1.5	1707	5.1	2307	1.4	◐
25	F	0547	4.9	1126	1.6	1807	4.9			
26	SA	0008	1.6	0655	4.7	1245	1.7	1930	4.7	
27	SU	0157	1.7	0820	4.7	1442	1.6	2103	4.9	
28	M	0329	1.5	0943	5.0	1605	1.3	2224	5.3	
29	TU	0438	1.2	1052	5.3	1718	0.9	2327	5.7	
30	W	0539	1.0	1147	5.6	1820	0.6			
31	TH	0019	6.0	0633	0.9	1235	5.9	1913	0.3	○

Chart Datum: 2·90 metres below Ordnance Datum (Newlyn)
HAT is 6·3 metres above Chart Datum

TIME ZONE (UT)
For Summer Time add ONE hour in **non-shaded areas**

SHEERNESS

LAT 51°27′N LONG 0°45′E

TIMES AND HEIGHTS OF HIGH AND LOW WATERS

Dates in amber are **SPRINGS**
Dates in grey are **NEAPS**

2023

SEPTEMBER

Date	Day	Time	m	Time	m	Time	m	Time	m	Moon
1	F	0106	6.2	0720	0.7	1318	6.0	2000	0.2	
2	SA	0150	6.2	0803	0.7	1400	6.1	2042	0.1	
3	SU	0233	6.2	0843	0.7	1440	6.1	2120	0.3	
4	M	0313	6.0	0919	0.8	1520	6.0	2155	0.5	
5	TU	0353	5.8	0953	1.0	1600	5.8	2225	0.8	
6	W	0434	5.5	1027	1.2	1643	5.5	2256	1.2	◑
7	TH	0517	5.1	1107	1.4	1734	5.1	2337	1.5	
8	F	0611	4.8	1204	1.6	1843	4.7			
9	SA	0044	1.8	0725	4.5	1338	1.8	2015	4.6	
10	SU	0223	2.0	0854	4.5	1518	1.6	2144	4.8	
11	M	0345	1.8	1009	4.8	1633	1.3	2247	5.1	
12	TU	0447	1.6	1104	5.1	1726	1.1	2334	5.4	
13	W	0531	1.4	1146	5.4	1806	0.9			
14	TH	0011	5.5	0607	1.2	1221	5.5	1840	0.8	
15	F	0044	5.6	0638	1.1	1252	5.6	1910	0.8	●
16	SA	0113	5.6	0708	1.0	1321	5.7	1941	0.7	
17	SU	0142	5.7	0739	1.0	1349	5.7	2012	0.7	
18	M	0211	5.7	0812	1.0	1419	5.7	2043	0.8	
19	TU	0241	5.6	0841	1.1	1449	5.6	2110	0.9	
20	W	0312	5.5	0907	1.2	1521	5.5	2131	1.1	
21	TH	0346	5.4	0930	1.3	1557	5.4	2154	1.3	
22	F	0424	5.2	1005	1.4	1643	5.2	2234	1.5	◐
23	SA	0514	4.9	1101	1.6	1745	4.9	2345	1.7	
24	SU	0623	4.7	1228	1.7	1911	4.7			
25	M	0140	1.8	0756	4.6	1431	1.5	2051	4.9	
26	TU	0312	1.6	0925	4.9	1555	1.2	2211	5.4	
27	W	0421	1.3	1033	5.3	1706	0.8	2311	5.8	
28	TH	0521	1.0	1126	5.7	1804	0.5			
29	F	0000	6.1	0611	0.9	1211	5.9	1852	0.3	○
30	SA	0044	6.2	0656	0.7	1252	6.1	1934	0.2	

OCTOBER

Date	Day	Time	m	Time	m	Time	m	Time	m	Moon
1	SU	0125	6.2	0737	0.7	1332	6.2	2012	0.3	
2	M	0204	6.1	0815	0.7	1412	6.2	2047	0.5	
3	TU	0242	5.9	0851	0.8	1451	6.0	2118	0.7	
4	W	0319	5.7	0924	1.0	1531	5.7	2145	1.0	
5	TH	0356	5.4	0956	1.2	1612	5.4	2213	1.4	
6	F	0435	5.1	1033	1.4	1702	5.0	2253	1.7	◑
7	SA	0523	4.7	1125	1.7	1809	4.6	2355	2.0	
8	SU	0636	4.4	1302	1.8	1940	4.5			
9	M	0143	2.2	0812	4.4	1449	1.7	2110	4.7	
10	TU	0310	2.0	0932	4.7	1557	1.4	2214	5.0	
11	W	0411	1.7	1028	5.0	1648	1.1	2300	5.3	
12	TH	0456	1.4	1110	5.3	1729	0.9	2337	5.5	
13	F	0533	1.2	1146	5.5	1803	0.8			
14	SA	0009	5.6	0606	1.1	1217	5.6	1835	0.8	●
15	SU	0039	5.7	0638	1.0	1248	5.7	1907	0.8	
16	M	0109	5.7	0712	1.0	1319	5.7	1940	0.8	
17	TU	0140	5.8	0746	1.0	1351	5.7	2012	0.9	
18	W	0212	5.7	0818	1.0	1424	5.7	2041	1.0	
19	TH	0245	5.6	0847	1.1	1501	5.6	2106	1.2	
20	F	0321	5.4	0917	1.2	1542	5.4	2138	1.3	
21	SA	0402	5.2	0959	1.3	1633	5.2	2227	1.6	
22	SU	0455	4.9	1101	1.5	1739	4.9	2342	1.8	◐
23	M	0607	4.7	1236	1.5	1905	4.9			
24	TU	0125	1.8	0738	4.7	1421	1.3	2037	5.1	
25	W	0249	1.6	0902	5.0	1539	1.0	2150	5.5	
26	TH	0355	1.3	1006	5.4	1644	0.7	2247	5.8	
27	F	0452	1.1	1058	5.7	1738	0.5	2335	5.9	
28	SA	0541	0.9	1143	5.9	1822	0.5			○
29	SU	0017	6.0	0626	0.8	1225	6.0	1903	0.5	
30	M	0057	6.0	0708	0.7	1306	6.1	1939	0.5	
31	TU	0136	5.9	0748	0.7	1346	6.0	2012	0.7	

NOVEMBER

Date	Day	Time	m	Time	m	Time	m	Time	m	Moon
1	W	0213	5.8	0826	0.8	1427	5.9	2042	0.9	
2	TH	0249	5.6	0900	1.0	1508	5.6	2110	1.2	
3	F	0324	5.3	0932	1.2	1550	5.3	2139	1.5	
4	SA	0400	5.0	1006	1.4	1637	4.9	2217	1.8	
5	SU	0445	4.7	1053	1.6	1736	4.6	2312	2.0	◑
6	M	0549	4.5	1207	1.7	1851	4.5			
7	TU	0035	2.2	0715	4.4	1357	1.7	2012	4.5	
8	W	0214	2.1	0834	4.6	1505	1.4	2119	4.8	
9	TH	0319	1.8	0935	4.9	1557	1.2	2210	5.1	
10	F	0408	1.5	1023	5.1	1641	1.0	2252	5.3	
11	SA	0451	1.3	1104	5.4	1720	0.9	2329	5.5	
12	SU	0529	1.2	1141	5.5	1757	0.9			
13	M	0004	5.6	0607	1.1	1216	5.6	1834	0.9	●
14	TU	0038	5.7	0645	1.0	1252	5.7	1910	0.9	
15	W	0113	5.7	0724	1.0	1329	5.7	1945	0.9	
16	TH	0149	5.7	0802	0.9	1408	5.7	2020	1.0	
17	F	0226	5.6	0840	1.0	1450	5.6	2056	1.1	
18	SA	0306	5.4	0921	1.0	1537	5.5	2138	1.3	
19	SU	0352	5.2	1010	1.1	1632	5.3	2231	1.5	
20	M	0448	5.0	1115	1.2	1738	5.1	2340	1.7	◐
21	TU	0557	4.9	1238	1.2	1855	5.1			
22	W	0100	1.7	0716	4.9	1359	1.1	2012	5.2	
23	TH	0215	1.5	0831	5.1	1510	0.9	2120	5.4	
24	F	0319	1.4	0934	5.3	1612	0.8	2218	5.6	
25	SA	0417	1.2	1028	5.5	1706	0.7	2308	5.7	
26	SU	0509	1.0	1117	5.7	1750	0.7	2352	5.7	
27	M	0558	0.9	1203	5.8	1830	0.8			○
28	TU	0033	5.7	0644	0.8	1246	5.8	1907	0.8	
29	W	0112	5.7	0727	0.8	1329	5.8	1942	0.9	
30	TH	0150	5.6	0808	0.8	1411	5.7	2014	1.1	

DECEMBER

Date	Day	Time	m	Time	m	Time	m	Time	m	Moon
1	F	0226	5.4	0844	0.9	1452	5.5	2044	1.3	
2	SA	0301	5.3	0917	1.1	1533	5.2	2114	1.5	
3	SU	0337	5.1	0949	1.2	1616	5.0	2150	1.6	
4	M	0418	4.9	1029	1.4	1704	4.8	2236	1.8	
5	TU	0508	4.7	1121	1.5	1759	4.6	2334	1.9	◑
6	W	0611	4.6	1230	1.5	1901	4.6			
7	TH	0045	2.0	0722	4.6	1349	1.5	2006	4.6	
8	F	0204	1.9	0828	4.7	1454	1.4	2106	4.8	
9	SA	0309	1.7	0926	4.9	1548	1.2	2159	5.1	
10	SU	0403	1.5	1018	5.1	1636	1.1	2247	5.3	
11	M	0452	1.3	1105	5.3	1721	1.0	2332	5.5	
12	TU	0538	1.1	1150	5.5	1804	1.0			●
13	W	0013	5.6	0624	1.0	1233	5.6	1846	0.9	
14	TH	0054	5.6	0709	0.9	1316	5.7	1928	0.9	
15	F	0135	5.6	0755	0.8	1400	5.7	2010	0.9	
16	SA	0217	5.6	0843	0.7	1447	5.7	2053	1.0	
17	SU	0301	5.5	0932	0.7	1537	5.7	2139	1.1	
18	M	0349	5.4	1023	0.8	1630	5.5	2229	1.3	
19	TU	0442	5.3	1118	0.8	1728	5.4	2324	1.4	◐
20	W	0540	5.2	1219	0.9	1832	5.2			
21	TH	0025	1.5	0646	5.1	1324	1.0	1939	5.2	
22	F	0132	1.5	0754	5.1	1429	1.0	2045	5.2	
23	SA	0238	1.4	0900	5.2	1532	1.0	2146	5.2	
24	SU	0342	1.3	1002	5.3	1631	1.0	2242	5.3	
25	M	0443	1.2	1058	5.4	1721	1.1	2332	5.4	
26	TU	0540	1.0	1150	5.5	1805	1.1			
27	W	0017	5.4	0631	0.9	1237	5.5	1845	1.1	○
28	TH	0058	5.5	0717	0.8	1321	5.5	1921	1.1	
29	F	0137	5.4	0758	0.8	1402	5.5	1955	1.2	
30	SA	0213	5.4	0834	0.9	1440	5.4	2026	1.2	
31	SU	0247	5.3	0906	1.0	1517	5.3	2056	1.3	

Chart Datum: 2·90 metres below Ordnance Datum (Newlyn)
HAT is 6·3 metres above Chart Datum

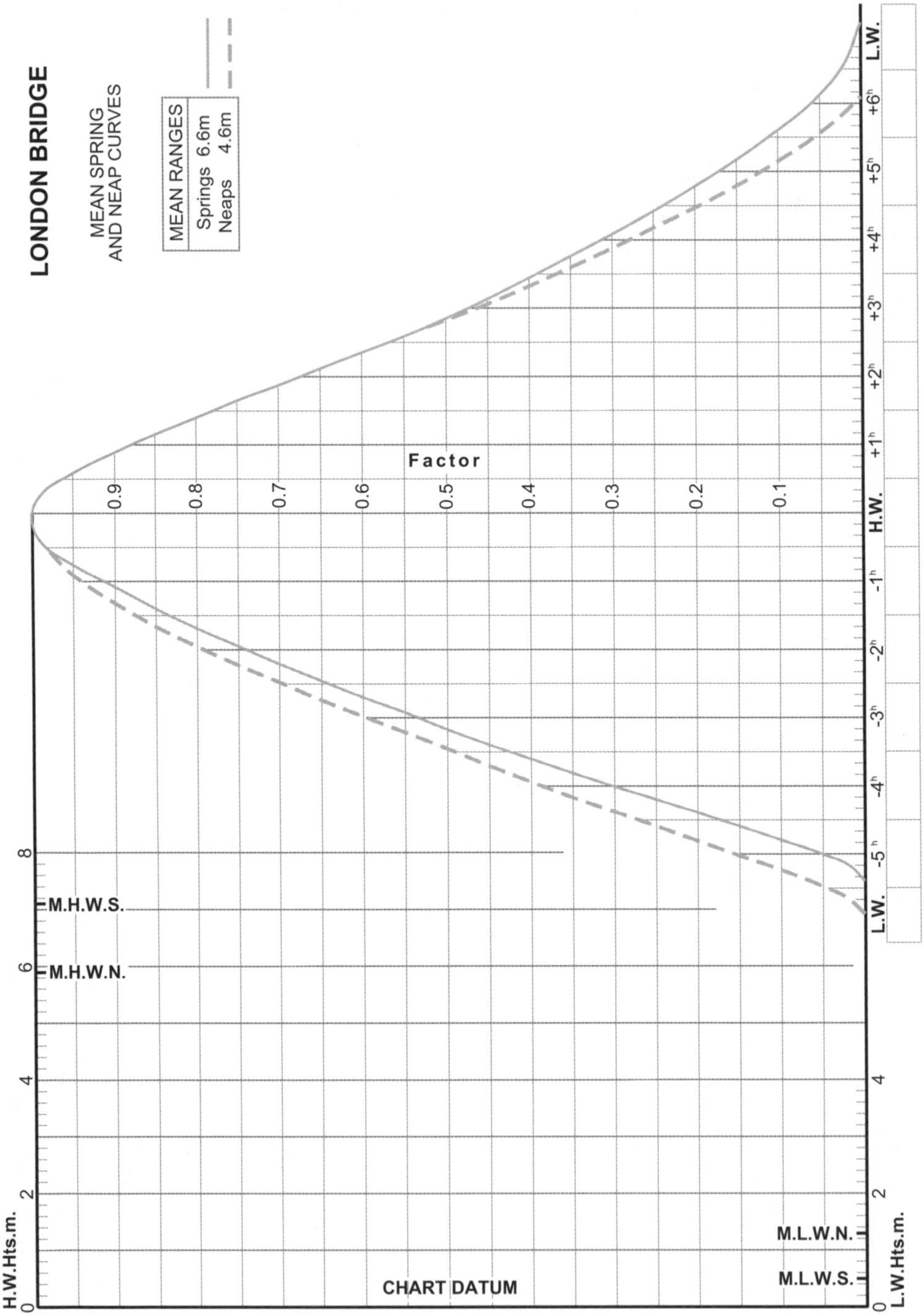
LONDON BRIDGE
MEAN SPRING AND NEAP CURVES
MEAN RANGES
Springs 6.6m
Neaps 4.6m
Factor
0.9
0.8
0.7
0.6
0.5
0.4
0.3
0.2
0.1
L.W.
-5h
-4h
-3h
-2h
-1h
H.W.
+1h
+2h
+3h
+4h
+5h
+6h
L.W.
H.W.Hts.m.
0
2
4
6
8
M.H.W.S.
M.H.W.N.
CHART DATUM
M.L.W.N.
M.L.W.S.
L.W.Hts.m.
0
2
4

TIME ZONE (UT)
For Summer Time add ONE hour in **non-shaded areas**

LONDON BRIDGE

LAT 51°30′N LONG 0°05′W

TIMES AND HEIGHTS OF HIGH AND LOW WATERS

Dates in amber are **SPRINGS**
Dates in grey are **NEAPS**

2023

JANUARY

Date	Day	Time	m	Time	m	Time	m	Time	m
1	SU	0242	1.5	0853	6.3	1519	0.9	2132	6.3
2	M	0347	1.5	0955	6.3	1617	1.1	2235	6.2
3	TU	0453	1.4	1058	6.3	1717	1.1	2338	6.3
4	W	0558	1.2	1158	6.4	1817	1.2		
5	TH	0031	6.4	0656	1.0	1248	6.6	1909	1.1
6	F	0117	6.5	0746	0.9	1333	6.7	○ 1953	1.1
7	SA	0156	6.5	0829	0.8	1414	6.7	2031	1.1
8	SU	0232	6.6	0907	0.8	1451	6.7	2105	1.2
9	M	0306	6.6	0943	0.8	1525	6.7	2137	1.2
10	TU	0337	6.6	1016	0.7	1557	6.7	2211	1.2
11	W	0409	6.5	1048	0.7	1630	6.6	2245	1.2
12	TH	0441	6.5	1119	0.8	1704	6.5	2318	1.2
13	F	0514	6.4	1146	0.8	1740	6.4	2349	1.3
14	SA	0551	6.3	1214	0.9	1820	6.2		
15	SU	0024	1.4	0633	6.2	1249	1.0	◑ 1907	6.1
16	M	0107	1.5	0723	6.1	1336	1.1	2007	5.9
17	TU	0205	1.7	0830	6.0	1441	1.2	2127	5.9
18	W	0324	1.7	0957	6.1	1616	1.3	2241	6.1
19	TH	0504	1.5	1112	6.4	1735	1.1	2350	6.4
20	F	0623	1.1	1217	6.8	1848	1.0		
21	SA	0052	6.6	0738	0.8	1316	7.1	● 1959	0.9
22	SU	0147	6.8	0843	0.5	1411	7.3	2059	0.8
23	M	0238	7.0	0939	0.2	1502	7.4	2151	0.7
24	TU	0326	7.1	1028	0.0	1550	7.5	2236	0.6
25	W	0411	7.1	1111	-0.1	1637	7.4	2316	0.6
26	TH	0454	7.1	1149	0.0	1723	7.2	2353	0.7
27	F	0537	7.0	1223	0.2	1809	6.9		
28	SA	0029	0.9	0622	6.8	1255	0.5	◐ 1857	6.5
29	SU	0107	1.2	0710	6.6	1332	0.8	1947	6.2
30	M	0152	1.4	0804	6.3	1420	1.1	2042	6.0
31	TU	0253	1.6	0907	6.1	1523	1.4	2145	5.8

FEBRUARY

Date	Day	Time	m	Time	m	Time	m	Time	m
1	W	0405	1.6	1018	6.0	1632	1.5	2302	5.8
2	TH	0518	1.4	1132	6.1	1743	1.4		
3	F	0010	6.0	0630	1.2	1233	6.3	1848	1.3
4	SA	0101	6.3	0726	0.9	1322	6.6	1939	1.2
5	SU	0144	6.5	0812	0.7	1403	6.7	○ 2022	1.2
6	M	0221	6.6	0853	0.7	1439	6.7	2100	1.1
7	TU	0254	6.7	0930	0.6	1510	6.7	2134	1.1
8	W	0324	6.7	1004	0.5	1539	6.8	2207	1.0
9	TH	0353	6.7	1036	0.5	1609	6.8	2239	1.0
10	F	0423	6.7	1104	0.6	1640	6.7	2308	1.1
11	SA	0453	6.6	1127	0.7	1714	6.5	2334	1.2
12	SU	0526	6.5	1149	0.8	1750	6.3		
13	M	0002	1.3	0604	6.4	1217	0.9	◑ 1832	6.1
14	TU	0038	1.4	0651	6.3	1256	1.0	1924	5.9
15	W	0128	1.6	0751	6.1	1353	1.3	2042	5.7
16	TH	0243	1.7	0921	6.0	1543	1.6	2213	5.8
17	F	0441	1.6	1050	6.2	1718	1.4	2334	6.1
18	SA	0612	1.2	1206	6.6	1843	1.1		
19	SU	0042	6.5	0737	0.7	1308	7.0	1955	0.8
20	M	0138	6.8	0838	0.2	1401	7.3	● 2051	0.6
21	TU	0225	7.0	0929	-0.1	1449	7.4	2139	0.5
22	W	0309	7.2	1013	-0.3	1533	7.5	2222	0.4
23	TH	0350	7.4	1052	-0.2	1616	7.4	2259	0.5
24	F	0429	7.4	1125	0.0	1656	7.1	2332	0.6
25	SA	0508	7.2	1150	0.3	1735	6.8		
26	SU	0000	0.8	0547	6.9	1211	0.6	1814	6.4
27	M	0028	1.1	0628	6.6	1236	1.0	◐ 1855	6.1
28	TU	0100	1.3	0716	6.2	1313	1.4	1944	5.7

MARCH

Date	Day	Time	m	Time	m	Time	m	Time	m
1	W	0149	1.6	0818	5.8	1418	1.8	2049	5.4
2	TH	0316	1.8	0938	5.6	1554	1.9	2219	5.4
3	F	0442	1.6	1105	5.8	1717	1.7	2343	5.7
4	SA	0558	1.3	1212	6.1	1825	1.4		
5	SU	0037	6.1	0700	0.9	1301	6.4	1917	1.2
6	M	0120	6.4	0747	0.7	1341	6.6	2001	1.1
7	TU	0158	6.6	0828	0.6	1415	6.7	○ 2041	1.1
8	W	0230	6.7	0906	0.5	1445	6.7	2117	1.0
9	TH	0300	6.8	0940	0.5	1513	6.8	2151	0.9
10	F	0329	6.9	1013	0.5	1543	6.8	2224	0.9
11	SA	0358	6.9	1040	0.5	1614	6.7	2252	1.0
12	SU	0429	6.8	1101	0.7	1647	6.6	2316	1.1
13	M	0503	6.7	1122	0.8	1723	6.3	2343	1.2
14	TU	0541	6.6	1151	0.9	1803	6.1		
15	W	0017	1.3	0629	6.3	1229	1.2	◑ 1856	5.8
16	TH	0105	1.5	0732	6.0	1328	1.6	2014	5.5
17	F	0223	1.7	0906	5.8	1531	1.8	2154	5.6
18	SA	0428	1.5	1038	6.1	1708	1.5	2322	6.0
19	SU	0612	1.0	1157	6.6	1835	1.1		
20	M	0029	6.5	0726	0.4	1256	7.0	1940	0.8
21	TU	0121	6.9	0820	0.0	1345	7.2	● 2032	0.6
22	W	0205	7.1	0907	-0.1	1429	7.3	2117	0.5
23	TH	0245	7.3	0947	-0.1	1509	7.3	2158	0.4
24	F	0323	7.5	1023	0.0	1548	7.2	2234	0.5
25	SA	0400	7.4	1050	0.3	1624	7.0	2304	0.6
26	SU	0437	7.3	1109	0.6	1659	6.7	2328	0.8
27	M	0514	6.9	1126	0.8	1732	6.3	2351	1.0
28	TU	0552	6.5	1152	1.1	1808	6.0		
29	W	0021	1.3	0636	6.1	1226	1.5	◐ 1851	5.6
30	TH	0103	1.6	0733	5.6	1320	1.9	1954	5.3
31	F	0219	1.8	0857	5.4	1508	2.2	2130	5.2

APRIL

Date	Day	Time	m	Time	m	Time	m	Time	m
1	SA	0404	1.7	1025	5.5	1643	1.9	2259	5.5
2	SU	0517	1.3	1136	5.9	1749	1.6		
3	M	0000	6.0	0617	1.0	1227	6.3	1843	1.3
4	TU	0045	6.3	0709	0.8	1307	6.5	1929	1.2
5	W	0123	6.6	0753	0.7	1341	6.6	2011	1.1
6	TH	0157	6.7	0832	0.6	1411	6.7	○ 2050	1.0
7	F	0228	6.9	0909	0.5	1443	6.8	2127	0.9
8	SA	0300	7.0	0942	0.5	1516	6.8	2202	0.9
9	SU	0333	7.0	1010	0.6	1550	6.8	2233	0.9
10	M	0407	7.0	1034	0.7	1625	6.6	2300	1.0
11	TU	0444	6.8	1101	0.8	1702	6.3	2329	1.0
12	W	0527	6.6	1135	1.0	1745	6.0		
13	TH	0006	1.1	0619	6.3	1220	1.3	◑ 1843	5.7
14	F	0058	1.3	0729	6.0	1329	1.7	2005	5.5
15	SA	0229	1.5	0901	6.0	1522	1.8	2140	5.7
16	SU	0418	1.2	1025	6.2	1651	1.4	2302	6.1
17	M	0553	0.8	1138	6.6	1811	1.1		
18	TU	0006	6.5	0700	0.3	1236	6.9	1913	0.8
19	W	0056	6.9	0751	0.1	1323	7.1	2004	0.6
20	TH	0138	7.1	0835	0.1	1403	7.1	● 2049	0.6
21	F	0216	7.3	0914	0.2	1441	7.1	2129	0.5
22	SA	0253	7.4	0946	0.4	1517	7.1	2204	0.5
23	SU	0331	7.4	1008	0.6	1552	6.9	2233	0.6
24	M	0408	7.2	1024	0.8	1625	6.6	2255	0.8
25	TU	0446	6.8	1049	1.0	1657	6.3	2320	1.0
26	W	0523	6.4	1119	1.2	1730	6.0	2351	1.2
27	TH	0603	6.0	1153	1.5	1809	5.7	◐	
28	F	0029	1.4	0653	5.6	1239	1.9	1904	5.4
29	SA	0132	1.7	0807	5.4	1400	2.2	2034	5.2
30	SU	0314	1.7	0933	5.5	1545	2.1	2203	5.4

Chart Datum: 3·20 metres below Ordnance Datum (Newlyn)
HAT is 7·7 metres above Chart Datum

TIME ZONE (UT)
For Summer Time add ONE hour in **non-shaded areas**

LONDON BRIDGE

LAT 51°30'N LONG 0°05'W

TIMES AND HEIGHTS OF HIGH AND LOW WATERS

Dates in amber are **SPRINGS**
Dates in grey are **NEAPS**

2023

MAY

Day	Time	m	Day	Time	m
1 M	0427 1041 1657 2308	1.3 5.8 1.7 5.8	**16** TU	0515 1111 1735 2335	0.7 6.6 1.1 6.6
2 TU	0525 1136 1754 2359	1.0 6.1 1.4 6.2	**17** W	0622 1209 1838	0.5 6.8 0.9
3 W	0618 1221 1845	0.8 6.4 1.3	**18** TH	0026 0715 1256 1932	6.8 0.5 6.8 0.8
4 TH	0041 0707 1300 1934	6.5 0.7 6.6 1.1	**19** F	0110 0759 1337 ● 2018	7.0 0.5 6.9 0.7
5 F	0119 0752 1337 ○ 2019	6.8 0.7 6.7 1.0	**20** SA	0149 0836 1415 2059	7.1 0.6 6.9 0.6
6 SA	0156 0833 1415 2101	6.9 0.7 6.8 0.9	**21** SU	0228 0906 1450 2135	7.2 0.7 6.8 0.6
7 SU	0233 0911 1453 2141	7.1 0.7 6.8 0.8	**22** M	0307 0927 1525 2205	7.2 0.8 6.7 0.7
8 M	0312 0944 1532 2217	7.1 0.7 6.7 0.7	**23** TU	0345 0952 1559 2231	7.0 0.9 6.5 0.8
9 TU	0352 1016 1612 2251	7.0 0.8 6.5 0.8	**24** W	0423 1023 1632 2259	6.7 1.1 6.3 0.9
10 W	0435 1052 1654 2326	6.9 0.9 6.3 0.8	**25** TH	0500 1056 1706 2332	6.4 1.2 6.0 1.1
11 TH	0523 1134 1743	6.6 1.1 6.0	**26** F	0539 1132 1744	6.1 1.4 5.8
12 F	0008 0621 1226 ◑ 1844	0.9 6.4 1.4 5.9	**27** SA	0010 0623 1215 ◐ 1831	1.2 5.8 1.7 5.6
13 SA	0108 0733 1341 2002	1.1 6.2 1.6 5.8	**28** SU	0100 0718 1313 1933	1.3 5.6 1.9 5.5
14 SU	0236 0851 1506 2121	1.1 6.2 1.5 6.0	**29** M	0209 0831 1424 2102	1.4 5.6 1.9 5.5
15 M	0358 1003 1623 2232	0.9 6.4 1.3 6.3	**30** TU	0324 0940 1540 2211	1.3 5.8 1.8 5.8
			31 W	0428 1039 1652 2307	1.1 6.0 1.6 6.2

JUNE

Day	Time	m	Day	Time	m
1 TH	0524 1133 1755 2358	0.9 6.3 1.3 6.5	**16** F	0632 1231 1900	0.8 6.6 0.9
2 F	0618 1222 1853	0.8 6.5 1.1	**17** SA	0046 0722 1316 1951	6.8 0.9 6.6 0.7
3 SA	0044 0711 1309 1948	6.8 0.8 6.7 1.0	**18** SU	0130 0803 1357 ● 2035	6.9 0.9 6.6 0.7
4 SU	0129 0801 1354 ○ 2039	7.0 0.7 6.8 0.8	**19** M	0212 0838 1434 2115	6.9 1.0 6.6 0.7
5 M	0214 0848 1439 2126	7.1 0.7 6.8 0.6	**20** TU	0253 0908 1510 2150	6.9 1.1 6.6 0.7
6 TU	0300 0932 1524 2211	7.2 0.8 6.7 0.5	**21** W	0331 0938 1544 2221	6.8 1.1 6.5 0.8
7 W	0346 1015 1610 2255	7.1 0.8 6.6 0.5	**22** TH	0408 1011 1618 2252	6.6 1.2 6.4 0.8
8 TH	0434 1058 1656 2338	7.0 0.9 6.5 0.5	**23** F	0444 1047 1652 2325	6.4 1.2 6.3 0.8
9 F	0526 1145 1746	6.9 1.0 6.4	**24** SA	0519 1124 1727 2359	6.3 1.3 6.1 0.9
10 SA	0025 0623 1237 ◑ 1844	0.5 6.7 1.1 6.3	**25** SU	0557 1201 1806	6.1 1.4 6.0
11 SU	0121 0726 1337 1948	0.6 6.5 1.2 6.3	**26** M	0035 0640 1242 ◐ 1852	1.0 6.0 1.5 5.9
12 M	0223 0831 1443 2055	0.6 6.5 1.3 6.3	**27** TU	0116 0730 1330 1949	1.1 5.8 1.7 5.8
13 TU	0326 0934 1550 2158	0.6 6.5 1.2 6.4	**28** W	0208 0837 1429 2106	1.2 5.8 1.7 5.8
14 W	0428 1038 1657 2300	0.7 6.5 1.2 6.5	**29** TH	0315 0947 1545 2218	1.2 5.9 1.6 6.1
15 TH	0532 1139 1802 2356	0.8 6.5 1.0 6.7	**30** F	0430 1051 1709 2320	1.1 6.2 1.4 6.4

JULY

Day	Time	m	Day	Time	m
1 SA	0536 1152 1819	0.9 6.4 1.1	**16** SU	0028 0652 1302 1931	6.6 1.1 6.4 0.8
2 SU	0016 0638 1247 1924	6.7 0.8 6.6 0.9	**17** M	0119 0743 1346 ● 2019	6.7 1.1 6.5 0.7
3 M	0110 0740 1340 ○ 2025	7.0 0.8 6.7 0.6	**18** TU	0204 0826 1426 2102	6.8 1.1 6.6 0.6
4 TU	0201 0839 1430 2121	7.2 0.8 6.8 0.4	**19** W	0245 0904 1501 2140	6.8 1.1 6.6 0.6
5 W	0252 0933 1518 2213	7.3 0.7 6.9 0.2	**20** TH	0321 0938 1534 2213	6.8 1.1 6.6 0.6
6 TH	0341 1022 1605 2301	7.3 0.7 6.9 0.1	**21** F	0354 1009 1605 2244	6.7 1.1 6.6 0.6
7 F	0430 1106 1651 2344	7.3 0.7 6.9 0.0	**22** SA	0425 1042 1635 2314	6.6 1.1 6.5 0.6
8 SA	0519 1149 1737	7.2 0.7 6.8	**23** SU	0456 1114 1706 2342	6.5 1.1 6.4 0.7
9 SU	0025 0611 1232 1827	0.1 7.0 0.8 6.7	**24** M	0528 1145 1740	6.4 1.3 6.3
10 M	0107 0705 1318 ◑ 1921	0.2 6.7 1.0 6.6	**25** TU	0007 0604 1214 ◐ 1817	0.9 6.2 1.4 6.1
11 TU	0153 0801 1411 2020	0.5 6.5 1.1 6.5	**26** W	0035 0645 1250 1902	1.0 6.0 1.5 6.0
12 W	0245 0859 1511 2121	0.7 6.4 1.3 6.4	**27** TH	0113 0737 1339 2001	1.1 5.8 1.6 5.9
13 TH	0341 1001 1616 2224	0.9 6.2 1.3 6.4	**28** F	0207 0852 1448 2127	1.3 5.7 1.7 5.9
14 F	0442 1107 1725 2329	1.1 6.2 1.2 6.4	**29** SA	0336 1014 1632 2246	1.4 5.9 1.6 6.2
15 SA	0549 1209 1833	1.2 6.3 1.0	**30** SU	0505 1126 1753 2355	1.2 6.2 1.2 6.6
			31 M	0617 1231 1909	1.0 6.5 0.8

AUGUST

Day	Time	m	Day	Time	m
1 TU	0055 0731 1327 ○ 2019	6.9 0.9 6.7 0.5	**16** W	0151 0812 1410 ● 2043	6.8 1.1 6.6 0.6
2 W	0151 0836 1418 2118	7.2 0.8 6.9 0.1	**17** TH	0229 0851 1444 2120	6.8 1.1 6.7 0.5
3 TH	0241 0930 1505 2208	7.4 0.6 7.1 -0.1	**18** F	0302 0926 1515 2153	6.8 1.1 6.7 0.5
4 F	0329 1018 1550 2252	7.5 0.5 7.2 -0.3	**19** SA	0331 0958 1543 2223	6.8 1.0 6.8 0.5
5 SA	0415 1059 1633 2332	7.5 0.5 7.2 -0.2	**20** SU	0358 1029 1610 2251	6.7 1.0 6.7 0.6
6 SU	0500 1137 1715	7.3 0.5 7.2	**21** M	0426 1058 1640 2316	6.7 1.1 6.6 0.7
7 M	0006 0546 1213 1758	0.0 7.0 0.7 7.0	**22** TU	0457 1124 1711 2335	6.5 1.2 6.5 0.9
8 TU	0037 0633 1249 ◑ 1844	0.3 6.7 0.9 6.8	**23** W	0530 1148 1745 2358	6.3 1.4 6.3 1.0
9 W	0111 0722 1331 1937	0.6 6.3 1.2 6.5	**24** TH	0607 1217 1827 ◐	6.0 1.5 6.2
10 TH	0153 0816 1426 2039	1.0 6.0 1.4 6.2	**25** F	0030 0654 1259 1922	1.1 5.8 1.6 6.0
11 F	0252 0918 1535 2149	1.4 5.8 1.5 6.0	**26** SA	0119 0801 1404 2043	1.4 5.6 1.8 5.8
12 SA	0403 1034 1651 2306	1.6 5.8 1.4 6.1	**27** SU	0245 0940 1606 2220	1.7 5.6 1.7 6.0
13 SU	0520 1150 1811	1.5 6.0 1.1	**28** M	0445 1105 1737 2338	1.6 5.9 1.2 6.5
14 M	0014 0633 1246 1914	6.4 1.3 6.3 0.8	**29** TU	0607 1216 1905	1.2 6.4 0.7
15 TU	0107 0727 1331 2002	6.6 1.2 6.5 0.6	**30** W	0042 0726 1312 2011	6.9 0.9 6.8 0.2
			31 TH	0137 0826 1401 ○ 2104	7.3 0.7 7.0 -0.1

Chart Datum: 3·20 metres below Ordnance Datum (Newlyn)
HAT is 7·7 metres above Chart Datum

TIME ZONE (UT)
For Summer Time add ONE hour in **non-shaded areas**

LONDON BRIDGE

LAT 51°30′N LONG 0°05′W

TIMES AND HEIGHTS OF HIGH AND LOW WATERS

Dates in amber are **SPRINGS**
Dates in grey are **NEAPS**

2023

SEPTEMBER

Date	Day	Time	m	Time	m	Time	m	Time	m	Moon
1	F	0225	7.4	0916	0.5	1445	7.3	2150	-0.3	
2	SA	0309	7.5	1001	0.5	1526	7.4	2231	-0.3	
3	SU	0352	7.4	1040	0.4	1606	7.5	2306	-0.1	
4	M	0433	7.2	1116	0.6	1645	7.3	2335	0.2	
5	TU	0513	6.9	1147	0.8	1725	7.1	2358	0.6	
6	W	0553	6.5	1216	1.0	1806	6.7			◑
7	TH	0021	1.0	0634	6.1	1248	1.3	1854	6.3	
8	F	0055	1.4	0722	5.7	1335	1.6	1955	5.9	
9	SA	0154	1.8	0827	5.4	1453	1.8	2116	5.7	
10	SU	0328	2.0	0959	5.4	1621	1.6	2242	5.8	
11	M	0456	1.8	1123	5.7	1743	1.2	2354	6.2	
12	TU	0609	1.5	1222	6.1	1846	0.9			
13	W	0046	6.5	0703	1.2	1306	6.4	1934	0.7	
14	TH	0127	6.7	0747	1.1	1344	6.6	2014	0.6	
15	F	0202	6.7	0827	1.1	1417	6.7	2050	0.6	●
16	SA	0233	6.7	0902	1.1	1446	6.8	2123	0.6	
17	SU	0259	6.8	0936	1.0	1513	6.9	2154	0.6	
18	M	0326	6.8	1007	1.0	1541	6.9	2221	0.7	
19	TU	0355	6.7	1036	1.1	1611	6.8	2243	0.8	
20	W	0427	6.6	1101	1.2	1643	6.7	2302	1.0	
21	TH	0459	6.3	1123	1.3	1719	6.5	2327	1.1	
22	F	0535	6.1	1152	1.4	1802	6.3			◐
23	SA	0001	1.3	0622	5.8	1234	1.5	1859	6.0	
24	SU	0050	1.6	0729	5.5	1338	1.7	2023	5.8	
25	M	0225	2.0	0912	5.4	1550	1.7	2202	6.0	
26	TU	0429	1.7	1044	5.8	1727	1.1	2321	6.5	
27	W	0554	1.3	1155	6.4	1850	0.6			
28	TH	0024	7.0	0707	0.9	1250	6.8	1950	0.1	
29	F	0116	7.3	0803	0.7	1336	7.1	2039	-0.1	○
30	SA	0201	7.4	0852	0.6	1417	7.4	2123	-0.1	

OCTOBER

Date	Day	Time	m	Time	m	Time	m	Time	m	Moon
1	SU	0243	7.4	0935	0.5	1457	7.5	2201	0.1	
2	M	0323	7.3	1014	0.5	1536	7.5	2233	0.3	
3	TU	0401	7.1	1048	0.6	1614	7.4	2255	0.6	
4	W	0438	6.8	1116	0.8	1653	7.1	2312	0.9	
5	TH	0513	6.4	1140	1.1	1733	6.6	2336	1.3	
6	F	0548	6.0	1209	1.3	1818	6.2			◑
7	SA	0009	1.6	0630	5.6	1249	1.6	1914	5.7	
8	SU	0100	2.1	0730	5.2	1404	1.9	2037	5.4	
9	M	0243	2.3	0910	5.1	1545	1.7	2204	5.6	
10	TU	0422	2.1	1038	5.4	1659	1.4	2316	6.0	
11	W	0531	1.7	1142	5.9	1800	1.0			
12	TH	0010	6.3	0625	1.4	1229	6.3	1850	0.8	
13	F	0052	6.6	0712	1.2	1308	6.6	1933	0.7	
14	SA	0126	6.7	0753	1.2	1341	6.7	2012	0.7	●
15	SU	0156	6.7	0831	1.1	1411	6.8	2047	0.7	
16	M	0224	6.8	0907	1.1	1440	6.9	2119	0.7	
17	TU	0255	6.8	0941	1.0	1512	7.0	2147	0.8	
18	W	0327	6.8	1012	1.0	1545	6.9	2210	0.9	
19	TH	0401	6.6	1039	1.1	1621	6.8	2236	1.0	
20	F	0435	6.4	1105	1.1	1701	6.6	2308	1.2	
21	SA	0514	6.1	1139	1.2	1749	6.3	2348	1.4	
22	SU	0604	5.8	1224	1.4	1850	6.1			◐
23	M	0043	1.8	0714	5.5	1332	1.6	2015	5.9	
24	TU	0229	2.0	0852	5.6	1536	1.4	2143	6.2	
25	W	0408	1.7	1018	5.9	1704	1.0	2257	6.6	
26	TH	0526	1.3	1126	6.4	1820	0.6			
27	F	0000	6.9	0636	1.0	1221	6.8	1918	0.3	
28	SA	0050	7.1	0733	0.8	1307	7.1	2007	0.2	○
29	SU	0135	7.2	0822	0.7	1348	7.3	2049	0.3	
30	M	0215	7.2	0906	0.6	1428	7.4	2125	0.5	
31	TU	0253	7.1	0945	0.6	1507	7.4	2153	0.7	

NOVEMBER

Date	Day	Time	m	Time	m	Time	m	Time	m	Moon
1	W	0330	6.9	1019	0.7	1547	7.3	2211	0.9	
2	TH	0406	6.7	1045	0.9	1627	6.9	2233	1.2	
3	F	0440	6.3	1109	1.1	1706	6.5	2303	1.4	
4	SA	0513	6.0	1139	1.3	1748	6.1	2337	1.7	
5	SU	0549	5.7	1217	1.5	1837	5.7			◑
6	M	0022	2.0	0639	5.4	1316	1.7	1947	5.4	
7	TU	0136	2.3	0802	5.2	1454	1.8	2110	5.5	
8	W	0321	2.3	0940	5.3	1608	1.5	2219	5.7	
9	TH	0438	2.0	1046	5.7	1706	1.2	2316	6.1	
10	F	0535	1.6	1140	6.1	1758	1.0			
11	SA	0003	6.3	0626	1.4	1224	6.4	1845	0.9	
12	SU	0043	6.5	0713	1.3	1302	6.7	1929	0.8	
13	M	0119	6.7	0757	1.1	1337	6.9	2009	0.9	●
14	TU	0154	6.8	0838	1.0	1412	7.0	2045	0.9	
15	W	0231	6.8	0918	1.0	1450	7.0	2118	0.9	
16	TH	0308	6.7	0954	0.9	1528	7.0	2149	1.0	
17	F	0346	6.6	1027	0.9	1610	6.9	2224	1.1	
18	SA	0425	6.4	1101	0.9	1655	6.7	2305	1.2	
19	SU	0509	6.2	1140	1.0	1747	6.5	2353	1.4	
20	M	0603	6.0	1231	1.1	1850	6.3			◐
21	TU	0055	1.7	0710	5.8	1349	1.2	2006	6.2	
22	W	0220	1.8	0832	5.9	1515	1.1	2121	6.3	
23	TH	0340	1.6	0948	6.1	1628	0.9	2228	6.5	
24	F	0453	1.4	1053	6.4	1738	0.7	2331	6.7	
25	SA	0601	1.1	1151	6.7	1840	0.6			
26	SU	0024	6.8	0701	0.9	1239	6.9	1931	0.7	
27	M	0110	6.9	0753	0.8	1323	7.1	2014	0.7	○
28	TU	0151	6.9	0839	0.7	1405	7.2	2050	0.9	
29	W	0230	6.8	0920	0.7	1446	7.2	2118	1.0	
30	TH	0307	6.7	0956	0.8	1528	7.0	2140	1.2	

DECEMBER

Date	Day	Time	m	Time	m	Time	m	Time	m	Moon
1	F	0343	6.5	1025	0.9	1608	6.8	2209	1.3	
2	SA	0418	6.3	1051	1.1	1647	6.4	2243	1.4	
3	SU	0452	6.1	1122	1.2	1726	6.1	2320	1.6	
4	M	0527	5.9	1159	1.3	1807	5.9			
5	TU	0001	1.8	0609	5.7	1243	1.4	1857	5.7	◑
6	W	0051	2.0	0703	5.5	1342	1.5	2002	5.6	
7	TH	0153	2.1	0824	5.4	1456	1.5	2113	5.7	
8	F	0306	2.1	0944	5.6	1605	1.4	2214	5.9	
9	SA	0430	1.9	1044	5.9	1703	1.2	2310	6.1	
10	SU	0535	1.6	1137	6.3	1757	1.1			
11	M	0001	6.4	0631	1.3	1225	6.6	1848	1.0	
12	TU	0048	6.6	0724	1.1	1309	6.8	1936	1.0	●
13	W	0133	6.7	0814	1.0	1353	7.0	2022	1.0	
14	TH	0217	6.7	0902	0.8	1437	7.0	2106	1.0	
15	F	0301	6.7	0948	0.7	1522	7.1	2149	1.0	
16	SA	0344	6.7	1033	0.6	1608	7.1	2233	1.0	
17	SU	0428	6.6	1116	0.6	1656	7.0	2319	1.1	
18	M	0513	6.5	1159	0.6	1747	6.8			
19	TU	0007	1.2	0603	6.4	1247	0.7	1845	6.6	◐
20	W	0100	1.3	0700	6.3	1343	0.7	1948	6.5	
21	TH	0200	1.4	0807	6.3	1444	0.8	2053	6.4	
22	F	0307	1.5	0914	6.3	1547	0.9	2156	6.4	
23	SA	0416	1.4	1019	6.4	1651	0.9	2300	6.4	
24	SU	0525	1.3	1121	6.5	1757	1.0			
25	M	0000	6.5	0632	1.1	1218	6.7	1857	1.0	
26	TU	0053	6.5	0729	0.9	1309	6.8	1946	1.1	
27	W	0139	6.6	0819	0.7	1355	6.9	2029	1.1	○
28	TH	0221	6.6	0904	0.7	1438	6.9	2105	1.2	
29	F	0259	6.6	0945	0.8	1519	6.8	2135	1.3	
30	SA	0334	6.5	1018	0.8	1557	6.7	2204	1.3	
31	SU	0407	6.4	1046	0.9	1632	6.5	2236	1.3	

Chart Datum: 3·20 metres below Ordnance Datum (Newlyn)
HAT is 7·7 metres above Chart Datum

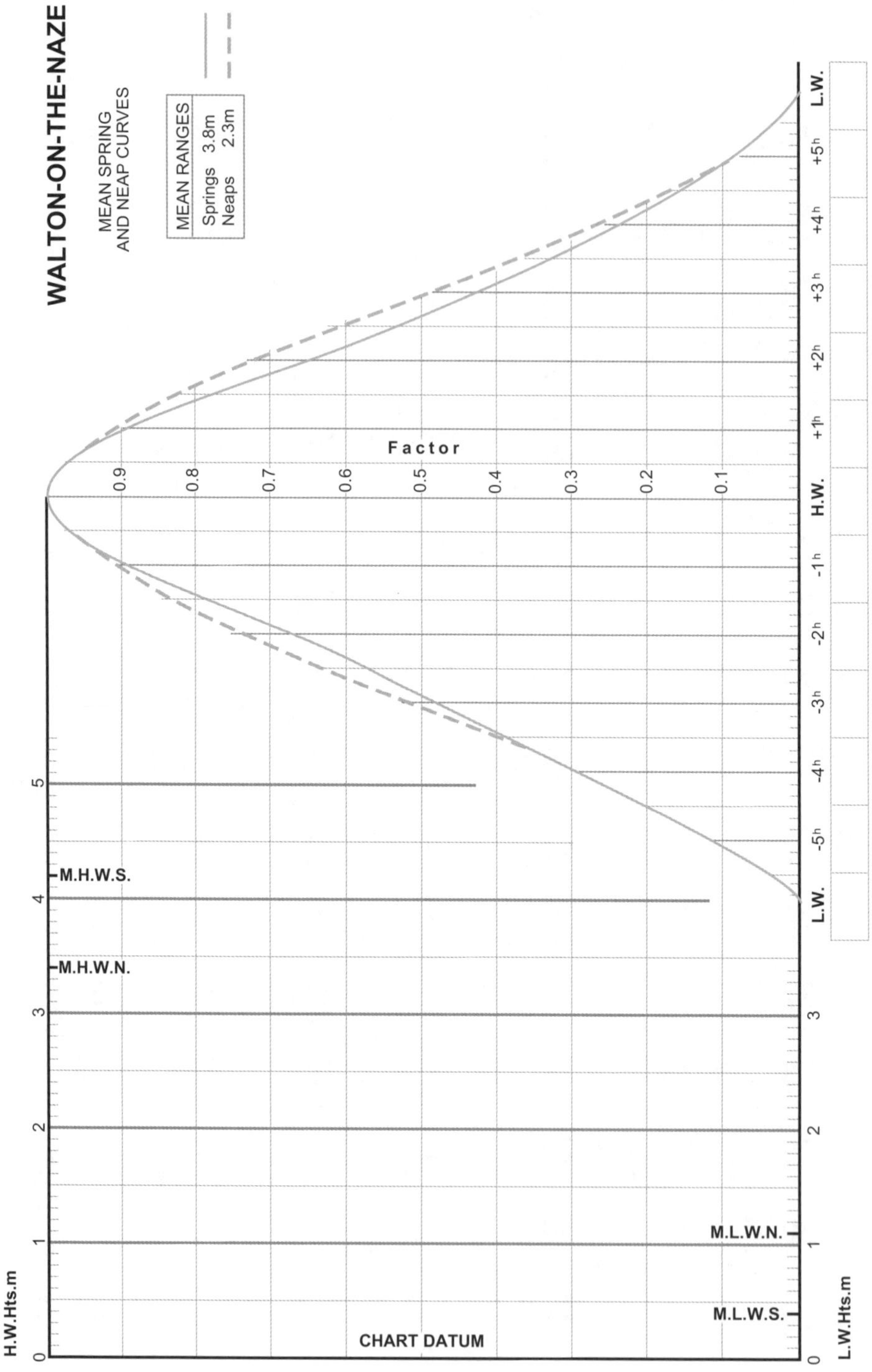
WALTON-ON-THE-NAZE
MEAN SPRING
AND NEAP CURVES
MEAN RANGES
Springs 3.8m
Neaps 2.3m
Factor
0.9
0.8
0.7
0.6
0.5
0.4
0.3
0.2
0.1
L.W.
+5h
+4h
+3h
+2h
+1h
H.W.
-1h
-2h
-3h
-4h
-5h
L.W.
H.W.Hts.m
M.H.W.S.
M.H.W.N.
CHART DATUM
M.L.W.N.
M.L.W.S.
L.W.Hts.m

TIME ZONE (UT)
For Summer Time add ONE hour in **non-shaded areas**

WALTON-ON-THE-NAZE

LAT 51°51′N LONG 1°17′E

TIMES AND HEIGHTS OF HIGH AND LOW WATERS

Dates in amber are **SPRINGS**
Dates in grey are **NEAPS**

2023

JANUARY

Date	Day	Time	m	Time	m	Time	m	Time	m
1	SU	0025	1.2	0647	3.7	1316	0.7	1934	3.7
2	M	0132	1.2	0754	3.7	1417	0.8	2038	3.7
3	TU	0237	1.1	0855	3.7	1515	0.9	2133	3.8
4	W	0338	1.0	0948	3.8	1605	0.9	2221	3.8
5	TH	0431	0.8	1034	3.9	1647	0.9	2303	3.9
6	F ○	0516	0.7	1116	3.9	1725	0.9	2342	4.0
7	SA	0556	0.6	1154	4.0	1801	0.9		
8	SU	0017	4.0	0634	0.5	1231	4.0	1835	0.9
9	M	0052	4.0	0708	0.5	1307	4.0	1905	0.9
10	TU	0125	4.0	0740	0.5	1342	4.0	1934	0.9
11	W	0158	4.0	0812	0.5	1417	3.9	2006	0.9
12	TH	0232	3.9	0845	0.5	1452	3.8	2041	1.0
13	F	0307	3.8	0920	0.6	1530	3.7	2120	1.1
14	SA	0345	3.8	1000	0.7	1613	3.7	2204	1.2
15	SU ◑	0429	3.7	1047	0.7	1704	3.6	2300	1.3
16	M	0523	3.6	1148	0.8	1806	3.5		
17	TU	0013	1.3	0632	3.6	1301	0.8	1918	3.5
18	W	0138	1.2	0746	3.6	1412	0.8	2030	3.6
19	TH	0250	1.0	0858	3.8	1516	0.8	2139	3.8
20	F	0353	0.8	1002	4.0	1614	0.7	2239	3.9
21	SA ●	0453	0.6	1059	4.2	1709	0.7	2333	4.1
22	SU	0549	0.4	1152	4.4	1801	0.7		
23	M	0022	4.2	0643	0.2	1242	4.5	1850	0.7
24	TU	0110	4.3	0733	0.1	1331	4.5	1937	0.7
25	W	0156	4.3	0821	0.1	1420	4.4	2021	0.7
26	TH	0241	4.3	0906	0.1	1508	4.2	2104	0.8
27	F	0325	4.2	0950	0.2	1556	4.0	2149	0.9
28	SA ◐	0410	4.1	1034	0.4	1647	3.8	2238	1.0
29	SU	0459	3.9	1123	0.6	1741	3.6	2336	1.1
30	M	0555	3.7	1218	0.9	1843	3.4		
31	TU	0042	1.2	0706	3.5	1322	1.0	1956	3.4

FEBRUARY

Date	Day	Time	m	Time	m	Time	m	Time	m
1	W	0158	1.2	0822	3.5	1438	1.1	2107	3.5
2	TH	0321	1.0	0928	3.6	1548	1.1	2203	3.6
3	F	0423	0.8	1021	3.7	1635	1.0	2249	3.8
4	SA	0507	0.7	1105	3.8	1713	1.0	2329	3.9
5	SU ○	0544	0.5	1143	3.9	1747	0.9		
6	M	0004	4.0	0617	0.5	1218	4.0	1819	0.9
7	TU	0037	4.0	0648	0.4	1252	4.0	1848	0.8
8	W	0110	4.1	0719	0.4	1325	4.0	1917	0.8
9	TH	0142	4.1	0749	0.4	1357	4.0	1947	0.8
10	F	0212	4.0	0818	0.4	1429	3.9	2019	0.8
11	SA	0243	4.0	0848	0.5	1503	3.8	2053	0.9
12	SU	0316	3.9	0920	0.6	1541	3.8	2131	1.0
13	M ◑	0354	3.9	0959	0.7	1626	3.7	2220	1.1
14	TU	0443	3.8	1055	0.8	1723	3.5	2328	1.2
15	W	0547	3.6	1217	1.0	1837	3.4		
16	TH	0103	1.2	0712	3.5	1348	1.0	2004	3.4
17	F	0231	1.0	0842	3.6	1502	0.9	2128	3.6
18	SA	0344	0.7	0955	3.9	1607	0.8	2232	3.8
19	SU	0449	0.5	1054	4.1	1703	0.7	2324	4.0
20	M ●	0543	0.2	1144	4.3	1751	0.7		
21	TU	0010	4.2	0633	0.1	1231	4.4	1837	0.6
22	W	0054	4.4	0718	0.0	1316	4.5	1919	0.6
23	TH	0135	4.5	0759	0.0	1359	4.4	1959	0.6
24	F	0216	4.4	0837	0.1	1442	4.2	2038	0.7
25	SA	0255	4.3	0911	0.3	1524	4.0	2117	0.8
26	SU	0334	4.1	0946	0.5	1606	3.7	2158	0.9
27	M ◐	0416	3.9	1027	0.8	1653	3.5	2248	1.0
28	TU	0507	3.6	1121	1.1	1749	3.3	2354	1.2

MARCH

Date	Day	Time	m	Time	m	Time	m	Time	m
1	W	0617	3.3	1232	1.3	1904	3.2		
2	TH	0117	1.2	0748	3.3	1400	1.4	2035	3.2
3	F	0301	1.1	0907	3.4	1528	1.3	2140	3.4
4	SA	0407	0.8	1004	3.6	1617	1.1	2228	3.6
5	SU	0448	0.6	1048	3.8	1654	1.0	2307	3.8
6	M	0521	0.5	1124	3.9	1726	0.9	2342	3.9
7	TU ○	0551	0.4	1158	3.9	1756	0.8		
8	W	0014	4.0	0621	0.4	1229	4.0	1825	0.7
9	TH	0045	4.1	0650	0.3	1301	4.0	1854	0.7
10	F	0116	4.1	0719	0.3	1332	4.0	1925	0.7
11	SA	0147	4.1	0747	0.3	1404	4.0	1956	0.7
12	SU	0217	4.1	0815	0.4	1437	3.9	2029	0.8
13	M	0250	4.0	0846	0.5	1513	3.8	2107	0.8
14	TU	0328	4.0	0925	0.7	1556	3.6	2154	0.9
15	W ◑	0417	3.8	1021	0.9	1651	3.4	2303	1.1
16	TH	0523	3.6	1154	1.2	1809	3.2		
17	F	0046	1.1	0657	3.4	1334	1.2	1951	3.2
18	SA	0221	0.9	0838	3.6	1451	1.0	2119	3.5
19	SU	0337	0.6	0949	3.9	1555	0.9	2219	3.8
20	M	0438	0.3	1043	4.1	1647	0.7	2307	4.1
21	TU ●	0527	0.1	1130	4.3	1732	0.6	2350	4.3
22	W	0611	0.0	1212	4.4	1814	0.6		
23	TH	0030	4.4	0652	0.0	1252	4.4	1855	0.5
24	F	0108	4.5	0728	0.1	1333	4.3	1934	0.5
25	SA	0146	4.4	0801	0.2	1412	4.1	2011	0.6
26	SU	0222	4.3	0830	0.4	1449	3.9	2047	0.7
27	M	0259	4.1	0901	0.7	1526	3.7	2124	0.8
28	TU	0339	3.8	0937	0.9	1607	3.5	2209	0.9
29	W ◐	0428	3.5	1030	1.2	1659	3.3	2310	1.1
30	TH	0536	3.3	1146	1.4	1812	3.1		
31	F	0033	1.2	0710	3.2	1319	1.5	1943	3.1

APRIL

Date	Day	Time	m	Time	m	Time	m	Time	m
1	SA	0214	1.1	0833	3.3	1447	1.4	2100	3.3
2	SU	0328	0.9	0933	3.5	1543	1.2	2153	3.5
3	M	0412	0.7	1017	3.7	1622	1.0	2233	3.7
4	TU	0446	0.5	1054	3.8	1655	0.9	2308	3.9
5	W	0516	0.4	1127	3.9	1726	0.8	2341	4.0
6	TH ○	0546	0.4	1159	4.0	1756	0.7		
7	F	0013	4.1	0617	0.3	1232	4.1	1829	0.6
8	SA	0046	4.2	0646	0.3	1305	4.1	1902	0.6
9	SU	0120	4.2	0715	0.4	1340	4.0	1935	0.6
10	M	0154	4.2	0746	0.5	1415	3.9	2011	0.7
11	TU	0231	4.1	0821	0.6	1453	3.8	2052	0.7
12	W	0313	4.0	0906	0.8	1538	3.6	2145	0.8
13	TH ◑	0406	3.8	1012	1.1	1636	3.4	2301	0.9
14	F	0518	3.5	1148	1.3	1759	3.2		
15	SA	0044	0.9	0658	3.5	1319	1.2	1941	3.3
16	SU	0210	0.7	0828	3.7	1433	1.1	2059	3.6
17	M	0321	0.5	0933	4.0	1533	0.9	2156	3.9
18	TU	0417	0.3	1024	4.1	1623	0.8	2242	4.1
19	W	0503	0.2	1107	4.2	1706	0.7	2323	4.3
20	TH ●	0543	0.1	1148	4.3	1748	0.6		
21	F	0001	4.4	0620	0.2	1226	4.3	1830	0.5
22	SA	0039	4.4	0654	0.3	1304	4.2	1910	0.5
23	SU	0116	4.4	0725	0.4	1341	4.1	1948	0.5
24	M	0152	4.2	0755	0.6	1416	3.9	2023	0.6
25	TU	0229	4.0	0824	0.8	1451	3.7	2058	0.7
26	W	0309	3.8	0859	1.0	1528	3.5	2139	0.8
27	TH ◐	0356	3.5	0947	1.2	1617	3.3	2234	1.0
28	F	0500	3.3	1057	1.4	1727	3.2	2351	1.1
29	SA	0624	3.2	1230	1.5	1846	3.1		
30	SU	0117	1.0	0741	3.3	1354	1.4	1959	3.3

Chart Datum: 2·16 metres below Ordnance Datum (Newlyn)
HAT is 4·7 metres above Chart Datum

TIME ZONE (UT)
For Summer Time add ONE hour in **non-shaded areas**

WALTON-ON-THE-NAZE

LAT 51°51′N LONG 1°17′E

TIMES AND HEIGHTS OF HIGH AND LOW WATERS

Dates in amber are **SPRINGS**
Dates in grey are **NEAPS**

2023

MAY

Date	Day	Time	m	Date	Day	Time	m
1	M	0228	0.9	16	TU	0255	0.4
		0843	3.5			0907	4.0
		1455	1.2			1505	1.0
		2059	3.5			2126	3.9
2	TU	0320	0.7	17	W	0349	0.3
		0932	3.7			0959	4.1
		1540	1.0			1556	0.8
		2146	3.7			2214	4.1
3	W	0400	0.6	18	TH	0434	0.3
		1012	3.8			1043	4.1
		1617	0.9			1642	0.7
		2226	3.9			2256	4.2
4	TH	0436	0.5	19	F	0514	0.4
		1049	3.9			1123	4.1
		1652	0.8			1726	0.6
		2303	4.0			● 2335	4.3
5	F	0510	0.4	20	SA	0550	0.4
		1125	4.0			1202	4.1
		1728	0.7			1809	0.5
		○ 2340	4.2				
6	SA	0543	0.4	21	SU	0013	4.3
		1203	4.1			0625	0.5
		1804	0.6			1239	4.1
						1851	0.5
7	SU	0018	4.2	22	M	0051	4.2
		0617	0.4			0658	0.7
		1241	4.1			1316	4.0
		1843	0.6			1929	0.5
8	M	0057	4.3	23	TU	0129	4.1
		0651	0.5			0730	0.8
		1321	4.1			1351	3.9
		1922	0.6			2005	0.6
9	TU	0137	4.2	24	W	0207	4.0
		0728	0.6			0801	0.9
		1401	4.0			1426	3.8
		2004	0.6			2039	0.7
10	W	0220	4.2	25	TH	0247	3.8
		0812	0.7			0835	1.0
		1445	3.8			1503	3.6
		2052	0.6			2118	0.7
11	TH	0309	4.0	26	F	0332	3.6
		0907	0.9			0918	1.2
		1535	3.6			1549	3.5
		2153	0.7			2207	0.8
12	F	0407	3.8	27	SA	0427	3.4
		1017	1.1			1013	1.3
		1639	3.5			1648	3.4
		◑ 2313	0.7			◐ 2309	0.9
13	SA	0523	3.7	28	SU	0534	3.3
		1139	1.2			1125	1.4
		1757	3.4			1755	3.3
14	SU	0036	0.6	29	M	0022	0.9
		0649	3.7			0642	3.3
		1257	1.2			1249	1.4
		1918	3.5			1900	3.4
15	M	0150	0.5	30	TU	0129	0.9
		0805	3.8			0741	3.4
		1405	1.1			1358	1.3
		2029	3.7			1959	3.5
				31	W	0225	0.7
						0836	3.6
						1450	1.1
						2053	3.7

JUNE

Date	Day	Time	m	Date	Day	Time	m
1	TH	0312	0.7	16	F	0406	0.6
		0925	3.8			1019	4.0
		1536	1.0			1622	0.8
		2142	3.9			2232	4.1
2	F	0355	0.6	17	SA	0449	0.7
		1011	3.9			1103	4.0
		1620	0.8			1710	0.7
		2227	4.0			2315	4.1
3	SA	0436	0.6	18	SU	0527	0.7
		1055	4.0			1144	4.0
		1703	0.7			1755	0.6
		2312	4.2			● 2355	4.1
4	SU	0516	0.5	19	M	0605	0.8
		1140	4.1			1222	4.0
		1747	0.6			1837	0.5
		○ 2356	4.3				
5	M	0557	0.6	20	TU	0034	4.1
		1225	4.1			0641	0.8
		1832	0.5			1259	4.0
						1917	0.5
6	TU	0041	4.3	21	W	0113	4.0
		0640	0.6			0715	0.9
		1310	4.1			1335	4.0
		1919	0.5			1952	0.6
7	W	0128	4.3	22	TH	0152	4.0
		0726	0.7			0747	1.0
		1356	4.0			1410	3.9
		2009	0.4			2026	0.6
8	TH	0217	4.3	23	F	0231	3.8
		0816	0.8			0819	1.0
		1445	4.0			1447	3.8
		2103	0.4			2101	0.6
9	F	0310	4.1	24	SA	0311	3.7
		0911	0.9			0857	1.1
		1538	3.9			1527	3.7
		2203	0.4			2141	0.7
10	SA	0409	4.0	25	SU	0354	3.6
		1012	1.0			0940	1.2
		1636	3.8			1611	3.6
		◑ 2309	0.4			2227	0.8
11	SU	0515	3.9	26	M	0442	3.5
		1119	1.1			1030	1.3
		1740	3.8			1702	3.6
						◐ 2322	0.8
12	M	0016	0.4	27	TU	0537	3.5
		0624	3.8			1131	1.4
		1226	1.1			1800	3.5
		1847	3.8				
13	TU	0120	0.5	28	W	0025	0.9
		0732	3.8			0639	3.5
		1331	1.1			1246	1.3
		1953	3.8			1902	3.6
14	W	0221	0.5	29	TH	0129	0.9
		0836	3.9			0740	3.5
		1433	1.0			1359	1.2
		2053	3.9			2004	3.7
15	TH	0318	0.6	30	F	0227	0.8
		0931	3.9			0841	3.7
		1530	0.9			1458	1.1
		2146	4.0			2103	3.8

JULY

Date	Day	Time	m	Date	Day	Time	m
1	SA	0321	0.7	16	SU	0434	1.0
		0938	3.8			1049	3.9
		1553	0.9			1703	0.7
		2159	4.0			2302	4.0
2	SU	0411	0.7	17	M	0515	1.0
		1033	3.9			1131	3.9
		1645	0.7			1748	0.6
		2251	4.1			● 2345	4.0
3	M	0500	0.7	18	TU	0553	0.9
		1124	4.0			1210	4.0
		1736	0.6			1827	0.5
		○ 2342	4.3				
4	TU	0548	0.7	19	W	0023	4.0
		1214	4.1			0628	0.9
		1828	0.5			1246	4.0
						1903	0.5
5	W	0031	4.4	20	TH	0100	4.0
		0637	0.7			0701	0.9
		1302	4.2			1320	4.1
		1920	0.3			1935	0.5
6	TH	0121	4.4	21	F	0137	4.0
		0726	0.7			0731	0.9
		1350	4.2			1354	4.0
		2011	0.3			2006	0.5
7	F	0212	4.4	22	SA	0212	3.9
		0814	0.8			0801	0.9
		1438	4.2			1427	4.0
		2102	0.2			2037	0.5
8	SA	0303	4.3	23	SU	0246	3.9
		0903	0.9			0833	1.0
		1527	4.2			1501	3.9
		2153	0.2			2109	0.6
9	SU	0356	4.2	24	M	0320	3.8
		0954	0.9			0909	1.1
		1617	4.1			1535	3.8
		2247	0.3			2144	0.7
10	M	0452	4.0	25	TU	0358	3.7
		1049	1.0			0949	1.2
		1710	4.0			1614	3.8
		◑ 2343	0.4			◐ 2224	0.8
11	TU	0551	3.8	26	W	0442	3.6
		1149	1.1			1037	1.3
		1809	3.9			1702	3.7
						2317	0.9
12	W	0040	0.6	27	TH	0539	3.5
		0654	3.7			1142	1.3
		1253	1.1			1804	3.6
		1914	3.8				
13	TH	0140	0.7	28	F	0030	1.0
		0801	3.7			0649	3.5
		1359	1.1			1309	1.3
		2021	3.8			1917	3.6
14	F	0244	0.9	29	SA	0149	1.0
		0905	3.7			0802	3.5
		1508	1.0			1428	1.2
		2122	3.8			2031	3.7
15	SA	0344	0.9	30	SU	0255	1.0
		1001	3.8			0914	3.7
		1611	0.9			1533	0.9
		2216	3.9			2139	3.9
				31	M	0355	0.9
						1018	3.8
						1633	0.7
						2239	4.1

AUGUST

Date	Day	Time	m	Date	Day	Time	m
1	TU	0451	0.8	16	W	0538	1.0
		1113	4.0			1154	4.0
		1729	0.5			1809	0.5
		○ 2332	4.3			●	
2	W	0541	0.8	17	TH	0008	4.0
		1203	4.2			0610	0.9
		1822	0.3			1227	4.1
						1840	0.5
3	TH	0022	4.5	18	F	0042	4.1
		0630	0.7			0640	0.9
		1250	4.3			1259	4.1
		1912	0.2			1910	0.5
4	F	0110	4.5	19	SA	0114	4.1
		0716	0.7			0709	0.9
		1336	4.4			1330	4.2
		1959	0.1			1938	0.5
5	SA	0158	4.5	20	SU	0146	4.0
		0800	0.7			0738	0.9
		1420	4.5			1400	4.1
		2044	0.1			2006	0.5
6	SU	0245	4.4	21	M	0216	4.0
		0843	0.8			0808	0.9
		1504	4.4			1430	4.1
		2127	0.2			2033	0.6
7	M	0332	4.2	22	TU	0247	3.9
		0927	0.9			0840	1.0
		1547	4.3			1500	4.0
		2210	0.4			2101	0.7
8	TU	0420	4.0	23	W	0321	3.8
		1014	1.0			0914	1.1
		1634	4.1			1535	3.9
		◑ 2257	0.6			2134	0.8
9	W	0512	3.8	24	TH	0401	3.7
		1108	1.1			0956	1.2
		1727	3.9			1618	3.8
		2350	0.9			◐ 2221	1.0
10	TH	0612	3.6	25	F	0452	3.5
		1212	1.2			1056	1.3
		1834	3.7			1717	3.7
						2336	1.2
11	F	0053	1.1	26	SA	0602	3.4
		0724	3.4			1230	1.3
		1326	1.2			1837	3.5
		1953	3.6				
12	SA	0212	1.2	27	SU	0119	1.2
		0841	3.5			0730	3.4
		1454	1.1			1405	1.2
		2106	3.7			2011	3.6
13	SU	0332	1.2	28	M	0238	1.1
		0945	3.6			0859	3.5
		1607	0.9			1519	0.9
		2205	3.8			2129	3.9
14	M	0425	1.1	29	TU	0344	1.0
		1035	3.8			1007	3.8
		1657	0.7			1623	0.6
		2253	3.9			2229	4.2
15	TU	0504	1.1	30	W	0439	0.9
		1117	3.9			1100	4.1
		1736	0.6			1718	0.4
		2333	4.0			2320	4.4
				31	TH	0527	0.8
						1146	4.3
						1807	0.2
						○	

Chart Datum: 2·16 metres below Ordnance Datum (Newlyn)
HAT is 4·7 metres above Chart Datum

TIME ZONE (UT)
For Summer Time add ONE hour in **non-shaded areas**

WALTON-ON-THE-NAZE

LAT 51°51′N LONG 1°17′E

TIMES AND HEIGHTS OF HIGH AND LOW WATERS

Dates in amber are **SPRINGS**
Dates in grey are **NEAPS**

2023

SEPTEMBER

Date	Day	Time	m	Time	m	Time	m	Time	m
1	F	0006	4.5	0612	0.7	1229	4.5	1853	0.1
2	SA	0051	4.6	0655	0.7	1312	4.6	1935	0.1
3	SU	0135	4.5	0737	0.7	1353	4.6	2015	0.2
4	M	0218	4.4	0818	0.7	1433	4.5	2051	0.4
5	TU	0301	4.2	0858	0.8	1513	4.3	2126	0.6
6	W	0344	3.9	0941	0.9	1555	4.1	◑ 2206	0.9
7	TH	0430	3.7	1030	1.0	1646	3.8	2258	1.2
8	F	0526	3.4	1132	1.2	1755	3.5		
9	SA	0008	1.4	0642	3.3	1252	1.2	1927	3.4
10	SU	0139	1.5	0813	3.3	1438	1.2	2049	3.6
11	M	0314	1.4	0923	3.5	1551	0.9	2149	3.8
12	TU	0406	1.2	1013	3.7	1637	0.7	2234	3.9
13	W	0443	1.1	1053	3.9	1711	0.6	2311	4.0
14	TH	0514	1.0	1128	4.0	1740	0.5	2344	4.1
15	F ●	0544	0.9	1159	4.1	1808	0.5		
16	SA	0015	4.1	0614	0.9	1229	4.2	1837	0.5
17	SU	0045	4.1	0642	0.8	1259	4.2	1904	0.5
18	M	0115	4.1	0711	0.8	1329	4.2	1930	0.6
19	TU	0145	4.1	0741	0.8	1359	4.1	1955	0.6
20	W	0216	4.0	0813	0.9	1430	4.1	2023	0.7
21	TH	0249	3.9	0847	1.0	1505	4.0	2057	0.9
22	F	0328	3.7	0929	1.0	1550	3.9	◐ 2144	1.1
23	SA	0417	3.5	1029	1.2	1650	3.7	2305	1.4
24	SU	0529	3.3	1209	1.2	1815	3.5		
25	M	0100	1.4	0708	3.3	1349	1.1	2001	3.6
26	TU	0221	1.2	0843	3.5	1504	0.8	2117	3.9
27	W	0326	1.0	0948	3.8	1606	0.5	2214	4.2
28	TH	0418	0.9	1038	4.1	1657	0.3	2301	4.4
29	F	0504	0.8	1122	4.4	1743	0.1	○ 2344	4.5
30	SA	0547	0.7	1203	4.5	1825	0.1		

OCTOBER

Date	Day	Time	m	Time	m	Time	m	Time	m
1	SU	0026	4.5	0630	0.6	1242	4.6	1904	0.2
2	M	0107	4.5	0711	0.6	1321	4.6	1939	0.3
3	TU	0147	4.3	0752	0.6	1400	4.5	2012	0.6
4	W	0227	4.1	0831	0.7	1439	4.3	2043	0.8
5	TH	0305	3.9	0911	0.8	1520	4.0	2120	1.1
6	F	0346	3.6	0956	1.0	1609	3.7	◑ 2210	1.4
7	SA	0438	3.4	1055	1.1	1719	3.4	2323	1.6
8	SU	0553	3.2	1214	1.2	1853	3.3		
9	M	0056	1.7	0726	3.2	1353	1.2	2017	3.5
10	TU	0230	1.5	0843	3.4	1512	1.0	2118	3.7
11	W	0329	1.3	0937	3.6	1559	0.8	2202	3.9
12	TH	0409	1.2	1017	3.8	1633	0.6	2238	4.0
13	F	0442	1.0	1052	4.0	1703	0.6	2311	4.1
14	SA	0513	0.9	1123	4.1	1732	0.5	● 2341	4.1
15	SU	0543	0.8	1155	4.2	1800	0.5		
16	M	0012	4.2	0614	0.8	1226	4.2	1828	0.6
17	TU	0044	4.2	0646	0.8	1258	4.2	1854	0.6
18	W	0116	4.1	0718	0.8	1332	4.2	1922	0.7
19	TH	0150	4.0	0751	0.8	1407	4.1	1955	0.8
20	F	0226	3.9	0829	0.8	1447	4.0	2036	1.0
21	SA	0306	3.7	0917	0.9	1536	3.9	2132	1.2
22	SU	0358	3.5	1024	1.0	1640	3.7	◐ 2300	1.4
23	M	0513	3.3	1204	1.0	1809	3.6		
24	TU	0040	1.4	0652	3.3	1331	0.8	1946	3.7
25	W	0157	1.3	0818	3.6	1442	0.6	2056	4.0
26	TH	0259	1.1	0920	3.9	1541	0.4	2151	4.2
27	F	0351	0.9	1010	4.2	1630	0.3	2237	4.4
28	SA	0437	0.8	1054	4.4	1714	0.3	○ 2319	4.4
29	SU	0521	0.7	1134	4.5	1754	0.3		
30	M	0000	4.4	0605	0.6	1214	4.6	1831	0.4
31	TU	0039	4.4	0648	0.5	1252	4.5	1906	0.6

NOVEMBER

Date	Day	Time	m	Time	m	Time	m	Time	m
1	W	0118	4.2	0729	0.6	1331	4.4	1938	0.8
2	TH	0156	4.1	0808	0.7	1411	4.2	2010	1.0
3	F	0232	3.9	0847	0.8	1452	3.9	2044	1.2
4	SA	0309	3.6	0929	0.9	1540	3.6	2130	1.4
5	SU	0356	3.4	1021	1.0	1644	3.4	◑ 2235	1.6
6	M	0505	3.2	1132	1.1	1807	3.3		
7	TU	0001	1.7	0626	3.2	1255	1.1	1922	3.4
8	W	0131	1.6	0739	3.3	1407	1.0	2026	3.5
9	TH	0236	1.4	0840	3.5	1502	0.8	2115	3.7
10	F	0325	1.2	0928	3.7	1544	0.7	2156	3.9
11	SA	0404	1.1	1007	3.9	1620	0.7	2231	4.0
12	SU	0439	0.9	1044	4.0	1653	0.6	2306	4.1
13	M	0513	0.8	1120	4.2	1725	0.6	● 2341	4.1
14	TU	0548	0.8	1157	4.2	1756	0.6		
15	W	0018	4.2	0625	0.7	1234	4.3	1828	0.7
16	TH	0056	4.1	0702	0.7	1313	4.3	1903	0.8
17	F	0135	4.1	0742	0.7	1355	4.2	1944	0.9
18	SA	0216	3.9	0827	0.7	1441	4.1	2034	1.0
19	SU	0301	3.8	0922	0.7	1534	3.9	2136	1.2
20	M	0357	3.6	1033	0.8	1640	3.8	◐ 2253	1.3
21	TU	0509	3.5	1155	0.7	1801	3.7		
22	W	0013	1.3	0630	3.5	1308	0.6	1920	3.8
23	TH	0125	1.2	0746	3.7	1413	0.5	2028	4.0
24	F	0227	1.1	0849	3.9	1511	0.4	2125	4.1
25	SA	0322	1.0	0941	4.1	1601	0.4	2213	4.2
26	SU	0413	0.8	1027	4.2	1646	0.5	2256	4.2
27	M	0500	0.7	1110	4.3	1726	0.6	○ 2337	4.2
28	TU	0546	0.6	1151	4.4	1805	0.6		
29	W	0017	4.2	0631	0.5	1231	4.3	1842	0.8
30	TH	0056	4.1	0714	0.5	1311	4.2	1916	0.9

DECEMBER

Date	Day	Time	m	Time	m	Time	m	Time	m
1	F	0133	4.0	0753	0.6	1351	4.1	1949	1.1
2	SA	0209	3.9	0830	0.7	1433	3.9	2023	1.2
3	SU	0246	3.7	0908	0.8	1517	3.7	2102	1.3
4	M	0328	3.6	0952	0.8	1609	3.5	2152	1.4
5	TU	0422	3.4	1048	0.9	1712	3.4	◑ 2253	1.5
6	W	0528	3.4	1155	1.0	1817	3.4		
7	TH	0014	1.6	0633	3.4	1303	1.0	1918	3.4
8	F	0133	1.5	0735	3.4	1402	0.9	2014	3.5
9	SA	0232	1.3	0831	3.6	1452	0.8	2105	3.7
10	SU	0321	1.1	0922	3.8	1537	0.8	2151	3.8
11	M	0405	1.0	1008	3.9	1618	0.7	2235	4.0
12	TU	0447	0.8	1051	4.1	1658	0.7	● 2318	4.1
13	W	0529	0.7	1135	4.2	1736	0.7		
14	TH	0001	4.1	0612	0.6	1218	4.3	1816	0.7
15	F	0045	4.1	0657	0.5	1304	4.3	1859	0.8
16	SA	0130	4.1	0744	0.5	1350	4.3	1946	0.8
17	SU	0216	4.0	0834	0.4	1440	4.2	2037	1.0
18	M	0304	4.0	0928	0.4	1533	4.1	2133	1.1
19	TU	0356	3.9	1028	0.5	1633	3.9	◐ 2234	1.2
20	W	0455	3.8	1133	0.5	1738	3.8	2341	1.2
21	TH	0559	3.8	1237	0.5	1847	3.8		
22	F	0048	1.2	0708	3.8	1338	0.6	1955	3.8
23	SA	0153	1.1	0815	3.8	1437	0.6	2057	3.8
24	SU	0255	1.0	0915	3.9	1533	0.7	2152	3.9
25	M	0354	0.9	1007	4.0	1624	0.8	2240	4.0
26	TU	0447	0.7	1054	4.1	1709	0.8	2324	4.0
27	W ○	0537	0.6	1138	4.1	1750	0.9		
28	TH	0004	4.0	0623	0.5	1219	4.1	1828	0.9
29	F	0043	4.0	0704	0.5	1259	4.1	1904	1.0
30	SA	0120	4.0	0741	0.5	1338	4.0	1936	1.0
31	SU	0155	3.9	0815	0.6	1417	3.9	2006	1.1

Chart Datum: 2·16 metres below Ordnance Datum (Newlyn)
HAT is 4·7 metres above Chart Datum

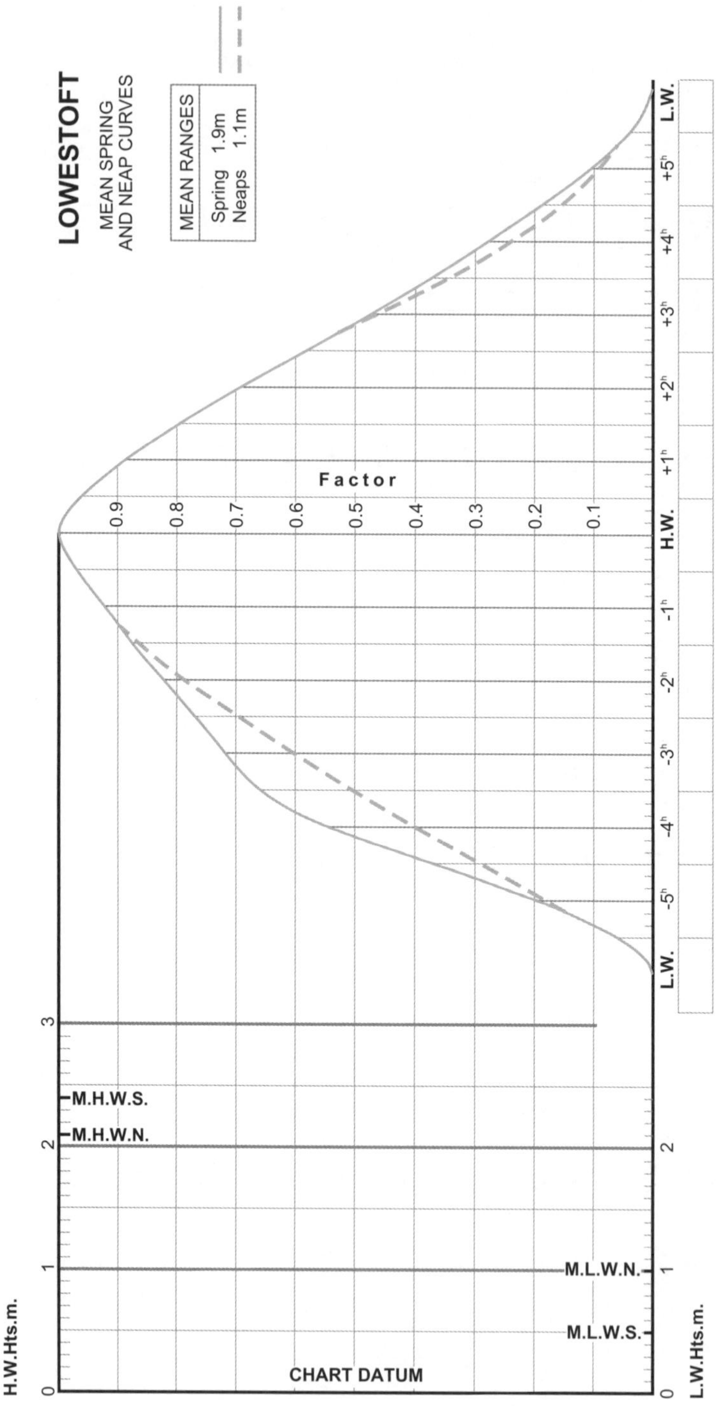
LOWESTOFT
MEAN SPRING
AND NEAP CURVES
MEAN RANGES
Spring 1.9m
Neaps 1.1m
Factor
0.9
0.8
0.7
0.6
0.5
0.4
0.3
0.2
0.1
L.W.
-5h
-4h
-3h
-2h
-1h
H.W.
+1h
+2h
+3h
+4h
+5h
L.W.
H.W.Hts.m.
0
1
2
3
M.H.W.S.
M.H.W.N.
M.L.W.N.
M.L.W.S.
CHART DATUM
L.W.Hts.m.
0
1
2

TIME ZONE (UT)

For Summer Time add ONE hour in **non-shaded areas**

LOWESTOFT

LAT 52°28′N LONG 1°45′E

TIMES AND HEIGHTS OF HIGH AND LOW WATERS

Dates in amber are **SPRINGS**
Dates in grey are **NEAPS**

2023

JANUARY

Date	Day	Time	m	Time	m	Time	m	Time	m
1	SU	0410	2.4	1107	0.8	1752	2.2	2316	1.3
2	M	0521	2.3	1206	0.8	1845	2.2		
3	TU	0024	1.2	0626	2.3	1259	0.9	1932	2.3
4	W	0124	1.1	0730	2.3	1347	1.0	2012	2.3
5	TH	0216	1.0	0829	2.3	1430	1.0	2049	2.4
6	F	0302	0.9	0918	2.3	1508	1.0	○ 2123	2.4
7	SA	0344	0.8	1000	2.3	1541	1.0	2155	2.5
8	SU	0422	0.7	1037	2.3	1611	1.0	2227	2.5
9	M	0458	0.7	1111	2.3	1640	1.0	2301	2.5
10	TU	0532	0.7	1144	2.2	1712	1.0	2336	2.5
11	W	0607	0.7	1217	2.2	1747	1.0		
12	TH	0013	2.5	0644	0.7	1252	2.2	1826	1.1
13	F	0052	2.5	0722	0.8	1331	2.1	1908	1.1
14	SA	0133	2.4	0804	0.8	1416	2.1	1955	1.2
15	SU	0217	2.4	0854	0.9	1515	2.1	◑ 2048	1.3
16	M	0309	2.3	0956	0.9	1644	2.1	2154	1.3
17	TU	0420	2.3	1108	0.9	1746	2.2	2322	1.2
18	W	0538	2.3	1212	0.9	1838	2.2		
19	TH	0034	1.1	0642	2.3	1307	0.8	1927	2.3
20	F	0135	0.9	0743	2.4	1401	0.8	2015	2.4
21	SA	0234	0.7	0845	2.5	1454	0.8	● 2102	2.5
22	SU	0331	0.5	0942	2.5	1546	0.8	2148	2.6
23	M	0425	0.4	1033	2.6	1634	0.8	2234	2.7
24	TU	0515	0.3	1121	2.5	1718	0.8	2319	2.7
25	W	0602	0.2	1209	2.4	1800	0.8		
26	TH	0003	2.7	0648	0.3	1256	2.3	1840	0.9
27	F	0048	2.7	0734	0.4	1348	2.2	1921	1.0
28	SA	0134	2.6	0823	0.6	1454	2.1	◐ 2007	1.1
29	SU	0226	2.5	0920	0.8	1608	2.1	2103	1.2
30	M	0336	2.3	1027	0.9	1708	2.1	2232	1.3
31	TU	0500	2.2	1136	1.1	1807	2.1		

FEBRUARY

Date	Day	Time	m	Time	m	Time	m	Time	m
1	W	0000	1.2	0618	2.2	1237	1.1	1905	2.2
2	TH	0111	1.1	0739	2.2	1334	1.1	1954	2.2
3	F	0208	0.9	0835	2.2	1421	1.1	2034	2.3
4	SA	0253	0.8	0916	2.3	1459	1.1	2107	2.4
5	SU	0332	0.7	0951	2.3	1530	1.0	○ 2137	2.4
6	M	0407	0.7	1021	2.3	1558	1.0	2208	2.5
7	TU	0440	0.6	1049	2.3	1626	0.9	2241	2.5
8	W	0512	0.6	1117	2.3	1657	0.9	2316	2.5
9	TH	0544	0.6	1148	2.3	1730	0.9	2350	2.5
10	F	0616	0.6	1220	2.2	1804	0.9		
11	SA	0024	2.5	0650	0.7	1255	2.2	1841	1.0
12	SU	0101	2.4	0725	0.7	1334	2.1	1922	1.0
13	M	0142	2.4	0808	0.8	1421	2.1	◑ 2011	1.1
14	TU	0232	2.3	0901	0.9	1526	2.1	2113	1.2
15	W	0343	2.2	1022	1.0	1657	2.1	2249	1.2
16	TH	0518	2.2	1149	1.0	1804	2.1		
17	F	0017	1.0	0635	2.3	1253	1.0	1902	2.2
18	SA	0124	0.8	0747	2.4	1351	0.9	1955	2.3
19	SU	0227	0.6	0847	2.4	1447	0.9	2045	2.5
20	M	0323	0.4	0935	2.5	1536	0.8	● 2131	2.6
21	TU	0413	0.2	1019	2.5	1620	0.7	2215	2.7
22	W	0458	0.1	1102	2.5	1700	0.7	2258	2.8
23	TH	0540	0.2	1143	2.4	1738	0.7	2341	2.8
24	F	0620	0.3	1224	2.3	1815	0.8		
25	SA	0023	2.7	0701	0.5	1306	2.2	1853	0.9
26	SU	0107	2.5	0741	0.7	1350	2.1	1935	1.0
27	M	0158	2.4	0827	0.9	1447	2.0	◐ 2027	1.1
28	TU	0309	2.2	0930	1.1	1607	2.0	2149	1.2

MARCH

Date	Day	Time	m	Time	m	Time	m	Time	m
1	W	0445	2.1	1108	1.3	1715	2.0	2342	1.1
2	TH	0615	2.1	1223	1.3	1823	2.1		
3	F	0053	1.0	0736	2.2	1324	1.2	1926	2.2
4	SA	0149	0.9	0824	2.2	1410	1.2	2009	2.2
5	SU	0232	0.8	0859	2.3	1444	1.1	2041	2.3
6	M	0308	0.7	0929	2.3	1512	1.0	2111	2.4
7	TU	0341	0.6	0954	2.3	1538	0.9	○ 2143	2.5
8	W	0412	0.5	1020	2.3	1607	0.8	2216	2.5
9	TH	0444	0.5	1048	2.3	1638	0.8	2250	2.5
10	F	0515	0.5	1118	2.3	1710	0.8	2324	2.5
11	SA	0546	0.5	1150	2.3	1742	0.8	2358	2.5
12	SU	0618	0.6	1225	2.3	1817	0.8		
13	M	0034	2.4	0652	0.7	1302	2.2	1857	0.9
14	TU	0117	2.4	0733	0.8	1348	2.1	1946	1.0
15	W	0212	2.3	0826	1.0	1446	2.1	◑ 2050	1.0
16	TH	0333	2.2	0946	1.2	1608	2.0	2240	1.0
17	F	0520	2.2	1135	1.2	1730	2.1		
18	SA	0007	0.9	0642	2.3	1243	1.1	1835	2.2
19	SU	0114	0.7	0749	2.4	1343	1.0	1933	2.3
20	M	0215	0.5	0838	2.4	1434	0.9	2023	2.5
21	TU	0307	0.3	0919	2.5	1519	0.8	● 2108	2.6
22	W	0353	0.2	0958	2.5	1559	0.7	2152	2.7
23	TH	0434	0.2	1037	2.5	1637	0.6	2236	2.7
24	F	0513	0.2	1115	2.4	1714	0.6	2318	2.7
25	SA	0549	0.4	1152	2.3	1751	0.7		
26	SU	0000	2.6	0625	0.6	1229	2.2	1829	0.7
27	M	0045	2.4	0701	0.8	1307	2.2	1911	0.8
28	TU	0137	2.3	0739	1.0	1350	2.1	2000	1.0
29	W	0253	2.1	0826	1.3	1447	2.1	◐ 2116	1.1
30	TH	0430	2.0	1034	1.4	1609	2.0	2315	1.0
31	F	0554	2.1	1201	1.4	1723	2.0		

APRIL

Date	Day	Time	m	Time	m	Time	m	Time	m
1	SA	0020	0.9	0710	2.1	1259	1.3	1831	2.1
2	SU	0112	0.8	0757	2.2	1342	1.2	1923	2.2
3	M	0155	0.7	0831	2.2	1414	1.1	2002	2.3
4	TU	0232	0.7	0857	2.3	1441	1.0	2036	2.4
5	W	0305	0.6	0922	2.3	1509	0.9	2111	2.4
6	TH	0338	0.5	0948	2.3	1541	0.8	○ 2146	2.5
7	F	0411	0.5	1017	2.4	1615	0.7	2222	2.5
8	SA	0444	0.5	1049	2.4	1649	0.7	2258	2.5
9	SU	0517	0.5	1123	2.4	1724	0.7	2336	2.5
10	M	0550	0.6	1159	2.3	1801	0.7		
11	TU	0016	2.4	0627	0.8	1238	2.3	1844	0.8
12	W	0105	2.3	0711	0.9	1325	2.2	1938	0.8
13	TH	0209	2.2	0806	1.1	1424	2.1	◑ 2052	0.9
14	F	0349	2.2	0930	1.3	1538	2.1	2240	0.8
15	SA	0526	2.2	1119	1.3	1658	2.1	2354	0.7
16	SU	0639	2.3	1226	1.2	1807	2.2		
17	M	0056	0.5	0736	2.4	1323	1.1	1905	2.3
18	TU	0154	0.4	0820	2.4	1412	0.9	1956	2.5
19	W	0243	0.3	0857	2.4	1455	0.8	2044	2.6
20	TH	0326	0.3	0934	2.4	1535	0.7	● 2129	2.6
21	F	0406	0.3	1010	2.4	1614	0.6	2214	2.6
22	SA	0443	0.4	1047	2.4	1653	0.6	2258	2.5
23	SU	0518	0.6	1123	2.4	1731	0.6	2343	2.4
24	M	0551	0.8	1158	2.3	1809	0.7		
25	TU	0029	2.3	0624	0.9	1233	2.3	1851	0.8
26	W	0122	2.2	0659	1.1	1314	2.2	1940	0.9
27	TH	0237	2.1	0740	1.3	1404	2.1	◐ 2048	1.0
28	F	0403	2.0	0835	1.5	1507	2.1	2235	1.0
29	SA	0515	2.0	1115	1.5	1623	2.1	2337	0.9
30	SU	0622	2.1	1212	1.4	1731	2.1		

Chart Datum: 1·50 metres below Ordnance Datum (Newlyn)
HAT is 2·9 metres above Chart Datum

TIME ZONE (UT)
For Summer Time add ONE hour in **non-shaded areas**

LOWESTOFT

LAT 52°28′N LONG 1°45′E

TIMES AND HEIGHTS OF HIGH AND LOW WATERS

Dates in amber are **SPRINGS**
Dates in grey are **NEAPS**

2023

MAY

Day		Time	m	Time	m	Time	m	Time	m
1	M	0026	0.8	0714	2.2	1254	1.3	1827	2.2
2	TU	0108	0.7	0750	2.2	1328	1.1	1914	2.2
3	W	0147	0.7	0818	2.3	1401	1.0	1956	2.3
4	TH	0223	0.6	0846	2.3	1435	0.9	2036	2.4
5	F	0300	0.5	0916	2.4	1513	0.8	○ 2115	2.4
6	SA	0337	0.5	0948	2.4	1552	0.7	2155	2.5
7	SU	0414	0.5	1023	2.4	1632	0.7	2237	2.5
8	M	0452	0.6	1100	2.4	1712	0.6	2320	2.4
9	TU	0531	0.7	1140	2.4	1756	0.7		
10	W	0009	2.4	0613	0.9	1223	2.3	1846	0.7
11	TH	0106	2.3	0701	1.0	1313	2.3	1946	0.7
12	F	0218	2.2	0758	1.2	1411	2.2	◑ 2104	0.7
13	SA	0400	2.2	0916	1.3	1516	2.2	2226	0.6
14	SU	0517	2.2	1048	1.3	1629	2.2	2332	0.6
15	M	0620	2.3	1154	1.2	1737	2.3		
16	TU	0031	0.5	0713	2.3	1251	1.1	1837	2.4
17	W	0126	0.5	0756	2.3	1343	1.0	1931	2.4
18	TH	0215	0.5	0833	2.4	1430	0.8	2021	2.5
19	F	0258	0.5	0909	2.4	1514	0.7	● 2110	2.5
20	SA	0338	0.5	0946	2.4	1556	0.6	2158	2.5
21	SU	0415	0.7	1023	2.4	1636	0.6	2246	2.4
22	M	0449	0.8	1059	2.4	1716	0.6	2332	2.3
23	TU	0521	0.9	1133	2.4	1755	0.7		
24	W	0018	2.2	0553	1.0	1208	2.3	1837	0.7
25	TH	0108	2.1	0626	1.2	1247	2.3	1922	0.8
26	F	0206	2.1	0705	1.3	1334	2.3	2017	0.9
27	SA	0320	2.0	0753	1.4	1426	2.2	◐ 2130	0.9
28	SU	0427	2.0	0851	1.4	1526	2.2	2241	0.9
29	M	0525	2.1	1024	1.4	1634	2.2	2334	0.8
30	TU	0615	2.1	1144	1.3	1736	2.2		
31	W	0018	0.8	0658	2.2	1233	1.2	1830	2.2

JUNE

Day		Time	m	Time	m	Time	m	Time	m
1	TH	0101	0.7	0735	2.2	1318	1.1	1918	2.3
2	F	0143	0.7	0810	2.3	1402	1.0	2003	2.3
3	SA	0225	0.6	0846	2.4	1447	0.8	2049	2.4
4	SU	0307	0.6	0923	2.4	1532	0.7	○ 2135	2.4
5	M	0351	0.6	1001	2.4	1619	0.6	2224	2.5
6	TU	0434	0.7	1043	2.5	1707	0.6	2315	2.4
7	W	0519	0.8	1127	2.5	1757	0.5		
8	TH	0009	2.4	0605	0.9	1213	2.5	1851	0.5
9	F	0108	2.3	0654	1.0	1303	2.4	1950	0.5
10	SA	0216	2.3	0747	1.2	1356	2.4	◑ 2054	0.5
11	SU	0344	2.2	0848	1.3	1453	2.4	2201	0.5
12	M	0453	2.2	1002	1.3	1559	2.4	2304	0.6
13	TU	0551	2.2	1114	1.2	1710	2.4		
14	W	0002	0.6	0644	2.3	1218	1.2	1813	2.4
15	TH	0057	0.6	0730	2.3	1317	1.0	1911	2.4
16	F	0147	0.7	0810	2.3	1410	0.9	2008	2.4
17	SA	0233	0.8	0849	2.4	1459	0.8	2103	2.4
18	SU	0314	0.8	0927	2.4	1544	0.7	● 2154	2.3
19	M	0352	0.9	1003	2.5	1626	0.7	2241	2.3
20	TU	0426	0.9	1039	2.5	1706	0.6	2324	2.3
21	W	0458	1.0	1113	2.4	1744	0.7		
22	TH	0004	2.2	0528	1.1	1148	2.4	1823	0.7
23	F	0043	2.1	0601	1.1	1226	2.4	1901	0.7
24	SA	0124	2.1	0638	1.2	1307	2.4	1943	0.8
25	SU	0209	2.1	0721	1.2	1351	2.3	2030	0.8
26	M	0310	2.0	0809	1.3	1440	2.3	◐ 2125	0.9
27	TU	0423	2.0	0905	1.3	1535	2.2	2228	0.9
28	W	0519	2.1	1017	1.3	1643	2.2	2328	0.8
29	TH	0608	2.2	1139	1.3	1748	2.2		
30	F	0020	0.8	0654	2.2	1240	1.2	1844	2.3

JULY

Day		Time	m	Time	m	Time	m	Time	m
1	SA	0109	0.8	0737	2.3	1334	1.0	1938	2.3
2	SU	0157	0.8	0819	2.4	1426	0.9	2031	2.4
3	M	0245	0.7	0901	2.4	1519	0.7	○ 2126	2.4
4	TU	0334	0.7	0944	2.5	1612	0.5	2220	2.5
5	W	0423	0.8	1029	2.6	1703	0.4	2313	2.5
6	TH	0510	0.8	1115	2.6	1754	0.3		
7	F	0003	2.5	0556	0.9	1200	2.6	1845	0.3
8	SA	0055	2.4	0641	1.0	1246	2.6	1935	0.3
9	SU	0152	2.3	0726	1.1	1334	2.6	2029	0.4
10	M	0306	2.2	0815	1.2	1426	2.5	◑ 2127	0.6
11	TU	0418	2.2	0913	1.2	1529	2.4	2230	0.7
12	W	0516	2.2	1030	1.3	1646	2.4	2333	0.8
13	TH	0611	2.2	1149	1.2	1756	2.3		
14	F	0031	0.9	0703	2.3	1258	1.1	1906	2.3
15	SA	0126	1.0	0751	2.3	1400	0.9	2015	2.3
16	SU	0216	1.0	0833	2.4	1452	0.8	2109	2.3
17	M	0300	1.0	0911	2.4	1536	0.7	● 2153	2.3
18	TU	0338	1.0	0947	2.5	1616	0.7	2232	2.3
19	W	0411	1.0	1020	2.5	1653	0.6	2308	2.3
20	TH	0440	1.0	1053	2.5	1728	0.6	2340	2.3
21	F	0508	1.0	1127	2.5	1801	0.6		
22	SA	0010	2.2	0539	1.0	1202	2.5	1834	0.7
23	SU	0043	2.2	0614	1.1	1239	2.5	1908	0.7
24	M	0118	2.1	0652	1.1	1317	2.4	1945	0.8
25	TU	0158	2.1	0735	1.2	1359	2.4	◐ 2028	0.9
26	W	0248	2.1	0824	1.3	1447	2.3	2121	0.9
27	TH	0405	2.1	0923	1.3	1550	2.2	2232	1.0
28	F	0518	2.1	1048	1.3	1712	2.2	2344	1.0
29	SA	0614	2.2	1212	1.2	1820	2.3		
30	SU	0043	1.0	0705	2.3	1313	1.0	1925	2.3
31	M	0137	0.9	0754	2.4	1412	0.8	2028	2.4

AUGUST

Day		Time	m	Time	m	Time	m	Time	m
1	TU	0231	0.9	0841	2.5	1509	0.6	○ 2124	2.5
2	W	0323	0.8	0927	2.6	1603	0.4	2213	2.6
3	TH	0412	0.8	1012	2.7	1653	0.3	2300	2.6
4	F	0457	0.8	1057	2.8	1740	0.2	2345	2.5
5	SA	0539	0.8	1140	2.8	1824	0.2		
6	SU	0030	2.4	0620	0.9	1224	2.8	1909	0.3
7	M	0117	2.3	0700	1.0	1309	2.7	1955	0.5
8	TU	0211	2.2	0744	1.1	1359	2.6	◑ 2045	0.7
9	W	0324	2.2	0836	1.2	1503	2.4	2149	0.9
10	TH	0433	2.2	0951	1.2	1631	2.3	2304	1.1
11	F	0533	2.2	1131	1.2	1751	2.2		
12	SA	0013	1.2	0634	2.2	1249	1.1	1919	2.2
13	SU	0116	1.2	0731	2.3	1352	0.9	2020	2.3
14	M	0209	1.2	0816	2.4	1441	0.8	2104	2.3
15	TU	0251	1.2	0853	2.4	1521	0.7	2140	2.3
16	W	0325	1.1	0925	2.5	1557	0.7	● 2212	2.3
17	TH	0353	1.0	0956	2.6	1630	0.6	2241	2.3
18	F	0420	1.0	1028	2.6	1702	0.6	2308	2.3
19	SA	0447	0.9	1101	2.6	1732	0.6	2336	2.3
20	SU	0517	0.9	1135	2.6	1802	0.6		
21	M	0006	2.3	0549	1.0	1209	2.6	1832	0.7
22	TU	0039	2.3	0624	1.0	1244	2.5	1905	0.8
23	W	0116	2.2	0703	1.1	1323	2.4	1943	0.9
24	TH	0200	2.2	0750	1.2	1410	2.3	◐ 2031	1.0
25	F	0256	2.2	0847	1.2	1514	2.3	2137	1.1
26	SA	0418	2.2	1012	1.3	1650	2.2	2315	1.2
27	SU	0534	2.2	1152	1.1	1812	2.3		
28	M	0025	1.1	0635	2.3	1258	0.9	1925	2.4
29	TU	0124	1.1	0729	2.4	1400	0.7	2025	2.5
30	W	0219	1.0	0819	2.5	1457	0.5	2113	2.6
31	TH	0310	0.9	0905	2.7	1548	0.3	○ 2156	2.6

Chart Datum: 1·50 metres below Ordnance Datum (Newlyn)
HAT is 2·9 metres above Chart Datum

TIME ZONE (UT)
For Summer Time add ONE hour in **non-shaded areas**

LOWESTOFT

LAT 52°28′N LONG 1°45′E

TIMES AND HEIGHTS OF HIGH AND LOW WATERS

Dates in amber are **SPRINGS**
Dates in grey are **NEAPS**

2023

SEPTEMBER

Date	Day	Time	m	Time	m	Time	m	Time	m
1	F	0355	0.8	0950	2.8	1634	0.2	2238	2.6
2	SA	0437	0.8	1033	2.9	1716	0.2	2319	2.5
3	SU	0516	0.8	1117	2.9	1757	0.3		
4	M	0000	2.5	0555	0.8	1200	2.8	1837	0.4
5	TU	0041	2.4	0634	0.9	1245	2.7	1918	0.7
6	W	0125	2.3	0717	1.0	1335	2.5	◑ 2001	0.9
7	TH	0217	2.2	0808	1.1	1445	2.3	2057	1.2
8	F	0332	2.2	0923	1.2	1623	2.2	2235	1.3
9	SA	0445	2.2	1117	1.2	1750	2.2	2359	1.4
10	SU	0552	2.2	1232	1.0	1914	2.3		
11	M	0104	1.3	0659	2.3	1330	0.9	2007	2.3
12	TU	0154	1.3	0748	2.4	1416	0.8	2045	2.4
13	W	0230	1.2	0824	2.4	1454	0.7	2116	2.4
14	TH	0300	1.1	0854	2.5	1527	0.7	2143	2.4
15	F	0327	1.0	0925	2.6	1558	0.6	● 2208	2.4
16	SA	0353	0.9	0958	2.6	1628	0.6	2234	2.4
17	SU	0422	0.9	1032	2.7	1658	0.6	2302	2.4
18	M	0453	0.9	1106	2.6	1727	0.6	2334	2.4
19	TU	0525	0.9	1140	2.6	1757	0.7		
20	W	0006	2.4	0600	1.0	1215	2.5	1830	0.8
21	TH	0043	2.3	0638	1.0	1256	2.4	1907	1.0
22	F	0126	2.3	0724	1.1	1347	2.3	◐ 1955	1.1
23	SA	0220	2.2	0825	1.2	1459	2.3	2101	1.3
24	SU	0331	2.2	1000	1.2	1649	2.2	2253	1.3
25	M	0454	2.2	1138	1.0	1813	2.3		
26	TU	0009	1.3	0603	2.3	1243	0.8	1920	2.4
27	W	0108	1.2	0700	2.4	1343	0.6	2011	2.5
28	TH	0201	1.1	0751	2.6	1437	0.4	2054	2.6
29	F	0249	0.9	0838	2.7	1525	0.3	○ 2133	2.6
30	SA	0332	0.8	0924	2.9	1608	0.2	2211	2.6

OCTOBER

Date	Day	Time	m	Time	m	Time	m	Time	m
1	SU	0412	0.7	1008	2.9	1648	0.3	2250	2.6
2	M	0452	0.7	1053	2.9	1727	0.4	2329	2.5
3	TU	0531	0.7	1138	2.8	1804	0.6		
4	W	0008	2.4	0612	0.8	1224	2.6	1841	0.9
5	TH	0048	2.4	0656	0.9	1318	2.4	1920	1.1
6	F	0133	2.3	0747	1.0	1435	2.3	◑ 2007	1.4
7	SA	0229	2.2	0902	1.1	1610	2.2	2136	1.5
8	SU	0346	2.2	1052	1.1	1731	2.2	2333	1.5
9	M	0459	2.2	1159	1.0	1847	2.3		
10	TU	0034	1.5	0604	2.3	1252	0.9	1938	2.3
11	W	0121	1.4	0659	2.3	1337	0.8	2015	2.4
12	TH	0156	1.3	0740	2.4	1415	0.7	2044	2.4
13	F	0226	1.1	0815	2.5	1448	0.7	2108	2.4
14	SA	0253	1.0	0850	2.6	1519	0.6	● 2132	2.4
15	SU	0323	0.9	0926	2.6	1551	0.6	2200	2.5
16	M	0355	0.9	1002	2.6	1622	0.6	2231	2.5
17	TU	0430	0.9	1038	2.6	1654	0.7	2304	2.5
18	W	0505	0.9	1115	2.5	1727	0.8	2339	2.5
19	TH	0541	0.9	1154	2.5	1802	0.9		
20	F	0017	2.4	0623	0.9	1240	2.4	1843	1.0
21	SA	0101	2.4	0714	1.0	1338	2.3	1935	1.2
22	SU	0156	2.3	0821	1.0	1501	2.2	◐ 2042	1.4
23	M	0303	2.3	1000	1.0	1652	2.3	2228	1.4
24	TU	0418	2.3	1121	0.8	1804	2.4	2345	1.3
25	W	0530	2.4	1222	0.7	1903	2.5		
26	TH	0042	1.2	0630	2.5	1318	0.5	1950	2.5
27	F	0134	1.1	0722	2.6	1410	0.4	2029	2.5
28	SA	0222	1.0	0811	2.7	1457	0.4	○ 2107	2.6
29	SU	0306	0.8	0859	2.8	1539	0.4	2144	2.6
30	M	0349	0.7	0946	2.8	1619	0.5	2223	2.6
31	TU	0431	0.7	1034	2.7	1656	0.6	2301	2.5

NOVEMBER

Date	Day	Time	m	Time	m	Time	m	Time	m
1	W	0512	0.7	1121	2.6	1732	0.8	2339	2.5
2	TH	0554	0.8	1211	2.4	1807	1.0		
3	F	0017	2.4	0639	0.9	1307	2.3	1844	1.2
4	SA	0059	2.4	0730	0.9	1420	2.2	1925	1.4
5	SU	0148	2.3	0837	1.0	1543	2.1	◑ 2017	1.6
6	M	0248	2.3	1011	1.0	1654	2.2	2237	1.6
7	TU	0359	2.2	1116	1.0	1801	2.2	2345	1.5
8	W	0505	2.3	1207	0.9	1855	2.3		
9	TH	0032	1.4	0602	2.3	1251	0.8	1934	2.3
10	F	0110	1.3	0651	2.4	1329	0.8	2004	2.4
11	SA	0142	1.2	0734	2.4	1404	0.7	2030	2.4
12	SU	0216	1.1	0814	2.5	1439	0.7	2058	2.5
13	M	0252	1.0	0854	2.5	1514	0.7	● 2129	2.5
14	TU	0330	0.9	0934	2.5	1550	0.7	2203	2.5
15	W	0410	0.8	1015	2.5	1627	0.7	2238	2.5
16	TH	0451	0.8	1057	2.5	1705	0.8	2317	2.5
17	F	0534	0.8	1144	2.4	1746	1.0	2359	2.5
18	SA	0621	0.8	1237	2.4	1831	1.1		
19	SU	0046	2.4	0718	0.8	1339	2.3	1923	1.2
20	M	0140	2.4	0826	0.8	1504	2.3	◐ 2027	1.4
21	TU	0240	2.4	0946	0.8	1639	2.3	2149	1.4
22	W	0346	2.4	1056	0.7	1743	2.3	2308	1.4
23	TH	0457	2.4	1155	0.6	1837	2.4		
24	F	0008	1.3	0600	2.5	1250	0.6	1923	2.4
25	SA	0104	1.1	0656	2.6	1342	0.6	2004	2.5
26	SU	0156	1.0	0748	2.6	1429	0.6	2042	2.5
27	M	0245	0.8	0841	2.6	1512	0.6	○ 2121	2.5
28	TU	0332	0.7	0932	2.6	1552	0.7	2200	2.5
29	W	0416	0.7	1023	2.5	1630	0.9	2238	2.5
30	TH	0500	0.7	1113	2.4	1706	1.0	2316	2.5

DECEMBER

Date	Day	Time	m	Time	m	Time	m	Time	m
1	F	0542	0.7	1202	2.3	1739	1.1	2353	2.5
2	SA	0625	0.8	1253	2.2	1812	1.2		
3	SU	0032	2.4	0712	0.8	1347	2.2	1850	1.3
4	M	0116	2.4	0804	0.9	1455	2.1	1933	1.4
5	TU	0206	2.3	0908	1.0	1604	2.1	◑ 2025	1.5
6	W	0301	2.3	1018	1.0	1704	2.1	2132	1.5
7	TH	0405	2.3	1114	0.9	1756	2.2	2314	1.5
8	F	0510	2.3	1201	0.9	1840	2.2		
9	SA	0012	1.4	0607	2.3	1243	0.9	1918	2.3
10	SU	0058	1.2	0656	2.3	1323	0.8	1952	2.3
11	M	0141	1.1	0743	2.4	1403	0.8	2026	2.4
12	TU	0225	1.0	0828	2.4	1444	0.8	● 2102	2.5
13	W	0310	0.9	0914	2.4	1526	0.8	2140	2.5
14	TH	0356	0.8	1001	2.5	1609	0.8	2220	2.5
15	F	0444	0.7	1051	2.5	1653	0.9	2302	2.5
16	SA	0533	0.6	1142	2.4	1737	0.9	2347	2.5
17	SU	0624	0.6	1235	2.4	1823	1.1		
18	M	0034	2.5	0719	0.6	1332	2.3	1912	1.2
19	TU	0123	2.5	0817	0.6	1442	2.2	◐ 2005	1.2
20	W	0216	2.5	0920	0.6	1611	2.2	2106	1.3
21	TH	0314	2.5	1025	0.7	1713	2.2	2219	1.3
22	F	0425	2.4	1126	0.7	1807	2.3	2333	1.2
23	SA	0535	2.4	1223	0.7	1856	2.3		
24	SU	0038	1.1	0638	2.4	1317	0.8	1941	2.4
25	M	0138	1.0	0738	2.4	1407	0.8	2023	2.4
26	TU	0234	0.9	0838	2.4	1453	0.9	2103	2.5
27	W	0323	0.7	0933	2.4	1535	0.9	○ 2143	2.5
28	TH	0409	0.7	1022	2.4	1613	1.0	2221	2.5
29	F	0452	0.7	1107	2.3	1647	1.0	2258	2.5
30	SA	0532	0.7	1148	2.3	1717	1.1	2333	2.5
31	SU	0610	0.7	1227	2.2	1747	1.1		

Chart Datum: 1·50 metres below Ordnance Datum (Newlyn)
HAT is 2·9 metres above Chart Datum

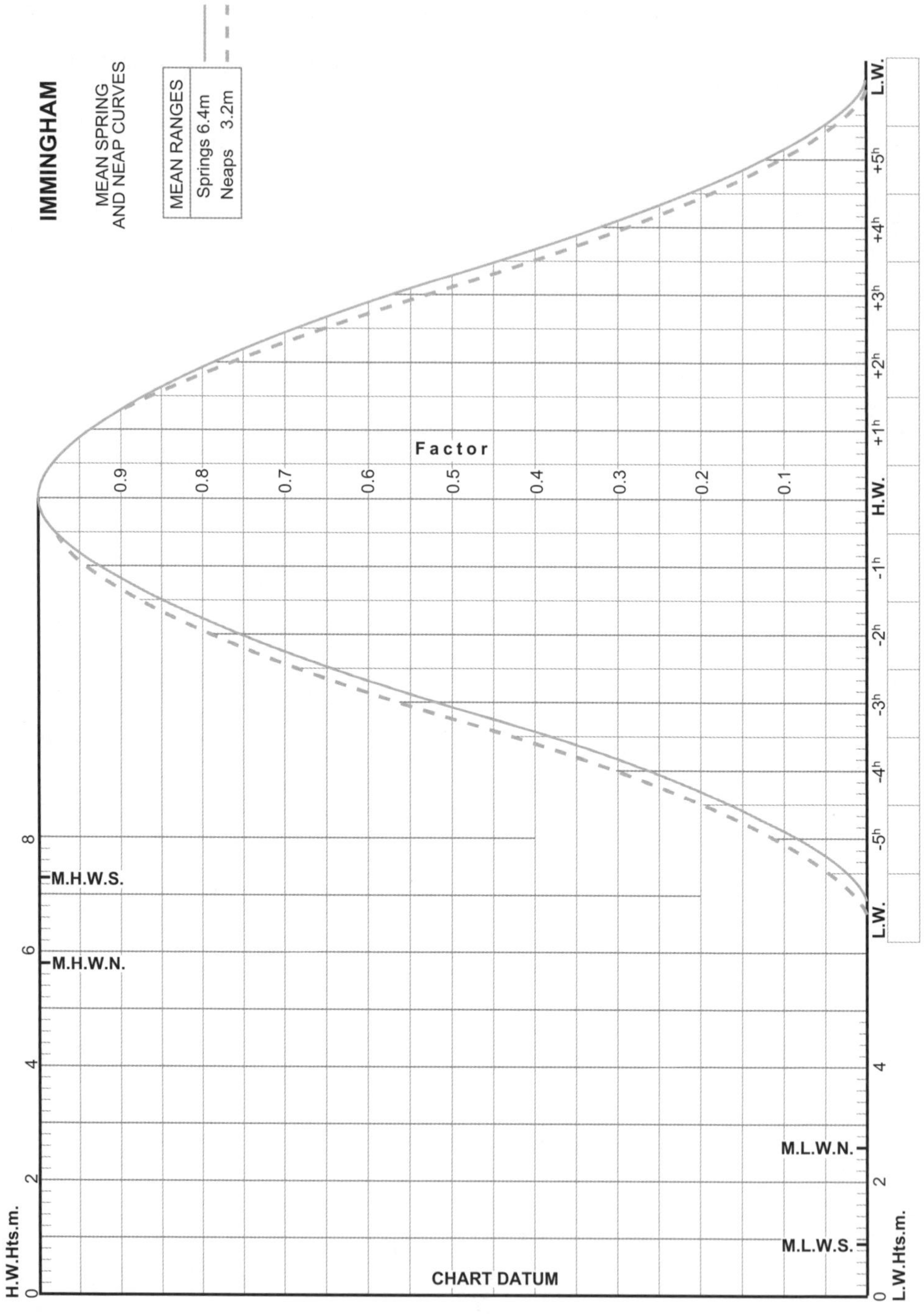
IMMINGHAM
MEAN SPRING AND NEAP CURVES
MEAN RANGES
Springs 6.4m
Neaps 3.2m
Factor
0.9
0.8
0.7
0.6
0.5
0.4
0.3
0.2
0.1
L.W.
-5h
-4h
-3h
-2h
-1h
H.W.
+1h
+2h
+3h
+4h
+5h
L.W.
H.W.Hts.m.
0
2
4
6
8
M.H.W.S.
M.H.W.N.
CHART DATUM
L.W.Hts.m.
0
2
4
M.L.W.S.
M.L.W.N.

TIME ZONE (UT)
For Summer Time add ONE hour in **non-shaded areas**

IMMINGHAM

LAT 53°38′N LONG 0°11′W

TIMES AND HEIGHTS OF HIGH AND LOW WATERS

Dates in amber are **SPRINGS**
Dates in grey are **NEAPS**

2023

JANUARY

Date	Day	Moon	Time	m	Time	m	Time	m	Time	m
1	SU		0042	6.3	0722	2.0	1343	5.9	1940	2.6
2	M		0148	6.2	0824	2.1	1442	6.0	2049	2.5
3	TU		0251	6.2	0920	2.1	1535	6.2	2148	2.3
4	W		0350	6.3	1010	2.1	1622	6.4	2240	2.0
5	TH		0441	6.4	1055	2.0	1704	6.6	2326	1.8
6	F	○	0527	6.5	1137	1.9	1742	6.7		
7	SA		0009	1.6	0609	6.5	1215	1.8	1819	6.8
8	SU		0048	1.5	0646	6.6	1251	1.8	1853	6.9
9	M		0125	1.5	0721	6.5	1324	1.8	1926	6.9
10	TU		0159	1.6	0755	6.5	1354	1.9	1957	6.8
11	W		0231	1.6	0829	6.4	1425	1.9	2028	6.7
12	TH		0302	1.7	0904	6.3	1457	2.1	2100	6.5
13	F		0336	1.9	0941	6.1	1533	2.2	2137	6.4
14	SA		0415	2.0	1024	6.0	1616	2.4	2222	6.3
15	SU	◑	0504	2.1	1115	5.8	1710	2.6	2318	6.1
16	M		0604	2.2	1220	5.7	1817	2.7		
17	TU		0025	6.0	0713	2.3	1335	5.8	1934	2.6
18	W		0145	6.1	0825	2.2	1445	6.0	2050	2.4
19	TH		0303	6.3	0932	2.0	1547	6.3	2201	2.0
20	F		0411	6.6	1033	1.7	1642	6.7	2305	1.5
21	SA	●	0513	6.9	1130	1.5	1732	7.0		
22	SU		0003	1.1	0610	7.1	1222	1.2	1820	7.3
23	M		0057	0.8	0703	7.3	1311	1.1	1906	7.5
24	TU		0146	0.5	0751	7.3	1356	1.1	1950	7.6
25	W		0233	0.5	0837	7.2	1439	1.2	2033	7.5
26	TH		0317	0.7	0921	7.0	1520	1.4	2117	7.3
27	F		0400	1.0	1006	6.6	1601	1.7	2203	7.0
28	SA	◐	0443	1.4	1054	6.3	1643	2.1	2255	6.6
29	SU		0528	1.9	1147	5.9	1732	2.5	2356	6.2
30	M		0621	2.4	1247	5.7	1835	2.8		
31	TU		0106	5.8	0730	2.6	1352	5.6	2006	2.8

FEBRUARY

Date	Day	Moon	Time	m	Time	m	Time	m	Time	m
1	W		0221	5.7	0845	2.7	1458	5.7	2127	2.6
2	TH		0333	5.8	0947	2.5	1556	6.0	2225	2.2
3	F		0432	6.0	1037	2.3	1644	6.3	2314	1.9
4	SA		0518	6.3	1121	2.1	1725	6.6	2357	1.6
5	SU	○	0557	6.4	1202	1.9	1802	6.8		
6	M		0036	1.4	0632	6.5	1239	1.7	1836	6.9
7	TU		0113	1.3	0704	6.6	1312	1.7	1909	6.9
8	W		0146	1.3	0735	6.6	1341	1.6	1940	6.9
9	TH		0216	1.4	0806	6.6	1409	1.7	2009	6.9
10	F		0243	1.4	0836	6.6	1436	1.7	2037	6.8
11	SA		0308	1.5	0907	6.5	1507	1.8	2109	6.7
12	SU		0337	1.7	0941	6.3	1542	2.0	2148	6.6
13	M	◑	0415	1.9	1024	6.0	1626	2.2	2237	6.3
14	TU		0508	2.2	1120	5.8	1729	2.5	2342	6.0
15	W		0626	2.5	1239	5.6	1856	2.6		
16	TH		0112	5.8	0755	2.5	1415	5.7	2029	2.5
17	F		0258	6.0	0916	2.3	1530	6.1	2153	2.0
18	SA		0414	6.4	1023	1.9	1630	6.6	2301	1.4
19	SU		0515	6.8	1121	1.5	1721	7.1	2357	0.9
20	M	●	0607	7.2	1212	1.2	1807	7.4		
21	TU		0047	0.5	0654	7.4	1257	0.9	1852	7.7
22	W		0133	0.3	0736	7.4	1340	0.8	1933	7.8
23	TH		0214	0.3	0814	7.3	1419	0.9	2013	7.7
24	F		0252	0.5	0851	7.1	1456	1.1	2052	7.5
25	SA		0327	1.0	0926	6.7	1529	1.5	2132	7.1
26	SU		0359	1.5	1002	6.3	1603	1.9	2215	6.5
27	M	◐	0433	2.1	1043	5.9	1643	2.3	2309	6.0
28	TU		0517	2.6	1143	5.5	1738	2.7		

MARCH

Date	Day	Moon	Time	m	Time	m	Time	m	Time	m
1	W		0025	5.5	0622	3.0	1304	5.3	1901	3.0
2	TH		0156	5.3	0804	3.1	1424	5.4	2111	2.7
3	F		0317	5.5	0928	2.8	1530	5.8	2209	2.3
4	SA		0418	5.9	1021	2.4	1622	6.2	2255	1.9
5	SU		0502	6.2	1104	2.1	1703	6.5	2336	1.5
6	M		0537	6.4	1144	1.8	1738	6.7		
7	TU	○	0014	1.3	0609	6.6	1220	1.6	1812	6.9
8	W		0050	1.2	0639	6.7	1253	1.5	1844	7.0
9	TH		0123	1.1	0709	6.8	1322	1.4	1915	7.0
10	F		0152	1.1	0739	6.8	1349	1.4	1944	7.1
11	SA		0218	1.2	0807	6.8	1416	1.4	2013	7.0
12	SU		0241	1.3	0836	6.7	1444	1.5	2045	6.9
13	M		0308	1.5	0909	6.5	1517	1.7	2124	6.6
14	TU		0342	1.9	0950	6.2	1600	2.0	2214	6.2
15	W	◑	0434	2.3	1045	5.8	1705	2.4	2323	5.8
16	TH		0558	2.7	1206	5.5	1841	2.6		
17	F		0117	5.6	0740	2.8	1358	5.6	2024	2.4
18	SA		0305	5.9	0907	2.4	1516	6.1	2149	1.8
19	SU		0413	6.4	1013	1.9	1614	6.6	2251	1.2
20	M		0507	6.9	1106	1.4	1703	7.1	2342	0.7
21	TU	●	0552	7.2	1154	1.1	1747	7.5		
22	W		0028	0.4	0634	7.4	1237	0.8	1830	7.7
23	TH		0110	0.3	0711	7.4	1318	0.7	1911	7.7
24	F		0148	0.4	0745	7.3	1355	0.8	1950	7.6
25	SA		0222	0.7	0816	7.1	1429	1.0	2027	7.4
26	SU		0252	1.1	0846	6.8	1459	1.4	2103	6.9
27	M		0319	1.6	0915	6.4	1530	1.8	2141	6.4
28	TU		0350	2.2	0949	6.0	1608	2.2	2229	5.8
29	W	◐	0431	2.7	1037	5.6	1701	2.6	2348	5.3
30	TH		0533	3.1	1213	5.3	1820	2.9		
31	F		0131	5.2	0708	3.3	1349	5.3	2040	2.8

APRIL

Date	Day	Moon	Time	m	Time	m	Time	m	Time	m
1	SA		0250	5.4	0900	3.0	1459	5.7	2139	2.3
2	SU		0349	5.8	0954	2.5	1550	6.1	2224	1.9
3	M		0432	6.2	1037	2.1	1631	6.4	2304	1.5
4	TU		0507	6.5	1115	1.8	1706	6.7	2342	1.3
5	W		0537	6.7	1152	1.6	1740	6.8		
6	TH	○	0019	1.1	0608	6.8	1225	1.4	1814	7.0
7	F		0053	1.0	0639	6.9	1256	1.3	1847	7.1
8	SA		0123	1.0	0710	7.0	1327	1.3	1920	7.1
9	SU		0152	1.1	0740	6.9	1357	1.3	1953	7.1
10	M		0219	1.3	0811	6.8	1430	1.4	2030	6.9
11	TU		0250	1.5	0847	6.6	1507	1.6	2113	6.5
12	W		0329	1.9	0930	6.3	1555	1.9	2209	6.1
13	TH	◑	0425	2.4	1029	5.9	1709	2.3	2330	5.6
14	F		0551	2.8	1156	5.6	1844	2.3		
15	SA		0135	5.6	0730	2.8	1342	5.8	2019	2.0
16	SU		0257	6.1	0850	2.4	1454	6.2	2132	1.5
17	M		0358	6.5	0951	1.9	1550	6.7	2228	1.0
18	TU		0446	6.9	1042	1.4	1638	7.1	2316	0.7
19	W		0528	7.1	1129	1.1	1723	7.4		
20	TH	●	0000	0.6	0606	7.2	1212	0.9	1806	7.5
21	F		0041	0.6	0641	7.2	1253	0.9	1847	7.5
22	SA		0118	0.7	0714	7.1	1330	0.9	1927	7.3
23	SU		0150	1.0	0745	7.0	1404	1.1	2004	7.0
24	M		0219	1.4	0813	6.8	1435	1.4	2040	6.7
25	TU		0247	1.8	0842	6.5	1507	1.7	2117	6.2
26	W		0319	2.2	0915	6.1	1545	2.1	2203	5.7
27	TH	◐	0358	2.7	0959	5.7	1638	2.5	2314	5.3
28	F		0456	3.0	1118	5.4	1751	2.7		
29	SA		0051	5.2	0618	3.2	1301	5.4	1925	2.6
30	SU		0207	5.4	0756	3.1	1413	5.6	2046	2.3

Chart Datum: 3·90 metres below Ordnance Datum (Newlyn)
HAT is 8·0 metres above Chart Datum

TIME ZONE (UT)
For Summer Time add ONE hour in **non-shaded areas**

IMMINGHAM

LAT 53°38′N LONG 0°11′W

TIMES AND HEIGHTS OF HIGH AND LOW WATERS

Dates in amber are **SPRINGS**
Dates in grey are **NEAPS**

2023

MAY

Day		Time	m	Time	m	Time	m	Time	m	Moon
1	M	0305	5.7	0907	2.7	1506	5.9	2137	1.9	
2	TU	0350	6.1	0954	2.3	1548	6.3	2221	1.6	
3	W	0426	6.4	1036	1.9	1626	6.5	2302	1.4	
4	TH	0500	6.6	1114	1.7	1704	6.8	2341	1.2	
5	F	0534	6.8	1152	1.5	1742	6.9			○
6	SA	0019	1.1	0609	6.9	1229	1.3	1821	7.1	
7	SU	0054	1.1	0644	7.0	1306	1.2	1900	7.1	
8	M	0129	1.1	0719	7.0	1344	1.2	1941	7.0	
9	TU	0205	1.3	0756	6.9	1425	1.3	2025	6.8	
10	W	0243	1.6	0836	6.7	1510	1.5	2115	6.5	
11	TH	0329	2.0	0925	6.4	1607	1.7	2218	6.1	
12	F	0429	2.4	1027	6.1	1720	1.9	2350	5.8	◑
13	SA	0546	2.6	1151	5.9	1840	1.9			
14	SU	0121	5.9	0708	2.6	1316	6.1	1957	1.7	
15	M	0232	6.2	0821	2.3	1424	6.4	2102	1.4	
16	TU	0330	6.5	0921	1.9	1521	6.7	2157	1.1	
17	W	0418	6.7	1014	1.6	1611	6.9	2245	1.0	
18	TH	0459	6.9	1102	1.3	1658	7.1	2330	1.0	
19	F	0536	7.0	1148	1.2	1743	7.1			●
20	SA	0011	1.1	0612	7.0	1230	1.1	1827	7.1	
21	SU	0048	1.2	0647	6.9	1309	1.2	1908	6.9	
22	M	0123	1.4	0719	6.9	1345	1.3	1947	6.7	
23	TU	0154	1.6	0750	6.7	1419	1.5	2024	6.4	
24	W	0224	1.9	0821	6.5	1453	1.7	2101	6.1	
25	TH	0257	2.2	0855	6.3	1532	2.0	2145	5.8	
26	F	0336	2.5	0938	6.0	1621	2.3	2240	5.5	
27	SA	0426	2.8	1038	5.7	1722	2.4	2352	5.4	◐
28	SU	0530	3.0	1156	5.6	1828	2.4			
29	M	0103	5.5	0643	2.9	1307	5.6	1935	2.3	
30	TU	0204	5.7	0753	2.8	1406	5.9	2035	2.0	
31	W	0256	5.9	0854	2.5	1457	6.1	2129	1.8	

JUNE

Day		Time	m	Time	m	Time	m	Time	m	Moon
1	TH	0341	6.2	0946	2.1	1544	6.4	2217	1.6	
2	F	0422	6.5	1034	1.8	1629	6.6	2303	1.4	
3	SA	0503	6.7	1120	1.6	1715	6.8	2347	1.3	
4	SU	0543	6.9	1206	1.3	1802	7.0			○
5	M	0030	1.2	0624	7.0	1252	1.1	1849	7.0	
6	TU	0113	1.2	0705	7.1	1338	1.0	1938	7.0	
7	W	0156	1.3	0748	7.0	1426	1.0	2028	6.9	
8	TH	0241	1.5	0833	6.9	1517	1.1	2122	6.6	
9	F	0330	1.8	0924	6.7	1614	1.3	2227	6.3	
10	SA	0426	2.1	1023	6.5	1715	1.4	2340	6.2	◑
11	SU	0529	2.3	1133	6.4	1820	1.5			
12	M	0050	6.1	0637	2.3	1243	6.3	1925	1.6	
13	TU	0154	6.2	0744	2.3	1349	6.4	2026	1.6	
14	W	0252	6.3	0848	2.1	1450	6.5	2123	1.6	
15	TH	0344	6.4	0946	1.9	1546	6.6	2215	1.5	
16	F	0429	6.5	1038	1.7	1638	6.7	2302	1.6	
17	SA	0509	6.6	1127	1.5	1727	6.7	2345	1.6	
18	SU	0548	6.7	1213	1.4	1813	6.7			●
19	M	0025	1.6	0625	6.8	1255	1.4	1855	6.6	
20	TU	0102	1.7	0701	6.8	1334	1.4	1934	6.5	
21	W	0136	1.8	0735	6.7	1410	1.5	2011	6.4	
22	TH	0208	1.9	0808	6.6	1445	1.7	2046	6.2	
23	F	0241	2.1	0842	6.5	1521	1.8	2124	6.0	
24	SA	0316	2.2	0920	6.3	1601	2.0	2207	5.9	
25	SU	0356	2.4	1004	6.1	1647	2.1	2257	5.7	
26	M	0444	2.6	1057	5.9	1738	2.2	2355	5.7	◐
27	TU	0541	2.7	1158	5.8	1835	2.2			
28	W	0057	5.7	0646	2.7	1302	5.9	1936	2.2	
29	TH	0159	5.8	0753	2.6	1405	6.0	2037	2.0	
30	F	0256	6.0	0858	2.3	1506	6.2	2136	1.9	

JULY

Day		Time	m	Time	m	Time	m	Time	m	Moon
1	SA	0349	6.3	0959	2.0	1603	6.5	2231	1.7	
2	SU	0438	6.6	1056	1.7	1659	6.7	2324	1.5	
3	M	0525	6.8	1151	1.3	1754	6.9			○
4	TU	0014	1.3	0611	7.1	1244	1.0	1847	7.1	
5	W	0103	1.2	0657	7.2	1336	0.8	1939	7.1	
6	TH	0150	1.2	0742	7.3	1426	0.7	2030	7.1	
7	F	0236	1.3	0828	7.3	1515	0.7	2121	6.9	
8	SA	0322	1.5	0916	7.2	1605	0.9	2214	6.7	
9	SU	0410	1.7	1008	7.0	1655	1.1	2310	6.4	
10	M	0501	2.0	1105	6.7	1749	1.4			◑
11	TU	0007	6.2	0558	2.2	1207	6.5	1846	1.8	
12	W	0107	6.0	0703	2.4	1312	6.2	1949	2.0	
13	TH	0207	5.9	0815	2.4	1420	6.1	2051	2.1	
14	F	0307	6.0	0923	2.3	1526	6.1	2149	2.2	
15	SA	0400	6.2	1022	2.0	1626	6.2	2240	2.1	
16	SU	0447	6.4	1114	1.8	1719	6.3	2326	2.0	
17	M	0529	6.6	1201	1.6	1804	6.4			●
18	TU	0008	1.9	0608	6.7	1244	1.4	1844	6.5	
19	W	0047	1.8	0645	6.8	1323	1.4	1920	6.5	
20	TH	0123	1.8	0719	6.8	1359	1.4	1953	6.5	
21	F	0155	1.8	0752	6.8	1432	1.5	2025	6.4	
22	SA	0225	1.9	0824	6.7	1504	1.6	2058	6.3	
23	SU	0254	2.0	0856	6.6	1534	1.7	2132	6.2	
24	M	0326	2.1	0930	6.4	1607	1.9	2209	6.1	
25	TU	0403	2.3	1009	6.3	1647	2.0	2254	5.9	◐
26	W	0449	2.5	1057	6.1	1738	2.2	2350	5.7	
27	TH	0549	2.6	1159	5.9	1842	2.3			
28	F	0102	5.7	0702	2.7	1316	5.9	1954	2.4	
29	SA	0217	5.8	0820	2.5	1440	6.0	2106	2.2	
30	SU	0324	6.1	0935	2.2	1552	6.3	2211	1.9	
31	M	0421	6.5	1044	1.7	1655	6.6	2310	1.7	

AUGUST

Day		Time	m	Time	m	Time	m	Time	m	Moon
1	TU	0512	6.9	1144	1.2	1753	7.0			○
2	W	0003	1.4	0600	7.2	1239	0.8	1846	7.2	
3	TH	0053	1.2	0646	7.5	1329	0.5	1934	7.3	
4	F	0139	1.0	0730	7.6	1415	0.3	2019	7.3	
5	SA	0222	1.0	0814	7.7	1459	0.4	2102	7.2	
6	SU	0304	1.2	0857	7.5	1542	0.7	2145	6.9	
7	M	0345	1.4	0943	7.3	1624	1.1	2229	6.5	
8	TU	0426	1.8	1032	6.8	1707	1.7	2319	6.1	◑
9	W	0513	2.2	1130	6.4	1757	2.2			
10	TH	0017	5.8	0613	2.6	1238	5.9	1903	2.6	
11	F	0123	5.6	0741	2.8	1355	5.7	2023	2.8	
12	SA	0232	5.7	0909	2.6	1514	5.8	2131	2.7	
13	SU	0336	6.0	1011	2.2	1621	6.0	2225	2.4	
14	M	0428	6.3	1102	1.9	1712	6.2	2311	2.2	
15	TU	0511	6.6	1146	1.6	1752	6.4	2353	1.9	
16	W	0549	6.8	1227	1.4	1826	6.6			●
17	TH	0031	1.8	0624	6.9	1305	1.3	1858	6.6	
18	F	0106	1.7	0658	7.0	1339	1.2	1928	6.7	
19	SA	0137	1.7	0729	7.0	1410	1.3	1957	6.7	
20	SU	0204	1.7	0800	6.9	1437	1.4	2026	6.6	
21	M	0229	1.8	0828	6.8	1501	1.6	2055	6.5	
22	TU	0255	1.9	0857	6.7	1526	1.7	2126	6.3	
23	W	0327	2.0	0931	6.5	1557	2.0	2203	6.1	
24	TH	0406	2.3	1015	6.2	1642	2.3	2253	5.8	◐
25	F	0503	2.6	1115	5.9	1753	2.6			
26	SA	0005	5.6	0626	2.8	1244	5.7	1923	2.7	
27	SU	0147	5.7	0758	2.6	1435	5.8	2049	2.5	
28	M	0306	6.0	0927	2.2	1552	6.3	2200	2.1	
29	TU	0406	6.5	1038	1.6	1653	6.8	2259	1.7	
30	W	0457	7.0	1135	1.0	1745	7.1	2350	1.3	
31	TH	0543	7.4	1226	0.5	1832	7.4			○

Chart Datum: 3·90 metres below Ordnance Datum (Newlyn)
HAT is 8·0 metres above Chart Datum

TIME ZONE (UT)
For Summer Time add ONE hour in **non-shaded areas**

IMMINGHAM

LAT 53°38'N LONG 0°11'W

TIMES AND HEIGHTS OF HIGH AND LOW WATERS

Dates in amber are **SPRINGS**
Dates in grey are **NEAPS**

2023

SEPTEMBER

Date	Day	Time	m	Time	m	Time	m	Time	m	Moon
1	F	0036	1.0	0628	7.7	1311	0.3	1915	7.5	
2	SA	0120	0.9	0710	7.9	1354	0.2	1954	7.5	
3	SU	0200	0.9	0751	7.9	1434	0.4	2031	7.3	
4	M	0238	1.0	0832	7.7	1510	0.8	2107	7.0	
5	TU	0314	1.4	0914	7.3	1544	1.4	2144	6.6	
6	W	0349	1.8	0958	6.8	1618	2.0	2226	6.1	◑
7	TH	0428	2.3	1053	6.2	1700	2.6	2323	5.7	
8	F	0522	2.7	1208	5.6	1802	3.1			
9	SA	0041	5.5	0659	3.0	1337	5.4	1954	3.2	
10	SU	0202	5.5	0858	2.7	1502	5.6	2115	3.0	
11	M	0311	5.9	0956	2.3	1608	5.9	2207	2.6	
12	TU	0405	6.3	1041	1.8	1653	6.3	2251	2.2	
13	W	0447	6.6	1122	1.5	1728	6.5	2331	1.9	
14	TH	0523	6.9	1201	1.3	1759	6.7			
15	F	0007	1.7	0557	7.0	1236	1.2	1829	6.8	●
16	SA	0041	1.6	0629	7.1	1310	1.2	1857	6.9	
17	SU	0111	1.6	0701	7.1	1340	1.2	1925	6.9	
18	M	0138	1.6	0731	7.1	1406	1.3	1953	6.8	
19	TU	0202	1.6	0759	7.0	1428	1.5	2020	6.7	
20	W	0228	1.7	0828	6.9	1451	1.7	2050	6.5	
21	TH	0258	1.9	0903	6.6	1520	2.0	2126	6.3	
22	F	0337	2.2	0949	6.2	1605	2.4	2215	5.9	◐
23	SA	0436	2.6	1054	5.8	1720	2.9	2330	5.6	
24	SU	0609	2.8	1246	5.5	1904	3.0			
25	M	0126	5.6	0751	2.6	1436	5.9	2037	2.7	
26	TU	0248	6.1	0922	2.0	1545	6.4	2146	2.2	
27	W	0346	6.7	1024	1.3	1639	6.9	2240	1.7	
28	TH	0435	7.2	1116	0.8	1726	7.3	2328	1.3	
29	F	0520	7.6	1202	0.5	1808	7.5			○
30	SA	0013	1.0	0603	7.8	1245	0.3	1847	7.5	

OCTOBER

Date	Day	Time	m	Time	m	Time	m	Time	m	Moon
1	SU	0055	0.8	0645	7.9	1326	0.4	1923	7.5	
2	M	0134	0.9	0726	7.8	1402	0.7	1957	7.3	
3	TU	0211	1.1	0806	7.6	1435	1.1	2029	7.0	
4	W	0244	1.4	0846	7.1	1504	1.6	2102	6.6	
5	TH	0316	1.8	0928	6.6	1534	2.2	2137	6.2	
6	F	0353	2.3	1020	6.0	1613	2.8	2226	5.7	◑
7	SA	0446	2.7	1140	5.5	1712	3.3	2357	5.4	
8	SU	0614	3.0	1314	5.3	1858	3.5			
9	M	0129	5.5	0830	2.8	1433	5.5	2046	3.1	
10	TU	0239	5.8	0926	2.3	1535	5.9	2139	2.7	
11	W	0333	6.2	1009	1.9	1619	6.3	2221	2.2	
12	TH	0415	6.6	1048	1.5	1654	6.6	2300	1.9	
13	F	0450	6.8	1125	1.3	1725	6.8	2336	1.7	
14	SA	0523	7.0	1201	1.2	1753	6.9			●
15	SU	0009	1.6	0557	7.1	1235	1.2	1824	7.0	
16	M	0041	1.5	0630	7.1	1306	1.2	1854	7.0	
17	TU	0110	1.5	0702	7.1	1333	1.4	1923	7.0	
18	W	0138	1.5	0734	7.0	1359	1.5	1952	6.9	
19	TH	0209	1.6	0808	6.9	1427	1.7	2024	6.7	
20	F	0243	1.8	0848	6.6	1502	2.1	2103	6.4	
21	SA	0327	2.1	0940	6.1	1552	2.5	2156	6.0	
22	SU	0434	2.4	1054	5.7	1708	2.9	2314	5.7	◐
23	M	0606	2.5	1257	5.7	1847	3.0			
24	TU	0103	5.8	0741	2.3	1422	6.0	2014	2.7	
25	W	0221	6.3	0859	1.7	1525	6.5	2120	2.2	
26	TH	0318	6.8	0957	1.2	1616	6.9	2213	1.7	
27	F	0408	7.2	1047	0.9	1659	7.2	2301	1.3	
28	SA	0453	7.5	1133	0.7	1739	7.4	2346	1.1	○
29	SU	0537	7.7	1215	0.7	1816	7.4			
30	M	0029	1.0	0621	7.7	1254	0.8	1852	7.3	
31	TU	0109	1.0	0703	7.5	1330	1.1	1925	7.2	

NOVEMBER

Date	Day	Time	m	Time	m	Time	m	Time	m	Moon
1	W	0146	1.2	0744	7.3	1402	1.4	1958	7.0	
2	TH	0220	1.5	0824	6.9	1431	1.9	2029	6.7	
3	F	0252	1.8	0906	6.4	1502	2.3	2103	6.3	
4	SA	0330	2.2	0955	5.9	1541	2.8	2146	5.9	
5	SU	0422	2.6	1107	5.5	1635	3.2	2301	5.6	◑
6	M	0537	2.8	1235	5.3	1755	3.4			
7	TU	0040	5.5	0720	2.8	1347	5.5	1939	3.3	
8	W	0153	5.7	0833	2.4	1447	5.8	2051	2.9	
9	TH	0248	6.1	0921	2.1	1534	6.2	2139	2.5	
10	F	0332	6.4	1003	1.8	1612	6.5	2219	2.1	
11	SA	0410	6.6	1043	1.5	1645	6.7	2257	1.9	
12	SU	0447	6.8	1121	1.4	1718	6.9	2334	1.7	
13	M	0524	7.0	1158	1.3	1751	7.0			●
14	TU	0009	1.5	0602	7.1	1232	1.3	1826	7.1	
15	W	0045	1.5	0640	7.1	1306	1.4	1859	7.1	
16	TH	0121	1.4	0719	7.0	1340	1.5	1934	7.0	
17	F	0159	1.5	0801	6.8	1416	1.8	2011	6.8	
18	SA	0241	1.6	0847	6.6	1458	2.1	2055	6.6	
19	SU	0333	1.9	0945	6.2	1551	2.4	2150	6.3	
20	M	0439	2.1	1103	5.9	1700	2.7	2303	6.1	◐
21	TU	0557	2.1	1237	5.9	1822	2.8			
22	W	0030	6.1	0716	1.9	1350	6.1	1939	2.6	
23	TH	0144	6.4	0825	1.7	1452	6.4	2045	2.2	
24	F	0245	6.7	0923	1.4	1544	6.7	2142	1.9	
25	SA	0339	7.0	1015	1.2	1629	6.9	2234	1.6	
26	SU	0428	7.2	1102	1.2	1710	7.1	2322	1.4	
27	M	0516	7.3	1146	1.2	1748	7.1			○
28	TU	0006	1.2	0603	7.2	1226	1.3	1826	7.1	
29	W	0049	1.2	0647	7.1	1303	1.5	1902	7.1	
30	TH	0128	1.3	0729	6.9	1337	1.7	1936	6.9	

DECEMBER

Date	Day	Time	m	Time	m	Time	m	Time	m	Moon
1	F	0204	1.5	0810	6.6	1408	2.0	2009	6.8	
2	SA	0239	1.8	0849	6.3	1441	2.2	2043	6.5	
3	SU	0317	2.0	0932	6.0	1518	2.5	2123	6.2	
4	M	0403	2.3	1025	5.7	1603	2.8	2216	5.9	
5	TU	0500	2.5	1131	5.5	1702	3.1	2329	5.7	◑
6	W	0605	2.6	1240	5.5	1812	3.1			
7	TH	0042	5.7	0712	2.5	1341	5.7	1925	3.0	
8	F	0144	5.9	0813	2.3	1435	5.9	2031	2.8	
9	SA	0238	6.1	0908	2.1	1522	6.2	2126	2.5	
10	SU	0326	6.3	0956	1.9	1605	6.4	2214	2.1	
11	M	0412	6.6	1041	1.7	1645	6.7	2259	1.9	
12	TU	0456	6.8	1124	1.5	1725	6.9	2343	1.6	●
13	W	0541	6.9	1206	1.5	1804	7.0			
14	TH	0027	1.4	0627	7.0	1247	1.4	1844	7.1	
15	F	0112	1.3	0713	7.0	1329	1.5	1924	7.1	
16	SA	0158	1.2	0801	6.9	1411	1.6	2006	7.1	
17	SU	0246	1.3	0851	6.7	1457	1.8	2052	6.9	
18	M	0337	1.4	0946	6.5	1547	2.1	2144	6.8	
19	TU	0434	1.5	1052	6.3	1644	2.3	2245	6.6	◐
20	W	0536	1.7	1202	6.1	1748	2.4	2355	6.5	
21	TH	0640	1.8	1308	6.1	1857	2.5			
22	F	0104	6.4	0746	1.8	1410	6.2	2008	2.4	
23	SA	0210	6.5	0848	1.8	1507	6.3	2113	2.2	
24	SU	0313	6.6	0945	1.8	1559	6.5	2211	1.9	
25	M	0410	6.7	1036	1.7	1645	6.6	2304	1.7	
26	TU	0503	6.7	1123	1.7	1727	6.8	2352	1.5	
27	W	0553	6.8	1206	1.7	1807	6.9			○
28	TH	0037	1.4	0638	6.7	1245	1.7	1846	7.0	
29	F	0119	1.4	0719	6.7	1321	1.8	1922	6.9	
30	SA	0156	1.5	0757	6.5	1354	1.9	1955	6.9	
31	SU	0231	1.6	0832	6.4	1426	2.0	2028	6.7	

Chart Datum: 3·90 metres below Ordnance Datum (Newlyn)
HAT is 8·0 metres above Chart Datum

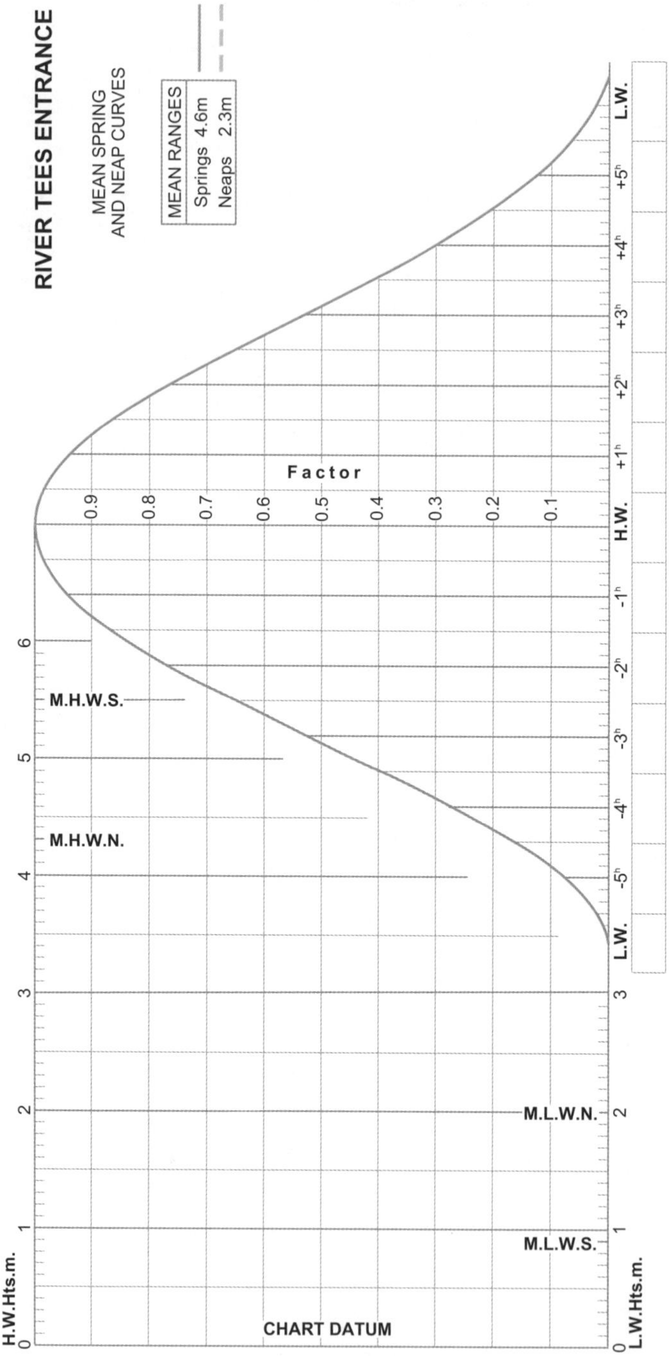
RIVER TEES ENTRANCE
MEAN SPRING
AND NEAP CURVES
MEAN RANGES
Springs 4.6m
Neaps 2.3m
Factor
H.W.
L.W.
M.H.W.S.
M.H.W.N.
M.L.W.N.
M.L.W.S.
CHART DATUM
H.W.Hts.m.
L.W.Hts.m.

TIME ZONE (UT)
For Summer Time add ONE hour in **non-shaded areas**

RIVER TEES

LAT 54°38′N LONG 1°09′W

TIMES AND HEIGHTS OF HIGH AND LOW WATERS

Dates in amber are **SPRINGS**
Dates in grey are **NEAPS**

2023

JANUARY

Date	Day	Time	m	Time	m	Time	m	Time	m
1	SU	0512	1.6	1128	4.4	1734	2.1	2335	4.6
2	M	0619	1.7	1231	4.5	1840	2.0		
3	TU	0041	4.6	0718	1.7	1324	4.6	1937	1.8
4	W	0139	4.7	0805	1.7	1411	4.8	2026	1.6
5	TH	0229	4.7	0847	1.6	1452	4.9	2108	1.4
6	F	0312	4.8	0924	1.6	1528	5.0	○ 2147	1.3
7	SA	0351	4.9	0958	1.6	1602	5.1	2224	1.2
8	SU	0427	4.9	1030	1.5	1634	5.1	2300	1.2
9	M	0503	4.9	1102	1.5	1706	5.1	2335	1.2
10	TU	0537	4.9	1134	1.6	1740	5.1		
11	W	0009	1.2	0614	4.8	1208	1.6	1817	5.0
12	TH	0044	1.3	0652	4.7	1245	1.8	1855	4.9
13	F	0122	1.4	0734	4.6	1325	1.9	1937	4.8
14	SA	0204	1.5	0821	4.5	1409	2.0	2024	4.6
15	SU	0254	1.6	0914	4.4	1504	2.1	◑ 2120	4.5
16	M	0353	1.7	1013	4.3	1612	2.2	2225	4.5
17	TU	0501	1.8	1116	4.4	1728	2.1	2335	4.5
18	W	0610	1.7	1220	4.5	1839	1.9		
19	TH	0044	4.7	0717	1.5	1319	4.7	1946	1.5
20	F	0150	4.9	0817	1.3	1415	5.0	2046	1.2
21	SA	0249	5.2	0912	1.1	1507	5.3	● 2142	0.8
22	SU	0344	5.4	1003	1.0	1556	5.5	2233	0.5
23	M	0435	5.5	1051	0.9	1643	5.7	2322	0.3
24	TU	0524	5.5	1136	0.9	1729	5.7		
25	W	0008	0.3	0612	5.4	1219	1.0	1815	5.7
26	TH	0052	0.4	0700	5.2	1302	1.2	1901	5.5
27	F	0137	0.7	0748	5.0	1346	1.5	1949	5.2
28	SA	0223	1.1	0838	4.7	1434	1.7	◐ 2041	4.9
29	SU	0315	1.5	0932	4.4	1532	2.0	2142	4.6
30	M	0417	1.9	1034	4.2	1644	2.2	2252	4.3
31	TU	0534	2.1	1145	4.2	1807	2.2		

FEBRUARY

Date	Day	Time	m	Time	m	Time	m	Time	m
1	W	0011	4.2	0650	2.1	1256	4.3	1919	2.0
2	TH	0125	4.3	0748	2.0	1352	4.5	2014	1.7
3	F	0219	4.5	0833	1.9	1438	4.7	2058	1.5
4	SA	0302	4.7	0911	1.7	1516	4.9	2136	1.3
5	SU	0340	4.8	0945	1.6	1549	5.1	○ 2211	1.1
6	M	0414	4.9	1017	1.4	1620	5.2	2244	1.0
7	TU	0446	5.0	1048	1.4	1649	5.2	2316	1.0
8	W	0516	5.0	1118	1.3	1719	5.2	2346	1.0
9	TH	0547	5.0	1149	1.3	1750	5.2		
10	F	0017	1.0	0621	4.9	1220	1.4	1823	5.1
11	SA	0051	1.1	0657	4.8	1254	1.5	1858	5.0
12	SU	0128	1.3	0738	4.6	1331	1.7	1940	4.8
13	M	0210	1.5	0826	4.4	1417	1.9	◑ 2034	4.6
14	TU	0304	1.7	0925	4.3	1520	2.0	2144	4.4
15	W	0416	1.9	1035	4.2	1647	2.1	2308	4.3
16	TH	0542	2.0	1151	4.3	1820	1.9		
17	F	0032	4.5	0705	1.8	1302	4.6	1940	1.5
18	SA	0145	4.8	0810	1.5	1404	4.9	2042	1.0
19	SU	0245	5.1	0905	1.2	1457	5.3	2136	0.6
20	M	0336	5.4	0952	0.9	1543	5.6	● 2223	0.3
21	TU	0422	5.5	1036	0.8	1627	5.8	2307	0.1
22	W	0506	5.6	1118	0.7	1709	5.9	2348	0.1
23	TH	0548	5.5	1157	0.8	1750	5.8		
24	F	0026	0.3	0630	5.3	1234	0.9	1832	5.6
25	SA	0104	0.7	0711	5.0	1311	1.2	1916	5.3
26	SU	0142	1.1	0754	4.7	1351	1.5	2004	4.9
27	M	0223	1.6	0842	4.4	1441	1.9	◐ 2101	4.4
28	TU	0317	2.1	0940	4.1	1554	2.2	2213	4.1

MARCH

Date	Day	Time	m	Time	m	Time	m	Time	m
1	W	0441	2.4	1056	4.0	1733	2.2	2343	4.0
2	TH	0621	2.4	1224	4.1	1859	2.0		
3	F	0108	4.1	0728	2.2	1330	4.3	1956	1.7
4	SA	0204	4.4	0814	2.0	1417	4.6	2039	1.4
5	SU	0244	4.6	0852	1.7	1455	4.9	2116	1.2
6	M	0320	4.8	0926	1.5	1528	5.0	2149	1.0
7	TU	0351	5.0	0956	1.3	1557	5.2	○ 2220	0.9
8	W	0420	5.1	1026	1.2	1624	5.2	2250	0.8
9	TH	0448	5.1	1055	1.1	1651	5.3	2319	0.7
10	F	0517	5.1	1124	1.1	1720	5.3	2349	0.8
11	SA	0548	5.1	1155	1.1	1751	5.2		
12	SU	0021	0.9	0622	5.0	1226	1.2	1828	5.1
13	M	0056	1.1	0700	4.8	1303	1.4	1911	4.9
14	TU	0137	1.5	0746	4.5	1348	1.7	2008	4.6
15	W	0230	1.8	0847	4.3	1453	1.9	◑ 2125	4.3
16	TH	0348	2.1	1006	4.1	1631	2.0	2258	4.2
17	F	0530	2.1	1132	4.2	1817	1.8		
18	SA	0030	4.4	0657	1.9	1250	4.5	1935	1.3
19	SU	0141	4.8	0759	1.5	1351	4.9	2032	0.8
20	M	0234	5.1	0849	1.2	1440	5.3	2120	0.4
21	TU	0319	5.4	0933	0.9	1524	5.6	● 2203	0.2
22	W	0401	5.5	1014	0.7	1605	5.8	2243	0.1
23	TH	0441	5.5	1052	0.6	1644	5.8	2320	0.2
24	F	0519	5.4	1129	0.7	1724	5.7	2355	0.5
25	SA	0556	5.3	1204	0.8	1804	5.5		
26	SU	0029	0.8	0633	5.0	1239	1.1	1846	5.1
27	M	0102	1.3	0711	4.7	1317	1.4	1932	4.7
28	TU	0137	1.7	0754	4.4	1403	1.8	2027	4.3
29	W	0221	2.2	0849	4.1	1513	2.1	◐ 2138	4.0
30	TH	0343	2.5	1006	3.9	1656	2.2	2311	3.8
31	F	0542	2.5	1141	4.0	1825	2.0		

APRIL

Date	Day	Time	m	Time	m	Time	m	Time	m
1	SA	0037	4.0	0655	2.3	1254	4.2	1923	1.7
2	SU	0133	4.3	0743	2.0	1343	4.5	2006	1.4
3	M	0214	4.6	0821	1.7	1422	4.8	2043	1.1
4	TU	0249	4.8	0855	1.4	1455	5.0	2117	0.9
5	W	0319	5.0	0926	1.2	1524	5.1	2148	0.8
6	TH	0347	5.1	0957	1.1	1553	5.2	○ 2218	0.7
7	F	0416	5.2	1027	1.0	1621	5.3	2249	0.7
8	SA	0446	5.2	1059	0.9	1653	5.3	2321	0.7
9	SU	0518	5.2	1131	0.9	1728	5.3	2356	0.9
10	M	0553	5.0	1207	1.1	1810	5.1		
11	TU	0033	1.2	0634	4.8	1247	1.3	1900	4.8
12	W	0116	1.5	0724	4.6	1339	1.5	2004	4.5
13	TH	0213	1.9	0828	4.3	1451	1.8	◑ 2124	4.2
14	F	0339	2.2	0949	4.2	1633	1.8	2257	4.2
15	SA	0520	2.1	1117	4.3	1808	1.5		
16	SU	0023	4.5	0639	1.9	1232	4.6	1917	1.1
17	M	0126	4.8	0736	1.5	1330	5.0	2010	0.7
18	TU	0214	5.1	0824	1.2	1418	5.3	2056	0.5
19	W	0257	5.3	0907	0.9	1500	5.5	2137	0.4
20	TH	0336	5.4	0947	0.8	1540	5.6	● 2215	0.4
21	F	0413	5.4	1025	0.7	1619	5.6	2251	0.5
22	SA	0448	5.3	1102	0.7	1659	5.4	2324	0.8
23	SU	0523	5.2	1138	0.9	1739	5.2	2357	1.1
24	M	0558	5.0	1214	1.1	1821	4.9		
25	TU	0028	1.5	0636	4.7	1253	1.4	1908	4.6
26	W	0102	1.8	0718	4.5	1339	1.7	2000	4.3
27	TH	0144	2.2	0809	4.2	1443	1.9	◐ 2105	4.0
28	F	0252	2.5	0918	4.0	1611	2.1	2227	3.9
29	SA	0443	2.5	1045	4.0	1734	1.9	2347	4.0
30	SU	0603	2.4	1201	4.2	1834	1.7		

Chart Datum: 2·85 metres below Ordnance Datum (Newlyn)
HAT is 6·1 metres above Chart Datum

TIME ZONE (UT)
For Summer Time add ONE hour in **non-shaded areas**

RIVER TEES

LAT 54°38'N LONG 1°09'W

TIMES AND HEIGHTS OF HIGH AND LOW WATERS

Dates in amber are **SPRINGS**
Dates in grey are **NEAPS**

2023

MAY

Date	Day	Time	m	Time	m	Time	m	Time	m
1	M	0047	4.2	0657	2.1	1254	4.4	1922	1.4
2	TU	0131	4.5	0739	1.8	1336	4.7	2002	1.2
3	W	0207	4.7	0816	1.5	1413	4.9	2038	1.0
4	TH	0239	4.9	0850	1.3	1446	5.1	2112	0.8
5	F	0311	5.1	0925	1.1	1520	5.2	○ 2146	0.7
6	SA	0344	5.2	1000	0.9	1555	5.3	2221	0.7
7	SU	0418	5.2	1036	0.9	1634	5.3	2258	0.8
8	M	0455	5.2	1115	0.9	1717	5.2	2337	1.0
9	TU	0536	5.1	1157	1.0	1806	5.0		
10	W	0020	1.2	0622	4.9	1245	1.1	1903	4.8
11	TH	0109	1.6	0715	4.7	1344	1.3	2009	4.5
12	F	0212	1.9	0820	4.5	1500	1.5	◑ 2125	4.4
13	SA	0334	2.1	0937	4.4	1624	1.4	2246	4.4
14	SU	0457	2.0	1056	4.5	1743	1.3		
15	M	0000	4.5	0608	1.8	1205	4.7	1848	1.0
16	TU	0059	4.8	0706	1.5	1303	5.0	1941	0.8
17	W	0148	5.0	0756	1.3	1352	5.2	2028	0.7
18	TH	0231	5.1	0840	1.1	1437	5.3	2110	0.7
19	F	0310	5.2	0922	1.0	1519	5.3	● 2148	0.8
20	SA	0347	5.2	1002	0.9	1559	5.3	2224	0.9
21	SU	0422	5.1	1040	0.9	1640	5.2	2258	1.1
22	M	0456	5.1	1118	1.0	1721	5.0	2331	1.3
23	TU	0531	5.0	1157	1.1	1803	4.8		
24	W	0003	1.6	0610	4.8	1237	1.3	1848	4.6
25	TH	0039	1.8	0652	4.6	1322	1.6	1936	4.3
26	F	0121	2.1	0740	4.4	1416	1.7	2031	4.2
27	SA	0217	2.3	0837	4.3	1520	1.9	◐ 2134	4.1
28	SU	0334	2.4	0944	4.2	1629	1.9	2242	4.1
29	M	0452	2.3	1053	4.2	1731	1.7	2343	4.2
30	TU	0554	2.2	1153	4.4	1825	1.6		
31	W	0034	4.4	0646	1.9	1243	4.6	1913	1.4

JUNE

Date	Day	Time	m	Time	m	Time	m	Time	m
1	TH	0118	4.6	0731	1.7	1328	4.8	1956	1.2
2	F	0158	4.8	0813	1.4	1411	5.0	2037	1.0
3	SA	0237	5.0	0855	1.2	1453	5.1	2118	0.9
4	SU	0317	5.1	0938	1.0	1538	5.2	○ 2201	0.9
5	M	0358	5.2	1022	0.8	1625	5.3	2244	0.9
6	TU	0441	5.3	1108	0.8	1715	5.2	2329	1.1
7	W	0527	5.2	1157	0.8	1808	5.1		
8	TH	0017	1.3	0616	5.1	1250	0.9	1905	4.9
9	F	0109	1.5	0710	5.0	1349	1.0	2006	4.7
10	SA	0209	1.7	0810	4.9	1453	1.1	◑ 2111	4.6
11	SU	0315	1.9	0917	4.8	1600	1.2	2218	4.5
12	M	0423	1.9	1026	4.7	1708	1.2	2325	4.5
13	TU	0530	1.8	1133	4.8	1813	1.2		
14	W	0026	4.6	0633	1.7	1234	4.8	1911	1.2
15	TH	0120	4.7	0728	1.5	1330	4.9	2002	1.2
16	F	0207	4.9	0818	1.3	1420	5.0	2046	1.2
17	SA	0249	4.9	0903	1.2	1505	5.0	2127	1.3
18	SU	0328	5.0	0945	1.1	1548	5.0	● 2204	1.3
19	M	0404	5.0	1025	1.1	1629	4.9	2239	1.4
20	TU	0438	5.0	1105	1.1	1708	4.9	2313	1.5
21	W	0513	5.0	1143	1.2	1748	4.8	2347	1.6
22	TH	0550	4.9	1222	1.3	1828	4.7		
23	F	0022	1.7	0630	4.8	1302	1.4	1910	4.5
24	SA	0101	1.9	0713	4.7	1344	1.5	1955	4.4
25	SU	0145	2.0	0800	4.5	1431	1.6	2045	4.3
26	M	0237	2.1	0853	4.4	1525	1.7	◐ 2140	4.2
27	TU	0339	2.2	0951	4.4	1623	1.8	2238	4.2
28	W	0446	2.2	1052	4.4	1723	1.7	2335	4.3
29	TH	0548	2.0	1152	4.5	1821	1.6		
30	F	0030	4.5	0646	1.8	1249	4.7	1917	1.4

JULY

Date	Day	Time	m	Time	m	Time	m	Time	m
1	SA	0122	4.7	0740	1.6	1343	4.9	2009	1.3
2	SU	0211	4.9	0833	1.3	1436	5.1	2100	1.1
3	M	0258	5.1	0924	1.0	1528	5.2	○ 2149	1.0
4	TU	0345	5.3	1015	0.8	1620	5.3	2238	1.0
5	W	0432	5.4	1106	0.6	1711	5.4	2326	1.0
6	TH	0519	5.5	1156	0.5	1803	5.3		
7	F	0013	1.1	0607	5.5	1246	0.5	1856	5.2
8	SA	0101	1.2	0658	5.4	1337	0.7	1949	5.0
9	SU	0151	1.4	0751	5.2	1430	0.9	2044	4.8
10	M	0245	1.6	0848	5.0	1527	1.1	◑ 2142	4.6
11	TU	0345	1.8	0951	4.8	1629	1.4	2244	4.5
12	W	0451	1.9	1058	4.6	1736	1.6	2350	4.4
13	TH	0601	1.9	1208	4.6	1843	1.7		
14	F	0053	4.5	0707	1.8	1314	4.6	1942	1.7
15	SA	0148	4.6	0804	1.6	1411	4.7	2031	1.7
16	SU	0235	4.8	0853	1.4	1459	4.8	2113	1.6
17	M	0315	4.9	0936	1.3	1540	4.9	● 2151	1.6
18	TU	0352	5.0	1015	1.2	1618	4.9	2225	1.5
19	W	0425	5.1	1051	1.1	1654	4.9	2258	1.5
20	TH	0458	5.1	1127	1.1	1729	4.9	2330	1.5
21	F	0530	5.1	1201	1.1	1803	4.9		
22	SA	0002	1.5	0605	5.0	1234	1.2	1840	4.8
23	SU	0035	1.6	0642	4.9	1310	1.3	1918	4.7
24	M	0112	1.7	0721	4.8	1348	1.5	2001	4.5
25	TU	0152	1.9	0805	4.7	1433	1.6	◐ 2049	4.4
26	W	0240	2.0	0857	4.5	1526	1.8	2144	4.3
27	TH	0341	2.1	0959	4.4	1630	1.9	2246	4.3
28	F	0456	2.1	1109	4.4	1740	1.8	2351	4.3
29	SA	0611	2.0	1221	4.5	1849	1.7		
30	SU	0054	4.5	0720	1.7	1328	4.8	1953	1.5
31	M	0152	4.8	0822	1.3	1427	5.0	2049	1.3

AUGUST

Date	Day	Time	m	Time	m	Time	m	Time	m
1	TU	0244	5.1	0918	0.9	1521	5.3	○ 2141	1.1
2	W	0333	5.4	1010	0.6	1612	5.5	2229	0.9
3	TH	0419	5.6	1058	0.3	1700	5.6	2315	0.9
4	F	0505	5.8	1145	0.2	1747	5.6	2358	0.9
5	SA	0550	5.8	1230	0.3	1834	5.4		
6	SU	0040	1.0	0636	5.7	1313	0.5	1921	5.2
7	M	0123	1.2	0723	5.4	1359	0.9	2009	4.9
8	TU	0210	1.5	0815	5.1	1448	1.3	◑ 2102	4.6
9	W	0304	1.8	0914	4.7	1546	1.7	2201	4.3
10	TH	0412	2.0	1025	4.4	1659	2.0	2311	4.2
11	F	0535	2.1	1147	4.3	1822	2.1		
12	SA	0028	4.3	0655	1.9	1307	4.4	1929	2.1
13	SU	0132	4.5	0757	1.7	1405	4.5	2019	1.9
14	M	0221	4.7	0844	1.5	1450	4.7	2100	1.8
15	TU	0302	4.9	0923	1.3	1528	4.9	2135	1.6
16	W	0337	5.1	0959	1.1	1602	5.0	● 2208	1.5
17	TH	0408	5.2	1032	1.0	1634	5.0	2238	1.4
18	F	0437	5.2	1103	1.0	1704	5.1	2307	1.3
19	SA	0506	5.2	1133	1.0	1733	5.1	2337	1.3
20	SU	0535	5.2	1203	1.0	1805	5.0		
21	M	0007	1.4	0607	5.1	1234	1.2	1840	4.9
22	TU	0039	1.5	0641	5.0	1309	1.3	1918	4.7
23	W	0113	1.7	0720	4.8	1349	1.6	2002	4.5
24	TH	0155	1.9	0810	4.6	1439	1.8	◐ 2057	4.3
25	F	0252	2.1	0917	4.4	1546	2.1	2205	4.2
26	SA	0416	2.2	1041	4.3	1712	2.1	2321	4.2
27	SU	0552	2.0	1207	4.4	1836	2.0		
28	M	0035	4.5	0712	1.6	1321	4.7	1944	1.7
29	TU	0138	4.9	0815	1.2	1420	5.1	2039	1.3
30	W	0230	5.3	0908	0.7	1510	5.4	2127	1.0
31	TH	0317	5.6	0956	0.4	1556	5.6	○ 2212	0.8

Chart Datum: 2·85 metres below Ordnance Datum (Newlyn)
HAT is 6·1 metres above Chart Datum

TIME ZONE (UT)
For Summer Time add ONE hour in **non-shaded areas**

RIVER TEES

LAT 54°38'N LONG 1°09'W

TIMES AND HEIGHTS OF HIGH AND LOW WATERS

Dates in amber are **SPRINGS**
Dates in grey are **NEAPS**

2023

SEPTEMBER

Date	Time	m	Date	Time	m
1 F	0401	5.9	16 SA	0410	5.3
	1041	0.1		1033	0.9
	1640	5.7		1633	5.2
	2254	0.7		2239	1.2
2 SA	0443	6.0	17 SU	0436	5.3
	1123	0.1		1101	0.9
	1723	5.7		1700	5.2
	2334	0.7		2308	1.2
3 SU	0525	5.9	18 M	0503	5.3
	1203	0.3		1130	1.0
	1805	5.5		1730	5.2
				2338	1.2
4 M	0012	0.8	19 TU	0533	5.2
	0608	5.8		1201	1.1
	1242	0.6		1802	5.0
	1847	5.3			
5 TU	0051	1.1	20 W	0009	1.4
	0653	5.5		0607	5.1
	1322	1.0		1235	1.3
	1931	4.9		1839	4.9
6 W	0133	1.4	21 TH	0043	1.5
	0742	5.0		0648	4.9
	1406	1.6		1314	1.6
	◑ 2019	4.6		1922	4.6
7 TH	0224	1.8	22 F	0125	1.8
	0840	4.6		0742	4.6
	1500	2.1		1403	2.0
	2117	4.3		◐ 2019	4.4
8 F	0335	2.1	23 SA	0224	2.0
	0955	4.2		0856	4.3
	1621	2.4		1516	2.3
	2232	4.1		2134	4.2
9 SA	0514	2.2	24 SU	0359	2.1
	1129	4.1		1029	4.2
	1801	2.5		1658	2.3
				2259	4.2
10 SU	0001	4.1	25 M	0546	1.9
	0642	2.0		1202	4.4
	1256	4.2		1826	2.1
	1911	2.3			
11 M	0111	4.4	26 TU	0018	4.5
	0741	1.7		0704	1.5
	1350	4.5		1313	4.8
	1959	2.0		1929	1.7
12 TU	0200	4.7	27 W	0120	5.0
	0824	1.4		0801	1.0
	1430	4.7		1406	5.2
	2038	1.8		2020	1.3
13 W	0239	5.0	28 TH	0211	5.4
	0900	1.2		0849	0.6
	1505	4.9		1452	5.5
	2111	1.6		2105	1.0
14 TH	0312	5.1	29 F	0255	5.7
	0933	1.0		0934	0.3
	1537	5.1		1534	5.7
	2142	1.4		○ 2147	0.8
15 F	0342	5.3	30 SA	0337	5.9
	1004	0.9		1016	0.2
	1606	5.2		1614	5.7
	● 2211	1.3		2227	0.7

OCTOBER

Date	Time	m	Date	Time	m
1 SU	0417	6.0	16 M	0405	5.3
	1055	0.2		1029	0.9
	1654	5.7		1627	5.3
	2306	0.7		2241	1.1
2 M	0458	5.9	17 TU	0435	5.3
	1133	0.5		1100	1.0
	1733	5.5		1658	5.3
	2344	0.8		2313	1.1
3 TU	0540	5.7	18 W	0508	5.3
	1209	0.8		1133	1.1
	1811	5.2		1732	5.1
				2347	1.3
4 W	0022	1.1	19 TH	0547	5.1
	0625	5.3		1209	1.4
	1245	1.3		1811	4.9
	1852	4.9			
5 TH	0103	1.4	20 F	0025	1.4
	0714	4.9		0635	4.9
	1324	1.8		1250	1.7
	1937	4.6		1858	4.7
6 F	0152	1.8	21 SA	0113	1.7
	0811	4.4		0735	4.6
	1412	2.3		1343	2.1
	◑ 2032	4.3		1957	4.5
7 SA	0303	2.1	22 SU	0219	1.9
	0926	4.1		0852	4.3
	1538	2.6		1501	2.3
	2149	4.1		◐ 2113	4.3
8 SU	0445	2.2	23 M	0357	1.9
	1102	4.0		1023	4.3
	1727	2.7		1643	2.3
	2322	4.1		2238	4.4
9 M	0611	2.0	24 TU	0532	1.7
	1227	4.2		1150	4.5
	1838	2.4		1803	2.1
				2355	4.7
10 TU	0035	4.4	25 W	0642	1.3
	0708	1.7		1255	4.9
	1320	4.5		1903	1.7
	1927	2.1			
11 W	0126	4.6	26 TH	0056	5.1
	0750	1.5		0737	0.9
	1359	4.7		1344	5.2
	2005	1.8		1954	1.4
12 TH	0205	4.9	27 F	0146	5.4
	0826	1.2		0824	0.6
	1433	4.9		1428	5.4
	2039	1.6		2039	1.1
13 F	0239	5.1	28 SA	0231	5.6
	0900	1.1		0908	0.5
	1504	5.1		1509	5.6
	2111	1.4		○ 2121	0.9
14 SA	0310	5.2	29 SU	0313	5.8
	0930	0.9		0948	0.5
	1532	5.2		1548	5.6
	● 2141	1.2		2202	0.8
15 SU	0338	5.3	30 M	0354	5.8
	1000	0.9		1027	0.6
	1559	5.3		1625	5.5
	2210	1.1		2241	0.8
			31 TU	0436	5.6
				1103	0.8
				1703	5.4
				2320	0.9

NOVEMBER

Date	Time	m	Date	Time	m
1 W	0519	5.4	16 TH	0456	5.2
	1139	1.2		1113	1.2
	1740	5.2		1714	5.2
	2359	1.1		2336	1.1
2 TH	0603	5.1	17 F	0542	5.1
	1214	1.5		1154	1.4
	1819	5.0		1757	5.1
3 F	0041	1.4	18 SA	0021	1.3
	0652	4.7		0635	4.9
	1250	1.9		1240	1.7
	1903	4.7		1847	4.9
4 SA	0130	1.7	19 SU	0115	1.4
	0747	4.4		0737	4.6
	1334	2.3		1337	2.0
	1954	4.4		1946	4.7
5 SU	0234	2.0	20 M	0223	1.6
	0854	4.1		0848	4.5
	1444	2.6		1452	2.2
	◑ 2101	4.2		◐ 2056	4.6
6 M	0357	2.1	21 TU	0343	1.6
	1015	4.0		1006	4.4
	1627	2.7		1615	2.2
	2225	4.2		2212	4.6
7 TU	0518	2.0	22 W	0502	1.5
	1134	4.1		1122	4.6
	1746	2.5		1728	2.0
	2341	4.3		2324	4.8
8 W	0619	1.8	23 TH	0610	1.2
	1233	4.4		1225	4.8
	1840	2.3		1831	1.8
9 TH	0037	4.5	24 F	0026	5.0
	0706	1.6		0708	1.0
	1316	4.6		1317	5.0
	1924	2.0		1925	1.5
10 F	0121	4.7	25 SA	0120	5.2
	0746	1.4		0758	0.9
	1353	4.8		1403	5.2
	2001	1.7		2013	1.3
11 SA	0159	4.9	26 SU	0209	5.4
	0822	1.2		0843	0.9
	1425	5.0		1445	5.3
	2035	1.5		2059	1.1
12 SU	0233	5.1	27 M	0254	5.4
	0855	1.1		0924	0.9
	1456	5.2		1525	5.3
	2109	1.3		○ 2142	1.0
13 M	0306	5.2	28 TU	0338	5.4
	0927	1.0		1004	1.0
	1527	5.3		1603	5.3
	● 2143	1.2		2223	1.0
14 TU	0340	5.3	29 W	0422	5.3
	1001	1.0		1041	1.2
	1600	5.3		1640	5.3
	2218	1.1		2304	1.0
15 W	0416	5.3	30 TH	0505	5.1
	1036	1.0		1117	1.4
	1635	5.3		1717	5.2
	2256	1.1		2344	1.2

DECEMBER

Date	Time	m	Date	Time	m
1 F	0548	4.9	16 SA	0542	5.2
	1151	1.7		1150	1.4
	1755	5.0		1749	5.3
2 SA	0026	1.3	17 SU	0023	0.9
	0634	4.7		0635	5.0
	1227	1.9		1238	1.5
	1837	4.9		1839	5.2
3 SU	0111	1.5	18 M	0116	1.0
	0722	4.5		0732	4.9
	1307	2.2		1332	1.7
	1924	4.7		1933	5.1
4 M	0201	1.8	19 TU	0214	1.1
	0816	4.3		0833	4.7
	1358	2.4		1432	1.9
	2017	4.5		◐ 2034	4.9
5 TU	0300	1.9	20 W	0317	1.3
	0917	4.2		0937	4.6
	1508	2.5		1539	2.0
	◑ 2120	4.3		2139	4.8
6 W	0407	2.0	21 TH	0423	1.4
	1022	4.1		1043	4.6
	1626	2.5		1647	2.0
	2229	4.3		2247	4.8
7 TH	0511	1.9	22 F	0532	1.4
	1125	4.2		1149	4.6
	1734	2.4		1754	1.9
	2332	4.4		2355	4.8
8 F	0608	1.8	23 SA	0637	1.4
	1218	4.4		1249	4.7
	1829	2.2		1858	1.7
9 SA	0026	4.5	24 SU	0058	4.9
	0657	1.6		0735	1.4
	1303	4.6		1341	4.9
	1916	1.9		1955	1.5
10 SU	0114	4.7	25 M	0155	5.0
	0740	1.5		0825	1.3
	1344	4.8		1428	5.0
	1959	1.7		2045	1.3
11 M	0158	4.9	26 TU	0246	5.0
	0821	1.3		0909	1.4
	1422	5.0		1511	5.1
	2040	1.4		2131	1.2
12 TU	0240	5.0	27 W	0333	5.0
	0900	1.2		0949	1.4
	1501	5.1		1550	5.2
	● 2122	1.2		○ 2214	1.1
13 W	0323	5.2	28 TH	0415	5.0
	0940	1.1		1027	1.5
	1540	5.3		1627	5.2
	2204	1.1		2254	1.1
14 TH	0407	5.2	29 F	0456	5.0
	1022	1.1		1102	1.5
	1621	5.3		1702	5.2
	2248	1.0		2333	1.1
15 F	0453	5.2	30 SA	0535	4.9
	1105	1.2		1136	1.6
	1704	5.3		1738	5.1
	2334	0.9			
			31 SU	0010	1.2
				0615	4.8
				1208	1.7
				1815	5.0

Chart Datum: 2·85 metres below Ordnance Datum (Newlyn)
HAT is 6·1 metres above Chart Datum

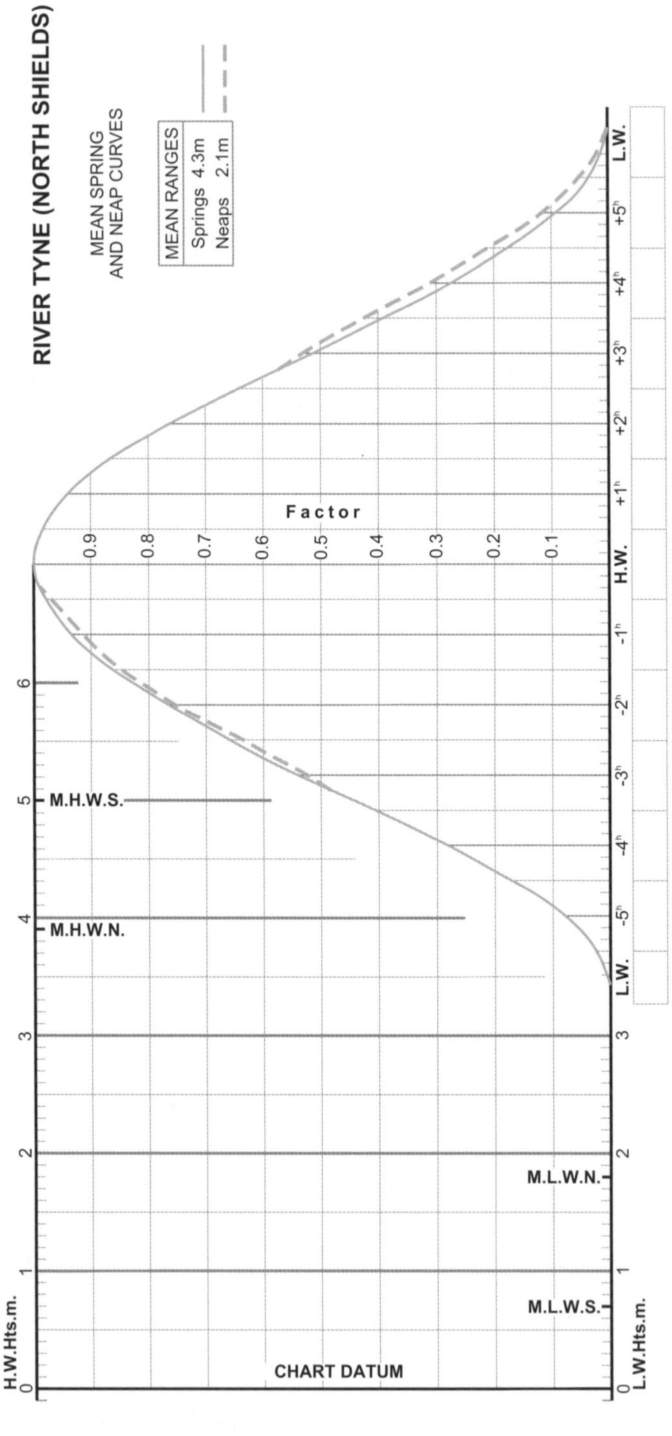
RIVER TYNE (NORTH SHIELDS)
MEAN SPRING AND NEAP CURVES
MEAN RANGES
Springs 4.3m
Neaps 2.1m
Factor
0.9
0.8
0.7
0.6
0.5
0.4
0.3
0.2
0.1
L.W.
-5h
-4h
-3h
-2h
-1h
H.W.
+1h
+2h
+3h
+4h
+5h
L.W.
H.W.Hts.m.
0
1
2
3
4
5
6
M.H.W.S.
M.H.W.N.
M.L.W.N.
M.L.W.S.
CHART DATUM
L.W.Hts.m.

TIME ZONE (UT)
For Summer Time add ONE hour in **non-shaded areas**

NORTH SHIELDS

LAT 55°00′N LONG 1°26′W

TIMES AND HEIGHTS OF HIGH AND LOW WATERS

Dates in amber are **SPRINGS**
Dates in grey are **NEAPS**

2023

JANUARY

Date	Time	m
1 SU	0502	1.5
	1116	4.2
	1723	2.0
	2327	4.4
2 M	0606	1.6
	1218	4.3
	1830	1.9
3 TU	0032	4.4
	0704	1.6
	1311	4.4
	1929	1.7
4 W	0129	4.4
	0753	1.6
	1358	4.5
	2018	1.5
5 TH	0218	4.5
	0834	1.5
	1438	4.7
	2101	1.4
6 F	0301	4.6
	0911	1.5
	1515	4.8
	○ 2139	1.2
7 SA	0339	4.6
	0946	1.5
	1549	4.8
	2215	1.2
8 SU	0415	4.7
	1018	1.4
	1622	4.9
	2249	1.1
9 M	0450	4.7
	1050	1.4
	1654	4.9
	2323	1.1
10 TU	0524	4.6
	1122	1.5
	1727	4.8
	2358	1.1
11 W	0600	4.5
	1154	1.5
	1802	4.8
12 TH	0033	1.2
	0637	4.4
	1228	1.6
	1839	4.7
13 F	0111	1.3
	0717	4.3
	1306	1.8
	1919	4.5
14 SA	0153	1.4
	0802	4.2
	1349	1.9
	2005	4.4
15 SU	0242	1.6
	0854	4.1
	1443	2.0
	◑ 2101	4.3
16 M	0341	1.7
	0955	4.1
	1554	2.1
	2206	4.2
17 TU	0449	1.7
	1102	4.1
	1714	2.0
	2320	4.3
18 W	0559	1.6
	1210	4.3
	1828	1.8
19 TH	0034	4.4
	0705	1.5
	1311	4.5
	1935	1.5
20 F	0140	4.7
	0805	1.3
	1405	4.7
	2034	1.1
21 SA	0237	4.9
	0859	1.1
	1453	5.0
	● 2128	0.8
22 SU	0329	5.1
	0949	1.0
	1540	5.2
	2219	0.5
23 M	0419	5.2
	1036	0.9
	1625	5.3
	2308	0.3
24 TU	0508	5.2
	1120	0.9
	1711	5.4
	2355	0.3
25 W	0556	5.1
	1204	1.0
	1757	5.3
26 TH	0041	0.4
	0645	4.9
	1245	1.2
	1845	5.2
27 F	0127	0.7
	0734	4.6
	1329	1.4
	1935	4.9
28 SA	0214	1.1
	0825	4.4
	1418	1.7
	◐ 2030	4.6
29 SU	0306	1.4
	0921	4.1
	1517	1.9
	2133	4.3
30 M	0407	1.7
	1024	4.0
	1633	2.1
	2246	4.1
31 TU	0520	1.9
	1137	4.0
	1758	2.0

FEBRUARY

Date	Time	m
1 W	0007	4.0
	0636	2.0
	1245	4.1
	1913	1.9
2 TH	0117	4.1
	0737	1.9
	1341	4.3
	2008	1.6
3 F	0210	4.3
	0823	1.8
	1426	4.5
	2052	1.4
4 SA	0253	4.4
	0901	1.6
	1503	4.6
	2128	1.2
5 SU	0329	4.6
	0934	1.5
	1536	4.8
	○ 2202	1.0
6 M	0401	4.7
	1005	1.3
	1606	4.9
	2234	0.9
7 TU	0432	4.7
	1035	1.3
	1636	4.9
	2305	0.9
8 W	0502	4.7
	1104	1.2
	1706	4.9
	2336	0.9
9 TH	0533	4.7
	1134	1.2
	1736	4.9
10 F	0007	0.9
	0606	4.6
	1203	1.3
	1809	4.8
11 SA	0040	1.0
	0640	4.5
	1235	1.4
	1844	4.7
12 SU	0115	1.2
	0718	4.4
	1311	1.6
	1925	4.6
13 M	0155	1.4
	0804	4.2
	1357	1.7
	◑ 2017	4.4
14 TU	0248	1.6
	0902	4.1
	1501	1.9
	2125	4.2
15 W	0403	1.8
	1016	4.0
	1634	2.0
	2253	4.1
16 TH	0531	1.8
	1140	4.1
	1809	1.8
17 F	0024	4.2
	0653	1.7
	1254	4.3
	1927	1.4
18 SA	0136	4.5
	0758	1.4
	1353	4.6
	2029	1.0
19 SU	0233	4.9
	0851	1.1
	1442	5.0
	2121	0.6
20 M	0322	5.1
	0938	0.9
	1527	5.3
	● 2209	0.3
21 TU	0407	5.2
	1021	0.7
	1609	5.4
	2253	0.1
22 W	0450	5.2
	1101	0.7
	1651	5.5
	2335	0.1
23 TH	0532	5.1
	1140	0.8
	1734	5.4
24 F	0014	0.3
	0614	4.9
	1217	0.9
	1817	5.2
25 SA	0053	0.7
	0655	4.7
	1255	1.2
	1902	4.9
26 SU	0131	1.1
	0739	4.4
	1336	1.5
	1952	4.6
27 M	0213	1.5
	0829	4.1
	1427	1.8
	◐ 2051	4.2
28 TU	0308	1.9
	0930	3.9
	1542	2.0
	2207	3.9

MARCH

Date	Time	m
1 W	0429	2.2
	1050	3.8
	1725	2.1
	2342	3.8
2 TH	0609	2.3
	1216	3.9
	1856	1.9
3 F	0102	3.9
	0721	2.1
	1320	4.1
	1952	1.6
4 SA	0156	4.2
	0807	1.8
	1406	4.3
	2033	1.4
5 SU	0235	4.4
	0844	1.6
	1443	4.6
	2108	1.1
6 M	0308	4.5
	0915	1.4
	1514	4.7
	2139	0.9
7 TU	0338	4.7
	0945	1.2
	1543	4.9
	○ 2209	0.8
8 W	0406	4.8
	1013	1.1
	1611	5.0
	2239	0.7
9 TH	0435	4.8
	1041	1.0
	1639	5.0
	2309	0.7
10 F	0504	4.8
	1110	1.0
	1709	5.0
	2339	0.7
11 SA	0534	4.7
	1139	1.0
	1740	4.9
12 SU	0009	0.9
	0607	4.7
	1210	1.2
	1817	4.8
13 M	0042	1.1
	0645	4.5
	1246	1.3
	1859	4.6
14 TU	0121	1.4
	0730	4.3
	1332	1.6
	1954	4.3
15 W	0214	1.7
	0828	4.1
	1439	1.8
	◑ 2109	4.1
16 TH	0336	2.0
	0948	3.9
	1620	1.9
	2248	4.0
17 F	0520	2.0
	1121	4.0
	1803	1.6
18 SA	0023	4.2
	0646	1.8
	1240	4.3
	1921	1.2
19 SU	0130	4.5
	0748	1.4
	1338	4.6
	2018	0.8
20 M	0221	4.9
	0836	1.1
	1425	5.0
	2106	0.4
21 TU	0305	5.1
	0919	0.8
	1508	5.3
	● 2149	0.2
22 W	0346	5.2
	0959	0.6
	1548	5.4
	2230	0.1
23 TH	0424	5.2
	1037	0.6
	1628	5.5
	2308	0.2
24 F	0502	5.1
	1114	0.6
	1708	5.3
	2343	0.5
25 SA	0539	4.9
	1150	0.8
	1750	5.1
26 SU	0017	0.8
	0618	4.7
	1225	1.0
	1833	4.8
27 M	0051	1.2
	0657	4.4
	1305	1.3
	1921	4.4
28 TU	0128	1.7
	0742	4.1
	1352	1.7
	2019	4.0
29 W	0216	2.1
	0840	3.9
	1501	2.0
	◐ 2133	3.7
30 TH	0336	2.4
	0959	3.7
	1644	2.1
	2306	3.7
31 F	0531	2.4
	1132	3.7
	1820	1.9

APRIL

Date	Time	m
1 SA	0032	3.8
	0651	2.2
	1245	4.0
	1919	1.6
2 SU	0126	4.1
	0738	1.9
	1333	4.2
	2000	1.3
3 M	0204	4.3
	0814	1.6
	1410	4.5
	2035	1.1
4 TU	0236	4.5
	0846	1.3
	1442	4.7
	2107	0.9
5 W	0306	4.7
	0916	1.1
	1511	4.8
	2137	0.7
6 TH	0334	4.8
	0945	1.0
	1540	5.0
	○ 2208	0.6
7 F	0404	4.9
	1015	0.9
	1610	5.0
	2239	0.6
8 SA	0434	4.9
	1046	0.9
	1643	5.0
	2311	0.7
9 SU	0506	4.8
	1118	0.9
	1718	4.9
	2344	0.9
10 M	0541	4.7
	1153	1.0
	1759	4.8
11 TU	0019	1.1
	0621	4.6
	1234	1.2
	1849	4.6
12 W	0103	1.4
	0710	4.4
	1327	1.4
	1951	4.3
13 TH	0202	1.8
	0812	4.1
	1442	1.6
	◑ 2114	4.0
14 F	0331	2.0
	0935	4.0
	1622	1.6
	2249	4.0
15 SA	0512	2.0
	1106	4.1
	1754	1.4
16 SU	0012	4.3
	0630	1.7
	1220	4.4
	1903	1.0
17 M	0113	4.6
	0726	1.4
	1317	4.7
	1957	0.7
18 TU	0201	4.8
	0813	1.1
	1403	5.0
	2043	0.4
19 W	0242	5.0
	0855	0.9
	1445	5.2
	2124	0.3
20 TH	0320	5.1
	0934	0.7
	1525	5.3
	● 2202	0.4
21 F	0356	5.1
	1012	0.6
	1605	5.2
	2238	0.5
22 SA	0433	5.0
	1049	0.7
	1645	5.1
	2312	0.8
23 SU	0509	4.9
	1126	0.8
	1727	4.9
	2345	1.1
24 M	0545	4.7
	1203	1.0
	1810	4.6
25 TU	0017	1.4
	0624	4.5
	1242	1.3
	1858	4.3
26 W	0053	1.8
	0707	4.2
	1329	1.6
	1953	4.0
27 TH	0139	2.1
	0801	4.0
	1430	1.8
	◐ 2059	3.8
28 F	0247	2.3
	0911	3.8
	1553	1.9
	2217	3.7
29 SA	0430	2.4
	1033	3.8
	1720	1.8
	2336	3.8
30 SU	0554	2.2
	1149	3.9
	1825	1.6

Chart Datum: 2·60 metres below Ordnance Datum (Newlyn)
HAT is 5·7 metres above Chart Datum

TIME ZONE (UT)
For Summer Time add ONE hour in **non-shaded areas**

NORTH SHIELDS

LAT 55°00'N LONG 1°26'W

TIMES AND HEIGHTS OF HIGH AND LOW WATERS

Dates in amber are **SPRINGS**
Dates in grey are **NEAPS**

2023

MAY

Date	Day	Time	m
1	M	0036 0650 1244 1912	4.0 1.9 4.1 1.4
2	TU	0120 0731 1326 1951	4.2 1.7 4.4 1.1
3	W	0155 0807 1402 2027	4.4 1.4 4.6 0.9
4	TH	0228 0841 1435 2101	4.6 1.2 4.7 0.8
5	F	0300 0914 1509 ○ 2136	4.8 1.0 4.9 0.7
6	SA	0333 0949 1544 2211	4.9 0.9 5.0 0.7
7	SU	0406 1025 1623 2247	4.9 0.8 5.0 0.8
8	M	0443 1104 1706 2326	4.9 0.8 4.9 1.0
9	TU	0523 1147 1754	4.8 0.9 4.8
10	W	0008 0609 1235 1850	1.2 4.7 1.0 4.5
11	TH	0059 0702 1335 1957	1.5 4.5 1.2 4.3
12	F	0203 0807 1449 ◑ 2115	1.8 4.3 1.3 4.2
13	SA	0325 0924 1614 2236	1.9 4.2 1.3 4.2
14	SU	0450 1043 1731 2348	1.9 4.3 1.1 4.3
15	M	0559 1153 1835	1.7 4.5 0.9
16	TU	0046 0656 1250 1929	4.5 1.4 4.7 0.8
17	W	0134 0745 1338 2015	4.7 1.2 4.8 0.7
18	TH	0216 0829 1422 2056	4.8 1.0 5.0 0.7
19	F	0255 0911 1505 ● 2134	4.9 0.9 5.0 0.8
20	SA	0331 0951 1547 2210	4.9 0.8 5.0 0.9
21	SU	0408 1030 1628 2245	4.9 0.8 4.8 1.1
22	M	0444 1108 1711 2318	4.8 0.9 4.7 1.3
23	TU	0521 1146 1753 2352	4.7 1.1 4.5 1.5
24	W	0559 1226 1838	4.5 1.2 4.3
25	TH	0028 0641 1309 1928	1.7 4.4 1.4 4.1
26	F	0111 0730 1401 2023	2.0 4.2 1.6 3.9
27	SA	0206 0828 1503 ◐ 2124	2.1 4.0 1.7 3.8
28	SU	0319 0933 1613 2229	2.2 3.9 1.7 3.8
29	M	0438 1039 1718 2331	2.2 4.0 1.6 3.9
30	TU	0544 1140 1813	2.0 4.1 1.5
31	W	0024 0637 1232 1901	4.1 1.8 4.3 1.3

JUNE

Date	Day	Time	m
1	TH	0109 0722 1318 1944	4.3 1.6 4.5 1.1
2	F	0149 0804 1400 2026	4.5 1.3 4.6 1.0
3	SA	0228 0845 1442 2107	4.7 1.1 4.8 0.9
4	SU	0306 0927 1526 ○ 2149	4.9 0.9 4.9 0.8
5	M	0345 1011 1612 2232	4.9 0.8 5.0 0.9
6	TU	0427 1058 1701 2318	5.0 0.7 4.9 1.0
7	W	0512 1147 1754	4.9 0.7 4.8
8	TH	0005 0602 1239 1852	1.2 4.8 0.8 4.7
9	F	0057 0656 1338 1955	1.4 4.7 0.9 4.5
10	SA	0156 0757 1442 ◑ 2101	1.6 4.6 1.0 4.4
11	SU	0303 0904 1551 2208	1.7 4.5 1.1 4.3
12	M	0414 1013 1658 2314	1.8 4.5 1.1 4.3
13	TU	0521 1120 1801	1.7 4.5 1.1
14	W	0013 0623 1221 1858	4.4 1.6 4.6 1.1
15	TH	0106 0718 1317 1948	4.5 1.4 4.6 1.1
16	F	0152 0809 1406 2032	4.6 1.2 4.7 1.1
17	SA	0234 0855 1452 2112	4.7 1.1 4.7 1.2
18	SU	0313 0937 1536 ● 2150	4.8 1.0 4.7 1.2
19	M	0350 1017 1617 2225	4.8 1.0 4.7 1.3
20	TU	0427 1056 1657 2259	4.8 1.0 4.6 1.4
21	W	0503 1133 1737 2333	4.7 1.0 4.5 1.5
22	TH	0539 1210 1816	4.6 1.1 4.4
23	F	0008 0618 1248 1859	1.6 4.5 1.2 4.2
24	SA	0046 0700 1331 1944	1.7 4.4 1.3 4.1
25	SU	0129 0746 1418 2033	1.9 4.3 1.5 4.0
26	M	0219 0838 1512 ◐ 2127	2.0 4.2 1.6 3.9
27	TU	0320 0934 1611 2225	2.1 4.1 1.6 4.0
28	W	0429 1034 1712 2325	2.1 4.1 1.6 4.1
29	TH	0536 1136 1810	1.9 4.2 1.5
30	F	0021 0636 1236 1905	4.2 1.7 4.3 1.3

JULY

Date	Day	Time	m
1	SA	0113 0731 1332 1957	4.4 1.5 4.5 1.2
2	SU	0201 0823 1425 2047	4.6 1.2 4.7 1.1
3	M	0246 0914 1515 ○ 2136	4.8 0.9 4.9 1.0
4	TU	0331 1004 1605 2224	5.0 0.7 5.0 0.9
5	W	0416 1054 1656 2311	5.1 0.5 5.1 1.0
6	TH	0502 1144 1748 2358	5.1 0.4 5.0 1.0
7	F	0551 1234 1841	5.1 0.4 4.9
8	SA	0045 0642 1326 1936	1.2 5.1 0.6 4.7
9	SU	0135 0737 1420 2033	1.4 4.9 0.8 4.5
10	M	0229 0835 1517 ◑ 2131	1.5 4.7 1.0 4.3
11	TU	0331 0938 1619 2234	1.7 4.6 1.3 4.2
12	W	0439 1046 1724 2338	1.8 4.4 1.4 4.2
13	TH	0550 1156 1828	1.8 4.3 1.5
14	F	0039 0659 1302 1928	4.3 1.6 4.3 1.6
15	SA	0133 0757 1359 2017	4.4 1.5 4.4 1.5
16	SU	0220 0846 1447 2059	4.5 1.3 4.5 1.5
17	M	0301 0929 1529 ● 2136	4.7 1.1 4.6 1.4
18	TU	0337 1007 1606 2211	4.8 1.0 4.6 1.4
19	W	0412 1042 1642 2243	4.8 1.0 4.6 1.4
20	TH	0445 1115 1716 2314	4.8 0.9 4.6 1.4
21	F	0517 1149 1750 2346	4.8 1.0 4.5 1.4
22	SA	0551 1222 1825	4.8 1.0 4.4
23	SU	0018 0627 1258 1903	1.5 4.7 1.1 4.3
24	M	0053 0705 1336 1943	1.6 4.6 1.3 4.2
25	TU	0132 0747 1419 ◐ 2030	1.7 4.4 1.4 4.1
26	W	0219 0837 1511 2125	1.9 4.3 1.6 4.0
27	TH	0321 0937 1615 2229	2.0 4.2 1.7 4.0
28	F	0440 1049 1727 2338	2.0 4.1 1.7 4.1
29	SA	0559 1207 1836	1.9 4.2 1.6
30	SU	0044 0709 1317 1940	4.3 1.6 4.4 1.4
31	M	0141 0811 1416 2035	4.6 1.2 4.7 1.2

AUGUST

Date	Day	Time	m
1	TU	0231 0905 1508 ○ 2126	4.9 0.8 5.0 1.0
2	W	0317 0956 1557 2213	5.1 0.5 5.2 0.9
3	TH	0402 1045 1644 2258	5.3 0.2 5.2 0.8
4	F	0447 1131 1731 2341	5.4 0.2 5.2 0.8
5	SA	0532 1217 1818	5.4 0.2 5.0
6	SU	0023 0619 1301 1907	1.0 5.3 0.4 4.8
7	M	0106 0709 1347 1956	1.1 5.1 0.8 4.6
8	TU	0152 0802 1436 ◑ 2050	1.4 4.8 1.2 4.3
9	W	0247 0903 1534 2151	1.7 4.5 1.6 4.1
10	TH	0359 1014 1645 2302	1.9 4.2 1.9 4.0
11	F	0524 1137 1805	1.9 4.1 2.0
12	SA	0016 0648 1255 1916	4.1 1.8 4.1 1.9
13	SU	0119 0751 1354 2008	4.3 1.6 4.3 1.8
14	M	0207 0838 1439 2048	4.5 1.3 4.4 1.6
15	TU	0247 0916 1516 2122	4.7 1.1 4.6 1.5
16	W	0321 0950 1549 ● 2153	4.8 1.0 4.7 1.3
17	TH	0352 1021 1619 2222	4.9 0.9 4.7 1.2
18	F	0422 1051 1649 2251	5.0 0.8 4.7 1.2
19	SA	0451 1121 1719 2320	5.0 0.8 4.7 1.2
20	SU	0522 1152 1750 2349	4.9 0.9 4.6 1.3
21	M	0553 1223 1822	4.9 1.0 4.5
22	TU	0020 0627 1256 1859	1.4 4.7 1.2 4.4
23	W	0054 0705 1333 1941	1.5 4.6 1.4 4.3
24	TH	0136 0753 1420 ◐ 2034	1.7 4.4 1.7 4.1
25	F	0234 0857 1528 2143	1.9 4.2 1.9 4.0
26	SA	0400 1021 1657 2306	2.0 4.0 2.0 4.0
27	SU	0538 1155 1822	1.9 4.1 1.8
28	M	0025 0659 1311 1930	4.3 1.5 4.5 1.6
29	TU	0126 0802 1408 2024	4.6 1.1 4.8 1.2
30	W	0216 0854 1456 2112	5.0 0.6 5.1 1.0
31	TH	0300 0942 1541 ○ 2155	5.3 0.3 5.3 0.8

Chart Datum: 2·60 metres below Ordnance Datum (Newlyn)
HAT is 5·7 metres above Chart Datum

TIME ZONE (UT)
For Summer Time add ONE hour in **non-shaded areas**

NORTH SHIELDS

LAT 55°00'N LONG 1°26'W

TIMES AND HEIGHTS OF HIGH AND LOW WATERS

Dates in amber are **SPRINGS**
Dates in grey are **NEAPS**

2023

SEPTEMBER

Date	Day	Time	m	Time	m	Time	m	Time	m
1	F	0343	5.5	1026	0.1	1624	5.4	2236	0.7
2	SA	0425	5.6	1109	0.1	1706	5.3	2316	0.7
3	SU	0508	5.6	1150	0.2	1748	5.1	2355	0.8
4	M	0552	5.4	1230	0.5	1830	4.9		
5	TU	0035	1.0	0638	5.1	1309	1.0	1915	4.6
6	W	0117	1.3	0730	4.7	1352	1.5	◑ 2006	4.3
7	TH	0209	1.7	0830	4.3	1446	1.9	2107	4.1
8	F	0323	2.0	0946	4.0	1605	2.2	2224	3.9
9	SA	0504	2.1	1120	3.9	1747	2.3	2351	4.0
10	SU	0637	1.9	1245	4.0	1903	2.1		
11	M	0059	4.2	0736	1.6	1340	4.2	1951	1.9
12	TU	0148	4.5	0818	1.3	1420	4.4	2028	1.7
13	W	0225	4.7	0852	1.1	1453	4.6	2059	1.5
14	TH	0257	4.8	0923	0.9	1522	4.8	2129	1.3
15	F	0326	5.0	0953	0.8	1550	4.8	● 2157	1.2
16	SA	0354	5.1	1021	0.7	1618	4.9	2224	1.1
17	SU	0422	5.1	1050	0.8	1646	4.9	2252	1.1
18	M	0451	5.1	1120	0.8	1715	4.8	2321	1.2
19	TU	0522	5.0	1149	1.0	1747	4.7	2352	1.3
20	W	0555	4.8	1220	1.2	1821	4.6		
21	TH	0026	1.4	0636	4.6	1256	1.5	1904	4.4
22	F	0109	1.7	0728	4.4	1344	1.8	◐ 1959	4.2
23	SA	0211	1.9	0839	4.1	1459	2.1	2114	4.0
24	SU	0346	2.0	1014	4.0	1643	2.2	2246	4.1
25	M	0530	1.8	1151	4.2	1813	1.9		
26	TU	0008	4.3	0649	1.4	1301	4.6	1917	1.6
27	W	0108	4.7	0747	0.9	1353	4.9	2007	1.2
28	TH	0156	5.1	0836	0.5	1438	5.2	2051	1.0
29	F	0239	5.4	0920	0.2	1518	5.3	○ 2132	0.7
30	SA	0320	5.6	1002	0.1	1557	5.4	2211	0.6

OCTOBER

Date	Day	Time	m	Time	m	Time	m	Time	m
1	SU	0400	5.7	1042	0.2	1636	5.3	2250	0.7
2	M	0442	5.6	1119	0.5	1715	5.1	2328	0.8
3	TU	0525	5.3	1156	0.8	1754	4.9		
4	W	0007	1.0	0612	5.0	1232	1.3	1836	4.6
5	TH	0049	1.4	0702	4.6	1311	1.7	1924	4.4
6	F	0140	1.7	0803	4.2	1400	2.2	◑ 2023	4.1
7	SA	0250	2.0	0919	3.9	1520	2.5	2142	3.9
8	SU	0433	2.1	1050	3.8	1715	2.5	2313	3.9
9	M	0606	1.9	1216	4.0	1833	2.3		
10	TU	0026	4.1	0703	1.7	1310	4.2	1921	2.0
11	W	0115	4.4	0744	1.4	1349	4.4	1957	1.7
12	TH	0153	4.6	0818	1.2	1421	4.6	2028	1.5
13	F	0225	4.8	0849	1.0	1450	4.8	2058	1.3
14	SA	0254	5.0	0919	0.9	1518	4.9	● 2127	1.2
15	SU	0323	5.1	0949	0.8	1546	5.0	2156	1.1
16	M	0352	5.1	1018	0.8	1615	5.0	2227	1.1
17	TU	0423	5.1	1049	0.9	1645	5.0	2258	1.1
18	W	0457	5.0	1120	1.1	1718	4.9	2332	1.2
19	TH	0536	4.8	1154	1.3	1756	4.7		
20	F	0011	1.4	0622	4.6	1234	1.6	1842	4.5
21	SA	0101	1.6	0721	4.4	1328	1.9	1940	4.3
22	SU	0210	1.8	0838	4.1	1449	2.2	◐ 2057	4.1
23	M	0343	1.8	1011	4.1	1631	2.2	2227	4.2
24	TU	0517	1.6	1137	4.3	1753	2.0	2345	4.5
25	W	0628	1.2	1242	4.6	1853	1.6		
26	TH	0044	4.8	0724	0.9	1331	4.9	1942	1.3
27	F	0132	5.1	0812	0.6	1414	5.1	2025	1.0
28	SA	0215	5.4	0855	0.4	1453	5.2	○ 2107	0.8
29	SU	0257	5.5	0935	0.4	1531	5.3	2147	0.8
30	M	0339	5.5	1013	0.6	1608	5.2	2227	0.8
31	TU	0421	5.3	1050	0.8	1646	5.1	2307	0.9

NOVEMBER

Date	Day	Time	m	Time	m	Time	m	Time	m
1	W	0505	5.1	1125	1.2	1724	4.9	2347	1.1
2	TH	0551	4.8	1201	1.5	1805	4.7		
3	F	0029	1.4	0641	4.5	1237	1.9	1850	4.4
4	SA	0117	1.6	0738	4.2	1323	2.2	1945	4.2
5	SU	0219	1.9	0845	3.9	1430	2.5	◑ 2055	4.0
6	M	0341	2.0	1001	3.8	1610	2.6	2214	4.0
7	TU	0505	1.9	1119	3.9	1735	2.4	2330	4.1
8	W	0609	1.8	1221	4.1	1831	2.2		
9	TH	0027	4.3	0656	1.5	1305	4.3	1914	1.9
10	F	0110	4.5	0735	1.3	1341	4.5	1951	1.6
11	SA	0147	4.7	0810	1.2	1413	4.7	2024	1.4
12	SU	0220	4.8	0843	1.0	1445	4.9	2057	1.3
13	M	0253	5.0	0916	1.0	1516	5.0	● 2131	1.2
14	TU	0327	5.0	0950	1.0	1548	5.0	2206	1.1
15	W	0404	5.0	1025	1.0	1622	5.0	2243	1.1
16	TH	0444	5.0	1102	1.2	1659	4.9	2324	1.1
17	F	0529	4.8	1142	1.4	1741	4.8		
18	SA	0010	1.2	0621	4.7	1228	1.6	1831	4.7
19	SU	0105	1.4	0722	4.5	1325	1.9	1930	4.5
20	M	0212	1.5	0836	4.3	1439	2.1	◐ 2042	4.4
21	TU	0332	1.5	0955	4.3	1604	2.1	2200	4.4
22	W	0451	1.4	1109	4.4	1719	1.9	2313	4.6
23	TH	0558	1.2	1212	4.6	1820	1.7		
24	F	0014	4.8	0656	1.0	1304	4.7	1913	1.5
25	SA	0107	5.0	0745	0.9	1349	4.9	2001	1.2
26	SU	0155	5.1	0830	0.8	1430	5.0	2046	1.1
27	M	0240	5.2	0911	0.9	1509	5.1	○ 2129	1.0
28	TU	0324	5.1	0950	1.0	1547	5.1	2211	0.9
29	W	0408	5.0	1027	1.2	1625	5.0	2253	1.0
30	TH	0452	4.9	1103	1.4	1703	4.9	2333	1.1

DECEMBER

Date	Day	Time	m	Time	m	Time	m	Time	m
1	F	0537	4.7	1138	1.6	1742	4.8		
2	SA	0013	1.3	0623	4.5	1213	1.9	1824	4.6
3	SU	0057	1.5	0711	4.2	1254	2.1	1911	4.4
4	M	0146	1.7	0804	4.1	1344	2.3	2007	4.2
5	TU	0244	1.8	0904	3.9	1450	2.4	◑ 2110	4.1
6	W	0351	1.9	1007	3.9	1610	2.4	2216	4.1
7	TH	0456	1.8	1111	4.0	1721	2.3	2320	4.2
8	F	0554	1.7	1207	4.1	1818	2.1		
9	SA	0016	4.3	0644	1.6	1254	4.3	1907	1.9
10	SU	0104	4.5	0728	1.4	1335	4.5	1949	1.6
11	M	0147	4.6	0809	1.3	1414	4.7	2030	1.4
12	TU	0229	4.8	0849	1.2	1450	4.9	● 2111	1.2
13	W	0310	4.9	0929	1.1	1528	5.0	2153	1.1
14	TH	0353	5.0	1011	1.1	1607	5.0	2237	1.0
15	F	0439	5.0	1053	1.2	1648	5.1	2323	0.9
16	SA	0527	4.9	1138	1.3	1734	5.0		
17	SU	0012	0.9	0620	4.8	1225	1.5	1823	4.9
18	M	0105	1.0	0717	4.6	1318	1.7	1918	4.8
19	TU	0203	1.1	0820	4.5	1417	1.8	◐ 2020	4.7
20	W	0308	1.2	0925	4.4	1525	1.9	2127	4.6
21	TH	0415	1.3	1031	4.3	1636	1.9	2236	4.6
22	F	0521	1.3	1136	4.4	1743	1.8	2344	4.6
23	SA	0624	1.3	1235	4.5	1846	1.7		
24	SU	0047	4.7	0721	1.3	1327	4.6	1944	1.5
25	M	0143	4.7	0811	1.3	1413	4.7	2035	1.3
26	TU	0233	4.8	0855	1.3	1455	4.9	2121	1.1
27	W	0319	4.8	0936	1.3	1534	4.9	○ 2204	1.0
28	TH	0402	4.8	1013	1.4	1612	4.9	2244	1.0
29	F	0443	4.7	1048	1.5	1648	4.9	2322	1.1
30	SA	0522	4.7	1121	1.5	1724	4.8	2358	1.1
31	SU	0600	4.5	1154	1.6	1801	4.7		

Chart Datum: 2·60 metres below Ordnance Datum (Newlyn)
HAT is 5·7 metres above Chart Datum

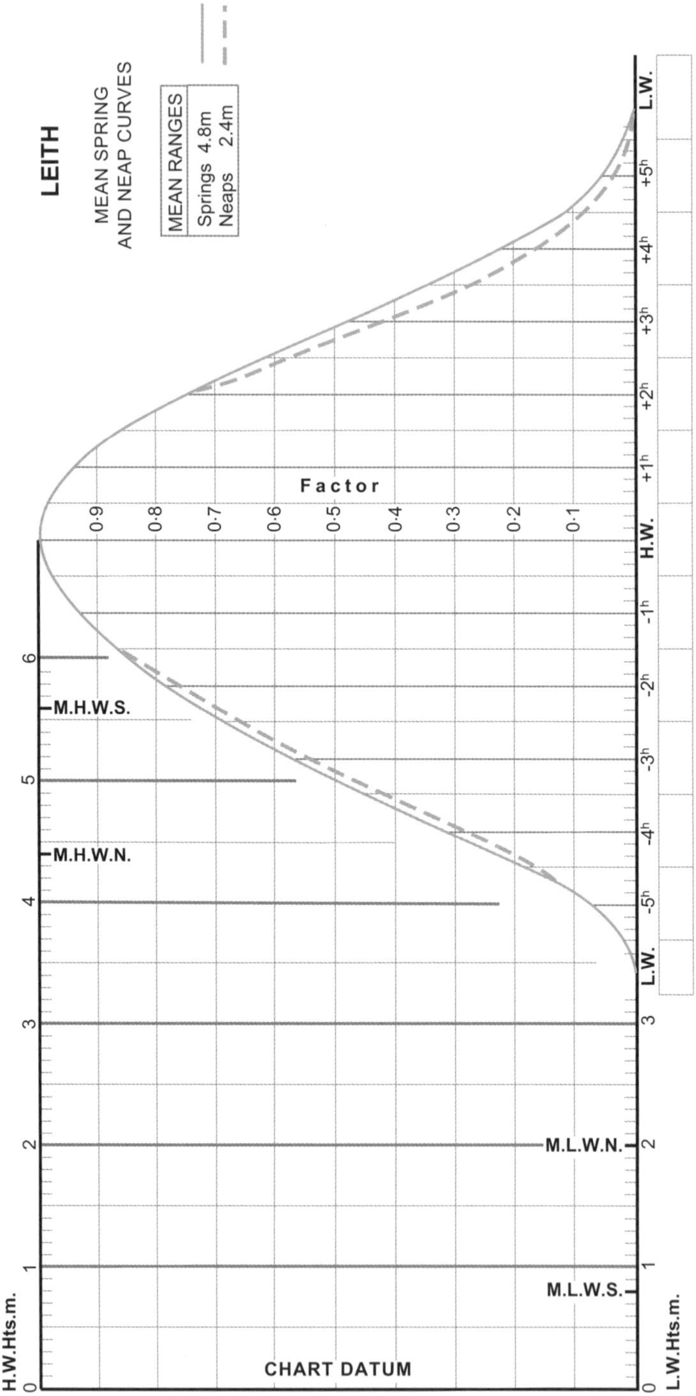
LEITH
MEAN SPRING
AND NEAP CURVES
MEAN RANGES
Springs 4.8m
Neaps 2.4m
Factor
0·9
0·8
0·7
0·6
0·5
0·4
0·3
0·2
0·1
L.W.
-5h
-4h
-3h
-2h
-1h
H.W.
+1h
+2h
+3h
+4h
+5h
L.W.
M.H.W.S.
M.H.W.N.
M.L.W.N.
M.L.W.S.
CHART DATUM
H.W.Hts.m.
L.W.Hts.m.
0
1
2
3
4
5
6

TIME ZONE (UT)
For Summer Time add ONE hour in **non-shaded areas**

SCOTLAND – LEITH

LAT 55°59′N LONG 3°11′W

TIMES AND HEIGHTS OF HIGH AND LOW WATERS

Dates in amber are **SPRINGS**
Dates in grey are **NEAPS**

2023

JANUARY

Date	Day	Time	m	Time	m	Time	m	Time	m	Moon
1	SU	0355	1.7	1015	4.7	1602	2.1	2236	4.8	
2	M	0502	1.8	1116	4.7	1707	2.0	2338	4.8	
3	TU	0559	1.8	1214	4.8	1807	1.8			
4	W	0036	4.9	0644	1.7	1305	4.9	1859	1.6	
5	TH	0127	4.9	0720	1.7	1349	5.1	1943	1.4	
6	F	0211	5.0	0752	1.6	1428	5.2	2021	1.3	○
7	SA	0249	5.1	0824	1.5	1504	5.2	2056	1.2	
8	SU	0325	5.1	0855	1.5	1537	5.2	2128	1.2	
9	M	0358	5.1	0927	1.5	1609	5.2	2201	1.2	
10	TU	0432	5.1	1000	1.5	1642	5.2	2234	1.2	
11	W	0508	5.0	1032	1.6	1717	5.1	2309	1.3	
12	TH	0546	4.9	1104	1.7	1753	5.0	2345	1.4	
13	F	0627	4.8	1135	1.9	1832	4.9			
14	SA	0022	1.5	0712	4.7	1212	2.0	1917	4.7	
15	SU	0107	1.7	0802	4.6	1306	2.2	2011	4.6	◑
16	M	0204	1.8	0901	4.5	1426	2.3	2119	4.6	
17	TU	0320	1.9	1007	4.5	1558	2.2	2235	4.6	
18	W	0444	1.8	1114	4.7	1715	1.9	2347	4.8	
19	TH	0554	1.6	1217	4.9	1820	1.6			
20	F	0050	5.1	0655	1.4	1313	5.2	1922	1.2	
21	SA	0146	5.4	0751	1.2	1402	5.5	2021	0.8	●
22	SU	0236	5.7	0843	1.0	1449	5.7	2116	0.5	
23	M	0324	5.8	0932	0.9	1536	5.8	2206	0.3	
24	TU	0412	5.8	1017	0.8	1622	5.9	2252	0.3	
25	W	0500	5.7	1100	0.9	1710	5.8	2336	0.4	
26	TH	0548	5.5	1139	1.1	1759	5.6			
27	F	0017	0.8	0639	5.2	1214	1.4	1852	5.3	
28	SA	0055	1.2	0732	4.9	1253	1.7	1949	5.0	◐
29	SU	0136	1.6	0829	4.6	1347	2.0	2052	4.7	
30	M	0235	2.0	0928	4.4	1507	2.2	2157	4.5	
31	TU	0406	2.2	1033	4.4	1638	2.2	2308	4.4	

FEBRUARY

Date	Day	Time	m	Time	m	Time	m	Time	m	Moon
1	W	0528	2.2	1145	4.5	1755	2.0			
2	TH	0020	4.5	0626	2.1	1249	4.7	1855	1.8	
3	F	0118	4.7	0707	1.9	1338	4.9	1939	1.5	
4	SA	0202	4.9	0740	1.7	1417	5.0	2014	1.3	
5	SU	0238	5.0	0811	1.5	1451	5.2	2046	1.1	○
6	M	0310	5.1	0843	1.4	1522	5.3	2116	1.0	
7	TU	0340	5.2	0915	1.3	1552	5.3	2148	0.9	
8	W	0411	5.2	0947	1.2	1623	5.3	2220	0.9	
9	TH	0444	5.2	1016	1.2	1653	5.3	2249	1.0	
10	F	0518	5.1	1040	1.3	1725	5.2	2315	1.1	
11	SA	0554	5.0	1100	1.5	1800	5.1	2339	1.3	
12	SU	0634	4.8	1129	1.6	1840	4.9			
13	M	0010	1.5	0719	4.7	1211	1.8	1929	4.7	◑
14	TU	0059	1.8	0813	4.5	1314	2.1	2034	4.5	
15	W	0216	2.0	0922	4.4	1501	2.2	2203	4.5	
16	TH	0420	2.1	1043	4.5	1702	2.0	2330	4.7	
17	F	0547	1.9	1158	4.7	1819	1.6			
18	SA	0041	5.0	0651	1.5	1300	5.1	1924	1.1	
19	SU	0137	5.4	0744	1.2	1350	5.4	2018	0.6	
20	M	0225	5.7	0832	0.9	1435	5.7	2107	0.2	●
21	TU	0309	5.8	0916	0.7	1519	5.9	2151	0.1	
22	W	0353	5.9	0957	0.6	1603	6.0	2232	0.1	
23	TH	0437	5.7	1036	0.6	1647	5.9	2310	0.3	
24	F	0520	5.5	1109	0.9	1732	5.7	2343	0.7	
25	SA	0605	5.2	1136	1.2	1819	5.3			
26	SU	0006	1.2	0651	4.9	1205	1.5	1911	5.0	
27	M	0032	1.7	0742	4.5	1251	1.9	2010	4.6	◐
28	TU	0120	2.1	0840	4.3	1407	2.2	2116	4.3	

MARCH

Date	Day	Time	m	Time	m	Time	m	Time	m	Moon
1	W	0251	2.5	0947	4.2	1616	2.3	2233	4.2	
2	TH	0503	2.5	1108	4.2	1750	2.1			
3	F	0003	4.3	0613	2.3	1229	4.4	1848	1.8	
4	SA	0105	4.6	0654	2.0	1320	4.7	1927	1.5	
5	SU	0146	4.8	0726	1.7	1358	5.0	1959	1.2	
6	M	0218	5.0	0755	1.5	1430	5.2	2028	1.0	
7	TU	0247	5.1	0826	1.2	1500	5.3	2057	0.8	○
8	W	0315	5.2	0858	1.1	1529	5.4	2127	0.7	
9	TH	0345	5.3	0928	1.0	1558	5.4	2157	0.7	
10	F	0416	5.3	0955	1.0	1627	5.4	2224	0.8	
11	SA	0449	5.2	1013	1.1	1659	5.3	2243	0.9	
12	SU	0524	5.1	1032	1.2	1735	5.2	2301	1.2	
13	M	0602	5.0	1101	1.3	1817	5.0	2332	1.4	
14	TU	0646	4.7	1143	1.6	1908	4.8			
15	W	0021	1.8	0739	4.5	1246	1.9	2015	4.5	◑
16	TH	0151	2.2	0851	4.3	1458	2.1	2149	4.4	
17	F	0420	2.2	1023	4.4	1705	1.8	2321	4.6	
18	SA	0540	1.9	1144	4.7	1819	1.4			
19	SU	0031	5.0	0639	1.5	1245	5.1	1916	0.9	
20	M	0124	5.4	0727	1.1	1333	5.5	2005	0.5	
21	TU	0207	5.6	0811	0.8	1415	5.8	2048	0.2	●
22	W	0248	5.8	0853	0.5	1457	5.9	2128	0.1	
23	TH	0329	5.8	0933	0.5	1540	6.0	2206	0.2	
24	F	0410	5.6	1009	0.5	1623	5.8	2240	0.5	
25	SA	0451	5.4	1041	0.8	1706	5.6	2306	0.9	
26	SU	0532	5.2	1105	1.1	1751	5.2	2321	1.3	
27	M	0614	4.8	1131	1.4	1838	4.8	2346	1.8	
28	TU	0700	4.5	1212	1.8	1933	4.5			
29	W	0030	2.2	0756	4.3	1321	2.2	2037	4.2	◐
30	TH	0152	2.6	0903	4.1	1554	2.3	2149	4.0	
31	F	0429	2.6	1021	4.1	1723	2.1	2326	4.1	

APRIL

Date	Day	Time	m	Time	m	Time	m	Time	m	Moon
1	SA	0538	2.4	1150	4.3	1815	1.8			
2	SU	0035	4.4	0621	2.0	1246	4.6	1855	1.5	
3	M	0114	4.7	0655	1.7	1324	4.9	1927	1.2	
4	TU	0146	4.9	0727	1.4	1357	5.1	1957	1.0	
5	W	0215	5.1	0759	1.2	1428	5.3	2027	0.8	
6	TH	0244	5.3	0832	1.0	1459	5.4	2059	0.7	○
7	F	0315	5.3	0903	0.9	1529	5.4	2129	0.6	
8	SA	0348	5.4	0930	0.9	1602	5.4	2156	0.7	
9	SU	0422	5.3	0952	0.9	1638	5.4	2216	0.9	
10	M	0458	5.2	1014	1.1	1718	5.2	2238	1.2	
11	TU	0538	5.0	1048	1.2	1804	5.0	2314	1.6	
12	W	0624	4.8	1137	1.5	1900	4.8			
13	TH	0015	2.0	0721	4.5	1302	1.8	2012	4.5	◑
14	F	0219	2.3	0838	4.4	1522	1.9	2143	4.5	
15	SA	0409	2.2	1009	4.5	1657	1.5	2307	4.7	
16	SU	0519	1.9	1125	4.8	1802	1.1			
17	M	0012	5.0	0613	1.5	1222	5.1	1856	0.8	
18	TU	0102	5.3	0659	1.1	1309	5.4	1941	0.5	
19	W	0144	5.5	0743	0.8	1352	5.7	2022	0.3	
20	TH	0224	5.6	0826	0.6	1434	5.8	2101	0.3	●
21	F	0303	5.6	0906	0.5	1517	5.7	2137	0.5	
22	SA	0343	5.5	0944	0.6	1600	5.6	2208	0.8	
23	SU	0423	5.3	1017	0.8	1644	5.4	2230	1.1	
24	M	0503	5.1	1043	1.1	1727	5.1	2246	1.5	
25	TU	0542	4.8	1109	1.4	1812	4.8	2314	1.9	
26	W	0626	4.6	1150	1.7	1902	4.5	2359	2.2	
27	TH	0718	4.3	1250	2.0	1959	4.2			◐
28	F	0110	2.5	0822	4.2	1441	2.2	2103	4.1	
29	SA	0325	2.6	0932	4.1	1631	2.0	2215	4.1	
30	SU	0444	2.4	1046	4.2	1724	1.8	2330	4.3	

Chart Datum: 2·90 metres below Ordnance Datum (Newlyn)
HAT is 6·3 metres above Chart Datum

TIME ZONE (UT)
For Summer Time add ONE hour in **non-shaded areas**

SCOTLAND – LEITH

LAT 55°59′N LONG 3°11′W

TIMES AND HEIGHTS OF HIGH AND LOW WATERS

Dates in amber are **SPRINGS**
Dates in grey are **NEAPS**

2023

MAY

Date	Time	m	Date	Time	m
1 M	0532 1151 1806	2.1 4.5 1.5	16 TU	0538 1156 1826	1.5 5.1 0.9
2 TU	0021 0612 1237 1842	4.6 1.8 4.7 1.3	17 W	0035 0627 1245 1912	5.2 1.2 5.3 0.8
3 W	0100 0649 1316 1916	4.9 1.5 5.0 1.0	18 TH	0119 0714 1331 1954	5.3 1.0 5.4 0.7
4 TH	0136 0724 1351 1950	5.1 1.2 5.2 0.9	19 F	0200 0800 1415 ● 2032	5.4 0.8 5.5 0.8
5 F	0210 0759 1427 ○ 2024	5.3 1.0 5.3 0.8	20 SA	0240 0843 1459 2107	5.4 0.8 5.4 0.9
6 SA	0245 0834 1503 2059	5.4 0.9 5.4 0.7	21 SU	0321 0922 1542 2137	5.3 0.8 5.3 1.1
7 SU	0321 0909 1541 2133	5.4 0.8 5.5 0.8	22 M	0400 0957 1625 2200	5.2 1.0 5.2 1.4
8 M	0358 0944 1622 2208	5.4 0.9 5.4 1.1	23 TU	0438 1027 1706 2224	5.1 1.2 5.0 1.6
9 TU	0438 1022 1708 2246	5.3 1.0 5.3 1.3	24 W	0517 1057 1748 2256	4.9 1.4 4.8 1.8
10 W	0522 1111 1759 2339	5.1 1.2 5.1 1.7	25 TH	0558 1136 1833 2339	4.7 1.6 4.6 2.1
11 TH	0612 1217 1858	4.9 1.4 4.8	26 F	0646 1226 1923	4.5 1.8 4.4
12 F	0053 0714 1339 ◑ 2011	2.0 4.7 1.5 4.7	27 SA	0037 0741 1330 ◐ 2018	2.3 4.4 1.9 4.3
13 SA	0219 0831 1514 2130	2.1 4.6 1.5 4.7	28 SU	0156 0842 1500 2117	2.4 4.3 2.0 4.2
14 SU	0341 0951 1631 2243	2.0 4.7 1.3 4.8	29 M	0329 0945 1615 2218	2.4 4.3 1.8 4.3
15 M	0444 1059 1733 2345	1.8 4.9 1.1 5.0	30 TU	0432 1046 1706 2317	2.2 4.4 1.6 4.5
			31 W	0521 1142 1749	1.9 4.6 1.4

JUNE

Date	Time	m	Date	Time	m
1 TH	0009 0605 1231 1831	4.8 1.6 4.9 1.2	16 F	0056 0650 1314 1925	5.0 1.3 5.1 1.2
2 F	0055 0646 1316 1911	5.0 1.4 5.1 1.1	17 SA	0141 0740 1402 2004	5.1 1.1 5.2 1.2
3 SA	0137 0727 1359 1953	5.2 1.2 5.3 1.0	18 SU	0224 0825 1446 ● 2039	5.2 1.0 5.2 1.3
4 SU	0218 0811 1441 ○ 2037	5.3 1.0 5.4 0.9	19 M	0304 0905 1528 2110	5.2 1.0 5.1 1.4
5 M	0258 0858 1526 2123	5.4 0.8 5.5 1.0	20 TU	0343 0940 1608 2139	5.1 1.1 5.1 1.5
6 TU	0340 0948 1612 2211	5.4 0.8 5.5 1.1	21 W	0419 1012 1646 2209	5.1 1.1 5.0 1.5
7 W	0425 1040 1701 2301	5.4 0.8 5.4 1.3	22 TH	0456 1044 1724 2242	5.0 1.2 4.9 1.7
8 TH	0513 1133 1754 2354	5.3 0.9 5.3 1.5	23 F	0534 1120 1804 2320	4.9 1.3 4.7 1.8
9 F	0606 1231 1853	5.2 1.0 5.1	24 SA	0615 1201 1847	4.8 1.5 4.6
10 SA	0050 0706 1334 ◑ 1959	1.7 5.0 1.2 4.9	25 SU	0003 0701 1248 1935	2.0 4.6 1.6 4.5
11 SU	0154 0816 1444 2106	1.8 4.9 1.2 4.8	26 M	0057 0750 1343 ◐ 2027	2.1 4.5 1.7 4.4
12 M	0301 0925 1554 2211	1.9 4.9 1.3 4.8	27 TU	0204 0847 1447 2123	2.2 4.5 1.8 4.4
13 TU	0404 1029 1657 2312	1.8 4.9 1.3 4.9	28 W	0318 0948 1555 2223	2.2 4.5 1.8 4.5
14 W	0502 1128 1753	1.6 5.0 1.3	29 TH	0425 1050 1656 2323	2.1 4.6 1.6 4.7
15 TH	0006 0558 1223 1843	4.9 1.5 5.1 1.2	30 F	0522 1150 1751	1.8 4.7 1.5

JULY

Date	Time	m	Date	Time	m
1 SA	0018 0614 1246 1843	4.9 1.6 5.0 1.3	16 SU	0129 0731 1355 1943	5.0 1.4 4.9 1.6
2 SU	0109 0706 1338 1934	5.1 1.3 5.2 1.2	17 M	0213 0815 1438 ● 2017	5.1 1.2 5.0 1.5
3 M	0157 0759 1427 ○ 2026	5.3 1.0 5.4 1.0	18 TU	0252 0853 1515 2049	5.1 1.1 5.1 1.4
4 TU	0242 0854 1515 2117	5.4 0.7 5.6 1.0	19 W	0328 0925 1550 2120	5.2 1.0 5.1 1.4
5 W	0327 0948 1603 2207	5.6 0.5 5.7 1.0	20 TH	0401 0956 1623 2153	5.2 1.0 5.1 1.4
6 TH	0414 1040 1652 2255	5.6 0.4 5.6 1.0	21 F	0434 1028 1658 2225	5.2 1.0 5.0 1.4
7 F	0502 1130 1743 2342	5.6 0.5 5.5 1.2	22 SA	0508 1100 1734 2257	5.1 1.1 4.9 1.5
8 SA	0553 1219 1837	5.5 0.6 5.3	23 SU	0544 1133 1812 2327	5.0 1.2 4.8 1.7
9 SU	0028 0649 1309 1934	1.4 5.3 0.9 5.1	24 M	0621 1208 1854	4.9 1.4 4.7
10 M	0117 0749 1403 ◑ 2034	1.6 5.2 1.2 4.8	25 TU	0000 0702 1246 ◐ 1940	1.8 4.7 1.6 4.6
11 TU	0214 0854 1505 2135	1.8 5.0 1.5 4.7	26 W	0044 0750 1336 2033	2.0 4.6 1.8 4.5
12 W	0321 0958 1615 2237	1.9 4.8 1.7 4.7	27 TH	0152 0850 1443 2135	2.2 4.5 1.9 4.5
13 TH	0431 1102 1722 2339	1.9 4.7 1.7 4.7	28 F	0323 1004 1609 2243	2.2 4.5 1.9 4.5
14 F	0538 1207 1819	1.7 4.8 1.7	29 SA	0449 1119 1727 2349	2.0 4.6 1.8 4.7
15 SA	0038 0639 1305 1905	4.8 1.6 4.8 1.7	30 SU	0557 1227 1829	1.7 4.9 1.6
			31 M	0049 0658 1325 1926	5.0 1.3 5.2 1.3

AUGUST

Date	Time	m	Date	Time	m
1 TU	0141 0756 1416 ○ 2018	5.3 0.9 5.5 1.1	16 W	0237 0838 1458 ● 2030	5.2 1.1 5.1 1.4
2 W	0228 0851 1503 2107	5.6 0.5 5.8 0.8	17 TH	0309 0907 1528 2102	5.3 0.9 5.2 1.2
3 TH	0313 0942 1549 2154	5.8 0.2 5.9 0.7	18 F	0339 0936 1558 2133	5.3 0.8 5.2 1.2
4 F	0358 1029 1635 2238	5.9 0.1 5.8 0.7	19 SA	0409 1006 1629 2203	5.3 0.8 5.2 1.2
5 SA	0444 1113 1722 2319	5.9 0.2 5.6 0.9	20 SU	0440 1034 1703 2228	5.3 0.9 5.1 1.3
6 SU	0532 1155 1810 2358	5.8 0.5 5.4 1.1	21 M	0512 1100 1738 2248	5.2 1.0 5.0 1.4
7 M	0622 1234 1902	5.5 0.9 5.1	22 TU	0545 1123 1815 2312	5.1 1.3 4.9 1.6
8 TU	0035 0717 1313 ◑ 1957	1.4 5.2 1.3 4.8	23 W	0623 1149 1857 2348	4.9 1.5 4.7 1.8
9 W	0123 0820 1403 2057	1.8 4.9 1.8 4.6	24 TH	0709 1230 1947 ◐	4.7 1.8 4.6
10 TH	0235 0927 1526 2201	2.0 4.6 2.1 4.5	25 F	0044 0809 1341 2051	2.1 4.5 2.1 4.4
11 F	0410 1038 1700 2312	2.1 4.5 2.2 4.5	26 SA	0227 0930 1544 2210	2.3 4.4 2.2 4.4
12 SA	0535 1155 1809	2.0 4.5 2.1	27 SU	0436 1059 1720 2328	2.1 4.6 2.0 4.7
13 SU	0023 0643 1300 1856	4.6 1.7 4.7 2.0	28 M	0555 1214 1823	1.7 4.9 1.7
14 M	0119 0731 1348 1930	4.9 1.5 4.9 1.8	29 TU	0033 0657 1313 1916	5.0 1.2 5.3 1.3
15 TU	0201 0808 1426 2000	5.1 1.2 5.0 1.6	30 W	0125 0751 1401 2003	5.4 0.7 5.7 1.0
			31 TH	0209 0839 1445 ○ 2049	5.7 0.3 5.9 0.7

Chart Datum: 2·90 metres below Ordnance Datum (Newlyn)
HAT is 6·3 metres above Chart Datum

TIME ZONE (UT)
For Summer Time add ONE hour in **non-shaded areas**

SCOTLAND – LEITH

LAT 55°59′N LONG 3°11′W

TIMES AND HEIGHTS OF HIGH AND LOW WATERS

Dates in amber are **SPRINGS**
Dates in grey are **NEAPS**

2023

SEPTEMBER

Date	Time	m	Date	Time	m
1 F	0252	6.0	16 SA	0311	5.4
	0925	0.0		0909	0.8
	1527	6.0		1528	5.3
	2132	0.5		2109	1.1
2 SA	0336	6.1	17 SU	0340	5.4
	1007	0.0		0937	0.8
	1611	5.9		1559	5.3
	2213	0.6		2137	1.1
3 SU	0420	6.1	18 M	0410	5.4
	1047	0.2		1003	0.8
	1655	5.7		1631	5.3
	2251	0.7		2157	1.2
4 M	0506	5.9	19 TU	0442	5.3
	1124	0.5		1022	1.0
	1740	5.4		1705	5.2
	2324	1.0		2214	1.3
5 TU	0554	5.5	20 W	0516	5.2
	1154	1.1		1039	1.2
	1827	5.1		1741	5.0
	2355	1.4		2240	1.5
6 W	0646	5.1	21 TH	0557	5.0
	1220	1.6		1105	1.5
	1918	4.8		1823	4.8
◑				2317	1.7
7 TH	0037	1.8	22 F	0646	4.8
	0747	4.7		1147	1.9
	1301	2.1		1913	4.6
	2018	4.5	◐		
8 F	0151	2.2	23 SA	0013	2.0
	0855	4.4		0748	4.5
	1427	2.5		1307	2.3
	2126	4.3		2020	4.4
9 SA	0404	2.3	24 SU	0221	2.2
	1012	4.3		0914	4.4
	1648	2.5		1543	2.4
	2244	4.3		2148	4.4
10 SU	0538	2.0	25 M	0437	2.0
	1142	4.4		1046	4.6
	1759	2.3		1711	2.1
				2310	4.7
11 M	0005	4.5	26 TU	0549	1.5
	0635	1.7		1201	5.0
	1248	4.6		1808	1.7
	1841	2.1			
12 TU	0100	4.8	27 W	0014	5.1
	0715	1.5		0646	1.0
	1331	4.9		1255	5.4
	1911	1.8		1856	1.3
13 W	0140	5.1	28 TH	0103	5.5
	0746	1.2		0734	0.6
	1404	5.1		1340	5.7
	1938	1.5		1940	0.9
14 TH	0213	5.2	29 F	0146	5.9
	0813	1.0		0819	0.2
	1432	5.2		1421	5.9
	2008	1.3	○	2023	0.7
15 F	0242	5.4	30 SA	0228	6.1
	0840	0.9		0901	0.1
	1500	5.3		1502	5.9
●	2039	1.1		2106	0.5

OCTOBER

Date	Time	m	Date	Time	m
1 SU	0311	6.1	16 M	0311	5.5
	0941	0.1		0905	0.8
	1543	5.9		1528	5.4
	2146	0.6		2109	1.0
2 M	0355	6.0	17 TU	0343	5.4
	1018	0.4		0930	0.9
	1626	5.7		1601	5.4
	2223	0.8		2132	1.1
3 TU	0441	5.8	18 W	0418	5.4
	1049	0.8		0950	1.1
	1709	5.4		1636	5.3
	2254	1.1		2154	1.2
4 W	0528	5.4	19 TH	0456	5.2
	1110	1.3		1012	1.4
	1753	5.1		1715	5.1
	2321	1.4		2224	1.4
5 TH	0619	5.0	20 F	0541	5.0
	1130	1.8		1044	1.7
	1842	4.7		1759	4.9
				2308	1.7
6 F	0001	1.8	21 SA	0634	4.8
	0717	4.6		1133	2.1
	1212	2.3		1852	4.7
◑	1941	4.4			
7 SA	0111	2.2	22 SU	0025	2.0
	0823	4.3		0740	4.6
	1331	2.7		1333	2.4
	2050	4.3	◐	2002	4.5
8 SU	0352	2.3	23 M	0239	2.0
	0937	4.2		0905	4.5
	1617	2.7		1530	2.4
	2207	4.3		2131	4.6
9 M	0512	2.1	24 TU	0423	1.7
	1109	4.3		1030	4.7
	1722	2.5		1646	2.1
	2329	4.5		2249	4.8
10 TU	0602	1.8	25 W	0529	1.3
	1218	4.6		1139	5.1
	1804	2.2		1740	1.7
				2349	5.2
11 W	0025	4.8	26 TH	0622	0.9
	0640	1.5		1232	5.4
	1259	4.8		1827	1.3
	1837	1.9			
12 TH	0106	5.0	27 F	0038	5.5
	0711	1.3		0709	0.6
	1330	5.0		1315	5.6
	1908	1.6		1912	1.0
13 F	0139	5.2	28 SA	0122	5.8
	0739	1.1		0752	0.5
	1358	5.2		1356	5.8
	1939	1.3	○	1956	0.8
14 SA	0209	5.4	29 SU	0205	5.9
	0807	0.9		0833	0.4
	1427	5.3		1437	5.8
●	2011	1.1		2040	0.7
15 SU	0240	5.4	30 M	0250	5.9
	0836	0.8		0912	0.5
	1457	5.4		1518	5.7
	2041	1.1		2122	0.7
			31 TU	0335	5.8
				0947	0.8
				1559	5.5
				2200	0.9

NOVEMBER

Date	Time	m	Date	Time	m
1 W	0421	5.6	16 TH	0401	5.4
	1015	1.2		0938	1.2
	1641	5.3		1614	5.4
	2232	1.2		2158	1.2
2 TH	0507	5.2	17 F	0444	5.3
	1032	1.6		1013	1.5
	1724	5.0		1656	5.2
	2300	1.5		2243	1.3
3 F	0556	4.9	18 SA	0533	5.2
	1057	2.0		1100	1.8
	1811	4.8		1744	5.1
	2339	1.8		2343	1.5
4 SA	0648	4.6	19 SU	0628	5.0
	1139	2.3		1210	2.1
	1905	4.5		1839	4.9
5 SU	0037	2.1	20 M	0059	1.7
	0747	4.3		0734	4.8
	1246	2.7		1334	2.3
◑	2010	4.4	◐	1949	4.8
6 M	0249	2.3	21 TU	0227	1.7
	0852	4.2		0850	4.7
	1500	2.8		1458	2.2
	2119	4.3		2109	4.8
7 TU	0418	2.1	22 W	0351	1.5
	1003	4.2		1004	4.8
	1624	2.6		1608	2.0
	2230	4.4		2221	5.0
8 W	0510	1.9	23 TH	0456	1.3
	1115	4.4		1109	5.0
	1713	2.3		1705	1.8
	2332	4.6		2321	5.2
9 TH	0550	1.7	24 F	0552	1.1
	1207	4.7		1203	5.2
	1753	2.0		1756	1.5
10 F	0019	4.9	25 SA	0013	5.4
	0626	1.4		0641	1.0
	1244	4.9		1250	5.4
	1830	1.7		1845	1.2
11 SA	0058	5.1	26 SU	0102	5.6
	0658	1.2		0726	0.9
	1319	5.1		1334	5.5
	1906	1.5		1933	1.0
12 SU	0134	5.2	27 M	0148	5.6
	0730	1.1		0807	0.9
	1352	5.3		1416	5.6
	1940	1.3	○	2020	0.9
13 M	0209	5.4	28 TU	0234	5.6
	0802	1.0		0845	1.0
	1426	5.4		1458	5.5
●	2014	1.1		2104	0.9
14 TU	0245	5.4	29 W	0320	5.5
	0834	1.0		0920	1.2
	1501	5.5		1539	5.4
	2047	1.1		2144	1.0
15 W	0321	5.5	30 TH	0405	5.3
	0906	1.1		0947	1.5
	1536	5.4		1620	5.3
	2121	1.1		2217	1.2

DECEMBER

Date	Time	m	Date	Time	m
1 F	0449	5.1	16 SA	0436	5.5
	1010	1.7		1030	1.4
	1701	5.1		1645	5.4
	2247	1.4		2304	1.0
2 SA	0533	4.9	17 SU	0526	5.4
	1039	1.9		1120	1.5
	1743	4.9		1734	5.3
	2322	1.6		2357	1.1
3 SU	0619	4.7	18 M	0619	5.2
	1119	2.2		1212	1.7
	1830	4.7		1828	5.2
4 M	0007	1.8	19 TU	0054	1.2
	0708	4.5		0719	5.0
	1209	2.4		1310	1.9
	1925	4.5	◐	1930	5.1
5 TU	0106	2.0	20 W	0157	1.4
	0801	4.4		0824	4.9
	1319	2.6		1414	2.0
◑	2024	4.4		2040	5.0
6 W	0230	2.1	21 TH	0306	1.5
	0858	4.3		0931	4.8
	1454	2.6		1522	2.0
	2126	4.4		2149	5.0
7 TH	0352	2.0	22 F	0415	1.5
	0958	4.4		1035	4.9
	1609	2.4		1627	1.9
	2226	4.5		2253	5.0
8 F	0448	1.9	23 SA	0519	1.5
	1056	4.5		1134	4.9
	1703	2.2		1728	1.7
	2322	4.6		2353	5.1
9 SA	0533	1.7	24 SU	0615	1.5
	1150	4.7		1229	5.1
	1749	1.9		1826	1.5
10 SU	0013	4.8	25 M	0048	5.2
	0615	1.5		0704	1.4
	1237	5.0		1318	5.2
	1831	1.7		1920	1.3
11 M	0100	5.0	26 TU	0140	5.2
	0654	1.4		0747	1.4
	1320	5.2		1404	5.3
	1912	1.5		2010	1.2
12 TU	0143	5.2	27 W	0228	5.3
	0733	1.3		0826	1.4
	1401	5.3		1447	5.3
●	1953	1.3	○	2054	1.1
13 W	0225	5.4	28 TH	0312	5.3
	0813	1.2		0900	1.4
	1440	5.4		1527	5.3
	2036	1.1		2133	1.1
14 TH	0307	5.5	29 F	0353	5.2
	0856	1.2		0929	1.5
	1519	5.5		1606	5.3
	2123	1.0		2206	1.1
15 F	0350	5.5	30 SA	0432	5.1
	0942	1.2		0956	1.6
	1601	5.5		1642	5.2
	2212	0.9		2235	1.2
			31 SU	0509	5.0
				1026	1.7
				1719	5.1
				2305	1.3

Chart Datum: 2·90 metres below Ordnance Datum (Newlyn)
HAT is 6·3 metres above Chart Datum

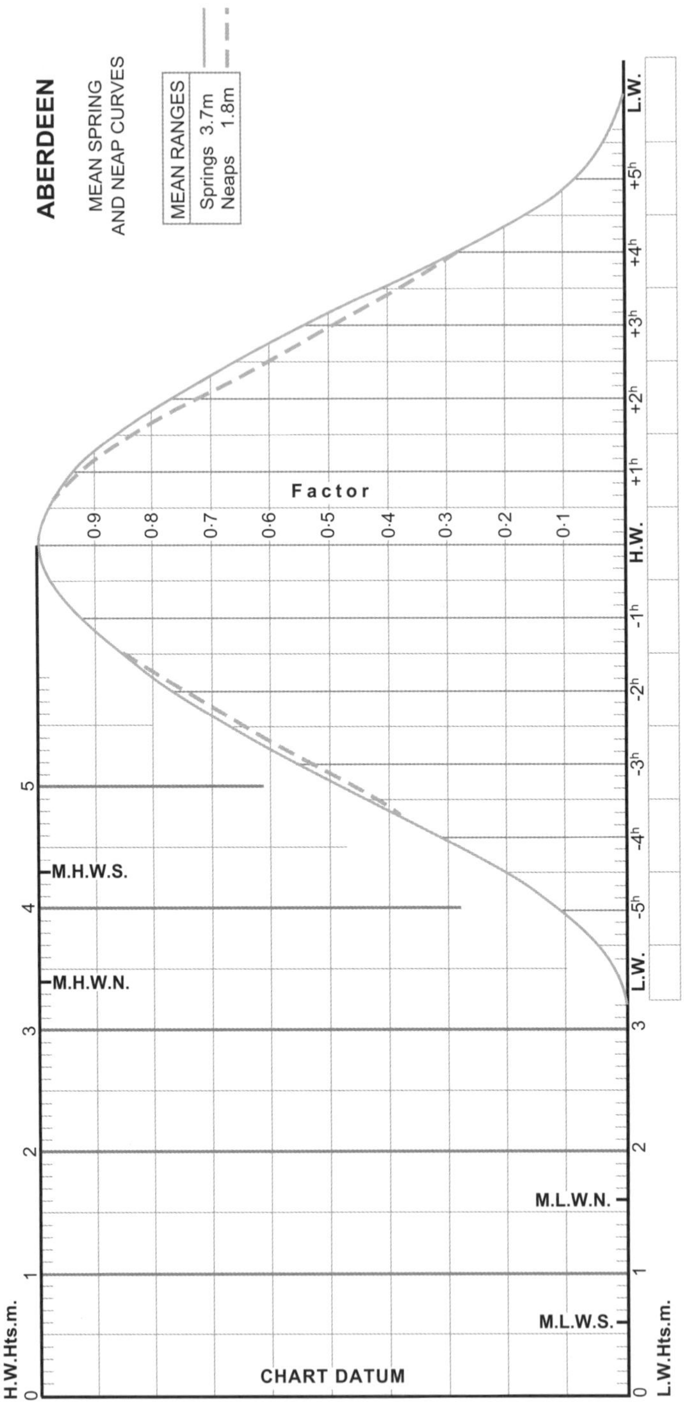
ABERDEEN
MEAN SPRING
AND NEAP CURVES
MEAN RANGES
Springs 3.7m
Neaps 1.8m
Factor
0·9
0·8
0·7
0·6
0·5
0·4
0·3
0·2
0·1
L.W.
-5h
-4h
-3h
-2h
-1h
H.W.
+1h
+2h
+3h
+4h
+5h
L.W.
H.W.Hts.m.
M.H.W.S.
M.H.W.N.
M.L.W.N.
M.L.W.S.
CHART DATUM
L.W.Hts.m.

TIME ZONE (UT)
For Summer Time add ONE hour in **non-shaded areas**

SCOTLAND – ABERDEEN

LAT 57°09′N LONG 2°04′W

TIMES AND HEIGHTS OF HIGH AND LOW WATERS

Dates in amber are **SPRINGS**
Dates in grey are **NEAPS**

2023

JANUARY

Date	Day	Time	m	Time	m	Time	m	Time	m
1	SU	0239	1.4	0913	3.6	1501	1.8	2122	3.7
2	M	0347	1.5	1015	3.6	1611	1.7	2228	3.7
3	TU	0445	1.5	1107	3.7	1708	1.6	2324	3.8
4	W	0532	1.5	1152	3.9	1756	1.4		
5	TH	0012	3.8	0613	1.4	1231	4.0	1838	1.3
6	F ○	0054	3.9	0649	1.4	1308	4.1	1916	1.2
7	SA	0133	3.9	0724	1.4	1342	4.1	1952	1.1
8	SU	0209	3.9	0757	1.4	1414	4.1	2026	1.0
9	M	0244	3.9	0829	1.4	1446	4.1	2100	1.0
10	TU	0319	3.9	0901	1.4	1519	4.1	2135	1.1
11	W	0354	3.8	0934	1.4	1553	4.0	2211	1.1
12	TH	0432	3.7	1009	1.5	1630	3.9	2249	1.2
13	F	0513	3.6	1047	1.6	1711	3.8	2331	1.3
14	SA	0559	3.5	1131	1.7	1759	3.7		
15	SU ◑	0020	1.4	0652	3.5	1227	1.8	1858	3.6
16	M	0119	1.5	0752	3.5	1337	1.9	2004	3.6
17	TU	0225	1.5	0858	3.5	1453	1.8	2116	3.6
18	W	0334	1.5	1004	3.6	1607	1.6	2229	3.8
19	TH	0442	1.4	1105	3.8	1713	1.4	2334	4.0
20	F	0541	1.2	1158	4.1	1810	1.1		
21	SA ●	0031	4.2	0634	1.1	1246	4.3	1903	0.7
22	SU	0123	4.4	0723	0.9	1332	4.4	1952	0.5
23	M	0213	4.4	0809	0.9	1418	4.6	2041	0.4
24	TU	0302	4.4	0854	0.9	1503	4.6	2129	0.3
25	W	0350	4.3	0938	1.0	1550	4.5	2216	0.5
26	TH	0438	4.1	1022	1.1	1638	4.4	2303	0.7
27	F	0528	3.9	1108	1.3	1729	4.2	2352	1.0
28	SA ◐	0619	3.7	1159	1.5	1824	3.9		
29	SU	0044	1.3	0716	3.5	1258	1.7	1928	3.7
30	M	0144	1.6	0821	3.4	1411	1.8	2042	3.5
31	TU	0300	1.8	0934	3.4	1542	1.8	2204	3.4

FEBRUARY

Date	Day	Time	m	Time	m	Time	m	Time	m
1	W	0421	1.8	1041	3.5	1654	1.7	2313	3.5
2	TH	0517	1.7	1135	3.7	1745	1.5		
3	F	0005	3.6	0601	1.6	1218	3.8	1828	1.3
4	SA	0047	3.7	0637	1.5	1255	3.9	1904	1.1
5	SU ○	0123	3.8	0711	1.4	1328	4.1	1938	1.0
6	M	0155	3.9	0742	1.2	1359	4.1	2009	0.9
7	TU	0226	4.0	0812	1.2	1429	4.2	2041	0.8
8	W	0256	4.0	0841	1.1	1458	4.2	2112	0.8
9	TH	0327	3.9	0911	1.1	1529	4.2	2143	0.9
10	F	0400	3.9	0941	1.2	1602	4.1	2216	1.0
11	SA	0434	3.8	1014	1.3	1638	4.0	2251	1.1
12	SU	0513	3.7	1051	1.4	1720	3.9	2333	1.3
13	M ◑	0601	3.6	1139	1.6	1813	3.7		
14	TU	0027	1.5	0701	3.4	1245	1.7	1925	3.5
15	W	0140	1.6	0814	3.4	1413	1.8	2049	3.5
16	TH	0306	1.7	0933	3.5	1549	1.6	2217	3.6
17	F	0432	1.5	1047	3.7	1706	1.3	2330	3.9
18	SA	0535	1.3	1146	3.9	1804	0.9		
19	SU	0026	4.1	0626	1.1	1235	4.2	1855	0.5
20	M ●	0115	4.3	0712	0.9	1319	4.5	1941	0.3
21	TU	0200	4.4	0754	0.7	1402	4.6	2025	0.2
22	W	0243	4.4	0835	0.7	1444	4.7	2108	0.2
23	TH	0325	4.3	0914	0.7	1527	4.6	2148	0.4
24	F	0406	4.1	0953	0.8	1610	4.4	2228	0.7
25	SA	0449	3.9	1033	1.1	1656	4.2	2309	1.0
26	SU	0534	3.7	1117	1.3	1747	3.8	2354	1.4
27	M ◐	0625	3.5	1212	1.6	1848	3.5		
28	TU	0049	1.7	0728	3.3	1325	1.8	2004	3.3

MARCH

Date	Day	Time	m	Time	m	Time	m	Time	m
1	W	0207	2.0	0846	3.2	1514	1.9	2139	3.2
2	TH	0359	2.0	1010	3.3	1639	1.7	2259	3.3
3	F	0502	1.9	1113	3.5	1729	1.5	2351	3.5
4	SA	0544	1.7	1159	3.7	1809	1.2		
5	SU	0030	3.7	0620	1.5	1235	3.8	1843	1.0
6	M	0102	3.8	0651	1.3	1306	4.0	1914	0.9
7	TU ○	0132	3.9	0720	1.1	1336	4.1	1944	0.7
8	W	0200	4.0	0749	1.0	1404	4.2	2014	0.6
9	TH	0229	4.0	0817	0.9	1433	4.2	2043	0.6
10	F	0258	4.0	0846	0.9	1503	4.2	2113	0.7
11	SA	0328	4.0	0915	0.9	1536	4.2	2144	0.8
12	SU	0401	3.9	0947	1.0	1612	4.0	2217	1.0
13	M	0439	3.8	1024	1.2	1655	3.9	2258	1.2
14	TU	0524	3.6	1111	1.4	1750	3.7	2353	1.5
15	W ◑	0624	3.4	1221	1.6	1908	3.5		
16	TH	0115	1.7	0745	3.3	1359	1.7	2041	3.4
17	F	0258	1.8	0912	3.4	1545	1.5	2216	3.6
18	SA	0426	1.6	1032	3.6	1659	1.1	2325	3.8
19	SU	0525	1.3	1131	3.9	1753	0.7		
20	M	0016	4.1	0612	1.0	1218	4.2	1840	0.4
21	TU ●	0059	4.3	0654	0.8	1300	4.4	1922	0.2
22	W	0139	4.4	0733	0.6	1341	4.6	2002	0.2
23	TH	0217	4.4	0811	0.6	1421	4.6	2040	0.2
24	F	0255	4.3	0848	0.6	1502	4.5	2117	0.5
25	SA	0332	4.1	0925	0.7	1543	4.3	2152	0.8
26	SU	0410	3.9	1003	0.9	1627	4.0	2228	1.1
27	M	0451	3.7	1044	1.2	1716	3.7	2308	1.5
28	TU	0537	3.5	1136	1.5	1816	3.4		
29	W ◐	0000	1.8	0638	3.3	1247	1.7	1930	3.2
30	TH	0119	2.1	0754	3.1	1431	1.8	2103	3.1
31	F	0323	2.1	0925	3.2	1609	1.6	2230	3.2

APRIL

Date	Day	Time	m	Time	m	Time	m	Time	m
1	SA	0434	1.9	1038	3.3	1700	1.4	2322	3.4
2	SU	0517	1.7	1126	3.5	1738	1.2		
3	M	0000	3.6	0551	1.4	1204	3.7	1811	1.0
4	TU	0031	3.8	0622	1.2	1235	3.9	1843	0.8
5	W	0100	3.9	0651	1.0	1305	4.1	1912	0.7
6	TH ○	0129	4.0	0720	0.9	1335	4.2	1942	0.6
7	F	0158	4.1	0750	0.8	1406	4.2	2013	0.6
8	SA	0228	4.1	0821	0.8	1439	4.2	2044	0.7
9	SU	0300	4.1	0853	0.8	1515	4.1	2117	0.8
10	M	0335	4.0	0928	0.9	1556	4.0	2153	1.0
11	TU	0414	3.8	1010	1.1	1644	3.8	2239	1.3
12	W	0502	3.7	1105	1.2	1747	3.6	2342	1.6
13	TH ◑	0606	3.5	1223	1.4	1910	3.4		
14	F	0111	1.8	0730	3.3	1401	1.4	2041	3.4
15	SA	0252	1.8	0855	3.4	1536	1.2	2208	3.6
16	SU	0410	1.6	1013	3.6	1642	0.9	2309	3.8
17	M	0504	1.3	1110	3.9	1733	0.6	2356	4.0
18	TU	0549	1.0	1157	4.2	1817	0.4		
19	W	0036	4.2	0631	0.8	1238	4.3	1858	0.3
20	TH ●	0113	4.2	0709	0.6	1318	4.4	1936	0.4
21	F	0149	4.2	0747	0.6	1358	4.4	2012	0.5
22	SA	0225	4.2	0824	0.6	1439	4.3	2046	0.7
23	SU	0301	4.1	0902	0.7	1521	4.1	2120	1.0
24	M	0338	3.9	0940	0.9	1605	3.8	2155	1.3
25	TU	0416	3.7	1022	1.2	1653	3.6	2234	1.6
26	W	0459	3.5	1111	1.4	1751	3.3	2322	1.9
27	TH ◐	0556	3.3	1214	1.6	1857	3.2		
28	F	0034	2.1	0707	3.2	1337	1.7	2012	3.1
29	SA	0212	2.1	0825	3.2	1509	1.6	2134	3.2
30	SU	0342	1.9	0942	3.3	1612	1.4	2234	3.3

Chart Datum: 2·25 metres below Ordnance Datum (Newlyn)
HAT is 4·8 metres above Chart Datum

TIME ZONE (UT)
For Summer Time add ONE hour in **non-shaded areas**

SCOTLAND – ABERDEEN

LAT 57°09′N LONG 2°04′W

TIMES AND HEIGHTS OF HIGH AND LOW WATERS

Dates in amber are **SPRINGS**
Dates in grey are **NEAPS**

2023

MAY

Date	Day	Phase	Time	m	Time	m	Time	m	Time	m
1	M		0433	1.7	1039	3.5	1655	1.2	2316	3.5
2	TU		0511	1.5	1121	3.6	1731	1.0	2352	3.7
3	W		0545	1.3	1157	3.8	1804	0.8		
4	TH		0023	3.9	0618	1.1	1231	4.0	1837	0.7
5	F	○	0055	4.0	0650	0.9	1305	4.1	1910	0.6
6	SA		0127	4.1	0724	0.8	1341	4.2	1945	0.6
7	SU		0201	4.1	0800	0.7	1419	4.2	2021	0.7
8	M		0237	4.1	0838	0.7	1501	4.1	2100	0.9
9	TU		0316	4.0	0921	0.8	1549	4.0	2144	1.1
10	W		0400	3.9	1012	0.9	1645	3.8	2237	1.4
11	TH		0453	3.7	1114	1.1	1754	3.6	2344	1.6
12	F	◑	0600	3.6	1230	1.2	1909	3.5		
13	SA		0106	1.7	0717	3.5	1353	1.1	2029	3.5
14	SU		0228	1.7	0833	3.6	1512	1.0	2144	3.6
15	M		0339	1.5	0945	3.7	1615	0.9	2243	3.8
16	TU		0435	1.3	1044	3.9	1707	0.7	2330	3.9
17	W		0523	1.1	1133	4.0	1752	0.7		
18	TH		0010	4.0	0607	0.9	1216	4.1	1832	0.6
19	F	●	0048	4.1	0648	0.8	1259	4.2	1910	0.7
20	SA		0124	4.1	0727	0.7	1341	4.1	1946	0.8
21	SU		0201	4.1	0806	0.8	1423	4.0	2021	1.0
22	M		0237	4.0	0845	0.8	1505	3.9	2056	1.2
23	TU		0313	3.9	0924	1.0	1548	3.7	2131	1.4
24	W		0351	3.8	1005	1.1	1634	3.6	2210	1.6
25	TH		0433	3.6	1050	1.3	1725	3.4	2255	1.7
26	F		0523	3.5	1144	1.4	1820	3.3	2352	1.9
27	SA	◐	0623	3.4	1247	1.5	1920	3.2		
28	SU		0104	2.0	0727	3.3	1355	1.5	2024	3.2
29	M		0220	1.9	0832	3.3	1500	1.4	2128	3.3
30	TU		0326	1.8	0935	3.4	1555	1.3	2222	3.5
31	W		0418	1.6	1029	3.6	1641	1.1	2306	3.6

JUNE

Date	Day	Phase	Time	m	Time	m	Time	m	Time	m
1	TH		0501	1.4	1115	3.7	1722	1.0	2345	3.8
2	F		0542	1.2	1157	3.9	1802	0.9		
3	SA		0023	4.0	0622	1.0	1239	4.0	1842	0.8
4	SU	○	0100	4.1	0703	0.8	1322	4.1	1924	0.8
5	M		0139	4.2	0747	0.7	1407	4.2	2007	0.8
6	TU		0221	4.2	0833	0.7	1456	4.1	2053	1.0
7	W		0305	4.1	0922	0.7	1549	4.1	2142	1.1
8	TH		0353	4.1	1016	0.7	1647	3.9	2236	1.3
9	F		0448	4.0	1117	0.8	1750	3.8	2337	1.4
10	SA	◑	0550	3.8	1222	0.9	1854	3.7		
11	SU		0044	1.6	0657	3.8	1329	0.9	2002	3.6
12	M		0152	1.6	0804	3.7	1437	1.0	2109	3.6
13	TU		0259	1.5	0912	3.8	1542	1.0	2210	3.7
14	W		0403	1.4	1016	3.8	1639	1.0	2302	3.7
15	TH		0458	1.3	1112	3.9	1727	1.0	2347	3.8
16	F		0547	1.1	1201	3.9	1810	1.0		
17	SA		0028	3.9	0633	1.0	1247	3.9	1850	1.1
18	SU	●	0106	4.0	0715	0.9	1330	3.9	1928	1.1
19	M		0143	4.0	0754	0.9	1412	3.9	2003	1.2
20	TU		0220	4.0	0833	0.9	1453	3.8	2038	1.3
21	W		0255	4.0	0910	0.9	1533	3.7	2113	1.4
22	TH		0331	3.9	0948	1.0	1613	3.6	2149	1.4
23	F		0410	3.8	1028	1.1	1655	3.5	2228	1.5
24	SA		0452	3.7	1111	1.2	1740	3.4	2312	1.7
25	SU		0540	3.6	1159	1.3	1830	3.4		
26	M	◐	0003	1.8	0633	3.5	1253	1.4	1924	3.3
27	TU		0105	1.8	0730	3.4	1351	1.4	2021	3.3
28	W		0212	1.8	0830	3.4	1450	1.4	2120	3.4
29	TH		0316	1.7	0932	3.5	1548	1.3	2218	3.6
30	F		0416	1.6	1034	3.6	1643	1.2	2309	3.7

JULY

Date	Day	Phase	Time	m	Time	m	Time	m	Time	m
1	SA		0511	1.3	1129	3.8	1734	1.1	2356	3.9
2	SU		0601	1.1	1221	4.0	1823	1.0		
3	M	○	0040	4.1	0651	0.9	1311	4.1	1912	0.9
4	TU		0124	4.2	0739	0.6	1401	4.2	1959	0.9
5	W		0209	4.3	0829	0.5	1452	4.3	2046	0.9
6	TH		0255	4.3	0919	0.4	1543	4.2	2134	1.0
7	F		0344	4.3	1010	0.4	1636	4.1	2223	1.1
8	SA		0435	4.2	1104	0.5	1731	3.9	2315	1.2
9	SU		0530	4.1	1158	0.7	1826	3.8		
10	M	◑	0010	1.4	0629	4.0	1255	0.9	1925	3.6
11	TU		0111	1.5	0731	3.8	1356	1.1	2029	3.5
12	W		0218	1.6	0840	3.7	1503	1.3	2134	3.5
13	TH		0332	1.6	0952	3.6	1612	1.4	2235	3.6
14	F		0441	1.5	1058	3.6	1709	1.4	2328	3.7
15	SA		0536	1.3	1155	3.7	1756	1.4		
16	SU		0014	3.8	0624	1.2	1242	3.8	1837	1.3
17	M	●	0054	3.9	0705	1.0	1324	3.8	1914	1.3
18	TU		0131	4.0	0743	0.9	1402	3.8	1948	1.3
19	W		0205	4.0	0818	0.9	1437	3.9	2021	1.2
20	TH		0238	4.1	0852	0.9	1511	3.8	2053	1.2
21	F		0311	4.0	0926	0.9	1546	3.8	2125	1.3
22	SA		0344	4.0	1000	0.9	1621	3.7	2158	1.3
23	SU		0420	3.9	1036	1.0	1659	3.6	2234	1.4
24	M		0458	3.8	1114	1.1	1740	3.5	2314	1.5
25	TU	◐	0542	3.7	1158	1.3	1828	3.4		
26	W		0003	1.7	0634	3.6	1250	1.4	1924	3.4
27	TH		0106	1.8	0737	3.5	1353	1.5	2026	3.4
28	F		0221	1.8	0847	3.5	1503	1.5	2134	3.5
29	SA		0339	1.7	1003	3.5	1615	1.5	2239	3.6
30	SU		0451	1.4	1113	3.7	1718	1.3	2335	3.9
31	M		0549	1.1	1211	4.0	1812	1.1		

AUGUST

Date	Day	Phase	Time	m	Time	m	Time	m	Time	m
1	TU	○	0025	4.1	0642	0.8	1303	4.2	1902	0.9
2	W		0111	4.3	0731	0.5	1352	4.4	1948	0.8
3	TH		0156	4.5	0818	0.3	1440	4.4	2032	0.8
4	F		0240	4.6	0905	0.2	1526	4.4	2116	0.8
5	SA		0326	4.6	0952	0.2	1613	4.2	2159	0.9
6	SU		0412	4.5	1038	0.4	1700	4.0	2244	1.1
7	M		0502	4.3	1125	0.7	1750	3.8	2333	1.3
8	TU	◑	0556	4.0	1215	1.1	1845	3.6		
9	W		0030	1.5	0658	3.8	1312	1.4	1947	3.5
10	TH		0139	1.7	0810	3.5	1423	1.7	2058	3.4
11	F		0309	1.7	0934	3.4	1552	1.8	2212	3.5
12	SA		0432	1.6	1052	3.5	1657	1.7	2313	3.6
13	SU		0529	1.4	1150	3.6	1745	1.6		
14	M		0001	3.8	0614	1.2	1234	3.7	1824	1.5
15	TU		0040	3.9	0652	1.0	1311	3.8	1858	1.3
16	W	●	0114	4.0	0726	0.9	1344	3.9	1930	1.2
17	TH		0146	4.1	0757	0.8	1414	3.9	2000	1.1
18	F		0215	4.2	0828	0.7	1444	4.0	2029	1.1
19	SA		0245	4.2	0858	0.8	1514	3.9	2058	1.1
20	SU		0315	4.2	0928	0.8	1545	3.9	2127	1.2
21	M		0347	4.1	0959	0.9	1618	3.8	2159	1.3
22	TU		0422	4.0	1032	1.1	1655	3.7	2234	1.4
23	W		0501	3.8	1110	1.3	1738	3.6	2317	1.6
24	TH	◐	0551	3.7	1159	1.5	1833	3.5		
25	F		0017	1.7	0658	3.5	1307	1.7	1944	3.4
26	SA		0143	1.8	0820	3.4	1433	1.8	2101	3.4
27	SU		0319	1.7	0949	3.5	1602	1.7	2217	3.6
28	M		0441	1.4	1106	3.8	1709	1.4	2320	3.9
29	TU		0540	1.0	1203	4.1	1801	1.2		
30	W		0009	4.2	0630	0.6	1251	4.3	1847	0.9
31	TH	○	0054	4.4	0716	0.3	1336	4.5	1930	0.7

Chart Datum: 2·25 metres below Ordnance Datum (Newlyn)
HAT is 4·8 metres above Chart Datum

TIME ZONE (UT)
For Summer Time add ONE hour in **non-shaded areas**

SCOTLAND – ABERDEEN

LAT 57°09′N LONG 2°04′W

TIMES AND HEIGHTS OF HIGH AND LOW WATERS

Dates in amber are **SPRINGS**
Dates in grey are **NEAPS**

2023

SEPTEMBER

Date	Day	Time	m	Time	m	Time	m	Time	m
1	F	0137	4.7	0800	0.1	1418	4.5	2011	0.6
2	SA	0219	4.8	0843	0.1	1500	4.5	2051	0.7
3	SU	0301	4.7	0924	0.2	1542	4.3	2131	0.8
4	M	0345	4.6	1005	0.5	1625	4.1	2212	1.0
5	TU	0432	4.3	1047	0.9	1710	3.9	2258	1.2
6	W	0525	4.0	1132	1.3	1802	3.6	◑ 2353	1.5
7	TH	0628	3.6	1228	1.7	1904	3.4		
8	F	0106	1.8	0744	3.4	1344	2.0	2021	3.3
9	SA	0251	1.8	0918	3.3	1536	2.1	2146	3.4
10	SU	0421	1.6	1042	3.4	1644	1.9	2253	3.6
11	M	0514	1.4	1137	3.6	1728	1.7	2340	3.8
12	TU	0554	1.2	1216	3.7	1804	1.5		
13	W	0017	3.9	0629	1.0	1248	3.9	1836	1.3
14	TH	0050	4.1	0700	0.9	1317	4.0	1905	1.2
15	F	0119	4.2	0729	0.8	1345	4.1	● 1933	1.1
16	SA	0147	4.3	0758	0.7	1412	4.1	2001	1.0
17	SU	0216	4.3	0826	0.7	1441	4.1	2029	1.0
18	M	0246	4.3	0854	0.8	1510	4.1	2058	1.1
19	TU	0318	4.2	0924	0.9	1542	4.0	2128	1.2
20	W	0353	4.1	0955	1.1	1618	3.9	2203	1.3
21	TH	0434	3.9	1032	1.3	1700	3.7	2248	1.5
22	F	0526	3.7	1122	1.6	1755	3.6	◐ 2352	1.7
23	SA	0639	3.5	1239	1.9	1912	3.4		
24	SU	0127	1.8	0810	3.4	1421	1.9	2038	3.5
25	M	0312	1.6	0944	3.6	1554	1.8	2159	3.7
26	TU	0430	1.2	1056	3.9	1656	1.5	2301	4.0
27	W	0525	0.8	1149	4.2	1744	1.2	2350	4.3
28	TH	0611	0.5	1233	4.4	1826	0.9		
29	F	0032	4.5	0655	0.3	1313	4.5	○ 1907	0.7
30	SA	0113	4.7	0736	0.2	1351	4.5	1946	0.6

OCTOBER

Date	Day	Time	m	Time	m	Time	m	Time	m
1	SU	0155	4.8	0815	0.3	1430	4.5	2024	0.6
2	M	0236	4.7	0853	0.5	1509	4.3	2104	0.8
3	TU	0320	4.5	0931	0.8	1549	4.1	2144	1.0
4	W	0406	4.2	1009	1.2	1631	3.9	2229	1.2
5	TH	0459	3.9	1051	1.6	1720	3.7	2323	1.5
6	F	0602	3.5	1144	1.9	1823	3.5	◑	
7	SA	0035	1.8	0718	3.3	1302	2.2	1939	3.3
8	SU	0219	1.8	0849	3.2	1502	2.2	2106	3.4
9	M	0353	1.7	1015	3.4	1616	2.1	2219	3.5
10	TU	0444	1.5	1107	3.6	1659	1.8	2308	3.7
11	W	0523	1.3	1145	3.7	1734	1.6	2346	3.9
12	TH	0556	1.1	1216	3.9	1805	1.4		
13	F	0018	4.1	0627	0.9	1244	4.0	1835	1.2
14	SA	0048	4.2	0656	0.8	1312	4.1	● 1904	1.1
15	SU	0117	4.3	0724	0.8	1340	4.2	1933	1.0
16	M	0148	4.3	0753	0.8	1409	4.2	2002	1.0
17	TU	0220	4.3	0823	0.9	1440	4.2	2033	1.0
18	W	0254	4.2	0854	1.0	1513	4.1	2107	1.1
19	TH	0333	4.1	0929	1.2	1551	4.0	2147	1.3
20	F	0419	3.9	1010	1.5	1635	3.8	2238	1.4
21	SA	0518	3.7	1107	1.7	1733	3.6	2350	1.6
22	SU	0637	3.5	1231	2.0	1854	3.5	◐	
23	M	0124	1.6	0804	3.5	1410	2.0	2018	3.6
24	TU	0258	1.4	0931	3.7	1533	1.8	2135	3.8
25	W	0409	1.1	1037	3.9	1632	1.5	2237	4.0
26	TH	0502	0.8	1127	4.2	1720	1.2	2326	4.3
27	F	0548	0.6	1209	4.3	1802	1.0		
28	SA	0009	4.5	0630	0.5	1247	4.4	○ 1843	0.8
29	SU	0051	4.6	0710	0.5	1324	4.5	1923	0.7
30	M	0133	4.6	0748	0.6	1402	4.4	2002	0.7
31	TU	0216	4.5	0825	0.8	1439	4.3	2042	0.9

NOVEMBER

Date	Day	Time	m	Time	m	Time	m	Time	m
1	W	0300	4.3	0901	1.1	1518	4.2	2124	1.0
2	TH	0347	4.1	0938	1.4	1559	4.0	2208	1.3
3	F	0438	3.8	1018	1.7	1644	3.8	2259	1.5
4	SA	0538	3.5	1107	2.0	1742	3.6		
5	SU	0003	1.7	0644	3.3	1216	2.2	◑ 1852	3.4
6	M	0124	1.8	0758	3.3	1349	2.3	2007	3.4
7	TU	0252	1.7	0917	3.3	1519	2.2	2122	3.5
8	W	0356	1.6	1018	3.5	1615	1.9	2220	3.6
9	TH	0439	1.4	1101	3.7	1655	1.7	2304	3.8
10	F	0515	1.2	1136	3.8	1729	1.5	2341	4.0
11	SA	0548	1.1	1208	4.0	1802	1.3		
12	SU	0015	4.1	0620	1.0	1239	4.1	1834	1.2
13	M	0048	4.2	0652	0.9	1310	4.2	● 1907	1.1
14	TU	0123	4.3	0725	0.9	1342	4.3	1941	1.0
15	W	0200	4.3	0759	1.0	1416	4.3	2018	1.0
16	TH	0240	4.2	0836	1.1	1453	4.2	2059	1.1
17	F	0324	4.1	0917	1.3	1534	4.1	2146	1.1
18	SA	0416	4.0	1005	1.5	1622	4.0	2242	1.3
19	SU	0519	3.8	1105	1.7	1723	3.8	2352	1.3
20	M	0632	3.7	1221	1.9	1837	3.7	◐	
21	TU	0112	1.4	0748	3.6	1343	1.9	1952	3.8
22	W	0230	1.3	0903	3.7	1457	1.8	2103	3.9
23	TH	0338	1.1	1008	3.9	1600	1.6	2207	4.0
24	F	0434	1.0	1059	4.0	1652	1.4	2301	4.2
25	SA	0523	0.9	1144	4.2	1739	1.2	2349	4.3
26	SU	0606	0.8	1224	4.3	1823	1.0		
27	M	0034	4.4	0647	0.9	1302	4.3	○ 1906	0.9
28	TU	0118	4.4	0726	1.0	1340	4.3	1948	0.9
29	W	0203	4.3	0803	1.1	1418	4.3	2029	1.0
30	TH	0247	4.1	0840	1.3	1456	4.2	2110	1.1

DECEMBER

Date	Day	Time	m	Time	m	Time	m	Time	m
1	F	0333	4.0	0917	1.5	1535	4.0	2152	1.2
2	SA	0419	3.8	0955	1.7	1617	3.9	2237	1.4
3	SU	0509	3.6	1037	1.9	1705	3.7	2328	1.5
4	M	0603	3.4	1129	2.0	1802	3.6		
5	TU	0027	1.6	0700	3.3	1235	2.1	◑ 1904	3.5
6	W	0132	1.7	0802	3.3	1350	2.1	2008	3.5
7	TH	0237	1.7	0906	3.4	1501	2.1	2113	3.5
8	F	0336	1.6	1004	3.5	1559	1.9	2211	3.7
9	SA	0425	1.4	1050	3.7	1646	1.7	2300	3.8
10	SU	0507	1.3	1130	3.9	1727	1.5	2343	3.9
11	M	0546	1.2	1208	4.0	1807	1.3		
12	TU	0023	4.1	0625	1.1	1244	4.2	● 1847	1.2
13	W	0105	4.2	0705	1.1	1321	4.3	1928	1.0
14	TH	0148	4.2	0746	1.1	1400	4.3	2012	0.9
15	F	0233	4.2	0829	1.1	1441	4.3	2058	0.9
16	SA	0322	4.2	0914	1.2	1525	4.3	2148	0.9
17	SU	0415	4.1	1003	1.4	1615	4.2	2242	0.9
18	M	0513	4.0	1057	1.5	1711	4.1	2342	1.0
19	TU	0614	3.8	1158	1.7	1813	4.0	◐	
20	W	0046	1.1	0718	3.7	1305	1.7	1920	3.9
21	TH	0152	1.2	0825	3.7	1413	1.7	2028	3.9
22	F	0259	1.2	0931	3.7	1522	1.7	2137	3.9
23	SA	0404	1.2	1031	3.8	1627	1.5	2241	4.0
24	SU	0501	1.2	1122	3.9	1723	1.3	2337	4.0
25	M	0549	1.2	1207	4.1	1812	1.2		
26	TU	0027	4.1	0633	1.2	1248	4.1	1858	1.1
27	W	0114	4.1	0712	1.3	1327	4.2	○ 1940	1.0
28	TH	0157	4.1	0750	1.3	1405	4.2	2020	1.0
29	F	0238	4.0	0825	1.4	1441	4.2	2058	1.0
30	SA	0318	3.9	0859	1.4	1517	4.1	2135	1.1
31	SU	0357	3.8	0934	1.5	1554	4.0	2212	1.2

Chart Datum: 2·25 metres below Ordnance Datum (Newlyn)
HAT is 4·8 metres above Chart Datum

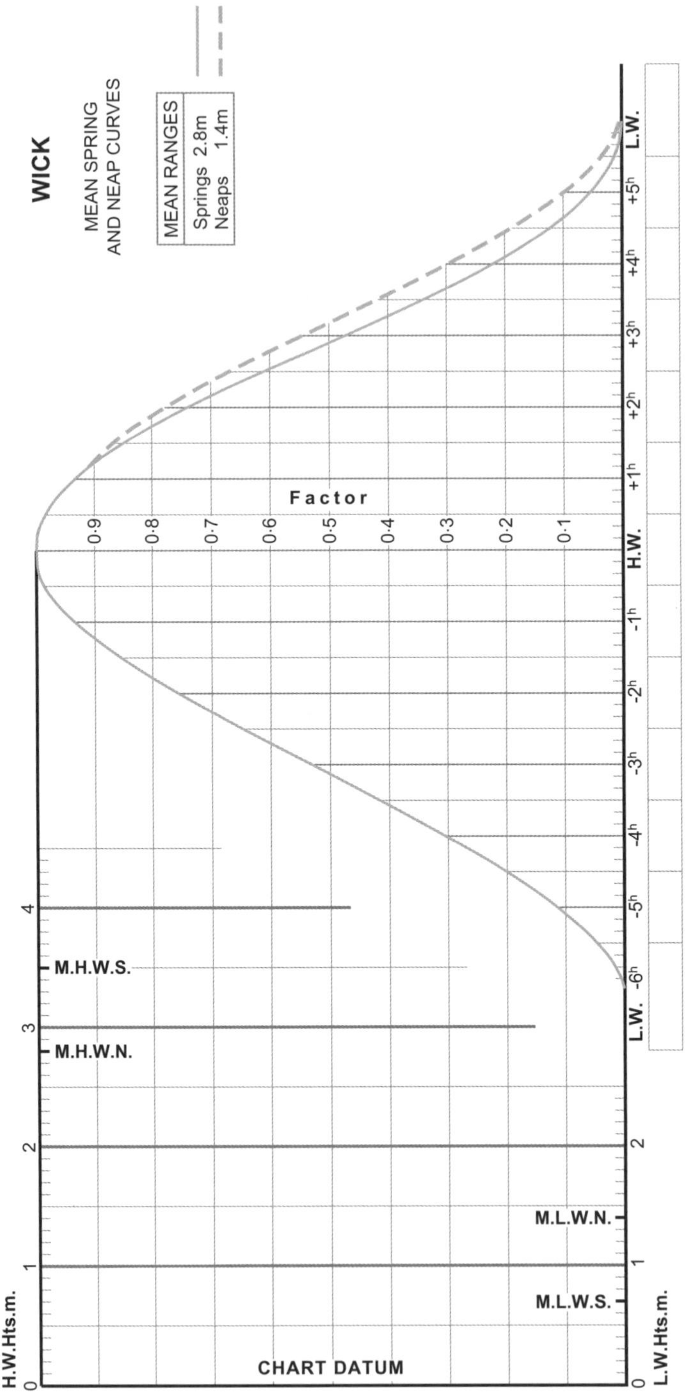
WICK
MEAN SPRING
AND NEAP CURVES
MEAN RANGES
Springs 2.8m
Neaps 1.4m
Factor
0·9
0·8
0·7
0·6
0·5
0·4
0·3
0·2
0·1
L.W. -6h -5h -4h -3h -2h -1h H.W. +1h +2h +3h +4h +5h L.W.
H.W.Hts.m.
M.H.W.S.
M.H.W.N.
M.L.W.N.
M.L.W.S.
CHART DATUM
L.W.Hts.m.
0
1
2
3
4

TIME ZONE (UT)

For Summer Time add ONE hour in **non-shaded areas**

SCOTLAND – WICK

LAT 58°26′N LONG 3°05′W

TIMES AND HEIGHTS OF HIGH AND LOW WATERS

Dates in amber are **SPRINGS**
Dates in grey are **NEAPS**

2023

JANUARY

Day	Time	m	Day	Time	m
1 SU	0038	1.2	16 M	0535	2.8
	0654	2.9		1122	1.6
	1251	1.6		1748	2.9
	1901	3.1			
2 M	0142	1.2	17 TU	0021	1.3
	0757	2.9		0642	2.8
	1400	1.5		1242	1.6
	2009	3.1		1901	3.0
3 TU	0234	1.3	18 W	0129	1.3
	0854	3.0		0748	3.0
	1456	1.4		1357	1.4
	2110	3.1		2014	3.1
4 W	0318	1.3	19 TH	0233	1.2
	0941	3.2		0851	3.1
	1543	1.2		1503	1.2
	2201	3.1		2123	3.2
5 TH	0356	1.3	20 F	0330	1.1
	1022	3.3		0948	3.3
	1624	1.1		1559	0.9
	2245	3.2		2224	3.4
6 F	0432	1.2	21 SA	0421	1.0
	1100	3.4		1040	3.5
	1703	1.0		1651	0.7
	○ 2324	3.2		● 2318	3.5
7 SA	0506	1.2	22 SU	0508	0.9
	1135	3.4		1128	3.7
	1739	1.0		1740	0.5
8 SU	0000	3.2	23 M	0008	3.6
	0539	1.2		0554	0.8
	1209	3.4		1215	3.8
	1814	0.9		1829	0.4
9 M	0035	3.2	24 TU	0057	3.6
	0611	1.2		0638	0.8
	1242	3.4		1301	3.8
	1849	0.9		1916	0.3
10 TU	0109	3.1	25 W	0144	3.5
	0643	1.2		0721	0.9
	1315	3.4		1347	3.8
	1923	0.9		2003	0.4
11 W	0144	3.1	26 TH	0230	3.3
	0716	1.2		0803	1.0
	1348	3.3		1433	3.7
	1958	1.0		2050	0.6
12 TH	0220	3.0	27 F	0317	3.2
	0749	1.3		0846	1.1
	1424	3.2		1521	3.5
	2036	1.1		2139	0.9
13 F	0259	2.9	28 SA	0406	3.0
	0826	1.4		0935	1.3
	1503	3.2		1613	3.2
	2118	1.1		◐ 2234	1.1
14 SA	0343	2.8	29 SU	0500	2.8
	0908	1.5		1037	1.5
	1548	3.1		1713	3.0
	2210	1.2		2338	1.4
15 SU	0434	2.8	30 M	0601	2.7
	1002	1.6		1159	1.6
	1642	3.0		1822	2.9
	◑ 2314	1.3			
			31 TU	0057	1.5
				0712	2.7
				1336	1.5
				1943	2.8

FEBRUARY

Day	Time	m	Day	Time	m
1 W	0212	1.5	16 TH	0102	1.4
	0824	2.8		0715	2.8
	1446	1.4		1344	1.4
	2057	2.8		2002	2.9
2 TH	0305	1.5	17 F	0224	1.3
	0921	3.0		0830	3.0
	1536	1.3		1500	1.1
	2152	2.9		2120	3.1
3 F	0346	1.4	18 SA	0325	1.1
	1007	3.1		0934	3.2
	1617	1.1		1555	0.8
	2235	3.0		2219	3.3
4 SA	0422	1.3	19 SU	0413	1.0
	1045	3.3		1028	3.5
	1652	1.0		1643	0.5
	2312	3.1		2310	3.5
5 SU	0454	1.2	20 M	0457	0.8
	1121	3.3		1115	3.7
	1725	0.9		1728	0.3
	○ 2346	3.2		● 2356	3.6
6 M	0525	1.1	21 TU	0538	0.7
	1154	3.4		1201	3.8
	1757	0.8		1811	0.2
7 TU	0018	3.2	22 W	0039	3.6
	0555	1.0		0618	0.6
	1225	3.4		1243	3.9
	1828	0.7		1853	0.2
8 W	0049	3.2	23 TH	0120	3.5
	0625	1.0		0656	0.7
	1255	3.4		1325	3.8
	1859	0.7		1934	0.4
9 TH	0120	3.2	24 F	0200	3.3
	0654	1.0		0734	0.8
	1326	3.4		1407	3.6
	1930	0.8		2012	0.6
10 F	0152	3.1	25 SA	0240	3.2
	0725	1.0		0811	0.9
	1358	3.3		1449	3.4
	2002	0.8		2051	0.9
11 SA	0225	3.0	26 SU	0321	3.0
	0757	1.1		0852	1.1
	1432	3.2		1535	3.1
	2036	0.9		2133	1.2
12 SU	0303	3.0	27 M	0407	2.8
	0832	1.2		0944	1.3
	1512	3.1		1632	2.8
	2116	1.1		◐ 2230	1.5
13 M	0348	2.9	28 TU	0507	2.7
	0915	1.3		1111	1.5
	1601	3.0		1745	2.6
	◑ 2210	1.2		2358	1.7
14 TU	0443	2.8			
	1019	1.5			
	1707	2.9			
	2333	1.4			
15 W	0555	2.8			
	1204	1.5			
	1832	2.8			

MARCH

Day	Time	m	Day	Time	m
1 W	0623	2.6	16 TH	0523	2.7
	1313	1.5		1156	1.4
	1918	2.6		1826	2.7
2 TH	0150	1.7	17 F	0054	1.5
	0750	2.7		0653	2.7
	1431	1.4		1343	1.2
	2044	2.7		2004	2.8
3 F	0251	1.6	18 SA	0218	1.3
	0858	2.8		0814	2.9
	1520	1.2		1453	0.9
	2137	2.8		2116	3.0
4 SA	0332	1.4	19 SU	0314	1.1
	0945	3.0		0919	3.2
	1558	1.0		1543	0.6
	2217	2.9		2208	3.3
5 SU	0405	1.3	20 M	0358	0.9
	1024	3.1		1011	3.4
	1631	0.9		1627	0.3
	2252	3.0		2254	3.4
6 M	0435	1.1	21 TU	0438	0.7
	1058	3.3		1057	3.6
	1701	0.7		1708	0.2
	2323	3.1		● 2335	3.5
7 TU	0503	1.0	22 W	0516	0.6
	1130	3.4		1140	3.8
	1731	0.6		1747	0.1
	○ 2354	3.2			
8 W	0531	0.9	23 TH	0014	3.5
	1201	3.4		0553	0.5
	1800	0.6		1221	3.8
				1825	0.2
9 TH	0023	3.2	24 F	0052	3.4
	0600	0.8		0630	0.5
	1231	3.4		1301	3.7
	1830	0.6		1900	0.4
10 F	0053	3.2	25 SA	0128	3.3
	0630	0.8		0706	0.6
	1301	3.4		1340	3.5
	1859	0.6		1934	0.7
11 SA	0123	3.2	26 SU	0203	3.2
	0700	0.8		0743	0.8
	1332	3.4		1420	3.2
	1930	0.7		2007	1.0
12 SU	0155	3.1	27 M	0239	3.0
	0732	0.9		0821	1.0
	1407	3.3		1503	3.0
	2003	0.8		2042	1.3
13 M	0231	3.0	28 TU	0321	2.8
	0807	1.0		0910	1.2
	1448	3.1		1557	2.7
	2041	1.0		2128	1.5
14 TU	0314	2.9	29 W	0415	2.6
	0850	1.2		1035	1.4
	1539	2.9		1711	2.5
	2132	1.3		◐ 2258	1.7
15 W	0408	2.8	30 TH	0534	2.5
	0953	1.3		1234	1.4
	1649	2.8		1846	2.4
	◑ 2304	1.5			
			31 F	0111	1.7
				0703	2.6
				1359	1.3
				2017	2.5

APRIL

Day	Time	m	Day	Time	m
1 SA	0222	1.6	16 SU	0200	1.3
	0820	2.7		0754	2.9
	1449	1.1		1435	0.7
	2109	2.7		2059	3.0
2 SU	0304	1.4	17 M	0253	1.1
	0911	2.9		0857	3.2
	1526	0.9		1523	0.5
	2148	2.9		2148	3.2
3 M	0336	1.2	18 TU	0335	0.9
	0951	3.0		0948	3.4
	1559	0.8		1604	0.3
	2221	3.0		2230	3.3
4 TU	0406	1.0	19 W	0414	0.7
	1026	3.2		1034	3.5
	1629	0.7		1642	0.3
	2252	3.1		2310	3.4
5 W	0434	0.9	20 TH	0451	0.6
	1059	3.3		1117	3.6
	1658	0.5		1719	0.3
	2323	3.2		● 2347	3.4
6 TH	0503	0.8	21 F	0529	0.5
	1131	3.4		1157	3.6
	1728	0.5		1754	0.4
	○ 2353	3.3			
7 F	0533	0.7	22 SA	0022	3.4
	1203	3.4		0607	0.5
	1758	0.5		1237	3.5
				1829	0.6
8 SA	0024	3.3	23 SU	0057	3.3
	0605	0.7		0644	0.6
	1236	3.4		1316	3.3
	1830	0.5		1901	0.8
9 SU	0056	3.3	24 M	0131	3.2
	0638	0.7		0721	0.8
	1311	3.3		1355	3.1
	1903	0.7		1933	1.1
10 M	0130	3.2	25 TU	0206	3.0
	0713	0.8		0802	1.0
	1350	3.2		1438	2.8
	1939	0.9		2008	1.3
11 TU	0208	3.1	26 W	0246	2.9
	0753	0.9		0852	1.1
	1436	3.0		1530	2.6
	2022	1.1		2051	1.5
12 W	0253	3.0	27 TH	0336	2.7
	0844	1.0		1007	1.3
	1533	2.8		1638	2.5
	2120	1.3		◐ 2208	1.7
13 TH	0350	2.8	28 F	0446	2.6
	1006	1.2		1137	1.3
	1652	2.7		1800	2.4
	◑ 2303	1.5		2354	1.7
14 F	0508	2.7	29 SA	0608	2.5
	1202	1.2		1303	1.2
	1829	2.7		1920	2.5
15 SA	0045	1.5	30 SU	0126	1.6
	0637	2.7		0721	2.6
	1333	1.0		1401	1.1
	1956	2.8		2022	2.6

Chart Datum: 1·71 metres below Ordnance Datum (Newlyn)
HAT is 4·0 metres above Chart Datum

TIME ZONE (UT)
For Summer Time add ONE hour in **non-shaded areas**

SCOTLAND – WICK

LAT 58°26′N LONG 3°05′W

TIMES AND HEIGHTS OF HIGH AND LOW WATERS

Dates in amber are **SPRINGS**
Dates in grey are **NEAPS**

2023

MAY

Date	Time	m	Date	Time	m
1 M	0218 0820 1443 2105	1.4 2.7 0.9 2.8	16 TU	0223 0829 1457 2121	1.1 3.1 0.6 3.1
2 TU	0256 0906 1518 2141	1.2 2.9 0.8 2.9	17 W	0308 0923 1538 2204	0.9 3.2 0.5 3.2
3 W	0329 0945 1551 2215	1.1 3.0 0.7 3.1	18 TH	0350 1011 1616 2243	0.8 3.3 0.5 3.3
4 TH	0401 1022 1623 2248	0.9 3.2 0.6 3.2	19 F	0430 1055 1652 ● 2321	0.7 3.4 0.6 3.3
5 F	0433 1059 1655 ○ 2322	0.8 3.3 0.5 3.3	20 SA	0509 1137 1728 2357	0.6 3.3 0.7 3.3
6 SA	0507 1137 1729 2357	0.7 3.3 0.5 3.3	21 SU	0549 1218 1802	0.6 3.2 0.8
7 SU	0543 1216 1806	0.6 3.4 0.6	22 M	0032 0629 1257 1837	3.3 0.7 3.1 1.0
8 M	0033 0623 1258 1845	3.3 0.6 3.3 0.8	23 TU	0107 0709 1337 1910	3.2 0.8 3.0 1.2
9 TU	0112 0705 1343 1927	3.3 0.7 3.2 0.9	24 W	0143 0750 1419 1946	3.1 0.9 2.8 1.3
10 W	0155 0754 1436 2018	3.2 0.8 3.0 1.2	25 TH	0222 0837 1506 2029	3.0 1.0 2.7 1.4
11 TH	0244 0857 1539 2126	3.0 0.9 2.8 1.4	26 F	0308 0936 1601 2126	2.8 1.1 2.5 1.6
12 F	0345 1025 1656 ◑ 2256	2.9 1.0 2.7 1.4	27 SA	0403 1043 1706 ◐ 2246	2.7 1.2 2.5 1.6
13 SA	0459 1152 1817	2.8 0.9 2.7	28 SU	0510 1151 1812	2.6 1.2 2.5
14 SU	0019 0617 1308 1931	1.4 2.9 0.8 2.8	29 M	0003 0616 1254 1913	1.6 2.6 1.1 2.6
15 M	0129 0727 1408 2031	1.3 3.0 0.7 3.0	30 TU	0109 0716 1347 2006	1.5 2.7 1.0 2.7
			31 W	0202 0810 1431 2052	1.3 2.8 0.9 2.9

JUNE

Date	Time	m	Date	Time	m
1 TH	0246 0859 1511 2134	1.2 3.0 0.8 3.0	16 F	0332 0953 1554 2221	1.0 3.1 0.9 3.1
2 F	0326 0946 1549 2214	1.0 3.1 0.7 3.2	17 SA	0417 1040 1632 2301	0.9 3.1 0.9 3.2
3 SA	0406 1031 1627 2254	0.9 3.2 0.7 3.3	18 SU	0459 1124 1709 ● 2338	0.8 3.1 1.0 3.3
4 SU	0447 1117 1708 ○ 2335	0.7 3.3 0.7 3.4	19 M	0540 1205 1744	0.8 3.1 1.0
5 M	0530 1203 1750	0.6 3.3 0.7	20 TU	0014 0619 1243 1820	3.3 0.8 3.0 1.1
6 TU	0017 0617 1251 1836	3.4 0.6 3.3 0.8	21 W	0049 0658 1321 1854	3.2 0.8 3.0 1.2
7 W	0101 0707 1342 1925	3.4 0.6 3.2 1.0	22 TH	0125 0736 1359 1929	3.2 0.8 2.9 1.2
8 TH	0148 0802 1437 2018	3.3 0.6 3.1 1.1	23 F	0202 0816 1439 2007	3.1 0.9 2.8 1.3
9 F	0240 0906 1537 2120	3.2 0.7 3.0 1.2	24 SA	0242 0900 1523 2049	3.0 1.0 2.7 1.4
10 SA	0338 1016 1643 ◑ 2230	3.1 0.7 2.9 1.3	25 SU	0325 0951 1612 2141	2.9 1.1 2.6 1.5
11 SU	0442 1126 1748 2340	3.1 0.8 2.8 1.3	26 M	0415 1047 1707 ◐ 2248	2.8 1.1 2.6 1.5
12 M	0549 1234 1853	3.0 0.8 2.8	27 TU	0512 1147 1806 2358	2.7 1.1 2.6 1.5
13 TU	0048 0655 1336 1955	1.3 3.0 0.8 2.9	28 W	0613 1245 1904	2.7 1.1 2.7
14 W	0151 0759 1429 2050	1.2 3.0 0.8 3.0	29 TH	0103 0716 1341 2001	1.4 2.8 1.1 2.8
15 TH	0245 0900 1514 2138	1.1 3.1 0.8 3.1	30 F	0204 0817 1433 2054	1.3 2.9 1.0 3.0

JULY

Date	Time	m	Date	Time	m
1 SA	0258 0916 1522 2144	1.1 3.0 0.9 3.1	16 SU	0412 1032 1620 2246	1.0 3.0 1.2 3.2
2 SU	0348 1012 1609 2232	0.9 3.2 0.9 3.3	17 M	0453 1115 1656 ● 2324	0.9 3.0 1.1 3.3
3 M	0436 1104 1656 ○ 2319	0.7 3.3 0.8 3.4	18 TU	0530 1153 1730	0.8 3.1 1.1
4 TU	0525 1156 1743	0.6 3.4 0.8	19 W	0000 0606 1229 1803	3.3 0.7 3.1 1.1
5 W	0005 0615 1246 1830	3.5 0.4 3.4 0.8	20 TH	0033 0640 1302 1836	3.3 0.7 3.0 1.1
6 TH	0052 0706 1336 1918	3.5 0.4 3.4 0.9	21 F	0107 0714 1336 1908	3.3 0.7 3.0 1.1
7 F	0140 0758 1428 2006	3.5 0.4 3.3 1.0	22 SA	0140 0748 1410 1940	3.2 0.8 2.9 1.1
8 SA	0229 0852 1520 2056	3.5 0.5 3.1 1.1	23 SU	0213 0822 1446 2014	3.2 0.9 2.9 1.2
9 SU	0321 0949 1614 2152	3.4 0.6 3.0 1.2	24 M	0249 0900 1525 2051	3.1 1.0 2.8 1.3
10 M	0416 1049 1711 ◑ 2255	3.2 0.8 2.8 1.3	25 TU	0329 0944 1610 ◐ 2138	3.0 1.1 2.7 1.4
11 TU	0517 1152 1811	3.1 0.9 2.8	26 W	0417 1039 1704 2246	2.9 1.2 2.7 1.5
12 W	0006 0622 1300 1916	1.3 3.0 1.1 2.8	27 TH	0517 1147 1808	2.8 1.2 2.7
13 TH	0123 0733 1403 2020	1.3 2.9 1.2 2.8	28 F	0011 0630 1256 1916	1.5 2.8 1.3 2.8
14 F	0231 0844 1457 2116	1.2 2.9 1.2 3.0	29 SA	0130 0746 1406 2021	1.4 2.8 1.2 2.9
15 SA	0326 0943 1541 2204	1.1 2.9 1.2 3.1	30 SU	0242 0859 1507 2122	1.2 3.0 1.1 3.1
			31 M	0340 1002 1600 2216	0.9 3.2 1.0 3.3

AUGUST

Date	Time	m	Date	Time	m
1 TU	0430 1057 1647 ○ 2305	0.7 3.3 0.9 3.5	16 W	0512 1135 1712 ● 2340	0.8 3.1 1.1 3.4
2 W	0518 1147 1732 2353	0.4 3.5 0.8 3.7	17 TH	0544 1207 1742	0.7 3.1 1.0
3 TH	0605 1235 1816	0.2 3.5 0.7	18 F	0012 0615 1237 1812	3.4 0.6 3.2 0.9
4 F	0039 0652 1321 1859	3.8 0.2 3.5 0.7	19 SA	0042 0645 1307 1841	3.4 0.6 3.1 0.9
5 SA	0124 0738 1406 1941	3.8 0.2 3.4 0.8	20 SU	0113 0715 1338 1911	3.4 0.7 3.1 1.0
6 SU	0209 0824 1452 2024	3.7 0.4 3.2 0.9	21 M	0143 0745 1409 1941	3.3 0.8 3.0 1.1
7 M	0256 0911 1538 2111	3.5 0.6 3.0 1.1	22 TU	0216 0817 1444 2015	3.2 0.9 3.0 1.2
8 TU	0346 1003 1629 ◑ 2208	3.3 0.9 2.9 1.3	23 W	0253 0852 1525 2055	3.1 1.1 2.9 1.3
9 W	0443 1103 1728 2327	3.0 1.2 2.7 1.4	24 TH	0338 0939 1616 ◐ 2150	2.9 1.2 2.8 1.5
10 TH	0551 1219 1836	2.8 1.4 2.7	25 F	0438 1053 1721 2332	2.8 1.4 2.7 1.5
11 F	0105 0713 1345 1953	1.4 2.7 1.5 2.8	26 SA	0600 1228 1841	2.7 1.5 2.8
12 SA	0226 0837 1447 2058	1.3 2.7 1.5 2.9	27 SU	0117 0732 1355 1958	1.4 2.8 1.4 2.9
13 SU	0321 0937 1532 2149	1.2 2.8 1.4 3.1	28 M	0236 0853 1500 2105	1.1 3.0 1.2 3.1
14 M	0404 1023 1609 2230	1.0 3.0 1.3 3.2	29 TU	0332 0955 1549 2200	0.8 3.2 1.0 3.4
15 TU	0440 1101 1641 2307	0.9 3.0 1.2 3.3	30 W	0419 1045 1633 2249	0.5 3.4 0.8 3.6
			31 TH	0503 1131 1714 ○ 2335	0.3 3.6 0.7 3.8

Chart Datum: 1·71 metres below Ordnance Datum (Newlyn)
HAT is 4·0 metres above Chart Datum

TIME ZONE (UT)
For Summer Time add ONE hour in **non-shaded areas**

SCOTLAND – WICK

LAT 58°26′N LONG 3°05′W

TIMES AND HEIGHTS OF HIGH AND LOW WATERS

Dates in amber are **SPRINGS**
Dates in grey are **NEAPS**

2023

SEPTEMBER

Date	Time	m	Date	Time	m
1 F	0546 1215 1754	0.1 3.6 0.6	16 SA	0543 1208 1744	0.6 3.3 0.9
2 SA	0018 0628 1256 1834	3.9 0.1 3.6 0.6	17 SU	0014 0612 1236 1813	3.5 0.6 3.3 0.9
3 SU	0101 0709 1337 1913	3.9 0.2 3.5 0.7	18 M	0044 0641 1305 1842	3.5 0.7 3.3 0.9
4 M	0144 0749 1417 1952	3.7 0.5 3.3 0.9	19 TU	0114 0710 1336 1913	3.4 0.8 3.2 1.0
5 TU	0227 0829 1459 2034	3.5 0.8 3.1 1.1	20 W	0147 0741 1410 1947	3.3 0.9 3.1 1.1
6 W	0314 0911 1545 ◑ 2128	3.2 1.1 2.9 1.3	21 TH	0226 0816 1450 2028	3.1 1.1 3.0 1.3
7 TH	0411 1007 1643 2255	2.9 1.5 2.8 1.5	22 F	0314 0901 1541 ◐ 2125	3.0 1.4 2.9 1.4
8 F	0524 1134 1757	2.7 1.7 2.7	23 SA	0419 1020 1650 2324	2.8 1.6 2.8 1.5
9 SA	0053 0658 1328 1923	1.5 2.6 1.7 2.7	24 SU	0552 1218 1818	2.7 1.6 2.8
10 SU	0215 0828 1434 2036	1.3 2.7 1.6 2.9	25 M	0113 0730 1347 1940	1.3 2.8 1.5 3.0
11 M	0305 0923 1516 2126	1.2 2.8 1.5 3.1	26 TU	0225 0846 1446 2046	1.0 3.1 1.3 3.2
12 TU	0343 1003 1549 2207	1.0 3.0 1.3 3.2	27 W	0316 0940 1531 2140	0.7 3.3 1.0 3.5
13 W	0416 1038 1619 2242	0.9 3.1 1.2 3.3	28 TH	0400 1026 1611 2228	0.4 3.5 0.8 3.7
14 TH	0445 1109 1647 2314	0.7 3.2 1.0 3.4	29 F	0441 1109 1650 ○ 2312	0.3 3.6 0.7 3.9
15 F	0514 1139 1715 ● 2344	0.7 3.2 0.9 3.5	30 SA	0521 1149 1728 2355	0.2 3.7 0.6 3.9

OCTOBER

Date	Time	m	Date	Time	m
1 SU	0559 1228 1807	0.3 3.6 0.6	16 M	0539 1205 1746	0.7 3.4 0.9
2 M	0036 0637 1305 1846	3.9 0.4 3.5 0.7	17 TU	0016 0609 1235 1818	3.5 0.8 3.4 0.9
3 TU	0118 0714 1343 1925	3.7 0.7 3.4 0.9	18 W	0051 0641 1308 1853	3.4 0.9 3.4 1.0
4 W	0200 0749 1421 2006	3.4 1.0 3.2 1.1	19 TH	0128 0715 1345 1931	3.3 1.1 3.3 1.1
5 TH	0246 0825 1504 2059	3.1 1.4 3.0 1.3	20 F	0212 0754 1428 2018	3.2 1.3 3.1 1.2
6 F	0342 0912 1559 ◑ 2228	2.8 1.7 2.8 1.5	21 SA	0306 0846 1522 2129	3.0 1.5 3.0 1.4
7 SA	0458 1042 1716	2.6 1.9 2.7	22 SU	0417 1016 1633 ◐ 2327	2.8 1.7 2.9 1.4
8 SU	0022 0632 1252 1843	1.5 2.6 1.9 2.8	23 M	0551 1205 1759	2.8 1.7 2.9
9 M	0145 0800 1405 1959	1.4 2.7 1.7 2.9	24 TU	0058 0718 1325 1917	1.2 2.9 1.5 3.1
10 TU	0234 0853 1447 2052	1.2 2.8 1.6 3.0	25 W	0204 0826 1421 2022	0.9 3.1 1.3 3.3
11 W	0311 0932 1519 2133	1.0 3.0 1.4 3.2	26 TH	0254 0918 1506 2116	0.7 3.3 1.1 3.5
12 TH	0343 1005 1549 2208	0.9 3.1 1.2 3.3	27 F	0336 1002 1547 2204	0.5 3.5 0.9 3.7
13 F	0412 1036 1617 2241	0.8 3.2 1.1 3.4	28 SA	0416 1043 1626 ○ 2249	0.4 3.6 0.8 3.8
14 SA	0441 1106 1646 ● 2313	0.7 3.3 1.0 3.5	29 SU	0454 1122 1705 2332	0.4 3.6 0.7 3.8
15 SU	0510 1135 1715 2344	0.7 3.4 0.9 3.5	30 M	0531 1200 1745	0.6 3.6 0.7
			31 TU	0014 0608 1236 1825	3.7 0.7 3.5 0.8

NOVEMBER

Date	Time	m	Date	Time	m
1 W	0056 0643 1313 1906	3.5 1.0 3.4 0.9	16 TH	0035 0621 1249 1843	3.4 1.0 3.5 0.9
2 TH	0138 0718 1350 1949	3.3 1.3 3.3 1.1	17 F	0119 0701 1330 1929	3.3 1.2 3.4 1.0
3 F	0224 0753 1432 2042	3.1 1.5 3.1 1.3	18 SA	0208 0748 1417 2026	3.2 1.3 3.3 1.1
4 SA	0317 0836 1523 2156	2.8 1.7 3.0 1.4	19 SU	0306 0846 1512 2144	3.0 1.5 3.2 1.2
5 SU	0425 0947 1632 ◑ 2324	2.7 1.9 2.8 1.5	20 M	0417 1008 1620 ◐ 2311	2.9 1.6 3.1 1.2
6 M	0544 1130 1750	2.6 1.9 2.8	21 TU	0536 1134 1736	2.9 1.6 3.1
7 TU	0048 0702 1304 1902	1.4 2.7 1.8 2.9	22 W	0028 0650 1248 1847	1.1 3.0 1.5 3.2
8 W	0146 0804 1400 2001	1.3 2.8 1.7 3.0	23 TH	0134 0755 1349 1952	0.9 3.1 1.4 3.3
9 TH	0228 0849 1439 2048	1.1 2.9 1.5 3.1	24 F	0226 0849 1439 2049	0.8 3.2 1.2 3.4
10 F	0303 0925 1513 2128	1.0 3.1 1.3 3.2	25 SA	0311 0936 1524 2142	0.8 3.4 1.0 3.5
11 SA	0335 0959 1545 2205	0.9 3.2 1.2 3.3	26 SU	0352 1018 1607 2230	0.7 3.5 0.9 3.6
12 SU	0407 1031 1617 2241	0.9 3.3 1.1 3.4	27 M	0431 1058 1649 ○ 2315	0.8 3.5 0.8 3.6
13 M	0438 1104 1650 ● 2318	0.8 3.4 1.0 3.5	28 TU	0508 1137 1731 2359	0.9 3.5 0.8 3.5
14 TU	0510 1137 1725 2356	0.8 3.5 0.9 3.5	29 W	0545 1214 1813	1.0 3.5 0.9
15 W	0544 1212 1802	0.9 3.5 0.9	30 TH	0041 0621 1251 1855	3.4 1.2 3.5 1.0

DECEMBER

Date	Time	m	Date	Time	m
1 F	0122 0657 1329 1938	3.2 1.3 3.4 1.1	16 SA	0116 0657 1323 1934	3.4 1.1 3.5 0.8
2 SA	0205 0733 1409 2025	3.0 1.5 3.2 1.2	17 SU	0207 0746 1411 2030	3.3 1.2 3.5 0.8
3 SU	0252 0813 1454 2119	2.9 1.6 3.1 1.3	18 M	0302 0839 1503 2133	3.2 1.4 3.4 0.9
4 M	0345 0903 1547 2222	2.8 1.7 3.0 1.4	19 TU	0402 0941 1602 ◐ 2241	3.1 1.5 3.3 1.0
5 TU	0446 1013 1650 ◑ 2328	2.7 1.8 2.9 1.4	20 W	0506 1051 1707 2350	3.0 1.5 3.2 1.0
6 W	0550 1132 1755	2.7 1.8 2.9	21 TH	0611 1202 1813	2.9 1.5 3.2
7 TH	0033 0652 1245 1856	1.4 2.7 1.7 2.9	22 F	0057 0716 1312 1921	1.0 3.0 1.5 3.2
8 F	0130 0748 1345 1952	1.3 2.8 1.6 3.0	23 SA	0158 0817 1415 2027	1.1 3.1 1.3 3.2
9 SA	0216 0836 1432 2043	1.2 3.0 1.5 3.1	24 SU	0250 0911 1510 2127	1.1 3.2 1.2 3.3
10 SU	0256 0918 1513 2129	1.1 3.1 1.3 3.2	25 M	0335 0959 1559 2220	1.1 3.3 1.1 3.3
11 M	0334 0957 1552 2214	1.0 3.3 1.2 3.3	26 TU	0416 1042 1644 2307	1.1 3.4 1.0 3.3
12 TU	0411 1036 1631 ● 2258	1.0 3.4 1.0 3.4	27 W	0454 1122 1726 ○ 2350	1.2 3.5 0.9 3.3
13 W	0449 1115 1712 2343	1.0 3.5 0.9 3.5	28 TH	0531 1200 1806	1.2 3.5 0.9
14 TH	0529 1156 1756	1.0 3.6 0.8	29 F	0030 0607 1237 1845	3.3 1.2 3.5 0.9
15 F	0028 0612 1238 1843	3.5 1.0 3.6 0.8	30 SA	0108 0641 1313 1923	3.2 1.3 3.4 0.9
			31 SU	0145 0715 1349 2001	3.1 1.3 3.3 1.0

Chart Datum: 1·71 metres below Ordnance Datum (Newlyn)
HAT is 4·0 metres above Chart Datum

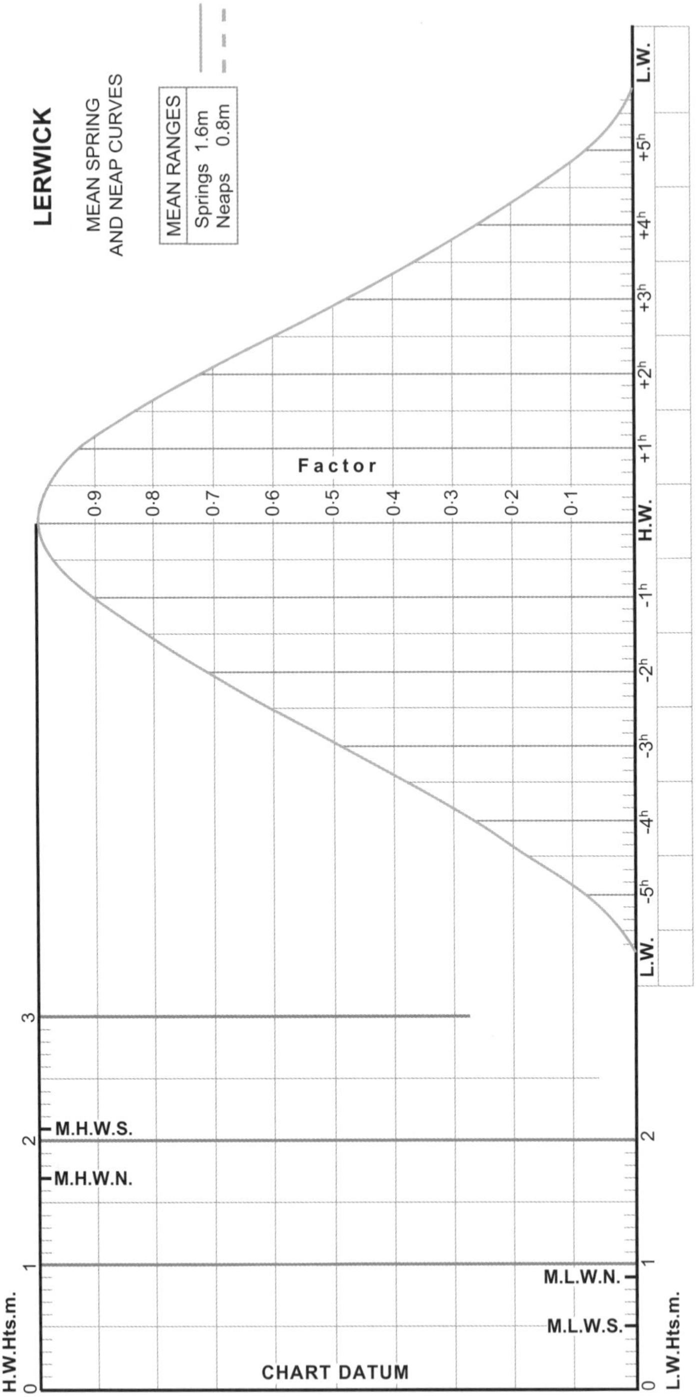
LERWICK
MEAN SPRING AND NEAP CURVES
MEAN RANGES
Springs 1.6m
Neaps 0.8m
Factor
0·9
0·8
0·7
0·6
0·5
0·4
0·3
0·2
0·1
L.W.
-5h
-4h
-3h
-2h
-1h
H.W.
+1h
+2h
+3h
+4h
+5h
L.W.
H.W.Hts.m.
M.H.W.S.
M.H.W.N.
CHART DATUM
M.L.W.N.
M.L.W.S.
L.W.Hts.m.
0
1
2
3

TIME ZONE (UT)
For Summer Time add ONE hour in **non-shaded areas**

SCOTLAND – LERWICK

LAT 60°09′N LONG 1°08′W

TIMES AND HEIGHTS OF HIGH AND LOW WATERS

Dates in amber are **SPRINGS**
Dates in grey are **NEAPS**

2023

JANUARY

Date	Day	Time	m	Time	m	Time	m	Time	m
1	SU	0023	0.8	0633	1.8	1240	1.0	1846	1.9
2	M	0125	0.9	0734	1.8	1347	1.0	1952	1.9
3	TU	0218	0.9	0827	1.9	1442	0.9	2050	1.9
4	W	0303	0.9	0914	2.0	1530	0.8	2140	1.9
5	TH	0343	0.9	0956	2.1	1612	0.8	2225	2.0
6	F	0420	0.9	1035	2.1	1650	0.7	○ 2304	2.0
7	SA	0454	0.9	1111	2.2	1725	0.7	2342	2.0
8	SU	0528	0.9	1145	2.2	1800	0.7		
9	M	0017	2.0	0600	0.9	1218	2.2	1835	0.7
10	TU	0051	2.0	0632	0.9	1251	2.1	1909	0.7
11	W	0125	1.9	0704	0.9	1324	2.1	1946	0.7
12	TH	0200	1.9	0738	0.9	1400	2.0	2024	0.7
13	F	0239	1.8	0816	1.0	1440	2.0	2107	0.8
14	SA	0323	1.8	0901	1.0	1527	1.9	2156	0.8
15	SU	0415	1.7	0956	1.1	1623	1.8	◑ 2257	0.9
16	M	0514	1.7	1111	1.1	1728	1.8		
17	TU	0007	0.9	0622	1.8	1239	1.1	1845	1.8
18	W	0115	0.9	0730	1.9	1348	1.0	1959	1.9
19	TH	0215	0.8	0829	2.0	1448	0.8	2103	2.0
20	F	0311	0.8	0923	2.1	1543	0.6	2201	2.1
21	SA	0403	0.7	1014	2.2	1634	0.5	● 2257	2.2
22	SU	0451	0.7	1104	2.3	1722	0.3	2350	2.3
23	M	0537	0.6	1153	2.4	1810	0.2		
24	TU	0039	2.2	0622	0.6	1240	2.4	1856	0.2
25	W	0126	2.2	0705	0.6	1326	2.4	1943	0.3
26	TH	0211	2.1	0749	0.7	1412	2.3	2029	0.5
27	F	0256	1.9	0834	0.8	1459	2.2	2119	0.6
28	SA	0342	1.8	0923	0.9	1549	2.0	◐ 2215	0.8
29	SU	0434	1.7	1027	1.0	1648	1.8	2327	0.9
30	M	0537	1.7	1159	1.0	1805	1.7		
31	TU	0048	1.0	0653	1.7	1327	1.0	1929	1.7

FEBRUARY

Date	Day	Time	m	Time	m	Time	m	Time	m
1	W	0157	1.1	0801	1.8	1433	0.9	2040	1.7
2	TH	0251	1.0	0857	1.9	1524	0.9	2133	1.8
3	F	0334	1.0	0942	2.0	1604	0.8	2215	1.9
4	SA	0411	0.9	1022	2.1	1639	0.7	2252	1.9
5	SU	0444	0.9	1058	2.1	1711	0.6	○ 2327	2.0
6	M	0514	0.8	1131	2.1	1742	0.5	2359	2.0
7	TU	0543	0.7	1203	2.2	1812	0.5		
8	W	0029	2.0	0613	0.7	1232	2.1	1844	0.5
9	TH	0059	1.9	0642	0.7	1302	2.1	1916	0.5
10	F	0129	1.9	0713	0.7	1333	2.1	1950	0.6
11	SA	0203	1.9	0748	0.8	1408	2.0	2027	0.7
12	SU	0241	1.8	0827	0.9	1450	1.9	2110	0.8
13	M	0327	1.8	0915	0.9	1542	1.8	◑ 2203	0.9
14	TU	0424	1.7	1020	1.0	1649	1.7	2316	0.9
15	W	0533	1.7	1159	1.0	1815	1.7		
16	TH	0048	1.0	0657	1.7	1333	0.9	1948	1.8
17	F	0204	0.9	0812	1.9	1441	0.7	2100	1.9
18	SA	0305	0.8	0912	2.0	1537	0.5	2158	2.0
19	SU	0355	0.7	1004	2.2	1625	0.3	2250	2.2
20	M	0439	0.6	1053	2.3	1709	0.2	● 2336	2.2
21	TU	0521	0.5	1139	2.4	1752	0.1		
22	W	0020	2.2	0601	0.4	1222	2.4	1834	0.1
23	TH	0101	2.1	0641	0.5	1304	2.4	1915	0.2
24	F	0140	2.0	0721	0.5	1345	2.3	1955	0.4
25	SA	0218	1.9	0802	0.6	1427	2.1	2037	0.6
26	SU	0257	1.8	0846	0.8	1512	1.9	2121	0.8
27	M	0341	1.7	0942	0.9	1605	1.7	◐ 2219	1.0
28	TU	0435	1.6	1118	1.0	1720	1.6		

MARCH

Date	Day	Time	m	Time	m	Time	m	Time	m
1	W	0002	1.1	0602	1.6	1305	1.0	1912	1.5
2	TH	0135	1.1	0734	1.7	1417	0.9	2030	1.6
3	F	0236	1.1	0836	1.8	1507	0.8	2119	1.7
4	SA	0319	1.0	0922	1.9	1544	0.7	2156	1.8
5	SU	0353	0.9	1000	1.9	1616	0.6	2229	1.9
6	M	0423	0.8	1035	2.0	1645	0.5	2301	1.9
7	TU	0451	0.7	1108	2.1	1714	0.4	○ 2332	2.0
8	W	0518	0.6	1138	2.1	1743	0.4		
9	TH	0000	2.0	0547	0.5	1206	2.1	1814	0.4
10	F	0028	2.0	0617	0.5	1236	2.1	1845	0.4
11	SA	0057	2.0	0649	0.6	1307	2.1	1918	0.5
12	SU	0129	1.9	0724	0.6	1342	2.0	1955	0.6
13	M	0205	1.9	0804	0.7	1424	1.9	2036	0.7
14	TU	0248	1.8	0852	0.8	1517	1.8	2129	0.9
15	W	0343	1.7	0959	0.9	1631	1.7	◑ 2245	1.0
16	TH	0457	1.6	1147	0.9	1810	1.6		
17	F	0040	1.0	0634	1.6	1326	0.8	1950	1.7
18	SA	0158	0.9	0759	1.8	1432	0.6	2055	1.8
19	SU	0254	0.8	0859	1.9	1524	0.4	2147	2.0
20	M	0339	0.6	0949	2.1	1608	0.2	2232	2.1
21	TU	0420	0.5	1035	2.2	1648	0.1	● 2314	2.1
22	W	0459	0.4	1118	2.3	1728	0.1	2353	2.1
23	TH	0537	0.3	1159	2.3	1806	0.1		
24	F	0030	2.1	0616	0.3	1238	2.3	1844	0.3
25	SA	0105	2.0	0655	0.4	1317	2.1	1921	0.5
26	SU	0139	1.9	0734	0.5	1358	2.0	1957	0.7
27	M	0215	1.8	0817	0.7	1441	1.8	2034	0.9
28	TU	0254	1.7	0911	0.8	1532	1.6	2121	1.0
29	W	0343	1.6	1040	0.9	1640	1.5	◐ 2307	1.2
30	TH	0452	1.5	1226	0.9	1846	1.4		
31	F	0100	1.1	0656	1.5	1341	0.8	2003	1.5

APRIL

Date	Day	Time	m	Time	m	Time	m	Time	m
1	SA	0207	1.0	0803	1.6	1432	0.7	2048	1.6
2	SU	0250	0.9	0849	1.7	1510	0.6	2123	1.7
3	M	0322	0.8	0928	1.8	1541	0.5	2156	1.8
4	TU	0351	0.7	1003	1.9	1610	0.4	2227	1.9
5	W	0420	0.6	1035	2.0	1640	0.3	2258	1.9
6	TH	0449	0.5	1107	2.0	1711	0.3	○ 2327	2.0
7	F	0520	0.4	1138	2.1	1742	0.3	2357	2.0
8	SA	0552	0.4	1211	2.1	1815	0.4		
9	SU	0028	2.0	0628	0.4	1245	2.0	1851	0.5
10	M	0101	2.0	0707	0.5	1325	1.9	1930	0.6
11	TU	0138	1.9	0751	0.6	1412	1.8	2015	0.7
12	W	0222	1.8	0845	0.7	1514	1.7	2112	0.9
13	TH	0320	1.7	0959	0.7	1633	1.6	◑ 2238	1.0
14	F	0439	1.6	1149	0.7	1815	1.6		
15	SA	0030	1.0	0619	1.6	1312	0.6	1940	1.7
16	SU	0140	0.9	0740	1.7	1413	0.4	2037	1.8
17	M	0232	0.7	0838	1.9	1502	0.3	2124	1.9
18	TU	0316	0.6	0927	2.0	1544	0.2	2207	2.0
19	W	0356	0.4	1012	2.1	1623	0.2	2246	2.0
20	TH	0435	0.3	1054	2.2	1701	0.2	● 2323	2.0
21	F	0514	0.3	1135	2.2	1737	0.3	2358	2.0
22	SA	0552	0.3	1214	2.1	1813	0.4		
23	SU	0031	2.0	0632	0.4	1253	2.0	1849	0.6
24	M	0104	1.9	0712	0.5	1334	1.8	1923	0.7
25	TU	0140	1.8	0756	0.6	1418	1.7	1959	0.9
26	W	0219	1.7	0849	0.7	1507	1.5	2043	1.0
27	TH	0306	1.6	1004	0.8	1608	1.4	◐ 2212	1.1
28	F	0406	1.5	1128	0.8	1745	1.4	2358	1.1
29	SA	0538	1.5	1241	0.8	1911	1.5		
30	SU	0111	1.0	0713	1.5	1338	0.7	2001	1.5

Chart Datum: 1·22 metres below Ordnance Datum (Local)
HAT is 2·5 metres above Chart Datum

TIME ZONE (UT)
For Summer Time add ONE hour in **non-shaded areas**

SCOTLAND – LERWICK

LAT 60°09′N LONG 1°08′W

TIMES AND HEIGHTS OF HIGH AND LOW WATERS

Dates in amber are **SPRINGS**
Dates in grey are **NEAPS**

2023

MAY

Date	Day	Time	m	Time	m	Time	m	Time	m
1	M	0201	0.9	0805	1.6	1420	0.6	2040	1.6
2	TU	0239	0.8	0846	1.7	1456	0.5	2114	1.7
3	W	0312	0.7	0923	1.8	1530	0.4	2147	1.8
4	TH	0345	0.6	0958	1.9	1604	0.4	2220	1.9
5	F	0419	0.5	1034	2.0	1638	0.3	○ 2254	2.0
6	SA	0454	0.4	1111	2.0	1714	0.4	2328	2.0
7	SU	0531	0.4	1150	2.0	1751	0.4		
8	M	0003	2.0	0612	0.4	1232	2.0	1831	0.5
9	TU	0041	2.0	0657	0.4	1320	1.9	1915	0.6
10	W	0124	1.9	0747	0.5	1416	1.8	2006	0.8
11	TH	0214	1.8	0848	0.5	1522	1.7	2109	0.9
12	F	0317	1.7	1004	0.6	1636	1.6	◑ 2232	0.9
13	SA	0432	1.7	1134	0.6	1800	1.6		
14	SU	0001	0.9	0557	1.7	1247	0.5	1912	1.6
15	M	0109	0.8	0712	1.8	1347	0.4	2007	1.7
16	TU	0203	0.7	0810	1.9	1436	0.4	2055	1.8
17	W	0250	0.6	0902	1.9	1519	0.3	2138	1.9
18	TH	0333	0.5	0948	2.0	1558	0.4	2217	2.0
19	F	0414	0.4	1033	2.0	1636	0.4	● 2254	2.0
20	SA	0454	0.4	1115	2.0	1712	0.5	2330	2.0
21	SU	0535	0.4	1156	1.9	1748	0.6		
22	M	0004	2.0	0616	0.4	1236	1.9	1824	0.7
23	TU	0039	1.9	0657	0.5	1317	1.8	1900	0.8
24	W	0116	1.9	0741	0.6	1400	1.7	1937	0.9
25	TH	0156	1.8	0829	0.7	1445	1.6	2021	1.0
26	F	0241	1.7	0926	0.7	1535	1.5	2122	1.0
27	SA	0333	1.6	1030	0.7	1634	1.4	◐ 2244	1.0
28	SU	0433	1.6	1134	0.7	1749	1.4	2358	1.0
29	M	0547	1.5	1232	0.7	1857	1.5		
30	TU	0058	0.9	0702	1.6	1323	0.6	1946	1.6
31	W	0147	0.8	0755	1.7	1408	0.6	2027	1.7

JUNE

Date	Day	Time	m	Time	m	Time	m	Time	m
1	TH	0230	0.7	0840	1.8	1449	0.5	2107	1.8
2	F	0311	0.6	0923	1.9	1530	0.5	2145	1.9
3	SA	0351	0.5	1006	1.9	1610	0.5	2225	2.0
4	SU	0433	0.4	1051	2.0	1651	0.5	○ 2305	2.1
5	M	0517	0.4	1138	2.0	1735	0.5	2348	2.1
6	TU	0603	0.3	1229	2.0	1820	0.6		
7	W	0032	2.1	0653	0.3	1323	1.9	1909	0.7
8	TH	0121	2.0	0747	0.4	1420	1.8	2002	0.7
9	F	0215	1.9	0845	0.4	1518	1.7	2100	0.8
10	SA	0314	1.9	0951	0.4	1620	1.7	◑ 2205	0.9
11	SU	0418	1.8	1104	0.5	1727	1.6	2320	0.9
12	M	0527	1.8	1215	0.5	1832	1.6		
13	TU	0031	0.8	0638	1.8	1316	0.5	1931	1.7
14	W	0133	0.7	0742	1.8	1409	0.5	2023	1.8
15	TH	0228	0.7	0838	1.8	1455	0.6	2110	1.8
16	F	0316	0.6	0930	1.9	1537	0.6	2153	1.9
17	SA	0401	0.5	1018	1.9	1616	0.6	2233	2.0
18	SU	0443	0.5	1103	1.9	1654	0.7	● 2311	2.0
19	M	0524	0.5	1144	1.9	1731	0.7	2348	2.0
20	TU	0604	0.5	1224	1.8	1808	0.8		
21	W	0024	2.0	0644	0.5	1302	1.8	1844	0.8
22	TH	0100	1.9	0723	0.5	1341	1.7	1920	0.8
23	F	0138	1.9	0804	0.6	1420	1.7	1957	0.9
24	SA	0217	1.8	0847	0.6	1501	1.6	2040	0.9
25	SU	0301	1.7	0935	0.7	1546	1.6	2130	0.9
26	M	0349	1.7	1029	0.7	1638	1.5	◐ 2235	1.0
27	TU	0445	1.6	1129	0.7	1737	1.5	2350	1.0
28	W	0547	1.6	1228	0.7	1840	1.6		
29	TH	0055	0.9	0657	1.7	1322	0.7	1939	1.7
30	F	0151	0.8	0759	1.7	1413	0.7	2029	1.8

JULY

Date	Day	Time	m	Time	m	Time	m	Time	m
1	SA	0242	0.7	0854	1.8	1502	0.6	2117	1.9
2	SU	0331	0.6	0947	1.9	1550	0.6	2203	2.0
3	M	0419	0.5	1040	2.0	1638	0.6	○ 2250	2.1
4	TU	0508	0.3	1133	2.1	1725	0.6	2338	2.2
5	W	0557	0.3	1227	2.1	1813	0.6		
6	TH	0027	2.2	0647	0.2	1318	2.0	1900	0.6
7	F	0117	2.2	0737	0.2	1409	1.9	1948	0.6
8	SA	0207	2.1	0829	0.3	1459	1.8	2037	0.7
9	SU	0259	2.0	0923	0.4	1551	1.7	2131	0.8
10	M	0353	1.9	1024	0.5	1646	1.7	◑ 2234	0.8
11	TU	0454	1.8	1134	0.6	1748	1.6	2352	0.9
12	W	0603	1.8	1243	0.7	1853	1.7		
13	TH	0109	0.8	0717	1.7	1345	0.8	1954	1.7
14	F	0214	0.8	0823	1.7	1439	0.8	2048	1.8
15	SA	0309	0.7	0922	1.8	1525	0.8	2137	1.9
16	SU	0356	0.6	1012	1.8	1606	0.8	2220	2.0
17	M	0437	0.6	1055	1.8	1644	0.8	● 2259	2.0
18	TU	0515	0.5	1133	1.9	1719	0.8	2336	2.0
19	W	0550	0.5	1209	1.9	1753	0.8		
20	TH	0010	2.0	0625	0.5	1243	1.8	1825	0.7
21	F	0043	2.0	0658	0.5	1316	1.8	1856	0.7
22	SA	0116	2.0	0732	0.5	1349	1.8	1928	0.8
23	SU	0149	1.9	0808	0.6	1423	1.7	2003	0.8
24	M	0226	1.9	0847	0.6	1502	1.7	2043	0.9
25	TU	0308	1.8	0930	0.7	1548	1.6	◐ 2131	0.9
26	W	0358	1.7	1023	0.8	1641	1.6	2235	1.0
27	TH	0457	1.7	1130	0.8	1742	1.6		
28	F	0003	1.0	0609	1.7	1242	0.9	1853	1.7
29	SA	0120	0.9	0729	1.7	1346	0.8	1959	1.8
30	SU	0223	0.8	0838	1.8	1446	0.8	2056	1.9
31	M	0319	0.6	0938	1.9	1539	0.7	2149	2.1

AUGUST

Date	Day	Time	m	Time	m	Time	m	Time	m
1	TU	0411	0.4	1033	2.1	1628	0.6	○ 2239	2.2
2	W	0459	0.3	1125	2.1	1714	0.5	2328	2.3
3	TH	0546	0.1	1215	2.2	1758	0.5		
4	F	0015	2.3	0631	0.1	1301	2.1	1841	0.5
5	SA	0101	2.3	0716	0.2	1346	2.0	1924	0.5
6	SU	0147	2.3	0802	0.3	1430	1.9	2008	0.6
7	M	0234	2.2	0849	0.5	1515	1.8	2056	0.7
8	TU	0323	2.0	0941	0.7	1603	1.7	◑ 2154	0.8
9	W	0419	1.8	1045	0.8	1701	1.7	2319	0.9
10	TH	0530	1.7	1210	1.0	1814	1.7		
11	F	0054	0.9	0700	1.6	1328	1.0	1931	1.7
12	SA	0208	0.9	0820	1.7	1429	1.0	2033	1.8
13	SU	0304	0.8	0918	1.7	1517	1.0	2123	1.9
14	M	0347	0.7	1002	1.8	1556	0.9	2205	2.0
15	TU	0424	0.6	1039	1.9	1630	0.8	2243	2.1
16	W	0456	0.5	1114	1.9	1701	0.7	● 2317	2.1
17	TH	0527	0.5	1146	1.9	1730	0.7	2349	2.1
18	F	0557	0.4	1216	1.9	1759	0.7		
19	SA	0019	2.1	0628	0.5	1245	1.9	1828	0.7
20	SU	0048	2.1	0659	0.5	1314	1.9	1858	0.7
21	M	0118	2.0	0731	0.5	1344	1.9	1931	0.7
22	TU	0151	2.0	0806	0.6	1420	1.8	2008	0.8
23	W	0230	1.9	0845	0.7	1502	1.8	2052	0.9
24	TH	0318	1.8	0933	0.9	1554	1.7	◐ 2152	1.0
25	F	0421	1.7	1038	1.0	1658	1.7	2323	1.0
26	SA	0540	1.7	1213	1.0	1816	1.7		
27	SU	0105	0.9	0717	1.7	1335	1.0	1939	1.8
28	M	0215	0.8	0833	1.8	1438	0.9	2043	2.0
29	TU	0311	0.6	0931	2.0	1529	0.7	2136	2.1
30	W	0359	0.4	1022	2.1	1614	0.6	2225	2.3
31	TH	0444	0.2	1109	2.2	1656	0.5	○ 2311	2.4

Chart Datum: 1·22 metres below Ordnance Datum (Local)
HAT is 2·5 metres above Chart Datum

TIME ZONE (UT)
For Summer Time add ONE hour in **non-shaded areas**

SCOTLAND – LERWICK

LAT 60°09′N LONG 1°08′W

TIMES AND HEIGHTS OF HIGH AND LOW WATERS

Dates in amber are **SPRINGS**
Dates in grey are **NEAPS**

2023

SEPTEMBER

Date	Day	Time	m	Time	m	Time	m	Time	m
1	F	0526	0.1	1153	2.2	1736	0.4	2355	2.4
2	SA	0608	0.1	1236	2.2	1816	0.4		
3	SU	0038	2.4	0649	0.2	1315	2.1	1858	0.5
4	M	0121	2.3	0731	0.4	1355	2.0	1940	0.6
5	TU	0205	2.2	0813	0.6	1435	1.9	2026	0.7
6	W	0252	2.0	0858	0.8	1520	1.8	◑ 2122	0.9
7	TH	0347	1.8	0955	1.0	1613	1.7	2255	1.0
8	F	0500	1.6	1137	1.2	1731	1.7		
9	SA	0042	1.0	0653	1.6	1311	1.2	1909	1.7
10	SU	0155	0.9	0815	1.7	1415	1.1	2015	1.8
11	M	0248	0.8	0904	1.7	1500	1.0	2103	1.9
12	TU	0327	0.7	0940	1.8	1536	0.9	2142	2.0
13	W	0359	0.6	1014	1.9	1606	0.8	2218	2.1
14	TH	0429	0.5	1045	2.0	1634	0.7	2250	2.1
15	F	0457	0.5	1115	2.0	1702	0.7	● 2321	2.2
16	SA	0526	0.4	1144	2.0	1730	0.6	2350	2.2
17	SU	0554	0.4	1211	2.0	1759	0.6		
18	M	0018	2.2	0625	0.5	1238	2.0	1830	0.6
19	TU	0048	2.1	0657	0.6	1308	2.0	1904	0.7
20	W	0121	2.0	0731	0.7	1342	2.0	1942	0.8
21	TH	0201	2.0	0810	0.8	1423	1.9	2029	0.9
22	F	0252	1.8	0858	1.0	1514	1.8	◐ 2132	1.0
23	SA	0401	1.7	1008	1.1	1624	1.7	2312	1.0
24	SU	0531	1.7	1204	1.1	1752	1.7		
25	M	0057	0.9	0718	1.7	1327	1.0	1925	1.8
26	TU	0203	0.7	0825	1.9	1424	0.9	2028	2.0
27	W	0255	0.5	0917	2.0	1511	0.7	2118	2.2
28	TH	0340	0.3	1003	2.2	1553	0.6	2204	2.3
29	F	0422	0.2	1045	2.2	1632	0.5	○ 2248	2.4
30	SA	0502	0.2	1126	2.3	1712	0.4	2331	2.5

OCTOBER

Date	Day	Time	m	Time	m	Time	m	Time	m
1	SU	0541	0.2	1205	2.2	1752	0.4		
2	M	0013	2.4	0620	0.3	1241	2.2	1833	0.5
3	TU	0055	2.3	0659	0.5	1318	2.1	1915	0.6
4	W	0138	2.1	0738	0.8	1356	2.0	2001	0.7
5	TH	0225	1.9	0819	1.0	1438	1.9	2058	0.9
6	F	0320	1.7	0910	1.2	1530	1.8	◑ 2230	1.0
7	SA	0431	1.6	1056	1.3	1642	1.7		
8	SU	0012	1.0	0631	1.6	1240	1.3	1835	1.7
9	M	0125	0.9	0748	1.7	1346	1.2	1943	1.8
10	TU	0216	0.8	0832	1.7	1431	1.1	2031	1.9
11	W	0254	0.7	0907	1.8	1505	0.9	2110	2.0
12	TH	0325	0.6	0939	1.9	1535	0.8	2145	2.1
13	F	0354	0.6	1010	2.0	1603	0.7	2218	2.1
14	SA	0423	0.5	1040	2.1	1631	0.7	● 2249	2.2
15	SU	0452	0.5	1109	2.1	1701	0.6	2319	2.2
16	M	0522	0.5	1137	2.1	1733	0.6	2351	2.2
17	TU	0554	0.6	1207	2.1	1807	0.6		
18	W	0024	2.2	0628	0.7	1239	2.1	1845	0.7
19	TH	0102	2.1	0705	0.8	1315	2.1	1927	0.8
20	F	0146	2.0	0747	0.9	1357	2.0	2019	0.9
21	SA	0244	1.8	0840	1.1	1451	1.9	2128	0.9
22	SU	0400	1.7	0957	1.2	1606	1.8	◐ 2312	0.9
23	M	0532	1.7	1152	1.2	1736	1.8		
24	TU	0040	0.8	0705	1.8	1306	1.0	1904	1.9
25	W	0143	0.6	0805	1.9	1401	0.9	2005	2.1
26	TH	0233	0.5	0854	2.0	1447	0.8	2055	2.2
27	F	0317	0.4	0937	2.1	1529	0.6	2141	2.3
28	SA	0357	0.3	1018	2.2	1609	0.5	○ 2226	2.4
29	SU	0436	0.3	1057	2.3	1650	0.5	2309	2.4
30	M	0515	0.4	1134	2.3	1730	0.5	2351	2.3
31	TU	0553	0.6	1210	2.2	1812	0.5		

NOVEMBER

Date	Day	Time	m	Time	m	Time	m	Time	m
1	W	0034	2.2	0631	0.7	1246	2.2	1856	0.6
2	TH	0118	2.1	0709	0.9	1325	2.1	1943	0.8
3	F	0205	1.9	0748	1.1	1407	2.0	2039	0.9
4	SA	0257	1.7	0836	1.2	1457	1.9	2154	1.0
5	SU	0359	1.6	1000	1.3	1558	1.8	◑ 2317	1.0
6	M	0528	1.6	1139	1.3	1728	1.7		
7	TU	0028	1.0	0652	1.6	1253	1.2	1854	1.8
8	W	0125	0.9	0744	1.7	1345	1.1	1947	1.8
9	TH	0208	0.8	0823	1.8	1424	1.0	2030	1.9
10	F	0243	0.7	0859	1.9	1457	0.9	2107	2.0
11	SA	0315	0.7	0931	2.0	1529	0.8	2142	2.1
12	SU	0347	0.6	1003	2.1	1602	0.7	2217	2.2
13	M	0420	0.6	1036	2.2	1636	0.7	● 2253	2.2
14	TU	0454	0.6	1109	2.2	1712	0.6	2330	2.2
15	W	0529	0.7	1143	2.2	1751	0.6		
16	TH	0010	2.2	0608	0.8	1219	2.2	1834	0.7
17	F	0055	2.1	0650	0.9	1300	2.2	1922	0.7
18	SA	0148	2.0	0737	1.0	1346	2.1	2019	0.8
19	SU	0250	1.9	0835	1.1	1445	2.0	2127	0.8
20	M	0359	1.8	0946	1.1	1556	1.9	◐ 2252	0.8
21	TU	0516	1.8	1116	1.1	1714	1.9		
22	W	0011	0.7	0634	1.8	1231	1.0	1833	2.0
23	TH	0114	0.7	0734	1.9	1331	0.9	1936	2.1
24	F	0207	0.6	0825	2.0	1422	0.8	2031	2.2
25	SA	0253	0.6	0910	2.1	1507	0.7	2120	2.2
26	SU	0335	0.6	0952	2.2	1551	0.6	2208	2.2
27	M	0414	0.6	1032	2.2	1634	0.6	○ 2253	2.2
28	TU	0453	0.7	1110	2.2	1717	0.6	2338	2.2
29	W	0532	0.8	1148	2.2	1800	0.6		
30	TH	0021	2.1	0611	0.9	1225	2.2	1844	0.7

DECEMBER

Date	Day	Time	m	Time	m	Time	m	Time	m
1	F	0104	2.0	0649	1.0	1305	2.1	1929	0.8
2	SA	0148	1.9	0728	1.1	1346	2.0	2018	0.8
3	SU	0233	1.8	0810	1.2	1430	2.0	2111	0.9
4	M	0322	1.7	0904	1.2	1520	1.9	2211	0.9
5	TU	0417	1.7	1015	1.2	1617	1.8	◑ 2315	1.0
6	W	0526	1.6	1133	1.2	1727	1.8		
7	TH	0015	0.9	0638	1.7	1239	1.2	1844	1.8
8	F	0108	0.9	0731	1.8	1332	1.1	1940	1.9
9	SA	0153	0.8	0813	1.9	1417	1.0	2026	1.9
10	SU	0234	0.8	0852	2.0	1457	0.9	2108	2.0
11	M	0314	0.8	0930	2.1	1537	0.8	2151	2.1
12	TU	0353	0.7	1008	2.2	1617	0.7	● 2234	2.2
13	W	0433	0.7	1047	2.2	1659	0.6	2319	2.2
14	TH	0514	0.7	1128	2.3	1743	0.6		
15	F	0006	2.2	0558	0.8	1210	2.3	1831	0.6
16	SA	0057	2.1	0644	0.8	1256	2.2	1921	0.6
17	SU	0150	2.1	0732	0.9	1346	2.2	2014	0.6
18	M	0246	2.0	0824	1.0	1441	2.1	2112	0.6
19	TU	0343	1.9	0922	1.0	1540	2.1	◐ 2219	0.7
20	W	0445	1.8	1029	1.0	1645	2.0	2332	0.7
21	TH	0552	1.8	1146	1.0	1756	2.0		
22	F	0041	0.7	0657	1.8	1259	1.0	1907	2.0
23	SA	0140	0.8	0754	1.9	1400	0.9	2010	2.0
24	SU	0232	0.8	0846	2.0	1454	0.8	2107	2.0
25	M	0318	0.8	0933	2.1	1543	0.7	2200	2.1
26	TU	0401	0.8	1017	2.2	1628	0.7	2249	2.1
27	W	0441	0.9	1058	2.2	1711	0.6	○ 2332	2.1
28	TH	0520	0.9	1137	2.2	1752	0.6		
29	F	0013	2.0	0558	0.9	1214	2.2	1832	0.6
30	SA	0051	2.0	0634	0.9	1251	2.2	1911	0.7
31	SU	0128	1.9	0708	1.0	1327	2.1	1950	0.7

Chart Datum: 1·22 metres below Ordnance Datum (Local)
HAT is 2·5 metres above Chart Datum

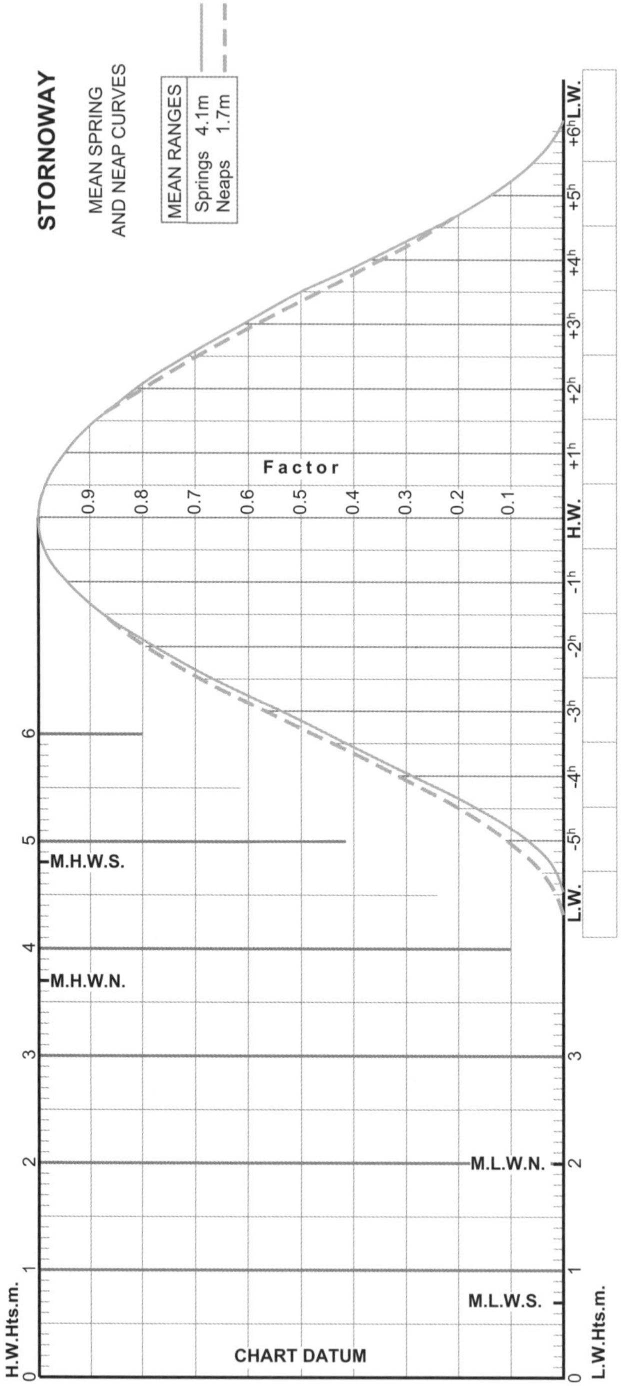
STORNOWAY
MEAN SPRING
AND NEAP CURVES
MEAN RANGES
Springs 4.1m
Neaps 1.7m
Factor
0.9
0.8
0.7
0.6
0.5
0.4
0.3
0.2
0.1
L.W.
-5h
-4h
-3h
-2h
-1h
H.W.
+1h
+2h
+3h
+4h
+5h
+6h
L.W.
H.W.Hts.m.
0
1
2
3
4
5
6
M.H.W.S.
M.H.W.N.
M.L.W.N.
M.L.W.S.
CHART DATUM
L.W.Hts.m.

TIME ZONE (UT)
For Summer Time add ONE hour in **non-shaded areas**

SCOTLAND – STORNOWAY

LAT 58°12′N LONG 6°23′W

TIMES AND HEIGHTS OF HIGH AND LOW WATERS

Dates in amber are **SPRINGS**
Dates in grey are **NEAPS**

2023

JANUARY

Date	Day	Time	m	Time	m	Time	m	Time	m	Moon
1	SU	0250	3.8	0833	2.1	1458	4.1	2115	1.8	
2	M	0353	3.9	0945	2.0	1559	4.1	2217	1.8	
3	TU	0445	4.1	1047	1.9	1652	4.2	2308	1.7	
4	W	0527	4.3	1139	1.7	1737	4.2	2351	1.6	
5	TH	0603	4.4	1223	1.6	1817	4.3			
6	F	0029	1.5	0637	4.5	1302	1.5	1854	4.4	○
7	SA	0104	1.5	0708	4.6	1338	1.4	1929	4.4	
8	SU	0138	1.4	0738	4.7	1413	1.3	2002	4.4	
9	M	0211	1.4	0807	4.7	1447	1.3	2035	4.3	
10	TU	0243	1.4	0838	4.6	1521	1.3	2108	4.2	
11	W	0316	1.5	0910	4.5	1556	1.4	2145	4.1	
12	TH	0351	1.6	0946	4.4	1633	1.5	2226	4.0	
13	F	0429	1.7	1027	4.3	1713	1.7	2315	3.8	
14	SA	0511	1.9	1116	4.1	1800	1.8			
15	SU	0016	3.7	0604	2.0	1216	4.0	1857	1.9	◑
16	M	0126	3.7	0709	2.2	1329	3.9	2006	1.9	
17	TU	0235	3.8	0826	2.2	1445	4.0	2120	1.8	
18	W	0339	4.0	0943	2.0	1555	4.1	2226	1.7	
19	TH	0436	4.3	1050	1.7	1659	4.3	2323	1.4	
20	F	0527	4.6	1148	1.3	1754	4.5			
21	SA	0014	1.2	0614	4.9	1240	1.0	1845	4.8	●
22	SU	0101	1.0	0700	5.2	1330	0.7	1932	4.9	
23	M	0147	0.8	0744	5.3	1417	0.5	2018	4.9	
24	TU	0231	0.8	0829	5.3	1503	0.5	2103	4.8	
25	W	0314	0.8	0914	5.2	1547	0.6	2149	4.5	
26	TH	0358	1.0	1001	5.0	1632	0.8	2237	4.2	
27	F	0443	1.3	1053	4.7	1717	1.2	2332	4.0	
28	SA	0531	1.6	1153	4.3	1806	1.6			◐
29	SU	0041	3.7	0628	1.9	1304	4.0	1904	1.9	
30	M	0201	3.6	0740	2.2	1422	3.8	2019	2.1	
31	TU	0321	3.7	0915	2.2	1539	3.7	2147	2.1	

FEBRUARY

Date	Day	Time	m	Time	m	Time	m	Time	m	Moon
1	W	0427	3.8	1036	2.1	1642	3.8	2253	2.0	
2	TH	0515	4.0	1133	1.9	1731	4.0	2340	1.8	
3	F	0554	4.2	1216	1.6	1810	4.1			
4	SA	0018	1.6	0627	4.4	1253	1.4	1844	4.3	
5	SU	0053	1.5	0655	4.6	1326	1.2	1914	4.4	○
6	M	0125	1.3	0722	4.7	1358	1.1	1943	4.4	
7	TU	0156	1.2	0748	4.7	1428	1.0	2011	4.4	
8	W	0226	1.1	0815	4.8	1458	1.0	2040	4.4	
9	TH	0256	1.1	0844	4.7	1528	1.1	2111	4.3	
10	F	0327	1.2	0915	4.6	1600	1.2	2146	4.2	
11	SA	0400	1.3	0949	4.4	1634	1.3	2226	4.0	
12	SU	0438	1.5	1030	4.3	1713	1.5	2316	3.9	
13	M	0521	1.7	1121	4.0	1800	1.8			◑
14	TU	0026	3.7	0618	2.0	1237	3.8	1907	2.0	
15	W	0152	3.7	0739	2.2	1418	3.7	2042	2.0	
16	TH	0314	3.8	0921	2.1	1550	3.8	2213	1.9	
17	F	0422	4.1	1044	1.7	1700	4.1	2316	1.5	
18	SA	0517	4.5	1145	1.2	1752	4.4			
19	SU	0006	1.2	0603	4.9	1234	0.8	1837	4.7	
20	M	0051	0.9	0646	5.2	1320	0.4	1918	4.9	●
21	TU	0133	0.6	0726	5.4	1402	0.2	1957	4.9	
22	W	0214	0.5	0806	5.4	1442	0.2	2035	4.8	
23	TH	0253	0.5	0847	5.3	1521	0.4	2113	4.6	
24	F	0332	0.7	0928	5.0	1559	0.7	2153	4.3	
25	SA	0412	1.0	1012	4.6	1638	1.1	2235	4.0	
26	SU	0454	1.4	1104	4.1	1718	1.5	2332	3.7	
27	M	0543	1.8	1218	3.8	1805	2.0			◐
28	TU	0106	3.5	0650	2.2	1348	3.5	1914	2.3	

MARCH

Date	Day	Time	m	Time	m	Time	m	Time	m	Moon
1	W	0242	3.5	0847	2.3	1516	3.4	2116	2.4	
2	TH	0400	3.6	1028	2.1	1627	3.6	2238	2.2	
3	F	0455	3.9	1120	1.9	1716	3.8	2324	1.9	
4	SA	0533	4.1	1200	1.6	1753	4.0			
5	SU	0001	1.6	0605	4.3	1233	1.3	1823	4.2	
6	M	0033	1.4	0632	4.5	1304	1.1	1851	4.4	
7	TU	0104	1.2	0657	4.7	1333	0.9	1916	4.5	○
8	W	0133	1.0	0721	4.8	1401	0.8	1943	4.6	
9	TH	0202	0.9	0747	4.8	1429	0.7	2010	4.6	
10	F	0231	0.8	0815	4.8	1458	0.8	2039	4.5	
11	SA	0301	0.9	0845	4.7	1528	0.9	2112	4.4	
12	SU	0334	1.0	0919	4.5	1600	1.1	2149	4.2	
13	M	0411	1.3	0959	4.2	1637	1.4	2237	4.0	
14	TU	0453	1.6	1053	3.9	1722	1.7	2348	3.7	
15	W	0549	1.9	1223	3.6	1828	2.0			◑
16	TH	0127	3.6	0718	2.1	1418	3.5	2025	2.2	
17	F	0256	3.8	0921	1.9	1550	3.7	2207	1.9	
18	SA	0407	4.1	1041	1.5	1654	4.1	2306	1.5	
19	SU	0501	4.5	1135	1.0	1741	4.4	2352	1.1	
20	M	0545	4.9	1220	0.6	1820	4.7			
21	TU	0033	0.7	0625	5.2	1300	0.3	1856	4.9	●
22	W	0113	0.5	0703	5.3	1338	0.2	1931	4.9	
23	TH	0151	0.4	0740	5.3	1415	0.2	2005	4.8	
24	F	0229	0.4	0818	5.1	1451	0.4	2039	4.6	
25	SA	0306	0.6	0857	4.8	1526	0.7	2113	4.4	
26	SU	0344	0.9	0938	4.4	1601	1.1	2150	4.1	
27	M	0424	1.3	1027	3.9	1637	1.6	2234	3.8	
28	TU	0509	1.8	1140	3.6	1718	2.0			
29	W	0002	3.5	0612	2.1	1314	3.3	1816	2.3	◐
30	TH	0153	3.4	0813	2.3	1443	3.3	2026	2.5	
31	F	0317	3.5	1001	2.1	1557	3.4	2208	2.3	

APRIL

Date	Day	Time	m	Time	m	Time	m	Time	m	Moon
1	SA	0418	3.7	1051	1.8	1648	3.7	2255	1.9	
2	SU	0500	3.9	1129	1.5	1724	3.9	2331	1.6	
3	M	0531	4.2	1201	1.2	1753	4.1			
4	TU	0003	1.4	0559	4.4	1231	1.0	1820	4.3	
5	W	0034	1.1	0624	4.6	1300	0.8	1845	4.5	
6	TH	0104	0.9	0650	4.7	1329	0.6	1912	4.6	○
7	F	0134	0.8	0717	4.8	1357	0.6	1940	4.7	
8	SA	0205	0.7	0747	4.7	1427	0.6	2011	4.6	
9	SU	0237	0.8	0821	4.6	1459	0.8	2046	4.5	
10	M	0313	0.9	0900	4.4	1534	1.0	2127	4.3	
11	TU	0352	1.1	0948	4.1	1613	1.4	2220	4.0	
12	W	0439	1.5	1058	3.8	1702	1.7	2340	3.8	
13	TH	0542	1.8	1241	3.5	1816	2.1			◑
14	F	0115	3.7	0724	1.9	1418	3.5	2019	2.1	
15	SA	0238	3.9	0915	1.7	1539	3.7	2148	1.8	
16	SU	0345	4.1	1023	1.3	1637	4.0	2243	1.5	
17	M	0438	4.5	1113	0.9	1720	4.3	2329	1.1	
18	TU	0521	4.8	1156	0.6	1757	4.6			
19	W	0010	0.8	0601	5.0	1234	0.4	1831	4.7	
20	TH	0049	0.6	0639	5.0	1311	0.3	1904	4.8	●
21	F	0128	0.5	0716	5.0	1347	0.4	1937	4.7	
22	SA	0205	0.6	0754	4.8	1421	0.6	2010	4.6	
23	SU	0243	0.8	0833	4.5	1455	0.9	2044	4.4	
24	M	0321	1.0	0915	4.1	1529	1.2	2120	4.1	
25	TU	0401	1.4	1006	3.8	1605	1.6	2204	3.9	
26	W	0447	1.7	1114	3.5	1646	1.9	2313	3.6	
27	TH	0546	2.0	1235	3.3	1739	2.2			◐
28	F	0053	3.5	0720	2.1	1353	3.3	1917	2.4	
29	SA	0216	3.5	0903	2.0	1507	3.4	2107	2.3	
30	SU	0322	3.6	1003	1.8	1603	3.6	2206	2.0	

Chart Datum: 2·71 metres below Ordnance Datum (Local)
HAT is 5·5 metres above Chart Datum

TIME ZONE (UT)
For Summer Time add ONE hour in **non-shaded areas**

SCOTLAND – STORNOWAY

LAT 58°12′N LONG 6°23′W

TIMES AND HEIGHTS OF HIGH AND LOW WATERS

Dates in amber are **SPRINGS**
Dates in grey are **NEAPS**

2023

MAY

Date	Time	m	Date	Time	m
1 M	0411 1044 1643 2248	3.8 1.5 3.8 1.7	16 TU	0411 1043 1655 2301	4.4 1.0 4.2 1.2
2 TU	0447 1119 1715 2324	4.0 1.2 4.0 1.4	17 W	0457 1128 1733 2346	4.5 0.8 4.4 1.0
3 W	0518 1152 1744 2358	4.2 1.0 4.3 1.2	18 TH	0539 1208 1808	4.6 0.7 4.5
4 TH	0547 1223 1812	4.4 0.8 4.5	19 F	0028 0619 1246 ● 1843	0.9 4.7 0.7 4.6
5 F	0031 0618 1255 ○ 1842	1.0 4.6 0.7 4.6	20 SA	0108 0658 1321 1917	0.8 4.6 0.8 4.6
6 SA	0105 0650 1327 1915	0.8 4.7 0.6 4.7	21 SU	0147 0738 1356 1951	0.9 4.4 1.0 4.5
7 SU	0141 0727 1401 1951	0.7 4.6 0.7 4.7	22 M	0226 0819 1431 2026	1.0 4.2 1.1 4.4
8 M	0219 0808 1438 2032	0.8 4.5 0.8 4.6	23 TU	0305 0902 1507 2104	1.2 4.0 1.4 4.2
9 TU	0300 0857 1518 2120	0.9 4.3 1.1 4.4	24 W	0346 0950 1544 2147	1.4 3.8 1.6 4.0
10 W	0345 0959 1603 2222	1.1 4.0 1.4 4.2	25 TH	0430 1045 1625 2241	1.6 3.6 1.8 3.8
11 TH	0440 1118 1659 2340	1.3 3.7 1.7 4.0	26 F	0522 1148 1714 2350	1.8 3.4 2.1 3.7
12 F	0551 1242 1819 ◑	1.5 3.6 2.0	27 SA	0627 1255 1820 ◐	1.9 3.4 2.2
13 SA	0059 0722 1401 1956	3.9 1.6 3.6 2.0	28 SU	0105 0743 1401 1944	3.6 1.9 3.4 2.2
14 SU	0212 0847 1513 2113	4.0 1.4 3.8 1.8	29 M	0212 0851 1501 2056	3.6 1.8 3.5 2.1
15 M	0317 0952 1611 2212	4.2 1.2 4.0 1.5	30 TU	0308 0945 1551 2152	3.7 1.6 3.7 1.9
			31 W	0354 1029 1631 2238	3.9 1.4 3.9 1.6

JUNE

Date	Time	m	Date	Time	m
1 TH	0434 1109 1707 2320	4.1 1.2 4.2 1.4	16 F	0525 1146 1754	4.3 1.2 4.3
2 F	0512 1147 1742	4.3 1.0 4.4	17 SA	0013 0609 1226 1831	1.2 4.3 1.2 4.4
3 SA	0000 0551 1224 1818	1.1 4.4 0.9 4.6	18 SU	0057 0650 1304 ● 1906	1.2 4.3 1.2 4.5
4 SU	0041 0633 1303 ○ 1857	1.0 4.5 0.8 4.7	19 M	0137 0730 1340 1940	1.1 4.2 1.2 4.5
5 M	0124 0718 1344 1940	0.8 4.5 0.8 4.8	20 TU	0216 0809 1416 2014	1.1 4.1 1.3 4.4
6 TU	0208 0808 1426 2027	0.8 4.4 0.9 4.7	21 W	0254 0848 1451 2049	1.2 4.0 1.4 4.3
7 W	0255 0904 1512 2120	0.8 4.3 1.1 4.6	22 TH	0332 0928 1528 2126	1.3 3.9 1.5 4.2
8 TH	0347 1006 1602 2220	0.9 4.1 1.3 4.4	23 F	0412 1010 1606 2208	1.4 3.8 1.6 4.1
9 F	0443 1113 1659 2326	1.1 3.9 1.5 4.3	24 SA	0454 1058 1647 2256	1.5 3.6 1.8 3.9
10 SA	0547 1222 1806 ◑	1.2 3.8 1.7	25 SU	0540 1153 1735 2352	1.7 3.5 1.9 3.8
11 SU	0034 0656 1331 1919	4.2 1.3 3.7 1.8	26 M	0632 1254 1833 ◐	1.7 3.5 2.0
12 M	0141 0806 1439 2031	4.2 1.4 3.8 1.7	27 TU	0056 0732 1356 1941	3.7 1.8 3.5 2.1
13 TU	0246 0912 1540 2137	4.2 1.3 3.9 1.6	28 W	0200 0835 1455 2049	3.7 1.7 3.7 2.0
14 W	0345 1010 1631 2235	4.2 1.3 4.0 1.5	29 TH	0259 0934 1547 2151	3.8 1.6 3.8 1.8
15 TH	0437 1101 1715 2327	4.2 1.2 4.2 1.3	30 F	0354 1027 1634 2246	3.9 1.5 4.1 1.6

JULY

Date	Time	m	Date	Time	m
1 SA	0446 1116 1719 2337	4.1 1.3 4.3 1.3	16 SU	0008 0606 1214 1824	1.5 4.1 1.5 4.4
2 SU	0537 1203 1802	4.3 1.1 4.6	17 M	0051 0645 1253 ● 1857	1.3 4.1 1.4 4.5
3 M	0026 0627 1249 ○ 1847	1.1 4.4 1.0 4.8	18 TU	0129 0720 1328 1928	1.2 4.2 1.3 4.5
4 TU	0115 0717 1334 1933	0.8 4.5 0.9 4.9	19 W	0205 0754 1402 1958	1.1 4.2 1.3 4.5
5 W	0204 0808 1420 2020	0.7 4.6 0.9 5.0	20 TH	0239 0826 1435 2028	1.1 4.2 1.3 4.5
6 TH	0252 0859 1507 2110	0.6 4.5 0.9 4.9	21 F	0312 0858 1508 2059	1.1 4.1 1.3 4.4
7 F	0342 0951 1554 2202	0.6 4.4 1.1 4.8	22 SA	0346 0932 1542 2132	1.2 4.0 1.4 4.3
8 SA	0432 1047 1644 2259	0.8 4.2 1.2 4.6	23 SU	0420 1010 1617 2209	1.3 3.9 1.5 4.2
9 SU	0524 1148 1738	1.0 3.9 1.5	24 M	0456 1054 1655 2252	1.4 3.8 1.7 4.0
10 M	0001 0619 1253 ◑ 1839	4.4 1.2 3.8 1.7	25 TU	0536 1148 1741 ◐ 2345	1.6 3.7 1.9 3.8
11 TU	0107 0720 1402 1948	4.2 1.5 3.7 1.8	26 W	0625 1254 1837	1.7 3.6 2.0
12 W	0216 0827 1511 2104	4.0 1.6 3.7 1.9	27 TH	0053 0726 1404 1949	3.7 1.9 3.6 2.1
13 TH	0325 0938 1613 2218	3.9 1.7 3.9 1.8	28 F	0212 0841 1510 2111	3.7 1.9 3.8 2.0
14 F	0427 1040 1704 2318	3.9 1.7 4.0 1.6	29 SA	0329 0956 1611 2225	3.8 1.8 4.0 1.8
15 SA	0520 1131 1746	4.0 1.6 4.2	30 SU	0437 1058 1704 2326	3.9 1.6 4.3 1.4
			31 M	0534 1152 1751	4.2 1.3 4.6

AUGUST

Date	Time	m	Date	Time	m
1 TU	0019 0624 1239 ○ 1837	1.0 4.5 1.0 4.9	16 W	0114 0701 1312 ● 1907	1.1 4.3 1.3 4.6
2 W	0108 0710 1325 1920	0.7 4.7 0.8 5.2	17 TH	0145 0730 1343 1933	1.0 4.4 1.2 4.7
3 TH	0155 0755 1409 2004	0.4 4.8 0.7 5.3	18 F	0215 0757 1413 1959	0.9 4.4 1.1 4.7
4 F	0240 0839 1452 2048	0.3 4.7 0.7 5.2	19 SA	0245 0825 1443 2027	0.9 4.4 1.1 4.6
5 SA	0324 0923 1535 2134	0.3 4.6 0.8 5.0	20 SU	0314 0854 1513 2056	1.0 4.3 1.2 4.5
6 SU	0407 1010 1619 2225	0.5 4.3 1.0 4.7	21 M	0344 0926 1545 2128	1.1 4.2 1.3 4.4
7 M	0451 1103 1706 2323	0.9 4.1 1.3 4.4	22 TU	0415 1003 1620 2205	1.3 4.0 1.5 4.2
8 TU	0537 1208 1759 ◑	1.3 3.8 1.7	23 W	0451 1050 1700 2252	1.5 3.9 1.7 3.9
9 W	0033 0631 1325 1907	4.0 1.7 3.7 2.0	24 TH	0533 1156 1751 ◐	1.7 3.7 2.0
10 TH	0152 0739 1446 2040	3.8 2.0 3.6 2.1	25 F	0002 0630 1323 1904	3.7 2.0 3.6 2.2
11 F	0312 0911 1558 2214	3.7 2.1 3.8 2.0	26 SA	0149 0759 1446 2049	3.6 2.1 3.7 2.1
12 SA	0422 1030 1654 2316	3.7 2.0 4.0 1.8	27 SU	0324 0941 1556 2219	3.7 2.0 4.0 1.8
13 SU	0516 1123 1736	3.8 1.8 4.2	28 M	0436 1051 1651 2321	3.9 1.7 4.4 1.3
14 M	0002 0557 1203 1811	1.6 4.0 1.6 4.4	29 TU	0529 1142 1738	4.3 1.3 4.8
15 TU	0040 0631 1239 1840	1.3 4.2 1.5 4.5	30 W	0010 0614 1227 1820	0.9 4.6 1.0 5.1
			31 TH	0055 0654 1309 ○ 1900	0.5 4.9 0.7 5.4

Chart Datum: 2·71 metres below Ordnance Datum (Local)
HAT is 5·5 metres above Chart Datum

TIME ZONE (UT)
For Summer Time add ONE hour in **non-shaded areas**

SCOTLAND – STORNOWAY

LAT 58°12′N LONG 6°23′W

TIMES AND HEIGHTS OF HIGH AND LOW WATERS

Dates in amber are **SPRINGS**
Dates in grey are **NEAPS**

2023

SEPTEMBER

Date	Time	m	Date	Time	m
1 F	0137	0.2	16 SA	0145	0.8
	0732	5.0		0726	4.6
	1350	0.5		1346	1.0
	1940	5.5		1929	4.8
2 SA	0218	0.1	17 SU	0212	0.8
	0811	4.9		0751	4.6
	1430	0.5		1414	1.0
	2021	5.4		1955	4.8
3 SU	0257	0.2	18 M	0240	0.9
	0849	4.8		0819	4.6
	1510	0.6		1444	1.0
	2103	5.1		2023	4.7
4 M	0336	0.5	19 TU	0308	1.0
	0930	4.5		0850	4.4
	1551	0.9		1516	1.2
	2149	4.7		2055	4.5
5 TU	0415	1.0	20 W	0339	1.2
	1015	4.2		0925	4.3
	1634	1.3		1551	1.4
	2243	4.3		2132	4.2
6 W	0456	1.4	21 TH	0414	1.5
	1115	3.9		1009	4.0
	1724	1.7		1631	1.7
◑				2221	3.9
7 TH	0001	3.8	22 F	0455	1.8
	0543	1.9		1116	3.8
	1248	3.6		1723	2.0
	1831	2.1	◐	2349	3.6
8 F	0132	3.6	23 SA	0552	2.1
	0649	2.3		1259	3.7
	1420	3.6		1843	2.2
	2026	2.3			
9 SA	0259	3.5	24 SU	0150	3.5
	0848	2.4		0740	2.3
	1539	3.7		1428	3.8
	2211	2.1		2048	2.1
10 SU	0411	3.6	25 M	0322	3.7
	1019	2.2		0935	2.1
	1635	3.9		1539	4.1
	2305	1.8		2213	1.7
11 M	0502	3.8	26 TU	0428	4.0
	1107	2.0		1038	1.7
	1716	4.2		1633	4.5
	2344	1.5		2307	1.2
12 TU	0538	4.0	27 W	0515	4.4
	1144	1.7		1125	1.3
	1747	4.4		1718	4.9
				2352	0.7
13 W	0017	1.3	28 TH	0554	4.7
	0608	4.2		1207	0.9
	1217	1.5		1757	5.2
	1815	4.6			
14 TH	0048	1.1	29 F	0033	0.4
	0635	4.4		0631	5.0
	1248	1.2		1247	0.6
	1840	4.7	○	1836	5.4
15 F	0117	0.9	30 SA	0112	0.2
	0700	4.5		0706	5.1
	1317	1.1		1326	0.5
●	1904	4.8		1915	5.5

OCTOBER

Date	Time	m	Date	Time	m
1 SU	0150	0.2	16 M	0139	0.8
	0741	5.0		0721	4.8
	1405	0.5		1346	1.0
	1954	5.3		1927	4.8
2 M	0227	0.4	17 TU	0208	0.9
	0817	4.9		0750	4.7
	1444	0.7		1418	1.0
	2034	5.0		1958	4.7
3 TU	0304	0.7	18 W	0238	1.0
	0853	4.6		0822	4.6
	1524	1.0		1452	1.2
	2118	4.6		2034	4.5
4 W	0341	1.2	19 TH	0311	1.3
	0933	4.3		0901	4.4
	1607	1.4		1530	1.4
	2212	4.1		2119	4.2
5 TH	0419	1.6	20 F	0349	1.5
	1024	4.0		0950	4.2
	1655	1.8		1615	1.7
	2333	3.7		2223	3.9
6 F	0503	2.1	21 SA	0434	1.9
	1204	3.7		1105	4.0
	1802	2.2		1713	1.9
◑					
7 SA	0106	3.5	22 SU	0006	3.6
	0603	2.4		0539	2.2
	1343	3.6		1243	3.9
	2003	2.3	◐	1845	2.1
8 SU	0231	3.4	23 M	0145	3.6
	0807	2.6		0734	2.3
	1503	3.7		1406	4.0
	2145	2.1		2038	1.9
9 M	0344	3.6	24 TU	0306	3.8
	0948	2.4		0913	2.1
	1602	3.9		1514	4.3
	2235	1.9		2152	1.5
10 TU	0434	3.8	25 W	0408	4.1
	1037	2.1		1012	1.7
	1643	4.1		1609	4.6
	2312	1.6		2243	1.1
11 W	0509	4.0	26 TH	0453	4.5
	1113	1.8		1100	1.3
	1715	4.3		1654	4.9
	2344	1.3		2327	0.8
12 TH	0538	4.3	27 F	0531	4.7
	1146	1.5		1142	1.0
	1742	4.5		1734	5.2
13 F	0014	1.1	28 SA	0007	0.6
	0604	4.5		0607	4.9
	1216	1.3		1223	0.8
	1808	4.7	○	1814	5.3
14 SA	0043	0.9	29 SU	0046	0.5
	0629	4.6		0641	5.0
	1246	1.1		1303	0.7
●	1833	4.8		1853	5.2
15 SU	0111	0.9	30 M	0123	0.6
	0655	4.7		0716	5.0
	1316	1.0		1343	0.7
	1859	4.8		1932	5.1
			31 TU	0200	0.7
				0751	4.9
				1423	0.9
				2014	4.8

NOVEMBER

Date	Time	m	Date	Time	m
1 W	0236	1.0	16 TH	0217	1.1
	0827	4.7		0809	4.8
	1504	1.2		1438	1.2
	2059	4.4		2031	4.5
2 TH	0312	1.4	17 F	0255	1.3
	0906	4.4		0854	4.6
	1547	1.5		1522	1.3
	2152	4.0		2127	4.2
3 F	0351	1.8	18 SA	0338	1.6
	0953	4.1		0949	4.4
	1635	1.8		1613	1.5
	2301	3.7		2237	4.0
4 SA	0433	2.1	19 SU	0429	1.9
	1106	3.9		1101	4.2
	1737	2.1		1717	1.7
5 SU	0022	3.5	20 M	0000	3.8
	0529	2.4		0538	2.1
	1244	3.7		1221	4.2
◑	1907	2.3	◐	1839	1.8
6 M	0140	3.5	21 TU	0122	3.8
	0700	2.6		0709	2.2
	1404	3.7		1336	4.2
	2044	2.2		2005	1.7
7 TU	0253	3.6	22 W	0236	3.9
	0844	2.5		0833	2.0
	1509	3.9		1443	4.4
	2145	2.0		2116	1.5
8 W	0349	3.7	23 TH	0338	4.1
	0947	2.2		0937	1.8
	1558	4.0		1540	4.6
	2228	1.7		2212	1.3
9 TH	0429	4.0	24 F	0428	4.4
	1031	2.0		1031	1.5
	1635	4.2		1630	4.7
	2303	1.5		2300	1.1
10 F	0502	4.2	25 SA	0509	4.6
	1108	1.7		1119	1.3
	1706	4.4		1715	4.9
	2336	1.3		2343	1.0
11 SA	0531	4.4	26 SU	0547	4.7
	1142	1.5		1204	1.1
	1734	4.6		1758	4.9
12 SU	0007	1.1	27 M	0023	0.9
	0559	4.6		0624	4.9
	1214	1.3		1247	1.0
	1803	4.7	○	1840	4.9
13 M	0038	1.0	28 TU	0102	1.0
	0627	4.8		0700	4.9
	1248	1.2		1329	1.0
●	1834	4.7		1921	4.7
14 TU	0109	1.0	29 W	0139	1.1
	0657	4.9		0736	4.8
	1322	1.1		1410	1.1
	1908	4.7		2004	4.5
15 W	0142	1.0	30 TH	0216	1.3
	0731	4.9		0814	4.7
	1359	1.1		1451	1.3
	1946	4.6		2048	4.3

DECEMBER

Date	Time	m	Date	Time	m
1 F	0253	1.5	16 SA	0249	1.2
	0852	4.5		0852	4.9
	1534	1.5		1522	1.1
	2134	4.1		2130	4.4
2 SA	0331	1.7	17 SU	0335	1.4
	0934	4.3		0945	4.8
	1618	1.7		1613	1.2
	2225	3.9		2229	4.2
3 SU	0412	2.0	18 M	0426	1.6
	1023	4.1		1045	4.6
	1709	1.9		1710	1.4
	2323	3.7		2335	4.0
4 M	0500	2.2	19 TU	0525	1.8
	1126	4.0		1150	4.5
	1808	2.1		1813	1.5
			◐		
5 TU	0029	3.6	20 W	0045	3.9
	0600	2.4		0633	1.9
	1241	3.8		1259	4.4
◑	1918	2.1		1921	1.6
6 W	0139	3.6	21 TH	0156	3.9
	0715	2.4		0746	2.0
	1353	3.8		1407	4.3
	2028	2.1		2031	1.6
7 TH	0244	3.7	22 F	0304	4.0
	0831	2.4		0858	1.9
	1454	3.9		1512	4.3
	2127	1.9		2137	1.6
8 F	0337	3.8	23 SA	0404	4.1
	0933	2.2		1004	1.8
	1544	4.0		1612	4.4
	2214	1.7		2235	1.5
9 SA	0420	4.0	24 SU	0454	4.3
	1022	2.0		1102	1.6
	1625	4.2		1705	4.5
	2255	1.6		2325	1.4
10 SU	0457	4.3	25 M	0538	4.5
	1105	1.8		1154	1.5
	1703	4.3		1753	4.5
	2333	1.4			
11 M	0531	4.5	26 TU	0009	1.4
	1146	1.5		0618	4.7
	1740	4.5		1240	1.3
				1837	4.5
12 TU	0009	1.3	27 W	0049	1.3
	0606	4.7		0655	4.7
	1226	1.3		1323	1.3
●	1819	4.6	○	1918	4.5
13 W	0047	1.2	28 TH	0127	1.3
	0642	4.8		0730	4.8
	1307	1.2		1404	1.2
	1901	4.6		1956	4.4
14 TH	0125	1.1	29 F	0204	1.4
	0721	4.9		0804	4.7
	1349	1.1		1442	1.3
	1947	4.6		2033	4.3
15 F	0206	1.1	30 SA	0240	1.4
	0805	4.9		0838	4.7
	1434	1.1		1520	1.3
	2036	4.5		2110	4.2
			31 SU	0315	1.5
				0912	4.5
				1557	1.5
				2147	4.1

Chart Datum: 2·71 metres below Ordnance Datum (Local)
HAT is 5·5 metres above Chart Datum

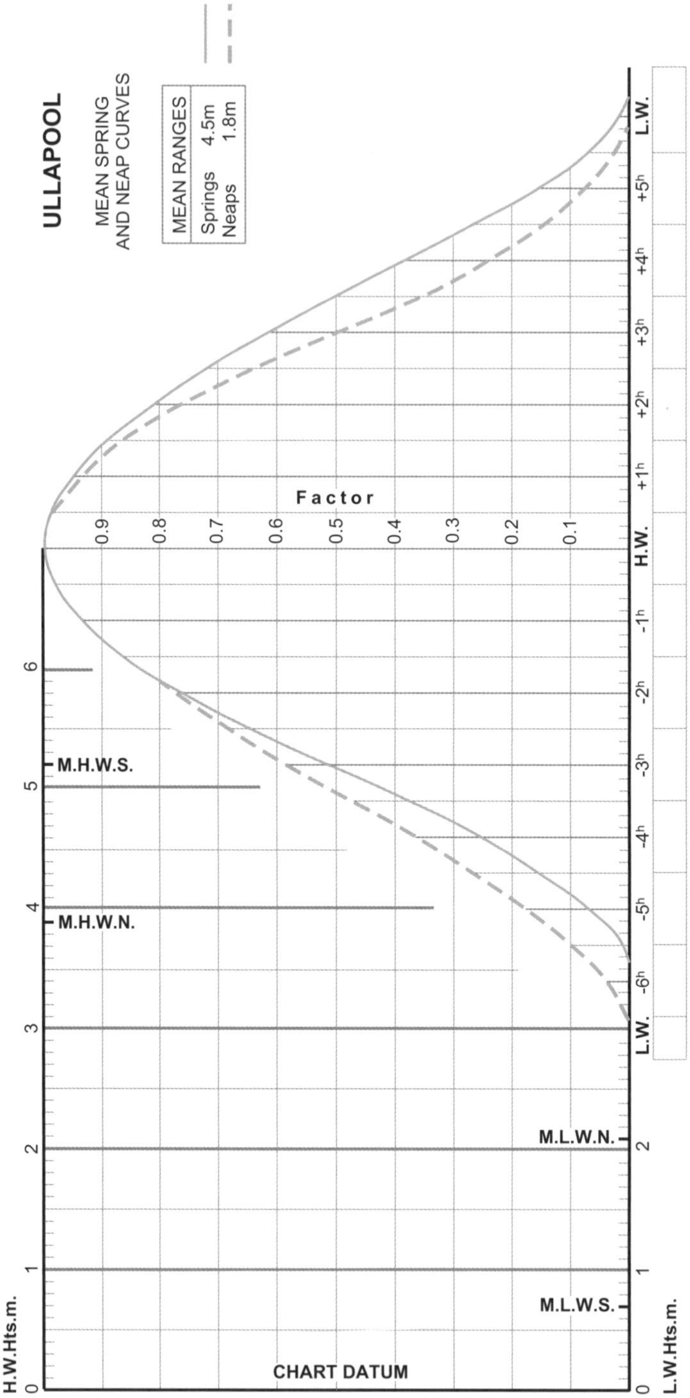
ULLAPOOL
MEAN SPRING AND NEAP CURVES
MEAN RANGES
Springs 4.5m
Neaps 1.8m
H.W.Hts.m.
0
1
2
3
4
5
6
M.H.W.S.
M.H.W.N.
M.L.W.N.
M.L.W.S.
CHART DATUM
L.W.Hts.m.
Factor
0.9
0.8
0.7
0.6
0.5
0.4
0.3
0.2
0.1
L.W.
-6h
-5h
-4h
-3h
-2h
-1h
H.W.
+1h
+2h
+3h
+4h
+5h
L.W.

TIME ZONE (UT)
For Summer Time add ONE hour in **non-shaded areas**

SCOTLAND – ULLAPOOL

LAT 57°54′N LONG 5°09′W

TIMES AND HEIGHTS OF HIGH AND LOW WATERS

Dates in amber are **SPRINGS**
Dates in grey are **NEAPS**

2023

JANUARY

Date	Time m	Date	Time m
1 SU	0253 4.2 0843 2.2 1506 4.4 2119 2.0	16 M	0129 4.1 0719 2.3 1337 4.2 2010 2.1
2 M	0357 4.3 0954 2.1 1608 4.4 2222 1.9	17 TU	0238 4.1 0835 2.3 1451 4.2 2124 2.0
3 TU	0448 4.4 1054 2.0 1700 4.5 2314 1.8	18 W	0342 4.3 0950 2.1 1601 4.4 2231 1.8
4 W	0531 4.6 1145 1.8 1745 4.6 2358 1.7	19 TH	0440 4.6 1056 1.8 1704 4.6 2329 1.5
5 TH	0608 4.7 1229 1.7 1825 4.6	20 F	0532 4.9 1154 1.4 1800 4.9
6 F	0036 1.6 0642 4.9 1307 1.5 ○ 1902 4.7	21 SA	0021 1.3 0620 5.2 1246 1.0 ● 1851 5.1
7 SA	0112 1.6 0714 4.9 1344 1.5 1937 4.7	22 SU	0109 1.0 0706 5.5 1336 0.7 1939 5.3
8 SU	0146 1.5 0744 5.0 1419 1.4 2010 4.7	23 M	0155 0.9 0751 5.7 1423 0.6 2024 5.3
9 M	0219 1.5 0813 5.0 1452 1.4 2042 4.7	24 TU	0239 0.8 0836 5.7 1509 0.5 2110 5.2
10 TU	0252 1.5 0844 4.9 1526 1.4 2116 4.6	25 W	0323 0.9 0921 5.6 1553 0.6 2155 5.0
11 W	0325 1.6 0916 4.8 1600 1.5 2151 4.5	26 TH	0407 1.1 1008 5.3 1637 0.9 2244 4.7
12 TH	0400 1.7 0952 4.7 1636 1.6 2232 4.3	27 F	0452 1.3 1100 5.0 1723 1.3 2338 4.4
13 F	0437 1.8 1032 4.5 1716 1.8 2320 4.2	28 SA	0540 1.7 1159 4.6 1812 1.7 ◐
14 SA	0520 2.0 1120 4.4 1803 1.9	29 SU	0044 4.1 0638 2.0 1309 4.3 1910 2.0
15 SU	0020 4.1 0613 2.2 1221 4.3 ◑ 1900 2.0	30 M	0202 4.0 0751 2.3 1428 4.1 2025 2.3
		31 TU	0324 4.0 0921 2.4 1547 4.0 2152 2.3

FEBRUARY

Date	Time m	Date	Time m
1 W	0430 4.1 1041 2.2 1650 4.1 2259 2.2	16 TH	0316 4.1 0928 2.2 1554 4.1 2218 2.0
2 TH	0520 4.3 1137 2.0 1738 4.3 2347 2.0	17 F	0427 4.4 1049 1.8 1705 4.5 2323 1.7
3 F	0559 4.5 1221 1.8 1817 4.5	18 SA	0523 4.8 1150 1.3 1758 4.8
4 SA	0026 1.7 0632 4.7 1258 1.5 1851 4.6	19 SU	0014 1.3 0610 5.2 1240 0.9 1843 5.1
5 SU	0101 1.6 0701 4.9 1331 1.3 ○ 1922 4.8	20 M	0059 0.9 0653 5.5 1325 0.5 ● 1924 5.3
6 M	0133 1.4 0728 5.0 1403 1.2 1951 4.8	21 TU	0141 0.6 0733 5.7 1408 0.3 2003 5.4
7 TU	0204 1.3 0755 5.1 1434 1.1 2019 4.8	22 W	0222 0.5 0813 5.8 1448 0.3 2042 5.3
8 W	0234 1.2 0822 5.1 1503 1.1 2047 4.8	23 TH	0301 0.6 0854 5.6 1527 0.4 2120 5.1
9 TH	0304 1.2 0850 5.0 1533 1.1 2118 4.7	24 F	0341 0.8 0935 5.3 1605 0.7 2200 4.7
10 F	0335 1.3 0921 4.9 1604 1.2 2152 4.6	25 SA	0420 1.1 1019 4.9 1644 1.2 2243 4.4
11 SA	0408 1.4 0955 4.8 1638 1.4 2231 4.4	26 SU	0503 1.5 1111 4.4 1725 1.6 2340 4.1
12 SU	0445 1.6 1036 4.6 1718 1.6 2321 4.2	27 M	0552 2.0 1222 4.0 1813 2.1 ◐
13 M	0530 1.9 1128 4.3 1806 1.9 ◑	28 TU	0105 3.8 0659 2.3 1351 3.8 1924 2.5
14 TU	0030 4.1 0628 2.1 1244 4.1 1914 2.1		
15 W	0155 4.0 0748 2.3 1423 4.0 2047 2.2		

MARCH

Date	Time m	Date	Time m
1 W	0245 3.8 0850 2.5 1524 3.7 2122 2.5	16 TH	0130 3.9 0726 2.2 1421 3.8 2033 2.3
2 TH	0406 3.9 1029 2.3 1634 3.9 2244 2.3	17 F	0301 4.0 0925 2.1 1555 4.0 2213 2.0
3 F	0500 4.1 1124 2.0 1722 4.1 2332 2.0	18 SA	0414 4.3 1045 1.6 1700 4.4 2313 1.6
4 SA	0539 4.4 1203 1.7 1759 4.4	19 SU	0508 4.8 1140 1.1 1746 4.8
5 SU	0008 1.7 0611 4.6 1237 1.4 1830 4.6	20 M	0000 1.2 0553 5.2 1225 0.7 1826 5.1
6 M	0041 1.5 0638 4.8 1309 1.1 1858 4.8	21 TU	0042 0.8 0632 5.5 1306 0.3 ● 1902 5.3
7 TU	0112 1.2 0704 5.0 1338 0.9 ○ 1924 4.9	22 W	0121 0.5 0710 5.7 1344 0.2 1937 5.3
8 W	0141 1.0 0728 5.1 1407 0.8 1950 5.0	23 TH	0159 0.4 0748 5.6 1421 0.2 2011 5.3
9 TH	0210 0.9 0754 5.1 1434 0.8 2017 5.0	24 F	0237 0.5 0825 5.4 1457 0.4 2046 5.0
10 F	0238 0.9 0821 5.1 1503 0.8 2046 4.9	25 SA	0314 0.7 0904 5.1 1532 0.8 2121 4.8
11 SA	0309 1.0 0851 5.0 1533 0.9 2118 4.8	26 SU	0352 1.0 0945 4.7 1608 1.2 2158 4.4
12 SU	0341 1.1 0926 4.8 1606 1.2 2155 4.6	27 M	0432 1.4 1034 4.2 1645 1.7 2243 4.1
13 M	0418 1.4 1006 4.6 1644 1.5 2242 4.3	28 TU	0517 1.9 1144 3.9 1728 2.1
14 TU	0501 1.7 1100 4.2 1730 1.8 2353 4.0	29 W	0004 3.8 0619 2.3 1315 3.6 ◐ 1830 2.5
15 W	0558 2.0 1230 3.9 1838 2.2 ◑	30 TH	0153 3.6 0811 2.4 1449 3.6 2038 2.6
		31 F	0325 3.7 1000 2.2 1604 3.7 2214 2.4

APRIL

Date	Time m	Date	Time m
1 SA	0425 3.9 1054 1.9 1653 4.0 2302 2.0	16 SU	0354 4.4 1028 1.4 1642 4.4 2252 1.5
2 SU	0506 4.2 1132 1.6 1729 4.2 2339 1.7	17 M	0446 4.7 1118 1.0 1726 4.7 2337 1.1
3 M	0538 4.4 1206 1.3 1759 4.5	18 TU	0530 5.1 1202 0.7 1802 5.0
4 TU	0011 1.4 0606 4.7 1236 1.0 1826 4.7	19 W	0018 0.8 0609 5.3 1241 0.4 1837 5.1
5 W	0042 1.1 0631 4.9 1305 0.8 1852 4.9	20 TH	0058 0.6 0646 5.4 1318 0.4 ● 1911 5.2
6 TH	0111 0.9 0657 5.0 1334 0.7 ○ 1919 5.0	21 F	0136 0.5 0723 5.3 1353 0.5 1944 5.1
7 F	0141 0.8 0724 5.1 1403 0.6 1947 5.1	22 SA	0213 0.6 0801 5.1 1428 0.7 2017 4.9
8 SA	0212 0.8 0754 5.1 1433 0.7 2018 5.0	23 SU	0250 0.8 0840 4.8 1503 1.0 2051 4.7
9 SU	0244 0.8 0828 5.0 1506 0.8 2052 4.9	24 M	0328 1.1 0923 4.5 1538 1.3 2128 4.4
10 M	0320 1.0 0907 4.7 1541 1.1 2133 4.6	25 TU	0408 1.5 1013 4.1 1615 1.7 2212 4.1
11 TU	0400 1.2 0955 4.4 1621 1.5 2226 4.3	26 W	0453 1.8 1118 3.8 1658 2.1 2318 3.9
12 W	0447 1.5 1104 4.1 1712 1.9 2346 4.1	27 TH	0551 2.1 1236 3.6 1754 2.4 ◐
13 TH	0551 1.9 1245 3.8 1828 2.2 ◑	28 F	0053 3.7 0721 2.3 1357 3.6 1934 2.5
14 F	0120 4.0 0730 2.0 1421 3.8 2029 2.2	29 SA	0222 3.7 0902 2.2 1513 3.7 2117 2.4
15 SA	0244 4.1 0918 1.8 1544 4.1 2156 1.9	30 SU	0332 3.8 1005 1.9 1608 3.9 2215 2.1

Chart Datum: 2·75 metres below Ordnance Datum (Newlyn)
HAT is 5·9 metres above Chart Datum

TIME ZONE (UT)
For Summer Time add ONE hour in **non-shaded areas**

SCOTLAND – ULLAPOOL

LAT 57°54′N LONG 5°09′W

Dates in amber are **SPRINGS**
Dates in grey are **NEAPS**

2023

TIMES AND HEIGHTS OF HIGH AND LOW WATERS

MAY

Date	Time	m	Date	Time	m
1 M	0420 1048 1648 2257	4.0 1.6 4.1 1.8	16 TU	0420 1049 1700 2310	4.6 1.1 4.6 1.2
2 TU	0456 1124 1721 2332	4.3 1.4 4.4 1.5	17 W	0506 1134 1739 2354	4.8 0.9 4.8 1.0
3 W	0526 1157 1750	4.5 1.1 4.6	18 TH	0547 1215 1814	4.9 0.8 4.9
4 TH	0005 0555 1229 1819	1.2 4.7 0.9 4.8	19 F	0036 0627 1252 ● 1849	0.9 5.0 0.8 4.9
5 F	0038 0625 1301 ○ 1849	1.0 4.9 0.7 5.0	20 SA	0115 0706 1329 1923	0.8 4.9 0.9 4.9
6 SA	0112 0658 1334 1921	0.8 5.0 0.7 5.1	21 SU	0154 0746 1404 1958	0.9 4.8 1.0 4.8
7 SU	0148 0734 1408 1957	0.8 5.0 0.7 5.0	22 M	0233 0827 1440 2033	1.0 4.6 1.2 4.6
8 M	0226 0816 1446 2038	0.8 4.8 0.9 4.9	23 TU	0311 0910 1516 2111	1.2 4.3 1.4 4.4
9 TU	0307 0905 1526 2127	0.9 4.6 1.2 4.7	24 W	0352 0957 1554 2154	1.4 4.1 1.7 4.2
10 W	0353 1006 1613 2229	1.2 4.3 1.5 4.4	25 TH	0435 1051 1637 2246	1.7 3.9 1.9 4.0
11 TH	0447 1124 1711 2347	1.4 4.1 1.8 4.2	26 F	0526 1151 1727 2354	1.9 3.7 2.2 3.9
12 F	0557 1246 1831 ◑	1.6 3.9 2.1	27 SA	0629 1258 1834 ◐	2.0 3.7 2.3
13 SA	0106 0726 1405 2007	4.2 1.7 3.9 2.0	28 SU	0109 0745 1405 1957	3.8 2.0 3.7 2.3
14 SU	0220 0851 1518 2123	4.2 1.6 4.1 1.8	29 M	0219 0855 1506 2108	3.8 1.9 3.8 2.2
15 M	0326 0957 1615 2221	4.4 1.3 4.3 1.5	30 TU	0316 0949 1556 2202	4.0 1.8 4.0 1.9
			31 W	0403 1034 1636 2246	4.1 1.5 4.3 1.7

JUNE

Date	Time	m	Date	Time	m
1 TH	0442 1114 1712 2328	4.3 1.3 4.5 1.4	16 F	0533 1152 1759	4.6 1.3 4.6
2 F	0520 1153 1747	4.6 1.1 4.7	17 SA	0020 0617 1233 1837	1.3 4.6 1.2 4.7
3 SA	0007 0559 1231 1824	1.2 4.7 1.0 4.9	18 SU	0103 0658 1312 ● 1912	1.2 4.6 1.3 4.8
4 SU	0048 0640 1311 ○ 1903	1.0 4.8 0.9 5.0	19 M	0143 0738 1349 1947	1.2 4.6 1.3 4.7
5 M	0131 0726 1352 1946	0.8 4.9 0.9 5.1	20 TU	0222 0817 1425 2021	1.2 4.5 1.4 4.7
6 TU	0215 0816 1435 2034	0.8 4.8 1.0 5.0	21 W	0300 0856 1501 2056	1.3 4.4 1.5 4.6
7 W	0303 0912 1522 2128	0.9 4.7 1.2 4.9	22 TH	0337 0935 1538 2133	1.3 4.3 1.6 4.4
8 TH	0353 1013 1613 2228	1.0 4.5 1.4 4.7	23 F	0416 1017 1616 2214	1.5 4.1 1.7 4.3
9 F	0450 1119 1710 2334	1.1 4.3 1.6 4.5	24 SA	0457 1103 1658 2301	1.6 4.0 1.9 4.1
10 SA	0552 1226 1817 ◑	1.3 4.1 1.8	25 SU	0543 1157 1746 2358	1.7 3.9 2.0 4.0
11 SU	0042 0701 1335 1930	4.4 1.4 4.1 1.8	26 M	0635 1258 1844 ◐	1.9 3.8 2.1
12 M	0149 0811 1443 2042	4.4 1.5 4.1 1.8	27 TU	0103 0735 1400 1951	3.9 1.9 3.8 2.2
13 TU	0255 0917 1545 2146	4.4 1.5 4.2 1.7	28 W	0207 0839 1458 2058	3.9 1.9 4.0 2.1
14 W	0354 1016 1636 2244	4.4 1.4 4.4 1.5	29 TH	0307 0939 1551 2159	4.0 1.8 4.1 1.9
15 TH	0446 1107 1720 2334	4.5 1.3 4.5 1.4	30 F	0402 1033 1638 2253	4.2 1.6 4.4 1.7

JULY

Date	Time	m	Date	Time	m
1 SA	0453 1123 1723 2344	4.4 1.4 4.6 1.4	16 SU	0013 0613 1222 1829	1.5 4.4 1.6 4.6
2 SU	0544 1210 1808	4.6 1.2 4.9	17 M	0056 0653 1301 ● 1903	1.4 4.5 1.5 4.7
3 M	0033 0634 1256 ○ 1853	1.1 4.8 1.0 5.1	18 TU	0135 0728 1337 1934	1.3 4.5 1.4 4.8
4 TU	0122 0724 1343 1940	0.9 4.9 0.9 5.2	19 W	0210 0801 1412 2004	1.2 4.6 1.3 4.8
5 W	0210 0815 1429 2028	0.7 4.9 0.9 5.2	20 TH	0244 0833 1445 2034	1.1 4.5 1.3 4.8
6 TH	0259 0906 1516 2118	0.6 4.9 1.0 5.2	21 F	0317 0905 1517 2105	1.2 4.5 1.4 4.7
7 F	0348 0959 1604 2210	0.7 4.7 1.1 5.0	22 SA	0350 0939 1550 2138	1.2 4.4 1.5 4.6
8 SA	0438 1054 1654 2307	0.8 4.5 1.3 4.8	23 SU	0424 1016 1625 2215	1.3 4.3 1.6 4.4
9 SU	0529 1153 1749	1.0 4.3 1.5	24 M	0500 1059 1704 2258	1.5 4.1 1.8 4.3
10 M	0009 0625 1257 ◑ 1850	4.6 1.3 4.1 1.7	25 TU	0540 1152 1750 ◐ 2352	1.7 4.0 1.9 4.1
11 TU	0115 0725 1405 1958	4.4 1.6 4.0 1.9	26 W	0629 1258 1847	1.9 3.9 2.1
12 W	0224 0833 1515 2113	4.2 1.8 4.1 1.9	27 TH	0102 0731 1406 1958	4.0 2.0 3.9 2.2
13 TH	0333 0943 1617 2224	4.2 1.8 4.2 1.9	28 F	0220 0846 1512 2118	3.9 2.0 4.0 2.1
14 F	0435 1047 1708 2324	4.2 1.8 4.3 1.7	29 SA	0334 1001 1614 2231	4.0 1.9 4.3 1.9
15 SA	0528 1139 1751	4.3 1.7 4.5	30 SU	0443 1105 1709 2332	4.2 1.7 4.6 1.5
			31 M	0540 1159 1757	4.5 1.4 4.9

AUGUST

Date	Time	m	Date	Time	m
1 TU	0025 0631 1247 ○ 1843	1.1 4.8 1.1 5.2	16 W	0119 0708 1321 ● 1914	1.2 4.6 1.4 4.9
2 W	0114 0717 1333 1927	0.7 5.1 0.8 5.5	17 TH	0150 0737 1352 1940	1.1 4.7 1.2 5.0
3 TH	0201 0801 1418 2011	0.4 5.2 0.7 5.6	18 F	0221 0804 1422 2006	1.0 4.8 1.2 5.0
4 F	0246 0845 1501 2055	0.3 5.1 0.7 5.5	19 SA	0250 0832 1451 2033	1.0 4.7 1.2 4.9
5 SA	0330 0930 1544 2142	0.4 5.0 0.8 5.3	20 SU	0318 0901 1521 2102	1.0 4.7 1.2 4.8
6 SU	0413 1017 1628 2232	0.6 4.7 1.0 5.0	21 M	0348 0933 1552 2135	1.1 4.5 1.4 4.7
7 M	0457 1110 1715 2330	0.9 4.4 1.4 4.6	22 TU	0420 1009 1628 2212	1.3 4.4 1.6 4.4
8 TU	0543 1212 1809 ◑	1.3 4.2 1.7	23 W	0456 1055 1708 2259	1.6 4.2 1.8 4.2
9 W	0039 0637 1326 1917	4.3 1.8 4.0 2.1	24 TH	0539 1159 1800 ◐	1.8 4.0 2.1
10 TH	0157 0746 1449 2046	4.0 2.1 3.9 2.2	25 F	0010 0638 1325 1914	4.0 2.1 3.9 2.3
11 F	0319 0916 1602 2217	3.9 2.2 4.0 2.1	26 SA	0154 0806 1447 2055	3.8 2.3 4.0 2.2
12 SA	0429 1036 1658 2320	4.0 2.1 4.2 1.9	27 SU	0327 0947 1600 2223	4.0 2.1 4.3 1.9
13 SU	0523 1130 1741	4.1 1.9 4.4	28 M	0441 1057 1657 2325	4.2 1.8 4.6 1.4
14 M	0006 0604 1211 1816	1.6 4.3 1.7 4.6	29 TU	0535 1149 1744	4.6 1.4 5.0
15 TU	0044 0638 1248 1846	1.4 4.5 1.5 4.8	30 W	0015 0619 1234 1827	0.9 5.0 1.0 5.4
			31 TH	0100 0659 1317 ○ 1907	0.5 5.2 0.7 5.7

Chart Datum: 2·75 metres below Ordnance Datum (Newlyn)
HAT is 5·9 metres above Chart Datum

TIME ZONE (UT)
For Summer Time add ONE hour in **non-shaded areas**

SCOTLAND – ULLAPOOL

LAT 57°54′N LONG 5°09′W

TIMES AND HEIGHTS OF HIGH AND LOW WATERS

Dates in amber are **SPRINGS**
Dates in grey are **NEAPS**

2023

SEPTEMBER

Day	Time	m	Day	Time	m
1	0143	0.2	16	0150	0.9
	0738	5.4		0732	5.0
F	1358	0.5	SA	1353	1.0
	1947	5.8		1935	5.1
2	0223	0.1	17	0217	0.9
	0817	5.3		0758	5.0
SA	1438	0.5	SU	1422	1.0
	2028	5.7		2001	5.1
3	0303	0.3	18	0245	0.9
	0856	5.2		0826	4.9
SU	1518	0.6	M	1451	1.1
	2110	5.4		2030	5.0
4	0342	0.6	19	0314	1.1
	0936	4.9		0856	4.8
M	1559	0.9	TU	1522	1.2
	2156	5.0		2102	4.8
5	0421	1.0	20	0345	1.3
	1022	4.5		0930	4.6
TU	1642	1.4	W	1557	1.5
	2250	4.5		2139	4.5
6	0503	1.5	21	0420	1.6
	1121	4.2		1014	4.4
W	1732	1.8	TH	1638	1.8
◑				2229	4.2
7	0005	4.1	22	0503	1.9
	0552	2.0		1119	4.1
TH	1247	3.9	F	1731	2.1
	1839	2.2	◐	2355	3.9
8	0135	3.8	23	0603	2.3
	0659	2.4		1301	4.0
F	1423	3.8	SA	1851	2.3
	2027	2.4			
9	0306	3.8	24	0152	3.8
	0855	2.5		0749	2.4
SA	1544	4.0	SU	1432	4.0
	2212	2.2		2051	2.2
10	0418	3.9	25	0326	4.0
	1026	2.4		0942	2.2
SU	1641	4.2	M	1545	4.3
	2307	1.9		2216	1.8
11	0507	4.1	26	0432	4.4
	1115	2.1		1045	1.8
M	1721	4.4	TU	1640	4.8
	2347	1.6		2312	1.3
12	0544	4.4	27	0520	4.8
	1152	1.8		1132	1.3
TU	1753	4.6	W	1725	5.2
				2357	0.8
13	0021	1.4	28	0559	5.1
	0614	4.6		1215	0.9
W	1225	1.5	TH	1805	5.5
	1821	4.8			
14	0052	1.1	29	0038	0.4
	0641	4.8		0636	5.4
TH	1256	1.3	F	1254	0.6
	1846	5.0	○	1843	5.8
15	0122	1.0	30	0118	0.2
	0707	4.9		0712	5.5
F	1325	1.1	SA	1334	0.5
●	1911	5.1		1922	5.8

OCTOBER

Day	Time	m	Day	Time	m
1	0156	0.2	16	0144	0.9
	0747	5.4		0727	5.1
SU	1412	0.5	M	1353	1.0
	2000	5.6		1934	5.1
2	0233	0.4	17	0213	0.9
	0823	5.3		0756	5.1
M	1451	0.7	TU	1424	1.1
	2041	5.3		2005	5.0
3	0310	0.8	18	0244	1.1
	0900	5.0		0829	5.0
TU	1531	1.0	W	1459	1.2
	2125	4.9		2041	4.8
4	0348	1.2	19	0318	1.3
	0940	4.6		0906	4.8
W	1614	1.5	TH	1537	1.5
	2218	4.4		2125	4.5
5	0427	1.7	20	0356	1.6
	1031	4.2		0955	4.5
TH	1702	1.9	F	1622	1.7
	2335	4.0		2228	4.2
6	0513	2.2	21	0443	2.0
	1201	3.9		1108	4.2
F	1808	2.3	SA	1721	2.0
◑					
7	0106	3.7	22	0009	4.0
	0617	2.6		0551	2.3
SA	1345	3.8	SU	1247	4.1
	2000	2.5	◐	1850	2.2
8	0238	3.7	23	0147	3.9
	0820	2.7		0744	2.5
SU	1511	3.9	M	1412	4.2
	2144	2.3		2041	2.0
9	0350	3.9	24	0310	4.1
	0956	2.5		0921	2.2
M	1610	4.1	TU	1522	4.5
	2237	2.0		2155	1.6
10	0438	4.1	25	0412	4.5
	1044	2.2		1021	1.8
TU	1650	4.4	W	1617	4.8
	2315	1.7		2248	1.2
11	0514	4.4	26	0458	4.8
	1121	1.9		1108	1.4
W	1722	4.6	TH	1702	5.2
	2349	1.4		2333	0.9
12	0543	4.6	27	0536	5.1
	1154	1.6		1150	1.0
TH	1749	4.8	F	1742	5.5
13	0019	1.2	28	0013	0.6
	0610	4.8		0612	5.3
F	1224	1.3	SA	1231	0.8
	1815	5.0	○	1821	5.6
14	0048	1.0	29	0052	0.5
	0636	5.0		0647	5.4
SA	1254	1.2	SU	1311	0.7
●	1840	5.1		1900	5.6
15	0116	0.9	30	0130	0.6
	0701	5.1		0722	5.4
SU	1323	1.1	M	1350	0.7
	1906	5.2		1939	5.4
			31	0206	0.8
				0757	5.2
			TU	1430	0.9
				2021	5.1

NOVEMBER

Day	Time	m	Day	Time	m
1	0243	1.1	16	0224	1.2
	0834	5.0		0815	5.1
W	1510	1.2	TH	1445	1.2
	2106	4.7		2038	4.8
2	0321	1.5	17	0303	1.4
	0913	4.7		0859	4.9
TH	1553	1.6	F	1529	1.4
	2158	4.3		2133	4.6
3	0400	1.9	18	0346	1.7
	1000	4.4		0955	4.7
F	1641	1.9	SA	1619	1.6
	2305	4.0		2243	4.3
4	0445	2.2	19	0439	2.0
	1109	4.1		1107	4.5
SA	1741	2.3	SU	1722	1.8
5	0022	3.8	20	0004	4.2
	0543	2.5		0550	2.2
SU	1243	3.9	M	1227	4.4
◑	1908	2.4	◐	1843	1.9
6	0143	3.8	21	0124	4.1
	0716	2.7		0720	2.3
M	1411	3.9	TU	1342	4.4
	2043	2.3		2009	1.8
7	0259	3.9	22	0240	4.2
	0855	2.6		0843	2.1
TU	1519	4.1	W	1450	4.6
	2147	2.1		2120	1.6
8	0354	4.1	23	0343	4.5
	0956	2.3		0946	1.9
W	1607	4.3	TH	1549	4.8
	2231	1.9		2217	1.4
9	0435	4.3	24	0432	4.7
	1039	2.0		1039	1.6
TH	1643	4.5	F	1638	5.0
	2308	1.6		2305	1.2
10	0507	4.5	25	0514	4.9
	1116	1.8		1127	1.3
F	1713	4.7	SA	1723	5.2
	2341	1.4		2349	1.0
11	0536	4.8	26	0552	5.1
	1149	1.5		1211	1.1
SA	1742	4.9	SU	1805	5.3
12	0012	1.2	27	0029	1.0
	0605	5.0		0630	5.2
SU	1222	1.3	M	1254	1.1
	1811	5.0	○	1847	5.2
13	0043	1.1	28	0109	1.0
	0633	5.1		0706	5.2
M	1255	1.2	TU	1335	1.1
●	1841	5.1		1929	5.1
14	0115	1.0	29	0147	1.2
	0703	5.2		0743	5.1
TU	1329	1.1	W	1416	1.2
	1915	5.1		2011	4.9
15	0148	1.1	30	0224	1.4
	0737	5.2		0820	5.0
W	1405	1.1	TH	1457	1.4
	1953	5.0		2055	4.7

DECEMBER

Day	Time	m	Day	Time	m
1	0302	1.6	16	0258	1.3
	0858	4.8		0859	5.2
F	1539	1.6	SA	1528	1.2
	2141	4.4		2137	4.8
2	0341	1.8	17	0344	1.5
	0940	4.6		0952	5.0
SA	1623	1.8	SU	1619	1.3
	2231	4.2		2236	4.6
3	0423	2.1	18	0436	1.7
	1028	4.4		1051	4.9
SU	1712	2.0	M	1715	1.4
	2327	4.0		2340	4.4
4	0511	2.3	19	0535	1.9
	1129	4.2		1157	4.7
M	1811	2.2	TU	1818	1.6
			◐		
5	0032	3.9	20	0048	4.3
	0612	2.5		0643	2.0
TU	1244	4.1	W	1305	4.6
◑	1920	2.3		1926	1.7
6	0142	3.9	21	0159	4.3
	0728	2.6		0756	2.1
W	1359	4.0	TH	1414	4.6
	2031	2.2		2035	1.7
7	0249	4.0	22	0308	4.3
	0843	2.5		0907	2.0
TH	1502	4.1	F	1520	4.6
	2131	2.1		2141	1.7
8	0343	4.1	23	0408	4.5
	0943	2.3		1012	1.9
F	1551	4.3	SA	1620	4.7
	2219	1.9		2240	1.6
9	0425	4.4	24	0458	4.7
	1030	2.1		1110	1.7
SA	1633	4.4	SU	1713	4.8
	2300	1.7		2331	1.5
10	0502	4.6	25	0542	4.8
	1113	1.8		1201	1.5
SU	1710	4.6	M	1800	4.8
	2338	1.5			
11	0536	4.8	26	0016	1.5
	1153	1.6		0623	5.0
M	1747	4.8	TU	1246	1.4
				1844	4.9
12	0015	1.4	27	0057	1.4
	0611	5.0		0700	5.1
TU	1232	1.4	W	1329	1.3
●	1826	4.9	○	1925	4.9
13	0053	1.2	28	0136	1.4
	0648	5.2		0736	5.1
W	1313	1.2	TH	1409	1.3
	1908	5.0		2004	4.8
14	0133	1.2	29	0213	1.5
	0728	5.3		0810	5.0
TH	1356	1.1	F	1447	1.3
	1954	5.0		2041	4.7
15	0214	1.2	30	0249	1.5
	0811	5.3		0844	4.9
F	1440	1.1	SA	1525	1.4
	2043	4.9		2117	4.6
			31	0325	1.6
				0918	4.8
			SU	1602	1.5
				2154	4.4

Chart Datum: 2·75 metres below Ordnance Datum (Newlyn)
HAT is 5·9 metres above Chart Datum

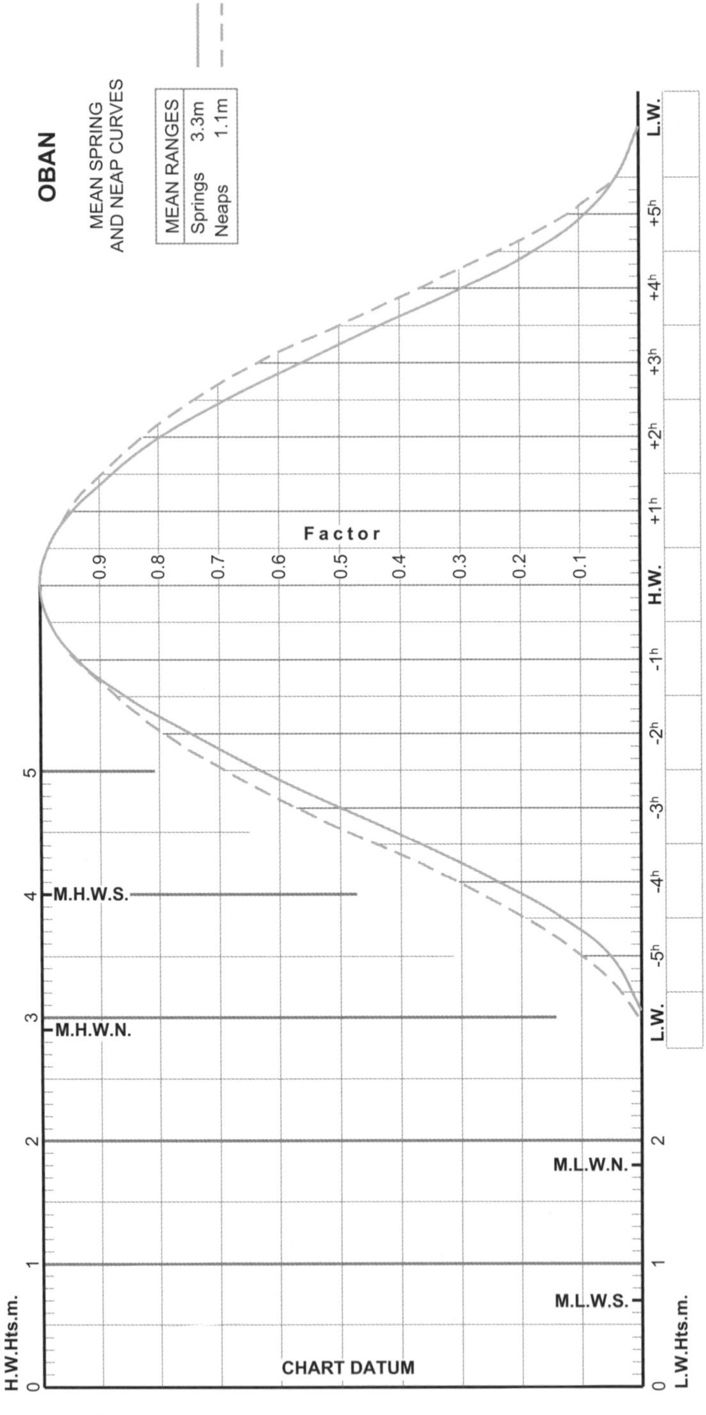
OBAN
MEAN SPRING
AND NEAP CURVES
MEAN RANGES
Springs 3.3m
Neaps 1.1m
Factor
0.9
0.8
0.7
0.6
0.5
0.4
0.3
0.2
0.1
L.W.
-5h
-4h
-3h
-2h
-1h
H.W.
+1h
+2h
+3h
+4h
+5h
L.W.
H.W.Hts.m.
M.H.W.S.
M.H.W.N.
M.L.W.N.
M.L.W.S.
CHART DATUM
L.W.Hts.m.

TIME ZONE (UT)
For Summer Time add ONE hour in **non-shaded areas**

SCOTLAND – OBAN

LAT 56°25′N LONG 5°29′W

TIMES AND HEIGHTS OF HIGH AND LOW WATERS

Dates in amber are **SPRINGS**
Dates in grey are **NEAPS**

2023

JANUARY

Date	Day	Time	m	Time	m	Time	m	Time	m
1	SU	0101	2.9	0715	1.5	1358	3.2	1956	1.7
2	M	0210	3.0	0829	1.6	1458	3.3	2055	1.7
3	TU	0303	3.1	0935	1.6	1545	3.4	2144	1.6
4	W	0347	3.3	1029	1.5	1624	3.5	2226	1.5
5	TH	0428	3.5	1114	1.5	1700	3.6	2306	1.4
6	F	0507	3.7	1154	1.5	1736	3.7	○ 2345	1.3
7	SA	0545	3.8	1231	1.5	1813	3.7		
8	SU	0024	1.2	0623	3.9	1306	1.5	1849	3.8
9	M	0102	1.2	0659	3.9	1341	1.5	1925	3.7
10	TU	0138	1.2	0734	3.8	1415	1.6	1959	3.6
11	W	0212	1.3	0807	3.8	1448	1.7	2031	3.5
12	TH	0244	1.4	0840	3.7	1518	1.8	2103	3.4
13	F	0318	1.5	0914	3.5	1550	1.9	2140	3.2
14	SA	0357	1.6	0954	3.4	1634	1.9	2224	3.1
15	SU	0446	1.7	1044	3.3	1737	2.0	◑ 2322	3.0
16	M	0546	1.7	1150	3.2	1851	1.9		
17	TU	0043	3.0	0657	1.7	1323	3.2	2004	1.8
18	W	0224	3.1	0812	1.6	1452	3.3	2110	1.6
19	TH	0332	3.4	0925	1.4	1555	3.5	2207	1.3
20	F	0426	3.7	1030	1.1	1647	3.7	2259	1.0
21	SA	0513	3.9	1128	0.9	1733	3.8	● 2347	0.8
22	SU	0558	4.1	1219	0.7	1817	3.9		
23	M	0033	0.6	0643	4.2	1307	0.6	1859	3.9
24	TU	0118	0.5	0726	4.2	1352	0.6	1940	3.8
25	W	0203	0.5	0809	4.1	1437	0.8	2020	3.7
26	TH	0248	0.6	0851	3.9	1521	1.0	2059	3.5
27	F	0334	0.8	0935	3.7	1606	1.2	2140	3.3
28	SA	0422	1.1	1022	3.4	1653	1.5	◐ 2224	3.0
29	SU	0514	1.4	1121	3.1	1747	1.7	2325	2.9
30	M	0616	1.7	1256	2.9	1850	1.8		
31	TU	0104	2.8	0741	1.8	1441	2.9	2004	1.9

FEBRUARY

Date	Day	Time	m	Time	m	Time	m	Time	m
1	W	0232	2.9	0929	1.8	1554	3.0	2118	1.8
2	TH	0335	3.1	1033	1.7	1631	3.2	2214	1.6
3	F	0421	3.3	1117	1.6	1701	3.4	2257	1.4
4	SA	0501	3.5	1154	1.4	1732	3.6	2336	1.2
5 ○	SU	0538	3.7	1227	1.3	1806	3.7		
6	M	0012	1.0	0614	3.8	1256	1.3	1840	3.8
7	TU	0046	1.0	0647	3.9	1325	1.2	1911	3.8
8	W	0118	0.9	0718	3.9	1354	1.2	1939	3.8
9	TH	0147	1.0	0745	3.9	1418	1.3	2004	3.7
10	F	0213	1.0	0812	3.8	1436	1.4	2030	3.5
11	SA	0242	1.1	0840	3.7	1501	1.5	2102	3.4
12	SU	0317	1.3	0914	3.5	1539	1.6	2140	3.3
13	M	0402	1.4	0957	3.3	1632	1.8	◑ 2229	3.1
14	TU	0502	1.6	1055	3.1	1752	1.9	2344	2.9
15	W	0624	1.7	1238	2.9	1926	1.8		
16	TH	0206	3.0	0755	1.7	1457	3.1	2051	1.6
17	F	0333	3.3	0924	1.4	1606	3.3	2159	1.3
18	SA	0427	3.6	1033	1.1	1653	3.6	2253	0.9
19	SU	0511	4.0	1127	0.8	1733	3.8	2340	0.6
20 ●	M	0552	4.2	1212	0.6	1809	3.9		
21	TU	0023	0.4	0631	4.3	1254	0.4	1846	4.0
22	W	0105	0.3	0710	4.3	1334	0.5	1921	3.9
23	TH	0146	0.3	0747	4.2	1412	0.6	1955	3.8
24	F	0226	0.4	0823	4.0	1449	0.8	2027	3.6
25	SA	0306	0.7	0858	3.7	1527	1.1	2059	3.4
26	SU	0347	1.1	0935	3.3	1609	1.4	2133	3.2
27	M	0433	1.4	1018	3.0	1659	1.6	◐ 2215	2.9
28	TU	0529	1.8	1126	2.7	1801	1.9	2331	2.7

MARCH

Date	Day	Time	m	Time	m	Time	m	Time	m
1	W	0651	2.0	1437	2.6	1918	1.9		
2	TH	0214	2.7	0938	1.9	1556	2.8	2054	1.8
3	F	0345	2.9	1032	1.7	1628	3.0	2201	1.6
4	SA	0415	3.2	1109	1.5	1649	3.3	2244	1.3
5	SU	0448	3.4	1139	1.3	1716	3.5	2319	1.1
6	M	0521	3.7	1207	1.1	1746	3.7	2352	0.9
7 ○	TU	0554	3.8	1233	1.0	1818	3.8		
8	W	0022	0.8	0625	3.9	1258	0.9	1846	3.9
9	TH	0051	0.7	0653	4.0	1323	0.9	1910	3.8
10	F	0117	0.7	0717	3.9	1344	1.0	1933	3.8
11	SA	0143	0.8	0742	3.8	1403	1.1	2000	3.7
12	SU	0213	0.9	0811	3.7	1430	1.2	2031	3.5
13	M	0249	1.1	0844	3.5	1508	1.4	2109	3.3
14	TU	0335	1.3	0925	3.2	1558	1.6	2158	3.1
15	W	0438	1.6	1023	2.9	1722	1.8	◑ 2319	2.9
16	TH	0615	1.7	1238	2.7	1907	1.8		
17	F	0211	3.0	0757	1.6	1507	2.9	2038	1.5
18	SA	0324	3.3	0927	1.3	1603	3.2	2147	1.2
19	SU	0414	3.7	1027	1.0	1644	3.5	2239	0.8
20	M	0455	4.0	1113	0.7	1719	3.7	2324	0.5
21 ●	TU	0533	4.2	1154	0.5	1750	3.9		
22	W	0005	0.3	0610	4.3	1231	0.4	1823	4.0
23	TH	0045	0.2	0645	4.3	1307	0.4	1855	4.0
24	F	0124	0.3	0719	4.2	1342	0.6	1926	3.9
25	SA	0202	0.5	0752	3.9	1416	0.8	1955	3.7
26	SU	0239	0.8	0824	3.6	1452	1.0	2025	3.5
27	M	0317	1.2	0857	3.3	1534	1.3	2059	3.3
28	TU	0400	1.5	0935	2.9	1623	1.6	2139	3.0
29	W	0457	1.9	1030	2.6	1726	1.8	◐ 2240	2.7
30	TH	0623	2.1	1406	2.5	1842	1.9		
31	F	0157	2.7	0929	2.0	1518	2.7	2016	1.8

APRIL

Date	Day	Time	m	Time	m	Time	m	Time	m
1	SA	0319	2.9	1012	1.7	1553	3.0	2129	1.6
2	SU	0350	3.1	1042	1.5	1619	3.2	2213	1.3
3	M	0420	3.4	1109	1.3	1646	3.4	2248	1.0
4	TU	0452	3.6	1134	1.1	1717	3.6	2320	0.8
5	W	0524	3.8	1159	0.9	1747	3.8	2350	0.7
6 ○	TH	0554	3.9	1224	0.8	1813	3.8		
7	F	0018	0.6	0622	4.0	1248	0.8	1838	3.8
8	SA	0048	0.6	0648	3.9	1312	0.8	1904	3.8
9	SU	0119	0.7	0716	3.8	1339	0.9	1935	3.7
10	M	0154	0.8	0749	3.7	1412	1.0	2011	3.6
11	TU	0236	1.0	0827	3.4	1454	1.2	2054	3.4
12	W	0328	1.3	0913	3.1	1551	1.5	2151	3.1
13	TH	0443	1.5	1023	2.8	1717	1.6	◑ 2327	2.9
14	F	0618	1.6	1316	2.7	1852	1.6		
15	SA	0154	3.1	0756	1.5	1448	2.9	2019	1.4
16	SU	0301	3.4	0914	1.2	1541	3.1	2125	1.1
17	M	0349	3.7	1006	0.9	1620	3.4	2216	0.8
18	TU	0431	3.9	1049	0.7	1652	3.6	2301	0.5
19	W	0508	4.1	1128	0.6	1723	3.8	2343	0.4
20 ●	TH	0544	4.2	1204	0.5	1754	3.9		
21	F	0022	0.4	0618	4.1	1238	0.6	1826	3.9
22	SA	0101	0.5	0651	4.0	1312	0.7	1858	3.9
23	SU	0138	0.7	0723	3.8	1347	0.9	1929	3.8
24	M	0215	1.0	0756	3.5	1424	1.1	2001	3.6
25	TU	0253	1.4	0831	3.2	1506	1.3	2038	3.3
26	W	0338	1.7	0911	2.9	1556	1.6	2121	3.1
27	TH	0436	1.9	1008	2.7	1655	1.8	◐ 2222	2.9
28	F	0559	2.1	1312	2.6	1803	1.9		
29	SA	0033	2.8	0838	2.0	1422	2.7	1921	1.8
30	SU	0224	2.9	0927	1.8	1505	2.9	2032	1.6

Chart Datum: 2·10 metres below Ordnance Datum (Newlyn)
HAT is 4·5 metres above Chart Datum

TIME ZONE (UT)
For Summer Time add ONE hour in **non-shaded areas**

SCOTLAND – OBAN

LAT 56°25′N LONG 5°29′W

Dates in amber are **SPRINGS**
Dates in grey are **NEAPS**

2023

TIMES AND HEIGHTS OF HIGH AND LOW WATERS

MAY

Day		Moon	Time m
1	M		0306 3.1; 0959 1.6; 1538 3.1; 2123 1.4
2	TU		0341 3.3; 1025 1.3; 1609 3.3; 2202 1.2
3	W		0415 3.5; 1051 1.1; 1641 3.5; 2237 1.0
4	TH		0448 3.7; 1118 1.0; 1711 3.7; 2311 0.8
5	F	○	0520 3.8; 1146 0.8; 1739 3.8; 2346 0.7
6	SA		0551 3.9; 1215 0.8; 1808 3.8
7	SU		0023 0.6; 0623 3.9; 1247 0.8; 1842 3.8
8	M		0103 0.7; 0659 3.8; 1323 0.8; 1920 3.7
9	TU		0146 0.8; 0738 3.6; 1406 0.9; 2003 3.6
10	W		0237 1.0; 0824 3.3; 1455 1.1; 2054 3.4
11	TH		0337 1.2; 0920 3.0; 1556 1.3; 2158 3.2
12	F	◑	0449 1.4; 1037 2.8; 1709 1.4; 2332 3.1
13	SA		0611 1.5; 1249 2.7; 1830 1.4
14	SU		0122 3.2; 0736 1.4; 1414 2.9; 1949 1.3
15	M		0228 3.4; 0845 1.2; 1508 3.1; 2056 1.1
16	TU		0320 3.6; 0937 1.1; 1548 3.3; 2150 0.9
17	W		0403 3.7; 1020 0.9; 1621 3.5; 2237 0.8
18	TH		0442 3.8; 1058 0.8; 1654 3.7; 2320 0.7
19	F	●	0518 3.9; 1134 0.8; 1727 3.8
20	SA		0001 0.8; 0554 3.8; 1209 0.8; 1802 3.8
21	SU		0040 0.9; 0628 3.8; 1245 0.9; 1836 3.8
22	M		0119 1.1; 0703 3.6; 1323 1.0; 1911 3.7
23	TU		0157 1.3; 0739 3.4; 1402 1.2; 1947 3.6
24	W		0237 1.5; 0817 3.2; 1445 1.3; 2026 3.4
25	TH		0322 1.7; 0901 3.0; 1531 1.5; 2110 3.2
26	F		0416 1.9; 0954 2.9; 1622 1.7; 2203 3.1
27	SA	◐	0522 2.0; 1113 2.7; 1718 1.8; 2311 3.0
28	SU		0643 2.0; 1305 2.8; 1818 1.8
29	M		0041 3.0; 0800 1.9; 1404 2.9; 1918 1.7
30	TU		0156 3.1; 0851 1.7; 1448 3.0; 2014 1.5
31	W		0247 3.2; 0929 1.5; 1526 3.2; 2104 1.4

JUNE

Day		Moon	Time m
1	TH		0330 3.4; 1004 1.3; 1602 3.4; 2150 1.1
2	F		0410 3.6; 1037 1.1; 1637 3.6; 2235 1.0
3	SA		0449 3.7; 1112 0.9; 1712 3.7; 2320 0.8
4	SU	○	0528 3.8; 1150 0.8; 1750 3.8
5	M		0006 0.7; 0609 3.8; 1230 0.7; 1831 3.8
6	TU		0054 0.7; 0652 3.7; 1314 0.7; 1916 3.8
7	W		0144 0.8; 0737 3.5; 1401 0.8; 2004 3.7
8	TH		0238 0.9; 0827 3.3; 1453 0.9; 2057 3.6
9	F		0336 1.0; 0922 3.1; 1549 1.0; 2157 3.4
10	SA	◑	0439 1.2; 1028 2.9; 1651 1.2; 2312 3.3
11	SU		0547 1.3; 1155 2.8; 1759 1.3
12	M		0038 3.3; 0659 1.4; 1320 2.9; 1912 1.3
13	TU		0150 3.3; 0805 1.4; 1423 3.0; 2021 1.3
14	W		0249 3.4; 0902 1.3; 1512 3.1; 2122 1.2
15	TH		0338 3.4; 0949 1.2; 1552 3.3; 2215 1.2
16	F		0422 3.5; 1031 1.2; 1630 3.5; 2303 1.1
17	SA		0501 3.6; 1110 1.1; 1708 3.6; 2347 1.2
18	SU	●	0538 3.6; 1148 1.1; 1745 3.7
19	M		0027 1.2; 0615 3.6; 1226 1.1; 1823 3.7
20	TU		0107 1.3; 0652 3.5; 1306 1.1; 1900 3.7
21	W		0146 1.4; 0730 3.5; 1345 1.2; 1938 3.7
22	TH		0225 1.5; 0809 3.4; 1425 1.3; 2016 3.6
23	F		0306 1.6; 0848 3.2; 1505 1.4; 2055 3.4
24	SA		0349 1.8; 0930 3.1; 1545 1.5; 2135 3.3
25	SU		0436 1.8; 1016 3.0; 1629 1.6; 2220 3.2
26	M	◐	0529 1.9; 1111 2.9; 1717 1.7; 2313 3.1
27	TU		0628 1.9; 1222 2.9; 1811 1.7
28	W		0019 3.1; 0729 1.8; 1337 2.9; 1911 1.6
29	TH		0137 3.2; 0826 1.7; 1437 3.1; 2012 1.5
30	F		0245 3.3; 0917 1.5; 1528 3.2; 2112 1.4

JULY

Day		Moon	Time m
1	SA		0342 3.4; 1004 1.3; 1615 3.5; 2211 1.1
2	SU		0432 3.6; 1050 1.1; 1700 3.7; 2306 0.9
3	M	○	0519 3.7; 1135 0.8; 1745 3.8; 2359 0.8
4	TU		0605 3.7; 1221 0.7; 1830 4.0
5	W		0050 0.7; 0650 3.7; 1307 0.6; 1916 4.0
6	TH		0141 0.6; 0736 3.6; 1354 0.6; 2002 3.9
7	F		0231 0.7; 0821 3.5; 1442 0.6; 2050 3.8
8	SA		0322 0.9; 0909 3.3; 1533 0.8; 2141 3.6
9	SU		0415 1.0; 1001 3.1; 1626 1.0; 2238 3.4
10	M	◑	0511 1.2; 1100 3.0; 1724 1.2; 2346 3.2
11	TU		0610 1.4; 1214 2.9; 1828 1.4
12	W		0105 3.1; 0715 1.5; 1332 2.9; 1942 1.5
13	TH		0220 3.1; 0821 1.6; 1439 3.0; 2100 1.5
14	F		0326 3.1; 0921 1.5; 1533 3.1; 2207 1.5
15	SA		0417 3.2; 1012 1.4; 1617 3.3; 2301 1.4
16	SU		0458 3.3; 1055 1.3; 1658 3.5; 2345 1.4
17	M	●	0534 3.4; 1136 1.2; 1737 3.6
18	TU		0023 1.3; 0610 3.5; 1214 1.1; 1815 3.7
19	W		0059 1.3; 0645 3.6; 1252 1.0; 1851 3.8
20	TH		0134 1.3; 0720 3.6; 1328 1.0; 1925 3.8
21	F		0208 1.4; 0754 3.6; 1403 1.1; 1959 3.7
22	SA		0242 1.4; 0826 3.5; 1435 1.2; 2030 3.6
23	SU		0313 1.5; 0856 3.3; 1506 1.3; 2101 3.5
24	M		0342 1.6; 0929 3.2; 1541 1.4; 2135 3.4
25	TU	◐	0417 1.7; 1007 3.1; 1623 1.6; 2215 3.3
26	W		0508 1.8; 1056 3.0; 1716 1.7; 2308 3.1
27	TH		0617 1.9; 1206 2.9; 1822 1.7
28	F		0024 3.0; 0733 1.8; 1357 2.9; 1937 1.7
29	SA		0217 3.1; 0844 1.6; 1516 3.2; 2053 1.5
30	SU		0335 3.3; 0947 1.4; 1611 3.4; 2204 1.3
31	M		0432 3.5; 1040 1.1; 1659 3.7; 2305 1.0

AUGUST

Day		Moon	Time m
1	TU	○	0519 3.6; 1128 0.8; 1743 4.0; 2358 0.7
2	W		0603 3.8; 1213 0.5; 1825 4.2
3	TH		0045 0.5; 0644 3.8; 1257 0.4; 1908 4.2
4	F		0131 0.5; 0724 3.8; 1341 0.3; 1949 4.2
5	SA		0215 0.5; 0803 3.7; 1425 0.4; 2031 4.0
6	SU		0258 0.7; 0843 3.5; 1510 0.6; 2113 3.8
7	M		0342 0.9; 0923 3.3; 1557 0.9; 2158 3.5
8	TU	◑	0429 1.2; 1008 3.1; 1648 1.2; 2250 3.1
9	W		0522 1.5; 1106 2.9; 1747 1.5
10	TH		0010 2.9; 0625 1.7; 1242 2.8; 1903 1.8
11	F		0206 2.8; 0739 1.8; 1422 2.8; 2101 1.8
12	SA		0344 2.9; 0901 1.7; 1547 3.0; 2218 1.7
13	SU		0432 3.0; 1002 1.5; 1618 3.2; 2305 1.6
14	M		0458 3.2; 1047 1.3; 1652 3.5; 2342 1.4
15	TU		0525 3.4; 1125 1.1; 1726 3.7
16	W	●	0013 1.3; 0556 3.6; 1200 1.0; 1801 3.8
17	TH		0043 1.2; 0628 3.7; 1234 0.9; 1834 3.9
18	F		0112 1.1; 0700 3.8; 1306 0.9; 1905 3.9
19	SA		0142 1.1; 0729 3.8; 1335 0.9; 1933 3.9
20	SU		0209 1.2; 0754 3.7; 1402 1.0; 1959 3.8
21	M		0231 1.3; 0819 3.5; 1428 1.2; 2024 3.7
22	TU		0250 1.4; 0847 3.4; 1500 1.3; 2053 3.5
23	W		0319 1.6; 0921 3.2; 1539 1.5; 2129 3.4
24	TH	◐	0404 1.7; 1006 3.1; 1632 1.7; 2217 3.1
25	F		0520 1.9; 1113 2.9; 1751 1.8; 2338 2.9
26	SA		0659 1.9; 1358 2.9; 1923 1.8
27	SU		0232 2.9; 0828 1.7; 1518 3.2; 2054 1.6
28	M		0347 3.2; 0938 1.4; 1609 3.6; 2208 1.3
29	TU		0435 3.4; 1032 1.0; 1652 3.9; 2302 0.9
30	W		0514 3.7; 1117 0.7; 1731 4.2; 2348 0.6
31	TH	○	0550 3.9; 1200 0.4; 1810 4.4

Chart Datum: 2·10 metres below Ordnance Datum (Newlyn)
HAT is 4·5 metres above Chart Datum

TIME ZONE (UT)
For Summer Time add ONE hour in **non-shaded areas**

SCOTLAND – OBAN

LAT 56°25′N LONG 5°29′W

TIMES AND HEIGHTS OF HIGH AND LOW WATERS

Dates in amber are **SPRINGS**
Dates in grey are **NEAPS**

2023

SEPTEMBER

Date	Day	Time	m	Time	m	Time	m	Time	m
1	F	0030	0.4	0626	4.0	1242	0.2	1848	4.4
2	SA	0110	0.4	0701	4.0	1323	0.2	1925	4.3
3	SU	0149	0.5	0735	3.9	1403	0.4	2002	4.1
4	M	0227	0.7	0809	3.7	1445	0.6	2038	3.8
5	TU	0306	0.9	0843	3.5	1527	1.0	2115	3.4
6	W	0349	1.2	0920	3.2	1615	1.4	◑ 2158	3.1
7	TH	0440	1.5	1004	3.0	1713	1.7	2302	2.7
8	F	0543	1.8	1146	2.7	1836	2.0		
9	SA	0213	2.6	0703	1.9	1526	2.8	2123	2.0
10	SU	0343	2.8	0842	1.8	1619	3.0	2219	1.8
11	M	0420	3.0	0947	1.5	1614	3.3	2253	1.6
12	TU	0438	3.2	1029	1.3	1635	3.5	2322	1.4
13	W	0501	3.5	1105	1.1	1705	3.7	2350	1.2
14	TH	0530	3.7	1138	0.9	1736	3.9		
15	F	0015	1.1	0601	3.8	1208	0.8	● 1807	4.0
16	SA	0041	1.0	0631	3.9	1237	0.8	1836	4.0
17	SU	0108	1.0	0656	3.9	1304	0.8	1901	4.0
18	M	0132	1.0	0719	3.8	1329	0.9	1925	3.9
19	TU	0151	1.2	0743	3.7	1355	1.1	1950	3.8
20	W	0213	1.3	0812	3.6	1428	1.3	2020	3.6
21	TH	0245	1.5	0848	3.4	1510	1.5	2055	3.3
22	F	0329	1.7	0933	3.1	1608	1.8	◐ 2143	3.0
23	SA	0446	1.9	1048	2.9	1743	1.9	2325	2.8
24	SU	0639	1.9	1401	3.0	1926	1.9		
25	M	0241	2.9	0813	1.7	1505	3.4	2058	1.6
26	TU	0338	3.2	0923	1.3	1552	3.7	2200	1.2
27	W	0420	3.5	1014	0.9	1632	4.1	2246	0.8
28	TH	0455	3.7	1058	0.6	1709	4.3	2327	0.6
29	F ○	0527	3.9	1140	0.4	1745	4.5		
30	SA	0005	0.4	0559	4.1	1220	0.3	1821	4.5

OCTOBER

Date	Day	Time	m	Time	m	Time	m	Time	m
1	SU	0042	0.4	0632	4.1	1300	0.3	1856	4.3
2	M	0118	0.5	0705	4.0	1340	0.5	1930	4.1
3	TU	0154	0.7	0737	3.8	1419	0.8	2003	3.8
4	W	0233	1.0	0810	3.6	1500	1.2	2038	3.4
5	TH	0315	1.3	0845	3.4	1547	1.6	2116	3.0
6	F	0406	1.6	0929	3.1	1647	2.0	◑ 2212	2.7
7	SA	0509	1.8	1047	2.8	1822	2.2		
8	SU	0149	2.6	0628	1.9	1439	2.9	2113	2.0
9	M	0304	2.8	0805	1.8	1530	3.1	2155	1.8
10	TU	0340	3.0	0914	1.6	1542	3.3	2224	1.6
11	W	0403	3.3	0958	1.4	1606	3.6	2250	1.4
12	TH	0429	3.5	1034	1.1	1634	3.8	2315	1.2
13	F	0458	3.7	1105	1.0	1705	3.9	2340	1.1
14	SA ●	0528	3.9	1135	0.9	1735	4.1		
15	SU	0005	1.0	0557	3.9	1203	0.9	1803	4.1
16	M	0031	0.9	0622	3.9	1232	0.9	1829	4.0
17	TU	0056	1.0	0647	3.9	1301	1.0	1855	3.9
18	W	0121	1.1	0715	3.8	1333	1.1	1925	3.8
19	TH	0151	1.2	0749	3.7	1411	1.3	1959	3.6
20	F	0229	1.4	0830	3.5	1500	1.5	2040	3.3
21	SA	0319	1.6	0923	3.2	1609	1.8	2139	3.0
22	SU	0440	1.8	1052	3.1	1745	1.9	◐ 2344	2.7
23	M	0618	1.8	1336	3.2	1922	1.8		
24	TU	0219	2.9	0747	1.6	1438	3.5	2041	1.5
25	W	0314	3.2	0856	1.3	1525	3.8	2136	1.2
26	TH	0354	3.5	0949	1.0	1606	4.1	2220	0.9
27	F	0427	3.7	1034	0.7	1643	4.3	2300	0.7
28	SA	0458	3.9	1117	0.6	1718	4.4	○ 2337	0.6
29	SU	0530	4.1	1159	0.5	1753	4.3		
30	M	0013	0.7	0604	4.1	1238	0.6	1828	4.2
31	TU	0049	0.7	0638	4.1	1318	0.9	1902	4.0

NOVEMBER

Date	Day	Time	m	Time	m	Time	m	Time	m
1	W	0126	0.9	0712	3.9	1358	1.1	1936	3.7
2	TH	0205	1.1	0747	3.7	1439	1.5	2012	3.4
3	F	0248	1.4	0825	3.5	1527	1.8	2053	3.1
4	SA	0338	1.6	0911	3.3	1626	2.1	2147	2.8
5	SU ◑	0437	1.8	1018	3.0	1752	2.2		
6	M	0053	2.7	0546	1.9	1316	3.0	2017	2.1
7	TU	0205	2.8	0705	1.9	1423	3.1	2110	1.9
8	W	0249	3.0	0819	1.7	1458	3.3	2142	1.7
9	TH	0322	3.2	0911	1.6	1528	3.5	2209	1.5
10	F	0352	3.4	0950	1.4	1558	3.7	2235	1.4
11	SA	0423	3.6	1025	1.2	1630	3.9	2301	1.2
12	SU	0454	3.8	1057	1.1	1702	4.0	2329	1.1
13	M	0524	3.9	1130	1.0	1732	4.0	● 2358	1.0
14	TU	0553	3.9	1205	1.0	1803	4.0		
15	W	0029	1.0	0624	3.9	1242	1.0	1836	3.9
16	TH	0103	1.1	0659	3.9	1323	1.1	1913	3.8
17	F	0142	1.2	0740	3.8	1409	1.3	1955	3.5
18	SA	0227	1.3	0828	3.6	1505	1.5	2044	3.3
19	SU	0322	1.4	0927	3.4	1613	1.6	2148	3.0
20	M	0430	1.6	1048	3.3	1732	1.7	◐ 2322	2.9
21	TU	0550	1.6	1251	3.4	1855	1.7		
22	W	0133	3.0	0710	1.5	1401	3.5	2007	1.5
23	TH	0236	3.2	0821	1.3	1454	3.7	2104	1.3
24	F	0321	3.4	0920	1.2	1539	3.9	2150	1.2
25	SA	0357	3.6	1010	1.0	1619	4.0	2231	1.0
26	SU	0431	3.8	1056	0.9	1656	4.1	2310	1.0
27	M	0506	3.9	1140	0.9	1732	4.1	○ 2348	0.9
28	TU	0542	4.0	1222	1.0	1807	4.0		
29	W	0025	1.0	0619	4.0	1303	1.2	1844	3.8
30	TH	0104	1.1	0656	3.9	1343	1.4	1920	3.7

DECEMBER

Date	Day	Time	m	Time	m	Time	m	Time	m
1	F	0145	1.2	0734	3.8	1425	1.6	1959	3.5
2	SA	0228	1.4	0814	3.6	1510	1.8	2040	3.3
3	SU	0314	1.5	0858	3.5	1602	2.0	2129	3.1
4	M	0404	1.7	0950	3.3	1703	2.2	2233	2.9
5	TU ◑	0459	1.8	1055	3.2	1818	2.2		
6	W	0018	2.9	0558	1.9	1223	3.1	1937	2.1
7	TH	0141	3.0	0659	1.9	1345	3.2	2034	2.0
8	F	0230	3.1	0758	1.8	1436	3.4	2115	1.8
9	SA	0310	3.3	0850	1.6	1518	3.5	2149	1.6
10	SU	0347	3.4	0937	1.5	1557	3.7	2223	1.4
11	M	0423	3.6	1020	1.3	1635	3.8	2257	1.3
12	TU	0459	3.8	1104	1.2	1712	3.9	● 2333	1.1
13	W	0536	3.9	1148	1.1	1750	3.9		
14	TH	0011	1.0	0614	3.9	1233	1.0	1829	3.9
15	F	0052	1.0	0655	4.0	1320	1.0	1911	3.8
16	SA	0136	1.0	0740	3.9	1409	1.1	1956	3.6
17	SU	0223	1.0	0828	3.8	1503	1.2	2044	3.4
18	M	0315	1.1	0923	3.7	1600	1.4	2139	3.2
19	TU	0412	1.2	1026	3.5	1703	1.5	◐ 2244	3.0
20	W	0517	1.4	1148	3.4	1811	1.6		
21	TH	0007	3.0	0628	1.4	1313	3.4	1920	1.6
22	F	0135	3.0	0741	1.4	1421	3.5	2024	1.6
23	SA	0239	3.2	0851	1.4	1517	3.6	2119	1.5
24	SU	0329	3.4	0951	1.3	1604	3.6	2206	1.4
25	M	0411	3.6	1044	1.3	1646	3.7	2249	1.3
26	TU	0451	3.7	1132	1.3	1724	3.7	2330	1.2
27	W ○	0531	3.8	1215	1.3	1801	3.8		
28	TH	0010	1.1	0610	3.9	1256	1.3	1837	3.7
29	F	0050	1.1	0648	3.9	1335	1.4	1913	3.7
30	SA	0130	1.1	0725	3.9	1414	1.6	1950	3.6
31	SU	0210	1.2	0802	3.8	1452	1.7	2027	3.5

Chart Datum: 2·10 metres below Ordnance Datum (Newlyn)
HAT is 4·5 metres above Chart Datum

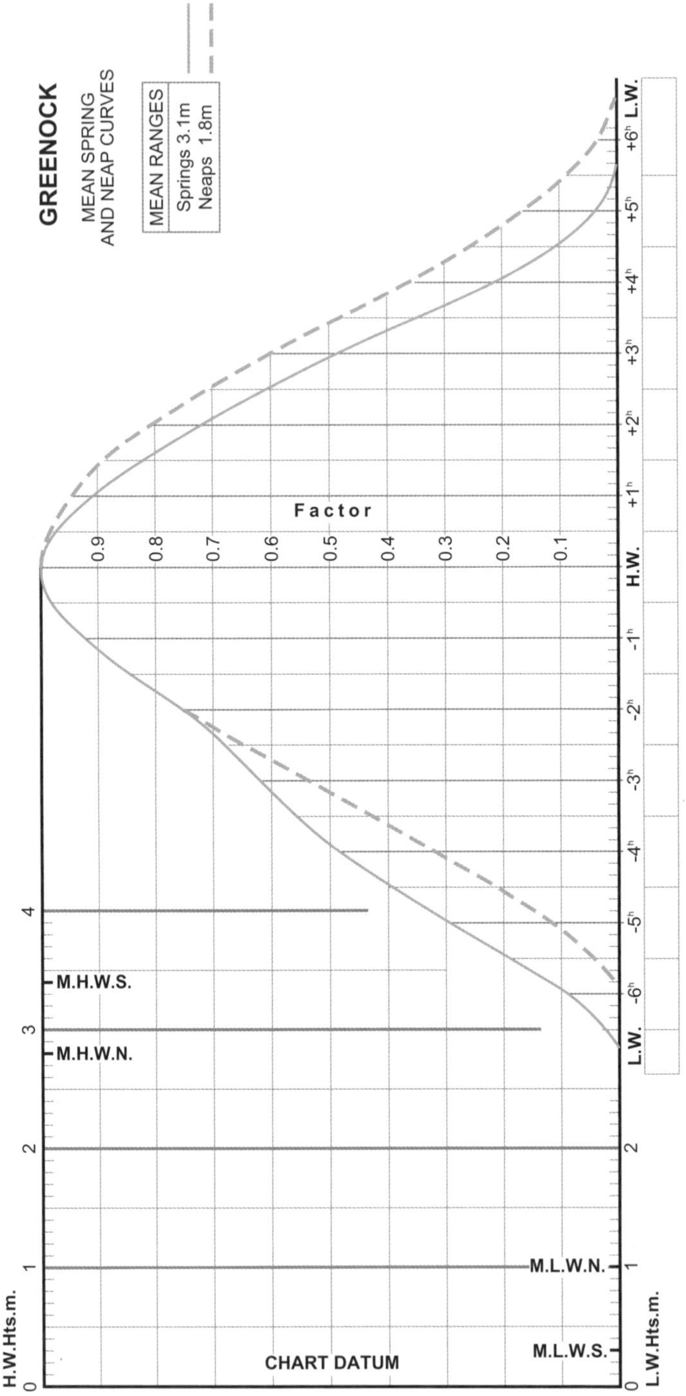
GREENOCK
MEAN SPRING AND NEAP CURVES
MEAN RANGES
Springs 3.1m
Neaps 1.8m
Factor
0.9
0.8
0.7
0.6
0.5
0.4
0.3
0.2
0.1
L.W.
-6h
-5h
-4h
-3h
-2h
-1h
H.W.
+1h
+2h
+3h
+4h
+5h
+6h
L.W.
H.W.Hts.m.
0
1
2
3
4
M.H.W.S.
M.H.W.N.
M.L.W.N.
M.L.W.S.
CHART DATUM
L.W.Hts.m.

TIME ZONE (UT)
For Summer Time add ONE hour in **non-shaded areas**

SCOTLAND – GREENOCK

LAT 55°57′N LONG 4°46′W

TIMES AND HEIGHTS OF HIGH AND LOW WATERS

Dates in amber are **SPRINGS**
Dates in grey are **NEAPS**

2023

JANUARY

Day		Time	m	Time	m	Time	m	Time	m
1	SU	0106	0.6	0738	3.0	1325	1.1	2002	3.2
2	M	0206	0.7	0843	3.0	1431	1.0	2112	3.2
3	TU	0301	0.7	0943	3.1	1529	0.9	2215	3.2
4	W	0352	0.7	1036	3.2	1618	0.8	2309	3.2
5	TH	0437	0.7	1121	3.4	1702	0.7	2357	3.2
6	F ○	0519	0.7	1201	3.5	1740	0.7		
7	SA	0039	3.2	0558	0.7	1236	3.6	1815	0.7
8	SU	0116	3.2	0634	0.7	1310	3.6	1848	0.7
9	M	0150	3.2	0709	0.7	1344	3.7	1921	0.7
10	TU	0225	3.2	0744	0.8	1417	3.6	1955	0.7
11	W	0301	3.1	0820	0.8	1453	3.6	2032	0.7
12	TH	0338	3.1	0858	0.8	1530	3.6	2111	0.7
13	F	0417	3.1	0939	0.9	1609	3.5	2155	0.7
14	SA	0457	3.0	1025	1.0	1652	3.4	2244	0.8
15	SU	0540	2.9	1117	1.1	1739	3.3	◑ 2340	0.8
16	M	0632	2.9	1217	1.1	1836	3.1		
17	TU	0041	0.9	0740	2.8	1324	1.1	1946	3.1
18	W	0148	0.9	0902	2.9	1434	1.0	2105	3.1
19	TH	0254	0.8	1011	3.0	1538	0.8	2218	3.2
20	F	0354	0.7	1107	3.3	1634	0.5	2322	3.3
21	SA ●	0449	0.6	1156	3.5	1725	0.3		
22	SU	0019	3.4	0541	0.5	1243	3.6	1813	0.1
23	M	0113	3.4	0630	0.4	1329	3.7	1901	0.0
24	TU	0204	3.4	0717	0.4	1414	3.8	1948	0.0
25	W	0252	3.4	0805	0.4	1459	3.8	2036	0.0
26	TH	0337	3.4	0852	0.5	1544	3.8	2126	0.2
27	F	0419	3.3	0940	0.6	1629	3.7	2219	0.3
28	SA	0500	3.2	1030	0.7	1715	3.5	◐ 2316	0.5
29	SU	0542	3.1	1126	0.9	1803	3.2		
30	M	0021	0.7	0628	2.9	1235	1.0	1901	3.0
31	TU	0130	0.9	0725	2.8	1358	1.1	2022	2.8

FEBRUARY

Day		Time	m	Time	m	Time	m	Time	m
1	W	0235	0.9	0849	2.8	1508	1.0	2202	2.8
2	TH	0332	0.9	1011	3.0	1603	0.9	2304	2.9
3	F	0422	0.8	1106	3.2	1649	0.7	2352	3.0
4	SA	0506	0.7	1149	3.4	1728	0.6		
5	SU	0032	3.1	0545	0.6	1225	3.5	○ 1802	0.6
6	M	0108	3.1	0620	0.6	1258	3.5	1833	0.5
7	TU	0140	3.1	0651	0.6	1328	3.5	1902	0.5
8	W	0211	3.1	0721	0.6	1359	3.6	1930	0.5
9	TH	0241	3.1	0752	0.6	1432	3.6	2002	0.5
10	F	0312	3.2	0827	0.6	1507	3.6	2037	0.4
11	SA	0343	3.2	0905	0.6	1544	3.5	2118	0.5
12	SU	0416	3.1	0948	0.7	1622	3.4	2204	0.5
13	M	0452	3.0	1037	0.8	1704	3.3	◑ 2257	0.7
14	TU	0532	2.9	1135	0.9	1754	3.1	2359	0.9
15	W	0625	2.8	1245	1.0	1900	2.9		
16	TH	0111	1.0	0806	2.7	1407	0.9	2038	2.9
17	F	0233	1.0	0952	2.9	1525	0.7	2215	3.0
18	SA	0345	0.8	1055	3.2	1625	0.4	2321	3.2
19	SU	0442	0.6	1145	3.4	1714	0.1		
20	M	0015	3.3	0531	0.4	1231	3.6	● 1800	-0.1
21	TU	0105	3.4	0616	0.3	1316	3.7	1843	-0.2
22	W	0151	3.4	0659	0.2	1400	3.8	1926	-0.2
23	TH	0232	3.4	0742	0.2	1443	3.8	2009	-0.1
24	F	0310	3.4	0824	0.3	1524	3.7	2052	0.1
25	SA	0345	3.3	0905	0.3	1603	3.6	2138	0.3
26	SU	0420	3.3	0949	0.5	1642	3.4	2227	0.6
27	M	0456	3.1	1037	0.7	1723	3.1	◐ 2327	0.9
28	TU	0537	3.0	1138	0.9	1811	2.8		

MARCH

Day		Time	m	Time	m	Time	m	Time	m
1	W	0049	1.1	0626	2.8	1322	1.1	1916	2.6
2	TH	0209	1.1	0735	2.7	1446	1.0	2157	2.6
3	F	0312	1.0	0946	2.8	1543	0.8	2253	2.8
4	SA	0403	0.9	1047	3.0	1628	0.6	2335	3.0
5	SU	0446	0.7	1130	3.2	1705	0.5		
6	M	0012	3.1	0524	0.6	1205	3.3	1739	0.4
7	TU	0046	3.1	0556	0.5	1237	3.4	○ 1808	0.4
8	W	0118	3.1	0625	0.5	1306	3.4	1833	0.4
9	TH	0148	3.1	0652	0.5	1335	3.4	1859	0.4
10	F	0215	3.2	0721	0.4	1408	3.5	1930	0.3
11	SA	0242	3.2	0755	0.4	1444	3.5	2006	0.3
12	SU	0311	3.2	0834	0.4	1520	3.5	2047	0.3
13	M	0342	3.2	0918	0.5	1558	3.4	2134	0.5
14	TU	0416	3.1	1008	0.6	1639	3.2	2228	0.7
15	W	0454	3.0	1109	0.8	1728	3.0	◑ 2332	0.9
16	TH	0545	2.8	1224	0.9	1833	2.8		
17	F	0051	1.1	0717	2.6	1357	0.8	2037	2.7
18	SA	0226	1.0	0938	2.8	1516	0.5	2219	2.9
19	SU	0339	0.8	1039	3.1	1612	0.2	2315	3.1
20	M	0431	0.5	1128	3.4	1658	-0.1		
21	TU	0003	3.3	0516	0.3	1213	3.6	● 1741	-0.2
22	W	0047	3.3	0557	0.2	1258	3.7	1821	-0.2
23	TH	0127	3.4	0637	0.1	1340	3.7	1900	-0.1
24	F	0204	3.4	0715	0.1	1421	3.7	1939	0.0
25	SA	0237	3.4	0752	0.2	1459	3.6	2018	0.2
26	SU	0310	3.4	0831	0.2	1536	3.5	2100	0.4
27	M	0344	3.3	0911	0.4	1613	3.2	2145	0.7
28	TU	0419	3.2	0956	0.6	1653	3.0	2239	0.9
29	W	0459	3.0	1053	0.9	1739	2.7	◐ 2357	1.2
30	TH	0547	2.8	1235	1.1	1842	2.4		
31	F	0134	1.3	0650	2.7	1413	1.0	2131	2.5

APRIL

Day		Time	m	Time	m	Time	m	Time	m
1	SA	0242	1.1	0859	2.7	1511	0.8	2224	2.7
2	SU	0334	0.9	1012	2.9	1555	0.6	2304	2.9
3	M	0417	0.7	1056	3.1	1632	0.4	2340	3.0
4	TU	0453	0.5	1132	3.2	1705	0.4		
5	W	0014	3.1	0525	0.5	1204	3.3	1734	0.3
6	TH	0047	3.1	0553	0.4	1234	3.3	○ 1759	0.3
7	F	0117	3.2	0621	0.4	1307	3.4	1828	0.3
8	SA	0144	3.2	0653	0.3	1343	3.4	1902	0.2
9	SU	0212	3.3	0730	0.3	1421	3.5	1942	0.2
10	M	0243	3.3	0811	0.3	1500	3.5	2027	0.3
11	TU	0316	3.3	0858	0.4	1540	3.3	2116	0.5
12	W	0352	3.2	0952	0.5	1624	3.2	2213	0.8
13	TH	0434	3.1	1059	0.7	1717	2.9	◑ 2321	1.0
14	F	0529	2.8	1222	0.7	1832	2.7		
15	SA	0045	1.1	0720	2.7	1350	0.6	2050	2.7
16	SU	0215	1.0	0917	2.9	1458	0.3	2205	2.9
17	M	0322	0.8	1016	3.2	1551	0.1	2256	3.1
18	TU	0413	0.5	1105	3.4	1636	-0.1	2340	3.3
19	W	0456	0.3	1150	3.5	1717	-0.1		
20	TH	0020	3.3	0536	0.2	1234	3.6	● 1756	-0.1
21	F	0057	3.3	0613	0.1	1316	3.5	1833	0.0
22	SA	0132	3.4	0649	0.2	1356	3.5	1910	0.2
23	SU	0204	3.4	0724	0.2	1433	3.4	1949	0.3
24	M	0238	3.4	0801	0.3	1510	3.3	2030	0.5
25	TU	0312	3.4	0841	0.4	1548	3.1	2115	0.7
26	W	0348	3.3	0927	0.6	1630	2.9	2207	1.0
27	TH	0427	3.1	1024	0.8	1719	2.6	◐ 2313	1.2
28	F	0514	2.9	1146	1.0	1823	2.5		
29	SA	0037	1.3	0616	2.8	1319	0.9	2011	2.5
30	SU	0153	1.2	0743	2.7	1422	0.8	2131	2.7

Chart Datum: 1·62 metres below Ordnance Datum (Newlyn)
HAT is 3·9 metres above Chart Datum

TIME ZONE (UT)
For Summer Time add ONE hour in **non-shaded areas**

SCOTLAND – GREENOCK

LAT 55°57′N LONG 4°46′W

TIMES AND HEIGHTS OF HIGH AND LOW WATERS

Dates in amber are **SPRINGS**
Dates in grey are **NEAPS**

2023

MAY

Day	Time	m	Day	Time	m
1 M	0251 0915 1510 2218	1.0 2.9 0.6 2.9	16 TU	0254 0946 1523 2224	0.7 3.2 0.1 3.1
2 TU	0337 1007 1549 2258	0.8 3.0 0.5 3.0	17 W	0348 1037 1610 2309	0.5 3.4 0.1 3.2
3 W	0415 1046 1624 2336	0.6 3.1 0.4 3.1	18 TH	0433 1124 1652 2350	0.4 3.4 0.1 3.3
4 TH	0448 1122 1655	0.5 3.2 0.3	19 F ●	0514 1210 1731	0.3 3.4 0.2
5 F ○	0011 0520 1159 1726	3.2 0.4 3.3 0.3	20 SA	0027 0552 1252 1810	3.3 0.3 3.4 0.3
6 SA	0043 0554 1238 1801	3.2 0.3 3.3 0.3	21 SU	0102 0627 1332 1848	3.4 0.3 3.3 0.4
7 SU	0114 0631 1320 1842	3.3 0.2 3.4 0.3	22 M	0136 0702 1411 1927	3.4 0.3 3.2 0.5
8 M	0147 0712 1403 1926	3.4 0.2 3.4 0.3	23 TU	0210 0739 1448 2009	3.5 0.3 3.1 0.6
9 TU	0222 0757 1446 2016	3.4 0.2 3.4 0.4	24 W	0246 0820 1528 2054	3.5 0.4 3.0 0.8
10 W	0300 0849 1531 2110	3.4 0.3 3.3 0.6	25 TH	0322 0906 1611 2144	3.4 0.6 2.8 0.9
11 TH	0340 0948 1622 2210	3.3 0.4 3.1 0.8	26 F	0400 1000 1701 2238	3.2 0.7 2.7 1.0
12 F ◑	0428 1059 1723 2318	3.2 0.5 2.9 0.9	27 SA ◐	0445 1105 1800 2339	3.1 0.8 2.6 1.1
13 SA	0532 1217 1849	3.0 0.5 2.8	28 SU	0539 1215 1908	2.9 0.8 2.6
14 SU	0033 0715 1329 2026	1.0 2.9 0.4 2.8	29 M	0044 0645 1318 2019	1.1 2.8 0.8 2.7
15 M	0149 0845 1431 2133	0.9 3.0 0.2 3.0	30 TU	0148 0757 1413 2119	1.1 2.9 0.6 2.8
			31 W	0243 0901 1458 2209	0.9 3.0 0.5 2.9

JUNE

Day	Time	m	Day	Time	m
1 TH	0330 0953 1539 2254	0.7 3.1 0.4 3.0	16 F	0412 1101 1630 2321	0.5 3.2 0.3 3.2
2 F	0411 1041 1618 2334	0.6 3.2 0.4 3.1	17 SA	0457 1150 1713	0.5 3.2 0.4
3 SA	0451 1127 1658	0.4 3.2 0.3	18 SU ●	0001 0537 1235 1754	3.3 0.4 3.1 0.5
4 SU ○	0012 0532 1214 1741	3.2 0.3 3.3 0.3	19 M	0038 0614 1316 1834	3.4 0.4 3.1 0.6
5 M	0050 0615 1302 1827	3.4 0.2 3.3 0.4	20 TU	0114 0649 1355 1913	3.4 0.4 3.0 0.6
6 TU	0128 0701 1350 1917	3.5 0.2 3.3 0.4	21 W	0149 0726 1432 1953	3.5 0.4 3.0 0.7
7 W	0209 0750 1440 2010	3.5 0.1 3.3 0.5	22 TH	0224 0804 1511 2035	3.5 0.5 2.9 0.7
8 TH	0251 0844 1531 2105	3.5 0.2 3.2 0.6	23 F	0259 0846 1553 2118	3.4 0.5 2.9 0.8
9 F	0337 0943 1626 2203	3.5 0.2 3.1 0.7	24 SA	0336 0931 1638 2203	3.3 0.6 2.8 0.8
10 SA ◑	0428 1048 1728 2303	3.3 0.3 3.0 0.8	25 SU	0417 1021 1725 2251	3.2 0.6 2.8 0.9
11 SU	0531 1155 1835	3.2 0.3 2.9	26 M ◐	0503 1116 1815 2343	3.1 0.7 2.8 1.0
12 M	0007 0649 1259 1945	0.8 3.1 0.3 2.9	27 TU	0556 1213 1910	3.0 0.7 2.7
13 TU	0115 0806 1359 2048	0.8 3.1 0.3 2.9	28 W	0041 0657 1310 2010	1.0 2.9 0.7 2.8
14 W	0221 0912 1454 2145	0.8 3.2 0.3 3.0	29 TH	0142 0803 1405 2113	1.0 2.9 0.6 2.8
15 TH	0320 1009 1544 2235	0.7 3.2 0.3 3.1	30 F	0242 0908 1457 2210	0.9 3.0 0.6 2.9

JULY

Day	Time	m	Day	Time	m
1 SA	0338 1008 1547 2301	0.7 3.1 0.5 3.1	16 SU	0444 1142 1700 2345	0.6 3.0 0.6 3.2
2 SU	0428 1103 1636 2348	0.5 3.2 0.4 3.2	17 M ●	0527 1229 1742	0.5 3.0 0.6
3 M ○	0516 1157 1726	0.3 3.2 0.4	18 TU	0024 0605 1309 1822	3.3 0.5 3.0 0.6
4 TU	0032 0604 1250 1817	3.4 0.1 3.3 0.4	19 W	0059 0639 1345 1858	3.4 0.4 3.0 0.6
5 W	0116 0652 1344 1908	3.5 0.0 3.3 0.4	20 TH	0132 0711 1419 1933	3.5 0.4 2.9 0.6
6 TH	0200 0741 1437 1959	3.6 0.0 3.2 0.4	21 F	0204 0744 1453 2009	3.5 0.4 3.0 0.6
7 F	0245 0832 1529 2051	3.6 0.0 3.2 0.4	22 SA	0238 0819 1528 2046	3.5 0.5 3.0 0.6
8 SA	0332 0926 1621 2144	3.6 0.0 3.2 0.5	23 SU	0313 0855 1605 2124	3.5 0.5 3.0 0.7
9 SU	0421 1023 1711 2237	3.5 0.1 3.1 0.6	24 M	0350 0935 1642 2207	3.4 0.5 2.9 0.7
10 M ◑	0514 1124 1801 2335	3.4 0.2 3.0 0.7	25 TU ◐	0429 1021 1722 2253	3.3 0.6 2.9 0.8
11 TU	0612 1226 1852	3.2 0.3 2.9	26 W	0514 1114 1807 2347	3.1 0.7 2.8 1.0
12 W	0038 0719 1327 1951	0.8 3.1 0.5 2.9	27 TH	0607 1213 1902	3.0 0.8 2.8
13 TH	0148 0834 1427 2058	0.9 3.0 0.5 2.9	28 F	0050 0714 1317 2014	1.0 2.9 0.8 2.8
14 F	0256 0947 1522 2204	0.8 3.0 0.6 3.0	29 SA	0201 0831 1423 2133	1.0 2.9 0.8 2.9
15 SA	0355 1049 1613 2259	0.7 3.0 0.6 3.1	30 SU	0312 0946 1526 2238	0.8 3.0 0.7 3.1
			31 M	0413 1052 1623 2331	0.5 3.1 0.6 3.3

AUGUST

Day	Time	m	Day	Time	m
1 TU ○	0504 1151 1715	0.2 3.2 0.5	16 W ●	0012 0549 1256 1804	3.4 0.4 3.0 0.6
2 W	0018 0552 1245 1805	3.4 0.0 3.2 0.4	17 TH	0045 0621 1328 1837	3.4 0.4 3.0 0.6
3 TH	0104 0638 1337 1853	3.6 -0.1 3.3 0.3	18 F	0114 0649 1358 1907	3.5 0.4 3.0 0.6
4 F	0149 0724 1427 1940	3.7 -0.2 3.3 0.3	19 SA	0143 0717 1427 1937	3.5 0.4 3.0 0.6
5 SA	0234 0810 1513 2028	3.7 -0.1 3.3 0.3	20 SU	0214 0745 1456 2009	3.5 0.4 3.1 0.6
6 SU	0318 0858 1556 2115	3.7 0.0 3.2 0.4	21 M	0248 0817 1527 2046	3.5 0.4 3.1 0.6
7 M	0402 0949 1637 2204	3.6 0.1 3.2 0.5	22 TU	0323 0854 1559 2126	3.5 0.4 3.1 0.7
8 TU ◑	0446 1045 1716 2256	3.5 0.3 3.1 0.6	23 W	0400 0937 1634 2212	3.4 0.5 3.0 0.8
9 W	0533 1149 1758 2358	3.2 0.6 3.0 0.8	24 TH ◐	0439 1028 1714 2307	3.2 0.7 2.9 0.9
10 TH	0626 1258 1847	3.0 0.7 2.9	25 F	0526 1129 1804	3.0 0.9 2.8
11 F	0117 0743 1405 1954	1.0 2.7 0.8 2.8	26 SA	0012 0631 1240 1920	1.1 2.9 1.0 2.7
12 SA	0238 0942 1506 2139	1.0 2.7 0.8 2.9	27 SU	0133 0802 1401 2106	1.0 2.8 1.0 2.8
13 SU	0342 1048 1559 2246	0.8 2.8 0.8 3.1	28 M	0258 0941 1515 2222	0.8 2.9 0.9 3.1
14 M	0432 1137 1646 2333	0.7 2.9 0.7 3.2	29 TU	0402 1051 1614 2316	0.5 3.1 0.6 3.3
15 TU	0514 1219 1727	0.5 3.0 0.6	30 W	0451 1146 1703	0.1 3.2 0.5
			31 TH ○	0003 0536 1235 1749	3.5 -0.1 3.3 0.3

Chart Datum: 1·62 metres below Ordnance Datum (Newlyn)
HAT is 3·9 metres above Chart Datum

TIME ZONE (UT)
For Summer Time add ONE hour in **non-shaded areas**

SCOTLAND – GREENOCK

LAT 55°57′N LONG 4°46′W

TIMES AND HEIGHTS OF HIGH AND LOW WATERS

Dates in amber are **SPRINGS**
Dates in grey are **NEAPS**

2023

SEPTEMBER

Date	Day	Time	m	Time	m	Time	m	Time	m
1	F	0049	3.7	0618	-0.2	1321	3.3	1832	0.2
2	SA	0133	3.8	0700	-0.2	1405	3.3	1916	0.2
3	SU	0216	3.8	0743	-0.1	1445	3.4	1959	0.3
4	M	0258	3.8	0826	0.1	1521	3.3	2042	0.3
5	TU	0338	3.7	0912	0.3	1557	3.3	2126	0.5
6	W	0417	3.5	1002	0.6	1634	3.2	◑ 2215	0.7
7	TH	0458	3.2	1104	0.8	1714	3.1	2314	0.9
8	F	0545	2.9	1229	1.1	1801	2.9		
9	SA	0054	1.1	0650	2.6	1345	1.1	1903	2.8
10	SU	0221	1.1	0942	2.6	1448	1.1	2115	2.8
11	M	0323	0.9	1037	2.8	1541	0.9	2226	3.1
12	TU	0411	0.7	1119	3.0	1626	0.7	2311	3.3
13	W	0450	0.5	1156	3.1	1705	0.6	2349	3.4
14	TH	0524	0.4	1229	3.1	1739	0.6		
15	F	0020	3.5	0554	0.4	1300	3.2	● 1809	0.6
16	SA	0049	3.5	0620	0.4	1328	3.2	1835	0.6
17	SU	0117	3.5	0644	0.4	1355	3.2	1903	0.6
18	M	0148	3.5	0711	0.4	1422	3.2	1935	0.6
19	TU	0222	3.6	0743	0.4	1451	3.3	2012	0.6
20	W	0258	3.6	0821	0.5	1522	3.3	2054	0.6
21	TH	0335	3.5	0905	0.6	1557	3.2	2142	0.8
22	F	0414	3.3	0957	0.8	1635	3.1	◐ 2239	0.9
23	SA	0500	3.1	1100	1.1	1725	2.9	2350	1.1
24	SU	0604	2.8	1219	1.2	1842	2.8		
25	M	0122	1.0	0753	2.7	1352	1.2	2050	2.9
26	TU	0248	0.7	0946	2.9	1508	1.0	2205	3.2
27	W	0346	0.4	1045	3.2	1601	0.7	2256	3.5
28	TH	0433	0.1	1132	3.3	1647	0.5	2343	3.7
29	F	0515	-0.1	1215	3.4	1729	0.3	○	
30	SA	0027	3.8	0555	-0.1	1256	3.4	1809	0.2

OCTOBER

Date	Day	Time	m	Time	m	Time	m	Time	m
1	SU	0111	3.8	0635	-0.1	1334	3.5	1849	0.2
2	M	0154	3.8	0714	0.1	1410	3.5	1929	0.3
3	TU	0234	3.7	0754	0.3	1445	3.5	2009	0.4
4	W	0312	3.6	0836	0.5	1521	3.5	2051	0.5
5	TH	0350	3.4	0923	0.8	1558	3.4	2137	0.8
6	F	0431	3.1	1019	1.1	1639	3.2	◑ 2237	1.0
7	SA	0518	2.8	1149	1.3	1727	3.0		
8	SU	0024	1.2	0625	2.5	1317	1.4	1830	2.9
9	M	0153	1.1	0919	2.6	1421	1.2	2025	2.9
10	TU	0252	0.9	1009	2.9	1513	1.0	2150	3.1
11	W	0339	0.7	1047	3.1	1558	0.8	2236	3.3
12	TH	0418	0.6	1121	3.2	1636	0.7	2313	3.4
13	F	0451	0.5	1155	3.3	1708	0.6	2346	3.5
14	SA	0520	0.5	1226	3.3	1737	0.6	●	
15	SU	0016	3.5	0547	0.5	1255	3.3	1804	0.6
16	M	0047	3.5	0612	0.5	1323	3.4	1833	0.6
17	TU	0122	3.6	0642	0.5	1351	3.4	1908	0.6
18	W	0200	3.6	0718	0.5	1422	3.5	1948	0.6
19	TH	0238	3.6	0800	0.6	1455	3.5	2032	0.7
20	F	0317	3.5	0846	0.8	1532	3.4	2124	0.8
21	SA	0359	3.3	0941	1.0	1613	3.3	2226	0.9
22	SU	0448	3.1	1047	1.2	1706	3.1	◐ 2344	1.0
23	M	0558	2.9	1210	1.4	1829	3.0		
24	TU	0114	0.9	0800	2.8	1340	1.3	2028	3.1
25	W	0228	0.6	0931	3.1	1449	1.0	2139	3.3
26	TH	0323	0.4	1023	3.3	1542	0.7	2231	3.6
27	F	0409	0.1	1108	3.4	1627	0.5	2318	3.7
28	SA	0451	0.0	1149	3.5	1708	0.4	○	
29	SU	0004	3.8	0531	0.1	1227	3.5	1747	0.3
30	M	0048	3.8	0610	0.2	1304	3.6	1825	0.3
31	TU	0130	3.7	0649	0.3	1339	3.6	1903	0.4

NOVEMBER

Date	Day	Time	m	Time	m	Time	m	Time	m
1	W	0211	3.6	0728	0.5	1415	3.6	1942	0.5
2	TH	0249	3.5	0810	0.7	1452	3.6	2024	0.6
3	F	0329	3.3	0855	0.9	1530	3.5	2111	0.8
4	SA	0411	3.0	0948	1.2	1611	3.4	2209	1.0
5	SU	0501	2.8	1059	1.4	1658	3.2	◑ 2332	1.2
6	M	0609	2.6	1226	1.5	1758	3.0		
7	TU	0104	1.2	0804	2.6	1337	1.4	1920	3.0
8	W	0207	1.0	0916	2.9	1434	1.2	2049	3.1
9	TH	0256	0.8	1001	3.1	1521	1.0	2145	3.2
10	F	0337	0.7	1040	3.2	1600	0.9	2228	3.3
11	SA	0413	0.6	1117	3.3	1634	0.8	2305	3.4
12	SU	0445	0.6	1152	3.4	1706	0.7	2341	3.5
13	M	0514	0.6	1224	3.4	1737	0.6	●	
14	TU	0019	3.5	0546	0.6	1255	3.5	1812	0.6
15	W	0100	3.5	0621	0.6	1327	3.6	1850	0.6
16	TH	0141	3.5	0702	0.6	1401	3.6	1934	0.6
17	F	0224	3.5	0748	0.7	1439	3.6	2022	0.6
18	SA	0307	3.4	0839	0.9	1519	3.6	2117	0.7
19	SU	0354	3.3	0935	1.0	1605	3.4	2221	0.8
20	M	0449	3.1	1040	1.2	1702	3.3	◐ 2335	0.8
21	TU	0602	3.0	1154	1.3	1821	3.2		
22	W	0051	0.7	0738	3.0	1311	1.2	1954	3.2
23	TH	0158	0.6	0855	3.1	1420	1.1	2106	3.4
24	F	0254	0.4	0951	3.3	1517	0.8	2203	3.5
25	SA	0343	0.3	1038	3.4	1605	0.7	2254	3.6
26	SU	0428	0.3	1121	3.5	1649	0.5	2342	3.6
27	M	0510	0.3	1201	3.5	1729	0.5	○	
28	TU	0028	3.6	0551	0.4	1238	3.6	1808	0.5
29	W	0112	3.5	0631	0.5	1315	3.7	1846	0.5
30	TH	0153	3.4	0711	0.7	1352	3.7	1925	0.6

DECEMBER

Date	Day	Time	m	Time	m	Time	m	Time	m
1	F	0233	3.3	0753	0.8	1430	3.7	2007	0.7
2	SA	0313	3.2	0837	1.0	1508	3.6	2053	0.8
3	SU	0356	3.0	0925	1.1	1548	3.5	2144	0.9
4	M	0445	2.9	1018	1.2	1633	3.3	2244	1.0
5	TU	0541	2.8	1119	1.3	1724	3.2	◑ 2353	1.1
6	W	0648	2.8	1227	1.4	1824	3.1		
7	TH	0100	1.1	0758	2.8	1332	1.3	1931	3.1
8	F	0158	1.0	0900	3.0	1429	1.2	2037	3.1
9	SA	0247	0.9	0952	3.1	1517	1.1	2134	3.2
10	SU	0330	0.8	1038	3.2	1559	0.9	2224	3.3
11	M	0409	0.7	1119	3.3	1638	0.8	2311	3.4
12	TU	0446	0.7	1157	3.4	1716	0.7	● 2357	3.4
13	W	0525	0.6	1233	3.5	1756	0.6		
14	TH	0043	3.5	0608	0.6	1310	3.6	1840	0.5
15	F	0130	3.5	0653	0.7	1349	3.7	1926	0.5
16	SA	0216	3.4	0742	0.7	1430	3.7	2016	0.5
17	SU	0304	3.4	0833	0.8	1514	3.7	2110	0.5
18	M	0354	3.3	0927	0.9	1602	3.6	2209	0.5
19	TU	0448	3.2	1025	0.9	1657	3.5	◐ 2312	0.6
20	W	0547	3.1	1127	1.0	1801	3.4		
21	TH	0018	0.6	0655	3.0	1235	1.1	1914	3.3
22	F	0124	0.6	0805	3.0	1345	1.0	2028	3.3
23	SA	0224	0.6	0911	3.1	1450	0.9	2135	3.3
24	SU	0319	0.6	1008	3.2	1546	0.8	2235	3.4
25	M	0409	0.6	1058	3.3	1635	0.7	2329	3.4
26	TU	0456	0.6	1142	3.5	1719	0.6		
27	W	0018	3.4	0540	0.6	1222	3.5	○ 1800	0.6
28	TH	0104	3.3	0621	0.7	1300	3.6	1837	0.6
29	F	0145	3.3	0700	0.7	1337	3.7	1914	0.6
30	SA	0223	3.2	0739	0.8	1413	3.7	1952	0.6
31	SU	0300	3.1	0818	0.8	1450	3.6	2032	0.7

Chart Datum: 1·62 metres below Ordnance Datum (Newlyn)
HAT is 3·9 metres above Chart Datum

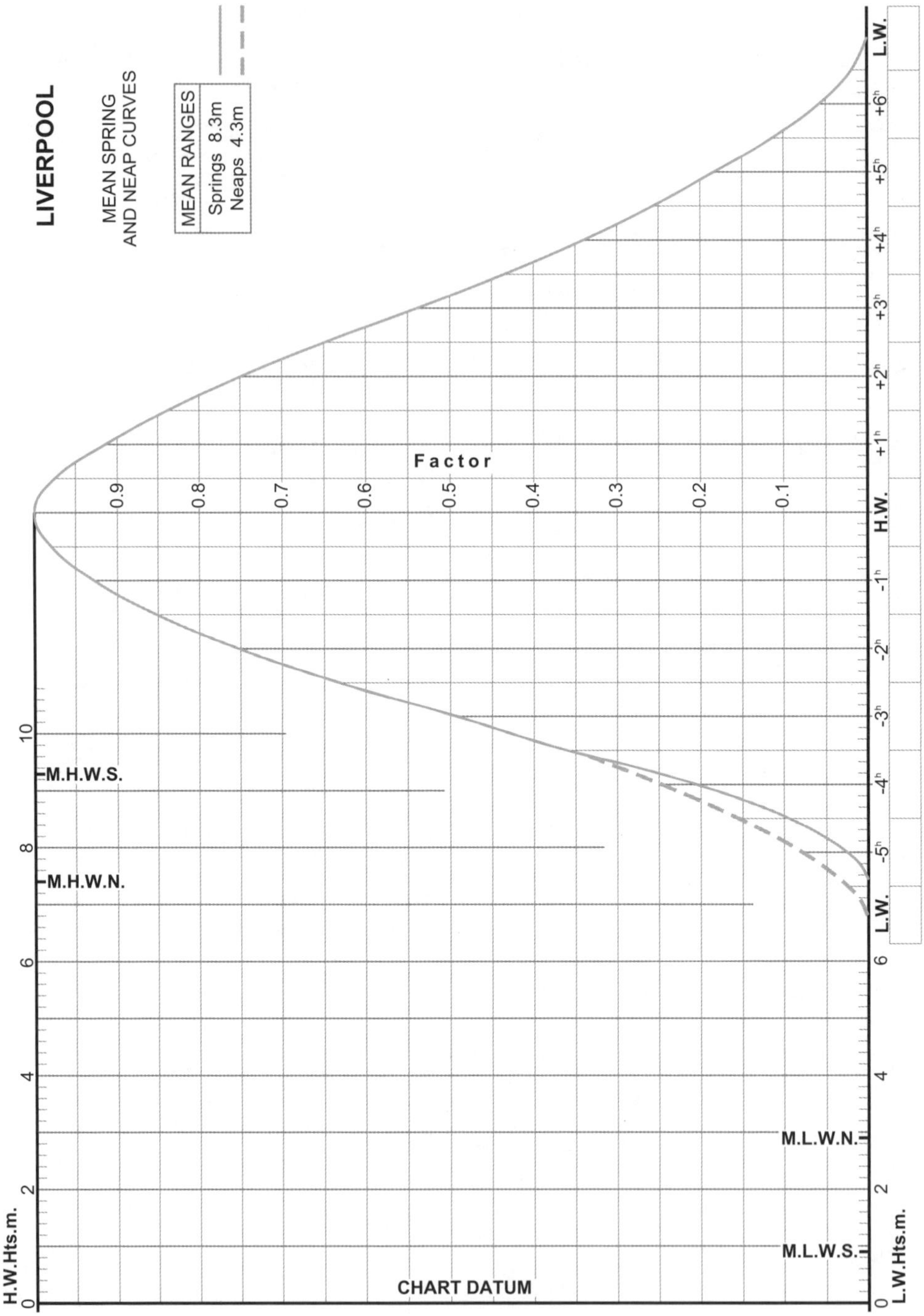
LIVERPOOL
MEAN SPRING
AND NEAP CURVES
MEAN RANGES
Springs 8.3m
Neaps 4.3m
Factor
0.9
0.8
0.7
0.6
0.5
0.4
0.3
0.2
0.1
L.W.
-5h
-4h
-3h
-2h
-1h
H.W.
+1h
+2h
+3h
+4h
+5h
+6h
L.W.
H.W.Hts.m.
0
2
4
6
8
10
M.H.W.S.
M.H.W.N.
CHART DATUM
M.L.W.S.
M.L.W.N.
L.W.Hts.m.

TIME ZONE (UT)
For Summer Time add ONE hour in **non-shaded areas**

LIVERPOOL (GLADSTONE DOCK)

LAT 53°27′N LONG 3°01′W

TIMES AND HEIGHTS OF HIGH AND LOW WATERS

Dates in amber are **SPRINGS**
Dates in grey are **NEAPS**

2023

JANUARY

Date	Day	Time	m	Time	m	Time	m	Time	m
1	SU	0045	2.5	0632	7.7	1310	3.0	1854	8.0
2	M	0149	2.6	0739	7.7	1416	2.9	1958	8.0
3	TU	0248	2.6	0837	7.9	1517	2.7	2056	8.1
4	W	0340	2.5	0927	8.2	1610	2.5	2145	8.3
5	TH	0425	2.4	1010	8.4	1655	2.3	2229	8.4
6	F	0504	2.3	1048	8.6	1736	2.1	○ 2308	8.5
7	SA	0539	2.2	1123	8.8	1813	2.0	2344	8.6
8	SU	0612	2.1	1157	8.8	1847	2.0		
9	M	0017	8.6	0645	2.1	1229	8.8	1920	2.0
10	TU	0050	8.5	0718	2.2	1302	8.8	1953	2.0
11	W	0124	8.4	0753	2.2	1336	8.6	2028	2.2
12	TH	0159	8.3	0830	2.4	1410	8.5	2104	2.3
13	F	0236	8.1	0908	2.6	1447	8.3	2143	2.5
14	SA	0316	7.9	0951	2.9	1530	8.1	2227	2.8
15	SU	0405	7.7	1040	3.1	1622	7.9	◑ 2322	3.0
16	M	0504	7.5	1142	3.3	1728	7.7		
17	TU	0033	3.0	0616	7.5	1258	3.2	1845	7.7
18	W	0152	2.8	0729	7.8	1418	2.9	1959	8.0
19	TH	0301	2.5	0835	8.2	1527	2.4	2105	8.4
20	F	0401	2.1	0934	8.7	1629	1.9	2204	8.8
21	SA	0457	1.6	1027	9.2	1727	1.3	● 2258	9.2
22	SU	0549	1.3	1118	9.6	1821	0.9	2349	9.4
23	M	0639	1.1	1207	9.8	1912	0.6		
24	TU	0037	9.5	0727	1.0	1254	9.9	1959	0.6
25	W	0123	9.4	0812	1.1	1340	9.8	2044	0.8
26	TH	0208	9.1	0855	1.4	1426	9.5	2127	1.2
27	F	0253	8.7	0937	1.8	1512	9.1	2210	1.7
28	SA	0339	8.3	1022	2.3	1601	8.5	◐ 2256	2.3
29	SU	0431	7.8	1114	2.8	1658	8.0	2351	2.9
30	M	0534	7.4	1219	3.2	1806	7.5		
31	TU	0058	3.2	0651	7.2	1337	3.3	1925	7.4

FEBRUARY

Date	Day	Time	m	Time	m	Time	m	Time	m
1	W	0212	3.3	0808	7.4	1453	3.1	2037	7.5
2	TH	0317	3.1	0909	7.8	1555	2.8	2135	7.8
3	F	0409	2.8	0957	8.1	1645	2.4	2220	8.2
4	SA	0452	2.5	1036	8.5	1726	2.1	2257	8.4
5	SU	0528	2.2	1111	8.7	1802	1.9	○ 2331	8.6
6	M	0601	2.0	1143	8.9	1834	1.7		
7	TU	0001	8.7	0633	1.8	1213	9.0	1905	1.6
8	W	0032	8.8	0705	1.7	1244	9.0	1936	1.6
9	TH	0102	8.8	0737	1.7	1313	8.9	2007	1.7
10	F	0133	8.7	0810	1.9	1343	8.8	2039	1.8
11	SA	0205	8.5	0843	2.1	1414	8.6	2110	2.1
12	SU	0239	8.3	0918	2.4	1451	8.4	2145	2.4
13	M	0321	8.0	0958	2.7	1537	8.1	◑ 2230	2.8
14	TU	0414	7.7	1054	3.1	1639	7.7	2338	3.1
15	W	0529	7.4	1214	3.2	1808	7.4		
16	TH	0114	3.2	0700	7.5	1352	3.0	1942	7.6
17	F	0239	2.8	0819	7.9	1513	2.5	2059	8.1
18	SA	0348	2.2	0924	8.6	1621	1.7	2200	8.7
19	SU	0447	1.6	1019	9.2	1720	1.1	2251	9.2
20	M	0540	1.1	1107	9.7	1811	0.5	● 2338	9.6
21	TU	0627	0.8	1152	10.0	1857	0.2		
22	W	0020	9.7	0711	0.6	1235	10.1	1939	0.2
23	TH	0101	9.6	0751	0.7	1316	9.9	2018	0.5
24	F	0140	9.3	0829	1.0	1356	9.6	2055	1.0
25	SA	0218	8.9	0905	1.5	1436	9.1	2129	1.7
26	SU	0257	8.4	0943	2.1	1518	8.5	2206	2.4
27	M	0340	7.8	1027	2.8	1609	7.8	◐ 2251	3.1
28	TU	0438	7.3	1128	3.4	1718	7.1	2359	3.6

MARCH

Date	Day	Time	m	Time	m	Time	m	Time	m
1	W	0559	6.9	1258	3.6	1850	6.9		
2	TH	0134	3.7	0736	7.0	1430	3.4	2020	7.1
3	F	0255	3.4	0848	7.4	1538	2.9	2120	7.6
4	SA	0353	3.0	0937	7.9	1627	2.4	2203	8.0
5	SU	0435	2.5	1015	8.4	1706	2.0	2238	8.4
6	M	0510	2.1	1049	8.7	1740	1.7	2309	8.7
7	TU	0542	1.8	1120	8.9	1811	1.4	○ 2338	8.9
8	W	0613	1.6	1149	9.1	1841	1.3		
9	TH	0006	9.0	0645	1.4	1218	9.1	1912	1.2
10	F	0035	9.0	0717	1.3	1246	9.1	1943	1.3
11	SA	0105	8.9	0749	1.5	1315	9.0	2012	1.5
12	SU	0136	8.8	0820	1.7	1347	8.8	2041	1.9
13	M	0210	8.5	0852	2.0	1424	8.5	2114	2.3
14	TU	0251	8.2	0932	2.5	1511	8.1	2158	2.8
15	W	0345	7.7	1027	2.9	1617	7.5	◑ 2306	3.2
16	TH	0506	7.3	1154	3.2	1756	7.2		
17	F	0052	3.3	0645	7.4	1340	2.9	1937	7.5
18	SA	0225	2.9	0808	7.9	1503	2.3	2053	8.1
19	SU	0336	2.2	0912	8.6	1610	1.5	2150	8.8
20	M	0434	1.6	1004	9.2	1705	0.9	2236	9.3
21	TU	0523	1.0	1049	9.7	1752	0.4	● 2318	9.6
22	W	0607	0.7	1131	10.0	1834	0.2	2357	9.6
23	TH	0647	0.5	1211	10.0	1912	0.3		
24	F	0034	9.5	0725	0.6	1249	9.8	1947	0.7
25	SA	0109	9.3	0800	1.0	1326	9.4	2020	1.2
26	SU	0144	8.9	0835	1.5	1403	8.9	2050	1.8
27	M	0219	8.4	0909	2.1	1442	8.3	2120	2.5
28	TU	0300	7.9	0947	2.8	1530	7.6	2158	3.2
29	W	0353	7.3	1042	3.4	1636	6.9	◐ 2259	3.8
30	TH	0513	6.8	1216	3.7	1812	6.6		
31	F	0045	4.0	0652	6.8	1355	3.5	1948	6.9

APRIL

Date	Day	Time	m	Time	m	Time	m	Time	m
1	SA	0220	3.7	0810	7.2	1502	2.9	2049	7.4
2	SU	0319	3.1	0902	7.8	1552	2.4	2132	7.9
3	M	0403	2.6	0942	8.2	1631	1.9	2206	8.3
4	TU	0439	2.1	1016	8.6	1706	1.6	2237	8.7
5	W	0513	1.7	1047	8.9	1739	1.3	2306	8.9
6	TH	0546	1.4	1118	9.1	1812	1.1	○ 2336	9.1
7	F	0620	1.2	1148	9.2	1844	1.1		
8	SA	0006	9.1	0654	1.2	1219	9.2	1917	1.2
9	SU	0038	9.1	0728	1.3	1252	9.1	1948	1.4
10	M	0112	8.9	0801	1.5	1328	8.8	2020	1.8
11	TU	0150	8.7	0837	1.9	1411	8.5	2056	2.3
12	W	0236	8.3	0921	2.3	1504	8.0	2145	2.8
13	TH	0337	7.8	1023	2.7	1619	7.4	◑ 2259	3.2
14	F	0503	7.5	1154	2.9	1756	7.3		
15	SA	0041	3.2	0634	7.6	1330	2.6	1928	7.6
16	SU	0208	2.8	0750	8.1	1447	2.0	2037	8.2
17	M	0316	2.1	0851	8.7	1550	1.4	2129	8.7
18	TU	0411	1.6	0941	9.2	1641	0.9	2213	9.1
19	W	0459	1.1	1025	9.5	1725	0.7	2253	9.3
20	TH	0541	0.8	1105	9.7	1805	0.6	● 2330	9.4
21	F	0620	0.8	1145	9.6	1841	0.7		
22	SA	0005	9.3	0658	0.9	1222	9.4	1915	1.1
23	SU	0040	9.1	0733	1.2	1259	9.1	1946	1.5
24	M	0114	8.8	0807	1.6	1335	8.6	2015	2.0
25	TU	0149	8.4	0841	2.2	1415	8.1	2045	2.6
26	W	0229	8.0	0918	2.7	1501	7.5	2122	3.2
27	TH	0319	7.4	1008	3.2	1601	7.0	◐ 2215	3.7
28	F	0430	7.0	1127	3.5	1723	6.7	2341	3.9
29	SA	0558	6.9	1300	3.4	1851	6.8		
30	SU	0118	3.7	0715	7.2	1409	3.0	1958	7.2

Chart Datum: 4·93 metres below Ordnance Datum (Newlyn)
HAT is 10·3m above Chart Datum

TIME ZONE (UT)
For Summer Time add ONE hour in **non-shaded areas**

LIVERPOOL (GLADSTONE DOCK)

LAT 53°27'N LONG 3°01'W

TIMES AND HEIGHTS OF HIGH AND LOW WATERS

Dates in amber are **SPRINGS**
Dates in grey are **NEAPS**

2023

MAY

Date	Day	Time	m	Time	m	Time	m	Time	m
1	M	0225	3.3	0812	7.6	1501	2.5	2045	7.7
2	TU	0314	2.7	0857	8.0	1545	2.1	2123	8.2
3	W	0357	2.3	0934	8.4	1625	1.7	2157	8.5
4	TH	0436	1.8	1009	8.7	1703	1.4	2230	8.8
5	F	0515	1.5	1043	9.0	1740	1.2	○ 2304	9.0
6	SA	0554	1.3	1119	9.1	1817	1.2	2339	9.2
7	SU	0632	1.2	1156	9.1	1853	1.2		
8	M	0016	9.2	0711	1.3	1236	9.0	1930	1.5
9	TU	0056	9.0	0750	1.5	1319	8.8	2008	1.8
10	W	0141	8.8	0833	1.7	1409	8.4	2051	2.2
11	TH	0234	8.4	0924	2.1	1509	8.0	2147	2.7
12	F	0340	8.0	1031	2.4	1624	7.6	◑ 2301	3.0
13	SA	0457	7.9	1153	2.4	1746	7.6		
14	SU	0025	2.9	0614	8.0	1310	2.2	1904	7.8
15	M	0140	2.6	0724	8.3	1419	1.9	2009	8.2
16	TU	0245	2.2	0823	8.6	1519	1.5	2101	8.5
17	W	0341	1.8	0914	8.9	1610	1.3	2146	8.8
18	TH	0430	1.5	0959	9.1	1655	1.2	2226	9.0
19	F	0514	1.3	1041	9.2	1734	1.2	● 2304	9.1
20	SA	0554	1.2	1121	9.1	1810	1.3	2341	9.0
21	SU	0633	1.3	1200	8.9	1844	1.5		
22	M	0016	8.9	0710	1.5	1237	8.7	1917	1.9
23	TU	0051	8.7	0746	1.9	1315	8.4	1948	2.2
24	W	0127	8.4	0821	2.2	1354	8.0	2020	2.6
25	TH	0207	8.1	0858	2.6	1437	7.6	2058	3.0
26	F	0253	7.7	0942	2.9	1529	7.3	2145	3.3
27	SA	0351	7.4	1040	3.1	1632	7.0	◐ 2248	3.6
28	SU	0500	7.2	1151	3.2	1742	7.0		
29	M	0001	3.6	0610	7.3	1300	3.0	1849	7.2
30	TU	0113	3.3	0710	7.5	1401	2.7	1945	7.5
31	W	0215	2.9	0802	7.8	1454	2.3	2032	7.9

JUNE

Date	Day	Time	m	Time	m	Time	m	Time	m
1	TH	0309	2.5	0848	8.2	1542	2.0	2114	8.3
2	F	0358	2.1	0930	8.5	1627	1.7	2155	8.7
3	SA	0445	1.7	1012	8.8	1711	1.5	2236	9.0
4	SU	0530	1.5	1055	9.0	1753	1.4	○ 2317	9.1
5	M	0615	1.3	1140	9.0	1836	1.4		
6	TU	0001	9.2	0700	1.2	1227	9.0	1919	1.5
7	W	0048	9.2	0747	1.3	1317	8.9	2004	1.7
8	TH	0139	9.0	0837	1.4	1411	8.6	2053	2.0
9	F	0234	8.8	0931	1.6	1510	8.3	2148	2.3
10	SA	0335	8.6	1031	1.8	1613	8.0	◑ 2251	2.5
11	SU	0439	8.4	1135	2.0	1720	7.9	2357	2.6
12	M	0545	8.3	1240	2.0	1828	7.9		
13	TU	0104	2.5	0650	8.3	1344	2.0	1934	8.0
14	W	0209	2.4	0751	8.4	1444	2.0	2030	8.2
15	TH	0309	2.2	0847	8.5	1538	1.9	2120	8.4
16	F	0403	2.0	0937	8.6	1625	1.9	2204	8.6
17	SA	0451	1.8	1022	8.6	1707	1.9	2244	8.7
18	SU	0535	1.8	1105	8.6	1745	1.9	● 2323	8.7
19	M	0616	1.8	1144	8.6	1821	2.0	2359	8.7
20	TU	0654	1.8	1222	8.5	1854	2.1		
21	W	0034	8.6	0730	2.0	1258	8.3	1927	2.2
22	TH	0110	8.5	0804	2.1	1335	8.2	2001	2.4
23	F	0147	8.3	0839	2.3	1414	7.9	2038	2.6
24	SA	0227	8.1	0918	2.5	1456	7.7	2120	2.9
25	SU	0312	7.9	1001	2.7	1543	7.5	2208	3.1
26	M	0402	7.6	1052	2.8	1637	7.3	◐ 2303	3.2
27	TU	0459	7.5	1150	2.9	1737	7.3		
28	W	0006	3.2	0601	7.5	1256	2.9	1840	7.4
29	TH	0115	3.1	0704	7.6	1401	2.7	1940	7.7
30	F	0222	2.8	0803	7.9	1501	2.4	2035	8.1

JULY

Date	Day	Time	m	Time	m	Time	m	Time	m
1	SA	0323	2.4	0858	8.2	1555	2.0	2126	8.5
2	SU	0419	2.0	0950	8.6	1646	1.7	2215	8.9
3	M	0512	1.6	1041	8.9	1736	1.5	○ 2303	9.2
4	TU	0604	1.3	1132	9.1	1824	1.3	2352	9.4
5	W	0655	1.0	1222	9.2	1913	1.3		
6	TH	0041	9.5	0746	0.9	1313	9.1	2001	1.3
7	F	0132	9.4	0835	0.9	1403	9.0	2048	1.5
8	SA	0223	9.3	0924	1.1	1455	8.7	2137	1.8
9	SU	0315	9.0	1013	1.4	1547	8.4	2227	2.1
10	M	0410	8.7	1105	1.8	1644	8.0	◑ 2323	2.4
11	TU	0508	8.4	1202	2.2	1747	7.8		
12	W	0024	2.6	0613	8.1	1304	2.5	1855	7.7
13	TH	0133	2.7	0720	7.9	1409	2.6	2001	7.8
14	F	0242	2.7	0825	7.9	1510	2.6	2059	8.0
15	SA	0344	2.5	0923	8.0	1603	2.5	2149	8.2
16	SU	0438	2.3	1012	8.2	1649	2.3	2232	8.5
17	M	0525	2.1	1055	8.3	1729	2.2	● 2311	8.6
18	TU	0606	1.9	1133	8.4	1805	2.2	2346	8.7
19	W	0642	1.9	1208	8.5	1838	2.1		
20	TH	0019	8.7	0715	1.8	1241	8.5	1911	2.1
21	F	0052	8.7	0746	1.9	1314	8.4	1943	2.1
22	SA	0125	8.6	0818	1.9	1348	8.3	2018	2.2
23	SU	0158	8.5	0851	2.1	1422	8.1	2054	2.4
24	M	0233	8.3	0926	2.3	1459	7.9	2133	2.6
25	TU	0310	8.0	1005	2.6	1541	7.7	◐ 2217	2.9
26	W	0356	7.8	1051	2.8	1634	7.5	2311	3.1
27	TH	0454	7.6	1154	3.0	1740	7.4		
28	F	0021	3.2	0609	7.5	1312	3.0	1855	7.5
29	SA	0143	3.1	0728	7.6	1428	2.8	2006	7.9
30	SU	0257	2.6	0838	8.0	1532	2.3	2108	8.4
31	M	0401	2.1	0939	8.4	1630	1.9	2202	8.9

AUGUST

Date	Day	Time	m	Time	m	Time	m	Time	m
1	TU	0501	1.5	1034	8.9	1724	1.5	○ 2253	9.4
2	W	0556	1.0	1125	9.3	1815	1.2	2342	9.7
3	TH	0648	0.6	1213	9.5	1903	1.0		
4	F	0028	9.9	0735	0.4	1259	9.5	1949	0.9
5	SA	0115	9.9	0820	0.5	1344	9.3	2032	1.1
6	SU	0200	9.7	0902	0.8	1428	9.0	2114	1.4
7	M	0246	9.3	0944	1.3	1513	8.5	2157	1.9
8	TU	0333	8.8	1027	1.9	1601	8.1	◑ 2245	2.4
9	W	0427	8.2	1117	2.6	1700	7.6	2345	2.9
10	TH	0533	7.7	1221	3.1	1814	7.3		
11	F	0102	3.2	0653	7.4	1338	3.2	1936	7.4
12	SA	0225	3.1	0812	7.4	1452	3.1	2045	7.7
13	SU	0335	2.8	0916	7.7	1552	2.9	2138	8.1
14	M	0431	2.4	1005	8.0	1640	2.6	2220	8.4
15	TU	0515	2.1	1044	8.3	1718	2.3	2256	8.7
16	W	0552	1.9	1118	8.5	1751	2.1	● 2328	8.9
17	TH	0624	1.7	1148	8.7	1821	1.9	2359	9.0
18	F	0653	1.6	1218	8.7	1851	1.8		
19	SA	0028	9.0	0722	1.6	1248	8.7	1922	1.8
20	SU	0058	8.9	0751	1.6	1317	8.6	1954	1.9
21	M	0126	8.8	0821	1.8	1348	8.5	2027	2.1
22	TU	0156	8.6	0852	2.1	1420	8.3	2100	2.4
23	W	0229	8.3	0925	2.4	1457	8.0	2138	2.7
24	TH	0310	8.0	1004	2.8	1545	7.7	◐ 2227	3.1
25	F	0406	7.6	1102	3.2	1654	7.4	2340	3.3
26	SA	0529	7.3	1233	3.4	1825	7.4		
27	SU	0117	3.2	0709	7.4	1405	3.1	1949	7.8
28	M	0241	2.7	0830	7.9	1516	2.5	2056	8.4
29	TU	0350	2.0	0933	8.5	1617	1.9	2151	9.1
30	W	0451	1.3	1025	9.1	1712	1.3	2239	9.6
31	TH	0544	0.7	1111	9.5	1801	0.9	○ 2325	10.0

Chart Datum: 4·93 metres below Ordnance Datum (Newlyn)
HAT is 10·3m above Chart Datum

TIME ZONE (UT)
For Summer Time add ONE hour in **non-shaded areas**

LIVERPOOL (GLADSTONE DOCK)

LAT 53°27′N LONG 3°01′W

TIMES AND HEIGHTS OF HIGH AND LOW WATERS

Dates in amber are **SPRINGS**
Dates in grey are **NEAPS**

2023

SEPTEMBER

Date	Time	m	Date	Time	m
1 F	0631 1154 1845	0.3 9.7 0.7	16 SA	0624 1150 1826	1.4 9.0 1.6
2 SA	0008 0715 1236 1927	10.2 0.2 9.7 0.7	17 SU	0000 0653 1217 1858	9.1 1.4 9.0 1.6
3 SU	0050 0755 1316 2007	10.1 0.4 9.5 0.9	18 M	0028 0723 1246 1930	9.1 1.5 8.9 1.7
4 M	0131 0832 1355 2045	9.8 0.8 9.1 1.3	19 TU	0055 0752 1315 2001	9.0 1.7 8.7 1.9
5 TU	0212 0909 1435 2124	9.3 1.5 8.6 2.0	20 W	0125 0822 1347 2033	8.7 2.0 8.5 2.3
6 W	0256 0946 1519 ◑ 2209	8.6 2.2 8.1 2.6	21 TH	0159 0853 1425 2110	8.5 2.4 8.2 2.7
7 TH	0346 1030 1615 2309	7.9 3.0 7.5 3.2	22 F	0242 0932 1515 ◐ 2202	8.0 2.9 7.8 3.1
8 F	0454 1135 1735	7.2 3.6 7.1	23 SA	0342 1033 1630 2321	7.5 3.4 7.4 3.4
9 SA	0037 0628 1311 1912	3.5 6.9 3.8 7.1	24 SU	0517 1212 1810	7.1 3.6 7.4
10 SU	0211 0801 1437 2028	3.3 7.1 3.5 7.5	25 M	0105 0702 1349 1936	3.2 7.3 3.2 7.9
11 M	0321 0904 1538 2119	2.9 7.6 3.1 8.0	26 TU	0230 0823 1502 2041	2.5 8.0 2.5 8.6
12 TU	0412 0948 1622 2159	2.4 8.1 2.6 8.5	27 W	0337 0921 1601 2134	1.7 8.7 1.8 9.3
13 W	0452 1023 1657 2232	2.0 8.4 2.3 8.8	28 TH	0434 1008 1653 2219	1.1 9.3 1.3 9.8
14 TH	0525 1053 1727 2303	1.7 8.7 2.0 9.0	29 F	0523 1050 1739 ○ 2302	0.6 9.6 0.9 10.1
15 F	0555 1122 1756 ● 2332	1.5 8.9 1.8 9.1	30 SA	0606 1130 1821 2343	0.3 9.8 0.7 10.2

OCTOBER

Date	Time	m	Date	Time	m
1 SU	0647 1209 1901	0.4 9.7 0.7	16 M	0623 1147 1833 2359	1.4 9.1 1.5 9.1
2 M	0023 0724 1246 1939	10.0 0.7 9.5 1.0	17 TU	0655 1218 1906	1.5 9.1 1.7
3 TU	0102 0759 1322 2017	9.6 1.2 9.1 1.5	18 W	0030 0726 1250 1940	9.0 1.7 8.9 1.9
4 W	0141 0833 1400 2055	9.1 1.8 8.6 2.1	19 TH	0104 0758 1326 2016	8.8 2.1 8.7 2.2
5 TH	0223 0907 1441 2138	8.4 2.6 8.1 2.8	20 F	0144 0833 1408 2058	8.4 2.5 8.3 2.6
6 F	0312 0947 1535 ◑ 2237	7.7 3.3 7.5 3.4	21 SA	0234 0918 1505 2155	8.0 3.0 7.9 3.0
7 SA	0419 1048 1656	7.0 3.9 7.0	22 SU	0342 1025 1625 ◐ 2319	7.5 3.4 7.6 3.2
8 SU	0010 0556 1234 1835	3.7 6.7 4.1 7.0	23 M	0516 1201 1757	7.3 3.5 7.6
9 M	0142 0732 1406 1953	3.5 7.0 3.8 7.4	24 TU	0054 0650 1330 1916	2.9 7.6 3.1 8.1
10 TU	0248 0834 1505 2045	3.0 7.5 3.3 7.9	25 W	0211 0804 1439 2018	2.3 8.2 2.5 8.7
11 W	0336 0917 1547 2125	2.5 8.0 2.8 8.4	26 TH	0314 0859 1537 2110	1.6 8.7 1.9 9.3
12 TH	0415 0951 1623 2159	2.1 8.4 2.3 8.7	27 F	0408 0944 1627 2155	1.1 9.2 1.4 9.7
13 F	0449 1021 1655 2230	1.7 8.7 2.0 9.0	28 SA	0455 1025 1713 ○ 2238	0.8 9.5 1.1 9.9
14 SA	0521 1050 1727 ● 2300	1.5 8.9 1.7 9.1	29 SU	0538 1104 1755 2319	0.7 9.6 1.0 9.9
15 SU	0552 1118 1759 2329	1.4 9.1 1.6 9.2	30 M	0617 1142 1835 2359	0.9 9.6 1.0 9.7
			31 TU	0653 1219 1914	1.1 9.4 1.3

NOVEMBER

Date	Time	m	Date	Time	m
1 W	0038 0728 1255 1953	9.3 1.6 9.0 1.7	16 TH	0014 0707 1234 1928	9.0 1.8 9.1 1.8
2 TH	0117 0802 1332 2031	8.8 2.2 8.6 2.3	17 F	0055 0744 1316 2010	8.8 2.1 8.9 2.1
3 F	0158 0834 1413 2113	8.2 2.8 8.2 2.9	18 SA	0142 0826 1405 2059	8.5 2.4 8.6 2.3
4 SA	0245 0912 1504 2207	7.6 3.4 7.7 3.4	19 SU	0237 0917 1506 2200	8.1 2.8 8.2 2.6
5 SU	0345 1005 1615 ◑ 2327	7.1 3.9 7.2 3.6	20 M	0345 1023 1619 ◐ 2315	7.8 3.1 8.0 2.7
6 M	0507 1132 1741	6.8 4.1 7.1	21 TU	0504 1143 1735	7.6 3.2 8.1
7 TU	0050 0634 1306 1857	3.5 6.9 3.9 7.3	22 W	0032 0623 1300 1846	2.5 7.8 2.9 8.3
8 W	0155 0742 1410 1956	3.1 7.3 3.5 7.7	23 TH	0142 0733 1407 1949	2.2 8.1 2.5 8.7
9 TH	0246 0831 1459 2041	2.7 7.8 3.0 8.1	24 F	0244 0830 1507 2043	1.8 8.5 2.1 9.0
10 F	0329 0909 1539 2120	2.3 8.2 2.6 8.5	25 SA	0339 0918 1600 2132	1.6 8.9 1.8 9.3
11 SA	0407 0943 1618 2154	2.0 8.6 2.2 8.8	26 SU	0427 1001 1648 2217	1.4 9.1 1.5 9.4
12 SU	0444 1015 1655 2228	1.7 8.8 1.9 8.9	27 M	0510 1042 1732 ○ 2300	1.4 9.2 1.4 9.3
13 M	0519 1047 1733 ● 2301	1.6 9.0 1.7 9.1	28 TU	0550 1121 1815 2341	1.5 9.2 1.5 9.2
14 TU	0555 1121 1811 2336	1.5 9.2 1.6 9.1	29 W	0627 1159 1856	1.7 9.1 1.6
15 W	0631 1156 1849	1.6 9.2 1.7	30 TH	0021 0704 1236 1936	8.9 2.0 8.9 1.9

DECEMBER

Date	Time	m	Date	Time	m
1 F	0100 0737 1313 2014	8.6 2.3 8.7 2.3	16 SA	0053 0740 1313 2012	9.0 1.8 9.2 1.6
2 SA	0140 0811 1353 2053	8.2 2.7 8.3 2.7	17 SU	0142 0826 1404 2103	8.8 2.1 9.0 1.8
3 SU	0223 0847 1438 2137	7.8 3.1 8.0 3.0	18 M	0236 0916 1500 2157	8.5 2.3 8.8 2.0
4 M	0312 0931 1533 2231	7.5 3.5 7.6 3.3	19 TU	0334 1013 1600 ◐ 2256	8.2 2.6 8.6 2.1
5 TU	0411 1029 1639 ◑ 2336	7.2 3.7 7.4 3.4	20 W	0437 1115 1703 2359	8.0 2.7 8.4 2.3
6 W	0519 1140 1747	7.0 3.8 7.4	21 TH	0545 1222 1810	7.9 2.8 8.4
7 TH	0043 0628 1253 1851	3.3 7.1 3.7 7.5	22 F	0104 0654 1329 1916	2.3 7.9 2.7 8.4
8 F	0144 0729 1357 1947	3.0 7.4 3.3 7.8	23 SA	0209 0758 1436 2017	2.3 8.1 2.5 8.5
9 SA	0237 0819 1451 2034	2.7 7.8 2.9 8.1	24 SU	0309 0854 1536 2113	2.2 8.4 2.3 8.6
10 SU	0324 0902 1540 2118	2.4 8.2 2.5 8.4	25 M	0402 0944 1630 2204	2.1 8.6 2.0 8.7
11 M	0408 0942 1625 2159	2.1 8.6 2.2 8.6	26 TU	0449 1028 1719 2250	2.0 8.8 1.9 8.8
12 TU	0451 1021 1710 ● 2240	1.9 8.9 1.9 8.8	27 W	0532 1110 1804 ○ 2332	2.0 8.9 1.8 8.8
13 W	0532 1100 1754 2322	1.7 9.1 1.7 9.0	28 TH	0611 1148 1846	2.0 9.0 1.8
14 TH	0614 1142 1839	1.7 9.2 1.6	29 F	0011 0647 1224 1924	8.7 2.1 8.9 1.9
15 F	0006 0657 1226 1925	9.0 1.7 9.3 1.5	30 SA	0047 0721 1259 2000	8.6 2.3 8.8 2.1
			31 SU	0123 0753 1335 2033	8.4 2.4 8.6 2.3

Chart Datum: 4·93 metres below Ordnance Datum (Newlyn)
HAT is 10·3m above Chart Datum

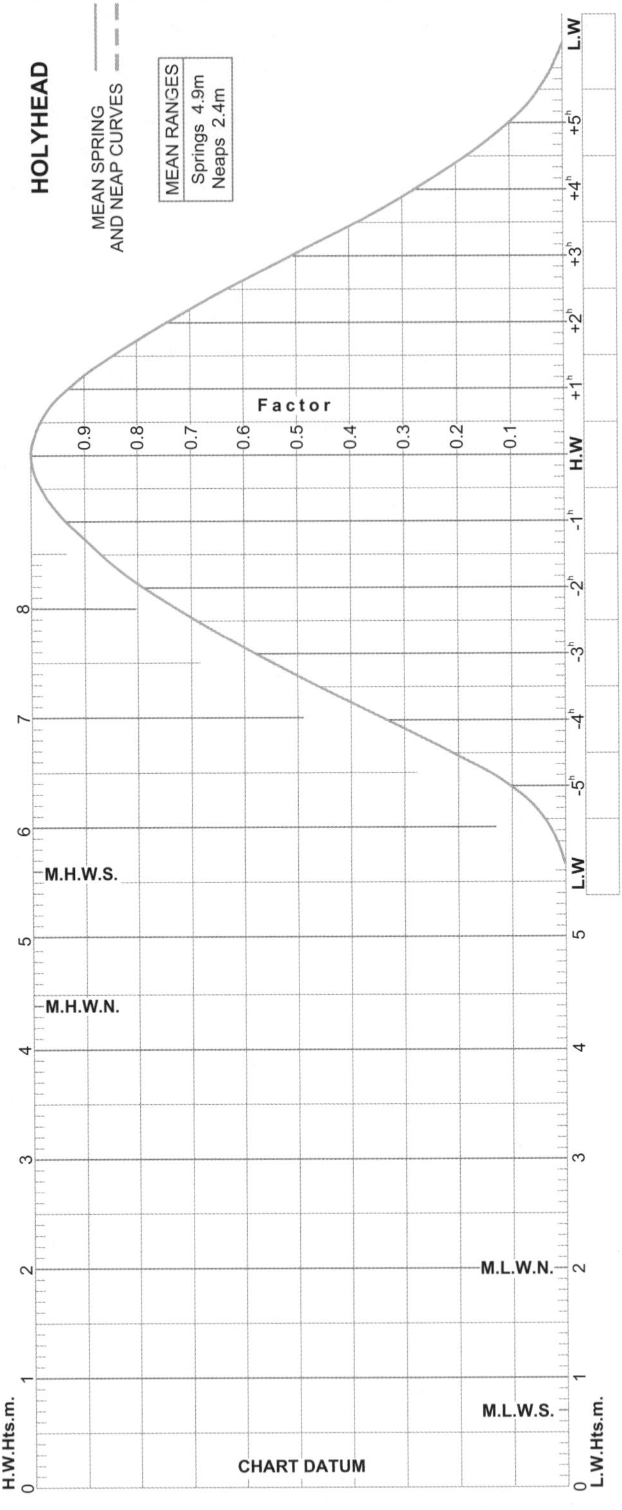
HOLYHEAD
MEAN SPRING AND NEAP CURVES
MEAN RANGES
Springs 4.9m
Neaps 2.4m
Factor
0.9
0.8
0.7
0.6
0.5
0.4
0.3
0.2
0.1
L.W
-5h
-4h
-3h
-2h
-1h
H.W
+1h
+2h
+3h
+4h
+5h
L.W
M.H.W.S.
M.H.W.N.
M.L.W.N.
M.L.W.S.
CHART DATUM
H.W.Hts.m.
L.W.Hts.m.
0
1
2
3
4
5
6
7
8

TIME ZONE (UT)
For Summer Time add ONE hour in **non-shaded areas**

WALES – HOLYHEAD

LAT 53°19′N LONG 4°37′W

TIMES AND HEIGHTS OF HIGH AND LOW WATERS

Dates in amber are **SPRINGS**
Dates in grey are **NEAPS**

2023

JANUARY

Date	Time	m	Date	Time	m
1 SU	0602 1200 1815	4.6 2.0 4.9	16 M	0433 1036 1652 2323	4.5 2.1 4.7 1.9
2 M	0037 0706 1304 1920	1.7 4.7 1.9 4.9	17 TU	0546 1149 1808	4.5 2.1 4.7
3 TU	0135 0800 1403 2016	1.7 4.9 1.8 4.9	18 W	0032 0656 1259 1920	1.8 4.7 1.9 4.9
4 W	0226 0847 1453 2104	1.7 5.0 1.6 5.0	19 TH	0136 0757 1402 2024	1.6 5.0 1.6 5.1
5 TH	0309 0927 1537 2145	1.6 5.2 1.5 5.1	20 F	0233 0851 1459 2120	1.3 5.3 1.2 5.4
6 F	0347 1004 1616 ○ 2223	1.5 5.3 1.4 5.1	21 SA	0325 0940 1552 ● 2211	1.1 5.6 0.8 5.6
7 SA	0422 1038 1651 2258	1.4 5.4 1.3 5.1	22 SU	0414 1028 1642 2300	0.9 5.9 0.5 5.7
8 SU	0455 1110 1725 2331	1.4 5.4 1.3 5.1	23 M	0501 1115 1731 2348	0.7 6.0 0.4 5.7
9 M	0527 1143 1759	1.4 5.4 1.3	24 TU	0547 1202 1818	0.7 6.1 0.4
10 TU	0004 0601 1216 1834	5.1 1.4 5.4 1.3	25 W	0034 0634 1248 1907	5.6 0.8 6.0 0.5
11 W	0039 0636 1251 1910	5.0 1.5 5.3 1.4	26 TH	0121 0720 1335 1955	5.4 0.9 5.8 0.8
12 TH	0116 0713 1328 1948	4.9 1.6 5.2 1.5	27 F	0208 0809 1424 2045	5.2 1.2 5.5 1.1
13 F	0155 0752 1407 2030	4.8 1.8 5.1 1.6	28 SA	0259 0901 1516 ◐ 2140	4.9 1.5 5.2 1.5
14 SA	0238 0837 1452 2118	4.7 1.9 4.9 1.7	29 SU	0356 1003 1617 2244	4.6 1.9 4.8 1.9
15 SU	0330 0931 1546 ◑ 2216	4.6 2.0 4.8 1.8	30 M	0505 1116 1731 2355	4.4 2.1 4.6 2.1
			31 TU	0625 1234 1853	4.4 2.1 4.5

FEBRUARY

Date	Time	m	Date	Time	m
1 W	0107 0738 1346 2004	2.1 4.5 2.0 4.6	16 TH	0001 0626 1238 1908	2.0 4.5 1.9 4.6
2 TH	0210 0833 1444 2057	2.0 4.8 1.8 4.7	17 F	0120 0741 1353 2020	1.8 4.8 1.5 4.9
3 F	0258 0916 1528 2139	1.8 5.0 1.6 4.9	18 SA	0225 0840 1453 2116	1.4 5.2 1.1 5.3
4 SA	0337 0952 1605 2213	1.6 5.2 1.3 5.0	19 SU	0317 0930 1544 2203	1.1 5.6 0.6 5.5
5 SU	0410 1024 1637 ○ 2244	1.4 5.3 1.2 5.1	20 M	0403 1015 1630 ● 2247	0.7 5.9 0.3 5.7
6 M	0440 1054 1708 2314	1.3 5.4 1.1 5.2	21 TU	0446 1059 1714 2329	0.5 6.1 0.2 5.8
7 TU	0510 1124 1738 2344	1.2 5.5 1.0 5.2	22 W	0528 1142 1756	0.4 6.2 0.2
8 W	0540 1155 1809	1.1 5.5 1.0	23 TH	0010 0610 1224 1839	5.7 0.5 6.1 0.4
9 TH	0015 0612 1227 1841	5.2 1.1 5.5 1.1	24 F	0051 0652 1307 1921	5.5 0.7 5.8 0.7
10 F	0047 0645 1259 1913	5.2 1.2 5.4 1.2	25 SA	0132 0735 1350 2004	5.2 1.0 5.5 1.1
11 SA	0121 0720 1334 1949	5.1 1.3 5.3 1.3	26 SU	0214 0822 1436 2051	4.9 1.4 5.1 1.6
12 SU	0158 0759 1412 2031	4.9 1.5 5.1 1.5	27 M	0301 0917 1530 ◐ 2149	4.6 1.8 4.6 2.0
13 M	0241 0846 1459 ◑ 2124	4.7 1.7 4.9 1.7	28 TU	0404 1030 1646 2307	4.3 2.1 4.3 2.3
14 TU	0337 0948 1603 2235	4.6 2.0 4.6 1.9			
15 W	0455 1110 1734	4.4 2.1 4.5			

MARCH

Date	Time	m	Date	Time	m
1 W	0533 1201 1827	4.2 2.3 4.2	16 TH	0426 1053 1726 2346	4.4 2.0 4.3 2.1
2 TH	0036 0710 1326 1952	2.4 4.3 2.1 4.3	17 F	0608 1229 1906	4.5 1.8 4.5
3 F	0151 0813 1427 2045	2.2 4.6 1.8 4.6	18 SA	0111 0727 1344 2014	1.9 4.8 1.4 4.9
4 SA	0241 0857 1509 2123	1.9 4.8 1.5 4.8	19 SU	0213 0825 1441 2105	1.4 5.2 0.9 5.3
5 SU	0318 0932 1543 2154	1.6 5.1 1.2 5.0	20 M	0303 0913 1528 2147	1.0 5.6 0.5 5.5
6 M	0349 1002 1613 2222	1.4 5.3 1.0 5.2	21 TU	0345 0956 1610 ● 2226	0.7 5.9 0.2 5.7
7 TU	0417 1030 1642 ○ 2249	1.1 5.4 0.9 5.3	22 W	0425 1037 1650 2305	0.4 6.1 0.2 5.7
8 W	0446 1059 1710 2317	1.0 5.5 0.8 5.3	23 TH	0505 1118 1730 2343	0.3 6.1 0.2 5.7
9 TH	0515 1129 1739 2347	0.9 5.6 0.8 5.4	24 F	0544 1159 1808	0.4 5.9 0.5
10 F	0545 1200 1809	0.9 5.6 0.8	25 SA	0020 0625 1239 1847	5.5 0.6 5.7 0.8
11 SA	0018 0617 1231 1841	5.3 0.9 5.5 1.0	26 SU	0058 0706 1319 1927	5.3 0.9 5.3 1.2
12 SU	0050 0651 1305 1916	5.2 1.1 5.3 1.1	27 M	0136 0750 1402 2009	5.0 1.3 4.9 1.7
13 M	0126 0730 1343 1957	5.1 1.3 5.1 1.4	28 TU	0219 0841 1452 2101	4.7 1.8 4.5 2.1
14 TU	0208 0818 1431 2050	4.9 1.5 4.8 1.7	29 W	0313 0949 1605 ◐ 2215	4.4 2.1 4.1 2.5
15 W	0304 0922 1540 ◑ 2207	4.6 1.8 4.5 2.0	30 TH	0437 1123 1751 2355	4.2 2.3 4.0 2.5
			31 F	0622 1251 1922	4.2 2.1 4.2

APRIL

Date	Time	m	Date	Time	m
1 SA	0117 0736 1353 2015	2.3 4.4 1.8 4.5	16 SU	0054 0707 1327 1958	1.8 4.9 1.2 4.9
2 SU	0209 0822 1436 2052	2.0 4.7 1.5 4.7	17 M	0153 0803 1421 2044	1.4 5.2 0.8 5.2
3 M	0247 0858 1510 2123	1.7 5.0 1.2 5.0	18 TU	0241 0850 1506 2124	1.0 5.6 0.5 5.4
4 TU	0318 0929 1540 2150	1.4 5.2 1.0 5.2	19 W	0323 0932 1546 2202	0.7 5.8 0.4 5.6
5 W	0346 0958 1608 2218	1.1 5.4 0.8 5.3	20 TH	0402 1013 1625 ● 2239	0.5 5.9 0.4 5.6
6 TH	0415 1028 1637 ○ 2247	0.9 5.5 0.7 5.4	21 F	0441 1054 1702 2316	0.5 5.8 0.5 5.6
7 F	0446 1059 1707 2318	0.8 5.6 0.7 5.5	22 SA	0521 1135 1740 2354	0.6 5.7 0.7 5.5
8 SA	0518 1132 1739 2351	0.7 5.6 0.8 5.4	23 SU	0601 1215 1817	0.8 5.4 1.0
9 SU	0552 1207 1813	0.8 5.5 0.9	24 M	0030 0642 1254 1855	5.3 1.0 5.1 1.4
10 M	0025 0630 1244 1852	5.4 0.9 5.3 1.1	25 TU	0107 0725 1335 1936	5.0 1.4 4.8 1.7
11 TU	0105 0714 1328 1938	5.2 1.2 5.0 1.4	26 W	0148 0814 1424 2025	4.8 1.7 4.4 2.1
12 W	0151 0807 1423 2037	4.9 1.4 4.7 1.8	27 TH	0238 0916 1529 ◐ 2129	4.5 2.0 4.1 2.4
13 TH	0253 0918 1543 ◑ 2200	4.7 1.7 4.4 2.1	28 F	0348 1036 1659 2257	4.3 2.1 4.0 2.5
14 F	0418 1051 1730 2336	4.5 1.8 4.4 2.1	29 SA	0517 1158 1826	4.2 2.1 4.1
15 SA	0552 1219 1856	4.6 1.6 4.6	30 SU	0020 0635 1301 1926	2.4 4.4 1.8 4.4

Chart Datum: 3·05 metres below Ordnance Datum (Newlyn)
HAT is 6·3m above Chart Datum

TIME ZONE (UT)
For Summer Time add ONE hour in **non-shaded areas**

WALES – HOLYHEAD

LAT 53°19′N LONG 4°37′W

TIMES AND HEIGHTS OF HIGH AND LOW WATERS

Dates in amber are **SPRINGS**
Dates in grey are **NEAPS**

2023

MAY

Date	Day	Time	m	Date	Day	Time	m
1		0118	2.1	16		0125	1.4
		0731	4.6			0736	5.2
	M	1348	1.5		TU	1355	0.9
		2008	4.6			2018	5.1
2		0201	1.8	17		0215	1.2
		0812	4.9			0825	5.4
	TU	1426	1.3		W	1441	0.8
		2042	4.9			2059	5.3
3		0237	1.5	18		0259	0.9
		0848	5.1			0910	5.5
	W	1459	1.1		TH	1522	0.8
		2113	5.1			2138	5.4
4		0310	1.2	19		0341	0.8
		0922	5.3			0952	5.5
	TH	1531	0.9		F	1601	0.8
		2144	5.3			● 2216	5.4
5		0343	1.0	20		0422	0.8
		0956	5.4			1034	5.5
	F	1604	0.8		SA	1639	0.9
		○ 2216	5.4			2254	5.4
6		0417	0.8	21		0503	0.9
		1031	5.5			1115	5.3
	SA	1638	0.7		SU	1716	1.0
		2251	5.5			2332	5.4
7		0454	0.8	22		0543	1.0
		1109	5.5			1155	5.1
	SU	1715	0.8		M	1753	1.2
		2329	5.5				
8		0534	0.8	23		0008	5.2
		1150	5.4			0624	1.2
	M	1755	0.9		TU	1234	4.9
						1832	1.5
9		0009	5.4	24		0045	5.1
		0619	0.9			0706	1.4
	TU	1235	5.2		W	1315	4.7
		1840	1.2			1912	1.7
10		0055	5.3	25		0125	4.9
		0709	1.1			0752	1.6
	W	1327	5.0		TH	1400	4.5
		1933	1.5			1957	2.0
11		0148	5.1	26		0211	4.7
		0809	1.3			0844	1.8
	TH	1429	4.7		F	1454	4.3
		2037	1.8			2050	2.2
12		0252	4.9	27		0306	4.5
		0922	1.5			0945	1.9
	F	1550	4.5		SA	1601	4.2
		◑ 2155	1.9			◐ 2155	2.3
13		0410	4.8	28		0414	4.4
		1042	1.5			1053	1.9
	SA	1718	4.5		SU	1714	4.2
		2316	1.9			2307	2.3
14		0530	4.8	29		0524	4.4
		1158	1.3			1156	1.8
	SU	1832	4.7		M	1818	4.3
15		0027	1.7	30		0012	2.2
		0639	5.0			0627	4.6
	M	1301	1.1		TU	1249	1.7
		1931	4.9			1911	4.5
				31		0105	1.9
						0719	4.7
					W	1335	1.5
						1955	4.8

JUNE

Date	Day	Time	m	Date	Day	Time	m
1		0150	1.6	16		0241	1.3
		0804	4.9			0852	5.1
	TH	1416	1.3		F	1502	1.2
		2034	5.0			2119	5.2
2		0232	1.4	17		0327	1.2
		0846	5.1			0938	5.2
	F	1455	1.1		SA	1543	1.2
		2111	5.2			2159	5.3
3		0312	1.1	18		0410	1.1
		0927	5.3			1021	5.1
	SA	1535	0.9		SU	1622	1.2
		2150	5.4			● 2238	5.3
4		0354	0.9	19		0451	1.1
		1009	5.4			1101	5.1
	SU	1616	0.9		M	1659	1.3
		○ 2231	5.5			2315	5.3
5		0438	0.8	20		0530	1.1
		1054	5.4			1140	5.0
	M	1659	0.9		TU	1735	1.4
		2314	5.6			2351	5.2
6		0524	0.8	21		0608	1.2
		1142	5.4			1217	4.9
	TU	1745	1.0		W	1812	1.5
7		0000	5.6	22		0027	5.2
		0615	0.8			0647	1.3
	W	1232	5.3		TH	1254	4.8
		1836	1.1			1850	1.6
8		0050	5.5	23		0104	5.1
		0709	0.9			0727	1.4
	TH	1327	5.1		F	1334	4.7
		1930	1.3			1930	1.7
9		0145	5.3	24		0144	4.9
		0808	1.0			0810	1.5
	F	1429	4.9		SA	1418	4.5
		2031	1.5			2014	1.9
10		0245	5.2	25		0229	4.8
		0913	1.1			0857	1.7
	SA	1537	4.7		SU	1507	4.4
		◑ 2137	1.7			2104	2.0
11		0351	5.1	26		0319	4.7
		1020	1.2			0949	1.8
	SU	1648	4.6		M	1604	4.3
		2246	1.7			◐ 2201	2.1
12		0500	5.0	27		0417	4.6
		1128	1.3			1047	1.8
	M	1757	4.7		TU	1707	4.4
		2353	1.7			2304	2.1
13		0606	5.0	28		0521	4.6
		1230	1.3			1147	1.8
	TU	1858	4.8		W	1809	4.5
14		0055	1.5	29		0007	2.0
		0708	5.1			0624	4.6
	W	1326	1.2		TH	1244	1.7
		1951	4.9			1907	4.6
15		0150	1.4	30		0105	1.8
		0803	5.1			0722	4.8
	TH	1417	1.2		F	1337	1.5
		2037	5.0			1958	4.9

JULY

Date	Day	Time	m	Date	Day	Time	m
1		0159	1.6	16		0321	1.4
		0816	4.9			0932	4.9
	SA	1427	1.3		SU	1533	1.5
		2045	5.1			2149	5.1
2		0250	1.3	17		0404	1.3
		0907	5.1			1013	5.0
	SU	1515	1.1		M	1611	1.4
		2131	5.3			● 2226	5.3
3		0339	1.0	18		0442	1.2
		0957	5.3			1050	5.0
	M	1602	1.0		TU	1645	1.3
		○ 2217	5.5			2301	5.3
4		0428	0.8	19		0516	1.1
		1046	5.4			1124	5.0
	TU	1649	0.9		W	1718	1.3
		2304	5.7			2333	5.3
5		0518	0.6	20		0550	1.1
		1136	5.5			1157	5.0
	W	1738	0.8		TH	1751	1.3
		2352	5.8				
6		0609	0.5	21		0006	5.3
		1227	5.4			0624	1.1
	TH	1827	0.9		F	1229	5.0
						1825	1.4
7		0041	5.8	22		0040	5.3
		0701	0.6			0658	1.2
	F	1318	5.3		SA	1304	4.9
		1918	1.0			1901	1.5
8		0132	5.7	23		0115	5.2
		0754	0.7			0734	1.3
	SA	1411	5.1		SU	1340	4.8
		2011	1.2			1938	1.6
9		0225	5.5	24		0152	5.0
		0849	0.9			0812	1.5
	SU	1507	4.9		M	1420	4.7
		2107	1.4			2019	1.8
10		0322	5.3	25		0232	4.9
		0948	1.2			0855	1.6
	M	1609	4.7		TU	1505	4.6
		◑ 2210	1.6			◐ 2107	1.9
11		0424	5.1	26		0319	4.7
		1051	1.4			0946	1.8
	TU	1715	4.6		W	1601	4.4
		2317	1.7			2205	2.1
12		0532	4.9	27		0419	4.6
		1156	1.6			1048	1.9
	W	1823	4.6		TH	1710	4.4
						2315	2.1
13		0026	1.8	28		0533	4.5
		0642	4.8			1159	1.9
	TH	1259	1.7		F	1824	4.5
		1927	4.7				
14		0132	1.7	29		0030	2.0
		0748	4.8			0652	4.6
	F	1358	1.6		SA	1307	1.8
		2022	4.8			1931	4.7
15		0231	1.6	30		0138	1.7
		0844	4.8			0800	4.8
	SA	1449	1.6		SU	1408	1.5
		2108	5.0			2027	5.0
				31		0237	1.3
						0858	5.1
					M	1502	1.2
						2118	5.4

AUGUST

Date	Day	Time	m	Date	Day	Time	m
1		0330	0.9	16		0425	1.1
		0949	5.3			1032	5.1
	TU	1551	1.0		W	1627	1.3
		○ 2205	5.7			● 2240	5.4
2		0419	0.6	17		0455	1.0
		1037	5.5			1102	5.1
	W	1638	0.8		TH	1656	1.2
		2251	5.9			2310	5.5
3		0507	0.4	18		0524	1.0
		1124	5.6			1130	5.2
	TH	1723	0.6		F	1726	1.1
		2337	6.0			2340	5.5
4		0553	0.3	19		0554	1.0
		1210	5.6			1200	5.2
	F	1808	0.6		SA	1757	1.2
5		0022	6.0	20		0011	5.4
		0640	0.3			0625	1.0
	SA	1255	5.5		SU	1231	5.1
		1855	0.7			1829	1.2
6		0109	5.9	21		0042	5.3
		0727	0.5			0656	1.2
	SU	1341	5.3		M	1304	5.0
		1942	1.0			1902	1.4
7		0157	5.7	22		0115	5.2
		0816	0.9			0729	1.3
	M	1430	5.0		TU	1339	4.9
		2033	1.3			1939	1.6
8		0248	5.3	23		0151	5.0
		0909	1.3			0808	1.5
	TU	1524	4.7		W	1419	4.8
		◑ 2131	1.6			2023	1.8
9		0346	4.9	24		0234	4.8
		1009	1.7			0855	1.8
	W	1629	4.5		TH	1510	4.6
		2242	1.9			◐ 2120	2.0
10		0457	4.6	25		0332	4.6
		1120	2.0			1000	2.0
	TH	1747	4.4		F	1621	4.4
						2238	2.2
11		0001	2.0	26		0458	4.4
		0623	4.4			1126	2.1
	F	1235	2.1		SA	1752	4.5
		1907	4.5				
12		0120	2.0	27		0008	2.1
		0742	4.5			0638	4.5
	SA	1346	2.0		SU	1250	2.0
		2011	4.7			1913	4.7
13		0225	1.8	28		0126	1.7
		0842	4.6			0754	4.8
	SU	1440	1.8		M	1357	1.6
		2059	4.9			2013	5.1
14		0313	1.5	29		0227	1.2
		0926	4.8			0851	5.1
	M	1522	1.6		TU	1451	1.3
		2137	5.1			2103	5.5
15		0352	1.3	30		0318	0.8
		1001	5.0			0938	5.4
	TU	1557	1.5		W	1537	0.9
		2210	5.3			2148	5.9
				31		0404	0.4
						1021	5.7
					TH	1620	0.6
						○ 2231	6.1

Chart Datum: 3·05 metres below Ordnance Datum (Newlyn)
HAT is 6·3m above Chart Datum

TIME ZONE (UT)
For Summer Time add ONE hour in **non-shaded areas**

WALES – HOLYHEAD

LAT 53°19′N LONG 4°37′W

TIMES AND HEIGHTS OF HIGH AND LOW WATERS

Dates in amber are **SPRINGS**
Dates in grey are **NEAPS**

2023

SEPTEMBER

Date	Time	m	Date	Time	m
1 F	0447	0.2	16 SA	0453	0.9
	1103	5.8		1100	5.4
	1702	0.5		1657	1.0
	2315	6.2		2310	5.6
2 SA	0530	0.1	17 SU	0521	0.9
	1145	5.8		1129	5.4
	1744	0.5		1726	1.0
	2358	6.2		2340	5.5
3 SU	0612	0.3	18 M	0550	1.0
	1226	5.6		1159	5.3
	1826	0.6		1757	1.1
4 M	0041	6.0	19 TU	0011	5.5
	0656	0.6		0620	1.1
	1308	5.4		1231	5.3
	1911	0.9		1831	1.3
5 TU	0126	5.6	20 W	0043	5.3
	0740	1.0		0653	1.3
	1352	5.1		1305	5.1
	1959	1.3		1908	1.5
6 W	0214	5.2	21 TH	0119	5.1
	0828	1.5		0732	1.6
	1441	4.8		1345	4.9
	◑ 2056	1.7		1953	1.7
7 TH	0310	4.8	22 F	0204	4.8
	0925	2.0		0821	1.9
	1543	4.5		1437	4.7
	2209	2.1		◐ 2053	2.0
8 F	0426	4.4	23 SA	0308	4.5
	1042	2.3		0931	2.2
	1710	4.3		1553	4.5
	2340	2.2		2220	2.2
9 SA	0607	4.2	24 SU	0449	4.3
	1212	2.4		1109	2.3
	1846	4.4		1734	4.5
				2358	2.0
10 SU	0106	2.1	25 M	0635	4.5
	0735	4.4		1238	2.1
	1330	2.3		1856	4.8
	1954	4.7			
11 M	0209	1.8	26 TU	0115	1.6
	0830	4.6		0746	4.9
	1424	2.0		1343	1.7
	2040	4.9		1956	5.3
12 TU	0254	1.5	27 W	0212	1.1
	0908	4.8		0837	5.3
	1502	1.7		1433	1.2
	2115	5.2		2044	5.7
13 W	0328	1.3	28 TH	0300	0.7
	0939	5.0		0920	5.6
	1534	1.5		1516	0.9
	2145	5.4		2127	6.0
14 TH	0358	1.1	29 F	0342	0.4
	1007	5.2		0959	5.8
	1601	1.3		1557	0.6
	2213	5.5		○ 2208	6.2
15 F	0426	1.0	30 SA	0423	0.2
	1033	5.3		1038	5.8
	1629	1.1		1637	0.4
	● 2241	5.6		2250	6.2

OCTOBER

Date	Time	m	Date	Time	m
1 SU	0503	0.3	16 M	0448	0.9
	1117	5.8		1058	5.5
	1718	0.5		1658	1.0
	2333	6.1		2311	5.6
2 M	0543	0.5	17 TU	0518	1.0
	1157	5.7		1130	5.5
	1800	0.7		1731	1.1
				2345	5.5
3 TU	0015	5.9	18 W	0551	1.1
	0624	0.8		1204	5.4
	1237	5.5		1807	1.2
	1844	1.0			
4 W	0058	5.5	19 TH	0020	5.3
	0706	1.3		0628	1.4
	1318	5.2		1242	5.3
	1931	1.4		1849	1.4
5 TH	0144	5.0	20 F	0102	5.1
	0751	1.7		0711	1.6
	1404	4.9		1326	5.1
	2026	1.8		1940	1.7
6 F	0239	4.6	21 SA	0154	4.8
	0845	2.2		0806	2.0
	1502	4.6		1424	4.8
	◑ 2138	2.2		2047	1.9
7 SA	0355	4.2	22 SU	0307	4.5
	1000	2.5		0922	2.3
	1627	4.4		1543	4.7
	2310	2.3		◐ 2215	2.0
8 SU	0541	4.1	23 M	0450	4.4
	1138	2.6		1057	2.3
	1807	4.4		1716	4.7
				2345	1.8
9 M	0035	2.2	24 TU	0622	4.7
	0707	4.3		1219	2.0
	1257	2.5		1833	5.0
	1918	4.6			
10 TU	0137	1.9	25 W	0055	1.4
	0800	4.6		0726	5.0
	1351	2.2		1320	1.7
	2005	4.9		1931	5.4
11 W	0220	1.6	26 TH	0150	1.0
	0837	4.9		0815	5.3
	1430	1.8		1410	1.3
	2041	5.1		2019	5.7
12 TH	0254	1.3	27 F	0236	0.7
	0907	5.1		0856	5.6
	1501	1.6		1453	0.9
	2112	5.3		2103	5.9
13 F	0324	1.1	28 SA	0318	0.5
	0934	5.2		0935	5.7
	1530	1.3		1534	0.7
	2141	5.5		○ 2145	6.1
14 SA	0352	1.0	29 SU	0358	0.5
	1001	5.4		1013	5.8
	1558	1.2		1615	0.6
	● 2209	5.6		2228	6.1
15 SU	0419	0.9	30 M	0437	0.6
	1029	5.5		1052	5.8
	1627	1.1		1656	0.7
	2240	5.6		2310	5.9
			31 TU	0517	0.8
				1132	5.7
				1739	0.9
				2353	5.6

NOVEMBER

Date	Time	m	Date	Time	m
1 W	0557	1.1	16 TH	0532	1.2
	1212	5.5		1147	5.6
	1823	1.2		1756	1.2
2 TH	0036	5.3	17 F	0010	5.3
	0638	1.5		0615	1.4
	1252	5.3		1230	5.4
	1910	1.5		1844	1.3
3 F	0121	4.9	18 SA	0059	5.1
	0721	1.9		0704	1.6
	1335	5.0		1320	5.3
	2002	1.8		1939	1.5
4 SA	0212	4.6	19 SU	0156	4.9
	0811	2.2		0802	1.9
	1427	4.7		1420	5.1
	2106	2.1		2046	1.7
5 SU	0319	4.3	20 M	0309	4.7
	0915	2.5		0914	2.1
	1538	4.5		1532	5.0
	◑ 2225	2.3		◐ 2203	1.7
6 M	0447	4.2	21 TU	0435	4.6
	1041	2.7		1034	2.1
	1703	4.5		1650	5.0
	2343	2.2		2320	1.6
7 TU	0611	4.3	22 W	0553	4.8
	1202	2.6		1148	2.0
	1818	4.6		1801	5.2
8 W	0045	2.0	23 TH	0026	1.4
	0711	4.5		0656	5.0
	1301	2.3		1250	1.7
	1914	4.8		1902	5.4
9 TH	0133	1.7	24 F	0122	1.2
	0753	4.8		0748	5.2
	1345	2.0		1343	1.4
	1957	5.0		1955	5.6
10 F	0212	1.5	25 SA	0211	1.0
	0828	5.0		0832	5.4
	1421	1.7		1431	1.2
	2033	5.2		2042	5.7
11 SA	0245	1.3	26 SU	0255	0.9
	0858	5.2		0913	5.5
	1454	1.5		1516	1.0
	2106	5.4		2127	5.7
12 SU	0316	1.2	27 M	0337	0.9
	0928	5.4		0953	5.6
	1526	1.3		1559	0.9
	2139	5.5		○ 2212	5.7
13 M	0347	1.1	28 TU	0418	1.0
	0959	5.5		1034	5.7
	1600	1.2		1643	1.0
	● 2213	5.5		2255	5.6
14 TU	0419	1.1	29 W	0458	1.1
	1032	5.6		1114	5.6
	1635	1.1		1726	1.1
	2249	5.5		2338	5.4
15 W	0454	1.1	30 TH	0537	1.3
	1108	5.6		1153	5.5
	1713	1.1		1809	1.3
	2327	5.5			

DECEMBER

Date	Time	m	Date	Time	m
1 F	0019	5.2	16 SA	0007	5.4
	0617	1.6		0610	1.2
	1232	5.3		1225	5.7
	1853	1.5		1842	1.0
2 SA	0101	4.9	17 SU	0057	5.3
	0657	1.8		0700	1.4
	1312	5.1		1315	5.6
	1939	1.7		1936	1.1
3 SU	0146	4.7	18 M	0152	5.1
	0741	2.1		0754	1.6
	1357	4.9		1410	5.4
	2029	1.9		2034	1.3
4 M	0238	4.5	19 TU	0254	4.9
	0832	2.3		0855	1.7
	1449	4.7		1510	5.3
	2128	2.1		◐ 2138	1.4
5 TU	0340	4.3	20 W	0402	4.8
	0933	2.5		1001	1.8
	1553	4.6		1616	5.2
	◑ 2233	2.1		2245	1.5
6 W	0451	4.3	21 TH	0512	4.7
	1043	2.5		1111	1.9
	1702	4.6		1725	5.2
	2337	2.1		2352	1.5
7 TH	0558	4.4	22 F	0619	4.8
	1151	2.4		1217	1.8
	1806	4.7		1831	5.2
8 F	0033	1.9	23 SA	0053	1.5
	0655	4.6		0720	4.9
	1248	2.2		1319	1.6
	1902	4.8		1933	5.2
9 SA	0121	1.8	24 SU	0149	1.4
	0741	4.8		0812	5.1
	1336	2.0		1415	1.5
	1950	5.0		2029	5.3
10 SU	0203	1.6	25 M	0240	1.4
	0821	5.0		0859	5.3
	1418	1.7		1506	1.3
	2032	5.1		2119	5.3
11 M	0242	1.4	26 TU	0325	1.3
	0858	5.2		0942	5.4
	1459	1.5		1553	1.2
	2113	5.3		2204	5.3
12 TU	0320	1.3	27 W	0407	1.3
	0935	5.4		1023	5.5
	1539	1.3		1637	1.2
	● 2153	5.4		○ 2247	5.3
13 W	0359	1.2	28 TH	0446	1.3
	1014	5.6		1102	5.5
	1621	1.1		1717	1.2
	2235	5.5		2327	5.2
14 TH	0439	1.1	29 F	0523	1.4
	1054	5.7		1139	5.5
	1704	1.0		1756	1.2
	2320	5.5			
15 F	0523	1.1	30 SA	0004	5.1
	1138	5.7		0559	1.5
	1751	1.0		1215	5.4
				1834	1.3
			31 SU	0040	5.0
				0636	1.6
				1250	5.3
				1912	1.4

Chart Datum: 3·05 metres below Ordnance Datum (Newlyn)
HAT is 6·3m above Chart Datum

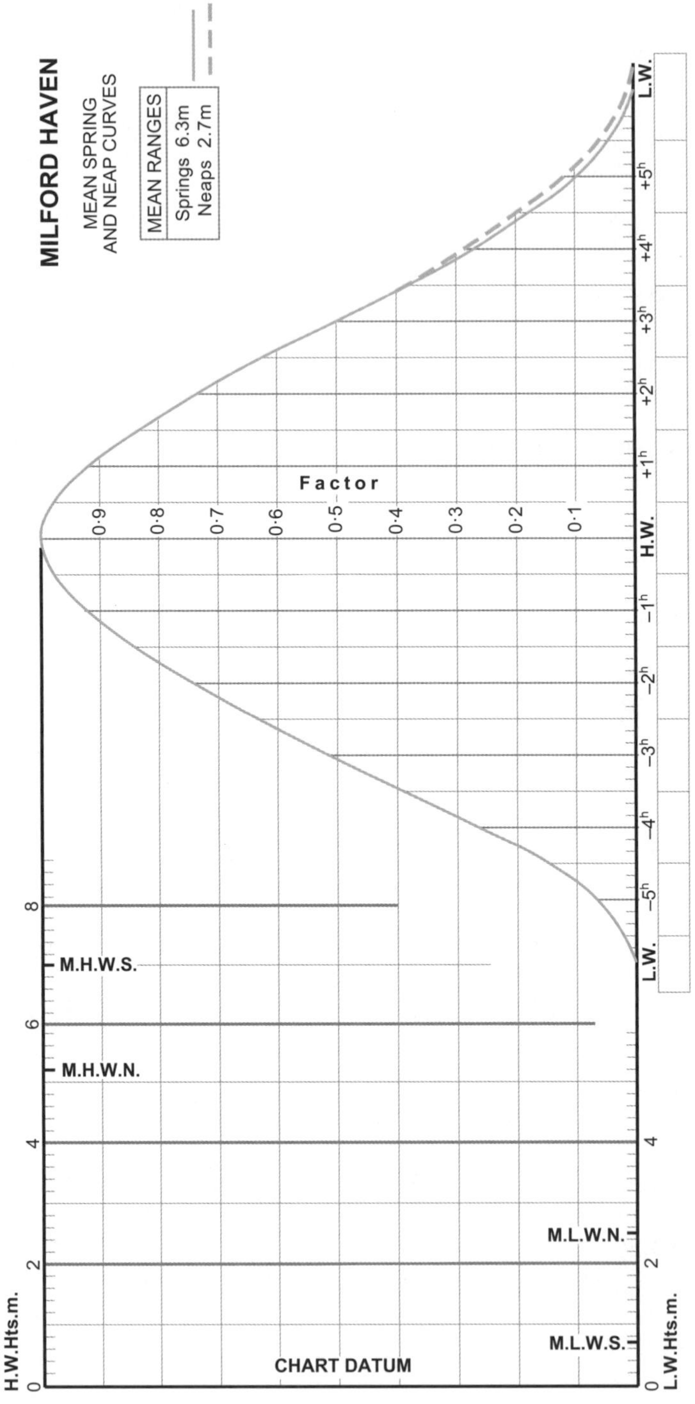
MILFORD HAVEN
MEAN SPRING AND NEAP CURVES
MEAN RANGES
Springs 6.3m
Neaps 2.7m
Factor
0·9 0·8 0·7 0·6 0·5 0·4 0·3 0·2 0·1
L.W. −5h −4h −3h −2h −1h H.W. +1h +2h +3h +4h +5h L.W.
H.W.Hts.m.
0 2 4 6 8
M.H.W.S.
M.H.W.N.
M.L.W.N.
M.L.W.S.
CHART DATUM
L.W.Hts.m.

TIME ZONE (UT)
For Summer Time add ONE hour in **non-shaded areas**

WALES – MILFORD HAVEN

LAT 51°42′N LONG 5°03′W

TIMES AND HEIGHTS OF HIGH AND LOW WATERS

Dates in amber are **SPRINGS**
Dates in grey are **NEAPS**

2023

JANUARY

Date	Day	Time	m	Time	m	Time	m	Time	m
1	SU	0117	5.5	0745	2.2	1349	5.8	2020	2.2
2	M	0225	5.6	0853	2.2	1454	5.8	2122	2.1
3	TU	0327	5.7	0953	2.1	1553	5.9	2216	2.0
4	W	0422	5.9	1045	1.9	1645	6.0	2302	1.8
5	TH	0509	6.2	1129	1.8	1730	6.2	2343	1.7
6	F	0550	6.3	1209	1.6	1810	6.3	○	
7	SA	0020	1.6	0627	6.5	1245	1.5	1847	6.3
8	SU	0055	1.5	0702	6.5	1320	1.5	1922	6.4
9	M	0129	1.5	0735	6.5	1353	1.5	1955	6.3
10	TU	0201	1.5	0808	6.5	1425	1.5	2027	6.2
11	W	0234	1.6	0841	6.4	1458	1.6	2101	6.1
12	TH	0307	1.7	0915	6.3	1533	1.8	2136	5.9
13	F	0344	1.9	0952	6.1	1610	1.9	2215	5.7
14	SA	0424	2.1	1034	5.9	1653	2.1	2301	5.5
15	SU	0511	2.3	1124	5.7	1745	2.3	◑ 2358	5.4
16	M	0611	2.4	1226	5.5	1854	2.4		
17	TU	0108	5.4	0729	2.4	1340	5.5	2014	2.3
18	W	0223	5.5	0849	2.2	1455	5.7	2128	2.0
19	TH	0333	5.9	0959	1.9	1603	6.1	2232	1.7
20	F	0434	6.4	1100	1.4	1704	6.5	2328	1.3
21	SA	0530	6.8	1156	1.0	1759	6.8	●	
22	SU	0019	0.9	0623	7.2	1247	0.6	1850	7.1
23	M	0108	0.7	0712	7.4	1337	0.4	1939	7.2
24	TU	0155	0.6	0800	7.5	1424	0.4	2024	7.1
25	W	0240	0.6	0845	7.4	1509	0.6	2108	6.9
26	TH	0324	0.8	0930	7.1	1552	0.9	2151	6.6
27	F	0407	1.2	1014	6.7	1634	1.3	2235	6.2
28	SA	0451	1.6	1100	6.3	1720	1.8	◐ 2323	5.7
29	SU	0540	2.0	1153	5.8	1812	2.2		
30	M	0020	5.4	0644	2.4	1256	5.4	1921	2.5
31	TU	0133	5.2	0807	2.6	1413	5.2	2043	2.6

FEBRUARY

Date	Day	Time	m	Time	m	Time	m	Time	m
1	W	0255	5.2	0928	2.5	1530	5.3	2153	2.4
2	TH	0405	5.5	1030	2.2	1632	5.6	2247	2.1
3	F	0457	5.9	1119	1.9	1719	5.9	2331	1.8
4	SA	0538	6.2	1159	1.6	1758	6.2		
5	SU	0008	1.5	0615	6.4	1234	1.4	○ 1834	6.3
6	M	0042	1.4	0648	6.6	1306	1.3	1906	6.5
7	TU	0113	1.2	0719	6.7	1336	1.2	1936	6.5
8	W	0144	1.2	0750	6.7	1406	1.1	2007	6.5
9	TH	0215	1.1	0820	6.7	1436	1.2	2037	6.4
10	F	0246	1.2	0850	6.6	1507	1.3	2108	6.3
11	SA	0317	1.4	0922	6.4	1538	1.5	2141	6.1
12	SU	0351	1.6	0958	6.2	1613	1.8	2219	5.8
13	M	0430	1.9	1040	5.9	1655	2.1	◑ 2308	5.5
14	TU	0521	2.2	1137	5.5	1755	2.4		
15	W	0016	5.3	0638	2.5	1257	5.3	1930	2.5
16	TH	0148	5.3	0822	2.4	1432	5.4	2109	2.3
17	F	0315	5.6	0947	2.0	1554	5.8	2221	1.8
18	SA	0425	6.2	1053	1.4	1658	6.3	2319	1.2
19	SU	0522	6.8	1148	0.8	1751	6.8		
20	M	0010	0.8	0613	7.3	1237	0.4	● 1839	7.2
21	TU	0056	0.4	0659	7.6	1322	0.2	1922	7.3
22	W	0139	0.3	0742	7.7	1404	0.1	2003	7.3
23	TH	0220	0.3	0823	7.5	1444	0.3	2042	7.1
24	F	0258	0.6	0902	7.2	1520	0.7	2119	6.7
25	SA	0334	1.0	0940	6.8	1555	1.2	2156	6.3
26	SU	0410	1.5	1019	6.2	1631	1.8	2235	5.8
27	M	0450	2.0	1102	5.6	1713	2.3	◐ 2322	5.3
28	TU	0542	2.5	1159	5.1	1815	2.7		

MARCH

Date	Day	Time	m	Time	m	Time	m	Time	m
1	W	0035	4.9	0713	2.9	1329	4.8	1959	2.9
2	TH	0221	4.9	0904	2.8	1510	4.9	2131	2.7
3	F	0346	5.3	1014	2.4	1616	5.3	2229	2.2
4	SA	0438	5.7	1101	1.9	1701	5.8	2312	1.8
5	SU	0518	6.1	1139	1.6	1737	6.1	2348	1.5
6	M	0552	6.4	1212	1.3	1810	6.4		
7	TU	0020	1.2	0624	6.6	1242	1.1	○ 1841	6.6
8	W	0051	1.0	0654	6.8	1312	0.9	1911	6.7
9	TH	0121	0.9	0724	6.9	1341	0.9	1940	6.8
10	F	0151	0.9	0753	6.9	1410	0.9	2009	6.7
11	SA	0221	0.9	0823	6.8	1439	1.0	2039	6.6
12	SU	0252	1.1	0854	6.6	1510	1.3	2112	6.4
13	M	0325	1.4	0929	6.3	1543	1.6	2149	6.0
14	TU	0403	1.8	1011	5.9	1624	2.0	2236	5.6
15	W	0454	2.2	1107	5.5	1724	2.4	◑ 2348	5.3
16	TH	0615	2.5	1236	5.1	1909	2.6		
17	F	0131	5.2	0813	2.4	1424	5.2	2059	2.3
18	SA	0306	5.6	0939	1.9	1548	5.7	2211	1.8
19	SU	0415	6.2	1042	1.2	1647	6.4	2306	1.1
20	M	0508	6.8	1133	0.7	1735	6.9	2354	0.7
21	TU	0554	7.3	1219	0.3	1818	7.2	●	
22	W	0036	0.3	0638	7.6	1259	0.1	1859	7.3
23	TH	0116	0.2	0718	7.6	1338	0.2	1936	7.3
24	F	0153	0.3	0756	7.4	1413	0.4	2012	7.1
25	SA	0229	0.6	0832	7.1	1447	0.8	2046	6.8
26	SU	0302	1.0	0907	6.6	1519	1.3	2120	6.3
27	M	0335	1.5	0942	6.1	1550	1.8	2155	5.8
28	TU	0410	2.0	1021	5.5	1626	2.3	2237	5.3
29	W	0457	2.5	1113	5.0	1720	2.8	◐ 2342	4.9
30	TH	0622	2.9	1242	4.6	1906	3.0		
31	F	0138	4.8	0827	2.9	1436	4.8	2055	2.8

APRIL

Date	Day	Time	m	Time	m	Time	m	Time	m
1	SA	0310	5.1	0941	2.4	1545	5.2	2156	2.4
2	SU	0404	5.6	1029	2.0	1629	5.7	2240	1.9
3	M	0444	6.0	1106	1.6	1705	6.1	2316	1.5
4	TU	0519	6.4	1140	1.2	1738	6.4	2349	1.2
5	W	0551	6.6	1211	1.0	1809	6.6		
6	TH	0021	1.0	0623	6.8	1241	0.9	○ 1840	6.8
7	F	0052	0.8	0654	6.9	1312	0.8	1911	6.9
8	SA	0125	0.8	0725	6.9	1343	0.8	1942	6.9
9	SU	0157	0.8	0758	6.9	1415	1.0	2015	6.7
10	M	0231	1.0	0833	6.6	1448	1.2	2051	6.5
11	TU	0308	1.3	0911	6.3	1525	1.6	2132	6.1
12	W	0352	1.7	0958	5.8	1612	2.0	2226	5.7
13	TH	0450	2.1	1102	5.4	1720	2.4	◑ 2344	5.4
14	F	0619	2.4	1235	5.1	1908	2.6		
15	SA	0124	5.4	0805	2.2	1416	5.3	2045	2.2
16	SU	0251	5.8	0923	1.7	1531	5.8	2152	1.6
17	M	0354	6.3	1021	1.2	1626	6.4	2244	1.1
18	TU	0445	6.8	1110	0.7	1711	6.8	2330	0.7
19	W	0530	7.1	1153	0.5	1753	7.0		
20	TH	0010	0.5	0612	7.3	1231	0.4	● 1831	7.2
21	F	0049	0.5	0650	7.3	1308	0.5	1908	7.1
22	SA	0126	0.6	0727	7.1	1343	0.7	1943	6.9
23	SU	0201	0.8	0803	6.8	1416	1.0	2016	6.7
24	M	0235	1.2	0837	6.4	1448	1.4	2050	6.3
25	TU	0308	1.6	0913	6.0	1520	1.9	2126	5.9
26	W	0344	2.1	0952	5.5	1556	2.3	2208	5.5
27	TH	0430	2.5	1041	5.0	1646	2.7	◐ 2307	5.1
28	F	0542	2.8	1156	4.7	1813	3.0		
29	SA	0038	4.9	0725	2.8	1339	4.7	1954	2.8
30	SU	0212	5.1	0845	2.5	1452	5.1	2103	2.5

Chart Datum: 3·71 metres below Ordnance Datum (Newlyn)
HAT is 7·9m above Chart Datum

TIME ZONE (UT)
For Summer Time add ONE hour in **non-shaded areas**

WALES – MILFORD HAVEN

LAT 51°42'N LONG 5°03'W

TIMES AND HEIGHTS OF HIGH AND LOW WATERS

Dates in amber are **SPRINGS**
Dates in grey are **NEAPS**

2023

MAY

Date	Day	Time	m	Time	m	Time	m	Time	m
1	M	0313	5.4	0939	2.1	1542	5.5	2153	2.0
2	TU	0358	5.8	1021	1.7	1622	5.9	2234	1.7
3	W	0436	6.2	1058	1.4	1658	6.3	2311	1.3
4	TH	0512	6.5	1133	1.1	1732	6.6	2347	1.1
5	F ○	0547	6.7	1208	1.0	1807	6.8		
6	SA	0023	0.9	0624	6.9	1243	0.9	1843	6.9
7	SU	0100	0.8	0700	6.9	1319	0.9	1920	6.9
8	M	0138	0.9	0739	6.8	1357	1.0	1959	6.8
9	TU	0219	1.0	0820	6.6	1437	1.3	2041	6.6
10	W	0303	1.3	0906	6.3	1521	1.6	2130	6.2
11	TH	0354	1.6	1000	5.9	1615	2.0	2231	5.9
12	F ◑	0458	1.9	1108	5.5	1727	2.2	2346	5.7
13	SA	0620	2.0	1230	5.4	1857	2.3		
14	SU	0108	5.7	0744	1.9	1352	5.5	2018	2.0
15	M	0222	6.0	0854	1.6	1500	5.9	2122	1.6
16	TU	0324	6.3	0951	1.3	1555	6.2	2215	1.3
17	W	0416	6.6	1040	1.1	1642	6.5	2302	1.1
18	TH	0502	6.8	1123	0.9	1725	6.7	2344	0.9
19	F ●	0545	6.8	1203	0.9	1804	6.8		
20	SA	0023	0.9	0625	6.8	1240	1.0	1842	6.8
21	SU	0101	1.0	0703	6.7	1316	1.1	1918	6.7
22	M	0138	1.2	0740	6.5	1351	1.3	1954	6.5
23	TU	0214	1.4	0816	6.2	1425	1.6	2029	6.2
24	W	0249	1.7	0853	5.9	1459	1.9	2107	6.0
25	TH	0327	2.0	0932	5.6	1536	2.2	2148	5.7
26	F	0410	2.3	1018	5.3	1623	2.5	2239	5.4
27	SA ◐	0506	2.5	1115	5.0	1725	2.7	2342	5.2
28	SU	0618	2.6	1226	4.9	1843	2.7		
29	M	0056	5.2	0731	2.5	1341	5.1	1954	2.5
30	TU	0205	5.4	0833	2.2	1441	5.4	2053	2.2
31	W	0300	5.7	0926	1.9	1530	5.7	2144	1.9

JUNE

Date	Day	Time	m	Time	m	Time	m	Time	m
1	TH	0347	6.0	1012	1.6	1613	6.1	2230	1.6
2	F	0431	6.3	1055	1.4	1655	6.4	2314	1.3
3	SA	0514	6.6	1137	1.2	1737	6.7	2358	1.1
4	SU ○	0558	6.7	1220	1.0	1820	6.9		
5	M	0041	0.9	0643	6.8	1302	1.0	1905	6.9
6	TU	0127	0.9	0729	6.8	1347	1.0	1951	6.9
7	W	0214	1.0	0817	6.6	1433	1.2	2040	6.7
8	TH	0303	1.1	0908	6.4	1522	1.4	2133	6.5
9	F	0357	1.3	1003	6.1	1617	1.7	2230	6.3
10	SA ◑	0457	1.5	1102	5.8	1720	1.9	2333	6.1
11	SU	0603	1.7	1208	5.7	1830	1.9		
12	M	0039	6.0	0711	1.7	1316	5.7	1941	1.9
13	TU	0146	6.0	0816	1.7	1421	5.8	2046	1.8
14	W	0248	6.1	0916	1.6	1520	5.9	2144	1.7
15	TH	0345	6.2	1009	1.5	1613	6.1	2235	1.5
16	F	0437	6.3	1056	1.4	1701	6.3	2322	1.4
17	SA	0523	6.3	1139	1.4	1744	6.4		
18	SU ●	0004	1.4	0607	6.4	1219	1.4	1825	6.5
19	M	0044	1.4	0646	6.3	1257	1.4	1903	6.5
20	TU	0122	1.4	0724	6.3	1333	1.5	1939	6.4
21	W	0159	1.5	0801	6.1	1408	1.6	2015	6.3
22	TH	0234	1.6	0837	6.0	1443	1.7	2051	6.1
23	F	0310	1.8	0913	5.8	1518	1.9	2129	6.0
24	SA	0348	1.9	0953	5.6	1558	2.1	2210	5.8
25	SU	0430	2.1	1036	5.4	1643	2.3	2256	5.6
26	M ◐	0520	2.3	1127	5.2	1738	2.4	2350	5.4
27	TU	0618	2.4	1226	5.2	1842	2.4		
28	W	0051	5.4	0723	2.3	1331	5.3	1950	2.4
29	TH	0157	5.5	0827	2.2	1434	5.5	2054	2.1
30	F	0258	5.7	0927	1.9	1532	5.9	2152	1.8

JULY

Date	Day	Time	m	Time	m	Time	m	Time	m
1	SA	0355	6.0	1022	1.6	1625	6.2	2247	1.5
2	SU	0449	6.3	1113	1.4	1716	6.6	2339	1.2
3	M ○	0541	6.6	1203	1.1	1806	6.8		
4	TU	0030	0.9	0633	6.8	1252	1.0	1856	7.0
5	W	0120	0.8	0723	6.8	1340	0.9	1946	7.1
6	TH	0210	0.7	0813	6.8	1428	0.9	2035	7.1
7	F	0259	0.7	0901	6.7	1517	1.0	2125	6.9
8	SA	0348	0.9	0950	6.5	1606	1.2	2215	6.7
9	SU	0439	1.2	1041	6.2	1657	1.5	2307	6.4
10	M ◑	0531	1.5	1134	5.9	1753	1.8		
11	TU	0003	6.1	0629	1.8	1234	5.7	1857	2.0
12	W	0105	5.8	0733	2.0	1339	5.5	2007	2.1
13	TH	0212	5.7	0840	2.1	1447	5.6	2116	2.1
14	F	0318	5.7	0943	2.0	1551	5.7	2217	2.0
15	SA	0419	5.8	1037	1.9	1646	6.0	2309	1.8
16	SU	0511	6.0	1124	1.7	1732	6.2	2354	1.6
17	M ●	0555	6.1	1205	1.6	1813	6.3		
18	TU	0033	1.5	0635	6.2	1243	1.5	1851	6.4
19	W	0109	1.4	0711	6.3	1318	1.4	1925	6.5
20	TH	0143	1.4	0745	6.3	1351	1.4	1958	6.5
21	F	0216	1.4	0817	6.2	1423	1.5	2030	6.4
22	SA	0247	1.5	0849	6.1	1455	1.6	2103	6.3
23	SU	0320	1.6	0922	6.0	1529	1.7	2137	6.1
24	M	0354	1.8	0957	5.8	1605	1.9	2214	5.9
25	TU ◐	0431	2.0	1037	5.6	1647	2.1	2257	5.7
26	W	0515	2.2	1126	5.4	1738	2.3	2351	5.5
27	TH	0613	2.4	1229	5.3	1847	2.5		
28	F	0059	5.4	0730	2.4	1344	5.3	2010	2.4
29	SA	0218	5.5	0851	2.3	1459	5.6	2126	2.1
30	SU	0331	5.7	1000	1.9	1605	6.0	2231	1.6
31	M	0435	6.2	1059	1.5	1703	6.5	2328	1.2

AUGUST

Date	Day	Time	m	Time	m	Time	m	Time	m
1	TU ○	0532	6.6	1152	1.1	1756	7.0		
2	W	0021	0.8	0625	6.9	1242	0.8	1846	7.3
3	TH	0111	0.5	0713	7.1	1329	0.6	1934	7.5
4	F	0158	0.3	0759	7.1	1415	0.5	2020	7.5
5	SA	0243	0.4	0843	7.0	1459	0.6	2105	7.3
6	SU	0327	0.6	0926	6.8	1542	0.9	2149	6.9
7	M	0409	1.0	1010	6.4	1625	1.3	2234	6.5
8	TU ◑	0452	1.5	1055	6.0	1712	1.8	2323	6.0
9	W	0541	2.0	1148	5.6	1809	2.2		
10	TH	0021	5.5	0644	2.4	1256	5.3	1928	2.5
11	F	0137	5.2	0806	2.6	1420	5.2	2058	2.5
12	SA	0300	5.2	0925	2.5	1539	5.4	2208	2.3
13	SU	0411	5.5	1026	2.2	1637	5.8	2301	2.0
14	M	0502	5.8	1113	1.9	1721	6.1	2343	1.7
15	TU	0543	6.1	1152	1.6	1759	6.4		
16	W ●	0019	1.4	0619	6.3	1226	1.4	1833	6.6
17	TH	0051	1.3	0651	6.4	1258	1.3	1904	6.7
18	F	0122	1.2	0722	6.5	1329	1.2	1934	6.7
19	SA	0151	1.2	0751	6.5	1358	1.2	2004	6.7
20	SU	0219	1.2	0820	6.4	1428	1.3	2033	6.6
21	M	0248	1.3	0849	6.3	1459	1.4	2103	6.4
22	TU	0318	1.5	0920	6.1	1530	1.7	2135	6.2
23	W	0350	1.8	0955	5.9	1606	2.0	2213	5.9
24	TH ◐	0428	2.1	1038	5.6	1652	2.3	2303	5.5
25	F	0520	2.4	1139	5.3	1759	2.6		
26	SA	0015	5.2	0644	2.7	1308	5.2	1943	2.6
27	SU	0153	5.2	0832	2.5	1442	5.5	2115	2.2
28	M	0321	5.6	0949	2.0	1555	6.0	2223	1.6
29	TU	0428	6.2	1049	1.5	1653	6.7	2319	1.0
30	W	0522	6.7	1141	1.0	1744	7.2		
31	TH ○	0008	0.5	0611	7.1	1227	0.6	1831	7.6

Chart Datum: 3·71 metres below Ordnance Datum (Newlyn)
HAT is 7·9m above Chart Datum

TIME ZONE (UT)
For Summer Time add ONE hour in **non-shaded areas**

WALES – MILFORD HAVEN

LAT 51°42′N LONG 5°03′W

TIMES AND HEIGHTS OF HIGH AND LOW WATERS

Dates in amber are **SPRINGS**
Dates in grey are **NEAPS**

2023

SEPTEMBER

Date	Day	Time	m	Time	m	Time	m	Time	m
1	F	0054	0.2	0655	7.4	1311	0.3	1915	7.7
2	SA	0137	0.1	0737	7.4	1353	0.3	1957	7.7
3	SU	0218	0.3	0817	7.3	1433	0.5	2038	7.4
4	M	0257	0.6	0856	6.9	1512	0.9	2117	7.0
5	TU	0334	1.1	0934	6.5	1550	1.4	2157	6.4
6	W	0411	1.7	1014	6.0	1631	2.0	◑ 2241	5.8
7	TH	0453	2.2	1102	5.5	1723	2.5	2337	5.2
8	F	0553	2.7	1212	5.1	1852	2.9		
9	SA	0104	4.9	0735	3.0	1358	5.0	2046	2.8
10	SU	0248	5.0	0912	2.7	1526	5.3	2158	2.4
11	M	0359	5.4	1011	2.3	1621	5.8	2245	2.0
12	TU	0444	5.8	1054	1.9	1701	6.2	2323	1.6
13	W	0521	6.2	1130	1.6	1735	6.5	2356	1.4
14	TH	0553	6.4	1203	1.3	1807	6.7		
15	F	0025	1.2	0624	6.6	1232	1.1	● 1837	6.8
16	SA	0054	1.1	0653	6.7	1301	1.1	1905	6.9
17	SU	0122	1.0	0721	6.8	1331	1.0	1934	6.9
18	M	0150	1.1	0749	6.7	1400	1.1	2002	6.8
19	TU	0218	1.2	0818	6.6	1430	1.3	2032	6.6
20	W	0247	1.5	0849	6.4	1501	1.6	2104	6.3
21	TH	0318	1.8	0923	6.1	1537	2.0	2142	5.9
22	F	0356	2.2	1006	5.7	1625	2.3	◐ 2234	5.5
23	SA	0450	2.6	1111	5.3	1738	2.7	2355	5.1
24	SU	0625	2.8	1252	5.2	1936	2.6		
25	M	0146	5.2	0824	2.6	1433	5.6	2108	2.1
26	TU	0316	5.7	0939	2.0	1544	6.2	2211	1.5
27	W	0417	6.3	1035	1.4	1638	6.8	2303	0.9
28	TH	0506	6.9	1123	0.9	1725	7.4	2349	0.5
29	F	0549	7.3	1207	0.5	1808	7.7	○	
30	SA	0031	0.2	0631	7.5	1248	0.3	1850	7.7

OCTOBER

Date	Day	Time	m	Time	m	Time	m	Time	m
1	SU	0111	0.2	0710	7.5	1328	0.4	1930	7.6
2	M	0149	0.4	0748	7.3	1405	0.6	2009	7.3
3	TU	0225	0.8	0825	7.0	1442	1.0	2046	6.8
4	W	0300	1.3	0901	6.5	1518	1.6	2124	6.2
5	TH	0335	1.9	0939	6.0	1557	2.1	2205	5.6
6	F	0413	2.4	1024	5.5	1647	2.7	◑ 2259	5.1
7	SA	0509	2.9	1131	5.0	1818	3.1		
8	SU	0029	4.7	0657	3.2	1325	4.9	2019	2.9
9	M	0221	4.9	0842	2.9	1455	5.3	2129	2.5
10	TU	0329	5.3	0941	2.5	1549	5.7	2214	2.1
11	W	0413	5.8	1024	2.0	1628	6.2	2251	1.7
12	TH	0449	6.2	1059	1.6	1703	6.5	2323	1.4
13	F	0521	6.5	1132	1.4	1734	6.7	2353	1.2
14	SA	0551	6.7	1203	1.2	1804	6.9	●	
15	SU	0022	1.1	0621	6.8	1233	1.1	1834	7.0
16	M	0052	1.0	0651	6.9	1303	1.1	1905	7.0
17	TU	0121	1.1	0721	6.9	1335	1.1	1936	6.9
18	W	0152	1.2	0753	6.8	1408	1.3	2009	6.6
19	TH	0224	1.5	0827	6.5	1443	1.6	2045	6.3
20	F	0259	1.8	0906	6.2	1525	2.0	2128	5.9
21	SA	0343	2.2	0955	5.8	1620	2.3	2227	5.5
22	SU	0445	2.6	1108	5.5	1741	2.6	◐ 2355	5.2
23	M	0626	2.8	1246	5.4	1930	2.4		
24	TU	0138	5.3	0810	2.5	1416	5.8	2050	2.0
25	W	0257	5.8	0919	1.9	1522	6.4	2150	1.4
26	TH	0354	6.4	1013	1.4	1615	6.9	2240	1.0
27	F	0442	6.8	1100	1.0	1701	7.3	2324	0.7
28	SA	0525	7.2	1143	0.7	1744	7.5	○	
29	SU	0005	0.5	0605	7.3	1223	0.6	1825	7.5
30	M	0044	0.6	0644	7.3	1303	0.7	1905	7.3
31	TU	0121	0.8	0722	7.1	1341	0.9	1943	7.0

NOVEMBER

Date	Day	Time	m	Time	m	Time	m	Time	m
1	W	0157	1.1	0758	6.9	1418	1.3	2020	6.6
2	TH	0232	1.6	0835	6.5	1455	1.8	2059	6.1
3	F	0307	2.0	0914	6.1	1534	2.2	2140	5.6
4	SA	0346	2.5	0958	5.6	1623	2.7	2231	5.2
5	SU	0437	2.9	1058	5.2	1737	2.9	◑ 2345	4.9
6	M	0603	3.1	1227	5.1	1917	2.9		
7	TU	0123	4.9	0741	3.0	1357	5.2	2034	2.7
8	W	0237	5.2	0850	2.7	1458	5.6	2127	2.3
9	TH	0328	5.6	0939	2.3	1544	5.9	2208	1.9
10	F	0408	6.0	1019	1.9	1622	6.3	2244	1.6
11	SA	0443	6.3	1056	1.6	1657	6.5	2318	1.4
12	SU	0516	6.6	1131	1.4	1731	6.7	2351	1.2
13	M	0550	6.8	1205	1.2	1805	6.9	●	
14	TU	0024	1.2	0624	6.9	1240	1.2	1841	6.9
15	W	0059	1.2	0659	6.9	1317	1.2	1917	6.8
16	TH	0135	1.3	0737	6.8	1356	1.3	1957	6.6
17	F	0213	1.5	0817	6.7	1438	1.5	2040	6.4
18	SA	0256	1.8	0904	6.4	1527	1.8	2131	6.0
19	SU	0346	2.1	1000	6.1	1626	2.1	2234	5.7
20	M	0450	2.4	1110	5.8	1742	2.2	◐ 2350	5.5
21	TU	0615	2.5	1229	5.8	1906	2.1		
22	W	0112	5.6	0740	2.3	1345	6.0	2019	1.9
23	TH	0224	5.9	0848	1.9	1450	6.3	2120	1.5
24	F	0323	6.2	0945	1.6	1546	6.6	2212	1.3
25	SA	0414	6.6	1035	1.3	1636	6.9	2259	1.1
26	SU	0500	6.8	1120	1.1	1721	7.0	2341	1.0
27	M	0543	6.9	1203	1.1	1804	7.0	○	
28	TU	0021	1.1	0624	7.0	1244	1.1	1846	6.9
29	W	0100	1.2	0703	6.9	1323	1.3	1925	6.7
30	TH	0137	1.4	0741	6.7	1402	1.5	2004	6.4

DECEMBER

Date	Day	Time	m	Time	m	Time	m	Time	m
1	F	0214	1.7	0819	6.5	1440	1.8	2042	6.1
2	SA	0250	2.0	0858	6.2	1519	2.1	2122	5.8
3	SU	0327	2.3	0939	5.9	1601	2.4	2207	5.4
4	M	0411	2.5	1027	5.6	1654	2.6	2300	5.2
5	TU	0508	2.8	1126	5.4	1800	2.7	◑	
6	W	0005	5.0	0621	2.8	1236	5.3	1913	2.7
7	TH	0120	5.1	0735	2.8	1347	5.4	2018	2.5
8	F	0225	5.3	0838	2.5	1445	5.6	2113	2.3
9	SA	0316	5.6	0930	2.2	1534	5.9	2159	2.0
10	SU	0401	6.0	1017	1.9	1618	6.2	2242	1.7
11	M	0442	6.3	1100	1.6	1700	6.4	2323	1.5
12	TU	0522	6.6	1142	1.4	1742	6.6	●	
13	W	0003	1.3	0604	6.8	1224	1.2	1825	6.8
14	TH	0044	1.2	0646	6.9	1307	1.1	1909	6.8
15	F	0126	1.2	0730	7.0	1352	1.1	1954	6.7
16	SA	0210	1.3	0817	6.9	1439	1.2	2042	6.6
17	SU	0257	1.4	0906	6.7	1529	1.4	2133	6.3
18	M	0347	1.6	0959	6.5	1623	1.5	2228	6.1
19	TU	0443	1.8	1057	6.3	1724	1.7	◐ 2328	5.9
20	W	0548	2.0	1200	6.1	1830	1.9		
21	TH	0034	5.7	0658	2.1	1307	6.1	1938	1.9
22	F	0143	5.7	0809	2.0	1413	6.1	2044	1.9
23	SA	0248	5.9	0914	1.9	1516	6.2	2144	1.8
24	SU	0348	6.1	1013	1.7	1614	6.3	2237	1.6
25	M	0441	6.3	1105	1.6	1706	6.4	2324	1.5
26	TU	0529	6.5	1151	1.5	1753	6.5		
27	W	0006	1.4	0613	6.6	1234	1.4	○ 1836	6.5
28	TH	0047	1.4	0653	6.7	1314	1.4	1915	6.5
29	F	0124	1.4	0731	6.6	1351	1.5	1952	6.4
30	SA	0200	1.5	0807	6.5	1427	1.6	2028	6.2
31	SU	0234	1.7	0842	6.4	1501	1.7	2103	6.0

Chart Datum: 3·71 metres below Ordnance Datum (Newlyn)
HAT is 7·9m above Chart Datum

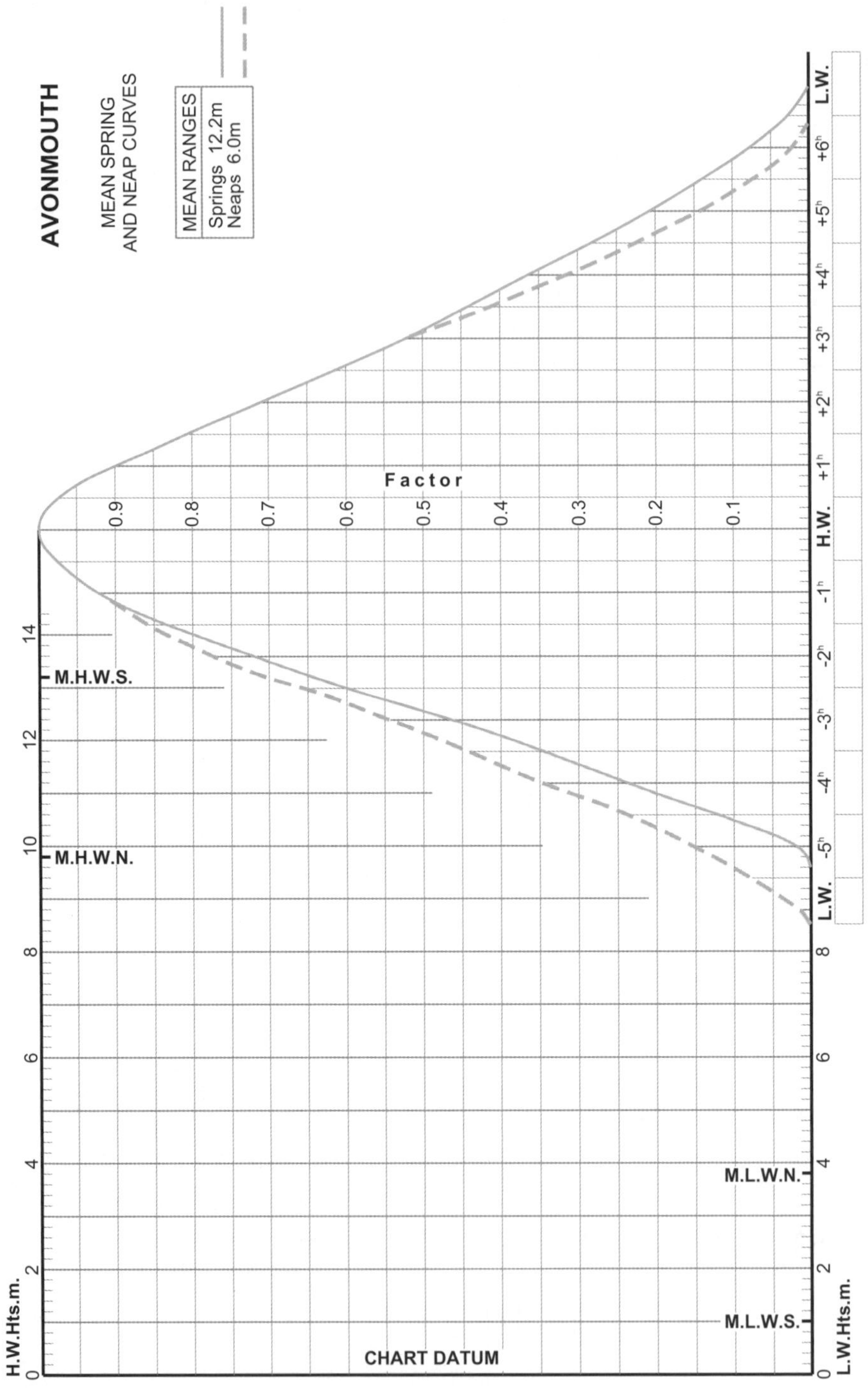
AVONMOUTH
MEAN SPRING
AND NEAP CURVES
MEAN RANGES
Springs 12.2m
Neaps 6.0m
Factor
H.W.Hts.m.
L.W.Hts.m.
M.H.W.S.
M.H.W.N.
M.L.W.N.
M.L.W.S.
CHART DATUM
L.W.
H.W.

TIME ZONE (UT)
For Summer Time add ONE hour in **non-shaded areas**

AVONMOUTH

LAT 51°30′N LONG 2°44′W

TIMES AND HEIGHTS OF HIGH AND LOW WATERS

Dates in amber are **SPRINGS**
Dates in grey are **NEAPS**

2023

JANUARY

Date	Day	Time	m	Time	m	Time	m	Time	m	Moon
1	SU	0205	10.6	0817	3.5	1441	10.8	2053	3.3	
2	M	0310	10.5	0932	3.6	1543	10.9	2205	3.3	
3	TU	0410	10.8	1042	3.3	1640	11.1	2308	2.9	
4	W	0504	11.2	1139	2.8	1732	11.4			
5	TH	0001	2.5	0553	11.7	1229	2.4	1820	11.8	
6	F	0050	2.1	0637	12.0	1316	2.2	1903	12.0	○
7	SA	0135	2.0	0718	12.3	1400	2.1	1943	12.0	
8	SU	0217	1.9	0757	12.3	1441	2.2	2021	12.0	
9	M	0254	2.1	0833	12.2	1516	2.4	2056	11.8	
10	TU	0325	2.3	0907	12.0	1544	2.6	2128	11.7	
11	W	0350	2.4	0938	11.8	1608	2.6	2159	11.5	
12	TH	0416	2.5	1009	11.6	1635	2.6	2230	11.3	
13	F	0448	2.6	1042	11.4	1709	2.7	2305	11.1	
14	SA	0525	2.7	1122	11.2	1748	2.8	2348	10.8	
15	SU	0609	3.0	1211	10.9	1835	3.2			◑
16	M	0041	10.4	0703	3.4	1311	10.6	1933	3.5	
17	TU	0148	10.2	0813	3.7	1424	10.4	2054	3.7	
18	W	0309	10.3	0949	3.6	1547	10.7	2234	3.4	
19	TH	0430	11.0	1111	3.0	1702	11.4	2347	2.7	
20	F	0535	11.9	1217	2.2	1804	12.2			
21	SA	0048	2.1	0631	12.7	1317	1.6	1900	12.9	●
22	SU	0146	1.5	0723	13.4	1414	1.1	1952	13.4	
23	M	0240	1.1	0813	13.8	1507	0.8	2041	13.6	
24	TU	0329	0.9	0900	14.0	1554	0.6	2127	13.6	
25	W	0412	0.9	0945	13.9	1635	0.7	2209	13.4	
26	TH	0449	1.1	1028	13.5	1710	1.1	2249	12.9	
27	F	0520	1.6	1108	12.8	1741	1.7	2328	12.1	
28	SA	0549	2.2	1150	11.9	1812	2.3			◐
29	SU	0007	11.3	0623	2.8	1236	11.0	1850	3.0	
30	M	0055	10.4	0706	3.5	1338	10.2	1940	3.6	
31	TU	0206	9.8	0808	4.0	1457	9.8	2050	4.0	

FEBRUARY

Date	Day	Time	m	Time	m	Time	m	Time	m	Moon
1	W	0327	9.8	0938	4.1	1608	10.0	2220	3.8	
2	TH	0435	10.2	1107	3.6	1709	10.5	2331	3.2	
3	F	0531	10.9	1205	2.9	1801	11.2			
4	SA	0026	2.5	0620	11.6	1256	2.3	1847	11.7	
5	SU	0115	2.0	0703	12.1	1344	2.0	1928	12.0	○
6	M	0202	1.8	0742	12.4	1429	1.9	2006	12.2	
7	TU	0245	1.8	0819	12.4	1509	2.0	2041	12.2	
8	W	0321	1.9	0852	12.4	1542	2.1	2112	12.1	
9	TH	0348	2.1	0922	12.3	1603	2.3	2140	12.0	
10	F	0407	2.1	0950	12.2	1620	2.2	2208	11.9	
11	SA	0430	2.1	1019	12.0	1645	2.2	2239	11.7	
12	SU	0500	2.2	1055	11.8	1717	2.3	2316	11.4	
13	M	0536	2.5	1137	11.3	1756	2.7			◑
14	TU	0001	10.8	0621	3.0	1230	10.6	1845	3.4	
15	W	0102	10.2	0721	3.7	1342	10.1	1955	4.0	
16	TH	0228	9.9	0904	4.0	1520	10.1	2209	3.9	
17	F	0410	10.4	1057	3.3	1651	10.8	2336	3.0	
18	SA	0524	11.5	1209	2.3	1757	11.9			
19	SU	0041	2.0	0623	12.6	1310	1.4	1852	12.9	
20	M	0138	1.2	0713	13.6	1406	0.7	1941	13.7	●
21	TU	0231	0.6	0801	14.2	1457	0.2	2026	14.0	
22	W	0318	0.3	0845	14.4	1540	0.1	2108	14.1	
23	TH	0357	0.3	0926	14.3	1617	0.3	2146	13.8	
24	F	0430	0.7	1003	13.8	1645	0.9	2220	13.2	
25	SA	0453	1.3	1037	13.0	1707	1.5	2250	12.4	
26	SU	0512	1.9	1108	12.0	1729	2.2	2320	11.4	
27	M	0537	2.6	1142	10.9	1759	2.9	2356	10.4	◐
28	TU	0612	3.4	1228	9.8	1842	3.8			

MARCH

Date	Day	Time	m	Time	m	Time	m	Time	m	Moon
1	W	0049	9.5	0708	4.2	1355	9.0	1953	4.4	
2	TH	0240	9.0	0839	4.6	1539	9.1	2132	4.4	
3	F	0408	9.6	1040	4.1	1647	9.9	2306	3.5	
4	SA	0509	10.5	1145	3.1	1741	10.9			
5	SU	0004	2.6	0559	11.4	1236	2.3	1826	11.7	
6	M	0055	1.9	0641	12.1	1324	1.8	1906	12.2	
7	TU	0143	1.6	0720	12.5	1410	1.6	1942	12.4	○
8	W	0227	1.5	0756	12.6	1451	1.6	2017	12.5	
9	TH	0305	1.6	0829	12.6	1525	1.8	2047	12.5	
10	F	0334	1.7	0858	12.6	1547	2.0	2115	12.4	
11	SA	0351	1.9	0926	12.5	1600	2.0	2142	12.3	
12	SU	0410	1.8	0956	12.4	1620	2.0	2213	12.1	
13	M	0436	1.9	1031	12.0	1649	2.1	2249	11.6	
14	TU	0509	2.2	1111	11.4	1725	2.6	2333	10.9	
15	W	0550	2.9	1203	10.5	1811	3.4			◑
16	TH	0033	10.0	0650	3.7	1318	9.7	1922	4.2	
17	F	0208	9.5	0850	4.2	1515	9.7	2208	4.1	
18	SA	0402	10.2	1052	3.2	1645	10.8	2328	2.9	
19	SU	0514	11.5	1158	2.0	1746	12.0			
20	M	0027	1.7	0609	12.8	1255	1.0	1837	13.1	
21	TU	0121	0.9	0657	13.8	1347	0.3	1922	13.9	●
22	W	0211	0.3	0741	14.3	1435	0.0	2004	14.2	
23	TH	0255	0.1	0822	14.4	1516	0.0	2043	14.1	
24	F	0333	0.2	0900	14.2	1550	0.4	2118	13.7	
25	SA	0403	0.8	0934	13.6	1615	1.0	2148	13.1	
26	SU	0422	1.4	1004	12.7	1631	1.7	2214	12.3	
27	M	0437	2.0	1032	11.8	1649	2.2	2240	11.4	
28	TU	0459	2.5	1101	10.7	1715	2.9	2311	10.4	
29	W	0530	3.3	1138	9.6	1752	3.8	2354	9.4	◐
30	TH	0619	4.2	1248	8.7	1901	4.6			
31	F	0147	8.7	0758	4.8	1505	8.7	2052	4.7	

APRIL

Date	Day	Time	m	Time	m	Time	m	Time	m	Moon
1	SA	0335	9.3	0957	4.2	1616	9.6	2235	3.8	
2	SU	0438	10.2	1116	3.2	1709	10.6	2336	2.8	
3	M	0527	11.2	1207	2.3	1754	11.6			
4	TU	0026	2.0	0610	12.0	1254	1.8	1834	12.2	
5	W	0113	1.6	0649	12.5	1340	1.6	1911	12.5	
6	TH	0157	1.5	0725	12.7	1421	1.5	1946	12.7	○
7	F	0236	1.5	0759	12.8	1456	1.6	2018	12.7	
8	SA	0308	1.6	0831	12.8	1522	1.8	2049	12.7	
9	SU	0331	1.6	0903	12.7	1539	1.8	2120	12.5	
10	M	0352	1.7	0937	12.5	1601	1.9	2153	12.2	
11	TU	0419	1.8	1014	12.0	1630	2.1	2232	11.7	
12	W	0453	2.2	1057	11.2	1707	2.7	2319	10.8	
13	TH	0537	2.9	1152	10.3	1756	3.5			◑
14	F	0024	10.0	0643	3.8	1315	9.6	1918	4.3	
15	SA	0212	9.7	0903	3.8	1510	9.9	2157	3.7	
16	SU	0348	10.6	1032	2.8	1626	11.0	2306	2.6	
17	M	0453	11.7	1134	1.8	1724	12.2			
18	TU	0001	1.5	0546	12.8	1228	1.0	1813	13.1	
19	W	0053	0.8	0633	13.6	1318	0.4	1856	13.7	
20	TH	0141	0.4	0715	13.9	1404	0.3	1936	13.9	●
21	F	0225	0.4	0756	13.9	1445	0.4	2014	13.7	
22	SA	0304	0.7	0833	13.6	1519	0.8	2047	13.3	
23	SU	0334	1.2	0906	13.0	1543	1.4	2117	12.7	
24	M	0353	1.7	0936	12.2	1600	1.9	2144	12.0	
25	TU	0409	2.2	1003	11.4	1619	2.4	2210	11.3	
26	W	0432	2.6	1032	10.6	1645	2.9	2241	10.4	
27	TH	0503	3.2	1108	9.7	1721	3.6	2323	9.6	◐
28	F	0549	4.0	1208	9.0	1821	4.4			
29	SA	0047	9.0	0718	4.5	1407	8.8	2006	4.6	
30	SU	0247	9.2	0854	4.2	1528	9.5	2137	4.0	

Chart Datum: 6·50 metres below Ordnance Datum (Newlyn)
HAT is 14·7m above Chart Datum

TIME ZONE (UT)
For Summer Time add ONE hour in **non-shaded areas**

AVONMOUTH

LAT 51°30′N LONG 2°44′W

TIMES AND HEIGHTS OF HIGH AND LOW WATERS

Dates in amber are **SPRINGS**
Dates in grey are **NEAPS**

2023

MAY

Day	Time	m	Day	Time	m
1 M	0352 1018 1625 2248	10.0 3.4 10.4 3.1	16 TU	0421 1058 1652 2327	11.8 1.9 11.9 1.8
2 TU	0444 1121 1713 2344	10.9 2.7 11.3 2.4	17 W	0515 1153 1741	12.5 1.4 12.6
3 W	0529 1213 1755	11.7 2.1 12.0	18 TH	0019 0603 1243 1826	1.3 12.9 1.1 13.0
4 TH	0033 0612 1300 1835	1.9 12.2 1.8 12.4	19 F	0108 0647 1330 ● 1907	1.1 13.1 1.0 13.1
5 F	0119 0651 1343 ○ 1913	1.6 12.6 1.6 12.7	20 SA	0152 0728 1412 1945	1.1 13.1 1.1 13.0
6 SA	0201 0729 1422 1949	1.5 12.8 1.6 12.9	21 SU	0233 0807 1448 2021	1.3 12.8 1.4 12.7
7 SU	0238 0807 1455 2026	1.4 12.8 1.6 12.9	22 M	0307 0843 1517 2053	1.7 12.3 1.8 12.3
8 M	0311 0845 1524 2103	1.4 12.8 1.7 12.7	23 TU	0331 0915 1538 2124	2.1 11.8 2.2 11.7
9 TU	0342 0925 1553 2143	1.6 12.5 1.9 12.3	24 W	0352 0946 1601 2154	2.5 11.2 2.5 11.2
10 W	0416 1008 1626 2227	1.8 12.0 2.2 11.7	25 TH	0417 1018 1630 2227	2.8 10.6 2.9 10.6
11 TH	0455 1056 1708 2320	2.3 11.3 2.8 11.0	26 F	0451 1055 1707 2308	3.1 10.1 3.3 10.1
12 F ◑	0546 1156 1804	2.9 10.5 3.4	27 SA ◐	0536 1145 1758	3.5 9.6 3.8
13 SA	0029 0701 1317 1941	10.4 3.3 10.1 3.8	28 SU	0008 0639 1254 1913	9.7 3.8 9.4 4.1
14 SU	0203 0840 1446 2123	10.4 3.2 10.4 3.3	29 M	0130 0755 1415 2032	9.6 3.8 9.6 3.9
15 M	0320 0956 1554 2230	11.0 2.6 11.1 2.5	30 TU	0246 0908 1524 2144	10.0 3.5 10.1 3.4
			31 W	0347 1017 1621 2250	10.6 3.1 10.8 2.8

JUNE

Day	Time	m	Day	Time	m
1 TH	0441 1121 1712 2347	11.3 2.6 11.6 2.3	16 F	0532 1208 1755	12.0 2.0 12.1
2 F	0531 1216 1758	11.9 2.2 12.2	17 SA	0035 0620 1257 1840	1.9 12.1 1.8 12.3
3 SA	0038 0618 1305 1843	1.9 12.3 1.8 12.6	18 SU	0123 0705 1342 ● 1921	1.8 12.2 1.8 12.3
4 SU	0127 0703 1351 ○ 1926	1.6 12.7 1.6 12.9	19 M	0207 0746 1424 2000	1.9 12.1 1.9 12.2
5 M	0213 0748 1435 2010	1.4 12.8 1.5 13.0	20 TU	0247 0826 1459 2037	2.1 11.8 2.1 12.0
6 TU	0257 0834 1516 2054	1.3 12.8 1.6 12.9	21 W	0320 0902 1528 2112	2.4 11.6 2.3 11.7
7 W	0340 0921 1555 2141	1.4 12.6 1.7 12.6	22 TH	0347 0936 1554 2145	2.6 11.3 2.5 11.4
8 TH	0423 1009 1636 2229	1.6 12.3 2.0 12.2	23 F	0412 1008 1622 2218	2.7 11.0 2.7 11.1
9 F	0508 1059 1722 2322	1.9 11.8 2.4 11.7	24 SA	0443 1042 1656 2253	2.8 10.7 2.9 10.8
10 SA ◑	0558 1154 1816	2.2 11.3 2.8	25 SU	0520 1120 1736 2336	2.9 10.5 3.1 10.5
11 SU	0024 0657 1258 1922	11.3 2.5 10.9 3.0	26 M ◐	0605 1207 1826	3.1 10.2 3.4
12 M	0135 0802 1408 2036	11.1 2.6 10.9 3.0	27 TU	0029 0659 1304 1929	10.3 3.3 10.1 3.6
13 TU	0243 0909 1514 2146	11.2 2.6 11.0 2.8	28 W	0133 0802 1411 2041	10.2 3.4 10.1 3.6
14 W	0344 1015 1613 2249	11.4 2.4 11.3 2.5	29 TH	0242 0915 1523 2158	10.4 3.4 10.5 3.3
15 TH	0440 1114 1707 2345	11.7 2.2 11.7 2.1	30 F	0351 1032 1629 2307	10.8 3.1 11.1 2.7

JULY

Day	Time	m	Day	Time	m
1 SA	0454 1138 1727	11.4 2.6 11.8	16 SU	0008 0559 1230 1820	2.7 11.3 2.4 11.7
2 SU	0006 0551 1236 1820	2.2 12.0 2.1 12.4	17 M	0059 0647 1319 ● 1904	2.3 11.6 2.1 12.0
3 M	0102 0644 1330 ○ 1910	1.7 12.5 1.8 12.9	18 TU	0148 0731 1406 1946	2.2 11.8 2.0 12.1
4 TU	0157 0736 1423 1959	1.4 12.8 1.5 13.2	19 W	0233 0812 1448 2024	2.1 11.8 2.1 12.1
5 W	0250 0827 1513 2048	1.2 13.0 1.4 13.3	20 TH	0313 0849 1524 2059	2.2 11.8 2.2 12.0
6 TH	0340 0917 1559 2136	1.1 13.0 1.3 13.3	21 F	0346 0922 1552 2131	2.4 11.6 2.4 11.8
7 F	0426 1004 1642 2223	1.1 12.9 1.4 13.0	22 SA	0410 0952 1614 2201	2.5 11.5 2.5 11.6
8 SA	0509 1050 1722 2311	1.2 12.6 1.7 12.6	23 SU	0431 1021 1639 2230	2.6 11.3 2.5 11.4
9 SU	0550 1136 1803	1.5 12.1 2.1	24 M	0458 1052 1711 2304	2.6 11.1 2.6 11.2
10 M	0000 0632 1226 ◑ 1847	12.1 1.9 11.5 2.5	25 TU	0531 1128 1749 ◐ 2346	2.6 10.9 2.9 10.9
11 TU	0057 0718 1323 1939	11.5 2.4 11.0 3.0	26 W	0612 1214 1835	2.9 10.5 3.3
12 W	0200 0812 1428 2046	11.0 2.9 10.6 3.4	27 TH	0039 0703 1313 1938	10.5 3.3 10.2 3.7
13 TH	0305 0920 1534 2206	10.7 3.2 10.5 3.4	28 F	0147 0812 1429 2108	10.2 3.7 10.1 3.8
14 F	0408 1034 1635 2313	10.7 3.2 10.8 3.1	29 SA	0308 0949 1554 2237	10.3 3.6 10.5 3.2
15 SA	0506 1136 1730	11.0 2.8 11.2	30 SU	0428 1112 1706 2348	10.9 3.1 11.3 2.5
			31 M	0535 1219 1805	11.6 2.4 12.3

AUGUST

Day	Time	m	Day	Time	m
1 TU	0050 0634 1320 ○ 1859	1.8 12.4 1.8 13.0	16 W	0131 0714 1349 ● 1929	2.0 11.9 1.8 12.4
2 W	0150 0727 1417 1949	1.3 13.0 1.3 13.6	17 TH	0218 0753 1434 2006	1.8 12.1 1.8 12.5
3 TH	0245 0818 1509 2038	0.8 13.4 0.9 13.9	18 F	0300 0828 1513 2040	1.9 12.1 1.9 12.4
4 F	0335 0905 1554 2123	0.5 13.6 0.7 14.0	19 SA	0335 0900 1543 2110	2.1 12.0 2.1 12.2
5 SA	0418 0949 1633 2206	0.5 13.6 0.8 13.7	20 SU	0400 0928 1601 2136	2.3 11.9 2.3 12.0
6 SU	0455 1029 1707 2247	0.7 13.2 1.2 13.2	21 M	0413 0953 1617 2202	2.4 11.7 2.3 11.9
7 M	0527 1108 1736 2328	1.2 12.5 1.8 12.3	22 TU	0430 1020 1642 2232	2.4 11.6 2.4 11.6
8 TU ◑	0556 1147 1805	1.9 11.7 2.5	23 W	0457 1053 1714 2310	2.5 11.3 2.6 11.2
9 W	0011 0630 1231 1844	11.4 2.6 10.8 3.3	24 TH	0531 1135 1753 ◐ 2359	2.8 10.7 3.1 10.5
10 TH	0108 0714 1334 1939	10.4 3.4 10.0 4.0	25 F	0615 1230 1847	3.4 10.1 3.8
11 F	0226 0817 1457 2111	9.8 4.0 9.7 4.3	26 SA	0106 0718 1349 2020	9.9 4.0 9.7 4.3
12 SA	0342 0953 1610 2251	9.8 4.0 10.0 3.8	27 SU	0240 0918 1535 2225	9.8 4.2 10.1 3.7
13 SU	0447 1113 1712 2351	10.2 3.4 10.7 3.1	28 M	0418 1104 1655 2341	10.5 3.4 11.2 2.6
14 M	0543 1210 1804	10.9 2.7 11.5	29 TU	0528 1212 1755	11.6 2.4 12.4
15 TU	0042 0632 1301 1849	2.4 11.5 2.2 12.1	30 W	0043 0624 1311 1847	1.6 12.6 1.5 13.4
			31 TH	0140 0714 1406 ○ 1935	0.9 13.5 0.9 14.1

Chart Datum: 6·50 metres below Ordnance Datum (Newlyn)
HAT is 14·7m above Chart Datum

TIME ZONE (UT)
For Summer Time add ONE hour in **non-shaded areas**

AVONMOUTH

LAT 51°30'N LONG 2°44'W

TIMES AND HEIGHTS OF HIGH AND LOW WATERS

Dates in amber are **SPRINGS**
Dates in grey are **NEAPS**

2023

SEPTEMBER

Day	Time	m	Time	m	Time	m	Time	m
1 F	0232	0.3	0801	13.9	1455	0.5	2020	14.5
2 SA	0319	0.1	0844	14.1	1538	0.4	2102	14.4
3 SU	0359	0.2	0924	13.9	1613	0.7	2142	14.0
4 M	0431	0.7	1001	13.4	1641	1.2	2218	13.3
5 TU	0455	1.4	1034	12.6	1701	2.0	2251	12.2
6 W	0515	2.2	1105	11.6	1723	2.7	◑ 2326	11.1
7 TH	0542	3.0	1140	10.5	1754	3.5		
8 F	0009	9.9	0621	3.9	1232	9.5	1844	4.5
9 SA	0143	9.0	0726	4.6	1429	9.0	2020	5.0
10 SU	0322	9.1	0919	4.7	1551	9.6	2240	4.2
11 M	0429	9.8	1056	3.7	1652	10.5	2335	3.1
12 TU	0523	10.8	1151	2.7	1743	11.5		
13 W	0022	2.3	0609	11.7	1239	2.0	1826	12.2
14 TH	0108	1.7	0649	12.2	1326	1.6	1904	12.6
15 F	0153	1.5	0726	12.5	1411	1.5	● 1940	12.8
16 SA	0235	1.6	0800	12.5	1450	1.7	2012	12.7
17 SU	0311	1.8	0831	12.4	1521	1.9	2042	12.5
18 M	0336	2.2	0858	12.2	1540	2.2	2108	12.3
19 TU	0347	2.4	0923	12.0	1553	2.3	2134	12.1
20 W	0402	2.4	0951	11.8	1616	2.3	2206	11.8
21 TH	0427	2.4	1024	11.5	1646	2.6	2244	11.3
22 F	0500	2.8	1106	10.8	1723	3.1	◐ 2332	10.4
23 SA	0541	3.5	1202	10.0	1815	4.0		
24 SU	0040	9.6	0644	4.3	1328	9.5	1955	4.6
25 M	0234	9.5	0924	4.5	1529	10.0	2223	3.7
26 TU	0412	10.5	1058	3.3	1644	11.3	2331	2.4
27 W	0516	11.8	1159	2.1	1740	12.7		
28 TH	0027	1.3	0608	13.0	1253	1.2	1829	13.7
29 F	0120	0.6	0654	13.8	1344	0.6	○ 1914	14.4
30 SA	0209	0.2	0737	14.2	1430	0.3	1957	14.6

OCTOBER

Day	Time	m	Time	m	Time	m	Time	m
1 SU	0253	0.1	0818	14.2	1512	0.4	2037	14.4
2 M	0330	0.4	0855	13.9	1546	0.9	2114	13.8
3 TU	0400	1.1	0929	13.3	1611	1.6	2147	13.0
4 W	0420	1.8	0959	12.4	1627	2.3	2217	11.9
5 TH	0437	2.5	1027	11.5	1647	2.9	2247	10.8
6 F	0502	3.2	1058	10.4	1715	3.7	◑ 2323	9.6
7 SA	0536	4.1	1143	9.4	1800	4.6		
8 SU	0040	8.6	0639	4.9	1358	8.8	1940	5.2
9 M	0256	8.8	0839	5.0	1523	9.4	2214	4.5
10 TU	0400	9.7	1029	4.0	1622	10.4	2307	3.3
11 W	0452	10.7	1122	2.9	1711	11.4	2353	2.4
12 TH	0536	11.6	1210	2.1	1753	12.2		
13 F	0037	1.8	0616	12.3	1254	1.7	1832	12.6
14 SA	0121	1.5	0653	12.6	1338	1.6	● 1908	12.8
15 SU	0202	1.6	0727	12.7	1417	1.7	1941	12.8
16 M	0238	1.8	0759	12.6	1450	1.9	2012	12.7
17 TU	0305	2.0	0829	12.5	1514	2.1	2042	12.5
18 W	0323	2.2	0858	12.3	1534	2.2	2113	12.3
19 TH	0341	2.3	0930	12.1	1558	2.3	2148	11.9
20 F	0408	2.5	1007	11.6	1630	2.6	2229	11.2
21 SA	0442	2.9	1051	10.9	1710	3.2	2321	10.4
22 SU	0527	3.6	1151	10.1	1807	4.0	◐	
23 M	0033	9.7	0635	4.4	1326	9.7	2011	4.3
24 TU	0230	9.7	0916	4.3	1514	10.4	2202	3.4
25 W	0353	10.7	1034	3.1	1621	11.6	2306	2.2
26 TH	0453	11.9	1132	2.0	1716	12.7		
27 F	0000	1.3	0543	12.9	1224	1.3	1804	13.6
28 SA	0050	0.7	0628	13.6	1314	0.8	○ 1849	14.1
29 SU	0138	0.5	0710	13.9	1400	0.7	1931	14.1
30 M	0221	0.5	0750	13.9	1441	0.9	2011	13.8
31 TU	0259	0.9	0827	13.5	1516	1.3	2048	13.3

NOVEMBER

Day	Time	m	Time	m	Time	m	Time	m
1 W	0329	1.5	0901	12.9	1543	2.0	2122	12.5
2 TH	0350	2.1	0932	12.2	1601	2.6	2152	11.6
3 F	0410	2.7	1001	11.4	1623	3.1	2222	10.7
4 SA	0435	3.3	1033	10.5	1653	3.7	2259	9.8
5 SU	0509	3.9	1116	9.7	1737	4.4	◑ 2358	9.0
6 M	0605	4.6	1248	9.1	1859	4.9		
7 TU	0203	8.8	0744	4.9	1437	9.4	2040	4.6
8 W	0314	9.5	0919	4.3	1538	10.1	2209	3.8
9 TH	0409	10.4	1032	3.4	1628	11.0	2306	3.0
10 F	0456	11.2	1126	2.7	1713	11.7	2355	2.3
11 SA	0538	11.9	1213	2.2	1754	12.2		
12 SU	0040	1.9	0617	12.4	1257	1.9	1833	12.6
13 M	0122	1.8	0654	12.7	1339	1.8	● 1911	12.7
14 TU	0201	1.8	0730	12.8	1417	1.8	1947	12.7
15 W	0235	1.9	0805	12.7	1451	1.9	2024	12.6
16 TH	0305	2.0	0841	12.6	1522	2.0	2102	12.4
17 F	0333	2.2	0920	12.3	1555	2.2	2143	12.0
18 SA	0405	2.5	1003	11.8	1632	2.6	2229	11.4
19 SU	0444	2.9	1052	11.3	1718	3.0	2323	10.8
20 M	0533	3.5	1153	10.7	1821	3.5	◐	
21 TU	0032	10.3	0646	3.9	1316	10.5	1953	3.6
22 W	0202	10.3	0836	3.8	1442	10.9	2120	3.1
23 TH	0318	10.9	0955	3.1	1548	11.6	2227	2.4
24 F	0419	11.7	1057	2.4	1645	12.3	2325	1.8
25 SA	0512	12.4	1151	1.8	1736	12.9		
26 SU	0017	1.4	0600	12.9	1241	1.4	1823	13.2
27 M	0105	1.2	0643	13.2	1329	1.3	○ 1906	13.3
28 TU	0150	1.2	0724	13.2	1413	1.5	1948	13.1
29 W	0230	1.5	0803	13.0	1452	1.8	2028	12.6
30 TH	0305	1.9	0840	12.6	1523	2.3	2105	12.1

DECEMBER

Day	Time	m	Time	m	Time	m	Time	m
1 F	0332	2.3	0915	12.1	1548	2.7	2138	11.5
2 SA	0355	2.7	0948	11.5	1612	3.1	2211	10.9
3 SU	0422	3.1	1022	10.9	1643	3.4	2247	10.3
4 M	0457	3.5	1102	10.3	1724	3.7	2332	9.8
5 TU	0542	3.9	1155	9.9	1819	4.1	◑	
6 W	0032	9.5	0647	4.2	1310	9.7	1929	4.2
7 TH	0152	9.5	0803	4.2	1427	9.9	2042	4.0
8 F	0303	9.9	0916	3.9	1530	10.4	2154	3.6
9 SA	0402	10.5	1025	3.4	1624	11.0	2259	3.0
10 SU	0454	11.2	1125	2.8	1714	11.6	2355	2.5
11 M	0540	11.9	1217	2.3	1800	12.1		
12 TU	0044	2.1	0624	12.4	1304	1.9	● 1845	12.5
13 W	0129	1.9	0707	12.7	1350	1.7	1929	12.7
14 TH	0213	1.8	0749	12.9	1435	1.7	2013	12.7
15 F	0255	1.8	0833	12.9	1519	1.7	2058	12.6
16 SA	0335	1.9	0917	12.8	1601	1.8	2144	12.4
17 SU	0415	2.1	1004	12.5	1644	2.0	2231	12.1
18 M	0456	2.4	1052	12.1	1729	2.3	2320	11.7
19 TU	0543	2.7	1146	11.7	1820	2.6	◐	
20 W	0015	11.2	0638	3.0	1248	11.3	1919	2.8
21 TH	0121	10.9	0744	3.2	1400	11.2	2026	3.0
22 F	0233	10.8	0901	3.3	1508	11.2	2138	3.0
23 SA	0340	11.0	1015	3.1	1611	11.5	2246	2.7
24 SU	0440	11.4	1118	2.7	1708	11.8	2344	2.4
25 M	0533	11.9	1213	2.3	1800	12.1		
26 TU	0036	2.1	0621	12.3	1303	2.1	1848	12.3
27 W	0125	1.9	0706	12.5	1351	2.0	○ 1933	12.4
28 TH	0210	1.9	0748	12.5	1435	2.1	2015	12.2
29 F	0250	2.0	0828	12.4	1514	2.3	2054	12.0
30 SA	0324	2.3	0904	12.2	1545	2.6	2128	11.7
31 SU	0351	2.5	0938	11.8	1610	2.8	2200	11.4

Chart Datum: 6·50 metres below Ordnance Datum (Newlyn)
HAT is 14·7m above Chart Datum

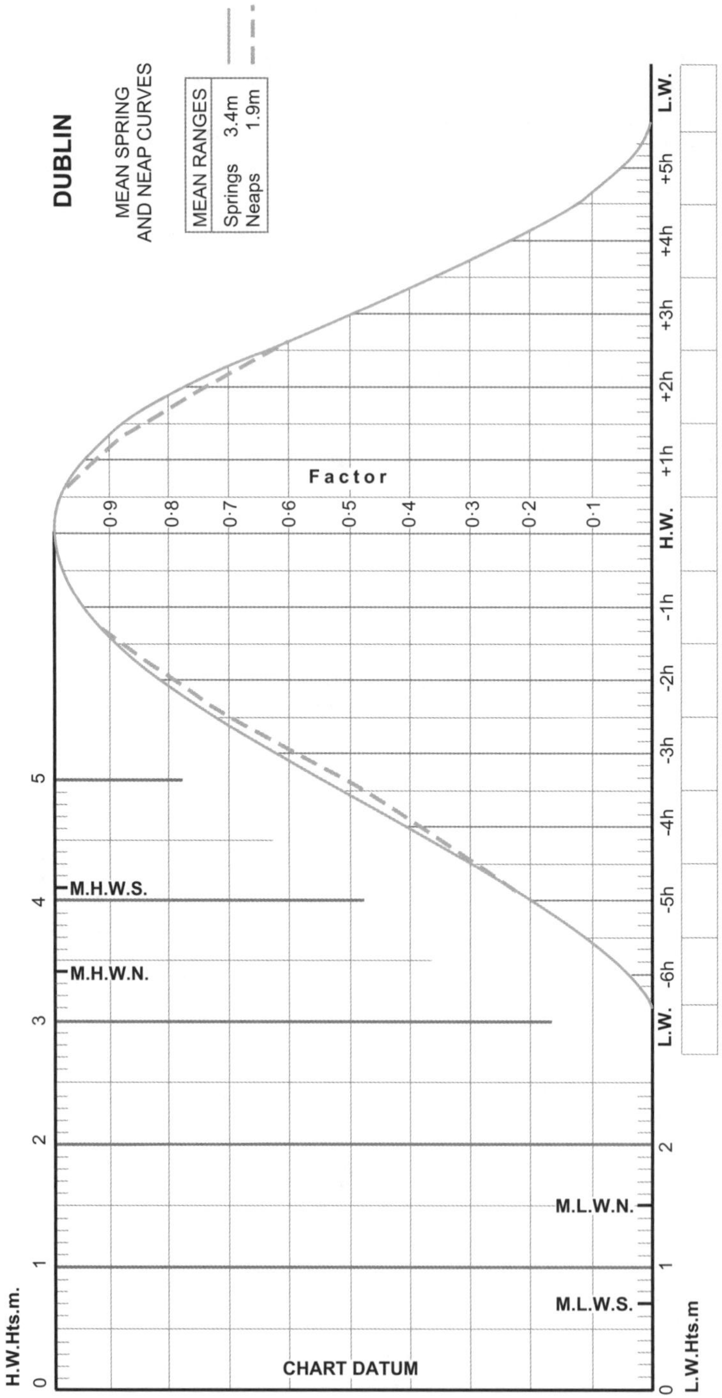
DUBLIN
MEAN SPRING AND NEAP CURVES
MEAN RANGES
Springs 3.4m
Neaps 1.9m
Factor
0·9
0·8
0·7
0·6
0·5
0·4
0·3
0·2
0·1
L.W.
-6h
-5h
-4h
-3h
-2h
-1h
H.W.
+1h
+2h
+3h
+4h
+5h
L.W.
H.W.Hts.m.
M.H.W.S.
M.H.W.N.
CHART DATUM
M.L.W.N.
M.L.W.S.
L.W.Hts.m
0
1
2
3
4
5

TIME ZONE (UT)
For Summer Time add ONE hour in **non-shaded areas**

IRELAND – DUBLIN (NORTH WALL)

LAT 53°21′N LONG 6°13′W

TIMES AND HEIGHTS OF HIGH AND LOW WATERS

Dates in amber are **SPRINGS**
Dates in grey are **NEAPS**

2023

JANUARY

Day	Time	m	Day	Time	m
1 SU	0028 0723 1250 1933	1.2 3.6 1.5 3.7	16 M	0601 1135 1818	3.4 1.5 3.5
2 M	0135 0823 1357 2037	1.2 3.6 1.4 3.7	17 TU	0020 0706 1245 1928	1.3 3.4 1.5 3.5
3 TU	0236 0919 1458 2135	1.3 3.7 1.3 3.7	18 W	0127 0810 1353 2037	1.2 3.5 1.4 3.6
4 W	0329 1008 1550 2226	1.2 3.8 1.2 3.7	19 TH	0229 0909 1455 2140	1.1 3.7 1.1 3.8
5 TH	0412 1049 1634 2307	1.2 3.9 1.1 3.7	20 F	0325 1001 1550 2235	1.0 3.9 0.8 3.9
6 F	0450 1124 1714 ○ 2342	1.2 3.9 1.0 3.7	21 SA	0415 1050 1641 ● 2326	0.8 4.1 0.6 4.0
7 SA	0523 1157 1750	1.2 3.9 1.0	22 SU	0501 1137 1729	0.7 4.3 0.4
8 SU	0014 0555 1228 1826	3.7 1.1 4.0 1.0	23 M	0014 0546 1223 1817	4.1 0.6 4.4 0.3
9 M	0047 0626 1301 1859	3.7 1.1 3.9 1.0	24 TU	0102 0631 1310 1906	4.1 0.6 4.4 0.3
10 TU	0121 0656 1335 1933	3.6 1.1 3.9 1.0	25 W	0150 0717 1359 1955	4.0 0.7 4.3 0.4
11 W	0158 0730 1413 2008	3.6 1.2 3.9 1.0	26 TH	0241 0807 1450 2047	3.9 0.8 4.2 0.6
12 TH	0238 0808 1454 2047	3.6 1.2 3.8 1.0	27 F	0333 0900 1543 2140	3.7 1.0 4.0 0.8
13 F	0322 0851 1538 2130	3.5 1.3 3.7 1.1	28 SA	0429 0957 1641 ◐ 2236	3.6 1.2 3.8 1.1
14 SA	0409 0938 1625 2219	3.4 1.4 3.6 1.1	29 SU	0530 1059 1746 2338	3.4 1.4 3.6 1.3
15 SU	0502 1032 1718 ◑ 2316	3.4 1.5 3.5 1.2	30 M	0635 1208 1856	3.4 1.5 3.5
			31 TU	0051 0742 1326 2007	1.5 3.4 1.5 3.4

FEBRUARY

Day	Time	m	Day	Time	m
1 W	0211 0845 1442 2114	1.5 3.5 1.4 3.4	16 TH	0056 0741 1333 2024	1.4 3.4 1.3 3.4
2 TH	0314 0942 1539 2211	1.5 3.6 1.3 3.5	17 F	0214 0851 1447 2132	1.3 3.6 1.1 3.6
3 F	0400 1028 1623 2254	1.4 3.7 1.1 3.5	18 SA	0318 0949 1546 2229	1.1 3.8 0.7 3.8
4 SA	0436 1106 1700 2327	1.2 3.8 1.0 3.6	19 SU	0408 1039 1635 2317	0.8 4.1 0.4 4.0
5 SU	0508 1139 1732 ○ 2357	1.1 3.9 0.9 3.6	20 M	0451 1125 1719 ●	0.6 4.3 0.2
6 M	0537 1208 1802	1.0 3.9 0.8	21 TU	0001 0533 1207 1802	4.0 0.5 4.4 0.1
7 TU	0024 0603 1237 1831	3.6 1.0 3.9 0.8	22 W	0043 0613 1250 1845	4.0 0.4 4.4 0.1
8 W	0053 0629 1308 1859	3.7 0.9 3.9 0.8	23 TH	0124 0654 1334 1928	4.0 0.5 4.3 0.3
9 TH	0125 0659 1343 1930	3.7 0.9 3.9 0.7	24 F	0206 0739 1420 2013	3.8 0.6 4.1 0.5
10 F	0202 0734 1421 2007	3.7 0.9 3.9 0.8	25 SA	0250 0827 1508 2101	3.7 0.8 3.9 0.8
11 SA	0242 0813 1502 2048	3.7 1.0 3.8 0.8	26 SU	0338 0920 1600 2151	3.5 1.0 3.7 1.1
12 SU	0326 0857 1547 2134	3.6 1.1 3.7 1.0	27 M	0434 1020 1703 ◐ 2248	3.4 1.2 3.4 1.4
13 M	0414 0947 1638 ◑ 2227	3.5 1.2 3.5 1.2	28 TU	0544 1127 1819 2358	3.2 1.4 3.2 1.7
14 TU	0511 1047 1739 2333	3.4 1.4 3.4 1.3			
15 W	0622 1206 1859	3.3 1.4 3.3			

MARCH

Day	Time	m	Day	Time	m
1 W	0658 1251 1937	3.2 1.5 3.1	16 TH	0551 1152 1849	3.3 1.3 3.2
2 TH	0140 0810 1423 2053	1.7 3.3 1.4 3.2	17 F	0040 0721 1326 2018	1.5 3.3 1.2 3.4
3 F	0255 0914 1521 2153	1.6 3.5 1.2 3.3	18 SA	0205 0836 1441 2127	1.3 3.5 0.9 3.6
4 SA	0342 1004 1603 2234	1.4 3.6 1.0 3.5	19 SU	0308 0937 1537 2221	1.1 3.8 0.6 3.8
5 SU	0416 1043 1636 2306	1.2 3.8 0.9 3.5	20 M	0356 1027 1623 2306	0.8 4.0 0.3 3.9
6 M	0446 1115 1705 2333	1.0 3.8 0.8 3.6	21 TU	0437 1110 1704 ● 2345	0.5 4.2 0.1 4.0
7 TU	0512 1143 1732 ○ 2357	0.9 3.9 0.7 3.7	22 W	0515 1151 1743	0.4 4.3 0.1
8 W	0535 1209 1756	0.8 3.9 0.6	23 TH	0020 0553 1229 1821	4.0 0.3 4.3 0.2
9 TH	0022 0559 1238 1824	3.7 0.7 3.9 0.6	24 F	0055 0632 1310 1900	3.9 0.4 4.2 0.4
10 F	0052 0628 1312 1856	3.8 0.6 3.9 0.6	25 SA	0132 0714 1352 1941	3.8 0.5 4.0 0.6
11 SA	0127 0703 1351 1933	3.8 0.6 3.9 0.6	26 SU	0212 0800 1438 2025	3.7 0.7 3.8 0.9
12 SU	0207 0742 1432 2014	3.8 0.7 3.8 0.7	27 M	0256 0852 1528 2113	3.6 0.9 3.6 1.2
13 M	0251 0827 1518 2101	3.7 0.8 3.7 0.9	28 TU	0346 0950 1628 2208	3.4 1.1 3.3 1.5
14 TU	0339 0919 1611 2157	3.5 1.0 3.5 1.2	29 W	0452 1055 1745 ◐ 2316	3.2 1.3 3.1 1.7
15 W	0437 1024 1718 ◑ 2309	3.4 1.2 3.3 1.4	30 TH	0616 1214 1906	3.2 1.4 3.0
			31 F	0044 0733 1347 2022	1.8 3.2 1.4 3.1

APRIL

Day	Time	m	Day	Time	m
1 SA	0220 0839 1448 2121	1.7 3.4 1.2 3.3	16 SU	0146 0819 1424 2113	1.3 3.6 0.8 3.6
2 SU	0310 0931 1530 2203	1.4 3.5 1.0 3.4	17 M	0247 0920 1518 2205	1.1 3.8 0.5 3.8
3 M	0345 1012 1602 2235	1.2 3.7 0.8 3.6	18 TU	0335 1010 1603 2249	0.8 4.0 0.3 3.9
4 TU	0414 1045 1631 2302	1.0 3.8 0.7 3.7	19 W	0417 1055 1644 2326	0.6 4.1 0.3 3.9
5 W	0439 1113 1656 2325	0.8 3.8 0.6 3.7	20 TH	0456 1134 1722 ● 2359	0.5 4.1 0.3 3.9
6 TH	0503 1139 1722 ○ 2350	0.7 3.9 0.5 3.8	21 F	0534 1212 1759	0.4 4.1 0.4
7 F	0529 1210 1751	0.6 3.9 0.5	22 SA	0030 0614 1250 1836	3.9 0.5 4.0 0.6
8 SA	0021 0600 1245 1826	3.9 0.5 3.9 0.5	23 SU	0106 0655 1331 1914	3.8 0.6 3.9 0.8
9 SU	0058 0637 1326 1905	3.9 0.5 3.9 0.6	24 M	0144 0741 1416 1956	3.7 0.7 3.7 1.0
10 M	0140 0720 1412 1950	3.9 0.6 3.8 0.8	25 TU	0227 0831 1504 2043	3.6 0.9 3.5 1.2
11 TU	0226 0810 1502 2041	3.8 0.8 3.7 1.0	26 W	0314 0927 1601 2138	3.5 1.1 3.3 1.5
12 W	0318 0910 1601 2144	3.6 1.0 3.5 1.3	27 TH	0414 1029 1711 ◐ 2242	3.3 1.2 3.1 1.7
13 TH	0420 1024 1716 ◑ 2300	3.5 1.1 3.3 1.5	28 F	0533 1137 1828 2356	3.2 1.3 3.0 1.7
14 F	0537 1151 1847	3.4 1.2 3.3	29 SA	0650 1252 1938	3.2 1.3 3.1
15 SA	0027 0705 1316 2009	1.5 3.4 1.0 3.4	30 SU	0116 0756 1356 2035	1.7 3.3 1.2 3.2

Chart Datum: 0·20 metres above Ordnance Datum (Dublin)
HAT is 4·5m above Chart Datum

TIME ZONE (UT)
For Summer Time add ONE hour in **non-shaded areas**

IRELAND – DUBLIN (NORTH WALL)

LAT 53°21′N LONG 6°13′W

TIMES AND HEIGHTS OF HIGH AND LOW WATERS

Dates in amber are **SPRINGS**
Dates in grey are **NEAPS**

2023

MAY

Date	Day	Time	m
1	M	0217 0849 1443 2120	1.5 3.4 1.0 3.4
2	TU	0259 0932 1519 2156	1.3 3.6 0.8 3.5
3	W	0332 1007 1550 2225	1.1 3.7 0.7 3.7
4	TH	0400 1038 1619 2250	0.9 3.8 0.6 3.8
5	F	0429 1109 1650 ○ 2320	0.7 3.9 0.5 3.9
6	SA	0501 1145 1724 2355	0.6 3.9 0.5 4.0
7	SU	0537 1225 1802	0.5 3.9 0.6
8	M	0035 0620 1310 1846	4.0 0.6 3.9 0.7
9	TU	0121 0709 1401 1935	3.9 0.6 3.8 0.9
10	W	0212 0806 1457 2033	3.9 0.8 3.7 1.1
11	TH	0308 0912 1602 2138	3.8 0.9 3.5 1.3
12	F	0413 1026 1716 ◑ 2251	3.7 1.0 3.4 1.4
13	SA	0528 1142 1834	3.6 1.0 3.4
14	SU	0006 0646 1254 1947	1.4 3.6 0.9 3.5
15	M	0116 0755 1358 2049	1.3 3.7 0.7 3.6
16	TU	0217 0856 1453 2141	1.1 3.9 0.6 3.7
17	W	0309 0950 1540 2227	0.9 3.9 0.6 3.8
18	TH	0355 1037 1623 2306	0.8 4.0 0.6 3.8
19	F	0438 1119 1702 ● 2340	0.7 4.0 0.6 3.8
20	SA	0519 1157 1739	0.7 3.9 0.7
21	SU	0011 0600 1235 1816	3.8 0.7 3.8 0.8
22	M	0045 0642 1314 1853	3.8 0.7 3.7 1.0
23	TU	0124 0727 1357 1933	3.8 0.8 3.6 1.1
24	W	0205 0815 1443 2018	3.7 0.9 3.5 1.3
25	TH	0251 0906 1534 2109	3.6 1.0 3.3 1.4
26	F	0343 1001 1632 2208	3.5 1.2 3.2 1.6
27	SA	0445 1059 1738 ◐ 2311	3.4 1.2 3.1 1.6
28	SU	0555 1158 1843	3.3 1.2 3.1
29	M	0014 0700 1255 1941	1.6 3.3 1.2 3.2
30	TU	0112 0755 1346 2028	1.5 3.4 1.1 3.4
31	W	0201 0842 1429 2109	1.4 3.5 1.0 3.5

JUNE

Date	Day	Time	m
1	TH	0243 0924 1508 2144	1.2 3.6 0.8 3.7
2	F	0321 1004 1545 2218	1.0 3.8 0.7 3.8
3	SA	0358 1044 1623 2256	0.8 3.9 0.7 3.9
4	SU	0438 1127 1703 ○ 2336	0.7 3.9 0.6 4.0
5	M	0522 1213 1746	0.6 3.9 0.7
6	TU	0020 0611 1302 1833	4.1 0.6 3.9 0.8
7	W	0109 0704 1356 1925	4.1 0.6 3.8 0.9
8	TH	0203 0804 1453 2023	4.0 0.7 3.7 1.0
9	F	0301 0908 1556 2125	4.0 0.7 3.6 1.2
10	SA	0404 1014 1702 ◑ 2230	3.9 0.8 3.6 1.3
11	SU	0511 1120 1809 2336	3.8 0.8 3.5 1.3
12	M	0620 1225 1915	3.8 0.9 3.5
13	TU	0042 0728 1327 2017	1.3 3.8 0.9 3.6
14	W	0145 0830 1425 2113	1.2 3.8 0.9 3.7
15	TH	0243 0928 1518 2203	1.1 3.8 0.9 3.7
16	F	0336 1020 1604 2246	1.0 3.8 0.9 3.8
17	SA	0424 1106 1646 2322	1.0 3.8 0.9 3.8
18	SU	0507 1145 1723 ● 2355	0.9 3.7 1.0 3.8
19	M	0549 1221 1759	0.9 3.7 1.0
20	TU	0028 0630 1257 1834	3.9 0.9 3.6 1.1
21	W	0104 0711 1336 1911	3.8 0.9 3.6 1.1
22	TH	0143 0754 1417 1951	3.8 0.9 3.5 1.2
23	F	0225 0838 1501 2034	3.7 1.0 3.4 1.3
24	SA	0309 0925 1547 2121	3.7 1.1 3.3 1.4
25	SU	0357 1013 1638 2214	3.6 1.1 3.3 1.5
26	M	0450 1104 1733 ◐ 2310	3.5 1.2 3.2 1.5
27	TU	0548 1156 1832	3.4 1.2 3.3
28	W	0008 0649 1249 1928	1.5 3.4 1.2 3.3
29	TH	0104 0748 1341 2020	1.5 3.5 1.1 3.5
30	F	0157 0844 1430 2108	1.3 3.6 1.0 3.6

JULY

Date	Day	Time	m
1	SA	0247 0937 1517 2154	1.1 3.7 0.9 3.8
2	SU	0336 1027 1603 2238	0.9 3.8 0.8 4.0
3	M	0424 1115 1648 ○ 2323	0.7 3.9 0.7 4.1
4	TU	0513 1204 1734	0.6 4.0 0.7
5	W	0009 0603 1253 1821	4.2 0.5 4.0 0.7
6	TH	0057 0656 1345 1911	4.2 0.4 3.9 0.8
7	F	0149 0751 1439 2004	4.2 0.5 3.9 0.9
8	SA	0244 0849 1535 2101	4.2 0.6 3.8 1.0
9	SU	0342 0949 1634 2200	4.1 0.7 3.6 1.1
10	M	0443 1049 1736 ◑ 2301	4.0 0.8 3.6 1.3
11	TU	0549 1151 1839	3.8 1.0 3.5
12	W	0006 0658 1254 1943	1.3 3.7 1.1 3.5
13	TH	0114 0805 1359 2044	1.4 3.7 1.2 3.6
14	F	0222 0909 1459 2139	1.3 3.6 1.2 3.6
15	SA	0323 1006 1549 2226	1.2 3.6 1.2 3.7
16	SU	0415 1054 1632 2306	1.1 3.6 1.2 3.8
17	M	0458 1133 1709 ● 2339	1.0 3.6 1.1 3.9
18	TU	0537 1206 1742	1.0 3.6 1.1
19	W	0010 0614 1237 1814	3.9 0.9 3.6 1.1
20	TH	0042 0649 1310 1845	3.9 0.9 3.6 1.1
21	F	0116 0723 1345 1918	3.9 0.9 3.6 1.1
22	SA	0153 0759 1423 1953	3.9 0.9 3.5 1.1
23	SU	0233 0836 1503 2033	3.8 1.0 3.5 1.2
24	M	0316 0916 1547 2116	3.7 1.0 3.4 1.3
25	TU	0402 1002 1635 ◐ 2205	3.6 1.1 3.4 1.4
26	W	0453 1053 1729 2302	3.5 1.2 3.3 1.5
27	TH	0553 1154 1833	3.4 1.3 3.3
28	F	0009 0704 1259 1940	1.5 3.4 1.3 3.4
29	SA	0121 0817 1402 2042	1.4 3.5 1.3 3.6
30	SU	0226 0920 1500 2136	1.2 3.6 1.1 3.8
31	M	0324 1015 1551 2225	1.0 3.8 0.9 4.0

AUGUST

Date	Day	Time	m
1	TU	0416 1105 1637 ○ 2310	0.7 3.9 0.7 4.2
2	W	0504 1152 1721 2355	0.4 4.0 0.6 4.3
3	TH	0551 1238 1805	0.3 4.1 0.6
4	F	0040 0639 1324 1850	4.4 0.2 4.0 0.6
5	SA	0127 0729 1413 1938	4.4 0.3 3.9 0.7
6	SU	0217 0820 1503 2029	4.3 0.5 3.8 0.9
7	M	0310 0914 1555 2125	4.1 0.7 3.7 1.0
8	TU	0407 1010 1654 ◑ 2225	3.9 0.9 3.5 1.2
9	W	0513 1110 1759 2331	3.7 1.2 3.4 1.4
10	TH	0627 1217 1908	3.5 1.4 3.4
11	F	0047 0742 1334 2015	1.5 3.4 1.5 3.5
12	SA	0210 0854 1444 2117	1.5 3.4 1.5 3.6
13	SU	0317 0955 1536 2208	1.3 3.5 1.4 3.7
14	M	0405 1043 1617 2248	1.1 3.5 1.3 3.8
15	TU	0444 1118 1651 2320	1.0 3.6 1.2 3.9
16	W	0518 1147 1721 ● 2349	0.9 3.6 1.0 3.9
17	TH	0549 1214 1749	0.8 3.6 1.0
18	F	0017 0618 1241 1816	4.0 0.8 3.7 0.9
19	SA	0047 0645 1311 1843	4.0 0.8 3.7 0.9
20	SU	0120 0715 1346 1916	3.9 0.8 3.7 0.9
21	M	0158 0749 1424 1953	3.9 0.8 3.7 1.0
22	TU	0238 0828 1505 2034	3.8 0.9 3.6 1.1
23	W	0322 0913 1551 2121	3.7 1.1 3.5 1.2
24	TH	0412 1004 1644 ◐ 2218	3.5 1.2 3.4 1.4
25	F	0513 1109 1750 2333	3.4 1.4 3.3 1.5
26	SA	0635 1229 1909	3.3 1.5 3.3
27	SU	0101 0803 1346 2023	1.5 3.4 1.4 3.5
28	M	0218 0911 1450 2121	1.2 3.6 1.2 3.8
29	TU	0319 1006 1541 2211	0.9 3.8 0.9 4.1
30	W	0409 1054 1625 2255	0.5 4.0 0.7 4.3
31	TH	0453 1137 1705 ○ 2337	0.2 4.1 0.5 4.4

Chart Datum: 0·20 metres above Ordnance Datum (Dublin)
HAT is 4·5m above Chart Datum

TIME ZONE (UT)
For Summer Time add ONE hour in **non-shaded areas**

IRELAND – DUBLIN (NORTH WALL)

LAT 53°21′N LONG 6°13′W

TIMES AND HEIGHTS OF HIGH AND LOW WATERS

Dates in amber are **SPRINGS**
Dates in grey are **NEAPS**

2023

SEPTEMBER

Date	Day	Time	m	Time	m	Time	m	Time	m
1	F	0535	0.1	1218	4.1	1745	0.4		
2	SA	0018	4.5	0617	0.1	1259	4.1	1827	0.5
3	SU	0101	4.4	0701	0.3	1341	4.0	1911	0.6
4	M	0147	4.3	0747	0.5	1425	3.8	1959	0.8
5	TU	0236	4.1	0836	0.8	1513	3.7	2052	1.0
6	W	0330	3.8	0930	1.1	1608	3.5	◑ 2152	1.2
7	TH	0436	3.5	1028	1.4	1715	3.4	2259	1.4
8	F	0557	3.3	1137	1.7	1831	3.3		
9	SA	0021	1.6	0720	3.2	1307	1.7	1946	3.4
10	SU	0158	1.5	0840	3.3	1426	1.7	2053	3.6
11	M	0301	1.3	0942	3.4	1517	1.5	2146	3.7
12	TU	0346	1.1	1025	3.5	1556	1.3	2225	3.9
13	W	0421	0.9	1056	3.6	1628	1.1	2257	3.9
14	TH	0451	0.8	1123	3.7	1656	1.0	2325	4.0
15	F	0519	0.7	1147	3.7	1721	0.9	● 2350	4.0
16	SA	0543	0.7	1211	3.8	1745	0.8		
17	SU	0017	4.0	0608	0.7	1238	3.8	1812	0.8
18	M	0049	4.0	0636	0.7	1311	3.8	1844	0.8
19	TU	0126	3.9	0711	0.8	1349	3.8	1920	0.9
20	W	0206	3.8	0751	0.9	1431	3.7	2003	1.0
21	TH	0252	3.7	0837	1.1	1518	3.6	2052	1.2
22	F	0344	3.5	0932	1.3	1612	3.4	◐ 2154	1.4
23	SA	0450	3.3	1043	1.6	1721	3.3	2319	1.5
24	SU	0623	3.2	1212	1.6	1847	3.4		
25	M	0054	1.4	0754	3.4	1334	1.5	2004	3.6
26	TU	0212	1.1	0902	3.6	1437	1.2	2105	3.9
27	W	0309	0.7	0955	3.8	1526	0.9	2154	4.1
28	TH	0355	0.4	1039	4.0	1608	0.7	2238	4.3
29	F	0436	0.2	1119	4.1	1647	0.5	○ 2318	4.4
30	SA	0515	0.1	1156	4.1	1725	0.4	2358	4.4

OCTOBER

Date	Day	Time	m	Time	m	Time	m	Time	m
1	SU	0554	0.2	1233	4.1	1805	0.4		
2	M	0038	4.3	0634	0.4	1311	4.0	1848	0.5
3	TU	0122	4.2	0716	0.6	1353	3.9	1934	0.7
4	W	0210	4.0	0802	0.9	1438	3.7	2027	1.0
5	TH	0302	3.7	0853	1.2	1530	3.6	2126	1.2
6	F	0406	3.4	0952	1.5	1635	3.4	◑ 2233	1.4
7	SA	0527	3.2	1100	1.8	1754	3.4	2352	1.5
8	SU	0652	3.2	1227	1.9	1911	3.4		
9	M	0127	1.5	0813	3.3	1354	1.7	2019	3.5
10	TU	0231	1.3	0913	3.4	1447	1.5	2113	3.7
11	W	0315	1.1	0953	3.6	1526	1.3	2154	3.8
12	TH	0349	0.9	1025	3.7	1558	1.1	2228	3.9
13	F	0419	0.8	1053	3.8	1626	1.0	2257	4.0
14	SA	0445	0.7	1117	3.8	1651	0.9	● 2323	4.0
15	SU	0509	0.7	1140	3.9	1715	0.8	2350	4.0
16	M	0534	0.7	1208	3.9	1744	0.8		
17	TU	0022	4.0	0605	0.7	1242	3.9	1818	0.8
18	W	0101	3.9	0641	0.8	1322	3.9	1857	0.9
19	TH	0144	3.8	0723	1.0	1406	3.8	1944	1.0
20	F	0234	3.7	0813	1.2	1456	3.7	2040	1.2
21	SA	0332	3.5	0914	1.5	1554	3.6	2150	1.3
22	SU	0445	3.4	1031	1.6	1705	3.5	◐ 2315	1.4
23	M	0615	3.3	1157	1.6	1826	3.5		
24	TU	0042	1.2	0738	3.5	1314	1.5	1941	3.7
25	W	0153	1.0	0843	3.7	1414	1.2	2042	3.9
26	TH	0248	0.7	0935	3.9	1504	1.0	2134	4.1
27	F	0335	0.4	1020	4.0	1548	0.8	2220	4.3
28	SA	0417	0.3	1100	4.1	1629	0.6	○ 2302	4.3
29	SU	0456	0.3	1136	4.1	1708	0.5	2342	4.3
30	M	0534	0.4	1212	4.1	1749	0.6		
31	TU	0022	4.2	0612	0.6	1249	4.0	1832	0.6

NOVEMBER

Date	Day	Time	m	Time	m	Time	m	Time	m
1	W	0105	4.0	0652	0.8	1329	4.0	1918	0.8
2	TH	0152	3.8	0735	1.1	1413	3.8	2009	1.0
3	F	0243	3.6	0824	1.3	1503	3.7	2106	1.2
4	SA	0343	3.4	0922	1.6	1602	3.6	2207	1.3
5	SU	0455	3.2	1027	1.8	1714	3.5	◑ 2316	1.4
6	M	0612	3.2	1140	1.9	1828	3.4		
7	TU	0033	1.4	0724	3.2	1259	1.8	1934	3.5
8	W	0141	1.3	0823	3.4	1401	1.6	2029	3.6
9	TH	0231	1.2	0908	3.5	1446	1.4	2115	3.7
10	F	0309	1.0	0946	3.7	1522	1.2	2153	3.8
11	SA	0340	0.9	1017	3.8	1552	1.1	2225	3.9
12	SU	0409	0.8	1045	3.9	1620	1.0	2255	3.9
13	M	0436	0.8	1111	4.0	1649	0.9	● 2327	4.0
14	TU	0507	0.8	1143	4.0	1722	0.8		
15	W	0003	4.0	0542	0.8	1220	4.0	1801	0.8
16	TH	0046	3.9	0622	0.9	1303	4.0	1846	0.9
17	F	0133	3.8	0707	1.1	1351	4.0	1937	0.9
18	SA	0227	3.7	0801	1.3	1444	3.9	2038	1.0
19	SU	0329	3.6	0905	1.4	1544	3.8	2147	1.1
20	M	0440	3.5	1017	1.5	1651	3.8	◐ 2302	1.1
21	TU	0557	3.5	1132	1.5	1802	3.8		
22	W	0016	1.1	0710	3.6	1242	1.5	1912	3.8
23	TH	0123	0.9	0814	3.7	1344	1.3	2016	4.0
24	F	0222	0.8	0909	3.9	1439	1.1	2112	4.0
25	SA	0312	0.7	0958	4.0	1528	1.0	2204	4.1
26	SU	0358	0.6	1041	4.0	1613	0.8	2250	4.1
27	M	0439	0.7	1120	4.1	1657	0.8	○ 2332	4.1
28	TU	0518	0.8	1157	4.1	1739	0.8		
29	W	0012	4.0	0556	0.9	1233	4.0	1822	0.8
30	TH	0054	3.9	0635	1.0	1312	4.0	1907	0.9

DECEMBER

Date	Day	Time	m	Time	m	Time	m	Time	m
1	F	0137	3.8	0715	1.2	1354	3.9	1954	1.0
2	SA	0224	3.6	0800	1.3	1440	3.8	2044	1.1
3	SU	0316	3.4	0851	1.5	1530	3.7	2138	1.2
4	M	0415	3.3	0949	1.7	1628	3.6	2235	1.3
5	TU	0520	3.2	1052	1.7	1732	3.5	◑ 2335	1.4
6	W	0625	3.2	1157	1.8	1836	3.4		
7	TH	0035	1.4	0725	3.3	1258	1.7	1935	3.5
8	F	0131	1.3	0816	3.4	1352	1.6	2026	3.5
9	SA	0218	1.2	0900	3.6	1437	1.4	2111	3.6
10	SU	0258	1.1	0938	3.7	1515	1.3	2152	3.7
11	M	0334	1.0	1012	3.8	1551	1.1	2231	3.8
12	TU	0410	0.9	1047	4.0	1628	1.0	● 2310	3.9
13	W	0446	0.9	1124	4.1	1708	0.8	2352	3.9
14	TH	0526	0.9	1205	4.1	1751	0.8		
15	F	0037	3.9	0610	0.9	1250	4.1	1840	0.7
16	SA	0127	3.9	0657	1.0	1339	4.1	1932	0.7
17	SU	0221	3.8	0750	1.1	1432	4.1	2030	0.8
18	M	0319	3.7	0849	1.2	1529	4.0	2131	0.8
19	TU	0421	3.7	0952	1.3	1629	4.0	◐ 2236	0.9
20	W	0528	3.6	1059	1.4	1734	3.9	2343	1.0
21	TH	0635	3.6	1206	1.4	1841	3.9		
22	F	0049	1.0	0740	3.7	1312	1.4	1948	3.8
23	SA	0153	1.0	0840	3.7	1414	1.3	2052	3.8
24	SU	0252	1.0	0935	3.8	1512	1.2	2151	3.9
25	M	0343	1.0	1025	3.9	1604	1.1	2243	3.9
26	TU	0428	1.0	1108	4.0	1650	1.0	2327	3.8
27	W	0508	1.0	1146	4.0	1733	0.9	○	
28	TH	0006	3.8	0545	1.0	1220	4.0	1814	0.9
29	F	0042	3.7	0620	1.1	1256	4.0	1854	0.9
30	SA	0120	3.7	0656	1.1	1333	4.0	1934	0.9
31	SU	0159	3.6	0734	1.2	1413	3.9	2016	1.0

Chart Datum: 0·20 metres above Ordnance Datum (Dublin)
HAT is 4·5m above Chart Datum

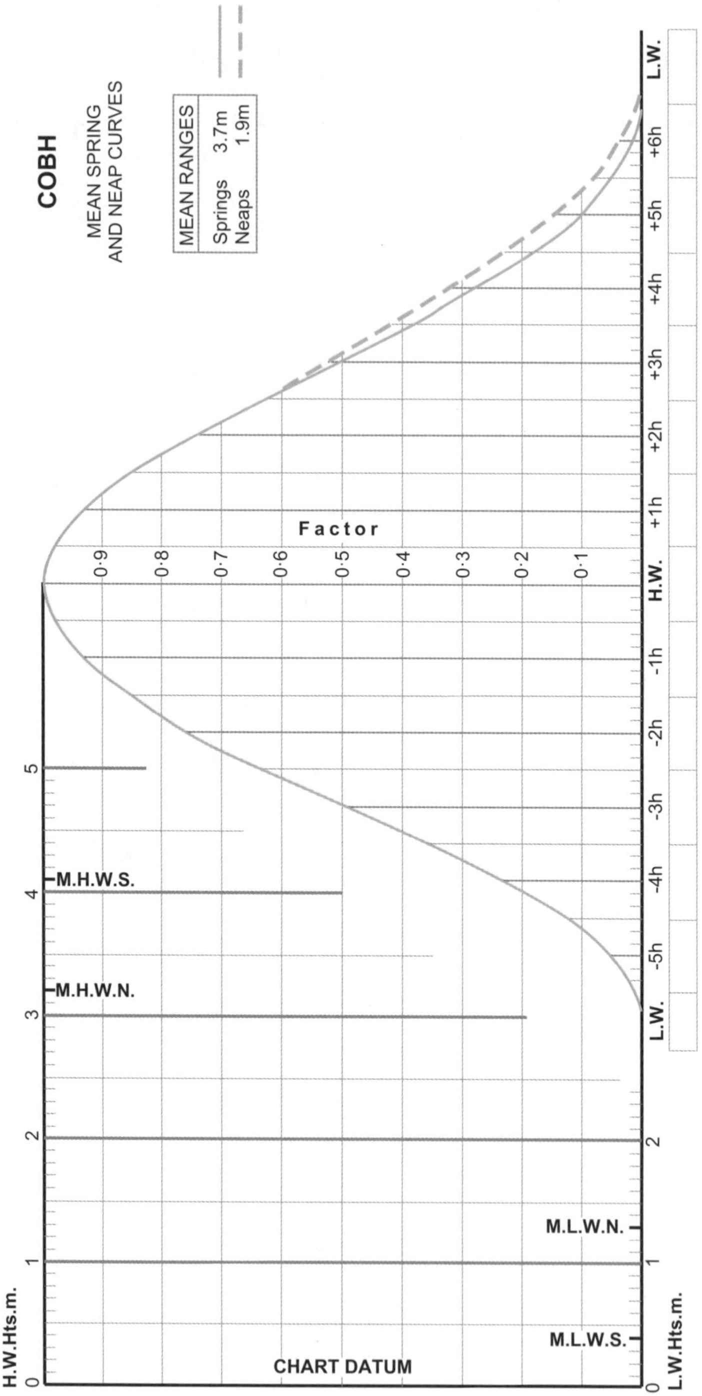
COBH
MEAN SPRING
AND NEAP CURVES
MEAN RANGES
Springs 3.7m
Neaps 1.9m
Factor
0·9
0·8
0·7
0·6
0·5
0·4
0·3
0·2
0·1
L.W.
-5h
-4h
-3h
-2h
-1h
H.W.
+1h
+2h
+3h
+4h
+5h
+6h
L.W.
H.W.Hts.m.
0
1
2
3
4
5
M.H.W.S.
M.H.W.N.
CHART DATUM
M.L.W.S.
M.L.W.N.
L.W.Hts.m.
0
1
2

TIME ZONE (UT)
For Summer Time add ONE hour in **non-shaded areas**

IRELAND – COBH

LAT 51°51′N LONG 8°18′W

TIMES AND HEIGHTS OF HIGH AND LOW WATERS

Dates in amber are **SPRINGS**
Dates in grey are **NEAPS**

2023

JANUARY

Date	Day	Time	m	Time	m	Time	m	Time	m
1	SU	0020	3.4	0707	1.1	1259	3.5	1937	1.2
2	M	0126	3.4	0811	1.1	1401	3.5	2037	1.1
3	TU	0229	3.5	0910	1.1	1458	3.6	2133	1.1
4	W	0326	3.6	1004	1.0	1549	3.7	2223	1.0
5	TH	0416	3.8	1051	1.0	1636	3.8	2306	0.9
6	F	0500	3.9	1131	0.9	1717	3.8	○ 2343	0.9
7	SA	0540	4.0	1206	0.9	1753	3.9		
8	SU	0015	0.8	0616	4.0	1236	0.9	1827	3.9
9	M	0045	0.8	0649	4.0	1308	0.9	1859	3.9
10	TU	0116	0.9	0722	3.9	1341	1.0	1932	3.8
11	W	0150	0.9	0756	3.9	1418	1.1	2007	3.8
12	TH	0228	1.0	0833	3.8	1457	1.1	2046	3.7
13	F	0310	1.1	0913	3.8	1538	1.2	2128	3.7
14	SA	0355	1.2	0957	3.7	1624	1.3	2216	3.6
15	SU	0446	1.3	1047	3.6	1719	1.4	◑ 2312	3.5
16	M	0547	1.3	1146	3.5	1826	1.4		
17	TU	0016	3.5	0657	1.3	1251	3.5	1938	1.3
18	W	0125	3.5	0809	1.2	1400	3.5	2048	1.2
19	TH	0236	3.6	0919	1.1	1509	3.7	2152	1.0
20	F	0343	3.8	1023	0.8	1612	3.8	2250	0.7
21	SA	0443	4.0	1119	0.6	1708	4.0	● 2342	0.5
22	SU	0536	4.2	1209	0.4	1758	4.1		
23	M	0029	0.3	0625	4.3	1255	0.3	1846	4.2
24	TU	0115	0.2	0712	4.3	1341	0.3	1931	4.1
25	W	0201	0.3	0758	4.2	1426	0.4	2016	4.0
26	TH	0247	0.4	0844	4.1	1511	0.5	2100	3.9
27	F	0334	0.5	0929	3.9	1557	0.7	2145	3.7
28	SA	0421	0.7	1016	3.7	1644	0.9	◐ 2232	3.6
29	SU	0513	1.0	1106	3.5	1737	1.1	2325	3.4
30	M	0611	1.2	1205	3.3	1839	1.3		
31	TU	0032	3.2	0720	1.3	1314	3.2	1950	1.4

FEBRUARY

Date	Day	Time	m	Time	m	Time	m	Time	m
1	W	0149	3.2	0833	1.3	1425	3.3	2102	1.3
2	TH	0300	3.4	0941	1.2	1527	3.4	2204	1.1
3	F	0358	3.6	1036	1.0	1619	3.6	2253	0.9
4	SA	0445	3.8	1118	0.9	1703	3.8	2331	0.8
5	SU	0525	3.9	1153	0.8	1740	3.9	○	
6	M	0002	0.7	0601	4.0	1222	0.7	1814	3.9
7	TU	0029	0.7	0634	4.0	1250	0.7	1845	3.9
8	W	0057	0.7	0703	4.0	1320	0.8	1914	3.9
9	TH	0128	0.7	0733	3.9	1353	0.8	1945	3.9
10	F	0202	0.8	0805	3.9	1427	0.9	2017	3.8
11	SA	0239	0.9	0839	3.9	1502	1.0	2053	3.8
12	SU	0319	1.0	0918	3.8	1540	1.1	2134	3.7
13	M	0404	1.1	1003	3.6	1626	1.3	◑ 2225	3.6
14	TU	0500	1.3	1059	3.5	1730	1.4	2331	3.4
15	W	0613	1.4	1211	3.3	1856	1.4		
16	TH	0050	3.3	0738	1.3	1333	3.3	2022	1.3
17	F	0215	3.4	0901	1.1	1455	3.4	2137	1.0
18	SA	0332	3.7	1012	0.8	1604	3.7	2238	0.6
19	SU	0433	4.0	1108	0.5	1659	4.0	2329	0.3
20	M	0524	4.2	1156	0.2	1746	4.1	●	
21	TU	0014	0.1	0610	4.3	1239	0.1	1829	4.2
22	W	0057	0.1	0653	4.4	1321	0.1	1911	4.2
23	TH	0139	0.1	0734	4.3	1401	0.2	1950	4.1
24	F	0220	0.2	0814	4.1	1441	0.4	2029	4.0
25	SA	0301	0.4	0854	3.9	1521	0.6	2107	3.8
26	SU	0343	0.6	0934	3.7	1601	0.8	2148	3.6
27	M	0427	0.9	1017	3.4	1647	1.1	◐ 2234	3.3
28	TU	0521	1.2	1110	3.2	1746	1.3	2337	3.1

MARCH

Date	Day	Time	m	Time	m	Time	m	Time	m
1	W	0628	1.4	1226	3.0	1902	1.5		
2	TH	0112	3.0	0752	1.4	1357	3.0	2030	1.4
3	F	0237	3.2	0917	1.3	1507	3.2	2145	1.2
4	SA	0338	3.4	1017	1.0	1601	3.5	2236	0.9
5	SU	0425	3.7	1059	0.8	1644	3.7	2313	0.7
6	M	0504	3.9	1133	0.7	1720	3.8	2342	0.6
7	TU	0538	4.0	1200	0.6	1753	3.9	○	
8	W	0007	0.6	0609	4.0	1226	0.6	1822	3.9
9	TH	0032	0.5	0637	4.0	1254	0.6	1850	3.9
10	F	0102	0.6	0704	4.0	1325	0.6	1918	3.9
11	SA	0135	0.6	0734	3.9	1357	0.7	1948	3.9
12	SU	0211	0.7	0808	3.9	1431	0.8	2023	3.8
13	M	0250	0.8	0845	3.8	1509	1.0	2103	3.7
14	TU	0335	1.0	0930	3.6	1555	1.1	2154	3.5
15	W	0431	1.2	1028	3.3	1659	1.3	◑ 2302	3.3
16	TH	0547	1.3	1146	3.1	1829	1.4		
17	F	0029	3.2	0718	1.3	1318	3.1	2003	1.3
18	SA	0206	3.4	0847	1.1	1447	3.3	2122	0.9
19	SU	0322	3.7	0958	0.7	1553	3.7	2223	0.5
20	M	0418	4.0	1052	0.4	1643	4.0	2312	0.2
21	TU	0506	4.2	1137	0.1	1727	4.1	● 2355	0.0
22	W	0548	4.3	1218	0.0	1808	4.2		
23	TH	0035	0.0	0629	4.3	1256	0.1	1846	4.2
24	F	0114	0.1	0707	4.2	1334	0.2	1922	4.1
25	SA	0153	0.2	0743	4.1	1411	0.3	1958	4.0
26	SU	0230	0.4	0820	3.9	1448	0.6	2033	3.8
27	M	0309	0.7	0856	3.6	1526	0.8	2111	3.6
28	TU	0351	0.9	0936	3.4	1608	1.1	2155	3.3
29	W	0442	1.2	1025	3.1	1705	1.3	◐ 2254	3.1
30	TH	0549	1.4	1136	2.9	1823	1.5		
31	F	0033	2.9	0712	1.5	1324	2.9	1951	1.4

APRIL

Date	Day	Time	m	Time	m	Time	m	Time	m
1	SA	0209	3.1	0837	1.3	1440	3.1	2109	1.2
2	SU	0308	3.3	0940	1.0	1532	3.4	2201	0.9
3	M	0354	3.6	1024	0.8	1614	3.6	2239	0.7
4	TU	0433	3.8	1058	0.6	1650	3.8	2309	0.6
5	W	0507	3.9	1128	0.5	1723	3.9	2336	0.5
6	TH	0537	3.9	1157	0.5	1752	3.9	○	
7	F	0004	0.5	0605	4.0	1226	0.5	1822	3.9
8	SA	0036	0.5	0635	4.0	1259	0.5	1852	4.0
9	SU	0111	0.5	0708	3.9	1333	0.6	1926	3.9
10	M	0149	0.6	0745	3.8	1411	0.7	2004	3.9
11	TU	0232	0.7	0827	3.7	1453	0.9	2048	3.7
12	W	0322	0.9	0916	3.5	1545	1.0	2143	3.5
13	TH	0422	1.1	1018	3.3	1654	1.2	◑ 2253	3.3
14	F	0538	1.2	1137	3.1	1820	1.3		
15	SA	0023	3.2	0707	1.2	1309	3.1	1949	1.1
16	SU	0155	3.4	0831	0.9	1431	3.4	2103	0.8
17	M	0303	3.7	0936	0.6	1531	3.7	2201	0.5
18	TU	0356	4.0	1028	0.3	1621	3.9	2250	0.2
19	W	0442	4.1	1113	0.2	1704	4.1	2333	0.1
20	TH	0524	4.2	1154	0.1	1744	4.2	●	
21	F	0012	0.1	0604	4.2	1231	0.2	1821	4.1
22	SA	0050	0.2	0640	4.1	1308	0.3	1856	4.0
23	SU	0127	0.4	0715	3.9	1344	0.5	1930	3.9
24	M	0203	0.6	0750	3.8	1420	0.7	2006	3.7
25	TU	0241	0.8	0826	3.6	1457	0.9	2044	3.5
26	W	0323	1.0	0905	3.4	1539	1.1	2128	3.3
27	TH	0412	1.2	0952	3.1	1634	1.3	◐ 2223	3.1
28	F	0516	1.4	1055	3.0	1746	1.4	2343	3.0
29	SA	0630	1.4	1228	2.9	1904	1.4		
30	SU	0119	3.1	0743	1.3	1351	3.1	2013	1.2

Chart Datum: 0·13 metres above Ordnance Datum (Dublin)
HAT is 4·5m above Chart Datum

TIME ZONE (UT)
For Summer Time add ONE hour in **non-shaded areas**

IRELAND – COBH

LAT 51°51′N LONG 8°18′W

TIMES AND HEIGHTS OF HIGH AND LOW WATERS

Dates in amber are **SPRINGS**
Dates in grey are **NEAPS**

2023

MAY

Date	Day	Time	m	Date	Day	Time	m
1		0222	3.3	16		0234	3.7
		0843	1.1			0907	0.6
	M	1446	3.3		TU	1501	3.7
		2107	1.0			2134	0.5
2		0310	3.5	17		0328	3.9
		0932	0.9			1000	0.5
	TU	1530	3.5		W	1552	3.8
		2150	0.8			2224	0.4
3		0350	3.7	18		0416	4.0
		1012	0.7			1047	0.4
	W	1609	3.7		TH	1638	4.0
		2227	0.7			2309	0.3
4		0426	3.8	19		0459	4.0
		1050	0.6			1129	0.4
	TH	1645	3.8		F	1720	4.0
		2302	0.5		●	2350	0.4
5		0500	3.9	20		0539	4.0
		1126	0.5			1208	0.4
	F	1720	3.9		SA	1758	4.0
	○	2337	0.5				
6		0535	3.9	21		0028	0.5
		1202	0.5			0617	3.9
	SA	1755	4.0		SU	1245	0.5
						1834	3.9
7		0014	0.5	22		0104	0.6
		0612	3.9			0652	3.8
	SU	1240	0.5		M	1321	0.6
		1833	4.0			1909	3.8
8		0055	0.5	23		0140	0.7
		0651	3.9			0727	3.7
	M	1320	0.6		TU	1357	0.8
		1912	4.0			1945	3.7
9		0138	0.6	24		0217	0.9
		0734	3.8			0803	3.6
	TU	1404	0.6		W	1434	0.9
		1956	3.9			2024	3.6
10		0226	0.7	25		0258	1.0
		0821	3.7			0843	3.4
	W	1453	0.8		TH	1516	1.1
		2046	3.7			2107	3.4
11		0320	0.8	26		0345	1.2
		0916	3.5			0928	3.3
	TH	1549	0.9		F	1605	1.2
		2145	3.6			2157	3.3
12		0422	1.0	27		0440	1.3
		1018	3.3			1022	3.2
	F	1655	1.0		SA	1705	1.3
	◑	2254	3.4		◐	2256	3.2
13		0533	1.0	28		0544	1.3
		1132	3.2			1127	3.1
	SA	1812	1.0		SU	1811	1.3
14		0015	3.4	29		0006	3.2
		0653	1.0			0648	1.3
	SU	1251	3.3		M	1238	3.2
		1930	0.9			1914	1.2
15		0131	3.5	30		0114	3.3
		0807	0.8			0746	1.1
	M	1403	3.5		TU	1341	3.3
		2037	0.7			2009	1.1
				31		0209	3.4
						0838	1.0
					W	1434	3.5
						2058	0.9

JUNE

Date	Day	Time	m	Date	Day	Time	m
1		0257	3.6	16		0347	3.7
		0927	0.9			1021	0.7
	TH	1521	3.6		F	1612	3.8
		2145	0.8			2247	0.6
2		0342	3.7	17		0435	3.8
		1014	0.7			1107	0.7
	F	1607	3.8		SA	1658	3.8
		2231	0.6			2330	0.6
3		0426	3.8	18		0518	3.8
		1059	0.6			1149	0.7
	SA	1651	3.9		SU	1740	3.8
		2316	0.5		●		
4		0511	3.9	19		0009	0.7
		1144	0.5			0558	3.8
	SU	1735	4.0		M	1226	0.7
	○					1818	3.8
5		0001	0.5	20		0044	0.7
		0556	3.9			0634	3.7
	M	1228	0.5		TU	1301	0.7
		1821	4.0			1854	3.8
6		0046	0.5	21		0119	0.8
		0642	3.9			0709	3.7
	TU	1314	0.5		W	1336	0.8
		1907	4.0			1929	3.7
7		0134	0.5	22		0154	0.9
		0730	3.8			0745	3.6
	W	1402	0.5		TH	1411	0.9
		1956	3.9			2006	3.7
8		0225	0.6	23		0233	1.0
		0821	3.7			0823	3.5
	TH	1453	0.6		F	1449	1.0
		2048	3.8			2046	3.6
9		0319	0.7	24		0315	1.1
		0916	3.6			0905	3.5
	F	1548	0.7		SA	1532	1.1
		2145	3.7			2129	3.5
10		0417	0.8	25		0401	1.2
		1013	3.5			0950	3.4
	SA	1648	0.8		SU	1619	1.1
	◑	2246	3.6			2216	3.4
11		0520	0.8	26		0453	1.2
		1115	3.4			1041	3.4
	SU	1754	0.8		M	1712	1.2
		2352	3.6		◐	2308	3.4
12		0628	0.9	27		0550	1.2
		1221	3.4			1137	3.3
	M	1901	0.8		TU	1812	1.2
13		0058	3.6	28		0006	3.4
		0734	0.8			0650	1.2
	TU	1326	3.5		W	1237	3.4
		2006	0.8			1913	1.2
14		0159	3.6	29		0106	3.4
		0834	0.8			0750	1.1
	W	1426	3.6		TH	1338	3.4
		2104	0.7			2013	1.1
15		0255	3.7	30		0206	3.5
		0929	0.7			0847	1.0
	TH	1521	3.7		F	1437	3.6
		2158	0.7			2111	0.9

JULY

Date	Day	Time	m	Date	Day	Time	m
1		0303	3.6	16		0415	3.6
		0944	0.9			1051	0.9
	SA	1534	3.7		SU	1641	3.7
		2207	0.8			2315	0.8
2		0400	3.7	17		0501	3.7
		1039	0.7			1134	0.8
	SU	1630	3.9		M	1725	3.8
		2301	0.6		●	2354	0.8
3		0454	3.8	18		0542	3.7
		1130	0.6			1211	0.7
	M	1722	4.0		TU	1803	3.8
	○	2352	0.5				
4		0545	3.9	19		0027	0.8
		1219	0.4			0619	3.7
	TU	1811	4.1		W	1243	0.7
						1839	3.8
5		0040	0.4	20		0058	0.8
		0635	4.0			0653	3.7
	W	1306	0.4		TH	1313	0.7
		1900	4.1			1912	3.8
6		0128	0.4	21		0130	0.8
		0724	3.9			0726	3.7
	TH	1354	0.3		F	1345	0.8
		1949	4.1			1945	3.8
7		0217	0.4	22		0204	0.9
		0813	3.9			0800	3.7
	F	1444	0.4		SA	1418	0.9
		2039	4.0			2019	3.7
8		0308	0.5	23		0241	1.0
		0903	3.8			0836	3.6
	SA	1534	0.5		SU	1455	0.9
		2130	3.9			2055	3.7
9		0359	0.6	24		0320	1.0
		0954	3.7			0915	3.6
	SU	1626	0.6		M	1535	1.0
		2222	3.8			2135	3.6
10		0453	0.7	25		0402	1.1
		1046	3.6			0957	3.5
	M	1722	0.7		TU	1620	1.1
	◑	2317	3.6		◐	2220	3.6
11		0551	0.9	26		0450	1.2
		1143	3.5			1046	3.5
	TU	1822	0.8		W	1713	1.2
						2313	3.5
12		0017	3.5	27		0549	1.3
		0653	1.0			1145	3.4
	W	1244	3.4		TH	1818	1.3
		1927	0.9				
13		0120	3.4	28		0015	3.4
		0757	1.0			0701	1.3
	TH	1349	3.4		F	1252	3.4
		2031	1.0			1932	1.2
14		0223	3.4	29		0125	3.4
		0859	1.0			0814	1.2
	F	1453	3.5		SA	1403	3.5
		2133	0.9			2043	1.1
15		0322	3.5	30		0235	3.5
		0959	0.9			0921	1.0
	SA	1551	3.6		SU	1513	3.6
		2229	0.9			2150	0.9
				31		0342	3.6
						1023	0.8
					M	1615	3.8
						2249	0.6

AUGUST

Date	Day	Time	m	Date	Day	Time	m
1		0441	3.8	16		0525	3.8
		1117	0.5			1154	0.7
	TU	1710	4.0		W	1745	3.9
	○	2340	0.4		●		
2		0533	4.0	17		0008	0.7
		1206	0.3			0600	3.8
	W	1759	4.2		TH	1221	0.6
						1819	3.9
3		0028	0.2	18		0034	0.7
		0622	4.1			0632	3.8
	TH	1251	0.2		F	1246	0.7
		1846	4.2			1848	3.9
4		0113	0.2	19		0102	0.7
		0708	4.1			0701	3.8
	F	1337	0.1		SA	1314	0.7
		1932	4.2			1916	3.9
5		0159	0.2	20		0132	0.8
		0753	4.0			0731	3.8
	SA	1422	0.2		SU	1345	0.7
		2017	4.1			1946	3.8
6		0244	0.3	21		0206	0.9
		0838	3.9			0802	3.7
	SU	1508	0.3		M	1419	0.8
		2102	4.0			2018	3.8
7		0330	0.5	22		0240	0.9
		0923	3.8			0836	3.7
	M	1554	0.5		TU	1456	0.9
		2148	3.8			2054	3.7
8		0416	0.7	23		0318	1.1
		1009	3.6			0915	3.6
	TU	1642	0.7		W	1537	1.1
	◑	2236	3.6			2136	3.6
9		0507	0.9	24		0401	1.2
		1100	3.4			1001	3.5
	W	1737	1.0		TH	1627	1.2
		2331	3.4		◐	2227	3.5
10		0606	1.1	25		0458	1.3
		1201	3.3			1102	3.4
	TH	1843	1.2		F	1734	1.4
						2334	3.3
11		0040	3.2	26		0619	1.4
		0717	1.2			1218	3.3
	F	1317	3.2		SA	1858	1.4
		1959	1.2				
12		0155	3.2	27		0055	3.2
		0833	1.2			0747	1.3
	SA	1433	3.3		SU	1342	3.3
		2115	1.2			2023	1.2
13		0303	3.3	28		0219	3.4
		0944	1.1			0903	1.1
	SU	1536	3.4		M	1501	3.6
		2216	1.0			2135	0.9
14		0359	3.5	29		0331	3.6
		1039	0.9			1007	0.7
	M	1626	3.6		TU	1603	3.9
		2303	0.9			2235	0.6
15		0445	3.6	30		0428	3.9
		1121	0.8			1100	0.4
	TU	1709	3.8		W	1655	4.1
		2339	0.8			2324	0.3
				31		0517	4.1
						1147	0.2
					TH	1741	4.3
					○		

Chart Datum: 0·13 metres above Ordnance Datum (Dublin)
HAT is 4·5m above Chart Datum

TIME ZONE (UT)
For Summer Time add ONE hour in **non-shaded areas**

IRELAND – COBH

LAT 51°51'N LONG 8°18'W

TIMES AND HEIGHTS OF HIGH AND LOW WATERS

Dates in amber are **SPRINGS**
Dates in grey are **NEAPS**

2023

SEPTEMBER

Date	Day	Time	m	Time	m	Time	m	Time	m
1	F	0009	0.1	0602	4.2	1231	0.0	1825	4.4
2	SA	0051	0.1	0645	4.2	1313	0.0	1907	4.3
3	SU	0133	0.1	0727	4.1	1355	0.1	1948	4.2
4	M	0214	0.3	0808	4.0	1437	0.3	2029	4.0
5	TU	0256	0.5	0849	3.8	1519	0.6	2110	3.8
6	W	0339	0.7	0931	3.6	1604	0.8	◑ 2154	3.5
7	TH	0426	1.0	1018	3.4	1656	1.1	2245	3.2
8	F	0524	1.3	1120	3.1	1802	1.4	2359	3.0
9	SA	0641	1.4	1253	3.0	1928	1.4		
10	SU	0134	3.0	0812	1.4	1418	3.2	2058	1.3
11	M	0247	3.2	0929	1.1	1519	3.4	2159	1.1
12	TU	0341	3.4	1021	0.9	1606	3.7	2242	0.9
13	W	0424	3.7	1059	0.7	1646	3.8	2316	0.7
14	TH	0502	3.8	1130	0.6	1721	3.9	2342	0.7
15	F ●	0535	3.9	1154	0.6	1751	4.0		
16	SA	0005	0.6	0604	3.9	1216	0.6	1819	4.0
17	SU	0031	0.7	0632	3.9	1242	0.6	1844	3.9
18	M	0101	0.7	0659	3.9	1313	0.7	1912	3.9
19	TU	0133	0.8	0729	3.8	1347	0.8	1943	3.9
20	W	0207	0.9	0802	3.8	1424	0.9	2019	3.8
21	TH	0244	1.0	0840	3.7	1507	1.1	2101	3.6
22	F	0329	1.2	0929	3.5	1600	1.3	◐ 2156	3.4
23	SA	0430	1.4	1034	3.3	1710	1.4	2309	3.2
24	SU	0556	1.5	1158	3.2	1839	1.4		
25	M	0038	3.2	0729	1.3	1332	3.3	2008	1.2
26	TU	0209	3.4	0847	1.0	1450	3.6	2120	0.9
27	W	0318	3.7	0949	0.6	1547	4.0	2216	0.5
28	TH	0410	4.0	1041	0.3	1636	4.2	2304	0.3
29	F	0456	4.2	1126	0.1	1719	4.4	○ 2346	0.1
30	SA	0539	4.3	1208	0.0	1800	4.4		

OCTOBER

Date	Day	Time	m	Time	m	Time	m	Time	m
1	SU	0026	0.1	0620	4.3	1248	0.1	1840	4.3
2	M	0106	0.2	0659	4.2	1328	0.2	1919	4.2
3	TU	0145	0.4	0737	4.0	1408	0.4	1957	4.0
4	W	0225	0.6	0816	3.8	1449	0.7	2035	3.7
5	TH	0307	0.9	0857	3.6	1532	1.0	2116	3.5
6	F	0353	1.1	0943	3.3	1623	1.3	◑ 2205	3.2
7	SA	0451	1.4	1045	3.1	1729	1.5	2316	3.0
8	SU	0609	1.5	1226	3.0	1855	1.6		
9	M	0105	2.9	0742	1.4	1354	3.1	2025	1.4
10	TU	0221	3.2	0857	1.2	1452	3.4	2125	1.2
11	W	0312	3.4	0946	1.0	1537	3.6	2207	0.9
12	TH	0354	3.7	1024	0.8	1615	3.8	2240	0.8
13	F	0430	3.8	1054	0.7	1649	3.9	2308	0.7
14	SA	0503	3.9	1120	0.6	1719	4.0	● 2334	0.7
15	SU	0533	4.0	1146	0.6	1746	4.0		
16	M	0002	0.7	0602	4.0	1214	0.7	1814	4.0
17	TU	0034	0.7	0631	4.0	1248	0.7	1844	4.0
18	W	0107	0.8	0704	3.9	1324	0.8	1919	3.9
19	TH	0144	0.9	0740	3.9	1405	0.9	1958	3.8
20	F	0226	1.0	0824	3.7	1453	1.1	2045	3.6
21	SA	0318	1.2	0918	3.6	1550	1.3	2144	3.4
22	SU	0424	1.3	1025	3.4	1702	1.4	◐ 2258	3.2
23	M	0546	1.4	1150	3.3	1827	1.4		
24	TU	0027	3.2	0713	1.2	1320	3.5	1952	1.1
25	W	0152	3.5	0828	0.9	1430	3.8	2059	0.8
26	TH	0256	3.8	0927	0.6	1525	4.0	2153	0.6
27	F	0348	4.0	1018	0.4	1613	4.2	2240	0.4
28	SA	0434	4.2	1104	0.3	1656	4.3	○ 2323	0.3
29	SU	0516	4.3	1147	0.2	1737	4.3		
30	M	0003	0.3	0557	4.3	1226	0.3	1816	4.2
31	TU	0042	0.4	0635	4.2	1306	0.5	1853	4.1

NOVEMBER

Date	Day	Time	m	Time	m	Time	m	Time	m
1	W	0120	0.6	0713	4.0	1345	0.7	1929	3.9
2	TH	0159	0.8	0751	3.8	1424	0.9	2006	3.7
3	F	0240	1.0	0831	3.6	1507	1.2	2047	3.5
4	SA	0325	1.2	0918	3.4	1556	1.4	2134	3.2
5	SU	0422	1.4	1015	3.2	1658	1.6	◑ 2235	3.1
6	M	0533	1.5	1137	3.1	1813	1.6		
7	TU	0006	3.0	0653	1.5	1305	3.2	1929	1.5
8	W	0131	3.2	0802	1.3	1407	3.4	2029	1.3
9	TH	0227	3.4	0854	1.1	1454	3.6	2116	1.1
10	F	0312	3.6	0936	1.0	1534	3.8	2155	0.9
11	SA	0351	3.8	1012	0.8	1610	3.9	2230	0.8
12	SU	0427	3.9	1046	0.8	1644	4.0	2305	0.7
13	M	0502	4.0	1120	0.7	1716	4.0	● 2340	0.7
14	TU	0536	4.0	1156	0.7	1750	4.0		
15	W	0015	0.7	0613	4.1	1233	0.7	1827	4.0
16	TH	0054	0.8	0651	4.0	1314	0.8	1907	3.9
17	F	0136	0.8	0733	4.0	1400	0.9	1951	3.8
18	SA	0224	1.0	0822	3.8	1451	1.0	2043	3.7
19	SU	0319	1.1	0918	3.7	1549	1.2	2143	3.5
20	M	0422	1.2	1024	3.6	1656	1.2	◐ 2251	3.4
21	TU	0535	1.2	1138	3.5	1812	1.2		
22	W	0008	3.4	0652	1.1	1254	3.6	1928	1.1
23	TH	0123	3.5	0802	0.9	1400	3.8	2032	0.9
24	F	0226	3.8	0902	0.7	1457	4.0	2127	0.7
25	SA	0321	3.9	0955	0.6	1547	4.1	2217	0.6
26	SU	0410	4.1	1044	0.5	1634	4.1	2302	0.6
27	M	0456	4.1	1128	0.5	1717	4.1	○ 2344	0.6
28	TU	0538	4.2	1210	0.6	1756	4.1		
29	W	0023	0.6	0618	4.1	1248	0.7	1834	4.0
30	TH	0101	0.7	0656	4.0	1326	0.8	1910	3.9

DECEMBER

Date	Day	Time	m	Time	m	Time	m	Time	m
1	F	0139	0.9	0734	3.9	1404	1.0	1946	3.7
2	SA	0217	1.0	0813	3.7	1444	1.2	2025	3.6
3	SU	0300	1.2	0857	3.6	1529	1.3	2109	3.4
4	M	0348	1.3	0946	3.4	1621	1.5	2200	3.3
5	TU	0446	1.4	1043	3.3	1721	1.5	◑ 2302	3.2
6	W	0551	1.5	1149	3.3	1826	1.5		
7	TH	0012	3.2	0656	1.4	1256	3.4	1927	1.4
8	F	0119	3.4	0753	1.3	1353	3.5	2021	1.3
9	SA	0215	3.5	0844	1.2	1442	3.6	2110	1.1
10	SU	0304	3.7	0932	1.0	1528	3.8	2156	1.0
11	M	0350	3.8	1017	0.9	1611	3.9	2241	0.9
12	TU	0435	4.0	1102	0.8	1654	4.0	● 2324	0.8
13	W	0519	4.1	1145	0.7	1736	4.0		
14	TH	0006	0.7	0602	4.1	1228	0.7	1819	4.0
15	F	0049	0.7	0647	4.1	1312	0.7	1904	4.0
16	SA	0134	0.7	0733	4.1	1359	0.8	1951	3.9
17	SU	0222	0.8	0823	4.0	1449	0.8	2042	3.8
18	M	0315	0.8	0916	3.9	1543	0.9	2136	3.7
19	TU	0411	0.9	1013	3.8	1640	1.0	◐ 2234	3.6
20	W	0512	1.0	1113	3.7	1744	1.1	2337	3.5
21	TH	0619	1.0	1218	3.7	1852	1.1		
22	F	0043	3.5	0728	1.0	1323	3.7	1958	1.1
23	SA	0150	3.6	0832	1.0	1425	3.7	2059	1.0
24	SU	0252	3.7	0932	0.9	1522	3.8	2155	0.9
25	M	0349	3.8	1027	0.8	1614	3.9	2246	0.8
26	TU	0440	3.9	1115	0.8	1701	3.9	2330	0.8
27	W	0525	4.0	1158	0.8	1743	3.9	○	
28	TH	0010	0.7	0606	4.0	1235	0.8	1821	3.9
29	F	0046	0.8	0644	4.0	1311	0.9	1856	3.9
30	SA	0121	0.8	0720	3.9	1345	1.0	1930	3.8
31	SU	0156	0.9	0757	3.8	1420	1.1	2006	3.7

Chart Datum: 0·13 metres above Ordnance Datum (Dublin)
HAT is 4·5m above Chart Datum

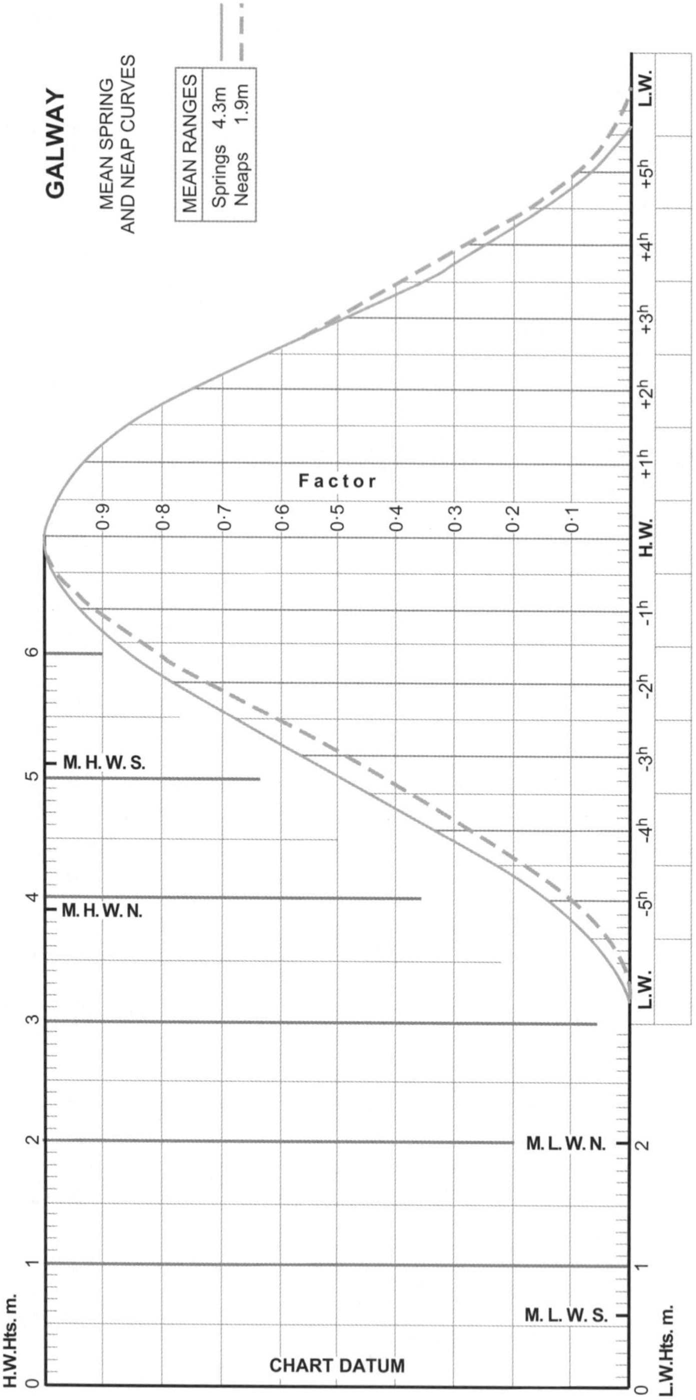
GALWAY
MEAN SPRING AND NEAP CURVES
MEAN RANGES
Springs 4.3m
Neaps 1.9m
Factor
0·9
0·8
0·7
0·6
0·5
0·4
0·3
0·2
0·1
L.W.
-5h
-4h
-3h
-2h
-1h
H.W.
+1h
+2h
+3h
+4h
+5h
L.W.
H.W.Hts. m.
M. H. W. S.
M. H. W. N.
CHART DATUM
M. L. W. N.
M. L. W. S.
L.W.Hts. m.

TIME ZONE (UT)
For Summer Time add ONE hour in **non-shaded areas**

IRELAND – GALWAY

LAT 53°16′N LONG 9°03′W

TIMES AND HEIGHTS OF HIGH AND LOW WATERS

Dates in amber are **SPRINGS**
Dates in grey are **NEAPS**

2023

JANUARY

Date	Day	Time	m
1	SU	0033 0635 1300 1906	4.2 1.9 4.2 1.8
2	M	0139 0743 1404 2006	4.2 1.9 4.2 1.8
3	TU	0234 0840 1459 2056	4.3 1.8 4.3 1.8
4	W	0321 0928 1546 2137	4.5 1.6 4.4 1.7
5	TH	0403 1007 1628 2213	4.6 1.5 4.6 1.6
6	F	0441 1042 1707 ○ 2248	4.8 1.4 4.7 1.5
7	SA	0518 1115 1745 2324	4.9 1.3 4.7 1.4
8	SU	0556 1150 1823	4.9 1.2 4.8
9	M	0000 0632 1225 1859	1.4 4.9 1.2 4.7
10	TU	0034 0708 1300 1936	1.4 4.9 1.2 4.6
11	W	0108 0741 1335 2012	1.5 4.7 1.3 4.5
12	TH	0144 0814 1411 2049	1.6 4.6 1.4 4.4
13	F	0223 0853 1452 2131	1.7 4.5 1.6 4.2
14	SA	0308 0940 1538 2220	1.9 4.3 1.7 4.1
15	SU	0400 1034 1632 ◑ 2316	2.0 4.2 1.9 4.1
16	M	0500 1136 1735	2.1 4.2 1.9
17	TU	0018 0614 1244 1855	4.2 2.1 4.2 1.9
18	W	0125 0742 1356 2015	4.3 1.9 4.4 1.7
19	TH	0229 0848 1502 2113	4.6 1.5 4.6 1.5
20	F	0326 0942 1558 2203	4.9 1.2 4.9 1.2
21	SA	0418 1030 1650 ● 2250	5.2 0.9 5.2 1.0
22	SU	0508 1117 1740 2335	5.5 0.6 5.3 0.8
23	M	0557 1202 1828	5.6 0.5 5.4
24	TU	0019 0645 1246 1916	0.8 5.7 0.5 5.3
25	W	0103 0732 1330 2003	0.8 5.5 0.6 5.2
26	TH	0148 0819 1415 2050	1.0 5.3 0.9 4.9
27	F	0235 0907 1503 2139	1.3 5.0 1.2 4.6
28	SA	0329 0957 1557 ◐ 2231	1.6 4.6 1.6 4.3
29	SU	0433 1055 1702 2332	1.9 4.2 1.9 4.1
30	M	0548 1211 1816	2.1 4.0 2.1
31	TU	0056 0703 1340 1928	4.0 2.1 3.9 2.2

FEBRUARY

Date	Day	Time	m
1	W	0213 0813 1447 2030	4.0 2.0 4.0 2.1
2	TH	0309 0911 1538 2120	4.2 1.8 4.2 1.9
3	F	0354 0954 1620 2200	4.5 1.6 4.4 1.7
4	SA	0433 1029 1657 2236	4.7 1.4 4.6 1.5
5	SU	0509 1101 1732 ○ 2310	4.8 1.2 4.8 1.3
6	M	0544 1133 1807 2343	5.0 1.0 4.8 1.2
7	TU	0618 1205 1840	5.0 0.9 4.9
8	W	0015 0650 1236 1912	1.1 5.0 0.9 4.8
9	TH	0046 0717 1308 1941	1.1 4.9 1.0 4.7
10	F	0120 0744 1342 2012	1.2 4.8 1.1 4.6
11	SA	0156 0818 1420 2049	1.3 4.7 1.2 4.5
12	SU	0237 0901 1502 2135	1.5 4.5 1.5 4.3
13	M	0323 0954 1551 ◑ 2232	1.7 4.3 1.7 4.1
14	TU	0418 1059 1649 2338	1.9 4.1 2.0 4.0
15	W	0527 1214 1809	2.1 4.0 2.1
16	TH	0055 0724 1339 2011	4.1 2.0 4.1 1.9
17	F	0213 0847 1455 2112	4.4 1.6 4.4 1.6
18	SA	0317 0940 1552 2200	4.8 1.1 4.8 1.2
19	SU	0410 1026 1642 2243	5.2 0.7 5.2 0.8
20	M	0457 1107 1727 ● 2323	5.5 0.4 5.4 0.6
21	TU	0543 1147 1811	5.7 0.2 5.5
22	W	0002 0627 1225 1853	0.5 5.8 0.2 5.5
23	TH	0041 0709 1302 1935	0.5 5.6 0.4 5.3
24	F	0119 0751 1341 2016	0.7 5.3 0.7 5.0
25	SA	0200 0834 1422 2058	1.0 5.0 1.1 4.7
26	SU	0245 0919 1508 2143	1.4 4.6 1.6 4.3
27	M	0343 1009 1609 ◐ 2233	1.8 4.1 2.0 4.0
28	TU	0508 1109 1739 2336	2.1 3.8 2.3 3.8

MARCH

Date	Day	Time	m
1	W	0629 1323 1855	2.2 3.7 2.4
2	TH	0158 0742 1436 2002	3.8 2.1 3.8 2.2
3	F	0257 0846 1525 2056	4.0 1.9 4.1 2.0
4	SA	0341 0930 1605 2138	4.3 1.6 4.3 1.6
5	SU	0418 1004 1640 2215	4.6 1.3 4.6 1.4
6	M	0452 1037 1712 2248	4.8 1.0 4.8 1.1
7	TU	0524 1109 1744 ○ 2320	4.9 0.8 4.9 0.9
8	W	0555 1139 1814 2350	5.0 0.7 4.9 0.8
9	TH	0624 1208 1842	5.0 0.7 4.9
10	F	0020 0649 1239 1909	0.8 5.0 0.7 4.9
11	SA	0054 0716 1314 1939	0.9 4.9 0.8 4.8
12	SU	0130 0750 1351 2015	1.0 4.8 1.0 4.6
13	M	0210 0832 1432 2059	1.2 4.5 1.3 4.4
14	TU	0256 0926 1520 2157	1.5 4.2 1.7 4.1
15	W	0351 1035 1620 ◑ 2309	1.8 3.9 2.0 3.9
16	TH	0503 1158 1751	2.0 3.8 2.2
17	F	0036 0735 1336 2013	4.0 1.9 4.0 1.9
18	SA	0205 0844 1451 2106	4.3 1.4 4.4 1.5
19	SU	0308 0931 1543 2149	4.7 0.9 4.8 1.0
20	M	0357 1012 1627 2227	5.2 0.5 5.2 0.6
21	TU	0441 1049 1708 ● 2304	5.5 0.2 5.4 0.4
22	W	0523 1124 1747 2339	5.6 0.1 5.5 0.3
23	TH	0604 1158 1826	5.6 0.2 5.4
24	F	0014 0644 1231 1904	0.4 5.5 0.5 5.3
25	SA	0050 0724 1307 1943	0.6 5.2 0.8 5.0
26	SU	0128 0805 1345 2023	1.0 4.8 1.2 4.7
27	M	0210 0849 1427 2106	1.3 4.4 1.7 4.3
28	TU	0301 0937 1519 2155	1.8 4.0 2.1 4.0
29	W	0435 1032 1708 ◐ 2252	2.1 3.7 2.4 3.7
30	TH	0558 1259 1826	2.2 3.5 2.4
31	F	0131 0707 1413 1930	3.6 2.1 3.7 2.2

APRIL

Date	Day	Time	m
1	SA	0232 0807 1501 2025	3.9 1.8 4.0 1.9
2	SU	0315 0854 1539 2109	4.2 1.5 4.3 1.6
3	M	0351 0933 1612 2147	4.4 1.2 4.5 1.3
4	TU	0424 1007 1643 2221	4.6 0.9 4.7 1.0
5	W	0455 1039 1712 2252	4.8 0.7 4.9 0.8
6	TH	0525 1108 1741 ○ 2321	4.9 0.6 4.9 0.7
7	F	0553 1138 1809 2353	5.0 0.6 5.0 0.6
8	SA	0621 1211 1838	5.0 0.6 5.0
9	SU	0029 0654 1247 1912	0.7 4.9 0.8 4.9
10	M	0108 0732 1326 1952	0.8 4.7 1.0 4.7
11	TU	0150 0818 1410 2039	1.0 4.5 1.4 4.4
12	W	0239 0915 1501 2139	1.3 4.1 1.7 4.1
13	TH	0338 1027 1609 ◑ 2254	1.6 3.9 2.1 4.0
14	F	0458 1153 1800	1.8 3.8 2.1
15	SA	0024 0724 1330 1957	4.0 1.6 4.0 1.8
16	SU	0151 0826 1436 2048	4.3 1.2 4.4 1.3
17	M	0250 0912 1523 2129	4.7 0.8 4.8 0.9
18	TU	0337 0951 1605 2206	5.0 0.5 5.1 0.6
19	W	0420 1025 1644 2241	5.3 0.4 5.3 0.5
20	TH	0501 1057 1722 ● 2315	5.4 0.4 5.3 0.4
21	F	0541 1129 1759 2349	5.3 0.5 5.3 0.5
22	SA	0620 1202 1835	5.2 0.7 5.1
23	SU	0024 0700 1238 1914	0.7 4.9 1.0 4.9
24	M	0103 0741 1316 1955	1.0 4.7 1.4 4.6
25	TU	0146 0825 1357 2038	1.4 4.3 1.7 4.3
26	W	0236 0912 1445 2127	1.7 4.0 2.1 4.1
27	TH	0359 1005 1634 ◐ 2221	2.0 3.8 2.4 3.8
28	F	0523 1108 1752 2324	2.1 3.6 2.4 3.7
29	SA	0628 1330 1854	2.0 3.6 2.2
30	SU	0146 0726 1421 1949	3.7 1.8 3.9 2.0

Chart Datum: 0·20 metres above Ordnance Datum (Dublin)
HAT is 5·9m above Chart Datum

TIME ZONE (UT)
For Summer Time add ONE hour in **non-shaded areas**

IRELAND – GALWAY

LAT 53°16′N LONG 9°03′W

TIMES AND HEIGHTS OF HIGH AND LOW WATERS

Dates in amber are **SPRINGS**
Dates in grey are **NEAPS**

2023

MAY

Date	Day	Time	m	Time	m	Time	m	Time	m
1	M	0235	4.0	0815	1.5	1500	4.1	2034	1.7
2	TU	0313	4.2	0857	1.3	1533	4.4	2114	1.4
3	W	0346	4.5	0933	1.0	1603	4.6	2149	1.1
4	TH	0417	4.7	1006	0.9	1632	4.8	2220	0.9
5	F	0448	4.8	1036	0.7	1704	5.0	○ 2252	0.7
6	SA	0522	4.9	1108	0.7	1737	5.0	2328	0.6
7	SU	0558	5.0	1145	0.7	1814	5.0		
8	M	0008	0.7	0640	4.9	1225	0.9	1856	5.0
9	TU	0051	0.8	0725	4.7	1309	1.1	1941	4.8
10	W	0138	1.0	0816	4.5	1358	1.4	2033	4.5
11	TH	0232	1.2	0915	4.2	1456	1.7	2135	4.3
12	F	0335	1.4	1024	4.0	1609	1.9	◑ 2246	4.1
13	SA	0454	1.6	1143	4.0	1746	1.9		
14	SU	0007	4.1	0645	1.5	1305	4.1	1923	1.7
15	M	0124	4.3	0754	1.2	1407	4.4	2019	1.4
16	TU	0224	4.6	0843	1.0	1456	4.7	2103	1.1
17	W	0313	4.8	0924	0.8	1539	4.9	2143	0.9
18	TH	0358	4.9	0959	0.8	1619	5.0	2219	0.8
19	F	0440	5.0	1032	0.8	1657	5.1	● 2253	0.8
20	SA	0521	5.0	1104	0.9	1734	5.1	2329	0.8
21	SU	0601	4.9	1139	1.1	1812	5.0		
22	M	0006	1.0	0641	4.7	1216	1.3	1852	4.8
23	TU	0046	1.1	0722	4.5	1256	1.5	1932	4.6
24	W	0129	1.4	0805	4.3	1337	1.8	2015	4.4
25	TH	0216	1.6	0850	4.1	1423	2.0	2101	4.2
26	F	0314	1.8	0939	3.9	1529	2.2	2151	4.0
27	SA	0429	1.9	1033	3.8	1703	2.3	◐ 2246	3.8
28	SU	0539	1.9	1134	3.7	1810	2.2	2347	3.8
29	M	0639	1.8	1254	3.8	1906	2.0		
30	TU	0106	3.9	0731	1.7	1356	4.0	1954	1.8
31	W	0210	4.1	0816	1.5	1437	4.3	2036	1.5

JUNE

Date	Day	Time	m	Time	m	Time	m	Time	m
1	TH	0253	4.3	0855	1.3	1514	4.5	2114	1.3
2	F	0333	4.6	0931	1.1	1551	4.8	2150	1.0
3	SA	0413	4.8	1006	1.0	1630	5.0	2228	0.9
4	SU	0456	4.9	1045	0.9	1713	5.1	○ 2310	0.7
5	M	0541	5.0	1127	0.9	1758	5.1	2355	0.7
6	TU	0629	4.9	1213	1.0	1845	5.1		
7	W	0042	0.7	0719	4.8	1301	1.1	1935	5.0
8	TH	0132	0.8	0812	4.7	1353	1.3	2029	4.8
9	F	0227	1.0	0909	4.5	1452	1.5	2126	4.6
10	SA	0327	1.2	1011	4.3	1558	1.7	◑ 2230	4.4
11	SU	0434	1.3	1118	4.2	1713	1.7	2340	4.3
12	M	0549	1.4	1229	4.2	1833	1.7		
13	TU	0051	4.3	0707	1.4	1333	4.3	1941	1.5
14	W	0155	4.4	0807	1.3	1427	4.5	2035	1.4
15	TH	0250	4.5	0856	1.3	1514	4.6	2122	1.2
16	F	0338	4.6	0937	1.3	1557	4.8	2203	1.1
17	SA	0423	4.6	1013	1.3	1638	4.8	2240	1.1
18	SU	0506	4.7	1048	1.3	1717	4.9	● 2316	1.1
19	M	0546	4.7	1125	1.3	1756	4.9	2354	1.1
20	TU	0626	4.6	1203	1.4	1835	4.8		
21	W	0032	1.2	0706	4.5	1241	1.5	1915	4.7
22	TH	0111	1.3	0746	4.4	1319	1.6	1954	4.6
23	F	0151	1.4	0827	4.3	1358	1.8	2035	4.4
24	SA	0233	1.6	0910	4.2	1440	1.9	2118	4.2
25	SU	0317	1.7	0956	4.0	1529	2.1	2205	4.1
26	M	0407	1.8	1045	3.9	1629	2.1	◐ 2256	4.0
27	TU	0507	1.9	1139	3.9	1744	2.1	2352	4.0
28	W	0617	1.8	1237	4.0	1856	2.0		
29	TH	0054	4.0	0722	1.7	1335	4.2	1953	1.8
30	F	0157	4.2	0815	1.6	1429	4.5	2042	1.5

JULY

Date	Day	Time	m	Time	m	Time	m	Time	m
1	SA	0255	4.4	0902	1.4	1519	4.7	2128	1.2
2	SU	0347	4.7	0947	1.2	1607	5.0	2214	1.0
3	M	0438	4.9	1033	1.0	1656	5.2	○ 2301	0.8
4	TU	0528	5.0	1119	1.0	1745	5.3	2348	0.6
5	W	0618	5.1	1206	0.9	1834	5.4		
6	TH	0036	0.6	0708	5.0	1254	1.0	1924	5.3
7	F	0124	0.6	0759	4.9	1343	1.1	2015	5.1
8	SA	0214	0.7	0851	4.8	1435	1.2	2108	4.9
9	SU	0306	1.0	0945	4.6	1533	1.4	2204	4.7
10	M	0403	1.2	1044	4.4	1637	1.6	◑ 2305	4.4
11	TU	0506	1.5	1148	4.2	1748	1.7		
12	W	0016	4.2	0616	1.7	1258	4.2	1902	1.8
13	TH	0128	4.1	0728	1.8	1402	4.2	2010	1.7
14	F	0232	4.2	0830	1.8	1457	4.4	2107	1.6
15	SA	0326	4.3	0920	1.7	1545	4.5	2154	1.4
16	SU	0413	4.4	1001	1.6	1627	4.7	2232	1.3
17	M	0456	4.5	1037	1.5	1706	4.8	● 2305	1.2
18	TU	0535	4.6	1112	1.4	1744	4.9	2339	1.1
19	W	0612	4.6	1147	1.3	1821	4.9		
20	TH	0012	1.1	0649	4.6	1222	1.3	1858	4.8
21	F	0047	1.1	0725	4.6	1256	1.4	1932	4.7
22	SA	0122	1.1	0800	4.5	1330	1.5	2005	4.6
23	SU	0157	1.3	0835	4.4	1406	1.6	2039	4.4
24	M	0234	1.4	0914	4.2	1447	1.7	2120	4.3
25	TU	0316	1.6	0958	4.1	1534	1.9	◐ 2209	4.1
26	W	0404	1.7	1050	4.0	1628	2.0	2307	4.0
27	TH	0459	1.9	1148	4.0	1734	2.1		
28	F	0011	4.0	0608	1.9	1252	4.1	1906	2.0
29	SA	0121	4.1	0744	1.9	1358	4.3	2025	1.7
30	SU	0232	4.3	0851	1.6	1459	4.7	2121	1.3
31	M	0333	4.6	0942	1.3	1553	5.0	2210	0.9

AUGUST

Date	Day	Time	m	Time	m	Time	m	Time	m
1	TU	0426	4.9	1029	1.0	1643	5.3	○ 2256	0.6
2	W	0516	5.1	1113	0.8	1732	5.5	2340	0.4
3	TH	0604	5.3	1156	0.7	1819	5.6		
4	F	0023	0.3	0651	5.3	1239	0.6	1907	5.6
5	SA	0106	0.3	0737	5.2	1323	0.8	1953	5.4
6	SU	0149	0.6	0823	5.0	1409	1.0	2041	5.1
7	M	0236	0.9	0911	4.7	1459	1.3	2131	4.7
8	TU	0326	1.3	1001	4.4	1558	1.6	◑ 2226	4.3
9	W	0426	1.7	1059	4.1	1712	1.9	2336	4.0
10	TH	0539	2.0	1220	3.9	1831	2.0		
11	F	0110	3.8	0657	2.1	1347	4.0	1949	1.9
12	SA	0224	3.9	0808	2.1	1449	4.2	2057	1.8
13	SU	0320	4.1	0905	1.9	1537	4.4	2144	1.5
14	M	0405	4.3	0947	1.7	1618	4.6	2217	1.3
15	TU	0444	4.5	1021	1.5	1654	4.8	2247	1.1
16	W	0519	4.6	1054	1.3	1729	4.9	● 2317	0.9
17	TH	0553	4.7	1126	1.1	1803	4.9	2348	0.9
18	F	0626	4.8	1158	1.1	1836	4.9		
19	SA	0019	0.8	0658	4.7	1229	1.1	1905	4.8
20	SU	0051	0.9	0727	4.7	1301	1.1	1931	4.7
21	M	0124	1.0	0756	4.5	1336	1.3	2000	4.6
22	TU	0200	1.2	0830	4.4	1414	1.4	2038	4.4
23	W	0239	1.4	0912	4.2	1458	1.7	2128	4.2
24	TH	0324	1.7	1005	4.1	1550	1.9	◐ 2230	4.0
25	F	0418	1.9	1109	4.0	1653	2.1	2342	3.8
26	SA	0527	2.1	1221	4.0	1843	2.0		
27	SU	0101	3.9	0742	2.0	1339	4.2	2023	1.7
28	M	0225	4.2	0848	1.7	1448	4.6	2116	1.2
29	TU	0327	4.6	0936	1.2	1543	5.0	2202	0.7
30	W	0416	5.0	1019	0.8	1631	5.4	2243	0.3
31	TH	0501	5.3	1059	0.5	1716	5.7	○ 2323	0.1

Chart Datum: 0·20 metres above Ordnance Datum (Dublin)
HAT is 5·9m above Chart Datum

TIME ZONE (UT)
For Summer Time add ONE hour in **non-shaded areas**

IRELAND – GALWAY

LAT 53°16′N LONG 9°03′W

TIMES AND HEIGHTS OF HIGH AND LOW WATERS

Dates in amber are **SPRINGS**
Dates in grey are **NEAPS**

2023

SEPTEMBER

Day	Time m	Day	Time m
1 F	0545 5.4 1138 0.4 1800 5.8	16 SA	0557 4.9 1131 0.9 1808 4.9 2349 0.7
2 SA	0001 0.1 0627 5.5 1216 0.4 1843 5.7	17 SU	0626 4.8 1201 0.9 1834 4.9
3 SU	0039 0.2 0709 5.3 1256 0.6 1927 5.4	18 M	0019 0.7 0653 4.8 1233 0.9 1858 4.8
4 M	0118 0.5 0751 5.1 1337 0.9 2011 5.0	19 TU	0053 0.9 0719 4.7 1308 1.1 1928 4.6
5 TU	0200 0.9 0834 4.7 1423 1.3 2057 4.6	20 W	0129 1.1 0752 4.6 1347 1.3 2008 4.4
6 W	0246 1.4 0920 4.4 1520 1.7 ◑ 2149 4.2	21 TH	0208 1.4 0834 4.3 1430 1.5 2058 4.2
7 TH	0346 1.9 1011 4.1 1643 2.0 2252 3.8	22 F	0253 1.7 0930 4.1 1522 1.8 ◐ 2206 3.9
8 F	0511 2.2 1117 3.8 1806 2.1	23 SA	0349 2.0 1040 3.9 1630 2.0 2324 3.7
9 SA	0102 3.6 0631 2.3 1336 3.8 1924 2.0	24 SU	0508 2.2 1159 3.9 1904 2.0
10 SU	0216 3.8 0742 2.2 1437 4.1 2038 1.8	25 M	0055 3.8 0743 2.0 1327 4.2 2015 1.5
11 M	0307 4.0 0840 2.0 1522 4.3 2119 1.5	26 TU	0223 4.2 0839 1.6 1438 4.6 2104 1.0
12 TU	0348 4.3 0922 1.7 1600 4.6 2149 1.2	27 W	0317 4.7 0922 1.1 1529 5.1 2145 0.5
13 W	0424 4.5 0957 1.4 1634 4.7 2219 1.0	28 TH	0400 5.1 1001 0.7 1613 5.4 2223 0.2
14 TH	0456 4.7 1029 1.1 1707 4.9 2249 0.8	29 F	0441 5.4 1038 0.4 1655 5.7 ○ 2259 0.1
15 F	0527 4.8 1101 1.0 1738 4.9 ● 2319 0.7	30 SA	0521 5.5 1114 0.3 1737 5.7 2334 0.1

OCTOBER

Day	Time m	Day	Time m
1 SU	0600 5.5 1151 0.4 1818 5.6	16 M	0552 4.9 1133 0.8 1805 4.9 2350 0.8
2 M	0009 0.4 0640 5.3 1228 0.6 1900 5.3	17 TU	0620 4.9 1207 0.8 1834 4.8
3 TU	0046 0.7 0719 5.1 1308 0.9 1943 4.9	18 W	0025 0.9 0651 4.8 1245 1.0 1909 4.7
4 W	0126 1.1 0801 4.8 1352 1.3 2029 4.5	19 TH	0103 1.1 0728 4.7 1326 1.2 1953 4.4
5 TH	0210 1.6 0845 4.4 1447 1.7 2119 4.1	20 F	0145 1.4 0813 4.5 1412 1.4 2047 4.1
6 F	0308 2.1 0935 4.1 1618 2.0 ◑ 2218 3.7	21 SA	0233 1.8 0910 4.2 1508 1.7 2156 3.9
7 SA	0446 2.4 1034 3.8 1739 2.1	22 SU	0336 2.1 1022 4.0 1623 1.9 ◐ 2314 3.8
8 SU	0043 3.6 0604 2.4 1311 3.7 1848 2.0	23 M	0507 2.2 1143 4.0 1848 1.8
9 M	0153 3.8 0709 2.3 1411 4.0 1950 1.8	24 TU	0048 3.9 0724 2.0 1311 4.2 1955 1.4
10 TU	0242 4.0 0806 2.0 1455 4.2 2037 1.5	25 W	0206 4.3 0818 1.5 1418 4.6 2042 0.9
11 W	0321 4.3 0850 1.7 1533 4.5 2114 1.2	26 TH	0256 4.7 0901 1.1 1508 5.0 2122 0.6
12 TH	0355 4.5 0928 1.4 1606 4.7 2148 1.0	27 F	0338 5.1 0939 0.8 1552 5.3 2158 0.4
13 F	0426 4.7 1001 1.1 1637 4.8 2219 0.8	28 SA	0417 5.3 1015 0.6 1634 5.5 ○ 2233 0.4
14 SA	0455 4.8 1033 1.0 1708 4.9 ● 2249 0.7	29 SU	0456 5.4 1051 0.5 1715 5.4 2306 0.5
15 SU	0523 4.9 1102 0.8 1737 4.9 2318 0.7	30 M	0534 5.4 1127 0.6 1756 5.3 2342 0.7
		31 TU	0613 5.3 1205 0.8 1838 5.1

NOVEMBER

Day	Time m	Day	Time m
1 W	0019 1.0 0653 5.0 1246 1.0 1921 4.8	16 TH	0003 1.0 0634 5.0 1228 1.0 1902 4.7
2 TH	0059 1.4 0734 4.8 1331 1.4 2006 4.4	17 F	0046 1.2 0717 4.8 1313 1.1 1950 4.5
3 F	0144 1.8 0819 4.5 1425 1.7 2055 4.1	18 SA	0132 1.5 0806 4.7 1404 1.3 2045 4.3
4 SA	0240 2.1 0907 4.2 1544 2.0 2150 3.8	19 SU	0226 1.8 0903 4.4 1503 1.5 2149 4.1
5 SU	0412 2.4 1002 3.9 1703 2.1 ◑ 2300 3.6	20 M	0332 2.0 1009 4.3 1615 1.7 ◐ 2301 4.0
6 M	0529 2.4 1109 3.8 1807 2.0	21 TU	0454 2.0 1122 4.2 1750 1.6
7 TU	0109 3.7 0632 2.3 1325 3.9 1905 1.9	22 W	0021 4.1 0638 1.9 1241 4.3 1917 1.4
8 W	0202 3.9 0727 2.1 1415 4.1 1955 1.6	23 TH	0132 4.4 0745 1.6 1349 4.6 2011 1.2
9 TH	0243 4.2 0814 1.8 1455 4.3 2037 1.4	24 F	0227 4.6 0834 1.3 1443 4.8 2055 1.0
10 F	0317 4.4 0855 1.5 1529 4.5 2114 1.2	25 SA	0312 4.9 0916 1.0 1531 5.0 2134 0.9
11 SA	0348 4.6 0931 1.3 1601 4.7 2148 1.0	26 SU	0354 5.1 0956 0.9 1615 5.1 2210 0.9
12 SU	0417 4.8 1004 1.1 1633 4.8 2218 0.9	27 M	0434 5.2 1034 0.9 1658 5.1 ○ 2246 1.0
13 M	0448 4.9 1035 1.0 1706 4.9 ● 2250 0.9	28 TU	0514 5.2 1112 0.9 1740 5.0 2323 1.1
14 TU	0520 5.0 1109 0.9 1741 4.9 2325 0.9	29 W	0553 5.1 1151 1.0 1823 4.9
15 W	0555 5.0 1147 0.9 1819 4.9	30 TH	0002 1.3 0634 5.0 1232 1.2 1905 4.7

DECEMBER

Day	Time m	Day	Time m
1 F	0043 1.5 0715 4.8 1315 1.4 1949 4.5	16 SA	0038 1.2 0710 5.1 1307 1.0 1945 4.8
2 SA	0126 1.8 0758 4.6 1403 1.6 2034 4.3	17 SU	0127 1.3 0759 5.0 1358 1.1 2037 4.6
3 SU	0215 2.0 0843 4.4 1459 1.8 2122 4.1	18 M	0220 1.5 0852 4.8 1453 1.2 2134 4.5
4 M	0316 2.2 0933 4.2 1606 2.0 2216 3.9	19 TU	0319 1.7 0951 4.6 1553 1.4 ◐ 2235 4.3
5 TU	0434 2.3 1027 4.0 1715 2.0 ◑ 2316 3.8	20 W	0425 1.8 1055 4.5 1701 1.5 2343 4.3
6 W	0543 2.3 1128 3.9 1816 2.0	21 TH	0540 1.8 1206 4.4 1817 1.6
7 TH	0033 3.9 0643 2.2 1247 3.9 1910 1.9	22 F	0053 4.3 0659 1.7 1318 4.4 1931 1.5
8 F	0139 4.0 0735 2.0 1355 4.1 1958 1.7	23 SA	0156 4.5 0805 1.6 1420 4.5 2029 1.5
9 SA	0224 4.3 0820 1.8 1441 4.3 2040 1.5	24 SU	0249 4.6 0859 1.4 1514 4.6 2116 1.4
10 SU	0302 4.5 0901 1.6 1521 4.5 2118 1.4	25 M	0337 4.8 0945 1.3 1602 4.8 2158 1.4
11 M	0338 4.7 0938 1.4 1600 4.7 2153 1.2	26 TU	0420 4.9 1027 1.2 1648 4.8 2236 1.4
12 TU	0416 4.9 1014 1.2 1641 4.9 ● 2229 1.2	27 W	0502 5.0 1106 1.1 1731 4.9 ○ 2314 1.4
13 W	0456 5.1 1053 1.0 1723 5.0 2309 1.1	28 TH	0542 5.1 1143 1.1 1812 4.8 2351 1.4
14 TH	0538 5.2 1136 0.9 1808 5.0 2352 1.1	29 F	0621 5.0 1220 1.2 1852 4.8
15 F	0623 5.2 1220 0.9 1855 4.9	30 SA	0029 1.5 0700 4.9 1257 1.2 1931 4.7
		31 SU	0107 1.6 0739 4.8 1336 1.4 2011 4.5

Chart Datum: 0·20 metres above Ordnance Datum (Dublin)
HAT is 5·9m above Chart Datum

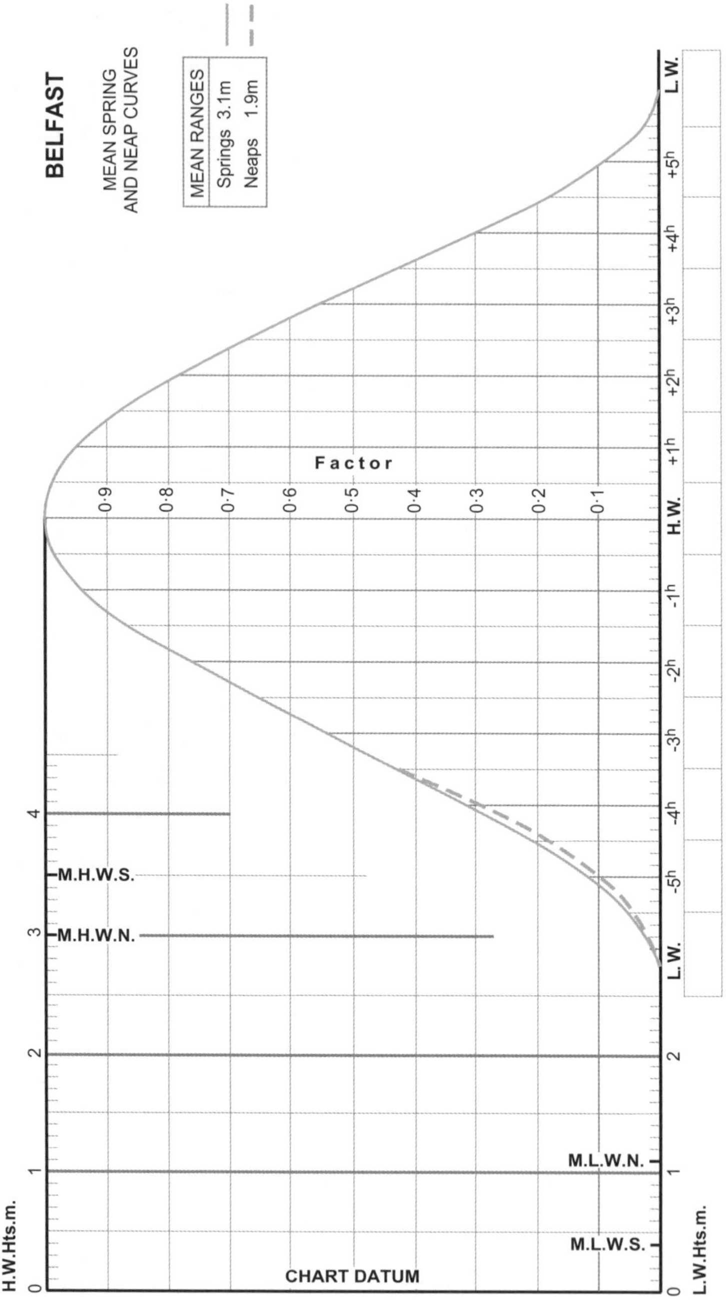
BELFAST
MEAN SPRING
AND NEAP CURVES
MEAN RANGES
Springs 3.1m
Neaps 1.9m
Factor
0·9
0·8
0·7
0·6
0·5
0·4
0·3
0·2
0·1
L.W.
-5h
-4h
-3h
-2h
-1h
H.W.
+1h
+2h
+3h
+4h
+5h
L.W.
H.W.Hts.m.
0
1
2
3
4
M.H.W.S.
M.H.W.N.
M.L.W.N.
M.L.W.S.
CHART DATUM
L.W.Hts.m.

TIME ZONE (UT)
For Summer Time add ONE hour in **non-shaded areas**

NORTHERN IRELAND – BELFAST

LAT 54°36'N LONG 5°55'W

TIMES AND HEIGHTS OF HIGH AND LOW WATERS

Dates in amber are **SPRINGS**
Dates in grey are **NEAPS**

2023

JANUARY

Date	Day	Time	m	Time	m	Time	m	Time	m
1	SU	0023	0.8	0643	3.0	1234	1.1	1902	3.3
2	M	0124	0.8	0743	3.1	1339	1.1	2006	3.2
3	TU	0219	0.9	0837	3.2	1439	1.0	2103	3.2
4	W	0308	0.9	0927	3.3	1531	1.0	2154	3.2
5	TH	0351	0.9	1012	3.4	1616	0.9	2238	3.2
6	F	0430	0.9	1053	3.5	1654	0.8	○ 2318	3.2
7	SA	0506	0.9	1131	3.6	1730	0.8	2354	3.2
8	SU	0541	0.9	1206	3.6	1804	0.7		
9	M	0026	3.1	0617	0.9	1239	3.6	1839	0.7
10	TU	0059	3.1	0652	0.9	1313	3.6	1914	0.7
11	W	0132	3.1	0730	0.9	1347	3.5	1951	0.7
12	TH	0206	3.0	0809	0.9	1422	3.5	2030	0.7
13	F	0245	3.0	0850	0.9	1501	3.4	2113	0.7
14	SA	0329	3.0	0935	1.0	1546	3.3	2201	0.8
15	SU	0420	2.9	1026	1.1	1639	3.2	◑ 2255	0.9
16	M	0520	2.9	1126	1.2	1743	3.1	2359	0.9
17	TU	0627	2.9	1240	1.2	1853	3.1		
18	W	0111	0.9	0733	3.0	1356	1.1	2002	3.2
19	TH	0217	0.8	0835	3.1	1459	0.9	2104	3.3
20	F	0313	0.8	0931	3.3	1552	0.7	2201	3.4
21	SA	0404	0.7	1024	3.5	1642	0.5	● 2254	3.5
22	SU	0452	0.6	1114	3.6	1731	0.3	2345	3.5
23	M	0540	0.6	1203	3.7	1819	0.2		
24	TU	0036	3.4	0628	0.6	1252	3.8	1907	0.2
25	W	0128	3.4	0716	0.6	1341	3.8	1956	0.2
26	TH	0219	3.3	0804	0.6	1430	3.7	2046	0.3
27	F	0310	3.2	0853	0.7	1520	3.6	2138	0.5
28	SA	0400	3.1	0945	0.8	1611	3.4	◐ 2237	0.7
29	SU	0452	3.0	1044	1.0	1707	3.2	2342	0.9
30	M	0550	2.9	1155	1.1	1814	3.1		
31	TU	0047	1.0	0659	2.9	1307	1.1	1937	2.9

FEBRUARY

Date	Day	Time	m	Time	m	Time	m	Time	m
1	W	0148	1.0	0808	3.0	1414	1.1	2046	3.0
2	TH	0244	1.0	0907	3.1	1514	0.9	2141	3.0
3	F	0332	1.0	0956	3.3	1601	0.8	2227	3.1
4	SA	0413	0.9	1038	3.4	1639	0.7	2306	3.1
5	SU	0448	0.8	1116	3.5	1712	0.6	○ 2341	3.1
6	M	0522	0.8	1151	3.5	1744	0.6		
7	TU	0012	3.0	0556	0.7	1221	3.5	1817	0.6
8	W	0039	3.0	0630	0.7	1247	3.5	1850	0.5
9	TH	0059	3.0	0705	0.7	1314	3.5	1923	0.5
10	F	0128	3.1	0739	0.7	1348	3.5	1958	0.5
11	SA	0205	3.1	0816	0.7	1427	3.4	2036	0.5
12	SU	0246	3.0	0856	0.8	1511	3.3	2120	0.6
13	M	0331	3.0	0942	0.9	1601	3.2	◑ 2211	0.8
14	TU	0426	2.9	1039	1.0	1705	3.1	2313	1.0
15	W	0537	2.8	1158	1.1	1822	3.0		
16	TH	0038	1.1	0657	2.8	1342	1.0	1941	3.0
17	F	0205	1.0	0814	3.0	1450	0.8	2054	3.1
18	SA	0306	0.8	0920	3.2	1545	0.5	2154	3.2
19	SU	0358	0.6	1014	3.4	1635	0.3	2245	3.3
20	M	0444	0.5	1102	3.6	1720	0.1	● 2332	3.4
21	TU	0528	0.5	1148	3.7	1804	0.0		
22	W	0018	3.4	0611	0.4	1234	3.8	1847	0.1
23	TH	0104	3.3	0653	0.4	1320	3.7	1930	0.2
24	F	0150	3.3	0735	0.5	1406	3.7	2012	0.3
25	SA	0235	3.2	0819	0.5	1451	3.5	2057	0.5
26	SU	0320	3.1	0905	0.7	1538	3.3	2147	0.8
27	M	0406	3.1	0958	0.8	1628	3.1	◐ 2254	1.0
28	TU	0457	2.9	1113	1.0	1726	2.9		

MARCH

Date	Day	Time	m	Time	m	Time	m	Time	m
1	W	0008	1.2	0559	2.8	1236	1.1	1900	2.7
2	TH	0116	1.2	0729	2.9	1347	1.0	2031	2.7
3	F	0217	1.1	0843	3.0	1450	0.9	2126	2.8
4	SA	0310	1.0	0935	3.2	1539	0.7	2209	2.9
5	SU	0352	0.9	1016	3.3	1615	0.6	2246	3.0
6	M	0426	0.7	1053	3.4	1646	0.5	2319	3.0
7	TU	0459	0.7	1126	3.4	1717	0.5	○ 2348	3.0
8	W	0531	0.6	1152	3.4	1748	0.4		
9	TH	0007	3.0	0604	0.6	1212	3.4	1820	0.4
10	F	0023	3.1	0637	0.5	1241	3.4	1852	0.4
11	SA	0054	3.1	0709	0.5	1317	3.4	1926	0.4
12	SU	0131	3.2	0744	0.5	1358	3.4	2004	0.5
13	M	0212	3.1	0824	0.6	1444	3.3	2048	0.6
14	TU	0257	3.1	0911	0.8	1538	3.1	2139	0.8
15	W	0352	2.9	1011	0.9	1646	2.9	◑ 2244	1.1
16	TH	0506	2.8	1142	1.1	1806	2.8		
17	F	0023	1.2	0634	2.8	1334	0.9	1932	2.8
18	SA	0156	1.0	0801	2.9	1439	0.6	2049	3.0
19	SU	0256	0.8	0909	3.2	1533	0.3	2144	3.2
20	M	0346	0.6	1000	3.4	1620	0.1	2230	3.3
21	TU	0431	0.5	1045	3.6	1703	0.0	● 2313	3.4
22	W	0511	0.4	1129	3.7	1743	0.0	2356	3.4
23	TH	0550	0.4	1212	3.7	1821	0.1		
24	F	0038	3.3	0628	0.4	1255	3.6	1859	0.3
25	SA	0120	3.3	0707	0.4	1339	3.5	1938	0.4
26	SU	0201	3.3	0748	0.5	1422	3.4	2019	0.6
27	M	0243	3.2	0832	0.6	1507	3.2	2104	0.9
28	TU	0327	3.1	0921	0.8	1555	3.0	2201	1.1
29	W	0416	3.0	1031	1.0	1651	2.7	◐ 2326	1.3
30	TH	0513	2.9	1201	1.1	1803	2.6		
31	F	0038	1.3	0625	2.8	1313	1.0	2006	2.6

APRIL

Date	Day	Time	m	Time	m	Time	m	Time	m
1	SA	0142	1.2	0805	2.9	1414	0.9	2100	2.7
2	SU	0238	1.1	0902	3.0	1503	0.7	2141	2.9
3	M	0322	0.9	0944	3.2	1541	0.6	2215	3.0
4	TU	0358	0.7	1019	3.3	1614	0.5	2246	3.0
5	W	0431	0.6	1050	3.3	1646	0.4	2312	3.1
6	TH	0503	0.6	1114	3.4	1717	0.4	○ 2329	3.1
7	F	0535	0.5	1139	3.4	1749	0.4	2352	3.2
8	SA	0608	0.5	1212	3.4	1822	0.4		
9	SU	0025	3.3	0643	0.5	1252	3.4	1859	0.4
10	M	0105	3.3	0720	0.5	1337	3.4	1940	0.6
11	TU	0149	3.3	0804	0.6	1429	3.2	2026	0.7
12	W	0238	3.2	0855	0.7	1529	3.1	2122	1.0
13	TH	0338	3.0	1003	0.9	1641	2.9	◑ 2233	1.1
14	F	0452	2.9	1151	0.9	1802	2.8		
15	SA	0014	1.2	0621	2.9	1318	0.7	1928	2.9
16	SU	0137	1.1	0748	3.0	1422	0.5	2034	3.0
17	M	0238	0.8	0851	3.3	1514	0.2	2125	3.2
18	TU	0328	0.6	0940	3.5	1559	0.1	2209	3.3
19	W	0411	0.5	1025	3.6	1639	0.1	2251	3.4
20	TH	0451	0.4	1107	3.6	1717	0.2	● 2332	3.4
21	F	0528	0.4	1149	3.6	1754	0.3		
22	SA	0011	3.4	0606	0.4	1231	3.5	1831	0.5
23	SU	0051	3.4	0644	0.5	1312	3.4	1909	0.6
24	M	0131	3.4	0724	0.5	1355	3.2	1949	0.8
25	TU	0212	3.4	0807	0.6	1439	3.1	2033	1.0
26	W	0256	3.3	0855	0.8	1527	2.9	2124	1.1
27	TH	0343	3.2	0956	0.9	1621	2.7	◐ 2236	1.3
28	F	0437	3.0	1119	1.0	1723	2.6	2354	1.3
29	SA	0539	2.9	1231	1.0	1852	2.6		
30	SU	0059	1.3	0653	2.9	1331	0.9	2014	2.7

Chart Datum: 2·01 metres below Ordnance Datum (Belfast)
HAT is 3·9m above Chart Datum

TIME ZONE (UT)
For Summer Time add ONE hour in **non-shaded areas**

NORTHERN IRELAND – BELFAST

LAT 54°36′N LONG 5°55′W

TIMES AND HEIGHTS OF HIGH AND LOW WATERS

Dates in amber are **SPRINGS**
Dates in grey are **NEAPS**

2023

MAY

Day	Time	m	Day	Time	m
1	0156	1.1	16	0208	0.9
	0806	3.0		0826	3.3
M	1421	0.7	TU	1447	0.3
	2057	2.9		2100	3.2
2	0244	1.0	17	0302	0.7
	0856	3.1		0917	3.4
TU	1502	0.6	W	1533	0.3
	2131	3.0		2145	3.3
3	0324	0.8	18	0348	0.6
	0935	3.2		1004	3.5
W	1537	0.5	TH	1614	0.3
	2203	3.1		2228	3.3
4	0359	0.7	19	0430	0.6
	1008	3.3		1047	3.5
TH	1611	0.4	F	1652	0.4
	2231	3.2		● 2309	3.4
5	0433	0.6	20	0510	0.6
	1039	3.4		1129	3.4
F	1644	0.4	SA	1730	0.6
	○ 2256	3.3		2348	3.4
6	0508	0.6	21	0549	0.6
	1112	3.4		1209	3.3
SA	1719	0.4	SU	1808	0.7
	2327	3.3			
7	0544	0.5	22	0026	3.4
	1151	3.4		0628	0.6
SU	1757	0.5	M	1248	3.2
				1847	0.8
8	0005	3.4	23	0105	3.5
	0624	0.5		0707	0.6
M	1236	3.4	TU	1329	3.1
	1839	0.6		1927	0.9
9	0050	3.4	24	0146	3.5
	0707	0.5		0748	0.7
TU	1327	3.3	W	1413	3.0
	1925	0.7		2009	1.0
10	0139	3.4	25	0229	3.4
	0757	0.5		0832	0.7
W	1425	3.2	TH	1500	2.9
	2018	0.8		2056	1.1
11	0233	3.3	26	0314	3.3
	0856	0.6		0922	0.8
TH	1529	3.0	F	1552	2.8
	2120	1.0		2149	1.2
12	0334	3.2	27	0403	3.2
	1011	0.7		1022	0.9
F	1640	2.9	SA	1649	2.7
	◑ 2232	1.1		◐ 2252	1.2
13	0444	3.1	28	0458	3.0
	1137	0.7		1131	0.9
SA	1756	2.9	SU	1750	2.7
	2351	1.1			
14	0606	3.1	29	0000	1.2
	1254	0.6		0559	3.0
SU	1909	3.0	M	1237	0.9
				1854	2.7
15	0105	1.0	30	0102	1.2
	0725	3.2		0703	3.0
M	1355	0.4	TU	1331	0.8
	2009	3.1		1951	2.9
			31	0156	1.1
				0800	3.1
			W	1417	0.7
				2038	3.0

JUNE

Day	Time	m	Day	Time	m
1	0243	0.9	16	0326	0.8
	0848	3.2		0945	3.3
TH	1457	0.6	F	1550	0.6
	2118	3.1		2207	3.3
2	0325	0.8	17	0413	0.7
	0931	3.3		1031	3.3
F	1536	0.5	SA	1631	0.7
	2155	3.2		2249	3.4
3	0405	0.7	18	0456	0.7
	1011	3.4		1114	3.2
SA	1615	0.5	SU	1711	0.8
	2231	3.3		● 2329	3.4
4	0446	0.6	19	0536	0.7
	1053	3.4		1153	3.2
SU	1656	0.5	M	1750	0.8
	○ 2310	3.4			
5	0528	0.5	20	0007	3.5
	1138	3.4		0614	0.7
M	1739	0.6	TU	1230	3.1
	2354	3.5		1828	0.9
6	0613	0.5	21	0044	3.5
	1228	3.4		0651	0.7
TU	1827	0.7	W	1308	3.0
				1906	0.9
7	0043	3.5	22	0123	3.5
	0703	0.4		0728	0.7
W	1323	3.3	TH	1348	3.0
	1919	0.7		1945	1.0
8	0135	3.5	23	0203	3.5
	0757	0.4		0806	0.7
TH	1422	3.2	F	1432	2.9
	2015	0.8		2026	1.0
9	0230	3.5	24	0244	3.4
	0856	0.5		0847	0.7
F	1525	3.1	SA	1520	2.9
	2114	0.9		2111	1.0
10	0328	3.4	25	0326	3.3
	1002	0.5		0933	0.8
SA	1630	3.0	SU	1610	2.8
	◑ 2217	0.9		2159	1.1
11	0431	3.3	26	0412	3.2
	1111	0.5		1024	0.8
SU	1736	3.0	M	1704	2.8
	2322	1.0		◐ 2252	1.1
12	0542	3.3	27	0506	3.1
	1220	0.5		1121	0.9
M	1840	3.0	TU	1759	2.8
				2352	1.2
13	0028	1.0	28	0606	3.0
	0655	3.3		1225	0.9
TU	1322	0.5	W	1855	2.9
	1939	3.1			
14	0133	0.9	29	0058	1.1
	0759	3.3		0708	3.1
W	1417	0.5	TH	1326	0.8
	2032	3.2		1948	3.0
15	0233	0.8	30	0201	1.0
	0855	3.3		0807	3.1
TH	1506	0.5	F	1420	0.7
	2121	3.2		2038	3.1

JULY

Day	Time	m	Day	Time	m
1	0255	0.9	16	0401	0.8
	0900	3.3		1021	3.1
SA	1508	0.7	SU	1614	0.9
	2124	3.2		2234	3.4
2	0345	0.7	17	0444	0.7
	0950	3.4		1104	3.1
SU	1554	0.6	M	1653	0.9
	2210	3.4		● 2315	3.4
3	0432	0.6	18	0522	0.7
	1039	3.4		1142	3.1
M	1640	0.6	TU	1730	0.9
	○ 2257	3.5		2351	3.5
4	0519	0.4	19	0556	0.7
	1129	3.4		1216	3.0
TU	1728	0.6	W	1805	0.9
	2345	3.5			
5	0606	0.3	20	0026	3.5
	1221	3.4		0629	0.6
W	1817	0.7	TH	1248	3.0
				1841	0.9
6	0035	3.6	21	0100	3.5
	0656	0.3		0702	0.6
TH	1315	3.3	F	1322	3.0
	1909	0.7		1916	0.9
7	0127	3.6	22	0134	3.4
	0748	0.3		0736	0.6
F	1411	3.2	SA	1358	3.0
	2002	0.7		1954	0.9
8	0219	3.6	23	0208	3.4
	0841	0.3		0812	0.6
SA	1508	3.2	SU	1435	3.0
	2055	0.7		2033	0.9
9	0312	3.6	24	0244	3.4
	0938	0.4		0851	0.6
SU	1605	3.1	M	1516	2.9
	2151	0.8		2115	0.9
10	0408	3.5	25	0324	3.3
	1039	0.5		0935	0.7
M	1703	3.1	TU	1602	2.9
	◑ 2250	0.9		◐ 2202	1.0
11	0508	3.3	26	0412	3.2
	1144	0.6		1025	0.8
TU	1803	3.0	W	1657	2.9
	2355	0.9		2256	1.1
12	0617	3.2	27	0511	3.1
	1249	0.7		1124	0.9
W	1903	3.0	TH	1758	2.9
13	0103	1.0	28	0002	1.2
	0730	3.1		0622	3.0
TH	1348	0.8	F	1236	1.0
	2003	3.1		1902	2.9
14	0209	1.0	29	0128	1.1
	0835	3.1		0732	3.0
F	1443	0.8	SA	1351	0.9
	2059	3.2		2003	3.0
15	0309	0.9	30	0237	0.9
	0932	3.1		0838	3.1
SA	1531	0.8	SU	1451	0.8
	2149	3.3		2101	3.2
			31	0333	0.7
				0936	3.3
			M	1542	0.7
				2154	3.4

AUGUST

Day	Time	m	Day	Time	m
1	0423	0.5	16	0502	0.6
	1028	3.4		1126	3.0
TU	1630	0.6	W	1707	0.9
	○ 2244	3.5		● 2332	3.5
2	0510	0.3	17	0531	0.6
	1118	3.4		1157	3.0
W	1716	0.6	TH	1739	0.8
	2332	3.6			
3	0555	0.2	18	0003	3.5
	1207	3.4		0601	0.6
TH	1803	0.6	F	1225	3.0
				1812	0.8
4	0021	3.7	19	0030	3.4
	0642	0.1		0631	0.6
F	1257	3.4	SA	1247	3.0
	1850	0.6		1846	0.8
5	0110	3.7	20	0057	3.4
	0728	0.1		0703	0.5
SA	1348	3.3	SU	1313	3.1
	1938	0.6		1920	0.8
6	0159	3.7	21	0128	3.4
	0815	0.2		0736	0.5
SU	1439	3.3	M	1346	3.1
	2026	0.6		1956	0.8
7	0249	3.6	22	0204	3.4
	0905	0.4		0812	0.6
M	1531	3.2	TU	1425	3.1
	2117	0.7		2035	0.8
8	0340	3.5	23	0245	3.3
	1001	0.6		0852	0.7
TU	1622	3.1	W	1508	3.1
	◑ 2213	0.8		2119	0.9
9	0434	3.3	24	0333	3.2
	1106	0.8		0940	0.8
W	1718	3.0	TH	1601	3.0
	2322	1.0		◐ 2211	1.1
10	0537	3.1	25	0432	3.1
	1216	1.0		1038	1.0
TH	1821	3.0	F	1708	2.9
				2320	1.2
11	0037	1.1	26	0549	2.9
	0702	2.9		1153	1.2
F	1322	1.1	SA	1824	2.9
	1934	3.0			
12	0149	1.0	27	0112	1.2
	0822	2.9		0709	2.9
SA	1422	1.1	SU	1335	1.1
	2039	3.1		1938	3.0
13	0256	0.9	28	0226	0.9
	0922	3.0		0823	3.0
SU	1515	1.0	M	1441	1.0
	2132	3.3		2044	3.2
14	0351	0.8	29	0322	0.6
	1009	3.0		0926	3.2
M	1558	0.9	TU	1532	0.8
	2217	3.4		2140	3.4
15	0431	0.7	30	0411	0.3
	1050	3.0		1017	3.4
TU	1634	0.9	W	1618	0.6
	2257	3.5		2229	3.6
			31	0455	0.2
				1103	3.4
			TH	1700	0.5
				○ 2315	3.7

Chart Datum: 2·01 metres below Ordnance Datum (Belfast)
HAT is 3·9m above Chart Datum

TIME ZONE (UT)
For Summer Time add ONE hour in **non-shaded areas**

NORTHERN IRELAND – BELFAST

LAT 54°36′N LONG 5°55′W

TIMES AND HEIGHTS OF HIGH AND LOW WATERS

Dates in amber are **SPRINGS**
Dates in grey are **NEAPS**

2023

SEPTEMBER

Date	Day	Time	m	Time	m	Time	m	Time	m
1	F	0537	0.1	1148	3.5	1742	0.5		
2	SA	0001	3.8	0619	0.1	1233	3.4	1825	0.5
3	SU	0048	3.8	0700	0.2	1320	3.4	1908	0.5
4	M	0135	3.7	0742	0.3	1407	3.4	1953	0.6
5	TU	0223	3.6	0827	0.5	1455	3.3	2041	0.7
6	W	0311	3.4	0916	0.8	1543	3.2	◑ 2135	0.9
7	TH	0402	3.2	1020	1.0	1635	3.1	2247	1.1
8	F	0501	2.9	1142	1.3	1735	3.0		
9	SA	0011	1.2	0630	2.7	1253	1.3	1857	3.0
10	SU	0126	1.1	0809	2.8	1358	1.3	2016	3.1
11	M	0236	1.0	0907	2.9	1454	1.1	2111	3.3
12	TU	0331	0.8	0952	3.0	1537	1.0	2154	3.4
13	W	0407	0.7	1028	3.1	1611	0.9	2232	3.4
14	TH	0434	0.6	1101	3.1	1641	0.8	2305	3.5
15	F	0501	0.6	1130	3.1	1711	0.8	● 2333	3.5
16	SA	0529	0.6	1153	3.1	1743	0.8	2354	3.5
17	SU	0559	0.6	1208	3.2	1814	0.7		
18	M	0019	3.5	0629	0.6	1234	3.2	1847	0.7
19	TU	0053	3.5	0701	0.6	1308	3.3	1921	0.8
20	W	0132	3.5	0737	0.6	1348	3.3	2000	0.8
21	TH	0216	3.4	0819	0.8	1432	3.2	2046	0.9
22	F	0307	3.2	0907	1.0	1524	3.1	◐ 2141	1.1
23	SA	0412	3.0	1007	1.2	1635	3.0	2258	1.2
24	SU	0532	2.9	1129	1.3	1759	2.9		
25	M	0102	1.1	0655	2.9	1323	1.3	1920	3.0
26	TU	0211	0.8	0815	3.0	1426	1.0	2031	3.3
27	W	0305	0.5	0914	3.3	1517	0.8	2125	3.5
28	TH	0352	0.3	1001	3.4	1600	0.7	2212	3.7
29	F	0434	0.2	1043	3.5	1640	0.6	○ 2256	3.8
30	SA	0513	0.1	1126	3.5	1719	0.5	2340	3.8

OCTOBER

Date	Day	Time	m	Time	m	Time	m	Time	m
1	SU	0551	0.2	1209	3.5	1758	0.5		
2	M	0025	3.8	0630	0.4	1252	3.5	1840	0.6
3	TU	0111	3.7	0710	0.5	1336	3.5	1924	0.6
4	W	0157	3.5	0752	0.8	1421	3.4	2010	0.8
5	TH	0244	3.3	0839	1.0	1508	3.3	2103	0.9
6	F	0334	3.1	0936	1.3	1558	3.2	◑ 2213	1.1
7	SA	0430	2.9	1100	1.4	1655	3.1	2339	1.2
8	SU	0545	2.7	1217	1.5	1805	3.0		
9	M	0052	1.2	0744	2.7	1322	1.4	1938	3.1
10	TU	0158	1.0	0841	2.8	1420	1.3	2038	3.2
11	W	0251	0.9	0923	3.0	1505	1.1	2123	3.3
12	TH	0328	0.8	0958	3.1	1541	1.0	2159	3.4
13	F	0358	0.7	1028	3.2	1612	0.9	2231	3.5
14	SA	0427	0.6	1056	3.2	1643	0.8	● 2258	3.5
15	SU	0457	0.6	1118	3.3	1714	0.8	2321	3.5
16	M	0527	0.6	1136	3.4	1746	0.8	2350	3.5
17	TU	0558	0.6	1205	3.4	1819	0.7		
18	W	0027	3.5	0633	0.7	1242	3.4	1856	0.8
19	TH	0110	3.5	0712	0.8	1324	3.4	1938	0.8
20	F	0159	3.4	0756	0.9	1412	3.3	2027	0.9
21	SA	0256	3.2	0848	1.1	1509	3.2	2129	1.1
22	SU	0405	3.0	0954	1.3	1619	3.1	◐ 2258	1.1
23	M	0523	2.9	1121	1.4	1741	3.1		
24	TU	0041	1.0	0647	3.0	1257	1.3	1905	3.2
25	W	0148	0.7	0800	3.1	1402	1.1	2013	3.4
26	TH	0242	0.5	0854	3.3	1454	0.9	2107	3.6
27	F	0328	0.3	0939	3.5	1538	0.7	2153	3.7
28	SA	0409	0.3	1022	3.6	1618	0.6	○ 2237	3.8
29	SU	0447	0.3	1103	3.6	1657	0.6	2321	3.8
30	M	0525	0.5	1145	3.6	1737	0.6		
31	TU	0004	3.7	0604	0.6	1226	3.6	1819	0.6

NOVEMBER

Date	Day	Time	m	Time	m	Time	m	Time	m
1	W	0049	3.6	0644	0.8	1309	3.6	1902	0.7
2	TH	0133	3.4	0727	1.0	1352	3.6	1948	0.8
3	F	0219	3.2	0812	1.2	1437	3.5	2039	0.9
4	SA	0308	3.1	0904	1.3	1526	3.4	2140	1.1
5	SU	0402	2.9	1012	1.5	1620	3.2	◑ 2256	1.2
6	M	0504	2.7	1129	1.5	1720	3.1		
7	TU	0007	1.2	0634	2.7	1236	1.5	1832	3.1
8	W	0109	1.1	0754	2.8	1335	1.4	1944	3.1
9	TH	0202	1.0	0840	3.0	1424	1.2	2037	3.3
10	F	0244	0.9	0916	3.1	1505	1.1	2118	3.4
11	SA	0320	0.8	0949	3.3	1541	0.9	2154	3.4
12	SU	0352	0.7	1020	3.4	1614	0.9	2226	3.5
13	M	0425	0.7	1047	3.4	1649	0.8	● 2256	3.5
14	TU	0459	0.7	1113	3.5	1724	0.8	2331	3.5
15	W	0535	0.7	1146	3.5	1802	0.7		
16	TH	0012	3.5	0614	0.8	1227	3.5	1844	0.8
17	F	0100	3.4	0657	0.9	1313	3.5	1930	0.8
18	SA	0153	3.3	0747	1.0	1405	3.5	2026	0.8
19	SU	0253	3.2	0844	1.2	1502	3.4	2132	0.9
20	M	0400	3.1	0950	1.3	1607	3.3	◐ 2250	0.9
21	TU	0514	3.0	1105	1.3	1722	3.3		
22	W	0008	0.8	0629	3.0	1220	1.2	1842	3.3
23	TH	0115	0.7	0734	3.2	1327	1.1	1949	3.4
24	F	0211	0.6	0828	3.3	1424	1.0	2045	3.6
25	SA	0300	0.5	0917	3.4	1514	0.8	2135	3.6
26	SU	0344	0.5	1001	3.5	1559	0.8	2221	3.6
27	M	0425	0.6	1044	3.6	1643	0.7	○ 2306	3.6
28	TU	0506	0.7	1126	3.6	1725	0.7	2349	3.5
29	W	0546	0.8	1207	3.7	1807	0.7		
30	TH	0031	3.4	0627	1.0	1248	3.7	1849	0.8

DECEMBER

Date	Day	Time	m	Time	m	Time	m	Time	m
1	F	0114	3.3	0708	1.1	1329	3.6	1932	0.8
2	SA	0157	3.2	0750	1.2	1413	3.6	2017	0.9
3	SU	0243	3.0	0836	1.2	1458	3.5	2106	1.0
4	M	0333	2.9	0927	1.3	1547	3.4	2200	1.0
5	TU	0427	2.8	1024	1.4	1640	3.2	◑ 2303	1.1
6	W	0527	2.8	1131	1.4	1739	3.1		
7	TH	0008	1.1	0631	2.8	1237	1.4	1842	3.1
8	F	0107	1.0	0732	2.9	1335	1.3	1941	3.2
9	SA	0157	1.0	0823	3.1	1425	1.2	2033	3.3
10	SU	0240	0.9	0907	3.2	1509	1.0	2118	3.4
11	M	0320	0.8	0947	3.3	1549	0.9	2159	3.4
12	TU	0359	0.8	1023	3.4	1630	0.8	● 2239	3.5
13	W	0438	0.8	1058	3.5	1711	0.7	2321	3.5
14	TH	0520	0.8	1137	3.6	1753	0.7		
15	F	0006	3.5	0604	0.8	1220	3.6	1840	0.6
16	SA	0055	3.4	0652	0.9	1308	3.6	1930	0.6
17	SU	0149	3.3	0743	0.9	1359	3.6	2024	0.6
18	M	0247	3.2	0838	1.0	1453	3.6	2123	0.6
19	TU	0348	3.1	0936	1.0	1552	3.5	◐ 2226	0.7
20	W	0452	3.1	1038	1.1	1657	3.4	2333	0.7
21	TH	0558	3.1	1144	1.1	1810	3.4		
22	F	0038	0.7	0702	3.1	1252	1.1	1921	3.4
23	SA	0139	0.7	0800	3.2	1356	1.0	2024	3.4
24	SU	0234	0.7	0854	3.3	1455	0.9	2120	3.4
25	M	0324	0.8	0944	3.4	1547	0.8	2211	3.4
26	TU	0409	0.8	1031	3.5	1634	0.8	2258	3.4
27	W	0452	0.9	1114	3.6	1717	0.7	○ 2341	3.3
28	TH	0533	0.9	1155	3.6	1758	0.7		
29	F	0021	3.2	0612	1.0	1233	3.7	1837	0.7
30	SA	0058	3.1	0650	1.0	1311	3.6	1914	0.7
31	SU	0136	3.1	0727	1.0	1350	3.6	1951	0.7

Chart Datum: 2·01 metres below Ordnance Datum (Belfast)
HAT is 3·9m above Chart Datum

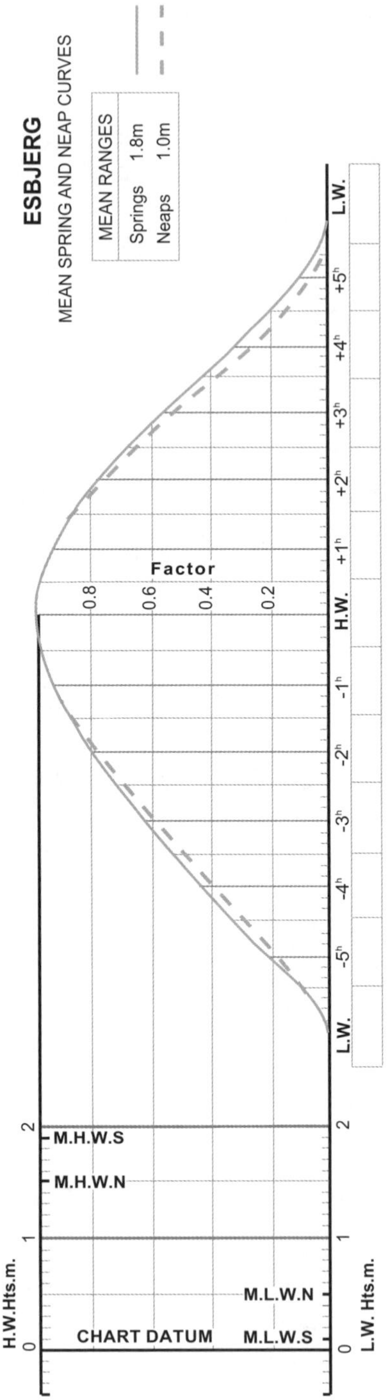
ESBJERG
MEAN SPRING AND NEAP CURVES
MEAN RANGES
Springs 1.8m
Neaps 1.0m
Factor
0.8
0.6
0.4
0.2
L.W.
-5h
-4h
-3h
-2h
-1h
H.W.
+1h
+2h
+3h
+4h
+5h
L.W.
H.W.Hts.m.
L.W. Hts.m.
M.H.W.S
M.H.W.N
M.L.W.N
M.L.W.S
CHART DATUM
0
1
2

TIME ZONE -0100 (Danish Standard Time) **Subtract 1 hour for UT** For Danish Summer Time add ONE hour in **non-shaded areas**

DENMARK – ESBJERG

LAT 55°28′N LONG 8°27′E

TIMES AND HEIGHTS OF HIGH AND LOW WATERS

Dates in amber are **SPRINGS** Dates in grey are **NEAPS**

2023

JANUARY

Day	Time	m	Day	Time	m
1 SU	0319 0955 1610 2243	0.4 2.1 0.3 1.8	16 M	0220 0831 1505 2116	0.4 2.0 0.4 1.8
2 M	0425 1103 1710 2342	0.4 2.0 0.4 1.8	17 TU	0321 0935 1607 2222	0.4 2.0 0.4 1.8
3 TU	0531 1207 1808	0.4 2.0 0.4	18 W	0430 1047 1714 2332	0.5 1.9 0.4 1.8
4 W	0039 0633 1307 1901	1.9 0.4 1.9 0.4	19 TH	0543 1206 1821	0.4 1.9 0.4
5 TH	0130 0730 1359 1949	1.9 0.3 1.9 0.4	20 F	0043 0654 1323 1922	1.9 0.4 1.9 0.4
6 F	0216 0819 1444 2031	2.0 0.3 1.9 0.4	21 SA	0147 0757 1429 ● 2017	2.0 0.3 1.9 0.3
7 SA	0256 0904 1524 ○ 2110	2.0 0.3 1.9 0.4	22 SU	0244 0852 1527 2107	2.0 0.2 1.9 0.3
8 SU	0331 0943 1558 2146	2.1 0.3 1.8 0.3	23 M	0334 0943 1617 2154	2.1 0.1 1.9 0.3
9 M	0401 1019 1627 2219	2.1 0.3 1.8 0.3	24 TU	0420 1030 1702 2239	2.2 0.1 1.9 0.2
10 TU	0429 1053 1655 2252	2.1 0.3 1.8 0.3	25 W	0503 1116 1744 2323	2.2 0.1 1.9 0.2
11 W	0457 1127 1724 2326	2.1 0.3 1.8 0.3	26 TH	0545 1202 1826	2.2 0.1 1.8
12 TH	0529 1201 1758	2.1 0.3 1.8	27 F	0008 0629 1248 1909	0.2 2.2 0.2 1.8
13 F	0002 0605 1238 1837	0.3 2.1 0.3 1.8	28 SA	0055 0717 1337 ◐ 1956	0.2 2.2 0.2 1.8
14 SA	0042 0647 1321 1923	0.4 2.1 0.3 1.8	29 SU	0145 0811 1429 2050	0.3 2.1 0.3 1.8
15 SU	0128 0736 1409 ◑ 2015	0.4 2.1 0.3 1.8	30 M	0241 0913 1526 2152	0.4 2.0 0.4 1.8
			31 TU	0346 1024 1630 2258	0.5 1.9 0.5 1.8

FEBRUARY

Day	Time	m	Day	Time	m
1 W	0459 1137 1736	0.5 1.8 0.5	16 TH	0357 1018 1641 2256	0.5 1.8 0.5 1.8
2 TH	0004 0612 1243 1837	1.8 0.5 1.8 0.5	17 F	0521 1154 1758	0.5 1.8 0.5
3 F	0103 0714 1339 1929	1.9 0.4 1.8 0.5	18 SA	0021 0641 1319 1905	1.9 0.4 1.8 0.5
4 SA	0155 0805 1428 2014	2.0 0.4 1.8 0.4	19 SU	0134 0745 1425 2003	2.0 0.3 1.9 0.4
5 SU	0239 0849 1509 ○ 2054	2.0 0.3 1.9 0.4	20 M	0233 0840 1519 ● 2052	2.1 0.1 1.9 0.3
6 M	0317 0927 1545 2129	2.1 0.3 1.9 0.3	21 TU	0323 0928 1604 2138	2.2 0.1 1.9 0.2
7 TU	0349 1001 1616 2202	2.1 0.3 1.9 0.3	22 W	0408 1013 1644 2221	2.2 0.0 1.9 0.1
8 W	0416 1033 1642 2234	2.1 0.3 1.9 0.3	23 TH	0448 1055 1720 2302	2.2 0.1 1.9 0.1
9 TH	0442 1104 1708 2306	2.1 0.3 1.9 0.3	24 F	0526 1136 1755 2344	2.2 0.1 1.9 0.1
10 F	0510 1136 1737 2340	2.1 0.3 1.9 0.3	25 SA	0604 1218 1830	2.2 0.2 1.9
11 SA	0542 1210 1809	2.1 0.3 1.9	26 SU	0027 0645 1300 1910	0.2 2.1 0.3 1.9
12 SU	0017 0620 1249 1849	0.3 2.1 0.3 1.8	27 M	0113 0731 1346 ◐ 1956	0.3 2.0 0.4 1.8
13 M	0059 0705 1334 ◑ 1936	0.3 2.1 0.3 1.8	28 TU	0204 0826 1438 2053	0.4 1.9 0.5 1.8
14 TU	0148 0757 1426 2032	0.3 2.0 0.4 1.8			
15 W	0246 0900 1528 2138	0.4 1.9 0.5 1.8			

MARCH

Day	Time	m	Day	Time	m
1 W	0306 0939 1543 2207	0.5 1.8 0.7 1.8	16 TH	0223 0839 1459 2108	0.4 1.8 0.6 1.8
2 TH	0428 1104 1659 2326	0.6 1.7 0.7 1.8	17 F	0340 1010 1619 2236	0.5 1.7 0.6 1.8
3 F	0550 1216 1810	0.6 1.7 0.6	18 SA	0511 1157 1741	0.5 1.7 0.6
4 SA	0034 0654 1315 1907	1.8 0.5 1.8 0.5	19 SU	0009 0629 1313 1849	1.9 0.4 1.8 0.5
5 SU	0129 0744 1405 1952	1.9 0.4 1.8 0.5	20 M	0121 0730 1412 1945	2.0 0.2 1.9 0.4
6 M	0216 0826 1448 2032	2.0 0.3 1.9 0.4	21 TU	0219 0822 1502 ● 2033	2.1 0.1 1.9 0.2
7 TU	0255 0903 1524 ○ 2107	2.1 0.3 1.9 0.3	22 W	0308 0908 1544 2118	2.2 0.1 2.0 0.2
8 W	0329 0936 1556 2140	2.1 0.2 1.9 0.3	23 TH	0350 0949 1620 2159	2.2 0.1 2.0 0.1
9 TH	0357 1007 1623 2212	2.1 0.2 1.9 0.2	24 F	0428 1029 1652 2239	2.2 0.1 1.9 0.1
10 F	0423 1037 1648 2244	2.1 0.2 1.9 0.2	25 SA	0503 1108 1722 2319	2.2 0.2 1.9 0.1
11 SA	0451 1109 1714 2318	2.1 0.2 1.9 0.2	26 SU	0537 1145 1753 2359	2.1 0.3 1.9 0.2
12 SU	0522 1144 1744 2355	2.1 0.3 1.9 0.2	27 M	0613 1224 1827	2.0 0.4 1.9
13 M	0558 1222 1820	2.1 0.3 1.9	28 TU	0042 0653 1304 1908	0.3 1.9 0.5 1.9
14 TU	0036 0641 1305 1904	0.3 2.0 0.4 1.9	29 W	0130 0741 1350 ◐ 1959	0.4 1.8 0.6 1.8
15 W	0124 0734 1356 ◑ 1959	0.3 1.9 0.5 1.8	30 TH	0229 0847 1450 2108	0.5 1.7 0.7 1.8
			31 F	0353 1025 1614 2239	0.6 1.6 0.8 1.8

APRIL

Day	Time	m	Day	Time	m
1 SA	0519 1142 1734 2355	0.6 1.6 0.7 1.8	16 SU	0501 1149 1722 2354	0.4 1.7 0.6 1.9
2 SU	0623 1242 1833	0.5 1.7 0.6	17 M	0611 1254 1827	0.3 1.8 0.5
3 M	0054 0712 1333 1921	1.9 0.4 1.8 0.5	18 TU	0101 0708 1350 1922	2.0 0.2 1.9 0.3
4 TU	0143 0753 1417 2002	2.0 0.3 1.9 0.4	19 W	0158 0758 1437 2011	2.1 0.1 1.9 0.2
5 W	0224 0830 1455 2038	2.0 0.3 1.9 0.3	20 TH	0248 0843 1518 ● 2055	2.2 0.1 2.0 0.2
6 TH	0300 0904 1529 ○ 2113	2.1 0.2 2.0 0.3	21 F	0330 0924 1553 2137	2.2 0.2 2.0 0.1
7 F	0332 0937 1558 2147	2.1 0.2 1.9 0.2	22 SA	0408 1002 1623 2217	2.1 0.2 1.9 0.1
8 SA	0402 1010 1625 2222	2.1 0.2 1.9 0.2	23 SU	0441 1039 1651 2257	2.0 0.3 1.9 0.2
9 SU	0432 1044 1653 2258	2.0 0.3 1.9 0.2	24 M	0512 1115 1720 2336	2.0 0.4 2.0 0.2
10 M	0505 1120 1723 2337	2.0 0.3 1.9 0.2	25 TU	0544 1150 1752	1.9 0.4 1.9
11 TU	0543 1159 1800	1.9 0.4 1.9	26 W	0017 0620 1228 1831	0.3 1.8 0.5 1.9
12 W	0021 0628 1244 1844	0.3 1.9 0.5 1.9	27 TH	0102 0704 1310 ◐ 1918	0.4 1.7 0.6 1.9
13 TH	0112 0724 1337 ◑ 1941	0.3 1.8 0.6 1.8	28 F	0156 0801 1402 2016	0.6 1.6 0.7 1.8
14 F	0216 0839 1443 2055	0.4 1.7 0.6 1.8	29 SA	0309 0926 1514 2133	0.6 1.6 0.8 1.8
15 SA	0337 1023 1604 2228	0.5 1.7 0.7 1.8	30 SU	0430 1051 1637 2257	0.6 1.6 0.7 1.8

Chart Datum: 0·69 metres below Dansk Normal Null
HAT is 2·2 metres above Chart Datum

TIME ZONE -0100
(Danish Standard Time)
Subtract 1 hour for UT
For Danish Summer Time add ONE hour in **non-shaded areas**

DENMARK – ESBJERG

LAT 55°28′N LONG 8°26′E

TIMES AND HEIGHTS OF HIGH AND LOW WATERS

Dates in amber are **SPRINGS**
Dates in grey are **NEAPS**

2023

MAY

Day	Time	m	Time	m	Time	m	Time	m
1 M	0534	0.6	1155	1.7	1744	0.6		
2 TU	0002	1.9	0626	0.5	1249	1.8	1837	0.5
3 W	0056	1.9	0710	0.4	1336	1.9	1922	0.4
4 TH	0143	2.0	0750	0.3	1418	1.9	2004	0.3
5 F	0226	2.0	0829	0.2	1456	2.0	○ 2043	0.3
6 SA	0304	2.0	0906	0.2	1530	1.9	2122	0.3
7 SU	0341	2.0	0943	0.3	1602	1.9	2201	0.2
8 M	0418	2.0	1021	0.3	1634	1.9	2242	0.2
9 TU	0456	1.9	1101	0.4	1708	1.9	2325	0.3
10 W	0539	1.8	1143	0.4	1748	1.9		
11 TH	0013	0.3	0628	1.8	1231	0.5	1836	1.9
12 F	0109	0.3	0731	1.7	1326	0.6	◑ 1936	1.9
13 SA	0214	0.4	0852	1.7	1431	0.6	2052	1.9
14 SU	0328	0.4	1015	1.7	1544	0.6	2215	1.9
15 M	0440	0.3	1124	1.7	1655	0.5	2330	2.0
16 TU	0544	0.3	1224	1.8	1759	0.4		
17 W	0036	2.1	0640	0.2	1319	1.9	1855	0.3
18 TH	0134	2.1	0730	0.2	1407	1.9	1946	0.3
19 F	0225	2.1	0816	0.2	1449	1.9	● 2033	0.2
20 SA	0310	2.0	0858	0.3	1526	1.9	2117	0.2
21 SU	0348	2.0	0936	0.3	1557	1.9	2158	0.2
22 M	0422	1.9	1013	0.4	1625	2.0	2238	0.3
23 TU	0451	1.8	1048	0.4	1653	2.0	2317	0.3
24 W	0521	1.8	1123	0.5	1725	2.0	2357	0.4
25 TH	0554	1.7	1159	0.5	1801	2.0		
26 F	0039	0.5	0634	1.7	1238	0.6	1845	1.9
27 SA	0125	0.5	0724	1.6	1324	0.6	◐ 1935	1.9
28 SU	0220	0.6	0825	1.6	1421	0.7	2035	1.9
29 M	0324	0.6	0937	1.6	1528	0.7	2142	1.8
30 TU	0428	0.6	1048	1.7	1638	0.6	2252	1.9
31 W	0526	0.5	1149	1.7	1740	0.6	2356	1.9

JUNE

Day	Time	m	Time	m	Time	m	Time	m
1 TH	0618	0.4	1243	1.8	1835	0.5		
2 F	0054	1.9	0707	0.3	1333	1.9	1926	0.4
3 SA	0147	2.0	0752	0.3	1419	1.9	2013	0.3
4 SU	0237	2.0	0837	0.3	1501	1.9	○ 2059	0.3
5 M	0324	1.9	0920	0.3	1540	1.9	2145	0.3
6 TU	0410	1.9	1003	0.4	1619	1.9	2231	0.2
7 W	0455	1.8	1046	0.4	1659	1.9	2318	0.2
8 TH	0543	1.8	1132	0.4	1743	2.0		
9 F	0009	0.3	0635	1.7	1220	0.5	1833	2.0
10 SA	0103	0.3	0734	1.7	1314	0.5	◑ 1932	2.0
11 SU	0203	0.3	0839	1.7	1413	0.5	2039	2.0
12 M	0306	0.3	0944	1.7	1517	0.5	2150	2.0
13 TU	0409	0.3	1047	1.8	1622	0.5	2300	2.0
14 W	0510	0.3	1146	1.8	1727	0.4		
15 TH	0006	2.0	0608	0.3	1242	1.8	1827	0.4
16 F	0107	2.0	0701	0.4	1334	1.9	1923	0.3
17 SA	0203	2.0	0749	0.4	1421	1.9	2014	0.3
18 SU	0251	1.9	0834	0.4	1501	1.9	● 2101	0.3
19 M	0332	1.9	0914	0.4	1536	1.9	2143	0.3
20 TU	0407	1.8	0951	0.4	1606	2.0	2223	0.3
21 W	0437	1.7	1027	0.5	1634	2.0	2301	0.4
22 TH	0504	1.7	1101	0.5	1703	2.0	2337	0.4
23 F	0534	1.7	1136	0.5	1737	2.0		
24 SA	0014	0.4	0608	1.7	1212	0.5	1815	2.0
25 SU	0053	0.5	0649	1.7	1253	0.5	1859	2.0
26 M	0136	0.5	0737	1.7	1339	0.5	◐ 1949	1.9
27 TU	0225	0.5	0832	1.7	1433	0.5	2045	1.9
28 W	0321	0.5	0933	1.7	1534	0.6	2147	1.9
29 TH	0421	0.5	1037	1.7	1639	0.5	2254	1.9
30 F	0523	0.5	1141	1.8	1746	0.5		

JULY

Day	Time	m	Time	m	Time	m	Time	m
1 SA	0003	1.9	0622	0.4	1243	1.8	1849	0.4
2 SU	0112	1.9	0718	0.4	1341	1.9	1947	0.4
3 M	0215	1.9	0811	0.4	1433	1.9	○ 2041	0.3
4 TU	0312	1.9	0900	0.4	1522	2.0	2132	0.2
5 W	0404	1.9	0947	0.4	1607	2.0	2220	0.2
6 TH	0453	1.8	1032	0.4	1651	2.0	2308	0.2
7 F	0539	1.8	1118	0.4	1735	2.1	2357	0.2
8 SA	0625	1.8	1205	0.4	1823	2.1		
9 SU	0046	0.2	0714	1.8	1254	0.4	1914	2.1
10 M	0138	0.2	0805	1.8	1347	0.4	◑ 2012	2.1
11 TU	0233	0.3	0901	1.8	1444	0.4	2116	2.0
12 W	0331	0.4	1000	1.8	1546	0.4	2224	2.0
13 TH	0432	0.4	1102	1.8	1653	0.4	2335	1.9
14 F	0534	0.5	1203	1.8	1801	0.4		
15 SA	0042	1.9	0633	0.5	1302	1.8	1904	0.4
16 SU	0141	1.8	0726	0.5	1354	1.9	1959	0.4
17 M	0232	1.8	0813	0.5	1439	1.9	● 2047	0.4
18 TU	0315	1.8	0855	0.5	1518	2.0	2129	0.3
19 W	0351	1.8	0933	0.5	1550	2.0	2207	0.3
20 TH	0422	1.7	1008	0.4	1617	2.0	2242	0.4
21 F	0447	1.7	1041	0.4	1644	2.0	2314	0.4
22 SA	0513	1.8	1114	0.4	1713	2.0	2346	0.4
23 SU	0542	1.8	1147	0.4	1747	2.0		
24 M	0019	0.4	0616	1.8	1224	0.4	1825	2.0
25 TU	0057	0.4	0656	1.8	1304	0.4	◐ 1909	2.0
26 W	0139	0.4	0743	1.8	1351	0.4	2000	2.0
27 TH	0229	0.4	0836	1.8	1445	0.5	2058	1.9
28 F	0326	0.5	0937	1.8	1549	0.5	2205	1.9
29 SA	0432	0.5	1044	1.8	1703	0.5	2322	1.8
30 SU	0543	0.5	1157	1.8	1819	0.5		
31 M	0047	1.8	0650	0.5	1308	1.9	1928	0.4

AUGUST

Day	Time	m	Time	m	Time	m	Time	m
1 TU	0201	1.9	0749	0.4	1411	1.9	○ 2026	0.3
2 W	0301	1.9	0842	0.4	1505	2.0	2118	0.2
3 TH	0353	1.9	0930	0.3	1552	2.1	2205	0.1
4 F	0438	1.9	1015	0.3	1636	2.1	2251	0.1
5 SA	0520	1.9	1059	0.2	1719	2.1	2335	0.1
6 SU	0559	1.8	1143	0.2	1802	2.1		
7 M	0020	0.2	0639	1.8	1229	0.2	1847	2.1
8 TU	0106	0.2	0722	1.8	1317	0.3	◑ 1938	2.1
9 W	0155	0.3	0811	1.8	1409	0.3	2035	2.0
10 TH	0249	0.5	0907	1.8	1510	0.4	2145	1.9
11 F	0350	0.6	1013	1.8	1621	0.5	2304	1.8
12 SA	0458	0.6	1124	1.8	1739	0.5		
13 SU	0017	1.7	0606	0.6	1231	1.8	1848	0.5
14 M	0119	1.7	0705	0.6	1329	1.9	1944	0.4
15 TU	0211	1.8	0754	0.5	1417	1.9	2030	0.4
16 W	0254	1.8	0836	0.5	1457	2.0	● 2109	0.3
17 TH	0331	1.8	0913	0.4	1531	2.0	2144	0.3
18 F	0401	1.8	0947	0.4	1558	2.0	2216	0.3
19 SA	0426	1.8	1019	0.3	1623	2.0	2246	0.3
20 SU	0450	1.8	1050	0.3	1650	2.0	2316	0.3
21 M	0515	1.8	1122	0.3	1720	2.0	2347	0.3
22 TU	0545	1.9	1156	0.3	1755	2.0		
23 W	0022	0.3	0620	1.9	1234	0.3	1836	2.0
24 TH	0102	0.4	0702	1.9	1319	0.3	◐ 1924	2.0
25 F	0149	0.4	0752	1.8	1410	0.4	2022	1.9
26 SA	0245	0.5	0853	1.8	1514	0.5	2132	1.8
27 SU	0353	0.6	1003	1.8	1636	0.5	2300	1.7
28 M	0514	0.6	1124	1.8	1802	0.4		
29 TU	0037	1.8	0629	0.6	1246	1.9	1912	0.3
30 W	0148	1.8	0731	0.5	1352	2.0	2009	0.2
31 TH	0245	1.9	0823	0.3	1447	2.1	○ 2059	0.1

Chart Datum: 0·69 metres below Dansk Normal Null
HAT is 2·2 metres above Chart Datum

TIME ZONE -0100
(Danish Standard Time)
Subtract 1 hour for UT
For Danish Summer Time add ONE hour in **non-shaded areas**

DENMARK – ESBJERG

LAT 55°28′N LONG 8°26′E

TIMES AND HEIGHTS OF HIGH AND LOW WATERS

Dates in amber are **SPRINGS**
Dates in grey are **NEAPS**

2023

SEPTEMBER

Date	Time	m	Date	Time	m
1	0333	1.9	16	0335	1.9
	0910	0.3		0922	0.3
F	1534	2.2	SA	1534	2.0
	2144	0.1		2146	0.3
2	0414	1.9	17	0401	1.9
	0954	0.2		0953	0.3
SA	1616	2.2	SU	1600	2.0
	2227	0.1		2216	0.3
3	0451	1.9	18	0425	1.9
	1037	0.1		1025	0.3
SU	1656	2.2	M	1627	2.0
	2308	0.1		2246	0.3
4	0526	1.9	19	0450	1.9
	1119	0.1		1057	0.3
M	1735	2.1	TU	1657	2.0
	2349	0.2		2318	0.3
5	0601	1.9	20	0518	1.9
	1202	0.2		1132	0.3
TU	1816	2.1	W	1731	2.0
				2353	0.3
6	0031	0.3	21	0551	1.9
	0638	1.9		1210	0.3
W	1247	0.2	TH	1811	1.9
◑	1901	2.0			
7	0116	0.4	22	0033	0.4
	0721	1.9		0631	1.9
TH	1336	0.3	F	1255	0.3
	1954	1.9	◐	1859	1.9
8	0205	0.5	23	0120	0.5
	0813	1.8		0721	1.9
F	1435	0.4	SA	1349	0.4
	2102	1.7		2000	1.8
9	0305	0.7	24	0217	0.6
	0920	1.8		0823	1.8
SA	1553	0.5	SU	1457	0.5
	2233	1.7		2117	1.7
10	0421	0.7	25	0329	0.7
	1044	1.8		0939	1.8
SU	1718	0.6	M	1625	0.5
	2350	1.7		2301	1.7
11	0538	0.7	26	0454	0.6
	1159	1.8		1108	1.9
M	1827	0.5	TU	1749	0.4
12	0052	1.7	27	0027	1.8
	0640	0.6		0609	0.5
TU	1259	1.9	W	1229	2.0
	1920	0.4		1854	0.2
13	0143	1.8	28	0131	1.9
	0729	0.5		0710	0.4
W	1349	2.0	TH	1333	2.1
	2004	0.3		1948	0.1
14	0227	1.8	29	0223	1.9
	0811	0.4		0801	0.3
TH	1431	2.0	F	1426	2.2
	2042	0.3	○	2035	0.1
15	0303	1.9	30	0308	2.0
	0848	0.4		0848	0.2
F	1505	2.0	SA	1513	2.2
●	2115	0.3		2119	0.1

OCTOBER

Date	Time	m	Date	Time	m
1	0347	2.0	16	0334	2.0
	0932	0.1		0927	0.3
SU	1554	2.2	M	1537	2.0
	2200	0.1		2147	0.2
2	0421	2.0	17	0401	2.0
	1013	0.1		1001	0.3
M	1632	2.1	TU	1607	2.0
	2240	0.2		2220	0.3
3	0453	2.0	18	0428	1.9
	1055	0.1		1036	0.3
TU	1709	2.1	W	1639	2.0
	2318	0.3		2254	0.3
4	0525	2.0	19	0457	1.9
	1136	0.2		1113	0.3
W	1746	2.0	TH	1715	1.9
	2358	0.4		2331	0.4
5	0559	2.0	20	0531	1.9
	1220	0.2		1155	0.3
TH	1827	1.9	F	1757	1.8
6	0038	0.5	21	0013	0.4
	0640	1.9		0612	1.9
F	1308	0.4	SA	1243	0.3
◑	1915	1.8		1849	1.8
7	0124	0.6	22	0102	0.5
	0729	1.9		0704	1.9
SA	1406	0.5	SU	1341	0.4
	2019	1.6	◐	1954	1.7
8	0219	0.7	23	0201	0.6
	0831	1.8		0809	1.9
SU	1524	0.6	M	1454	0.4
	2155	1.6		2122	1.7
9	0337	0.8	24	0316	0.6
	0957	1.8		0929	1.9
M	1649	0.6	TU	1617	0.4
	2315	1.6		2257	1.7
10	0501	0.7	25	0436	0.6
	1119	1.8		1055	2.0
TU	1755	0.5	W	1729	0.3
11	0016	1.7	26	0008	1.8
	0606	0.6		0546	0.5
W	1222	1.9	TH	1209	2.0
	1847	0.4		1830	0.2
12	0108	1.8	27	0106	1.9
	0657	0.5		0645	0.4
TH	1314	2.0	F	1311	2.1
	1930	0.3		1923	0.1
13	0152	1.9	28	0157	1.9
	0740	0.4		0737	0.2
F	1357	2.0	SA	1405	2.2
	2008	0.3	○	2010	0.1
14	0231	1.9	29	0241	2.0
	0818	0.3		0825	0.2
SA	1434	2.1	SU	1452	2.2
●	2042	0.2		2053	0.1
15	0305	2.0	30	0319	2.0
	0853	0.3		0910	0.1
SU	1507	2.1	M	1534	2.1
	2115	0.2		2134	0.2
			31	0353	2.0
				0952	0.1
			TU	1611	2.0
				2213	0.2

NOVEMBER

Date	Time	m	Date	Time	m
1	0424	2.0	16	0411	2.0
	1034	0.1		1021	0.2
W	1646	2.0	TH	1631	1.9
	2250	0.3		2236	0.3
2	0455	2.0	17	0444	2.0
	1116	0.2		1102	0.3
TH	1721	1.9	F	1711	1.8
	2328	0.4		2317	0.4
3	0529	2.0	18	0521	2.0
	1159	0.3		1148	0.3
F	1759	1.8	SA	1757	1.8
4	0007	0.5	19	0001	0.4
	0608	2.0		0605	2.0
SA	1245	0.4	SU	1240	0.3
	1844	1.7		1852	1.7
5	0049	0.6	20	0052	0.5
	0655	1.9		0659	2.0
SU	1340	0.5	M	1339	0.3
◑	1941	1.6	◐	2000	1.7
6	0141	0.7	21	0152	0.5
	0752	1.9		0804	2.0
M	1449	0.6	TU	1447	0.3
	2101	1.6		2120	1.7
7	0248	0.7	22	0300	0.6
	0904	1.9		0919	2.0
TU	1604	0.6	W	1558	0.3
	2224	1.6		2234	1.7
8	0407	0.7	23	0411	0.5
	1024	1.9		1036	2.0
W	1708	0.5	TH	1703	0.2
	2329	1.7		2339	1.8
9	0517	0.6	24	0517	0.4
	1132	1.9		1146	2.1
TH	1801	0.4	F	1802	0.2
10	0023	1.8	25	0036	1.9
	0613	0.5		0618	0.3
F	1228	2.0	SA	1249	2.1
	1847	0.3		1855	0.2
11	0111	1.9	26	0128	1.9
	0701	0.4		0713	0.3
SA	1317	2.0	SU	1345	2.1
	1928	0.3		1944	0.2
12	0154	2.0	27	0214	2.0
	0743	0.4		0804	0.2
SU	1400	2.0	M	1434	2.1
	2007	0.2	○	2029	0.2
13	0232	2.0	28	0255	2.0
	0824	0.3		0851	0.2
M	1439	2.0	TU	1518	2.0
●	2044	0.2		2111	0.3
14	0307	2.0	29	0331	2.0
	0902	0.3		0936	0.2
TU	1517	2.0	W	1557	1.9
	2121	0.2		2150	0.3
15	0339	2.0	30	0404	2.0
	0941	0.2		1019	0.2
W	1553	2.0	TH	1631	1.8
	2158	0.3		2228	0.4

DECEMBER

Date	Time	m	Date	Time	m
1	0435	2.0	16	0437	2.0
	1101	0.3		1056	0.2
F	1704	1.8	SA	1715	1.8
	2305	0.4		2307	0.4
2	0508	2.1	17	0518	2.1
	1143	0.3		1144	0.2
SA	1739	1.7	SU	1802	1.8
	2343	0.4		2353	0.4
3	0545	2.0	18	0603	2.1
	1226	0.4		1234	0.2
SU	1819	1.7	M	1854	1.8
4	0023	0.5	19	0042	0.4
	0628	2.0		0655	2.1
M	1313	0.4	TU	1329	0.2
	1907	1.7	◐	1952	1.7
5	0109	0.5	20	0137	0.4
	0718	2.0		0754	2.1
TU	1406	0.5	W	1427	0.2
◑	2006	1.6		2056	1.7
6	0202	0.6	21	0236	0.4
	0815	1.9		0900	2.1
W	1504	0.5	TH	1529	0.3
	2115	1.6		2200	1.8
7	0305	0.6	22	0341	0.4
	0919	1.9		1010	2.1
TH	1605	0.5	F	1631	0.3
	2224	1.7		2303	1.8
8	0412	0.6	23	0447	0.4
	1027	1.9		1120	2.1
F	1703	0.5	SA	1731	0.3
	2326	1.8			
9	0516	0.6	24	0003	1.9
	1131	1.9		0551	0.4
SA	1756	0.4	SU	1227	2.0
				1829	0.3
10	0022	1.8	25	0100	1.9
	0614	0.5		0653	0.3
SU	1230	2.0	M	1328	2.0
	1845	0.3		1921	0.3
11	0112	1.9	26	0152	2.0
	0706	0.4		0749	0.3
M	1324	2.0	TU	1422	2.0
	1932	0.3		2009	0.3
12	0158	2.0	27	0238	2.0
	0755	0.3		0839	0.3
TU	1415	2.0	W	1509	1.9
	2016	0.3	○	2053	0.4
13	0241	2.0	28	0318	2.0
	0841	0.3		0925	0.2
W	1502	2.0	TH	1549	1.8
●	2059	0.3		2133	0.4
14	0321	2.0	29	0352	2.1
	0926	0.2		1008	0.3
TH	1547	1.9	F	1623	1.8
	2141	0.3		2211	0.4
15	0359	2.0	30	0424	2.1
	1011	0.2		1048	0.3
F	1630	1.9	SA	1654	1.8
	2223	0.3		2248	0.4
			31	0454	2.1
				1126	0.3
			SU	1724	1.7
				2324	0.4

Chart Datum: 0·69 metres below Dansk Normal Null
HAT is 2·2 metres above Chart Datum

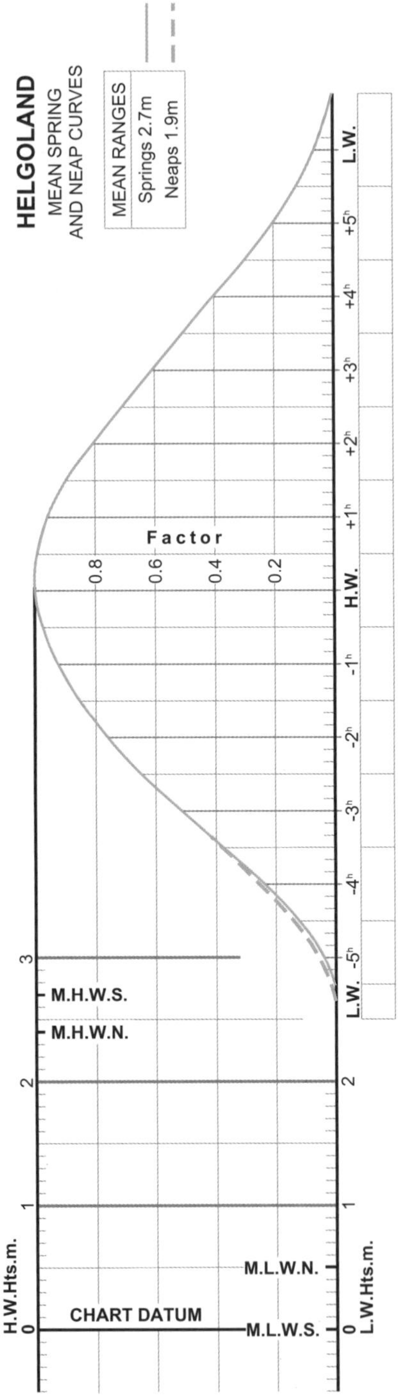
HELGOLAND
MEAN SPRING
AND NEAP CURVES
MEAN RANGES
Springs 2.7m
Neaps 1.9m
Factor
0.8
0.6
0.4
0.2
L.W.
-5h
-4h
-3h
-2h
-1h
H.W.
+1h
+2h
+3h
+4h
+5h
L.W.
H.W.Hts.m.
L.W.Hts.m.
0
1
2
3
M.H.W.S.
M.H.W.N.
M.L.W.N.
M.L.W.S.
CHART DATUM

TIME ZONE -0100
(German Standard Time)
Subtract 1 hour for UT
For German Summer Time add ONE hour in **non-shaded areas**

GERMANY – HELGOLAND

LAT 54°11'N LONG 7°53'E

TIMES AND HEIGHTS OF HIGH AND LOW WATERS

Dates in amber are **SPRINGS**
Dates in grey are **NEAPS**

2023

JANUARY

Date	Time	m	Time	m	Time	m	Time	m
1 SU	0057	0.9	0645	3.1	1340	0.8	1926	2.8
2 M	0205	0.9	0753	3.1	1446	0.9	2033	2.8
3 TU	0316	0.9	0902	3.0	1550	0.9	2135	2.9
4 W	0421	0.8	1003	3.0	1647	0.9	2228	3.0
5 TH	0516	0.8	1054	3.0	1735	0.8	2314	3.1
6 F	0603	0.6	1139	3.0	1818	0.7	2355	3.1
7 SA ○	0644	0.5	1220	2.9	1855	0.6		
8 SU	0032	3.1	0722	0.5	1257	2.9	1930	0.6
9 M	0108	3.1	0757	0.5	1332	2.9	2003	0.6
10 TU	0142	3.1	0831	0.5	1405	2.9	2034	0.6
11 W	0214	3.1	0902	0.6	1438	2.9	2105	0.6
12 TH	0245	3.1	0936	0.6	1513	2.8	2140	0.7
13 F	0321	3.1	1013	0.6	1552	2.8	2218	0.7
14 SA	0359	3.1	1049	0.6	1630	2.8	2256	0.7
15 SU	0438	3.0	1126	0.7	1709	2.8	◑ 2340	0.8
16 M	0524	2.9	1213	0.7	1801	2.7		
17 TU	0039	0.8	0626	2.8	1319	0.8	1909	2.7
18 W	0154	0.8	0742	2.8	1435	0.8	2023	2.8
19 TH	0314	0.8	0859	2.9	1550	0.7	2134	2.9
20 F	0429	0.7	1011	3.0	1659	0.6	2238	3.0
21 SA	0535	0.5	1114	3.0	1800	0.6	● 2335	3.1
22 SU	0632	0.4	1211	3.1	1854	0.6		
23 M	0028	3.3	0726	0.4	1303	3.1	1945	0.6
24 TU	0118	3.4	0819	0.3	1353	3.1	2033	0.5
25 W	0206	3.4	0907	0.3	1441	3.0	2117	0.4
26 TH	0252	3.4	0951	0.3	1524	3.0	2157	0.4
27 F	0336	3.3	1033	0.4	1606	2.9	2238	0.5
28 SA	0421	3.2	1113	0.6	1648	2.9	◐ 2321	0.6
29 SU	0506	3.1	1153	0.7	1733	2.8		
30 M	0007	0.7	0556	3.0	1240	0.8	1826	2.8
31 TU	0108	0.8	0659	2.9	1346	0.9	1935	2.7

FEBRUARY

Date	Time	m	Time	m	Time	m	Time	m
1 W	0226	0.8	0817	2.8	1504	0.9	2053	2.8
2 TH	0348	0.8	0934	2.8	1618	0.9	2203	2.9
3 F	0457	0.7	1037	2.8	1718	0.8	2257	3.0
4 SA	0550	0.6	1127	2.8	1804	0.6	2341	3.0
5 SU ○	0632	0.5	1208	2.8	1843	0.5		
6 M	0019	3.0	0709	0.4	1244	2.9	1917	0.5
7 TU	0053	3.1	0743	0.4	1317	2.9	1950	0.4
8 W	0126	3.1	0815	0.4	1348	2.9	2019	0.4
9 TH	0156	3.1	0845	0.4	1418	2.9	2049	0.5
10 F	0226	3.1	0916	0.4	1450	2.9	2122	0.5
11 SA	0259	3.1	0949	0.5	1524	2.9	2156	0.5
12 SU	0333	3.1	1020	0.5	1556	2.9	2226	0.5
13 M	0404	3.0	1046	0.5	1625	2.8	◑ 2258	0.6
14 TU	0441	2.9	1123	0.7	1709	2.7	2351	0.7
15 W	0539	2.8	1227	0.8	1818	2.7		
16 TH	0112	0.8	0703	2.7	1356	0.8	1945	2.7
17 F	0247	0.7	0836	2.7	1527	0.7	2112	2.8
18 SA	0416	0.5	1000	2.8	1648	0.6	2227	3.0
19 SU	0530	0.4	1110	2.9	1754	0.5	2328	3.1
20 M ●	0630	0.3	1206	3.0	1847	0.5		
21 TU	0020	3.3	0720	0.2	1254	3.0	1934	0.4
22 W	0106	3.3	0807	0.2	1337	3.1	2018	0.3
23 TH	0150	3.3	0850	0.2	1419	3.0	2058	0.3
24 F	0232	3.3	0929	0.3	1458	2.9	2135	0.3
25 SA	0312	3.2	1004	0.3	1534	2.9	2211	0.3
26 SU	0350	3.1	1036	0.5	1609	2.9	2244	0.4
27 M	0428	3.0	1105	0.6	1644	2.8	◐ 2321	0.5
28 TU	0509	2.8	1144	0.8	1730	2.7		

MARCH

Date	Time	m	Time	m	Time	m	Time	m
1 W	0015	0.7	0608	2.7	1247	0.9	1840	2.7
2 TH	0136	0.8	0731	2.6	1416	1.0	2009	2.7
3 F	0313	0.8	0902	2.6	1547	0.9	2134	2.8
4 SA	0436	0.6	1018	2.7	1657	0.7	2238	2.9
5 SU	0533	0.5	1110	2.7	1745	0.6	2322	3.0
6 M	0613	0.4	1149	2.8	1823	0.5	2358	3.0
7 TU ○	0647	0.3	1223	2.8	1857	0.4		
8 W	0032	3.1	0721	0.3	1255	2.9	1930	0.3
9 TH	0103	3.1	0753	0.3	1325	2.9	2000	0.3
10 F	0134	3.1	0822	0.3	1354	2.9	2029	0.3
11 SA	0203	3.1	0851	0.3	1424	3.0	2100	0.3
12 SU	0234	3.1	0922	0.4	1455	2.9	2133	0.3
13 M	0307	3.0	0951	0.4	1525	2.9	2203	0.4
14 TU	0339	2.9	1018	0.5	1556	2.8	2236	0.4
15 W	0418	2.8	1055	0.6	1640	2.7	◑ 2329	0.6
16 TH	0518	2.6	1201	0.8	1751	2.7		
17 F	0053	0.6	0646	2.6	1335	0.8	1925	2.7
18 SA	0235	0.5	0825	2.6	1514	0.7	2059	2.8
19 SU	0408	0.4	0952	2.7	1637	0.6	2215	3.0
20 M	0522	0.3	1100	2.8	1741	0.4	2315	3.1
21 TU ●	0618	0.2	1152	2.9	1832	0.4		
22 W	0005	3.2	0704	0.2	1235	3.0	1916	0.3
23 TH	0047	3.3	0744	0.2	1313	3.0	1955	0.3
24 F	0127	3.3	0822	0.2	1350	3.0	2032	0.2
25 SA	0206	3.2	0857	0.3	1427	3.0	2109	0.2
26 SU	0244	3.1	0930	0.3	1501	2.9	2142	0.3
27 M	0320	3.0	0958	0.5	1532	2.9	2213	0.3
28 TU	0354	2.9	1024	0.6	1605	2.8	2246	0.5
29 W	0433	2.7	1100	0.8	1648	2.8	◐ 2334	0.7
30 TH	0529	2.6	1200	1.0	1754	2.7		
31 F	0052	0.8	0649	2.5	1329	1.0	1924	2.7

APRIL

Date	Time	m	Time	m	Time	m	Time	m
1 SA	0231	0.8	0823	2.5	1506	0.9	2055	2.7
2 SU	0400	0.6	0945	2.6	1622	0.7	2205	2.8
3 M	0501	0.5	1040	2.7	1713	0.6	2250	3.0
4 TU	0540	0.3	1118	2.8	1751	0.5	2326	3.0
5 W	0614	0.3	1151	2.9	1827	0.4		
6 TH	0001	3.0	0649	0.2	1224	2.9	○ 1903	0.3
7 F	0034	3.1	0722	0.2	1256	3.0	1935	0.3
8 SA	0106	3.1	0753	0.3	1325	3.0	2005	0.3
9 SU	0137	3.1	0823	0.3	1355	3.0	2037	0.3
10 M	0209	3.0	0854	0.3	1427	3.0	2112	0.2
11 TU	0245	2.9	0927	0.3	1502	2.9	2150	0.2
12 W	0326	2.8	1003	0.4	1542	2.8	2232	0.3
13 TH	0414	2.7	1049	0.6	1633	2.8	◑ 2330	0.4
14 F	0518	2.6	1157	0.7	1745	2.8		
15 SA	0052	0.5	0643	2.5	1328	0.7	1915	2.8
16 SU	0229	0.4	0817	2.5	1502	0.7	2045	2.9
17 M	0356	0.3	0938	2.6	1620	0.5	2157	3.0
18 TU	0502	0.3	1039	2.8	1719	0.4	2253	3.1
19 W	0553	0.2	1128	2.9	1808	0.4	2341	3.2
20 TH ●	0637	0.2	1209	3.0	1851	0.3		
21 F	0023	3.2	0714	0.3	1246	3.0	1929	0.3
22 SA	0102	3.2	0749	0.3	1320	3.1	2006	0.3
23 SU	0140	3.1	0823	0.4	1356	3.1	2042	0.3
24 M	0217	3.0	0856	0.4	1431	3.0	2116	0.3
25 TU	0253	2.9	0926	0.5	1504	3.0	2149	0.4
26 W	0329	2.8	0955	0.6	1538	3.0	2223	0.5
27 TH	0409	2.7	1031	0.8	1620	2.9	◐ 2308	0.7
28 F	0500	2.6	1125	0.9	1719	2.8		
29 SA	0015	0.8	0610	2.5	1243	1.0	1837	2.8
30 SU	0141	0.8	0734	2.5	1413	0.9	2002	2.8

Chart Datum: 1·68 metres below Normal Null (German reference level)
HAT is 3·0 metres above Chart Datum

TIME ZONE -0100
(German Standard Time)
Subtract 1 hour for UT
For German Summer Time add ONE hour in **non-shaded areas**

GERMANY – HELGOLAND

LAT 54°11′N LONG 7°53′E

TIMES AND HEIGHTS OF HIGH AND LOW WATERS

Dates in amber are **SPRINGS**
Dates in grey are **NEAPS**

2023

MAY

Date	Day	Time	m	Time	m	Time	m	Time	m
1	M	0306	0.6	0853	2.6	1530	0.7	2113	2.8
2	TU	0410	0.4	0952	2.7	1625	0.6	2203	2.9
3	W	0453	0.3	1033	2.8	1707	0.5	2244	3.0
4	TH	0531	0.3	1110	2.9	1749	0.4	2323	3.0
5	F ○	0610	0.3	1147	3.0	1829	0.3		
6	SA	0000	3.1	0647	0.2	1222	3.0	1905	0.3
7	SU	0035	3.1	0722	0.3	1255	3.1	1941	0.3
8	M	0111	3.1	0757	0.3	1330	3.1	2018	0.2
9	TU	0150	3.0	0834	0.3	1407	3.0	2059	0.2
10	W	0233	2.9	0914	0.3	1449	3.0	2145	0.2
11	TH	0323	2.8	0959	0.4	1539	3.0	2238	0.3
12	F ◑	0419	2.7	1053	0.6	1637	2.9	2339	0.4
13	SA	0524	2.6	1159	0.7	1746	2.9		
14	SU	0053	0.4	0640	2.6	1319	0.7	1905	2.9
15	M	0215	0.4	0801	2.6	1443	0.6	2025	3.0
16	TU	0332	0.4	0913	2.7	1554	0.6	2132	3.1
17	W	0432	0.4	1011	2.8	1650	0.5	2226	3.2
18	TH	0521	0.4	1057	3.0	1739	0.5	2314	3.2
19	F ●	0604	0.4	1140	3.0	1825	0.4	2359	3.2
20	SA	0644	0.4	1219	3.1	1906	0.4		
21	SU	0039	3.1	0720	0.5	1254	3.1	1943	0.4
22	M	0117	3.1	0755	0.5	1331	3.1	2020	0.4
23	TU	0155	3.0	0830	0.5	1407	3.1	2056	0.4
24	W	0232	2.9	0902	0.6	1442	3.1	2131	0.5
25	TH	0309	2.8	0935	0.6	1518	3.1	2206	0.6
26	F	0349	2.7	1012	0.8	1559	3.0	2248	0.7
27	SA ◐	0436	2.7	1059	0.9	1649	2.9	2341	0.8
28	SU	0532	2.6	1200	0.9	1750	2.9		
29	M	0047	0.7	0638	2.6	1312	0.8	1859	2.8
30	TU	0158	0.6	0747	2.6	1423	0.7	2007	2.9
31	W	0302	0.5	0848	2.7	1523	0.7	2104	2.9

JUNE

Date	Day	Time	m	Time	m	Time	m	Time	m
1	TH	0354	0.4	0938	2.8	1615	0.6	2154	3.0
2	F	0441	0.4	1024	2.9	1706	0.5	2242	3.0
3	SA	0529	0.4	1108	3.0	1753	0.4	2327	3.1
4	SU ○	0613	0.3	1150	3.1	1837	0.4		
5	M	0009	3.1	0656	0.3	1230	3.1	1921	0.3
6	TU	0053	3.1	0739	0.4	1312	3.1	2007	0.3
7	W	0140	3.0	0824	0.4	1357	3.2	2055	0.2
8	TH	0230	2.9	0910	0.4	1445	3.1	2146	0.2
9	F	0322	2.8	0959	0.5	1538	3.1	2241	0.3
10	SA ◑	0419	2.7	1053	0.6	1636	3.1	2339	0.4
11	SU	0520	2.7	1154	0.6	1738	3.1		
12	M	0042	0.4	0625	2.7	1300	0.6	1845	3.1
13	TU	0149	0.5	0732	2.7	1412	0.6	1955	3.1
14	W	0256	0.5	0838	2.8	1520	0.6	2101	3.1
15	TH	0356	0.5	0937	2.9	1620	0.6	2158	3.1
16	F	0448	0.6	1027	3.0	1713	0.6	2250	3.1
17	SA	0536	0.6	1114	3.1	1803	0.5	2338	3.1
18	SU ●	0620	0.5	1157	3.1	1848	0.4		
19	M	0022	3.0	0700	0.5	1236	3.1	1927	0.4
20	TU	0102	3.0	0736	0.5	1314	3.2	2005	0.4
21	W	0140	2.9	0812	0.6	1350	3.2	2041	0.5
22	TH	0216	2.9	0845	0.6	1425	3.2	2114	0.5
23	F	0251	2.8	0917	0.6	1459	3.1	2149	0.6
24	SA	0328	2.8	0953	0.7	1537	3.1	2228	0.6
25	SU	0411	2.8	1035	0.8	1620	3.1	2310	0.7
26	M ◐	0455	2.8	1120	0.8	1705	3.0	2355	0.7
27	TU	0542	2.7	1211	0.8	1757	2.9		
28	W	0047	0.7	0636	2.7	1311	0.8	1856	2.9
29	TH	0148	0.6	0738	2.8	1416	0.8	2001	2.9
30	F	0251	0.6	0839	2.8	1522	0.8	2105	3.0

JULY

Date	Day	Time	m	Time	m	Time	m	Time	m
1	SA	0353	0.6	0938	2.9	1626	0.7	2206	3.0
2	SU	0454	0.5	1034	3.0	1725	0.5	2302	3.1
3	M ○	0549	0.5	1125	3.1	1819	0.4	2354	3.1
4	TU	0640	0.5	1214	3.2	1910	0.3		
5	W	0044	3.1	0730	0.4	1302	3.3	2003	0.3
6	TH	0135	3.1	0819	0.4	1352	3.3	2054	0.2
7	F	0226	3.0	0906	0.4	1440	3.3	2143	0.2
8	SA	0316	2.9	0952	0.4	1529	3.3	2233	0.3
9	SU	0407	2.8	1042	0.5	1622	3.2	2324	0.4
10	M ◑	0459	2.8	1134	0.5	1717	3.2		
11	TU	0015	0.5	0553	2.7	1228	0.6	1813	3.1
12	W	0108	0.6	0650	2.7	1330	0.7	1917	3.0
13	TH	0210	0.7	0755	2.8	1441	0.7	2026	3.0
14	F	0317	0.8	0902	2.9	1552	0.7	2134	3.0
15	SA	0420	0.8	1003	3.0	1655	0.7	2233	3.0
16	SU	0515	0.7	1055	3.1	1749	0.6	2324	3.0
17	M ●	0603	0.6	1141	3.1	1835	0.5		
18	TU	0009	2.9	0646	0.6	1223	3.1	1916	0.4
19	W	0050	2.9	0723	0.5	1301	3.2	1952	0.5
20	TH	0126	2.9	0757	0.6	1335	3.2	2025	0.5
21	F	0159	2.9	0828	0.6	1407	3.2	2055	0.6
22	SA	0230	2.9	0857	0.6	1438	3.2	2126	0.6
23	SU	0303	2.9	0931	0.7	1512	3.2	2202	0.6
24	M	0341	2.9	1008	0.7	1550	3.2	2236	0.7
25	TU ◐	0417	2.9	1043	0.8	1625	3.1	2307	0.7
26	W	0451	2.9	1118	0.8	1703	3.0	2343	0.8
27	TH	0532	2.8	1207	0.9	1754	2.9		
28	F	0039	0.8	0632	2.8	1316	0.9	1905	2.9
29	SA	0154	0.8	0746	2.8	1438	0.9	2025	2.9
30	SU	0314	0.8	0902	2.9	1558	0.7	2141	3.0
31	M	0429	0.7	1010	3.0	1709	0.6	2248	3.0

AUGUST

Date	Day	Time	m	Time	m	Time	m	Time	m
1	TU ○	0535	0.6	1110	3.1	1810	0.4	2346	3.1
2	W	0631	0.5	1204	3.3	1904	0.3		
3	TH	0038	3.1	0722	0.5	1253	3.4	1956	0.3
4	F	0127	3.1	0810	0.4	1341	3.4	2046	0.2
5	SA	0214	3.0	0855	0.3	1427	3.4	2130	0.2
6	SU	0258	2.9	0937	0.3	1511	3.3	2212	0.3
7	M	0342	2.9	1019	0.4	1557	3.2	2254	0.4
8	TU ◑	0425	2.8	1102	0.5	1645	3.1	2334	0.5
9	W	0510	2.8	1147	0.6	1734	3.0		
10	TH	0018	0.7	0601	2.8	1244	0.7	1834	2.9
11	F	0118	0.9	0707	2.8	1359	0.8	1950	2.8
12	SA	0236	1.0	0826	2.8	1525	0.8	2112	2.8
13	SU	0356	0.9	0943	2.9	1642	0.8	2222	2.9
14	M	0502	0.8	1043	3.0	1739	0.7	2315	2.9
15	TU	0551	0.7	1130	3.1	1823	0.5	2357	2.9
16	W ●	0631	0.6	1209	3.1	1900	0.5		
17	TH	0034	2.9	0707	0.6	1244	3.2	1934	0.5
18	F	0107	3.0	0739	0.6	1316	3.2	2004	0.5
19	SA	0137	3.0	0808	0.6	1345	3.3	2032	0.6
20	SU	0205	3.0	0835	0.6	1413	3.3	2059	0.6
21	M	0234	3.0	0905	0.7	1444	3.2	2130	0.6
22	TU	0307	3.0	0939	0.7	1518	3.2	2200	0.7
23	W	0339	3.0	1010	0.7	1549	3.1	2226	0.7
24	TH ◐	0407	3.0	1038	0.8	1621	3.0	2255	0.8
25	F	0443	2.9	1121	0.9	1711	2.9	2349	1.0
26	SA	0544	2.8	1234	1.0	1827	2.8		
27	SU	0114	1.0	0708	2.8	1409	0.9	2000	2.8
28	M	0249	0.9	0838	2.9	1542	0.7	2128	2.8
29	TU	0415	0.8	0956	3.0	1700	0.5	2240	2.9
30	W	0524	0.6	1059	3.2	1802	0.4	2338	3.0
31	TH ○	0620	0.5	1152	3.3	1854	0.3		

Chart Datum: 1·68 metres below Normal Null (German reference level)
HAT is 3·0 metres above Chart Datum

TIME ZONE -0100
(German Standard Time)
Subtract 1 hour for UT
For German Summer Time add ONE hour in **non-shaded areas**

GERMANY – HELGOLAND

LAT 54°11′N LONG 7°53′E

TIMES AND HEIGHTS OF HIGH AND LOW WATERS

Dates in amber are **SPRINGS**
Dates in grey are **NEAPS**

2023

SEPTEMBER

Date	Day	Time	m	Time	m	Time	m	Time	m
1	F	0027	3.1	0708	0.4	1238	3.4	1940	0.3
2	SA	0110	3.1	0752	0.4	1323	3.4	2024	0.3
3	SU	0152	3.0	0834	0.3	1406	3.4	2105	0.3
4	M	0232	3.0	0913	0.3	1447	3.3	2142	0.4
5	TU	0310	2.9	0950	0.4	1528	3.2	2215	0.5
6	W	0347	2.9	1027	0.5	1609	3.1	◑ 2248	0.7
7	TH	0426	2.9	1107	0.6	1654	2.9	2328	0.9
8	F	0513	2.8	1159	0.8	1753	2.7		
9	SA	0028	1.1	0621	2.8	1318	1.0	1913	2.6
10	SU	0154	1.1	0749	2.8	1455	1.0	2046	2.7
11	M	0329	1.1	0919	2.9	1624	0.9	2206	2.8
12	TU	0444	0.9	1027	3.0	1725	0.7	2301	2.9
13	W	0533	0.8	1112	3.1	1803	0.6	2338	2.9
14	TH	0609	0.7	1146	3.1	1835	0.5		
15	F	0009	3.0	0642	0.6	1219	3.2	● 1906	0.5
16	SA	0040	3.0	0714	0.6	1250	3.2	1936	0.5
17	SU	0109	3.1	0743	0.6	1319	3.2	2003	0.5
18	M	0136	3.1	0810	0.6	1346	3.2	2029	0.6
19	TU	0203	3.1	0838	0.6	1415	3.2	2056	0.6
20	W	0232	3.1	0909	0.6	1446	3.1	2125	0.7
21	TH	0303	3.0	0941	0.7	1519	3.0	2153	0.7
22	F	0335	3.0	1013	0.7	1556	2.9	◐ 2226	0.9
23	SA	0415	2.9	1059	0.8	1650	2.8	2324	1.0
24	SU	0518	2.8	1215	0.9	1810	2.7		
25	M	0052	1.1	0648	2.8	1355	0.8	1947	2.6
26	TU	0233	1.0	0823	2.9	1532	0.7	2118	2.7
27	W	0401	0.8	0943	3.1	1649	0.5	2229	2.9
28	TH	0508	0.7	1044	3.2	1747	0.4	2322	3.0
29	F	0601	0.6	1134	3.3	1834	0.4	○	
30	SA	0007	3.1	0647	0.5	1218	3.4	1915	0.4

OCTOBER

Date	Day	Time	m	Time	m	Time	m	Time	m
1	SU	0046	3.1	0728	0.4	1259	3.4	1954	0.4
2	M	0124	3.1	0807	0.4	1341	3.3	2032	0.5
3	TU	0202	3.1	0846	0.4	1421	3.2	2107	0.5
4	W	0238	3.1	0922	0.4	1459	3.1	2138	0.6
5	TH	0312	3.0	0956	0.6	1537	3.0	2209	0.8
6	F	0349	3.0	1034	0.7	1621	2.8	◑ 2247	1.0
7	SA	0435	2.9	1124	0.9	1717	2.7	2345	1.2
8	SU	0541	2.8	1238	1.1	1836	2.6		
9	M	0111	1.2	0708	2.8	1414	1.1	2008	2.6
10	TU	0248	1.1	0841	2.9	1547	0.9	2133	2.7
11	W	0409	1.0	0954	3.0	1651	0.8	2230	2.8
12	TH	0500	0.8	1040	3.1	1729	0.6	2305	2.9
13	F	0535	0.7	1113	3.1	1758	0.6	2335	3.0
14	SA	0609	0.6	1145	3.1	1830	0.5	●	
15	SU	0006	3.0	0643	0.6	1219	3.2	1901	0.5
16	M	0037	3.1	0714	0.6	1249	3.2	1930	0.5
17	TU	0106	3.1	0743	0.6	1318	3.2	1958	0.6
18	W	0133	3.1	0812	0.6	1348	3.1	2026	0.6
19	TH	0203	3.1	0844	0.6	1421	3.1	2057	0.7
20	F	0236	3.1	0921	0.6	1501	3.0	2133	0.8
21	SA	0316	3.0	1003	0.7	1547	2.8	2216	0.9
22	SU	0405	3.0	1056	0.8	1647	2.7	◐ 2317	1.0
23	M	0511	2.9	1211	0.9	1806	2.7		
24	TU	0042	1.1	0636	2.9	1344	0.8	1937	2.6
25	W	0218	1.0	0807	3.0	1516	0.7	2102	2.7
26	TH	0342	0.9	0924	3.1	1628	0.6	2208	2.9
27	F	0445	0.7	1022	3.3	1721	0.6	2258	3.0
28	SA	0535	0.7	1110	3.4	1806	0.5	○ 2341	3.1
29	SU	0621	0.6	1155	3.4	1845	0.6		
30	M	0019	3.1	0702	0.5	1236	3.3	1923	0.6
31	TU	0056	3.2	0742	0.5	1316	3.3	1959	0.6

NOVEMBER

Date	Day	Time	m	Time	m	Time	m	Time	m
1	W	0133	3.2	0821	0.5	1357	3.1	2036	0.7
2	TH	0211	3.1	0858	0.5	1436	3.0	2109	0.7
3	F	0247	3.1	0934	0.6	1514	2.9	2141	0.8
4	SA	0323	3.1	1011	0.8	1556	2.8	2218	1.0
5	SU	0407	3.0	1057	1.0	1648	2.7	◑ 2311	1.1
6	M	0505	2.9	1201	1.1	1756	2.6		
7	TU	0025	1.2	0620	2.9	1323	1.1	1916	2.6
8	W	0151	1.1	0743	2.9	1447	0.9	2035	2.6
9	TH	0311	1.0	0857	2.9	1554	0.8	2137	2.8
10	F	0408	0.9	0950	3.0	1638	0.7	2218	2.9
11	SA	0449	0.8	1029	3.1	1712	0.6	2253	3.0
12	SU	0528	0.8	1106	3.1	1749	0.6	2328	3.0
13	M	0607	0.7	1143	3.1	1825	0.6	●	
14	TU	0003	3.1	0643	0.7	1218	3.1	1858	0.6
15	W	0035	3.1	0717	0.6	1252	3.1	1932	0.6
16	TH	0108	3.2	0752	0.6	1329	3.1	2006	0.7
17	F	0144	3.2	0831	0.6	1409	3.0	2044	0.7
18	SA	0223	3.1	0914	0.6	1455	3.0	2126	0.8
19	SU	0309	3.1	1003	0.6	1547	2.9	2216	0.9
20	M	0403	3.1	1100	0.7	1648	2.8	◐ 2317	1.0
21	TU	0507	3.1	1209	0.8	1759	2.7		
22	W	0031	1.0	0622	3.1	1328	0.8	1917	2.7
23	TH	0154	1.0	0742	3.1	1448	0.8	2033	2.8
24	F	0312	0.9	0856	3.2	1556	0.7	2137	2.9
25	SA	0414	0.8	0955	3.3	1649	0.7	2228	3.1
26	SU	0507	0.8	1046	3.3	1736	0.7	2313	3.1
27	M	0556	0.7	1133	3.3	1819	0.7	○ 2354	3.2
28	TU	0641	0.6	1217	3.2	1857	0.7		
29	W	0033	3.2	0722	0.5	1258	3.1	1935	0.7
30	TH	0112	3.2	0802	0.6	1339	3.0	2014	0.7

DECEMBER

Date	Day	Time	m	Time	m	Time	m	Time	m
1	F	0152	3.2	0842	0.6	1419	3.0	2049	0.7
2	SA	0229	3.2	0918	0.6	1457	2.9	2122	0.8
3	SU	0304	3.1	0954	0.7	1536	2.8	2158	0.9
4	M	0344	3.1	1035	0.9	1621	2.8	2243	1.0
5	TU	0432	3.0	1125	1.0	1714	2.7	◑ 2338	1.1
6	W	0529	3.0	1225	1.0	1815	2.7		
7	TH	0044	1.0	0635	2.9	1332	0.9	1921	2.7
8	F	0155	1.0	0743	2.9	1437	0.8	2025	2.8
9	SA	0259	1.0	0844	3.0	1532	0.8	2119	2.9
10	SU	0354	0.9	0937	3.0	1621	0.8	2206	3.0
11	M	0444	0.9	1025	3.1	1708	0.7	2250	3.0
12	TU	0532	0.8	1110	3.1	1752	0.7	2331	3.1
13	W	0616	0.7	1153	3.1	1833	0.7	●	
14	TH	0011	3.2	0657	0.6	1234	3.1	1915	0.7
15	F	0052	3.2	0742	0.6	1319	3.1	1958	0.6
16	SA	0135	3.2	0828	0.5	1406	3.0	2042	0.6
17	SU	0219	3.3	0915	0.5	1454	3.0	2126	0.7
18	M	0307	3.3	1005	0.5	1545	2.9	2216	0.7
19	TU	0400	3.2	1059	0.6	1641	2.8	◐ 2311	0.8
20	W	0457	3.2	1157	0.7	1740	2.8		
21	TH	0012	0.8	0559	3.1	1300	0.7	1845	2.8
22	F	0121	0.8	0708	3.1	1408	0.8	1953	2.8
23	SA	0234	0.8	0820	3.1	1516	0.8	2100	2.9
24	SU	0343	0.8	0927	3.2	1617	0.9	2158	3.0
25	M	0444	0.8	1025	3.2	1711	0.8	2249	3.1
26	TU	0538	0.7	1117	3.1	1759	0.8	2336	3.1
27	W	0627	0.6	1204	3.1	1842	0.7	○	
28	TH	0019	3.1	0711	0.5	1247	3.0	1921	0.7
29	F	0059	3.2	0751	0.5	1328	3.0	1959	0.7
30	SA	0138	3.2	0830	0.6	1406	2.9	2034	0.7
31	SU	0214	3.2	0904	0.6	1440	2.9	2105	0.7

Chart Datum: 1·68 metres below Normal Null (German reference level)
HAT is 3·0 metres above Chart Datum

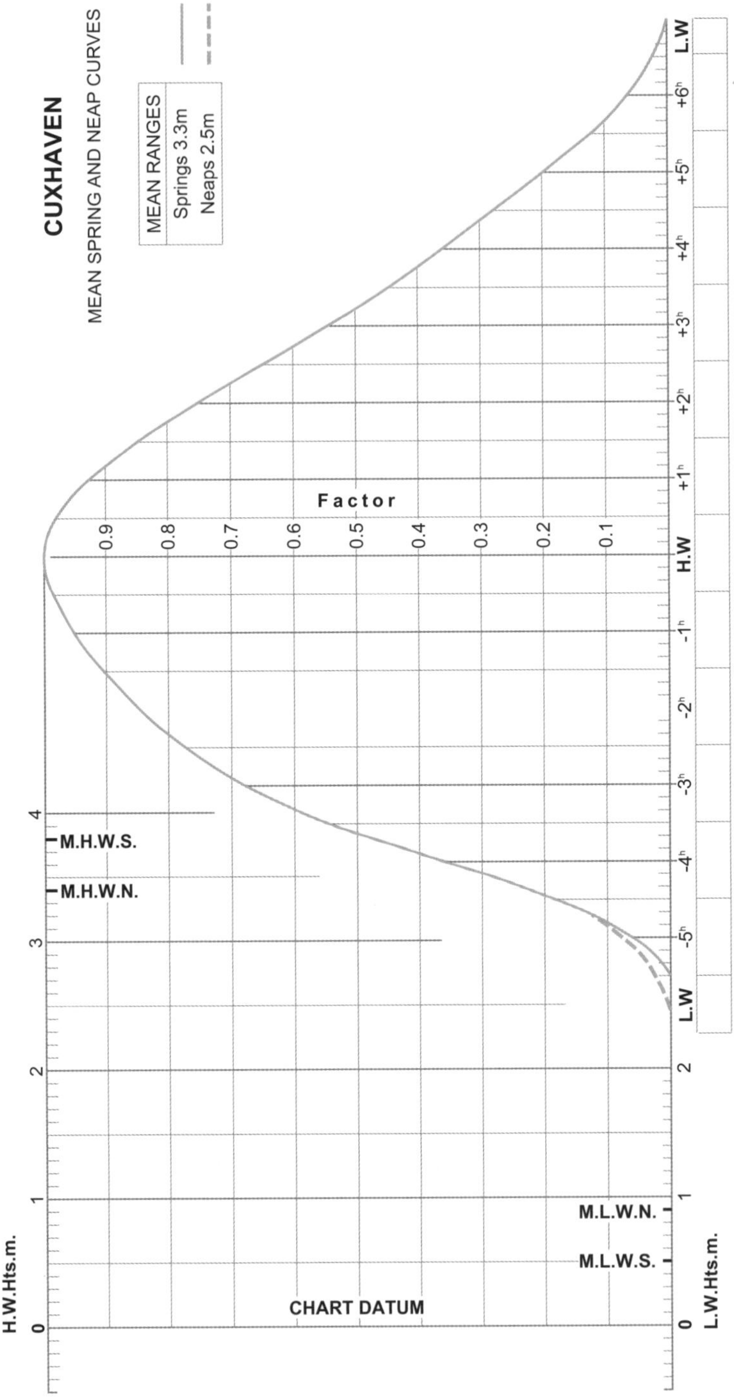
CUXHAVEN
MEAN SPRING AND NEAP CURVES
MEAN RANGES
Springs 3.3m
Neaps 2.5m
Factor
0.9
0.8
0.7
0.6
0.5
0.4
0.3
0.2
0.1
L.W
-5h
-4h
-3h
-2h
-1h
H.W
+1h
+2h
+3h
+4h
+5h
+6h
L.W
H.W.Hts.m.
0
1
2
3
4
M.H.W.S.
M.H.W.N.
CHART DATUM
M.L.W.N.
M.L.W.S.
L.W.Hts.m.

TIME ZONE -0100
(German Standard Time)
Subtract 1 hour for UT
For German Summer Time add ONE hour in **non-shaded areas**

GERMANY – CUXHAVEN

LAT 53°52′N LONG 8°43′E

TIMES AND HEIGHTS OF HIGH AND LOW WATERS

Dates in amber are **SPRINGS**
Dates in grey are **NEAPS**

2023

JANUARY

Date	Day	Time	m	Time	m	Time	m	Time	m	Moon
1	SU	0208	0.8	0755	3.7	1452	0.8	2036	3.3	
2	M	0315	0.8	0903	3.6	1558	0.9	2142	3.4	
3	TU	0427	0.8	1012	3.6	1704	0.9	2245	3.4	
4	W	0534	0.8	1113	3.6	1802	0.9	2339	3.6	
5	TH	0631	0.7	1206	3.6	1853	0.8			
6	F	0025	3.6	0720	0.6	1252	3.5	1936	0.6	
7	SA	0107	3.6	0802	0.5	1334	3.4	2014	0.5	○
8	SU	0144	3.6	0840	0.4	1412	3.4	2049	0.5	
9	M	0220	3.7	0917	0.4	1447	3.4	2122	0.5	
10	TU	0253	3.7	0951	0.5	1520	3.4	2152	0.5	
11	W	0325	3.7	1021	0.5	1552	3.4	2223	0.6	
12	TH	0357	3.7	1053	0.5	1627	3.4	2257	0.6	
13	F	0432	3.7	1129	0.6	1704	3.4	2334	0.7	
14	SA	0509	3.6	1203	0.6	1741	3.3			
15	SU	0010	0.7	0547	3.5	1237	0.6	1820	3.3	◑
16	M	0051	0.7	0633	3.4	1321	0.7	1911	3.2	
17	TU	0148	0.8	0734	3.4	1425	0.7	2018	3.2	
18	W	0303	0.8	0850	3.4	1543	0.7	2133	3.3	
19	TH	0425	0.7	1009	3.4	1703	0.6	2246	3.4	
20	F	0543	0.6	1123	3.5	1816	0.6	2352	3.6	
21	SA	0653	0.5	1228	3.5	1919	0.5			●
22	SU	0050	3.7	0752	0.4	1325	3.6	2015	0.5	
23	M	0141	3.8	0847	0.4	1419	3.7	2107	0.5	
24	TU	0231	3.9	0940	0.3	1510	3.7	2156	0.5	
25	W	0319	4.0	1030	0.3	1557	3.6	2239	0.4	
26	TH	0405	3.9	1114	0.3	1639	3.5	2318	0.4	
27	F	0448	3.9	1153	0.4	1720	3.4	2357	0.5	
28	SA	0531	3.8	1231	0.5	1801	3.4			◐
29	SU	0035	0.6	0616	3.7	1307	0.6	1843	3.3	
30	M	0116	0.6	0705	3.6	1350	0.8	1934	3.3	
31	TU	0213	0.7	0808	3.4	1452	0.9	2042	3.3	

FEBRUARY

Date	Day	Time	m	Time	m	Time	m	Time	m	Moon
1	W	0330	0.8	0924	3.3	1610	0.9	2159	3.3	
2	TH	0454	0.8	1041	3.3	1728	0.8	2309	3.4	
3	F	0607	0.6	1146	3.3	1831	0.7			
4	SA	0005	3.5	0704	0.5	1238	3.3	1920	0.5	
5	SU	0050	3.5	0748	0.4	1320	3.3	2000	0.4	○
6	M	0129	3.6	0827	0.3	1358	3.4	2036	0.4	
7	TU	0204	3.6	0903	0.3	1431	3.4	2109	0.4	
8	W	0237	3.7	0936	0.3	1502	3.4	2139	0.4	
9	TH	0307	3.7	1005	0.4	1532	3.4	2208	0.4	
10	F	0337	3.7	1035	0.4	1604	3.4	2240	0.4	
11	SA	0410	3.7	1107	0.4	1638	3.4	2314	0.5	
12	SU	0443	3.7	1136	0.4	1708	3.4	2342	0.5	
13	M	0513	3.6	1159	0.5	1737	3.4			◑
14	TU	0010	0.5	0549	3.4	1230	0.6	1818	3.2	
15	W	0057	0.6	0647	3.3	1331	0.7	1926	3.2	
16	TH	0216	0.7	0810	3.2	1459	0.8	2054	3.2	
17	F	0353	0.6	0944	3.2	1636	0.7	2222	3.4	
18	SA	0527	0.5	1110	3.3	1803	0.6	2339	3.5	
19	SU	0646	0.4	1222	3.4	1913	0.5			
20	M	0041	3.7	0749	0.3	1320	3.5	2009	0.4	●
21	TU	0132	3.8	0842	0.2	1409	3.6	2057	0.4	
22	W	0218	4.0	0929	0.2	1454	3.6	2140	0.3	
23	TH	0301	4.0	1012	0.2	1535	3.6	2220	0.3	
24	F	0344	3.9	1051	0.2	1613	3.5	2256	0.2	
25	SA	0424	3.8	1125	0.3	1648	3.5	2329	0.3	
26	SU	0502	3.7	1155	0.4	1721	3.4	2359	0.4	
27	M	0538	3.5	1220	0.6	1754	3.3			◐
28	TU	0029	0.5	0619	3.4	1252	0.7	1838	3.2	

MARCH

Date	Day	Time	m	Time	m	Time	m	Time	m	Moon
1	W	0116	0.6	0716	3.2	1349	0.9	1946	3.2	
2	TH	0234	0.7	0838	3.1	1516	0.9	2113	3.2	
3	F	0412	0.7	1008	3.1	1650	0.8	2238	3.3	
4	SA	0541	0.6	1125	3.2	1807	0.7	2343	3.4	
5	SU	0645	0.4	1220	3.2	1900	0.5			
6	M	0030	3.5	0729	0.3	1300	3.3	1940	0.4	
7	TU	0107	3.5	0806	0.2	1336	3.4	2016	0.3	○
8	W	0142	3.6	0841	0.2	1408	3.4	2050	0.3	
9	TH	0214	3.7	0913	0.2	1439	3.5	2120	0.3	
10	F	0244	3.7	0942	0.3	1508	3.5	2149	0.3	
11	SA	0314	3.7	1010	0.3	1537	3.5	2219	0.3	
12	SU	0346	3.7	1040	0.3	1608	3.5	2251	0.3	
13	M	0418	3.6	1109	0.3	1638	3.4	2320	0.3	
14	TU	0450	3.5	1132	0.4	1707	3.4	2347	0.4	
15	W	0527	3.3	1203	0.5	1750	3.3			◑
16	TH	0034	0.5	0627	3.2	1303	0.7	1900	3.2	
17	F	0155	0.5	0754	3.1	1437	0.7	2033	3.2	
18	SA	0339	0.5	0933	3.1	1621	0.6	2208	3.3	
19	SU	0518	0.3	1102	3.2	1751	0.5	2327	3.5	
20	M	0637	0.2	1212	3.3	1900	0.4			
21	TU	0027	3.7	0737	0.2	1307	3.4	1954	0.3	●
22	W	0116	3.8	0825	0.1	1352	3.5	2038	0.3	
23	TH	0159	3.9	0906	0.2	1430	3.6	2117	0.2	
24	F	0238	3.9	0943	0.2	1506	3.6	2153	0.2	
25	SA	0318	3.8	1018	0.2	1541	3.5	2228	0.2	
26	SU	0357	3.7	1049	0.3	1614	3.5	2300	0.2	
27	M	0433	3.6	1116	0.4	1644	3.4	2328	0.3	
28	TU	0506	3.4	1140	0.6	1715	3.4	2354	0.4	
29	W	0544	3.2	1208	0.7	1756	3.3			◐
30	TH	0036	0.6	0637	3.0	1300	0.9	1901	3.2	
31	F	0149	0.8	0756	2.9	1425	0.9	2029	3.2	

APRIL

Date	Day	Time	m	Time	m	Time	m	Time	m	Moon
1	SA	0329	0.7	0930	2.9	1606	0.8	2159	3.2	
2	SU	0505	0.5	1052	3.1	1731	0.6	2310	3.4	
3	M	0613	0.4	1150	3.2	1827	0.5	2358	3.5	
4	TU	0657	0.2	1229	3.3	1908	0.4			
5	W	0035	3.5	0732	0.2	1303	3.4	1946	0.3	
6	TH	0111	3.6	0808	0.2	1338	3.5	2022	0.3	○
7	F	0145	3.6	0842	0.2	1410	3.5	2055	0.3	
8	SA	0217	3.7	0912	0.2	1439	3.6	2125	0.2	
9	SU	0249	3.7	0942	0.2	1509	3.6	2156	0.2	
10	M	0322	3.6	1012	0.2	1540	3.5	2230	0.2	
11	TU	0359	3.5	1044	0.3	1614	3.5	2305	0.2	
12	W	0438	3.3	1116	0.4	1654	3.4	2343	0.3	
13	TH	0525	3.2	1157	0.5	1745	3.3			◑
14	F	0036	0.4	0629	3.1	1300	0.6	1856	3.3	
15	SA	0155	0.4	0754	3.0	1431	0.7	2025	3.3	
16	SU	0334	0.4	0927	3.0	1610	0.6	2155	3.4	
17	M	0507	0.3	1050	3.1	1733	0.5	2309	3.6	
18	TU	0618	0.2	1153	3.3	1837	0.4			
19	W	0005	3.7	0712	0.2	1243	3.4	1928	0.4	
20	TH	0053	3.8	0757	0.2	1326	3.5	2012	0.3	●
21	F	0136	3.8	0836	0.3	1402	3.6	2050	0.3	
22	SA	0215	3.8	0911	0.3	1436	3.6	2126	0.3	
23	SU	0253	3.7	0943	0.4	1510	3.6	2201	0.3	
24	M	0330	3.6	1015	0.4	1543	3.6	2234	0.3	
25	TU	0407	3.5	1043	0.5	1615	3.6	2303	0.4	
26	W	0442	3.3	1109	0.6	1648	3.5	2333	0.5	
27	TH	0520	3.2	1140	0.8	1729	3.4			◐
28	F	0013	0.6	0610	3.1	1227	0.9	1827	3.3	
29	SA	0116	0.8	0719	3.0	1342	0.9	1944	3.3	
30	SU	0242	0.7	0842	3.0	1514	0.8	2109	3.3	

Chart Datum: 2·06 metres below Normal Null (German reference level)
HAT is 4·1 metres above Chart Datum

TIME ZONE -0100
(German Standard Time)
Subtract 1 hour for UT
For German Summer Time add ONE hour in **non-shaded areas**

GERMANY – CUXHAVEN

LAT 53°52'N LONG 8°43'E

TIMES AND HEIGHTS OF HIGH AND LOW WATERS

Dates in amber are **SPRINGS**
Dates in grey are **NEAPS**

2023

MAY

Date	Day	Time	m	Time	m	Time	m	Time	m	Moon
1	M	0411	0.5	1002	3.1	1638	0.6	2220	3.4	
2	TU	0520	0.3	1102	3.2	1738	0.5	2312	3.5	
3	W	0608	0.2	1145	3.4	1824	0.4	2353	3.6	
4	TH	0648	0.2	1223	3.4	1907	0.4			
5	F	0033	3.6	0728	0.2	1301	3.5	1948	0.3	○
6	SA	0111	3.6	0806	0.2	1336	3.6	2025	0.3	
7	SU	0148	3.6	0840	0.2	1410	3.6	2100	0.3	
8	M	0225	3.6	0915	0.2	1444	3.6	2137	0.2	
9	TU	0305	3.5	0951	0.2	1521	3.6	2217	0.2	
10	W	0349	3.4	1029	0.3	1603	3.5	2301	0.2	
11	TH	0437	3.3	1112	0.4	1652	3.5	2350	0.2	
12	F	0533	3.1	1203	0.5	1750	3.5			◑
13	SA	0048	0.3	0637	3.1	1307	0.6	1859	3.5	
14	SU	0201	0.4	0753	3.1	1427	0.7	2017	3.5	
15	M	0325	0.4	0915	3.1	1552	0.6	2137	3.6	
16	TU	0445	0.3	1028	3.2	1707	0.5	2244	3.7	
17	W	0548	0.3	1126	3.4	1806	0.5	2338	3.8	
18	TH	0638	0.4	1213	3.5	1857	0.5			
19	F	0027	3.8	0724	0.4	1256	3.6	1944	0.4	●
20	SA	0112	3.8	0805	0.4	1335	3.7	2025	0.4	
21	SU	0153	3.7	0841	0.4	1410	3.7	2102	0.4	
22	M	0231	3.6	0914	0.5	1444	3.7	2138	0.4	
23	TU	0309	3.5	0947	0.5	1519	3.7	2213	0.4	
24	W	0346	3.4	1018	0.5	1553	3.7	2246	0.5	
25	TH	0423	3.3	1048	0.6	1629	3.6	2319	0.5	
26	F	0502	3.2	1123	0.7	1709	3.6	2359	0.6	
27	SA	0548	3.2	1206	0.8	1759	3.5			◐
28	SU	0049	0.7	0643	3.1	1305	0.8	1900	3.4	
29	M	0153	0.7	0749	3.1	1417	0.8	2009	3.4	
30	TU	0305	0.5	0858	3.1	1531	0.7	2116	3.4	
31	W	0411	0.4	1000	3.2	1635	0.6	2214	3.5	

JUNE

Date	Day	Time	m	Time	m	Time	m	Time	m	Moon
1	TH	0507	0.3	1051	3.4	1730	0.6	2305	3.6	
2	F	0557	0.3	1137	3.5	1823	0.5	2353	3.6	
3	SA	0646	0.3	1222	3.6	1912	0.4			
4	SU	0039	3.6	0731	0.3	1304	3.7	1957	0.3	○
5	M	0123	3.6	0814	0.3	1345	3.7	2040	0.3	
6	TU	0208	3.6	0856	0.3	1427	3.7	2125	0.2	
7	W	0256	3.6	0941	0.3	1511	3.7	2213	0.2	
8	TH	0347	3.4	1026	0.3	1559	3.7	2303	0.2	
9	F	0439	3.3	1114	0.4	1651	3.7	2357	0.2	
10	SA	0535	3.2	1207	0.5	1749	3.7			◑
11	SU	0054	0.3	0635	3.2	1305	0.6	1851	3.7	
12	M	0155	0.4	0739	3.2	1411	0.6	1959	3.7	
13	TU	0301	0.5	0847	3.2	1522	0.6	2108	3.7	
14	W	0409	0.5	0954	3.3	1631	0.6	2214	3.7	
15	TH	0510	0.5	1053	3.4	1733	0.6	2311	3.8	
16	F	0604	0.6	1143	3.6	1828	0.6			
17	SA	0003	3.7	0653	0.6	1229	3.7	1919	0.5	
18	SU	0052	3.7	0739	0.5	1312	3.7	2005	0.4	●
19	M	0137	3.6	0819	0.5	1350	3.7	2045	0.4	
20	TU	0216	3.6	0854	0.5	1427	3.8	2123	0.4	
21	W	0254	3.5	0928	0.5	1502	3.8	2158	0.5	
22	TH	0330	3.4	1000	0.5	1536	3.8	2231	0.5	
23	F	0405	3.4	1032	0.6	1610	3.7	2305	0.6	
24	SA	0442	3.4	1107	0.7	1649	3.7	2343	0.6	
25	SU	0524	3.3	1148	0.8	1731	3.6			
26	M	0023	0.6	0608	3.3	1231	0.8	1817	3.6	◐
27	TU	0106	0.6	0656	3.3	1321	0.8	1908	3.5	
28	W	0156	0.6	0750	3.2	1420	0.8	2008	3.5	
29	TH	0256	0.6	0851	3.3	1526	0.8	2112	3.5	
30	F	0401	0.5	0953	3.4	1634	0.7	2216	3.5	

JULY

Date	Day	Time	m	Time	m	Time	m	Time	m	Moon
1	SA	0506	0.5	1052	3.5	1741	0.6	2318	3.6	
2	SU	0609	0.5	1148	3.6	1842	0.5			
3	M	0015	3.6	0706	0.4	1240	3.7	1937	0.4	○
4	TU	0108	3.6	0758	0.4	1329	3.8	2029	0.3	
5	W	0159	3.7	0848	0.4	1417	3.9	2121	0.3	
6	TH	0252	3.6	0938	0.4	1506	3.9	2214	0.2	
7	F	0344	3.5	1025	0.4	1554	3.9	2303	0.2	
8	SA	0433	3.4	1110	0.4	1643	3.9	2352	0.3	
9	SU	0523	3.3	1157	0.5	1735	3.8			
10	M	0041	0.3	0615	3.3	1247	0.5	1830	3.8	◑
11	TU	0130	0.4	0708	3.3	1339	0.6	1927	3.7	
12	W	0221	0.6	0806	3.3	1439	0.7	2031	3.6	
13	TH	0321	0.7	0910	3.3	1549	0.7	2140	3.6	
14	F	0428	0.7	1017	3.4	1701	0.7	2247	3.6	
15	SA	0533	0.8	1118	3.6	1806	0.7	2346	3.6	
16	SU	0631	0.7	1210	3.7	1902	0.6			
17	M	0038	3.6	0720	0.6	1255	3.7	1950	0.5	●
18	TU	0124	3.5	0803	0.5	1336	3.7	2032	0.4	
19	W	0205	3.5	0840	0.5	1413	3.8	2111	0.4	
20	TH	0241	3.5	0914	0.5	1447	3.8	2145	0.5	
21	F	0313	3.5	0945	0.5	1519	3.8	2214	0.5	
22	SA	0344	3.5	1014	0.6	1550	3.8	2244	0.6	
23	SU	0418	3.5	1047	0.7	1624	3.8	2319	0.6	
24	M	0455	3.5	1125	0.7	1702	3.7	2354	0.6	
25	TU	0532	3.4	1159	0.7	1737	3.7			◐
26	W	0023	0.7	0606	3.4	1231	0.8	1814	3.6	
27	TH	0055	0.7	0647	3.4	1316	0.8	1906	3.5	
28	F	0148	0.8	0746	3.3	1423	0.9	2016	3.4	
29	SA	0302	0.8	0900	3.4	1546	0.8	2136	3.4	
30	SU	0425	0.7	1016	3.5	1709	0.7	2253	3.5	
31	M	0544	0.6	1125	3.6	1824	0.5			

AUGUST

Date	Day	Time	m	Time	m	Time	m	Time	m	Moon
1	TU	0002	3.6	0652	0.5	1226	3.7	1928	0.4	○
2	W	0101	3.6	0750	0.5	1319	3.9	2024	0.3	
3	TH	0154	3.7	0842	0.4	1407	4.0	2117	0.3	
4	F	0244	3.7	0931	0.4	1455	4.0	2207	0.2	
5	SA	0332	3.6	1015	0.3	1541	4.0	2252	0.2	
6	SU	0416	3.5	1056	0.3	1625	3.9	2333	0.3	
7	M	0459	3.4	1136	0.4	1711	3.9			
8	TU	0013	0.4	0542	3.4	1217	0.5	1758	3.7	◑
9	W	0051	0.5	0625	3.3	1258	0.6	1848	3.6	
10	TH	0131	0.7	0715	3.3	1350	0.7	1948	3.4	
11	F	0227	0.9	0821	3.3	1502	0.8	2103	3.4	
12	SA	0343	0.9	0940	3.3	1629	0.9	2224	3.4	
13	SU	0505	0.9	1056	3.5	1750	0.8	2335	3.4	
14	M	0614	0.8	1156	3.6	1852	0.6			
15	TU	0029	3.4	0706	0.7	1243	3.7	1938	0.5	
16	W	0112	3.4	0748	0.5	1321	3.7	2018	0.4	●
17	TH	0149	3.5	0824	0.5	1356	3.7	2054	0.4	
18	F	0222	3.5	0858	0.5	1429	3.8	2126	0.5	
19	SA	0252	3.6	0927	0.5	1458	3.8	2152	0.5	
20	SU	0320	3.6	0954	0.6	1526	3.9	2219	0.6	
21	M	0349	3.6	1023	0.6	1557	3.8	2249	0.6	
22	TU	0422	3.6	1057	0.7	1630	3.8	2320	0.6	
23	W	0454	3.5	1127	0.7	1701	3.7	2343	0.7	
24	TH	0522	3.5	1153	0.8	1733	3.5			◐
25	F	0008	0.8	0558	3.4	1231	0.9	1822	3.4	
26	SA	0057	0.9	0657	3.3	1339	0.9	1938	3.3	
27	SU	0220	0.9	0821	3.3	1515	0.8	2111	3.3	
28	M	0358	0.8	0952	3.4	1652	0.7	2240	3.3	
29	TU	0529	0.7	1112	3.5	1816	0.5	2355	3.4	
30	W	0643	0.5	1215	3.7	1922	0.4			
31	TH	0054	3.5	0742	0.5	1307	3.9	2016	0.3	○

Chart Datum: 2·06 metres below Normal Null (German reference level)
HAT is 4·1 metres above Chart Datum

TIME ZONE -0100
(German Standard Time)
Subtract 1 hour for UT
For German Summer Time add ONE hour in **non-shaded areas**

GERMANY – CUXHAVEN

LAT 53°52′N LONG 8°43′E

TIMES AND HEIGHTS OF HIGH AND LOW WATERS

Dates in amber are **SPRINGS**
Dates in grey are **NEAPS**

2023

SEPTEMBER

Day	Time	m	Time	m	Time	m	Time	m
1 F	0143	3.6	0831	0.4	1353	4.0	2103	0.3
2 SA	0228	3.7	0915	0.3	1437	4.0	2148	0.3
3 SU	0310	3.6	0955	0.3	1520	4.0	2227	0.3
4 M	0349	3.5	1033	0.3	1602	3.9	2303	0.3
5 TU	0427	3.5	1108	0.3	1643	3.8	2335	0.5
6 W ◑	0503	3.4	1142	0.5	1723	3.6		
7 TH	0006	0.6	0541	3.3	1217	0.6	1807	3.4
8 F	0040	0.8	0626	3.3	1303	0.8	1905	3.2
9 SA	0134	1.0	0733	3.2	1418	1.0	2025	3.1
10 SU	0256	1.1	0900	3.3	1556	1.0	2158	3.1
11 M	0433	1.1	1030	3.4	1730	0.9	2319	3.3
12 TU	0554	0.9	1139	3.5	1838	0.7		
13 W	0014	3.4	0649	0.7	1225	3.6	1921	0.5
14 TH	0052	3.4	0727	0.6	1259	3.7	1954	0.5
15 F	0124	3.5	0801	0.5	1332	3.7	● 2027	0.5
16 SA	0155	3.5	0834	0.5	1403	3.8	2058	0.5
17 SU	0225	3.6	0904	0.5	1432	3.8	2125	0.5
18 M	0252	3.6	0931	0.6	1459	3.8	2150	0.6
19 TU	0319	3.6	0958	0.6	1528	3.8	2216	0.6
20 W	0348	3.6	1028	0.6	1559	3.7	2244	0.6
21 TH	0418	3.6	1058	0.6	1632	3.6	2310	0.7
22 F	0449	3.5	1127	0.7	1708	3.4	◐ 2339	0.8
23 SA	0528	3.4	1208	0.8	1800	3.2		
24 SU	0032	1.0	0632	3.3	1320	0.8	1921	3.1
25 M	0159	1.0	0801	3.3	1500	0.8	2059	3.1
26 TU	0343	0.9	0937	3.4	1643	0.6	2231	3.2
27 W	0517	0.7	1059	3.6	1806	0.5	2344	3.4
28 TH	0629	0.6	1200	3.7	1908	0.4		
29 F	0040	3.5	0725	0.5	1250	3.9	○ 1957	0.4
30 SA	0125	3.6	0811	0.5	1333	4.0	2040	0.4

OCTOBER

Day	Time	m	Time	m	Time	m	Time	m
1 SU	0204	3.7	0852	0.4	1414	4.0	2119	0.4
2 M	0242	3.7	0930	0.4	1456	3.9	2155	0.4
3 TU	0319	3.6	1007	0.4	1537	3.8	2228	0.5
4 W	0354	3.6	1041	0.4	1616	3.7	2258	0.6
5 TH	0428	3.5	1112	0.5	1653	3.5	2326	0.8
6 F	0503	3.4	1144	0.7	1734	3.3	◑ 2358	0.9
7 SA	0547	3.3	1228	0.9	1829	3.1		
8 SU	0050	1.1	0650	3.3	1338	1.0	1946	3.0
9 M	0211	1.2	0817	3.3	1516	1.1	2119	3.0
10 TU	0351	1.1	0950	3.3	1654	0.9	2244	3.1
11 W	0519	1.0	1104	3.4	1805	0.7	2343	3.3
12 TH	0617	0.8	1152	3.6	1847	0.5		
13 F	0019	3.4	0654	0.7	1226	3.6	1918	0.5
14 SA	0049	3.5	0728	0.6	1259	3.7	● 1950	0.5
15 SU	0121	3.5	0803	0.5	1332	3.7	2023	0.5
16 M	0153	3.6	0835	0.5	1403	3.7	2053	0.5
17 TU	0222	3.6	0904	0.6	1432	3.7	2120	0.6
18 W	0249	3.6	0933	0.6	1502	3.7	2147	0.6
19 TH	0318	3.6	1004	0.6	1536	3.6	2216	0.6
20 F	0351	3.6	1038	0.6	1615	3.4	2249	0.7
21 SA	0430	3.5	1117	0.6	1659	3.3	2329	0.8
22 SU ◐	0518	3.4	1206	0.7	1757	3.2		
23 M	0027	1.0	0624	3.4	1318	0.8	1916	3.1
24 TU	0152	1.0	0749	3.4	1453	0.8	2048	3.1
25 W	0330	1.0	0920	3.5	1630	0.7	2215	3.2
26 TH	0459	0.8	1038	3.6	1746	0.6	2323	3.4
27 F	0606	0.7	1137	3.8	1843	0.5		
28 SA	0015	3.5	0659	0.6	1226	3.9	○ 1929	0.5
29 SU	0059	3.6	0745	0.6	1310	3.9	2010	0.5
30 M	0137	3.7	0826	0.5	1352	3.9	2048	0.5
31 TU	0213	3.7	0905	0.5	1432	3.8	2123	0.6

NOVEMBER

Day	Time	m	Time	m	Time	m	Time	m
1 W	0249	3.7	0942	0.5	1513	3.7	2157	0.6
2 TH	0325	3.7	1018	0.5	1553	3.5	2228	0.7
3 F	0400	3.6	1050	0.6	1630	3.4	2257	0.8
4 SA	0436	3.6	1123	0.7	1710	3.3	2330	0.9
5 SU ◑	0518	3.5	1205	0.9	1800	3.1		
6 M	0018	1.1	0614	3.4	1305	1.0	1905	3.0
7 TU	0127	1.1	0728	3.3	1426	1.0	2025	3.0
8 W	0255	1.1	0852	3.3	1555	0.9	2145	3.1
9 TH	0420	0.9	1006	3.4	1707	0.7	2248	3.2
10 F	0523	0.8	1100	3.5	1755	0.6	2331	3.4
11 SA	0607	0.8	1141	3.6	1831	0.6		
12 SU	0006	3.5	0647	0.7	1219	3.6	1908	0.6
13 M	0042	3.5	0727	0.6	1257	3.6	● 1946	0.5
14 TU	0118	3.6	0804	0.6	1332	3.7	2020	0.6
15 W	0151	3.7	0838	0.6	1407	3.7	2053	0.6
16 TH	0224	3.7	0913	0.6	1444	3.6	2127	0.6
17 F	0259	3.7	0950	0.5	1525	3.5	2204	0.6
18 SA	0338	3.6	1032	0.5	1610	3.4	2244	0.7
19 SU	0423	3.6	1119	0.6	1700	3.3	2332	0.8
20 M ◐	0516	3.6	1213	0.6	1759	3.2		
21 TU	0030	0.9	0619	3.6	1320	0.7	1908	3.2
22 W	0144	1.0	0734	3.6	1440	0.7	2027	3.2
23 TH	0308	0.9	0854	3.6	1603	0.7	2145	3.2
24 F	0429	0.8	1008	3.7	1714	0.7	2251	3.4
25 SA	0535	0.8	1108	3.8	1810	0.7	2343	3.6
26 SU	0629	0.7	1200	3.9	1858	0.7		
27 M	0029	3.7	0719	0.7	1248	3.9	○ 1942	0.6
28 TU	0111	3.7	0803	0.6	1332	3.8	2022	0.6
29 W	0149	3.7	0844	0.5	1414	3.7	2058	0.6
30 TH	0227	3.7	0923	0.5	1455	3.6	2134	0.6

DECEMBER

Day	Time	m	Time	m	Time	m	Time	m
1 F	0305	3.7	1001	0.5	1535	3.5	2208	0.7
2 SA	0341	3.7	1036	0.6	1613	3.4	2239	0.7
3 SU	0416	3.7	1110	0.7	1651	3.3	2312	0.9
4 M	0455	3.6	1147	0.8	1733	3.2	2353	1.0
5 TU ◑	0542	3.5	1234	0.9	1823	3.2		
6 W	0046	1.0	0638	3.4	1332	0.9	1923	3.1
7 TH	0152	1.0	0743	3.4	1440	0.9	2030	3.1
8 F	0304	0.9	0851	3.4	1547	0.8	2135	3.2
9 SA	0411	0.9	0953	3.4	1646	0.7	2230	3.4
10 SU	0509	0.9	1047	3.5	1737	0.7	2317	3.5
11 M	0601	0.8	1137	3.6	1826	0.7		
12 TU	0002	3.6	0651	0.7	1223	3.6	1912	0.6
13 W	0045	3.6	0736	0.6	1306	3.6	● 1954	0.6
14 TH	0125	3.7	0817	0.6	1349	3.7	2036	0.6
15 F	0206	3.8	0902	0.5	1435	3.6	2119	0.6
16 SA	0249	3.8	0948	0.5	1522	3.6	2203	0.6
17 SU	0334	3.8	1035	0.4	1610	3.5	2247	0.6
18 M	0420	3.8	1124	0.5	1659	3.4	2334	0.7
19 TU ◐	0512	3.8	1216	0.5	1753	3.3		
20 W	0027	0.8	0608	3.7	1312	0.6	1850	3.3
21 TH	0126	0.8	0710	3.7	1414	0.7	1954	3.3
22 F	0234	0.8	0819	3.7	1522	0.7	2103	3.3
23 SA	0347	0.8	0930	3.7	1631	0.8	2211	3.4
24 SU	0458	0.8	1037	3.7	1734	0.8	2311	3.5
25 M	0601	0.8	1137	3.7	1830	0.8		
26 TU	0003	3.7	0657	0.7	1230	3.7	1920	0.7
27 W	0050	3.7	0747	0.5	1319	3.6	○ 2004	0.6
28 TH	0132	3.7	0830	0.5	1403	3.6	2043	0.6
29 F	0212	3.7	0911	0.5	1443	3.5	2119	0.6
30 SA	0250	3.8	0950	0.5	1520	3.5	2153	0.6
31 SU	0325	3.8	1024	0.6	1555	3.4	2224	0.6

Chart Datum: 2·06 metres below Normal Null (German reference level)
HAT is 4·1 metres above Chart Datum

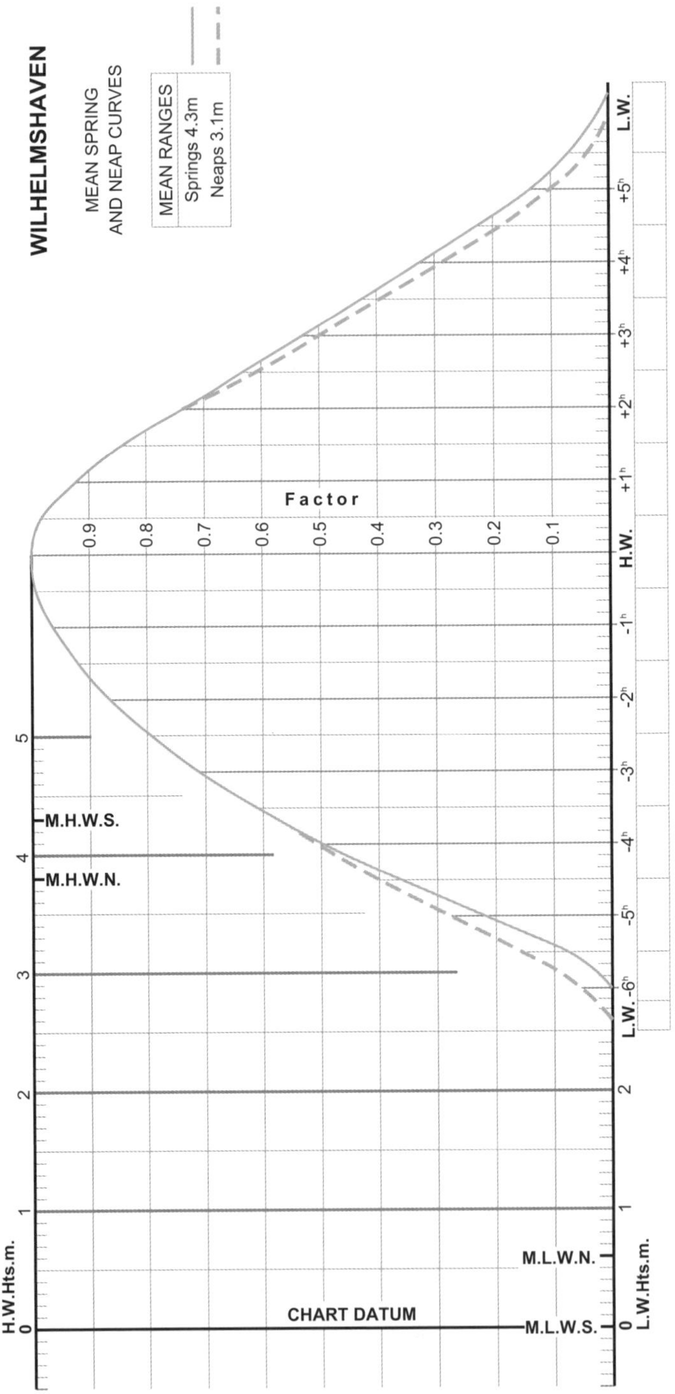
WILHELMSHAVEN
MEAN SPRING
AND NEAP CURVES
MEAN RANGES
Springs 4.3m
Neaps 3.1m
Factor
0.9
0.8
0.7
0.6
0.5
0.4
0.3
0.2
0.1
L.W. -6h
-5h
-4h
-3h
-2h
-1h
H.W.
+1h
+2h
+3h
+4h
+5h
L.W.
H.W.Hts.m.
0
1
2
3
4
5
M.H.W.S.
M.H.W.N.
CHART DATUM
M.L.W.S.
M.L.W.N.
L.W.Hts.m.

TIME ZONE -0100
(German Standard Time)
Subtract 1 hour for UT
For German Summer Time add ONE hour in **non-shaded areas**

GERMANY – WILHELMSHAVEN

LAT 53°31'N LONG 8°09'E

TIMES AND HEIGHTS OF HIGH AND LOW WATERS

Dates in amber are **SPRINGS**
Dates in grey are **NEAPS**

2023

JANUARY

Day	Time	m	Time	m	Time	m	Time	m
1 SU	0109	1.0	0738	4.7	1353	1.0	2015	4.3
2 M	0215	1.1	0845	4.6	1459	1.1	2122	4.3
3 TU	0326	1.1	0954	4.6	1607	1.1	2225	4.4
4 W	0433	1.0	1056	4.6	1707	1.0	2320	4.5
5 TH	0531	0.9	1149	4.6	1757	0.9		
6 F	0008	4.6	0621	0.8	1237	4.5	1840	0.8
7 SA ○	0049	4.6	0704	0.6	1319	4.4	1919	0.7
8 SU	0127	4.7	0742	0.6	1357	4.4	1955	0.7
9 M	0202	4.7	0819	0.6	1432	4.4	2029	0.6
10 TU	0236	4.7	0853	0.6	1504	4.4	2100	0.6
11 W	0307	4.7	0925	0.6	1536	4.4	2130	0.7
12 TH	0339	4.7	0956	0.7	1610	4.3	2203	0.8
13 F	0414	4.7	1031	0.7	1647	4.3	2240	0.8
14 SA	0452	4.6	1106	0.7	1723	4.3	2316	0.8
15 SU ◑	0530	4.5	1140	0.8	1802	4.2	2355	0.9
16 M	0615	4.4	1223	0.9	1853	4.2		
17 TU	0049	1.0	0716	4.3	1325	0.9	2001	4.2
18 W	0203	1.1	0832	4.3	1442	1.0	2117	4.3
19 TH	0324	1.0	0951	4.4	1602	0.9	2230	4.4
20 F	0442	0.9	1107	4.5	1717	0.8	2337	4.6
21 SA ●	0551	0.7	1214	4.6	1823	0.7		
22 SU	0035	4.7	0653	0.5	1314	4.6	1921	0.7
23 M	0128	4.9	0749	0.4	1408	4.7	2014	0.7
24 TU	0218	5.0	0843	0.4	1500	4.7	2102	0.6
25 W	0307	5.0	0932	0.3	1546	4.6	2144	0.5
26 TH	0352	5.0	1016	0.4	1627	4.5	2221	0.5
27 F	0435	4.9	1056	0.5	1706	4.4	2259	0.6
28 SA ◐	0518	4.9	1135	0.6	1745	4.4	2337	0.7
29 SU	0601	4.7	1212	0.8	1824	4.3		
30 M	0018	0.8	0649	4.5	1255	1.0	1915	4.2
31 TU	0113	1.0	0751	4.4	1355	1.1	2024	4.2

FEBRUARY

Day	Time	m	Time	m	Time	m	Time	m
1 W	0228	1.1	0909	4.3	1513	1.2	2142	4.3
2 TH	0352	1.0	1027	4.3	1631	1.1	2253	4.4
3 F	0506	0.9	1132	4.3	1733	0.9	2350	4.5
4 SA	0603	0.7	1223	4.4	1821	0.8		
5 SU ○	0035	4.6	0648	0.5	1306	4.3	1903	0.6
6 M	0113	4.6	0727	0.5	1344	4.4	1941	0.5
7 TU	0149	4.7	0804	0.5	1418	4.4	2016	0.5
8 W	0222	4.7	0838	0.5	1449	4.4	2047	0.5
9 TH	0252	4.8	0908	0.5	1518	4.4	2116	0.5
10 F	0322	4.8	0939	0.5	1550	4.4	2147	0.6
11 SA	0355	4.8	1011	0.5	1623	4.4	2219	0.6
12 SU	0429	4.7	1040	0.5	1653	4.4	2248	0.6
13 M ◑	0459	4.6	1104	0.6	1721	4.3	2315	0.7
14 TU	0534	4.4	1135	0.8	1802	4.2	2359	0.9
15 W	0631	4.3	1232	1.0	1911	4.1		
16 TH	0114	1.0	0754	4.2	1359	1.1	2039	4.2
17 F	0249	0.9	0929	4.2	1534	1.0	2208	4.3
18 SA	0421	0.7	1057	4.3	1701	0.8	2325	4.5
19 SU	0540	0.5	1212	4.4	1814	0.7		
20 M ●	0028	4.7	0647	0.4	1312	4.6	1914	0.6
21 TU	0121	4.9	0743	0.3	1402	4.7	2004	0.5
22 W	0208	5.0	0832	0.3	1446	4.7	2047	0.4
23 TH	0253	5.1	0916	0.2	1527	4.6	2125	0.3
24 F	0335	5.0	0955	0.3	1603	4.5	2200	0.3
25 SA	0415	4.9	1029	0.4	1636	4.4	2232	0.4
26 SU	0451	4.7	1100	0.5	1707	4.4	2302	0.5
27 M ◐	0525	4.6	1127	0.7	1737	4.3	2333	0.6
28 TU	0603	4.3	1200	0.9	1820	4.2		

MARCH

Day	Time	m	Time	m	Time	m	Time	m
1 W	0019	0.9	0701	4.1	1255	1.2	1929	4.1
2 TH	0134	1.1	0823	4.0	1420	1.2	2059	4.1
3 F	0311	1.1	0955	4.0	1553	1.1	2225	4.3
4 SA	0440	0.9	1112	4.2	1709	0.9	2330	4.4
5 SU	0545	0.6	1206	4.3	1801	0.7		
6 M	0016	4.5	0628	0.5	1247	4.3	1842	0.6
7 TU ○	0054	4.6	0705	0.4	1324	4.4	1921	0.5
8 W	0129	4.6	0741	0.4	1357	4.5	1957	0.4
9 TH	0202	4.7	0815	0.4	1428	4.5	2028	0.4
10 F	0232	4.8	0846	0.4	1457	4.5	2057	0.4
11 SA	0302	4.8	0915	0.4	1526	4.5	2126	0.4
12 SU	0334	4.7	0945	0.4	1557	4.5	2156	0.4
13 M	0407	4.6	1012	0.4	1626	4.5	2223	0.4
14 TU	0438	4.5	1036	0.5	1654	4.4	2250	0.5
15 W ◑	0514	4.3	1107	0.7	1736	4.2	2334	0.7
16 TH	0613	4.1	1205	1.0	1846	4.1		
17 F	0051	0.8	0741	4.0	1336	1.1	2020	4.2
18 SA	0232	0.8	0921	4.1	1519	1.0	2155	4.3
19 SU	0411	0.6	1052	4.2	1649	0.8	2315	4.6
20 M	0531	0.4	1204	4.4	1800	0.6		
21 TU ●	0017	4.7	0634	0.3	1301	4.5	1858	0.5
22 W	0108	4.9	0727	0.2	1346	4.6	1945	0.4
23 TH	0151	5.0	0811	0.2	1423	4.7	2024	0.3
24 F	0232	5.0	0849	0.3	1458	4.6	2059	0.3
25 SA	0311	4.9	0924	0.3	1532	4.6	2133	0.3
26 SU	0349	4.7	0956	0.4	1603	4.5	2204	0.3
27 M	0423	4.6	1024	0.5	1631	4.4	2232	0.4
28 TU	0453	4.4	1048	0.7	1700	4.4	2300	0.6
29 W ◐	0528	4.2	1117	0.9	1739	4.2	2341	0.9
30 TH	0621	4.0	1209	1.2	1844	4.1		
31 F	0052	1.1	0741	3.9	1332	1.3	2015	4.1

APRIL

Day	Time	m	Time	m	Time	m	Time	m
1 SA	0228	1.1	0917	3.9	1511	1.2	2148	4.2
2 SU	0403	0.9	1040	4.1	1634	0.9	2258	4.4
3 M	0512	0.6	1137	4.2	1730	0.7	2345	4.5
4 TU	0556	0.4	1216	4.4	1811	0.6		
5 W	0023	4.6	0632	0.3	1253	4.4	1850	0.5
6 TH ○	0059	4.6	0709	0.3	1329	4.5	1929	0.4
7 F	0134	4.7	0745	0.3	1401	4.6	2003	0.3
8 SA	0207	4.8	0817	0.3	1431	4.6	2033	0.3
9 SU	0239	4.7	0847	0.3	1501	4.6	2103	0.3
10 M	0312	4.7	0916	0.3	1532	4.6	2134	0.3
11 TU	0349	4.5	0946	0.4	1605	4.5	2206	0.3
12 W	0428	4.4	1018	0.5	1643	4.4	2243	0.4
13 TH ◑	0514	4.2	1059	0.7	1732	4.3	2334	0.5
14 F	0616	4.1	1202	0.9	1842	4.3		
15 SA	0051	0.7	0742	4.0	1330	1.0	2013	4.3
16 SU	0227	0.6	0917	4.0	1508	0.9	2144	4.5
17 M	0401	0.5	1041	4.2	1632	0.7	2258	4.7
18 TU	0514	0.4	1145	4.3	1737	0.6	2357	4.8
19 W	0611	0.3	1237	4.5	1831	0.5		
20 TH ●	0046	4.9	0701	0.3	1319	4.6	1919	0.4
21 F	0129	4.9	0743	0.3	1355	4.7	1958	0.4
22 SA	0208	4.9	0819	0.4	1427	4.7	2033	0.3
23 SU	0245	4.8	0851	0.4	1500	4.7	2106	0.3
24 M	0323	4.6	0922	0.5	1532	4.6	2139	0.4
25 TU	0358	4.5	0951	0.6	1602	4.6	2210	0.5
26 W	0430	4.3	1018	0.8	1633	4.5	2240	0.6
27 TH ◐	0505	4.2	1050	0.9	1712	4.4	2320	0.8
28 F	0553	4.0	1139	1.1	1810	4.3		
29 SA	0020	1.0	0703	3.9	1251	1.2	1930	4.2
30 SU	0143	1.0	0829	3.9	1420	1.1	2056	4.3

Chart Datum: 2·7 metres below Normal Null (German reference level)
HAT is 5·1 metres above Chart Datum

TIME ZONE -0100
(German Standard Time)
Subtract 1 hour for UT
For German Summer Time add ONE hour in **non-shaded areas**

GERMANY – WILHELMSHAVEN

LAT 53°31′N LONG 8°09′E

TIMES AND HEIGHTS OF HIGH AND LOW WATERS

Dates in amber are **SPRINGS**
Dates in grey are **NEAPS**

2023

MAY

Date	Day	Time	m	Time	m	Time	m	Time	m	Moon
1	M	0310	0.8	0950	4.1	1542	0.9	2208	4.4	
2	TU	0419	0.6	1050	4.2	1642	0.8	2259	4.5	
3	W	0507	0.4	1133	4.4	1727	0.6	2341	4.6	
4	TH	0548	0.4	1213	4.5	1811	0.5			
5	F	0023	4.6	0629	0.3	1253	4.6	1854	0.4	○
6	SA	0102	4.7	0709	0.3	1330	4.7	1933	0.4	
7	SU	0139	4.7	0746	0.3	1404	4.7	2008	0.3	
8	M	0217	4.7	0820	0.3	1438	4.7	2042	0.3	
9	TU	0257	4.6	0855	0.3	1515	4.7	2119	0.2	
10	W	0340	4.4	0932	0.4	1555	4.6	2200	0.3	
11	TH	0428	4.3	1014	0.5	1642	4.6	2248	0.3	
12	F	0522	4.2	1104	0.7	1737	4.5	2346	0.5	◑
13	SA	0626	4.1	1209	0.9	1845	4.5			
14	SU	0058	0.6	0741	4.1	1327	0.9	2005	4.5	
15	M	0221	0.6	0903	4.1	1452	0.9	2126	4.6	
16	TU	0342	0.5	1017	4.2	1607	0.8	2234	4.8	
17	W	0448	0.4	1115	4.4	1708	0.7	2329	4.9	
18	TH	0541	0.5	1204	4.6	1801	0.6			
19	F	0019	4.9	0629	0.5	1248	4.7	1850	0.5	●
20	SA	0105	4.9	0713	0.5	1326	4.7	1933	0.4	
21	SU	0146	4.8	0750	0.5	1400	4.8	2009	0.4	
22	M	0223	4.7	0823	0.6	1434	4.8	2044	0.4	
23	TU	0301	4.6	0855	0.6	1509	4.7	2119	0.5	
24	W	0338	4.4	0927	0.7	1542	4.7	2153	0.5	
25	TH	0412	4.3	0958	0.8	1615	4.7	2227	0.7	
26	F	0448	4.2	1033	0.9	1654	4.6	2306	0.8	
27	SA	0531	4.1	1118	1.0	1743	4.5	2355	0.9	◐
28	SU	0626	4.1	1216	1.1	1844	4.4			
29	M	0057	0.9	0734	4.0	1325	1.0	1955	4.4	
30	TU	0206	0.8	0845	4.1	1436	0.9	2103	4.4	
31	W	0312	0.6	0947	4.2	1541	0.8	2201	4.5	

JUNE

Date	Day	Time	m	Time	m	Time	m	Time	m	Moon
1	TH	0409	0.5	1039	4.4	1636	0.8	2252	4.6	
2	F	0459	0.5	1127	4.5	1728	0.7	2342	4.6	
3	SA	0549	0.4	1214	4.6	1819	0.5			
4	SU	0030	4.7	0637	0.4	1258	4.7	1904	0.4	○
5	M	0115	4.7	0720	0.4	1339	4.8	1947	0.4	
6	TU	0201	4.7	0803	0.4	1422	4.8	2031	0.3	
7	W	0250	4.6	0847	0.4	1506	4.8	2116	0.2	
8	TH	0340	4.5	0930	0.5	1552	4.8	2204	0.3	
9	F	0431	4.4	1016	0.6	1642	4.8	2256	0.3	
10	SA	0526	4.3	1108	0.7	1738	4.8	2353	0.4	◑
11	SU	0624	4.2	1207	0.8	1840	4.7			
12	M	0056	0.5	0726	4.2	1313	0.8	1947	4.7	
13	TU	0202	0.6	0833	4.2	1423	0.8	2057	4.7	
14	W	0310	0.6	0940	4.3	1533	0.8	2203	4.8	
15	TH	0415	0.6	1040	4.4	1637	0.8	2301	4.8	
16	F	0511	0.7	1131	4.6	1733	0.7	2354	4.8	
17	SA	0600	0.7	1219	4.7	1825	0.6			
18	SU	0043	4.7	0647	0.6	1302	4.7	1912	0.5	●
19	M	0129	4.6	0728	0.6	1340	4.8	1952	0.5	
20	TU	0209	4.6	0804	0.6	1417	4.8	2030	0.5	
21	W	0246	4.5	0838	0.6	1453	4.8	2106	0.5	
22	TH	0321	4.4	0911	0.7	1526	4.8	2140	0.6	
23	F	0354	4.4	0943	0.7	1558	4.8	2214	0.7	
24	SA	0429	4.3	1019	0.8	1635	4.7	2251	0.7	
25	SU	0508	4.3	1100	0.9	1717	4.7	2332	0.8	
26	M	0551	4.2	1144	0.9	1801	4.6			◐
27	TU	0014	0.8	0638	4.2	1232	1.0	1852	4.5	
28	W	0103	0.8	0734	4.2	1329	1.0	1952	4.4	
29	TH	0202	0.8	0836	4.3	1434	1.0	2056	4.5	
30	F	0306	0.7	0939	4.4	1542	0.9	2201	4.6	

JULY

Date	Day	Time	m	Time	m	Time	m	Time	m	Moon
1	SA	0412	0.7	1040	4.5	1647	0.8	2305	4.6	
2	SU	0515	0.6	1139	4.6	1748	0.6			
3	M	0005	4.6	0613	0.5	1233	4.8	1844	0.5	○
4	TU	0100	4.7	0706	0.5	1323	4.9	1936	0.4	
5	W	0153	4.7	0757	0.5	1412	5.0	2027	0.3	
6	TH	0247	4.7	0846	0.5	1501	5.0	2118	0.2	
7	F	0339	4.6	0931	0.4	1548	5.0	2207	0.2	
8	SA	0427	4.5	1014	0.5	1637	5.0	2255	0.3	
9	SU	0515	4.4	1101	0.6	1728	4.9	2345	0.4	
10	M	0604	4.3	1151	0.7	1821	4.8			◑
11	TU	0035	0.5	0654	4.3	1243	0.8	1916	4.7	
12	W	0127	0.7	0749	4.3	1342	0.8	2018	4.7	
13	TH	0227	0.8	0853	4.3	1452	0.9	2128	4.6	
14	F	0335	0.9	1001	4.4	1605	0.9	2236	4.6	
15	SA	0442	0.9	1104	4.5	1712	0.9	2336	4.6	
16	SU	0539	0.8	1158	4.7	1808	0.7			
17	M	0028	4.6	0628	0.7	1245	4.7	1858	0.6	●
18	TU	0116	4.5	0712	0.6	1326	4.7	1941	0.5	
19	W	0156	4.5	0752	0.6	1404	4.8	2020	0.5	
20	TH	0232	4.5	0827	0.6	1438	4.9	2055	0.6	
21	F	0304	4.5	0859	0.7	1509	4.9	2126	0.6	
22	SA	0334	4.5	0928	0.7	1538	4.9	2156	0.7	
23	SU	0405	4.4	1001	0.8	1612	4.8	2231	0.7	
24	M	0441	4.4	1038	0.8	1648	4.8	2305	0.7	
25	TU	0515	4.4	1113	0.9	1722	4.7	2335	0.7	◐
26	W	0547	4.4	1145	0.9	1757	4.6			
27	TH	0007	0.8	0628	4.3	1228	1.0	1848	4.5	
28	F	0057	0.9	0728	4.3	1333	1.1	1958	4.4	
29	SA	0209	1.0	0844	4.3	1454	1.1	2119	4.4	
30	SU	0331	0.9	1002	4.4	1615	0.9	2239	4.5	
31	M	0449	0.8	1114	4.6	1728	0.7	2351	4.6	

AUGUST

Date	Day	Time	m	Time	m	Time	m	Time	m	Moon
1	TU	0559	0.7	1217	4.8	1833	0.5			○
2	W	0054	4.7	0700	0.6	1312	4.9	1931	0.4	
3	TH	0149	4.7	0753	0.5	1402	5.1	2024	0.3	
4	F	0241	4.7	0841	0.5	1451	5.1	2114	0.2	
5	SA	0328	4.6	0924	0.4	1538	5.1	2159	0.2	
6	SU	0411	4.5	1003	0.4	1622	5.0	2240	0.3	
7	M	0451	4.4	1041	0.5	1705	4.9	2320	0.4	
8	TU	0531	4.4	1122	0.6	1749	4.8	2359	0.6	◑
9	W	0610	4.3	1204	0.7	1835	4.6			
10	TH	0040	0.8	0657	4.2	1255	0.9	1933	4.4	
11	F	0136	1.0	0801	4.2	1407	1.1	2049	4.3	
12	SA	0251	1.2	0922	4.3	1534	1.1	2211	4.3	
13	SU	0414	1.1	1040	4.4	1656	1.0	2322	4.4	
14	M	0524	1.0	1142	4.6	1759	0.8			
15	TU	0017	4.4	0615	0.8	1230	4.7	1847	0.7	
16	W	0101	4.4	0658	0.7	1310	4.7	1927	0.6	●
17	TH	0139	4.5	0737	0.6	1346	4.8	2004	0.5	
18	F	0213	4.5	0813	0.6	1419	4.9	2037	0.6	
19	SA	0242	4.6	0843	0.6	1447	4.9	2106	0.6	
20	SU	0309	4.6	0910	0.7	1515	4.9	2133	0.7	
21	M	0337	4.6	0939	0.7	1544	4.9	2203	0.7	
22	TU	0408	4.5	1011	0.8	1617	4.8	2233	0.7	
23	W	0438	4.5	1041	0.8	1646	4.7	2257	0.8	
24	TH	0504	4.4	1106	0.9	1715	4.6	2321	0.9	◐
25	F	0538	4.3	1142	1.1	1802	4.4			
26	SA	0008	1.1	0637	4.2	1247	1.2	1918	4.2	
27	SU	0126	1.2	0803	4.2	1419	1.1	2053	4.2	
28	M	0302	1.1	0936	4.4	1555	0.9	2225	4.3	
29	TU	0433	0.9	1057	4.6	1717	0.7	2343	4.5	
30	W	0549	0.8	1204	4.8	1825	0.5			
31	TH	0047	4.6	0651	0.6	1259	4.9	1923	0.4	○

Chart Datum: 2·7 metres below Normal Null (German reference level)
HAT is 5·1 metres above Chart Datum

TIME ZONE -0100
(German Standard Time)
Subtract 1 hour for UT
For German Summer Time add ONE hour in **non-shaded areas**

GERMANY – WILHELMSHAVEN

LAT 53°31'N LONG 8°09'E

TIMES AND HEIGHTS OF HIGH AND LOW WATERS

Dates in amber are **SPRINGS**
Dates in grey are **NEAPS**

2023

SEPTEMBER

Date	Day	Time	m	Time	m	Time	m	Time	m
1	F	0138	4.7	0743	0.5	1347	5.1	2013	0.3
2	SA	0223	4.7	0827	0.4	1433	5.1	2058	0.3
3	SU	0305	4.7	0906	0.4	1517	5.1	2138	0.3
4	M	0343	4.6	0942	0.3	1558	5.0	2214	0.4
5	TU	0418	4.5	1016	0.4	1636	4.8	2246	0.5
6	W	0450	4.4	1049	0.6	1713	4.6	◑ 2317	0.8
7	TH	0523	4.3	1124	0.8	1753	4.4	2351	1.0
8	F	0606	4.2	1210	1.0	1848	4.2		
9	SA	0044	1.3	0711	4.2	1323	1.2	2008	4.1
10	SU	0206	1.4	0840	4.2	1500	1.3	2141	4.1
11	M	0342	1.3	1012	4.3	1636	1.1	2303	4.2
12	TU	0504	1.1	1123	4.5	1745	0.9	2359	4.4
13	W	0558	0.9	1210	4.7	1828	0.7		
14	TH	0038	4.4	0637	0.8	1246	4.7	1902	0.6
15	F	0112	4.5	0713	0.7	1319	4.7	● 1937	0.6
16	SA	0144	4.5	0748	0.6	1351	4.8	2009	0.6
17	SU	0214	4.6	0820	0.6	1421	4.9	2038	0.6
18	M	0240	4.6	0847	0.6	1448	4.9	2104	0.6
19	TU	0306	4.6	0913	0.7	1515	4.8	2130	0.7
20	W	0334	4.6	0941	0.7	1545	4.7	2156	0.7
21	TH	0402	4.6	1009	0.8	1616	4.6	2221	0.8
22	F	0431	4.4	1037	0.9	1650	4.4	◐ 2250	1.0
23	SA	0508	4.3	1116	1.0	1740	4.2	2340	1.2
24	SU	0610	4.2	1224	1.1	1900	4.1		
25	M	0104	1.3	0740	4.2	1401	1.1	2039	4.1
26	TU	0246	1.2	0918	4.4	1542	0.9	2214	4.2
27	W	0420	1.0	1041	4.6	1706	0.7	2330	4.4
28	TH	0534	0.8	1146	4.8	1811	0.5		
29	F	0029	4.5	0633	0.7	1239	4.9	○ 1905	0.4
30	SA	0116	4.6	0722	0.6	1325	5.1	1951	0.4

OCTOBER

Date	Day	Time	m	Time	m	Time	m	Time	m
1	SU	0156	4.7	0804	0.5	1407	5.1	2031	0.4
2	M	0233	4.7	0841	0.4	1449	5.0	2108	0.5
3	TU	0308	4.6	0916	0.4	1530	4.9	2141	0.5
4	W	0341	4.6	0949	0.5	1606	4.7	2210	0.7
5	TH	0412	4.5	1020	0.6	1640	4.5	2237	0.9
6	F	0443	4.4	1052	0.9	1717	4.3	◑ 2310	1.1
7	SA	0524	4.3	1135	1.1	1810	4.1		
8	SU	0001	1.4	0627	4.2	1243	1.4	1926	3.9
9	M	0120	1.5	0755	4.2	1418	1.4	2100	4.0
10	TU	0258	1.5	0930	4.3	1556	1.2	2226	4.1
11	W	0426	1.2	1046	4.5	1709	1.0	2325	4.3
12	TH	0524	1.0	1134	4.6	1752	0.8		
13	F	0002	4.4	0602	0.9	1209	4.7	1824	0.7
14	SA	0034	4.5	0637	0.8	1243	4.7	● 1858	0.6
15	SU	0108	4.5	0715	0.7	1318	4.7	1933	0.6
16	M	0140	4.6	0749	0.7	1349	4.8	2005	0.6
17	TU	0208	4.7	0819	0.7	1418	4.8	2033	0.6
18	W	0235	4.7	0847	0.7	1448	4.7	2059	0.7
19	TH	0304	4.6	0915	0.7	1521	4.6	2126	0.7
20	F	0335	4.6	0946	0.8	1558	4.4	2158	0.9
21	SA	0411	4.5	1021	0.8	1641	4.3	2237	1.1
22	SU	0457	4.4	1109	1.0	1737	4.2	◐ 2334	1.3
23	M	0601	4.3	1219	1.1	1854	4.1		
24	TU	0055	1.4	0726	4.4	1351	1.1	2027	4.1
25	W	0231	1.3	0859	4.5	1527	0.9	2155	4.2
26	TH	0359	1.1	1019	4.7	1646	0.8	2305	4.4
27	F	0509	0.9	1121	4.9	1746	0.7	2359	4.6
28	SA	0605	0.8	1212	5.0	1837	0.6	○	
29	SU	0045	4.7	0654	0.7	1258	5.0	1922	0.6
30	M	0124	4.7	0737	0.6	1341	5.0	2001	0.6
31	TU	0159	4.8	0814	0.6	1421	4.9	2035	0.7

NOVEMBER

Date	Day	Time	m	Time	m	Time	m	Time	m
1	W	0234	4.7	0850	0.6	1502	4.7	2108	0.7
2	TH	0309	4.7	0924	0.6	1540	4.6	2139	0.8
3	F	0342	4.6	0957	0.7	1615	4.4	2207	1.0
4	SA	0415	4.6	1030	0.9	1651	4.2	2240	1.1
5	SU	0455	4.5	1111	1.1	1739	4.1	◑ 2328	1.3
6	M	0551	4.4	1209	1.3	1844	4.0		
7	TU	0036	1.5	0706	4.3	1328	1.4	2005	3.9
8	W	0201	1.4	0831	4.3	1455	1.2	2126	4.1
9	TH	0324	1.3	0946	4.4	1607	1.0	2229	4.2
10	F	0428	1.1	1040	4.5	1657	0.8	2312	4.4
11	SA	0513	1.0	1121	4.6	1736	0.8	2348	4.5
12	SU	0554	0.9	1201	4.6	1815	0.7		
13	M	0026	4.6	0636	0.8	1240	4.7	● 1855	0.7
14	TU	0103	4.7	0716	0.7	1316	4.7	1931	0.7
15	W	0136	4.7	0750	0.7	1351	4.7	2004	0.7
16	TH	0209	4.7	0823	0.7	1429	4.7	2038	0.7
17	F	0243	4.7	0858	0.7	1508	4.5	2111	0.8
18	SA	0321	4.7	0936	0.7	1552	4.4	2150	0.9
19	SU	0404	4.6	1020	0.8	1642	4.3	2236	1.0
20	M	0455	4.6	1114	0.9	1740	4.2	◐ 2334	1.2
21	TU	0558	4.6	1219	1.0	1848	4.2		
22	W	0045	1.3	0712	4.6	1337	1.0	2007	4.2
23	TH	0207	1.2	0833	4.6	1500	0.9	2124	4.2
24	F	0327	1.1	0948	4.7	1613	0.9	2230	4.4
25	SA	0435	1.0	1050	4.9	1713	0.8	2324	4.6
26	SU	0532	0.9	1143	4.9	1804	0.8		
27	M	0012	4.7	0623	0.8	1233	4.9	○ 1851	0.8
28	TU	0054	4.7	0710	0.7	1318	4.8	1932	0.7
29	W	0132	4.8	0750	0.6	1400	4.7	2008	0.8
30	TH	0209	4.8	0828	0.6	1442	4.6	2043	0.8

DECEMBER

Date	Day	Time	m	Time	m	Time	m	Time	m
1	F	0247	4.8	0906	0.6	1521	4.5	2116	0.8
2	SA	0322	4.7	0941	0.7	1556	4.4	2147	0.9
3	SU	0356	4.7	1015	0.8	1631	4.3	2221	1.0
4	M	0433	4.6	1052	1.0	1712	4.2	2302	1.2
5	TU	0519	4.5	1138	1.1	1802	4.1	◑ 2355	1.3
6	W	0616	4.4	1235	1.2	1903	4.0		
7	TH	0057	1.3	0722	4.4	1341	1.1	2010	4.1
8	F	0206	1.2	0830	4.4	1448	1.0	2114	4.2
9	SA	0314	1.2	0932	4.4	1548	0.9	2209	4.3
10	SU	0413	1.1	1026	4.5	1641	0.9	2258	4.5
11	M	0507	1.0	1117	4.6	1731	0.8	2345	4.6
12	TU	0557	0.9	1205	4.6	1819	0.8		
13	W	0029	4.7	0643	0.8	1249	4.7	● 1903	0.7
14	TH	0110	4.8	0725	0.7	1333	4.7	1945	0.7
15	F	0151	4.8	0808	0.6	1420	4.7	2027	0.7
16	SA	0233	4.8	0852	0.6	1507	4.6	2109	0.7
17	SU	0317	4.8	0937	0.5	1554	4.5	2150	0.8
18	M	0403	4.8	1024	0.6	1643	4.4	2236	0.9
19	TU	0454	4.8	1115	0.7	1736	4.3	◐ 2327	1.0
20	W	0550	4.8	1211	0.8	1833	4.3		
21	TH	0025	1.0	0652	4.7	1312	0.9	1935	4.2
22	F	0131	1.0	0801	4.7	1420	0.9	2043	4.3
23	SA	0244	1.0	0913	4.7	1531	1.0	2151	4.4
24	SU	0356	1.0	1020	4.7	1637	1.0	2251	4.5
25	M	0500	1.0	1120	4.7	1734	1.0	2344	4.6
26	TU	0558	0.8	1214	4.7	1825	0.9		
27	W	0032	4.7	0649	0.7	1304	4.6	○ 1910	0.8
28	TH	0115	4.7	0733	0.6	1348	4.5	1950	0.8
29	F	0154	4.8	0815	0.6	1428	4.5	2027	0.8
30	SA	0232	4.8	0854	0.6	1505	4.4	2101	0.8
31	SU	0307	4.8	0929	0.7	1538	4.4	2132	0.8

Chart Datum: 2·7 metres below Normal Null (German reference level)
HAT is 5·1 metres above Chart Datum

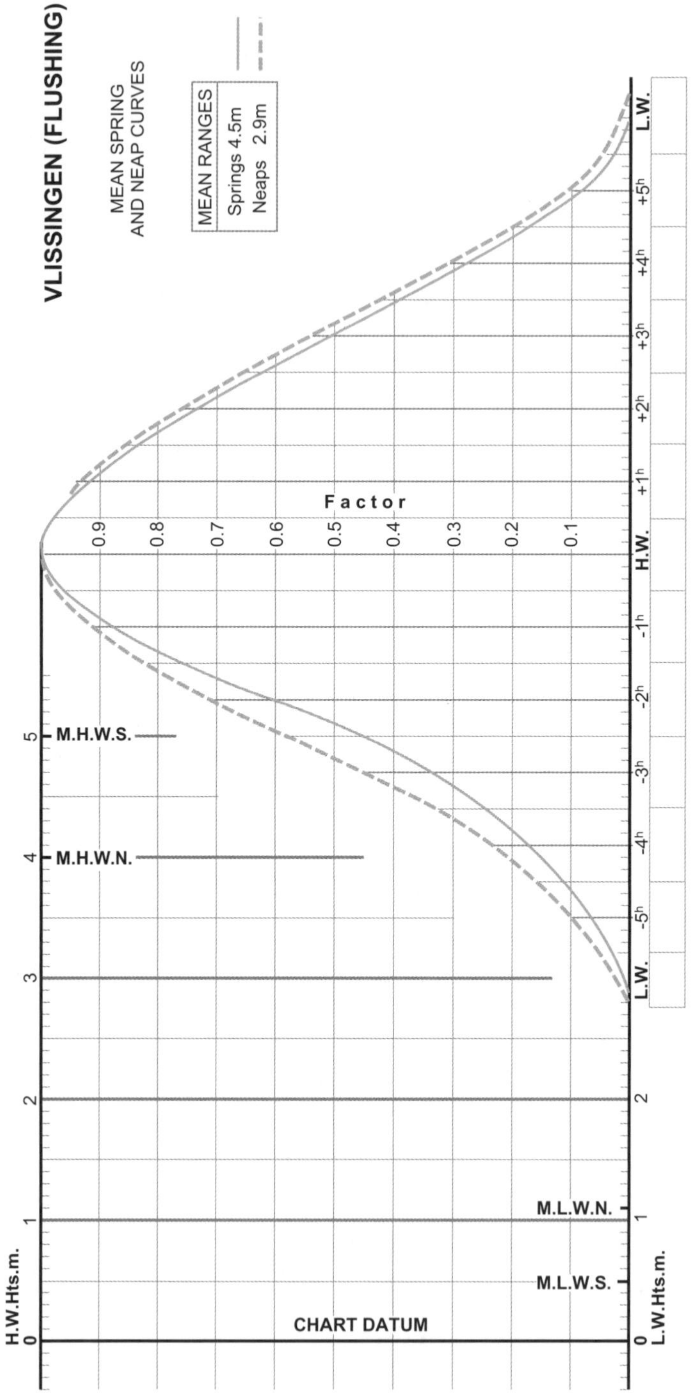
VLISSINGEN (FLUSHING)
MEAN SPRING AND NEAP CURVES
MEAN RANGES
Springs 4.5m
Neaps 2.9m
Factor
0.9 0.8 0.7 0.6 0.5 0.4 0.3 0.2 0.1
L.W. -5h -4h -3h -2h -1h H.W. +1h +2h +3h +4h +5h L.W.
H.W.Hts.m.
0 1 2 3 4 5
M.H.W.S.
M.H.W.N.
M.L.W.N.
M.L.W.S.
CHART DATUM
L.W.Hts.m.
0 1 2

TIME ZONE -0100
(Dutch Standard Time)
Subtract 1 hour for UT
For Dutch Summer Time add ONE hour in **non-shaded areas**

NETHERLANDS – VLISSINGEN

LAT 51°27′N LONG 3°36′E

TIMES AND HEIGHTS OF HIGH AND LOW WATERS

Dates in amber are **SPRINGS**
Dates in grey are **NEAPS**

2023

JANUARY

Date	Day	Time	m	Time	m	Time	m	Time	m
1	SU	0315	1.3	0926	4.2	1604	0.9	2213	4.3
2	M	0435	1.3	1034	4.2	1714	0.9	2316	4.3
3	TU	0540	1.2	1136	4.3	1808	0.9		
4	W	0013	4.4	0632	1.1	1232	4.4	1854	0.9
5	TH	0104	4.5	0717	1.0	1322	4.5	1934	1.0
6	F	0148	4.5	0758	0.9	1404	4.6	2010	1.0
7	SA	0226	4.5	0837	0.8	1440	4.6	○ 2045	1.0
8	SU	0259	4.6	0914	0.8	1513	4.7	2119	1.0
9	M	0330	4.6	0950	0.7	1547	4.7	2153	1.0
10	TU	0402	4.6	1026	0.7	1620	4.7	2227	1.0
11	W	0435	4.6	1100	0.7	1654	4.7	2259	1.0
12	TH	0509	4.6	1133	0.7	1728	4.6	2333	1.1
13	F	0545	4.5	1208	0.7	1807	4.5		
14	SA	0011	1.1	0625	4.4	1248	0.8	1853	4.4
15	SU	0056	1.1	0715	4.3	1337	0.8	◑ 1953	4.3
16	M	0151	1.2	0819	4.2	1437	0.9	2100	4.3
17	TU	0300	1.2	0930	4.2	1546	1.0	2209	4.3
18	W	0418	1.2	1039	4.3	1700	1.0	2316	4.4
19	TH	0532	1.1	1142	4.5	1808	0.9		
20	F	0015	4.6	0638	0.9	1239	4.7	1905	0.8
21	SA	0109	4.7	0735	0.6	1330	4.9	● 1956	0.7
22	SU	0158	4.9	0827	0.4	1419	5.1	2044	0.7
23	M	0244	5.0	0916	0.3	1506	5.2	2131	0.7
24	TU	0330	5.0	1004	0.2	1553	5.2	2216	0.7
25	W	0416	5.0	1051	0.2	1640	5.1	2300	0.8
26	TH	0502	5.0	1136	0.2	1729	5.0	2344	0.9
27	F	0550	4.9	1221	0.3	1820	4.8		
28	SA	0030	1.0	0640	4.7	1307	0.5	◐ 1915	4.6
29	SU	0121	1.1	0735	4.5	1359	0.7	2015	4.3
30	M	0222	1.2	0838	4.2	1503	1.0	2127	4.1
31	TU	0338	1.3	0954	4.1	1627	1.1	2244	4.0

FEBRUARY

Date	Day	Time	m	Time	m	Time	m	Time	m
1	W	0503	1.3	1111	4.1	1738	1.1	2351	4.1
2	TH	0609	1.2	1218	4.2	1832	1.1		
3	F	0048	4.2	0703	1.0	1312	4.4	1917	1.1
4	SA	0134	4.4	0746	0.9	1354	4.5	1954	1.0
5	SU	0211	4.5	0823	0.8	1427	4.6	○ 2028	1.0
6	M	0242	4.6	0857	0.7	1458	4.7	2101	0.9
7	TU	0311	4.7	0931	0.6	1528	4.8	2134	0.9
8	W	0342	4.8	1006	0.5	1559	4.9	2207	0.8
9	TH	0413	4.8	1039	0.5	1630	4.9	2238	0.8
10	F	0444	4.8	1110	0.5	1701	4.8	2309	0.8
11	SA	0516	4.8	1141	0.5	1735	4.8	2342	0.8
12	SU	0551	4.7	1216	0.5	1815	4.7		
13	M	0022	0.8	0634	4.6	1258	0.6	◑ 1906	4.5
14	TU	0111	0.9	0730	4.4	1354	0.8	2013	4.3
15	W	0217	1.1	0847	4.2	1506	1.0	2131	4.1
16	TH	0343	1.2	1010	4.2	1632	1.1	2251	4.1
17	F	0512	1.1	1126	4.3	1752	1.0		
18	SA	0002	4.3	0627	0.8	1230	4.6	1853	0.8
19	SU	0058	4.6	0726	0.6	1322	4.9	1945	0.7
20	M	0145	4.8	0816	0.3	1408	5.1	● 2031	0.6
21	TU	0229	5.0	0903	0.2	1451	5.2	2115	0.6
22	W	0311	5.1	0947	0.1	1535	5.3	2157	0.6
23	TH	0354	5.1	1029	0.1	1618	5.2	2238	0.6
24	F	0436	5.1	1110	0.2	1702	5.1	2318	0.7
25	SA	0519	5.0	1149	0.3	1747	4.8	2358	0.8
26	SU	0604	4.8	1229	0.5	1834	4.5		
27	M	0041	0.9	0652	4.5	1314	0.8	◐ 1925	4.2
28	TU	0137	1.1	0750	4.2	1415	1.1	2028	3.8

MARCH

Date	Day	Time	m	Time	m	Time	m	Time	m
1	W	0255	1.3	0909	3.9	1538	1.3	2210	3.6
2	TH	0422	1.3	1047	3.8	1704	1.3	2328	3.8
3	F	0542	1.2	1159	4.0	1809	1.2		
4	SA	0027	4.0	0642	1.0	1252	4.3	1858	1.1
5	SU	0112	4.3	0727	0.8	1332	4.5	1935	1.0
6	M	0147	4.5	0802	0.7	1404	4.7	2007	0.9
7	TU	0217	4.6	0834	0.6	1433	4.8	○ 2039	0.8
8	W	0245	4.8	0907	0.5	1502	4.9	2111	0.7
9	TH	0315	4.9	0939	0.4	1532	5.0	2143	0.7
10	F	0345	4.9	1012	0.4	1602	5.0	2215	0.7
11	SA	0415	4.9	1044	0.4	1633	4.9	2246	0.6
12	SU	0448	4.9	1116	0.4	1707	4.9	2319	0.6
13	M	0523	4.9	1150	0.5	1747	4.8	2358	0.6
14	TU	0605	4.8	1232	0.6	1835	4.5		
15	W	0048	0.8	0659	4.5	1328	0.8	◑ 1941	4.2
16	TH	0156	1.0	0820	4.2	1444	1.1	2107	3.9
17	F	0327	1.1	0954	4.1	1618	1.2	2237	3.9
18	SA	0503	1.0	1118	4.3	1742	1.1	2350	4.2
19	SU	0618	0.7	1221	4.6	1843	0.9		
20	M	0044	4.5	0714	0.5	1310	4.9	1931	0.7
21	TU	0128	4.8	0800	0.2	1352	5.1	● 2014	0.6
22	W	0209	5.0	0843	0.1	1432	5.2	2055	0.6
23	TH	0249	5.1	0924	0.1	1513	5.2	2135	0.5
24	F	0329	5.2	1004	0.1	1554	5.1	2214	0.6
25	SA	0409	5.1	1042	0.3	1634	5.0	2252	0.6
26	SU	0450	5.0	1118	0.4	1715	4.7	2329	0.7
27	M	0531	4.8	1154	0.7	1756	4.4		
28	TU	0009	0.8	0615	4.5	1235	0.9	1840	4.1
29	W	0058	1.0	0707	4.1	1331	1.2	◐ 1933	3.7
30	TH	0221	1.2	0821	3.8	1501	1.4	2110	3.4
31	F	0344	1.3	1016	3.7	1624	1.4	2257	3.6

APRIL

Date	Day	Time	m	Time	m	Time	m	Time	m
1	SA	0502	1.2	1129	3.9	1733	1.3	2355	3.9
2	SU	0608	1.0	1221	4.2	1826	1.1		
3	M	0039	4.2	0655	0.8	1300	4.5	1906	1.0
4	TU	0114	4.4	0731	0.6	1332	4.7	1939	0.8
5	W	0144	4.6	0804	0.5	1402	4.9	2011	0.7
6	TH	0213	4.8	0836	0.4	1431	5.0	○ 2043	0.7
7	F	0243	4.9	0909	0.4	1502	5.0	2117	0.6
8	SA	0315	5.0	0943	0.4	1534	5.0	2152	0.6
9	SU	0348	5.0	1018	0.4	1608	5.0	2227	0.5
10	M	0423	5.0	1053	0.4	1645	4.9	2304	0.5
11	TU	0502	5.0	1131	0.5	1727	4.7	2347	0.6
12	W	0547	4.8	1217	0.7	1817	4.4		
13	TH	0041	0.7	0645	4.4	1315	1.0	◑ 1927	4.0
14	F	0152	0.9	0813	4.1	1435	1.2	2055	3.8
15	SA	0323	1.0	0945	4.1	1611	1.2	2223	3.9
16	SU	0454	0.9	1107	4.3	1731	1.1	2333	4.2
17	M	0605	0.6	1206	4.6	1827	0.9		
18	TU	0024	4.5	0656	0.4	1252	4.9	1912	0.7
19	W	0106	4.7	0740	0.3	1332	5.0	1954	0.6
20	TH	0146	4.9	0821	0.2	1412	5.1	● 2034	0.6
21	F	0226	5.0	0900	0.2	1451	5.0	2113	0.5
22	SA	0305	5.1	0939	0.3	1531	4.9	2152	0.5
23	SU	0345	5.0	1015	0.5	1610	4.8	2230	0.6
24	M	0425	4.9	1051	0.6	1648	4.6	2308	0.7
25	TU	0504	4.7	1125	0.8	1726	4.3	2346	0.8
26	W	0547	4.4	1203	1.1	1807	4.1		
27	TH	0033	1.0	0637	4.1	1255	1.3	◐ 1856	3.8
28	F	0151	1.1	0744	3.8	1426	1.5	2004	3.5
29	SA	0306	1.2	0919	3.7	1541	1.4	2203	3.5
30	SU	0413	1.1	1045	3.9	1646	1.3	2310	3.8

Chart Datum: 2·56 metres below NAP Datum
HAT is 5·4 metres above Chart Datum

TIME ZONE -0100
(Dutch Standard Time)
Subtract 1 hour for UT
For Dutch Summer Time add ONE hour in **non-shaded areas**

NETHERLANDS – VLISSINGEN

LAT 51°27′N LONG 3°36′E

TIMES AND HEIGHTS OF HIGH AND LOW WATERS

Dates in amber are **SPRINGS**
Dates in grey are **NEAPS**

2023

MAY

Date	Day	Time	m	Time	m	Time	m	Time	m
1	M	0519	1.0	1138	4.2	1743	1.1	2356	4.1
2	TU	0612	0.8	1219	4.4	1827	1.0		
3	W	0032	4.4	0652	0.6	1254	4.7	1903	0.8
4	TH	0106	4.6	0727	0.5	1326	4.9	1938	0.7
5	F	0138	4.8	0802	0.5	1358	5.0	○ 2014	0.6
6	SA	0212	4.9	0838	0.4	1432	5.0	2052	0.6
7	SU	0247	5.0	0916	0.4	1509	5.0	2131	0.5
8	M	0325	5.0	0955	0.5	1547	4.9	2212	0.5
9	TU	0404	5.0	1035	0.5	1628	4.8	2256	0.5
10	W	0448	4.9	1118	0.7	1715	4.6	2344	0.5
11	TH	0538	4.7	1208	0.8	1811	4.3		
12	F	0042	0.6	0645	4.4	1309	1.0	◑ 1924	4.1
13	SA	0154	0.7	0809	4.3	1428	1.2	2042	3.9
14	SU	0314	0.8	0929	4.3	1555	1.2	2200	4.0
15	M	0435	0.7	1045	4.4	1709	1.1	2306	4.2
16	TU	0542	0.5	1143	4.6	1805	0.9	2359	4.5
17	W	0633	0.4	1230	4.8	1851	0.8		
18	TH	0044	4.6	0717	0.4	1312	4.9	1933	0.7
19	F	0126	4.8	0757	0.4	1353	4.9	● 2013	0.6
20	SA	0207	4.9	0836	0.4	1434	4.8	2054	0.6
21	SU	0247	4.9	0914	0.5	1513	4.7	2134	0.6
22	M	0327	4.8	0951	0.7	1551	4.6	2213	0.6
23	TU	0407	4.7	1027	0.8	1628	4.5	2252	0.7
24	W	0447	4.6	1103	1.0	1705	4.3	2332	0.8
25	TH	0528	4.4	1141	1.1	1745	4.1		
26	F	0018	0.9	0615	4.2	1227	1.3	1832	4.0
27	SA	0117	1.0	0712	4.0	1338	1.4	◐ 1929	3.8
28	SU	0223	1.0	0817	3.9	1454	1.4	2038	3.7
29	M	0323	1.0	0932	3.9	1554	1.3	2157	3.8
30	TU	0422	0.9	1040	4.1	1650	1.2	2258	4.0
31	W	0517	0.8	1129	4.4	1739	1.0	2344	4.3

JUNE

Date	Day	Time	m	Time	m	Time	m	Time	m
1	TH	0605	0.7	1211	4.6	1822	0.9		
2	F	0026	4.5	0647	0.6	1249	4.8	1904	0.8
3	SA	0105	4.7	0729	0.5	1328	4.9	1947	0.6
4	SU	0145	4.9	0810	0.5	1408	5.0	○ 2031	0.5
5	M	0225	5.0	0853	0.5	1449	4.9	2116	0.5
6	TU	0307	5.0	0937	0.6	1533	4.9	2203	0.4
7	W	0352	5.0	1022	0.7	1619	4.7	2251	0.4
8	TH	0440	4.9	1109	0.8	1709	4.6	2344	0.4
9	F	0536	4.7	1201	0.9	1807	4.4		
10	SA	0042	0.5	0642	4.6	1300	1.0	◑ 1912	4.3
11	SU	0145	0.5	0752	4.5	1409	1.1	2018	4.2
12	M	0251	0.6	0902	4.4	1522	1.2	2127	4.2
13	TU	0403	0.6	1012	4.5	1635	1.1	2233	4.3
14	W	0512	0.6	1113	4.5	1737	1.0	2331	4.4
15	TH	0606	0.6	1206	4.6	1828	0.9		
16	F	0022	4.5	0653	0.6	1255	4.7	1913	0.8
17	SA	0110	4.6	0735	0.6	1340	4.7	1956	0.7
18	SU	0155	4.7	0815	0.7	1423	4.6	● 2038	0.6
19	M	0237	4.7	0853	0.8	1502	4.6	2119	0.6
20	TU	0317	4.7	0930	0.9	1539	4.6	2159	0.6
21	W	0355	4.7	1006	1.0	1614	4.5	2238	0.6
22	TH	0433	4.6	1042	1.0	1649	4.4	2317	0.7
23	F	0512	4.5	1119	1.1	1726	4.3	2357	0.7
24	SA	0552	4.4	1158	1.2	1807	4.2		
25	SU	0039	0.8	0637	4.3	1241	1.3	1853	4.1
26	M	0126	0.8	0729	4.2	1335	1.3	◐ 1948	4.0
27	TU	0220	0.9	0827	4.1	1443	1.3	2051	4.0
28	W	0318	0.9	0929	4.2	1547	1.2	2155	4.1
29	TH	0417	0.9	1031	4.3	1645	1.1	2255	4.3
30	F	0516	0.8	1127	4.5	1741	1.0	2349	4.5

JULY

Date	Day	Time	m	Time	m	Time	m	Time	m
1	SA	0610	0.7	1217	4.7	1835	0.8		
2	SU	0037	4.7	0701	0.7	1304	4.8	1926	0.7
3	M	0124	4.9	0749	0.6	1350	4.9	○ 2016	0.5
4	TU	0210	5.0	0836	0.6	1436	4.9	2106	0.4
5	W	0256	5.1	0923	0.7	1522	4.9	2155	0.3
6	TH	0344	5.1	1010	0.7	1609	4.8	2245	0.3
7	F	0433	5.0	1058	0.8	1659	4.8	2336	0.3
8	SA	0526	4.9	1148	0.9	1751	4.7		
9	SU	0027	0.3	0624	4.8	1239	1.0	1847	4.6
10	M	0120	0.4	0724	4.7	1336	1.1	◑ 1946	4.5
11	TU	0216	0.5	0827	4.5	1439	1.1	2049	4.4
12	W	0321	0.7	0934	4.4	1552	1.2	2157	4.3
13	TH	0436	0.8	1042	4.4	1706	1.1	2304	4.3
14	F	0539	0.8	1144	4.4	1806	1.0		
15	SA	0007	4.4	0631	0.8	1241	4.5	1858	0.9
16	SU	0103	4.5	0717	0.9	1331	4.5	1944	0.8
17	M	0152	4.6	0758	0.9	1414	4.6	● 2026	0.7
18	TU	0232	4.7	0835	1.0	1451	4.6	2104	0.7
19	W	0308	4.7	0910	1.0	1524	4.6	2142	0.6
20	TH	0341	4.7	0946	1.0	1555	4.6	2219	0.6
21	F	0415	4.7	1021	1.0	1628	4.6	2255	0.6
22	SA	0448	4.7	1055	1.0	1702	4.6	2329	0.6
23	SU	0522	4.6	1127	1.1	1735	4.5		
24	M	0001	0.7	0557	4.5	1200	1.1	1812	4.4
25	TU	0035	0.7	0637	4.4	1238	1.1	◐ 1855	4.4
26	W	0117	0.8	0728	4.4	1327	1.1	1951	4.3
27	TH	0210	0.9	0831	4.3	1430	1.2	2101	4.2
28	F	0317	1.0	0938	4.2	1550	1.2	2211	4.2
29	SA	0432	1.0	1048	4.3	1707	1.1	2319	4.4
30	SU	0542	0.9	1152	4.5	1814	0.9		
31	M	0019	4.6	0642	0.8	1248	4.6	1912	0.7

AUGUST

Date	Day	Time	m	Time	m	Time	m	Time	m
1	TU	0111	4.8	0734	0.7	1337	4.8	○ 2005	0.5
2	W	0159	5.0	0823	0.7	1423	4.9	2055	0.3
3	TH	0245	5.2	0910	0.7	1508	5.0	2143	0.2
4	F	0331	5.2	0955	0.7	1553	5.0	2230	0.2
5	SA	0417	5.2	1040	0.8	1638	5.0	2316	0.2
6	SU	0504	5.1	1125	0.8	1725	4.9		
7	M	0000	0.3	0555	4.9	1210	0.9	1814	4.8
8	TU	0046	0.4	0649	4.7	1259	1.0	◑ 1908	4.6
9	W	0136	0.6	0747	4.5	1356	1.1	2009	4.4
10	TH	0235	0.9	0854	4.2	1509	1.2	2122	4.2
11	F	0355	1.1	1013	4.1	1635	1.3	2243	4.1
12	SA	0515	1.1	1126	4.1	1748	1.1	2356	4.3
13	SU	0615	1.1	1228	4.3	1847	1.0		
14	M	0056	4.5	0705	1.1	1318	4.5	1934	0.8
15	TU	0142	4.6	0744	1.0	1359	4.6	2013	0.7
16	W	0218	4.7	0818	1.0	1432	4.6	● 2047	0.7
17	TH	0249	4.8	0850	1.0	1502	4.7	2120	0.6
18	F	0319	4.8	0923	1.0	1531	4.8	2154	0.6
19	SA	0349	4.9	0956	0.9	1601	4.8	2227	0.6
20	SU	0419	4.9	1027	0.9	1631	4.8	2258	0.6
21	M	0449	4.8	1055	1.0	1701	4.8	2326	0.6
22	TU	0519	4.7	1125	0.9	1733	4.7	2357	0.7
23	W	0554	4.7	1200	0.9	1810	4.7		
24	TH	0034	0.7	0638	4.5	1245	1.0	◐ 1858	4.5
25	F	0124	0.9	0737	4.3	1344	1.1	2009	4.3
26	SA	0232	1.1	0856	4.1	1508	1.3	2137	4.1
27	SU	0400	1.2	1019	4.1	1643	1.2	2259	4.3
28	M	0524	1.1	1136	4.3	1801	1.0		
29	TU	0007	4.6	0628	1.0	1235	4.6	1902	0.7
30	W	0100	4.9	0721	0.8	1323	4.8	1953	0.4
31	TH	0146	5.1	0808	0.7	1406	5.0	○ 2039	0.3

Chart Datum: 2·56 metres below NAP Datum
HAT is 5·4 metres above Chart Datum

TIME ZONE -0100
(Dutch Standard Time)
Subtract 1 hour for UT
For Dutch Summer Time add
ONE hour in **non-shaded areas**

NETHERLANDS – VLISSINGEN

LAT 51°27′N LONG 3°36′E

TIMES AND HEIGHTS OF HIGH AND LOW WATERS

Dates in amber are **SPRINGS**
Dates in grey are **NEAPS**

2023

SEPTEMBER

Date	Time	m	Date	Time	m
1 F	0228 0852 1448 2124	5.3 0.7 5.1 0.2	16 SA	0250 0857 1501 2124	5.0 0.9 4.9 0.6
2 SA	0311 0935 1530 2207	5.3 0.7 5.2 0.2	17 SU	0319 0928 1530 2156	5.0 0.9 5.0 0.6
3 SU	0354 1017 1612 2249	5.3 0.7 5.2 0.3	18 M	0347 0958 1559 2226	5.0 0.9 5.0 0.6
4 M	0438 1058 1655 2330	5.1 0.8 5.1 0.4	19 TU	0416 1027 1629 2255	4.9 0.9 4.9 0.7
5 TU	0523 1139 1741	4.9 0.9 4.9	20 W	0448 1057 1702 2326	4.9 0.9 4.9 0.7
6 W	0010 0611 1223 ◑ 1830	0.6 4.7 1.0 4.7	21 TH	0523 1133 1740	4.8 0.9 4.8
7 TH	0055 0704 1317 1928	0.8 4.4 1.2 4.4	22 F	0004 0606 1218 ◐ 1826	0.8 4.6 0.9 4.6
8 F	0152 0809 1433 2047	1.1 4.0 1.3 4.0	23 SA	0054 0702 1320 1934	1.0 4.3 1.1 4.3
9 SA	0316 0944 1604 2224	1.4 3.8 1.4 4.0	24 SU	0205 0826 1449 2116	1.3 4.0 1.3 4.1
10 SU	0450 1107 1727 2341	1.4 3.9 1.2 4.2	25 M	0342 1000 1629 2246	1.4 3.9 1.2 4.2
11 M	0557 1210 1829	1.3 4.2 1.0	26 TU	0511 1121 1749 2355	1.3 4.2 0.9 4.6
12 TU	0038 0649 1258 1916	4.4 1.2 4.4 0.9	27 W	0616 1218 1848	1.1 4.5 0.7
13 W	0121 0726 1335 1952	4.7 1.1 4.6 0.8	28 TH	0045 0705 1303 1936	4.9 0.9 4.8 0.4
14 TH	0154 0757 1406 2023	4.8 1.0 4.7 0.7	29 F	0127 0749 1344 ○ 2019	5.1 0.8 5.0 0.3
15 F	0223 0826 1433 ● 2053	4.9 1.0 4.8 0.6	30 SA	0208 0831 1424 2101	5.3 0.7 5.2 0.2

OCTOBER

Date	Time	m	Date	Time	m
1 SU	0248 0912 1505 2142	5.3 0.7 5.3 0.3	16 M	0246 0859 1458 2124	5.0 0.8 5.0 0.6
2 M	0330 0953 1546 2221	5.2 0.7 5.2 0.4	17 TU	0317 0931 1530 2156	5.1 0.8 5.1 0.7
3 TU	0412 1033 1627 2259	5.1 0.8 5.1 0.6	18 W	0349 1004 1603 2229	5.0 0.8 5.1 0.7
4 W	0454 1112 1710 2337	4.9 0.9 4.9 0.8	19 TH	0423 1039 1639 2304	4.9 0.8 5.0 0.8
5 TH	0538 1153 1756	4.6 1.0 4.6	20 F	0501 1119 1720 2346	4.8 0.8 4.9 0.9
6 F	0018 0624 1243 ◑ 1851	1.1 4.2 1.2 4.3	21 SA	0546 1208 1810	4.5 0.9 4.6
7 SA	0112 0721 1401 2008	1.4 3.9 1.4 3.9	22 SU	0039 0645 1313 ◐ 1924	1.2 4.2 1.1 4.2
8 SU	0241 0901 1528 2157	1.6 3.6 1.4 3.8	23 M	0151 0811 1442 2103	1.4 3.9 1.2 4.1
9 M	0412 1038 1652 2314	1.6 3.7 1.3 4.1	24 TU	0328 0941 1615 2230	1.5 3.9 1.1 4.3
10 TU	0525 1140 1757	1.5 4.0 1.1	25 W	0455 1059 1733 2337	1.4 4.1 0.9 4.6
11 W	0008 0619 1226 1845	4.4 1.3 4.3 0.9	26 TH	0558 1155 1829	1.2 4.5 0.6
12 TH	0049 0657 1302 1921	4.6 1.1 4.5 0.8	27 F	0025 0646 1240 1915	4.9 1.0 4.8 0.5
13 F	0121 0728 1332 1951	4.8 1.0 4.7 0.7	28 SA	0106 0729 1321 ○ 1956	5.1 0.9 5.0 0.4
14 SA	0150 0757 1359 ● 2021	4.9 1.0 4.8 0.7	29 SU	0147 0810 1401 2037	5.2 0.8 5.1 0.4
15 SU	0218 0828 1428 2052	5.0 0.9 5.0 0.6	30 M	0227 0851 1442 2117	5.2 0.7 5.2 0.5
			31 TU	0308 0932 1523 2155	5.1 0.7 5.2 0.6

NOVEMBER

Date	Time	m	Date	Time	m
1 W	0349 1012 1605 2232	4.9 0.8 5.0 0.8	16 TH	0327 0948 1543 2210	5.0 0.7 5.1 0.8
2 TH	0430 1051 1647 2309	4.7 0.8 4.8 1.0	17 F	0406 1030 1624 2251	4.9 0.7 5.0 0.9
3 F	0511 1132 1731 2348	4.5 1.0 4.6 1.2	18 SA	0449 1116 1710 2336	4.7 0.7 4.8 1.0
4 SA	0554 1220 1823	4.2 1.1 4.2	19 SU	0538 1208 1806	4.5 0.8 4.6
5 SU	0037 0644 1329 ◑ 1929	1.5 3.9 1.3 3.9	20 M	0031 0641 1314 ◐ 1922	1.2 4.2 0.9 4.3
6 M	0159 0751 1445 2100	1.7 3.7 1.4 3.8	21 TU	0140 0758 1431 2044	1.4 4.0 1.0 4.3
7 TU	0320 0943 1556 2229	1.7 3.6 1.3 3.9	22 W	0305 0915 1550 2203	1.5 4.0 1.0 4.4
8 W	0429 1053 1706 2324	1.6 3.8 1.2 4.2	23 TH	0426 1028 1706 2309	1.4 4.2 0.8 4.6
9 TH	0530 1141 1759	1.4 4.1 1.0	24 F	0532 1126 1804	1.2 4.4 0.7
10 F	0006 0615 1219 1840	4.4 1.2 4.4 0.9	25 SA	0000 0623 1215 1851	4.7 1.1 4.7 0.6
11 SA	0041 0651 1252 1913	4.7 1.1 4.6 0.8	26 SU	0046 0708 1300 1934	4.9 0.9 4.8 0.6
12 SU	0113 0723 1323 1945	4.8 1.0 4.8 0.7	27 M	0129 0751 1343 ○ 2015	4.9 0.8 4.9 0.6
13 M	0143 0757 1356 ● 2019	4.9 0.9 4.9 0.7	28 TU	0211 0833 1426 2054	4.9 0.7 5.0 0.7
14 TU	0216 0832 1430 2054	5.0 0.8 5.0 0.7	29 W	0253 0915 1508 2133	4.9 0.7 5.0 0.8
15 W	0250 0909 1505 2131	5.0 0.7 5.1 0.7	30 TH	0334 0956 1550 2210	4.8 0.7 4.9 0.9

DECEMBER

Date	Time	m	Date	Time	m
1 F	0414 1036 1632 2246	4.6 0.8 4.7 1.1	16 SA	0356 1026 1616 2242	4.9 0.6 5.0 0.9
2 SA	0453 1117 1715 2325	4.5 0.9 4.5 1.3	17 SU	0442 1115 1705 2329	4.7 0.6 4.9 1.0
3 SU	0533 1201 1801	4.3 1.0 4.3	18 M	0533 1208 1802	4.6 0.6 4.7
4 M	0008 0617 1253 1852	1.4 4.1 1.1 4.1	19 TU	0022 0631 1306 ◐ 1908	1.1 4.4 0.7 4.6
5 TU	0105 0709 1356 ◑ 1952	1.6 3.9 1.2 4.0	20 W	0122 0735 1407 2017	1.2 4.3 0.7 4.4
6 W	0222 0811 1458 2102	1.6 3.8 1.2 3.9	21 TH	0229 0842 1514 2127	1.3 4.2 0.8 4.4
7 TH	0328 0927 1558 2217	1.6 3.8 1.2 4.0	22 F	0342 0951 1629 2235	1.3 4.2 0.8 4.4
8 F	0427 1036 1657 2311	1.5 4.0 1.1 4.2	23 SA	0457 1055 1735 2335	1.3 4.4 0.8 4.5
9 SA	0520 1126 1748 2354	1.3 4.2 1.0 4.5	24 SU	0558 1153 1827	1.1 4.5 0.8
10 SU	0606 1209 1831	1.2 4.4 0.9	25 M	0028 0649 1245 1913	4.6 1.0 4.6 0.8
11 M	0034 0648 1249 1910	4.7 1.0 4.7 0.8	26 TU	0117 0736 1334 1956	4.7 0.8 4.7 0.8
12 TU	0112 0728 1328 1950	4.8 0.9 4.8 0.7	27 W	0203 0820 1420 ○ 2036	4.7 0.7 4.8 0.8
13 W	0151 0810 1407 ● 2031	4.9 0.8 5.0 0.7	28 TH	0246 0902 1502 2114	4.7 0.7 4.8 0.9
14 TH	0231 0854 1448 2113	5.0 0.7 5.1 0.7	29 F	0325 0943 1541 2150	4.7 0.7 4.8 1.0
15 F	0312 0939 1530 2157	4.9 0.6 5.1 0.8	30 SA	0401 1022 1619 2227	4.6 0.7 4.7 1.1
			31 SU	0437 1100 1657 2303	4.6 0.7 4.6 1.1

Chart Datum: 2·56 metres below NAP Datum
HAT is 5·4 metres above Chart Datum

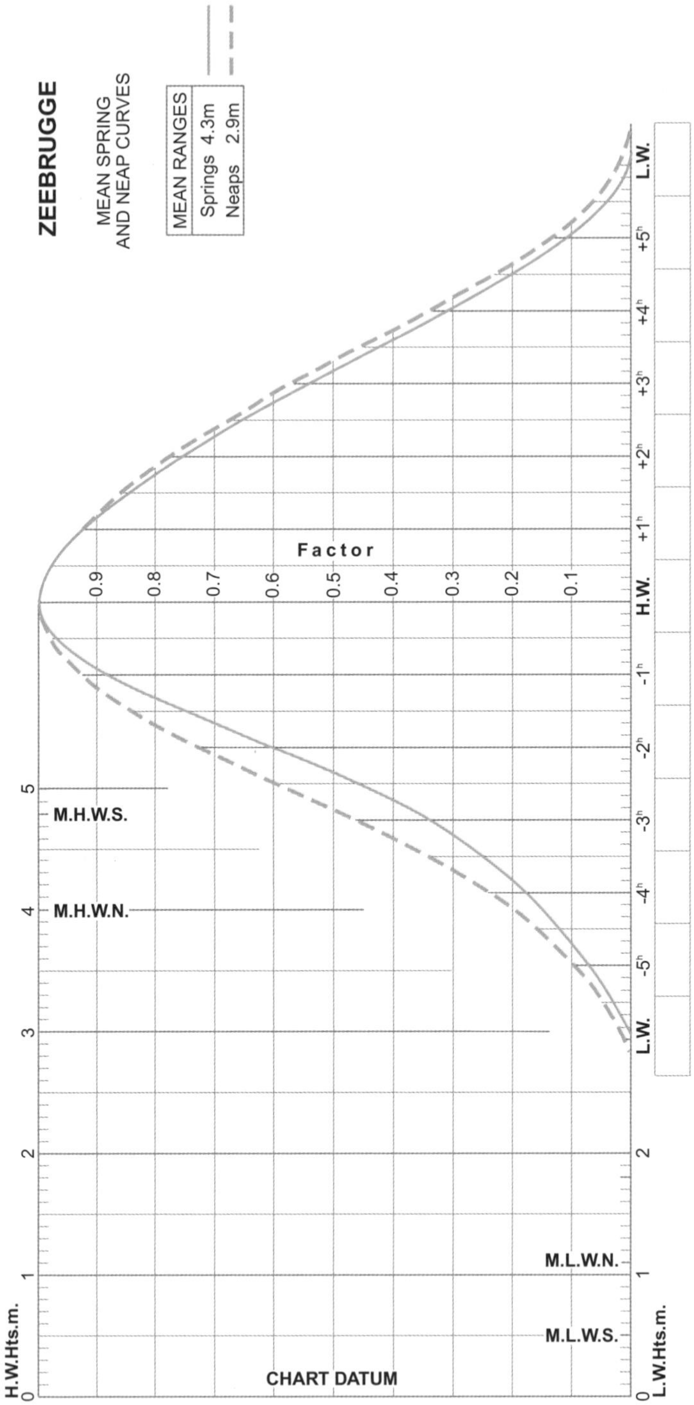
ZEEBRUGGE
MEAN SPRING AND NEAP CURVES
MEAN RANGES
Springs 4.3m
Neaps 2.9m
Factor
0.9
0.8
0.7
0.6
0.5
0.4
0.3
0.2
0.1
L.W.
-5h
-4h
-3h
-2h
-1h
H.W.
+1h
+2h
+3h
+4h
+5h
L.W.
M.H.W.S.
M.H.W.N.
M.L.W.N.
M.L.W.S.
CHART DATUM
H.W.Hts.m.
L.W.Hts.m.
0
1
2
3
4
5

TIME ZONE -0100
(Belgian Standard Time)
Subtract 1 hour for UT
For Belgian Summer Time add ONE hour in **non-shaded areas**

BELGIUM – ZEEBRUGGE

LAT 51°21'N LONG 3°12'E

TIMES AND HEIGHTS OF HIGH AND LOW WATERS

Dates in amber are **SPRINGS**
Dates in grey are **NEAPS**

2023

JANUARY

Date	Day	Time	m	Time	m	Time	m	Time	m
1	SU	0243	1.3	0857	4.2	1522	0.8	2141	4.2
2	M	0357	1.3	1007	4.2	1632	0.9	2250	4.2
3	TU	0511	1.2	1114	4.3	1738	0.9	2351	4.3
4	W	0611	1.1	1212	4.4	1832	0.9		
5	TH	0041	4.4	0658	0.9	1259	4.4	1916	1.0
6	F	0123	4.4	0738	0.9	1339	4.5	1952	1.0
7	SA ○	0159	4.4	0813	0.8	1414	4.4	2022	1.1
8	SU	0232	4.4	0844	0.8	1447	4.4	2047	1.1
9	M	0302	4.3	0913	0.8	1518	4.4	2114	1.1
10	TU	0331	4.3	0943	0.7	1548	4.5	2145	1.1
11	W	0400	4.4	1016	0.7	1621	4.5	2220	1.0
12	TH	0432	4.4	1052	0.7	1658	4.5	2259	1.1
13	F	0510	4.4	1133	0.8	1740	4.5	2342	1.1
14	SA	0555	4.3	1219	0.8	1830	4.4		
15	SU ◑	0033	1.2	0649	4.2	1316	0.9	1930	4.3
16	M	0137	1.3	0754	4.1	1427	1.0	2038	4.2
17	TU	0258	1.4	0904	4.1	1540	1.0	2147	4.1
18	W	0415	1.3	1014	4.1	1647	1.0	2255	4.1
19	TH	0521	1.2	1120	4.2	1746	0.9	2356	4.3
20	F	0619	1.0	1218	4.4	1840	0.9		
21	SA ●	0048	4.4	0709	0.8	1308	4.6	1928	0.8
22	SU	0133	4.5	0755	0.6	1354	4.8	2013	0.8
23	M	0216	4.6	0840	0.4	1439	4.9	2057	0.7
24	TU	0259	4.7	0925	0.3	1524	5.0	2142	0.7
25	W	0343	4.8	1012	0.2	1611	5.0	2228	0.7
26	TH	0429	4.8	1059	0.2	1700	4.9	2314	0.8
27	F	0518	4.7	1148	0.3	1752	4.7	2359	0.9
28	SA ◐	0610	4.5	1240	0.5	1847	4.5		
29	SU	0055	1.1	0707	4.3	1338	0.8	1948	4.2
30	M	0159	1.3	0812	4.1	1447	1.0	2059	3.9
31	TU	0323	1.4	0931	3.9	1603	1.2	2221	3.8

FEBRUARY

Date	Day	Time	m	Time	m	Time	m	Time	m
1	W	0446	1.4	1054	3.9	1717	1.2	2333	3.9
2	TH	0555	1.2	1159	4.1	1819	1.2		
3	F	0026	4.1	0647	1.0	1247	4.2	1906	1.1
4	SA	0108	4.2	0728	0.9	1325	4.3	1940	1.1
5	SU ○	0142	4.3	0801	0.8	1357	4.4	2004	1.1
6	M	0212	4.3	0827	0.7	1427	4.5	2027	1.0
7	TU	0239	4.4	0853	0.6	1455	4.6	2054	0.9
8	W	0307	4.5	0923	0.5	1525	4.7	2127	0.8
9	TH	0336	4.6	0956	0.5	1557	4.7	2202	0.8
10	F	0408	4.6	1031	0.5	1632	4.7	2238	0.8
11	SA	0444	4.7	1107	0.5	1710	4.7	2316	0.9
12	SU	0525	4.6	1146	0.6	1753	4.5	2358	1.0
13	M ◑	0611	4.5	1232	0.8	1844	4.3		
14	TU	0048	1.2	0707	4.2	1332	1.0	1947	4.0
15	W	0201	1.4	0819	4.0	1502	1.2	2109	3.8
16	TH	0346	1.4	0946	3.9	1623	1.2	2234	3.8
17	F	0503	1.2	1107	4.1	1730	1.1	2343	4.0
18	SA	0605	1.0	1208	4.3	1827	1.0		
19	SU	0035	4.2	0656	0.7	1257	4.6	1914	0.9
20	M ●	0117	4.5	0741	0.5	1340	4.8	1957	0.7
21	TU	0158	4.7	0824	0.2	1421	5.0	2039	0.6
22	W	0239	4.9	0907	0.1	1504	5.1	2122	0.5
23	TH	0321	5.0	0951	0.0	1549	5.1	2205	0.5
24	F	0405	5.0	1035	0.1	1634	4.9	2247	0.6
25	SA	0450	4.9	1119	0.2	1720	4.7	2330	0.8
26	SU	0536	4.6	1204	0.5	1808	4.4		
27	M ◐	0014	1.0	0625	4.3	1256	0.9	1901	4.0
28	TU	0109	1.3	0725	4.0	1410	1.3	2012	3.6

MARCH

Date	Day	Time	m	Time	m	Time	m	Time	m
1	W	0249	1.5	0851	3.7	1533	1.5	2145	3.5
2	TH	0413	1.5	1027	3.6	1648	1.5	2306	3.6
3	F	0525	1.3	1136	3.9	1755	1.4	2359	3.9
4	SA	0622	1.1	1224	4.1	1844	1.2		
5	SU	0043	4.1	0704	0.9	1300	4.3	1915	1.1
6	M	0115	4.2	0735	0.7	1331	4.4	1937	1.0
7	TU ○	0143	4.4	0759	0.6	1359	4.6	2001	0.9
8	W	0210	4.5	0826	0.5	1427	4.7	2030	0.7
9	TH	0238	4.7	0857	0.4	1458	4.8	2105	0.6
10	F	0309	4.8	0931	0.3	1530	4.9	2141	0.6
11	SA	0342	4.8	1007	0.3	1605	4.8	2217	0.6
12	SU	0418	4.8	1042	0.4	1642	4.7	2253	0.7
13	M	0457	4.7	1119	0.6	1723	4.5	2331	0.9
14	TU	0541	4.5	1201	0.8	1809	4.2		
15	W ◑	0017	1.1	0634	4.2	1257	1.1	1909	3.9
16	TH	0127	1.3	0748	3.9	1436	1.4	2042	3.6
17	F	0326	1.4	0931	3.8	1604	1.3	2218	3.6
18	SA	0443	1.2	1054	4.0	1713	1.2	2326	3.9
19	SU	0546	0.9	1154	4.4	1810	1.0		
20	M	0015	4.2	0637	0.6	1239	4.7	1856	0.8
21	TU ●	0056	4.5	0721	0.3	1320	4.9	1937	0.7
22	W	0136	4.8	0803	0.1	1401	5.0	2018	0.5
23	TH	0216	5.0	0845	0.0	1442	5.1	2059	0.4
24	F	0258	5.0	0927	0.0	1525	5.0	2140	0.4
25	SA	0340	5.0	1008	0.1	1607	4.8	2220	0.5
26	SU	0423	4.9	1049	0.4	1649	4.6	2259	0.7
27	M	0505	4.6	1129	0.7	1731	4.2	2337	0.9
28	TU	0548	4.2	1209	1.1	1815	3.9		
29	W ◐	0020	1.2	0639	3.9	1318	1.5	1918	3.5
30	TH	0215	1.5	0807	3.5	1457	1.7	2059	3.3
31	F	0335	1.5	0946	3.5	1607	1.6	2223	3.4

APRIL

Date	Day	Time	m	Time	m	Time	m	Time	m
1	SA	0441	1.3	1058	3.7	1711	1.5	2322	3.7
2	SU	0540	1.1	1147	4.0	1802	1.3		
3	M	0005	4.0	0624	0.9	1225	4.3	1836	1.1
4	TU	0039	4.2	0656	0.7	1257	4.5	1902	0.9
5	W	0108	4.4	0724	0.5	1326	4.7	1931	0.7
6	TH ○	0137	4.6	0755	0.4	1357	4.8	2005	0.6
7	F	0208	4.8	0829	0.3	1430	4.9	2041	0.5
8	SA	0242	4.9	0905	0.3	1504	4.9	2119	0.5
9	SU	0317	4.9	0942	0.4	1540	4.8	2156	0.6
10	M	0355	4.8	1019	0.5	1618	4.6	2233	0.7
11	TU	0435	4.7	1057	0.7	1658	4.4	2312	0.8
12	W	0520	4.5	1140	0.9	1746	4.1	2359	1.0
13	TH ◑	0615	4.2	1241	1.2	1848	3.8		
14	F	0122	1.2	0737	3.9	1421	1.4	2028	3.6
15	SA	0305	1.2	0918	3.9	1542	1.4	2156	3.7
16	SU	0417	1.0	1035	4.2	1649	1.2	2301	4.0
17	M	0520	0.7	1132	4.5	1747	1.0	2350	4.3
18	TU	0613	0.5	1218	4.7	1834	0.8		
19	W	0033	4.6	0658	0.3	1300	4.9	1916	0.7
20	TH ●	0114	4.8	0740	0.2	1340	4.9	1956	0.5
21	F	0155	4.9	0822	0.2	1421	4.9	2037	0.5
22	SA	0236	4.9	0902	0.2	1502	4.8	2116	0.5
23	SU	0318	4.9	0942	0.4	1543	4.6	2155	0.6
24	M	0359	4.7	1020	0.7	1622	4.4	2232	0.7
25	TU	0439	4.4	1054	1.0	1700	4.1	2307	0.9
26	W	0519	4.1	1127	1.2	1738	3.8	2345	1.2
27	TH ◐	0605	3.8	1208	1.5	1828	3.5		
28	F	0132	1.4	0721	3.6	1412	1.7	2005	3.3
29	SA	0252	1.4	0853	3.5	1519	1.7	2127	3.4
30	SU	0351	1.3	1004	3.7	1617	1.5	2229	3.6

Chart Datum: 0·23 metres below TAW Datum
HAT is 5·6 metres above Chart Datum

TIME ZONE -0100
(Belgian Standard Time)
Subtract 1 hour for UT
For Belgian Summer Time add ONE hour in **non-shaded areas**

BELGIUM – ZEEBRUGGE

LAT 51°21′N LONG 3°12′E

TIMES AND HEIGHTS OF HIGH AND LOW WATERS

Dates in amber are **SPRINGS**
Dates in grey are **NEAPS**

2023

MAY

Date	Day	Time	m	Time	m	Time	m	Time	m
1	M	0446	1.1	1057	4.0	1707	1.3	2316	3.9
2	TU	0532	0.9	1140	4.3	1749	1.1	2355	4.2
3	W	0611	0.7	1217	4.5	1825	0.9		
4	TH	0030	4.4	0647	0.5	1252	4.7	1901	0.7
5	F ○	0104	4.6	0723	0.4	1327	4.8	1939	0.6
6	SA	0140	4.8	0801	0.4	1403	4.8	2018	0.5
7	SU	0217	4.8	0841	0.4	1440	4.8	2058	0.5
8	M	0256	4.8	0920	0.5	1519	4.6	2138	0.6
9	TU	0336	4.7	1000	0.7	1559	4.5	2218	0.7
10	W	0420	4.6	1041	0.9	1643	4.3	2303	0.8
11	TH	0509	4.4	1130	1.1	1735	4.0	2359	0.9
12	F ◑	0611	4.2	1237	1.3	1843	3.8		
13	SA	0122	1.0	0734	4.1	1401	1.3	2011	3.8
14	SU	0240	0.9	0857	4.1	1513	1.3	2127	3.9
15	M	0347	0.8	1007	4.3	1618	1.2	2230	4.1
16	TU	0450	0.6	1106	4.5	1719	1.0	2324	4.4
17	W	0547	0.5	1156	4.6	1811	0.8		
18	TH	0011	4.6	0636	0.4	1240	4.7	1856	0.7
19	F ●	0055	4.7	0719	0.4	1323	4.7	1937	0.6
20	SA	0138	4.7	0801	0.4	1404	4.7	2018	0.6
21	SU	0219	4.7	0840	0.6	1444	4.6	2057	0.6
22	M	0301	4.6	0918	0.7	1523	4.4	2135	0.7
23	TU	0340	4.5	0952	0.9	1600	4.2	2210	0.8
24	W	0419	4.3	1024	1.1	1636	4.1	2245	0.9
25	TH	0457	4.1	1055	1.3	1712	3.9	2324	1.0
26	F	0540	3.9	1134	1.4	1756	3.7		
27	SA ◐	0024	1.2	0637	3.8	1235	1.6	1902	3.6
28	SU	0159	1.2	0753	3.7	1420	1.6	2022	3.6
29	M	0258	1.1	0902	3.8	1520	1.5	2126	3.7
30	TU	0351	1.0	1000	4.0	1613	1.3	2220	3.9
31	W	0441	0.9	1051	4.2	1703	1.1	2308	4.2

JUNE

Date	Day	Time	m	Time	m	Time	m	Time	m
1	TH	0527	0.7	1136	4.4	1749	0.9	2352	4.4
2	F	0611	0.6	1219	4.6	1833	0.8		
3	SA	0034	4.5	0654	0.5	1300	4.7	1916	0.7
4	SU ○	0115	4.7	0736	0.5	1340	4.7	1958	0.6
5	M	0157	4.7	0819	0.6	1421	4.6	2041	0.6
6	TU	0240	4.7	0901	0.7	1503	4.5	2125	0.6
7	W	0324	4.7	0945	0.8	1547	4.4	2210	0.6
8	TH	0412	4.6	1031	0.9	1635	4.3	2301	0.6
9	F	0505	4.5	1124	1.0	1729	4.2		
10	SA ◑	0000	0.7	0606	4.4	1226	1.1	1832	4.1
11	SU	0105	0.7	0717	4.3	1332	1.2	1943	4.1
12	M	0210	0.6	0827	4.3	1438	1.2	2052	4.1
13	TU	0314	0.6	0934	4.3	1544	1.2	2157	4.2
14	W	0419	0.6	1037	4.4	1651	1.1	2258	4.3
15	TH	0521	0.6	1135	4.4	1751	0.9	2353	4.4
16	F	0616	0.6	1226	4.5	1841	0.8		
17	SA	0043	4.5	0703	0.7	1311	4.5	1925	0.8
18	SU ●	0127	4.5	0745	0.8	1352	4.4	2005	0.7
19	M	0208	4.5	0822	0.9	1430	4.4	2043	0.7
20	TU	0247	4.5	0856	1.0	1507	4.3	2119	0.7
21	W	0324	4.4	0928	1.1	1541	4.2	2153	0.7
22	TH	0400	4.3	0958	1.1	1615	4.2	2228	0.8
23	F	0436	4.3	1031	1.2	1649	4.1	2305	0.8
24	SA	0514	4.2	1109	1.2	1727	4.1	2349	0.9
25	SU	0559	4.2	1155	1.3	1813	4.0		
26	M ◐	0045	1.0	0653	4.1	1254	1.3	1912	4.0
27	TU	0150	1.0	0756	4.1	1408	1.3	2018	4.0
28	W	0253	1.0	0859	4.1	1518	1.3	2122	4.0
29	TH	0351	0.9	0959	4.2	1620	1.2	2221	4.1
30	F	0447	0.9	1056	4.3	1716	1.1	2317	4.3

JULY

Date	Day	Time	m	Time	m	Time	m	Time	m
1	SA	0540	0.8	1150	4.4	1809	0.9		
2	SU	0009	4.4	0630	0.8	1239	4.4	1857	0.8
3	M ○	0057	4.6	0716	0.7	1324	4.5	1943	0.7
4	TU	0143	4.7	0801	0.7	1407	4.5	2028	0.6
5	W	0228	4.8	0846	0.8	1450	4.5	2114	0.5
6	TH	0314	4.8	0932	0.8	1535	4.6	2202	0.4
7	F	0402	4.8	1020	0.8	1622	4.5	2252	0.4
8	SA	0453	4.8	1110	0.9	1713	4.5	2344	0.4
9	SU	0548	4.7	1203	1.0	1808	4.5		
10	M ◑	0039	0.4	0648	4.5	1259	1.0	1909	4.4
11	TU	0137	0.5	0751	4.4	1400	1.1	2014	4.3
12	W	0240	0.7	0857	4.2	1510	1.2	2122	4.2
13	TH	0349	0.8	1008	4.2	1626	1.2	2235	4.2
14	F	0459	0.9	1117	4.2	1736	1.1	2342	4.3
15	SA	0602	0.9	1215	4.2	1832	1.0		
16	SU	0035	4.4	0652	1.0	1301	4.3	1917	0.9
17	M ●	0119	4.4	0733	1.0	1340	4.3	1956	0.8
18	TU	0157	4.4	0807	1.1	1415	4.3	2030	0.7
19	W	0232	4.4	0836	1.1	1448	4.3	2102	0.7
20	TH	0305	4.5	0904	1.1	1519	4.4	2134	0.6
21	F	0338	4.5	0935	1.0	1550	4.4	2207	0.6
22	SA	0411	4.5	1009	1.0	1622	4.4	2241	0.6
23	SU	0445	4.5	1045	1.0	1656	4.5	2318	0.7
24	M	0523	4.5	1124	1.0	1736	4.4	2358	0.7
25	TU ◐	0606	4.5	1207	1.1	1822	4.3		
26	W	0044	0.8	0657	4.3	1259	1.2	1918	4.2
27	TH	0144	1.0	0758	4.2	1410	1.3	2024	4.1
28	F	0301	1.1	0908	4.1	1539	1.3	2138	4.1
29	SA	0413	1.1	1021	4.0	1650	1.2	2250	4.1
30	SU	0516	1.0	1128	4.1	1750	1.0	2352	4.3
31	M	0611	0.9	1223	4.3	1842	0.8		

AUGUST

Date	Day	Time	m	Time	m	Time	m	Time	m
1	TU ○	0044	4.6	0700	0.9	1309	4.5	1929	0.6
2	W	0130	4.8	0746	0.8	1351	4.6	2014	0.4
3	TH	0214	4.9	0830	0.7	1433	4.7	2059	0.3
4	F	0258	5.0	0916	0.7	1517	4.9	2146	0.2
5	SA	0344	5.1	1002	0.7	1602	4.9	2233	0.1
6	SU	0432	5.0	1048	0.7	1650	4.9	2320	0.2
7	M	0522	4.9	1134	0.8	1739	4.8		
8	TU ◑	0009	0.4	0614	4.6	1223	0.9	1833	4.6
9	W	0103	0.6	0712	4.4	1320	1.1	1933	4.3
10	TH	0207	0.9	0818	4.1	1436	1.3	2048	4.0
11	F	0323	1.1	0938	3.9	1603	1.3	2215	4.0
12	SA	0439	1.2	1059	3.9	1718	1.2	2330	4.1
13	SU	0547	1.2	1200	4.1	1818	1.0		
14	M	0023	4.3	0640	1.2	1245	4.2	1904	0.9
15	TU	0104	4.4	0718	1.1	1321	4.3	1940	0.8
16	W ●	0138	4.5	0748	1.1	1353	4.4	2010	0.7
17	TH	0210	4.6	0813	1.0	1423	4.5	2038	0.6
18	F	0240	4.7	0840	0.9	1452	4.6	2108	0.5
19	SA	0311	4.8	0911	0.8	1522	4.7	2140	0.5
20	SU	0342	4.8	0945	0.8	1553	4.7	2213	0.5
21	M	0415	4.8	1020	0.8	1626	4.8	2247	0.5
22	TU	0449	4.8	1056	0.8	1703	4.7	2323	0.6
23	W	0528	4.7	1133	0.9	1744	4.6	2359	0.8
24	TH ◐	0613	4.5	1217	1.1	1834	4.4		
25	F	0053	1.0	0708	4.2	1315	1.3	1938	4.2
26	SA	0212	1.2	0823	3.9	1504	1.4	2104	4.0
27	SU	0348	1.3	0955	3.8	1628	1.3	2232	4.1
28	M	0456	1.2	1111	4.0	1732	1.1	2339	4.4
29	TU	0554	1.1	1206	4.3	1825	0.8		
30	W	0029	4.7	0644	0.9	1250	4.5	1912	0.5
31	TH ○	0113	4.9	0728	0.8	1331	4.8	1956	0.3

Chart Datum: 0·23 metres below TAW Datum
HAT is 5·6 metres above Chart Datum

TIME ZONE -0100
(Belgian Standard Time)
Subtract 1 hour for UT
For Belgian Summer Time add ONE hour in **non-shaded areas**

BELGIUM – ZEEBRUGGE

LAT 51°21′N LONG 3°12′E

TIMES AND HEIGHTS OF HIGH AND LOW WATERS

Dates in amber are **SPRINGS**
Dates in grey are **NEAPS**

2023

SEPTEMBER

Date	Day	Time	m	Time	m	Time	m	Time	m
1	F	0155	5.1	0812	0.6	1412	5.0	2040	0.1
2	SA	0238	5.3	0855	0.5	1455	5.1	2124	0.0
3	SU	0322	5.3	0939	0.5	1539	5.2	2209	0.1
4	M	0407	5.1	1022	0.6	1623	5.1	2253	0.2
5	TU	0453	4.9	1105	0.7	1709	4.9	2338	0.5
6	W	0540	4.6	1149	0.9	1758	4.6	◑	
7	TH	0026	0.9	0631	4.2	1239	1.2	1854	4.2
8	F	0132	1.2	0736	3.9	1407	1.4	2014	3.9
9	SA	0259	1.5	0907	3.6	1538	1.5	2153	3.8
10	SU	0414	1.5	1034	3.7	1651	1.3	2309	4.0
11	M	0523	1.4	1135	4.0	1752	1.1	2359	4.2
12	TU	0617	1.3	1220	4.2	1839	0.9		
13	W	0040	4.5	0654	1.2	1255	4.4	1914	0.7
14	TH	0112	4.6	0721	1.1	1325	4.6	1942	0.6
15	F	0142	4.8	0745	0.9	1354	4.7	● 2009	0.5
16	SA	0212	4.9	0813	0.8	1422	4.8	2039	0.4
17	SU	0242	5.0	0846	0.6	1452	4.9	2112	0.4
18	M	0313	5.0	0921	0.6	1524	4.9	2145	0.4
19	TU	0345	4.9	0955	0.7	1557	4.9	2219	0.5
20	W	0419	4.8	1030	0.7	1634	4.9	2254	0.7
21	TH	0457	4.7	1106	0.9	1715	4.7	2332	0.9
22	F	0539	4.5	1147	1.1	1803	4.5	◐	
23	SA	0020	1.1	0632	4.1	1245	1.3	1907	4.2
24	SU	0142	1.4	0751	3.8	1443	1.4	2046	4.0
25	M	0328	1.5	0937	3.8	1607	1.2	2217	4.1
26	TU	0437	1.3	1050	4.0	1710	1.0	2321	4.5
27	W	0535	1.1	1144	4.4	1804	0.6		
28	TH	0010	4.8	0625	0.9	1228	4.7	1851	0.4
29	F	0053	5.1	0709	0.7	1309	5.0	○ 1935	0.2
30	SA	0134	5.2	0751	0.6	1350	5.2	2018	0.1

OCTOBER

Date	Day	Time	m	Time	m	Time	m	Time	m
1	SU	0216	5.3	0833	0.5	1432	5.3	2101	0.1
2	M	0259	5.2	0915	0.5	1515	5.2	2144	0.2
3	TU	0342	5.1	0957	0.5	1559	5.1	2226	0.4
4	W	0425	4.8	1038	0.7	1642	4.8	2307	0.8
5	TH	0509	4.5	1118	0.9	1728	4.5	2349	1.1
6	F	0555	4.1	1204	1.2	1821	4.1	◑	
7	SA	0050	1.5	0656	3.8	1340	1.5	1941	3.8
8	SU	0229	1.7	0829	3.5	1506	1.5	2118	3.7
9	M	0340	1.7	0955	3.6	1613	1.3	2233	3.9
10	TU	0444	1.6	1058	3.9	1714	1.1	2326	4.2
11	W	0540	1.4	1144	4.2	1802	0.9		
12	TH	0007	4.5	0619	1.2	1221	4.4	1839	0.7
13	F	0040	4.7	0648	1.0	1252	4.6	1908	0.6
14	SA	0111	4.8	0716	0.8	1322	4.8	● 1937	0.5
15	SU	0142	5.0	0747	0.7	1352	4.9	2010	0.4
16	M	0213	5.0	0821	0.6	1424	5.0	2044	0.4
17	TU	0245	5.0	0857	0.6	1458	5.0	2119	0.5
18	W	0319	4.9	0933	0.7	1533	4.9	2155	0.7
19	TH	0354	4.8	1009	0.8	1611	4.8	2231	0.8
20	F	0433	4.6	1047	0.9	1654	4.7	2311	1.0
21	SA	0516	4.3	1131	1.1	1744	4.4	2359	1.3
22	SU	0612	4.0	1236	1.3	1855	4.1	◐	
23	M	0131	1.5	0739	3.8	1426	1.3	2035	4.1
24	TU	0305	1.5	0915	3.8	1541	1.1	2156	4.3
25	W	0412	1.3	1024	4.1	1644	0.8	2258	4.6
26	TH	0512	1.1	1119	4.4	1740	0.6	2348	4.9
27	F	0603	0.9	1205	4.7	1829	0.4		
28	SA	0033	5.0	0649	0.7	1248	5.0	○ 1914	0.3
29	SU	0115	5.1	0731	0.6	1330	5.1	1957	0.2
30	M	0157	5.1	0813	0.5	1413	5.1	2039	0.3
31	TU	0239	5.0	0855	0.5	1455	5.1	2120	0.5

NOVEMBER

Date	Day	Time	m	Time	m	Time	m	Time	m
1	W	0321	4.8	0936	0.6	1538	4.9	2200	0.7
2	TH	0402	4.6	1015	0.7	1621	4.7	2238	1.0
3	F	0444	4.3	1055	0.9	1705	4.4	2316	1.3
4	SA	0527	4.1	1139	1.2	1755	4.1		
5	SU	0003	1.6	0621	3.8	1307	1.4	◑ 1905	3.8
6	M	0147	1.8	0743	3.6	1427	1.4	2030	3.7
7	TU	0256	1.8	0902	3.6	1529	1.3	2141	3.9
8	W	0356	1.6	1007	3.8	1625	1.2	2238	4.1
9	TH	0450	1.4	1058	4.1	1715	1.0	2325	4.4
10	F	0536	1.2	1140	4.3	1757	0.8		
11	SA	0004	4.6	0612	1.0	1217	4.5	1832	0.7
12	SU	0039	4.8	0647	0.8	1251	4.7	1907	0.6
13	M	0113	4.9	0722	0.7	1325	4.8	● 1942	0.5
14	TU	0147	4.9	0800	0.7	1400	4.9	2019	0.6
15	W	0222	4.8	0838	0.7	1436	4.9	2057	0.7
16	TH	0258	4.7	0916	0.7	1515	4.8	2135	0.8
17	F	0336	4.6	0955	0.8	1557	4.7	2215	1.0
18	SA	0418	4.4	1038	0.9	1643	4.6	2300	1.1
19	SU	0506	4.2	1129	1.0	1739	4.4	2358	1.3
20	M	0606	4.1	1241	1.0	1851	4.3	◐	
21	TU	0118	1.4	0726	3.9	1402	1.0	2016	4.2
22	W	0235	1.4	0846	4.0	1511	0.9	2128	4.4
23	TH	0342	1.3	0953	4.2	1614	0.7	2231	4.5
24	F	0445	1.1	1051	4.4	1715	0.6	2326	4.7
25	SA	0542	1.0	1143	4.7	1809	0.5		
26	SU	0015	4.8	0632	0.8	1231	4.8	1856	0.5
27	M	0100	4.8	0717	0.7	1316	4.9	○ 1940	0.5
28	TU	0143	4.8	0759	0.7	1400	4.9	2021	0.6
29	W	0225	4.7	0840	0.6	1442	4.8	2101	0.8
30	TH	0306	4.6	0920	0.7	1524	4.7	2138	1.0

DECEMBER

Date	Day	Time	m	Time	m	Time	m	Time	m
1	F	0345	4.4	0959	0.8	1605	4.5	2214	1.2
2	SA	0424	4.3	1038	0.9	1647	4.4	2249	1.3
3	SU	0504	4.1	1122	1.0	1732	4.2	2328	1.5
4	M	0550	4.0	1222	1.2	1826	4.0		
5	TU	0027	1.6	0648	3.8	1337	1.2	◑ 1933	3.9
6	W	0156	1.7	0759	3.8	1438	1.2	2040	3.9
7	TH	0300	1.6	0904	3.8	1533	1.2	2140	4.0
8	F	0357	1.5	1002	3.9	1625	1.1	2234	4.2
9	SA	0449	1.3	1053	4.1	1713	1.0	2323	4.4
10	SU	0537	1.1	1139	4.3	1757	0.8		
11	M	0007	4.5	0620	1.0	1221	4.5	1839	0.8
12	TU	0048	4.6	0702	0.8	1302	4.6	1919	0.7
13	W	0126	4.6	0742	0.8	1342	4.7	● 1959	0.7
14	TH	0205	4.6	0822	0.7	1422	4.8	2040	0.8
15	F	0244	4.6	0904	0.7	1504	4.8	2122	0.9
16	SA	0325	4.5	0948	0.7	1549	4.7	2206	1.0
17	SU	0410	4.5	1035	0.7	1638	4.7	2255	1.1
18	M	0459	4.4	1129	0.7	1733	4.6	2351	1.2
19	TU	0556	4.3	1230	0.7	1837	4.5	◐	
20	W	0053	1.2	0701	4.2	1333	0.7	1947	4.4
21	TH	0159	1.3	0811	4.2	1438	0.7	2055	4.4
22	F	0306	1.3	0919	4.2	1544	0.8	2202	4.4
23	SA	0417	1.2	1025	4.3	1651	0.8	2307	4.4
24	SU	0526	1.1	1128	4.4	1753	0.8		
25	M	0005	4.5	0622	1.0	1224	4.5	1845	0.8
26	TU	0054	4.5	0710	0.8	1311	4.6	1930	0.8
27	W	0137	4.5	0752	0.8	1354	4.6	○ 2010	0.9
28	TH	0216	4.5	0831	0.7	1433	4.6	2046	1.0
29	F	0253	4.4	0909	0.7	1511	4.6	2120	1.1
30	SA	0329	4.4	0946	0.7	1549	4.5	2152	1.1
31	SU	0404	4.4	1023	0.7	1626	4.4	2225	1.2

Chart Datum: 0·23 metres below TAW Datum
HAT is 5·6 metres above Chart Datum

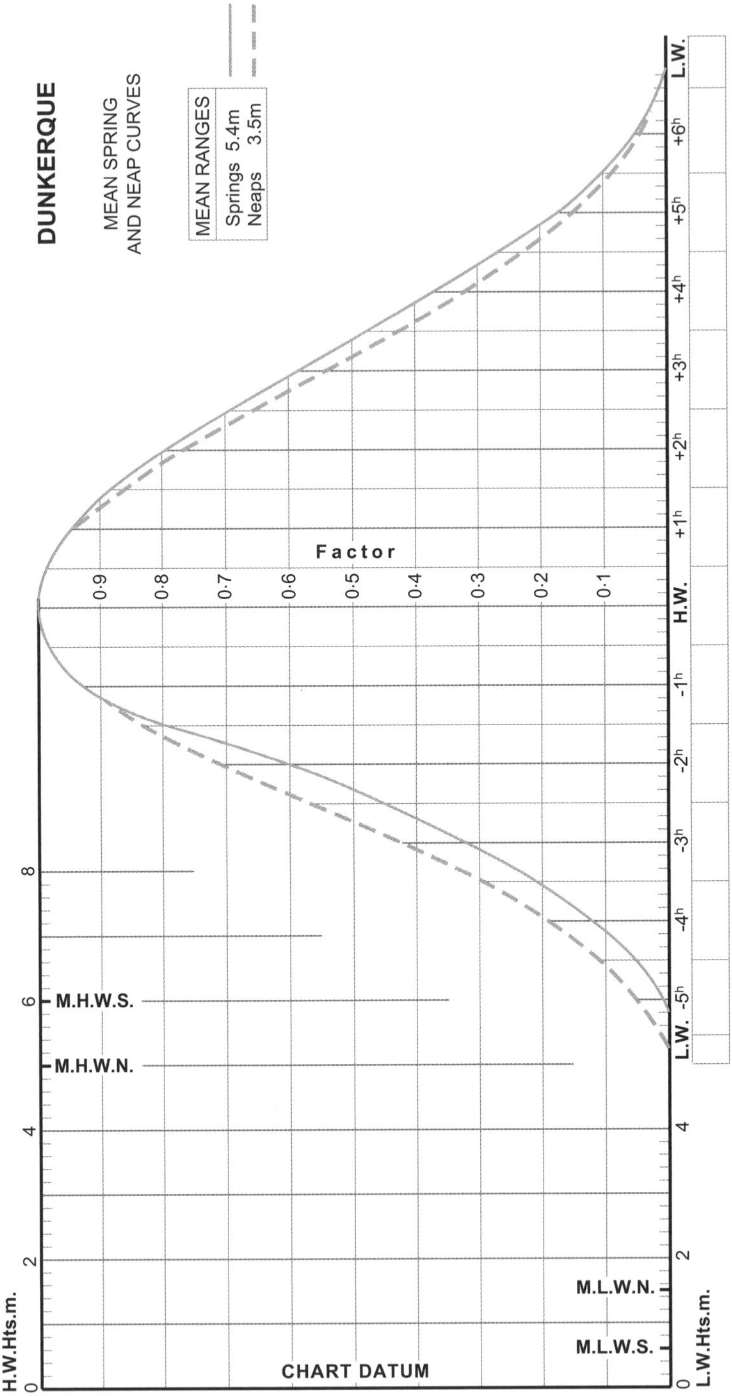
DUNKERQUE
MEAN SPRING
AND NEAP CURVES
MEAN RANGES
Springs 5.4m
Neaps 3.5m
Factor
0·9
0·8
0·7
0·6
0·5
0·4
0·3
0·2
0·1
L.W.
-5h
-4h
-3h
-2h
-1h
H.W.
+1h
+2h
+3h
+4h
+5h
+6h
L.W.
H.W.Hts.m.
0
2
4
6
8
M.H.W.S.
M.H.W.N.
CHART DATUM
M.L.W.S.
M.L.W.N.
L.W.Hts.m.

TIME ZONE -0100
(French Standard Time)
Subtract 1 hour for UT
For French Summer Time add ONE hour in **non-shaded areas**

FRANCE – DUNKERQUE

LAT 51°03'N LONG 2°22'E

TIMES AND HEIGHTS OF HIGH AND LOW WATERS

Dates in amber are **SPRINGS**
Dates in grey are **NEAPS**

2023

JANUARY

Date	Day	Time	m	Time	m	Time	m	Time	m
1	SU	0231	1.6	0810	5.1	1509	1.3	2055	5.1
2	M	0336	1.6	0914	5.1	1615	1.3	2154	5.1
3	TU	0441	1.5	1012	5.2	1717	1.3	2249	5.2
4	W	0539	1.4	1105	5.3	1809	1.2	2338	5.3
5	TH	0627	1.2	1153	5.4	1852	1.2		
6	F	0021	5.4	0709	1.1	1236	5.6	1929	1.1
7	SA ○	0059	5.5	0746	1.0	1314	5.6	2003	1.1
8	SU	0133	5.6	0822	0.9	1348	5.7	2037	1.1
9	M	0204	5.6	0857	0.9	1421	5.7	2111	1.1
10	TU	0235	5.6	0931	0.9	1454	5.6	2144	1.2
11	W	0309	5.6	1003	0.9	1530	5.6	2217	1.2
12	TH	0344	5.5	1036	1.0	1607	5.5	2250	1.3
13	F	0419	5.4	1111	1.1	1644	5.3	2327	1.4
14	SA	0457	5.2	1153	1.2	1728	5.2		
15	SU ◑	0010	1.5	0545	5.1	1241	1.3	1823	5.1
16	M	0102	1.6	0646	5.0	1340	1.4	1926	5.0
17	TU	0210	1.7	0752	5.0	1456	1.4	2034	5.0
18	W	0331	1.7	0903	5.1	1611	1.3	2147	5.1
19	TH	0443	1.5	1015	5.3	1718	1.2	2254	5.4
20	F	0549	1.2	1119	5.6	1819	1.0	2350	5.6
21	SA ●	0647	0.9	1213	5.9	1914	0.8		
22	SU	0040	5.8	0739	0.6	1304	6.1	2005	0.6
23	M	0128	6.0	0829	0.4	1353	6.2	2052	0.6
24	TU	0214	6.0	0917	0.3	1441	6.2	2139	0.6
25	W	0259	6.0	1004	0.3	1529	6.1	2224	0.7
26	TH	0343	5.9	1050	0.4	1616	5.9	2308	0.9
27	F	0427	5.8	1136	0.6	1703	5.7	2352	1.1
28	SA ◐	0513	5.6	1223	0.9	1754	5.4		
29	SU	0041	1.4	0607	5.3	1315	1.2	1854	5.1
30	M	0137	1.6	0714	5.0	1416	1.5	2004	4.8
31	TU	0242	1.7	0830	4.8	1526	1.6	2117	4.7

FEBRUARY

Date	Day	Time	m	Time	m	Time	m	Time	m
1	W	0400	1.8	0944	4.8	1648	1.6	2226	4.8
2	TH	0519	1.6	1051	5.0	1753	1.5	2325	5.0
3	F	0615	1.3	1145	5.2	1839	1.3		
4	SA	0011	5.3	0658	1.1	1228	5.4	1917	1.2
5	SU ○	0048	5.4	0733	0.9	1304	5.6	1949	1.1
6	M	0120	5.6	0806	0.8	1336	5.7	2021	1.0
7	TU	0149	5.7	0839	0.7	1405	5.7	2053	0.9
8	W	0217	5.7	0911	0.7	1434	5.8	2124	0.9
9	TH	0246	5.7	0942	0.7	1505	5.7	2154	0.9
10	F	0316	5.7	1013	0.7	1534	5.7	2224	1.0
11	SA	0343	5.6	1043	0.8	1603	5.6	2256	1.1
12	SU	0413	5.6	1119	0.9	1638	5.4	2332	1.2
13	M ◑	0453	5.4	1159	1.1	1727	5.2		
14	TU	0017	1.4	0550	5.2	1252	1.3	1836	5.0
15	W	0120	1.6	0707	5.0	1409	1.5	1956	4.8
16	TH	0249	1.7	0834	4.9	1540	1.5	2130	4.8
17	F	0419	1.6	1007	5.1	1704	1.3	2248	5.2
18	SA	0539	1.2	1116	5.5	1813	1.0	2345	5.5
19	SU	0640	0.8	1209	5.9	1906	0.7		
20	M ●	0032	5.8	0730	0.5	1256	6.1	1953	0.6
21	TU	0115	6.0	0816	0.2	1341	6.2	2036	0.5
22	W	0156	6.1	0900	0.1	1424	6.2	2118	0.5
23	TH	0236	6.1	0943	0.2	1506	6.1	2158	0.6
24	F	0315	6.1	1024	0.3	1547	5.9	2237	0.7
25	SA	0355	5.9	1103	0.5	1627	5.7	2315	1.0
26	SU	0436	5.7	1142	0.9	1709	5.4	2355	1.2
27	M ◐	0523	5.4	1226	1.2	1800	5.0		
28	TU	0045	1.5	0621	5.0	1322	1.6	1910	4.6

MARCH

Date	Day	Time	m	Time	m	Time	m	Time	m
1	W	0150	1.8	0745	4.6	1436	1.9	2038	4.4
2	TH	0316	1.9	0917	4.5	1616	1.9	2202	4.5
3	F	0454	1.7	1034	4.8	1731	1.6	2306	4.8
4	SA	0554	1.4	1129	5.1	1820	1.3	2351	5.1
5	SU	0637	1.1	1210	5.4	1856	1.1		
6	M	0027	5.4	0711	0.9	1244	5.6	1926	1.0
7	TU ○	0059	5.6	0742	0.7	1314	5.7	1956	0.8
8	W	0126	5.7	0813	0.6	1341	5.8	2027	0.8
9	TH	0152	5.8	0845	0.5	1408	5.9	2058	0.7
10	F	0218	5.9	0916	0.5	1435	5.9	2128	0.7
11	SA	0244	5.8	0946	0.5	1501	5.8	2157	0.8
12	SU	0310	5.8	1016	0.6	1530	5.7	2228	0.9
13	M	0342	5.7	1050	0.8	1606	5.6	2304	1.0
14	TU	0422	5.6	1130	1.0	1654	5.3	2349	1.3
15	W ◑	0519	5.2	1223	1.3	1806	4.9		
16	TH	0053	1.6	0645	4.9	1345	1.6	1939	4.6
17	F	0228	1.7	0827	4.8	1527	1.6	2125	4.7
18	SA	0408	1.5	1004	5.1	1656	1.3	2239	5.1
19	SU	0528	1.0	1107	5.6	1800	0.9	2332	5.5
20	M	0626	0.6	1157	5.9	1850	0.7		
21	TU ●	0015	5.8	0713	0.3	1241	6.1	1933	0.6
22	W	0053	6.0	0757	0.2	1320	6.2	2013	0.5
23	TH	0130	6.1	0837	0.2	1359	6.2	2052	0.5
24	F	0208	6.1	0916	0.2	1437	6.1	2129	0.6
25	SA	0246	6.1	0953	0.4	1515	5.9	2205	0.7
26	SU	0324	5.9	1029	0.6	1552	5.7	2241	0.9
27	M	0404	5.7	1104	1.0	1631	5.3	2319	1.1
28	TU	0447	5.3	1143	1.3	1716	4.9		
29	W ◐	0004	1.5	0541	4.9	1235	1.7	1820	4.5
30	TH	0105	1.8	0700	4.5	1349	2.0	1952	4.2
31	F	0231	2.0	0842	4.4	1532	2.0	2126	4.4

APRIL

Date	Day	Time	m	Time	m	Time	m	Time	m
1	SA	0413	1.8	1004	4.6	1654	1.7	2231	4.7
2	SU	0519	1.4	1058	5.0	1746	1.4	2318	5.1
3	M	0603	1.1	1139	5.3	1823	1.1	2355	5.4
4	TU	0638	0.8	1214	5.6	1854	0.9		
5	W	0028	5.6	0709	0.7	1244	5.7	1924	0.8
6	TH ○	0055	5.7	0741	0.6	1310	5.8	1956	0.7
7	F	0120	5.8	0814	0.5	1336	5.9	2029	0.7
8	SA	0146	5.9	0848	0.5	1404	5.9	2102	0.7
9	SU	0215	5.9	0921	0.5	1434	5.9	2134	0.7
10	M	0247	5.9	0953	0.6	1508	5.7	2209	0.8
11	TU	0324	5.8	1031	0.8	1549	5.5	2248	1.0
12	W	0411	5.5	1113	1.1	1645	5.2	2338	1.2
13	TH ◑	0519	5.2	1214	1.4	1805	4.8		
14	F	0049	1.5	0647	4.9	1344	1.6	1935	4.6
15	SA	0225	1.5	0826	4.9	1520	1.5	2113	4.8
16	SU	0357	1.3	0951	5.2	1639	1.2	2220	5.2
17	M	0509	0.9	1050	5.6	1739	0.9	2310	5.5
18	TU	0605	0.6	1138	5.9	1826	0.7	2351	5.8
19	W	0650	0.4	1218	6.0	1908	0.7		
20	TH ●	0027	5.9	0732	0.3	1255	6.0	1947	0.6
21	F	0103	6.0	0811	0.4	1331	6.0	2025	0.6
22	SA	0141	6.0	0848	0.5	1409	5.9	2102	0.6
23	SU	0220	6.0	0924	0.6	1446	5.8	2138	0.7
24	M	0259	5.8	0959	0.8	1523	5.6	2215	0.9
25	TU	0338	5.6	1034	1.1	1602	5.3	2252	1.1
26	W	0422	5.3	1113	1.4	1647	5.0	2335	1.4
27	TH ◐	0514	4.9	1201	1.7	1745	4.6		
28	F	0030	1.7	0621	4.6	1306	2.0	1859	4.4
29	SA	0143	1.8	0748	4.4	1437	2.0	2030	4.4
30	SU	0315	1.7	0915	4.6	1600	1.8	2142	4.6

Chart Datum: 2·69 metres below IGN Datum
HAT is 6·4 metres above Chart Datum

TIME ZONE -0100
(French Standard Time)
Subtract 1 hour for UT
For French Summer Time add ONE hour in **non-shaded areas**

FRANCE – DUNKERQUE

LAT 51°03'N LONG 2°22'E

TIMES AND HEIGHTS OF HIGH AND LOW WATERS

Dates in amber are **SPRINGS**
Dates in grey are **NEAPS**

2023

MAY

Date	Day	Time	m	Time	m	Time	m	Time	m	Moon
1	M	0425	1.4	1013	4.9	1656	1.5	2233	5.0	
2	TU	0515	1.1	1057	5.2	1739	1.2	2314	5.3	
3	W	0555	0.9	1134	5.5	1815	1.0	2348	5.5	
4	TH	0631	0.7	1206	5.6	1849	0.9			
5	F	0018	5.7	0707	0.6	1235	5.7	1925	0.8	○
6	SA	0047	5.8	0744	0.6	1305	5.8	2001	0.7	
7	SU	0118	5.9	0822	0.6	1339	5.9	2039	0.7	
8	M	0155	5.9	0900	0.6	1418	5.8	2118	0.7	
9	TU	0236	5.9	0940	0.7	1501	5.7	2200	0.8	
10	W	0324	5.7	1023	0.9	1554	5.5	2247	0.9	
11	TH	0423	5.5	1115	1.2	1657	5.2	2344	1.1	
12	F	0531	5.3	1222	1.4	1805	5.0			◑
13	SA	0057	1.3	0645	5.1	1344	1.5	1924	4.8	
14	SU	0220	1.2	0814	5.1	1503	1.4	2049	5.0	
15	M	0336	1.0	0928	5.3	1613	1.2	2151	5.2	
16	TU	0443	0.8	1025	5.5	1711	1.0	2240	5.5	
17	W	0538	0.6	1112	5.7	1759	0.9	2323	5.6	
18	TH	0625	0.6	1153	5.8	1842	0.8			
19	F	0002	5.8	0706	0.6	1231	5.8	1922	0.8	●
20	SA	0041	5.8	0745	0.7	1309	5.8	2001	0.7	
21	SU	0121	5.9	0823	0.7	1348	5.7	2039	0.7	
22	M	0202	5.8	0900	0.9	1427	5.6	2118	0.8	
23	TU	0242	5.7	0936	1.0	1505	5.5	2155	0.9	
24	W	0323	5.5	1013	1.2	1544	5.3	2234	1.1	
25	TH	0405	5.3	1052	1.4	1627	5.1	2314	1.3	
26	F	0453	5.0	1135	1.6	1718	4.8			
27	SA	0001	1.4	0548	4.8	1228	1.8	1815	4.7	◐
28	SU	0058	1.6	0650	4.7	1334	1.9	1920	4.6	
29	M	0208	1.6	0800	4.7	1452	1.8	2031	4.7	
30	TU	0321	1.4	0908	4.9	1556	1.6	2133	4.9	
31	W	0419	1.2	1002	5.1	1648	1.3	2222	5.2	

JUNE

Date	Day	Time	m	Time	m	Time	m	Time	m	Moon
1	TH	0508	1.0	1046	5.3	1733	1.2	2303	5.4	
2	F	0552	0.9	1125	5.5	1815	1.0	2341	5.6	
3	SA	0635	0.8	1201	5.6	1857	0.9			
4	SU	0018	5.7	0718	0.7	1241	5.8	1940	0.8	○
5	M	0059	5.9	0801	0.7	1324	5.8	2024	0.7	
6	TU	0145	5.9	0847	0.7	1412	5.8	2111	0.6	
7	W	0235	5.9	0935	0.8	1504	5.7	2200	0.6	
8	TH	0330	5.8	1026	0.9	1558	5.6	2251	0.7	
9	F	0427	5.7	1120	1.1	1652	5.4	2348	0.8	
10	SA	0526	5.5	1221	1.2	1751	5.2			◑
11	SU	0052	0.9	0631	5.3	1327	1.3	1859	5.1	
12	M	0200	1.0	0747	5.3	1433	1.3	2012	5.2	
13	TU	0307	0.9	0855	5.3	1537	1.3	2115	5.2	
14	W	0411	0.9	0953	5.4	1638	1.2	2209	5.4	
15	TH	0509	0.9	1045	5.4	1732	1.1	2258	5.5	
16	F	0601	0.9	1132	5.5	1820	1.0	2344	5.5	
17	SA	0646	0.9	1215	5.5	1904	0.9			
18	SU	0028	5.6	0727	1.0	1257	5.6	1945	0.9	●
19	M	0111	5.7	0806	1.0	1337	5.6	2025	0.8	
20	TU	0152	5.7	0844	1.0	1416	5.6	2103	0.8	
21	W	0232	5.6	0920	1.1	1452	5.5	2141	0.9	
22	TH	0310	5.5	0956	1.2	1528	5.4	2217	1.0	
23	F	0348	5.4	1032	1.3	1606	5.3	2253	1.1	
24	SA	0429	5.2	1110	1.4	1648	5.1	2332	1.2	
25	SU	0514	5.1	1151	1.5	1735	5.0			
26	M	0016	1.3	0604	5.0	1239	1.6	1827	4.9	◐
27	TU	0108	1.3	0658	4.9	1337	1.7	1923	4.9	
28	W	0211	1.4	0756	4.9	1447	1.7	2023	4.9	
29	TH	0320	1.3	0857	5.0	1553	1.5	2124	5.0	
30	F	0421	1.2	0956	5.1	1651	1.4	2220	5.2	

JULY

Date	Day	Time	m	Time	m	Time	m	Time	m	Moon
1	SA	0517	1.1	1050	5.3	1745	1.2	2312	5.4	
2	SU	0609	1.0	1140	5.5	1836	1.0			
3	M	0001	5.7	0700	0.9	1228	5.7	1926	0.8	○
4	TU	0050	5.9	0750	0.8	1316	5.8	2016	0.6	
5	W	0140	6.0	0840	0.7	1406	5.8	2105	0.5	
6	TH	0232	6.0	0930	0.7	1456	5.8	2155	0.4	
7	F	0324	6.0	1019	0.8	1545	5.8	2245	0.5	
8	SA	0416	5.9	1109	0.9	1634	5.7	2337	0.5	
9	SU	0509	5.7	1200	1.0	1726	5.5			
10	M	0031	0.7	0605	5.5	1255	1.2	1823	5.4	◑
11	TU	0129	0.9	0708	5.3	1355	1.3	1928	5.2	
12	W	0230	1.0	0814	5.2	1457	1.4	2036	5.1	
13	TH	0334	1.2	0919	5.1	1604	1.4	2141	5.1	
14	F	0443	1.3	1021	5.1	1711	1.3	2242	5.2	
15	SA	0544	1.2	1119	5.2	1807	1.2	2337	5.3	
16	SU	0635	1.2	1209	5.3	1854	1.0			
17	M	0024	5.5	0717	1.1	1251	5.4	1936	0.9	●
18	TU	0106	5.6	0754	1.1	1329	5.5	2013	0.8	
19	W	0144	5.6	0829	1.1	1403	5.6	2049	0.8	
20	TH	0219	5.6	0904	1.1	1434	5.6	2124	0.8	
21	F	0251	5.6	0937	1.1	1505	5.6	2157	0.8	
22	SA	0324	5.6	1009	1.1	1538	5.5	2228	0.9	
23	SU	0359	5.5	1041	1.2	1613	5.4	2301	0.9	
24	M	0435	5.4	1114	1.3	1649	5.3	2336	1.0	
25	TU	0514	5.2	1152	1.4	1730	5.2			◐
26	W	0019	1.2	0601	5.1	1238	1.5	1822	5.0	
27	TH	0111	1.4	0658	5.0	1337	1.7	1925	4.9	
28	F	0219	1.5	0803	4.9	1457	1.7	2035	4.9	
29	SA	0337	1.5	0916	4.9	1614	1.6	2151	5.1	
30	SU	0448	1.3	1029	5.1	1723	1.3	2259	5.4	
31	M	0554	1.1	1129	5.4	1824	1.0	2354	5.7	

AUGUST

Date	Day	Time	m	Time	m	Time	m	Time	m	Moon
1	TU	0651	0.9	1220	5.7	1918	0.7			○
2	W	0044	6.0	0742	0.7	1307	5.9	2007	0.5	
3	TH	0132	6.1	0829	0.6	1352	6.0	2054	0.3	
4	F	0219	6.2	0915	0.6	1438	6.0	2141	0.2	
5	SA	0307	6.2	1000	0.7	1522	6.0	2227	0.3	
6	SU	0354	6.0	1045	0.8	1606	5.9	2312	0.4	
7	M	0441	5.8	1129	1.0	1651	5.8	2359	0.7	
8	TU	0529	5.6	1216	1.2	1743	5.5			◑
9	W	0049	1.0	0624	5.3	1311	1.4	1844	5.2	
10	TH	0148	1.3	0731	5.0	1415	1.6	1959	5.0	
11	F	0257	1.6	0847	4.8	1532	1.7	2119	4.9	
12	SA	0421	1.6	1004	4.8	1656	1.6	2233	5.0	
13	SU	0532	1.5	1111	5.0	1757	1.3	2332	5.2	
14	M	0623	1.3	1200	5.3	1843	1.1			
15	TU	0017	5.4	0704	1.2	1239	5.5	1922	0.9	
16	W	0054	5.6	0738	1.1	1312	5.6	1956	0.8	●
17	TH	0128	5.7	0809	1.0	1342	5.7	2028	0.7	
18	F	0158	5.8	0840	1.0	1409	5.7	2059	0.7	
19	SA	0225	5.8	0911	1.0	1436	5.7	2130	0.7	
20	SU	0253	5.8	0941	1.0	1504	5.7	2159	0.7	
21	M	0322	5.7	1009	1.0	1531	5.6	2227	0.8	
22	TU	0349	5.6	1039	1.1	1557	5.5	2301	1.0	
23	W	0418	5.5	1112	1.3	1630	5.4	2337	1.1	
24	TH	0458	5.3	1153	1.5	1718	5.2			◐
25	F	0024	1.4	0600	5.0	1248	1.7	1834	4.9	
26	SA	0131	1.6	0722	4.8	1411	1.9	2003	4.8	
27	SU	0304	1.7	0854	4.8	1548	1.7	2139	5.0	
28	M	0432	1.5	1020	5.0	1711	1.4	2252	5.4	
29	TU	0545	1.2	1121	5.4	1815	0.9	2346	5.8	
30	W	0641	0.9	1208	5.7	1906	0.6			
31	TH	0032	6.1	0727	0.7	1251	6.0	1952	0.3	○

Chart Datum: 2·69 metres below IGN Datum
HAT is 6·4 metres above Chart Datum

TIME ZONE -0100
(French Standard Time)
Subtract 1 hour for UT
For French Summer Time add ONE hour in **non-shaded areas**

FRANCE – DUNKERQUE

LAT 51°03'N LONG 2°22'E

TIMES AND HEIGHTS OF HIGH AND LOW WATERS

Dates in amber are **SPRINGS**
Dates in grey are **NEAPS**

2023

SEPTEMBER

Day	Time	m	Day	Time	m
1	0116	6.3	16	0129	5.9
	0811	0.6		0811	0.9
F	1331	6.1	SA	1339	5.9
	2036	0.2		2029	0.7
2	0158	6.3	17	0153	5.9
	0853	0.6		0841	0.9
SA	1411	6.2	SU	1402	5.9
	2119	0.2		2059	0.7
3	0240	6.2	18	0218	5.9
	0934	0.7		0910	0.9
SU	1451	6.2	M	1427	5.9
	2200	0.3		2128	0.7
4	0323	6.1	19	0243	5.8
	1015	0.8		0938	1.0
M	1532	6.0	TU	1452	5.8
	2241	0.5		2156	0.8
5	0405	5.8	20	0309	5.8
	1055	1.0		1007	1.1
TU	1616	5.8	W	1520	5.7
	2322	0.8		2228	1.0
6	0449	5.5	21	0340	5.6
	1136	1.2		1040	1.2
W	1704	5.5	TH	1555	5.6
◑				2305	1.2
7	0007	1.2	22	0420	5.3
	0540	5.2		1122	1.4
TH	1226	1.5	F	1642	5.3
	1803	5.1	◐	2353	1.5
8	0103	1.7	23	0521	5.0
	0648	4.8		1219	1.7
F	1332	1.8	SA	1805	4.9
	1925	4.8			
9	0219	2.0	24	0105	1.8
	0815	4.5		0701	4.7
SA	1502	1.9	SU	1348	1.9
	2059	4.6		1951	4.8
10	0359	2.0	25	0247	1.9
	0945	4.6		0845	4.7
SU	1637	1.7	M	1533	1.7
	2221	4.9		2132	5.0
11	0514	1.7	26	0421	1.6
	1053	4.9		1009	5.1
M	1738	1.4	TU	1658	1.3
	2318	5.2		2240	5.5
12	0604	1.4	27	0531	1.2
	1139	5.2		1105	5.5
TU	1823	1.0	W	1759	0.8
	2358	5.5		2331	5.9
13	0643	1.2	28	0622	0.9
	1215	5.5		1149	5.8
W	1859	0.9	TH	1847	0.5
14	0032	5.7	29	0014	6.2
	0714	1.1		0706	0.7
TH	1246	5.7	F	1227	6.1
	1929	0.7	○	1931	0.3
15	0102	5.8	30	0053	6.3
	0742	1.0		0747	0.7
F	1314	5.8	SA	1304	6.2
●	1959	0.7		2012	0.3

OCTOBER

Day	Time	m	Day	Time	m
1	0132	6.3	16	0119	5.9
	0827	0.7		0809	0.9
SU	1342	6.3	M	1329	5.9
	2052	0.3		2028	0.7
2	0211	6.2	17	0144	6.0
	0906	0.7		0841	0.9
M	1421	6.2	TU	1356	6.0
	2131	0.5		2059	0.8
3	0250	6.0	18	0213	5.9
	0944	0.8		0912	1.0
TU	1502	6.1	W	1426	5.9
	2209	0.8		2130	0.9
4	0330	5.8	19	0244	5.8
	1022	1.0		0945	1.1
W	1544	5.8	TH	1459	5.8
	2247	1.1		2205	1.1
5	0412	5.5	20	0320	5.6
	1102	1.3		1021	1.2
TH	1631	5.5	F	1540	5.6
	2328	1.5		2245	1.3
6	0501	5.1	21	0407	5.3
	1149	1.6		1108	1.4
F	1729	5.0	SA	1637	5.3
◑				2338	1.6
7	0020	1.9	22	0520	4.9
	0606	4.7		1211	1.7
SA	1252	1.9	SU	1810	5.0
	1849	4.6	◐		
8	0136	2.2	23	0058	1.9
	0736	4.4		0653	4.7
SU	1423	2.1	M	1343	1.8
	2031	4.5		1944	4.9
9	0322	2.2	24	0238	1.8
	0912	4.5		0830	4.8
M	1602	1.8	TU	1519	1.6
	2152	4.8		2117	5.2
10	0440	1.9	25	0403	1.5
	1018	4.8		0947	5.2
TU	1706	1.5	W	1637	1.1
	2246	5.1		2220	5.6
11	0532	1.5	26	0507	1.2
	1104	5.2		1040	5.5
W	1751	1.1	TH	1735	0.7
	2326	5.5		2310	5.9
12	0610	1.2	27	0558	0.9
	1141	5.5		1123	5.8
TH	1826	0.9	F	1824	0.5
				2351	6.1
13	0000	5.7	28	0642	0.8
	0641	1.1		1200	6.0
F	1213	5.7	SA	1907	0.4
	1856	0.8	○		
14	0030	5.8	29	0028	6.2
	0709	1.0		0722	0.8
SA	1241	5.8	SU	1237	6.2
●	1925	0.7		1947	0.5
15	0055	5.9	30	0105	6.2
	0738	0.9		0801	0.8
SU	1305	5.9	M	1316	6.2
	1956	0.7		2026	0.6
			31	0144	6.1
				0840	0.8
			TU	1357	6.2
				2104	0.7

NOVEMBER

Day	Time	m	Day	Time	m
1	0223	5.9	16	0155	5.9
	0919	0.9		0855	0.9
W	1438	6.0	TH	1413	5.9
	2141	1.0		2116	1.0
2	0303	5.7	17	0234	5.8
	0957	1.0		0935	1.0
TH	1521	5.7	F	1456	5.8
	2219	1.3		2156	1.1
3	0345	5.4	18	0320	5.6
	1037	1.3		1019	1.1
F	1607	5.4	SA	1548	5.6
	2259	1.6		2243	1.4
4	0431	5.1	19	0416	5.3
	1122	1.6		1111	1.3
SA	1701	5.0	SU	1654	5.4
	2347	1.9		2342	1.6
5	0528	4.7	20	0523	5.1
	1216	1.8		1215	1.5
SU	1808	4.7	M	1805	5.2
◑			◐		
6	0051	2.2	21	0056	1.7
	0642	4.5		0636	4.9
M	1332	2.0	TU	1336	1.5
	1937	4.5		1926	5.1
7	0222	2.2	22	0218	1.7
	0814	4.5		0801	5.0
TU	1503	1.9	W	1456	1.3
	2102	4.7		2050	5.3
8	0343	2.0	23	0332	1.5
	0926	4.7		0914	5.2
W	1611	1.6	TH	1607	1.1
	2158	5.0		2152	5.5
9	0441	1.7	24	0436	1.3
	1017	5.1		1009	5.5
TH	1702	1.3	F	1707	0.8
	2243	5.3		2243	5.7
10	0525	1.4	25	0530	1.1
	1058	5.4		1055	5.7
F	1742	1.1	SA	1759	0.7
	2320	5.5		2327	5.9
11	0600	1.2	26	0617	1.0
	1134	5.6		1136	5.9
SA	1817	0.9	SU	1844	0.7
	2352	5.7			
12	0633	1.1	27	0007	5.9
	1204	5.7		0700	0.9
SU	1850	0.9	M	1217	6.0
			○	1926	0.8
13	0020	5.8	28	0047	5.9
	0706	1.0		0741	0.9
M	1231	5.8	TU	1259	6.0
●	1925	0.8		2005	0.8
14	0047	5.9	29	0127	5.9
	0741	1.0		0822	0.8
TU	1301	5.9	W	1342	6.0
	2001	0.8		2044	1.0
15	0119	5.9	30	0207	5.8
	0818	0.9		0901	0.9
W	1335	6.0	TH	1425	5.9
	2038	0.9		2122	1.1

DECEMBER

Day	Time	m	Day	Time	m
1	0248	5.6	16	0234	5.8
	0941	1.0		0934	0.8
F	1508	5.7	SA	1500	5.9
	2200	1.3		2158	1.0
2	0327	5.4	17	0323	5.7
	1020	1.2		1022	0.9
SA	1551	5.4	SU	1552	5.8
	2238	1.5		2247	1.2
3	0409	5.2	18	0414	5.5
	1101	1.4		1114	1.0
SU	1637	5.2	M	1648	5.6
	2320	1.8		2340	1.3
4	0456	5.0	19	0508	5.4
	1145	1.6		1211	1.1
M	1728	4.9	TU	1748	5.4
			◐		
5	0008	1.9	20	0040	1.4
	0550	4.8		0609	5.2
TU	1239	1.7	W	1316	1.1
◑	1828	4.8		1857	5.3
6	0109	2.0	21	0147	1.5
	0653	4.7		0719	5.2
W	1346	1.7	TH	1424	1.2
	1937	4.7		2011	5.3
7	0225	2.0	22	0254	1.5
	0804	4.7		0832	5.2
TH	1459	1.7	F	1532	1.1
	2048	4.8		2117	5.3
8	0333	1.8	23	0400	1.5
	0911	4.9		0935	5.3
F	1600	1.5	SA	1637	1.1
	2145	5.0		2216	5.4
9	0428	1.6	24	0502	1.3
	1005	5.1		1031	5.4
SA	1651	1.3	SU	1737	1.1
	2231	5.3		2308	5.5
10	0515	1.4	25	0558	1.2
	1049	5.3		1122	5.6
SU	1736	1.2	M	1828	1.0
	2312	5.4		2357	5.6
11	0557	1.3	26	0647	1.1
	1128	5.5		1210	5.7
M	1818	1.0	TU	1913	1.0
	2348	5.6			
12	0639	1.1	27	0041	5.6
	1205	5.7		0730	0.9
TU	1859	1.0	W	1255	5.8
			○	1954	1.0
13	0025	5.7	28	0121	5.7
	0720	1.0		0812	0.9
W	1243	5.8	TH	1338	5.8
●	1942	0.9		2032	1.1
14	0105	5.8	29	0200	5.7
	0803	0.9		0851	0.8
TH	1325	6.0	F	1419	5.8
	2025	0.9		2109	1.1
15	0148	5.9	30	0237	5.6
	0848	0.8		0928	0.9
F	1411	6.0	SA	1456	5.7
	2111	0.9		2144	1.2
			31	0311	5.5
				1004	1.0
			SU	1533	5.5
				2218	1.3

Chart Datum: 2·69 metres below IGN Datum
HAT is 6·4 metres above Chart Datum

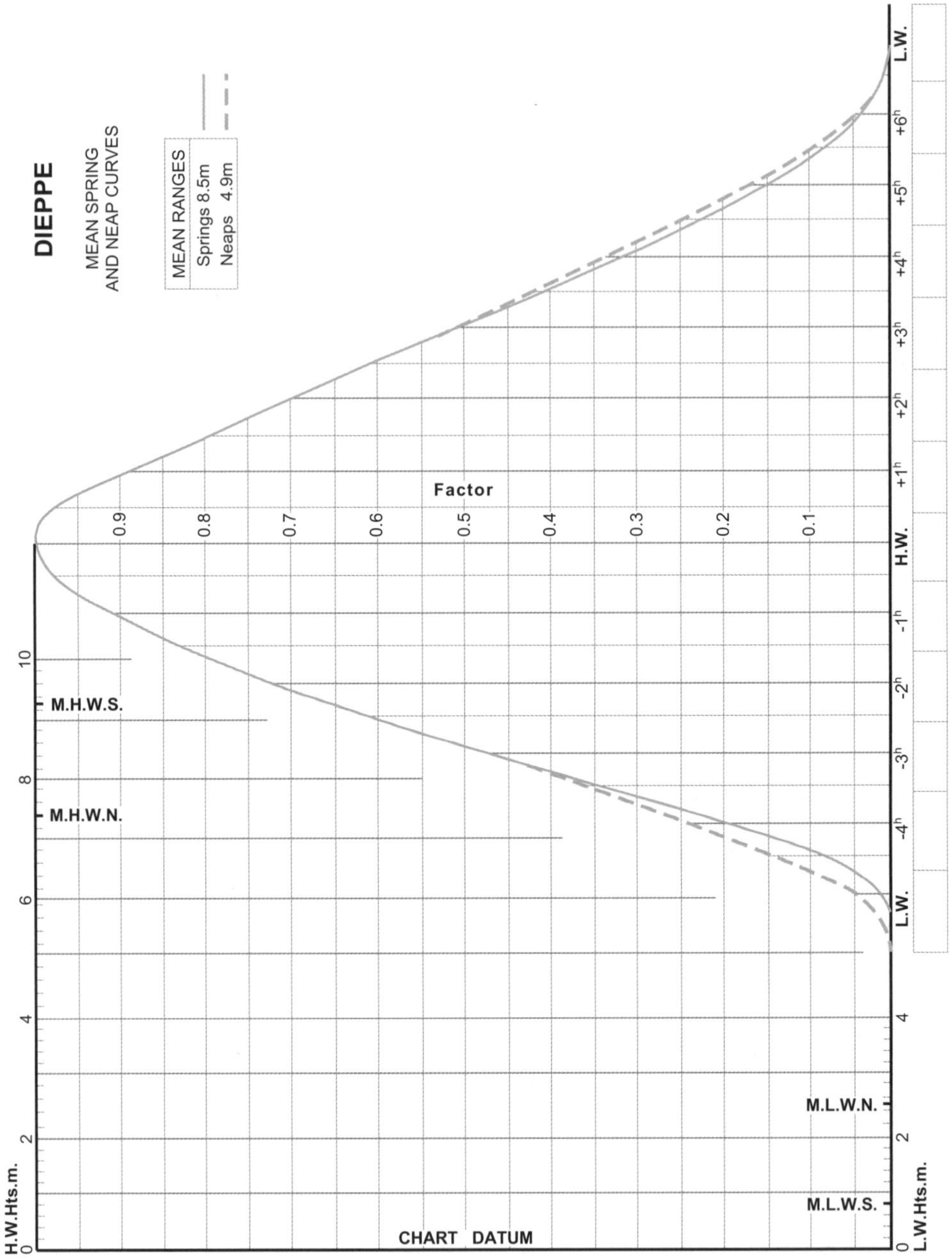
DIEPPE
MEAN SPRING
AND NEAP CURVES
MEAN RANGES
Springs 8.5m
Neaps 4.9m
Factor
0.9
0.8
0.7
0.6
0.5
0.4
0.3
0.2
0.1
L.W.
-4h
-3h
-2h
-1h
H.W.
+1h
+2h
+3h
+4h
+5h
+6h
L.W.
M.H.W.S.
M.H.W.N.
M.L.W.N.
M.L.W.S.
CHART DATUM
H.W.Hts.m.
L.W.Hts.m.
0
2
4
6
8
10

TIME ZONE -0100
(French Standard Time)
Subtract 1 hour for UT
For French Summer Time add ONE hour in **non-shaded areas**

FRANCE – DIEPPE

LAT 49°56′N LONG 1°05′E

TIMES AND HEIGHTS OF HIGH AND LOW WATERS

Dates in amber are **SPRINGS**
Dates in grey are **NEAPS**

2023

JANUARY

Date	Day	Time	m	Date	Day	Time	m
1	SU	0111 0655 1349 1928	2.3 7.6 2.4 7.5	16	M	0529 1220 1759	7.5 2.6 7.3
2	M	0216 0804 1456 2036	2.4 7.6 2.3 7.6	17	TU	0048 0640 1330 1918	2.6 7.4 2.6 7.3
3	TU	0321 0906 1558 2135	2.4 7.8 2.2 7.8	18	W	0205 0759 1450 2035	2.6 7.6 2.4 7.6
4	W	0419 0959 1650 2225	2.2 8.0 1.9 8.0	19	TH	0325 0908 1604 2141	2.3 8.0 1.9 8.1
5	TH	0507 1043 1735 2308	2.0 8.2 1.7 8.2	20	F	0433 1009 1706 2241	1.8 8.5 1.4 8.6
6	F	0550 1122 1815 2345	1.9 8.4 1.6 8.4	21	SA ●	0534 1105 1807 2336	1.4 8.9 1.0 9.0
7	SA ○	0629 1158 1853	1.7 8.5 1.5	22	SU	0633 1159 1904	1.1 9.3 0.7
8	SU	0021 0707 1233 1930	8.5 1.7 8.6 1.4	23	M	0028 0728 1249 1957	9.3 0.9 9.5 0.4
9	M	0056 0743 1308 2004	8.6 1.7 8.6 1.5	24	TU	0117 0819 1337 2045	9.5 0.7 9.6 0.4
10	TU	0130 0816 1342 2036	8.5 1.7 8.6 1.5	25	W	0203 0906 1423 2129	9.5 0.8 9.5 0.5
11	W	0204 0847 1416 2107	8.4 1.8 8.4 1.7	26	TH	0247 0948 1507 2207	9.2 1.0 9.2 0.9
12	TH	0238 0919 1450 2139	8.3 1.9 8.2 1.8	27	F	0330 1027 1551 2246	8.9 1.3 8.7 1.4
13	F	0312 0954 1526 2215	8.1 2.1 8.0 2.0	28	SA ◐	0413 1107 1636 2323	8.4 1.8 8.2 1.9
14	SA	0350 1035 1606 2256	7.9 2.3 7.7 2.2	29	SU	0500 1152 1728	7.9 2.3 7.6
15	SU ◑	0434 1122 1656 2346	7.6 2.5 7.5 2.5	30	M	0010 0557 1249 1835	2.4 7.4 2.7 7.1
				31	TU	0113 0712 1405 1958	2.9 7.0 2.9 6.9

FEBRUARY

Date	Day	Time	m	Date	Day	Time	m
1	W	0236 0835 1524 2114	3.0 7.1 2.7 7.1	16	TH	0122 0722 1416 2012	2.8 7.2 2.6 7.3
2	TH	0352 0941 1629 2211	2.7 7.4 2.3 7.5	17	F	0300 0850 1545 2130	2.6 7.6 2.1 7.8
3	F	0451 1030 1720 2256	2.3 7.8 1.9 8.0	18	SA	0419 1000 1656 2234	2.0 8.3 1.4 8.5
4	SA	0538 1110 1803 2333	2.0 8.2 1.6 8.3	19	SU	0526 1059 1800 2329	1.4 8.9 0.9 9.1
5	SU ○	0619 1146 1842	1.7 8.5 1.4	20	M ●	0626 1150 1857	0.9 9.4 0.4
6	M	0007 0655 1219 1917	8.5 1.5 8.7 1.2	21	TU	0017 0720 1237 1946	9.5 0.6 9.7 0.2
7	TU	0040 0729 1252 1951	8.7 1.4 8.8 1.2	22	W	0101 0806 1321 2029	9.7 0.4 9.8 0.2
8	W	0112 0802 1324 2021	8.8 1.3 8.9 1.1	23	TH	0143 0847 1402 2106	9.7 0.5 9.7 0.4
9	TH	0144 0831 1355 2050	8.8 1.3 8.8 1.2	24	F	0221 0923 1440 2137	9.4 0.7 9.4 0.8
10	F	0214 0901 1426 2118	8.7 1.4 8.7 1.3	25	SA	0258 0954 1518 2206	9.1 1.2 8.9 1.3
11	SA	0245 0931 1458 2147	8.6 1.6 8.5 1.6	26	SU	0334 1025 1555 2237	8.5 1.7 8.2 1.9
12	SU	0317 1004 1533 2220	8.4 1.8 8.2 1.9	27	M ◐	0411 1102 1638 2317	7.9 2.3 7.5 2.6
13	M ◑	0354 1043 1615 2302	8.1 2.1 7.8 2.2	28	TU	0459 1153 1740	7.2 2.8 6.8
14	TU	0440 1135 1711	7.7 2.4 7.4				
15	W	0000 0546 1244 1834	2.6 7.3 2.7 7.1				

MARCH

Date	Day	Time	m	Date	Day	Time	m
1	W	0016 0615 1312 1918	3.2 6.6 3.2 6.4	16	TH	0518 1219 1816	7.2 2.7 6.9
2	TH	0153 0804 1451 2055	3.4 6.5 3.1 6.7	17	F	0102 0706 1404 2005	3.0 7.0 2.6 7.2
3	F	0328 0923 1608 2154	3.1 7.0 2.6 7.3	18	SA	0250 0843 1535 2125	2.6 7.5 2.0 7.9
4	SA	0434 1012 1702 2236	2.5 7.6 2.0 7.9	19	SU	0411 0952 1647 2225	1.9 8.3 1.3 8.6
5	SU	0521 1051 1744 2311	2.0 8.1 1.6 8.3	20	M	0517 1047 1749 2314	1.3 9.0 0.8 9.2
6	M	0600 1125 1822 2345	1.6 8.5 1.3 8.7	21	TU ●	0613 1134 1840 2358	0.8 9.4 0.4 9.5
7	TU ○	0635 1158 1857	1.3 8.8 1.1	22	W	0701 1217 1924	0.5 9.7 0.2
8	W	0017 0708 1230 1928	8.9 1.1 9.0 0.9	23	TH	0038 0744 1257 2003	9.7 0.4 9.8 0.3
9	TH	0048 0740 1301 1958	9.0 1.0 9.1 0.9	24	F	0116 0820 1335 2036	9.6 0.5 9.6 0.5
10	F	0118 0811 1331 2027	9.1 1.0 9.1 0.9	25	SA	0151 0852 1411 2105	9.4 0.8 9.3 0.9
11	SA	0148 0839 1402 2055	9.1 1.1 9.0 1.1	26	SU	0225 0920 1445 2130	9.0 1.2 8.8 1.4
12	SU	0218 0908 1433 2122	8.9 1.2 8.8 1.3	27	M	0257 0948 1520 2158	8.5 1.7 8.1 2.0
13	M	0250 0939 1508 2152	8.7 1.5 8.4 1.7	28	TU	0330 1022 1558 2236	7.9 2.2 7.4 2.7
14	TU	0325 1017 1549 2234	8.3 1.9 7.9 2.2	29	W ◐	0412 1108 1654 2332	7.1 2.9 6.7 3.3
15	W ◑	0410 1108 1645 2334	7.7 2.3 7.3 2.7	30	TH	0522 1222 1832	6.4 3.3 6.3
				31	F	0110 0718 1409 2018	3.6 6.3 3.3 6.5

APRIL

Date	Day	Time	m	Date	Day	Time	m
1	SA	0252 0847 1530 2120	3.2 6.8 2.7 7.2	16	SU	0242 0830 1522 2109	2.4 7.7 1.8 8.1
2	SU	0358 0939 1626 2202	2.6 7.4 2.1 7.8	17	M	0356 0935 1629 2204	1.7 8.3 1.2 8.7
3	M	0446 1018 1710 2239	2.0 8.0 1.6 8.3	18	TU	0458 1026 1726 2251	1.2 8.9 0.8 9.1
4	TU	0526 1054 1749 2313	1.6 8.5 1.3 8.7	19	W	0550 1111 1814 2332	0.9 9.3 0.6 9.4
5	W	0604 1128 1825 2346	1.3 8.8 1.0 8.9	20	TH ●	0635 1153 1855	0.7 9.4 0.6
6	TH ○	0638 1201 1859	1.1 9.0 0.9	21	F	0011 0714 1231 1931	9.4 0.7 9.4 0.7
7	F	0018 0713 1233 1931	9.1 0.9 9.1 0.8	22	SA	0047 0749 1308 2002	9.4 0.8 9.3 0.9
8	SA	0049 0746 1305 2002	9.2 0.9 9.2 0.9	23	SU	0121 0821 1343 2032	9.2 1.0 9.0 1.2
9	SU	0121 0817 1338 2032	9.2 0.9 9.1 1.0	24	M	0155 0851 1418 2100	8.9 1.3 8.6 1.6
10	M	0154 0849 1414 2103	9.0 1.1 8.8 1.3	25	TU	0227 0920 1453 2130	8.4 1.7 8.0 2.1
11	TU	0229 0924 1452 2138	8.7 1.4 8.4 1.8	26	W	0301 0953 1532 2208	7.8 2.2 7.4 2.7
12	W	0309 1005 1537 2224	8.3 1.8 7.9 2.3	27	TH ◐	0342 1037 1623 2300	7.2 2.7 6.8 3.2
13	TH ◑	0359 1059 1641 2329	7.7 2.3 7.3 2.7	28	F	0444 1141 1744	6.6 3.2 6.5
14	F	0515 1215 1819	7.1 2.6 7.0	29	SA	0020 0619 1312 1916	3.4 6.4 3.2 6.6
15	SA	0102 0704 1359 1957	2.9 7.1 2.4 7.4	30	SU	0156 0746 1433 2025	3.2 6.7 2.8 7.1

Chart Datum: 4·43 metres below IGN Datum
HAT is 10·1 metres above Chart Datum

TIME ZONE -0100
(French Standard Time)
Subtract 1 hour for UT
For French Summer Time add ONE hour in **non-shaded areas**

FRANCE – DIEPPE

LAT 49°56′N LONG 1°05′E

TIMES AND HEIGHTS OF HIGH AND LOW WATERS

Dates in amber are **SPRINGS**
Dates in grey are **NEAPS**

2023

MAY

Date	Day	Time	m	Time	m	Time	m	Time	m	Moon
1	M	0302	2.7	0847	7.2	1532	2.3	2115	7.7	
2	TU	0355	2.1	0934	7.8	1622	1.8	2157	8.2	
3	W	0441	1.7	1015	8.3	1705	1.4	2235	8.6	
4	TH	0523	1.4	1053	8.6	1746	1.2	2312	8.8	
5	F	0603	1.2	1129	8.9	1825	1.0	2347	9.0	○
6	SA	0644	1.0	1205	9.0	1901	1.0			
7	SU	0022	9.1	0722	0.9	1242	9.1	1938	1.0	
8	M	0058	9.2	0758	0.9	1320	9.0	2014	1.1	
9	TU	0136	9.0	0836	1.0	1401	8.8	2052	1.4	
10	W	0218	8.7	0918	1.3	1446	8.4	2135	1.8	
11	TH	0305	8.3	1005	1.7	1540	7.9	2227	2.2	
12	F	0403	7.8	1103	2.0	1650	7.5	2335	2.5	◑
13	SA	0522	7.4	1220	2.2	1814	7.4			
14	SU	0101	2.5	0648	7.5	1344	2.0	1933	7.7	
15	M	0221	2.1	0803	7.8	1456	1.7	2040	8.1	
16	TU	0329	1.7	0907	8.3	1600	1.4	2135	8.5	
17	W	0428	1.4	0959	8.7	1654	1.2	2223	8.8	
18	TH	0520	1.2	1045	8.9	1741	1.1	2305	9.0	
19	F	0604	1.1	1127	9.0	1821	1.1	2344	9.0	●
20	SA	0643	1.1	1206	9.0	1858	1.1			
21	SU	0020	9.0	0720	1.1	1243	8.9	1932	1.2	
22	M	0055	8.9	0755	1.2	1320	8.7	2007	1.5	
23	TU	0131	8.6	0828	1.4	1357	8.4	2039	1.8	
24	W	0206	8.3	0901	1.7	1434	8.0	2112	2.1	
25	TH	0243	7.9	0935	2.1	1514	7.6	2149	2.5	
26	F	0324	7.4	1015	2.5	1600	7.2	2235	2.8	
27	SA	0416	7.0	1107	2.8	1659	6.9	2335	3.0	◐
28	SU	0522	6.8	1213	2.9	1808	6.9			
29	M	0046	3.0	0635	6.8	1323	2.7	1917	7.1	
30	TU	0156	2.7	0742	7.1	1428	2.4	2017	7.5	
31	W	0255	2.3	0840	7.6	1525	2.1	2108	7.9	

JUNE

Date	Day	Time	m	Time	m	Time	m	Time	m	Moon
1	TH	0349	1.9	0930	8.0	1617	1.7	2153	8.3	
2	F	0440	1.6	1015	8.3	1705	1.5	2236	8.6	
3	SA	0528	1.3	1058	8.6	1751	1.3	2317	8.8	
4	SU	0615	1.1	1141	8.8	1836	1.2	2359	9.0	○
5	M	0701	1.0	1224	9.0	1919	1.1			
6	TU	0042	9.1	0746	0.9	1310	9.0	2004	1.2	
7	W	0127	9.0	0831	0.9	1358	8.9	2050	1.3	
8	TH	0216	8.8	0919	1.1	1449	8.6	2139	1.5	
9	F	0309	8.5	1010	1.3	1544	8.3	2234	1.8	
10	SA	0407	8.2	1107	1.6	1645	8.1	2335	2.0	◑
11	SU	0511	7.9	1210	1.7	1749	7.9			
12	M	0041	2.0	0618	7.8	1314	1.8	1856	7.9	
13	TU	0148	2.0	0727	7.8	1420	1.8	2002	8.0	
14	W	0253	1.9	0832	8.0	1522	1.7	2102	8.2	
15	TH	0354	1.7	0931	8.2	1619	1.7	2155	8.4	
16	F	0448	1.6	1021	8.3	1709	1.6	2241	8.5	
17	SA	0535	1.5	1106	8.4	1752	1.6	2322	8.6	
18	SU	0617	1.4	1148	8.5	1832	1.5			●
19	M	0000	8.6	0657	1.4	1226	8.5	1910	1.5	
20	TU	0037	8.6	0735	1.4	1304	8.5	1948	1.6	
21	W	0114	8.5	0812	1.5	1341	8.4	2025	1.8	
22	TH	0151	8.3	0847	1.6	1418	8.2	2058	1.9	
23	F	0228	8.1	0920	1.8	1456	8.0	2132	2.2	
24	SA	0305	7.8	0955	2.1	1534	7.7	2210	2.3	
25	SU	0345	7.6	1035	2.3	1616	7.5	2255	2.5	
26	M	0431	7.3	1122	2.4	1706	7.3	2347	2.6	◐
27	TU	0526	7.2	1216	2.5	1804	7.3			
28	W	0046	2.6	0630	7.1	1318	2.5	1910	7.3	
29	TH	0150	2.5	0739	7.3	1425	2.4	2014	7.6	
30	F	0257	2.2	0843	7.6	1530	2.1	2112	8.0	

JULY

Date	Day	Time	m	Time	m	Time	m	Time	m	Moon
1	SA	0401	1.9	0940	8.0	1629	1.8	2204	8.3	
2	SU	0458	1.6	1033	8.4	1724	1.5	2254	8.7	
3	M	0552	1.2	1124	8.7	1817	1.3	2344	8.9	○
4	TU	0645	1.0	1214	9.0	1909	1.1			
5	W	0033	9.1	0738	0.8	1305	9.1	2001	1.0	
6	TH	0123	9.2	0830	0.7	1355	9.1	2051	1.0	
7	F	0213	9.2	0919	0.7	1444	9.1	2140	1.1	
8	SA	0303	9.0	1007	0.9	1533	8.8	2228	1.3	
9	SU	0353	8.7	1054	1.1	1622	8.5	2317	1.6	
10	M	0445	8.3	1143	1.5	1715	8.2			◑
11	TU	0008	1.9	0541	8.0	1235	1.9	1814	7.8	
12	W	0107	2.1	0646	7.6	1335	2.2	1921	7.6	
13	TH	0213	2.2	0757	7.5	1443	2.3	2030	7.6	
14	F	0321	2.2	0906	7.6	1548	2.2	2133	7.8	
15	SA	0423	2.0	1005	7.8	1645	2.1	2225	8.0	
16	SU	0515	1.8	1055	8.1	1734	1.9	2310	8.2	
17	M	0601	1.6	1137	8.3	1817	1.7	2349	8.4	●
18	TU	0642	1.5	1215	8.4	1857	1.6			
19	W	0025	8.5	0722	1.4	1250	8.5	1935	1.6	
20	TH	0100	8.6	0758	1.4	1325	8.6	2010	1.6	
21	F	0134	8.5	0832	1.4	1359	8.5	2042	1.6	
22	SA	0208	8.5	0902	1.5	1432	8.4	2111	1.8	
23	SU	0240	8.3	0931	1.6	1504	8.2	2142	1.9	
24	M	0313	8.1	1002	1.8	1537	8.0	2218	2.1	
25	TU	0348	7.8	1038	2.1	1615	7.8	2259	2.3	◐
26	W	0431	7.5	1122	2.4	1701	7.5	2350	2.5	
27	TH	0525	7.3	1217	2.6	1802	7.3			
28	F	0052	2.7	0637	7.1	1328	2.7	1921	7.3	
29	SA	0210	2.6	0801	7.3	1451	2.5	2038	7.6	
30	SU	0331	2.2	0914	7.7	1604	2.1	2143	8.1	
31	M	0436	1.7	1017	8.2	1707	1.7	2241	8.6	

AUGUST

Date	Day	Time	m	Time	m	Time	m	Time	m	Moon
1	TU	0537	1.3	1114	8.7	1806	1.3	2335	9.0	○
2	W	0638	0.9	1206	9.1	1904	1.0			
3	TH	0026	9.3	0734	0.5	1256	9.4	1956	0.7	
4	F	0114	9.5	0824	0.4	1342	9.5	2044	0.7	
5	SA	0200	9.6	0909	0.4	1426	9.4	2127	0.8	
6	SU	0244	9.4	0948	0.6	1509	9.2	2207	1.0	
7	M	0327	9.0	1027	1.0	1551	8.8	2246	1.5	
8	TU	0411	8.5	1104	1.6	1635	8.2	2328	1.9	◑
9	W	0501	7.9	1149	2.1	1728	7.7			
10	TH	0021	2.4	0603	7.3	1247	2.7	1838	7.2	
11	F	0133	2.7	0725	7.0	1407	2.9	2004	7.1	
12	SA	0255	2.7	0851	7.1	1528	2.7	2120	7.4	
13	SU	0407	2.4	0957	7.5	1633	2.4	2216	7.8	
14	M	0504	2.0	1045	8.0	1725	2.0	2259	8.2	
15	TU	0550	1.7	1124	8.3	1807	1.7	2335	8.4	
16	W	0630	1.4	1159	8.6	1844	1.5			●
17	TH	0008	8.6	0706	1.3	1231	8.7	1918	1.4	
18	F	0040	8.8	0739	1.2	1302	8.8	1949	1.3	
19	SA	0111	8.8	0809	1.2	1333	8.8	2020	1.4	
20	SU	0142	8.8	0837	1.2	1402	8.8	2046	1.4	
21	M	0211	8.7	0903	1.4	1431	8.6	2114	1.6	
22	TU	0240	8.5	0930	1.6	1501	8.4	2144	1.8	
23	W	0313	8.2	0959	1.9	1534	8.1	2219	2.1	
24	TH	0350	7.8	1037	2.3	1615	7.7	2305	2.5	◐
25	F	0439	7.4	1130	2.8	1711	7.2			
26	SA	0008	2.8	0552	7.0	1246	3.0	1840	7.0	
27	SU	0135	2.8	0736	7.0	1427	2.9	2017	7.3	
28	M	0312	2.4	0902	7.6	1549	2.3	2131	8.0	
29	TU	0423	1.7	1008	8.3	1656	1.6	2231	8.7	
30	W	0528	1.1	1104	8.9	1757	1.1	2324	9.2	
31	TH	0628	0.6	1153	9.4	1852	0.7			○

Chart Datum: 4·43 metres below IGN Datum
HAT is 10·1 metres above Chart Datum

TIME ZONE -0100
(French Standard Time)
Subtract 1 hour for UT
For French Summer Time add ONE hour in **non-shaded areas**

FRANCE – DIEPPE

LAT 49°56′N LONG 1°05′E

TIMES AND HEIGHTS OF HIGH AND LOW WATERS

Dates in amber are **SPRINGS**
Dates in grey are **NEAPS**

2023

SEPTEMBER

Date	Day	Time	m	Time	m	Time	m	Time	m	Moon
1	F	0011	9.6	0720	0.3	1238	9.7	1941	0.5	
2	SA	0056	9.8	0805	0.2	1320	9.8	2024	0.5	
3	SU	0138	9.8	0846	0.3	1400	9.6	2103	0.7	
4	M	0218	9.5	0919	0.7	1439	9.3	2137	1.0	
5	TU	0257	9.1	0953	1.2	1516	8.8	2210	1.5	
6	W	0336	8.4	1025	1.8	1555	8.1	2247	2.1	◑
7	TH	0420	7.7	1105	2.5	1642	7.4	2337	2.7	
8	F	0520	6.9	1203	3.1	1755	6.8			
9	SA	0053	3.2	0656	6.5	1338	3.4	1942	6.6	
10	SU	0232	3.1	0839	6.8	1512	3.1	2106	7.1	
11	M	0351	2.6	0941	7.4	1619	2.5	2158	7.7	
12	TU	0447	2.0	1025	8.0	1706	1.9	2238	8.2	
13	W	0529	1.6	1100	8.5	1745	1.6	2312	8.6	
14	TH	0606	1.3	1132	8.8	1820	1.4	2343	8.8	
15	F	0640	1.2	1203	8.9	1852	1.2			●
16	SA	0014	9.0	0711	1.1	1233	9.0	1922	1.2	
17	SU	0044	9.0	0740	1.1	1302	9.0	1953	1.2	
18	M	0113	9.0	0808	1.1	1331	9.0	2019	1.3	
19	TU	0141	8.9	0834	1.3	1359	8.9	2047	1.4	
20	W	0212	8.7	0900	1.6	1429	8.6	2116	1.7	
21	TH	0244	8.4	0928	2.0	1502	8.2	2149	2.1	
22	F	0322	7.9	1005	2.4	1543	7.7	2235	2.5	◐
23	SA	0412	7.3	1101	2.9	1643	7.2	2342	2.9	
24	SU	0532	6.9	1225	3.2	1823	6.9			
25	M	0118	2.9	0728	7.0	1416	2.9	2008	7.3	
26	TU	0302	2.4	0853	7.7	1539	2.2	2120	8.1	
27	W	0412	1.6	0955	8.5	1643	1.5	2216	8.8	
28	TH	0514	1.0	1046	9.2	1741	0.9	2305	9.4	
29	F	0609	0.6	1131	9.6	1832	0.6	2350	9.7	○
30	SA	0657	0.4	1214	9.8	1917	0.5			

OCTOBER

Date	Day	Time	m	Time	m	Time	m	Time	m	Moon
1	SU	0032	9.8	0738	0.4	1253	9.8	1957	0.6	
2	M	0111	9.7	0815	0.6	1331	9.6	2033	0.8	
3	TU	0149	9.4	0847	1.0	1407	9.2	2105	1.2	
4	W	0226	8.9	0917	1.5	1442	8.7	2136	1.7	
5	TH	0304	8.3	0948	2.1	1519	8.0	2210	2.3	
6	F	0345	7.5	1027	2.8	1603	7.3	2257	2.9	◑
7	SA	0442	6.8	1125	3.4	1714	6.6			
8	SU	0012	3.4	0619	6.4	1305	3.6	1904	6.4	
9	M	0156	3.3	0806	6.7	1440	3.2	2033	6.9	
10	TU	0316	2.8	0907	7.3	1544	2.6	2125	7.5	
11	W	0410	2.2	0950	7.9	1631	2.0	2204	8.1	
12	TH	0453	1.7	1025	8.4	1710	1.6	2238	8.5	
13	F	0531	1.4	1058	8.8	1746	1.4	2311	8.8	
14	SA	0606	1.2	1130	9.0	1820	1.2	2343	9.0	●
15	SU	0638	1.1	1201	9.1	1852	1.2			
16	M	0014	9.1	0709	1.1	1231	9.1	1925	1.2	
17	TU	0044	9.1	0739	1.2	1301	9.1	1954	1.2	
18	W	0115	9.0	0808	1.4	1332	9.0	2025	1.4	
19	TH	0149	8.8	0838	1.6	1406	8.7	2057	1.7	
20	F	0226	8.4	0911	2.0	1443	8.3	2135	2.0	
21	SA	0308	7.9	0954	2.5	1530	7.7	2225	2.5	
22	SU	0404	7.3	1054	2.9	1637	7.2	2335	2.8	◐
23	M	0533	7.0	1222	3.1	1820	7.0			
24	TU	0118	2.8	0717	7.3	1406	2.7	1951	7.5	
25	W	0245	2.2	0834	7.9	1522	2.0	2059	8.2	
26	TH	0353	1.5	0932	8.6	1623	1.4	2154	8.9	
27	F	0451	1.0	1021	9.2	1717	1.0	2241	9.3	
28	SA	0542	0.8	1105	9.5	1806	0.8	2325	9.5	○
29	SU	0627	0.7	1146	9.6	1849	0.7			
30	M	0006	9.6	0707	0.8	1225	9.5	1927	0.8	
31	TU	0045	9.4	0742	1.0	1302	9.4	2003	1.0	

NOVEMBER

Date	Day	Time	m	Time	m	Time	m	Time	m	Moon
1	W	0123	9.2	0816	1.3	1338	9.0	2036	1.4	
2	TH	0200	8.7	0847	1.7	1414	8.6	2108	1.8	
3	F	0238	8.2	0920	2.3	1452	8.0	2143	2.3	
4	SA	0320	7.6	0959	2.8	1536	7.3	2226	2.8	
5	SU	0413	7.0	1053	3.3	1638	6.8	2330	3.3	◑
6	M	0530	6.6	1215	3.5	1804	6.5			
7	TU	0057	3.3	0658	6.7	1342	3.3	1928	6.8	
8	W	0216	3.0	0809	7.1	1448	2.8	2030	7.3	
9	TH	0316	2.5	0859	7.7	1540	2.3	2117	7.8	
10	F	0404	2.0	0941	8.2	1625	1.9	2157	8.3	
11	SA	0447	1.7	1019	8.6	1706	1.6	2235	8.6	
12	SU	0526	1.5	1054	8.8	1744	1.4	2310	8.8	
13	M	0603	1.3	1128	9.0	1822	1.3	2345	8.9	●
14	TU	0638	1.3	1202	9.1	1859	1.2			
15	W	0020	9.0	0713	1.3	1237	9.1	1933	1.2	
16	TH	0056	9.0	0749	1.4	1313	9.0	2010	1.3	
17	F	0135	8.8	0826	1.7	1353	8.7	2050	1.5	
18	SA	0218	8.5	0907	2.0	1438	8.4	2135	1.8	
19	SU	0308	8.0	0957	2.3	1531	7.9	2228	2.2	
20	M	0410	7.6	1059	2.6	1641	7.5	2336	2.4	◐
21	TU	0529	7.4	1218	2.7	1804	7.5			
22	W	0100	2.4	0650	7.6	1342	2.4	1922	7.7	
23	TH	0217	2.0	0801	8.0	1453	2.0	2029	8.2	
24	F	0323	1.7	0902	8.5	1554	1.6	2126	8.6	
25	SA	0421	1.4	0953	8.9	1649	1.3	2216	8.9	
26	SU	0512	1.2	1039	9.1	1738	1.1	2302	9.0	
27	M	0557	1.2	1121	9.2	1821	1.1	2344	9.1	○
28	TU	0637	1.2	1201	9.2	1901	1.1			
29	W	0024	9.0	0715	1.3	1239	9.1	1938	1.2	
30	TH	0103	8.9	0751	1.5	1317	8.8	2015	1.4	

DECEMBER

Date	Day	Time	m	Time	m	Time	m	Time	m	Moon
1	F	0141	8.6	0827	1.8	1355	8.5	2050	1.7	
2	SA	0221	8.2	0903	2.2	1434	8.1	2125	2.1	
3	SU	0301	7.8	0940	2.5	1515	7.6	2203	2.5	
4	M	0346	7.4	1024	2.9	1603	7.2	2250	2.8	
5	TU	0439	7.1	1118	3.1	1703	6.9	2348	3.0	◑
6	W	0543	6.9	1224	3.2	1811	6.9			
7	TH	0056	3.0	0652	7.0	1334	3.0	1919	7.0	
8	F	0203	2.8	0755	7.4	1437	2.7	2019	7.4	
9	SA	0304	2.5	0849	7.8	1533	2.3	2111	7.8	
10	SU	0358	2.1	0936	8.2	1623	1.9	2157	8.2	
11	M	0446	1.8	1019	8.5	1709	1.6	2240	8.5	
12	TU	0530	1.6	1100	8.7	1755	1.4	2321	8.7	
13	W	0613	1.5	1140	8.9	1838	1.2			●
14	TH	0003	8.9	0656	1.4	1221	9.0	1922	1.1	
15	F	0046	9.0	0739	1.4	1305	9.1	2006	1.1	
16	SA	0131	8.9	0824	1.5	1351	8.9	2052	1.2	
17	SU	0220	8.7	0912	1.6	1440	8.7	2140	1.4	
18	M	0311	8.5	1002	1.8	1534	8.4	2231	1.6	
19	TU	0406	8.2	1058	2.0	1632	8.1	2327	1.8	◐
20	W	0507	8.0	1159	2.2	1735	7.9			
21	TH	0030	2.0	0613	7.9	1306	2.2	1844	7.8	
22	F	0136	2.1	0722	7.9	1416	2.1	1953	7.9	
23	SA	0245	2.1	0828	8.1	1522	2.0	2058	8.0	
24	SU	0349	1.9	0927	8.3	1622	1.7	2155	8.3	
25	M	0445	1.8	1019	8.5	1715	1.6	2245	8.5	
26	TU	0533	1.7	1105	8.7	1801	1.4	2330	8.6	
27	W	0616	1.6	1147	8.8	1843	1.3			○
28	TH	0012	8.7	0657	1.5	1226	8.8	1923	1.3	
29	F	0050	8.7	0736	1.6	1303	8.7	2001	1.4	
30	SA	0128	8.6	0814	1.7	1340	8.6	2037	1.5	
31	SU	0205	8.4	0849	1.9	1417	8.4	2109	1.7	

Chart Datum: 4·43 metres below IGN Datum
HAT is 10·1 metres above Chart Datum

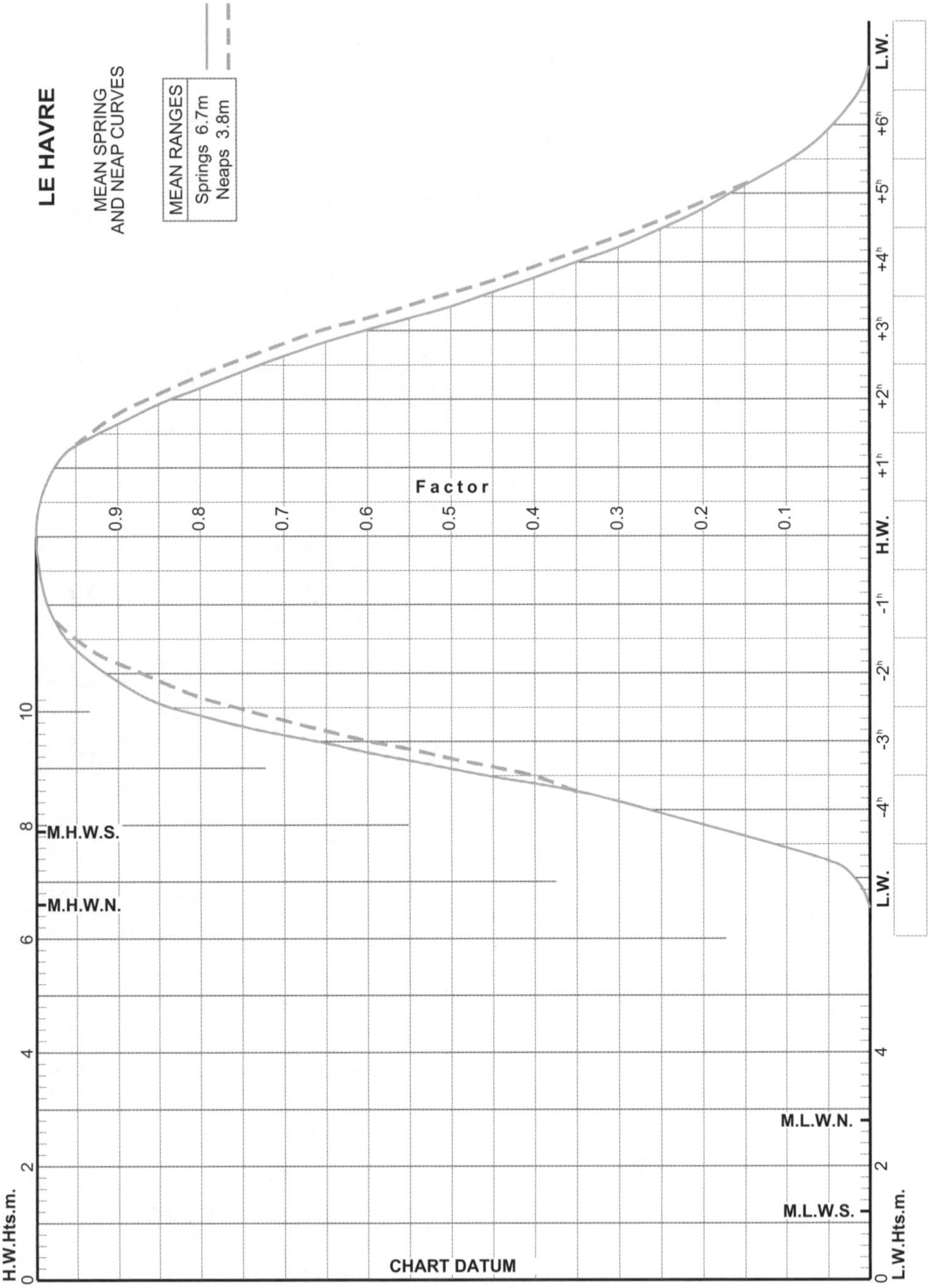
LE HAVRE
MEAN SPRING AND NEAP CURVES
MEAN RANGES
Springs 6.7m
Neaps 3.8m
Factor
0.9
0.8
0.7
0.6
0.5
0.4
0.3
0.2
0.1
L.W.
-4h
-3h
-2h
-1h
H.W.
+1h
+2h
+3h
+4h
+5h
+6h
L.W.
H.W.Hts.m.
0
2
4
6
8
10
M.H.W.S.
M.H.W.N.
CHART DATUM
L.W.Hts.m.
0
2
4
M.L.W.S.
M.L.W.N.

TIME ZONE -0100
(French Standard Time)
Subtract 1 hour for UT
For French Summer Time add ONE hour in **non-shaded areas**

FRANCE – LE HAVRE

LAT 49°29′N LONG 0°07′E

TIMES AND HEIGHTS OF HIGH AND LOW WATERS

Dates in amber are **SPRINGS**
Dates in grey are **NEAPS**

2023

JANUARY

Date	Day	Time	m	Time	m	Time	m	Time	m
1	SU	0018	2.6	0606	6.9	1254	2.8	1832	6.8
2	M	0121	2.7	0711	7.0	1401	2.7	1941	6.9
3	TU	0228	2.7	0811	7.1	1504	2.6	2041	7.0
4	W	0325	2.6	0902	7.2	1557	2.3	2131	7.2
5	TH	0415	2.4	0946	7.4	1643	2.1	2214	7.4
6	F	0459	2.2	1024	7.5	1724	2.0	2252	7.5
7	SA	0539	2.1	1058	7.6	1803	1.8	○ 2326	7.5
8	SU	0616	2.1	1131	7.6	1840	1.8		
9	M	0000	7.5	0652	2.1	1204	7.6	1914	1.8
10	TU	0033	7.5	0726	2.1	1237	7.6	1948	1.9
11	W	0107	7.4	0759	2.2	1311	7.5	2020	2.0
12	TH	0141	7.3	0831	2.3	1346	7.3	2052	2.2
13	F	0217	7.1	0906	2.5	1425	7.1	2127	2.4
14	SA	0258	7.0	0945	2.7	1507	6.9	2206	2.6
15	SU	0344	6.8	1030	2.9	1558	6.8	◑ 2255	2.8
16	M	0441	6.7	1126	3.0	1704	6.6	2355	2.9
17	TU	0552	6.7	1233	3.0	1824	6.7		
18	W	0111	2.9	0707	6.9	1359	2.8	1943	6.8
19	TH	0238	2.6	0816	7.2	1516	2.3	2052	7.2
20	F	0346	2.2	0916	7.5	1619	1.8	2150	7.6
21	SA	0446	1.8	1009	7.8	1718	1.4	● 2242	7.9
22	SU	0544	1.5	1059	8.1	1819	1.0	2331	8.1
23	M	0641	1.2	1148	8.2	1913	0.8		
24	TU	0019	8.2	0732	1.1	1235	8.3	2000	0.7
25	W	0106	8.1	0818	1.1	1321	8.2	2042	0.9
26	TH	0151	8.0	0900	1.4	1406	7.9	2121	1.2
27	F	0235	7.7	0939	1.7	1451	7.6	2158	1.7
28	SA	0320	7.3	1017	2.2	1537	7.2	◐ 2235	2.2
29	SU	0408	7.0	1100	2.7	1632	6.8	2320	2.8
30	M	0507	6.7	1157	3.0	1744	6.5		
31	TU	0022	3.1	0622	6.5	1312	3.2	1910	6.4

FEBRUARY

Date	Day	Time	m	Time	m	Time	m	Time	m
1	W	0142	3.3	0744	6.6	1430	3.0	2028	6.6
2	TH	0258	3.0	0848	6.8	1536	2.7	2123	6.9
3	F	0357	2.7	0936	7.1	1629	2.3	2205	7.2
4	SA	0447	2.4	1013	7.3	1714	2.0	2240	7.4
5	SU	0530	2.1	1046	7.5	1753	1.8	○ 2312	7.5
6	M	0610	1.9	1118	7.6	1830	1.6	2343	7.6
7	TU	0642	1.8	1149	7.7	1903	1.5		
8	W	0015	7.6	0713	1.7	1221	7.7	1933	1.5
9	TH	0046	7.6	0744	1.7	1253	7.7	2003	1.6
10	F	0118	7.6	0814	1.8	1325	7.6	2032	1.7
11	SA	0151	7.4	0845	2.0	1359	7.4	2102	2.0
12	SU	0225	7.2	0918	2.2	1434	7.2	2135	2.3
13	M	0301	7.0	0955	2.5	1515	6.9	◑ 2215	2.6
14	TU	0348	6.8	1043	2.8	1616	6.6	2311	3.0
15	W	0500	6.6	1149	3.1	1748	6.4		
16	TH	0031	3.2	0636	6.6	1328	3.0	1929	6.6
17	F	0218	2.9	0802	6.9	1459	2.4	2045	7.1
18	SA	0333	2.3	0907	7.4	1609	1.8	2143	7.5
19	SU	0440	1.8	1000	7.8	1716	1.3	2232	7.9
20	M	0542	1.3	1048	8.1	1813	0.8	● 2318	8.1
21	TU	0635	0.9	1134	8.3	1902	0.5		
22	W	0002	8.2	0720	0.8	1217	8.4	1944	0.5
23	TH	0044	8.2	0800	0.8	1259	8.3	2021	0.7
24	F	0125	8.1	0835	1.1	1340	8.0	2052	1.1
25	SA	0202	7.8	0907	1.5	1418	7.6	2121	1.7
26	SU	0238	7.4	0937	2.1	1457	7.2	2150	2.3
27	M	0316	7.0	1011	2.7	1543	6.7	◐ 2226	2.9
28	TU	0407	6.5	1100	3.2	1654	6.2	2326	3.5

MARCH

Date	Day	Time	m	Time	m	Time	m	Time	m
1	W	0530	6.2	1219	3.5	1840	6.1		
2	TH	0059	3.7	0715	6.2	1357	3.4	2013	6.3
3	F	0237	3.4	0833	6.4	1517	2.9	2109	6.7
4	SA	0344	2.9	0920	6.8	1613	2.4	2147	7.1
5	SU	0434	2.4	0955	7.2	1657	2.0	2219	7.4
6	M	0514	2.0	1025	7.4	1736	1.7	2249	7.6
7	TU	0552	1.7	1056	7.6	1810	1.4	○ 2319	7.7
8	W	0625	1.6	1127	7.8	1841	1.3	2350	7.7
9	TH	0652	1.5	1158	7.8	1910	1.3		
10	F	0021	7.8	0722	1.4	1230	7.8	1939	1.3
11	SA	0052	7.7	0752	1.5	1303	7.7	2009	1.5
12	SU	0124	7.6	0823	1.7	1336	7.5	2038	1.8
13	M	0156	7.4	0855	2.0	1410	7.3	2109	2.2
14	TU	0230	7.2	0930	2.3	1451	6.9	2148	2.7
15	W	0316	6.8	1016	2.8	1555	6.5	◑ 2244	3.1
16	TH	0433	6.4	1123	3.1	1739	6.3		
17	F	0013	3.3	0624	6.4	1316	3.0	1926	6.6
18	SA	0209	3.0	0754	6.8	1449	2.4	2037	7.1
19	SU	0325	2.3	0856	7.3	1601	1.7	2130	7.6
20	M	0433	1.7	0946	7.8	1704	1.2	2215	7.9
21	TU	0530	1.2	1030	8.1	1755	0.7	● 2258	8.1
22	W	0618	0.8	1113	8.2	1839	0.6	2338	8.2
23	TH	0658	0.7	1154	8.2	1918	0.6		
24	F	0017	8.1	0733	0.9	1233	8.1	1950	0.9
25	SA	0054	8.0	0805	1.1	1311	7.9	2019	1.3
26	SU	0128	7.7	0834	1.6	1347	7.5	2045	1.9
27	M	0200	7.4	0900	2.1	1423	7.1	2109	2.5
28	TU	0233	7.0	0929	2.7	1505	6.6	2142	3.1
29	W	0317	6.5	1013	3.2	1610	6.1	◐ 2241	3.6
30	TH	0438	6.0	1131	3.6	1802	5.9		
31	F	0017	3.9	0631	5.9	1315	3.6	1937	6.1

APRIL

Date	Day	Time	m	Time	m	Time	m	Time	m
1	SA	0204	3.5	0757	6.2	1440	3.1	2037	6.6
2	SU	0313	3.0	0848	6.7	1538	2.5	2115	7.0
3	M	0402	2.4	0923	7.1	1624	2.1	2146	7.3
4	TU	0443	2.0	0955	7.4	1704	1.7	2217	7.6
5	W	0522	1.7	1027	7.6	1739	1.5	2248	7.7
6	TH	0553	1.5	1059	7.7	1811	1.3	○ 2320	7.8
7	F	0624	1.4	1132	7.8	1841	1.3	2352	7.8
8	SA	0656	1.3	1206	7.8	1913	1.3		
9	SU	0025	7.8	0729	1.3	1241	7.7	1945	1.5
10	M	0059	7.7	0802	1.5	1318	7.5	2017	1.8
11	TU	0135	7.5	0836	1.8	1358	7.2	2051	2.2
12	W	0215	7.2	0913	2.2	1447	6.9	2133	2.7
13	TH	0308	6.8	1002	2.7	1557	6.5	◑ 2233	3.2
14	F	0430	6.5	1115	3.0	1743	6.4		
15	SA	0018	3.3	0617	6.5	1312	2.8	1914	6.7
16	SU	0158	2.8	0736	6.9	1435	2.3	2018	7.2
17	M	0309	2.2	0835	7.3	1541	1.7	2108	7.6
18	TU	0413	1.6	0924	7.7	1640	1.3	2152	7.8
19	W	0506	1.3	1007	7.9	1729	1.0	2232	8.0
20	TH	0551	1.1	1049	8.0	1810	0.9	● 2311	8.0
21	F	0629	1.0	1129	8.0	1847	1.1	2348	7.9
22	SA	0703	1.1	1207	7.9	1916	1.3		
23	SU	0023	7.8	0734	1.4	1244	7.7	1945	1.6
24	M	0056	7.6	0803	1.7	1320	7.4	2012	2.1
25	TU	0128	7.3	0830	2.1	1357	7.0	2039	2.6
26	W	0202	6.9	0859	2.6	1437	6.6	2113	3.1
27	TH	0243	6.5	0940	3.1	1534	6.2	◐ 2208	3.6
28	F	0348	6.1	1052	3.5	1712	6.0	2335	3.8
29	SA	0535	5.9	1220	3.5	1834	6.2		
30	SU	0103	3.6	0653	6.2	1339	3.2	1938	6.5

Chart Datum: 4·38 metres below IGN Datum
HAT is 8·4 metres above Chart Datum

TIME ZONE -0100
(French Standard Time)
Subtract 1 hour for UT
For French Summer Time add ONE hour in **non-shaded areas**

FRANCE – LE HAVRE

LAT 49°29'N LONG 0°07'E

TIMES AND HEIGHTS OF HIGH AND LOW WATERS

Dates in amber are **SPRINGS**
Dates in grey are **NEAPS**

2023

MAY

Date	Time	m	Time	m	Time	m	Time	m
1 M	0218	3.1	0753	6.5	1442	2.7	2025	6.9
2 TU	0311	2.6	0837	6.9	1533	2.3	2103	7.2
3 W	0358	2.2	0915	7.2	1617	1.9	2139	7.5
4 TH	0437	1.9	0952	7.5	1657	1.7	2214	7.6
5 F	0516	1.7	1028	7.6	1734	1.5	○ 2249	7.7
6 SA	0553	1.5	1105	7.7	1811	1.4	2324	7.8
7 SU	0630	1.4	1143	7.7	1848	1.5		
8 M	0001	7.8	0708	1.3	1224	7.7	1925	1.6
9 TU	0041	7.7	0745	1.5	1307	7.5	2002	1.9
10 W	0123	7.5	0824	1.8	1354	7.3	2041	2.2
11 TH	0211	7.3	0906	2.1	1449	7.0	2129	2.6
12 F	0310	6.9	1000	2.5	1601	6.7	◑ 2238	3.0
13 SA	0428	6.7	1124	2.7	1730	6.7		
14 SU	0016	2.9	0555	6.7	1254	2.5	1847	6.9
15 M	0133	2.6	0707	7.0	1406	2.2	1949	7.2
16 TU	0238	2.2	0806	7.3	1508	1.9	2040	7.5
17 W	0339	1.9	0857	7.5	1605	1.6	2124	7.6
18 TH	0433	1.6	0943	7.6	1654	1.5	2205	7.7
19 F	0518	1.5	1025	7.7	1737	1.5	● 2244	7.7
20 SA	0557	1.5	1106	7.6	1813	1.6	2320	7.7
21 SU	0632	1.5	1145	7.6	1845	1.7	2356	7.6
22 M	0705	1.6	1222	7.4	1917	2.0		
23 TU	0030	7.5	0738	1.8	1259	7.2	1948	2.3
24 W	0105	7.3	0809	2.2	1337	7.0	2020	2.6
25 TH	0140	7.0	0841	2.5	1416	6.7	2055	3.0
26 F	0220	6.7	0920	2.9	1503	6.5	2143	3.3
27 SA	0309	6.4	1015	3.1	1610	6.3	◐ 2248	3.5
28 SU	0422	6.2	1122	3.2	1727	6.3	2357	3.4
29 M	0542	6.2	1228	3.1	1830	6.5		
30 TU	0101	3.2	0645	6.4	1330	2.9	1924	6.8
31 W	0202	2.8	0739	6.7	1429	2.6	2012	7.0

JUNE

Date	Time	m	Time	m	Time	m	Time	m
1 TH	0258	2.5	0828	7.0	1523	2.3	2056	7.3
2 F	0349	2.1	0914	7.2	1613	2.0	2137	7.5
3 SA	0437	1.9	0958	7.4	1659	1.8	2218	7.6
4 SU	0523	1.6	1042	7.6	1744	1.7	○ 2300	7.7
5 M	0608	1.4	1127	7.7	1828	1.6	2344	7.8
6 TU	0652	1.4	1213	7.7	1912	1.7		
7 W	0030	7.8	0737	1.4	1302	7.6	1957	1.8
8 TH	0118	7.7	0823	1.6	1353	7.4	2045	2.1
9 F	0210	7.5	0913	1.8	1449	7.2	2140	2.3
10 SA	0307	7.2	1011	2.1	1552	7.0	◑ 2245	2.5
11 SU	0411	7.0	1117	2.2	1700	7.0	2352	2.6
12 M	0521	6.9	1222	2.3	1808	7.0		
13 TU	0057	2.5	0629	7.0	1325	2.3	1911	7.1
14 W	0200	2.4	0733	7.1	1427	2.2	2007	7.2
15 TH	0301	2.2	0830	7.2	1525	2.2	2057	7.3
16 F	0357	2.1	0921	7.3	1617	2.1	2141	7.4
17 SA	0445	1.9	1007	7.3	1703	2.1	2222	7.5
18 SU	0527	1.9	1050	7.4	1743	2.0	● 2300	7.5
19 M	0606	1.8	1129	7.4	1819	2.1	2336	7.5
20 TU	0643	1.8	1206	7.3	1856	2.1		
21 W	0011	7.4	0719	1.9	1243	7.3	1932	2.3
22 TH	0046	7.3	0754	2.1	1319	7.1	2007	2.4
23 F	0121	7.2	0828	2.2	1355	7.0	2041	2.6
24 SA	0158	7.0	0902	2.5	1433	6.8	2118	2.8
25 SU	0238	6.8	0940	2.7	1516	6.7	2202	3.0
26 M	0324	6.7	1025	2.8	1609	6.6	◐ 2253	3.1
27 TU	0421	6.5	1118	2.9	1711	6.6	2350	3.1
28 W	0528	6.5	1217	2.9	1815	6.7		
29 TH	0052	3.0	0635	6.6	1322	2.8	1915	6.8
30 F	0159	2.7	0738	6.8	1432	2.6	2012	7.1

JULY

Date	Time	m	Time	m	Time	m	Time	m
1 SA	0307	2.4	0839	7.0	1536	2.3	2105	7.3
2 SU	0406	2.0	0934	7.3	1632	2.0	2156	7.6
3 M	0500	1.7	1027	7.5	1725	1.8	○ 2245	7.8
4 TU	0553	1.4	1117	7.7	1818	1.6	2334	7.9
5 W	0646	1.3	1206	7.8	1910	1.5		
6 TH	0022	7.9	0739	1.2	1256	7.8	2002	1.5
7 F	0111	7.9	0829	1.2	1345	7.7	2051	1.6
8 SA	0200	7.8	0917	1.4	1435	7.6	2139	1.8
9 SU	0250	7.6	1003	1.6	1526	7.4	2226	2.1
10 M	0342	7.3	1049	2.0	1620	7.1	◑ 2317	2.4
11 TU	0440	7.0	1141	2.3	1721	6.9		
12 W	0015	2.6	0546	6.8	1240	2.6	1827	6.9
13 TH	0120	2.7	0659	6.7	1346	2.7	1935	6.9
14 F	0225	2.6	0809	6.8	1451	2.7	2035	7.0
15 SA	0326	2.5	0909	6.9	1548	2.6	2126	7.2
16 SU	0419	2.3	0958	7.1	1638	2.4	2209	7.3
17 M	0506	2.1	1040	7.3	1724	2.3	● 2247	7.4
18 TU	0549	1.9	1117	7.4	1806	2.2	2321	7.5
19 W	0629	1.8	1151	7.4	1843	2.1	2355	7.5
20 TH	0705	1.8	1224	7.4	1918	2.1		
21 F	0028	7.5	0739	1.8	1257	7.3	1951	2.1
22 SA	0100	7.5	0810	1.9	1329	7.3	2021	2.2
23 SU	0133	7.4	0839	2.1	1402	7.2	2052	2.4
24 M	0207	7.2	0908	2.2	1437	7.1	2124	2.5
25 TU	0245	7.0	0941	2.5	1516	6.9	◐ 2203	2.7
26 W	0328	6.8	1022	2.7	1603	6.8	2252	2.9
27 TH	0424	6.6	1116	3.0	1706	6.7	2353	3.1
28 F	0537	6.5	1224	3.1	1823	6.7		
29 SA	0110	3.0	0659	6.6	1353	3.0	1938	6.9
30 SU	0237	2.6	0817	6.9	1512	2.6	2046	7.2
31 M	0345	2.1	0923	7.3	1615	2.1	2143	7.6

AUGUST

Date	Time	m	Time	m	Time	m	Time	m
1 TU	0445	1.7	1017	7.6	1715	1.8	○ 2234	7.9
2 W	0546	1.3	1107	7.9	1814	1.4	2323	8.1
3 TH	0647	1.0	1155	8.0	1908	1.2		
4 F	0010	8.2	0737	0.8	1241	8.1	1956	1.1
5 SA	0056	8.2	0819	0.8	1326	8.0	2038	1.2
6 SU	0141	8.1	0859	1.0	1410	7.8	2117	1.5
7 M	0225	7.8	0936	1.5	1452	7.5	2155	1.9
8 TU	0309	7.4	1011	2.0	1536	7.2	◑ 2235	2.4
9 W	0358	7.0	1053	2.6	1629	6.9	2327	2.9
10 TH	0503	6.6	1150	3.1	1742	6.6		
11 F	0039	3.1	0631	6.4	1309	3.3	1909	6.5
12 SA	0157	3.1	0758	6.5	1428	3.2	2024	6.7
13 SU	0306	2.8	0903	6.8	1533	2.9	2118	7.0
14 M	0406	2.5	0950	7.1	1629	2.5	2159	7.3
15 TU	0456	2.1	1027	7.3	1714	2.2	2233	7.5
16 W	0537	1.9	1059	7.5	1754	2.0	● 2303	7.6
17 TH	0614	1.7	1129	7.5	1830	1.9	2334	7.7
18 F	0647	1.6	1159	7.6	1859	1.8		
19 SA	0005	7.7	0717	1.6	1230	7.6	1928	1.8
20 SU	0035	7.7	0745	1.6	1300	7.6	1956	1.9
21 M	0106	7.6	0812	1.8	1330	7.5	2025	2.0
22 TU	0137	7.4	0839	2.0	1402	7.3	2055	2.2
23 W	0211	7.2	0908	2.3	1435	7.1	2128	2.5
24 TH	0249	6.9	0943	2.7	1516	6.8	◐ 2212	2.9
25 F	0341	6.6	1032	3.1	1618	6.6	2311	3.1
26 SA	0502	6.4	1143	3.3	1749	6.5		
27 SU	0036	3.2	0643	6.4	1333	3.2	1923	6.7
28 M	0222	2.8	0811	6.9	1500	2.7	2037	7.2
29 TU	0332	2.1	0914	7.4	1605	2.1	2132	7.7
30 W	0438	1.5	1005	7.8	1708	1.6	2221	8.0
31 TH	0540	1.1	1051	8.1	1805	1.2	○ 2306	8.3

Chart Datum: 4·38 metres below IGN Datum
HAT is 8·4 metres above Chart Datum

TIME ZONE -0100
(French Standard Time)
Subtract 1 hour for UT
For French Summer Time add ONE hour in **non-shaded areas**

FRANCE – LE HAVRE

LAT 49°29'N LONG 0°07'E

TIMES AND HEIGHTS OF HIGH AND LOW WATERS

Dates in amber are **SPRINGS**
Dates in grey are **NEAPS**

2023

SEPTEMBER

Day	Time	m	Day	Time	m
1 F	0633 1135 1853 2351	0.7 8.2 0.9 8.4	16 SA	0620 1130 1833 2338	1.5 7.8 1.7 7.9
2 SA	0719 1218 1935	0.6 8.3 0.9	17 SU	0648 1200 1901	1.5 7.8 1.6
3 SU	0034 0757 1300 2013	8.4 0.7 8.2 1.1	18 M	0008 0716 1229 1930	7.9 1.5 7.7 1.7
4 M	0115 0831 1339 2048	8.2 1.1 7.9 1.4	19 TU	0039 0744 1259 2000	7.7 1.7 7.6 1.8
5 TU	0155 0902 1417 2119	7.8 1.6 7.6 2.0	20 W	0111 0814 1330 2031	7.6 1.9 7.5 2.1
6 W	0235 0931 1454 ◑ 2153	7.4 2.2 7.2 2.5	21 TH	0144 0843 1403 2104	7.3 2.3 7.2 2.4
7 TH	0320 1005 1542 2239	6.9 2.9 6.8 3.1	22 F	0223 0917 1445 ◐ 2146	7.0 2.8 6.9 2.8
8 F	0425 1102 1659 2358	6.4 3.5 6.3 3.5	23 SA	0321 1007 1554 2245	6.6 3.2 6.5 3.2
9 SA	0609 1235 1846	6.1 3.7 6.3	24 SU	0452 1123 1737	6.4 3.5 6.4
10 SU	0132 0747 1411 2011	3.4 6.3 3.5 6.5	25 M	0022 0643 1330 1916	3.3 6.5 3.3 6.8
11 M	0252 0850 1523 2103	3.0 6.7 3.0 6.9	26 TU	0213 0803 1449 2024	2.7 7.0 2.6 7.3
12 TU	0351 0931 1614 2139	2.5 7.1 2.5 7.3	27 W	0322 0859 1553 2116	2.0 7.6 1.9 7.8
13 W	0436 1003 1655 2209	2.1 7.4 2.1 7.5	28 TH	0424 0946 1652 2202	1.4 8.0 1.4 8.2
14 TH	0515 1032 1733 2238	1.8 7.6 1.9 7.7	29 F	0521 1029 1745 ○ 2245	0.9 8.2 1.0 8.4
15 F	0550 1100 1806 ● 2308	1.6 7.7 1.7 7.8	30 SA	0610 1111 1829 2327	0.7 8.3 0.9 8.4

OCTOBER

Day	Time	m	Day	Time	m
1 SU	0651 1151 1908	0.7 8.3 0.9	16 M	0617 1129 1832 2342	1.5 7.9 1.6 7.9
2 M	0008 0726 1230 1944	8.3 0.9 8.2 1.2	17 TU	0647 1200 1905	1.6 7.8 1.6
3 TU	0048 0758 1307 2016	8.1 1.3 7.9 1.5	18 W	0015 0719 1232 1938	7.8 1.7 7.7 1.7
4 W	0127 0827 1342 2045	7.7 1.9 7.6 2.1	19 TH	0051 0751 1307 2011	7.6 2.0 7.6 2.0
5 TH	0206 0854 1418 2116	7.3 2.5 7.2 2.6	20 F	0130 0825 1346 2047	7.3 2.4 7.3 2.4
6 F	0250 0927 1503 ◑ 2200	6.8 3.1 6.7 3.2	21 SA	0218 0904 1437 2132	7.0 2.8 6.9 2.8
7 SA	0354 1023 1621 2318	6.3 3.7 6.2 3.6	22 SU	0321 0958 1551 ◐ 2235	6.7 3.2 6.6 3.1
8 SU	0540 1201 1811	6.1 3.9 6.1	23 M	0454 1120 1731	6.5 3.5 6.6
9 M	0058 0713 1344 1938	3.6 6.3 3.6 6.4	24 TU	0024 0633 1320 1858	3.1 6.7 3.1 6.9
10 TU	0219 0819 1451 2031	3.1 6.7 3.0 6.8	25 W	0156 0742 1431 2002	2.5 7.2 2.4 7.4
11 W	0315 0858 1540 2107	2.6 7.1 2.5 7.2	26 TH	0301 0836 1531 2053	1.9 7.7 1.8 7.8
12 TH	0400 0929 1621 2137	2.1 7.4 2.1 7.5	27 F	0400 0921 1628 2138	1.4 8.0 1.4 8.1
13 F	0440 0958 1700 2208	1.8 7.7 1.9 7.7	28 SA	0453 1004 1718 ○ 2222	1.1 8.1 1.2 8.2
14 SA	0516 1028 1731 ● 2239	1.6 7.8 1.7 7.9	29 SU	0540 1044 1801 2304	1.0 8.2 1.1 8.2
15 SU	0547 1058 1802 2310	1.6 7.9 1.6 7.9	30 M	0620 1124 1839 2344	1.1 8.1 1.2 8.1
			31 TU	0654 1201 1914	1.3 8.0 1.4

NOVEMBER

Day	Time	m	Day	Time	m
1 W	0024 0726 1238 1947	7.9 1.7 7.8 1.7	16 TH	0659 1214 1921	1.8 7.8 1.7
2 TH	0103 0757 1313 2018	7.6 2.1 7.5 2.1	17 F	0041 0737 1256 2000	7.6 2.0 7.6 1.9
3 F	0143 0827 1350 2050	7.2 2.6 7.1 2.6	18 SA	0127 0816 1343 2040	7.4 2.3 7.4 2.2
4 SA	0227 0903 1434 2133	6.8 3.1 6.7 3.1	19 SU	0219 0900 1438 2129	7.2 2.7 7.1 2.5
5 SU	0326 0957 1542 ◑ 2240	6.4 3.6 6.3 3.5	20 M	0323 0958 1548 ◐ 2236	6.9 3.0 6.9 2.7
6 M	0455 1119 1719	6.2 3.8 6.2	21 TU	0444 1124 1712	6.8 3.1 6.8
7 TU	0003 0612 1244 1834	3.5 6.3 3.7 6.3	22 W	0009 0605 1253 1828	2.7 7.0 2.8 7.0
8 W	0120 0717 1359 1935	3.3 6.6 3.2 6.7	23 TH	0126 0711 1401 1932	2.4 7.3 2.4 7.3
9 TH	0222 0806 1453 2020	2.8 7.0 2.8 7.0	24 F	0231 0807 1502 2027	2.0 7.5 2.0 7.6
10 F	0313 0844 1539 2058	2.4 7.3 2.4 7.3	25 SA	0329 0855 1559 2116	1.7 7.8 1.7 7.8
11 SA	0357 0919 1620 2134	2.1 7.6 2.1 7.6	26 SU	0422 0939 1649 2201	1.6 7.9 1.5 7.9
12 SU	0436 0953 1655 2209	1.9 7.7 1.9 7.7	27 M	0508 1021 1733 ○ 2245	1.5 7.9 1.5 7.9
13 M	0512 1027 1731 ● 2244	1.8 7.8 1.7 7.8	28 TU	0550 1101 1812 2326	1.6 7.9 1.5 7.8
14 TU	0547 1101 1807 2320	1.7 7.9 1.6 7.8	29 W	0625 1139 1849	1.7 7.8 1.6
15 W	0623 1136 1844 2359	1.7 7.9 1.6 7.7	30 TH	0007 0701 1216 1925	7.7 1.9 7.7 1.8

DECEMBER

Day	Time	m	Day	Time	m
1 F	0046 0736 1253 1959	7.5 2.2 7.5 2.1	16 SA	0037 0733 1252 1959	7.7 1.9 7.8 1.6
2 SA	0126 0811 1331 2035	7.3 2.6 7.2 2.4	17 SU	0126 0818 1342 2046	7.6 2.0 7.7 1.8
3 SU	0207 0849 1411 2115	7.0 2.9 6.9 2.8	18 M	0218 0907 1435 2136	7.4 2.3 7.5 2.0
4 M	0254 0934 1500 2204	6.7 3.2 6.6 3.1	19 TU	0314 1003 1533 ◐ 2233	7.3 2.5 7.3 2.2
5 TU	0356 1030 1609 ◑ 2301	6.5 3.5 6.4 3.3	20 W	0417 1106 1639 2338	7.1 2.6 7.1 2.4
6 W	0505 1132 1723	6.5 3.5 6.4	21 TH	0525 1214 1749	7.1 2.7 7.1
7 TH	0003 0607 1235 1826	3.3 6.6 3.4 6.5	22 F	0045 0633 1323 1858	2.4 7.1 2.6 7.1
8 F	0105 0703 1339 1922	3.1 6.8 3.1 6.7	23 SA	0152 0735 1429 2002	2.4 7.2 2.4 7.2
9 SA	0208 0753 1440 2012	2.8 7.0 2.8 7.0	24 SU	0256 0830 1530 2058	2.3 7.4 2.2 7.3
10 SU	0305 0838 1533 2058	2.5 7.3 2.4 7.2	25 M	0353 0920 1624 2148	2.2 7.5 2.0 7.5
11 M	0354 0919 1620 2142	2.3 7.5 2.1 7.4	26 TU	0443 1005 1711 2234	2.1 7.6 1.8 7.6
12 TU	0439 1000 1703 2224	2.0 7.7 1.8 7.6	27 W	0527 1046 1753 ○ 2316	2.0 7.7 1.7 7.6
13 W	0522 1040 1747 ● 2307	1.9 7.8 1.6 7.7	28 TH	0606 1125 1832 2355	2.0 7.7 1.7 7.6
14 TH	0605 1122 1830 2351	1.8 7.9 1.5 7.8	29 F	0645 1201 1910	2.0 7.7 1.7
15 F	0648 1206 1914	1.8 7.9 1.5	30 SA	0032 0722 1237 1946	7.5 2.1 7.6 1.9
			31 SU	0108 0759 1312 2021	7.4 2.3 7.4 2.1

Chart Datum: 4·38 metres below IGN Datum
HAT is 8·4 metres above Chart Datum

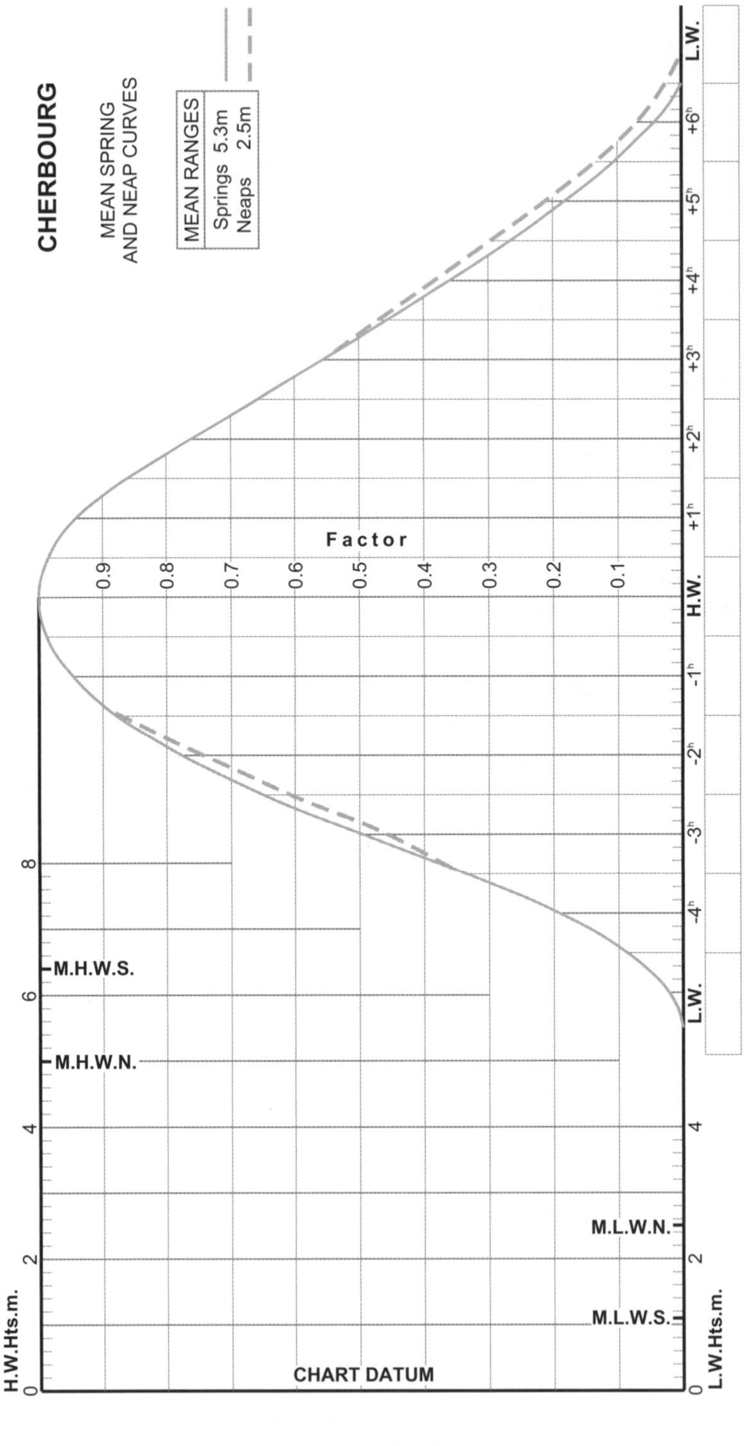

CHERBOURG
MEAN SPRING AND NEAP CURVES
MEAN RANGES
Springs 5.3m
Neaps 2.5m
Factor
0.9
0.8
0.7
0.6
0.5
0.4
0.3
0.2
0.1
L.W.
-4h
-3h
-2h
-1h
H.W.
+1h
+2h
+3h
+4h
+5h
+6h
L.W.
H.W.Hts.m.
0
2
4
6
8
M.H.W.S.
M.H.W.N.
CHART DATUM
M.L.W.N.
M.L.W.S.
L.W.Hts.m.
0
2
4

TIME ZONE -0100
(French Standard Time)
Subtract 1 hour for UT
For French Summer Time add ONE hour in **non-shaded areas**

FRANCE – CHERBOURG

LAT 49°39'N LONG 1°38'W

TIMES AND HEIGHTS OF HIGH AND LOW WATERS

Dates in amber are **SPRINGS**
Dates in grey are **NEAPS**

2023

JANUARY

Date	Day	Time	m	Time	m	Time	m	Time	m
1	SU	0406	5.3	1058	2.5	1630	5.3	2325	2.4
2	M	0511	5.3	1204	2.5	1737	5.3		
3	TU	0026	2.3	0610	5.4	1303	2.3	1838	5.4
4	W	0120	2.2	0701	5.6	1354	2.1	1930	5.6
5	TH	0208	2.1	0745	5.8	1438	1.9	2014	5.7
6	F	0249	2.0	0825	5.9	1518	1.8	2053	5.8
7	SA	0328	1.9	0901	6.0	1555	1.7	○ 2130	5.9
8	SU	0404	1.9	0935	6.1	1630	1.6	2204	5.9
9	M	0439	1.9	1009	6.1	1704	1.6	2237	5.9
10	TU	0513	1.9	1042	6.1	1737	1.7	2310	5.8
11	W	0546	2.0	1116	6.0	1810	1.8	2344	5.7
12	TH	0620	2.1	1150	5.8	1844	1.9		
13	F	0020	5.5	0657	2.2	1227	5.6	1921	2.1
14	SA	0059	5.4	0738	2.4	1308	5.4	2004	2.3
15	SU	0144	5.2	0828	2.6	1357	5.2	◑ 2057	2.4
16	M	0240	5.1	0929	2.7	1500	5.1	2203	2.5
17	TU	0349	5.1	1043	2.6	1617	5.1	2319	2.5
18	W	0509	5.3	1159	2.4	1742	5.3		
19	TH	0032	2.3	0619	5.6	1307	2.0	1851	5.6
20	F	0136	1.9	0717	5.9	1408	1.6	1950	6.0
21	SA	0235	1.6	0811	6.3	1505	1.2	● 2046	6.2
22	SU	0330	1.3	0903	6.6	1559	0.9	2139	6.4
23	M	0422	1.1	0954	6.8	1650	0.7	2229	6.5
24	TU	0510	1.1	1043	6.8	1737	0.7	2316	6.5
25	W	0556	1.1	1129	6.7	1822	0.8	2359	6.3
26	TH	0640	1.3	1213	6.5	1904	1.1		
27	F	0040	6.0	0723	1.6	1255	6.1	1946	1.5
28	SA	0121	5.7	0807	2.0	1338	5.7	◐ 2029	2.0
29	SU	0205	5.4	0857	2.4	1428	5.3	2120	2.4
30	M	0302	5.1	1000	2.7	1536	4.9	2228	2.7
31	TU	0419	4.9	1120	2.8	1703	4.8	2348	2.8

FEBRUARY

Date	Day	Time	m	Time	m	Time	m	Time	m
1	W	0540	5.0	1236	2.6	1823	5.0		
2	TH	0058	2.6	0644	5.2	1338	2.3	1921	5.2
3	F	0154	2.4	0733	5.5	1426	2.0	2006	5.5
4	SA	0240	2.1	0814	5.7	1507	1.8	2043	5.7
5	SU	0318	1.9	0850	5.9	1543	1.6	○ 2118	5.9
6	M	0353	1.7	0924	6.1	1617	1.4	2150	6.0
7	TU	0426	1.6	0956	6.2	1648	1.4	2220	6.0
8	W	0457	1.6	1027	6.2	1719	1.3	2251	6.0
9	TH	0528	1.6	1058	6.2	1749	1.4	2321	6.0
10	F	0559	1.6	1129	6.1	1819	1.5	2353	5.8
11	SA	0630	1.8	1200	5.9	1850	1.7		
12	SU	0024	5.7	0706	2.0	1233	5.7	1926	2.0
13	M	0059	5.4	0748	2.3	1313	5.4	◑ 2011	2.3
14	TU	0144	5.2	0842	2.5	1409	5.1	2114	2.6
15	W	0252	5.0	0958	2.7	1537	4.9	2243	2.7
16	TH	0436	5.0	1132	2.5	1730	5.0		
17	F	0015	2.5	0605	5.3	1254	2.1	1846	5.4
18	SA	0128	2.1	0709	5.8	1401	1.6	1947	5.9
19	SU	0230	1.6	0805	6.2	1459	1.1	2041	6.3
20	M	0324	1.2	0857	6.6	1551	0.7	● 2130	6.5
21	TU	0413	0.9	0944	6.9	1637	0.5	2215	6.7
22	W	0456	0.8	1029	6.9	1720	0.5	2256	6.6
23	TH	0537	0.8	1110	6.8	1759	0.6	2333	6.5
24	F	0615	1.0	1147	6.6	1835	1.0		
25	SA	0007	6.2	0651	1.4	1222	6.1	1909	1.5
26	SU	0039	5.8	0728	1.9	1258	5.6	1945	2.0
27	M	0114	5.4	0809	2.3	1339	5.1	◐ 2027	2.6
28	TU	0200	5.0	0904	2.7	1442	4.7	2129	3.0

MARCH

Date	Day	Time	m	Time	m	Time	m	Time	m
1	W	0319	4.7	1033	3.0	1634	4.5	2311	3.1
2	TH	0511	4.7	1211	2.8	1815	4.7		
3	F	0041	2.9	0629	4.9	1320	2.5	1911	5.1
4	SA	0141	2.5	0718	5.3	1409	2.1	1950	5.4
5	SU	0225	2.2	0757	5.6	1448	1.8	2024	5.7
6	M	0301	1.8	0832	5.9	1522	1.5	2056	5.9
7	TU	0334	1.6	0904	6.1	1554	1.3	○ 2128	6.1
8	W	0405	1.4	0935	6.3	1624	1.2	2157	6.2
9	TH	0435	1.3	1005	6.3	1654	1.1	2226	6.2
10	F	0505	1.3	1035	6.3	1723	1.2	2255	6.2
11	SA	0535	1.3	1105	6.2	1751	1.3	2325	6.1
12	SU	0605	1.5	1136	6.0	1822	1.6	2355	5.9
13	M	0639	1.7	1207	5.7	1856	1.9		
14	TU	0027	5.6	0719	2.1	1246	5.4	1940	2.3
15	W	0111	5.2	0813	2.4	1344	5.0	◑ 2045	2.7
16	TH	0222	4.9	0934	2.7	1529	4.7	2227	2.9
17	F	0425	4.9	1120	2.5	1732	4.9		
18	SA	0009	2.6	0557	5.2	1247	2.1	1843	5.4
19	SU	0123	2.1	0700	5.7	1352	1.5	1939	5.9
20	M	0220	1.5	0753	6.2	1446	1.0	2027	6.3
21	TU	0310	1.1	0841	6.6	1533	0.7	● 2111	6.6
22	W	0354	0.8	0925	6.8	1615	0.5	2151	6.7
23	TH	0434	0.7	1006	6.9	1654	0.6	2228	6.6
24	F	0512	0.8	1043	6.7	1729	0.8	2301	6.5
25	SA	0546	1.0	1118	6.4	1802	1.2	2332	6.2
26	SU	0619	1.4	1150	6.0	1833	1.6		
27	M	0001	5.8	0652	1.8	1223	5.5	1905	2.2
28	TU	0032	5.4	0729	2.3	1300	5.0	1943	2.7
29	W	0112	5.0	0819	2.7	1359	4.6	◐ 2042	3.1
30	TH	0223	4.6	0943	3.0	1558	4.4	2230	3.3
31	F	0428	4.5	1134	2.9	1750	4.6		

APRIL

Date	Day	Time	m	Time	m	Time	m	Time	m
1	SA	0011	3.0	0557	4.8	1246	2.6	1841	5.0
2	SU	0111	2.6	0646	5.1	1335	2.2	1918	5.4
3	M	0154	2.2	0725	5.5	1414	1.8	1952	5.7
4	TU	0230	1.9	0801	5.8	1449	1.5	2025	6.0
5	W	0303	1.6	0835	6.1	1521	1.3	2057	6.1
6	TH	0334	1.4	0907	6.3	1552	1.2	○ 2127	6.3
7	F	0406	1.2	0938	6.3	1624	1.1	2157	6.3
8	SA	0438	1.2	1009	6.3	1655	1.2	2228	6.3
9	SU	0511	1.2	1042	6.2	1726	1.3	2300	6.2
10	M	0544	1.4	1116	6.0	1759	1.6	2333	6.0
11	TU	0621	1.6	1154	5.7	1838	2.0		
12	W	0012	5.7	0705	2.0	1240	5.3	1927	2.4
13	TH	0103	5.3	0804	2.3	1346	4.9	◑ 2041	2.8
14	F	0221	4.9	0931	2.5	1543	4.8	2226	2.8
15	SA	0418	5.0	1113	2.4	1723	5.1	2359	2.5
16	SU	0540	5.3	1232	1.9	1827	5.5		
17	M	0106	2.0	0640	5.8	1332	1.5	1917	5.9
18	TU	0200	1.5	0731	6.2	1423	1.1	2002	6.3
19	W	0247	1.2	0817	6.5	1507	0.9	2044	6.4
20	TH	0329	1.0	0859	6.6	1547	0.8	● 2121	6.5
21	F	0408	0.9	0938	6.6	1624	0.9	2155	6.5
22	SA	0444	1.0	1014	6.4	1658	1.1	2228	6.3
23	SU	0518	1.2	1049	6.2	1729	1.5	2259	6.1
24	M	0550	1.5	1122	5.8	1801	1.9	2329	5.8
25	TU	0624	1.9	1156	5.4	1834	2.3		
26	W	0002	5.4	0700	2.3	1235	5.0	1913	2.7
27	TH	0041	5.0	0747	2.6	1330	4.7	◐ 2009	3.1
28	F	0142	4.7	0857	2.9	1503	4.5	2138	3.2
29	SA	0323	4.5	1034	2.9	1648	4.6	2316	3.1
30	SU	0455	4.7	1150	2.6	1749	4.9		

Chart Datum: 3·33 metres below IGN Datum
HAT is 7·0 metres above Chart Datum

TIME ZONE -0100
(French Standard Time)
Subtract 1 hour for UT
For French Summer Time add ONE hour in **non-shaded areas**

FRANCE – CHERBOURG

LAT 49°39'N LONG 1°38'W

TIMES AND HEIGHTS OF HIGH AND LOW WATERS

Dates in amber are **SPRINGS**
Dates in grey are **NEAPS**

2023

MAY

Date	Day	Time	m	Time	m	Time	m	Time	m
1	M	0019	2.7	0554	5.0	1244	2.3	1831	5.3
2	TU	0106	2.3	0639	5.4	1327	2.0	1909	5.6
3	W	0146	2.0	0719	5.7	1405	1.7	1945	5.9
4	TH	0223	1.7	0757	5.9	1441	1.5	2020	6.1
5	F	0259	1.5	0833	6.1	1517	1.3	○ 2054	6.2
6	SA	0336	1.3	0909	6.2	1553	1.2	2128	6.3
7	SU	0413	1.2	0945	6.2	1630	1.3	2203	6.3
8	M	0451	1.2	1024	6.2	1707	1.5	2241	6.2
9	TU	0531	1.3	1105	6.0	1747	1.7	2322	6.0
10	W	0614	1.6	1150	5.7	1834	2.0		
11	TH	0008	5.7	0705	1.9	1244	5.4	1931	2.4
12	F	0106	5.4	0809	2.1	1356	5.1	◑ 2046	2.6
13	SA	0224	5.2	0928	2.3	1533	5.0	2215	2.6
14	SU	0356	5.2	1053	2.1	1654	5.2	2334	2.3
15	M	0510	5.4	1204	1.9	1755	5.5		
16	TU	0037	2.0	0609	5.7	1302	1.6	1846	5.8
17	W	0130	1.7	0701	6.0	1352	1.4	1931	6.0
18	TH	0218	1.5	0749	6.1	1437	1.3	2013	6.2
19	F	0301	1.3	0832	6.2	1517	1.3	● 2050	6.2
20	SA	0341	1.3	0912	6.1	1554	1.4	2125	6.2
21	SU	0417	1.3	0949	6.0	1629	1.5	2159	6.1
22	M	0453	1.5	1025	5.9	1703	1.8	2233	6.0
23	TU	0527	1.6	1101	5.7	1737	2.0	2307	5.8
24	W	0602	1.9	1138	5.4	1813	2.3	2342	5.5
25	TH	0640	2.2	1218	5.1	1853	2.6		
26	F	0022	5.2	0723	2.4	1305	4.9	1942	2.8
27	SA	0113	5.0	0817	2.6	1408	4.7	◐ 2046	3.0
28	SU	0220	4.8	0924	2.7	1521	4.7	2200	3.0
29	M	0334	4.8	1036	2.7	1632	4.9	2310	2.8
30	TU	0441	4.9	1138	2.5	1729	5.1		
31	W	0006	2.5	0539	5.2	1230	2.2	1816	5.4

JUNE

Date	Day	Time	m	Time	m	Time	m	Time	m
1	TH	0055	2.2	0629	5.5	1317	1.9	1900	5.7
2	F	0140	1.9	0715	5.7	1401	1.7	1941	6.0
3	SA	0224	1.6	0800	5.9	1444	1.5	2022	6.1
4	SU	0308	1.4	0844	6.1	1528	1.5	○ 2103	6.3
5	M	0353	1.3	0928	6.1	1612	1.4	2146	6.3
6	TU	0438	1.2	1014	6.1	1657	1.5	2230	6.3
7	W	0525	1.2	1101	6.0	1745	1.7	2318	6.2
8	TH	0614	1.4	1152	5.8	1837	1.9		
9	F	0009	6.0	0708	1.6	1248	5.6	1934	2.1
10	SA	0106	5.8	0806	1.8	1351	5.4	◑ 2038	2.3
11	SU	0212	5.5	0911	1.9	1502	5.3	2147	2.3
12	M	0322	5.4	1019	2.0	1611	5.3	2257	2.3
13	TU	0430	5.4	1125	2.0	1713	5.4		
14	W	0001	2.2	0533	5.5	1225	1.9	1809	5.6
15	TH	0058	2.0	0631	5.6	1319	1.9	1900	5.7
16	F	0150	1.8	0723	5.7	1407	1.8	1945	5.9
17	SA	0236	1.7	0811	5.8	1451	1.8	2026	5.9
18	SU	0318	1.6	0853	5.8	1531	1.8	● 2103	6.0
19	M	0357	1.6	0932	5.8	1608	1.8	2139	6.0
20	TU	0434	1.6	1009	5.7	1645	1.9	2215	5.9
21	W	0510	1.7	1046	5.7	1720	2.0	2251	5.8
22	TH	0546	1.8	1122	5.5	1756	2.2	2327	5.7
23	F	0622	1.9	1159	5.4	1833	2.3		
24	SA	0004	5.5	0659	2.1	1237	5.2	1913	2.5
25	SU	0044	5.3	0739	2.3	1321	5.1	1959	2.6
26	M	0130	5.1	0826	2.4	1411	5.0	◐ 2053	2.7
27	TU	0224	5.0	0921	2.5	1509	5.0	2155	2.7
28	W	0325	5.0	1024	2.5	1612	5.0	2301	2.6
29	TH	0430	5.1	1130	2.4	1717	5.2		
30	F	0004	2.4	0537	5.2	1231	2.2	1816	5.5

JULY

Date	Day	Time	m	Time	m	Time	m	Time	m
1	SA	0102	2.1	0639	5.5	1327	2.0	1909	5.8
2	SU	0155	1.8	0735	5.7	1420	1.8	1959	6.0
3	M	0248	1.5	0828	6.0	1511	1.6	○ 2047	6.2
4	TU	0340	1.3	0919	6.1	1602	1.5	2136	6.4
5	W	0431	1.1	1010	6.2	1653	1.4	2226	6.5
6	TH	0522	1.0	1100	6.2	1743	1.4	2315	6.5
7	F	0611	1.0	1150	6.1	1833	1.5		
8	SA	0005	6.3	0700	1.2	1239	5.9	1923	1.7
9	SU	0054	6.1	0749	1.4	1328	5.7	2014	1.9
10	M	0145	5.8	0840	1.7	1421	5.5	◑ 2110	2.2
11	TU	0241	5.5	0937	2.1	1520	5.3	2214	2.4
12	W	0345	5.3	1040	2.3	1627	5.2	2323	2.4
13	TH	0456	5.2	1148	2.4	1734	5.3		
14	F	0029	2.3	0606	5.2	1251	2.4	1835	5.4
15	SA	0128	2.2	0707	5.3	1346	2.2	1926	5.6
16	SU	0219	2.0	0759	5.5	1434	2.1	2011	5.7
17	M	0304	1.8	0842	5.6	1516	2.0	● 2050	5.9
18	TU	0343	1.7	0920	5.7	1555	1.9	2126	6.0
19	W	0420	1.6	0955	5.8	1631	1.9	2201	6.0
20	TH	0455	1.6	1029	5.8	1704	1.9	2234	6.0
21	F	0527	1.6	1102	5.8	1737	1.9	2307	5.9
22	SA	0559	1.7	1134	5.7	1809	2.0	2339	5.8
23	SU	0630	1.8	1206	5.6	1842	2.1		
24	M	0013	5.7	0703	2.0	1240	5.5	1918	2.3
25	TU	0049	5.5	0739	2.2	1318	5.3	◐ 2001	2.5
26	W	0131	5.3	0823	2.4	1404	5.2	2054	2.6
27	TH	0223	5.1	0921	2.6	1504	5.0	2202	2.7
28	F	0332	5.0	1035	2.7	1621	5.1	2321	2.6
29	SA	0458	5.0	1155	2.5	1743	5.3		
30	SU	0034	2.3	0618	5.3	1305	2.3	1849	5.6
31	M	0138	1.9	0722	5.6	1406	1.9	1945	6.0

AUGUST

Date	Day	Time	m	Time	m	Time	m	Time	m
1	TU	0236	1.5	0819	6.0	1503	1.6	○ 2038	6.4
2	W	0332	1.1	0913	6.3	1556	1.3	2129	6.6
3	TH	0423	0.8	1003	6.5	1646	1.1	2218	6.8
4	F	0512	0.7	1051	6.5	1732	1.1	2305	6.8
5	SA	0557	0.7	1135	6.4	1816	1.2	2349	6.6
6	SU	0640	0.9	1216	6.2	1859	1.4		
7	M	0031	6.3	0721	1.3	1256	5.9	1942	1.8
8	TU	0112	5.9	0803	1.8	1337	5.6	◑ 2030	2.2
9	W	0159	5.5	0851	2.3	1426	5.2	2128	2.5
10	TH	0259	5.1	0952	2.6	1537	5.0	2245	2.7
11	F	0424	4.8	1113	2.8	1704	5.0		
12	SA	0006	2.7	0553	4.9	1232	2.7	1820	5.2
13	SU	0114	2.4	0702	5.1	1334	2.5	1916	5.4
14	M	0207	2.1	0751	5.4	1424	2.3	1959	5.7
15	TU	0251	1.9	0830	5.7	1504	2.0	2036	5.9
16	W	0328	1.7	0904	5.8	1540	1.8	● 2110	6.1
17	TH	0402	1.5	0936	6.0	1612	1.7	2142	6.2
18	F	0433	1.4	1006	6.0	1643	1.7	2212	6.2
19	SA	0503	1.4	1035	6.0	1712	1.6	2242	6.2
20	SU	0531	1.5	1104	6.0	1741	1.7	2311	6.1
21	M	0559	1.6	1133	5.9	1810	1.8	2341	5.9
22	TU	0627	1.8	1203	5.7	1842	2.0		
23	W	0012	5.7	0659	2.0	1235	5.5	1920	2.3
24	TH	0048	5.4	0738	2.4	1314	5.3	◐ 2008	2.6
25	F	0137	5.1	0832	2.7	1412	5.1	2117	2.8
26	SA	0252	4.9	0954	2.9	1543	4.9	2252	2.7
27	SU	0445	4.9	1136	2.8	1729	5.2		
28	M	0020	2.4	0613	5.3	1255	2.4	1839	5.6
29	TU	0128	1.9	0716	5.7	1358	1.9	1935	6.1
30	W	0227	1.3	0810	6.2	1453	1.4	2026	6.6
31	TH	0319	0.9	0900	6.5	1543	1.1	○ 2115	6.9

Chart Datum: 3·33 metres below IGN Datum
HAT is 7·0 metres above Chart Datum

TIME ZONE -0100
(French Standard Time)
Subtract 1 hour for UT
For French Summer Time add ONE hour in **non-shaded areas**

FRANCE – CHERBOURG

LAT 49°39'N LONG 1°38'W

TIMES AND HEIGHTS OF HIGH AND LOW WATERS

Dates in amber are **SPRINGS**
Dates in grey are **NEAPS**

2023

SEPTEMBER

Date	Day	Time	m	Time	m	Time	m	Time	m
1	F	0408	0.6	0947	6.7	1629	0.9	2201	7.0
2	SA	0452	0.5	1029	6.7	1711	0.8	2244	7.0
3	SU	0533	0.6	1109	6.6	1751	1.0	2324	6.8
4	M	0611	0.9	1145	6.4	1829	1.3		
5	TU	0001	6.4	0647	1.4	1219	6.0	1908	1.8
6	W	0038	5.9	0724	2.0	1254	5.6	◑ 1949	2.3
7	TH	0119	5.3	0806	2.5	1338	5.2	2044	2.7
8	F	0218	4.9	0905	3.0	1450	4.8	2209	3.0
9	SA	0400	4.6	1045	3.2	1640	4.8	2348	2.9
10	SU	0551	4.8	1219	3.0	1809	5.0		
11	M	0059	2.5	0652	5.1	1321	2.6	1901	5.4
12	TU	0149	2.2	0733	5.5	1406	2.3	1940	5.7
13	W	0228	1.8	0806	5.8	1443	2.0	2014	6.0
14	TH	0303	1.6	0838	6.0	1516	1.7	2047	6.2
15	F	0334	1.4	0909	6.2	1546	1.6	● 2117	6.3
16	SA	0404	1.3	0937	6.2	1615	1.5	2145	6.4
17	SU	0433	1.3	1005	6.3	1644	1.5	2214	6.4
18	M	0501	1.4	1032	6.2	1713	1.5	2242	6.3
19	TU	0528	1.5	1101	6.1	1742	1.7	2312	6.1
20	W	0556	1.7	1130	5.9	1813	1.9	2343	5.8
21	TH	0628	2.1	1201	5.7	1850	2.2		
22	F	0019	5.5	0707	2.4	1241	5.4	◐ 1938	2.5
23	SA	0111	5.1	0803	2.8	1343	5.0	2052	2.8
24	SU	0239	4.8	0938	3.1	1533	4.9	2239	2.8
25	M	0450	4.9	1130	2.9	1722	5.2		
26	TU	0011	2.3	0608	5.4	1247	2.3	1827	5.7
27	W	0116	1.7	0704	5.9	1345	1.8	1920	6.3
28	TH	0211	1.2	0753	6.3	1436	1.3	2009	6.7
29	F	0300	0.8	0838	6.7	1523	1.0	○ 2054	7.0
30	SA	0344	0.6	0921	6.8	1605	0.8	2137	7.0

OCTOBER

Date	Day	Time	m	Time	m	Time	m	Time	m
1	SU	0426	0.6	1000	6.8	1645	0.9	2217	6.9
2	M	0504	0.8	1037	6.7	1723	1.1	2255	6.7
3	TU	0539	1.2	1110	6.4	1759	1.4	2331	6.2
4	W	0613	1.7	1143	6.0	1835	1.9		
5	TH	0007	5.7	0648	2.2	1217	5.6	1914	2.3
6	F	0048	5.2	0728	2.7	1259	5.2	◑ 2005	2.8
7	SA	0147	4.8	0826	3.2	1410	4.8	2129	3.1
8	SU	0334	4.6	1012	3.4	1606	4.7	2317	3.0
9	M	0527	4.8	1151	3.1	1738	4.9		
10	TU	0026	2.6	0621	5.1	1251	2.7	1829	5.3
11	W	0115	2.3	0658	5.5	1334	2.3	1907	5.7
12	TH	0154	1.9	0731	5.8	1410	2.0	1942	6.0
13	F	0228	1.7	0804	6.1	1443	1.7	2015	6.2
14	SA	0300	1.5	0835	6.2	1514	1.6	● 2046	6.4
15	SU	0330	1.4	0905	6.3	1545	1.5	2116	6.4
16	M	0401	1.3	0933	6.4	1616	1.4	2146	6.4
17	TU	0431	1.4	1002	6.4	1647	1.5	2217	6.3
18	W	0501	1.6	1033	6.3	1719	1.6	2250	6.1
19	TH	0533	1.8	1106	6.1	1754	1.8	2327	5.8
20	F	0608	2.2	1143	5.8	1835	2.1		
21	SA	0011	5.5	0653	2.5	1231	5.4	1929	2.5
22	SU	0111	5.1	0758	2.9	1341	5.1	◐ 2048	2.7
23	M	0249	4.9	0937	3.0	1531	5.0	2230	2.6
24	TU	0441	5.1	1118	2.7	1704	5.4	2354	2.2
25	W	0549	5.5	1228	2.2	1806	5.8		
26	TH	0055	1.7	0641	6.0	1324	1.7	1857	6.3
27	F	0147	1.3	0728	6.4	1413	1.4	1945	6.6
28	SA	0234	1.0	0811	6.6	1458	1.1	○ 2030	6.8
29	SU	0317	0.9	0852	6.7	1540	1.0	2112	6.8
30	M	0357	1.0	0930	6.7	1619	1.1	2151	6.7
31	TU	0434	1.2	1005	6.6	1657	1.3	2229	6.4

NOVEMBER

Date	Day	Time	m	Time	m	Time	m	Time	m
1	W	0510	1.5	1039	6.3	1733	1.6	2306	6.1
2	TH	0544	1.9	1113	6.0	1809	1.9	2343	5.7
3	F	0620	2.4	1150	5.6	1848	2.3		
4	SA	0026	5.2	0701	2.8	1233	5.3	1937	2.7
5	SU	0123	4.9	0756	3.1	1336	4.9	◑ 2045	3.0
6	M	0248	4.7	0921	3.3	1508	4.7	2217	3.0
7	TU	0423	4.8	1056	3.2	1636	4.9	2332	2.8
8	W	0528	5.0	1201	2.9	1737	5.1		
9	TH	0026	2.5	0611	5.4	1248	2.5	1822	5.5
10	F	0109	2.1	0649	5.7	1329	2.2	1902	5.8
11	SA	0146	1.9	0725	6.0	1405	1.9	1939	6.0
12	SU	0222	1.7	0759	6.2	1440	1.7	2014	6.2
13	M	0256	1.5	0832	6.3	1515	1.5	● 2048	6.3
14	TU	0331	1.5	0905	6.4	1551	1.4	2123	6.3
15	W	0406	1.5	0938	6.4	1628	1.5	2159	6.2
16	TH	0443	1.7	1015	6.3	1706	1.5	2239	6.1
17	F	0521	1.9	1054	6.2	1747	1.7	2323	5.9
18	SA	0604	2.1	1140	5.9	1835	2.0		
19	SU	0013	5.6	0657	2.4	1233	5.6	1933	2.2
20	M	0117	5.3	0804	2.7	1343	5.4	◐ 2045	2.4
21	TU	0244	5.2	0927	2.8	1512	5.3	2208	2.3
22	W	0411	5.3	1050	2.6	1631	5.5	2324	2.1
23	TH	0517	5.6	1159	2.2	1735	5.8		
24	F	0026	1.8	0611	5.9	1256	1.9	1830	6.1
25	SA	0119	1.5	0659	6.2	1347	1.6	1920	6.3
26	SU	0207	1.4	0744	6.3	1434	1.4	2007	6.4
27	M	0251	1.4	0826	6.4	1518	1.3	○ 2050	6.4
28	TU	0332	1.4	0904	6.4	1558	1.4	2131	6.3
29	W	0410	1.6	0941	6.4	1637	1.5	2210	6.1
30	TH	0447	1.8	1017	6.2	1714	1.6	2248	5.9

DECEMBER

Date	Day	Time	m	Time	m	Time	m	Time	m
1	F	0524	2.0	1054	6.0	1751	1.9	2327	5.7
2	SA	0601	2.3	1132	5.7	1830	2.1		
3	SU	0009	5.4	0642	2.6	1213	5.4	1912	2.4
4	M	0056	5.1	0728	2.8	1302	5.2	2002	2.6
5	TU	0153	4.9	0825	3.0	1403	5.0	◑ 2102	2.8
6	W	0259	4.9	0934	3.1	1512	4.9	2212	2.8
7	TH	0408	4.9	1046	3.0	1620	5.0	2317	2.7
8	F	0508	5.1	1147	2.7	1721	5.2		
9	SA	0012	2.4	0558	5.4	1239	2.5	1814	5.4
10	SU	0100	2.2	0643	5.7	1324	2.2	1901	5.7
11	M	0144	2.0	0724	6.0	1407	1.9	1944	5.9
12	TU	0226	1.8	0804	6.2	1450	1.6	2027	6.1
13	W	0308	1.7	0844	6.3	1533	1.5	● 2108	6.2
14	TH	0350	1.6	0924	6.4	1617	1.4	2151	6.2
15	F	0434	1.6	1006	6.4	1702	1.4	2236	6.2
16	SA	0519	1.7	1052	6.3	1748	1.4	2324	6.0
17	SU	0608	1.9	1140	6.2	1838	1.5		
18	M	0016	5.8	0700	2.0	1233	6.0	1932	1.7
19	TU	0113	5.6	0757	2.2	1332	5.8	◐ 2030	1.9
20	W	0218	5.5	0901	2.4	1439	5.6	2134	2.1
21	TH	0328	5.4	1011	2.4	1550	5.5	2244	2.1
22	F	0435	5.4	1122	2.3	1659	5.5	2350	2.1
23	SA	0537	5.6	1227	2.2	1802	5.6		
24	SU	0051	2.0	0633	5.8	1325	2.0	1900	5.8
25	M	0144	1.9	0723	5.9	1416	1.8	1952	5.9
26	TU	0232	1.8	0808	6.1	1503	1.6	2038	6.0
27	W	0316	1.8	0849	6.2	1545	1.6	○ 2120	6.0
28	TH	0356	1.8	0927	6.2	1624	1.5	2158	6.0
29	F	0434	1.8	1004	6.2	1701	1.6	2235	5.9
30	SA	0510	1.9	1041	6.1	1737	1.7	2312	5.8
31	SU	0546	2.0	1117	5.9	1812	1.8	2348	5.6

Chart Datum: 3·33 metres below IGN Datum
HAT is 7·0 metres above Chart Datum

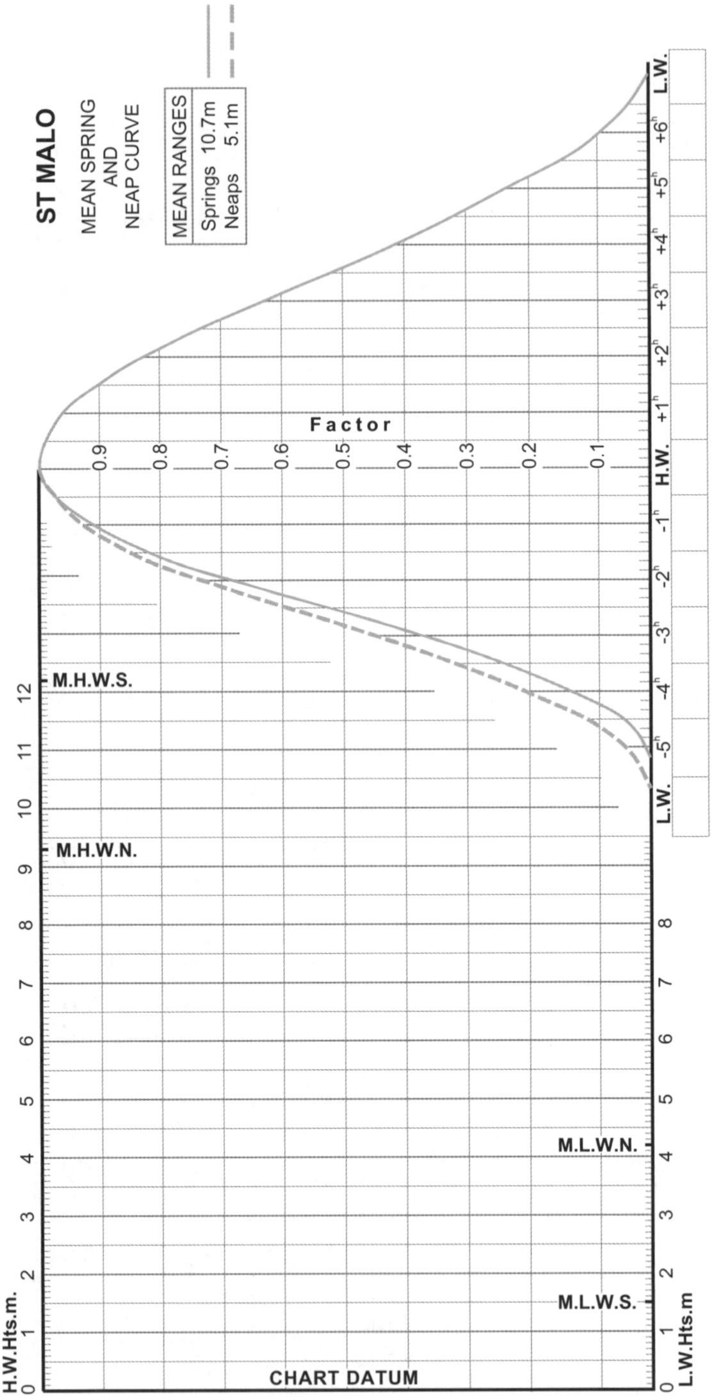
ST MALO
MEAN SPRING AND NEAP CURVE
MEAN RANGES
Springs 10.7m
Neaps 5.1m
Factor
0.9
0.8
0.7
0.6
0.5
0.4
0.3
0.2
0.1
L.W.
-5h
-4h
-3h
-2h
-1h
H.W.
+1h
+2h
+3h
+4h
+5h
+6h
L.W.
H.W.Hts.m.
M.H.W.S.
M.H.W.N.
CHART DATUM
M.L.W.N.
M.L.W.S.
L.W.Hts.m

TIME ZONE -0100
(French Standard Time)
Subtract 1 hour for UT
For French Summer Time add
ONE hour in **non-shaded areas**

FRANCE – ST MALO

LAT 48°38′N LONG 2°02′W

TIMES AND HEIGHTS OF HIGH AND LOW WATERS

Dates in amber are **SPRINGS**
Dates in grey are **NEAPS**

2023

JANUARY

Date	Day	Time	m	Time	m	Time	m	Time	m
1	SU	0202	9.5	0853	4.1	1438	9.6	2124	3.9
2	M	0312	9.5	1002	4.1	1547	9.7	2230	3.8
3	TU	0416	9.8	1106	3.8	1647	9.9	2330	3.6
4	W	0511	10.2	1201	3.4	1739	10.3		
5	TH	0020	3.3	0557	10.6	1249	3.1	1825	10.6
6	F	0104	3.0	0639	10.9	1330	2.8	1906	10.8
7	SA ○	0143	2.8	0716	11.2	1408	2.6	1943	10.9
8	SU	0220	2.7	0751	11.3	1445	2.5	2017	11.0
9	M	0256	2.6	0824	11.3	1519	2.5	2049	11.0
10	TU	0330	2.7	0856	11.3	1553	2.6	2121	10.9
11	W	0402	2.8	0929	11.1	1624	2.8	2154	10.6
12	TH	0434	3.1	1001	10.8	1656	3.1	2227	10.3
13	F	0507	3.4	1037	10.4	1729	3.4	2302	9.9
14	SA	0544	3.7	1114	10.0	1808	3.8	2342	9.6
15	SU ◑	0628	4.1	1201	9.6	1856	4.1		
16	M	0037	9.3	0724	4.3	1305	9.3	1958	4.3
17	TU	0151	9.1	0838	4.4	1427	9.3	2119	4.2
18	W	0312	9.4	1002	4.0	1546	9.7	2240	3.7
19	TH	0426	10.0	1116	3.3	1658	10.3	2349	3.1
20	F	0531	10.8	1222	2.5	1802	11.0		
21	SA ●	0053	2.4	0629	11.6	1324	1.8	1859	11.7
22	SU	0152	1.8	0722	12.2	1423	1.2	1951	12.2
23	M	0247	1.4	0811	12.7	1516	0.9	2040	12.5
24	TU	0337	1.1	0858	12.9	1604	0.7	2125	12.4
25	W	0422	1.2	0942	12.7	1648	1.0	2207	12.1
26	TH	0503	1.6	1024	12.2	1728	1.5	2246	11.5
27	F	0541	2.2	1104	11.5	1804	2.3	2325	10.8
28	SA ◐	0618	3.0	1145	10.6	1841	3.2		
29	SU	0006	10.0	0658	3.8	1232	9.7	1924	3.9
30	M	0058	9.3	0751	4.4	1337	9.0	2022	4.5
31	TU	0213	8.9	0907	4.7	1506	8.8	2142	4.7

FEBRUARY

Date	Day	Time	m	Time	m	Time	m	Time	m
1	W	0343	8.9	1033	4.5	1628	9.0	2301	4.4
2	TH	0453	9.4	1142	4.0	1728	9.6		
3	F	0002	3.8	0545	10.0	1234	3.4	1815	10.1
4	SA	0051	3.3	0627	10.6	1319	2.9	1855	10.6
5	SU ○	0133	2.8	0705	11.0	1358	2.5	1931	11.0
6	M	0210	2.5	0739	11.4	1435	2.3	2004	11.2
7	TU	0245	2.3	0811	11.6	1508	2.1	2035	11.4
8	W	0318	2.1	0842	11.7	1540	2.0	2105	11.4
9	TH	0349	2.1	0913	11.7	1609	2.1	2134	11.3
10	F	0418	2.3	0942	11.5	1637	2.4	2203	11.0
11	SA	0447	2.6	1012	11.1	1705	2.7	2231	10.6
12	SU	0517	3.0	1043	10.6	1736	3.2	2303	10.1
13	M ◑	0553	3.6	1119	10.0	1814	3.8	2344	9.6
14	TU	0640	4.1	1211	9.4	1908	4.3		
15	W	0048	9.1	0749	4.5	1335	8.9	2033	4.6
16	TH	0232	8.9	0930	4.4	1526	9.1	2216	4.3
17	F	0413	9.5	1100	3.6	1654	9.8	2338	3.4
18	SA	0526	10.5	1214	2.7	1759	10.8		
19	SU	0047	2.5	0624	11.5	1319	1.7	1854	11.7
20	M ●	0147	1.6	0714	12.4	1416	0.9	1942	12.4
21	TU	0239	0.9	0801	13.0	1506	0.4	2026	12.8
22	W	0325	0.6	0844	13.2	1549	0.3	2106	12.8
23	TH	0406	0.7	0923	13.1	1628	0.6	2143	12.5
24	F	0441	1.1	1000	12.5	1701	1.3	2217	11.9
25	SA	0512	1.9	1033	11.7	1730	2.2	2248	11.1
26	SU	0540	2.8	1106	10.6	1758	3.2	2319	10.2
27	M ◐	0610	3.8	1142	9.6	1830	4.1	2357	9.2
28	TU	0652	4.6	1235	8.6	1921	4.9		

MARCH

Date	Day	Time	m	Time	m	Time	m	Time	m
1	W	0105	8.5	0809	5.2	1426	8.1	2056	5.3
2	TH	0312	8.3	1006	5.1	1615	8.4	2241	4.9
3	F	0437	8.9	1125	4.4	1716	9.2	2347	4.2
4	SA	0528	9.7	1218	3.6	1758	10.0		
5	SU	0034	3.4	0609	10.4	1301	2.9	1835	10.6
6	M	0115	2.8	0645	11.0	1339	2.4	1909	11.1
7	TU ○	0152	2.3	0718	11.5	1415	2.0	1941	11.5
8	W	0226	1.9	0751	11.9	1448	1.7	2012	11.8
9	TH	0259	1.7	0821	12.0	1518	1.6	2041	11.9
10	F	0329	1.7	0851	12.0	1547	1.7	2110	11.8
11	SA	0358	1.8	0919	11.8	1614	2.0	2137	11.5
12	SU	0426	2.1	0948	11.4	1640	2.4	2204	11.1
13	M	0455	2.7	1018	10.9	1709	3.1	2234	10.5
14	TU	0528	3.3	1053	10.1	1744	3.8	2313	9.7
15	W ◑	0612	4.0	1142	9.3	1837	4.5		
16	TH	0015	9.0	0724	4.6	1315	8.6	2011	4.9
17	F	0221	8.7	0917	4.5	1527	8.8	2209	4.5
18	SA	0409	9.4	1054	3.7	1651	9.8	2333	3.4
19	SU	0517	10.5	1207	2.5	1750	10.9		
20	M	0038	2.3	0611	11.7	1307	1.5	1839	11.9
21	TU ●	0133	1.4	0658	12.5	1359	0.8	1923	12.5
22	W	0221	0.8	0741	13.0	1445	0.4	2003	12.9
23	TH	0304	0.6	0821	13.1	1525	0.4	2040	12.8
24	F	0341	0.7	0857	12.9	1559	0.8	2113	12.5
25	SA	0413	1.2	0931	12.3	1628	1.5	2144	11.9
26	SU	0440	2.0	1001	11.5	1653	2.4	2212	11.1
27	M	0504	2.9	1030	10.5	1717	3.4	2239	10.2
28	TU	0530	3.8	1102	9.5	1745	4.3	2314	9.3
29	W ◐	0606	4.7	1146	8.5	1831	5.2		
30	TH	0008	8.4	0716	5.4	1340	7.8	2008	5.7
31	F	0229	8.0	0930	5.4	1548	8.2	2211	5.3

APRIL

Date	Day	Time	m	Time	m	Time	m	Time	m
1	SA	0405	8.6	1055	4.6	1647	9.0	2317	4.4
2	SU	0457	9.4	1146	3.8	1727	9.8		
3	M	0003	3.5	0537	10.2	1228	3.0	1803	10.6
4	TU	0043	2.8	0613	10.9	1307	2.4	1837	11.2
5	W	0121	2.3	0648	11.5	1343	2.0	1911	11.6
6	TH ○	0157	1.9	0722	11.9	1418	1.7	1943	11.9
7	F	0232	1.6	0754	12.1	1451	1.6	2013	12.0
8	SA	0304	1.5	0825	12.1	1521	1.6	2043	12.0
9	SU	0336	1.7	0856	11.9	1551	1.9	2112	11.7
10	M	0406	2.0	0926	11.5	1619	2.4	2143	11.3
11	TU	0438	2.5	1002	10.9	1651	3.1	2218	10.6
12	W	0515	3.2	1042	10.0	1730	3.9	2303	9.7
13	TH ◑	0605	4.0	1141	9.2	1831	4.6		
14	F	0019	9.0	0724	4.5	1328	8.6	2015	4.9
15	SA	0221	8.9	0914	4.3	1520	9.1	2202	4.3
16	SU	0353	9.7	1042	3.4	1634	10.0	2317	3.3
17	M	0456	10.7	1148	2.4	1727	11.0		
18	TU	0017	2.3	0547	11.6	1244	1.6	1814	11.8
19	W	0109	1.6	0633	12.2	1334	1.2	1855	12.3
20	TH ●	0155	1.2	0714	12.5	1416	1.0	1934	12.5
21	F	0235	1.1	0753	12.5	1453	1.1	2009	12.4
22	SA	0310	1.3	0829	12.3	1525	1.5	2042	12.1
23	SU	0341	1.7	0901	11.8	1553	2.0	2112	11.6
24	M	0408	2.3	0932	11.1	1619	2.7	2139	11.0
25	TU	0434	3.0	1002	10.3	1644	3.5	2208	10.2
26	W	0502	3.8	1035	9.4	1714	4.3	2246	9.4
27	TH ◐	0538	4.6	1119	8.6	1758	5.1	2338	8.6
28	F	0637	5.2	1246	8.0	1917	5.5		
29	SA	0123	8.2	0822	5.3	1442	8.1	2110	5.4
30	SU	0302	8.5	0956	4.8	1553	8.8	2223	4.7

Chart Datum: 6·29 metres below IGN Datum
HAT is 13·6 metres above Chart Datum

TIME ZONE -0100
(French Standard Time)
Subtract 1 hour for UT
For French Summer Time add ONE hour in **non-shaded areas**

FRANCE – ST MALO

LAT 48°38'N LONG 2°02'W

TIMES AND HEIGHTS OF HIGH AND LOW WATERS

Dates in amber are **SPRINGS**
Dates in grey are **NEAPS**

2023

MAY

Date	Day	Time	m	Time	m	Time	m	Time	m
1	M	0403	9.2	1053	4.1	1639	9.5	2313	3.9
2	TU	0450	9.9	1139	3.4	1719	10.3	2357	3.2
3	W	0531	10.6	1222	2.8	1757	10.9		
4	TH	0039	2.6	0610	11.2	1303	2.3	1834	11.4
5	F	0120	2.1	0648	11.6	1343	1.9	○ 1909	11.8
6	SA	0200	1.8	0724	11.8	1420	1.8	1943	12.0
7	SU	0239	1.7	0800	11.9	1456	1.8	2018	12.0
8	M	0316	1.7	0836	11.8	1531	2.1	2054	11.8
9	TU	0353	2.0	0915	11.4	1607	2.5	2133	11.3
10	W	0432	2.5	0956	10.8	1646	3.1	2217	10.7
11	TH	0516	3.1	1047	10.1	1735	3.8	2314	10.0
12	F ◑	0613	3.6	1155	9.4	1842	4.3		
13	SA	0031	9.5	0730	4.0	1323	9.2	2012	4.4
14	SU	0202	9.5	0857	3.8	1451	9.5	2137	3.9
15	M	0321	9.9	1013	3.3	1600	10.1	2246	3.3
16	TU	0424	10.6	1116	2.7	1655	10.8	2345	2.6
17	W	0516	11.2	1212	2.2	1742	11.3		
18	TH	0037	2.2	0603	11.5	1300	2.0	1825	11.6
19	F	0123	2.0	0646	11.7	1343	1.9	● 1904	11.8
20	SA	0203	1.9	0726	11.7	1419	2.0	1940	11.8
21	SU	0239	2.0	0802	11.5	1451	2.2	2014	11.6
22	M	0311	2.3	0837	11.2	1522	2.5	2046	11.3
23	TU	0342	2.6	0910	10.7	1552	3.0	2117	10.8
24	W	0413	3.1	0943	10.2	1623	3.5	2151	10.3
25	TH	0445	3.7	1020	9.6	1657	4.1	2227	9.7
26	F	0521	4.2	1103	9.0	1738	4.6	2316	9.1
27	SA ◐	0608	4.6	1201	8.6	1834	5.0		
28	SU	0023	8.7	0712	4.9	1317	8.5	1948	5.1
29	M	0141	8.7	0829	4.7	1432	8.7	2105	4.8
30	TU	0251	9.0	0939	4.3	1534	9.2	2208	4.2
31	W	0349	9.6	1038	3.8	1625	9.9	2303	3.6

JUNE

Date	Day	Time	m	Time	m	Time	m	Time	m
1	TH	0440	10.2	1130	3.2	1711	10.5	2353	3.0
2	F	0528	10.7	1220	2.8	1754	11.0		
3	SA	0042	2.5	0613	11.1	1307	2.4	1836	11.5
4	SU	0130	2.1	0657	11.5	1353	2.1	○ 1918	11.8
5	M	0216	1.9	0741	11.6	1437	2.1	2001	11.9
6	TU	0302	1.8	0826	11.6	1520	2.1	2045	11.8
7	W	0347	1.9	0913	11.4	1605	2.4	2132	11.6
8	TH	0434	2.2	1002	11.1	1652	2.8	2223	11.1
9	F	0524	2.5	1055	10.6	1744	3.2	2318	10.7
10	SA ◑	0619	2.9	1152	10.1	1843	3.6		
11	SU	0020	10.2	0719	3.3	1257	9.8	1949	3.8
12	M	0128	10.0	0824	3.4	1407	9.7	2059	3.8
13	TU	0238	10.0	0931	3.4	1515	9.9	2206	3.5
14	W	0344	10.2	1035	3.2	1616	10.2	2308	3.3
15	TH	0442	10.4	1134	3.0	1709	10.6		
16	F	0003	3.0	0535	10.7	1225	2.9	1756	10.9
17	SA	0052	2.8	0622	10.8	1310	2.8	1839	11.1
18	SU	0134	2.7	0705	10.9	1349	2.7	● 1918	11.2
19	M	0213	2.6	0744	10.9	1426	2.7	1955	11.2
20	TU	0249	2.6	0821	10.8	1501	2.8	2029	11.1
21	W	0324	2.7	0856	10.6	1535	3.0	2103	10.9
22	TH	0358	3.0	0930	10.4	1609	3.3	2137	10.6
23	F	0431	3.3	1005	10.1	1642	3.6	2213	10.3
24	SA	0505	3.6	1042	9.8	1717	3.9	2251	9.9
25	SU	0541	3.9	1122	9.4	1757	4.2	2336	9.5
26	M ◐	0624	4.2	1211	9.1	1847	4.5		
27	TU	0029	9.3	0716	4.3	1311	9.0	1947	4.6
28	W	0135	9.2	0819	4.4	1419	9.1	2057	4.4
29	TH	0243	9.3	0930	4.2	1525	9.5	2207	4.0
30	F	0348	9.7	1039	3.8	1625	10.0	2311	3.5

JULY

Date	Day	Time	m	Time	m	Time	m	Time	m
1	SA	0448	10.2	1140	3.3	1720	10.6		
2	SU	0010	2.9	0545	10.7	1238	2.8	1813	11.1
3	M	0106	2.4	0639	11.2	1333	2.4	○ 1903	11.6
4	TU	0201	1.9	0731	11.5	1426	2.1	1953	12.0
5	W	0255	1.6	0822	11.8	1518	1.9	2042	12.2
6	TH	0347	1.5	0911	11.9	1607	1.9	2131	12.2
7	F	0436	1.5	0959	11.7	1654	2.0	2218	11.9
8	SA	0522	1.8	1046	11.3	1740	2.4	2305	11.5
9	SU	0608	2.2	1132	10.8	1826	2.9	2354	10.9
10	M ◑	0654	2.8	1221	10.3	1915	3.4		
11	TU	0047	10.3	0744	3.4	1317	9.8	2012	3.9
12	W	0150	9.8	0842	3.8	1424	9.5	2120	4.1
13	TH	0302	9.5	0949	4.0	1537	9.6	2230	4.0
14	F	0413	9.6	1057	3.9	1643	9.9	2334	3.7
15	SA	0515	9.9	1157	3.6	1738	10.3		
16	SU	0029	3.4	0608	10.2	1247	3.3	1824	10.6
17	M	0116	3.1	0653	10.5	1331	3.1	● 1905	10.9
18	TU	0157	2.8	0733	10.7	1410	2.9	1942	11.1
19	W	0235	2.7	0809	10.8	1447	2.8	2016	11.2
20	TH	0311	2.6	0842	10.9	1522	2.7	2049	11.3
21	F	0344	2.6	0913	10.9	1554	2.8	2120	11.2
22	SA	0414	2.7	0944	10.8	1624	2.9	2152	11.0
23	SU	0443	2.9	1015	10.5	1653	3.2	2222	10.6
24	M	0512	3.2	1046	10.2	1725	3.5	2256	10.2
25	TU	0544	3.6	1120	9.8	1802	3.9	◐ 2335	9.8
26	W	0624	4.0	1202	9.4	1849	4.3		
27	TH	0026	9.4	0715	4.3	1304	9.1	1953	4.5
28	F	0139	9.1	0827	4.5	1426	9.1	2118	4.4
29	SA	0305	9.2	0956	4.3	1549	9.5	2240	3.9
30	SU	0423	9.7	1113	3.7	1700	10.2	2349	3.2
31	M	0532	10.4	1220	3.0	1802	11.0		

AUGUST

Date	Day	Time	m	Time	m	Time	m	Time	m
1	TU	0053	2.4	0632	11.1	1323	2.4	○ 1856	11.8
2	W	0154	1.7	0726	11.8	1421	1.8	1947	12.4
3	TH	0250	1.1	0815	12.3	1513	1.3	2035	12.8
4	F	0341	0.8	0901	12.5	1600	1.2	2119	12.9
5	SA	0426	0.8	0944	12.4	1643	1.3	2202	12.6
6	SU	0506	1.2	1024	12.0	1721	1.8	2242	12.0
7	M	0544	1.9	1102	11.3	1758	2.6	2321	11.1
8	TU ◑	0619	2.7	1142	10.5	1836	3.4		
9	W	0005	10.2	0658	3.6	1227	9.8	1923	4.2
10	TH	0101	9.4	0750	4.4	1332	9.1	2032	4.7
11	F	0224	8.8	0905	4.8	1504	8.9	2202	4.7
12	SA	0356	8.9	1032	4.6	1628	9.3	2318	4.2
13	SU	0506	9.4	1141	4.1	1727	9.9		
14	M	0016	3.6	0558	10.0	1234	3.5	1812	10.5
15	TU	0103	3.1	0640	10.5	1318	3.0	1851	11.0
16	W	0143	2.7	0717	10.9	1357	2.7	● 1926	11.4
17	TH	0220	2.4	0750	11.2	1432	2.4	1958	11.6
18	F	0253	2.2	0821	11.4	1504	2.3	2028	11.7
19	SA	0324	2.2	0850	11.4	1533	2.3	2057	11.7
20	SU	0351	2.2	0918	11.3	1601	2.4	2126	11.5
21	M	0417	2.4	0945	11.1	1627	2.6	2153	11.2
22	TU	0442	2.8	1011	10.8	1655	3.1	2221	10.7
23	W	0510	3.2	1038	10.3	1726	3.6	2253	10.1
24	TH	0543	3.8	1113	9.7	1807	4.1	◐ 2336	9.5
25	F	0628	4.4	1205	9.2	1907	4.6		
26	SA	0047	8.9	0740	4.8	1340	8.8	2042	4.8
27	SU	0242	8.8	0930	4.8	1534	9.2	2223	4.2
28	M	0418	9.5	1101	4.0	1654	10.1	2339	3.1
29	TU	0527	10.5	1213	3.0	1754	11.2		
30	W	0045	2.1	0624	11.5	1315	2.0	1846	12.2
31	TH	0144	1.3	0713	12.3	1410	1.3	○ 1933	12.9

Chart Datum: 6·29 metres below IGN Datum
HAT is 13·6 metres above Chart Datum

TIME ZONE -0100
(French Standard Time)
Subtract 1 hour for UT
For French Summer Time add ONE hour in **non-shaded areas**

FRANCE – ST MALO

LAT 48°38′N LONG 2°02′W

TIMES AND HEIGHTS OF HIGH AND LOW WATERS

Dates in amber are **SPRINGS**
Dates in grey are **NEAPS**

2023

SEPTEMBER

Date	Day	Time	m	Time	m	Time	m	Time	m	Phase
1	F	0237	0.6	0759	12.8	1459	0.8	2018	13.3	
2	SA	0324	0.4	0841	13.0	1542	0.7	2059	13.3	
3	SU	0404	0.5	0920	12.8	1620	1.0	2137	12.9	
4	M	0440	1.1	0955	12.2	1654	1.7	2213	12.1	
5	TU	0511	2.0	1029	11.5	1724	2.6	2247	11.1	
6	W	0540	3.0	1100	10.6	1755	3.6	2323	10.0	◑
7	TH	0612	4.0	1139	9.6	1835	4.5			
8	F	0013	8.9	0659	4.9	1240	8.8	1946	5.2	
9	SA	0152	8.3	0826	5.4	1441	8.4	2142	5.2	
10	SU	0349	8.5	1017	5.1	1616	9.0	2306	4.4	
11	M	0455	9.2	1127	4.3	1711	9.8	2359	3.6	
12	TU	0540	10.0	1216	3.5	1752	10.6			
13	W	0042	3.0	0617	10.7	1257	2.9	1828	11.2	
14	TH	0120	2.5	0651	11.2	1333	2.5	1901	11.6	
15	F	0155	2.2	0723	11.6	1407	2.2	1933	11.9	●
16	SA	0227	2.0	0753	11.8	1439	2.0	2002	12.0	
17	SU	0257	1.9	0821	11.8	1508	2.0	2031	12.0	
18	M	0324	2.0	0848	11.8	1535	2.1	2058	11.9	
19	TU	0349	2.2	0914	11.5	1602	2.4	2125	11.5	
20	W	0414	2.6	0939	11.1	1629	2.8	2153	11.0	
21	TH	0440	3.2	1007	10.6	1700	3.5	2224	10.3	
22	F	0513	3.9	1041	9.9	1740	4.1	2307	9.4	◐
23	SA	0559	4.6	1134	9.1	1842	4.7			
24	SU	0025	8.7	0718	5.1	1329	8.6	2030	4.9	
25	M	0244	8.7	0925	4.9	1531	9.2	2217	4.1	
26	TU	0414	9.6	1055	3.9	1644	10.4	2330	2.9	
27	W	0516	10.8	1202	2.7	1739	11.5			
28	TH	0031	1.8	0607	11.8	1259	1.7	1827	12.5	
29	F	0126	1.0	0652	12.6	1350	1.0	1912	13.1	○
30	SA	0215	0.6	0735	13.0	1436	0.7	1954	13.4	

OCTOBER

Date	Day	Time	m	Time	m	Time	m	Time	m	Phase
1	SU	0258	0.5	0814	13.0	1517	0.8	2033	13.2	
2	M	0336	0.8	0850	12.8	1552	1.2	2109	12.7	
3	TU	0408	1.5	0923	12.2	1623	1.9	2142	11.8	
4	W	0436	2.3	0954	11.4	1651	2.8	2214	10.8	
5	TH	0502	3.3	1024	10.5	1719	3.8	2248	9.7	
6	F	0531	4.3	1058	9.5	1756	4.7	2335	8.7	◑
7	SA	0617	5.1	1154	8.6	1905	5.4			
8	SU	0121	8.0	0747	5.7	1410	8.3	2111	5.4	
9	M	0325	8.3	0950	5.3	1547	8.8	2236	4.6	
10	TU	0427	9.1	1057	4.5	1639	9.6	2326	3.8	
11	W	0508	10.0	1143	3.6	1719	10.4			
12	TH	0007	3.1	0543	10.7	1223	3.0	1755	11.1	
13	F	0045	2.5	0617	11.3	1300	2.5	1829	11.6	
14	SA	0121	2.2	0650	11.7	1335	2.1	1902	11.9	●
15	SU	0154	2.0	0721	11.9	1408	2.0	1933	12.1	
16	M	0226	1.9	0750	12.0	1440	1.9	2003	12.1	
17	TU	0256	2.0	0819	11.9	1511	2.0	2032	11.9	
18	W	0324	2.2	0847	11.7	1541	2.3	2102	11.5	
19	TH	0352	2.6	0916	11.3	1611	2.8	2135	11.0	
20	F	0422	3.2	0949	10.7	1647	3.4	2213	10.2	
21	SA	0459	3.9	1031	10.0	1732	4.1	2305	9.4	
22	SU	0552	4.6	1136	9.2	1842	4.6			◐
23	M	0038	8.8	0722	5.1	1335	8.9	2028	4.6	
24	TU	0236	9.0	0917	4.6	1514	9.6	2202	3.8	
25	W	0355	9.9	1038	3.6	1621	10.6	2310	2.7	
26	TH	0453	10.9	1140	2.6	1715	11.6			
27	F	0008	1.9	0541	11.8	1234	1.8	1802	12.3	
28	SA	0100	1.3	0625	12.4	1324	1.3	1846	12.8	○
29	SU	0146	1.0	0706	12.7	1408	1.2	1928	12.8	
30	M	0228	1.1	0745	12.7	1447	1.3	2006	12.6	
31	TU	0303	1.4	0820	12.4	1522	1.7	2042	12.1	

NOVEMBER

Date	Day	Time	m	Time	m	Time	m	Time	m	Phase
1	W	0335	2.0	0854	11.9	1553	2.2	2116	11.4	
2	TH	0404	2.7	0925	11.2	1623	3.0	2149	10.6	
3	F	0432	3.5	0957	10.5	1654	3.8	2225	9.7	
4	SA	0505	4.3	1032	9.6	1732	4.5	2311	8.9	
5	SU	0549	5.0	1125	8.8	1830	5.1			◑
6	M	0032	8.3	0702	5.5	1307	8.4	2004	5.3	
7	TU	0221	8.3	0846	5.4	1445	8.7	2136	4.9	
8	W	0333	8.9	1002	4.8	1547	9.3	2234	4.2	
9	TH	0421	9.6	1054	4.0	1633	10.0	2320	3.5	
10	F	0500	10.3	1137	3.4	1713	10.7			
11	SA	0001	2.9	0537	11.0	1218	2.8	1751	11.2	
12	SU	0041	2.5	0613	11.4	1258	2.4	1828	11.6	
13	M	0119	2.2	0648	11.7	1337	2.1	1903	11.8	●
14	TU	0155	2.1	0721	11.9	1414	2.0	1938	11.8	
15	W	0231	2.1	0754	11.9	1451	2.1	2013	11.8	
16	TH	0305	2.3	0829	11.8	1527	2.3	2050	11.5	
17	F	0340	2.6	0906	11.4	1606	2.6	2130	11.0	
18	SA	0418	3.1	0949	10.9	1649	3.1	2217	10.4	
19	SU	0504	3.7	1041	10.3	1741	3.6	2318	9.7	
20	M	0604	4.3	1150	9.7	1850	4.0			◐
21	TU	0038	9.3	0724	4.5	1317	9.6	2013	4.0	
22	W	0206	9.5	0852	4.2	1440	9.9	2131	3.5	
23	TH	0321	10.0	1006	3.6	1548	10.5	2239	2.9	
24	F	0420	10.7	1109	2.9	1645	11.2	2337	2.4	
25	SA	0511	11.3	1205	2.3	1735	11.6			
26	SU	0030	2.0	0557	11.8	1255	2.0	1821	11.9	
27	M	0116	1.9	0640	12.0	1340	1.9	1904	11.9	○
28	TU	0157	1.9	0720	12.0	1420	1.9	1945	11.8	
29	W	0234	2.1	0757	11.9	1456	2.1	2023	11.5	
30	TH	0308	2.4	0832	11.6	1530	2.5	2059	11.1	

DECEMBER

Date	Day	Time	m	Time	m	Time	m	Time	m	Phase
1	F	0341	2.8	0907	11.2	1604	2.9	2134	10.5	
2	SA	0414	3.4	0941	10.6	1639	3.5	2211	9.9	
3	SU	0449	3.9	1020	10.0	1716	4.1	2252	9.4	
4	M	0528	4.5	1103	9.4	1759	4.5	2344	8.9	
5	TU	0618	4.9	1202	9.0	1855	4.8			◑
6	W	0052	8.6	0722	5.1	1316	8.8	2004	4.9	
7	TH	0207	8.7	0836	4.9	1429	9.0	2115	4.6	
8	F	0313	9.1	0945	4.5	1531	9.4	2217	4.1	
9	SA	0407	9.7	1042	4.0	1624	10.0	2310	3.6	
10	SU	0454	10.3	1133	3.4	1711	10.5	2359	3.1	
11	M	0537	10.9	1221	2.9	1756	11.0			
12	TU	0045	2.7	0618	11.3	1308	2.4	1839	11.3	
13	W	0130	2.4	0659	11.6	1354	2.2	1921	11.6	●
14	TH	0213	2.2	0740	11.8	1439	2.0	2005	11.6	
15	F	0257	2.2	0823	11.9	1524	2.0	2049	11.6	
16	SA	0341	2.4	0908	11.8	1610	2.1	2136	11.3	
17	SU	0426	2.6	0955	11.5	1658	2.4	2225	10.9	
18	M	0515	3.0	1047	11.0	1749	2.8	2318	10.5	
19	TU	0608	3.4	1143	10.6	1843	3.1			◐
20	W	0016	10.1	0708	3.7	1246	10.2	1944	3.4	
21	TH	0122	9.8	0814	3.8	1356	10.0	2050	3.5	
22	F	0234	9.8	0924	3.8	1507	10.1	2158	3.4	
23	SA	0342	10.1	1033	3.5	1613	10.3	2303	3.2	
24	SU	0442	10.5	1136	3.1	1711	10.6			
25	M	0000	2.9	0534	10.9	1231	2.8	1803	10.9	
26	TU	0051	2.7	0622	11.2	1319	2.6	1850	11.1	
27	W	0135	2.6	0705	11.4	1401	2.4	1933	11.2	○
28	TH	0214	2.5	0744	11.5	1440	2.4	2012	11.2	
29	F	0251	2.5	0821	11.4	1517	2.4	2048	11.0	
30	SA	0327	2.7	0856	11.3	1552	2.6	2123	10.8	
31	SU	0401	2.9	0930	11.0	1626	2.9	2156	10.5	

Chart Datum: 6·29 metres below IGN Datum
HAT is 13·6 metres above Chart Datum

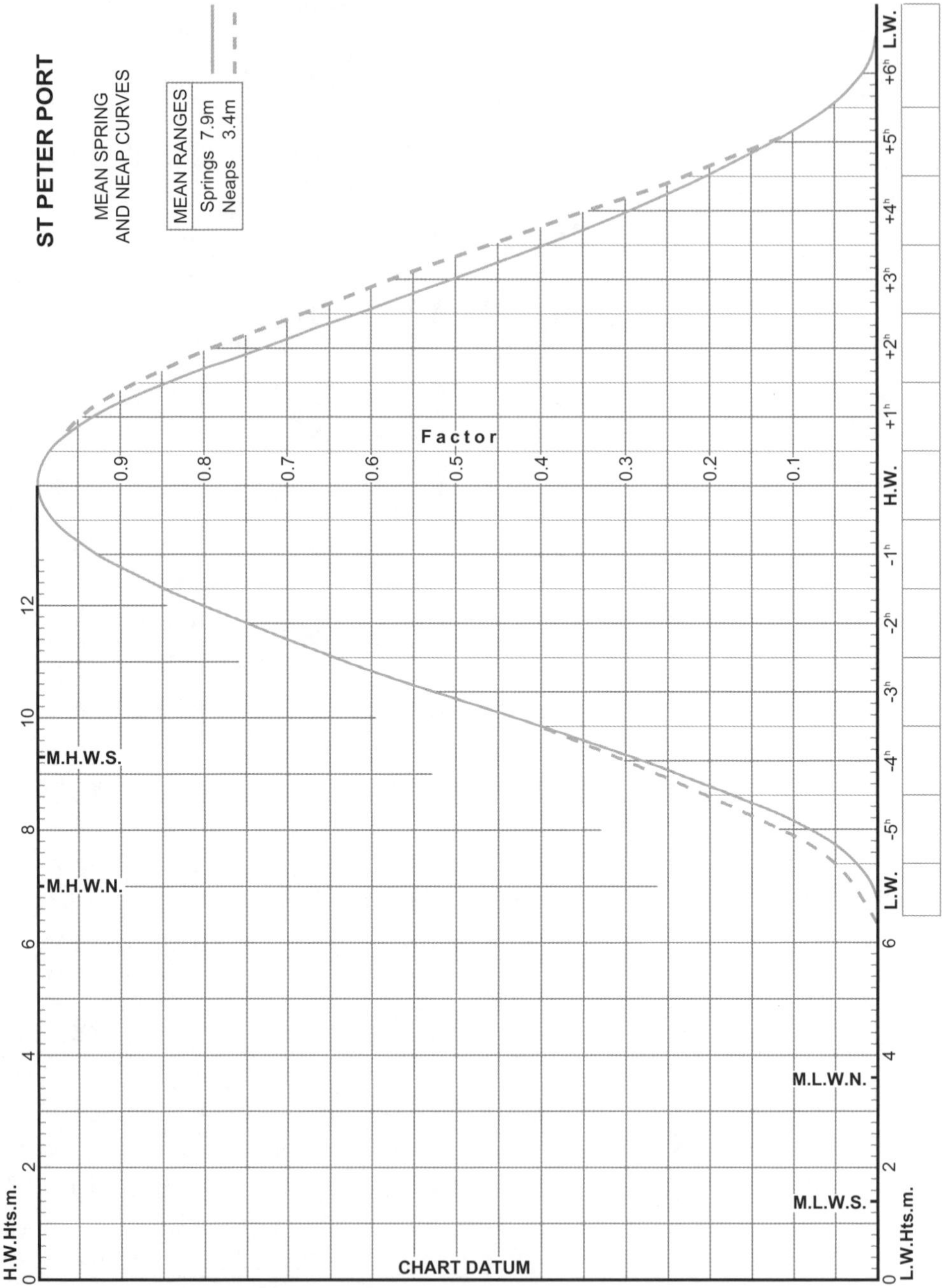
ST PETER PORT
MEAN SPRING AND NEAP CURVES
MEAN RANGES
Springs 7.9m
Neaps 3.4m
Factor
0.9
0.8
0.7
0.6
0.5
0.4
0.3
0.2
0.1
L.W.
-5h
-4h
-3h
-2h
-1h
H.W.
+1h
+2h
+3h
+4h
+5h
+6h
L.W.
H.W.Hts.m.
0
2
4
6
8
10
12
M.H.W.S.
M.H.W.N.
CHART DATUM
L.W.Hts.m.
0
2
4
6
M.L.W.S.
M.L.W.N.

TIME ZONE (UT)
For Summer Time add ONE hour in **non-shaded areas**

CHANNEL ISLES – ST PETER PORT

LAT 49°27′N LONG 2°32′W

TIMES AND HEIGHTS OF HIGH AND LOW WATERS

Dates in amber are **SPRINGS**
Dates in grey are **NEAPS**

2023

JANUARY

Date	Day	Time	m	Time	m	Time	m	Time	m
1	SU	0134	7.3	0804	3.4	1406	7.4	2035	3.2
2	M	0244	7.3	0914	3.4	1514	7.4	2139	3.2
3	TU	0345	7.5	1014	3.2	1612	7.6	2234	3.0
4	W	0436	7.8	1105	2.9	1701	7.8	2322	2.8
5	TH	0520	8.1	1150	2.6	1746	8.0		
6	F	0003	2.6	0601	8.4	1230	2.4	○ 1827	8.2
7	SA	0042	2.4	0640	8.6	1307	2.3	1905	8.3
8	SU	0117	2.3	0716	8.7	1343	2.2	1941	8.4
9	M	0151	2.3	0751	8.6	1416	2.2	2016	8.3
10	TU	0224	2.4	0824	8.5	1449	2.3	2048	8.2
11	W	0256	2.5	0856	8.3	1520	2.5	2120	8.0
12	TH	0328	2.7	0929	8.1	1552	2.7	2152	7.7
13	F	0402	3.0	1004	7.9	1626	2.9	2229	7.5
14	SA	0440	3.2	1045	7.6	1707	3.2	2313	7.3
15	SU ◑	0528	3.4	1135	7.4	1758	3.4		
16	M	0008	7.1	0630	3.6	1238	7.2	1906	3.5
17	TU	0120	7.1	0750	3.6	1355	7.2	2027	3.4
18	W	0242	7.3	0912	3.3	1515	7.4	2145	3.1
19	TH	0355	7.8	1023	2.8	1625	7.9	2253	2.6
20	F	0457	8.3	1126	2.2	1727	8.4	2353	2.1
21	SA ●	0553	8.9	1224	1.6	1823	8.8		
22	SU	0046	1.6	0645	9.4	1316	1.1	1915	9.2
23	M	0136	1.2	0734	9.7	1405	0.7	2003	9.5
24	TU	0223	1.0	0820	9.9	1451	0.6	2047	9.5
25	W	0307	1.0	0904	9.7	1534	0.8	2129	9.2
26	TH	0349	1.3	0947	9.4	1615	1.3	2210	8.8
27	F	0430	1.8	1028	8.8	1656	1.9	2250	8.2
28	SA	0511	2.4	1112	8.1	1738	2.6	◐ 2334	7.6
29	SU	0557	3.1	1201	7.4	1826	3.2		
30	M	0026	7.1	0655	3.6	1304	6.9	1928	3.7
31	TU	0141	6.7	0816	3.9	1432	6.7	2049	3.9

FEBRUARY

Date	Day	Time	m	Time	m	Time	m	Time	m
1	W	0310	6.8	0945	3.8	1550	6.8	2208	3.7
2	TH	0416	7.2	1049	3.4	1648	7.2	2305	3.3
3	F	0505	7.6	1137	2.9	1734	7.6	2350	2.9
4	SA	0548	8.1	1219	2.5	1814	8.0		
5	SU	0030	2.5	0627	8.4	1256	2.2	○ 1853	8.3
6	M	0106	2.2	0704	8.7	1331	1.9	1928	8.5
7	TU	0140	2.0	0738	8.8	1403	1.8	2001	8.6
8	W	0211	1.9	0810	8.8	1434	1.8	2032	8.6
9	TH	0241	1.9	0840	8.7	1502	1.9	2100	8.4
10	F	0310	2.1	0909	8.6	1529	2.1	2127	8.2
11	SA	0339	2.3	0939	8.3	1558	2.4	2158	8.0
12	SU	0410	2.6	1013	8.0	1631	2.7	2233	7.7
13	M	0449	3.0	1055	7.6	1713	3.1	◑ 2320	7.3
14	TU	0541	3.4	1152	7.2	1812	3.5		
15	W	0027	7.0	0659	3.6	1313	6.9	1942	3.7
16	TH	0204	7.0	0844	3.5	1455	7.0	2126	3.5
17	F	0339	7.4	1013	2.9	1619	7.5	2246	2.8
18	SA	0449	8.1	1120	2.2	1723	8.2	2347	2.1
19	SU	0545	8.9	1216	1.4	1816	8.9		
20	M	0038	1.4	0636	9.5	1305	0.7	● 1904	9.4
21	TU	0125	0.8	0722	10.0	1351	0.3	1948	9.8
22	W	0209	0.5	0804	10.2	1432	0.2	2028	9.8
23	TH	0248	0.5	0844	10.0	1511	0.5	2105	9.6
24	F	0325	0.9	0921	9.6	1546	1.0	2139	9.1
25	SA	0359	1.4	0956	8.9	1619	1.7	2211	8.4
26	SU	0432	2.2	1030	8.1	1651	2.5	2244	7.7
27	M	0506	3.0	1107	7.3	1728	3.3	◐ 2322	7.0
28	TU	0553	3.7	1158	6.6	1821	4.0		

MARCH

Date	Day	Time	m	Time	m	Time	m	Time	m
1	W	0022	6.5	0711	4.2	1338	6.2	1950	4.3
2	TH	0227	6.3	0915	4.2	1533	6.4	2144	4.1
3	F	0356	6.8	1033	3.6	1632	6.9	2249	3.5
4	SA	0448	7.3	1120	3.0	1716	7.5	2333	2.9
5	SU	0529	7.9	1159	2.5	1754	8.0		
6	M	0011	2.4	0607	8.4	1235	2.0	1831	8.4
7	TU	0046	1.9	0643	8.8	1309	1.7	○ 1906	8.7
8	W	0119	1.6	0717	9.0	1340	1.5	1938	8.9
9	TH	0150	1.5	0748	9.1	1410	1.4	2007	8.9
10	F	0220	1.5	0817	9.1	1437	1.5	2035	8.8
11	SA	0248	1.6	0846	8.9	1504	1.7	2101	8.6
12	SU	0315	1.9	0915	8.6	1531	2.1	2130	8.3
13	M	0345	2.2	0948	8.2	1603	2.5	2205	7.9
14	TU	0421	2.7	1028	7.7	1643	3.0	2249	7.4
15	W	0512	3.2	1125	7.1	1742	3.6	◑ 2357	6.9
16	TH	0634	3.7	1254	6.7	1921	3.9		
17	F	0146	6.8	0836	3.5	1453	6.9	2122	3.6
18	SA	0332	7.3	1007	2.8	1615	7.6	2238	2.8
19	SU	0438	8.1	1109	2.0	1712	8.3	2333	1.9
20	M	0531	8.9	1200	1.2	1800	9.0		
21	TU	0021	1.2	0618	9.6	1245	0.6	● 1844	9.6
22	W	0105	0.6	0701	10.0	1327	0.3	1924	9.8
23	TH	0146	0.4	0741	10.1	1406	0.3	2002	9.9
24	F	0223	0.5	0819	9.9	1442	0.5	2036	9.6
25	SA	0257	0.8	0853	9.5	1514	1.1	2107	9.1
26	SU	0328	1.4	0924	8.8	1543	1.8	2135	8.5
27	M	0357	2.2	0955	8.0	1611	2.6	2204	7.8
28	TU	0426	3.0	1027	7.2	1640	3.4	2237	7.1
29	W	0505	3.7	1112	6.5	1727	4.1	◐ 2328	6.5
30	TH	0622	4.2	1242	6.0	1901	4.5		
31	F	0124	6.2	0823	4.3	1501	6.2	2102	4.3

APRIL

Date	Day	Time	m	Time	m	Time	m	Time	m
1	SA	0321	6.6	0959	3.7	1602	6.8	2216	3.7
2	SU	0416	7.2	1047	3.1	1645	7.4	2301	3.0
3	M	0458	7.8	1126	2.5	1723	8.0	2339	2.4
4	TU	0536	8.3	1202	2.0	1800	8.5		
5	W	0015	1.9	0613	8.7	1236	1.6	1835	8.8
6	TH	0049	1.5	0647	9.0	1309	1.4	○ 1908	9.0
7	F	0122	1.3	0720	9.2	1340	1.3	1938	9.1
8	SA	0154	1.3	0751	9.2	1410	1.3	2008	9.0
9	SU	0224	1.4	0822	9.0	1439	1.6	2038	8.9
10	M	0255	1.7	0855	8.7	1510	2.0	2110	8.5
11	TU	0328	2.1	0931	8.2	1545	2.5	2148	8.1
12	W	0408	2.6	1016	7.6	1629	3.1	2238	7.5
13	TH	0505	3.2	1119	7.0	1735	3.6	◑ 2352	7.0
14	F	0636	3.5	1256	6.7	1922	3.8		
15	SA	0140	7.0	0830	3.3	1444	7.0	2110	3.4
16	SU	0314	7.5	0949	2.6	1556	7.7	2217	2.6
17	M	0416	8.2	1045	1.8	1648	8.4	2309	1.8
18	TU	0506	8.9	1134	1.2	1734	9.0	2356	1.3
19	W	0552	9.4	1218	0.8	1816	9.4		
20	TH	0039	0.9	0635	9.7	1259	0.6	● 1856	9.6
21	F	0119	0.7	0715	9.7	1337	0.7	1933	9.6
22	SA	0155	0.8	0752	9.5	1412	1.0	2006	9.3
23	SU	0229	1.2	0826	9.1	1443	1.5	2037	8.9
24	M	0300	1.7	0857	8.5	1512	2.1	2105	8.4
25	TU	0329	2.3	0928	7.9	1539	2.8	2135	7.8
26	W	0359	3.0	1002	7.2	1610	3.4	2210	7.2
27	TH	0438	3.6	1047	6.6	1655	4.0	◐ 2300	6.7
28	F	0548	4.0	1204	6.2	1819	4.4		
29	SA	0027	6.4	0726	4.1	1355	6.3	1958	4.3
30	SU	0215	6.5	0855	3.8	1510	6.7	2118	3.8

Chart Datum: 5·06 metres below Ordnance Datum (Local)
HAT is 10·3 metres above Chart Datum

TIME ZONE (UT)
For Summer Time add ONE hour in **non-shaded areas**

CHANNEL ISLES – ST PETER PORT

LAT 49°27'N LONG 2°31'W

TIMES AND HEIGHTS OF HIGH AND LOW WATERS

Dates in amber are **SPRINGS**
Dates in grey are **NEAPS**

2023

MAY

Date	Day	Time	m	Date	Day	Time	m
1	M	0323 0954 1559 2211	7.0 3.2 7.3 3.2	16	TU	0344 1014 1616 2239	8.2 2.0 8.3 2.1
2	TU	0412 1039 1641 2255	7.6 2.7 7.8 2.6	17	W	0436 1103 1703 2327	8.6 1.6 8.7 1.7
3	W	0454 1119 1720 2335	8.1 2.2 8.3 2.1	18	TH	0524 1148 1746	8.9 1.4 9.0
4	TH	0534 1157 1757	8.5 1.8 8.7	19	F ●	0010 0608 1230 1827	1.4 9.0 1.3 9.1
5	F ○	0014 0613 1234 1834	1.7 8.8 1.5 9.0	20	SA	0051 0649 1309 1905	1.4 9.0 1.4 9.1
6	SA	0051 0650 1310 1909	1.4 9.0 1.4 9.1	21	SU	0129 0727 1345 1940	1.4 8.9 1.6 8.9
7	SU	0128 0726 1345 1944	1.3 9.1 1.4 9.1	22	M	0204 0803 1418 2012	1.7 8.6 2.0 8.7
8	M	0204 0804 1421 2020	1.4 9.0 1.6 9.0	23	TU	0237 0837 1448 2044	2.0 8.2 2.4 8.3
9	TU	0241 0843 1458 2059	1.6 8.7 2.0 8.6	24	W	0309 0910 1519 2117	2.5 7.8 2.9 7.9
10	W	0322 0926 1540 2145	2.0 8.2 2.5 8.2	25	TH	0343 0947 1554 2154	2.9 7.3 3.3 7.4
11	TH	0410 1018 1631 2241	2.4 7.7 3.0 7.7	26	F	0423 1031 1637 2241	3.3 6.9 3.7 7.0
12	F ◑	0514 1125 1742 2355	2.9 7.2 3.4 7.4	27	SA ◐	0518 1129 1739 2343	3.7 6.6 4.0 6.8
13	SA	0639 1250 1916	3.1 7.1 3.5	28	SU	0630 1243 1856	3.8 6.6 4.0
14	SU	0122 0807 1415 2042	7.4 2.9 7.3 3.1	29	M	0059 0743 1356 2009	6.7 3.7 6.8 3.8
15	M	0242 0917 1522 2146	7.7 2.5 7.8 2.6	30	TU	0212 0847 1457 2111	7.0 3.4 7.1 3.4
				31	W	0312 0942 1548 2204	7.3 3.0 7.6 2.9

JUNE

Date	Day	Time	m	Date	Day	Time	m
1	TH	0404 1031 1635 2253	7.8 2.5 8.0 2.4	16	F	0457 1120 1719 2346	8.2 2.2 8.4 2.1
2	F	0452 1117 1718 2339	8.2 2.2 8.4 2.0	17	SA	0545 1205 1802	8.3 2.1 8.5
3	SA	0538 1201 1801	8.5 1.8 8.8	18	SU ●	0029 0629 1246 1843	2.0 8.4 2.1 8.6
4	SU ○	0023 0623 1245 1844	1.6 8.8 1.6 9.0	19	M	0109 0710 1324 1921	2.0 8.4 2.1 8.6
5	M	0108 0708 1328 1927	1.4 8.9 1.6 9.1	20	TU	0147 0748 1400 1956	2.1 8.3 2.3 8.5
6	TU	0152 0753 1411 2011	1.4 8.9 1.6 9.1	21	W	0222 0824 1433 2031	2.2 8.1 2.5 8.3
7	W	0237 0839 1456 2057	1.4 8.7 1.9 8.9	22	TH	0256 0859 1506 2105	2.4 7.9 2.7 8.0
8	TH	0325 0928 1544 2147	1.7 8.4 2.2 8.6	23	F	0330 0934 1540 2140	2.7 7.6 3.0 7.8
9	F	0417 1021 1637 2242	2.0 8.1 2.5 8.2	24	SA	0406 1011 1618 2219	2.9 7.4 3.3 7.5
10	SA ◑	0516 1120 1739 2344	2.3 7.8 2.9 7.9	25	SU	0446 1053 1701 2304	3.2 7.1 3.5 7.2
11	SU	0622 1226 1849	2.6 7.6 3.0	26	M ◐	0534 1142 1755 2357	3.4 7.0 3.6 7.1
12	M	0052 0731 1335 2002	7.7 2.7 7.5 3.0	27	TU	0632 1241 1859	3.5 6.9 3.7
13	TU	0202 0838 1441 2109	7.7 2.6 7.7 2.8	28	W	0100 0737 1346 2008	7.1 3.4 7.0 3.5
14	W	0308 0938 1540 2207	7.8 2.5 7.9 2.6	29	TH	0208 0843 1451 2114	7.2 3.3 7.3 3.2
15	TH	0406 1032 1632 2259	8.0 2.3 8.2 2.3	30	F	0314 0945 1551 2214	7.5 3.0 7.7 2.7

JULY

Date	Day	Time	m	Date	Day	Time	m
1	SA	0415 1042 1645 2310	7.8 2.6 8.1 2.3	16	SU	0530 1148 1746	7.8 2.7 8.1
2	SU	0511 1137 1738	8.2 2.2 8.6	17	M ●	0016 0616 1231 1828	2.5 8.0 2.5 8.4
3	M ○	0004 0606 1228 1829	1.8 8.6 1.9 9.0	18	TU	0057 0657 1310 1907	2.3 8.2 2.3 8.5
4	TU	0056 0658 1319 1918	1.5 8.8 1.6 9.2	19	W	0135 0735 1347 1943	2.1 8.3 2.2 8.6
5	W	0147 0748 1408 2006	1.2 9.0 1.4 9.4	20	TH	0210 0810 1420 2017	2.1 8.3 2.2 8.5
6	TH	0236 0837 1455 2054	1.1 9.1 1.4 9.4	21	F	0242 0843 1451 2049	2.1 8.2 2.3 8.4
7	F	0324 0924 1542 2141	1.1 8.9 1.6 9.2	22	SA	0312 0914 1522 2120	2.3 8.1 2.5 8.2
8	SA	0412 1011 1629 2229	1.4 8.7 1.9 8.8	23	SU	0342 0944 1552 2151	2.5 7.9 2.7 8.0
9	SU	0500 1100 1719 2319	1.8 8.3 2.3 8.3	24	M	0412 1016 1625 2226	2.8 7.6 3.0 7.7
10	M ◑	0551 1152 1813	2.2 7.9 2.7	25	TU ◐	0446 1053 1704 2308	3.0 7.4 3.3 7.4
11	TU	0015 0648 1249 1915	7.9 2.7 7.5 3.1	26	W	0530 1139 1755	3.3 7.2 3.5
12	W	0119 0751 1356 2026	7.5 3.0 7.3 3.3	27	TH	0001 0628 1240 1905	7.2 3.5 7.0 3.6
13	TH	0231 0859 1506 2137	7.3 3.2 7.3 3.2	28	F	0111 0745 1358 2029	7.1 3.6 7.1 3.5
14	F	0341 1004 1607 2239	7.3 3.1 7.5 3.0	29	SA	0234 0908 1517 2147	7.1 3.4 7.4 3.1
15	SA	0440 1100 1700 2330	7.5 3.0 7.8 2.7	30	SU	0352 1020 1626 2255	7.5 3.0 7.9 2.5
				31	M	0459 1124 1725 2355	8.0 2.4 8.5 1.9

AUGUST

Date	Day	Time	m	Date	Day	Time	m
1	TU ○	0557 1221 1819	8.5 1.9 9.1	16	W ●	0043 0640 1255 1850	2.2 8.3 2.2 8.7
2	W	0049 0651 1312 1910	1.3 9.0 1.4 9.5	17	TH	0118 0715 1329 1925	2.0 8.5 2.0 8.8
3	TH	0140 0740 1400 1957	0.8 9.4 1.0 9.8	18	F	0151 0749 1401 1957	1.8 8.6 1.9 8.9
4	F	0226 0825 1445 2041	0.6 9.5 0.9 9.9	19	SA	0220 0819 1430 2027	1.8 8.6 1.9 8.8
5	SA	0310 0908 1528 2124	0.6 9.5 1.0 9.7	20	SU	0247 0847 1457 2054	1.9 8.5 2.1 8.6
6	SU	0352 0949 1608 2205	0.9 9.2 1.4 9.2	21	M	0313 0913 1524 2121	2.1 8.3 2.3 8.4
7	M	0432 1029 1648 2247	1.5 8.6 2.0 8.5	22	TU	0338 0940 1551 2151	2.4 8.0 2.7 8.0
8	TU ◑	0514 1111 1731 2332	2.2 8.0 2.7 7.8	23	W	0407 1011 1624 2227	2.8 7.7 3.0 7.7
9	W	0600 1200 1824	2.9 7.4 3.4	24	TH ◐	0444 1052 1709 2317	3.2 7.4 3.4 7.2
10	TH	0030 0659 1306 1938	7.1 3.6 6.9 3.8	25	F	0537 1151 1816	3.6 7.0 3.7
11	F	0156 0819 1436 2115	6.7 3.9 6.8 3.9	26	SA	0030 0700 1320 2000	6.9 3.9 6.9 3.8
12	SA	0328 0946 1553 2230	6.7 3.8 7.0 3.5	27	SU	0213 0849 1502 2137	6.9 3.7 7.2 3.3
13	SU	0432 1049 1648 2322	7.1 3.4 7.5 3.1	28	M	0347 1013 1618 2248	7.3 3.1 7.9 2.5
14	M	0520 1137 1733	7.5 3.0 8.0	29	TU	0454 1117 1716 2346	8.0 2.4 8.7 1.7
15	TU	0005 0602 1218 1813	2.6 8.0 2.6 8.4	30	W	0548 1211 1808	8.8 1.6 9.4
				31	TH ○	0037 0638 1259 1855	1.0 9.4 1.0 9.9

Chart Datum: 5·06 metres below Ordnance Datum (Local)
HAT is 10·3 metres above Chart Datum

TIME ZONE (UT)
For Summer Time add ONE hour in **non-shaded areas**

CHANNEL ISLES – ST PETER PORT

LAT 49°27′N LONG 2°31′W

TIMES AND HEIGHTS OF HIGH AND LOW WATERS

Dates in amber are **SPRINGS**
Dates in grey are **NEAPS**

2023

SEPTEMBER

Date	Day	Time	m	Time	m	Time	m	Time	m
1	F	0123	0.5	0722	9.8	1344	0.6	1939	10.2
2	SA	0207	0.3	0804	9.9	1425	0.5	2020	10.2
3	SU	0247	0.4	0843	9.8	1504	0.7	2059	9.9
4	M	0324	0.8	0919	9.4	1540	1.3	2136	9.2
5	TU	0359	1.5	0954	8.7	1614	2.0	2211	8.4
6	W	0433	2.4	1028	8.0	1650	2.8	◑ 2248	7.6
7	TH	0511	3.3	1108	7.2	1735	3.6	2337	6.8
8	F	0606	4.0	1209	6.6	1851	4.2		
9	SA	0121	6.2	0740	4.4	1412	6.4	2104	4.3
10	SU	0320	6.4	0936	4.2	1540	6.8	2221	3.7
11	M	0420	7.0	1036	3.6	1632	7.4	2306	3.1
12	TU	0502	7.6	1119	3.0	1713	8.0	2344	2.6
13	W	0539	8.1	1157	2.5	1750	8.5		
14	TH	0019	2.1	0614	8.5	1231	2.1	1826	8.8
15	F	0052	1.8	0648	8.8	1304	1.8	● 1859	9.0
16	SA	0123	1.6	0720	8.9	1334	1.7	1930	9.1
17	SU	0151	1.6	0750	8.9	1403	1.7	1959	9.1
18	M	0218	1.7	0817	8.8	1430	1.8	2026	8.9
19	TU	0243	1.9	0842	8.6	1456	2.1	2053	8.6
20	W	0308	2.3	0909	8.3	1523	2.5	2123	8.2
21	TH	0337	2.7	0939	7.9	1556	2.9	2158	7.8
22	F	0413	3.2	1020	7.5	1640	3.4	◐ 2249	7.2
23	SA	0506	3.8	1123	7.0	1752	3.9		
24	SU	0010	6.7	0639	4.1	1304	6.8	1953	3.9
25	M	0212	6.8	0846	3.9	1456	7.2	2132	3.2
26	TU	0343	7.5	1006	3.1	1607	8.1	2237	2.3
27	W	0442	8.3	1103	2.2	1700	8.9	2329	1.5
28	TH	0530	9.0	1152	1.5	1748	9.6		
29	F	0016	0.9	0616	9.6	1237	0.9	○ 1833	10.0
30	SA	0059	0.5	0657	9.9	1320	0.6	1915	10.2

OCTOBER

Date	Day	Time	m	Time	m	Time	m	Time	m
1	SU	0140	0.4	0737	10.0	1400	0.6	1955	10.1
2	M	0218	0.6	0814	9.8	1437	0.9	2031	9.7
3	TU	0253	1.1	0848	9.3	1511	1.4	2105	9.1
4	W	0325	1.9	0919	8.7	1543	2.2	2138	8.3
5	TH	0356	2.7	0950	8.0	1615	3.0	2212	7.4
6	F	0429	3.5	1026	7.2	1657	3.8	◑ 2257	6.6
7	SA	0518	4.3	1121	6.6	1813	4.4		
8	SU	0037	6.1	0659	4.7	1333	6.3	2029	4.4
9	M	0254	6.4	0907	4.4	1510	6.7	2150	3.9
10	TU	0351	6.9	1007	3.8	1601	7.3	2234	3.2
11	W	0431	7.6	1048	3.1	1641	7.9	2311	2.7
12	TH	0507	8.1	1124	2.6	1718	8.4	2345	2.2
13	F	0541	8.6	1158	2.1	1753	8.8		
14	SA	0018	1.8	0615	8.9	1231	1.8	● 1828	9.0
15	SU	0049	1.6	0648	9.1	1303	1.6	1900	9.2
16	M	0119	1.6	0718	9.1	1334	1.6	1930	9.1
17	TU	0148	1.7	0746	9.0	1404	1.7	2000	9.0
18	W	0216	1.9	0815	8.8	1433	2.0	2031	8.7
19	TH	0245	2.3	0845	8.5	1504	2.4	2104	8.3
20	F	0317	2.7	0921	8.1	1542	2.8	2145	7.8
21	SA	0358	3.3	1008	7.6	1632	3.4	2242	7.2
22	SU	0458	3.8	1117	7.1	1752	3.8	◐	
23	M	0009	6.8	0640	4.1	1259	7.0	1948	3.6
24	TU	0204	7.0	0834	3.7	1438	7.5	2114	3.0
25	W	0323	7.7	0945	2.9	1544	8.2	2214	2.2
26	TH	0418	8.4	1039	2.2	1636	8.9	2304	1.6
27	F	0505	9.1	1127	1.5	1723	9.4	2350	1.1
28	SA	0548	9.5	1212	1.1	1807	9.8	○	
29	SU	0032	0.9	0630	9.8	1254	0.9	1850	9.8
30	M	0113	0.9	0709	9.8	1334	1.0	1929	9.7
31	TU	0150	1.1	0745	9.6	1411	1.3	2006	9.3

NOVEMBER

Date	Day	Time	m	Time	m	Time	m	Time	m
1	W	0225	1.6	0819	9.1	1445	1.8	2040	8.7
2	TH	0257	2.2	0851	8.6	1518	2.4	2113	8.1
3	F	0327	2.9	0924	8.0	1551	3.1	2149	7.4
4	SA	0400	3.6	1001	7.4	1633	3.7	2234	6.8
5	SU	0447	4.2	1053	6.8	1740	4.2	◑ 2351	6.3
6	M	0611	4.6	1226	6.5	1915	4.3		
7	TU	0147	6.4	0755	4.5	1408	6.7	2046	4.0
8	W	0259	6.8	0911	4.0	1510	7.1	2142	3.5
9	TH	0346	7.4	1000	3.4	1556	7.6	2225	3.0
10	F	0425	7.9	1041	2.9	1637	8.1	2303	2.5
11	SA	0502	8.3	1119	2.4	1715	8.5	2339	2.1
12	SU	0538	8.7	1156	2.1	1753	8.8		
13	M	0014	1.9	0614	9.0	1232	1.8	● 1829	9.0
14	TU	0049	1.8	0648	9.1	1308	1.7	1905	9.0
15	W	0123	1.8	0722	9.1	1343	1.7	1941	8.9
16	TH	0157	1.9	0757	9.0	1420	1.9	2018	8.7
17	F	0233	2.2	0834	8.7	1459	2.2	2059	8.3
18	SA	0313	2.6	0918	8.3	1544	2.6	2147	7.9
19	SU	0400	3.1	1011	7.9	1640	3.0	2247	7.4
20	M	0504	3.5	1119	7.5	1756	3.3	◐	
21	TU	0005	7.2	0632	3.7	1242	7.5	1923	3.2
22	W	0133	7.3	0803	3.4	1404	7.7	2040	2.9
23	TH	0248	7.7	0913	2.9	1511	8.1	2142	2.4
24	F	0346	8.3	1010	2.4	1607	8.6	2234	2.0
25	SA	0436	8.7	1101	2.0	1657	8.9	2322	1.7
26	SU	0521	9.1	1147	1.7	1743	9.1		
27	M	0006	1.6	0604	9.2	1231	1.5	○ 1827	9.2
28	TU	0048	1.6	0645	9.3	1312	1.6	1909	9.0
29	W	0127	1.7	0723	9.2	1351	1.8	1948	8.8
30	TH	0203	2.0	0759	8.9	1427	2.1	2024	8.4

DECEMBER

Date	Day	Time	m	Time	m	Time	m	Time	m
1	F	0237	2.4	0833	8.5	1502	2.5	2059	8.0
2	SA	0310	2.9	0908	8.1	1538	2.9	2136	7.5
3	SU	0345	3.4	0946	7.6	1617	3.4	2218	7.1
4	M	0426	3.8	1031	7.2	1706	3.7	2310	6.8
5	TU	0523	4.1	1130	6.9	1809	3.9	◑	
6	W	0019	6.6	0636	4.2	1242	6.8	1919	3.9
7	TH	0135	6.7	0750	4.1	1355	6.9	2026	3.7
8	F	0240	7.0	0855	3.7	1456	7.2	2124	3.4
9	SA	0333	7.5	0949	3.3	1548	7.6	2213	3.0
10	SU	0419	7.9	1037	2.8	1635	8.0	2259	2.6
11	M	0502	8.3	1122	2.4	1720	8.4	2342	2.3
12	TU	0543	8.7	1206	2.1	1803	8.6	●	
13	W	0024	2.0	0624	8.9	1249	1.8	1847	8.8
14	TH	0106	1.9	0706	9.1	1332	1.7	1931	8.9
15	F	0149	1.9	0749	9.1	1416	1.7	2015	8.8
16	SA	0232	2.0	0833	9.0	1502	1.8	2101	8.6
17	SU	0317	2.2	0920	8.8	1550	2.0	2150	8.3
18	M	0406	2.5	1011	8.5	1642	2.3	2243	8.0
19	TU	0501	2.8	1108	8.2	1740	2.6	◐ 2343	7.7
20	W	0606	3.1	1212	7.9	1845	2.8		
21	TH	0050	7.6	0718	3.2	1322	7.7	1955	2.9
22	F	0203	7.6	0832	3.1	1433	7.8	2103	2.8
23	SA	0310	7.8	0939	2.9	1537	7.9	2205	2.7
24	SU	0408	8.1	1037	2.6	1635	8.1	2259	2.5
25	M	0459	8.4	1129	2.4	1726	8.3	2348	2.3
26	TU	0546	8.6	1216	2.1	1813	8.4		
27	W	0032	2.2	0629	8.8	1259	2.0	○ 1857	8.5
28	TH	0113	2.2	0709	8.8	1340	2.0	1937	8.5
29	F	0151	2.2	0747	8.8	1417	2.1	2014	8.4
30	SA	0225	2.3	0823	8.6	1452	2.3	2049	8.2
31	SU	0258	2.6	0857	8.4	1525	2.5	2122	7.9

Chart Datum: 5·06 metres below Ordnance Datum (Local)
HAT is 10·3 metres above Chart Datum

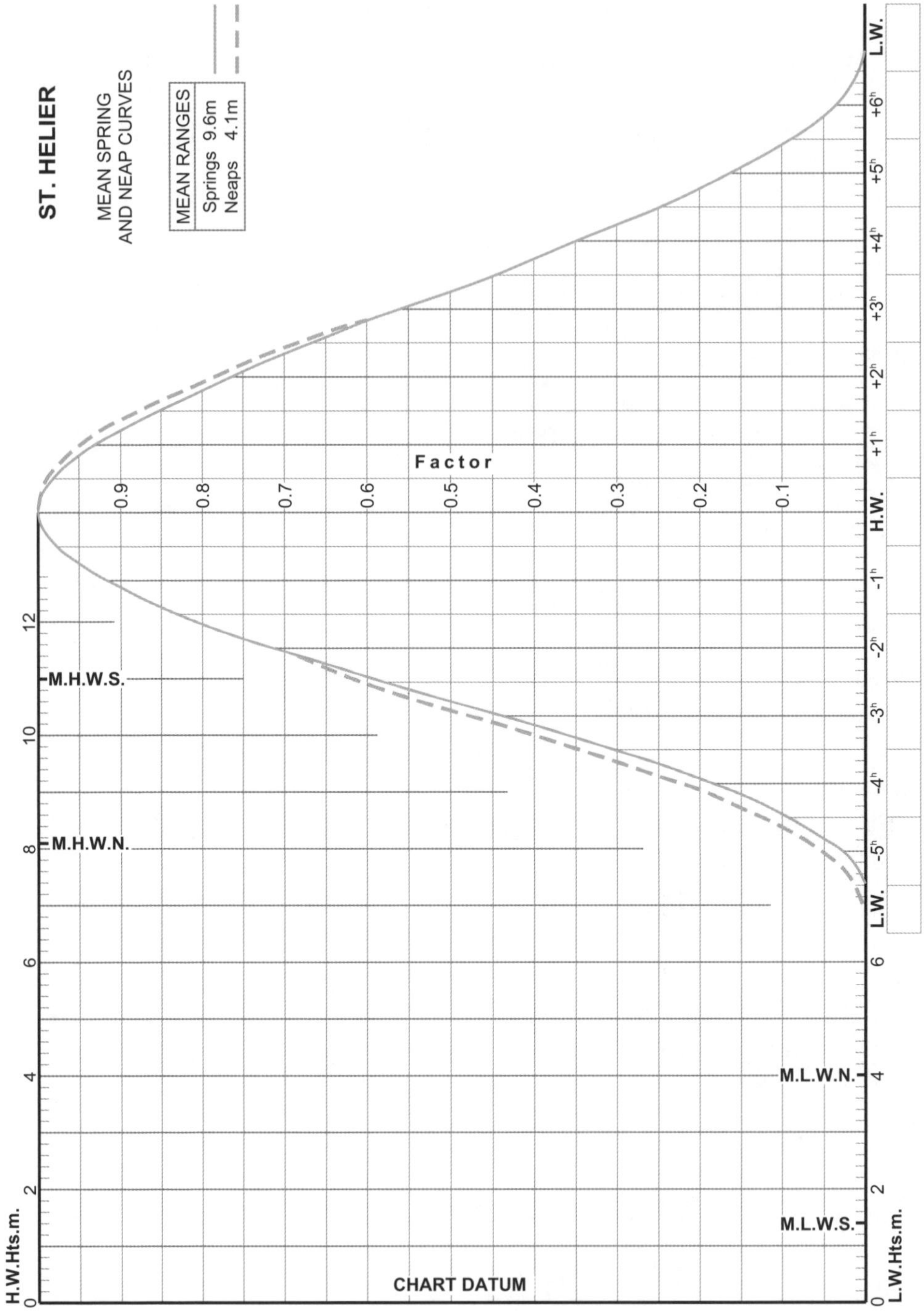
ST. HELIER
MEAN SPRING
AND NEAP CURVES
MEAN RANGES
Springs 9.6m
Neaps 4.1m
Factor
0.9
0.8
0.7
0.6
0.5
0.4
0.3
0.2
0.1
L.W.
-5h
-4h
-3h
-2h
-1h
H.W.
+1h
+2h
+3h
+4h
+5h
+6h
L.W.
H.W.Hts.m.
0
2
4
6
8
10
12
M.H.W.S.
M.H.W.N.
CHART DATUM
L.W.Hts.m.
M.L.W.S.
M.L.W.N.

TIME ZONE (UT)
For Summer Time add ONE hour in **non-shaded areas**

CHANNEL ISLES – ST HELIER

LAT 49°11′N LONG 2°07′W

TIMES AND HEIGHTS OF HIGH AND LOW WATERS

Dates in amber are **SPRINGS**
Dates in grey are **NEAPS**

2023

JANUARY

Date	Time	m	Date	Time	m
1	0117	8.5	16	0630	4.0
	0801	3.7		1221	8.3
SU	1351	8.6	M	1904	4.0
	2034	3.5			
2	0227	8.5	17	0106	8.2
	0910	3.6		0747	4.0
M	1501	8.6	TU	1339	8.3
	2139	3.5		2027	3.8
3	0331	8.8	18	0226	8.5
	1013	3.4		0910	3.6
TU	1602	8.8	W	1459	8.7
	2237	3.3		2147	3.4
4	0426	9.1	19	0340	9.0
	1108	3.1		1023	3.0
W	1655	9.1	TH	1611	9.3
	2327	3.0		2256	2.8
5	0512	9.5	20	0444	9.8
	1155	2.8		1128	2.3
TH	1740	9.4	F	1716	9.9
				2357	2.2
6	0009	2.8	21	0542	10.5
	0554	9.8		1228	1.6
F	1235	2.6	SA	1813	10.5
	○ 1820	9.6		●	
7	0048	2.6	22	0054	1.6
	0632	10.0		0637	11.0
SA	1312	2.4	SU	1324	1.1
	1857	9.8		1906	11.0
8	0123	2.5	23	0146	1.2
	0707	10.1		0726	11.4
SU	1346	2.3	M	1415	0.8
	1932	9.8		1955	11.2
9	0157	2.4	24	0235	1.1
	0740	10.1		0813	11.6
M	1419	2.3	TU	1503	0.7
	2005	9.8		2039	11.2
10	0229	2.5	25	0320	1.1
	0813	10.1		0857	11.4
TU	1451	2.4	W	1546	0.9
	2037	9.7		2121	10.9
11	0301	2.6	26	0402	1.4
	0845	9.9		0938	11.0
W	1523	2.6	TH	1626	1.4
	2109	9.5		2201	10.3
12	0333	2.8	27	0441	2.0
	0917	9.7		1018	10.3
TH	1555	2.8	F	1704	2.0
	2141	9.2		2239	9.7
13	0407	3.1	28	0519	2.6
	0951	9.3		1059	9.5
F	1630	3.1	SA	1742	2.8
	2216	8.9		◐ 2321	9.0
14	0445	3.4	29	0601	3.4
	1029	9.0		1145	8.7
SA	1709	3.5	SU	1827	3.6
	2258	8.5			
15	0530	3.8	30	0011	8.3
	1117	8.6		0656	4.0
SU	1758	3.8	M	1248	8.1
	◑ 2354	8.2		1930	4.1
			31	0125	7.9
				0815	4.3
			TU	1415	7.8
				2052	4.3

FEBRUARY

Date	Time	m	Date	Time	m
1	0252	8.0	16	0146	8.0
	0941	4.1		0837	3.9
W	1538	8.0	TH	1436	8.2
	2210	4.0		2124	3.8
2	0404	8.4	17	0323	8.6
	1050	3.7		1008	3.2
TH	1641	8.5	F	1605	8.9
	2310	3.5		2245	3.0
3	0458	9.0	18	0437	9.5
	1142	3.1		1120	2.3
F	1729	9.0	SA	1712	9.8
	2357	3.0		2351	2.1
4	0541	9.5	19	0536	10.4
	1224	2.7		1222	1.4
SA	1809	9.5	SU	1807	10.6
5	0037	2.6	20	0047	1.4
	0620	9.9		0628	11.2
SU	1302	2.3	M	1315	0.8
	○ 1845	9.8		● 1856	11.2
6	0113	2.3	21	0137	0.8
	0654	10.2		0715	11.7
M	1336	2.1	TU	1403	0.4
	1918	10.0		1940	11.5
7	0147	2.1	22	0222	0.6
	0727	10.4		0757	11.9
TU	1409	2.0	W	1446	0.3
	1949	10.1		2020	11.5
8	0218	2.0	23	0302	0.6
	0758	10.5		0837	11.8
W	1439	1.9	TH	1524	0.5
	2019	10.2		2057	11.2
9	0248	2.0	24	0338	1.0
	0828	10.5		0913	11.3
TH	1507	1.9	F	1558	1.1
	2048	10.1		2130	10.7
10	0317	2.1	25	0410	1.6
	0857	10.3		0947	10.5
F	1536	2.1	SA	1627	1.9
	2117	9.9		2201	9.9
11	0347	2.4	26	0440	2.5
	0927	10.0		1019	9.5
SA	1604	2.5	SU	1655	2.8
	2146	9.5		2233	9.1
12	0418	2.8	27	0510	3.3
	0958	9.5		1055	8.6
SU	1635	3.0	M	1728	3.7
	2218	9.1		◐ 2312	8.3
13	0453	3.3	28	0551	4.1
	1036	9.0		1146	7.7
M	1712	3.5	TU	1819	4.5
	◑ 2302	8.6			
14	0541	3.8			
	1130	8.4			
TU	1808	3.9			
15	0008	8.1			
	0656	4.1			
W	1252	8.0			
	1940	4.2			

MARCH

Date	Time	m	Date	Time	m
1	0018	7.6	16	0631	4.1
	0709	4.7		1232	7.8
W	1330	7.2	TH	1919	4.4
	2001	4.8			
2	0216	7.4	17	0132	7.8
	0911	4.6		0825	4.0
TH	1521	7.5	F	1435	8.0
	2148	4.5		2117	3.9
3	0346	7.9	18	0319	8.5
	1033	4.0		1001	3.1
F	1627	8.2	SA	1602	8.9
	2254	3.8		2238	3.0
4	0441	8.7	19	0429	9.5
	1124	3.2		1110	2.1
SA	1712	8.9	SU	1702	9.9
	2340	3.1		2339	2.0
5	0523	9.3	20	0523	10.5
	1205	2.6		1207	1.2
SU	1750	9.5	M	1752	10.7
6	0019	2.5	21	0031	1.2
	0601	9.9		0611	11.3
M	1242	2.2	TU	1257	0.6
	1825	9.9		● 1837	11.3
7	0055	2.1	22	0118	0.7
	0634	10.3		0655	11.8
TU	1317	1.8	W	1342	0.3
	○ 1856	10.3		1917	11.6
8	0128	1.8	23	0159	0.5
	0705	10.6		0734	11.9
W	1349	1.6	TH	1421	0.4
	1926	10.5		1954	11.6
9	0200	1.6	24	0236	0.6
	0736	10.8		0811	11.6
TH	1418	1.5	F	1455	0.7
	1955	10.6		2027	11.3
10	0229	1.5	25	0309	1.0
	0805	10.8		0845	11.1
F	1446	1.5	SA	1524	1.3
	2024	10.6		2057	10.7
11	0258	1.6	26	0337	1.7
	0835	10.7		0915	10.3
SA	1514	1.7	SU	1550	2.1
	2051	10.4		2125	9.9
12	0326	1.9	27	0403	2.5
	0903	10.3		0943	9.4
SU	1541	2.1	M	1615	3.0
	2119	9.9		2152	9.1
13	0356	2.4	28	0430	3.3
	0933	9.7		1014	8.4
M	1610	2.7	TU	1643	3.8
	2149	9.4		2226	8.3
14	0429	3.0	29	0506	4.1
	1009	9.1		1059	7.6
TU	1645	3.4	W	1729	4.6
	2230	8.7		◐ 2323	7.5
15	0515	3.6	30	0615	4.8
	1102	8.3		1249	7.0
W	1740	4.0	TH	1904	5.1
	◑ 2337	8.1			
			31	0136	7.2
				0827	4.8
			F	1454	7.3
				2113	4.7

APRIL

Date	Time	m	Date	Time	m
1	0315	7.7	16	0305	8.8
	1000	4.1		0945	2.9
SA	1557	8.1	SU	1545	9.1
	2222	4.0		2218	2.8
2	0410	8.5	17	0409	9.7
	1051	3.4		1049	2.0
SU	1641	8.8	M	1641	10.0
	2308	3.2		2316	1.9
3	0452	9.2	18	0501	10.5
	1132	2.7		1143	1.3
M	1718	9.5	TU	1728	10.7
	2348	2.5			
4	0529	9.8	19	0006	1.3
	1210	2.2		0547	11.1
TU	1752	10.0	W	1230	0.9
				1810	11.1
5	0025	2.1	20	0051	1.0
	0604	10.3		0629	11.4
W	1246	1.8	TH	1312	0.8
	1825	10.4		● 1849	11.3
6	0100	1.7	21	0131	0.9
	0636	10.6		0707	11.4
TH	1320	1.5	F	1349	0.9
	○ 1857	10.7		1924	11.2
7	0134	1.5	22	0206	1.1
	0708	10.9		0743	11.1
F	1352	1.4	SA	1422	1.2
	1927	10.8		1957	11.0
8	0206	1.4	23	0238	1.4
	0740	10.9		0816	10.6
SA	1422	1.4	SU	1451	1.7
	1958	10.8		2026	10.5
9	0236	1.4	24	0307	2.0
	0812	10.8		0847	10.0
SU	1452	1.6	M	1518	2.4
	2028	10.6		2055	9.8
10	0308	1.7	25	0334	2.6
	0844	10.4		0917	9.2
M	1522	2.1	TU	1545	3.1
	2059	10.1		2123	9.1
11	0340	2.2	26	0404	3.4
	0918	9.7		0949	8.4
TU	1554	2.7	W	1616	3.9
	2134	9.5		2158	8.4
12	0418	2.8	27	0441	4.0
	1000	9.0		1035	7.7
W	1635	3.4	TH	1701	4.5
	2221	8.8		◐ 2253	7.7
13	0511	3.5	28	0543	4.6
	1101	8.2		1205	7.2
TH	1738	4.0	F	1819	4.9
	◑ 2338	8.1			
14	0633	3.9	29	0038	7.3
	1241	7.8		0721	4.7
F	1921	4.2	SA	1358	7.3
				2007	4.8
15	0132	8.1	30	0220	7.7
	0820	3.7		0857	4.2
SA	1431	8.2	SU	1506	7.9
	2105	3.7		2126	4.1

Chart Datum: 5·88 metres below Ordnance Datum (Local)
HAT is 12·2 metres above Chart Datum

TIME ZONE (UT)
For Summer Time add ONE hour in **non-shaded areas**

CHANNEL ISLES – ST HELIER

LAT 49°11′N LONG 2°07′W

TIMES AND HEIGHTS OF HIGH AND LOW WATERS

Dates in amber are **SPRINGS**
Dates in grey are **NEAPS**

2023

MAY

Date	Day	Time	m	Time	m	Time	m	Time	m
1	M	0321	8.3	0957	3.6	1554	8.6	2219	3.4
2	TU	0407	9.0	1044	2.9	1635	9.3	2304	2.8
3	W	0447	9.6	1127	2.4	1712	9.8	2345	2.3
4	TH	0525	10.1	1208	2.0	1748	10.3		
5	F	0025	1.8	0602	10.5	1246	1.7	○ 1823	10.6
6	SA	0104	1.6	0639	10.7	1323	1.5	1859	10.8
7	SU	0141	1.4	0716	10.8	1358	1.5	1934	10.8
8	M	0217	1.4	0754	10.7	1433	1.7	2011	10.6
9	TU	0254	1.7	0833	10.3	1510	2.1	2050	10.2
10	W	0334	2.1	0917	9.7	1550	2.7	2135	9.6
11	TH	0421	2.6	1008	9.1	1640	3.2	2231	9.0
12	F	0520	3.1	1115	8.5	1748	3.7	◑ 2347	8.6
13	SA	0637	3.4	1240	8.3	1915	3.8		
14	SU	0116	8.6	0802	3.2	1405	8.6	2039	3.4
15	M	0235	9.0	0915	2.7	1513	9.2	2147	2.7
16	TU	0338	9.6	1016	2.2	1609	9.8	2244	2.2
17	W	0431	10.1	1110	1.8	1657	10.2	2335	1.8
18	TH	0518	10.5	1158	1.6	1740	10.5		
19	F	0021	1.6	0601	10.6	1240	1.6	● 1819	10.7
20	SA	0101	1.6	0641	10.6	1317	1.7	1855	10.7
21	SU	0138	1.7	0718	10.4	1351	1.9	1930	10.5
22	M	0211	1.9	0753	10.1	1423	2.2	2002	10.2
23	TU	0243	2.3	0827	9.7	1454	2.6	2034	9.7
24	W	0314	2.7	0900	9.1	1525	3.1	2107	9.2
25	TH	0347	3.2	0936	8.6	1600	3.6	2144	8.6
26	F	0426	3.7	1021	8.0	1643	4.1	2233	8.1
27	SA	0516	4.1	1121	7.7	1741	4.4	◐ 2341	7.8
28	SU	0622	4.3	1241	7.6	1855	4.5		
29	M	0103	7.8	0738	4.2	1355	7.9	2012	4.2
30	TU	0213	8.1	0848	3.8	1453	8.4	2117	3.7
31	W	0309	8.6	0946	3.3	1542	8.9	2212	3.2

JUNE

Date	Day	Time	m	Time	m	Time	m	Time	m
1	TH	0357	9.2	1038	2.8	1626	9.5	2301	2.6
2	F	0443	9.7	1126	2.4	1709	10.0	2349	2.1
3	SA	0527	10.2	1212	2.0	1751	10.4		
4	SU	0034	1.8	0613	10.5	1256	1.8	○ 1835	10.7
5	M	0119	1.5	0658	10.6	1339	1.7	1918	10.8
6	TU	0204	1.5	0744	10.6	1423	1.8	2004	10.7
7	W	0249	1.6	0832	10.3	1508	2.0	2051	10.5
8	TH	0336	1.8	0921	10.0	1555	2.3	2141	10.1
9	F	0427	2.1	1014	9.5	1647	2.7	2235	9.6
10	SA	0523	2.5	1111	9.1	1746	3.0	◑ 2337	9.3
11	SU	0624	2.8	1215	8.9	1852	3.2		
12	M	0044	9.0	0730	2.9	1323	8.8	2001	3.2
13	TU	0154	9.0	0835	2.9	1430	9.0	2107	3.0
14	W	0259	9.2	0937	2.7	1531	9.3	2208	2.8
15	TH	0358	9.4	1034	2.6	1624	9.6	2304	2.6
16	F	0450	9.6	1126	2.5	1711	9.8	2354	2.4
17	SA	0537	9.8	1212	2.4	1754	10.0		
18	SU	0037	2.3	0620	9.9	1252	2.4	● 1833	10.1
19	M	0116	2.3	0700	9.9	1329	2.4	1910	10.1
20	TU	0152	2.3	0737	9.8	1404	2.5	1946	10.0
21	W	0227	2.4	0813	9.6	1438	2.7	2020	9.8
22	TH	0301	2.6	0847	9.3	1511	2.9	2055	9.5
23	F	0334	2.9	0922	9.0	1545	3.2	2130	9.2
24	SA	0409	3.2	0959	8.7	1623	3.5	2209	8.8
25	SU	0448	3.5	1041	8.4	1706	3.8	2254	8.5
26	M	0534	3.7	1131	8.1	1758	4.0	◐ 2349	8.2
27	TU	0629	3.9	1233	8.0	1900	4.1		
28	W	0054	8.2	0734	3.9	1339	8.2	2010	3.9
29	TH	0202	8.4	0843	3.7	1443	8.5	2118	3.6
30	F	0306	8.8	0949	3.3	1541	9.1	2220	3.0

JULY

Date	Day	Time	m	Time	m	Time	m	Time	m
1	SA	0404	9.3	1048	2.8	1635	9.7	2317	2.5
2	SU	0501	9.8	1144	2.3	1728	10.2		
3	M	0012	2.0	0556	10.2	1237	2.0	○ 1820	10.6
4	TU	0106	1.6	0648	10.5	1329	1.7	1910	10.9
5	W	0158	1.3	0740	10.7	1419	1.5	2000	11.1
6	TH	0248	1.1	0829	10.7	1507	1.5	2048	11.0
7	F	0336	1.2	0917	10.6	1554	1.7	2135	10.8
8	SA	0423	1.4	1003	10.2	1641	2.0	2222	10.3
9	SU	0509	1.9	1050	9.8	1728	2.4	2311	9.8
10	M	0556	2.4	1139	9.3	1818	2.9	◑	
11	TU	0003	9.2	0649	2.9	1234	8.8	1917	3.3
12	W	0106	8.7	0749	3.3	1340	8.6	2024	3.6
13	TH	0217	8.5	0856	3.5	1451	8.6	2135	3.5
14	F	0328	8.6	1003	3.4	1556	8.8	2240	3.3
15	SA	0430	8.8	1103	3.2	1650	9.2	2336	3.0
16	SU	0522	9.2	1153	2.9	1737	9.5		
17	M	0022	2.7	0607	9.4	1236	2.7	● 1819	9.8
18	TU	0103	2.5	0648	9.6	1315	2.5	1857	10.0
19	W	0141	2.3	0724	9.8	1351	2.5	1932	10.1
20	TH	0215	2.3	0758	9.8	1424	2.4	2006	10.1
21	F	0246	2.3	0830	9.7	1456	2.5	2037	10.0
22	SA	0317	2.4	0901	9.6	1527	2.6	2109	9.8
23	SU	0347	2.6	0931	9.4	1559	2.9	2140	9.5
24	M	0419	2.9	1003	9.0	1632	3.2	2213	9.1
25	TU	0453	3.3	1038	8.7	1711	3.6	◐ 2253	8.7
26	W	0533	3.7	1123	8.3	1800	3.9	2346	8.3
27	TH	0627	4.0	1226	8.1	1907	4.1		
28	F	0058	8.1	0743	4.0	1346	8.2	2030	3.9
29	SA	0222	8.3	0908	3.8	1506	8.6	2149	3.4
30	SU	0340	8.8	1023	3.2	1615	9.3	2257	2.7
31	M	0447	9.5	1128	2.5	1715	10.1		

AUGUST

Date	Day	Time	m	Time	m	Time	m	Time	m
1	TU	0000	1.9	0547	10.2	1227	1.9	○ 1811	10.8
2	W	0058	1.3	0642	10.7	1322	1.4	1902	11.3
3	TH	0151	0.9	0731	11.1	1412	1.1	1950	11.6
4	F	0240	0.6	0817	11.3	1458	0.9	2035	11.6
5	SA	0325	0.6	0900	11.2	1541	1.1	2117	11.4
6	SU	0405	1.0	0940	10.8	1621	1.5	2158	10.8
7	M	0444	1.6	1018	10.1	1659	2.2	2237	10.0
8	TU	0521	2.4	1057	9.4	1739	3.0	◑ 2320	9.1
9	W	0602	3.2	1143	8.7	1827	3.7		
10	TH	0015	8.3	0657	3.9	1247	8.1	1939	4.2
11	F	0138	7.8	0816	4.3	1417	7.9	2110	4.2
12	SA	0311	7.9	0943	4.2	1540	8.3	2229	3.8
13	SU	0421	8.4	1051	3.7	1639	8.8	2326	3.2
14	M	0513	8.9	1142	3.1	1726	9.4		
15	TU	0011	2.7	0556	9.4	1224	2.7	1806	9.8
16	W	0050	2.4	0633	9.8	1301	2.4	● 1842	10.2
17	TH	0125	2.1	0706	10.0	1335	2.2	1914	10.4
18	F	0157	2.0	0737	10.2	1406	2.1	1945	10.5
19	SA	0227	1.9	0806	10.2	1435	2.1	2014	10.5
20	SU	0254	2.0	0834	10.2	1504	2.1	2042	10.3
21	M	0322	2.2	0901	9.9	1533	2.4	2110	10.0
22	TU	0349	2.5	0927	9.6	1602	2.8	2138	9.5
23	W	0417	3.0	0956	9.1	1634	3.3	2210	9.0
24	TH	0449	3.5	1032	8.6	1715	3.8	◐ 2256	8.4
25	F	0536	4.1	1129	8.1	1820	4.2		
26	SA	0010	7.9	0658	4.4	1304	7.9	1959	4.2
27	SU	0158	7.9	0846	4.2	1450	8.3	2134	3.6
28	M	0334	8.6	1012	3.4	1607	9.2	2248	2.7
29	TU	0443	9.5	1119	2.5	1708	10.2	2351	1.7
30	W	0539	10.4	1217	1.7	1800	11.1		
31	TH	0046	1.0	0629	11.1	1309	1.0	○ 1848	11.7

Chart Datum: 5·88 metres below Ordnance Datum (Local)
HAT is 12·2 metres above Chart Datum

TIME ZONE (UT)
For Summer Time add ONE hour in **non-shaded areas**

CHANNEL ISLES – ST HELIER

LAT 49°11′N LONG 2°07′W

TIMES AND HEIGHTS OF HIGH AND LOW WATERS

Dates in amber are **SPRINGS**
Dates in grey are **NEAPS**

2023

SEPTEMBER

Date	Day	Time	m	Time	m	Time	m	Time	m
1	F	0136	0.5	0714	11.6	1356	0.7	1933	12.0
2	SA	0221	0.3	0756	11.7	1439	0.6	2014	12.0
3	SU	0302	0.4	0835	11.5	1517	0.9	2052	11.6
4	M	0338	0.9	0910	11.0	1552	1.4	2128	10.8
5	TU	0411	1.7	0943	10.2	1625	2.3	2201	9.8
6	W	0441	2.7	1015	9.4	1657	3.2	◑ 2237	8.8
7	TH	0514	3.6	1053	8.5	1738	4.1	2326	7.8
8	F	0602	4.5	1153	7.7	1853	4.7		
9	SA	0105	7.2	0739	4.9	1353	7.4	2054	4.7
10	SU	0305	7.5	0931	4.6	1530	8.0	2220	4.0
11	M	0412	8.2	1038	3.9	1626	8.7	2310	3.3
12	TU	0457	9.0	1124	3.2	1708	9.4	2351	2.7
13	W	0534	9.6	1203	2.6	1744	10.0		
14	TH	0026	2.2	0609	10.0	1238	2.2	1818	10.4
15	F	0100	2.0	0640	10.3	1310	2.0	● 1849	10.6
16	SA	0131	1.8	0709	10.5	1341	1.8	1918	10.8
17	SU	0200	1.7	0737	10.6	1410	1.8	1947	10.8
18	M	0228	1.8	0804	10.6	1439	1.9	2014	10.6
19	TU	0254	2.0	0830	10.3	1507	2.2	2041	10.3
20	W	0321	2.4	0856	9.9	1535	2.6	2109	9.7
21	TH	0348	2.9	0923	9.4	1606	3.2	2141	9.1
22	F	0419	3.6	0959	8.8	1647	3.8	◐ 2226	8.4
23	SA	0508	4.2	1056	8.1	1757	4.3	2349	7.7
24	SU	0639	4.6	1249	7.8	1947	4.3		
25	M	0159	7.8	0839	4.3	1447	8.3	2127	3.5
26	TU	0332	8.7	1004	3.3	1559	9.4	2237	2.5
27	W	0432	9.7	1105	2.3	1654	10.5	2334	1.5
28	TH	0523	10.7	1159	1.5	1742	11.3		
29	F	0025	0.9	0609	11.3	1247	0.9	○ 1827	11.8
30	SA	0112	0.5	0651	11.7	1331	0.7	1909	12.0

OCTOBER

Date	Day	Time	m	Time	m	Time	m	Time	m
1	SU	0154	0.5	0729	11.7	1412	0.7	1948	11.9
2	M	0232	0.7	0805	11.5	1448	1.0	2024	11.3
3	TU	0305	1.3	0838	10.9	1520	1.7	2057	10.6
4	W	0335	2.1	0908	10.2	1550	2.5	2128	9.6
5	TH	0403	3.0	0937	9.3	1620	3.4	2201	8.6
6	F	0433	4.0	1011	8.4	1658	4.3	◑ 2246	7.7
7	SA	0518	4.8	1108	7.6	1811	4.9		
8	SU	0036	7.1	0659	5.2	1323	7.3	2026	4.9
9	M	0243	7.4	0904	4.8	1503	7.8	2150	4.2
10	TU	0344	8.2	1009	4.0	1557	8.6	2238	3.4
11	W	0426	8.9	1052	3.3	1637	9.4	2316	2.8
12	TH	0502	9.6	1130	2.7	1713	9.9	2352	2.3
13	F	0536	10.1	1205	2.2	1746	10.3		
14	SA	0026	2.0	0607	10.4	1239	1.9	● 1818	10.6
15	SU	0059	1.8	0637	10.6	1312	1.8	1848	10.8
16	M	0130	1.7	0706	10.8	1343	1.7	1919	10.8
17	TU	0200	1.8	0735	10.7	1414	1.8	1949	10.7
18	W	0229	2.0	0804	10.5	1444	2.1	2019	10.3
19	TH	0258	2.4	0834	10.1	1516	2.5	2052	9.8
20	F	0329	2.9	0906	9.6	1552	3.1	2130	9.1
21	SA	0407	3.6	0948	8.9	1640	3.7	2224	8.3
22	SU	0504	4.2	1056	8.2	1757	4.1	◐ 2357	7.8
23	M	0639	4.5	1250	8.0	1941	4.0		
24	TU	0154	8.1	0827	4.1	1431	8.6	2110	3.3
25	W	0313	8.9	0943	3.2	1537	9.6	2214	2.4
26	TH	0410	9.8	1042	2.3	1631	10.5	2309	1.6
27	F	0458	10.6	1133	1.6	1718	11.1	2358	1.1
28	SA ○	0542	11.1	1221	1.2	1801	11.5		
29	SU	0043	1.0	0623	11.4	1303	1.1	1843	11.5
30	M	0124	1.0	0701	11.4	1343	1.2	1921	11.3
31	TU	0200	1.3	0736	11.2	1418	1.5	1957	10.9

NOVEMBER

Date	Day	Time	m	Time	m	Time	m	Time	m
1	W	0233	1.8	0809	10.7	1451	2.0	2031	10.2
2	TH	0304	2.5	0840	10.1	1522	2.7	2104	9.4
3	F	0333	3.2	0911	9.3	1554	3.5	2139	8.5
4	SA	0405	4.0	0947	8.5	1633	4.2	2225	7.8
5	SU	0451	4.6	1041	7.8	1735	4.7	◑ 2350	7.3
6	M	0609	5.1	1222	7.4	1916	4.8		
7	TU	0143	7.4	0758	4.9	1406	7.7	2048	4.4
8	W	0253	8.0	0914	4.3	1508	8.3	2145	3.8
9	TH	0341	8.6	1004	3.7	1553	9.0	2229	3.2
10	F	0420	9.3	1047	3.0	1632	9.5	2309	2.7
11	SA	0456	9.8	1126	2.5	1708	10.0	2348	2.3
12	SU	0530	10.2	1205	2.2	1743	10.4		
13	M	0024	2.0	0604	10.5	1242	1.9	● 1818	10.6
14	TU	0100	1.9	0637	10.7	1318	1.8	1854	10.7
15	W	0135	1.9	0711	10.8	1353	1.8	1930	10.6
16	TH	0209	2.1	0747	10.6	1429	2.0	2008	10.3
17	F	0244	2.4	0824	10.3	1508	2.3	2049	9.8
18	SA	0323	2.8	0907	9.8	1552	2.8	2137	9.2
19	SU	0410	3.3	0959	9.2	1647	3.2	2238	8.7
20	M	0512	3.8	1107	8.7	1758	3.5	◐ 2356	8.4
21	TU	0632	4.0	1232	8.6	1921	3.5		
22	W	0122	8.5	0758	3.7	1355	8.9	2037	3.1
23	TH	0237	9.0	0910	3.1	1504	9.5	2141	2.5
24	F	0337	9.6	1011	2.6	1600	10.0	2238	2.1
25	SA	0428	10.1	1104	2.1	1651	10.4	2329	1.8
26	SU	0514	10.5	1153	1.8	1736	10.7		
27	M	0014	1.7	0556	10.8	1238	1.7	○ 1820	10.7
28	TU	0056	1.8	0636	10.8	1318	1.8	1900	10.6
29	W	0134	1.9	0713	10.7	1356	2.0	1938	10.3
30	TH	0209	2.2	0749	10.4	1431	2.3	2014	9.9

DECEMBER

Date	Day	Time	m	Time	m	Time	m	Time	m
1	F	0242	2.7	0823	10.0	1505	2.7	2050	9.3
2	SA	0315	3.2	0857	9.5	1539	3.2	2127	8.8
3	SU	0350	3.7	0934	8.9	1616	3.7	2209	8.3
4	M	0430	4.1	1019	8.4	1703	4.1	2302	7.9
5	TU ◑	0523	4.5	1118	8.0	1804	4.4		
6	W	0014	7.7	0633	4.7	1236	7.8	1918	4.4
7	TH	0133	7.8	0751	4.5	1353	8.0	2030	4.2
8	F	0236	8.2	0859	4.1	1453	8.4	2130	3.7
9	SA	0327	8.7	0955	3.6	1542	8.9	2221	3.3
10	SU	0411	9.2	1044	3.1	1627	9.4	2308	2.8
11	M	0452	9.7	1130	2.6	1710	9.9	2352	2.4
12	TU ●	0533	10.2	1215	2.2	1753	10.2		
13	W	0035	2.1	0614	10.5	1258	1.9	1837	10.4
14	TH	0117	2.0	0656	10.7	1341	1.7	1921	10.5
15	F	0159	2.0	0740	10.8	1424	1.7	2007	10.4
16	SA	0242	2.1	0825	10.6	1510	1.9	2054	10.2
17	SU	0327	2.3	0913	10.3	1557	2.1	2143	9.8
18	M	0416	2.6	1003	10.0	1649	2.4	2236	9.4
19	TU	0509	3.0	1058	9.5	1745	2.7	◐ 2333	9.1
20	W	0610	3.2	1200	9.2	1847	3.0		
21	TH	0038	8.8	0718	3.4	1309	9.0	1954	3.1
22	F	0148	8.8	0828	3.4	1420	9.0	2101	3.1
23	SA	0256	9.0	0935	3.1	1527	9.2	2204	2.9
24	SU	0357	9.4	1037	2.8	1626	9.5	2302	2.7
25	M	0450	9.7	1133	2.6	1718	9.7	2353	2.5
26	TU	0537	10.0	1222	2.3	1805	9.9		
27	W	0038	2.4	0620	10.2	1305	2.2	○ 1848	10.0
28	TH	0118	2.3	0700	10.3	1344	2.2	1927	10.0
29	F	0155	2.4	0737	10.3	1420	2.3	2004	9.8
30	SA	0230	2.5	0812	10.1	1454	2.5	2038	9.6
31	SU	0302	2.8	0846	9.8	1526	2.7	2112	9.3

Chart Datum: 5·88 metres below Ordnance Datum (Local)
HAT is 12·2 metres above Chart Datum

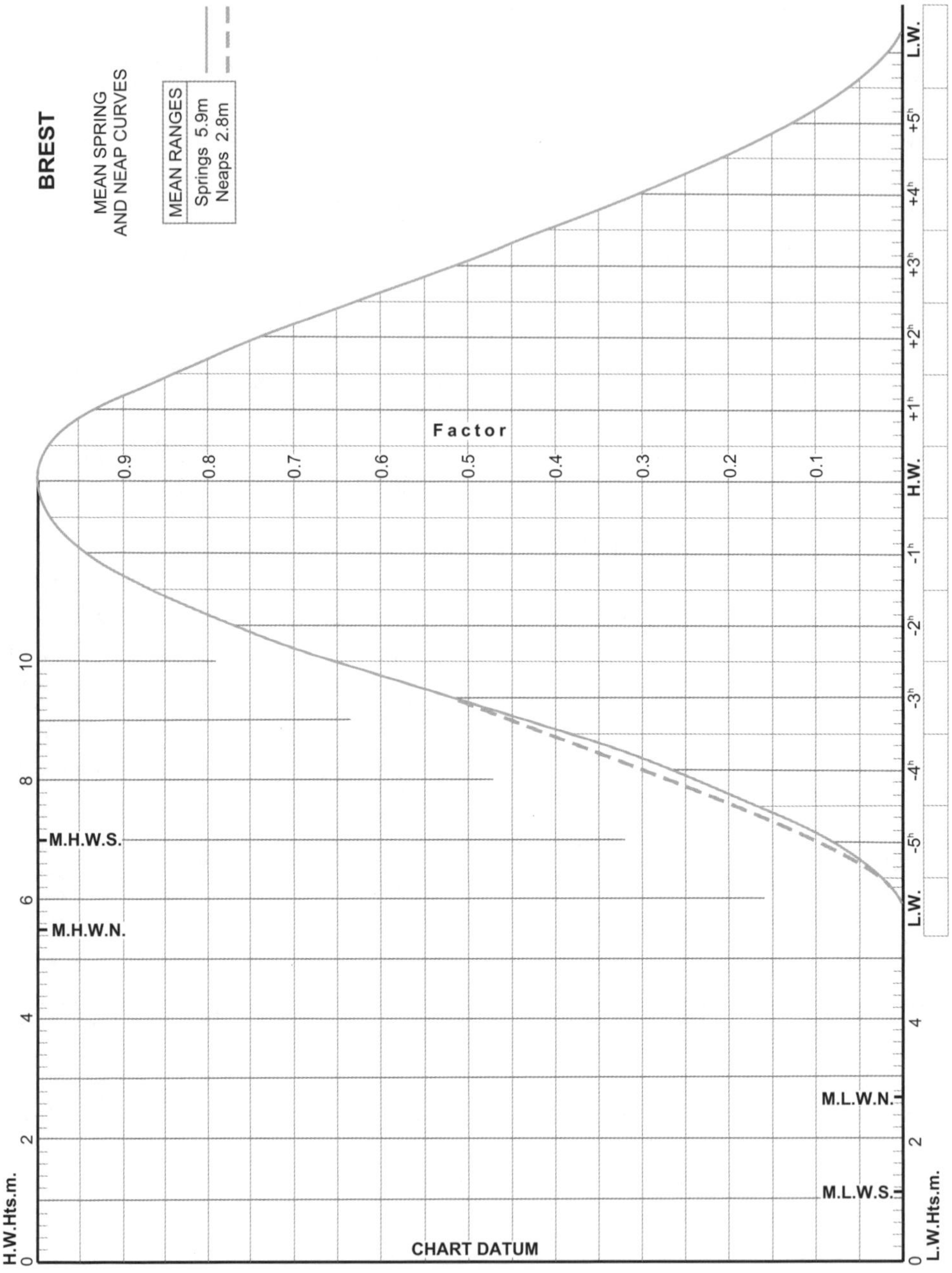
BREST
MEAN SPRING AND NEAP CURVES
MEAN RANGES
Springs 5.9m
Neaps 2.8m
Factor
0.9
0.8
0.7
0.6
0.5
0.4
0.3
0.2
0.1
L.W.
-5h
-4h
-3h
-2h
-1h
H.W.
+1h
+2h
+3h
+4h
+5h
L.W.
H.W.Hts.m.
0
2
4
6
8
10
M.H.W.S.
M.H.W.N.
CHART DATUM
L.W.Hts.m.
0
2
4
M.L.W.S.
M.L.W.N.

TIME ZONE -0100
(French Standard Time)
Subtract 1 hour for UT
For French Summer Time add ONE hour in **non-shaded areas**

FRANCE – BREST

LAT 48°23′N LONG 4°30′W

TIMES AND HEIGHTS OF HIGH AND LOW WATERS

Dates in amber are **SPRINGS**
Dates in grey are **NEAPS**

2023

JANUARY

Day	Time	m	Day	Time	m
1 SU	0010 0633 1241 1906	5.6 2.6 5.8 2.5	16 M	0510 1117 1749	2.7 5.6 2.7
2 M	0116 0740 1346 2008	5.7 2.5 5.8 2.4	17 TU	0001 0620 1230 1901	5.5 2.7 5.6 2.6
3 TU	0217 0841 1444 2103	5.8 2.4 5.9 2.3	18 W	0113 0734 1345 2011	5.7 2.5 5.8 2.4
4 W	0309 0934 1533 2150	6.0 2.2 6.1 2.2	19 TH	0221 0843 1453 2114	6.0 2.1 6.1 2.0
5 TH	0354 1019 1616 2232	6.2 2.0 6.2 2.1	20 F	0323 0945 1552 2211	6.5 1.7 6.5 1.6
6 F	0434 1059 1654 2309	6.4 1.9 6.3 2.0	21 SA	0418 1040 1646 ● 2304	6.9 1.2 6.9 1.3
7 SA	0510 1135 1730 ○ 2345	6.5 1.8 6.4 1.9	22 SU	0510 1132 1736 2354	7.3 0.9 7.1 1.0
8 SU	0545 1210 1804	6.6 1.8 6.4	23 M	0559 1221 1824	7.5 0.7 7.2
9 M	0019 0618 1244 1838	1.9 6.6 1.8 6.3	24 TU	0042 0646 1308 1910	0.9 7.6 0.7 7.1
10 TU	0053 0651 1317 1911	1.9 6.5 1.8 6.2	25 W	0129 0731 1355 1955	1.0 7.4 0.9 6.9
11 W	0127 0724 1351 1945	2.0 6.4 2.0 6.1	26 TH	0215 0816 1440 2039	1.2 7.1 1.2 6.6
12 TH	0202 0759 1426 2022	2.1 6.3 2.1 5.9	27 F	0301 0900 1527 2124	1.6 6.7 1.7 6.2
13 F	0239 0836 1505 2103	2.3 6.1 2.3 5.8	28 SA	0349 0947 1616 ◐ 2214	2.0 6.2 2.2 5.8
14 SA	0321 0919 1550 2152	2.4 5.9 2.5 5.6	29 SU	0442 1042 1711 2314	2.4 5.8 2.6 5.5
15 SU	0410 1011 1644 ◑ 2252	2.6 5.7 2.7 5.5	30 M	0544 1150 1818	2.8 5.4 2.9
			31 TU	0028 0700 1311 1933	5.3 2.9 5.3 2.9

FEBRUARY

Day	Time	m	Day	Time	m
1 W	0147 0818 1426 2042	5.4 2.8 5.4 2.7	16 TH	0039 0704 1324 1950	5.5 2.7 5.5 2.6
2 TH	0254 0920 1522 2135	5.7 2.5 5.7 2.5	17 F	0205 0829 1446 2104	5.8 2.3 5.9 2.2
3 F	0343 1007 1606 2218	6.0 2.2 6.0 2.2	18 SA	0313 0936 1546 2202	6.3 1.7 6.4 1.6
4 SA	0423 1046 1643 2256	6.2 2.0 6.2 2.0	19 SU	0409 1031 1638 2254	6.9 1.1 6.9 1.1
5 SU	0458 1121 1716 ○ 2330	6.5 1.7 6.4 1.8	20 M	0459 1120 1725 ● 2341	7.4 0.7 7.2 0.8
6 M	0531 1154 1748	6.6 1.6 6.5	21 TU	0545 1207 1808	7.7 0.5 7.4
7 TU	0002 0602 1225 1819	1.7 6.7 1.5 6.6	22 W	0026 0628 1250 1849	0.6 7.7 0.5 7.3
8 W	0034 0633 1256 1850	1.6 6.8 1.5 6.6	23 TH	0109 0709 1331 1928	0.7 7.6 0.7 7.1
9 TH	0106 0703 1326 1920	1.6 6.8 1.6 6.5	24 F	0150 0748 1411 2005	1.0 7.2 1.1 6.7
10 F	0138 0734 1358 1951	1.7 6.6 1.7 6.3	25 SA	0230 0825 1450 2042	1.4 6.7 1.7 6.3
11 SA	0211 0806 1431 2026	1.8 6.4 1.9 6.1	26 SU	0312 0904 1531 2123	1.9 6.2 2.2 5.8
12 SU	0249 0842 1511 2108	2.1 6.2 2.2 5.9	27 M	0358 0950 1620 ◐ 2216	2.4 5.6 2.8 5.4
13 M	0333 0927 1559 ◑ 2202	2.3 5.9 2.5 5.6	28 TU	0456 1056 1726 2336	2.9 5.1 3.1 5.1
14 TU	0427 1027 1701 2313	2.6 5.5 2.8 5.4			
15 W	0537 1149 1822	2.8 5.4 2.9			

MARCH

Day	Time	m	Day	Time	m
1 W	0617 1235 1857	3.2 4.9 3.2	16 TH	0515 1130 1803	2.8 5.2 3.0
2 TH	0119 0756 1411 2023	5.1 3.1 5.1 3.0	17 F	0025 0651 1320 1942	5.4 2.7 5.4 2.7
3 F	0238 0904 1509 2118	5.4 2.7 5.5 2.6	18 SA	0157 0821 1441 2055	5.8 2.3 5.9 2.1
4 SA	0326 0949 1549 2159	5.8 2.3 5.9 2.3	19 SU	0303 0925 1536 2150	6.4 1.6 6.5 1.5
5 SU	0405 1026 1623 2235	6.1 1.9 6.2 1.9	20 M	0355 1017 1623 2238	7.0 1.1 7.0 1.0
6 M	0437 1059 1655 2307	6.4 1.7 6.5 1.7	21 TU	0442 1103 1705 ● 2322	7.4 0.7 7.3 0.7
7 TU	0508 1130 1725 ○ 2339	6.7 1.4 6.7 1.5	22 W	0525 1146 1745	7.6 0.5 7.4
8 W	0539 1200 1754	6.9 1.3 6.8	23 TH	0004 0605 1225 1822	0.6 7.6 0.6 7.3
9 TH	0010 0608 1230 1823	1.3 7.0 1.3 6.8	24 F	0044 0642 1303 1857	0.7 7.5 0.8 7.1
10 F	0041 0638 1259 1853	1.3 7.0 1.3 6.8	25 SA	0122 0717 1339 1930	1.0 7.1 1.3 6.8
11 SA	0112 0707 1330 1923	1.4 6.8 1.5 6.6	26 SU	0159 0752 1414 2003	1.5 6.6 1.8 6.3
12 SU	0146 0739 1403 1957	1.6 6.6 1.7 6.4	27 M	0238 0827 1452 2040	2.0 6.1 2.3 5.8
13 M	0223 0815 1442 2037	1.8 6.3 2.1 6.0	28 TU	0321 0909 1536 2128	2.5 5.5 2.8 5.4
14 TU	0307 0858 1529 2130	2.2 5.9 2.5 5.7	29 W	0415 1011 1638 ◐ 2247	3.0 5.0 3.3 5.0
15 W	0402 0959 1633 ◑ 2247	2.5 5.5 2.9 5.4	30 TH	0534 1153 1812	3.3 4.8 3.4
			31 F	0037 0718 1340 1949	5.0 3.2 5.0 3.2

APRIL

Day	Time	m	Day	Time	m
1 SA	0205 0831 1439 2046	5.3 2.8 5.4 2.7	16 SU	0142 0806 1424 2037	5.9 2.1 6.0 2.0
2 SU	0254 0916 1518 2127	5.7 2.4 5.8 2.3	17 M	0243 0905 1516 2129	6.4 1.6 6.5 1.5
3 M	0331 0952 1552 2203	6.0 2.0 6.2 1.9	18 TU	0333 0955 1600 2216	6.9 1.2 6.9 1.1
4 TU	0404 1026 1623 2236	6.4 1.7 6.5 1.6	19 W	0418 1039 1641 2259	7.2 0.9 7.1 0.9
5 W	0437 1058 1654 2309	6.7 1.4 6.7 1.4	20 TH	0459 1120 1718 ● 2339	7.3 0.8 7.2 0.9
6 TH	0508 1129 1725 ○ 2341	6.9 1.3 6.9 1.2	21 F	0538 1158 1754	7.3 0.9 7.1
7 F	0540 1200 1755	7.0 1.2 7.0	22 SA	0017 0614 1234 1827	1.0 7.1 1.2 6.9
8 SA	0014 0611 1232 1826	1.2 7.0 1.2 6.9	23 SU	0054 0649 1309 1900	1.3 6.8 1.5 6.6
9 SU	0048 0643 1305 1859	1.3 6.9 1.4 6.8	24 M	0131 0723 1344 1934	1.6 6.4 1.9 6.3
10 M	0124 0718 1342 1936	1.5 6.6 1.7 6.5	25 TU	0210 0800 1421 2011	2.1 5.9 2.4 5.9
11 TU	0205 0758 1424 2020	1.7 6.3 2.1 6.1	26 W	0252 0842 1504 2057	2.5 5.5 2.8 5.4
12 W	0253 0847 1515 2119	2.1 5.8 2.5 5.7	27 TH	0343 0939 1600 ◐ 2206	2.9 5.1 3.2 5.1
13 TH	0353 0955 1625 ◑ 2242	2.5 5.4 2.9 5.4	28 F	0452 1104 1720 2339	3.1 4.9 3.3 5.0
14 F	0510 1131 1759	2.7 5.2 2.9	29 SA	0617 1235 1848	3.1 4.9 3.2
15 SA	0019 0645 1314 1931	5.5 2.6 5.5 2.6	30 SU	0101 0732 1343 1953	5.2 2.9 5.3 2.9

Chart Datum: 3·64 metres below IGN Datum
HAT is 7·9 metres above Chart Datum

TIME ZONE -0100
(French Standard Time)
Subtract 1 hour for UT
For French Summer Time add ONE hour in **non-shaded areas**

FRANCE – BREST

LAT 48°23′N LONG 4°30′W

TIMES AND HEIGHTS OF HIGH AND LOW WATERS

Dates in amber are **SPRINGS**
Dates in grey are **NEAPS**

2023

MAY

Date	Day	Time	m	Time	m	Time	m	Time	m
1	M	0159	5.5	0825	2.5	1430	5.6	2041	2.5
2	TU	0244	5.9	0907	2.1	1509	6.0	2121	2.1
3	W	0323	6.2	0945	1.8	1545	6.4	2159	1.7
4	TH	0359	6.5	1021	1.6	1620	6.7	2235	1.5
5	F	0435	6.7	1056	1.4	1654	6.9	○ 2312	1.3
6	SA	0510	6.9	1132	1.3	1728	7.0	2349	1.2
7	SU	0547	6.9	1208	1.3	1805	6.9		
8	M	0028	1.3	0625	6.8	1247	1.5	1844	6.8
9	TU	0110	1.4	0707	6.6	1329	1.7	1928	6.6
10	W	0157	1.7	0754	6.2	1418	2.1	2020	6.2
11	TH	0250	2.0	0851	5.8	1515	2.4	2124	5.9
12	F	0353	2.3	1002	5.5	1625	2.7	◑ 2241	5.7
13	SA	0508	2.4	1126	5.4	1748	2.7		
14	SU	0002	5.8	0628	2.3	1248	5.6	1906	2.4
15	M	0115	6.0	0739	2.0	1353	6.0	2009	2.0
16	TU	0214	6.3	0837	1.7	1446	6.3	2103	1.7
17	W	0306	6.6	0927	1.5	1532	6.6	2151	1.4
18	TH	0351	6.8	1012	1.4	1614	6.8	2234	1.3
19	F	0433	6.8	1053	1.3	1652	6.8	● 2315	1.3
20	SA	0513	6.8	1132	1.4	1728	6.8	2354	1.4
21	SU	0550	6.6	1208	1.6	1803	6.7		
22	M	0032	1.6	0626	6.4	1244	1.8	1838	6.5
23	TU	0109	1.8	0702	6.2	1320	2.1	1913	6.2
24	W	0148	2.1	0740	5.9	1358	2.4	1952	5.9
25	TH	0229	2.4	0822	5.5	1439	2.7	2036	5.6
26	F	0315	2.7	0912	5.3	1528	2.9	2130	5.4
27	SA	0409	2.9	1014	5.1	1628	3.1	◐ 2238	5.2
28	SU	0513	2.9	1124	5.1	1738	3.1	2349	5.2
29	M	0620	2.8	1231	5.2	1845	2.9		
30	TU	0052	5.4	0720	2.6	1329	5.5	1943	2.6
31	W	0147	5.7	0812	2.3	1418	5.8	2033	2.3

JUNE

Date	Day	Time	m	Time	m	Time	m	Time	m
1	TH	0235	6.0	0859	2.1	1502	6.2	2119	2.0
2	F	0320	6.3	0942	1.8	1544	6.5	2202	1.7
3	SA	0403	6.5	1025	1.6	1625	6.7	2246	1.4
4	SU	0446	6.7	1107	1.5	1707	6.9	○ 2330	1.3
5	M	0530	6.7	1151	1.4	1751	6.9		
6	TU	0015	1.2	0615	6.7	1236	1.5	1837	6.9
7	W	0103	1.3	0704	6.6	1324	1.6	1927	6.7
8	TH	0153	1.4	0756	6.3	1416	1.8	2021	6.5
9	F	0248	1.6	0853	6.1	1513	2.1	2121	6.3
10	SA	0347	1.9	0955	5.9	1616	2.2	◑ 2225	6.1
11	SU	0452	2.1	1102	5.7	1724	2.3	2332	6.0
12	M	0558	2.1	1210	5.7	1832	2.3		
13	TU	0039	6.0	0703	2.1	1315	5.8	1936	2.2
14	W	0141	6.1	0804	2.0	1413	6.0	2034	2.0
15	TH	0237	6.2	0858	1.9	1504	6.2	2126	1.9
16	F	0327	6.3	0947	1.9	1550	6.3	2214	1.8
17	SA	0412	6.3	1031	1.8	1631	6.4	2257	1.7
18	SU	0454	6.3	1111	1.8	1710	6.5	● 2337	1.7
19	M	0533	6.3	1149	1.9	1747	6.5		
20	TU	0015	1.8	0610	6.2	1225	1.9	1823	6.4
21	W	0052	1.8	0647	6.1	1302	2.0	1859	6.3
22	TH	0129	2.0	0723	6.0	1338	2.2	1935	6.1
23	F	0206	2.1	0800	5.8	1416	2.3	2013	5.9
24	SA	0245	2.3	0841	5.6	1456	2.5	2055	5.7
25	SU	0327	2.5	0926	5.4	1542	2.7	2143	5.6
26	M	0415	2.6	1019	5.3	1635	2.8	◐ 2240	5.4
27	TU	0511	2.7	1120	5.3	1736	2.8	2343	5.4
28	W	0613	2.7	1223	5.4	1841	2.7		
29	TH	0046	5.5	0715	2.5	1324	5.6	1943	2.5
30	F	0147	5.7	0813	2.3	1420	5.9	2041	2.2

JULY

Date	Day	Time	m	Time	m	Time	m	Time	m
1	SA	0244	6.0	0908	2.1	1514	6.2	2135	1.9
2	SU	0338	6.3	1000	1.8	1604	6.6	2226	1.5
3	M	0430	6.5	1050	1.5	1654	6.8	○ 2317	1.3
4	TU	0520	6.7	1139	1.4	1743	7.0		
5	W	0006	1.1	0610	6.8	1228	1.3	1832	7.1
6	TH	0056	1.0	0659	6.8	1318	1.3	1921	7.1
7	F	0146	1.0	0749	6.7	1408	1.4	2012	6.9
8	SA	0236	1.2	0839	6.4	1459	1.6	2103	6.7
9	SU	0328	1.5	0931	6.2	1553	1.9	2156	6.4
10	M	0423	1.9	1026	5.9	1650	2.1	◑ 2254	6.0
11	TU	0521	2.2	1127	5.7	1753	2.4	2358	5.8
12	W	0624	2.4	1233	5.6	1900	2.5		
13	TH	0106	5.7	0729	2.5	1340	5.7	2007	2.4
14	F	0212	5.7	0832	2.4	1442	5.8	2108	2.3
15	SA	0311	5.8	0928	2.3	1534	6.0	2200	2.1
16	SU	0400	6.0	1015	2.1	1619	6.2	2245	1.9
17	M	0442	6.1	1056	2.0	1658	6.3	● 2324	1.8
18	TU	0520	6.2	1134	1.9	1734	6.4		
19	W	0000	1.7	0555	6.3	1209	1.9	1808	6.5
20	TH	0034	1.7	0628	6.3	1243	1.9	1841	6.5
21	F	0107	1.7	0701	6.2	1316	1.9	1913	6.4
22	SA	0140	1.8	0733	6.1	1349	2.0	1945	6.3
23	SU	0212	2.0	0806	6.0	1423	2.1	2019	6.1
24	M	0247	2.2	0842	5.8	1501	2.3	2057	5.9
25	TU	0326	2.4	0924	5.6	1544	2.5	◐ 2142	5.7
26	W	0412	2.6	1017	5.5	1637	2.7	2239	5.5
27	TH	0510	2.7	1122	5.4	1743	2.8	2350	5.4
28	F	0621	2.8	1235	5.5	1857	2.7		
29	SA	0107	5.5	0735	2.6	1347	5.7	2011	2.4
30	SU	0220	5.7	0844	2.3	1453	6.1	2116	2.0
31	M	0325	6.1	0944	1.9	1551	6.5	2214	1.5

AUGUST

Date	Day	Time	m	Time	m	Time	m	Time	m
1	TU	0420	6.5	1038	1.5	1644	7.0	○ 2306	1.1
2	W	0511	6.9	1128	1.2	1733	7.3	2356	0.8
3	TH	0559	7.1	1217	0.9	1820	7.5		
4	F	0043	0.6	0645	7.1	1304	0.9	1906	7.5
5	SA	0129	0.7	0730	7.0	1349	1.0	1951	7.3
6	SU	0215	1.0	0813	6.8	1435	1.3	2035	6.9
7	M	0300	1.4	0857	6.4	1522	1.7	2121	6.4
8	TU	0347	1.9	0945	6.0	1613	2.2	◑ 2212	5.9
9	W	0440	2.4	1040	5.6	1713	2.6	2315	5.5
10	TH	0542	2.7	1151	5.4	1826	2.8		
11	F	0035	5.3	0658	2.9	1314	5.3	1948	2.8
12	SA	0158	5.3	0815	2.8	1431	5.6	2057	2.5
13	SU	0302	5.6	0915	2.5	1525	5.9	2150	2.2
14	M	0350	5.9	1002	2.3	1608	6.2	2232	2.0
15	TU	0429	6.1	1041	2.0	1644	6.4	2308	1.8
16	W	0503	6.3	1116	1.8	1717	6.6	● 2340	1.6
17	TH	0535	6.4	1148	1.7	1747	6.7		
18	F	0011	1.5	0605	6.5	1219	1.6	1817	6.7
19	SA	0041	1.5	0634	6.5	1249	1.6	1846	6.7
20	SU	0110	1.6	0703	6.5	1320	1.7	1915	6.6
21	M	0139	1.7	0732	6.3	1351	1.8	1945	6.4
22	TU	0210	1.9	0804	6.1	1425	2.1	2018	6.2
23	W	0245	2.2	0841	5.9	1506	2.3	2058	5.8
24	TH	0328	2.5	0928	5.6	1556	2.6	◐ 2152	5.5
25	F	0424	2.8	1035	5.4	1702	2.9	2309	5.3
26	SA	0540	3.0	1201	5.3	1826	2.9		
27	SU	0043	5.3	0711	2.8	1329	5.6	1954	2.5
28	M	0211	5.7	0831	2.4	1442	6.1	2105	1.9
29	TU	0317	6.2	0933	1.8	1540	6.7	2202	1.3
30	W	0409	6.7	1025	1.3	1630	7.2	2252	0.8
31	TH	0457	7.1	1113	0.9	1717	7.6	○ 2339	0.5

Chart Datum: 3·64 metres below IGN Datum
HAT is 7·9 metres above Chart Datum

TIME ZONE -0100
(French Standard Time)
Subtract 1 hour for UT
For French Summer Time add
ONE hour in **non-shaded areas**

FRANCE – BREST

LAT 48°23'N LONG 4°30'W

TIMES AND HEIGHTS OF HIGH AND LOW WATERS

Dates in amber are **SPRINGS**
Dates in grey are **NEAPS**

2023

SEPTEMBER

Date	Day	Time	m	Time	m	Time	m	Time	m
1	F	0541	7.4	1159	0.7	1801	7.8		
2	SA	0023	0.4	0623	7.4	1242	0.7	1843	7.7
3	SU	0106	0.6	0703	7.2	1325	0.9	1924	7.4
4	M	0147	1.0	0742	6.9	1407	1.2	2003	6.9
5	TU	0227	1.5	0820	6.5	1450	1.8	2044	6.3
6	W	0310	2.1	0902	6.0	1537	2.3	◑ 2131	5.7
7	TH	0358	2.6	0954	5.5	1635	2.8	2235	5.2
8	F	0501	3.1	1113	5.2	1755	3.1		
9	SA	0009	5.0	0629	3.2	1254	5.2	1932	3.0
10	SU	0147	5.1	0759	3.0	1417	5.5	2043	2.7
11	M	0249	5.5	0859	2.6	1508	5.9	2131	2.3
12	TU	0331	5.9	0942	2.3	1547	6.2	2209	1.9
13	W	0407	6.2	1018	2.0	1620	6.5	2242	1.7
14	TH	0438	6.5	1051	1.7	1651	6.7	2313	1.5
15	F	0507	6.6	1121	1.6	1720	6.8	● 2342	1.4
16	SA	0536	6.8	1151	1.5	1749	6.9		
17	SU	0011	1.4	0604	6.8	1221	1.5	1817	6.9
18	M	0039	1.4	0632	6.7	1251	1.5	1845	6.8
19	TU	0108	1.6	0701	6.6	1322	1.7	1915	6.6
20	W	0139	1.8	0732	6.4	1357	2.0	1948	6.3
21	TH	0215	2.2	0809	6.1	1439	2.3	2028	5.9
22	F	0258	2.5	0857	5.7	1531	2.6	◐ 2124	5.5
23	SA	0357	2.9	1008	5.4	1640	2.9	2250	5.2
24	SU	0520	3.1	1146	5.3	1812	2.9		
25	M	0038	5.3	0702	2.9	1321	5.7	1945	2.5
26	TU	0205	5.8	0821	2.4	1430	6.3	2052	1.8
27	W	0304	6.4	0918	1.7	1523	6.9	2145	1.2
28	TH	0352	6.9	1007	1.2	1611	7.4	2233	0.8
29	F	0436	7.3	1053	0.8	1655	7.7	○ 2317	0.5
30	SA	0518	7.5	1136	0.6	1737	7.8	2359	0.5

OCTOBER

Date	Day	Time	m	Time	m	Time	m	Time	m
1	SU	0557	7.5	1218	0.7	1817	7.6		
2	M	0039	0.8	0634	7.3	1258	1.0	1855	7.3
3	TU	0117	1.2	0710	7.0	1338	1.4	1932	6.8
4	W	0155	1.7	0746	6.5	1419	1.9	2011	6.2
5	TH	0235	2.3	0825	6.0	1505	2.5	2056	5.6
6	F	0321	2.8	0915	5.5	1602	3.0	◑ 2200	5.1
7	SA	0423	3.2	1035	5.1	1723	3.2	2339	4.9
8	SU	0554	3.4	1223	5.1	1902	3.1		
9	M	0119	5.1	0729	3.2	1346	5.4	2012	2.8
10	TU	0219	5.5	0828	2.8	1436	5.8	2058	2.4
11	W	0300	5.9	0910	2.4	1514	6.2	2135	2.0
12	TH	0334	6.2	0945	2.0	1547	6.5	2208	1.7
13	F	0405	6.5	1018	1.7	1618	6.7	2239	1.5
14	SA	0436	6.7	1050	1.5	1649	6.9	● 2310	1.4
15	SU	0505	6.9	1122	1.4	1719	7.0	2340	1.4
16	M	0535	6.9	1153	1.4	1749	6.9		
17	TU	0011	1.5	0605	6.9	1225	1.5	1819	6.8
18	W	0042	1.6	0636	6.8	1300	1.7	1852	6.6
19	TH	0116	1.9	0710	6.5	1339	1.9	1930	6.3
20	F	0156	2.2	0751	6.2	1424	2.3	2016	5.9
21	SA	0244	2.6	0845	5.8	1520	2.6	2119	5.5
22	SU	0348	2.9	1003	5.5	1634	2.8	◐ 2250	5.3
23	M	0514	3.1	1139	5.5	1805	2.7		
24	TU	0031	5.4	0650	2.8	1305	5.9	1929	2.3
25	W	0147	5.9	0801	2.3	1409	6.4	2031	1.8
26	TH	0242	6.4	0856	1.7	1501	6.9	2122	1.3
27	F	0329	6.9	0945	1.2	1548	7.3	2209	1.0
28	SA	0412	7.2	1030	1.0	1631	7.5	○ 2252	0.8
29	SU	0452	7.4	1113	0.9	1712	7.5	2333	0.9
30	M	0531	7.3	1154	1.0	1751	7.3		
31	TU	0012	1.1	0607	7.2	1234	1.2	1829	7.0

NOVEMBER

Date	Day	Time	m	Time	m	Time	m	Time	m
1	W	0050	1.5	0643	6.9	1313	1.6	1907	6.5
2	TH	0128	1.9	0720	6.5	1355	2.0	1946	6.1
3	F	0208	2.4	0759	6.0	1439	2.5	2031	5.6
4	SA	0252	2.8	0847	5.6	1533	2.9	2130	5.2
5	SU	0349	3.2	0956	5.3	1642	3.2	◑ 2252	5.0
6	M	0505	3.3	1125	5.2	1804	3.2		
7	TU	0018	5.1	0629	3.2	1246	5.3	1916	2.9
8	W	0125	5.4	0735	2.9	1344	5.6	2009	2.6
9	TH	0213	5.7	0824	2.6	1428	6.0	2050	2.3
10	F	0252	6.1	0904	2.2	1506	6.3	2128	2.0
11	SA	0328	6.4	0942	1.9	1542	6.5	2203	1.7
12	SU	0402	6.7	1018	1.7	1617	6.7	2238	1.6
13	M	0436	6.8	1054	1.5	1651	6.8	● 2312	1.5
14	TU	0509	6.9	1129	1.5	1726	6.9	2347	1.5
15	W	0544	6.9	1207	1.5	1802	6.8		
16	TH	0024	1.7	0621	6.8	1247	1.6	1842	6.6
17	F	0105	1.9	0702	6.6	1331	1.8	1926	6.3
18	SA	0150	2.1	0750	6.4	1421	2.1	2019	6.0
19	SU	0243	2.4	0849	6.1	1519	2.3	2125	5.7
20	M	0347	2.7	1000	5.9	1629	2.5	◐ 2243	5.5
21	TU	0504	2.7	1120	5.9	1747	2.4		
22	W	0005	5.7	0623	2.6	1236	6.1	1901	2.2
23	TH	0115	6.0	0732	2.2	1340	6.4	2002	1.9
24	F	0213	6.3	0830	1.9	1435	6.7	2056	1.6
25	SA	0302	6.6	0921	1.6	1524	6.9	2144	1.4
26	SU	0348	6.9	1008	1.4	1609	7.0	2229	1.3
27	M	0430	7.0	1053	1.3	1652	7.0	○ 2311	1.4
28	TU	0510	7.0	1135	1.4	1732	6.9	2351	1.5
29	W	0548	6.9	1215	1.5	1811	6.7		
30	TH	0029	1.7	0626	6.7	1255	1.7	1850	6.4

DECEMBER

Date	Day	Time	m	Time	m	Time	m	Time	m
1	F	0108	2.0	0703	6.5	1336	2.0	1929	6.1
2	SA	0147	2.3	0742	6.2	1417	2.3	2011	5.8
3	SU	0229	2.6	0825	5.9	1503	2.6	2059	5.5
4	M	0315	2.9	0915	5.6	1554	2.9	2156	5.2
5	TU	0410	3.1	1017	5.4	1655	3.0	◑ 2303	5.2
6	W	0515	3.1	1127	5.3	1801	3.0		
7	TH	0010	5.3	0623	3.0	1233	5.4	1902	2.8
8	F	0110	5.5	0724	2.8	1330	5.7	1956	2.6
9	SA	0201	5.8	0816	2.5	1420	5.9	2043	2.3
10	SU	0247	6.1	0903	2.2	1505	6.2	2126	2.0
11	M	0329	6.4	0947	1.9	1547	6.4	2208	1.8
12	TU	0410	6.6	1029	1.7	1629	6.6	2249	1.7
13	W	0450	6.8	1112	1.5	1711	6.7	● 2331	1.6
14	TH	0532	6.9	1155	1.4	1754	6.8		
15	F	0015	1.6	0616	7.0	1240	1.4	1840	6.7
16	SA	0100	1.6	0702	6.9	1327	1.5	1928	6.5
17	SU	0148	1.8	0752	6.7	1418	1.6	2020	6.3
18	M	0240	2.0	0846	6.5	1512	1.8	2117	6.1
19	TU	0337	2.2	0945	6.3	1612	2.1	◐ 2220	5.9
20	W	0440	2.3	1049	6.1	1717	2.2	2327	5.8
21	TH	0548	2.4	1158	6.0	1824	2.3		
22	F	0035	5.8	0657	2.4	1306	6.1	1929	2.2
23	SA	0140	6.0	0802	2.2	1408	6.2	2029	2.1
24	SU	0237	6.2	0900	2.0	1504	6.3	2123	2.0
25	M	0329	6.4	0953	1.8	1554	6.4	2211	1.8
26	TU	0415	6.6	1040	1.7	1639	6.5	2255	1.8
27	W	0457	6.7	1123	1.6	1720	6.5	○ 2336	1.8
28	TH	0537	6.7	1203	1.6	1759	6.5		
29	F	0015	1.8	0614	6.7	1241	1.7	1836	6.4
30	SA	0052	1.9	0650	6.6	1318	1.8	1912	6.2
31	SU	0128	2.0	0725	6.4	1354	2.0	1948	6.0

Chart Datum: 3·64 metres below IGN Datum
HAT is 7·9 metres above Chart Datum

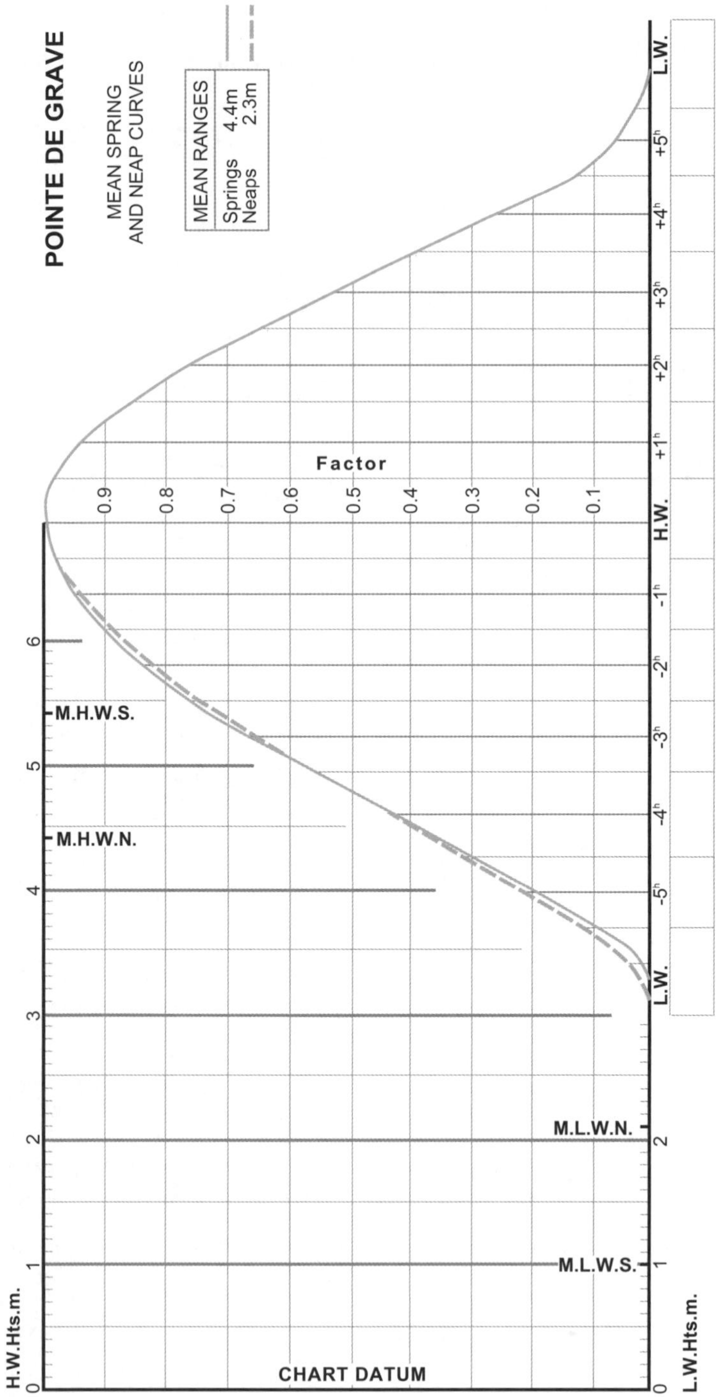
POINTE DE GRAVE
MEAN SPRING
AND NEAP CURVES
MEAN RANGES
Springs 4.4m
Neaps 2.3m
Factor
0.9
0.8
0.7
0.6
0.5
0.4
0.3
0.2
0.1
L.W.
-5h
-4h
-3h
-2h
-1h
H.W.
+1h
+2h
+3h
+4h
+5h
L.W.
H.W.Hts.m.
0
1
2
3
4
5
6
M.H.W.S.
M.H.W.N.
M.L.W.N.
M.L.W.S.
CHART DATUM
L.W.Hts.m.

TIME ZONE -0100 (French Standard Time) **Subtract 1 hour for UT** For French Summer Time add ONE hour in **non-shaded areas**

FRANCE – POINTE DE GRAVE

LAT 45°34′N LONG 1°04′W

TIMES AND HEIGHTS OF HIGH AND LOW WATERS

Dates in amber are **SPRINGS** Dates in grey are **NEAPS**

2023

JANUARY

Day	Time	m	Day	Time	m
1	0051	4.4	16	0501	2.1
	0620	2.0		1140	4.4
SU	1312	4.5	M	1741	2.1
	1854	2.0			
2	0152	4.5	17	0028	4.3
	0726	2.0		0610	2.1
M	1413	4.6	TU	1255	4.4
	1956	2.0		1852	2.1
3	0243	4.6	18	0137	4.5
	0827	1.9		0720	2.0
TU	1505	4.6	W	1409	4.6
	2051	1.9		2001	1.9
4	0328	4.7	19	0240	4.8
	0921	1.8		0829	1.8
W	1550	4.7	TH	1515	4.8
	2138	1.8		2104	1.7
5	0408	4.8	20	0337	5.1
	1007	1.7		0933	1.5
TH	1629	4.8	F	1612	5.0
	2219	1.7		2202	1.4
6	0444	4.9	21	0431	5.3
	1048	1.6		1031	1.2
F	1706	4.8	SA	1705	5.2
	2257	1.7	●	2254	1.2
7	0519	5.0	22	0522	5.5
	1126	1.6		1124	1.0
SA	1741	4.9	SU	1755	5.4
○	2332	1.6		2344	1.1
8	0552	5.0	23	0612	5.7
	1201	1.5		1213	0.8
SU	1814	4.8	M	1842	5.4
9	0007	1.6	24	0031	1.0
	0625	5.0		0700	5.7
M	1235	1.5	TU	1300	0.8
	1846	4.8		1929	5.3
10	0041	1.6	25	0117	1.0
	0657	5.0		0747	5.6
TU	1310	1.6	W	1344	0.9
	1918	4.7		2014	5.1
11	0116	1.7	26	0201	1.1
	0730	4.9		0833	5.4
W	1344	1.7	TH	1428	1.1
	1952	4.6		2059	4.9
12	0151	1.7	27	0246	1.3
	0806	4.8		0919	5.1
TH	1418	1.7	F	1512	1.4
	2030	4.5		2146	4.6
13	0228	1.8	28	0335	1.6
	0845	4.7		1009	4.7
F	1456	1.9	SA	1601	1.7
	2115	4.4	◐	2240	4.3
14	0310	1.9	29	0430	1.9
	0932	4.6		1109	4.4
SA	1540	2.0	SU	1659	2.0
	2211	4.3		2353	4.2
15	0400	2.1	30	0536	2.1
	1030	4.4		1227	4.2
SU	1635	2.1	M	1808	2.2
◑	2317	4.3			
			31	0117	4.2
				0652	2.2
			TU	1347	4.2
				1924	2.2

FEBRUARY

Day	Time	m	Day	Time	m
1	0222	4.3	16	0112	4.4
	0808	2.1		0655	2.1
W	1450	4.3	TH	1357	4.4
	2032	2.1		1942	2.1
2	0314	4.5	17	0227	4.6
	0909	2.0		0818	1.8
TH	1539	4.4	F	1509	4.7
	2125	2.0		2055	1.8
3	0356	4.7	18	0328	5.0
	0956	1.8		0927	1.5
F	1619	4.6	SA	1606	5.0
	2208	1.8		2154	1.4
4	0433	4.8	19	0421	5.3
	1036	1.6		1023	1.1
SA	1654	4.7	SU	1656	5.2
	2245	1.6		2245	1.1
5	0505	5.0	20	0510	5.6
	1112	1.5		1113	0.8
SU	1726	4.8	M	1741	5.4
○	2319	1.5	●	2332	0.9
6	0537	5.0	21	0556	5.8
	1146	1.4		1158	0.7
M	1756	4.9	TU	1823	5.4
	2353	1.4			
7	0607	5.1	22	0016	0.8
	1218	1.3		0639	5.8
TU	1826	4.9	W	1241	0.7
				1904	5.4
8	0025	1.4	23	0058	0.8
	0637	5.1		0721	5.6
W	1249	1.3	TH	1321	0.8
	1855	4.9		1943	5.2
9	0056	1.4	24	0138	1.0
	0706	5.1		0801	5.4
TH	1319	1.4	F	1359	1.1
	1925	4.9		2019	5.0
10	0127	1.4	25	0217	1.2
	0738	5.0		0840	5.0
F	1349	1.5	SA	1437	1.4
	1957	4.8		2055	4.7
11	0159	1.5	26	0259	1.5
	0812	4.9		0921	4.6
SA	1421	1.6	SU	1519	1.8
	2035	4.6		2137	4.4
12	0235	1.7	27	0348	1.9
	0853	4.7		1011	4.3
SU	1459	1.8	M	1610	2.1
	2121	4.5	◐	2239	4.1
13	0319	1.8	28	0452	2.2
	0944	4.5		1132	4.0
M	1546	2.0	TU	1720	2.4
◑	2223	4.3			
14	0415	2.0			
	1053	4.3			
TU	1651	2.2			
	2343	4.2			
15	0529	2.1			
	1224	4.2			
W	1815	2.2			

MARCH

Day	Time	m	Day	Time	m
1	0029	4.0	16	0506	2.2
	0617	2.4		1217	4.1
W	1320	3.9	TH	1755	2.3
	1850	2.5			
2	0158	4.1	17	0059	4.3
	0747	2.3		0647	2.1
TH	1432	4.1	F	1353	4.3
	2012	2.3		1934	2.2
3	0254	4.3	18	0215	4.7
	0851	2.1		0814	1.8
F	1523	4.3	SA	1501	4.7
	2106	2.1		2046	1.8
4	0338	4.5	19	0315	5.0
	0936	1.8		0916	1.4
SA	1601	4.5	SU	1553	5.0
	2148	1.8		2140	1.4
5	0413	4.8	20	0406	5.4
	1014	1.6		1007	1.0
SU	1633	4.7	M	1639	5.3
	2224	1.6		2228	1.1
6	0444	4.9	21	0452	5.6
	1049	1.4		1053	0.8
M	1702	4.9	TU	1719	5.4
	2258	1.4	●	2312	0.8
7	0513	5.1	22	0534	5.7
	1121	1.3		1136	0.7
TU	1731	5.0	W	1758	5.4
○	2330	1.3		2354	0.8
8	0542	5.2	23	0614	5.7
	1153	1.2		1215	0.8
W	1800	5.1	TH	1835	5.4
9	0002	1.2	24	0033	0.8
	0611	5.2		0652	5.5
TH	1223	1.2	F	1252	1.0
	1828	5.1		1909	5.2
10	0032	1.2	25	0110	1.0
	0640	5.2		0728	5.3
F	1252	1.2	SA	1327	1.2
	1857	5.0		1942	5.0
11	0102	1.2	26	0147	1.3
	0711	5.1		0803	4.9
SA	1321	1.3	SU	1402	1.5
	1928	5.0		2014	4.7
12	0134	1.3	27	0225	1.6
	0744	5.0		0839	4.6
SU	1352	1.5	M	1440	1.8
	2004	4.8		2051	4.4
13	0209	1.5	28	0310	2.0
	0824	4.7		0925	4.2
M	1429	1.7	TU	1526	2.2
	2048	4.6		2143	4.1
14	0251	1.7	29	0410	2.3
	0915	4.5		1041	3.9
TU	1515	2.0	W	1633	2.5
	2150	4.4	◐	2323	3.9
15	0347	2.0	30	0537	2.5
	1029	4.2		1241	3.8
W	1621	2.2	TH	1807	2.6
◑	2317	4.2			
			31	0116	4.0
				0711	2.4
			F	1358	4.0
				1934	2.4

APRIL

Day	Time	m	Day	Time	m
1	0220	4.2	16	0157	4.7
	0818	2.1		0757	1.7
SA	1450	4.2	SU	1442	4.7
	2032	2.2		2025	1.7
2	0305	4.5	17	0255	5.0
	0904	1.9		0855	1.4
SU	1528	4.5	M	1531	5.0
	2116	1.9		2117	1.4
3	0341	4.7	18	0345	5.3
	0942	1.6		0943	1.1
M	1600	4.7	TU	1614	5.2
	2153	1.6		2204	1.1
4	0412	4.9	19	0429	5.4
	1016	1.4		1027	1.0
TU	1630	4.9	W	1653	5.3
	2227	1.4		2247	1.0
5	0442	5.1	20	0509	5.5
	1049	1.3		1108	1.0
W	1700	5.0	TH	1730	5.3
	2300	1.3	●	2328	1.0
6	0513	5.2	21	0547	5.5
	1121	1.2		1146	1.0
TH	1729	5.1	F	1805	5.3
○	2333	1.2			
7	0543	5.2	22	0006	1.0
	1152	1.2		0624	5.3
F	1800	5.2	SA	1221	1.2
				1838	5.2
8	0006	1.1	23	0043	1.2
	0615	5.2		0659	5.1
SA	1223	1.2	SU	1255	1.4
	1832	5.2		1911	5.0
9	0039	1.2	24	0118	1.4
	0648	5.1		0733	4.8
SU	1256	1.3	M	1329	1.6
	1906	5.1		1944	4.8
10	0114	1.3	25	0156	1.7
	0726	5.0		0810	4.5
M	1331	1.5	TU	1407	1.9
	1946	4.9		2022	4.5
11	0152	1.4	26	0239	2.0
	0810	4.7		0855	4.2
TU	1411	1.7	W	1451	2.2
	2035	4.7		2111	4.3
12	0238	1.7	27	0334	2.2
	0907	4.4		1002	3.9
W	1501	2.0	TH	1553	2.5
	2140	4.5	◐	2228	4.1
13	0337	1.9	28	0450	2.4
	1030	4.2		1141	3.9
TH	1611	2.3	F	1715	2.6
◑	2312	4.3			
14	0500	2.1	29	0007	4.0
	1219	4.2		0611	2.4
F	1749	2.3	SA	1301	4.0
				1833	2.5
15	0046	4.5	30	0120	4.2
	0640	2.0		0721	2.2
SA	1342	4.4	SU	1357	4.2
	1919	2.1		1937	2.2

Chart Datum: 2·83 metres below IGN Datum
HAT is 6·1 metres above Chart Datum

TIME ZONE -0100
(French Standard Time)
Subtract 1 hour for UT
For French Summer Time add ONE hour in **non-shaded areas**

FRANCE – POINTE DE GRAVE

LAT 45°34′N LONG 1°04′W

TIMES AND HEIGHTS OF HIGH AND LOW WATERS

Dates in amber are **SPRINGS**
Dates in grey are **NEAPS**

2023

MAY

Date	Day	Time	m	Time	m	Time	m	Time	m
1	M	0214	4.4	0815	2.0	1440	4.4	2028	2.0
2	TU	0255	4.6	0858	1.7	1517	4.7	2110	1.7
3	W	0332	4.8	0935	1.5	1551	4.9	2148	1.5
4	TH	0407	5.0	1011	1.4	1625	5.0	2226	1.4
5	F	0442	5.1	1046	1.3	1659	5.2	○ 2303	1.2
6	SA	0517	5.2	1122	1.2	1734	5.2	2341	1.2
7	SU	0555	5.2	1159	1.3	1812	5.2		
8	M	0020	1.2	0635	5.1	1237	1.3	1854	5.1
9	TU	0100	1.2	0719	4.9	1318	1.5	1941	5.0
10	W	0145	1.4	0811	4.7	1404	1.7	2037	4.8
11	TH	0235	1.6	0915	4.4	1459	1.9	2145	4.6
12	F	0337	1.8	1039	4.3	1609	2.1	◑ 2307	4.6
13	SA	0455	1.9	1204	4.3	1734	2.1		
14	SU	0024	4.6	0618	1.8	1316	4.5	1851	1.9
15	M	0131	4.8	0727	1.7	1414	4.7	1954	1.7
16	TU	0230	5.0	0824	1.5	1504	4.9	2048	1.5
17	W	0320	5.1	0914	1.3	1547	5.0	2136	1.3
18	TH	0404	5.2	0958	1.3	1626	5.1	2221	1.2
19	F	0445	5.2	1039	1.3	1703	5.2	● 2303	1.2
20	SA	0524	5.2	1118	1.3	1739	5.1	2342	1.3
21	SU	0601	5.1	1153	1.4	1815	5.1		
22	M	0019	1.4	0637	4.9	1228	1.6	1849	5.0
23	TU	0056	1.6	0713	4.7	1304	1.7	1924	4.8
24	W	0134	1.7	0750	4.5	1342	1.9	2003	4.6
25	TH	0216	1.9	0833	4.3	1426	2.1	2048	4.4
26	F	0304	2.1	0927	4.1	1518	2.3	2145	4.3
27	SA	0403	2.2	1038	4.0	1623	2.4	◐ 2257	4.2
28	SU	0508	2.3	1151	4.0	1729	2.4		
29	M	0008	4.2	0612	2.2	1253	4.2	1831	2.2
30	TU	0108	4.3	0711	2.1	1344	4.4	1927	2.1
31	W	0200	4.5	0803	1.9	1429	4.6	2018	1.9

JUNE

Date	Day	Time	m	Time	m	Time	m	Time	m
1	TH	0247	4.7	0849	1.7	1511	4.8	2105	1.7
2	F	0331	4.9	0932	1.5	1552	5.0	2151	1.5
3	SA	0414	5.0	1014	1.4	1633	5.1	2235	1.3
4	SU	0458	5.1	1057	1.3	1716	5.2	○ 2321	1.2
5	M	0543	5.1	1140	1.3	1802	5.3		
6	TU	0006	1.1	0631	5.1	1225	1.3	1851	5.2
7	W	0053	1.2	0721	4.9	1312	1.4	1943	5.1
8	TH	0142	1.3	0816	4.8	1401	1.6	2040	5.0
9	F	0233	1.4	0918	4.6	1456	1.7	2142	4.9
10	SA	0331	1.5	1025	4.5	1558	1.8	◑ 2248	4.8
11	SU	0435	1.7	1134	4.4	1707	1.9	2354	4.7
12	M	0543	1.7	1241	4.5	1815	1.8		
13	TU	0100	4.7	0650	1.7	1343	4.6	1920	1.8
14	W	0201	4.7	0750	1.7	1436	4.7	2018	1.7
15	TH	0255	4.8	0844	1.6	1523	4.8	2111	1.6
16	F	0343	4.8	0932	1.6	1604	4.9	2200	1.5
17	SA	0426	4.9	1016	1.6	1643	5.0	2244	1.5
18	SU	0507	4.9	1056	1.6	1721	5.0	● 2325	1.5
19	M	0545	4.8	1134	1.6	1758	5.0		
20	TU	0004	1.5	0622	4.8	1210	1.6	1833	4.9
21	W	0041	1.6	0656	4.7	1247	1.7	1908	4.8
22	TH	0118	1.7	0731	4.6	1324	1.8	1944	4.7
23	F	0156	1.8	0808	4.4	1403	1.9	2023	4.6
24	SA	0236	1.9	0850	4.3	1446	2.0	2106	4.5
25	SU	0319	2.0	0939	4.2	1533	2.1	2157	4.4
26	M	0408	2.1	1039	4.2	1627	2.2	◐ 2257	4.3
27	TU	0504	2.1	1143	4.2	1727	2.2		
28	W	0000	4.3	0605	2.1	1245	4.3	1828	2.1
29	TH	0103	4.4	0705	2.0	1342	4.4	1928	2.0
30	F	0203	4.5	0803	1.9	1435	4.7	2026	1.8

JULY

Date	Day	Time	m	Time	m	Time	m	Time	m
1	SA	0301	4.7	0857	1.7	1525	4.9	2122	1.6
2	SU	0355	4.9	0950	1.5	1615	5.1	2216	1.4
3	M	0447	5.0	1040	1.4	1705	5.3	○ 2308	1.2
4	TU	0537	5.1	1129	1.3	1755	5.4	2358	1.0
5	W	0628	5.1	1218	1.2	1846	5.4		
6	TH	0047	1.0	0718	5.1	1305	1.2	1938	5.4
7	F	0135	1.0	0809	5.0	1353	1.3	2030	5.3
8	SA	0223	1.1	0900	4.8	1443	1.4	2122	5.1
9	SU	0312	1.3	0955	4.6	1535	1.5	2218	4.9
10	M	0405	1.5	1054	4.5	1634	1.7	◑ 2317	4.7
11	TU	0505	1.7	1200	4.4	1739	1.8		
12	W	0024	4.5	0610	1.9	1310	4.4	1847	1.9
13	TH	0134	4.4	0717	2.0	1413	4.4	1954	1.9
14	F	0236	4.5	0820	1.9	1505	4.6	2055	1.8
15	SA	0329	4.5	0915	1.8	1551	4.7	2148	1.7
16	SU	0414	4.6	1003	1.7	1631	4.8	2234	1.6
17	M	0455	4.7	1044	1.7	1708	4.9	● 2315	1.5
18	TU	0531	4.7	1122	1.6	1743	5.0	2352	1.5
19	W	0605	4.8	1157	1.6	1816	5.0		
20	TH	0027	1.5	0637	4.7	1232	1.6	1848	4.9
21	F	0100	1.5	0708	4.7	1305	1.6	1919	4.9
22	SA	0133	1.6	0739	4.6	1338	1.7	1952	4.8
23	SU	0205	1.6	0813	4.5	1412	1.7	2028	4.7
24	M	0238	1.8	0851	4.4	1449	1.8	2108	4.6
25	TU	0316	1.9	0937	4.3	1533	2.0	◐ 2157	4.4
26	W	0403	2.0	1036	4.2	1628	2.1	2259	4.3
27	TH	0502	2.1	1147	4.2	1735	2.2		
28	F	0013	4.3	0613	2.2	1301	4.3	1847	2.1
29	SA	0131	4.3	0726	2.1	1409	4.5	1958	1.9
30	SU	0242	4.5	0834	1.9	1509	4.8	2105	1.6
31	M	0344	4.8	0935	1.6	1603	5.1	2205	1.3

AUGUST

Date	Day	Time	m	Time	m	Time	m	Time	m
1	TU	0438	5.0	1030	1.3	1655	5.4	○ 2259	1.1
2	W	0529	5.2	1120	1.1	1745	5.6	2349	0.9
3	TH	0616	5.3	1207	1.0	1833	5.6		
4	F	0035	0.8	0702	5.3	1253	0.9	1920	5.6
5	SA	0120	0.8	0747	5.2	1337	1.0	2007	5.4
6	SU	0203	1.0	0831	5.0	1421	1.2	2053	5.2
7	M	0246	1.2	0917	4.7	1507	1.4	2141	4.9
8	TU	0332	1.5	1007	4.5	1559	1.7	◑ 2236	4.5
9	W	0425	1.9	1111	4.3	1702	2.0	2347	4.3
10	TH	0530	2.1	1239	4.2	1819	2.1		
11	F	0114	4.2	0648	2.2	1356	4.3	1939	2.1
12	SA	0225	4.2	0804	2.2	1454	4.4	2046	2.0
13	SU	0320	4.3	0904	2.0	1540	4.6	2138	1.8
14	M	0404	4.5	0951	1.8	1618	4.8	2221	1.6
15	TU	0440	4.7	1031	1.6	1651	4.9	2259	1.5
16	W	0512	4.8	1107	1.5	1722	5.0	● 2333	1.4
17	TH	0542	4.8	1140	1.4	1752	5.1		
18	F	0005	1.4	0611	4.9	1211	1.4	1821	5.1
19	SA	0035	1.4	0639	4.9	1241	1.4	1850	5.0
20	SU	0104	1.4	0707	4.8	1310	1.5	1919	5.0
21	M	0132	1.5	0737	4.8	1340	1.6	1951	4.9
22	TU	0201	1.6	0811	4.6	1413	1.7	2027	4.7
23	W	0234	1.8	0851	4.5	1452	1.9	2113	4.5
24	TH	0316	2.0	0946	4.3	1543	2.1	◐ 2215	4.3
25	F	0413	2.2	1102	4.2	1652	2.2	2341	4.2
26	SA	0533	2.3	1233	4.3	1820	2.2		
27	SU	0118	4.2	0703	2.2	1354	4.5	1946	2.0
28	M	0234	4.5	0823	1.9	1457	4.9	2057	1.6
29	TU	0334	4.8	0925	1.6	1551	5.2	2155	1.2
30	W	0425	5.1	1017	1.2	1640	5.5	2245	0.9
31	TH	0512	5.3	1105	1.0	1727	5.7	○ 2332	0.7

Chart Datum: 2·83 metres below IGN Datum
HAT is 6·1 metres above Chart Datum

TIME ZONE -0100
(French Standard Time)
Subtract 1 hour for UT
For French Summer Time add ONE hour in **non-shaded areas**

FRANCE – POINTE DE GRAVE

LAT 45°34′N LONG 1°04′W

TIMES AND HEIGHTS OF HIGH AND LOW WATERS

Dates in amber are **SPRINGS**
Dates in grey are **NEAPS**

2023

SEPTEMBER

Date	Day	Time	m	Date	Day	Time	m
1	F	0556	5.4	16	SA	0540	5.0
		1150	0.8			1144	1.3
		1812	5.8			1752	5.2
2	SA	0015	0.7	17	SU	0005	1.3
		0638	5.4			0608	5.1
		1233	0.8			1214	1.3
		1855	5.7			1819	5.2
3	SU	0056	0.8	18	M	0033	1.4
		0718	5.3			0636	5.0
		1314	0.9			1242	1.4
		1938	5.5			1848	5.1
4	M	0136	1.0	19	TU	0101	1.5
		0757	5.1			0706	5.0
		1354	1.1			1312	1.5
		2020	5.2			1920	4.9
5	TU	0215	1.3	20	W	0130	1.6
		0837	4.8			0739	4.8
		1436	1.5			1346	1.6
		2103	4.8			1956	4.7
6	W	0256	1.7	21	TH	0204	1.8
		0920	4.5			0819	4.6
		1524	1.8			1425	1.8
	◑	2155	4.4			2043	4.5
7	TH	0345	2.0	22	F	0247	2.0
		1020	4.2			0915	4.4
		1627	2.2			1516	2.1
		2313	4.1		◐	2152	4.2
8	F	0451	2.4	23	SA	0345	2.3
		1207	4.1			1037	4.2
		1754	2.4			1628	2.3
						2334	4.1
9	SA	0058	4.0	24	SU	0511	2.4
		0622	2.5			1221	4.3
		1339	4.2			1808	2.2
		1925	2.3				
10	SU	0212	4.1	25	M	0115	4.3
		0748	2.3			0653	2.3
		1438	4.4			1341	4.6
		2031	2.0			1939	1.9
11	M	0305	4.3	26	TU	0223	4.6
		0847	2.1			0811	1.9
		1522	4.6			1442	5.0
		2119	1.8			2045	1.5
12	TU	0344	4.5	27	W	0319	4.9
		0931	1.8			0908	1.5
		1557	4.8			1534	5.4
		2158	1.6			2137	1.2
13	W	0416	4.7	28	TH	0406	5.2
		1008	1.6			0958	1.2
		1627	5.0			1621	5.6
		2233	1.4			2224	0.9
14	TH	0445	4.9	29	F	0449	5.4
		1042	1.5			1044	0.9
		1656	5.1			1705	5.8
		2305	1.3		○	2308	0.8
15	F	0513	5.0	30	SA	0530	5.5
		1114	1.4			1127	0.8
		1724	5.2			1747	5.8
	●	2336	1.3			2349	0.8

OCTOBER

Date	Day	Time	m	Date	Day	Time	m
1	SU	0609	5.5	16	M	0538	5.2
		1208	0.8			1145	1.3
		1828	5.7			1753	5.2
2	M	0028	0.9	17	TU	0003	1.4
		0647	5.4			0609	5.2
		1247	1.0			1218	1.4
		1908	5.4			1824	5.1
3	TU	0106	1.2	18	W	0034	1.5
		0724	5.1			0642	5.1
		1326	1.3			1252	1.4
		1947	5.1			1859	5.0
4	W	0142	1.5	19	TH	0108	1.6
		0801	4.9			0719	4.9
		1406	1.6			1329	1.6
		2028	4.7			1941	4.7
5	TH	0222	1.8	20	F	0146	1.8
		0841	4.6			0805	4.7
		1452	2.0			1412	1.8
		2118	4.3			2034	4.5
6	F	0308	2.2	21	SA	0233	2.1
		0937	4.3			0907	4.5
		1553	2.3			1506	2.1
	◑	2239	4.0			2152	4.2
7	SA	0414	2.5	22	SU	0336	2.3
		1123	4.1			1033	4.4
		1722	2.5			1622	2.2
					◐	2339	4.2
8	SU	0030	3.9	23	M	0503	2.4
		0547	2.6			1209	4.5
		1305	4.1			1759	2.2
		1855	2.4				
9	M	0143	4.1	24	TU	0102	4.4
		0714	2.5			0637	2.2
		1406	4.3			1322	4.8
		2002	2.1			1921	1.9
10	TU	0233	4.3	25	W	0205	4.7
		0814	2.2			0748	1.9
		1451	4.6			1421	5.1
		2047	1.9			2021	1.5
11	W	0311	4.6	26	TH	0257	5.0
		0858	1.9			0844	1.5
		1525	4.8			1513	5.4
		2125	1.7			2112	1.2
12	TH	0342	4.8	27	F	0342	5.2
		0936	1.7			0933	1.2
		1555	5.0			1559	5.6
		2159	1.5			2158	1.0
13	F	0411	4.9	28	SA	0423	5.4
		1010	1.5			1019	1.1
		1624	5.1			1642	5.6
		2231	1.4		○	2241	1.0
14	SA	0440	5.1	29	SU	0503	5.5
		1042	1.4			1102	1.0
		1654	5.2			1723	5.6
	●	2302	1.3			2321	1.0
15	SU	0509	5.2	30	M	0542	5.4
		1114	1.3			1143	1.0
		1723	5.2			1804	5.5
		2332	1.3				
				31	TU	0000	1.2
						0620	5.3
						1223	1.2
						1843	5.2

NOVEMBER

Date	Day	Time	m	Date	Day	Time	m
1	W	0037	1.4	16	TH	0016	1.5
		0657	5.1			0629	5.2
		1301	1.4			1239	1.4
		1922	4.9			1853	5.0
2	TH	0114	1.7	17	F	0056	1.6
		0734	4.9			0714	5.1
		1341	1.7			1321	1.5
		2002	4.6			1941	4.7
3	F	0153	1.9	18	SA	0140	1.8
		0815	4.6			0806	4.9
		1426	2.0			1409	1.7
		2050	4.3			2041	4.5
4	SA	0239	2.2	19	SU	0231	2.0
		0907	4.4			0910	4.7
		1522	2.3			1506	1.9
		2200	4.0			2158	4.4
5	SU	0340	2.5	20	M	0333	2.1
		1025	4.2			1028	4.6
		1637	2.5			1615	2.0
	◑	2334	4.0		◐	2323	4.4
6	M	0458	2.6	21	TU	0449	2.2
		1200	4.1			1146	4.7
		1757	2.4			1735	2.0
7	TU	0049	4.1	22	W	0035	4.5
		0614	2.5			0608	2.1
		1312	4.3			1255	4.8
		1907	2.3			1849	1.8
8	W	0143	4.3	23	TH	0137	4.7
		0719	2.3			0717	1.8
		1403	4.5			1356	5.0
		2000	2.1			1951	1.6
9	TH	0225	4.5	24	F	0231	4.9
		0810	2.1			0815	1.6
		1443	4.7			1450	5.2
		2042	1.8			2043	1.4
10	F	0301	4.7	25	SA	0318	5.1
		0853	1.9			0907	1.4
		1517	4.9			1538	5.3
		2119	1.7			2131	1.3
11	SA	0334	4.9	26	SU	0401	5.2
		0931	1.7			0955	1.3
		1551	5.0			1623	5.3
		2154	1.5			2215	1.3
12	SU	0407	5.1	27	M	0442	5.3
		1007	1.5			1040	1.3
		1625	5.1			1705	5.3
		2228	1.5		○	2257	1.3
13	M	0440	5.2	28	TU	0522	5.3
		1043	1.4			1123	1.3
		1658	5.2			1746	5.2
	●	2302	1.4			2336	1.4
14	TU	0514	5.2	29	W	0601	5.2
		1120	1.4			1204	1.4
		1734	5.2			1825	5.1
		2338	1.4				
15	W	0550	5.2	30	TH	0014	1.6
		1158	1.3			0639	5.1
		1811	5.1			1244	1.5
						1904	4.9

DECEMBER

Date	Day	Time	m	Date	Day	Time	m
1	F	0052	1.7	16	SA	0050	1.5
		0717	5.0			0715	5.2
		1324	1.7			1318	1.3
		1943	4.6			1946	4.9
2	SA	0132	1.9	17	SU	0137	1.6
		0756	4.8			0808	5.1
		1406	1.9			1407	1.4
		2025	4.4			2042	4.7
3	SU	0216	2.1	18	M	0227	1.7
		0840	4.6			0906	5.0
		1454	2.1			1459	1.6
		2116	4.2			2144	4.6
4	M	0307	2.3	19	TU	0323	1.8
		0934	4.4			1008	4.9
		1549	2.3			1557	1.7
		2221	4.1		◐	2251	4.5
5	TU	0406	2.4	20	W	0425	1.9
		1041	4.3			1114	4.8
		1650	2.3			1702	1.8
	◑	2333	4.1			2359	4.5
6	W	0509	2.4	21	TH	0533	1.9
		1152	4.2			1221	4.8
		1754	2.3			1811	1.9
7	TH	0036	4.2	22	F	0105	4.6
		0611	2.4			0642	1.9
		1255	4.3			1328	4.8
		1854	2.2			1916	1.8
8	F	0130	4.4	23	SA	0206	4.7
		0708	2.2			0746	1.8
		1348	4.5			1430	4.8
		1947	2.1			2016	1.8
9	SA	0216	4.6	24	SU	0259	4.8
		0801	2.1			0845	1.7
		1436	4.6			1524	4.9
		2034	1.9			2109	1.7
10	SU	0257	4.8	25	M	0347	5.0
		0849	1.9			0939	1.6
		1519	4.8			1611	5.0
		2116	1.7			2158	1.6
11	M	0337	4.9	26	TU	0429	5.1
		0934	1.7			1028	1.5
		1600	5.0			1654	5.0
		2157	1.6			2242	1.6
12	TU	0417	5.1	27	W	0510	5.1
		1018	1.5			1113	1.5
		1641	5.1			1734	5.0
		2239	1.5		○	2323	1.6
13	W	0457	5.2	28	TH	0548	5.1
		1102	1.4			1154	1.5
		1724	5.1			1812	4.9
	●	2321	1.4				
14	TH	0540	5.3	29	F	0001	1.6
		1146	1.3			0625	5.1
		1808	5.1			1233	1.5
						1848	4.8
15	F	0005	1.4	30	SA	0039	1.6
		0626	5.3			0700	5.0
		1232	1.3			1310	1.6
		1855	5.0			1922	4.7
				31	SU	0116	1.7
						0734	4.9
						1346	1.7
						1956	4.6

Chart Datum: 2·83 metres below IGN Datum
HAT is 6·1 metres above Chart Datum

ADLARD
COLES
SHORE
GUIDE
CHANNEL COAST
OF FRANCE
Everything you need to know
when you step ashore
PAUL HEINEY
ADLARD COLES